Dramatic Justice

Dramatic Justice

Trial by Theater in the Age of the French Revolution

Yann Robert

PENN

UNIVERSITY OF PENNSYLVANIA PRESS

PHILADELPHIA

Published by
University of Pennsylvania Press
Philadelphia, Pennsylvania 19104-4112
www.upenn.edu/pennpress

Printed in the United States of America on acid-free paper
10 9 8 7 6 5 4 3 2 1

Library of Congress Cataloging-in-Publication Data

Names: Robert, Yann, author.
Title: Dramatic justice: trial by theater in the age of the French Revolution / Yann Robert.
Description: 1st edition. | Philadelphia: University of Pennsylvania Press, [2019] | Includes bibliographical references and index.
Identifiers: LCCN 2018018632| ISBN 9780812250756 (hardcopy: alk. paper)
Subjects: LCSH: Theater—Political aspects—France—History—18th century. | Justice, Administration of—France—History—18th century. | France—History—Revolution, 1789–1799.
Classification: LCC PN2633.R63 2019 | DDC 792.094409033—dc23
LC record available at https://lccn.loc.gov/2018018632

For Lori, Claire, and Nicolas, with love

Contents

Introduction

The year is 1793, and the king stands on trial. Gathered by the hundreds in a profoundly theatrical space—the *salle du manège*, formerly used for equestrian shows—spectators feasting on oranges and liqueurs observe the judges below, loudly jeering, applauding, and debating their every word. But what are they really watching? Are the men below actually judges? For months now, the deputies of the National Convention have tried, many reluctantly, to perform this role, to *act* as judges, despite lacking the training or credentials for it. They cannot even claim to be impartial: most have already publicly affirmed Louis XVI's guilt, giving the trial a seemingly scripted denouement (only the punishment remains unknown). Spectators, actors, and a script—it is easy to see why the proceedings against the king have traditionally been portrayed as a show trial, an early example of the political parodies of justice that the Jacobins would stage during the Terror to eliminate rival factions.

And yet . . . if the purpose of a show trial is to publicize the guilt of an accused, why, then, did the Jacobins fight so hard to have no trial at all, just a summary execution? Why did they repeatedly claim that the king had been found guilty during the 10 August insurrection—that he was, in fact, already dead—and that any trial would therefore amount to mere theater, an artificial repetition of the king's condemnation at the hands of the people? Once the trial of the century had nevertheless begun, why did they interrupt it to forbid the performance of a play, *L'Ami des lois*, that made it possible for a broader audience to participate in the king's judgment by reenacting key aspects of the case against him? It is true that *L'Ami des lois* and at least three other plays like it sided with the king, but if this was the sole reason behind the Jacobins' anger, why did they extend their refusal to dramatize the king's trial to performances aligned with their views, as when they rejected several proposals to commemorate the anniversary of the king's beheading with theatrical reenactments of his trial and execution? Lastly and, perhaps, most tellingly, why was it the Jacobins, not the Girondins, who most frequently accused their enemies of practicing a theatrical mode of justice?

These questions, to which I return in Chapter 7, reveal the need to rethink the standard narratives on the evolution of both theater and justice in eighteenth-century France. As we will see, the first narrative holds that theater, under the influence of bourgeois drama, began to drift toward pure entertainment and illusionism in the decades preceding the Revolution—further and further away, therefore, from any direct, judicial involvement in current affairs. The second narrative, a mirror image of the first, maintains that the justice system moved away from theatricality, as it shifted from an iconic, visual foundation (royal displays) to a rational, textual one (codes of law). The plays and trials of the Revolution hardly fit these two narratives, however. For that reason, they are typically discounted as a historical blip, an anomaly caused by the Jacobins' penchant for injecting politics everywhere, which blurred the line between theater and justice by turning the former into propaganda and the latter into show trials like the king's. Yet if, as their reaction to the king's trial and to its theatrical reenactments suggests, the Jacobins opposed the profound intertwining of justice and theater during the Revolution, where did it actually come from?

This book provides an answer, one that turns upside down the standard histories both of French theater and of French justice. Its first section ("Theater as Justice") uncovers, starting in the 1750s, numerous plans and attempts, including successful ones, to transform the theater into an instrument of justice, exposing criminals by name, recreating transgressions on stage, and reenacting contemporary trials. The next section ("Justice as Theater") reveals that many of the illustrious eighteenth-century figures who campaigned to reform the justice system explicitly modeled trials on the theater, even recommending that judges imitate the emotional, instinctual judgments of dramatic spectators and that lawyers seek private lessons from actors. The last section ("The Revolution's Performance of Justice") studies the realization of these parallel projects in the early years of the Revolution and the ensuing backlash as the Jacobins grew concerned that this new performance of justice placed greater emphasis on performance than it did on justice. This alternative history of justice and theater in France explains why the Jacobins attempted to limit the theatricality of the king's trial and not, as is commonly believed, to turn it into a show trial. They understood Louis XVI's trial as I do, not as a historical blip, but as its opposite: a culmination. In this account, the king's trial does not mark a beginning (the start of a momentary, aberrant mixing of justice and theater) but a peak, at once the apex of a fifty-year evolution that saw the theater grow ever-more judicial and justice ever-more theatrical *and* the start of its decline.

It is this half century of unparalleled experimentation, a time when thinkers set out to reinvent the very nature of a dramatic performance, of justice, and of the performance of justice, that this book seeks to revive, not only for what it can teach us about the past by challenging accepted narratives on French theater, law, and the Revolution, but also for the light it shines on contemporary issues and anxieties. To list only a few: this book traces the rise of such modern-day fears as celebrity lawyers, willing, like actors, to parrot any claim; illegitimate judges, easily misled, like dramatic spectators, by their vanity and sentimentality; a lawsuit culture, giving rise to never-ending trials; and a sensationalist mass media that transforms justice into gossip, entertainment, and revenge. These fears developed, in France, from the growing (con)fusion between theater and justice in the eighteenth century, giving rise to debates and innovations that survive to this day, on the stage as in the courtroom.

Theater as Justice

Few plays capture the intricate ties between Revolutionary drama and justice as fully as *L'Ami des lois*. Besides having interrupted the king's trial, it illustrates several key strands of "judicial theater"—a neologism I use to refer to public spectacles that reenact contemporary events on stage so as to expose, judge, and punish a transgression. Through its overt, virulent denunciation of living public figures (Maximilien Robespierre and Jean-Paul Marat) and their secret crimes, *L'Ami des lois* transforms the theater into a tribunal, and the audience into a jury. Itself, therefore, a kind of trial, it further functions as the trial of a trial, reproducing key aspects of the proceedings against the king in an attempt to influence the verdict. Such a play would have been unthinkable only fifty years earlier. As unremarkable as it may seem today, the idea that the theater could be used to recreate current affairs on stage constitutes a significant (and yet understudied) turning point in the history of French drama. For most of the seventeenth and eighteenth centuries, indeed, classical dogma and royal censorship worked together to ensure that official theaters would only stage historically distant, geographically remote, or entirely fictitious stories.[1] The abbé d'Aubignac, for instance, urged playwrights to maintain a clear divide between the world on stage and the one outside the auditorium by seeking their plots in times or countries with which the spectators had nothing in common.[2] Of course, seventeenth-century dramatic practice occasionally strayed from the wishes of early modern theorists and censors,[3] but all agreed on the importance of refraining from explicit depictions of the here and now, to such an extent, in fact, that many saw French classical theater as a continuation and highpoint of the evolution, begun in ancient Greece, from satirical plays denouncing actual events and individuals by name (Old Comedy) to more general and, as a result, fruitfully edifying critiques of abstract moral flaws (New Comedy).[4]

Starting in the 1750s, however, many reformers expressed an unprecedented desire for performances that would reproduce, with documentary-like precision, contemporary events and figures. At the heart of this evolution lies Denis Diderot's *Fils naturel*.[5] In Chapter 1, I engage in a close reading of this grippingly complex work, not only because it constitutes the earliest and most insightful exploration of reenactment, a theory central to my claims in this book, but also because, in typically Diderotian fashion, it ceaselessly challenges its own theory, thereby establishing a broad set of questions to which later, more historical chapters constantly return. Through the story of a patriarch who reaches for immortality by forcing his family to reenact a past event with flawless accuracy, Diderot sets out to discover what remains when one strips or tries to strip all theatricality from the theater. He attempts to imagine the conditions that would allow, and the consequences that would follow, a performance in which actors do not act (they "are" the characters), authors do not author (they strictly record), and beholders do not behold (they join or judge an event they deem real). Diderot even foresees the judicial implications of this new theory of reenactment, achieving the impressive feat of highlighting in a single work the diverse forms that judicial theater could—and would—take. In its initial form, a ruler (here, the patriarch) orders the reenactment of a transgression (an incestuous attraction) so as to condemn it again publicly, thereby deterring its repetition and enshrining his law in the souls of participants and spectators alike. The patriarch's death, however, by revealing the inherent mutability of the scenic arts, heralds a different kind of judicial theater, a fluid, egalitarian performance enabling a community to come together, relive and review a recent transgression, and achieve through its verdict a cathartic resolution, a reconciliation, or even a revision of the law. *Le Fils naturel* thus juxtaposes two competing notions of both theater and justice—fixed and autocratic vs. mutable and collective—thereby identifying the two poles that would shape all subsequent forms of judicial theater.

Ironically, Diderot would become one of the earliest victims of this new judicial vision of the theater when he was explicitly denounced as a criminal in Charles Palissot's infamous satire, *Les Philosophes*.[6] In fact, Palissot even cited Diderot's theories to defend a play that friends and foes alike instantly perceived as inaugurating a new kind of theater—one that would elicit ample discussion and imitation, as I show in Chapter 2. To grasp the implications of using theater as a space for legal accusations, eighteenth-century writers turned to the nearest equivalent known to them: the Old Comedy of ancient Greece. The once despised Aristophanes became the lens through which thinkers expressed excitement as well as unease at the evolution of theater into a popular tribunal. Some, such as Palissot, pointed to one side of Aristophanes (his authorship of *The Clouds*) and portrayed judicial theater as an official instrument of state discipline, targeting the people's hidden vices. Countering with a different Aristophanes (the intrepid author of *The Knights*), others presented judicial theater instead as a means of transparency, which would expose the crimes of the ruling class and enable ordinary people to pass judgment on contemporary affairs, figures, and trials—an increasingly common practice in eighteenth-century France, which actors encouraged by inviting famous litigants and lawyers as guests of honor to their performances. Yet another group, led by Jean-Jacques Rousseau, summoned a third Aristophanes (Socrates's killer) as proof that judicial theater inevitably results in slanderous accusations, trial by media, and the replacement of the rule of law by the rule of actors. These fears would haunt partisans of the new genre throughout the second half of the eighteenth century, leading many to conclude that the risk derived from the "theater," not the "judicial," in "judicial theater." In the hope of curbing such dangerous theatricality and, with it, the threat of fictitious accusations with little oversight and accountability, they sought to bring their judicial spectacles ever closer to the perfect reenactment—sans actor, author, and beholder—invented by Diderot. For instance, in a plan at once fantastical and entirely typical of the period, Nicolas-Edme Rétif de la Bretonne called for the monarchy to establish thousands of committees of elders, tasked with spying on their neighbors and forcing the guilty ones to reenact their own offenses, as their friends and family watched and jeered.[7]

Uniting these disparate visions of judicial theater is the conviction that theater should not simply seek to entertain, or even to impart abstract moral lessons, but should instead aim for a direct involvement in, and impact on, the real world. Such engagement may come as a surprise, challenging as it

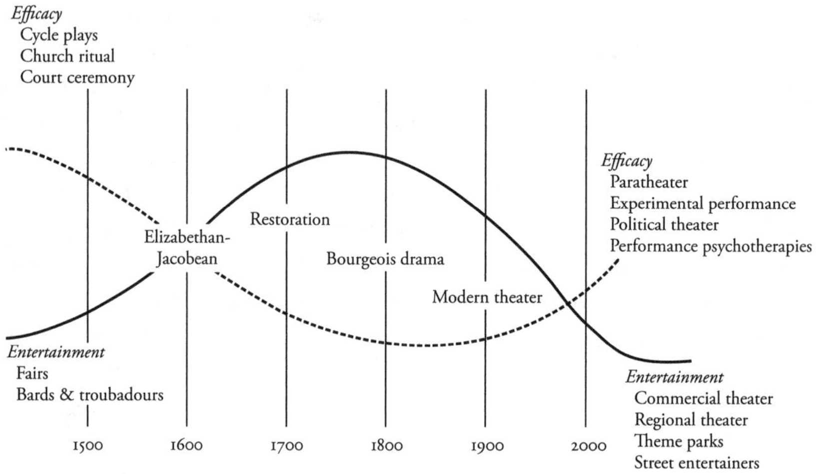

Figure 1. Diagram by Richard Schechner depicting the history of Western theater. *Source:* Richard Schechner, *Performance Theory* (London: Routledge, 2003), 133.

does the standard history of the theater. This dominant narrative is perfectly illustrated in a diagram by Richard Schechner (depicting the history of British theater, but the French tradition follows the same trajectory, according to Schechner).

This braid illustrates Schechner's seminal insight that instead of labeling performances as ritual or theater, one should see them as lying on a continuum between the two. To determine where a performance will fall, Schechner identifies a series of attributes, splitting them along two poles: "entertainment" and "efficacy." These attributes include the performance's objectives (fun or results), performers (acting or incarnating), spectators (critical outlook or direct participation), and authors (individual or collective creation).[8] Although all performances combine attributes from both poles, if most belong on the left (the "entertainment" pole), the performance lies on the theatrical end of the spectrum. If, as is the case with judicial reenactments, they mostly fall on the side of efficacy, the performance more closely resembles a ritual.

Looking at Schechner's braid, one would therefore anticipate finding judicial theater in the Middle Ages, and indeed, medieval spectacles included reenactments of trials and crimes, as well as overt denunciations of living figures.[9] Inversely, one would least expect judicial theater in the eighteenth century, which has the highest score on the entertainment scale while hitting near bottom in efficacy. In fact, Schechner considers the eighteenth century and its "development of bourgeois theater" to be the chief culprit in the disappearance of the "dominant efficacious mode of medieval performance."[10] This view is widely reflected in modern scholarship on eighteenth-century drama. In most histories of French theater, Diderot and the eighteenth century are credited primarily as the inventors of bourgeois drama and as precursors to the more realist, illusionist fare of the nineteenth century.[11] Tellingly, these are precisely the two theatrical traditions most often condemned as mere entertainment[12]—not without cause, as their formal innovations further solidified the division between the world on stage and the one off it. Indeed, scholars from Michael Fried to Paul Friedland (a chronological spread, not an alphabetical one!) have shown that the eighteenth century devised a conceptual framework that would later enable the creation of a structural divide between theater and reality.[13] Architectural and lighting reforms, new theories of realism and illusion, and Diderot's invention of the fourth wall promoted a new conception of the world on stage as distinct from the spectators', self-enclosed and complete, to be consumed silently rather than engaged directly. Friedland, in particular, presents this vision of the theater as evidence of a broader movement away from an older, ritualistic understanding of performance as embodiment: that is, as a presentation (not a representation) with the power to transform its participants and spectators.

Part of what makes judicial theater so fascinating, then, is that it turns on its head the standard account of eighteenth-century theatrical history as a progression away from ritual and toward pure entertainment. Naturally, some studies already offer a more nuanced picture of eighteenth-century theater. Scholars working on Diderot and Louis-Sébastien Mercier have not failed to notice the two playwrights' desire to use the theater to denounce and redress the social wrongs of their day.[14] Yet the passages they study concern broad social wrongs, not individual ones. As a result, they overlook the far more radical promotion of a theater that would go beyond general moral or social lessons to intervene directly in specific injustices, reenacting them and opening them up to popular judgment. Inversely, scholars have occasionally noted the period's interest in staging current events, but never as the primary subject of their research, and never in terms of the judicial function so often assigned to it. For instance, studies on society theater have revealed that the private troupes sometimes reenacted events from the performers' lives.[15] We also know that fairground theaters included vaudevilles, a term that in eighteenth-century France referred to brief songs with themes taken from current events.[16] Even official theaters did not always respect the classical stance against the representation of figures and events from France's past, with historical drama gaining in popularity as early as the 1730s.[17] It should be noted, however, that these plays resurrected distant events, and as such differed from the reenactments I study, which entertain the paradoxical aim of reviving something not yet dead—an ongoing event, or a past recent enough to still be experienced as the present.[18] Moreover, the examples above lack a clearly denunciatory function; they do not seek to put on trial and thereby transform the events and figures they reproduce.[19] Yet it is the combination of these two visions of the stage—as an instrument of justice and as a reenactment of current affairs—that for many eighteenth-century thinkers gave judicial theater its most appealing quality: the ability to produce concrete and immediate results. Despite its popularity, the very notion of judicial theater has been obscured by the longstanding account of eighteenth-century theatrical history as one of deritualization, and by the attendant emphasis on bourgeois drama and realist reforms. Bringing this unique conception of performance to light encourages us to refine our vision not just of eighteenth-century drama but of theater itself, by challenging divisions we sometimes take for granted: actor and character, stage and auditorium, representation and reality, and theater and ritual.

Justice as Theater

This book also inverts the standard narrative on the evolution of justice in France. Sarah Maza provides perhaps the best synopsis of this narrative when she argues that the legal system shifted from "a realm of display, of the visual, the iconic" to "the domain of the word, of textuality, of rationality."[20] Drawing from Michel Foucault, Jürgen Habermas, Joan Landes, and Marie-Hélène Huet—a list that leaves little doubt as to the narrative's pedigree and influence—Maza contends that early modern justice rested on a traditional order of figuration centered on the spectacular display of the king's body and authority, but that this order progressively gave way to a competing semiotic system, in which power resided in the written word of the law.[21] In short, according to most modern scholars, justice was moving away from the theatrical and toward the textual.

However, as Katherine Taylor observes in the introduction to her study of nineteenth-century courtroom architecture, this narrative fits the evolution of justice as an abstract concept (a written code having replaced the king as the basis of justice), yet it is utterly inaccurate with respect to its actual practice.[22] Trial proceedings, in fact, evolved in the opposite direction: not from theatrical to textual, but from textual to theatrical. Indeed, under the ancien régime, criminal proceedings were explicitly designed to be the least theatrical possible. They allowed neither spectators nor representation (i.e., lawyers *acting* for the litigants), thereby obviating two of the more obvious parallels between justice and theater. Nor was there, in any case, much of a spectacle to behold, given the proceedings never assembled the participants in one place and time for a climactic confrontation (the kind of performance we associate today with a trial). Instead, criminal cases followed what is known as the "inquisitorial model," meaning they unfolded as a series of private interrogations conducted by deeply involved and powerful judges.[23] An examining magistrate questioned the litigants and witnesses separately and compiled a dossier containing transcripts of the interrogations, forensic reports, and trial briefs. The dossier was then sent over to the judges, who reached a decision by applying fixed rules and mathematical formulas to the enclosed documents. Each text was assigned a numerical value, and these "fractions of proof" were added together to compose a verdict. What could have inspired such a convoluted system, which limited judgment to a primarily textual and mechanical exercise by denying judges the opportunity to see and hear vital interrogations directly? Looming behind these restrictions was the specter of theatricality: magistrates had to be prevented from judging in the manner of dramatic spectators through an emotional reaction to watching live disputes. Representation and spectators, physicality and orality, agonistic debates and emotional appeals—in short, all the characteristics of a performance—were thus deliberately excluded from trial proceedings.[24]

To be sure, even in the face of such precautions, some theatricality still crept into ancien régime justice. Civil trials and hearings at the Paris Parlement (in its role as a court of appeals) were not formally closed to the public and to lawyers in the way that criminal proceedings were, and certain cases drew considerable crowds and interest in the press. In such circumstances, lawyers sometimes borrowed narrative strategies from literary texts to make their pleas more dramatic, knowing this would make them the talk of the town. While criminal proceedings offered no such opportunity, lawyers could still seek to sway the judges and enhance their reputations by writing gripping accounts of the case, whether as pleas for a royal pardon or as trial briefs—documents that became remarkably popular and melodramatic in the eighteenth century.[25] As we will see, however, the judicial establishment, notably the Order of Barristers, vigorously opposed such practices. It is in fact telling that in criminal cases—even though, or rather because, they typically involved the most dramatic stories—what little theatricality existed was channeled through writing. While we may describe the narrative strategies in some trial briefs as dramatic, this did not make the trial or the briefs themselves theater, in the absence of spectators, actors, and oral delivery. Not until the 1750s and the Revolution (first in theory, then in practice) would live performance become the operating principle and foundation of justice.

Indeed, starting in the middle of the eighteenth century, reformers campaigned for the introduction of spectators, lawyers, and adversarial proceedings. In lieu of the inquisitorial model, they recommended adopting the "accusatorial model" characteristic, then as now, of Anglo-Saxon justice. In this model, a trial consists of a public clash between two rehearsed narratives. To ensure fairness, both parties are given the same advantages—speaking time, witnesses, knowledge of the case, and access to gifted orators (lawyers)—so that each may prepare the most persuasive narrative possible. These narratives are then delivered in a set form and sequence amounting to a veritable dramaturgy (testimony, direct and cross-examination, closing arguments, etc.). The result is a representation, not a repetition, of the original conflict, a staged translation that curbs its violence and makes it possible for a magistrate to pick a winning side. The judge's duties are thus more limited in the accusatorial model. No longer does he play a leading role in the composition of a single, "true" narrative through his interrogations or analyses of written documents; instead, he simply selects one of two premade narratives as the "truth." Excluded from the performance of justice, the judge becomes a silent spectator whose task it is to watch and assess, on the basis of subjective impressions, a spectacle staged for his benefit.

The accusatorial model thus clearly entails far more theatricality than the secret, textual trials of the ancien régime. One might have expected reformers to downplay this fact, but many embraced it instead, openly modeling their vision of legal proceedings on the theater. Long-forgotten debates from the period (May lawyers write or perform in plays? Should judges be barred from attending the theater? May actors testify in a tribunal? Should trial audiences be allowed to clap or hiss?) show the extent to which the reformers viewed the new proceedings through a theatrical lens. Indeed, this book is unique not only for studying the evolution of eighteenth-century legal practice as a shift toward theatricality, but also for revealing that thinkers of the period understood it precisely in those terms. For many reformers, theatricality was not, as we tend to think of it today, an accidental side effect or potential threat; it was the very core of liberal justice.

The term "liberal" warrants a note, as it was not used in its present-day acceptation in eighteenth-century France and is contested among political scientists today, who debate its applicability prior to the nineteenth century.[26] I employ it deliberately, as a useful anachronism, to refer to thinkers who espoused a set of key principles later associated with liberalism. These principles include publicity (as a deterrent and as a catalyst for greater public involvement), pluralism (especially in the form of free and adversarial debate), and individual rights (through equal protection before the law and alternatives to absolutism). In associating publicity, pluralism, and individual rights with a liberal worldview, I follow the example of such founding figures of modern liberalism as Benjamin Constant and John Stuart Mill. So ingrained has this association become, in fact, that many legal historians use the term "liberal" to describe the public and adversarial justice system championed by French reformers in the eighteenth century. Indeed, although this would likely surprise many political scientists, no scholars of history, law, or literature found it controversial, let alone unusual, when two recent studies presented early Revolutionary justice as the triumph of a "liberal model."[27]

Yet while I imitate legal historians by using "liberal" to describe eighteenth-century judicial reformers, I also seek, in the spirit (albeit not the manner) of political scientists, to complicate the term. In particular, I call attention to the way that it encourages a longstanding tendency to view the campaign to reform justice through the lens of a larger political conflict between two opposing conceptions of government and society. In this perspective, traditionalists defended the secretive, inquisitorial justice system of the ancien régime because it reflected the absolutist culture they supported, while liberal reformers, as apostles of publicity, pluralism, and individual rights, sought to open up and democratize the legal system.[28] With the Revolution, the liberal vision triumphed, and with it the reformers' conception of justice, destroying in the process the unjust and antiquated system of the past. Not coincidentally, perhaps, this political account reproduces the accusatorial model favored by liberal reformers in that it opposes two symmetrical, clearly delineated parties and ends their clash by selecting one side as victor and its vision as the sole truth.

In justice as in scholarship, however, sweeping binaries with fixed terms often risk distorting a story by obscuring crucial aspects of its particularity.

Imposing a political frame (liberalism vs. absolutism) upon the campaign to reform justice conceals the fact that many politically liberal thinkers expressed a profound anxiety that their own ideals, transferred to the courtroom, would bring about an overly dramatic mode of justice. This led them to take entirely unexpected positions, as when Mercier endorsed *lettres de cachet* (letters signed by the king ordering that a subject be imprisoned or exiled without a trial), or when he and several others challenged such key liberal principles as the universal right to a lawyer, public trials, and a fixed, comprehensive code of laws. Troubled by the secrecy of the status quo *and* by the theatricality of accusatorial justice, figures from both sides of the campaign set out to find innovative solutions. In fact, I contend that many aspects of the justice system in France today, including current forms of legal representation and judgment, find their roots in these compromises. By adopting a theatrical rather than political lens, this book proposes therefore a new history of justice, chronicling the rise of a modern legal system in France less as a tale of conquest (the triumph of liberal values over judicial absolutism) and more as a constant negotiation between two visions of justice, one (the ancien régime's inquisitorial model) too distant from the theater, the other (England's accusatorial model) too close to it.

This simultaneous attraction and unease toward dramatic justice is particularly evident in the king's trial, which revived disputes about the three reforms most desired by liberals—legal counsel for all, a new mode of judgment, and public trials—and yet also most feared for their theatricality, as I show in Chapters 3, 4, and 5, respectively. For instance, even as the National Convention gave Louis XVI not one but two attorneys, some Jacobin deputies fretted that lawyers might employ delaying tactics and manipulate naïve spectators into feeling compassion for the tyrant.[29] Even more interesting was Robespierre's warning that "if [Louis's defenders] plead his case, they can hope to make it prevail; otherwise, you would only be giving the world a ridiculous play."[30] If all agreed that the king was guilty, even the Girondins, then they turned his trial into theater by asking lawyers to defend the clearly culpable. This argument reveals Robespierre's unease with the transformation in the role of lawyers over his lifetime. As I show in Chapter 3, lawyers were once viewed as moral *vouchers*. Their membership in a selective Order of Barristers that excluded those prone to immorality or theatricality imbued them with an ethos and a legitimacy that they swore to lend only to clients they believed innocent. The reformers' calls for the order's abolition, in the belief that all men should be free to plead, coupled with their invention of a universal right to counsel, turned lawyers into *representatives*—men chosen for their eloquence, and with a duty to defend any party, even the patently guilty. This shift from a model locating truth in the lawyer's identity to one locating it in his speech elicited deep anxieties. Many feared that it would forever transform lawyers—not into liars (who still care about the truth, if only to hide it and claim they speak it), but worse, into actors (whose sole concern is persuasion, not truth, since everyone understands that they neither endorse their characters' words as truthful nor accept responsibility for them). What could then prevent ambitious youths from seeking unjust cases and employing histrionics and hyperbole for the sake of celebrity (as many believed was already happening)? What if a trial's verdict came to hinge more on the oratorical prowess and boldness of two lawyer-actors than on the merits of the case? Chapter 3 studies these anxieties, as well as the various attempts at appeasing them, extending to the very recent controversy on the way that French attorneys advertise their services.

The Jacobins also showed a surprising unease with the mode of judgment introduced by the Revolution. Especially striking is the number of deputies who demanded that the king respond in writing to a long list of accusations, and that he either only appear before his judges after they had read his answers or that he never appear at all.[31] Some deputies objected that both options meant the king's judges would assess his guilt before seeing and hearing him speak,[32] but this was almost certainly the point, considering the Jacobins' repeated warnings that a live debate would only yield confusion, hesitation, and misplaced compassion.[33] Such warnings, reminiscent of those by reactionaries before the Revolution, reveal the strength and persistence of the fears that greeted the shift toward a more theatrical mode of judgment in criminal cases. As I argue in Chapter 4, pre-Revolutionary judges most resembled authors, composing a single narrative in private through the careful analysis of written words. The legitimacy of their judgments rested upon this textual process and exclusive authorship: magistrates were a titled elite, (supposedly) handpicked by the king to serve as vessels for his divine justice, a mission they fulfilled by obeying hermeneutic rules from above, rather than subjective emotions from within. By contrast, the liberal conception of trials as a live, adversarial performance assigned a different role to judges, closer to that of dramatic spectators. Instead of anointed authors extracting an objective truth from snippets of text, judges would now be ordinary men who watched two preexisting, fictionalized narratives and picked the most credible through an instinctual, emotional response. This new mode of judgment led to widespread fears, even among reformers, that abandoning the notion of objective truth and the validation of exclusive titles and rules would leave judges vulnerable to accusations of arbitrariness, inconsistency, and credulous sentimentality. Other critics drew on Plato's famous denunciation of "theatrocracy" to warn that the conceit that all possess the right and the ability to judge, born in the theater and now making its way into the courtroom, would soon spread to the whole of society, delegitimizing judgment itself and ending in anarchy. These fears, I contend at the end of Chapter 4, inspired some lasting compromises, from the imposition of new limits on the timing and nature of judging, leading to what I have dubbed "modern delayed judgment," to the unique fusion of roles—at once author, actor, and spectator—that characterizes French magistrates today.

Belying their reputation as directors of show trials and apostles of transparency, Jacobin deputies also expressed anxiety at the sizeable audience watching the king's trial. They worried, of course, about being jeered. What if naïve spectators succumbed to the royalist claqueurs in the courtroom, or to the attempts outside it to paint the king as the victim in a sentimental drama?[34] More surprisingly, the Jacobins also criticized signs of approval, such as applause, for fear they would make it seem as if the trial was not an impartial act of justice but a partisan conflict that could be influenced by vocal factions in the crowd.[35] Better, they concluded, that the spectators be few in number, or entirely silent, or even absent, in keeping with Robespierre's order to "flee the spectacle of our debates."[36] In reaching these conclusions, the Jacobins were tapping into a preexisting undercurrent of antitheatrical anxiety, as they had when discussing lawyers and judges. Indeed, as I show in Chapter 5, even committed reformers worried that making criminal proceedings public would trigger a lawsuit culture. Was it not likely, after all, that public trials would come to supplant theatrical productions, luring spectators through sensationalism and sentimentalism and perverting justice by turning the litigants into caricatural monsters and martyrs? Would the frequent viewing of trials inspire some spectators to seek the spotlight for themselves by initiating needless proceedings? Might it not even increase crime, as spectators discovered rare transgressions or, inversely, the pervasiveness and thus normality of certain offenses? In response to these fears, there appeared in countless texts the same idyllic portrayal of primeval justice, in which a beloved patriarch settles disputes amicably, without spectators, procedures, judges, or lawyers. The simplicity and legitimacy of a trial based on biological ties, shared moral values, and the faithful, unrehearsed reenactment of the original conflict moved thinkers such as Montesquieu, Rétif, and Sylvain Maréchal to call for the revival of "domestic tribunals," the term they used to refer to a system in which fathers possess the right to try and convict their children in their own homes, in lieu of a public trial. As the popularity of this private conception of justice illustrates (various forms of "domestic tribunals" would in fact be instituted during the Revolution), the Jacobin deputies were far from the first to harbor mixed feelings about the publicity of liberal justice. Rather, they drew on half a century of cultural ambivalence, a forgotten history that, from the start, simultaneously recognized the benefits of a more dramatic justice and feared its impact on spectators and society.

The Revolution's Performance of Justice

In short, Chapters 3, 4, and 5 study the fears elicited by the rise of a more theatrical vision of justice as they crystalized around, challenged, and transformed three central characters in legal proceedings: lawyers, judges, and spectators. Chapter 6 focuses on the attempt in the early years of the Revolution to devise a performance of justice that would implement long-desired liberal reforms while shielding its participants from the harmful consequences of theatricality detailed in the preceding chapters. With the National Assembly hesitant to tackle too soon the complex and contentious establishment of an accusatorial justice system, it was on the dramatic stage that this new performance of justice initially made itself most visible. Dust had barely settled on the ruins of the Bastille when the theater was inundated with judicial plays. Some, labeled "aristophanic" in the press, reenacted the secret transgressions and ambitions of living public figures. Others, part of a popular genre I have dubbed "courtroom dramas," consisted of meticulous reenactments of recent or ongoing trials. Such plays served the usual functions of judicial theater—exposing and deterring crime, training spectators to become involved citizens and jurors, redressing miscarriages of justice, and enabling catharsis and reconciliation—but they also took on an additional role as "trial runs" for potential new performances of justice. By experimenting with the diverse ways proceedings could unfold—who spoke, when, for how long, as a series of monologues or as fragmented, heated disputes?—they set the stage for a series of little-known debates in the National Assembly on the proper "dramaturgy" of trials. Moved by the example of these judicial reenactments and by antitheatrical anxiety, the deputies proved reluctant to see proceedings (as most liberal reformers had) as a competition between two narratives studiously rehearsed and performed by litigants and their representatives. Instead, they championed lively, unstructured trials, more likely to reproduce the passion and spontaneity of the initial conflict. The closer the trial came to reenacting the conflict, the better the odds, they argued, that the litigants and witnesses would lose themselves in heated exchanges and speak with sincerity and emotion, instead of sticking to a prepared script and delivery—that is, instead of acting. In tribunals as in playhouses, therefore, the early Revolutionaries devised a new performance of justice grounded in the concept of reenactment, in the belief that only such a spectacle could be fair, adversarial, public—and yet untainted by theatricality.

This cultural faith in reenactment began to wane during the king's trial and *Ami des lois* scandal, a turning point for both judicial theater and theatrical justice—and, for that reason, the perfect transition from Chapter 6 to 7. The success of *L'Ami des lois* and plays like it renewed the usual fears of slander, trial by media, and vigilantism. These plays even led the Jacobins to cast doubt on the usefulness of publicly denouncing suspected schemers, as they grew concerned that the drive to unmask only produced, paradoxically, more and more masks. This anxiety explains the popularity of a (hitherto unstudied) series of plays written against denunciation—a surprising corpus, since denunciation is normally held to be one of the Jacobins' highest civic duties, and since it meant that the theater was here denouncing itself as a space of denunciation. Nor did the Jacobins find relief from their fears, as earlier Revolutionaries had done, in the fact that these denunciations took the form of reenactments. On the contrary, they argued that including real-life traitors and conspiracies on stage had the unintended consequence of keeping them and their anti-republican opinions alive. The same fears inspired them to question the value of reenactment in legal proceedings. In their eyes, trials that sought to resurrect past emotions and quarrels through lively, adversarial debates gave known conspirators a public stage and, thanks to the presumption of innocence, a legitimate voice with which to—quite literally—make their case against the Republic. Far from a source of certainty or catharsis, the spectacular reenactment of crimes and conflicts threatened the unity of the Republic by prolonging hatreds and ideologies best forgotten and by fueling a cycle of accusation and counteraccusation characteristic of a lawsuit culture. In response to these threats, the Jacobins established the infamous Revolutionary Tribunal and gradually restricted nearly every right introduced just years earlier: legal counsel, defense witnesses, a judgment based on free, adversarial debate rather than written dossiers, the presumption of innocence, and a trial by one's peers (since judges and juries were no longer chosen by the people or by chance, but by the government). Each of these steps, I contend, grew out of the Jacobins' fear of theatricality and resulted in an ironic twist: the proceedings at the Revolutionary Tribunal increasingly came to resemble the inquisitorial justice against which the Revolutionaries had once revolted. While the Jacobins' reign proved short-lived, their critique of the fusion between justice and theater did not: Chapter 7 concludes by retracing the efforts during the Directory to draw the curtain on judicial theater and theatrical justice.

Together, these chapters offer a fuller understanding of the famously militant theater of the Revolution and of the rise of the Terror by situating them within a wider historical evolution in the performance of justice, instead of treating them as anomalies resulting from an extreme politicization of the arts and the law. The value of this approach is particularly evident with respect to Revolutionary drama. For centuries, the latter was either ignored by scholars, because they struggled to reconcile it with the standard history of French theater, or was reduced to a simple illustration of the vicissitudes and excesses of Revolutionary politics.[37] Starting in the 1980s, studies on Revolutionary drama grew in both number and subtlety—giving rise to fascinating debates, notably between those who, like Susan Maslan, see the theater of the Revolution as a powerful site and symbol of direct democracy and those who, like Friedland, believe it illustrates a conception of representation that silences the people—yet even these studies largely retain a political lens.[38] Having grown dull from repeated use, this lens risks blinding us to other aspects of Revolutionary drama, notably by reinforcing the traditional perception of it as the product of a unique political moment, disconnected from the dramatic theories and practices that preceded it. In response, some scholars have recently begun to examine its links to the ancien régime. For instance, Cecilia Feilla has shown the importance of bourgeois drama and sentimental tropes in the theater of the Revolution, thereby adding to the more quantitative studies that first revealed the continued popularity of ancien régime plays and genres.[39] Yet what of the more topical plays, many of which were significant causes célèbres at the time, remain to this day the best (and often only) known dramatic works of the Revolution, and are therefore so central to our understanding of Revolutionary theater?[40] For them, the old answer persists—that they arose ex nihilo, the accidental offspring of an obsession with politics that turned everything it touched into propaganda.[41]

By contrast, this book seeks to draw attention to the continuity in dramatic theory and praxis pre- and post-storming of the Bastille.[42] Once inscribed in the broader history of judicial theater, the overt topicality of many of the Revolution's most consequential plays no longer appears to be the sign of an aberrant politicization. The same holds true for some of the most striking anecdotes from the period, ranging from actors tried and even executed for words they said while in character, to spectators watching their own lives reenacted, such as Anne Calas, who, if she truly attended one of the five plays about her family's trial staged in 1791, saw her father convicted and dragged to the scaffold twice. Indeed, while some of these consequential plays and dramatic anecdotes are clearly political in nature, many are not. What they all share, however, is a ritualistic vision of the theater as a mode of action on the present, made possible by its explicit reenactment of current events. By moving beyond the usual emphasis on politics, both as the supposed origin of Revolutionary drama's topicality and as the best lens for understanding it, this book offers a new perspective on the theater of the Revolution, viewing it not as an anomaly but as the result of an artistic and intellectual evolution that set the stage for a new judicial practice of the theater.

Likewise, a political lens often colors accounts of the Terror. Studies of Revolutionary justice typically portray the legal system instituted in the first years of the Revolution as a direct implementation of the Enlightenment project for a more rational, textual, egalitarian justice and the Terror as a temporary setback in that evolution, a thankfully brief period when the Jacobins' efforts to politicize the legal system prompted a return to autocratic, theatrical justice in the form of show trials. A closer attention to legal proceedings as performance, however, tells a different story: it was the early Revolutionaries who set out to turn trials into public performances (albeit ones whose theatricality they tried to curb), leading concerned Jacobins to attempt, through the creation of a Revolutionary Tribunal, to de-theatricalize justice. To their dismay, however, the Jacobins' efforts to protect justice from the theatricality at the heart of the liberal vision and in the hearts of masked traitors were widely seen, then as now, as steps in the opposite direction. Reviving prior restrictions on lawyers, witnesses, judges, and oral debates came across, in a public trial, as a heavy-handed scheme by the government to stage-manage the performance of justice so as to ensure it followed a prewritten script with a fixed ending. In an ironic twist, the more the Jacobins tried to de-theatricalize justice, the more it appeared theatrical! This book thus offers fresh insights into the rise and fall of the Terror by resituating both within a wider history: the search, ongoing to this day, for a theater-proof performance of justice.

A Closing Argument: The Panacea of Reenactment

To be clear: while I challenge prevailing narratives to contend that the theater became increasingly judicial and justice increasingly theatrical in the eighteenth century, I do not wish to make reductive generalizations about the nature of justice or theater—for instance, that all justice is theatrical, or all theater judicial, or even that the two became identical during the Revolution. Rather than conflating justice and theater by means of a tired metaphor, I seek to chart a parallel evolution in both realms, one that reveals similar struggles with, and solutions to, the new kinds of challenges raised by the growing popularity of liberal principles in the eighteenth century. More specifically, this book constantly returns to a key anxiety, then as now, at the heart of liberal thought—namely, that the desire to open all institutions to greater public supervision and democratic participation might rob them of their legitimacy by transforming them into purely theatrical spectacles. Hence, in the dramatic realm, plays that denounced current events and individuals satisfied the liberal longing for transparency and public engagement in ongoing affairs, but raised the specter, if their theatricality could not be contained, of groundless accusations, endless scandals and conflicts, and popular insurrections. Likewise, in the legal realm, the inclusion of spectators, lawyers, and live, oral debates fulfilled the same liberal ideals, yet introduced an essential theatricality into the courtroom and, with it, the threat of celebrity lawyers, illegitimate judges, and a lawsuit culture.

In the tribunal as in the theater, then, one finds the same anxiety, born of the thin line between publicity and theatricality. Indeed, both realms struggled with the same underlying challenge: how to perform justice without having it seem *just* a performance. And not surprisingly, both settled on the same solution: reenactment—a new conception of performance free from the lies and artificiality of mimesis. This dream of a nontheatrical performance, able to resurrect, and not just represent, an event or conflict, took on different forms, but it is the similarities of their ambitions that speak the loudest.

They speak of a desire for legitimizing rituals in a period usually known for undermining them. They speak, too, of the anxiety produced by a world governed by representation and public opinion, in which power depends not on the foliage of one's genealogical tree but on the persuasiveness of one's acting. They speak, lastly, of the longing to reduce, or at least disguise, the theatricality at the core of the liberal worldview, without sacrificing its greatest gift: publicity.

Impossible as a perfect reenactment—a truly nontheatrical performance—may be (something Diderot, its earliest theorist, acknowledges in *Le Fils naturel*), the dream of it contributed in ways previously unknown to the development of drama and justice in France. It inspired eighteenth-century thinkers to explore the limits of performance, resulting in some fascinating projects—imagine a theater without actors, spectators, or playwrights, or a legal system without lawyers, judges, or laws—that broadened the traditional conception of theater and justice and enabled lasting innovations. In fact, even the unattainability of a perfect reenactment should not be seen as a negative. By making it impossible to ignore the theatricality intrinsic to any performance—indeed, to any public, participative system—it encouraged the pursuit of a new equilibrium, one that acknowledged the necessity of theatricality, while at the same time seeking to control it. This delicate equilibrium is one that France continues to pursue today, as seen in recent debates, inspired by the influence of the far more theatrical American legal system, on whether and how to restrict the spread of a lawsuit culture, the playacting of celebrity-obsessed lawyers, and the impact on justice of mass media, notably of reality TV shows in the style of *Judge Judy*[43]—all phenomena, I argue, that find their roots in the eighteenth century.

PART I

Theater as Justice

Chapter 1

Fixing the Law

Reenactment in Diderot's *Fils naturel*

A New Performance for a New Time

Theater is out of the question, explains Dorval's father, Lysimond: "The point is not to erect a stage here, but to preserve the memory of an event that touches us, and to render it just as it first happened. . . . Every year we would recreate it ourselves, in this house, in this living room. What we once said, we would say again."[1] To satisfy this strange request, Dorval agrees to write *Le Fils naturel*, a dramatic work recounting the nascent love between Dorval and Rosalie, the wife-to-be of Clairville, Dorval's closest friend, the two lovers' decision to sacrifice their happiness in the name of friendship, and the startling revelation by Lysimond, returned propitiously after years abroad, that Dorval and Rosalie are actually his children and thus half-siblings. This unexpected disclosure dispels any lingering lust, jealousy, and distrust by retroactively convincing Dorval and Rosalie that their attraction for each other was little more than a sense of kinship and by binding the four main protagonists in perfectly symmetrical marital ties (Clairville is betrothed to Rosalie, Dorval's sister, just as Dorval is to marry Constance, Clairville's sister). The family now steadied by his presence, Lysimond demands that his children immortalize both the transgression (the incestuous love) that nearly tore them apart and his victory over it, synonymous with the restoration of the father's law, by means of a yearly reenactment so accurate that the family members repeat the same gestures and speeches, in the same setting (Clairville's living room) and in the same clothes as they had in reality. Yet Lysimond dies before the first performance, and his replacement, an old friend swaddled in his clothes, triggers such intense distress by reminding the other performers of their deceased father that they find themselves unable to continue. This incomplete performance is witnessed by a single beholder, hidden, unbeknownst to all but Dorval, behind a set of curtains. This state of concealment, together with the performance's realism, prompts him to surrender to such a powerful illusion that, forgetting he is just a spectator, he experiences the need to interact directly with the people and events before him.

So inventive and provocative is the performance dreamed up by Diderot, the real author of *Le Fils naturel*, that even modern readers may be surprised at the boldness of its innovations. Several influential studies, on subjects extending from dramaturgy and scenography to acting and reception, have shown the novelty of the reforms illustrated by the fictitious performance of *Le Fils naturel*.[2] Yet one of the performance's most striking innovations—its reenactment of very recent events—has failed to generate comparable interest, despite constituting a deliberate violation of classical dogma.[3] The notion that the theater could recreate as accurately as possible a contemporary incident has usually been portrayed, with good reason, as another one of Diderot's famous thought experiments, designed to see how close to reality one could bring the stage and its conventions. As we will see, however, reenactment soon grew into much more than just an abstract case study on the limits of realism. Over the next fifty years, there would appear countless plays reproducing current events and people on stage, as well as multiple projects seeking to go further still by turning Lysimond's dream (including his radical rejection of professional actors, aesthetically minded spectators, and artistic invention) into a national institution. The popularity of reenactment in the second half of the eighteenth century suggests that the unusual first performance of *Le Fils naturel*, so easily dismissed as fantastical or purely theoretical, ought to be taken seriously and regarded as the earliest illustration of a new kind of performance, closer to ritual than theater.

Before delving deeper into Diderot's text, it may prove worthwhile to reflect on possible contributing factors to the rise of an increasingly keen attraction for the reenactment of recent events. Without wishing to assign a single cause to a complex evolution, I contend that the interest in staging current events reflects a broader transformation in the Western world's relationship to the past, which also took place, according to Reinhart Koselleck, in the second half of the eighteenth century.[4] Although the bulk of Koselleck's evidence is drawn from early modern historiography, it highlights a shift in the perception of time that is equally pertinent to a new understanding of the evolution of eighteenth-century theater.[5] From the classical metaphor of *historia magistra vitae* (history is the teacher of life), as well as from other, largely semantic phenomena, Koselleck concludes that the seventeenth century experienced time as a cyclical process, comparable to the natural succession of seasons and regal dynasties. The past was understood as a vast reservoir of reiterated and reiterable events drawn from a plurality of individual histories (rather than one History) from which readers were expected to draw lessons through the recognition of parallels with their own situations. Such a model of history rested on an implicit faith in a continuous space of potential experience, as well as in the constancy of human nature, insofar as it posited a relationship between the past and the present that was less one of causality than it was one of analogy.

Starting in the middle of the eighteenth century, however, under the influence of Diderot and other *Encyclopédistes*, a new philosophy of history emerged, one in which the immediate past and the present were but preparations for a radically different future, unpredictable and yet predictably better. This conception of progress transformed the perception of time from a cyclical structure to a linear one. Because progress implied the existence of a driving force subjecting time itself to a constant renewal, it prompted a new relationship between the past and the future, in which the latter no longer resembled or repeated the former but opened up instead on an indeterminable horizon and a completely new experiential space. Accordingly, while the distant past lost much of its exemplary value, the immediate past acquired a new relevance, both as an indication of the accomplishments and direction of progress and as a lingering near present that needed to be worked through, its flaws highlighted, judged, and condemned, so that a new, better future could be set free. Indeed, as Koselleck notes, the *Encyclopédistes* often expressed the desire to "accelerate" the Enlightenment, with the result that even the most recent past became something to be exceeded, even exorcised.[6]

This shift in the conception of time appears to have influenced the representation and intended function of the past in eighteenth-century theater in much the same way it transformed the writing and meaning of historiography. Indeed, if classical rules opposed the dramatization of events taken from the nation's history, it was because theorists such as d'Aubignac, drawing heavily on Aristotle's *Poetics*,[7] deemed the preservation of a temporal divide between the spectators and the characters to be essential to the pedagogical aims of the theater. Historical events, especially recent ones, risked eliciting from the spectators an unmediated, visceral involvement in the particularities of the story (the domain of history, according to Aristotle) likely to prevent them from extracting more universal lessons and philosophical truths (the domain of poetry). Similarly, the settings of classical plays were deliberately kept indeterminate[8]—generic even—to encourage the spectators to view the world on stage not as a reenactment of a specific historical moment but rather as a universal, timeless space.[9] On the classical stage, as in classical historiography, events were thus never portrayed as links in a linear chain bridging the past and the present, but were depicted instead as eternal examples of political or ethical dilemmas bearing an analogical bond with those of the present. The utility of the theater (and of historiography) depended therefore on the spectators' ability to recognize these points of contiguity, identify the universal, atemporal laws illustrated by the story and then apply this knowledge in such a way as to enhance or reduce, as the case may be, the likelihood of a repetition of the play's outcome in their own time.

In the middle of the eighteenth century, this reflective relationship to the events on stage yielded increasingly to a more unmediated, emotional response, contingent on the spectator's immediate recognition of a basic identity between his own world and that of the stage. To quote Alain Ménil, the spectator's perspective shifted from "it's the same for me" to "it *is* me"—in other words, from a primarily analogical experience to a more direct involvement in the world of the play.[10] Promoting this experience of unity was the increasing realism of stage settings and costumes, as dramatists and decorators progressively redefined the space of representation from an atemporal, generic world to a fragment of the world inhabited by the audience. The rise of reenactments fits perfectly into that evolution, taking it, in fact, to its logical conclusion. By drawing their content from contemporary events, they achieve precisely what Mercier lamented classical tragedy, with its analogical conception of the past, could not: "History, from which the pompous tragedy emanates, is for the masses an effect without a cause; they do not see the connections."[11] Unlike classical plays, reenactments reveal causal relationships between the immediate past and the present. They allow the performers to reexperience their own role in a recent event, gain new insights into its sometimes-hidden roots, and reflect on its continued impact. And when they have spectators, reenactments seek less to impart universal laws to them than to enable them to actively intervene in and pass judgment on contemporary events, and in so doing shape their meaning and assign them a place in the linear narrative of history.

The shift toward a perception of time as linear and unpredictable thus likely contributed to the emergence of reenactments in one obvious way: by making the immediate past seem of the utmost relevance and worthy therefore of being dramatized. Yet the popularity of reenactments may also be linked to this shift in a different way—less as a symptom of it than as a remedy against it. The linear conception of time inevitably induces a certain anxiety, for it presents the future as experientially different from anything that preceded it, and for that reason, as impossible to predict and prepare. Transgressions become all the more alarming in light of the future's uncertainty. They belie the narrative of progress and raise the possibility that the perception of time as a force of constant and accelerating renewal will weaken longstanding laws and beliefs, leading to social chaos and collapse. Lysimond's reenactment is a response to precisely such a threat (incest) to his family's unity. Its aim is permanence: an end to the mercurial movement of time, synonymous with loss and difference (hence Lysimond's request that there be no acting, artistic invention, or outside spectators—nothing that could differentiate the reenactment from the event). By renewing year after year the judicial act (the prohibition of incest) through which Lysimond founded a united family, the reenactment seeks to bestow immortality to the patriarch and his law, thereby providing his descendants with the security of an everlasting stillness. Diderot deliberately pushes Lysimond's project beyond the limits of tenability, however, less to discredit it than to allow another conception of reenactment to emerge from its collapse. In this alternative model, reenactment ceases to be an instrument of fixity, wielded by a patriarch to enact his law, and becomes the very opposite: a way for members of a community to confront a recent transgression, reassess it, and gain control over it by playing (with) and amending their own roles within it, in an attempt to find forgiveness, or at least understanding and resolution. This second type of reenactment is easier to reconcile with the notions of linear time and progress, for it seeks to move beyond a transgression once and for all, not through the constant renewal of it and of its prohibition, but by the collective elaboration of new rules and values best able to free a new future from the shackles of the past. Through a single performance, then, Diderot identifies two very different kinds of reenactment, with nearly opposite views on the passage of both time and laws.

Fixing the Father's Law: Making It (and Him) Eternal

Let us begin by examining the first type of reenactment, as envisioned by Lysimond. From the start, the project bears witness both to his awareness of the looming specter of death (though he misjudges its proximity, promising that he would participate in the reenactment "once before dying") and to his refusal to surrender quietly to this fate.[12] Thanks to the reenactment, he tells Dorval, "I would survive myself, and go on and converse thus, generation after generation, with all of my descendants."[13] In Lysimond's vision, Dorval's and Rosalie's children, and their children's children, and their children's children's children, and so on ad infinitum will grow up watching the yearly reenactment—indeed, they will be its only spectators—until they are old enough to assume the role of their ancestors. More than simply, as Lysimond first suggests, preserving the *memory* of an important event, an objective that concedes implicitly the existence of a "before" and "after," the reenactment thus seeks to abolish time itself by bringing together the present members of the family and their posterity. It aims to continually reactivate the past in the present, precluding the possibility of a future in which Lysimond has ceased to exist and to rule.

This spectral quality of mimesis—its ability to give an otherworldly intransience to that which it represents—was primarily associated in the eighteenth century with the art of painting, which was deemed to possess, of all art forms, the closest relationship to the things themselves and therefore the greatest capacity to immortalize them. Many of the most influential aesthetic thinkers of the eighteenth century, including Jean-Baptiste Dubos, Edmund Burke, and Gotthold Ephraim Lessing, agreed that painting came closest to an unmediated transposition of reality, because it employed natural signs, affecting the senses of the beholder directly and requiring therefore little interpretative or imaginative exertion. Diderot largely agreed with such views, drawing heavily in his *Salons* from Burke's *Philosophical Enquiry into the Origin of Our Ideas of the Sublime and Beautiful*, although only after Burke had himself borrowed several ideas in his *Philosophical Enquiry* from Diderot's own *Lettre sur les sourds et muets*.[14] This letter is important, as it marks the first time that Diderot reflected on the differences between the visual and discursive arts, noting that if the former benefited from being straightforwardly representational ("painting shows the object itself"), this could also prove limiting, both for the artists, who unlike poets were restricted to the depiction of a unique moment, and for the beholders, who risked finding that such a precise art hampered their imaginations.[15] Hence, even before turning his attention to *Le Fils naturel*, Diderot had already discerned the principal elements in the opposition between painting and poetry on which Lessing's famous *Laocoon* would rest.

Diderot was thus well aware of the failings of painting as a support for a true reactivation of the past. To be sure, painting's spatiality afforded it a clear advantage over poetry, in that it rendered possible the resurrection of a given individual in a single image, thereby allowing its beholders to experience a multiplicity of characteristics, from distinct body parts to accouterment and stature, as they would in reality: all at once. Yet if poetry, limited in its descriptions by the successiveness of speech, could offer no such synchronicity, it could in return express the passage of time and seemed therefore better suited to the portrayal of the changing moral and physical states that together constitute a human life. Moreover, the greatest strength of painting—its ability to fix in tangible signs the outward appearance of a deceased being—also represented one of its principal weaknesses, as it struggled to match the capacity of poetry to convey through abstract signs the temperament and inner life of its subjects. Diderot attempted to address the first failing of painting (its inability to express time) in the opening pages of his *Essais sur la peinture* by advocating the creation of an academy in which aspiring painters could become acquainted with real people of various rank, wealth, and age, in lieu of paid models playing the part, as actors do, of priests, peasants, and noblemen. The painters would then be trained to identify and replicate the diverse marks on the body that signal their subjects' experiences: "the professor will take care to point out the accidents that daily functions, lifestyle, condition, and age have introduced in these forms."[16] This proposed amendment to portraiture, both in terms of the selection of its subjects and the realism of their portrayal, is reminiscent of Diderot's recommendation that the theater aspire to the faithful representation of "conditions"—that is, a character's profession, rank, or domestic role—in lieu of the generic personality traits that traditionally defined the protagonists of classical comedy. These proposals testify to Diderot's desire for artistic forms able to communicate the diverse ways in which one's identity is constructed in time—a diachronic conception of being at odds with the more deterministic interpretation of identity implied by classical comedy's fascination with immutable character traits. Indeed, Diderot suggested that reforming the art of portraiture might one day allow it to capture not only a unique moment but an entire life, to the extent that the mere sight of a body part would be enough for a connoisseur not only to identify the present occupation and age of the depicted individual but also to intuit his or her past experiences, joys, and sufferings.[17]

Nevertheless, Diderot remained skeptical of painting's ability to condense an entire lifetime into a single image, in part due to its limitations when contending with the subtle, ever-changing inner life of its subjects. Staring at his own portrait by Louis-Michel van Loo in 1767, he regretfully acknowledged that the artist had failed to satisfy the very same ideal that Lysimond had set for his own artistic commission—to serve as a medium for a conversation between himself and his descendants: "But what will my grandchildren say, when they come to compare my drab works with this cheerful, charming, effeminate, old dandy? I warn you, my children, it isn't me."[18] Diderot added that this failed attempt at intergenerational communication grew less from the painter's ineptitude than from the art of painting itself, which could not faithfully recreate the hundreds of fleeting emotions and the resulting physiognomies that together constitute a person. To communicate the changeability at the center of his being, Diderot felt it necessary to supplement van Loo's static representation with a discursive description of the characteristics (his energy, temperament, and sensibility) he perceived to be lacking from the portrait. Hence, while Diderot the reformer pursued the dream of a form of painting capable of conveying the passage of time, Diderot the art critic seemingly reached the conclusion that only a synthesis of visual and discursive elements could successfully spark in its beholder the genuine experience of knowing a person, insofar as such knowledge depends as much on visual as on linguistic cues.

This conclusion lies at the very center of Lysimond's project. Indeed, immediately after declaring his desire for immortality, Lysimond calls attention to the benefits of a multifaceted representation, in contrast with the more limited resources of portraiture: "Do you not think, Dorval, that a work that would pass down our own ideas, our true sentiments, the speeches we made during one of the most important occasions in our lives, would be more valuable than *family portraits, who show of us but one moment of our face.*"[19] Although Lysimond's argument reiterates the standard opposition between poetry and painting, it simultaneously undercuts it by introducing a third term, the theater, an art form occupying at once the domain of painting (space) and of poetry (time) and consisting therefore of a hitherto unexploited medium through which to preserve the past. In so doing, Lysimond echoes a vital, if undeveloped, insight of Remond de Sainte-Albine, perhaps the first Frenchman to assign drama a resurrective mission. Indeed, in his *Comédien* of 1747, Sainte-Albine praises the theater for its ability to breathe life into family portraits by lending them the exercise of speech and action, the two pillars of poetry: "In vain does painting boast of making canvas breathe. Only inanimate creations emerge from its hands. By contrast, dramatic poetry gives ideas and sentiments to the beings it engenders, and, with the help of playacting, lends them speech and action."[20] Such a synthesis of painting and poetry improves upon both art forms by providing the spectators with a truly lifelike experience, insofar as it appeals to all their senses: "Our imagination is almost always forced to compensate for the powerlessness of the other imitative arts. Only the actor's art demands no supplement from us."[21]

This understanding of the theater as a sequence of animated paintings constitutes a significant rupture with the classical model, one that Sainte-Albine intuits but leaves largely unexplored.[22] Diderot pursues this insight further, identifying the tableau as one of the keystones of an improved, resurrective theater. As Dorval puts it, "if a play were well made and performed, the stage would offer the spectator as many real tableaux as there are for a painter favorable moments in the story."[23] In these favorable (read: poignant) moments, Dorval proposes that speech and action be suspended, so as to compel the audience to focus its attention on the performers' bodies, on which can be seen the physical signs of the sincerity and intensity of their emotions (in Diderot's examples, almost always anguish at a witnessed or anticipated loss). Such signs, ranging from tears and groans to outright convulsions, incarnate for Diderot the last surviving examples of Étienne Bonnot de Condillac's *langage d'action*, a set of gestures and unarticulated sounds that precede the appearance of speech in both the development of the individual and of the species.[24] Because such gestures and sounds are universal and natural, they communicate emotions directly, without the mediation and sequentiality imposed by language. Frozen, like a tableau, in a state prior to articulation, such transparent signs possess the ability to bridge the gap between the characters' and the spectators' respective times, insofar as they trigger an emotional experience in the audience that is at once simultaneous and identical to the one felt by the characters on stage. Indeed, for Dorval, such is the superiority of the theater over both the visual and discursive arts that it can realistically convey, through the exercise of speech and action, the passage of time within the space of representation, even as it negates, through the inclusion of poignant tableaux, the effects of time outside of it. This dual relationship to time increases the likelihood that the spectators will experience the past events recreated before them as actually happening in the present—an experience that is precisely the aim of a reenactment.

Its aim, but also its precondition—indeed, for a reenactment to be successful, its creator must first undergo the very same experience. Dorval discovers this upon attempting to compose one of the most poignant scenes in *Le Fils naturel.* Drawing upon his theatrical erudition, he produces a string of grandiloquent homilies so deeply lacking in truth and emotion that they prompt Clairville to propose a new creative process: "all that's needed is to place oneself back in the situation and then listen to oneself."[25] By casting himself back into the past, Clairville yields to a genuine emotion, prompting him to uncover the primitive, unarticulated language of gestures, approvingly described by Dorval as "nature's tone."[26] The resulting scene, consisting of a tableau and a lengthy pantomime, is almost entirely lacking in speech, save for some monosyllabic exclamations and a few halting declarations. Clairville's self-resurrection thus ensures that lived experiences dictate both the spoken and the body language of the participants, in accordance with Lysimond's request for a performance indistinguishable from the event it reenacts. It would be difficult if not impossible to overstate the impact and originality of Diderot's promotion of lived experiences as an acting method, at a time when rigid conventions forbade players from kneeling, running, throwing themselves on the floor, raising their hands above their heads, turning their backs to the audience, or even exiting the small lighted space in the foreground of the stage.[27] Thanks to its proximity to actual events, still fresh in the memory of its participants, a reenactment is more likely than other types of performances, according to Diderot, to instill both writers and performers with the insight and the confidence necessary to break free from the unnatural conventions of classical theater.

Clairville's creative process is indeed just as applicable to performance as it is to composition. According to Diderot, performers, like writers, should draw simplicity and truth from an innate sensibility, as well as from a related talent without which "one cannot do anything worthwhile": the gift of self-alienation.[28] In later texts, notably his *Paradoxe sur le comédien*, Diderot would famously disavow the theory of creative self-alienation, at least with regards to theatrical performances, during which actors are not to feel but only feign.[29] In fact, *Le Paradoxe* also includes a repudiation of reenactments, when one of the protagonists defends the "protocol of the old Aeschylus," according to which a play must never draw its subject matter from a recent event, for fear that it might stir too intense an emotion.[30] When he wrote *Les Entretiens*, however, and for several years afterward, Diderot still valued creative self-alienation as an acting method, as evidenced by his praise of the young actress Mademoiselle Jodin for having been blessed with "a soul prone to alienation, that feels deeply, that transports itself to the play's setting, that becomes such and such, that sees and speaks to this or that character."[31] This gift makes it possible for performers like Mademoiselle Jodin to forget themselves as actors and identify completely with their characters—a feat that would be even easier, naturally, were they asked, like participants in a reenactment, to play themselves. Indeed, just as there is no artistic invention, no playwriting (understood as a technical, mediated act), but instead the transparent transcription of a lived experience, there is no acting in *Le Fils naturel.* Dorval and his kin identify with their former selves, losing sight of their current situation and causing the coincidence between past and present that Lysimond so desired. Sainte-Albine had intuited this—"The painter can only represent events. The actor, in a way, repeats and reproduces them"—but Lysimond goes further still.[32] In his eyes, in the same way that bread and wine do not stand for flesh and blood during a Catholic mass but actually become them, Dorval and his family are genuinely transformed into their former selves for the duration of the performance. Hence, for Lysimond, reenactments do more than simply repeat or reproduce a recent event (two concepts that distinguish between an original and a replica and thus implicitly concede the existence of time and difference), they truly resurrect it, halting thereby the very movement of time.

This sacramental conception of performance explains why the standard practice of holding repetitions is wholly absent from *Le Fils naturel* and the ensuing *Entretiens.* Truth be told, theatrical "repetitions" are improperly named, for while the term suggests sameness and stillness, the practice actually rests on a belief in progress, since it connects the achievement of mastery over body and text to a series, not of identical performances, but of steadily improving ones. Such an evolutive framework puts repetition at odds with Clairville's definition of artistic creation as a spontaneous, unmediated resurrection.[33] In fact, self-alienation stands at the very opposite extreme from self-mastery, the former relying on sensibility and identity, the latter, on reflection and difference. Accordingly, Diderot instructs Mademoiselle Jodin to forego private repetitions in front of a mirror, on the grounds that they are likely to direct her attention onto her exterior, thereby prompting her to attempt to exercise a rational mastery over her body, when it is her innate ability to achieve an internal coincidence with the character that ought to dictate her every movement.[34] Not only does repetition presume a faith in progress in strict opposition with spontaneity and fixity, the two principal characteristics, according to Lysimond, of the reenactive paradigm, it also promotes a fragmenting of the self—precisely that which *Le Fils naturel* seeks to prevent. Indeed, just as Dorval and his kin need not, in Lysimond's eyes, hold any repetitions in preparation for their roles, the performance is itself not a repetition, but a resurrection of the original event, with the result that the participants' experience is one not of division but of fusion with their former selves. It is clear, therefore, that *Le Fils naturel* does not originate from Lysimond's longing for repetition, as is commonly believed, but from the very opposite emotion, his dread of repetition—synonymous, in his mind, with change and fragmentation.

Nowhere is Lysimond's fear of repetition more evident than in the second justification he offers for his reenactment (the first being his desire for immortality): "Ah! my son, I never look at Rosalie without shuddering at the danger you faced. The more I see her, the more honest and beautiful I find her, and the more this danger seems grave to me. But the heavens that watch over us today may abandon us tomorrow."[35] Repetition thus poses a grave threat to the family, for several reasons. It cultivates and spreads illicit desires, as evidenced by Lysimond's use of the iterative "more" to describe the progression within him of a feeling toward his daughter alarmingly close to Dorval's own incestuous longings (the more he sees her, the more beautiful he finds her). As James Creech has noted, in fact, the incest within the play is itself the product of a love of repetition—more specifically, Dorval and Rosalie's desire to find in the other a mirror image of themselves.[36] Lastly—and Lysimond makes clear that this is the greatest danger—the concept of repetition opens up the possibility, if the classical perception of time is to be believed, that old conflicts and divisive desires (such as incest) will return in the future.

In view of Lysimond's fear of repetition, his decision to stage the past anew, notably by forcing future generations of innocent children to recreate the forbidden love between Dorval and Rosalie, may seem illogical. As Mona Ozouf has observed about the commemorative festivals of the French Revolution, however, ritualized reactivations of the past always constitute, along with an homage, a form of exorcism.[37] Commemorations often celebrate a foundational event, a fabled instance of harmony at the start of a new society. The event to be honored only works as a foundation, however, if it marks a rupture with a prior state of imperfection. Hence, for a commemoration to truly revive such an event, it must replicate the moment of rupture itself—a difficult feat it achieves by summoning the specter of past threats, but only in order to exorcize them promptly. Commemorations therefore provide a means to gain mastery over a distressful past, since they resurrect the precise event by which it was made past and thus denied persistence in the present. The same can be said of Lysimond's reenactment of the birth of a united family. Future generations will be compelled to experience incestuous desires vicariously, in the controlled setting of a ritualistic performance, so that Lysimond, whose absence nearly let an incestuous relationship occur in real life, may be eternally present, thanks to the reenactment, to forbid such perilous desires—thereby punishing and purging the very threat that he himself has revived. Indeed, as Lysimond reveals when he portrays his reenactment less as a celebration of unity than as a safeguard against past disunity, the act of resurrecting the foundation of a community is always partly synonymous with the transmission of a prohibition, that is, with the imposition of an external order on which the survival of the community depends.

In addition to the disunity that preceded the father's prohibition (the family's past, which continues, from the margins of history, to threaten its harmony), the performance of *Le Fils naturel* also seeks to exorcise the inevitable decline that will follow (the family's future) when the current state of domestic concord is rocked by the loss of the legislator responsible for engendering it: Lysimond. Indeed, as we saw earlier, Lysimond presents the reenactment as a way to triumph over his imminent death. In *Framed Narratives: Diderot's Genealogy of the Beholder*, Jay Caplan argues that the tableau operates in Diderot's aesthetics in much the same way a fetish does in psychoanalysis, insofar as both seek to suspend a painful loss by freezing the final moments before it in a fixed image: "the tableau in Diderot is a sort of fetishistic snapshot in which the transitoriness of the real world is magically transformed into an ideal fixity."[38] This particular operation is also at work in the first performance of *Le Fils naturel*, which seeks to exorcise the specter of death and disorder by ceaselessly resurrecting the state of domestic totality and equilibrium that preceded it. For Lysimond, reenactments are thus meant to serve two functions—first, to forestall the future, and second, to exorcize the past—with the result that their participants are left with an eternally fixed present, a state of harmony in which the father and his law reign supreme.

Fixing the Father's Law: Correcting It and the Future

Diderot does not, however, share Lysimond's faith in the capacity of reenactments to grant immortality to the father and his law. Indeed, as the epilogue teaches us, the father's prohibition against incest is never decreed during the first performance of *Le Fils naturel*, as the appearance of the old man tasked with replacing the defunct Lysimond provokes a stream of tears and prompts the play to be suspended before Lysimond (the character) has the opportunity to speak. This interruption has traditionally been interpreted as evidence of Diderot's awareness that no performance, however lifelike, can ever truly bridge the gap between reality and fiction.[39] As the sole "actor" in the performance, Lysimond's stand-in inadvertently reveals to Dorval and his kin that they too are participating in a fiction, with the result that they find themselves cast back into a fatherless reality—a disillusion rendered all the more upsetting by the fact that it closely follows a brief instant in which the family members, having identified with their characters, sincerely believed that the real Lysimond had entered the room. For many scholars, Béatrice Didier among them, the suspension of the performance signals Diderot's abandonment of the reenactive dream and foreshadows the central arguments of *Le Paradoxe*: "*Le Fils naturel*, like *Le Paradoxe*, are demonstrations of the need for a distanciation: the actors cannot be the individuals who lived through the tragedy."[40] Incompleteness need not signify failure, however, and certainly was unlikely to carry such a stigma for Diderot, a lifelong advocate, as we will see, of the indeterminate and *non finito* in art. While the first performance of *Le Fils naturel* calls into question the achievability of the principal qualities—permanence, stability, and order—attributed by Lysimond to reenactments, in no way does it indicate that Diderot had, by the end of *Le Fils naturel*, lost faith in the value of proximity, be it between actors and characters or between staged and current events. In fact, in his description of the play's first performance, Diderot not only draws attention to the incapacity of reenactments to halt the movement of time, he also transforms this apparent weakness into one of their greatest strengths—the capacity to exhibit time itself and in so doing interact with it.

Indeed, it is paradoxically the act of reenacting, intended to negate the passage of time, that ultimately gives it its visibility, in the same way that a sign always points to the absence it is meant to fill. The appearance of the faux father leads the participants to experience the passage of time directly, prompting them to discover the nonidentity of their present and former selves, as well as the impossibility of resurrecting the past. They are forced to confront, as never before, their own historicity. This experience of the world's and of one's own mutability is impressed all the more effectively on Dorval and his family because it belongs to the very essence of the theater. Unlike a portrait, a play exists only in the moment of its performance, each time in a unique form, as every production inevitably differs from the previous ones—a fluidity that becomes particularly apparent when a performer dies, as in *Le Fils naturel.* Those who, like Lysimond, value reenactments as a means of reviving the past naturally seek to reduce this variability, which they regard as the price to pay for the unsurpassed physicality and "presentness" of the theater. Yet such mutability need not be perceived in strictly negative terms, as it makes it possible for dramatic works to evolve with the passage of time, to an extent unmatched by any other art forms. In the actors' eyes, as well as in the spectators', never is a play complete in the way that a painting or a poem is. This principle holds especially true for Diderot's time, when it was still standard practice for members of the parterre to interrupt the play with boos, along with more specific instructions (such as the cry, "cut, cut"), so as to indicate to the playwright and actors the alterations required before the next performance.[41] Such a direct involvement reveals, in addition to the spectators' awareness of the theater's mutability, their embrace of it as a means to adapt dramatic performances to their present needs and desires. In the eighteenth century, far more than today, theater lovers—not only spectators but also actors, dramatists, and theorists—simply did not regard plays (understood here as both a written text and a performance) as fixed and finalized works of art, like a painting, but rather as constantly evolving, collaborative creations. Perhaps the best expression of this can be found in the widely praised (albeit never realized) proposal by the abbé de Saint-Pierre to devise a formal process through which old plays could be continually rewritten to reflect the customs and expectations of each new generation.[42]

Indeed, if the theater's changeability makes it more vulnerable to loss (such as the disappearance of a beloved performer), it also makes it more susceptible to revision. Even in the absence of spectators, the performance of a play can fundamentally alter its content and meaning. For instance, from a celebration of plenitude and constancy, *Le Fils naturel* becomes, before the end of its first performance, a mourning ritual. In its new function, it memorializes the recently deceased in much the same way a funeral rite does—less in hope of preserving the deceased's presence in the here and now than in order to draw a clear distinction between the dead and the living and thus between the past and the present. Indeed, the first performance of *Le Fils naturel* not only displays Lysimond's absence as a performer, it also erases his character from the text, a second, symbolic death that indicates a broader repudiation of the values the father incarnates—law, order, and fixity. Moreover, the absence of Lysimond's character transforms the meaning of the performance from a dogmatic prohibition of incest to a moving illustration of the power of friendship and virtue to overcome perilous passions (since Dorval and Rosalie triumphed over their feelings before even knowing their love was incestuous—a shocking truth they never discover in the abridged performance). *Le Fils naturel* thus exemplifies in a single work a more general evolution in the second half of the eighteenth century, which saw the standard fictional plot (notably in novels) shift from a narrative built around the father and his law to one in which a family of equals is created through love and self-sacrifice—what Lynn Hunt has called "the family romance of fraternity."[43] This transformation in the reenactment's content—from the fixed law of the father to the collective and fluid virtue of the family—brings about a similar change in its function. Lysimond's *Fils naturel* sought to enforce a strict obedience to timeless laws and as a result prohibited artistic creation, outside participation, and any other attempts to alter the performance and its meaning. By contrast, in the abridged version, the unity and purity of future generations depend on convincing individuals through a moral exemplar (like that of Dorval and Rosalie) to willingly sacrifice their own desires to the common good. The focus is not on permanence but on personal and collective growth—in other words, on an understanding of change as progress, rather than as a deviation from a fixed ideal. As a result, whereas Lysimond longed for the flawless resurrection in the present of a moment from the family's past, thus erasing all that preceded and followed it, Diderot comes to value reenactments as a way for participants and spectators alike to reexperience past actions and transgressive desires, acquire moral insights into them, and collectively rewrite their own pasts to better fit the needs and values of the present.

The extraordinary premiere that Diderot invents for his *Fils naturel* thus brings to light a conception of reenactment so markedly different from Lysimond's that their principal features stand in perfect opposition. As noted earlier, Lysimond's project springs from his belief that his family's unity is threatened by an absence (his imminent demise). This fear causes him to try to negate the lack through a reenactment that is not only fixed but also complete, thanks to the theater's unique ability to unfold in space as well as in time. In this alleged totality, Lysimond hopes to find a sanctuary from the incompleteness and inconsistency of the real world. The first performance of

Le Fils naturel demonstrates, however, that the theater is itself inhabited by the same lack, that it is, in fact, the art form least conducive to permanence. A dramatic performance can never fully negate the passage of time, because it too is altered by it, with the result that it always points, far more explicitly than a painting or a poem, to the very absence it seeks to fill. This is especially true of reenactments, whose proximity to reality has the paradoxical effect of accentuating the inevitable disparity between the past and the present. In fact, in foregrounding its own variability and indeterminacy, a reenactment reflects, better than any other art form, the nascent perception of time as a process of constant and unpredictable renewal. In many instances, as in *Le Fils naturel*, it even cultivates this perception in its participants, by prompting them to experience the recent past as a constitutive yet irretrievable part of the present, needing to be understood, judged, and worked through, before one can move forward. In this conception of reenactments, a lack is not perceived solely as a loss, but also as an invitation for both participants and spectators to complete the performance themselves by altering and rearranging elements of the past, and in so doing create a different performance—and a different future.

Much indicates, indeed, that Diderot neither desired nor deemed possible a truly complete art form, even going so far as to argue that "a poet who finishes everything . . . turns his back on nature."[44] Even before *Le Fils naturel*, he had tempered his praise for the visual arts with the warning that too flawless a reproduction risked hindering the spectator's imagination: "How is it possible that of the three arts that imitate nature, the one with the most arbitrary and least precise expression speaks the most intensely to the soul? Could it be that, showing objects less, it leaves more freedom to our imagination?"[45] Such a warning must have seemed particularly pertinent to the theater, the sole art form with the capacity to show objects as they appear in reality—at once in space and in time. As we saw, it was this very capacity that appealed to early advocates of reenactments, for it strengthened their faith in the possibility of a transition from imitation to reality, as illustrated in the following, sequential praise of the theater: "It is no longer an image, it is a portrait; it is even more: it is the object itself, the original."[46] A performance of this type, insofar as it claims to present reality, rather than represent it, demands of its spectators nothing less than complete belief, thus restricting the exercise of their creative faculties. Sainte-Albine had embraced precisely this unimaginative response when he noted approvingly that only the theater required no "supplement" from its viewers.[47] Diderot, however, condemns it, on the grounds that without imagination "one is neither a poet, nor a philosopher, nor a man of culture, nor a reasonable being, nor even a man."[48] Evidently, imagination consists for Diderot of a faculty with tremendous range, to such a degree, in fact, that he provides a vast array of definitions, reflecting the diversity of his interests (physiology, aesthetics, and sensationalist philosophy, to name only a few). Among these definitions, Margaret Gilman has identified several common traits, which taken together reveal a largely coherent vision of imagination as an active process of image combination, in contrast with memory, which Diderot defines as a purely reproductive and thus passive faculty.[49] The principal attribute of imagination is therefore its creativity, as it brings forth unique productions, unlike even the objects that inspired them, solely by combining, rearranging, and augmenting preexisting sensory images.

Hence, if indefinite or unfinished works of art most effectively stimulate the imagination, as Diderot believed, it is because they stir in the spectators the desire to construct a complete picture from the fragment they perceive, a task requiring the exercise of the very intellectual operations specific to imagination—combination, rearrangement, and augmentation. Accordingly, Diderot, more than any other French critic of his time, was drawn to incompleteness, particularly in painting, where it served to offset the visual arts' predisposition toward undue precision. In his *Salons*, he regularly praises the emotional impact of sketches,[50] which he credits to the imaginative freedom they allow: "What attaches us so strongly to sketches is perhaps that, being indeterminate, they leave more freedom to our imagination, which sees in them anything it pleases."[51] In the presence of a sketch, the beholder works in concert with the artist to create as stirring a work of art as possible. For Diderot, art is at its most powerful when collaborative, if only because, as he observes in his description of a sketch by Greuze, "I know better than anyone how to move myself by the experience I have of my own heart."[52] Moreover, a spectator's imaginative involvement heightens the emotional impact of a work of art because, while building upon the framework provided by the sketch, it creates an image that knows none of the formal limitations and conventions of art. In the words of Friedrich Melchior Grimm, Diderot's friend and admirer, "the most sublime genius cannot execute as well as the most mediocre imagination; the latter creates and invents as it pleases, whereas art finds, in the execution of its thoughts, hurdles at every step."[53] For Grimm as for Diderot, the execution of an idea or image into a work of art requires a series of concessions to the formal restrictions of one's art—a technical adaptation leading inevitably to a diminution of the image's emotional impact. A sketch partly succeeds in eluding this process of attenuation because its indeterminacy alludes to a forceful image unspoiled by execution, thereby prompting its beholders to recreate it in their imaginations, the sole canvas where fantasy is truly unchecked by artistic technique.

As a result, Diderot concludes in his *Salons* that a sketch, unlike a finished painting, has the power to transmit the artist's mental state without the alterations produced by reflection and artistic technique: "[A sketch] is the artist's moment of fervor and heat, pure verve, unadulterated by the artifice that reflection adds to everything."[54] A sketch remains necessarily incomplete, because it originates from an emotion so sincere and overwhelming as to be only expressible in the manner the artist experiences it—suddenly, impulsively, and transiently. Accordingly, for Diderot, a sketch's effectiveness as a creative catalyst derives less, as one might expect, from its spatial fragmentariness than it does from its temporal incompleteness. Indeed, a finished painting, a corner of which has been erased after being accidently covered in white paint, does not as a result become a sketch, because, in the absence of short, choppy strokes and other signs of precipitation, it fails to expose the movement of its own creation. By contrast, a blank in a true sketch is likely to be perceived as a space "in waiting," rather than as a loss or as an accident, because the sketch as a whole cultivates in its beholders the sense that they are witnessing the coming into being of a work of art rather than simply its fixed and final form.

For Diderot, therefore, a sketch is to a painting what a reenactment is to classical theater. Indeed, a clear parallel exists between the incompleteness of a sketch and the suspension of *Le Fils naturel.* As Clairville describes it, a reenactment, like a sketch, arises from the experience (indeed, the reliving) of an emotion so intense that it expresses itself instantly and artlessly—notably through interrupted gestures and unarticulated accents that are analogous to the halted, uneven strokes of a sketch. Insofar as a reenactment serves as a medium for genuine emotions incompatible with artistic technique, it always risks leading, like a sketch, to its own suspension. Lastly and most significantly, a reenactment, again like a sketch, encourages its spectators to become participants by convincing them that they are beholding an improvised spectacle, subject to modification. To be sure, the theater always operates, in the words of Jean-Christophe Bailly, "as a fragile coming-into-being, not something that is held or holds itself whole, like a painting, nor something that unfolds purely and simply, like a film, but something unstable, only holding by a thread."[55] Nevertheless, many dramatic genres neither embrace nor even recognize this essential instability in the way that a reenactment does. To grow convinced of this, one need only look at classical tragedies and comedies, in which strict rules governing acting and playwriting, along with the weight of tradition and the existence of character types, enforced a relative constancy, both between distinct plays and between individual performances of a given play. By contrast, a reenactment, like a sketch, openly presents itself as incomplete and indeterminate, as well as, crucially, as always coming into existence for the very first time.

Nowhere is this contrast more evident than in the epistolary exchange between Diderot and Marie-Jeanne Riccoboni, a famed novelist and actress. In a letter to Diderot, Riccoboni criticizes the reforms outlined in *Le Fils naturel* and *Les Entretiens*, largely on the basis that they contravene the classical ideals of clarity and constancy. Drawing on her experience of the stage, she offers, time and again, the same basic argument against Diderot's diverse proposals, namely that the theater should not become a space of indeterminacy and incompleteness. Whether in relation to sight (she claims that actors who turn their backs to the spectators or who recite from the center of the stage, rather than the foreground, are scarcely visible and thus ineffectual), or in relation to hearing (she argues that actors, were they to turn their heads while speaking, would not be heard by a quarter of the audience), she repeatedly displays an understanding of the theater as a totality, that is, as an art subjugated to an ideal of complete visibility and audibility. In his response, Diderot defends his vision of an indeterminate theater by arguing that situations in which the spectators lack a visual or textual element actually produce a greater emotional impact, because, like a sketch, they awaken the imagination: "Each actor is lost in his suffering, follows its impression, and the one whose movements I can barely see, bringing my imagination into play, pulls me in, strikes me, and saddens me, more than another whose action I can fully see."[56] Diderot's exchange with Riccoboni thus reveals the distance that separates his conception of theater not only from the classical model but also from the kind of reenactment envisioned by Lysimond. For Lysimond, a flawless portrayal of reality is essential to capturing the integrality of a past event, thus giving it the unity and fixity necessary for it to be infinitely reiterable. In his letter to Riccoboni, Diderot likewise promotes anchoring the stage to reality, but for the inverse reason—because to do so recreates the imprecision and mutability of life itself. Both Lysimond and Diderot thus seek a greater proximity between the dramatic arts and reality, but whereas

Lysimond looks to the dramatic arts to invest reality with permanence, Diderot turns to reality to endow the dramatic arts with impermanence.

Diderot's desire to stage the fluidity of reality leads him to praise improvisation, notably as it was practiced in the commedia dell'arte. In a chapter on pantomime, he applauds the actors of the Comédie-Italienne for surrendering to the fervor of their imagination, since "that which is impromptu has a character that the rehearsed work will never have."[57] The absence of a fixed script makes it easier for the actors to identify with their characters to the degree that they forget the spectators entirely and simply act as they would in reality.[58] Likewise, in *Les Entretiens*, Diderot argues that there exist in every performance moments that ought to be left largely unwritten, so that the participants on stage may produce their own text, one displaying all the characteristics of a sketch, since unrehearsed, undefined, and, crucially, unfinished: "screams, inarticulate sounds, broken voices, a few monosyllabic words that escape sporadically . . . the man jumps from one idea to another; he starts a multitude of speeches, none of which he finishes."[59] The emotional impact of such an improvised text stems first and foremost from its sincerity—in the 1750s, Diderot, like many of his contemporaries, believed heartfelt passions to be contagious—but it springs as well from the text's volatility and indefiniteness, which cultivate the spectators' sense that they are witnessing a truly unique, unpredictable happening. Indeed, if Diderot, in *Le Fils naturel* and *Les Entretiens*, accentuates the visuality of the theater, often at the expense of its textuality, it is partly because the script consists of the most invariable element of the theater, as well as the sole permanent one, and as such always threatens to remind the audience of the significant part played by meticulous planning and repetition in almost all performances.

In this regard, Diderot's conception of the dramatic arts constitutes the very inverse of classical theater. In the latter, the setting is kept deliberately indeterminate, a lack that, in concert with the contrasting clarity and precision of the text, incites the spectators to imagine a complete world on stage, thus achieving the ideal of hypotyposis. Conversely, in Diderot's ideal performance, the setting is carefully constructed, with the aim of depicting a real space, whereas the text frequently exhibits signs of opacity and incompletion, such as fractured sentences and ellipses, pointing, like a sketch, to something left unarticulated. The determinacy of the setting and the indeterminacy of the text operate jointly to inspire a new mode of reception, one in which the spectators imagine themselves within the scenic space, where they are free to converse with the play's characters and thereby "complete" the text of the play. In his seminal *Absorption and Theatricality: Painting and Beholder in the Age of Diderot*, Michael Fried studies Diderot's reiterated descriptions in his *Salons* of the very same experience, wherein the *philosophe* enters the world of a painting and engages in a conversation with its characters.[60] Fried notes that this fantasy of an absorption into the fiction rests on two main criteria. First, the fictional world must appear to the beholders sufficiently similar to their own that they may conceive themselves in it. This criterion explains Diderot's fondness for reenactments, the closest performance to reality and the most likely therefore to serve as a catalyst and support for the beholders' imaginations. Second, for the viewers to enter the scenic or pictorial space as characters, they must first be made to experience their exclusion from it as spectators. To that end, the world of the fiction must never acknowledge their presence, but must instead present itself as entirely self-contained, be it through the institution of the fourth wall or through the portrayal of characters so absorbed in their passions that they seem to ignore the beholders. Reenactments best fulfill this second criterion as well, insofar as they prompt the complete absorption of their participants, who identify so closely with their characters that they forget the spectators' presence. Moreover, by accentuating their own indeterminacy and unpredictability, particularly in relation to the script, reenactments not only stimulate the spectators' imaginations, as a sketch does, they also make it more likely that this imaginative act will consist of the self-projection identified by Fried, insofar as they induce the spectators to believe that they are the unknown observers of a chance event, rather than the intended addressees of a finished work of art.

Not surprisingly, this is precisely the experience of the lone spectator in *Le Fils naturel*: "the performance had been so true that, forgetting I was a spectator, and an unknown spectator, at various points I had been on the verge of leaving my place and adding a real character to the stage."[61] It is important to note that this experience differs from "sympathetic identification," the type of reception usually associated with Diderot and bourgeois drama, in which a spectator puts him or herself in the place of a suffering protagonist.[62] This mode of reception is indeed common in Diderot's writings, as evidenced by his advocacy of ordinary protagonists (who are easier to identify with) and his unreserved praise for compassion (which, he argues, guarantees that a spectator will always take the place of the innocent sufferer and never the villain's).[63] This makes it all the more significant, then, that when faced with a reenactment, not a bourgeois drama in an official theater, the spectator of *Le Fils naturel* reacts differently. Rather than entering the world of the stage through a preexisting character, he is moved to do so as himself, to interact with it and its inhabitants directly, in lieu of experiencing it vicariously. The veracity of the scenic world, as well as its seeming extemporaneity, kindles in the spectator a desire to add a new character and original dialogue to the story, effectively rewriting it. Such an imaginative, participative act differs from sympathetic identification, in which the spectators' experience is filtered through, and hence constricted by, the object of their compassion. Like Diderot in his *Salons*, the spectator of *Le Fils naturel* thus enjoys, in addition to the emotional gratification of being a character, the intellectual freedom and agency of being a participant.

In fact, as Marie-Hélène Huet argues in *Rehearsing the Revolution*, Diderot believed that people like to attend spectacles partly because they perceive in them the possibility of a transmutation from spectator to participant.[64] As evidence, Huet quotes a passage from Diderot's *Jacques le fataliste*: "The masses flock to executions to find a scene they can recount upon returning to their district. This scene or another, it matters not, so long as they get to play a role, assemble their neighbors around them, and make themselves heard."[65] Public executions thus trigger in their viewers an impulse similar to the one experienced by the hidden spectator of *Le Fils naturel*—the desire to become a character ("to play a role") by participating in the dramatic recreation of an important event ("a scene they can recount"). In fact, Diderot highlights this impulse again in his *Salon* of 1767, once more in response to an execution: "A spectator will leave Cato dying on stage to watch the execution of Lally. Mere matter of curiosity. If Lally were beheaded every day, one would stay with Cato. . . . The common man becomes upon his return the neighborhood Demosthenes. Eight days straight he perorates, all listen. He is a character."[66] Why are executions more effective than theatrical performances (even death-filled tragedies) at inspiring their spectators to take on a more active role, to become a "character," as both *Le Fils naturel* and the passage above put it? The difference lies, Diderot suggests, in the singularity of capital punishment. The spectators' impulse to participate depends upon their perception of the spectacle as a unique, unpredictable happening, deserving of their curiosity and that of their future listeners, unlike a staged production, such as Cato's death, which feels controlled, finished, reiterated, and reiterable. As we have seen, this provision need not disqualify the dramatic arts altogether, but it means that, for a performance to most effectively cultivate among its viewers the desire to become participants, it must foreground its own incompleteness and extemporaneity—that which makes it malleable, open to revision and change, as through the addition of new "characters."

Dorval's indeterminate, unfinished reenactment achieves this effect, and indeed, Diderot calls attention to the successful transformation of its sole spectator into a participant by ending *Les Entretiens* with an intimate dinner involving Dorval, his family, and the hidden spectator, who, despite being unknown to nearly everyone, observes that "in an instant [he] was one of the family."[67] Thanks to Dorval's reenactment, the spectator becomes a part of the family and of its story outside of the scenic space, just as he had previously imagined himself to be inside of it. Indeed, he credits the ease of his integration to the knowledge he garnered from watching the reenactment, as he identifies the family members he meets through the traits of their characters: "I recognized always the personality that Dorval had given to each of his characters. His tone was melancholic; Constance's, reasonable; Rosalie's, candid; Clairville's, passionate; and mine, amiable."[68] Reality is thus understood through its reenactment, but more significantly, it is also transformed by it, as evidenced by the spectator's self-inclusion among the list of characters, a sign that he has truly become, as he had wished during the performance, "a real character."[69] Dorval's reenactment makes the family accessible to new members; it opens up a new future, one in which performers and spectators participate equally. This marks a radical departure from Lysimond's vision of reenactment, which allowed neither spectators nor alterations. In fact, as Diderot reveals through his ending, reenactments can also function as instruments of change by encouraging their spectators to become participants, to interact with a defining event and rewrite it from their own present perspectives, thereby transforming not just the past but the future as well.

This holds true for the spectators-turned-participants and even truer for the performers, whose direct involvement in both the original event and its reenactment means they have the most to gain (and lose) from any revisions. Indeed, as time passes, and, with it, the fears and sufferings caused by the initial event, the cheerful and mercurial Clairville comes to regard the tale as "an everyday occurrence" and decides to rewrite the family's past as a comedy. Irritated, less by the act of rewriting itself than by the ridicule the resulting parody casts on him, the moody and austere Dorval takes his revenge by reworking the play once more, this time into a suicide-filled tragedy, exaggerating the perils faced by the family and causing great fright as to what might have been.[70] The same event thus takes on a different meaning with each revision, reflecting not only the personalities of their creators but also their different approaches to working through the past (whether by mitigating the severity of a peril until it is easier to dismiss, or by imagining and confronting its worst possible outcome).

As a matter of fact, a subtler yet even more significant and lasting act of rewriting had already taken place. Upon completing the script of *Le Fils naturel*, Dorval had passed it on to the other members of his family, so that they could, in accordance with Lysimond's request for a perfectly accurate reenactment, make any adjustments they felt necessary toward enhancing its truthfulness. To his surprise, however, "more to their present state than to their past situation, here they softened an expression; there, they moderated a sentiment; elsewhere, they explained away an incident. Rosalie wished to appear less guilty to Clairville; Clairville, to show an even greater passion for Rosalie; Constance, to display a little more tenderness for a man who is now her husband; and the veracity of the characters suffered from this in a few places."[71] As illustrated by the nature of their revisions, Clairville, Rosalie, and Constance do not consider Dorval's reenactment a fixed account, anchored to a unique "truth" defined by the past, but regard it rather as an incomplete and thus modifiable performance, in need of their input and participation. In aspiring toward less culpability, more passion, and more tenderness (for the right recipients), their alterations seek to bring about a cathartic resolution by erasing at the source any lingering incestuous and guilty feelings. Indeed, such revisions create a past that is easier to integrate into a historical narrative because, as Dorval notes, it reflects the present situation of the family members (their current happiness, values, and love interests) rather than a truth they no longer recognize. Hence, whereas Lysimond had hoped, through the constant, static resurrection of a prohibition, to protect the family from its shameful past, Clairville, Rosalie, and Constance seek to mobilize that past, revising it in such a way that its performance serves as a catalyst for the collective elaboration of a more harmonious future.

In this, they are successful. As we saw earlier, Diderot's book ends on the traditional scene of a family reunion, one achieved through a reenactment, as Lysimond had wanted, yet in no way similar to the limited, immutable gathering he had envisioned. Thanks to the incomplete reenactment of its birth, the family is actually able to expand, to redefine itself, with the departed father losing his place to a newcomer, the hidden spectator. Indeed, whereas Lysimond praises reenactments as the best example of the hardening and preserving faculties of the theater, the family's first performance shows the inverse attribute—the fragility of life—to be just as significant. In a single text, therefore, Diderot identifies the two principal kinds of reenactment, each associated with a different conception of theater and justice. The first holds performances and laws to be fixed, permanent, and single-authored; the second, to be fluid, evolving, and collaborative. The first—Lysimond's ideal reenactment—seeks to immortalize the laws of a patriarch as the foundation for a stable, legitimate, and autocratic order. It sets out to create a performance without actors, playwrights, and spectators, because they, as agents outside of the father's control, risk introducing individual creativity and artistic innovations, resulting in the very change and difference that the patriarch fears. The second—the reenactment as it actually transpires—includes actors, playwrights, and spectators, but blurs the distinction between them, insofar as they all become participants. Unpredictable, collective, more cathartic than punitive, this kind of reenactment allows its participants to interact with a transgression, judge and even revise it according to present values and beliefs (not eternal laws), and in so doing move beyond it. Diderot's brilliant work thus establishes the framework that for the rest of the century would shape the many attempts at creating a judicial theater, reenacting, like *Le Fils naturel*, real-life transgressions—but on a much larger scale.

Chapter 2

The Many Faces of Aristophanes

The Rise of a Judicial Theater

Diderot: Pioneer, Model, Victim?

Be careful what you wish for. Just three years after imagining a more topical, judicial brand of theater in *Le Fils naturel*, Diderot became one of its first victims. On May 2, 1760, Palissot's *Les Philosophes* had one of the best attended premieres in the history of the Comédie-Française.[1] As its critics stressed again and again, this prodigious success had less to do with its artistic merit (consisting as it did of an unimaginative rewriting of Molière's *Les Femmes savantes*) than with its overt caricature of Diderot and Rousseau, among others. To this day, Palissot's play is largely remembered as a particularly effective salvo in the then raging battle between the *philosophes* and their adversaries.[2] Certainly, it was perceived as such at the time, as shown by the fact that the dozens of pamphlets that greeted its premiere split, almost without exception, along expected ideological lines (with *anti-philosophes* loving the plays and *Encyclopédistes* hating it).[3] This is, in fact, what makes Louis Coste d'Arnobat's response to it so fascinating. In his pamphlet, he imagines Diderot reconciling with Palissot with these words: "I showed you the very genres you could select. Is it not to my genius that you owe the sublime idea of this drama, which I place between comedy and tragedy? Who other than I could have discovered the fallow space that separated the old comedy from the comédie larmoyante?"[4] A self-dubbed "friend of everyone," Coste d'Arnobat is better able to look past the animosity and partisanship of the rival factions and to notice, as a result, the similarities between Palissot's play and Diderot's theories. Against every interpretation—old *and* new—of *Les*

Philosophes, Coste d'Arnobat thus presents Palissot less as a rival of Diderot than as his disciple, the pioneer of a new theater built on insights garnered from reading *Le Fils naturel*.

Neither Diderot nor Palissot would have been likely to agree with this filiation, of course, yet Coste d'Arnobat is right, in my view, not only to portray *Les Philosophes* as a new kind of theater, falling somewhere between classical comedy, tragedy, and the tearjerkers of Nivelle de la Chaussée, but also to seek its roots in Diderot's thought. In fact, I contend that Palissot's play, by denouncing the transgressions of real-life individuals explicitly named on stage, was the first to bring to life the judicial theater that Diderot had only begun to envision in *Le Fils naturel*. As is often the case with pioneering works, Palissot's play proved to be especially controversial and influential, revealing dilemmas and pitfalls intrinsic to judicial theater and forcing its proponents to confront many vital questions. Among these: Who commissions a judicial play? Who legitimizes it and, by extension, its accusations? Can it expose any crime? Target any individual? What role should the audience play? And how will such a theater interact with justice, understood both as an abstract ideal and as an existing institution? These questions inspired a wide array of plays and projects for a judicial theater, with vastly divergent functions, including as an instrument of absolutist rule, a government watchdog, a sovereign court in which to appeal recent trials, and an intrusive system of moral policing.

"An Act of Justice": Palissot or the New Aristophanes

What could possibly connect Palissot's play to the dramatic vision of his favorite bête noire, Diderot? One response seems obvious: as in *Le Fils naturel*, Palissot includes real, living people as characters, in violation of the classical convention of setting plays in a historical or geographical elsewhere. Indeed, most participants in the quarrel noted the novelty (and, for many, the scandal) of seeing, on an official stage, such a transparently satirical play,[5] which left little doubt as to the real-life identity of the character Dortidius by attributing to him Diderot's published works (including *Le Fils naturel*). Palissot and his partisans were quick to mention, however, that Molière had done the very same thing, notably in *Les Femmes savantes* (the model for *Les Philosophes*), with the fictitious Trissotin a clear caricature of Charles Cotin. In response, the *philosophes* repeatedly drew attention to a key distinction between Molière and Palissot: "If the faults that Palissot attacks are merely ridiculous, he has the right to translate them to the stage; Molière, after all, placed well-known marquis and writers on it. But if he imputes dishonorable vices to his characters, if he identifies them personally, calls them, so to speak, by their name, it isn't in Molière that one should seek past examples."[6] What made Palissot's play so unique, they argued, so different from the satires of Molière, was not just the transparency of its attacks but also their target: odious vices punishable by law—crimes such as stealing and blasphemy—rather than harmless ridiculous traits, such as Cotin's (alleged) vanity and poetic ineptitude.

Even Élie-Catherine Fréron, a known accomplice of Palissot, condemned the playwright, somewhat disingenuously perhaps, for straying from the moderation shown by Molière: "It seemed, especially at the premiere, as if Palissot had set out to render odious the individuals he wanted to portray in his play, instead of only rendering them ridiculous. It would have been easy to do the latter, for it would have earned him unanimous plaudits. Indeed, it isn't for having put our philosophers on stage that he has been condemned; it is for having presented them in a guise more revolting than comical."[7] To be fair, Palissot's play was not entirely lacking in comic antics (Crispin's quadrupedalism comes to mind), but friends and foes alike were struck by its acerbic, denunciatory tone, as well as by Palissot's transformation of the stock character of the *philosophe*, a traditional object of ridicule in eighteenth-century comedies, into a seditious criminal.[8] In fact, the play was frequently condemned for the virulence and gravity of its attacks on the *philosophes*, which were submitted as evidence that the author's "intent to harm" had supplanted the classical aim of comedy: to improve morals.[9] As a result, critics engaged in a telling debate on *Les Philosophes*'s genre, in an attempt to determine whether a play which so clearly lacked "that playful tone that rebukes without causticity, / and strikes a ridiculous trait while preserving honor" could still be labeled a comedy.[10] Most concluded that it could not and that it heralded a new kind of theater in France.

Palissot could have contested the validity of this criticism, as some of his supporters did, but he opted instead for a surprising apologia of his play's indignant tone: "To the accusations of maliciousness leveled against me, I will respond only with Mr. Diderot's wise and remarkable words: 'I know it is often said of works where the authors gave in to their indignation: *This is horrible! One should not treat people so harshly!* . . . [Yet] posterity only sees folly, vice, and malice covered with ignominy, and *it rejoices at this act of justice.* . . . Only a reprehensible weakness keeps us from showing the intense and profound hatred for baseness, envy, and duplicity *that all honest men must feel.*' "[11] Palissot's homage is undoubtedly lacking in sincerity, seeking, as it does, to expose Diderot's hypocrisy, but it reveals more than Palissot likely intended, in that it hints at a basic homology between his play and the artistic vision of the men it lampooned. Indeed, the vast majority of *philosophes* agreed that the theater ought to condemn vices with the full force of indignation, instead of cheerfully mocking ridiculous traits—precisely the tone and target that now saw Palissot's play facing widespread criticism.

In rejecting classical comedy's embrace of ridicule, the *philosophes* challenged its raison d'être. In his *Lettre à d'Alembert,* Rousseau explains that comic playwrights, such as Molière, chose to portray vices in exaggerated forms—as ridiculous traits—because they aimed above all to elicit laughter. They justified this pursuit of laughter as vital to comedy's moral purpose—the oft-invoked "castigat ridendo mores"—since laughter proved that the spectators had correctly identified the ridiculous character's vice, distanced themselves from it, and begun as a result to preserve themselves from it. In his famous critique of Molière's *Misanthrope,* Rousseau dismantles this moral program by contesting its premise that ridiculous traits and vices are essentially linked, the former a direct symptom of the latter. On the contrary, he contends that they often exist in opposition to one another.[12] In the words of Mercier, "the virtuous man . . . is sometimes made to look ridiculous, while the vicious man, more adept, avoids this fate by concealing his every act."[13] Comedies teach spectators to become that skilled man who fears and eschews external behaviors perceived as ridiculous, the better to indulge in his inner vices: "comic hyperbole does not render objects detestable, it only makes them ridiculous, and from this results a great harm: we come to fear ridicule so much that vice no longer scares us."[14] Comedies thus provide a lesson in duplicity, transforming one vice into two. Nowhere is this more evident than in Diderot's *Neveu de Rameau,* when the titular character explains his love of classical comedy: "When I read *Tartuffe,* I tell myself: be a hypocrite, if you wish, but do not speak like a hypocrite. Keep the vices that are useful to you, but avoid a tone or an appearance that would make you look ridiculous."[15] Molière's *Tartuffe,* French theater's most illustrious condemnation of hypocrisy, therefore results, paradoxically, in even greater hypocrisy on the part of its spectators.

In fact, the vast majority of *philosophes* condemn *le ridicule* not only as the wrong target (in the play) but also as the wrong response (in the pit), on the grounds that laughter is intrinsically immoral. Louis-François Nouel de Buzonnière, author of the revealingly titled *Essai sur les moyens de rendre la comédie utile aux mœurs*, deplores that while laughing at a comedy, "each says to himself: I do not resemble this man here, I am more excellent than he. It follows that comedy, whose aim it is to improve morals, makes them worse, since it helps spread and strengthen egotism."[16] Laughter inevitably divides and excludes, instilling in the spectators an undeserved sense of superiority. The debate about the proper tone and target of comedy thus takes part in a broader conflict about laughter. In the 1750s and '60s, this war opposed the *chevaliers du bel esprit*, a small but prolific group of noblemen, self-appointed protectors of Gallic wit, raillery, and levity, and the *philosophes*, who favored a solemn, militant tone and worldview and condemned the culture of aristocratic laughter for its inequality, superficiality, cruelty, and conservatism.[17] Palissot belonged to the former; Rousseau and Diderot to the latter. While Rousseau's unease with laughter is legendary, Diderot's rejection of it may come as more of a surprise, given his penchant for mystification and persiflage. Yet as Jean Goldzink has shown, Diderot builds his vision of the theater in *Le Fils naturel* on the deliberate and explicit exclusion of laughter.[18]

In lieu of classical comedies, the *philosophes* championed a new kind of theater, tasked with representing modern vices accurately and exposing their social costs on stage. Stripped of any comic hyperbole, such plays would elicit righteous indignation and popular condemnation, instead of laughter, thereby impressing on guilty souls in the parterre the true depravity of their vice.[19] Even Rousseau, in spite of his general opposition to the theater, appears willing to make an exception for militant plays of the sort: "Certainly, plays based, like the Greeks', on the past misfortunes of the fatherland or on the present-day flaws of the people could provide their spectators with useful lessons."[20] Indeed, the *philosophes* hoped that a more solemn tone and lifelike depiction of vices would return the theater to its social function in ancient Greece: a scathing denunciation of the most shameful and detrimental flaws among its spectators. It is of course ironic to find this hope realized in the writings of Palissot. As a *chevalier du bel esprit*, he had sworn to combat the evolution from wit to serious, solemn topics, yet he seems to have succumbed to it. One of his earliest plays, *Le Cercle*, had ridiculed the *philosophes*, but in the style of Molière, harmlessly mocking their vanity, eccentricities, and intellectual poppycock, without accusing them of odious crimes. His next work, *Petites lettres sur de grands philosophes*, had adopted a far more personal and denunciatory tone, with much of his indignation leveled specifically at the recently published *Fils naturel.* In fact, there may be no better indication of the influence of Diderot's aesthetic treatise than the part it played in converting a man who had set out to disprove it. Three years later, Palissot would write *Les Philosophes* in the accusatory tone of his *Petites lettres,* rather than the more jocular one of *Le Cercle* (despite one scene in common, tellingly the most classically comedic of the play, showing a Rousseau-like figure crawling on all fours). Palissot was unlikely to admit it, but his career had followed the precise path that the *philosophes* had traced for the theater.

Of course, the aim here is not to reclaim Palissot as a closet *philosophe* (even if he was less ideologically rigid than his reputation today suggests).[21] Nor is it to question the sincerity of his hatred for bourgeois drama and for one of its founding texts, *Le Fils naturel.* Yet although Palissot truly disdained the maudlin and verbose bourgeois drama that he saw (like many today) as Diderot's principal contribution to French theater, he appears to have found other aspects of *Le Fils naturel* more to his liking—first, the notion that the theater could and should function as a tool of social activism, seeking to transform the here and now through the overt reenactment of contemporary issues and figures on stage; and second, the notion that the theater ought to target dangerous transgressions instead of harmless, ridiculous traits, in a solemn, indignant tone that Palissot ties explicitly, if sarcastically, to *Le Fils naturel.*[22] When combined, these two notions transform the theater from a superficial divertissement (classical comedy, in Diderot's eyes) or a moralistic sermon (bourgeois drama, in Palissot's) into—in the words of Diderot, reprised by Palissot in defense of his play—a veritable "act of justice." Indeed, in its denunciation of grievous crimes committed by real people (the *philosophes* stood accused of sedition and irreligion), Palissot's play truly inaugurated a new "judicial theater," the likes of which, the author of "Les Si et les mais" had reminded us, was not to be found in Molière.

To understand this new genre, the participants in the quarrel turned instead to the theater they deemed its closest equivalent—the satirical plays of Aristophanes. Both *philosophes* and *anti-philosophes* harked back almost obsessively to the Greek playwright and in particular to his most notorious play, *The Clouds,* in which he had publicly attacked his own philosopher-foe, Socrates. For Palissot's victims to liken him to Aristophanes was anything but unexpected—and not just because such a comparison carried the added benefit of equating them with Socrates! "Aristophanes" was one of the epithets most commonly used to belittle authors suspected of personal attacks, reflecting the near universal contempt in which the Greek was held for most of the early modern period.[23] To the vast majority of seventeenth-century thinkers, the plays of Aristophanes embodied not just one but three features of bad comedy. Their narrow topicality limited the universality of their moral and philosophical lessons and of their beauty.[24] Their satirical barbs were inspired by base, personal passions, such as hatred and vengeance, transforming the arts into a toxic battlefield of egos.[25] And last but not least, their brand of humor was crude and indecent, clearly intended for the Athenian rabble.[26] As a result, nearly every seventeenth-century thinker traced the birth of true comedy, the moral and sophisticated plays of Menander, to the passage of a law forbidding the representation of actual people on stage. They believed their own century to be carrying out a similar refinement of the theater, even praising Molière as "the French Menander." Not surprisingly, then, the *philosophes* seized on the opportunity to portray Palissot's play as a regression to the barbaric origins of the dramatic arts: "Isn't it shameful for France to have, in a way, ended up where Greece began?"[27] Like many others, the anonymous author went on to note that Aristophanes, by accusing Socrates of odious crimes, had laid the ground for the subsequent trial and execution of a wise and innocent man—a fate that, Voltaire worried, might now befall the modern *philosophes*.[28]

If the accusation was all too predictable, the response was anything but. Unlike prior satirists, who had denied any resemblance to Aristophanes, Palissot welcomed the comparison, decreeing with his customary modesty that his play had singlehandedly brought the theater back to its first institution.[29] Many of his allies followed suit. In a sign of the profound changes then taking place in the perception of the theater and of its social function, a large number of authors actually praised *Les Philosophes* for reviving the judicial theater of ancient Greece and, more specifically, Aristophanes's *The Clouds*. There had been, it is true, a few earlier attempts by Aristophanes's translators, chief among them Anne Dacier[30] and Pierre Brumoy,[31] to defend the subject of their labor. Yet while these attempts sketched the broad outline of a more flattering portrait of Aristophanes, which Palissot and his partisans would later appropriate, strip of all ambiguity, and disseminate, they remained as ambivalent as they were scarce. Certainly, no one before the *anti-philosophes* dared push Aristophanes's rehabilitation so far as to wish for his rebirth, and all struggled, above all, to justify his writing of *The Clouds* (Dacier does not even attempt to do so, while Brumoy merely argues that Aristophanes's play, while a vengeful, spiteful act, was not directly responsible for the death of Socrates more than two decades later). The *anti-philosophes* went much further: they argued that the play was the result of Socrates's many flaws, not of Aristophanes's. For instance, Ignace Hugary de Lamarche-Courmont asserted that Socrates had been "an agitator, an enemy of the State and of humanity, a false philosopher," as well as a dangerous atheist.[32] Of course, these accusations were precisely those leveled against the *philosophes*, so that, in defending Aristophanes, Lamarche-Courmont also vindicated Palissot.

The *anti-philosophes* dismissed another standard critique of Aristophanes's theater: that its primary ambition lay in amusing the rabble through lewd puns, burlesque caricatures, and farcical acts of shocking boorishness. Here, they could draw on Brumoy's hugely influential anthology, *Le Théâtre des Grecs*, for decades if not centuries the foremost introduction to Greek drama for would-be Hellenists.[33] In a lengthy preface, Brumoy admonishes his predecessors, Dacier and Jean Boivin, for their overly literal translations of Aristophanes's plays, including the many instances of lowbrow humor.[34] He prides himself on presenting his readers with a morally and aesthetically pleasing Aristophanes, a feat of whitewashing that he accomplishes by alternating between translations of acceptable verses and vague syntheses of the indecent episodes in the satirist's oeuvre (as a result, *The Clouds* spans only forty-four pages in Brumoy's collection). In so doing, Brumoy obliterates a good deal of the comic verve that had made Aristophanes such a popular playwright in his own time, but renders him more palatable to a period increasingly ill at ease with the idea that laughter was an acceptable end, in and of itself, for the theater. Brumoy thus rewrites *The Clouds* in a more solemn tone, transforming the play so that it read less like a grotesque caricature—but a relatively harmless one, precisely because of its comical excess—and more like a grave denunciation.

If Aristophanes was not motivated by personal vendetta or greed, nor by a longing for popular laughter and acclaim, why did he even write a satirical comedy? The *anti-philosophes* found an answer, and a justification, in an alternate depiction of Aristophanes as a protector of the common good. In this reading, already present in Dacier's preface, Aristophanes was nothing like the cruel jester, casting ridicule on private citizens, that most believed him to be, but was rather a serious and courageous poet, who had earned the esteem of his contemporaries by using his dramatic talent to expose the threat that specific individuals posed to society and its laws. This view of Aristophanes remained, however, largely marginal and ambivalent (even within

Dacier's work), for two main reasons. First, it seemed impossible to reconcile with his most notorious play, *The Clouds*, so beloved and innocent was the victim, Socrates. And second, it offered no clear distinction between the comedies of Aristophanes and the satirical tracts so common, and so reviled, in early modern France. As Romain Piana notes, satire had little support in the seventeenth and eighteenth centuries because it had no place in a society that understood justice as emanating from a sovereign being. However pure their intentions (to protect the state), the satires of Aristophanes, like those of lesser libelers, remained the works of private citizens, without official authority, and as such, illegitimate acts of justice. To quote Piana, "only through the transfer of an authority akin to the divine *auctoritas* can diabolical calumny be avoided."[35] This awareness of the razor-thin line between legitimate denunciation and slander inspired, according to Piana, Brumoy's major contribution to a more positive portrayal of Aristophanes. In his preface, Brumoy argued that Aristophanes wrote *for* the state—not only in defense of it but also on its behalf. Rather than a mere private citizen, Aristophanes was a censor, an official employed by the state, and thus legitimized by it, for its protection. The *anti-philosophes* embraced and developed this vision of Aristophanes with unparalleled vigor and certainty. Unlike Dacier and Brumoy, they even extended it to *The Clouds*, arguing that, as in all his other plays, Aristophanes had been charged by the state with exposing and punishing the machinations of a seditious freethinker, Socrates.

Not only did this new performance history for *The Clouds* offer Palissot and his allies yet another opportunity to nettle the *philosophes*, for whom Socrates was a model and idol, it also enabled them to turn one of the most frequent criticisms of Palissot's play—that it amounted to little more than a piece of government propaganda—into a positive. Indeed, many pamphlets responding to *Les Philosophes* made a special note of the government's unusual involvement in promoting its performance. Stories abounded, claiming that the foreign minister, Étienne François, Duc de Choiseul, had coerced the royal censors and that Fréron had threatened the reluctant actors. In his *Correspondance littéraire*, Grimm emphasized for his foreign readers how unprecedented this state-endorsed performance truly was.[36] While the monarchy had always kept a close watch on the theater, banning topical plays and encouraging allegorical depictions of its own grandeur, never before had it used its authority with such penal intent by ordering the performance of a play to punish individuals it considered a threat. To counter the *philosophes'* outcry, Palissot could point to the example of *The Clouds* and assert that the state's support, far from devaluing his act, actually gave it its legitimacy. He did so, notably, by inventing a fascinating dialogue between Aristophanes and Brumoy, in which the Greek playwright chastises his translator (unfairly, as we have seen) for not understanding the true nature of his state-sponsored denunciations: "My plays were not secret, obscure satires; they were performed on solemn days, before the assembled people and magistrates. They were intended to serve as punishment for those crimes against society upon which the Law had not imposed a penalty."[37] Palissot sees the presence and involvement of the magistrates—some *anti-philosophes* believed they had commissioned *The Clouds*; others, that they had examined it before the premiere—as evidence that Socrates had been tried and found guilty by the government, not by Aristophanes, whose play merely enacted the sentence.[38] (In that sense, the execution of Socrates twenty-three years later can be read as a reenactment, made necessary by the failure of the first dramatic enactment to silence Socrates). As Palissot notes, this means that Aristophanes's judicial theater was not intended to function as a trial, which allows for debate and the possibility of the accused's innocence, but as a special "punishment" for crimes against society, a judicial shaming with the same legitimacy as the public execution of a criminal, because it too emanated from the government.

In fact, Palissot goes on to claim, judicial theater served as an alternative to the official justice system by allowing the state to combat transgressions that posed a threat to society but were not included in the legal code. For Palissot, the raison d'état is the raison d'être of judicial theater: extralegal actions are sometimes necessary for the good of society and are completely legitimate, so long as they are undertaken by the proper authority. Fascinatingly, in a footnote to the passage above, Palissot links this vision of the theater, once again, to his archrival Diderot. He cites a passage from *De la Poésie dramatique*, published two years before the premiere of *Les Philosophes*, in which Diderot calls for the government to revive the judicial theater of Aristophanes because it is a more humane and effective way to punish certain transgressors than legal recourse, which risks transforming them into martyrs: "What is Aristophanes? An original jester. An author of this sort must be precious to the government, if it knows how to use him. It is to him that the fanatics who occasionally disturb society must be abandoned. If we expose them on stage, they won't fill our prisons."[39] Diderot champions here a new kind of theater, modeled on the satirical comedies of ancient Greece. He dreams of plays that are not superficial divertissements but state rituals, used by the government to punish real crimes (not ridiculous traits), especially those posing a threat to society, yet outside the purview of the legal system. *Les Philosophes*, Palissot slyly argues, had fulfilled Diderot's wishes; like *The Clouds*, it had condemned a sect of fanatical freethinkers sapping the foundations of the state. In so doing, it had restored the theater to its former role as a punitive arm of the government, working in tandem with the justice system.

Mercier's "Divine Weapon": A Third Aristophanes Is Born

Diderot thus found himself in a challenging position, the victim of a play that, in another context, he might have praised as a realization of his own judicial vision of the theater. Bertrand de Latour hinted at this dilemma when he argued that eighteenth-century *philosophes*, whom he despised almost as much as the theater, had a harder time defending themselves against satirical plays than previous targets such as Socrates, because they had previously celebrated the very art form now turned against them.[40] Indeed, after 1760, Diderot's thoughts on judicial theater appear a jumble of contradictions. In all likelihood as a result of his onstage persecution, Diderot paints a far less eulogistic portrait of Aristophanes in his *Mémoires pour Catherine II* than he had in *De la Poésie dramatique*, calling him and his successor Palissot "perverse."[41] And yet, in the very same text, he tries to convince Catherine II never to use force against leaders of religious sects, a tactic which, Diderot claims, only gives them renewed resolve and a sense of righteousness, by arguing that fanatics should instead be portrayed with scorn and derision on public stages.[42] So alluring was the dream of a state-run, satirical theater that even Diderot, the principal victim of the most egregious personal attack in pre-Revolutionary French theater, could still not bring himself to forget it completely. Or could he? In his *Paradoxe sur le comédien*, which he started writing in 1773, the same year as the *Mémoires pour Catherine II*, he abandons one of the key precepts from his own *Fils naturel* and praises "the protocol of the old Aeschylus"—as he calls the rule against putting real events and people on stage.[43]

Such inconsistencies echo the ambivalence that the *philosophes* felt, more broadly, toward satire. Hence, Voltaire wrote lengthy treatises condemning the maliciousness and ineffectiveness of satire, notably his *Mémoire sur la satire* and *Épître sur la calomnie*, and slammed Aristophanes in his *Dictionnaire philosophique*, even stating that the Athenians, for having esteemed his plays, deserved their subsequent enslavement![44] Yet he also relished the fame reaped from his own personal attacks on Rousseau and Fréron, including a satirical play, *L'Écossaise*, performed in response to *Les Philosophes*.[45] What's more, most *philosophes*, including Voltaire, were drawn to the English use of satirical tracts as a vital protection against corrupt political figures. They argued, like Louis de Jaucourt, that "it is less dangerous for a few honorable individuals to be unfairly defamed than for no one to dare enlighten the nation on the conduct of the powerful."[46] In fact, according to Volker Kapp, the term "satire" came to be understood in eighteenth-century France less and less in moral and personal terms and more and more as a means of civic involvement.[47] Voltaire both illustrates and extends this important distinction between private and public satire in his praise for the English model: "In England, it seems that the law gives each private individual the right to attack any official in his public character, but protects the reputation and the private conduct of all citizens."[48] For Voltaire, the ideal form of satire is doubly public: it targets governmental figures, rather than private citizens such as rival authors, and it focuses exclusively on crimes that impact the common good, not on the purely private vices of those in power.[49]

Not surprisingly, the *philosophes* made a similar distinction between different types of judicial theater. As we saw, years before Palissot's play, they had imagined a judicial theater overseen by the state and using satirical accusations to discredit private individuals and beliefs it deemed dangerous. The performance of *Les Philosophes*, however, made it impossible to ignore that such a theater could just as easily serve as a weapon against thinkers and artists promoting positive social change as it could against religious fanatics. This compelled the *philosophes* reluctant to abandon the dream of a judicial theater to seek an alternative portrait of Aristophanes. To find one, they needed to look no further than their own *Encyclopédie*, where Jean-François Marmontel had painted the many faces of Aristophanes, including the vile satirist who wrote obscene comedies for the rabble (the seventeenth century's vision), the state-commissioned censor who targeted private citizens (Palissot's vision), and a third Aristophanes, the author of "political satires," who exposed on stage the corruption of magistrates, the failings of generals, and the ill-conduct of rulers.[50] Written before *Les Philosophes*, Marmontel's article shows the least aversion toward the second Aristophanes, recognizing, as Diderot once had, the benefits of a system in which state-appointed playwrights could punish dangerous vices beyond the reach of the law.[51] Yet in the decades that followed Palissot's play, and as the *philosophes* faced ever-growing scrutiny and hostility from the government, they increasingly turned their attention to the plays of the third Aristophanes, particularly *The Knights*, which had exposed the seditious machinations of the politician Cleon. Thanks to its specific focus on the criminal acts of the ruling class, this form of judicial theater more closely resembled the English satire praised by Jaucourt and Voltaire and ensured that a play like Palissot's would never again be performed.

For many *philosophes*, in fact, *The Knights* amounted to a near-perfect inversion of *The Clouds* (claimed as a model by Palissot). In the latter, a public official had used the theater to expose a dangerous private citizen, whereas in the former, a private citizen had used the theater to expose a dangerous public official. Unlike Palissot, who wished to add judicial theater to the monarchy's disciplinary arsenal, the *philosophes* portrayed the early Athenian theater as a site of public engagement allowing enlightened authors to monitor and publicly denounce their rulers. So convinced, in fact, were many eighteenth-century thinkers of the essential link between civic participation and judicial theater that they argued that Athens's transition from a democracy to an aristocracy after the Peloponnesian War, and the resulting decline in the citizenry's political involvement, was the real reason behind the disappearance of Aristophanes's "political satires."[52] Though the parallel was left unstated, all likely understood that, as in Athens, the centralization of power in seventeenth-century France (into an absolute monarchy) had led to conventions against the dramatization of current events and people. This does not mean, of course, that the *philosophes*—very few of whom believed in democracy—were opposed to this evolution. While some wrote glowingly of the verve, freedom, and tangible impact of plays like *The Knights*, lamenting that the shift away from targeting public officials had culminated in the timid theater of the seventeenth century, filled with "languid moral tirades" and "tedious aphorisms,"[53] others stuck to the classical view that the disappearance of political satires had purified the theater, turning it into a more aesthetically pleasing and morally edifying art form.[54] Nevertheless, the very fact that they centered their debates on Aristophanes as a private censor of the government, rather than as the government censor favored by Palissot, is quite telling, especially when read side by side with their praise for the British vision of satire. Together, they reveal a desire to open the government to greater supervision and control by the wisest of citizens—men of letters.

Even as they remained mostly torn about Aristophanes, the *philosophes* thus called attention to a more liberal function for judicial theater. This inspired some of the more politically progressive among them, notably Mercier, to formulate in explicit terms a proposal for the revival of satirical plays modeled on those of the third Aristophanes. At first glance, Mercier may appear just as ambivalent as the others. Scattered in his voluminous oeuvre, one finds frequent attacks against satire, most quite typical: it irritates instead of amends,[55] it transforms the republic of letters into a factious arena, bursting with inflated egos and petty vendettas,[56] and it distracts authors from addressing serious matters by engaging them in superficial squabbles.[57] Yet for Mercier, these flaws are not inherent in satire but are the result of its cooption and corruption by the government. Indeed, he believes, not without reason,[58] that the shallow, divisive satire common in his time received covert protection and financial support from the state, which feared that a united republic of letters might otherwise have the time and freedom to examine the conduct and expose the crimes of public officials.[59] Rather than prohibit satire and risk becoming its prey, the government neutralized it by turning it against its own authors, ensuring that they tore each other apart, like Palissot and the *philosophes*, instead of investigating and exposing their rulers' transgressions. In response, Mercier reaches the bold and perhaps unprecedented conclusion that "the government must not concern itself with poetics."[60] Men of letters must be entirely free from governmental meddling, whether through censorship or patronage, for satire to attain its purest, most disinterested form, of genuine benefit to society.

To this condition, Mercier adds another: "It is only permissible to wield the stylus of satire against those the laws cannot reach, that is, against those public figures who, having everything, honors, wealth, authority, power, would be too dangerous if they did not at least fear the mirror of truth. But to target a private individual, who has no influence on public affairs, is to avenge one's vanity, to only see oneself, and to divert from its function a divine weapon."[61] Satire must not only be free of interference from the rich and powerful, it must choose them as its sole target. A "divine weapon," it must spare private citizens but hang like the sword of Damocles above the heads of public figures. The plays of the third Aristophanes fulfill these conditions, and it is therefore not surprising to find Mercier calling for the rebirth of such a "salutary institution." Were the judicial theater of antiquity revived in France, as Mercier believed it already had been in Britain, thanks to "the English Aristophanes," Samuel Foote, "the essence of comedy would be to carry the torch of truth into the shadowy lair where evil men plot their crimes, to break through opulence and majesty to reach the would-be tyrant, and to drag him trembling into the light."[62] The exclusive targeting of criminals from the rarefied world beyond the reach of the law allows Mercier to sidestep the authoritarian implications of Palissot's theater and defend the right to privacy of ordinary citizens (including the *philosophes*).

Crucially, it also guarantees that Mercier's judicial theater operates within the rule of law, in contrast with Palissot's extralegal vision. For Mercier, satirical plays serve as an extension to the justice system, not as an alternative to it. As a result, he assigns an innovative and remarkably ambitious mission to playwrights, whose role is no longer to entertain but rather to ensure that the laws apply to everyone, even those who, due to their social status, have long been able to commit crimes with impunity: "The poet will feel the need for all individuals to become once more equal before the laws."[63] This is why Mercier tends to depict satirical plays as trials and not, like Palissot, as punishments ordered by a supreme authority above the law. For instance, he calls judicial theater "a sovereign court"—a tribunal with jurisdiction over everyone, regardless of rank.[64] This sovereign court, Mercier explains, would open up a space where private citizens could come together, reveal and discuss purported abuses of power, and reach a verdict for or against their rulers.[65] It is not surprising that Mercier would locate this space in the theater. A unique site of assembly and direct participation—to quote Mercier, "a playhouse is our only meeting point where men can assemble and their voices rise together"[66]—the theater was particularly well suited to endowing the people with the task of a sovereign judge, accepting or rejecting accusations leveled against the rich and powerful.

Judicial theater thus entailed a new mode of audience involvement. That the eighteenth century's vision of dramatic judgment was changing, and how, can be seen in a fascinating campaign against applause. While it is possible to find a few condemnations of clapping in the first half of the eighteenth century, Diderot started an unprecedented movement against applause when he wrote in 1758: "the true applause you should seek to obtain is not the clapping that can suddenly be heard after a resounding verse, but the profound sigh that comes from the soul."[67] The exact same argument was subsequently reprised by Mercier, Rétif, the celebrated actor Jean Mauduit-Larive, and countless others,[68] becoming so ordinary, in fact, that by 1785, Jean-Baptiste-Antoine Suard could state: "The question has often been raised whether it would be useful to eliminate applause and ovations from our spectacles."[69] The reasons behind this aversion to applause (an unusual sentiment among actors and playwrights!) are diverse, but fall, I contend, under three categories, each associated with a different fear of fragmentation.

First, applause fragments the play. Hasty and loud, it interrupts poignant moments and speeches, breaking them into pieces before they have reached their full impact.[70] What's more, clapping often highlights a single aspect of the performance, such as the acting of a given performer or a particularly witty line. In so doing, Louis Charpentier argues, applause divides the theatrical experience into a series of discrete reactions to isolated, formal elements.[71] This fragmentation not only reveals an overly analytical relationship to the stage, it also cultivates it. Understanding a performance as a succession of elements to be applauded or hissed according to preexisting notions and rules inspires the spectators to engage in puerile debates about "the art of moving a spectator," with the ironic result that none is actually moved.[72] The same reasoning even leads Grimm to conclude that praise or applause for specific verses in a play constitutes in reality an involuntary critique of its overall emotional impact, since it shows that the performance failed to move the audience enough for it to abandon its fragmented and fragmenting vision of the theater.[73]

Second, applause fragments the theatrical space, separating the audience from the stage. As Mercier explains, "it is when a deep and somber silence reigns in the auditorium, when the spectator, broken-hearted and teary-eyed, has neither the idea nor the strength to applaud that, immersed in a victorious illusion, he forgets the actor and the art."[74] Applause is incompatible with the mode of reception praised in *Le Fils naturel*, in which the spectator forgets the theater and experiences the fiction on stage as a real, spontaneous event, for two reasons—first, as we saw earlier, because it directs the audience's attention to the formal, artistic qualities of the performance, and second, because it is an arbitrary expression of a purely aesthetic response, which reminds neighboring spectators that they too are watching a dramatic production. By making it difficult, if not impossible, to forget the theater, applause prevents Diderot's self-projection into the fiction: "The spectator, having given himself fully to the illusion, sees with displeasure that an unexpected sound pulls him out of Athens or Rome and coldly puts him back in his place."[75] The poor neighbor of the serial clapper is expelled from the world of the fiction, thereby deepening the divide between stage and auditorium. In fact, for Mercier and other theatrical reformers, the practice of clapping became a sign of an immoral distance, born of a refusal to invest emotionally and personally in the content of the play. That anyone confronted with the reenactment of genuine injustices could choose to engage in aesthetic contemplations struck these reformers as evidence of the superficiality and heartlessness of their time.[76]

Third, applause fragments the audience. Charpentier condemns it, and more broadly the analytical mindset that inspires it, for splintering the audience into cabals.[77] The enemies of applause often note that it is far less contagious than sincere displays of emotion such as tears and laughter. This is because a heartfelt emotional response to a play becomes itself a spectacle that generates emotions in neighboring spectators. To quote Marmontel, one cries first "from the direct impression of the touching object," but soon also "from seeing others cry."[78] Marmontel goes on to describe this sentimental contagion as "a kind of electricity,"[79] a popular metaphor that beautifully conveys the circulation of emotion from one spectator to the next, until all feel as one. By contrast, insofar as applause is perceived to express a subjective, analytical judgment, the sight or hearing of it appeals to the reason, not the emotion, of other spectators, and thereby invites disagreement. This claim stems from the belief, increasingly popular in the eighteenth century, that while all can sense beauty, none can fully define it or establish fixed rules to assess it. Consequently, judgments based on artistic conventions and models are likelier to breed conflict than ones based on sensation.[80] For this reason, Mercier and Marmontel, among others, proclaim the people gathered in the parterre a better judge than the elites in the galleries. The more popular, passionate parterre does not rely on rules or erudition but on "a superior instinct," a spontaneous, emotional reaction to beauty that ensures the spectators feel and judge in unison. Applause has the opposite effect; it cultivates the analytical mindset of the elites, spreading the division and endless pedantic squabbles all too common in the galleries.[81]

Eighteenth-century theatrical reformers dreamt of a different mode of reception, free of the fragmentation revealed and fostered by applause. Nowhere was this ambition more evident than in their support for a judicial theater. Immediately after endorsing the theater as a "sovereign court," Mercier states that it would bring the nation together in vocal denunciation of the political crimes and inequities of the day, its judgments so clear, direct and unanimous that they would resonate like the "thunder of posterity."[82] Indeed, more than any other genre, judicial theater presupposes an audience that is focused on content (not fixated on formal elements), participatory (not excluded from the stage), and united (not divided into cabals). Reenactments naturally encourage their spectators to pass judgment on the real figures and incidents depicted, rather than on how they are depicted. The audience's task is not to evaluate a work of art, but to exonerate or condemn an actual human being. This negation of a critical, aesthetic relationship to the theater echoes the one in *Le Fils naturel*: it too entails the erasure of the dramatic audience as such and its replacement by participants in a ritual ceremony.

Indeed, judicial theater seeks to inspire its spectators to participate directly and personally in the events on stage. In an insightful article, Pierre Frantz has shown that Mercier aspired to write historical dramas able to compete with the dominant narrative structure of classical tragedies, which he accused of suppressing the part played in French history by the common people, first by deifying sovereigns and aristocrats, and second by promoting a fatalistic understanding of history designed to accustom its plebeian audience to assume a passive stance toward political events.[83] Likewise, judicial theater challenges (even more effectively, in my view) this classical vision of theater and history by desacralizing present-day leaders, not just historical ones, and by rendering manifest, through the judgments of its spectators, the people's right and duty to participate directly in the unfolding history of the nation. According to Frantz, Mercier was also drawn to new dramatic genres like historical drama because of their narrative openness, which, unlike the formulaic, teleological structure of tragedies, freed the playwright to reenact a more authentic history, consisting of chaotic and random acts, performed by ordinary citizens as often as by monarchs. Judicial theater shares this conception of history, but goes even further by putting it into action, insofar as it gives everyday people the opportunity to write the history of their own time.

Lastly, judicial theater best unites its sundry spectators. Such a claim may seem odd, given the quarrel surrounding Palissot's play, but Mercier and other partisans of judicial theater truly believed that unlike critical debates on aesthetic issues, which invariably divided audiences, emotional judgments on current affairs were far likelier to foster unanimity: "This tribunal often issues sentences of great accuracy and sometimes of a subtlety beyond all expectations. Above all, it discerns, by a sort of instinct, the friends as well as the enemies of the common good. It is courteous, but it performs justice when necessary."[84] Spectators will argue over a clunky alexandrine but never over the guilt of a public enemy. That they listen to this "instinct" toward goodness has much to do with the electrical contagion described earlier, which amplifies their indignation and sorrow until it becomes impossible to ignore the voice of nature. In a deeply affected parterre, according to Mercier, "each spectator judges as a public individual, not as a private one: he forgets his personal interests and prejudices alike; he is just against himself."[85] A spectator moved by *public* emotions and focused on *public* matters and figures will best be able to overcome the *private* interests and prejudices (such as the desire to be seen as a connoisseur, or to show off one's membership in a particular cabal) that prevent the isolated, analytical spectator from listening to his instinct. Judicial theater thus enables the expression of a tangible public opinion, a potent, unified voice devoted to the cause of justice.

This vision of judicial theater mirrors Dorval's by the end of *Le Fils naturel.* From a fixed, autocratic ritual used by the powerful (Lysimond, the crown, etc.) to impose their law and punish transgressors, judicial theater develops into an open-ended trial, a free forum enabling a community to come together and discover, debate, and decide current affairs. Just as Dorval ultimately rejects his father's vision of reenactment as an instrument of permanence in favor of a more collaborative, evolutive model, Mercier criticizes the dramatic representation, notably in classical tragedies, of complete and inalterable events (since well known, historically distant, and portrayed as fate), preferring instead the reenactment of contemporary issues and figures, whose meaning and impact remain to be determined. Like Dorval, he welcomes this incompleteness because it encourages the spectators to intervene in the performance and transform it. Indeed, the play is only half of the judicial ritual imagined by Mercier; it levels an accusation but requires a verdict to complete it, lest it fail in its function. This verdict is no superficial aesthetic judgment, as with other plays; it is an integral part of the performance, serving as the play's ending and determining its social impact and meaning, as either a courageous censure or a contemptible slander. Mercier is confident that the theater can grow to be strictly the former, so long as it is placed within the hands of enlightened, moral playwrights, tasked with the role of government watchdogs.

Judicial Theater: In Practice

Mercier's vision of a judicial theater may seem fantastical, especially under an absolutist regime, yet there is much evidence, even beyond Palissot's *Philosophes*, that the use of the theater as a tribunal became increasingly common in the final decades of the ancien régime.[86] Against Mercier's expectations, however, the credit for this development does not really belong to enlightened men of letters. In fact, until the Revolution, no plays were performed, at least on a public stage, to denounce a government official. This was certainly not due to a lack of interest among eighteenth-century playwrights in assuming the role of intrepid "righters of wrongs." Mercier, for instance, tried to practice what he preached by writing *Charles II*, a play that dramatized, quite transparently, a recent transgression by the notoriously debauched Comte d'Artois, but it was never staged.[87] Several others wrote plays reenacting recent trials, notably the famous Calas affair, both to retry and exonerate the wrongly condemned and to denounce the perverse or corrupt magistrates responsible. In so doing, they realized Mercier's dream, in *L'An 2440*, of a dramatic recreation of Calas's judicial murder[88]—except for the fact that, once again, none of these plays were performed until the Revolution. Royal censorship would not have allowed it—nor, for that matter, any other judicial plays. Surprisingly, Fabre d'Églantine did succeed in having one performed in 1787. His *Augusta* was, according to the *Correspondance littéraire*, a thinly veiled reenactment of the infamous trial of the Chevalier de la Barre. Jakob Heinrich Meister underlined the production's uniqueness (its "interesting audacity") by claiming that it showed significant progress in the "morals" and "tolerance" of the French, but the play, poorly written to the point of confusion, did not outlast its premiere.[89] Not until the Revolution and the suspension of censorship would dramatists write plays denouncing corrupt officials in the expectation that they would be performed, with Jean-Louis Laya, in particular, often praised as a resurrection of the "true" Aristophanes (in an explicit contrast with Palissot, guilty of having revived the wrong Aristophanes).

If not the playwrights, however, what prompted the rise of a judicial theater in the final decades of the ancien régime? The answer: those features of the theater largely beyond the censors' control, none more so than the vagaries of reception. The public, indeed, appears to have found quite enticing the opportunity offered by judicial theater to pass judgment on current affairs, figures, and trials. This interest likely arose from a confluence of factors. As Maza has shown, the remarkable popularity of trial briefs (formerly dry, legal documents meant for the judges' eyes only, but increasingly mass-produced, highly melodramatic "memoirs" after 1760) led to a widespread obsession with legal matters, as well as a preference for creative works addressing current events directly.[90] In the same period, dramatic spectators grew more and more convinced that they had both a right and a duty to intervene loudly and frequently during performances, a belief strengthened by the new notion that their judgments served to give voice to a "public opinion."[91] As we saw earlier, many theatrical reformers not only welcomed this active participation, they called for it to focus on the content of plays, especially as it related to current affairs, rather than on the theater's formal, aesthetic qualities. Much suggests that their wish was coming true: for instance, Logan Connors has noted the rise in ideological judgments and a "language of denunciation" in and about the theater.[92] A fascination with justice, heightened participation, and a focus on topical content: together, they produced spectators eager to transform the theater into a tribunal where they could judge the present, whether the plays lent themselves to it or not.

One such instance came during a performance at the Comédie-Française of *Mustapha et Zéangir*, to which Victoire Salmon, a servant unfairly accused of poisoning her masters, had been invited as a guest of honor, along with her lawyer. The incident that ensued during Salmon's first ever outing to the theater is particularly interesting, because it reveals the many ways that the theater had grown to perform a judicial function. It began when Salmon lost herself in the fiction, reacting to the duplicity of the play's villain by crying aloud "He's lying, he's lying!" before turning to her lawyer and exclaiming "Ah! my god, papa; he's a false witness!"[93] She thus assumed the role of a moral judge (rather than an art critic), expressing a grave indignation at a criminal act (perjury)—precisely the relationship to the stage favored by partisans of a judicial theater. Yet the intensity of her response, resulting, as every spectator knew, from the remembrance of her own torment at the hands of dishonest accusers, led the rest of the audience to cease watching the play entirely and focus instead on the lamentations of the spellbound Salmon. It is telling that the audience abandoned the artistic, general fiction on stage for the more authentic and topical reenactment by Salmon of her previous part as a persecuted defendant during her trial. Through its tears of compassion and cheers of support, the audience transformed her into a character in a new performance, part theater, part trial, in which it played the role of a judge, proclaiming her innocence and condemning her accusers in a unified voice (thereby supporting Mercier's belief that one can judge a person's virtue by observing his or her reactions to a theatrical performance, and that spectators may disagree about aesthetic questions but will all instinctually know signs of innocence when they see them).

Yet the story did not end there. In a further twist, during the evening's second play, the actress Mademoiselle Contat paused mid-declamation, turned to face Salmon, and addressed to her three verses praising the unique beauty of triumphant truth. The entire audience greeted this initiative with thunderous cheer, and the other actors broke out of character to join in the applause.[94] By expressing her belief in Salmon's innocence, Contat not only transformed an unintentionally apropos performance into a deliberately topical one, she also reclaimed, in the process, the position of judge, restricting the spectators to the role of beholders assenting with another's verdict. The night thus ended on a suggestion of the ease with which judicial theater could be used to influence, if not manipulate, the expression of a supposedly public judgment. (On that note, it is ironic that the verses chosen by Contat appear in a speech highly critical of public opinion, which is portrayed as fickle, gullible, and hasty to condemn without proof.)[95] While there is no reason to think of Contat's intervention as anything but earnest, it exemplifies a broader desire among the theatrical establishment to retain control over these judicial events by staging them.

Indeed, the Salmon episode was far from an isolated, impromptu incident. It was, rather, one of the earliest attempts by a theatrical company to carry out a plan, found in both legal and dramatic pamphlets, to use the theater as a means to inspire public opinion to validate and thus legitimize the verdicts of recent trials. Hence, in *Du Théâtre*, Mercier had championed the reenactment of recently ended trials, so as to "confirm through the people's applause the triumph of the laws."[96] Similarly, Louis Philipon de La Madelaine had argued that a special area in public theaters ought to be reserved for those who had suffered the costs and indignities of a trial as the result of an unjust accusation, thereby allowing actors to parade them, and spectators to applaud them.[97] The troupe of the Comédie-Française invited Salmon precisely for that purpose—to display her innocence to spectators with the expectation that they would assent. The same applies to Catherine Estinès, also accused of being a poisoner and also, upon being exonerated, invited by a company in Toulouse to attend a play for the first time. Upon seeing the scaffold awaiting the play's female protagonist, Estinès began shuddering visibly. This reaction at a fate that could have been hers sent a chill throughout the audience, although the same spectators later broke out in wild acclamations at the appearance of Estinès's lawyers and at the play's happy ending.[98] According to Armand Fouquier, the practice of inviting recently exonerated defendants became sufficiently common for their presence on a given night to be advertised on playbills—a telling inclusion, insofar as it suggests that the actors regarded these invitations as staged spectacles, comparable to the evening's plays.[99] Such scriptedness—the fact that they were planned in advance, were repeated and repetitive, and had predictable outcomes—highlights one of judicial theater's most significant ambiguities, largely ignored by Mercier, but seized upon, as we will see, by Rousseau and others to condemn it. In staged ceremonies like the ones for Salmon and Estinès, one starts to wonder who actually does the judging. When innocence has already been attributed by the legal and theatrical establishments (the first through a trial and the second through its invitation), does the audience serve any real function, beyond validating the verdicts of more influential arbiters?

Yet although spectators gladly participated in these ritual displays of persecuted but victorious innocence, other incidents suggest that they saw themselves as independent judges, with the right and duty not only to praise correct verdicts but also to speak out against unjust ones, and against the government officials responsible. Meister thus observes in 1774 that the parterre's longstanding practice of creating "applications" had recently assumed a new judicial dimension, as spectators repeatedly distorted innocuous verses and situations into commentaries on the decisions of the tribunals: "Of late, the parterre of the Comédie-Française has usurped the right to applaud or hiss the court's sentences."[100] To praise (applaud) but also, and just as importantly, to condemn (hiss): Meister gives several examples of the latter, such as when a quip on "well-paid judges" in *La Réconciliation normande* was transformed by indignant spectators into a critique of the recent acquittal of the powerful Comte de Morangiès,[101] or when the audience of *Crispin rival de son maître* vented its anger at Louis Valentin Goëzman's treatment of Pierre-Augustin Caron de Beaumarchais by repeatedly calling out the judge's name whenever a character mentioned bribery, chicanery, or judicial ineptitude.[102] Nor did audiences limit their judgment to existing trials. For them, the theater was both an appellate court, reviewing prior legal decisions, *and* a trial court, where accusations against political figures under no formal litigation could be formulated and debated. For instance, in the same period as the examples above, the powerful and controversial Chancellor René Nicolas Charles Augustin de Maupeou became the target of frequent indictments by theatergoers.[103]

Like his idols Voltaire and Diderot and unlike the more radical Mercier, Meister stops short of fully embracing the slide toward a more judicial theater. He criticizes spectators for daring to judge with such limited knowledge of the evidence[104] and for showing such insolence toward their superiors—

conduct deserving of a trip to the Bastille.[105] Yet he immediately adds: "Even while acknowledging their fault, I must confess that I like seeing myself transported to Rome or Athens for an instant, to admire how much a taste for the arts, and especially for the theater, predisposes the mind to enjoy freedom."[106] Here we see, again, the attraction that *philosophes* like Meister felt for antiquity and for its vision of the dramatic arts as uniquely able to inspire and support a free, popular judgment. By the 1770s, many spectators, consciously or not, shared this judicial vision of the theater. Whether through applications or at the invitation of actors, they found in the theater a way to judge ongoing or recent trials. This mode of reception, while not, of course, entirely new, experienced so marked a growth that Meister flagged it as a novel, "usurped" right. Indeed, it became a common enough practice that, together with the dream, from Palissot to Mercier, of a rebirth of Aristophanes, it attracted the attention of some concerned authors, including Rousseau, who argued that the rise of a judicial conception of theater posed a grave threat to the very rule of law.

Acting Above the Law: Rousseau and the Case Against Judicial Theater

Who, in the end, really judges? This ambiguity, which I noted above, stems from one of the most troubling flaws in Mercier's judicial theater: the difficulty in tracing the legitimacy of any of its participants. In 1768, the abbé Joseph-Marie Gros de Besplas condemned the rise of judicial theater for precisely that reason: "Illicit personal attacks on stage have seen citizens brought before a tribunal of judges without the authority to judge anyone."[107] What, indeed, gave random spectators the right to judge a fellow citizen? Similarly, Latour denounced the playwrights' illegitimacy, noting that this distinguished them from official judges, imbued with the king's authority and entrusted with investigating all accusations before they became public, to ensure that they were honest, disinterested, and supported by evidence.[108] In the absence of anyone with the legitimate authority to separate the wheat from the chaff, all accusations would be entertained equally and publicly, including the most calumnious ones. Slander's threat was made even greater, Latour noted soon after rebuking Diderot for his praise of Aristophanes, by the theater's tendency to exaggerate faults and embroider narratives, so as to please its audience.[109] As expected, the partisans of judicial theater responded by defending the natural legitimacy of the people, as the voice of the nation, and by asserting that when assembled, the public possessed an innate ability to distinguish the truth. So long as the people sat in judgment, calumny would never triumph; true, it might find a public expression on stage, as in Palissot's *Philosophes*, but it would then be roundly jeered, and the false accuser discredited.[110]

The legitimacy of judicial theater thus depends on its audience, and on the latter's validation of the onstage accusations. Yet it is well known that while the *philosophes* praised public opinion as infallible and virtuous, they harbored a profound ambivalence toward the people. This was particularly true in the theater, where public opinion, so easy to applaud as an abstract concept, took on a far more concrete and threatening presence—that of a boisterous, volatile, socially diverse audience.[111] To be fair to Mercier, he proved far more consistent than most in his praise of the people, yet even he occasionally expressed unease at the presence in the polysemic "people" of the "populace," whose violent, erratic, hasty, often inaccurate judgments terrified him. This unease explains why Mercier sometimes painted, alongside his idealistic image of the "people" as an infallible judge, a strikingly different portrait: of a dangerous force to harness and command, or of a naïve child to mold and enlighten.[112] Such disparaging portrayals of the people naturally undermined the concept of judicial theater, playing into the hands of its critics, who, like Rousseau, stressed the dangers of placing the right to judge in the hands of everyday people.

Rousseau's name here may come as something of a surprise, given his oft-proclaimed admiration for a system of justice founded on free and public accusation, as in ancient Rome.[113] Individual privacy ranks well below collective transparency in Rousseau's list of priorities, and he often defends those who bring a criminal or sinner to the people's attention, even or perhaps especially when they do so outside of the legal system. For instance, in his *Lettre à d'Alembert*, he praises the gossipy women of Geneva for the surveillance and severe censorship that they exercise over their fellow citizens.[114] Yet in the very same text, he opposes the introduction of comedies in Geneva on the grounds that they will invariably come to do precisely what he earlier applauds Genevan women for doing: publicly denouncing specific individuals by name.

> As for comedy, let us not think of it: it would cause among us the most awful disorders. It would serve as an instrument of factions, parties, and

> vendettas. Our city is so small that even the most general comedy of manners would soon degenerate into satires and personal attacks. The example of ancient Athens, a city incomparably more populated than Geneva, offers a striking lesson. It is in the theater that the exile of many great men and the death of Socrates were prepared. It is because of its passion for the theater that Athens perished. These disasters justify all too well the sorrow Solon showed at Thespis's first performances.[115]

This passage contains a thoughtful, multifaceted critique of judicial theater, to which I will return, but one aspect of Rousseau's originality is immediately apparent. In an inversion of the standard historical progression described by Voltaire, Marmontel, and Jean-Jacques Barthélemy, according to whom the fall of Athenian democracy and the resulting decline in civic participation caused the disappearance of judicial theater, Rousseau argues instead that it was judicial theater that led to the demise of democracy and public engagement in Athens. For the *philosophes*, judicial theater is a fundamentally republican institution, whereas for Rousseau, it poses a grave threat to true republics (Athens and, by extension, Geneva) because it weakens their unity by dividing the people into factions and parties.

Interestingly, in portraying judicial theater as responsible for the collapse of Athenian democracy, Rousseau, like his adversaries, borrows from Brumoy's influential anthology, simply from different passages. Indeed, in *Le Théâtre des Grecs*, Brumoy contends that judicial theater served both as a fulcrum for Athenian democracy and as the root of its downfall. Satirical comedies were, he argues, indispensable, since "the republic of Athens sustained itself solely through the perpetual discord among those who handled its affairs, a unique counterweight that involved finding the cure in the sickness, and whose impetus came from eloquence and the theater."[116] Here, Brumoy perfectly sums up the claim, later reprised by Voltaire, Marmontel, and Barthélemy, that Aristophanes's judicial theater operated as a system of checks and balances. According to this interpretation, satirical comedies were designed to preserve a relative equality among citizens by publicly exposing any political figure given to such lofty ambitions as to threaten to replace the democratic regime by a dictatorship. The phrase "finding the cure in the sickness" hints, however, at Brumoy's ensuing criticism: while such plays provide a momentary remedy to democratic instability (caused by the lack of a fixed, legitimate ruler), they are also partly to blame for the very existence of this malady. At once medicine and poison, judicial theater impedes the will to power of great men only to encourage, as Brumoy goes on to explain, the creation of political factions, as lesser men realize that to wield power in a system founded on conflict and counterweight, they need to build alliances and secure the support of eloquent representatives. For Brumoy, such a deeply divisive and theatrical democracy is like a tree growing on putrid roots: while it needs them to survive, they will ultimately result in its collapse.

Brumoy's account—judicial theater is needed to steady a wobbly democracy, yet alters its foundations in a way that ensures its future downfall—unfolds according to the logic of the supplement so dear to Rousseau (in fact, the phrase "finding the cure in the sickness" has a distinctly Rousseauian ring to it).[117] For Rousseau as for Brumoy, satirical comedies herald the ascendancy of a toxic form of democracy, one rewarding factionalism over unity, artifice over transparency, and personal interests over the general will. This particular model of democracy resembles the "politics of contestation" characteristic of the English system, which some *philosophes* favored, but which Rousseau regarded with intense distrust and anxiety.[118] In brief, the British style of politics operated largely in accordance with the doctrine of "majority rule," with each eligible citizen encouraged to defend his private beliefs and interests in the political arena, in the belief that the most commendable politicians and causes would invariably accrue the greatest numerical support. Rousseau condemns this mathematical model in *Du Contrat social* for the same reasons that he opposes judicial theater: because it fosters discord among the people and leads to the creation of voting pacts, intrigues, and political parties. As is well known, Rousseau promotes an alternative form of democracy based on the general will, a pre- or a-political consensus that arises when each citizen voluntarily forfeits his private interests and votes in accordance with what he perceives to be in the best interest of the group. Political factions of any sort are incompatible with this vision; a party, even one that has the support of the majority, does not reflect the general will, but only the private interests and oratorical gifts of its members.[119]

Why does judicial theater (and not, say, the gossipy women of Geneva) cultivate this toxic, divisive vision of democracy? On a practical level, the unrivaled reach of dramatic denunciations makes them ideal weapons not only against, but also for, ambitious men, the latter eagerly seizing upon such an effective means to accuse and discredit rivals without the need for concrete evidence. The theater then becomes a political instrument that facilitates the rise of powerful factions, instead of a popular safeguard against it. On a more conceptual level, the very structure of theater mirrors the bad democracy that

Rousseau fears. Its distinction of actors and spectators endangers the unity of the citizenry. Worse, it rewards representation, the expression of ideas that are not one's own but those of a hidden other, with the most persuasive performer, not the sincerest one, sure to receive the most applause. In a perfect illustration of majority rule, success is determined by the number of spectators who applaud and by the intensity and duration of their acclamations. In short, theater teaches actors on the national stage (public officials) to tailor their message to the wishes of the majority over those of the whole community, and it teaches private citizens to seek likeminded allies, so as to produce the most noise possible and drown out the judgments of others. The resulting audience is the very inverse of the one that Mercier claims is created by judicial theater: divided, instead of united, and driven by private, instead of public, interests. In fact, this conflict-driven vision of judgment infects the justice system as well and creates a lawsuit culture, with Brumoy noting the Athenians' "obsession with trials,"[120] and Latour warning against the endless quarrels that would result from the establishment of a judicial theater in France.[121] It would therefore be foolish to seek legitimacy and protection from calumny in the audience of judicial theater; on the contrary, the general public becomes a less legitimate judge—more slanderous, unruly, and divided—by attending judicial plays.

As we saw earlier, this negative image of the people also haunts the writings of many *philosophes*. It inspired Mercier and others to seek a compromise, one that would preserve the right of the audience to judge and yet endow its judgments with a more legitimate origin. They found this compromise in the notion that it was ultimately men of letters (in other words, them) who formed public opinion, before it was expressed by the people. Hence, Marmontel claims that the parterre's judgments are worthy of trust because they originate from a small group of enlightened thinkers dispersed in the crowd, before being echoed and amplified by the common people, whose lack of education, prejudices, and vanity has left their minds malleable and open to the influence of their superiors.[122] Similarly, Mercier often asserts that men of letters determine the popular response to a play (and to the accusations it contains), although his focus is on the playwrights rather than the audience. A gifted dramatist, he argues, will find that spectators are "a wax pliable to the hand that molds it" or, in another hackneyed metaphor, "a kind of instrument he can make resonate as he pleases"—with a likely intentional pun on the homophones "raisonner" and "résonner" (reason and resonate), since Mercier immediately adds that this allows the playwright to gain mastery over the spectators' "reason."[123] In fact, men of letters have the ability to control more than just the reception of a particular play; they, as Mercier variously puts it, "hold the rudder of public opinion," "govern the ideas of the nation," and "form at last the national spirit."[124] In the wings or in the auditorium, they are the alchemists who distill popular opinion(s) into a purer, unanimous public opinion.

Yet if this compromise banishes the specter of an uncontrollable, divided people, it raises new issues in its place, particularly in the context of judicial theater. Can a judicial play still be compared to a trial if its author also determines its verdict? In this scenario, the playwright becomes a judge as well as an accuser, a status Mercier hints at when he praises men of letters as "substitutes for the magistracy" (a phrase he borrows from Jean-Baptiste-René Robinet).[125] In fact, Mercier never addresses one of the most troubling differences between a judicial play and a trial, namely that a playwright, unlike an accuser in a court of law, can shape the narrative as he sees fit, depicting the accused in the most damning light, without the latter being able to respond or demand evidence. Placing the legitimacy of the accusation entirely on the side of the accuser risks reducing the role of the spectators to that of mere assenters, present to observe and sanction a punitive act carried out by a sociocultural elite (the supposedly enlightened men of letters)—a performance closer to Palissot's vision than to a truly open-ended trial.[126] Many *philosophes*, given their embrace of enlightened despotism, may have been agreeable to such a compromise, if it meant judicial theater was governed by independent, progressive men of letters (not Palissot) with the people's best interest at heart. For Rousseau, however, shifting the responsibility for judgment (and the duty to fend off calumny) from the people to the theatrical establishment carried with it a different but equally dire threat.

In addition to fragmenting the people into factions, the judicial theater of ancient Greece, Rousseau writes in the passage from *La Lettre à d'Alembert* cited above, vindicated Solon's sorrow upon encountering the dramatic arts for the first time. This (likely apocryphal) dispute between the wise lawmaker and the Greek dramatist and actor Thespis was widely known in the early modern period, especially in antitheatrical circles. As narrated in Plutarch's *Parallel Lives,* Solon confronted Thespis following one of the actor's performances, inquiring whether he felt any shame at telling so many lies before so many people. When Thespis denied wrongdoing, claiming his speeches and actions were but a game, Solon replied, "But in praising and endorsing these games, where one lies knowingly, we do not take care that we will soon find them in our contracts and our very affairs."[127] This famous warning raised philosophical issues dear to Rousseau, notably the Platonic anxiety that mimesis, even in jest, might come to saturate and distort reality, weakening the tacit contracts and conventions that hold communities together.

With respect to judicial theater, however, Solon's admonition took on a more literal dimension: a warning that genuine "contracts," the legal agreements serving as one of the foundations of the justice system, were compromised by the theater. Invoking Solon was a way for Rousseau to revive the lawmaker's critique of the stage's inevitable usurpation of the tribunal—a reading substantiated by the reference in the same sentence to Socrates's trial and execution, which had been prepared, many believed, by Aristophanes's play. In fact, this understanding of Solon's admonition was far from unique to Rousseau. It inspired Suard's revealing, if slightly inaccurate, rewriting: "When Solon saw public theaters in Athens, he exclaimed: *these diversions will soon speak louder than the laws*."[128] Indeed, Suard goes on to repeatedly draw attention to the age-old rivalry between the arts and the laws: "An Englishman once said: make a people's laws, and let me make its songs; we will see which one of us will govern it . . . the ancient Greeks likely agreed, since they gave songs and laws the same name (nomos)."[129] Predictably for a man best known today for his part in censoring *Le Mariage de Figaro*, Suard endorses censorship as the sole practical response to the threat that judicial plays might come to wield an influence equal to or greater than the tribunals'.

Although Rousseau differs from Suard in the solution that he proposes (the interdiction of theater, rather than its censorship), he shares with him a profound distrust of judicial theater. In Rousseau's eyes, a truly satirical theater cannot lastingly operate as a parallel institution to the legal system without infringing upon it, gradually at first, but inexorably, until, to quote Suard (mis)quoting Solon, comedies speak louder than the laws themselves. His contemporaries' longing for a judicial theater betrays their blindness to the logic of the supplement, which means in this instance that a theater seeking to extend the reach of the tribunals will eventually come to supplant them. As evidence of this, Rousseau could point (as he does) to Socrates's execution, often cited in the period as proof of the ease with which theatrical accusations could not only instigate a trial but also infiltrate and distort it through their influence on public opinion—an early example of what is known today as trial by media.[130] To most eighteenth-century thinkers, in fact, Socrates symbolized the twin values of reason and law, and his death, the defeat of these values by the forces of theatricality. After all, had he not courageously refused during his trial to resort to the melodramatic appeals of the stage: "I respected you too much to try to touch you with my tears or with those of my children and my friends gathered about me. It is at the theater that one must arouse compassion through poignant images; here, only truth must make itself heard"?[131] To antitheatricalists like Rousseau, there was no better illustration of the frailty of truth, reason, and a formal legal system when faced with a satirical, denunciatory play of the kind written by Aristophanes.

Judicial theater infringes upon and eventually supplants the justice system, instead of working in tandem with it, as Mercier envisions, because it gives undue power to individuals (playwrights and actors) without holding them accountable for it. Mercier defends their legitimacy because they are more enlightened than regular magistrates (a subjective claim) and more transparent in their accusations, since the latter are made publicly (unlike in eighteenth-century trials). Throughout *La Lettre à d'Alembert*, however, Rousseau reminds us that the theater is the very antithesis of transparency. In particular, he condemns actors for uttering words that are not their own (but the author's) under an identity that is not their own (the character's), leading them to lose their individualities, to literally "self-destruct." This lack of transparency is especially troubling in judicial theater. Not only does it make it possible for actors to reenact slanderous accusations with impunity, by claiming their roles were assigned to them and do not necessarily reflect their own beliefs and values, but the true initiators of these accusations, the playwrights, are also offered the opportunity to conceal their identities, in name (under the cover of anonymity) and in body (under the cover of fenced boxes). This, in Rousseau's eyes, is what differentiates judicial theater from a Roman-like system of formal, public accusations, which he often praises and which rests entirely on the sincerity and personal involvement of the accuser—that is, on his or her answerability in cases of false allegations.[132] In the absence of such accountability, it is inevitable that actors and playwrights will come to speak louder than the laws, for who would choose the lengthy, unpredictable, and personally taxing and risky option of a formal trial, when one could gain a swift, easy, and certain vengeance by using another to put forth a dramatic accusation? This is precisely what had happened in ancient Greece, according to Rousseau and the abbé Gros de Besplas, who claimed that "poets, musicians, actors, dancers, and set designers having risen to the highest ranks in Athens, the laws lost all power."[133] Guilt and innocence were no longer determined in a courtroom, according to fixed laws and procedures, but by playwrights, actors, and other scenic artists.

Rousseau voices the fear in *La Lettre à d'Alembert* that the same fate awaits Geneva if it allows a public theater, giving us a more detailed account of the process through which the dramatic arts usurp the justice system. First, magistrates and their loved ones will grow familiar with actors, coming to admire the source of their pleasures to the point of "indulgence," even "protection." The actors, "certain of their impunity," will feel bold enough to elude the laws that curb their licentiousness. "Lastly, should the actors add enough art and intrigue to their success, I give it less than thirty years before they are the arbiters of the state." The actors come to govern the state—to be its "arbiters," that is, to replace the magistrates who indulged them—because judicial theater enables them to rule over the all-powerful tribunal of public opinion. As Rousseau goes on to explain, those wishing to serve in the government will be forced to seek their support, as they can, through their satirical plays, give some the fame needed to win an election, while accusing and discrediting others. "The rulers of a free people," Rousseau bitterly concludes, "will be the puppets of a gang of lowly actors."[134] Lest we think Rousseau was being, well, overdramatic, other writers feared this process was already unfolding in eighteenth-century France. Charpentier deplores that famous actors could commit crimes with impunity, and that on the rare occasions they were sent to jail, they were visited by a fawning court of political figures, aristocrats, and magistrates.[135] Latour even claims that his contemporaries had reached the next phase, with actors not only immune from prosecution but also deciding trials: "Actresses often tip the scales of trials in which they take an interest; the tribunal is on the stage. Nothing's easier than gaining their protection, when one wishes to purchase it."[136] Actors did not yet control the government (though that fear would soon become widespread, starting with the Revolution),[137] but they had, Latour believed, already begun to rule over the justice system.

Rousseau thus reveals that the two main strategies for legitimizing judicial theater—depicting it as democratic or as enlightened—both transform the justice system, coopting it and shaping it in their image, in ways that corrupt and ultimately abolish the rule of law. If judicial theater is placed in the hands of the people, justice turns popular—violent, unpredictable, and factious; if judicial theater is placed in the hands of the theatrical establishment, justice turns into theater—illusory, unaccountable, and manipulative.

Forced to Perform: Rétif and Reenactment

Rousseau condemns judicial theater, in short, for remaining theater—for the inclusion of professional actors and playwrights, and for the involvement of random spectators, drawn by a thirst for gossip and judgment. In a direct response to Rousseau's critique,[138] Rétif imagines a very different form of judicial theater: "Satirical comedies will expose to public laughter the individuals condemned to it by the Committee, which will itself give the playwrights their topics: vices and dangerous ridiculous traits against which the law has not spoken. In these critical plays, the sinful individual will be depicted plainly or condemned by the Supreme Senate to play his own role. He will thus personally receive the jeers of his fellow citizens."[139] This passage from *L'Andrographe* may seem not only dystopic but downright fantastical, with its strange vision of committees spying on private citizens, commissioning plays exposing their secret misdeeds, and forcing them to perform their own roles before friends and family. Yet Rétif's program of theatrical reforms should not be written off as pure fantasy. First, it represents over a decade of reflection, building upon ideas that Rétif had articulated twelve years prior in *La Mimographe*, notably the intriguing claim that the earliest and purest form of theater arose in small primeval tribes, when a father-king decided to punish his children by transcribing into dramatic form the specific immoral acts they had committed and obliging them to perform their own roles before the assembled tribe.[140] Second, it includes hundreds of pages of details and explanations designed to make it actionable, notably on the composition of the committees—wise elders, well known to those they monitor, and esteemed as moral fathers—and on their distribution—at least one per municipality, with the total in the thousands. Third, it is utterly earnest, as evidenced by Rétif's pride when he was informed (incorrectly) that the Polish prince Martin Lubomirski had carried out the program in *La Mimographe*, and by his repeated petitions to the French government for the institution of his reformed theater.[141] Fourth, it is far from unique, belonging instead to a general movement toward a new understanding of performance, in which spectacles are used to expose real offenses. Notably, it bears striking similarities to Diderot's *Fils naturel*, with both involving nonactors coerced by a paternal figure into reenacting recent transgressions in front of those most affected by them.[142]

Indeed, unlike Palissot, Mercier, and others, who turn Diderot's vision into a national tribunal, Rétif seeks to keep judicial theater as domestic and ritualistic as possible and to respond in this way to Rousseau's fears. Friends and families, not random spectators, gather to chastise someone they know well, not to judge an artistic representation or controversial public figure, lessening the risk that they will split into factions. More significantly still, Rétif's judicial theater employs no actors, ensuring a full accountability, since every word and deed on stage is truly that of its performer. In the absence of any gap between performer and character, the force of the law (as expressed by the jeers of the audience and the decree of the committee) falls not just on the character but on the performer as well, who experiences directly, physically even, the penalty for his or her sins. The legitimacy of these spectacles is further guaranteed by their provenance: "The satires will not be arbitrary; they will result from a judgment by the committee or even by the Supreme Senate to hinder certain acts that, without being crimes, are infinitely damaging."[143] Instead of arbitrary satires tainted by the artistic inventions of anonymous playwrights, they are direct transcriptions, expressing the official judgments of irreproachable father figures. As a result, judicial theater never becomes a site of gratuitous malice or political intrigue, because the playwrights and spectators are not the source of the accusations, but blameless participants in a legitimate punishment.[144]

Conceived as a punishment rather than as a trial, Rétif's judicial theater poses far less of a threat to the justice system than does Mercier's. Whereas the latter, according to Rousseau, parodies and eventually supplants legal proceedings, Rétif's judicial theater serves as their conclusion and confirmation. Its different focus—sins, not crimes—also makes it less likely to rival the justice system. Both passages cited above specifically forbid judicial theater from reenacting actual crimes, and Rétif notes elsewhere that the target should instead be hidden, personal vices, such as selfishness, ingratitude, and greed.[145] Illegal acts, when they occur, remain under the jurisdiction of official tribunals and continue to be treated and punished as crimes against the king himself. In this, Rétif departs from both Palissot and Mercier, for whom judicial theater is a means to condemn transgressions that pose a public threat to the state (whether committed by private citizens or political figures). By contrast, Rétif's judicial theater targets the domestic, politically harmless sins of unknown men and women. It consists of a completely different form of justice, targeting flaws instead of acts, and governed by moral principles instead of laws—wholly separate, as a result, from official tribunals, and unlikely to supplant them.

As we will see in Chapter 5, the notion of a domestic tribunal focusing on personal vices is characteristic of the second half of the eighteenth century. It reflects several key changes in the period's understanding of the performance and purpose of justice. First, it adds weight to Foucault's argument in *Surveiller et punir* that pre-Revolutionary justice saw a gradual shift in its preoccupation, from the most unusual and spectacular *crimes*, resulting in equally spectacular punishments, to the lesser, domestic *sins* of the general population, the detection of which required the establishment of a system of surveillance as intrusive as it was extensive.[146] Second, it echoes the period's evolving views on punishment. Scott Bryson and Maza, among others, have shown the development of a remarkably close symbiosis between penology and the new dramatic genres, chief among them bourgeois drama.[147] Drawing on Foucault, they argue that penal and theatrical representations (that is, public executions and plays) underwent a parallel evolution from a static reflection and glorification of the monarch's authority to a more dynamic spectacle directed at the indoctrination of its beholders. This evolution was partly inspired by liberal reformers following in Cesare Beccaria's footsteps, who questioned the reasoning behind the monarchy's spectacular punishments—namely, that the torture of criminals, by its gruesome excess, spread terror among the gathered people, deterring them from committing crimes. While they agreed on the importance of deterrence, they countered, in keeping with the sentimentalism of their age, that it would be better achieved if punishments more closely resembled simple, didactic narratives, providing background information to render the criminal more readily recognizable (and thus easier to identify with), showing the sorrows and social ills caused by the crime, and encouraging the audience to join in the judgment and thus internalize the law.

No text more clearly and perfectly combines these two (related) developments than Rétif's program for a judicial theater, with its overt surveillance and dramatization of private vices. Rather than a corporal punishment designed to inflict pain and terror, Rétif calls for a reenactment, a narrative retelling that reveals the sin's roots and its detrimental impact on the community, making it at once more understandable and more condemnable. Moreover, the spectators' bond with the principal participants, the knowledge that they share many similarities (and familial ties) with them, increases the likelihood that they will experience the moment of self-recognition and soul-searching so vital to moral improvement and the avoidance of a similar fate.

The reenactment further promotes this process of internalization by encouraging spectators to jeer the sinner, a public sanction of the punishment that reinforces their own adherence to the moral law that was broken. Such jeers inscribe the sin being reenacted within a narrative structure typical of bourgeois drama, in which hidden, domestic vices are invariably exposed and the sinners disgraced, in the end. In so doing, they act as a deterrent, not through the threat of violence, but through the promise of transparency—the warning that all vices eventually become known. As in *Le Fils naturel*, the aim is to prevent crime as well as punish it, to compel the individuals on stage (and by extension those watching) to amend their sinful inclinations, not from fear of a corporal punishment, but from the conviction that they will be found out and shamed.

This faith in transparency—both in the possibility of a total, unmitigated exposure and in its positive impact on society—constitutes yet another example of Rousseau's influence on Rétif. It justifies Rétif's committees of elderly spies, whose sage surveillance, rather like the gossipy women's in *La Lettre à d'Alembert*, compels all citizens to lead every moment of their lives as if their loved ones were watching, since they may one day be. It explains, as well, the emphasis that Rétif places on minor, domestic vices, in lieu of grave threats to the state, since for true transparency to come to pass, every sin, however insignificant, must be publicly exposed in an act of complete disclosure that erases the line between public and private. The same faith also inspires Rétif's focus on internal flaws, rather than criminal acts. In the name of transparency, Rétif's judicial theater aims to expose sins (selfishness, ingratitude, avarice) that often lead to inaction rather than crime, that can hide beneath and even sometimes encourage a public adherence to social conventions and laws, and that are therefore impossible to reveal and vanquish through legislation. Lastly, Rétif's belief in transparency accounts for his desire for a true reenactment, a ritualistic performance that will not be a theatrical (and thus, non-transparent) denunciation of a sin, but rather its resurrection by the very people responsible. Rétif thus hopes to find a judicial theater that, by ceasing to be theater, can bring Diderot's and Rousseau's visions together.

Perhaps because of this hybridity, Rétif's proposal really drives home the tremendous range of eighteenth-century conceptions of judicial theater and, more broadly, of art's function—a diversity especially striking in a period chiefly known today for its moralistic, mawkish fare. Like its putative pioneer Aristophanes, judicial theater proved to be highly malleable and prone to reflect the ideological worldviews of its advocates. For some, it constituted an instrument of absolutism, strengthening the crown against seditious free-thinkers; for others, a sovereign tribunal, founded on the liberal ideals of equality before the law, free and public debate, and popular judgment; and for Rétif, a key component in an intrusive, communal system of moral policing. As eighteenth-century theater grew increasingly judicial, in practice as well as in theory, more and more thinkers struggled with the real-life implications of these various models. Their fears could be summed up in one question: how could the theater act on the world, as so many wanted it to, without risking making the world more like theater? Rétif's turn to reenactment, to the dream of a nontheatrical performance, consists of an attempt to alleviate these fears, by inventing a spectacle (or, in his mind, reviving it from primeval times) that assigns a judicial function to theater without in the process turning justice into theater—into a space of deception, emotional manipulation, unbridled and unclaimed speech, and illegitimate, unruly participation by a factious people.

PART II

Justice as Theater

Chapter 3

Players at the Bar

The Birth of the Modern Lawyer

Turning Justice into Theater

If, as we just saw, eighteenth-century Frenchmen were drawn to a vision of the theater as a site of justice, the inverse longing—turning trials into a dramatic spectacle—tugged at them with an even more forceful pull. This desire is at its most evident in "De la décadence du barreau français," a manifesto written by Jacques Pierre Brissot, a young lawyer destined to play a leading role in the legal reforms of the Revolution.[1] Looking back to antiquity, Brissot asks: "Why not model our tribunal on the Roman Rostra? There, dominating an immense crowd, orators were not hindered in their movements nor condemned to an eternal rest."[2] Such a proposal entails a radical redesigning of courtroom space, one that overlaps in significant ways with the architectural transformations promoted by theatrical reformers in the second half of the eighteenth century.[3] Like the dramatic thinkers of his day, notably Diderot, Brissot highlights material obstacles to the staging of a stirring spectacle. In lieu of the narrow space that forced lawyers (like actors) to curb their movements, he calls for a large, elevated platform.[4] To the courtrooms of his day, small, somber, and rectangular like French theaters, he opposes the vast, circular auditoriums of the ancients, able to accommodate the population of an entire city even as they offered superior sight lines and acoustics.[5] Also on Brissot's list of grievances, as on that of dramatic reformers: the absurdity of the costumes, the lack of a school specializing in actio and declamation, and the imperfect lighting that, together with the absence of a rigid separation between the stage and the auditorium (lawyers, like actors, were lost among spectators seated on what ought to have been a self-enclosed stage), rendered the passion on the performer's face and in his eyes difficult to see.[6] The similarities in the vision of legal and theatrical reformers also extend beyond material concerns. Both condemn their predecessors for prioritizing the textual over the visual, as when Brissot criticizes lawyers who simply read or recite their speeches from memory, instead of performing them.[7] Both call for the use of simple, accessible language, in lieu of the verbose, derivative jargon of tragic playwrights and jurists.[8] And both reflect a sentimental worldview, notably in their support for emotional appeals (especially through public displays of suffering) and in their rejection of fixed rules and authorities.[9]

Such similarities are hardly surprising. Theatrical and legal reformers drew from a common archetype: antiquity, a time when justice and drama were closely related spectacles, performed in similar (and sometimes identical) amphitheaters, before the same spectators, and by men with a shared training in actio and declamation.[10] This conception of legal proceedings as a public performance had little in common, however, with criminal trials in the ancien régime. As we saw in the Introduction, criminal proceedings prior to the Revolution unfolded behind closed doors. An examining magistrate questioned the accused, plaintiff, and witnesses separately and secretly (without spectators, lawyers, or even the judges present) and compiled a dossier containing the transcripts of the interrogations, the reports of medical and forensic experts, and any trial briefs submitted to the court. The dossier was then passed on to the judges who read, collated, and evaluated the enclosed documents according to fixed rules. Each document was assigned a numerical value (near "full-proof" for a confession, "half-proof" for a reliable testimony, "quarter-proof" for a variety of other clues), and these fractions of truth were added together to compose a guilty verdict. Physical presence, speech, emotional appeals, (legal) representation, and spectators—in short, all the characteristics of a theatrical performance—were thus deliberately excluded from criminal trials. The reforms endorsed by Brissot and his allies sought to reintroduce all of these characteristics and therefore inevitably entailed bringing legal proceedings closer to a dramatic performance, but what is particularly striking in their writings is that they were wholly aware and supportive of this—a fact that should give pause to scholars who have argued that the reformers swung justice away from theatricality.[11] In fact, legal reformers frequently drew attention to the similarities between their conception of justice and the theater, with Brissot even praising playhouses as the only "school" where members of the legal profession could still find models.[12] Nowhere is this theatrical frame of reference as evident—and transformative—as in the new way that liberal reformers described the roles of lawyers.

In and of itself, the frequent call for the inclusion and sustained involvement of lawyers in criminal cases already signaled a different understanding of the way that justice ought to be performed. Under the ancien régime, lawyers played a limited role in legal proceedings. While they were allowed to speak before the court in civil cases, it was primarily to make a concluding speech, and solely (at least in theory) to address fine points of jurisprudence and legal precedent, *not* to discuss the facts of the case. In criminal proceedings, they were barred altogether from appearing in court. By contrast, the examining magistrate played a broad, active role, notably by interrogating witnesses and rival parties. When the accused appeared for the first time before his judges, near the end of the trial, it was to respond to the case that the examining magistrate had, without his knowledge, already built against him. Eighteenth-century jurists, particularly those opposed to the reform movement, often noted that since the role of the accused was limited to answering the simple, factual questions asked by his judges, no advanced knowledge or preparation was required. The accused was not expected to provide a counter-narrative, only to avow or disavow individual accusations, and hence had no need for a legal counsel to help him craft and deliver a compelling case. A lawyer, many argued, would only introduce delays and artifice in what was supposed to be a straightforward interrogation by impartial judges.[13] Such a performance of justice differs greatly from the accusatorial model practiced in antiquity and favored by many liberal reformers, notably in its lack of "agon." This concept, which the ancients used to describe formalized, public debates both in trials and in dramatic performances, constituted one of the principal links between the theater and justice of antiquity.[14] As Brissot often noted, the Romans perceived trials as an oratorical joust, in which two parties presented clashing narratives to judges tasked with selecting the most credible. This agonistic conception of legal proceedings informed many of the liberal reformers' demands. If the accused needed to be given advance knowledge of the charges and evidence against them, the right to call their own witnesses, and the help of a trained counsel, it was to ensure they could prepare and practice their own narrative most effectively. Whereas ancien régime jurists favored a process of investigation, collation, and addition, in which an authority figure is tasked with uncovering and elaborating a single narrative and then setting out to demonstrate, mathematically, its validity, most liberal reformers preferred a dialogical model, allowing both parties equal time and support to make the best possible case before disinterested judges.

This agonistic vision of trials entailed not only a more significant and sustained role for lawyers but a different one as well. Because the primary function of ancien régime lawyers, once a trial had begun, was to notify magistrates in writing of legal precedents and other fine points of jurisprudence supporting their client's case, the Order of Barristers considered the key qualities of its members to be an encyclopedic knowledge of France's complicated laws and customs, a precise, technical writing style, modesty and moderation in every endeavor, and loyalty to the order above any desire for personal fame or wealth. As a result, the order deterred and even occasionally disbarred those who, to quote Brissot, wrote in a "flowery style," pled with a "theatrical declamation," or committed the sin "of cultivating letters."[15] In fact, in the years prior to Brissot's manifesto, the Order of Barristers had engaged in a particularly aggressive backlash against the rise of a new breed of young, literary, fiery, and ambitious lawyers. Such illustrious names as Simon Linguet and François de Neufchâteau were dismissed from the bar, while nearly half of the new candidates in 1781 were turned away, according to Brissot, for reasons that included a perceived lack of moderation, a penchant for the dramatic, both in their legal writings and in their more creative works, and an overriding ambition for personal glory.[16]

It was this battle to define the very nature of a lawyer that, Brissot feared, the order was currently winning: "Alas! They are no more, those days when orators, combining strokes of eloquence with the charms of a moving declamation, communicated their fire, enthusiasm, and passions to their listeners, and electrified their souls."[17] By altering the performance of justice and eliminating the Order of Barristers (thereby allowing any gifted speaker to plead), Brissot hoped to turn the tide in the young lawyers' favor and resurrect in the process the great orators of antiquity. In his Roman-inspired vision of legal proceedings, lawyers did not simply dispense technical assistance from behind the scenes; they helped craft a compelling narrative concerning the facts of the case, which they then delivered publicly, with the skill and emotions necessary to sway the judges. To that end, they needed to possess a "first-rate sensibility," prowess in "the language of poetry," "the voice of *tragedians*," and "the pantomime of the greatest actors."[18] These attributes could be acquired by attending the theater, which had preserved in its practice the ancient arts of corporal eloquence, of heartrending declamation, and of the properly timed poetic flourish. Only by becoming more like modern actors could lawyers regain the exalted status of Roman orators.

The campaign to reform the legal system has usually been portrayed in political terms, with proponents and opponents assigned sides in a sweeping binary opposition between two perfectly opposed visions of government and society. In one corner stood reactionaries who defended the secretive, socially stratified legal system of the ancien régime because it reflected the conservative, absolutist culture they supported. In the other corner were liberal reformers who, inspired by ideals like publicity, pluralism, and individual rights, sought to open up and democratize the justice system by giving lay citizens a greater role in the courtroom.[19] This quest for a more public and egalitarian justice system led many reformers to openly and unreservedly model trials on the basic structure of a dramatic performance. However, as we will see in this chapter and the next (on judges), many others—not only reactionaries but, crucially, liberal thinkers as well—expressed a profound uneasiness at this theatricalization of justice. This shared anxiety calls into question the standard depiction of Enlightenment legal reforms as a conflict between clear-cut ideologies, culminating in the unmitigated victory of liberal ideals—a narrative of erasure and replacement, rather than of negotiation and compromise. On the contrary, the unease experienced by many reformers reveals that they, like the reactionaries, perceived the shift toward a more liberal justice as a perilous slide toward overly theatrical trials, an outcome no more desirable in their eyes than a perpetuation of the status quo. Their fears crystallized most visibly around the figures of the lawyer and the judge, whose conversion into "mere" actors and spectators threatened to undermine their authority and the legitimacy of the justice system as a whole. At every turn, the reformers struggled with the same dilemma: how could the liberal ideals of publicity and popular participation be applied to legal proceedings without turning them into staged spectacles akin to theatrical performances? This essential threat at the heart of liberal justice inspired original twists and solutions to age-old questions. In fact, countless aspects of the justice system in France today, and in particular the rise of modern forms of legal representation and judgment, find their roots in these solutions and are therefore less the result of a direct implementation of liberal values such as transparency and equality than they are a compromise between these ideals and a pervasive fear of theatricality.

The Lawyer-Actor Is Reborn

The figure of the lawyer-actor has of course a long and rich history, with none other than Cicero claiming that legal orators are just actors who perform real life.[20] The analogy between lawyers and actors may seem particularly obvious today. Aside, perhaps, from politicians, no other group is as frequently compared to actors. It is precisely the triteness of this analogy in ancient and modern societies that makes it all the more noteworthy that it was rarely, if ever, used in seventeenth-century France. In "Le Plaideur comme comédien: L'Art dramatique du procès," Dianne Dutton attempts to draw such a parallel, on the basis of broad, transhistorical similarities (the lawyer "represents" his client, "acting" for him before an audience) and the presence in legal manuals of sections on *actio* and *pronuntiatio*, that is, on the delivery of a plea.[21] Tellingly, however, all of her quotations likening lawyers to actors come from modern texts or from recent translations of ancient authors like Cicero, rather than from seventeenth-century sources. While it is true that seventeenth-century writers recognized the importance of gestures and declamation in legal pleas, in doing so they merely followed classical teachings, which included delivery as one of the five essential canons of rhetoric. In no texts from the period have I found the slightest suggestion that the bar's practice of actio was deemed analogous to playacting.[22] In fact, when lawyers were compared to anyone, it was almost always to preachers,[23] and never to actors, as if public speaking and acting occupied completely different realms of human experience. This held true not only discursively but physically as well: strict rules aimed to keep lawyers and actors from inhabiting the same spaces, thereby hindering any possible comparison. The actors' condition as *infâmes* (a form of ostracism to which we will return) forbade them access to the courtroom by denying them a legal status and, with it, the right to serve as an accuser, witness, lawyer, or magistrate in a tribunal.[24] As for lawyers, their order sought to thwart any interaction with the world of the theater, warning them against entering playhouses to attend performances (though it should be noted that many flouted these warnings). The order went so far, in fact, as to extend its prohibition to the domestic sphere, threatening to disbar any member guilty of having let thespians into his household by marrying an actress or even just the relative of an actor.[25] Admittedly, such draconian rules suggest an underlying anxiety at the very possibility that a parallel between lawyers and actors could be drawn, but they also ensured that the two were rarely, if ever, brought together, whether in discourse or in reality.

By contrast, starting in the 1750s, the comparison between lawyers and actors became increasingly common, to such an extent that the second half of the eighteenth century can be seen as marking the rebirth of a modern cliché. Unlike today, however, the analogy was not meant to belittle either profession. In fact, its resurgence occurred in texts on both lawyers and actors, exerting pressure from both ends to bring them closer together. For authors writing on actors, drawing a parallel with lawyers offered a means to defend players at a time when the long simmering dispute between pro- and antitheatricalists had been reignited by the publication of Rousseau's *Lettre à d'Alembert* in 1758. Among the many charges leveled by Rousseau against the theater was the essential immorality of actors, who publicly sold their bodies and words to the crowd, shedding their true selves to satisfy the desires of the spectators, and subjecting themselves to their judgment and jeers out of a longing for fame and wealth. In response, the actors' supporters frequently noted that lawyers too performed publicly in civil trials, acting for another in exchange for money, as well as in the hope of earning the admiration of an audience that could choose to boo them instead.[26] Such similarities meant, according to Barthélemy Graillard de Graville, that the legal profession was "most analogous to the actor's," despite the fact that only the latter incurred public infamy.[27] This recurring analogy between the two occupations, which highlighted the injustice of their very different standings, no doubt played a role in the lawyer François Huerne de la Mothe's decision in 1761, the same year as the publication of Graville's text, to take on the actress Mlle Clairon's case against the civil and religious ostracism endured by her peers. When the Order of Barristers, irate that Huerne de la Mothe's intervention implicitly aligned them with actors, dismissed him from the bar, he made the implicit explicit by embracing instead the career of a theatrical performer. While he met with little success in his new profession, he set a precedent that others, like the famous actor Grandmesnil, originally a lawyer in the Paris Parlement, followed to greater avail.

In the same years that theater aficionados began likening actors to lawyers, scholars of forensic rhetoric narrowed the gap between legal and theatrical performers from the other end, by arguing that lawyers should seek training from actors. The first to make this claim was Pierre Biarnoy de Merville, in 1711. His daring suggestion that young lawyers could learn proper elocution from actors was tempered if not contradicted, however, by his repetition in the same passage of the old, seventeenth-century belief that legal and dramatic declamations differed in essential ways.[28] Still, the seed had been sown, and by 1775, François Gourdin could state that Merville's informal proposal had turned into a frequent question: "can the Comédie-Française train a preacher or lawyer?"[29] Gourdin traces the real start of this debate to—once again—the middle of the eighteenth century and to a disagreement between two famous actors, Luigi Riccoboni and Poussin.[30] He attempts to reconcile them by concluding that while Riccoboni correctly argues that the acting of his time is too exaggerated to provide a suitable model for young lawyers, the latter would benefit from private lessons with actors, who would be free, behind closed doors, to eschew the unnatural conventions of the stage.[31] Gourdin hence suggests that while pleading and acting diverge in style and emphasis, they remain at their core the same practice.

Pierre-Louis-Claude Gin certainly shared this view; in *De l'Éloquence du barreau*, he states that lawyers ought to practice role-playing with professional actors because "through this exercise the soul grows accustomed to entering another's emotions."[32] In this perspective, judicial actio is more than a set of codified gestures and cadences, as was still the case, for instance, in Merville's *Règles pour former un avocat*, which fixes everything from the height of a shoulder shrug and the standard gesture when starting a plea (tenting one's fingers) to the fact that one's head should always be turned toward a hand motion, except when expressing indignation at an idea, as if pushing it away.[33] For Gin, a lawyer's actio should arise less from his training in a static oratorical choreography than from an actorly identification with his client. Climbing on stage does not mean internalizing a new set of rules (like, for instance, Merville's "proper elocution"); it means discovering new modes of feeling and speaking—"as" another, rather than just "for" another—and learning to control these borrowed emotions so as to communicate them most effectively.[34] Those who, like Gin, favored a theatrical formation for budding lawyers—and by the 1760s and 1770s, most thinkers who raised this once-inconceivable question sided with Gin—essentially redefined judicial actio from the use of a small set of acceptable movements, assimilated through legal training and classical erudition, to a form of playacting, in which gestures are the heartfelt expression of the lawyer's identification with his client. In so doing, they brought French lawyers and actors closer than ever before.

For the lawyer-actor parallel to have resurfaced in the second half of the eighteenth century is hardly surprising, considering the reformers' attempts to revive many aspects of the public, spectacular trials of antiquity. Cicero was on every lip, and few failed to mention his passion for the theater and his private lessons with the legendary actor Roscius.[35] This Cicero-mania shows how much the conception of legal practice had changed from previous centuries. David Bell has noted that, until the middle of the seventeenth century if not later, most lawyers rejected the example of Cicero and his dramatic eloquence, on the grounds that lawyers in a monarchy were tasked not with persuading a public of citizens, but with conveying the king's will, as expressed in his laws, to the judges charged with exercising it.[36] Convinced that their legitimacy derived from the rare insights into the king's logos that years of study had given them, they appealed incessantly for full noble status,[37] that is, for the kind of secure place in the absolutist hierarchy that would cement their role as the king's chosen vessels. Starting in the early eighteenth century, however, a growing number of lawyers began embracing the completely opposite notion that they embodied a natural order, unsullied by the hierarchical divisions of the monarchy. In an oft-cited speech, Henri François d'Aguesseau described the bar as a unique profession in which success is determined by one's talents and virtues and not by "luck of birth" or "prejudices of rank."[38] Later thinkers went even further, variously describing the bar as a "democracy," "a sort of absolutely independent little republic," and a sanctuary of "natural liberty"—that is, as a symbol for the liberal dream of a truly meritocratic society.[39]

If not in the king, however, where would lawyers find legitimacy? For some, the answer lay in a rigorous Order of Barristers, which would guarantee the probity and erudition of every lawyer by purging from its ranks unworthy individuals. Others, however, found in the vision of the courtroom as a Roman forum and of lawyers as Cicero a second solution, more compatible with the liberal ideals of transparency and free, open debate. As we saw earlier, Brissot and likeminded reformers called for tribunals to be opened to lay citizens, who would be invited to participate both as spectators and, if chosen by a client, as legal counsel. This vision, in which anyone, regardless of rank or training, was allowed to plead in court, meant the end of the legal profession as an exclusive order, but it conferred on lawyers the same gift as on their Roman ancestors: the legitimacy that comes from being freely chosen by a client on the basis of one's reputation. A man known to be lacking in morality or merit would never appear in court, for he would never find clients. Linguet and the generation of young, passionate, literary lawyers that came to the fore in the second half of the eighteenth century reflected this new vision. They proudly proclaimed their desire for glory, which they defined as the esteem of the public, and through their emphasis on poetic language, bodily eloquence, and sentimental appeals shifted the focus of legal practice from clarifying the king's logos (the laws) for his chosen enforcer (the judges) to winning over public opinion.

This redefinition of the role of lawyers in terms of public acclaim and emotional impact naturally reinforced the analogy to dramatic actors, but it also highlighted similarities extending beyond the significance of actio in both practices. In an absolutist society where, in theory at least, there could exist no debate, only obedience to the king's word, tribunals were almost unique in valuing the art of public speaking, argumentation, and persuasion above rank and privileges. The bar held a rare promise of social mobility; for gifted commoners, success in the tribunal could open doors to the highest society, purely based on their oratorical prowess (Gerbier, for instance, was visited by the king of Denmark, who wished to see him plead).[40] In many ways, the same held true of actors. Early modern troupes fixed their own membership and repertoire independently, according to a voting system that rewarded talent and seniority—an autonomous, participatory model that the seventeenth-century playwright and lawyer Samuel Chappuzeau labeled a "manner of republic."[41] Like lawyers, actors thus held an unusual, ill-defined place in the royal hierarchy, and yet enjoyed unparalleled access to the table and private chambers of the nation's greatest families, owing to their fame and to their gift for moving and persuading others through their speeches and bodies, with many aristocrats even lowering themselves to ask their inferiors to train them in this skill. Such social mobility partly explains why Brissot and others, who frequently deplored living in a society that did not reward oratorical genius with positions of power in the government, as it had in Cicero's time, embraced the parallel between lawyers and actors so explicitly and unambivalently. In their eyes, lawyers and actors stood as emblems of an alternative, liberal social order, in which all men held the right to engage in free, transparent debate, with public opinion determining the place in society of each individual, on the basis not of his birth but of his merit and eloquence.

Fearing the Lawyer-Actor

Naturally, not everyone welcomed this new order. When Chavray de Boissy likened the rising generation of lawyers to actors, his aim was not to laud them as self-made orators but to condemn their "pompous declamation, and their analogous voice, better suited to our theaters, if one wished to depict there the expression and action of a violent passion."[42] Critics of the new lawyers claimed that the lack of moderation in their expressions and emotions directly ensued from their obsession with the public reception of their pleas. They "played to the crowd" like actors did, with undue pathos, wit, and satire, and for the same reason: a thirst for "celebrity." Such an accusation is not surprising, given the middle of the eighteenth century saw the birth of celebrity culture. To those who despised this new phenomenon, "celebrity" was the antithesis of "glory" (the term used by the new lawyers to justify their desire for fame): it lacked the latter's legitimacy and permanence because it was based not on merit but on attracting the attention—positive or negative—of a superficial, mercurial public.[43] In fact, traditionalist lawyers argued that publicity, that most liberal of principles, fostered not only illegitimacy (a point to which we will return) but immorality as well. Drawing on antitheatrical discourse, they noted that performing for an audience corrupted actors in two seemingly contradictory ways. First, it provoked a loss of self, as the actors' dependence on the spectators for their livelihood required that they play any role and say anything that the audience desired, thus sacrificing their own values and beliefs to please others. Second, it fostered an obsession with the self, as the applause bred in the actors such arrogance that they came to see themselves as the equals of the aristocrats they portrayed on stage and mingled with offstage.[44] Love of publicity, traditionalist lawyers concluded, had corrupted Linguet (listed by Antoine Lilti as one of the first celebrities)[45] and his peers in much the same way it had actors. Again and again, they chastised their new colleagues for making scandalous statements for the sake of attention, and for lacking respect for their superiors inside and outside the order. Such theatrical conduct also showed contempt for the litigants, whose interests lawyer-actors sacrificed to their thirst for celebrity by seeking the public's applause instead of the judges' esteem.[46]

For the anonymous author of *Consultation sur la discipline des avocats*, pleading "to amuse the people" instead of "to enlighten the judges" had another, even direr consequence: it degraded the "nobility" of the legal profession.[47] Such an assertion suggests a deeper political anxiety produced by the theatricality at the core of the liberal vision of society and justice. Indeed, for every Brissot who hailed performers as symbols of social fluidity, many others denounced them as a threat to the social order—for the exact same reason. The abbé Gros de Besplas thus lamented that "the lowly actor is admitted to the most noble circles at court and in Paris: his pernicious talent serves as his lineage."[48] Like d'Aguesseau before him, the abbé noted that among performers, talent replaced filiation as the principal criterion determining one's place in the social hierarchy, but he condemned this situation as pernicious to the nobility and to a stable society. Naturally, fears of this nature have a history almost as long as the theater itself, having changed remarkably little since Plato first labeled the theater a menace to the orderly distribution of ranks and functions.[49] Yet the hundreds of pamphlets on the theater printed in the second half of the eighteenth century reveal a particularly intense resurgence of this anxiety. The political implications of acting were on everyone's mind, so much so that Paul-Antoine-Nicolas Nolivos de Saint-Cyr argued that they, not spiritual concerns, were the true motives behind the excommunication of actors in France. Religious ostracism, he explained, had been deemed necessary by the state to keep the theater from blurring the distinctions between ranks. First, it ensured aristocrats and wealthy bourgeois could not enter into a church-sanctioned marriage with the alluring actresses they frequented, thus preventing misalliances.[50] Second, it deterred young noblemen enthralled by the celebrity and freedom of actors from pursuing a career in the theater in lieu of "the offices and titles that parents wish to pass down to their children."[51] This fear echoes Plato's critique of acting as a form of depropriation. By disclosing to young men the possibility of, and pleasure in, performing social roles beyond the ones allotted to them by birth, acting threatened not only the self-replication of social groups and distinctions but their very existence, insofar as the actor's unique freedom to assume any role heralded a world in which no one possessed an exclusive claim to a particular function.

In such a world, power no longer lay in filiation, but rather in the ability to play a role convincingly. Brissot felt this would enable the rise of a true meritocracy, as in Rome, when eloquence was rewarded by public esteem and influence. Others were less sanguine, voicing, like Rousseau, the fear that actors would come to govern a society thus (dis)organized.[52] In fact, the resurgent antitheatricalism in the second half of the eighteenth century can be at least partly understood as the expression of a deeper anxiety relating to the implications of the liberal vision of society and justice, and notably the risk that it would bring about a crisis in legitimacy. In an absolutist regime, authority comes from one's identity—one's fixed place in the social order. By contrast, Brissot's liberal meritocracy situates authority not in the individual, and least of all in his title, but in his speech, as evaluated by its audience. For Rousseau and others, the theater represents an extreme example of this conception of speech as detached from personal legitimacy. Indeed, an actor's speech on stage is unique in that its audience does not evaluate it in relationship to the identity of its speaker. It is a requirement of the actor's trade that he be allowed, while in character, to utter words normally forbidden (whether to all or just to commoners like him), without being held personally accountable.[53] The result is a complete dissociation: the speaker is not judged on the basis of his speech (the words are the author's and the character's—doubly not "his"), just as the speech is not judged on the basis of its speaker (the actor's morality and social class are irrelevant). In response to such dissociated speech, the ancien régime exiled actors from society, confining them to a special category: *les infâmes*—a fitting designation, since *infâme* shares a root with *infans*, or, etymologically, "he who knows not how to speak."[54] In the eyes of many, the liberal vision of society and justice now raised the same peril as actors: the proliferation of an "empty" speech, disconnected from the speaker's legitimacy, and thus, unauthenticated and unaccountable. Not only did such speech offer no assurance of morality or truth, it also represented an unstable foundation for a society. Speech, unlike birth, is never fixed; it is infinitely reiterable and forever changing. In a social order founded on eloquence, all may speak, but none can claim a lasting legitimacy, for it only ever exists fleetingly—in the moment of speaking—and externally—in the opinions of others.

More than any other sites, the tribunal was supposed to offer a counterexample to and a rampart against the empty speech of the theater. In the prevailing view prior to the eighteenth century, the words spoken in a court of law were "full"—legitimate and effective—because of their speakers' identities: men of law who had been chosen by the king, the source of all truth and order, to express his infallible will. Reformers deprived lawyers and judges of the intrinsic legitimacy that came with being exclusive vessels of the king's logos, however, by reimagining the tribunal as a space where men of all backgrounds could plead before a public entrusted with evaluating speakers on the basis of their persuasiveness, not their identities. Locating authority in speeches rather than individuals, traditionalist lawyers and jurists argued, was precisely the reason why eighteenth-century justice increasingly resembled a performance, an oratorical contest between sophists choosing their words less from a belief in their veracity than from a desire for celebrity. In fact, so pervasive was this anxiety at the implications of dissociating speech from its speaker that it even affected many liberal reformers, as is suggested by their ambivalence on the question of *infâme* witnesses.

For centuries, the law had endeavored to keep empty speech out of the courtroom by prohibiting *les infâmes* (actors, criminals, heretics, and others) from testifying, on the grounds that their lack of a social identity stripped their words of any personal legitimacy. Although these restrictions were loosened slightly in 1670, when magistrates were given dispensation in grave cases to hear, if not necessarily count as evidence, the testimony of certain *infâmes*, Cesare Beccaria's proposal in 1764 that anyone who had seen a crime ought to be allowed to testify marked a radical departure from the traditional vision of testimony. Many reformers, including Brissot and Voltaire, warmly embraced this novel idea that the value of a testimony should be assessed on the basis of its content (are there contradictions, exaggerations, or outbursts that suggest dishonesty or impartiality?), rather than its speaker.[55] Such support for Beccaria's proposal is hardly surprising, considering how closely it dovetailed with liberal tenets such as the need for greater equality before the law, the benefits of free, public debate, and the ability of lay spectators to form an accurate opinion on a speech's veracity. Far more unexpected and, as a result, revealing is the number of liberal reformers who rejected this modern conception of testimony. For instance, Jean-Paul Marat suggested that, despite what other reformers sometimes seemed to believe, no speech contained in and of itself unequivocal proof of its own truthfulness. For such certainty, one would need to know the speaker's "heart," but as this was impossible, it became necessary, in order to protect the authority of human justice, to find an objective means of distinguishing legitimate testimonies from illegitimate ones. The identity of the witness—age, past crimes, current vices, and occupation—provided such a means, making it possible to recuse witnesses who, however sincere, lacked the public's trust.[56] Among other disqualifying attributes, Marat includes "the habit of lying": a clear reference to actors. In this, he again differs from the liberals in favor of Beccaria's proposal, who all dodge the issue of actors, even though performers were one of the largest and most visible subgroups among *les infâmes*.[57] Brissot, for example, supports the right to testify for such a long list of past and present "judicial mutes"—madmen, simpletons, children, women, blacks, Jews, heretics, beggars, servants, slaves, executioners, prisoners, and surgeons—that it is difficult to believe that the actors' noninclusion is a mere oversight.[58] Rather, this absence hints at an unspoken reluctance to extend the right to testify to actors. Together with Marat's more categorical opposition, it reveals that even reformers worried that once words, not self, became the locus of truth, tribunals would find themselves overrun by empty speech and actor-witnesses.

The same anxiety about the theatrical consequences of introducing liberal ideas in the courtroom is evident in another heretofore unstudied debate, in response to the question: Should a lawyer defend someone he believes to be guilty? One may be tempted, like Dutton in "Le Plaideur comme comédien," to present this question as timeless, born of the representative gap between lawyers and the clients for whom they speak, and the possibility this inevitably raises that a lawyer might, like an actor, feign a sincere conviction in words and claims he knows to be the lies of a guilty individual.[59] Yet while the question may indeed arise from an essential and thus transhistorical attribute of the legal profession, this should not obscure its particular history as a subject of debate. Indeed, although the topic of legal representation for the guilty appears in many texts prior to the eighteenth century, it only became a proper, two-sided debate with the emergence of the liberal conception of justice. Before then, all jurists, without exception, gave one, and only one, answer—a lawyer should never defend anyone he deemed culpable. In other words, they raised the topic, but without raising it as a question: not to examine or debate it, but only as a public declaration against the temptation of accepting any and all cases out of greed or ambition. So unanimous was their answer, and so central to the early modern vision of the legal profession, that it appeared in the sacred oath, dating as far back as the fourteenth century, that all lawyers took before joining the Order of Barristers. By taking this oath (as they were obliged to), lawyers promised not only to refuse cases they deemed unfounded, but also, should they change their minds about the justness of their cause during a trial, to abandon their client immediately.[60]

Such an oath is likely to seem deeply problematic to readers accustomed to the liberal vision of justice. From a contemporary perspective, early modern jurists appear to misconstrue the function of lawyers, which is to represent clients, not decide their guilt—a fundamental misunderstanding that is dangerous, insofar as it violates the right to be presumed innocent until convicted in court, as well as naïve, since it reveals a careless confusion between the roles of lawyers and judges. It should be noted, however, that early modern jurists were fully aware that by encouraging lawyers to decline unjust cases, they invested the legal profession with the function of the magistracy. In fact, they often hailed lawyers for their role as the nation's "first judges." There was therefore nothing careless or naïve in the attribution to lawyers of judicial duties; on the contrary, early modern jurists had given the issue careful, explicit consideration before concluding it was more beneficial than dangerous. Merville offers one reason why: "lawyers are the first judges, and their jurisdiction is in a way greater than the magistrates', even sovereign ones, since they smother many more trials at birth."[61] By judging and deterring guilty parties, lawyers kept frivolous lawsuits out of the legal system, thereby reducing expenses, wasted time, and prolonged conflicts. Hence, instead of condemning the "confusion" between lawyers and magistrates based on a liberal division of functions, one ought to see it as a window into an alternate conception of the legal profession and, more broadly, of the justice system. Notably, it reveals that the relationship between lawyers and clients exceeded mere representation. By accepting clients, a lawyer vouched for them, lending them not just his voice but his own personal legitimacy, which he laid on the line as a guarantee of their innocence.

This particular relationship explains the obsession in early modern treatises and manuals with the morality of lawyers—not only in their professional conduct but also in their personal lives. This obsession went well beyond mere rhetoric: the Order of Barristers kept a close watch over its members, dismissing those it found guilty of violating ethical rules, including private ones seemingly unconnected to legal practice, such as conjugal fidelity.[62] For Merville and others, absolute probity was essential to the legal profession, because: "A judge gladly listens to a lawyer from whom he fears no surprises, and the mere presence of a virtuous lawyer makes clear which side to take, as he has only ever sided with the truth. His speeches do not adorn his life; his life adorns his speeches. . . . He is not forced to arrange the facts artistically to make them credible in the judges' minds. The identity of the speaker, the esteem and the trust that one feels toward him, are more persuasive than his words; for true eloquence lies less in the mind than in the heart."[63] As the first sentence indicates, the morality of a lawyer determines his effectiveness. In a legal system that asks lawyers to determine the guilt of the parties and only defend the innocent, the verdict of a trial comes to depend heavily on the judges' opinion of the lawyers' virtue. Judges often know little about the two parties, but their familiarity with the lawyers' degree of probity makes up for this ignorance, as they can be confident that the most virtuous lawyer has chosen the side of innocence.[64] As Merville stresses repeatedly, the truth can thus be found in the speaker's identity rather than solely in his speech. Indeed, it is a lawyer's identity as a man of virtue that gives his words their legitimacy and allows a trust-based justice system, in which "art," here synonymous with artifice, has little power, since chicanery (the false eloquence of the mind) cannot vanquish the frank, simple speech of a lawyer whose persuasiveness comes from his well-known integrity (the true eloquence of the heart).

Defining lawyers as a select group of exceptionally moral individuals with the legitimacy to vouch for the innocence of others, rather than as skilled public speakers, helped protect the courtroom not only from false eloquence but also from outright lies. Present-day critics of the legal profession may scoff at this idea, but for many early modern jurists, the very existence of lawyers could be explained and justified by their ability to keep lies from entering the sacred halls of justice.[65] As Merville noted, a litigant, even when innocent, is always tempted to resort to casuistry and falsehoods, because his or her principal interest lies in winning the case. The lawyer's duty, his raison d'être, is to assess his client's story and present a sanitized version to the judges by eliminating from it all forms of deceit and manipulation.[66] A lawyer can be trusted to perform this essential role as a truth filter—discarding unjust cases and purifying just ones—because unlike his client, he has a greater personal investment in the proper functioning of justice than he does in a single trial's outcome. Nothing illustrates this better than the unanimously negative response to the question of whether a lawyer may rely on deception to save a client he knows beyond any doubt to be innocent, but who faces a likely conviction. Early modern jurists rejected this scenario, on the grounds that being caught employing the distortions typical of a litigant, even for a good cause, would harm the lawyer's reputation and credibility in the eyes of the judges, thereby limiting his ability to defend other innocent parties in the future.[67] In this view of justice, a lawyer is accountable for his speeches; he invests each and every word with his personal legitimacy, which he stands to lose (along with his livelihood) if he repeats his client's fabrications. Before 1750, in fact, jurists frequently warned lawyers against feeling too much compassion for a client, for fear that they would then deliver overly emotional, argumentative pleas and give the impression that they were speaking *as* their client (representing) instead of *for* their client (vouching).[68] D'Aguesseau, who was, as Jeffrey Ravel has shown, deeply wary of theatricality, expressed a similar anxiety when he asserted that a lawyer should "be true to his own character, and never speak with the voice of anyone other than himself."[69] Were a lawyer to let his identity vanish behind a client's, he would cease to speak in his own name and just repeat, like an actor in character, the arguments of others, without picking and endorsing them. This would in turn force judges to base their verdicts on claims that had not been legitimized by a man of known virtue and for which no one could be held responsible, with disastrous consequences: false eloquence, lies, and the collapse of trust-based justice. Indeed, as naïve as it may seem today, the oath never to defend the guilty served as the cornerstone of a different, but coherent conception of justice, which valued above all else authenticated, accountable speech, inextricably bound to its speaker—the very antithesis of the theater.

Accordingly, when liberal reformers declared that all litigants (including, implicitly, the guilty) should be entitled to a lawyer, especially in criminal cases where it was then forbidden, they undermined their predecessors' antitheatrical conception of justice. The liberals' proclamation of a universal right to legal counsel (many even called for the institution of free, state-funded attorneys)[70] reflected their belief in the presumption of innocence, which meant that lawyers could not reject any potential client, since guilt could never be assigned without a trial.[71] It also signaled a shift from a justice system rooted in identity, and thus restricted to a select group of legitimate individuals, to one founded on the greater egalitarianism of speech. Indeed, liberal reformers praised legal representation as an essential equalizer, which leveled the field between individuals of contrasting wealth, education, and eloquence, by ensuring that both parties made their arguments known to the judges through the mouths of speakers with comparable training and fluency.[72] The absence of lawyers left the poor and uneducated, with their jumbled and hesitant answers, far too vulnerable to the machinations of the more articulate and wealthier members of society. In this vision of justice, lawyers thus serve a function the very inverse of their former role, insofar as their purpose is now to detach words from their original speakers (the clients) to ensure each claim is evaluated on the basis of its judicial strength, irrespective of the claimant's identity. A lawyer's duty is no longer to speak *for* (judge and endorse), but rather to speak *as* his clients—that is, to make the same claims they would have, with the same aim (winning the case), but better, with the fluency and assuredness of an experienced orator.

In this new role, a lawyer's eloquence takes precedence over his morality. It thus comes as no surprise that many liberal reformers joined the new generation of lawyers in condemning the relentless attempts by the Order of Barristers to police the professional and personal ethics of its members. This so-called moral "censorship," Brissot, Linguet, and others argued, served in reality as a pretext for the exclusion of gifted orators, whose growing fame posed a threat to the livelihood of a stodgy legal profession.[73] In so doing, the liberals opened a breach between morality and eloquence that found its most explicit formulation in Giovanni Ferri's assertion, in a chapter advocating the removal of ethics from the study of rhetoric, that "speech can by itself appear worthy of belief, independently of its speaker."[74] Dissociating speech and speaker in this way would have been unthinkable for traditional jurists. Their entire vision of justice was rooted in identity, each verdict regarded as a divine truth, since uttered by the king's chosen vessels (the judges), and endorsed by a moral elite (lawyers) with the requisite legitimacy to ward off lies and manipulation. Yet the inequality and arbitrariness of a system that located truth solely in a few individuals, their much-vaunted legitimacy usually little more than an accident of birth, led the reformers to propose instead that all could plead, by which they meant both that every citizen would be entitled to a lawyer and that anyone could serve as that lawyer, irrespective of morality, rank, or membership in an exclusive order. The universal right to counsel thus played a key role in the evolution of the lawyers' (perceived) function from moral vouchers to eloquent representatives; not surprisingly, it also became, as a result, a locus for the anxiety that this transformation triggered.

Today, the universal right to a lawyer ranks among the least controversial of the liberal reforms, yet it raised a thorny issue in the eighteenth century, in that it required, particularly in clear-cut cases, that one of the two lawyers plead for a client whose innocence he doubted. Just as they had sidestepped the issue of witness-actors, however, most reformers failed to note this essential contradiction between the liberal right to counsel and the traditional oath never to defend the guilty. On the contrary, they continued to affirm that lawyers should act as the first judge of a client's guilt, often in the very same books that they endorsed the presumption of innocence. Hence, in Mercier's utopia *L'An 2440*, lawyers turn down unjust cases and vouch for the ones they accept.[75] While *L'An 2440* is not a legal treatise, its astounding popularity means its depiction of the ideal lawyer was among the most widely read in eighteenth-century France. Moreover, in his other, nonfiction writings, Mercier, like many reformers, including Linguet, frequently condemns the lawyers of his day for taking on cases they deem unjust—a practice that a universal right to counsel would make mandatory.[76] The liberal lawyer Mézard goes even further than mere criticism, noting that if "the litigants' defenders must be their first judges," as he still believed, it follows that lawyers should be punished for defending a clearly guilty party.[77] Nor was he alone in proposing to link the fates of client and lawyer,[78] a surprising idea at a time when the right to counsel and the presumption of innocence were first being seriously considered in France, and a clear indication, therefore, of the uneasiness, even among liberals, with seeming to sanction legal representation for the guilty.[79]

Gin was the first of a small group of reformers to grapple with this problem explicitly. Forced to choose between two incompatible ideals, Gin sided with the right to counsel. He conceded that a lawyer who believed a potential client to be guilty should inform him or her of this judgment, to avert a likely loss in court, but added that if the client persisted, the lawyer was then required to defend him or her with total commitment.[80] None before Gin (at least in France) had ever conceived of such a duty, which defied the lawyer's ancient oath but took the universal right to counsel to its only logical conclusion. To bolster his case, Gin also defined, again before anyone else, the division of legal roles that we still uphold today, notably in his claim that a lawyer who turns a client away should be ashamed "to have appointed himself the case's only judge."[81] Although a pioneer, Gin still made some concessions to the early modern vision of lawyers, as when he stated that a lawyer could refuse to plead for a litigant whose guilt was beyond dispute. Fourteen years later, Jacques-Vincent Delacroix dared to extend the right to counsel to nearly all litigants, including most caught in the act.[82] Yet even Delacroix felt it necessary to add certain stipulations, which reveal the true reasons for the collective reluctance to extend the right to counsel to the clearly guilty. "So as not to compromise the dignity of his ministry," a lawyer defending a criminal should, according to Delacroix, plead with the coldness and simplicity of a disinterested man, whose first responsibility is to the truth, and even confess his client's crimes, instead of denying or justifying them. As Delacroix tellingly puts it, "the lawyer would not identify with the accused, and would appear less his defender than that of the law and the truth."[83] In other words, a lawyer should never speak *as* (identify with) a manifestly guilty client—a surprising interdiction, considering liberals, including, as we saw earlier, both Gin and Delacroix, largely supported the evolution of the legal profession from guarantors of truth to eloquent spokespeople. Hence, although the universal right to a lawyer drew countless supporters when presented as a way of leveling the playing field between litigants of contrasting ranks and education, none, not even Delacroix, accepted as we do today that it also meant that obviously guilty individuals should be given the exact same legal representation as their innocent victims.

What might explain the liberal reformers' uneasiness with their own ideal of universal counsel? The answer goes beyond the expected one, namely that speaking *as* a guilty client turns lawyers into liars by forcing them to make claims they know to be false. After all, the anxiety concerns trials where the client's guilt is more than just suspected by the lawyer, it is evident to everyone—precisely the type of case where the fabrications of a clever attorney are least to be feared, since they will be quite apparent to all and unlikely to change the verdict, as they might in a more ambiguous case. As Delacroix's text suggests, the anxiety runs deeper; it has to do with "dignity," with the legitimacy of the legal profession as a whole, once it is no longer perceived to speak *for* the truth, but only *as* a client. What most concerns Delacroix and his contemporaries is not, paradoxically, that the universal right to counsel might produce more liars, but that it might produce none—because all lawyers will be transformed into actors. Indeed, despite the standard critique of actors as liars, the two are radically different, as eighteenth-century thinkers well knew, since even Rousseau had conceded as much in his *Lettre à d'Alembert*. Liars seek to deceive the public by claiming to be certain of a "fact" that they secretly believe to be false. As Harry Frankfurt has noted in *On Bullshit*, liars thus care deeply about the truth.[84] There are pragmatic reasons for this: liars must know the truth to compose the falsehood most likely to succeed in replacing and thus concealing it. More significant still are the philosophical reasons. Liars ultimately play the same game as truth tellers (albeit on opposite sides), in that both claim to be defenders of the truth. They invest their legitimacy in each falsehood, authenticating it and assuming responsibility for it. By contrast, actors do not genuinely seek to deceive the audience, who is a knowing participant in the dramatic fiction. The spectators accept that actors make no claim whatsoever—do not, in fact, pay any attention—to the truth of the statements they utter on stage. Actors never lie, because they do not endorse their own speech; their role is to heighten the impact of another's words, irrespective of their proximity to reality or to their own beliefs. This is precisely the role that the universal right to counsel assigns to lawyers, by requiring that they set aside their own beliefs regarding the truth of the case and relate the arguments of their client in the most compelling way possible. In such a system, lawyers cannot be liars, because they understand—as does their audience—that like theatrical performers they are not supposed to care about the truth, let alone speak it.

The liberal vision of lawyers thus goes beyond the adoption of a more dramatic actio (as existed in antiquity) by also instituting a "theatrical" relationship to truth for which I know no precedent (not even in antiquity). In so doing, it inaugurates a new breed of lawyer-actors. Indeed, the novel idea of a universal right to counsel casts lawyers together with actors as the only individuals allowed to dissociate their speech from their identities in the exercise of their functions. Duty bound to represent guilty parties as best they can, lawyers never vouch for the veracity of their claims, nor are they held accountable for them (if they prove to be inaccurate). Their words, like those of actors, are the definition of empty speech—statements unattached to any speaker willing to endorse them as the truth. Not surprisingly, however, the notion of lawyers as unbeholden to truth proved unpalatable even to the most devout liberals. This is undoubtedly why, even as they championed a system that grounds judgment in speech rather than identity, they asserted by way of reassurance that speech always reflects its speaker's identity. Drawing from Cicero and other writers of antiquity, they argued that one cannot speak well unless one is a moral and honest man, since true eloquence only comes to those inspired by love of virtue and a sincere belief in the veracity of one's cause.[85] As so often, the liberals here fall back upon publicity as the system's saving grace. The spectators do not need to know the speaker's rank, morality, or honesty, because they can reach the correct verdict solely by hearing him plead. A speech that the public deems eloquent reveals more than simply talent; it also proves the goodness of the speaker and that of his case. This perceived infallibility of public opinion allows the liberal reformers to reattach speech to its speaker and thereby dispel fears of an empty speech.

Such arguments left many unconvinced, including writers otherwise favorable to legal reforms. Marmontel, for instance, turns the liberals' standard reference to Rome against them, using it to refute the idea that lawyers derive their eloquence from their virtue and sincerity. Roman orators, he argues, were revered for their talent and for their victories, not for their morality.[86] Once a trial started, in fact, even the most virtuous orator "detached himself from himself, so as to give himself fully to his case: good or bad, just or unjust, defending it well and winning was his task, duty, and only religion."[87] Marmontel voices here precisely the anxiety raised by the universal right to counsel—that it not only encourages but effectively requires that lawyers detach themselves from themselves, sacrificing their identity, devotion to truth, and moral principles to their client's desire to win the case. Indeed, when a lawyer's principal duty becomes a "good defense," instead of a "defense of the good," his eloquence serves as evidence of his talent but of little else, and certainly not of his goodness or that of his case.

Marmontel warns of another downside to the increasingly popular belief among lawyers that they may plead any case that presents itself: "One no longer takes cases based on their real and absolute goodness, but based rather on their apparent goodness, relative to the minds of the judges."[88] The lawyer's transformation from moral voucher to gifted spokesperson brings with it a shift from *le vrai* (absolute, since intrinsic to the case) to *le vraisemblable* (relative, since located in the act of reception). Marmontel intuits here a fundamental weakness in the liberal vision of justice: that it requires abandoning the notion of objective truth as a guiding principle. Indeed, the accusatorial model endorsed by liberals gives both parties the same preparation time, counsel, and opportunities to speak in public, so as to allow them to create the most credible and poignant stories possible. According to this egalitarian vision, trials stage a conflict between two scripted performances, neither more intrinsically accurate or legitimate than the other, and which must therefore be evaluated as *subjective* narratives, on the assumption that the more persuasive of the two will most closely approach the truth (even though both may well contain falsehoods). This contrasts with the inquisitorial model of the ancien régime, in which men of law invested with the king's divine will undertake proceedings secretly and unilaterally to establish a singular, authoritative account. It is only then that the trial takes place, less to choose between conflicting narratives than to render manifest an *objective* truth, attributable to God himself. While every liberal condemned this model for its structural inequality, many were also concerned that the alternative vision of trials as a competition between two fictions would lead to "uncertain or constantly conflicting judgments."[89] By fostering an understanding of truth as relative, such a vision threatened to undermine the legitimacy of lawyers and judgments alike. Trials would come to be seen less as fixed rituals than as theatrical productions: endlessly reiterable and varying with each repetition, depending on the talent of the lawyer-actors and the mood of the spectator-judges.

The Birth of the Modern Lawyer

As I suggested earlier, the period's fear of lawyer-actors, like that of dramatic actors, grew partly out of an underlying anxiety that new liberal values were causing a loss of faith in absolutism, in both senses of the word: the existence of absolute values (such as truth) and the legitimacy of a social order eternally fixed by a divine ruler. Be they legal or theatrical, actors symbolized a new society governed by eloquence and public opinion and threatening to replace the existing order founded on identity and filiation. Some saw the promise of a meritocracy in the principle that any man could publicly perform a role of his choosing, but others worried instead that it would elicit a spate of empty speech and social fluidity, bringing an end to all order and legitimacy. So profound was this anxiety, in fact, that it gave rise to a series of fantastical and yet utterly sincere plans for sweeping societal reform. Remarkably similar in content, these long-forgotten plans started by targeting the clearest site of empty speech and social fluidity: the theater.[90] Yet unlike antitheatricalists who continued in the eighteenth century to call for a complete prohibition of the theater, they attempted to find in the theater a cure against the poison of its own theatricality.

Central to all these plans was the same radical idea: acting—as the root and symbol of a dangerous social fluidity—should be limited to those already destined by birth to perform on the world stage. Only the aristocracy would hence be allowed to perform, with the stage off-limits to everyone else. Louis Dancourt was the first to propose this idea in a letter to Fréron published in 1760.[91] Fréron responded by stressing the novelty of Dancourt's vision in a largely positive review in the *Année littéraire*.[92] For nearly a decade, no one took up Dancourt's proposal, until suddenly, between 1769 and 1772, it was championed (in slightly different forms) by numerous authors, including Rabelleau,[93] Rétif,[94] Louis Gachet,[95] and even Rousseau.[96] It continued to find supporters in the ensuing decades,[97] albeit less frequently and sometimes only as a passing wish, as in Diderot's *Paradoxe*.[98] For all their other differences, nearly all of these thinkers agreed that restricting acting to the nobility would benefit aristocrats as well as society: the theater would serve as a much needed school of declamation, eloquence, and poise for men and women whose public station required they master the arts of persuasion.

Of course, this was not an entirely novel idea. The Jesuits used theater in their schools partly because, they argued, it taught public speaking skills to the future lawyers and preachers of France. Yet they were often mocked for this claim, as when Jean-Baptiste de Boyer, Marquis d'Argens imagined a foreign rabbi responding to a Jesuit priest that such performances merely encouraged aspiring leaders to speak and behave with the grandiloquence and excessive sentimentality of actors and instilled in them a dangerous love of the stage that persisted beyond their studies.[99] Indeed, it is perhaps no coincidence that the eighteenth century saw the heyday of society theater. On these private stages, members of high society gathered to act in plays together, with a particular fondness for the roles of servants and peasants.[100] This predilection—illustrated most notoriously by Marie-Antoinette's shepherdess fantasy—drew frequent criticism, and understandably so, as it amounted to an especially shocking confirmation of the Platonic critique of theater as a form of depropriation. It revealed that even the ruling classes did not engage in playacting to improve their performance of the roles assigned to them by birth, but to find pleasure in experiencing roles of their own choosing, often diametrically opposed to their own. In so doing, however, they challenged the notion that an individual was destined to a single, inherited function, undermining both their own legitimacy and that of the roles themselves.

The plans for the creation of noble-actors differ from Jesuit and society theater, however, by imposing strict limitations on the roles performed, thereby easing the fear of depropriation. Rabelleau and Gachet both specify that the plays staged would be reenactments of recent or famous French military victories. Young noblemen drawn from military school would perform the role of their predecessors, thus gaining insight into heroism and the art of war. Rétif goes further still by requesting that the roles of the aristocratic heroes be assigned, whenever possible, to their nearest descendants.[101] Even Rousseau entertains this idea, which is especially surprising—and indicative of its popularity—given several of the plans for noble-actors were explicitly written to counter Rousseau's rejection of theater in his *Lettre à d'Alembert*. In the constitution he designs for Poland, Rousseau proposes the institution of open-air, martial competitions, with only aristocratic youths allowed to participate under the admiring gaze of the assembled people. Admittedly, these patrician spectacles differ from the others in that they are not theater, but nor are they Rousseauian festivals, given the social division they establish between performer and spectator. It is in fact telling that Rousseau cites as one of his models the theater of antiquity, which he praises for reenacting the heroic deeds of the spectators' ancestors, thereby nurturing love of country and of the great families that govern it.[102]

In *La Lanterne magique de l'histoire*, Anne Boës-Anthouard describes Rétif's project as an attempt to convince the people that the nobility's supremacy rests on merit, not privilege.[103] The same holds true for the other plans, even Rousseau's, whose famed republicanism is far from evident when he states that patrician spectacles would allow the nobility to publicize its "natural right to superiority."[104] It is indeed difficult to imagine a more effective way of exalting the aristocracy than the noble-only theater of Rétif and his fellow reformers. Not only does its content remind the spectators that titles, far from being arbitrary, reward past acts of heroism, but its performance by young nobles suggests that they have inherited the same virtues. After all—and the logic at play here is the very antithesis of depropriation—if only aristocrats play characters of such quality (rank *and* merit), it must be because no others are fit to do so. Yet it seems to me that such theater aims higher than just persuading its audience of the inheritability of aristocratic virtue: it also seeks to resurrect it. Nowhere is this more evident than in Rétif's request that young noblemen perform the part of their most celebrated biological ancestor. Rétif later adds that each youth should only play one role, so that after years of repetitions and public performances he will identify with his character to such a degree that the two will become one and the same, not only in the eyes of the audience but in his own mind as well.[105] At that point, he will truly *be*—on and offstage—the great man he at first only represented. The similarities with Lysimond's vision of the theater in Diderot's *Fils naturel* are striking.[106] Like Lysimond, Rétif dreams of a ritualistic performance, in which the descendants of a community's founding fathers reenact the latter's exploits with such precision and regularity that the patriarchs are literally brought back to life in their progeny. Through this resurrection, Rétif seeks to imbue each new generation of aristocrats with the values of their ancestors, as well as with the absolute legitimacy that each noble family enjoyed when it first earned its title.

The young aristocrat's complete identification with his character also ensures that he is no actor. Rétif is quite explicit on this point: through his reforms, he aims to invent "a theater without actors."[107] As we saw earlier, the fear of actors stems from the emptiness of their words. It is precisely this dissociation of identity and speech that Rétif seeks to negate through his aristocratic reenactments. As he makes clear, the constant repetition of the same role and of the same words constructs the young nobleman's identity. Such a claim bears a striking resemblance to modern theories of performativity and yet departs from them as well, in that for Rétif, the identity constructed is predetermined by birth and as such predates performance. Indeed, aristocratic reenactments are not meant to create new identities, but rather to resurrect through performative speech a fixed identity passed down through generations. Accordingly, a successful reenactment not only relegitimizes the young nobleman, it also binds his speech and his identity into an inseparable whole. There is of course something paradoxical in turning to the theater to combat social ills—the ruling class's loss of legitimacy and the rise of empty speech—that were partly caused, in Rétif's eyes, by the theater. Yet it reflects the awareness, shared by all of the plans' writers, that there are "young people destined to speak in public"—future lawyers and ministers—who in an age of public opinion will inevitably perform their social roles as if on a stage.[108] Having these youths, and only these youth, participate in closely regulated spectacles provides the people in the audience with a regular, visible reminder that public speaking is not open to all, but constitutes the birthright of those with an inherited virtue and legitimacy: the aristocracy. At the same time, through these performances, the young aristocrats practice a form of public speaking in which they become one with their role and their words, rediscovering an ancestral link between identity and speech. Patrician spectacles thus serve to convince both the people and the young aristocrats that the nobility rightly plays the first and only roles on the national stage, enacting but never acting.

So transformative are these patrician spectacles, in fact, that they are often presented as mandatory vocational training. Rabelleau, for instance, forbids anyone who did not spend his youth performing in these spectacles from holding an official position, notably in the justice system.[109] Like nearly every other supporter of an aristocratic theater, he considers it a first, formative step, teaching probity and "full" speech to young noblemen and preparing them for further public roles. Tellingly, the next step on the ladder of public speaking involves a stint in the legal profession. In his constitution for Poland, Rousseau stipulates that aristocratic youths must plead in a tribunal for at least three years—a literal "trial" period through which to show their faculties and, above all, their integrity—before they are allowed to vie for greater roles in public affairs, starting with the magistracy and ascending to increasingly influential positions in the government.[110] The two spectacles required of the young noblemen thus blend together in fascinating ways, with both the amphitheater and the tribunal offering future leaders a space in which to practice virtuous acts and speeches and develop a praiseworthy public persona.

Not surprisingly, given these similarities, the constraints placed on public performing also apply to public pleading, and for the same reasons: a fear of social fluidity and empty speech. Hence, in Rousseau's Polish paradise, the legal profession is restricted to men of noble birth. Of course, by early modern standards, the idea of noble-lawyers was far less scandalous than that of noble-actors. As we saw earlier, pre-1650 lawyers frequently asked the king to ennoble their order, a campaign that retained a certain degree of popularity in the eighteenth century, in spite—or because—of the liberal principle that all could plead. There is however a significant difference between a plan that rewards with a title anyone who succeeds in becoming a lawyer and one that decrees that only existing aristocrats will be allowed to practice law: the first acts as a potential driver of social mobility, whereas the second clearly hinders it. As a result, supporters of the latter did not look to France for a model, but further back, to Roman antiquity. Rétif, for instance, calls for the rebirth of Rome's earliest justice system, notably for the replacement of professional lawyers by "patrons, of known capacity and probity."[111] The term "patrons" refers to high-ranking Romans who entered into a hierarchical but mutually beneficial relationship with individuals of a lower status (called "clients"). One of the patrons' principal duties was to provide their clients with legal counsel and representation. Rousseau's advocacy of noble-lawyers not unlike the patrons of ancient Rome partly explains perhaps his surprising support in *Du Contrat social* for this most undemocratic of institutions, which he hails as "a masterpiece of politics and humanity."[112] Rétif's praise for Roman-style patronage is even more revealing, as it occurs immediately after he rebukes the lawyers of his time by asking in disbelief: "Can there be a democracy in a monarchical state?"[113] For Rétif, the qualities that make the legal profession a democracy—the autonomy and egalitarianism that eighteenth-century lawyers often identify as a point of pride—threaten the absolutist state. By contrast, following the Romans' example and restricting legal practice to the nobility would turn it into a charge inherited at birth, thereby transforming an emblem of social fluidity into a means of solidifying the patrimonial division between those who speak and those who watch.

Patrons sparked the interest of French jurists not only for their rank but also for their role within the justice system. Most eighteenth-century histories of the legal profession, notably those found in manuals for aspiring lawyers, give a similar account of Roman patronage.[114] All agree that the relationship between patron and client was not built on a legal contract or a monetary exchange, as the term "client" implies today, but on trust and virtue. Patrons served as sponsors to their clients, lending them, beyond their voice and money, their legitimacy and credibility. Their legal erudition and oratorical talent mattered less than their reputation and connections, since they came before the tribunal to vouch for their client (or abstained, if they thought him guilty). As a result, clients sought patrons known for their integrity to increase their odds of success, just as patrons sought moral clients to preserve their reputations. As the years passed, however, some patrons proved especially adept at pleading and attracted ever more clients as a result. Thus were born orators, whose studied eloquence soon supplanted the natural speech of patrons. Although eighteenth-century historical accounts often portray Roman orators as the pinnacle of the legal profession, because they combined the virtue of the patron with the artistry of the professional, it becomes clear as one continues to read that the rise of orators also produced unintended consequences by making justice less a matter of personal legitimacy than one of persuasiveness. In such a system, orators wielded such influence that kings themselves began to seek their support. With eloquence now a means to power, and legal representation a self-serving transaction, a new breed of plebeian speakers arose who more closely resembled "actors playing a role" than the patrons of yore.[115]

The eighteenth century's interest in the history of patronage thus needs no explanation: many saw it as a cautionary tale about recent changes in the legal profession, such as the rise of celebrity lawyers and the transition from vouching to representing. Indeed, while liberals like Brissot dreamed of resurrecting the orators of ancient Rome, others saw them as the beginning of Roman justice's slide into theatricality and campaigned instead for the rebirth of the patrons that the orators had supplanted. These writers wished to return to a time before pleading became a profession, a source of wealth and celebrity akin to acting—a time when public speaking was a privilege and duty reserved for those with the legitimacy to endorse the words they uttered. This fantasy that there once existed an idyllic era before theatricality, whose public performances were free of actors and invention and art, explains why so many eighteenth-century thinkers advocated limiting all forms of public speaking to the nobility: not just to relegitimize the latter, but also to relegitimize public speech itself, returning it to its former fullness.

Of course, the proposal to restrict representation (legal *and* theatrical) to the aristocracy could not have been further removed from Brissot's plan to allow all men of genius and virtue to plead. The French Revolution ensured that Brissot and likeminded liberals would be the ones to see their vision realized. Little more than a year had passed since the storming of the Bastille when the National Assembly dismantled the Order of Barristers, stripped lawyers of their privileges, and replaced them with *défenseurs officieux*—anyone enjoying a litigant's trust, regardless of training and integrity. The deputies' reasons for such a radical reform echoed Brissot's: a hatred of corporatism and a belief that choosing one's defender was, to quote Robespierre, a "natural right."[116] Again like Brissot, the deputies appealed to the example of Cicero. Robespierre in particular drew the usual idealized portrait of Roman orators, driven by love of justice, empathy for the wrongly accused, and a laudable ambition to acquire glory and rise to a higher station.[117] To the deputies concerned that lawyer-actors, unbeholden to truth and morality, might also gain access to the tribunals, the supporters of *défenseurs officieux* responded in typically liberal fashion by proclaiming their faith in publicity, which they hailed as an effective protection against the perils associated with the new, more theatrical performance of justice. First, they reiterated the belief we saw earlier that ordinary spectators—audience members, but also jurors (an institution related to the *défenseurs officieux* since both replaced legal professionals with amateurs)—possessed the ability to see through the manipulations of a dishonest or dissolute counsel. Let the people watch a live, oratorical contest in the courtroom and trust in their inner response: they will always be drawn toward the honest witness, the innocent litigant, and the counsel with the kind of eloquence only found in good men fighting a just cause. Then, having defeated the duplicitous defender during the trial, publicity would triumph over deception once more, by ensuring that he also began to acquire a reputation that would dissuade anyone from selecting him ever again—thereby recreating an order of sorts, but one open to everyone and based on merit and morality instead of privilege.[118]

Some deputies, however, questioned whether publicity would be enough to keep out charlatans. Against those who, like Robespierre and Brissot, attributed a near infallibility to public opinion, Pierre-Louis Prieur argued it was easy to imagine "a mob of schemers misleading the people through a false popularity."[119] If popularity could be thus falsified, was it truly wise, Joseph Prugnon wondered, for the deputies to entrust the interests of their fellow citizens "to men without titles and offering no guarantees?"[120] Therein lay the crux of the matter: the lack of guarantees in a justice system without an Order of Barristers. In the absence of any real disciplinary measures, since *défenseurs officieux* could neither be stripped of their identities (they lacked a title) nor of their livelihoods (they were not a profession), what stood to prevent them from behaving dishonestly?[121] *Défenseurs officieux* of questionable ethics would flood the tribunals in great numbers, the deputies warned, with a financial incentive to win the case at hand by any means necessary, and no counterincentive to build a lasting reputation as honest and moderate, since they would likely never again appear before the same judge, opposing counsel, and audience.

These fears proved largely prescient. Most historians agree that few of the *défenseurs officieux* turned out to be the eloquent, disinterested lovers of justice envisioned by Brissot and Robespierre.[122] Far more common were defenders who sought to win at all costs, because they deemed themselves, to quote one eighteenth-century critic, "nothing more than proxies"—that is, the representatives solely of their clients and of their selfish interests and not of a broader ideal or fellowship of lawyers.[123] Others, meanwhile, were driven by money. Michael P. Fitzsimmons even mentions greedy individuals entering prisons to solicit cases[124]—the birth in France of the ambulance chaser. Others sought to be the center of attention. Nicolas Derasse alludes to theater-like "scenes," in which *défenseurs officieux* engaged in scandalous, heated quarrels and ridiculed witnesses to amuse the audience.[125] Such playing to the crowd likely harmed their clients, but it helped the *défenseurs officieux* attain, in the words of Prieur, the "false popularity" they desired. Judges complained about the new counsels' immoderation, avarice, and dishonesty, as did some politicians (notably the Council of Ancients, which deplored "daily abuses"),[126] but it was not until the French Empire that the Order of Barristers was officially reestablished (1804), and not until the end of the Restoration (1830) that it regained the freedom, independence, and right to self-discipline it had possessed during the ancien régime.[127]

This brief history of the *défenseurs officieux* perfectly illustrates the struggle in the late eighteenth century between two competing visions of legal counsel—the traditional one, based on identity, in which a lawyer's membership in a select group makes it possible for him to vouch for his clients, and the liberal alternative, based on publicity and representation, in which lawyers are tasked with acting as their clients before the supposedly infallible court of public opinion. That the *défenseurs officieux* failed to establish themselves and were quickly replaced by an exclusive, self-disciplining order merits attention, as it shows that, contrary to expectations, today's legal profession did not arise from the triumph of a liberal worldview over the ancien régime's system of privilege. On the contrary, the birth of the modern lawyer can be traced to the failure of both visions or, more accurately perhaps, to the search for a compromise between the two. Indeed, there remains to this day a powerful, independent order, charged with establishing a set of rules for the legal profession and disciplining members who fail to follow them, notably through disbarment. A cursory glance at this code, which includes such terms as "probity," "honor," and "dignity," might lead one to think that little has changed since the ancien régime. Yet the rules specify explicitly that these virtues refer to the lawyer's professional conduct.[128] The code shows no interest in the private life and morality of its followers, nor in their social status or identity. Similarly absent is the requirement that lawyers only defend the innocent, for fear of harming their own standing as moral (and thus trustworthy) individuals. Indeed, the code reflects the order's adoption of many liberal ideals, including equal access to the profession and the universal right to counsel, regardless of guilt.[129] As the code makes clear, the duty of modern lawyers lies in representing their clients to the best of their abilities,[130] not in offering their own morality as a guarantee of their clients'.

Yet if the order is no longer needed to monitor and certify the morality of its members, what purpose does it serve today? One function strikes me as particularly crucial: the order is tasked, as it was under the ancien régime, with protecting the profession from the ever-looming threat of theatricality. This explains its emphasis on professional, interpersonal ethics concerned less with the personal morality of lawyers than with their public perception. "Moderation," "tact," and "politeness" are thus presented as indispensable values, in part because they combat the theatricality to which trials are prone. For the same reason, the order enforces strict restrictions on publicity. As we saw earlier, the Order of Barristers already condemned the pursuit of celebrity under the ancien régime, but the restored order of the nineteenth century went even further by explicitly banning all forms of advertisement, including wall plaques, letterhead, and interviews or articles in the press.[131] So significant was this issue that the order returned to it again and again, notably in 1972, 1991, and 2005, relaxing the restrictions slightly by allowing plaques (of a fixed size), letterhead, and the inclusion of "necessary information" (name, diplomas, specializations, and fees) in the phone book. Most of what we associate with publicity, however—the mention of past victories or famous clients, the promise of future triumphs, the claim of superiority over rival lawyers, and the use of mass media, such as newspaper ads, billboards, TV commercials, and appearances on radio or television shows—remained for centuries strictly forbidden. The reasons for this near-total ban on publicity are manifold, including the fear it might cultivate competitiveness among a supposedly united fellowship. Yet at its core, the ban represents a rejection not only of publicity's consequences but of publicity itself, owing to the way it erases the already fine line between lawyer and actor. Some blurring of this line is inevitable, the price to pay for the liberal principle of a universal right to counsel. In recognizing this right in its code of rules, the order concedes that its members must present arguments as persuasively as possible whether they believe them or not—in other words, that they must act. What the ban on publicity seeks to ensure, however, is that lawyers act for the right reasons: out of duty toward their clients and not out of a desire for celebrity or personal ambition (as was acceptable in the Revolutionaries' liberal vision). In that sense, the modern lawyer is a product of the late eighteenth century and of the clash it witnessed between two competing visions of the legal profession—one resolutely antitheatrical; the other unabashedly dramatic. From these two visions, and their failures, arose a new equilibrium, acknowledging theatricality as essential to the rights of the accused, but imposing strict restrictions upon it.

Interestingly, that two-hundred-year-old equilibrium is currently under threat, following an amendment to the order's code that many are calling a veritable "revolution."[132] As of 2014, French lawyers may now advertise their services without any restrictions as to form (all media are permissible, including billboards and TV commercials) and few restrictions as to content (boasting of one's superiority to other lawyers remains forbidden, but self-promotion is otherwise allowed). According to one of the largest newspapers in France, *Le Figaro*, this reform was opposed by many lawyers, who warned it might trigger "a downward spiral toward Americanism," emboldening celebrity-obsessed charlatans, degrading the dignity of the legal profession, and spurring the rise of a lawsuit culture.[133] If the frame of reference has changed (from Rome to America), the fears have not: these are precisely the arguments that traditionalist members of the order used two centuries prior in response to the proposed liberalization of their profession. Likewise, supporters of the reform sound remarkably close to Brissot, depicting the order as an assembly of pedantic reactionaries, paralyzed by the "weight of tradition," corrupted by "an elitist pride in their aristocratic origins," and opposed to publicity out of fear that more energetic and talented orators will steal the stage from them.[134] In one corner, arrogant would-be aristocrats; in the other, narcissistic would-be celebrities—how little have the adversaries (or their caricatures) evolved in two hundred years! There is even evidence of a generational divide between those opposed to publicity and liberalization (*les anciens*) and those in favor of it (*les jeunes diplômés*),[135] just as there had been centuries earlier, when Linguet and Brissot clashed with the order. By lifting the ban on publicity, the 2014 reform revived an eighteenth-century debate about the nature of the legal profession, leading to a resurgence of the age-old fear of the lawyer-actor, and likely requiring that a new equilibrium be found.

Chapter 4

Judges, Spectators, and Theatrocracy

The Judge as Spectator

The reformers' proposed alterations to the performance of criminal justice also entailed changes in its reception. As we saw earlier, ancien régime judges based their verdicts on a fixed set of rules that they applied to a dossier compiled by an examining magistrate. They assigned each testimony and forensic report a numerical value and added these fractions of proof together to compose a verdict. This reliance on written texts and mathematical formulas stemmed from a desire to eradicate subjective emotions from the act of judging. By reimagining criminal proceedings as public, adversarial spectacles, in which lawyers were tasked, in Brissot's words, with communicating their passions to the magistrates and electrifying their souls, the liberal reformers made clear that judges ought to place more weight on their emotional responses. This explains Gin's puzzling inclusion in his treatise on the eloquence of lawyers of several chapters analyzing the nature of the emotions one feels at the theater. Like many liberals, Gin views legal proceedings through the lens of a dramatic performance, one in which lawyers attempt to "interest" the judges in favor of their client by stirring in them the two famous tragic passions: pity, via touching portraits of the victim, and horror, via chilling depictions of the criminal.[1] In fact, extrapolating from Gin's musings on the theater, it becomes clear that lawyers play a vital role in his vision of legal proceedings because their eloquent speeches transform the suffering of the victim into a narrative, instead of showing it directly, a form of hypotyposis that, as in a classical tragedy, tempers the judges' emotions just enough to allow them to identify with the victim.[2] While Gin's analysis of the emotions felt by theatergoers is hardly original, his application of these aesthetic theories to legal judgment is unprecedented. To think of judges in such theatrical terms transforms their role in a trial from an active, hermeneutical involvement—comparing claims, piecing together a narrative, and using their deductive skills and knowledge of legal formulas to assign guilt—to a primarily passive, emotional one.

Indeed, in Gin's theatrical model, judges identify the innocent victim by first identifying *with* him: as firsthand witnesses of a judicial spectacle, they experience compassion for the blameless party and horror for the guilty one. Such faith in the forensic accuracy of compassion stems from the liberal reformers' belief in the existence of an innate sense of right and wrong. Hence, when the lawyer Mézard mocks the mathematical formulas of magistrates, pointedly asking: "Is persuasion determined by arithmetic? Can truth be weighed like matter?", it is because he believes that "all the methods prescribed by jurists have less value than our instinct toward virtue."[3] A judge's compassion not only derives from this instinct toward virtue, it gives it tangible form, revealing to the judge who listens to his emotions which client is deserving of pity and thus innocent (indeed, it was accepted dogma among sentimental authors like Diderot that a spectator always empathizes with the suffering virtuous, never with villains, however tormented they may be). This belief in an instinctual ability to identify (with) virtue forms the basis for the new mode of judgment championed by legal reformers under the name of *conviction intime*.[4] A judge's verdict, the reformers argued, should not be governed by external rules and mathematical formulas but by his own personal impression of the two parties and their competing narratives.

Ancien régime magistrates were required to focus solely on material evidence, provided to them in written form, in the belief that the ease with which it could be dissected and quantified made it more reliable than emotions or intuitions. In response, liberal reformers argued that such fragmentation was useless in assessing the truth of a case: "The proof of a fact is not a numerical object that can be broken down in such a way that its integral parts may exist detached from the whole."[5] Worse, it threatened to corrupt man's innate ability to distinguish guilt from innocence. As one reformer explained, "man is born with notions of what is just. Without any study, he senses the totality and the connections of this irrefutable principle," yet "these simple notions are lost, when combined into scientific calculations."[6] A simple man reaches more accurate verdicts than a professional magistrate because he evaluates a case in the same way he would any other story—as a whole and instinctively ("he *senses* the *totality*")—thereby eschewing the standard, scientific approach, which dissects the case into quantifiable pieces of truth but obscures as a result its overall verisimilitude and emotional impact. Like a theatrical spectator, he considers all forms of evidence, including sensorial impressions derived from seeing the parties interact, with these impressions combining in immeasurable ways to compose a more reliable conviction of the accused's guilt.

As the above suggests, by redefining *how* one judges, liberal reformers also sought to expand the definition of *who* could judge to include nearly any adult male.[7] This represented a radical departure from the existing system, which deemed the magistracy a lifetime position limited to a chosen few able to purchase the charge and title from the king or inherit them from a family member. Inspired by Montesquieu's ideal of a separation between the executive and judicial branches, the reformers condemned the notion that the Crown could grant a judge a permanent, infallible authority. The alternative they most frequently proposed—elected judges with limited terms—reveals that they regarded the power to judge as a temporary authority, open to men of all ranks, and contingent on public opinion: the same three principles behind their reconception of the legal profession. Indeed, as with lawyers, the liberal reformers called for merit, as determined by public opinion, to serve as the decisive criteria for entry into the magistracy.[8] The central role given to public opinion reflects the liberal reformers' contractual vision of justice, which maintains that the right to judge comes not from the king or from one's lineage, but from the people delegating their judicial sovereignty to a representative of their choice. Term limits and elections grow out of the same vision, as they keep magistrates accountable to the sole legitimate holder of the right to judge: the people. Furthermore, they ensure that judging, like pleading, never becomes a profession or privileged office, but always remains a temporary duty.[9] By contrast, according to liberal critics, the Crown's peddling of lifelong, titled offices justified the belief, among some judges, that they were an investment, thereby encouraging greed and bribery,[10] and, among others, that they (and the nobility they bestowed) were a sign of superiority, breeding the kind of arrogance and lack of empathy that silence one's instinctual sense of right and wrong. In short, as with pleading, liberal reformers aimed to transform judging into a more egalitarian practice, governed by merit and sincere emotions, instead of filiation and cold, esoteric rules. In so doing, however, they inspired—in friends and foes alike—an array of new fears about the implications of a theatrical model that not only reduced lawyers to actors, but also judges to spectators.

Fearing the Judge-Spectator

Latour, for instance, was so concerned about the impact of the theater on the figure of the judge that he devoted hundreds of pages to the matter. Some of his anxieties recall the ones regarding lawyers, revolving as they do around issues of legitimacy, social role, and acting. For example, he condemns the eagerness with which young judges performed as actors on private stages: "Do magistrates, who by their profession embody the king, respect themselves, respect their royal majesty enough, when they engage in such childish games?"[11] As Latour shrewdly emphasizes, ancien régime judges were held to be embodiments of the king. According to this conception of justice, magistrates acted as vessels chosen by the king to exercise his divine right to judge: "It is Your Majesty who, through this organ [the judges], listens to the grievances of the humblest citizen and gives him justice."[12] Judges did not speak in their own voice, according to their own sense of right and wrong, but rather made it possible, through their adherence to fixed rituals and laws, for the king to speak through them. It was this vital task of re-presenting the king (understood at the time in the etymological sense of making the king present)[13] that they undermined through their eagerness to represent (in the theatrical sense of the word). By performing other professions on stage, magistrates risked giving the impression that they also acted in the courtroom—that they could assume the role of a judge at any time and just as quickly abandon it for another. In so doing, they transformed the magistracy from a permanent and exclusive state of being with a direct link to the sovereign's will into just one social role among many others. This represented a considerable loss of legitimacy, since it implied that one became a judge through the performance of certain scripted gestures, rather than through the king's selection. In the same way that a judge could play any role, so could anyone play the role of a judge.

Moreover, if judges were no longer seen as embodiments of the king, it became possible to criticize their decisions. Like the actors they had become, judges could be subjected to the jeers and hisses of the general public. In fact, as we saw in Chapter 2, Latour's fears were in the process of being realized in the second half of the eighteenth century, as audiences increasingly turned to the theater, as well as to print, for the opportunity to comment on recent trials. As Maza suggests, the growing belief that the public enjoyed a right to judge, and that this right to judge extended to the decisions of its magistrates, "undermined the pristine authority of the courts."[14] Latour held the theater responsible for this transfer of authority from the magistracy to the general public, because it had revealed to the judges who acted on private stages a different mode of representation, one that drew its legitimacy from pleasing its audience, rather than from the true source of all justice, the king. This slide into theatricality, Latour and others argued, found an echo in the campaign to reform the legal system. They condemned the liberal notion that a judge received his power from the people, because, as Huet observes, "this delegation of powers instituted *representation* as opposed to *figuration*. The jury and the judge were not the image of a person [the king]; they were only, for the time of the trial, a temporary authority that was borrowed from the people and would ultimately be returned to the people."[15] To reactionaries like Latour, this shift from embodiment to representation, together with the rising power of public opinion, marked the final step in the demotion of magistrates to mere actors, whose sole claim to authority derived from their ability to convince an audience of their suitability for the role, and not, as it should, from any personal legitimacy.

Latour further blames this loss of legitimacy on the fact that, as well as actors, judges were frequent characters in early modern plays, owing to the popularity of comedies parodying legal proceedings.[16] In his eyes, the ridicule heaped on magistrates on stage constituted one of the principal reasons for the people's fast diminishing respect for their judges.[17] How could it be otherwise, when magistrates themselves had come to internalize the theater's derisive portrayal of their profession so completely that their own robes filled them with disgust? "Judges no longer dare wear clothes they have just mocked with the parterre. Would one dare attend the theater in a robe? He would be hissed."[18] Accustomed like Pavlovian dogs to jeering fictional characters in red robes, the spectators would extend the same treatment to anyone similarly attired. These robes, a perfect symbol of the judges' function as embodiments of the king in that they were literally hand-me-downs first worn by the sovereign himself,[19] were thus transformed by the theater into a mere costume, a comedic prop worn to elicit laughter rather than respect. Noting that the magistracy formed "a kind of priesthood," Latour requested that the police forbid the representation of judges on stage, as they did that of clergymen.[20] As this parallel suggests, Latour's opposition to the use of judges as characters extended beyond a simple critique of the derisive manner in which legal officials were portrayed in ancien régime comedies. For Latour, the very presence on stage of the magistracy amounted to an assault on the sacrality of justice. Legal rituals owed their sacred aura at least partly to being limited to specific surroundings, circumstances, and participants. Even a respectful representation of legal rituals, when performed by actors on a dramatic stage, severed them from the source of their power, reducing them to empty gestures, commonplace and ineffectual. The fear that repetition can reduce the sacrality of a ritual partly explains the reactionaries' opposition to public trials. To allow spectators inside the courtroom carried the risk that an increased familiarity with legal rituals would demystify them, turning once-revered judges into characters in a live performance, subject to the whims and criticisms of the public.

These examples notwithstanding, however, Latour's greatest concern was ultimately not that the theatromania and liberalism of his day would transform judges into actors or characters, but that they would turn magistrates into theatrical spectators, altering in the process the very essence of legal judgment. Accordingly, Latour focuses most of his outrage on the presence of so many magistrates at the theater, where they mixed with the other spectators and judged the plays on an equal footing. In so doing, they made visible—and thus strengthened—the dangerous notion that random members of the parterre possessed the same right to judge as men chosen by the king. As an antidote, Latour requests that the Crown forbid magistrates from attending the theater, or, were that unfeasible, that they at least be confined to an area in the center of the auditorium, a position reminiscent of the king's during court performances. By this architectural division, Latour hopes not only to reinforce visually the link between the king and his judges, but also to prevent the judgment of the magistrates from being confused with, or worse, influenced by, that of the parterre. As an example of such influence, Latour tells the story of a young magistrate whose approach to judging is corrupted by his love of theater. Abandoning his once-ardent pursuit of "the science of the Law," he stops reading the reports presented to him during trials, as he finds them lacking in wit and pathos. Increasingly ignorant and frivolous, he bases his verdicts solely on his subjective and emotional response to the parties, rather than on a methodical study of legal doctrines, precedents, and expert opinions, with predictably disastrous consequences.[21] Through this anecdote, Latour shows that the penchant for theatergoing among magistrates not only challenged their claim to the possession of an exclusive right to judge, it also introduced them to a superficial mode of judgment at odds with the one practiced in the courtroom.

In fact, Latour's story served as a warning not only against theatergoing but also, and more broadly, against the ideal of publicity so cherished by liberals. Whether in the tribunal or in the theater, the presence of an audience increased the risk that judges would begin to mimic its judgment. As evidence, one needed only to look at civil trials, which admitted spectators and had, by the second half of the eighteenth century, become a fashionable diversion. So popular had legal proceedings become, in fact, that Jean-François de La Harpe tempered his criticism of the 1773 theatrical season with the observation that, "in compensation, the tribunal has become a famous arena that attracts the attention of all of France. The scenes that take place there and the actors that distinguish themselves are equally worthy of curiosity."[22] Maza cites La Harpe's statement as evidence for one of her main arguments, namely that the courtroom was threatening to displace the theater, but it seems to me on the contrary to suggest that the legal system was increasingly being perceived as a type of dramatic spectacle.[23] If, as La Harpe claims, the same spectators who had once attended the theater now gravitated toward judicial spectacles, one might expect certain forms of conduct to have come along with them. Anecdotal reports indeed suggest that some trial spectators behaved as if attending a theatrical performance, leading one lawyer to interrupt his plea to remind his audience "that the tribunal isn't a theater, nor the orator an actor; and that a case where one must decide what is just is debased by applause reserved for what is only ingenious."[24] The spectators' applause (itself already a theatrical response) revealed an obsession with wit and oratorical flourishes far exceeding their interest in the justness of the case. Because of their publicity, civil courts thus cultivated a mode of judgment that Latour's story and the passage above both associated with the theater. In fact, even Marmontel, a supporter of public criminal proceedings, acknowledged this downside to trial audiences, noting that they introduced a second magistrate in the courtroom, one with a different approach to judging, since "it is more through sentiment than reason that the public decides." This encouraged lawyers to appeal to the spectators' emotions in hope of influencing the official judge, or, as Marmontel put it, to "want an intoxicated and passionate judge to drag down the other."[25] More than wit, then, it was the general public's susceptibility to emotional manipulation that concerned Marmontel. Like Latour, he worried that professional magistrates, trained to overcome this susceptibility, were being swayed by the example of lay spectators into adopting a theatrical mode of judgment based on subjective, emotional responses.

In its rejection of specialized knowledge in favor of personal impressions, this approach to judging echoed the new notion of *conviction intime*, and indeed, through the story of the young, theater-obsessed magistrate, Latour also signaled his opposition to the liberal campaign to redefine legal judgment. In one of the period's most widely read legal tracts, the prominent jurist Antoine-Louis Séguier condemned the reformers' claim that judges should be free to follow their intuitive sense of the accused's guilt, on the grounds that such disregard for judicial forms and precedents risked undermining the legitimacy of judges by making their verdicts appear arbitrary.[26] Like Séguier, Latour believed that judgments should arise from "the science of the Law"—a magistrate's arcane knowledge of the rules and procedures that, because they emanated from the king, gave each verdict its legitimacy. The reformers' belief that a verdict should originate instead from a judge's innate ability to discern guilt from innocence struck Latour as evidence that the mode of judgment that reigned in the theater—subjective, emotional, and available to all, irrespective of expertise—had begun to infiltrate the tribunal. The story of the young magistrate was meant to illustrate the dangers of such an approach to judging, ending as it did with a judge who no longer cared about the justness of the cases entrusted to him and simply ruled in favor of whichever party had most fully satiated his thirst for entertainment through witty or tear-jerking pleas. For Latour and reactionaries like him, a judge's emotions were not the forensically meaningful expressions of an instinct toward virtue, but rather the symptoms of a dramatic inebriation (to use Marmontel's image) overpowering rules and reason and leading the judge to speak not as the king but solely as himself—that is, arbitrarily. In fact, as we will see, the liberal faith in a universal intuition of right and wrong, requiring neither rules nor rank, entailed far greater risks than emotional manipulation and some wrong verdicts. Just as the hostility toward lawyer-actors reflected a more widespread Platonic anxiety about acting as a form of depropriation, the opposition to judge-spectators found its roots in another Platonic fear: theatrocracy. Indeed, Latour was but one eighteenth-century writer among many to worry that his contemporaries' infatuation with the theater was altering the nature of judgment so radically that society itself was under threat.

The Slide Toward Theatrocracy

As strange as it may seem to us, Latour understood the relationship between the popularity of the theater and the shift toward a more dramatic mode of judgment not in terms of analogy or symbiosis but in terms of causation: he genuinely believed that the theater was directly responsible for the (proposed) reforms to the legal system. In support of this conviction, he could appeal to no less an authority than Plato. Indeed, as proof of the threat that the theater posed to the rule of law, Latour referred his readers to Plato's famous account in *The Laws* of Athens's fall from a law-abiding patriarchy to a state of anarchy.[27] Plato's narrative opens with this idyllic description of the theater, as it existed before the fall:

> Now these and other types [of music] were definitely fixed, and it was not permissible to misuse one kind of melody for another. The competence to take cognizance of these rules, to pass verdicts in accord with them, and, in case of need, to penalize their infraction was not left, as it is today, to the catcalls and discordant outcries of the crowd, nor yet to the clapping of applauders; the educated made it their rule to hear the performances through in silence, and for the boys, their attendants, and the rabble at large, there was the discipline of the official's rod to enforce order. Thus the bulk of the populace was content to submit to this strict control in such matters without venturing to pronounce judgment by its clamors.[28]

According to Plato, there once existed in Athens a set of fixed conventions regulating the scenic arts, known only to an educated elite. Lacking in this training, the multitude knew better than to try to judge artistic productions, and was at any rate further dissuaded from breaking the silence in the amphitheater by the presence of armed officials.

This peaceful, regulated theater came to an end the day that poets began to value intuition above instruction, innovation above tradition, and the subjective above the universal:

> In course of time, an unmusical license set in with the appearance of poets who were men of native genius, but ignorant of what is right and legitimate in the realm of the Muses. Possessed by a frantic and unhallowed lust for pleasure, they contaminated laments with hymns and paeans with dithyrambs, actually imitated the strains of the flute on the harp, and created a universal confusion of forms. Thus their folly led them unintentionally to slander their profession by the assumption that in music there is no such thing as a right and a wrong, the right standard

> of judgment being the pleasure given to the hearer, be he high or low. By compositions of such a kind and discourse to the same effect, they naturally inspired the multitude with contempt of musical law, and a conceit of their own competence as judges. Thus our once silent audiences have found a voice, in the persuasion that they understand what is good and bad in art; the old "sovereignty of the best" in that sphere has given way to an evil "sovereignty of the audience."[29]

The new poets unwittingly signaled to the audience that "the right standard of judgment" resided not in a work of art's compliance to a fixed set of rules but solely in the pleasure it produced. This convinced each spectator that he or she was proficient as an artistic judge, leading them to grow increasingly outspoken, and turning the theater into a site where sovereignty no longer derived from the knowledge of "what is right and legitimate," but solely from the "discordant outcries of the crowd." It then became only a matter of time before the conceit that all citizens are able to judge infiltrated the tribunals: "So the next stage of the journey toward liberty will be refusal to submit to magistrates, and on this will follow emancipation from the authority and correction of parents and elders; then, as the goal of the race is approached, comes the effort to escape obedience to the law, and, when that goal is all but reached, contempt for oaths, for the plighted word, and all religion."[30] Having escaped from the theater, this conception of judgment as unhindered by rules and rank traveled up the great chain of being, challenging the legitimacy of each new authority it reached—fathers, elders, magistrates, even God himself. A community thus deprived of its patriarchs was doomed, according to Plato, to fall into a state of lawlessness, which he tellingly dubbed a "theatrocracy."

Latour believed—not without cause—that history was in the process of repeating itself in the second half of the eighteenth century.[31] Indeed, Plato's philosophical narrative is remarkably pertinent to the heated quarrels that greeted the invention by theatrical reformers of new genres like bourgeois drama and judicial theater. To their critics, these new genres were an assault on the reigning order of seventeenth-century French classicism. In fact, classical tragedies bore many similarities with Athenian theater before the fall. They too were governed by a set of conventions and allusions, a "representative code" that, because it was accessible only to the nation's sociocultural elite, served to partition audiences based on their response to the play.[32] Not surprisingly, the majority of French classical theorists praised the elite's refined mode of judgment, which found satisfaction in analyzing the play's beauty, as determined by its adherence to the representative code, and belittled the approach of the multitude, characterized by a purely sensual pleasure at the visual aspects of theater.[33] Like the new poets in Plato's story, however, theatrical reformers turned the established order upside down by maintaining that artistic creation should not conform to a preexisting code but should instead express freely the playwright's sensibility. In so doing, and even more overtly in their writings, they encouraged the audience to embrace a different mode of judgment. As we saw in Chapter 2, Diderot and his followers argued that a theatrical performance should not be treated as a composite of discrete fragments (writing, acting, staging, etc.), each satisfying or failing to satisfy set rules, but rather as a total experience, from which was born an instinctual pleasure—the most legitimate measure of a performance's worth. This evolution in the practice of judging clearly resembled the one longed for by legal reformers. Just as theatrical reformers affirmed the validity of natural, unmediated sentiments, thus inviting spectators of all backgrounds to ignore the opinions of connoisseurs and the fixed set of laws on which they relied, and to judge instead the merit of a performance based on their emotional reaction to it,[34] the notion of *conviction intime* redefined the basis of forensic judgment from arithmetic rules to an innate sense of guilt and innocence. In Latour's eyes, a battle that had begun in the theater was now being waged in the courtroom, just as Plato had foretold.

It may be tempting to regard this theatrocratic narrative as just another retelling of a story that has become central to our understanding of the eighteenth century: the story of the rise of public opinion. Modern historians following in the footsteps of Habermas have shown that public opinion initially manifested itself in apolitical forms, most notably as aesthetic criticism. The belief among a growing number of Frenchmen that individuals could, through a deliberative process that defied fixed rules and social distinctions, arrive at a public opinion about a work of art eventually led to calls for the extension of the same authority to political issues. Like Plato, historians have argued that this more egalitarian mode of judgment, once it entered the political realm, began to undermine the established order (here, absolutist monarchy). If public opinion expressed the will of the nation, then the king, formerly believed to embody and thus speak for the nation, now ruled in his own name, that is, arbitrarily. Yet while the theatrocratic narrative and the standard history of public opinion do indeed share many similarities, they also differ in significant ways. Whereas studies of public opinion focus primarily on its political implications, often with the aim of elucidating the origins of the French Revolution,[35] the theatrocratic narrative is concerned first and foremost with the influence of a new mode of judgment on the perception and practice of justice, as illustrated by Plato's mention of magistrates, oaths, and contracts.[36] The emphasis among modern historians on political repercussions, while legitimate, should not obscure the fact that the radical concept of an innate right to judge, which flourished in artistic milieus in the eighteenth century, was widely perceived at the time as having equally profound ramifications on the way that magistrates and, more broadly, the legal system operated.

Hence, while Ravel is right to stress that it became increasingly common in the second half of the eighteenth century to portray the parterre as representative of the nation, and audience intervention as the expression of a politically engaged public opinion, it should be noted that the theater was also frequently depicted as a popular tribunal, one that functioned differently from other courts and as a result possessed a degree of sovereignty over them.[37] In one telling example, several articles from the *Correspondance littéraire* concluded there was little value in analyzing the reception of plays by the king and his courtiers in Fontainebleau, because "such successes, always uncertain, have never been held to be legally established, since the Parisian public is universally regarded as the court of last resort for the verdicts reached by the royal court."[38] The public cherished this role as appellate judge, according to Grimm, who had already noted in an earlier article that part of the pleasure of attending the theater in Paris came from the opportunity "to successively revise all the trials that have been judged at court."[39] Meister, Grimm's successor at the head of the *Correspondance*, gave perhaps the best summary of this power relation, again in legal terms: "Fontainebleau is the Châtelet [a royal tribunal], and the Parisian parterre is the Parlement who overturns its sentences."[40] This analogy between the parterre and the Parlement is applicable to more than just the relationship between Parisian and court theaters. As we saw in Chapter 2, French audiences increasingly turned to the theater to express disagreement with the verdicts of the magistracy, at the same time as theatrical reformers promoted a vision of the theater as a popular, sovereign tribunal—two trends that bear witness to the desire for a parterre with the duties of an appellate court. In this vision of the theater, each spectator contributes to the expression of a definitive verdict on legal and artistic matters already judged by a royal court (in both the cultural and judicial meanings of the term "court"). The impact of this public judgment on the ones that preceded it is perfectly captured by Grimm's casual dismissal of the court's verdict on new plays as unworthy of transcription. The public revision of a prior judgment does not provide guidance or constructive criticism, as public opinion was often claimed to do with respect to the king's political decisions; instead, it renders all anterior judgments irrelevant and ineffectual. As Plato had foreseen, it thus undermines the legitimacy of the magistracy, by denying it—and any specific individual—the exclusive right to judge.

Partly as a result, the theatrocratic narrative deviates from the standard history of public opinion not only in its focus but also in its conclusion. Nearly all studies of public opinion present it as a catalyst in the transition from a political system based on the absolute power of a sovereign to a regime governed by laws and democratic processes. By contrast, the theatrocratic narrative adopts a far more expansive and pessimistic outlook on the social impact of freeing judgment from the complex rules and class restrictions that once regulated it. For Plato and his followers, this new mode of judgment threatens to erode not just a particular form of authority (absolutism), but authority itself. It does not inspire a transition from one order to another but results instead in the collapse of all order. Such a difference in outcome explains—or perhaps is explained by—a third distinction between the two narratives. Historians have traditionally identified the rise of public opinion as a contributing factor in a broader cultural shift from theatricality to textuality—that is, from an iconic order in which power lies in the spectacular display of a king's authority before docile subjects, to a linguistic order in which power resides in the ability to win the support of a critical public of readers. As a result, they have usually presented public opinion as a textual phenomenon, originating from the rapid expansion of printed material in the eighteenth century and developing through the reasoned, orderly exchanges that the practice of reading and writing cultivates.[41] By contrast, the theatrocratic narrative situates the rise of a new conception of judgment explicitly and exclusively in the theater. This theatrical origin is inseparable from the anarchy with which the narrative concludes. For Plato and Latour, there exists something in the theater, absent from the world of print, that makes free judgment especially dangerous, not just to absolutist authority but to authority in all its forms. Indeed, historians of public opinion mischaracterize the theatrical culture of the eighteenth century when they depict it as a symbol and foundation for the absolutist order. On the contrary, the theater can be (and often was) perceived as the site of a unique challenge to patriarchal authority.

Just as he had lamented the derisive portrayal of magistrates, Latour condemns the plays of his time for depicting father figures as ridiculous tyrants, while painting the young in a sympathetic light by presenting them as victims not of their own illicit passions but of the unjust rule of their elders.[42] This complaint, which Latour likely copied from Rousseau, was commonplace in the eighteenth century. Even partisans of the theater such as Rétif, Mercier, and Diderot expressed regret that plays depicted the illegitimacy and inevitable failure of paternal law far more frequently than its triumph. Fathers were also weakened by the theater in a more concrete way, insofar as they lost much of their power over their children when the latter chose to become actors. Rétif thus remarks that actors "have no family, they are no longer citizens: they have been stripped of their distinctive mark, the natural dependency of children on their fathers."[43] Rétif refers here to the actors' inclusion among the *infâmes*, which barred them from appearing in court, receiving religious sacraments, or holding a public office, essentially depriving them of a legal, religious, or civic identity. Unusually, however, Rétif does not tie the actors' ostracism to their craft as professional deceivers, but rather to the fact that they have lost their natural dependency on their fathers. As Rétif explains a few lines earlier, the moment a young actor climbs on stage, he agrees to submit to the judgment of the audience, whose orders he must follow, lest he starve. He thus takes the right to judge him out of the hands of the sole person to legitimately possess it, his father, and surrenders it to an anonymous, fickle audience, motivated by a desire for pleasure, rather than by a concern for his welfare. Such freedom from the influence of his father, who no longer determines his fate and who is furthermore forbidden by social norms from recognizing him as his progeny, harms not just the father and the young actor (described by Rétif as a "slave" to an uncaring public), but society as a whole. Indeed, for Rétif, actors constitute both a perfect symbol and a primary reason for the emergence of a post-patriarchal society, in which individuals allow themselves to be governed by the opinions of the majority, instead of the will of their superiors.

The theater's weakening of father figures ultimately derives therefore from the unique form of judgment it allows. In eighteenth-century France, the theater constituted an unusually democratic space in which the majority (the parterre) frequently imposed its verdict on the governing classes in the galleries. Unlike the metaphorical "public opinion" so frequently and effortlessly invoked in the pamphlets of the period, the judgment of dramatic spectators was tangible, immediate, and often belligerent (nothing like the docile theatrical subjects imagined by many historians of public opinion).[44] Moreover, whereas a text-centered public opinion remained for the most part circumscribed within an elite of educated readers, to the relief of the near totality of eighteenth-century thinkers, very few of whom genuinely believed that the judgments of the lower classes should play any part in the formation of a general will,[45] theatrical judgments could, and often did, involve the participation of a socially diverse audience. How plebeian spectators, traditionally denied the freedom to judge, inside as well as outside of the theater, reacted to this new right was a frequent source of concern in the eighteenth century. In the words of one anonymous author, "The praise that the people receive from actors, the absolute power that they wield over them, goes to their heads. Each spectator leaves the theater bolder and haughtier than he entered it. . . . At these performances, the servant sits next to his master. He comes to shake off his scruples and try his hand at insubordination."[46] The valets of the world tasted for the first time in the theater the power intrinsic to the act of judging and fell in love with it, to the point that they no longer obeyed their masters. Their judgments were not inspired by a longing for truth or social change, as public opinion claimed to be, but were motivated purely by the pleasure that came from ruling over another (a pleasure made even greater in the theater by the presence of the men—actors, playwrights, and masters—forced to submit to the parterre's verdict). Indeed, one finds in newspapers from the second half of the eighteenth century an increasingly frequent complaint that spectators sometimes waited scarcely more than a few minutes before beginning to hiss a play or actor—proof, in the eyes of the journalists, that many of their contemporaries went to the theater less out of a true appreciation for the arts than out of a desire to humiliate others.[47] Rétif shared this dim view of popular judgment and, like Plato and Latour, worried it was spreading beyond the theater: "The people test their strength at the theater; they are becoming impudent, impatient of the yoke of the laws, and they will soon shake off all the salutary shackles of sociability."[48] As this passage makes clear, the threat of the theater extended beyond the political realm. The compulsive need to judge that it created and cultivated within the people did not target a specific authority, such as the king, but authority itself. It instilled individual spectators with the conceit that no single being could ever have sovereignty over them, an overly egalitarian notion that would, Rétif feared, precipitate the demise of the rule of law and of the very ability to live in a society.

The Birth of Modern (Delayed) Judgment

Many eighteenth-century writers—antitheatricalists, such as Latour, but also, and more surprisingly, theatrical reformers, such as Rétif—thus expressed anxiety that the sudden growth in the theater's popularity among the lower classes (a phenomenon for which they even coined a derisive term: "theatromania") and the accompanying rise of a new, rule-free mode of judgment threatened to cast France into a state of anarchy. One obvious solution was to forbid judgments in the parterre through the use of force, but the crown had pursued this endeavor for centuries, with limited success.[49] In the late 1770s, a group of critics, nearly all admirers of French classical culture and politics, adopted a subtler and ultimately more effective strategy by initiating a campaign to seat the parterre.[50] Easily disguised as a movement seeking to improve the comfort of theatergoers, seating the parterre had the added benefit, in the eyes of reactionary critics, of limiting the affective flow between spectators, leading to a more tranquil, less interventionist audience. As a result, seated spectators would be more likely to follow the example of the elite and respond to performances analytically instead of emotionally. In the words of the architect Claude Nicolas Ledoux, "by extinguishing in this way what is falsely called the enthusiasm of the parterre, we will judge authors more accurately."[51] In fact, seating the parterre would do more than extend the elite's critical mode of judgment to the entire auditorium; it would also, in raising the entry price to the parterre, drive out the least fortunate members of the audience.

Not surprisingly, nearly every theatrical reformer vigorously (if unsuccessfully) opposed the campaign to seat the parterre. They joined voices in defense of plebeian spectators, on the grounds that commoners were in reality the best possible judges of a work of art, precisely because they lacked, to quote Marmontel, the "polished manners," "pretensions of vanity," and "prejudices of education" of their social superiors,[52] or as Mercier put it, "their metaphysics, their composed ideas, and their idiosyncratic systems."[53] Such unfamiliarity with aristocratic decorum and classical rules freed popular spectators to rely instead on their "naïve sensibility" and "common sense"[54] —a claim reminiscent of the liberal reformers' belief, discussed earlier, that simple men unhindered by legal formulas judged better than professional magistrates. Charpentier even concluded, in a passage addressed to all spectators, including himself and other intellectuals, that it would be preferable if "we were all commoners," or at least if "we took care to maintain ourselves in a kind of ignorance."[55]

If such a response and, more broadly, the terms of the debate on seating the parterre sound familiar, it is because the two parties were taking sides in a longstanding conflict, which had shaped (and constrained) discussions about audience participation ever since Plato. Both parties implicitly accepted a series of binary oppositions: on the one side, a traditional, highly regulated theater, intended to appeal to reason and to inspire an aesthetic judgment, and thus written for the elites; on the other, innovative, sentimental plays, written with the common people in mind and seeking to elicit an emotional, instinctual judgment. Tellingly however, although the two parties embraced completely antithetical visions of the perfect audience, they agreed on its basic right to pass a judgment on the performance as it unfolded. Indeed, despite differing as to the proper holders of this right (the elites or the people), they shared a vision of the theater as the site of a continuous exchange between the artists and the audience.

During the second half of the eighteenth century, however, there appeared a third movement, ignored until now, which broke free from this age-old vision and maintained instead that all judgment, regardless of its source and nature, should be forbidden in the theater. Again and again, in articles, pamphlets, and books, one finds expressions of the same desire for a way to persuade or compel spectators to postpone their verdicts until the end of the performance, if not later. As audience interventionism grew in the 1770s and 1780s, so did the frequency and intensity of the calls for the suspension of its judgments. Most authors, including Jacques Antoine Mague de Saint-Aubin and Jean Charles Levacher de Charnois,[56] demanded that judgment be withheld until the fall of the curtain; several others, Rétif among them,[57] proposed to wait until the fourth performance; and one critic, the royal censor Antoine Maillet-Duclairon,[58] even suggested that actors should only be judged after an entire year had passed. As a justification, many writers, including Rétif and Anne-Gabriel Meusnier de Querlon, pointed to similar practices in ancient Athens and Rome.[59] Plato himself had noted in his description of Athenian theater before its fall into theatrocracy that the educated elites, who enjoyed both the right and the ability to judge, nevertheless "made it their rule to hear the performances through in silence," so as not to set a perilous example for the rabble.[60] Indeed, the idea of delaying judgment pushed to its logical extreme the Platonic argument that the threat posed by audience interaction derived less from its content or target than from the act of judging itself, which bred in the spectators a dangerous conceit in their critical faculties. The supporters of a seated parterre had aimed to restrict the act of judgment to those with the proper instruction, but such a measure amounted to controlling the threat, not extinguishing it. Only a unanimous suspension of judgment could truly revive the theater of the pre-theatrocracy era, by ensuring that dramatic productions unfolded in complete silence.

Just as remarkable as the ambition to silence the entire auditorium is the innovative way that Rétif and his fellow reformers set out to achieve what must have seemed at the time an impossible task. In the words of Friedland, the second half of the eighteenth century "set about *inventing* the modern spectator": passive, silent, and fully captivated by the action on stage.[61] Friedland links this conception of the audience to Diderot's theorization of the fourth wall and to its implementation through architectural reforms, advances in lighting, and the ejection from the stage of the foppish noblemen who previously sat in the actors' midst. It is true, as we saw in Chapter 1, that Diderot and his disciples hoped that the fourth wall, along with the heightened verisimilitude of the new genres, would radically transform the spectators' relationship to the stage by inspiring in them the illusion that they were watching an unrehearsed, self-contained, actual event, rather than an artistic production. Modern scholars, influenced perhaps by the overall passivity of mainstream twentieth-century audiences and by Bertolt Brecht's famous critique of their lethargy, have tended to assume that dramatic illusion necessarily consists of a solitary, silent, nonparticipatory experience. The theatrocratic narrative challenges this assumption, however, by revealing that in the eighteenth century, the embrace of pathos and illusion was blamed not for dwindling audience participation but on the contrary for its sudden expansion, in quantity as well as intensity. In fact, both proponents and opponents of the new genres were far likelier to depict illusion as leading to an alternative mode of judgment than to the absence of one. For Diderot and his followers, dramatic illusion, because it entailed a "forgetting of the theater," was central to the shift away from the analytical judgment of the elites, focused on the formal qualities of the performance, toward a more authentic, emotional response to the play's content. This response expressed itself through tears and laughter, instead of applause and shouted criticisms, but was no less a judgment for being instinctual and emotional rather than studied and analytical.[62] Indeed, nothing demonstrated a performance's quality more irrefutably than when it succeeded in concealing its own theatricality, thereby inspiring intense emotions similar to those felt before a real event.

Not only did eighteenth-century thinkers not regard illusion as the antithesis of judgment, they did not even conceive of it as silent or solitary. On the contrary, nearly every theatrical reformer depicted illusion as a communal experience, the product of an overpowering emotion that only grew in intensity at the sight of other spectators' sentimental displays, be they tears, laughs, or screams directed at the characters. The constant motion of the crowd and the passionate outbursts of neighboring spectators operated like electronic amplifiers, blending and heightening sensations until the spectators no longer remembered that they were watching a theatrical production.[63] Accordingly, Diderot and the vast majority of his followers condemned all attempts at silencing the audience and explicitly championed a standing, lively parterre.[64] This even holds true with regards to their endorsement of the fourth wall. As Diderot conceived it—and this is too rarely emphasized—the fourth wall ensured that actors did not acknowledge the riotous displays of the parterre, *not* that these would be suspended. While it was essential, for the sake of the spectator's illusion, that actors never respond directly to the parterre's sentimental outbursts or applause (as they often did in the most artificial way imaginable: by pausing mid-sentence and curtsying), it was equally important that they be able to witness the effect of their acting on the audience, since this helped them refine their roles after each performance. Memoirs of former actors and treatises on the theater frequently draw attention to the crucial impact of the parterre's emotions on a performer's acting, not only in the long term (for the reason mentioned above) but also in the short term, since a particularly sensitive audience could electrify an actor, touching him so deeply that his own emotions, and thus his acting, became more sincere. Diderot therefore never intended for the fourth wall to produce today's silent, isolated spectator; quite the opposite, in fact: he viewed it as a cornerstone in a larger program of reform seeking to inspire a more expressive, authentic, and communal response to the theater.

It should come as no surprise that Rétif, the author of numerous sentimental dramas, drew many ideas from Diderot when developing his own conception of dramatic illusion. For instance, he too understands illusion as a "forgetting of the theater," a phenomenon he describes in *La Mimographe* as the greatest accomplishment of the scenic arts: "Dramatic pleasure is greater when the illusion is more complete; it would be as perfect as can be, if the spectator, forgetting the theater and the actor, saw only the action and the character."[65] Rétif goes on to lament—again like Diderot—that many of his contemporaries respond to the theater analytically rather than emotionally, in a manner that jeopardizes not only their own illusion but also that of their fellow spectators, since their applause and running commentary on the formal qualities of the play draw everyone's attention to the theatricality of the performance.[66] What Rétif adds next, however, alters the nature of illusion radically:

> SEPTIMANIE—Madam, could we not silence these childish spectators?
> ADELAÏDE—There is but one effective way to do this; it would be to convince them that the sensitive man does not applaud; he savors; he revels in being moved. To taste this tender voluptuousness, one must not go out of oneself, but withdraw within oneself: our century likes to flaunt emotions; such affectation is in fashion.[67]

This proposal by Adelaïde (the "mimographe" mentioned in the title), unremarkable as it may seem to a modern theatergoer, is in reality strikingly original, audacious even: it stands as one of the first portrayals—perhaps even *the* first in France—of illusion as a purely private experience, one for which a complete silence is both a prerequisite and a desired outcome. Whereas Diderot and Mercier believed illusion to be heightened by the emotional outbursts of nearby spectators, Rétif depicts illusion as a silent "turning inward," a solitary withdrawal into the world of one's emotions that even the slightest distraction endangers. Hence, for Rétif, sincere displays of emotion could prove as disruptive to illusion as conventional expressions of a more aesthetic judgment, like applause.

This redefinition of dramatic illusion as a solitary and silent self-immersion provided Rétif with the ideal justification for his true ambition: the suspension of all manifestations of judgment, including the thunderous emotional displays of the parterre. If the Greeks and Romans had devised strict policies regulating the timing of a spectator's participation, it was not, Rétif argued, so as to curb the emotions of each spectator, but rather so as to protect them: the wise ancients understood that a truly sensitive theatergoer "is indignant that one would dissipate his illusion" through premature applause.[68] Rétif could thus claim to act, if not in keeping with the spectators' wishes, at least in their best interest, when he proposed a draconian law prohibiting audience members not only from applauding or hissing during the first three performances of a play, but also from turning their backs to the stage or entering into a conversation with another spectator, under penalties ranging from a fine to corporal punishment and exile.[69] As the last two prohibitions make clear, the law sought to isolate each spectator from his neighbors, thereby enabling the "turning inward" essential to the experience of a theatrical illusion. In so doing, it established a network of barriers in the auditorium far more extensive and impervious than Diderot's fourth wall. Whereas the latter was a fiction designed to convince each spectator that the performers could not see the audience, Rétif's law imagined a theatrical space in which it was the spectators who no longer saw the audience. Yet for a theatergoer to forget the very existence of the other spectators required that complete silence reign in the parterre—a proposition that no one dared put forward in France until Rétif's bold assertion that "the slightest noise should be forbidden at the theater."[70] More than Diderot, therefore, it is Rétif who has the most convincing claim to the dubious honor of having invented the isolated and silent spectator of modern times.[71]

The rise of today's subdued audiences is often cited as evidence of a broader evolution culminating in the modern, alienated individual—unreflective, self-absorbed, uncomfortable with emotional displays, and excluded from the public sphere. Undoubtedly, spectators are far more passive than they once were, yet it is misleading to describe them as entirely bereft of judgment and authority. By the power of the purse, as well as that of word of mouth, they still determine the fate of nearly every play. Even Rétif never imagines that it could be otherwise, which is why he feels justified in writing, despite his calls for a silent audience: "I do not claim that one ought to deny the parterre their right to judge."[72] One may wonder, however: why not just abolish this right? Perhaps Rétif understood that once the slide toward theatrocracy had begun, and the conceit of judgment taken hold of the spectators, the use of force only made matters worse—or as Mercier put it: "I am convinced that the menacing sight of police officers only adds to the anger of the spectators, that it disturbs their pleasure, because they find a greater one in defying the policemen."[73] Whatever his reasons, Rétif's recognition of the parterre's "right to judge" may seem at odds with his attempts at restricting its judgments, yet taken together, they perfectly reflect the unprecedented focus in eighteenth-century France on *how*, *why*, and *when* theatrical audiences judge, rather than on *whether* they judge (they always do). This focus reveals the need for a nuanced understanding of audience behavior, less invested in the standard binary opposition between a judging (active) and a nonjudging (passive) public, and freer as a result to study the process through which judgment was gradually redefined (not abolished) to a limited range of expressions and timing.

For instance, the belief that spectators should postpone expressing their judgment on a performance until after it has ended has become so engrained in today's mainstream audiences, so seemingly natural, that its construction in the second half of the eighteenth century has failed to attract any attention. Yet the invention of the delayed judgment represents a momentous shift not only in the behavior of spectators but also in the very conception of the nature of theater. In the eighteenth century, spectators entertained a relationship to the stage drastically different from ours in that they deemed themselves to be integral participants in the play's production. The men in the parterre did not regard theatrical performances as finished works of art, to be consumed in silence or, if truly unpalatable, to be rejected in their entirety, but rather as ongoing creations, which they had a right and a duty to alter as they saw fit (one of the most popular cries, "cut, cut," was used to flag passages in need of pruning). In return, playwrights and actors took note of the spectators' reactions and revised the performance accordingly.[74] Voltaire did so with such frequency, in fact, that a humorous poem was written about it: "Despite his temerity, / Voltaire will obtain all our votes, / Since the parterre has the kindness / Of correcting each of his plays."[75] By contrast, the plea by Rétif and others to postpone judgment until the end of the performance betrayed their desire to redefine the theater as a fixed and finalized work of art, judgeable only as a totality. As they well knew, the simple act of suspending judgment transformed it from a specific contribution to the production, identifying a flaw for future amendment, to a largely perfunctory, since absolute, verdict on the performance as a whole. In the name of illusion, they encouraged spectators to surrender their longstanding right to judge every aspect of the performance and restrict themselves instead to a simple yay or nay vote, coming as a post factum verdict on a spectacle they had, up to that point, watched in silence.

The partisans of postponing judgment thus invented a new form of audience involvement, still prevailing to this day—not only in the theater but also in the justice system. Indeed, while the theory of delayed judgment first arose in relation to the theater, one of its earliest applications in France took place in the courtroom. As we saw earlier, legal reformers nearly all agreed that the presence of spectators was indispensable to the proper administration of justice. Making criminal proceedings public would help prevent miscarriages of justice, since a vigilant people would not fail to detect and denounce judicial errors and abuses.[76] Accordingly, the reformers envisioned a public of involved and informed citizens, interrupting trials to intervene directly and immediately, not unlike theatrical spectators of the period—a parallel that partly explains the reformers' attraction to theater as a model for a new performance of justice. Their dream was realized in the first few months of the Revolution, when the National Assembly decreed that all legal proceedings would henceforth be public.[77] In a striking reversal, however, the same deputies passed a law less than two years later imposing complete silence and stillness on judicial spectators:

> Art I. Citizens who attend proceedings in district, police, commerce, and criminal tribunals will sit their heads uncovered, in respect and in silence. . . .
>
> II. If one or more of the spectators interrupt this silence, give public signs of approval or disapproval, with regards to the defense or the verdict, create or incite turmoil in any manner, and if, after a warning by the bailiffs, they do not immediately return to order, they will be enjoined to leave.[78]

Although the impermanence of audience behavior makes it notoriously difficult to assess, it appears that most spectators adhered to this law. Indeed, in a recent article, Katherine Taylor shows that trial spectators in the early years of the Revolution were remarkably sedate. As evidence, she cites newspaper reports, including a telling incident that saw a judge respond to a solitary round of applause by reciting the new law, successfully restoring the silence that had been breached for the first and final time.[79]

The passage of this law suggests that the possibility of a direct, popular involvement in the tribunal elicited no less anxiety than it had in the theater—and for identical reasons. In fact, in an earlier text defending secret trials, Boucher d'Argis had employed the same arguments as those who denounced dramatic judgment as a source of theatrocracy: namely, that lay spectators judge too hastily, before a trial has run its course; that they are driven by the feeling of power that accompanies the act of judging, rather than by a desire for truth; and that they lack respect for the judgment of their superiors, sticking to their conclusions even after official magistrates have declared an accused innocent.[80] Indeed, it is telling that the authors of the law explicitly prohibited signs of approval (and not just of disapproval), as it suggests that their chief concern was less the content of the spectators' judgment than the fact that they were judging at all. The circumstances surrounding the law's passage confirm this: it was put forth during a larger debate on the perils of direct democracy and was introduced by the declaration that "Sovereignty, being one and indivisible, and belonging to the whole nation . . . no section of the people, whatever their denomination, may perform any action of the sovereign whole."[81] In the deputies' eyes, any judgment by the spectators of a trial, whether positive or negative, created within the courtroom a second center of sovereignty, thereby undermining the magistrates, the only individuals legitimately allowed to judge, since elected by, and acting for, the true sovereign: the whole people, not just a small section of it. The apparent contradiction of convening a public to decry judicial errors only to then silence it bears witness to the problem of legitimacy inherent in a representative system. In such a system, where the authority to judge comes not from within (one's rank) but from without (one's election), spectators must be present and informed to guarantee the legitimacy of the judges who represent them. Since any direct participation challenges the legitimacy of the magistracy, however, the same spectators must be compelled to express no judgments of their own, at least during the trial. In response, the National Assembly invented the modern judicial audience, with its paradoxical relationship to the performance of justice—at once central to it and forbidden from participating in it.[82]

As in the theater, however, it would be a mistake to portray such an audience as entirely powerless. Among the spectators were electors who effectively had the authority to dismiss a judge whose verdicts had displeased them by replacing him with a new magistrate once his term in office had come to an end. It was this right—to cast out judges they deemed illegitimate—that in turn gave legitimacy to the remaining magistrates and improved the odds that future verdicts would be more in line with public opinion. Yet the spectators' power only extended so far: not only were they unable to intervene directly in ongoing trials, they also could not revise past verdicts they deemed illegitimate. While they could deny reelection to the judges they held responsible, the cases themselves remained closed—fixed and finalized, much like dramatic works of art in Rétif's new vision of the theater. Indeed, the limited power granted to judicial spectators bore many similarities to the delayed judgment championed by Rétif and others in the theater. Both sets of audiences were compelled to let the legal or theatrical performance run its course without any input, and were only given in return a single, belated, yay or nay vote, meant to ensure that a mediocre performer (actor, author, or judge) would in time relinquish the spotlight. For this exceedingly narrow understanding of audience involvement to have appeared in the very same period as the institution of public criminal trials may seem paradoxical, yet it is far from surprising. It is precisely because the people were granted unprecedented access and insight into the workings of justice that a new mode of audience participation became necessary, so as to prevent the desire to judge awakened in each spectator at the sight of a trial from challenging the legitimacy of the magistracy and, with it, the entire justice system. The notion of a delayed judgment—here, the promise of future input through an election—provided an ideal solution because it could satisfy the spectators' longing to judge while limiting their ability to genuinely alter the performance. That this solution was adopted in many domains, including theater, justice, and politics,[83] suggests that the modern individual is perhaps less a being who does not judge than one who always judges too late for his or her verdict to have any effect.

Delayed Judgment and the New Magistrate

As we saw earlier, fears of a theatrical mode of judgment—and of it metastasizing—applied not only to trial spectators but to magistrates as well. Just as they had with courtroom audiences, these fears inspired attempts to limit the judges' involvement in legal proceedings. Such attempts were particularly surprising given the remarkably active role assigned to magistrates by the ancien régime's inquisitorial model of justice. Pre-Revolutionary judges were, in a very real sense, the primary authors of a trial's narrative. For instance, when they interrogated an accused, the latter was limited to brief, simple answers to specific questions and strictly forbidden from any digressions or unsolicited arguments. Liberal reformers found this infuriating, as it meant that the accused could offer *faits justificatifs* (evidence in favor of their innocence) only at the end of the trial, and only if they responded directly and overtly to a claim made by a witness or accuser. While the accused could request to confront key witnesses (whose names and motivations were usually unknown to them), the magistrates were under no obligation to accept, and even then, the two participants in the confrontation were prohibited from speaking to each other directly. Instead, the accused indicated errors or inconsistencies in the testimonies to the examining magistrate, who could then choose whether or not to ask the witness for a response.[84] Such a strangely convoluted process highlights the extent to which criminal proceedings at the time sought to avert agonistic, unregulated debate, as well as the judge's control over the trial's narrative, as he determined both what participants in the trial could answer and what they could ask. Indeed, for many jurists, the authorship of magistrates went beyond directing oral interrogations to encompass the proceedings as a whole. Like playwrights, judges selected a cast of characters (witnesses), extracted specific information from them, recorded and collated their statements, dissected them into meaningful (and quantifiable) fragments, and organized them into a coherent plot. In sum, they composed, in the privacy of their chambers, a single, credible narrative of events, to which they could then apply legal formulas. In the ancien régime vision of trials, it was precisely the magistrates' superior and exclusive knowledge of the written text (of the depositions and of the law) that allowed them to find the truth concealed by the oral deceptions and manipulations of the accused.[85]

Not surprisingly, liberal reformers condemned this vision for giving the magistracy an excessive and arbitrary authority (including in the etymological sense of being an author). Citing the jurist Pierre Ayrault, Joseph de Bernardi complained: "Our trials are just pieces or fragments. We judge without having seen or heard. We base our conscience and religion on paper, perhaps falsified, perhaps poorly engrossed, perhaps flawed."[86] In its rejection of the text and the fragment as loci of truth, this complaint echoed the critique of French classical theater by theatrical reformers such as Diderot. According to Bernardi and Diderot, ancien régime judges and spectators experienced trials and plays in the same way: as a series of textual fragments (depositions or verses) to be evaluated according to predetermined rules. Because of this obsession with the written word, which compelled them to read, collate, and analyze fragments, they became mired in trivial details and lost sight of the greater whole. By contrast, the liberal vision of trials as public, oral debates occurring in a single sitting and setting obviated the need for lengthy transcriptions and multiple, separate interrogations of the same individuals, thereby eliminating the two practices most responsible for fragmenting legal proceedings into a series of texts. The liberal model sought to allow magistrates a more comprehensive experience, since they would no longer read transcripts but see and hear the integrality of the proceedings, and to encourage them, as Diderot had the theatergoers of his time, to base their judgments not only on a speaker's words but also on nontextual cues, such as gestures and voice. In fact, the judges' experience was also less fragmented in its timing, because the liberal vision made it possible for them to weigh evidence of guilt and innocence simultaneously (since the parties now made claims and counterclaims concurrently, unlike under the ancien régime, when the case against the accused was developed by the judges themselves before they heard all of the evidence pointing toward innocence, such as *faits justificatifs*—an imbalance that liberals deplored, on the grounds that conceited judges often stuck to their first impression: guilt).[87]

As we saw with theatrical reformers, the shift away from an analytical focus on texts and fragments was not perceived as a restriction on judgment. Bernardi, for instance, calls for public, uninterrupted proceedings, yet presents judges as actively involved in the creation of each trial's narrative (albeit no longer as primary authors, and by means of oral debates rather than textual hermeneutics): "There are few people capable of rendering a story well, of expressing all of its circumstances with clarity, without being helped by someone. Most depositions would therefore be very imperfect, if they were not arranged by a judge from the interrogations he conducts."[88] By their questions and requests for clarification, magistrates still played a key role in the production of a coherent account of the events under litigation. Some legal reformers, however, reached a very different conclusion. As Rétif had done with Diderot's dramatic theories, they built on the widespread critique of the ancien régime's textual, fragmented mode of judgment to justify a far more sweeping condemnation of active, direct judgment in all its forms.

Hints of this more radical condemnation can be seen in the odd claim, popular among reformers, that judges should never ask captious, indirect, or misleading questions that might unsettle or surprise the accused and cause them to betray their guilt.[89] Under the ancien régime (and still to a large extent today), interrogation was understood as a means to break down the scripted story and rehearsed performance of the accused. Judges were expected to use their guile and greater knowledge of the case and of the law to set up traps for the accused, ensnare them in their own lies, and expose the truth. In reality, however, many liberals, like Joseph-Michel-Antoine Servan, warned that while "the judge believes he's discovered a culprit, he actually created him."[90] This is because, Julien Dentand noted, judges inevitably shape the accused's story, insofar as the questions they ask determine the parameters of the debate, notably by establishing which facts are significant, and can alter the perception of the accused by putting them at ease or on the defensive.[91] Hence, whereas for Bernardi the judges' interventions help the accused produce a clearer, more accurate narrative, for Dentand, they actually prevent the accused from controlling their own narrative and thereby distort it. In both views, the judges form the narrative, but in the first, this creative act leads to truth, while in the second, it obscures it. Worse, as Servan suggests above, the judges' questions create guilt far more often than innocence, since judges are never truly impartial. They usually presume the accused to be guilty, because, like theatrical spectators, they find more pleasure in condemning than in praising, and because their pride blinds them to the possible innocence of a man they deemed suspect enough to try in the first place.[92] This led many liberals to conclude that the active involvement of judges in trials did not improve their judgment but on the contrary impaired it.

Accordingly, some reformers proposed, for the first time in French legal history, that magistrates should play no direct role in interrogating the accused, accuser, and witnesses. Dentand recommends this explicitly in his *Essai de jurisprudence criminelle*,[93] while Marat affirms, against the standard practice of his time, that "it should not fall to judges to establish the proof of a crime, but only to examine impartially the evidence presented to them."[94] The ideal of impartiality plays a crucial role in justifying the new, diminished function assigned to judges. For Marat, a trial consists of a conflict between an accuser and an accused, unfolding before a neutral judge. In the name of equity and the presumption of innocence, both parties must be provided with the exact same support (legal representation, opportunities to speak, advanced knowledge of the charges and evidence, etc.) so that they may prepare and rehearse the most convincing narrative possible. For a magistrate to intervene and, through his questions and dissentions, interrupt or disrupt the litigants' performance risks undermining his impartiality. His involvement in challenging or corroborating specific claims may inspire him, consciously or not, to take a side, shaping thereby how the remainder of the trial unfolds and distorting his final judgment. Marat's and Dentand's proposals thus rest on the novel idea that it is essential to sever judgment from direct, active involvement, as if participation and impartiality were incompatible. Against the ancien régime's understanding of judging as a creative, hermeneutic act necessitating direct intervention in the proceedings, some reformers recast judgment as a largely passive, subjective form of reception. In this view, the magistrate no longer takes the lead or even participates in the creation of a narrative, but simply chooses the more compelling of the rehearsed narratives performed before him. Thus did the judge's role evolve in the writings of eighteenth-century jurists from head writer to spontaneous, direct contributor to, at last, passive spectator.

This evolution closely resembles the one we saw earlier in the figure of the theatrical spectator. On the judges' bench, as in the parterre, reformers invented a new kind of judgment, limited in timing, since requiring that judges not weigh in until the trial's (or the play's) end, as well as in scope, since consisting of an absolute, yay or nay, guilty or innocent vote, without the freedom to intervene at precise moments and transform the performances before them. Such similarities suggest a common source, a shared anxiety resulting from the period's redefinition of judgment, in the theater and the tribunal, as open to all and free of rules. Some reformers, like Bernardi, embraced these liberal ideals while preserving the traditional role of judges as active, immediate participants. For others, however, lifting longstanding restrictions on who can judge and how, while allowing untrained, power-hungry plebeians the same active involvement as their official predecessors, meant creating a breeding ground for theatrocracy. Indeed, what would prevent judges with no title to lose and no rules to follow from succumbing to the pleasure of finding a fellow man guilty, from intervening to criticize the accused and their answers with the same haste with which they heckled actors and playwrights at the theater, without giving them a full and impartial hearing? This was the fear, ubiquitous not only among reactionaries but also among liberals like Servan, that inspired the attempt to limit the timing and scope of the judges' interventions—to institute, as in the theater, a modern, delayed judgment.

One need only watch a trial in France today, however, to realize that these attempts proved less successful in the tribunal than in the theater. In fact, it often comes as a shock to Anglo-Saxon observers just how inquisitorial the French justice system remains. Its judges continue—as they never really ceased—to direct proceedings, question litigants, and participate directly in the early stages of the investigation, including through private interrogations. In her work on nineteenth-century judicial architecture, Taylor notes that modern French trials actually constitute a hybrid of the inquisitorial and accusatorial models, as illustrated by their division into three distinct phases: first, the one-sided, fragmented interrogation of the accused by a presiding magistrate with a superior knowledge of the text of the case and of the law;

then, a series of more open, adversarial debates involving judges, litigants, witnesses, and lawyers; and, by way of conclusion, two rehearsed speeches by the prosecution and the defense, delivered in silence and without interruption.[95] The first phase brings to mind the criminal trials of the ancien régime, with the judge as author; the second, the proceedings of antiquity (as imagined and celebrated by liberals), with the judge as participant; and the third, the approach favored by supporters of a delayed judgment, with the judge as spectator. Such hybridity reveals that today's French judges, like modern lawyers, are the product less of an unmitigated victory by the liberal conception of justice than of a process of negotiation and compromise. Of course, there is no denying that judging underwent some radical changes in response to liberal ideals such as equality and transparency, with judges forsaking fixed, arcane formulas in favor of a *conviction intime* derived from watching public, overtly dramatic trials. And yet, the preservation of examining magistrates, written dossiers, and inquisitorial interrogations testifies to the resiliency of the eighteenth-century fear that a loss of authorship meant a loss of authority, as judges declined from embodiments of divine justice to mere spectators. The modern magistracy thus finds its roots in the attempt at reconciling a pervasive anxiety about the theatricality of liberal justice, on the one hand, and a recognition of its necessity in order to protect the rights of the accused, on the other. The ensuing compromise assigned French judges a remarkably fluid function in the performance of justice, playing every role—author, actor, and spectator—and perhaps, as a result, playing none at all.

Chapter 5

From Parterre to Pater

Dreaming of Domestic Tribunals

The Resurrection of Domestic Tribunals

At a time when *lettres de cachet* were under constant attack, the least likely of voices came to their defense: none other than Louis-Sébastien Mercier. It is worth pausing here to emphasize just how astonishing it is to find Mercier praising *lettres de cachet* in not one but several articles of his widely read *Tableau de Paris.*[1] Although Mercier claimed (correctly, as historians have shown) that *lettres de cachet,* contrary to popular belief, rarely targeted political critics and freethinking authors,[2] his own life provided a counterexample: in 1775, Emmanuel-Félicité de Durfort, Duc de Duras had issued a *lettre de cachet* ordering Mercier's imprisonment for his subversive writings.[3] Even setting aside this likely source of personal hostility, Mercier did not lack philosophical incentives to oppose *lettres de cachet.* By the 1770s, they had long been transformed into one of the most notorious symbols of ancien régime injustice. Their secrecy, arbitrariness, and authoritarianism made them a perfect microcosm of early modern criminal proceedings, and for that reason, they have often been depicted as the very antithesis of the modern, liberal form of justice established during the Revolution.[4] Mercier is not known, however, for having been a fan of secrecy: in fact, he has been credited by Jürgen Habermas as the first writer to focus on the sociopolitical role of the then-emerging conception of public opinion.[5] Few authors spoke as highly and as frequently about the need for greater political transparency. Likewise, he fervently opposed arbitrariness and authoritarianism, favoring instead a constitutional monarchy in which everyone, including the king, was equal before the law.

Why, then, did Mercier defend such a secretive, arbitrary, and authoritarian practice? Ever the utilitarian, he emphasized its value to society: "Most of these incarcerations are outside the law, but they are nonetheless often made necessary by the circumstances, and they become a family decree. Maniacs, madmen, violent lunatics, etc., would cause infinite evils in society before ordinary laws could repress them."[6] Mercier understood that *lettres de cachet*, far from being, as Mirabeau and others claimed, the weapon of choice of a despotic government bent on crushing innocent writers, constituted in reality a veritable blessing for caring fathers and husbands who relied on them to quarantine family members they deemed a danger to themselves and to society. *Lettres de cachet* thus prevented imminent crimes instead of simply, like the laws, administering punishments for crimes that had already been committed.[7] Moreover, even when the family patriarch failed to prevent a relative's crime, *lettres de cachet* provided him with a way to avoid a trial and conviction that would dishonor the entire family (since in the eighteenth century serious crimes marked with infamy not only the culprits but also their children, spouses, parents, siblings, and even cousins).[8] But Mercier also defended *lettres de cachet* because he believed such "family decrees" to be the most reliable and legitimate form of justice: "What human tribunal would not listen to a father's accusing voice? Is he not a sacred judge? Our judicial forms are too crude to penetrate the secrecy of families."[9] No magistrate, no tribunal, could compete with a father turned judge, due to the latter's superior knowledge of the secrets in his family, but also, and more significantly, because of his "sacredness." Indeed, unlike other tribunals and magistrates, designated by Mercier as merely "human," a father could claim a divine right to judge, bestowed upon him by the biological and spiritual link between creator and child. At a time when many feared that a more theatrical practice of justice was undermining the legitimacy of the magistracy and, more broadly, the rule of law, *lettres de cachet* hinted at a possible solution, by attributing the right to judge to the *pater* not the *parterre*—that is, to the sole being with a genuinely natural authority.

Even opponents of *lettres de cachet* saw them as a vestige of a primeval, natural form of justice, in which each patriarch exercised complete authority over his family. In 1784, for its annual competition, the Royal Society of Arts and Sciences of Metz solicited treatises exploring the value of the notion of infamy and, in particular, of its extension to the relatives of convicted criminals. The two prize-winning essays, by the already-famous lawyer Pierre Louis de Lacretelle and by the soon-to-be immensely famous

Robespierre, argue that the revolting practice of *lettres de cachet* finds its raison d'être in the notion of infamy.[10] Both *lettres de cachet* and infamy belong, according to Lacretelle and a third contestant, the jurist Joseph de Bernardi, to a domestic mode of justice dating back to the very origins of society. Lacretelle and Bernardi paint a similar portrait of this primitive legal system in which each family operates as a sovereign court, with the patriarch as sole judge, while in the case of interfamilial conflicts, a wise elder, chosen by the heads of both families, serves as an arbiter and conciliator, with the task of avoiding bloodshed.[11] Lacretelle then tells a familiar story: little by little, the wise elders encroached on the father's jurisdiction. They began by declaring that guilty parties would be required to compensate not only the wronged family but also the whole of society—a key moment, according to Lacretelle, because it marked the birth of "the idea of a public sphere."[12] This transformed trials from a private attempt to reconcile two parties into an endeavor by a public official to punish individuals culpable of violating a communal set of laws. Lacretelle presents this development as a positive one: what individuals lost in liberty by accepting the shackle of fixed laws, they more than recovered in security, through new rights that protected them from the fickleness of paternal justice.[13] Such a claim makes evident the inspiration for Lacretelle's story: the theory of the social contract.[14] Under the impetus of the wise elders, the primeval vision of justice as an extension of the father's will had begun to yield to a contractual model in which covenanting brothers unanimously agree to be bound to a predetermined code of laws. Lacretelle argues that the institution of a liberal legal system will bring this evolution to its logical end, eradicating the last vestiges of paternal justice, such as *lettres de cachet* and infamy, and finally giving a voice in the dealing of justice to all citizens through their introduction into the courtroom as spectators and as jurors.

Yet in a surprising development that reveals the depth of the eighteenth century's fascination with a familial mode of justice, all three liberal contestants express interest in the creation of domestic tribunals. Robespierre raises the possibility of such an institution, calling it a "safeguard of morals," but never pursues the matter at greater length.[15] Lacretelle goes further, devoting several pages to the institution of a "family council," but it is Bernardi who proves the most eager of the three. In a passage reminiscent of Mercier's defense of *lettres de cachet,* he explains: "our laws have claimed the policing of families for themselves, stripping parents of that right: but what can they really do about what happens within families?"[16] Not only would a domestic tribunal be more effective in unearthing the crimes hidden in the private sphere, it would also reduce future crimes and create stronger family ties by encouraging parents to keep a close watch on the morals of their children.[17] While such advantages appealed to Bernardi and Lacretelle, both expressed anxiety at the idea of placing such power within the hands of a single man, leading them to propose several alterations to the domestic tribunal of primeval societies.[18] The right of the father to judge would instead be shared among the family,[19] the proceedings would unfold in public and according to predetermined forms so as to ensure their uniformity and fairness,[20] and a professional magistrate would review the verdict to ascertain that it conformed to national laws.[21] This nonpatriarchal, institutional version of the domestic tribunal enjoyed the support of many eighteenth-century thinkers—enough, in fact, for it to become a reality during the Revolution. That such a tribunal was often presented as the opposite of *lettres de cachet* reveals the distance it had traveled from its primeval, patriarchal origins. Its egalitarian attribution of the right to judge and its emphasis on predetermined, communal laws are evidence of a contractual basis, coming at the expense of the father's traditional authority. The family tribunals imagined by Lacretelle and Bernardi represent therefore less a revival of the domestic trials of primeval societies than an extension of the liberal reformers' theatrical model of justice into the private sphere (all the more intrusive, in fact, in that the family's arguments, once confidential, would now unfold as a *public* spectacle).

Yet to many in the eighteenth century—not only reactionaries but also liberals like Mercier, Maréchal, and Mézard—this egalitarian conception of domestic tribunals threatened to undermine the legitimacy of the justice system instead of strengthening it. Indeed, they blamed not only the theater (as we saw in Chapter 4) but also ongoing legal reforms for having weakened the authority of fathers. A well-meaning but misguided focus on individual rights had inspired laws allowing sons to testify against and even sue their own fathers (an "extraordinary contempt for paternal authority," to quote Mercier), all the while limiting the fathers' "Roman right" to discipline other family members—so much so, deplored Mercier, that it was no longer even permitted to beat one's own wife.[22] Such civil rights violated the natural order by infringing on the biologically justified rule of men over their children and wives. Even Robespierre, Lacretelle, and Bernardi noted the (relative) powerlessness of fathers in the eighteenth century, arguing that it made infamy all the more unfair, since it meant that fathers were dishonored for crimes that they could not have prevented.[23] Their solution—freeing fathers from blame by ending infamy, but also weakening them further by sharing the right to judge with other family members—only aggravated the problem, in Mercier's eyes, by disassociating the exercise of justice from its source and justification: the authority of fathers over their children. Hence, in 1789, Rétif greeted the Revolution with the warning that, after years of "domestic insubordination," there existed only one way to avoid a state of lawlessness (a theatrocracy): "one must strike at the root of the problem, and to ensure respect for the Fathers-of-the-nation, the laws, the king, the magistrates, all the delegates, one must reestablish on the most solid ground paternal and marital authority, in such a way that it be the supreme authority in the family."[24] For Rétif, the establishment of an effective justice system depended therefore on the resurrection of a genuine domestic tribunal, with the father as supreme judge.

In this regard, Rétif belongs to a remarkably large and diverse group of eighteenth-century thinkers who wished for the rebirth of truly patriarchal domestic tribunals. They found models for this dream in a variety of places. For some, domestic tribunals entail a revival of the ancient practice among French kings of rendering justice personally and directly in the presence of their "family": the assembled French nation.[25] Many others depict them instead as emblematic of a tribal past, before sovereign families merged into complex societies with professional judges and rulers. Maréchal thus inverts Lacretelle's narrative when he asks: "Instead of creating permanent magistrates or leaders, who, at the beginning, were only meant to resolve quarrels amicably and without delay, why not restrict ourselves to a domestic jurisdiction?"[26] Indeed, while supporters of this primeval model of justice nearly always describe it as "natural," they do not view it, as Lacretelle does (and as we may be tempted to), through the lens of natural right theory, that is, as a state of nature, whose universal, inalienable, but ultimately incomplete rights needed to be supplemented through a social contract. Their portrayal of domestic tribunals more closely resembles the myth of the golden age brilliantly studied by Dan Edelstein, notably in the lack of rulers (other than fathers), political or legal institutions, and written constitutions or laws. None are in fact needed (no more than a social contract) as everyone follows instead natural laws, defined not as individual rights, like liberty, but as moral precepts—mores—born of an instinctual sense of virtue and equity.[27] Lastly, a third group looked to antiquity. Mézard praises the Spartans for resolving all disputes through the arbitration of wise, elderly patriarchs (at least sixty years of age) rather than through fixed laws and professional judges.[28] Even more common are calls for the resurrection of the domestic tribunals of ancient Rome, especially in the wake of Montesquieu's *L'Esprit des lois*—if not the first text to study and applaud these tribunals, then certainly the most influential. Few texts sum up as perfectly the advantages that eighteenth-century thinkers, regardless of their preferred model, see in domestic tribunals. While Montesquieu concedes that the power wielded by Roman men over their wives and children was secretive, arbitrary (not bound by laws), and unlimited (extending even to capital punishment), he presents these traits as the source of the tribunals' effectiveness as a punitive *and* preventive measure.[29] Indeed, these ostensibly negative features gave domestic tribunals their unique qualities: privacy and rapidity, obviously, but also certainty (due to the patriarch's incontestable legitimacy) and morality (insofar as the patriarch targets vices as well as crimes and bases his judgment on ethical principles rather than fixed laws).

Rétif draws from all three models in his earnest and detailed proposal in *L'Andrographe* to build a new legal system around the figure of the father.[30] He recommends that, as in Rome, patriarchs be given complete power over their wives and children, including the right to punish them in the privacy of their own homes, without any obligation to notify a judge or even follow the laws. Rétif adds some original safeguards to the Roman model, however: the punishments cannot lastingly injure the wife's health or reputation, and, as in the primeval model, a sadistic father or husband can be denounced before wise elders (the same committee of elders, in fact, tasked with commissioning satirical plays to reform sinners).[31] If found guilty, a cruel father stands to lose his status as patriarch, with his family simply attributed to another man between forty-nine and sixty-five years of age.[32] Composed of villagers aged seventy years or older, the committees of elders function therefore as supervisors over paternal authority. Rétif repeatedly stresses, however, that they do not reinstate as a result an official legal system more powerful than paternal justice, because the elders also behave like fathers: "the Committees will be the natural judges of all citizens; they will resolve their affairs like genuine Fathers."[33] In fact, as Rétif himself notes, with nearly all quarrels resolved by patriarchs and only a small percentage requiring the intervention of elders equally lacking in legal training, the reforms in *L'Andrographe* mark the end of professional magistrates and their replacement by more moral, legitimate judges.[34]

It may be tempting to construe the dream of grounding justice in the figure of the father as an expression of support for absolutist monarchy. And indeed, the political model for this dream, with its celebration of the halcyon days when French kings, notably the revered Saint Louis, dispensed a paternal justice under an oak tree, clearly sets up an analogy between the omnipotence of a father-judge and that of an absolute monarch. That some of the period's most illustrious anti-absolutist thinkers, such as Mercier and Maréchal, also embraced domestic tribunals, however, should make us wary of positing a straightforwardly symbiotic relationship between paternal and royal authority. In fact, from a purely concrete, rather than figurative, perspective, one could argue that creating as many tribunals as there were households decentralized justice and set up spaces of power outside of the direct purview of the legal system and thus beyond the king's reach. Likewise, a historical perspective challenges the standard analogy between the absolute power of a father and that of a king, since according to Montesquieu, it was the institution of a monarchy in formerly republican Rome that brought an end to the practice of domestic tribunals. Such political ambiguity—neither clearly for nor clearly against absolutism—suggests that domestic tribunals appealed to eighteenth-century thinkers for another reason. Indeed, there is no explicitly political context when Grimm invokes an agrarian domestic tribunal to respond to *La Lettre à d'Alembert*. While he rejects Rousseau's plea that the theater be forbidden in large, civilized cities such as Geneva, he approves of such a measure in bucolic Swiss counties, where "the first magistrate is an old man of good sense, who cultivates his field like the others, who renders justice according to right reason, on a rock placed under an oak tree."[35] Though he judges under an oak tree, this magistrate is no king, but rather a wise elder reminiscent of the father figures that partisans of domestic justice often entrust with resolving interfamilial disputes. This rural justice, based on trust and proximity, rather than laws or representation, would vanish, according to Grimm, were theater allowed in the Swiss countryside.

This fear of the theater, and of its impact on a simpler, natural form of justice, illuminates the eighteenth century's strange attraction to domestic tribunals. In the figure of a benevolent patriarch resolving disputes among his relatives, eighteenth-century writers found a primeval, nontheatrical mode of justice, predating the institution of permanent tribunals, fixed forms, and professional magistrates. At a time when many liberal reformers, like Brissot, dreamed of overtly dramatic trials before mass audiences, the popularity of such small, private tribunals is telling. Domestic tribunals, like *lettres de cachet*, belong to an alternative conception of justice, one that solves many of the problems, including those studied in the two previous chapters, raised by the theatricality of liberal justice. In particular, the embrace of domestic tribunals hints at a general discomfort with three of the most essential principles of liberal justice: trials should be public; legal codes complete, precise, and binding; and judges restricted to a temporary, elected power, making them more accountable to the people. Indeed, in what follows, we will see that many in the eighteenth century, not only reactionaries but liberals as well, grew so concerned about the perils of theatricality that they came to defend, against all our expectations of the period, the virtues of secrecy, arbitrariness, and authoritarianism in the exercise of justice.

In Defense of Secrecy

Mercier wrote nearly all of his most successful plays in a period of five years, including *Jenneval* (1769), *Le Déserteur* (1770), *L'Indigent* (1772), *Le Juge* (1774), and *La Brouette du vinaigrier* (1774). These plays have much in common, as their plots center on families torn apart by legal conflicts (petty theft, desertion, inheritance, land appropriation, and marriage contracts) pitting, more often than not, father figures against their children. Maza cites two, *L'Indigent* and *Le Juge*, as textbook examples of a particular sentimental narrative hugely popular in eighteenth-century fiction and drama. In this narrative, wealthy noblemen, invariably selfish, duplicitous, and arrogant, use their influence and fortune to enlist corrupt judges in their attempts to swindle and exploit the hardworking and innocent poor. According to Maza, lawyers increasingly employed this narrative when composing their briefs for actual trials and in so doing contributed to the dissemination of the notion that the justice system of the ancien régime was a despotic instrument used by a depraved ruling class to avert the rise of a more egalitarian society.[36] Maza presents Mercier as an especially fervent believer in this narrative, and it is easy to see why. In his *Tableau de Paris*, Mercier states that when a destitute man climbs on the scaffold, one should always look upon him as a victim, not as a criminal, since his crimes pale in comparison to the inequities that the legal system supports and that compelled him to break the law in the first place.[37] This belief that the justice system of the ancien régime, through its secrecy and complexity, favors the ruling class, explains why Mercier advocates in *Du Théâtre* the creation of a denunciatory theater, exemplifying a new kind of justice, one that dares to expose publicly the crimes of the powerful and try them on the spot, with the jeers of the assembled people delivering an instant punishment. One would therefore expect Mercier's plays to follow such a model, by depicting a clear-cut conflict between perfectly wicked and virtuous characters, building toward a final, trial-like scene in which the wealthy villains' wrongdoings are made visible to all and swiftly followed by a suitable punishment.

Yet time and time again, Mercier confounds the expectations, not only of modern scholars but also of critics from his time. In a review of *Le Juge*, La Harpe regrets that the play, in which a count sues a farmer to take possession of his land based on an ancient land register, strays from the standard sentimental narrative. To La Harpe's dismay, the count is an honest man and not, as he ought to be, "a cruel man, the object of the spectators' aversion."[38] In fact, when one looks at Mercier's plays more closely, it becomes evident that he frequently and quite explicitly portrays the villains as virtuous men who have been temporarily corrupted by wealth and power. Even the exceptionally depraved de Lys in *L'Indigent* is described as "not evil" by Rémi, the play's wise elder, as early as the beginning of the third act.[39] La Harpe is equally dissatisfied with the farmer in *Le Juge*, noting that he is not your typical "judicial martyr," since the trial will ensure that he either recovers his house or wins many times its value in compensation, making it difficult for the spectators to feel pity for him. Another critic, writing in the *Journal encyclopédique*, expresses the same disappointment when he wishes that the play had been titled *Le Seigneur du village* and had focused on the inhumane treatment of a peasant by a feudal lord, rather than on the judge.[40] What both reviewers fail to realize, however, is that these deviations from the standard sentimental plot are entirely deliberate. In his preface to the play, Mercier gives a brief description of what *Le Juge* would have looked like, had he employed a sentimental frame: "one could have used the greatest weapons, achieved an emotional impact, created a spectacular performance, shown an innocent in chains about to fall under the sword of the Law, saved from his ordeal by a judge's resolve."[41] He explains that he opted instead for a conflict in which all parties possess admirable traits, as well as a legitimate claim to the disputed land, so as to examine an honest judge as he struggles with a difficult case. That Mercier explicitly refuses to stage a legal battle between an evil feudal lord and a virtuous commoner, even while recognizing the grandeur and pathos of such a narrative, reveals a surprising unease with the frequent representation of justice as a site of class conflict.

Indeed, it is telling that out of all the characters Mercier created, the one who most openly embraces this vision of justice is the villain in *Jenneval*,

Rosalie. In several lengthy speeches, she accuses the legal system of the ancien régime of protecting the rich and powerful before concluding that, were she to face Jenneval's wealthy uncle in court, "I will be sacrificed, as the weak and innocent always are."[42] Mercier thus places the standard sentimental narrative about justice in the mouth of a ruthless, immoral woman, who uses it to encourage Jenneval to bypass the legal system altogether and murder his uncle. In fact, such a narrative breeds distrust of the judicial apparatus not only among the weak but also among the powerful. In *Le Juge*, the count reacts to the loss of his trial by berating the judge, whom he accuses of having based his verdict on his compassion for the poor and hatred for the rich, rather than on the law. He asserts that eighteenth-century judges have internalized the sentimental narrative peddled by legal reformers so completely that wealthy participants in a trial are invariably found guilty.[43] Because they see justice in terms of class conflict, both Rosalie and the count develop an unwarranted sense of victimhood, which prompts them to forsake legal recourse in favor of violent measures. They come to see their adversaries as foes in a larger, Manichean war that justifies severing even the closest family ties, as the count sets out to throw his own son (the judge) and grandchildren out on the street, while Jenneval nearly succumbs to Rosalie's pleas that he murder the closest thing he has to a father. Mercier's plays thus highlight the dangers of applying a sentimental narrative to justice: by dividing the world into pure good and evil, it makes mediation (legal or otherwise) impossible, leaving violence as the sole course of action.

This does not mean, of course, that Mercier rejects all the beliefs central to that narrative, notably that money corrupts, that the system in place favors the rich, and that the simple, honest joys of the poor are preferable to the artificial pleasures of the wealthy. There is no denying that his heroes are usually poor and his villains affluent—although, as we have seen, not intrinsically "evil," but rather corrupted by wealth and power into committing evil acts. What Mercier's plays reveal, rather, is his discomfort with the practice of casting conflicts in sentimental, black-and-white terms and then publicizing them broadly, as the authors of trial briefs were doing at the time, to great commercial success. As Maza has noted, these writers used the sentimental narrative not only to pique interest in their cases but also to justify far-reaching appeals for legal reforms. They argued that only accusatorial proceedings, in which the two parties engage in a public, agonistic debate, would offer the transparency necessary to protect the people from the covert influence of the wealthy. They saw publicity as an undisputable good (thus justifying the publication of trial briefs formerly written only for magistrates), a safeguard against miscarriages of justice that had the added benefit of dissuading the wealthy from engaging in criminal acts by threatening them with public humiliation. In *Du Théâtre*, Mercier appears to share this faith in publicity; yet in his plays, the most admirable characters, including court officials like the magistrate in *Le Juge* and the notary public in *L'Indigent*, all advise, repeatedly and explicitly, against the public airing of disputes, particularly through legal proceedings. Tellingly, in fact, there are almost no depictions of trials in Mercier's plays, despite the popularity of such scenes in the period.[44] Instead of making legal proceedings public via the theater, Mercier shows through his characters that publicity only breeds further conflict and division. To turn every dispute into a public spectacle presenting a clear-cut opposition between moral absolutes leads to the fixation on social divisions, distrust of the judicial apparatus, and willingness to resort to violence exhibited by Rosalie and the count. Ironically, Mercier thus uses the theater to challenge the notion that justice ought to take the form of a public, agonistic trial—that it ought to resemble, in other words, a theatrical performance. This rejection of theatrical justice inspires Mercier and his characters to embrace an alternative form of conflict resolution. Most of his plays, including *Le Juge*, *L'Indigent*, and *Jenneval*, end not with a public trial but with a private reconciliation, brought about by a wise, benevolent figure invariably described by the characters as their "father."

The fear that public trials jeopardized social harmony, not only between the wealthy and the poor but between all members of society, was far more prevalent in Mercier's time than has previously been noted. Opponents of publicity have been given short shrift in historical accounts of the French justice system, perhaps because they have been seen as reactionaries fighting a losing battle against the forces of progress. Yet many liberal thinkers also expressed concern at the transformation of legal proceedings into spectacles for public consumption, a process already under way, as shown by the vast audiences at certain civil cases and the astonishing popularity of trial briefs, but which would reach new heights if spectators were allowed to attend criminal proceedings. To study the social impact of the growing obsession with judicial conflicts, opponents of public trials often turned to the remote hamlets of the French countryside, until recently untainted by direct knowledge of the legal system. For instance, Germain Rubigni paints an idyllic portrait of agrarian justice, complete with the standard depiction of a wise elder in the role of father-judge, before lamenting that it is rapidly losing ground to institutional justice: "the proliferation of tribunals in rural villages has introduced the disastrous practice of resorting to them without real or apparent motives."[45] Fascinatingly, Rubigni contends that it is not because of a surge in disputes that tribunals are built, but rather that it is because tribunals are built that there is a surge in disputes, often without motives. Tribunals, Rétif explains in a similar passage, breed a lawsuit culture: "Having a justice system means assured ruin for a village, because it teaches the peasants to plead."[46] The candid peasants discover the art of pleading, an exercise whose principal aim is to triumph over a rival by means of rhetorical tricks. Both Rétif and Rubigni note that peasants who become familiar with the legal system come to see justice in primarily adversarial terms. Whereas they formerly appealed to a wise elder to end a quarrel, they now turn to the tribunals as a means of perpetuating it, in the knowledge that a trial, lasting for months if not years, will offer them the opportunity to exact vengeance on their enemy over a prolonged period of time. As a result, judicial conflicts, particularly public ones, only entrench divisions deeper, leading to more quarrels and, in a never-ending loop, further trials.[47]

This vicious cycle is often highlighted by opponents of public trials. Whereas partisans of publicity argue that the more familiar the people become with the justice system, the fewer trials there will be, their rivals counter with the observation that the increased publicity of trials in the eighteenth century has only augmented their frequency. Rubigni portrays legal action as a veritable addiction, noting that once someone has become involved in a trial, quitting becomes impossible. This addiction even has physical symptoms: litigants are seized with "a kind of vertigo" and "their fibers experience violent tremors and shrivel, so great is the influence of the moral over the physical."[48] Their very nature is permanently transformed, losing, "like an alloy . . . its original, pure, honest constitution."[49] This loss of a primitive, unadulterated state echoes that of the peasants, whose natural, domestic justice is supplanted by the introduction of tribunals and a lawsuit culture. In a clever reversal of contractual theory, Rubigni maintains that it was not the discord of the primitive state that led to the institution of a legal system, but that it was the institution of a legal system that threw the primitive state into discord.

Many feared, in fact, that turning criminal proceedings into a public spectacle would not only engender further trials but also lead to an increase in crime. Such a notion is surprising, since the eighteenth century is usually portrayed as a period of near universal faith in the ability of exemplary justice to act as a deterrent. And indeed, many of those who opposed torture as it was practiced under the ancien régime still believed that a public trial and punishment could help prevent crime, if staged in the form of a moral spectacle seeking less to terrorize the beholders than to inspire them to identify with the criminal and apply to their own lives the lessons contained in his present misfortune.[50] In *Du Théâtre*, Mercier appears to share this belief in the preventive value of making crimes known, notably when he argues that a denunciatory theater, by revealing the sins of actual public figures, would deter other members of the ruling class from committing similar offenses by warning them that they too would one day have to endure the boos and taunts of the assembled people. Yet these are unique cases, crimes by public figures that affect everyone and need to be publicized lest they continue unimpeded. In his *Tableau de Paris*, Mercier repeatedly voices his concern at the idea of making the offenses of private citizens known to the masses. He praises *lettres de cachet* and more generally the secrecy of ancien régime justice for covering up the vast majority of murders, suicides, and injuries caused by speeding carriages and falling tiles. Were they all revealed, he argues, the public would lose faith in the policing of their city, leading some to anger and terror and others to a sense of impunity—both responses likely to inspire further criminal deeds.[51]

Mercier also fears that publicizing illicit acts would encourage some of the spectators to imitate behaviors that they would hear about regularly and come to regard as normal. Secrecy is particularly important in response to "unnatural" crimes, such as grave robbing, pederasty, and sodomy, which should never be tried and punished publicly, for fear that members of the audience will discover their existence: "there are vices about which censors must remain silent, because they might otherwise disclose them without correcting them."[52] However naïve such a belief may seem to us today, it was widely held in the eighteenth century and inspired judicial authorities to investigate and punish certain crimes—the ones supposedly unknown to the majority of people—with the utmost secrecy (*lettres de cachet* were especially useful in that regard).[53] It also explains why Mercier, the period's leading opponent of dramatic *bienséance* and notably of the convention forbidding violent acts from being performed on stage, wrote such a tame ending to his *Jenneval*. In *The London Merchant*, the play on which *Jenneval* is modeled, the protagonist murders his uncle before receiving a suitably moral punishment—execution. The *Journal encyclopédique* ventured an explanation for Mercier's alternate ending, in which Jenneval never kills his uncle: "Mercier studied the character of his spectators; he could not imagine a parricide among them. He saw the French as the first Athenian legislators saw the Greeks: they did not create any laws against children murdering their parents, because they did not presume man capable of such atrocity."[54] Such a comparison is fascinating not only for the equivalency it sets up between theater and justice—both of which must avoid publicizing certain crimes—but also because it extends the call for secrecy beyond trials and executions to the legal code itself. To make a law against killing one's father is to recognize the potentiality of such an act and thus, paradoxically, to give it legitimacy. This anecdote about Athenians and parricide appears frequently in eighteenth-century texts, usually in a positive light. For instance, Séguier defends the Athenians' practice on the basis that "certain crimes are so atrocious that it would be beyond imprudent to anticipate them; the law that would order their punishment would, in a way, realize them."[55] Séguier thus arrives at the intriguing conclusion that it is the law that creates crime, and not the other way around. At every stage of the judicial process—the writing of laws, the investigation of a crime,[56] the staging of its trial and of its punishment—publicity threatens to produce an increase in criminality. In response, Mercier affirms that it is vital "we remove from evil that which makes it most dangerous: its publicity."[57] Hence, the man described by Habermas as one of the most aggressive partisans of public opinion in the eighteenth century surprisingly comes out, in judicial matters at least, in favor of a near-total secrecy.

In Defense of Arbitrariness

The anecdote celebrating the Athenians' decision not to enact a law against parricide owed much of its popularity in the eighteenth century to the fact that it could be used to criticize the liberal reformers' campaign for the creation of a more complete and precise legal code. For instance, Séguier invokes the anecdote to refute Charles Dupaty's assertion (quoted in Séguier's pamphlet) that a good code of laws defines explicitly and systematically what is and is not a crime, in contrast with the legal code of the ancien régime, which lacks clarity and consistency because its laws were added gradually and haphazardly to fit whatever crime had just been committed. With the support of the Athenians' example, Séguier warns that a legal code that catalogs potential transgressions too precisely and thoroughly risks alerting the people to their existence, inspiring their imitation and, in some cases, even creating new crimes altogether.[58] This warning is in turn ridiculed by Julien Dentand in a pamphlet written explicitly as a response to Séguier's response to Dupaty's response to the famous trial of the Trois Roués. Coming to the defense of the liberal reformer Dupaty, Dentand mocks the notion that knowledge of the law will produce an increase in crime.[59] On the contrary, he argues that the legal code should be rewritten to ensure its intelligibility to all citizens—an ambition that leads him to champion the use of plain language, simple, invariable laws with few exceptions, and clearly stated punishments.[60] He, like many others, even demands that the Crown publish the resulting code of laws and supply each household with a free copy.[61] Likewise, he proposes that all legal proceedings be stripped of confusing rituals and displayed to the public, not only as a protection for the accused, but also for the benefit of the spectators, since there is no better way to commit the nation's laws to memory than to see them in action.[62] The conviction among many liberal reformers that it was of the utmost importance that the laws be known (or at least knowable) by every citizen derives from a deeper, fundamental opposition to arbitrariness. In a contractual model of justice, the laws must identify clearly and exhaustively every possible infraction, because a citizen cannot be punished for an action, however destructive, that the legal code—the "contract" one agrees to follow in exchange for social belonging and protection—has not defined as a crime.[63] Laws unknown to the public, or too vague, incomplete, or inconsistent, force—or at least encourage—a judge to act arbitrarily, by substituting his own will for the letter of the law.[64] To avoid this situation, the authors of the article "arbitraire" in the *Dictionnaire de jurisprudence* demand that "the laws decide clearly in all cases, and that there only remain for the judge to ensure they are executed."[65] A perfect code of laws, citing every conceivable crime and its punishment in clear, precise terms intelligible to all, would provide the most effective protection against arbitrariness.

Many of Mercier's plays, however, call into question the notion that the best form of justice is one that is based on—and constrained by—a written code of laws. In *Le Juge*, the count explains to the farmer that the land register he has in his possession guarantees his victory in court: "The law decides, written law, do you understand?"[66] Yet the count is here being deceitful, the judge having already informed him that he feels no such bondage to the written word and intends to side with the farmer. Indeed, the judge has been persuaded by the farmer's tearful arguments in an earlier scene that grounding justice in written laws and texts is unfair to the uneducated masses, who cannot read and have limited understanding of ownership titles, receipts, and other legal documents. For the same reason, the farmer laments the involvement of lawyers, whose endless briefs filled with legalese and trivial debates about obscure laws and precedents have transformed the case into a textual conflict he cannot participate in, let alone comprehend.[67] Few liberal reformers would have disputed this negative portrayal of ancien régime justice, which they would have seen as an illustration of the need for a more precise and coherent legal code, easier to understand for uneducated citizens like the farmer—a solution that Mercier himself endorses in some of his writings.[68] Yet another passage in *Le Juge* reveals a much deeper unease with the very existence of a legal code, however simplified and intelligible it may be. According to the judge, if the farmer and his forefathers never requested a record of ownership for their plot of land, it was less out of ignorance of written laws and contracts than out of a simple faith in the promise of the count's ancestors. The farmers belong to an ancient, agrarian culture in which social interactions are based on trust, not paper, because they are governed by a shared moral code rather than by laws.[69] As a result, the judge perceives his judgment as a broader philosophical choice between two legal cultures. To side with the count would be to assert the primacy of written laws and institutional justice, while ruling in the farmer's favor would mean upholding unwritten mores and patriarchal authority (the farmer repeatedly describes the land as his patrimony and reveals that his dying father made him promise never to part with it). In his review, La Harpe ridicules the idea of centering a play on so trivial a matter as the loss of a small plot of land, but such a literal reading misses the deeper cultural significance of the judge's decision. His verdict ultimately converts the count to the farmer's worldview, inspiring him to put an end to his textually justified, but morally unjustifiable, pursuit of the land (by not appealing) and to embrace instead the simple pleasures of paternity (by revealing that he is the judge's father).

Le Juge thus dramatizes the idea that a written code of laws is not only inferior to, but also incompatible with, good mores. In fact, Mercier frequently contrasts laws and mores in his nonliterary texts[70] in a way that reveals the marked influence of Montesquieu on his legal views.[71] This should come as little surprise: Montesquieu was, for nearly every eighteenth-century thinker, the go-to reference on the relationship between legal and moral codes. Among the many passages on the question in Montesquieu's oeuvre, the following one stands out, for reasons that will become clear later: "All that concerns mores . . . can hardly be comprised under a code of laws. It is easy to regulate through laws what we owe others, but it is difficult to include everything that we owe ourselves."[72] Montesquieu here identifies the principal shortcoming of legal codes: while they are able to limit the range of actions that one can take in relation to others, they are far less effective in regulating personal values and behaviors. In other words, laws are primarily negative (stating what one is not allowed to do—such as stealing money from the poor), unlike moral codes, which are also positive (stating what one should do—such as giving money to the poor). While laws can punish the criminal manifestations of certain vices, they cannot order virtue. Mercier makes a similar point in his *Tableau de Paris* when he argues that the French capital needs Roman-style "censors" because the laws are powerless to correct personal defects, such as vanity and debauchery, leading to behaviors that, while not illegal, are harmful to society, as for instance when the head of a household squanders his fortune on titles and courtesans.[73]

In fact, not only are written laws ineffectual against private sins, they often strengthen them. Many eighteenth-century thinkers, including liberal ones, note the counterintuitive fact that the more laws are enacted, the faster vice seems to multiply.[74] This is not simply because, as Séguier contends, knowledge of the laws often leads to the discovery and imitation of the crimes they forbid. Nor is it only because too great a familiarity with the law produces a lawsuit culture, in which justice becomes synonymous with vengeance. Mercier undoubtedly agrees with these critiques of written laws. In a humorous passage in *L'An 2440*, the citizens of his utopia explain that when besieged, they catapult volumes of jurisprudence into the camp of their enemies, who upon reading them soon proceed to destroy themselves.[75] Yet his anxiety about legal codes runs deeper: he fears that in addition to producing crimes, they gradually take the place of a people's mores, rendering them ineffective. The magistrate in *Le Juge* understands this. He senses that to rule against the farmer would destroy more than just a family; it would abolish an ancient culture and with it, its code of ethics, by teaching every peasant in the region to distrust the spoken word of others and value only written contracts.

Montesquieu's influence is here at its most evident. The judge's anxiety that written laws will supplant longstanding mores echoes the warnings of the wise elder in one of the most renowned passages in Montesquieu's oeuvre:

the story of the Troglodytes in *Les Lettres persanes*. In this parable, the Troglodytes, despite living happily in small, autonomous families, decide to ask the wisest, oldest man among them to become their king and devise the laws they will henceforth follow. As we saw earlier, a similar story frequently appears in the writings of liberal reformers (notably Lacretelle and Bernardi) who praise the enactment of fixed laws by wise elders as the event that marked the end of the arbitrary, paternal justice of primitive cultures and gave birth to the institutional legal system of modern societies. Montesquieu's version is different, however, in that the wise elder, much like the judge in Mercier's play, refuses to introduce written laws to a culture unacquainted with them. He accuses the Troglodytes of only wanting laws because they have grown weary of the sacrifices required by virtue. As the wise elder explains, enacting a legal code would do more than simply determine what is illegal; it would also, by extension, designate all other behavior as acceptable. Laws would become the standard by which the Troglodytes' conduct is evaluated—a much lower standard than their ancestors' mores, insofar as virtue requires action, whereas legality demands little more than inaction. This, according to the wise elder, is precisely what attracts the Troglodytes to the law. Wishing to feel virtuous, and yet unwilling to suffer the costs associated with virtue, they seek in the laws the assurance that goodness calls for no greater sacrifice than abstaining from illegal actions. The existence of a legal code would allow them to ask, when contemplating an action, "is it legal?" rather than the much more challenging and constraining question, "is it moral?" In fact, the plot in *Le Juge* revolves around the distinction between these two questions. Mercier explains in his preface that he purposefully invented a complicated lawsuit in which the judge has a personal interest in siding with the count, who has threatened to dismiss and evict him, and could easily justify such a verdict, both to his own conscience and to the community, by arguing it follows the letter of the law.[76] Yet all of the arguments pushing the judge toward the side of the count ultimately prove powerless against "that exclusive sentiment we call equity."[77] The judge constitutes therefore the very antithesis of the Troglodytes (the wise elder excepted). He bases his decision on moral principles, in full knowledge that this embrace of virtue will require great sacrifices and that the laws offer him a socially acceptable way out of his predicament. Heroically, he nevertheless refuses to adopt the law as his standard of judgment, as to do so would undermine not only the peasants' mores but his own as well.

In his writings, Montesquieu returns constantly to the threat posed by legalism to a people's mores. I selected the brief passage above, not only because it is representative of Montesquieu's thought, but also because it appears in a section of *L'Esprit des lois* devoted to the domestic tribunals of ancient Rome. In this section, Montesquieu presents domestic tribunals as superior to institutional justice, because a father bases his verdicts on purely moral considerations, rather than on fixed laws. Indeed, domestic tribunals were often celebrated in the eighteenth century as both symbols and safeguards of virtue. According to Montesquieu, sound mores could never have subsisted without domestic tribunals, just as domestic tribunals could not have survived without sound mores.[78] Paternal justice and good mores thus intertwined in a virtuous cycle, which should never have stopped spinning and yet came to a halt when, in a telling parallel with the Troglodytes' downfall, the Roman Republic and its powerful families were replaced by a monarchy and an ever-expanding code of laws.[79] The eighteenth century's fascination with domestic tribunals is therefore symptomatic of the same underlying anxiety about written laws and public, institutional justice that inspired Mercier to write *Le Juge* and to defend *lettres de cachet*. Together, they bring to light the surprisingly widespread desire, in a period usually known for its faith in the codification and standardization of the legal system, for a return to the simple, discretionary justice that existed before the enactment of a fixed code of laws. Behind this desire lies the dream of living in a culture like that of ancient Rome or the Troglodytes (both pre-monarchy), whose people were not guided by a fear of laws or rulers but by their love of virtue and their reverence for family. Hence, at a time when many liberals were campaigning for a more complete, precise, and public code of laws, others responded by extolling in their writings an alternative conception of justice, devoid of laws and freer as a result to target all forms of infraction, moral as well as criminal, and to steer the parties to better mores, instead of merely punishing them for crimes already committed.

Of course, the dream of a justice system operating via an unwritten moral code struck many as dangerously arbitrary. As we saw earlier, many liberal reformers opposed familial justice—whether in its primeval form (domestic tribunals) or in its final vestiges (*lettres de cachet*)—precisely because, in the absence of public trials and uniform laws, it could too easily become an instrument of patriarchal tyranny.[80] A spiteful father could, after all, declare just about any action a crime and punish it disproportionately. In fact, it is telling that the two attributes most attractive to supporters of domestic tribunals—their secrecy and their lack of a clear, fixed legal code—were the very features of ancien régime criminal justice that liberal reformers held most responsible for its arbitrariness. In their eyes, the history of legal proceedings tended away from the secret, arbitrary judgments characteristic of familial justice and toward the greater transparency and uniformity of institutional justice. Even Montesquieu, whose portrayal of domestic tribunals influenced generations of thinkers, conceded their arbitrariness.[81] Yet he appeared untroubled by this fact, which he argued was not only inevitable, since mores cannot be written into law, but also desirable, insofar as some freedom from the law was essential to a father's ability to prevent potential crimes, not just punish real ones. The accusation of arbitrariness leveled against familial justice put Mercier in a difficult position, however. How could a writer famous for his hostility to the arbitrariness of absolutism defend such arbitrary practices as *lettres de cachet* and a lawless justice system? More than a simple case of hypocrisy, this apparent inconsistency reveals that Mercier and other liberal thinkers relied on a different definition of arbitrariness when they promoted a justice system free from the tyranny of laws.

Indeed, arbitrariness strikes me as a deceptively ambiguous term, which was seldom defined because eighteenth-century writers believed they knew exactly what it meant, even as each one used it slightly differently. Consulting the *Encyclopédie* in search of a clear definition only leads to further surprises and ambiguities: "ARBITRARY, adj. broadly understood, that which is not defined or limited by any laws or formal constitutions, but which is left solely to the judgment and discretion of an individual. The punishment of a given crime is *arbitrary*. This word comes from the Latin *arbitrium*, or 'will.' The laws or measures through which the Creator acts are *arbitrary*—at least, all physical laws are."[82] François-Vincent Toussaint, the article's author, deems arbitrary any action that results from an individual exercising his or her will without observing collective laws or formal constitutions. As suggested by the first example of arbitrariness (an unfair punishment for a crime), this definition lent itself particularly well to the arguments of liberal reformers. Indeed, they used it to condemn the notion that judges, as embodiments of the king, possessed the right to determine unilaterally what constituted a crime and how to punish it. They argued that the exact nature of a crime, as well as its proper punishment, should not be left to the whims of individual judges but should instead be recorded in a written code of laws, serving to "define and limit" the wills of every citizen, even the king's. Modern readers might find the next example rather more puzzling, however. We do not tend to think of physical laws as arbitrary, or of their Creator (assuming, as Toussaint does, that such a deity exists) as the quintessential example of an arbitrary ruler.

Such an unexpected claim makes it abundantly clear that in Toussaint's definition the legitimacy of an action resides entirely in its accordance with man's laws, that is, with the collective will of the people. However immutable, systematic, and natural the laws of physics may be, they remain the expression of a singular will, unhindered by any communal, human laws, thereby making them arbitrary.[83]

If God himself is arbitrary, solely because his acts of creation are not defined by the laws of his creatures (and how could they be?), the same must hold true for paternal power, which places the will of the individual (the father) above that of the collective (the family). Yet as we saw earlier, many in the eighteenth century regarded fathers as the sole possessors of a truly legitimate, nonarbitrary authority. This reveals the existence of an alternative understanding of arbitrariness underlying the claims of defenders of paternal authority and of writers unwilling to consider the possibility that God's will could be arbitrary.[84] This understanding—in my opinion, the dominant one today—appears to have grown in popularity during the eighteenth century, becoming sufficiently established by 1835 to be added to the top of the list of definitions under the entry "arbitraire" in the *Dictionnaire de l'Académie française*: "That which is produced by the sole will of man, without a natural rule or foundation. *Most names given to things are purely arbitrary signs.*"[85] According to this definition, an arbitrary action is one that disregards the laws of nature. Hence, while every member of a society may agree on the name of a thing, such a name nevertheless remains arbitrary, because it derives solely from man's will and lacks therefore a natural basis. In this view, the collective rules of a people—its code of laws, tacit conventions, and language—are nearly all arbitrary. By contrast, as Montesquieu notes at the beginning of *L'Esprit des lois*, acts of divine creation, previously singled out for their arbitrariness, constitute in fact the least arbitrary of all phenomena, because they participate in a natural order composed of universal, immutable, systematic laws that are impervious to the vagaries of human volition.[86] Such a definition of arbitrariness could scarcely be more distant from the one employed by liberal reformers. In the latter, arbitrariness refers primarily to an action in violation of human laws, whereas in the former, it refers to an action taken solely in accordance with human laws, without any concern for those of nature.

The existence of conflicting definitions of arbitrariness offers a revealing analogy with—and perhaps an explanation for—the ambiguity in the eighteenth century surrounding the concept of arbitration (which has the same etymological root as arbitrary).[87] Then as now, the term "arbitration" referred to the decision by disputing parties to resolve their conflict without a trial, by presenting their claims before a mutually agreed-upon individual or group and promising to abide by the verdict. Many eighteenth-century legal thinkers—liberals as well as reactionaries—displayed a deep fascination with arbitration, especially in response to family quarrels, owing to its ability to prevent trivial disputes from metastasizing into costly, protracted trials.[88] As the *Encyclopédie* makes clear, however, arbitration did not mean the same thing to everyone: "In modern societies, there are ordinarily different types of arbiters. Some are obligated to proceed in strict accordance with the rigor of the law, and others are allowed by the parties to free themselves from the law and follow natural equity."[89] These two conceptions of arbitration mirror the two definitions of arbitrariness. One would therefore expect liberal reformers to have embraced the first, in which the arbiter's judgment is defined and limited by the nation's code of laws. While some did (Bernardi and Lacretelle, for instance), others were surprisingly drawn to the second definition, to the extent of praising explicitly the freedom it gave arbiters to disregard human laws and base their judgments instead on an older, more natural law: their instinctual sense of equity.[90] In fact, as Véronique Demars-Sion has shown, the distinction between the two conceptions of arbitration, dating back to the thirteenth century, was largely academic by the end of the early modern period, with the term "arbitration" primarily used to refer to a judgment based on mores and equity, rather than laws.[91] Hence, not only did "arbitrary" and "arbitration" both have two conflicting definitions, they also underwent a similar evolution, which saw the relationship to natural rather than human laws become increasingly central to their meaning.

The second conception of arbitration was attractive to many liberal reformers for the same reason as domestic tribunals, because of its proximity to nature. Hence, the authors of the *Dictionnaire de jurisprudence* describe arbitration as a primeval mode of justice, first practiced by father-kings within their tribes. As societies grew, it became necessary to create laws and tribunals, yet arbitration survived, "one of those primitive ideas that never vanishes," waiting for a more enlightened era to understand that "such a natural path" should always precede and seek to preclude the artificial, but sometimes necessary "legal avenues."[92] This defense of arbitration as prelegal and natural hinges upon the second definition of arbitrariness: an arbiter does not judge arbitrarily, despite his ignorance of human laws, because he consults his natural sense of equity and morality. This stands in clear opposition to one of the central tenets of the liberal vision of justice, namely that judges should adhere strictly to legal codes. Such a contradiction reveals that many liberal reformers felt a fascinating unease with their own legalistic principles, which could in certain situations force a judge to disregard his moral instinct and issue a lawful but unjust verdict.[93] Their willingness to consider a different, natural mode of justice suggests that they were not immune from the fear discussed earlier that too narrow an allegiance to written law negatively impacts society.

While it is revealing to find liberal reformers unexpectedly endorsing the second conception of arbitration, in that it speaks to the depth of the eighteenth century's attraction for a model of justice founded on natural equity rather than written law, it should be noted that many did not intend for arbitration to replace institutional justice and a precise, complete legal code, but only to supplement them in specific, limited cases (in civil disputes of minor import, where both parties voluntarily express the wish to avoid a public trial). Likewise, they refrained from pushing the second definition of arbitrariness to its logical conclusion: paternal arbitration. Lacretelle, Bernardi, and the authors of the *Dictionnaire de jurisprudence* all identify arbiters as relatives, friends, or neighbors, never exclusively as fathers. Yet if one accepts the second definition of arbitrariness, then paternal arbitration constitutes the least arbitrary form of conflict resolution, since a father's authority to judge his children derives from nature, not human laws. This explains why, against all expectations, some of the period's most liberal thinkers defended a patriarchal, lawless form of justice that seems to us the very definition of an arbitrary judgment. Mercier and the other partisans of domestic justice openly embraced one form of arbitrariness—an individual imposing his will above the nation's laws—to avoid the far greater arbitrariness of disregarding the natural order, which makes a creator the legitimate ruler over his creation. In this perspective, paternal authority legitimizes an otherwise arbitrary (since lawless) form of justice by ensuring that it conforms to the simple, natural way that trials unfolded in primitive times, before permanent tribunals, professional magistrates, and a fixed code of laws transformed them into theater.

In Defense of Authoritarianism

The idea of settling conflicts without resorting to written laws and institutional justice also derived much of its popularity from its supposed ability to guide opponents toward an amicable resolution. In the eighteenth century, conciliation was widely perceived to be the most desirable form of conflict resolution, including by liberal reformers. This is somewhat surprising, given conciliation dovetails uneasily with the legalistic principles of liberal justice. As treatises from the period make clear, a successful conciliation depends on finding a solution acceptable to both parties, even if this solution does not coincide with a strict application of the law.[94] To reach such a solution, conciliation encourages informal arguments on questions of morality and equity rather than ordered debates organized around points of jurisprudence. These ethical discussions highlight gray areas that trials avoid, notably the possibility that the parties both share some responsibility. The recognition of a certain degree of mutual guilt frees conciliators from the task of attributing right and wrong, in favor of guiding the two parties to an agreeable compromise. Tellingly, however, the very idea of partial guilt ranked high on the list of ancien régime principles loathed by liberal reformers, as evidenced by their opposition to *hors de cour* verdicts, in which magistrates neither convicted nor absolved a defendant whose guilt they suspected but could not legally establish, owing to insufficient fragments of proof. An ancien régime magistrate could thus find an accused fractionally guilty and impose a partial punishment. Liberal reformers supported instead the modern notion that a judge must choose between only two verdicts: wholly innocent or entirely guilty.[95] Anyone who had not broken an express law was utterly innocent, however immoral his or her actions. Conciliation thus entailed a departure from legalism on multiple levels; the unstructured proceedings, the attempt to find mutual guilt and, thereby, a compromise, and the extralegal nature of said compromise all clashed with a vision of justice as the systematic application of fixed rules and forms.

Why, then, did liberal reformers so eagerly embrace conciliation? They were drawn to the promise of a simpler, swifter justice, naturally, but above all, I contend, they admired the antiauthoritarianism of conciliation, seeing it as unique among methods of conflict resolution for requiring no imbalance of power (such as the one between judges and judged) and no imposition of one man's will over another (as in a disputed verdict). In their eyes, conciliation consisted of a mutual compromise, a voluntary sacrifice of pure self-interest in the name of a common good (avoiding a trial) and, as such, a perfect illustration of the social contract. Accordingly, liberal reformers constantly stress three contractual principles at the heart of their conception of conciliation. First, the parties should be allowed to select any conciliator they desire. In this view, a conciliator derives his legitimacy solely from the parties' approval (from the contract between them), not the king's divine justice or any special training. Second, the parties cannot be coerced into initiating conciliation proceedings, which, like a contract, can only be valid if both sides sign on willingly. Third, the parties must end the conciliation as they began it—voluntarily. No one should be compelled to accept a compromise, for it too, like the proceedings and the choice of conciliators, constitutes a kind of contract. Even as they praise conciliation for its antiauthoritarianism, however, many liberals show remarkably little faith in it. The *Dictionnaire de jurisprudence* lists centuries-worth of failed experiments illustrating the powerlessness of mediators to reconcile litigious parties, forcing its readers to confront the reality that conciliation proceedings nearly always prove to be little more than a brief detour on the road to a divisive and punitive verdict. What these repeated failures reveal is something that the liberals likely intuited (hence their lack of faith) but never addressed: the existence of a basic incompatibility between their own contractual ideals and the actual practice of conciliation. As we will see, notably where we might least expect it, in the works of Mercier, one of the greatest paradoxes about conciliation may be that an overtly authoritarian structure, not a contractual one, is best able to produce a successful, nonauthoritarian settlement.

Indeed, liberal treatises on conciliation show that the first contractual principle—the right of parties to select their own mediators—actually lowers the odds of a successful outcome. This is because, as eighteenth-century jurists often note, the parties are typically too divided to agree on any single mediator, leading each to choose half of a mediating body.[96] Consequently, however, the parties expect "their" mediators to protect their interests—that is, to behave like lawyers instead of neutral conciliators. The authors of the *Dictionnaire de jurisprudence* rail against this conflation of mediation and representation, on the grounds that it fosters the sophistry, delaying tactics, and avarice typical of official trials.[97] Unlike a conciliator tied to both parties by mutual respect and affection, lawyers have no personal investment in finding an amicable solution; on the contrary, their role is to pursue the best outcome for the party that chose them, in the knowledge this will also translate into a larger reward for them. Such an adversarial approach invariably leads to a stalemate and to the designation by the lawyer-mediators of a *surarbitre*, tasked with adjudicating between the two groups. The resulting proceedings thus scarcely resemble the conciliation desired by liberals, in which two parties negotiate freely and candidly before a mutually agreeable well-wisher. Rather, it calls to mind a contentious trial, complete with fixed, rehearsed narratives, trained rhetoricians, and a judge chosen by neither party yet empowered to select a victor and a loser.

The second contractual principle—that the initiation of conciliation proceedings must be entirely voluntary—can also be detrimental to an amicable resolution. The authors of the *Dictionnaire de jurisprudence* observe that people only seek outside intervention when engaged in a dispute they are unable to resolve themselves. This suggests an adversarial mindset, which makes it far more likely that the two parties will seek a judge than a mediator. In fact, in a conflictual situation of the sort, being open to a compromise is often perceived less as a sign of good faith than as evidence of a lack of confidence in one's own case.[98] As a result, in the absence of any pressure to seek conciliation, few ever will. A similar problem plagues the third contractual principle. If the parties know they can never be compelled to accept a compromise, and that they still can, if dissatisfied with the proposed settlement, demand a trial instead, they find themselves in a position of strength that diminishes their incentive to make any sacrifice. In fact, the authors of the *Dictionnaire de jurisprudence* reach the sad conclusion that parties who seek the intervention of mediators often do so not to prevent a trial but on the contrary to prolong their quarrel by adding a further trial to it, at no risk to them since they enjoy the right to appeal an unfavorable decision and can then begin making their way up the chain of official tribunals.[99]

This leaves liberal reformers in a bind. They believe that conciliation is the most ancient and natural form of justice and express outrage that trials, which they describe as a "cruel game," have become so frequent as to seem a perfectly normal and moral practice to everyone. Having accepted this narrative, however, how can they hope to renormalize the practice of conciliation in an already "degraded" culture, one that understands justice as a ruling by a public official rather than as a compromise among equals?[100] As the authors of the *Dictionnaire de jurisprudence* know from recording page after page of failed attempts, exhortations to peace seldom prove sufficient to convert a litigious man, let alone two. This knowledge leads them to consider violating their contractual ideals, notably when they champion the intervention of arbiters in all cases involving family members in the hope that such mandatory mediation will lead to a compromise. Although they acknowledge that this proposal for a compulsory domestic tribunal infringes upon individual rights, they contend that familial concord constitutes a societal good worthy of such a cost.[101] Besides, the infringement is, they argue, only temporary, since future generations, having learned within their families to seek private mediation instead of public trials, will eventually do the same *voluntarily* in all of their quarrels.[102] If sheer force of habit made trials seem "natural," why could it not have the same effect on conciliation?

It is telling, however, that liberals never explain why mandatory mediation should prove any more successful at producing an amicable resolution than the existing, voluntary options. After all, if parties who willingly entered into arbitration often failed to find a compromise, why would those forced to do so fare any better? In fact, the opposite appears to be true: requiring parties to consult mediators, instead of simply urging them to do so, lowers the prospect of a cordial settlement. This apparent paradox results in part from the first contractual principle: "since the will of the parties establishes the power of the mediators, if this will is not well stated and apparent, if it is not entirely free, it is as if null and void."[103] Because a mediator's authority derives solely from the will of the two parties, individuals who have not consented to mediation from the outset will inevitably be inclined to question the mediator's legitimacy and to oppose the concessions he advocates. Against expectations, therefore, increasing the use of mediation by making it systematic decreases the likelihood that it will yield many compromises. This is even truer when parties know that they are free to turn down all proposed settlements and that even the arbiter's subsequent ruling can be appealed in an official tribunal. Despite this, no eighteenth-century liberal reformer ever advocates a system imposing compromise as the sole possible outcome, even though it would have come closest to primeval, natural justice, before the "degradation" brought on by trials.[104] Such a system would have been far more effective in renormalizing conciliation, but it meant penalizing the truly innocent (who would be forced to abandon some of their rightful claims, as well as the public vindication of a not guilty verdict) and reintroducing the very authoritarianism (the imbalance between an all-powerful judge and two powerless parties) that conciliation was meant to avert.

In sum, liberal reformers reach an impasse, resulting from their perception of mediation in contractual terms, that is, as an exchange in which authority is never anchored in any one individual. As we have seen, when the power lies primarily with the parties, they have little incentive to consent to sacrifices demanded by a mediator whose authority they see as little more than a temporary, contingent extension of their own. Yet when the power lies primarily with the mediator, the parties are no likelier to agree to sacrifices they now regard as infringements on their rights. This impasse leaves liberal reformers at a loss to imagine how a successful conciliation might ever transpire. In their many volumes, there is indeed a remarkable lack of information on the steps that a mediator should take to produce an amicable resolution. In fairness to them, they are grappling with one of the most consequential, complicated, and yet rarely explicitly stated dilemmas confronting those who believe, as many Enlightenment thinkers do, that mankind, born good, has been denatured by society. If humanity has indeed been corrupted by civilization, notably by the replacement of an innate moral code (mores) by a system of laws, how can it return to natural virtue? Individuals cannot be expected to embrace virtue (or conciliation) spontaneously, since it no longer comes to them naturally. Yet attempts to impose virtue (or conciliation), especially through prescriptive laws, are destined to fail, because true virtue entails a sacrifice. Like a compromise, a virtuous action ceases to be one the moment it becomes mandatory, as there can be no sacrifice without freedom of choice. Humanity's primeval goodness, including its natural penchant for amicable resolutions, therefore appears unattainable, from within as from without.

It is to this central dilemma of the Enlightenment that Mercier's plays offer a solution. In contrast to the scholarly volumes of liberal reformers, they abound with detailed depictions of successful conciliations, almost always involving the lasting conversion to virtue of a depraved party. This capacity to imagine and then describe an amicable resolution to a heated conflict, a feat seemingly beyond legal scholars, stems from the fact that Mercier's plays, *because* they are plays, shift the terms of the debate from the legal to the artistic realm, from contract to example, and from mediator to father. Through his plays, Mercier does not simply tell, he shows, both how and why a true domestic tribunal, directed by a patriarch—that is, by a legitimate authority, not a contractually delegated one—is best able to produce a non-adversarial performance of justice, the example of which creates a possibility for sincere compromises.

As we noted earlier, among Mercier's many plays centering on a legal dispute, most end with a reconciliation, not a judgment. Many—notably *L'Indigent* and *Le Juge*—follow a nearly identical pattern in their progress toward an amicable resolution. Central to this outcome is the figure of a benevolent jurist (such as a judge or notary public) who attempts to mediate between the two parties. The notary in *L'Indigent*, for instance, explicitly states that he hopes to avoid a trial by healing de Lys's hardened heart.[105] The case could hardly be more clear-cut—Charlotte possesses enough evidence to prove that she is the long-lost sister of de Lys and is thus entitled to half of their father's fortune—and the notary asserts confidently that legal proceedings would yield a just resolution.[106] He fears, however, that a trial would divide not only the inheritance but the inheritors as well, by swelling de Lys's heart with hatred for the victor, his own sister. To persuade de Lys to cede half of his inheritance, the notary threatens him with the full authority of the law. He begins by reading, in a dramatic tone, the will of de Lys and Charlotte's father. This testament is to the notary what *Le Fils naturel* is to Lysimond: a means for a father to immortalize his will and express from beyond the grave "sacred laws" his children must follow.[107] Indeed, the notary takes the task of incarnating the father and his law very seriously, identifying so completely with his role that he "adopts" Charlotte, opening his house and wallet to her until she wins her case.[108] A remarkably forceful mediator, the notary tries to coerce de Lys into accepting an out-of-court settlement by warning the young libertine of the consequences of violating national and paternal laws.

This strategy fails, however, largely because the emphasis it places on laws and authority maintains an adversarial framework, ensuring that the mediation unfolds like a mini-trial. De Lys's corrupt lawyer thrives in such a framework, endlessly interrupting the notary to signal the ways that de Lys can use legal loopholes to discredit his sister. The more assertive the notary becomes, the more de Lys and his lawyer view the discussion less as a negotiation than as a legal competition with only one victor. The same problem confronts the benevolent jurist in *Le Juge*. The judge regards the count as a father (which, we later discover, he truly is), because the count has bestowed upon him his current position and arranged his marriage to the woman he loves. In return, the count makes clear that he looks to the judge as an instrument to impose his will upon the farmer, by means of a summary trial and favorable verdict. However, the judge resists both his father's increasingly insistent demands and the safety of a strict application of the law, pleading throughout the play for the two parties to seek a compromise in lieu of a trial. Yet every attempt to pressure the farmer into selling his land voluntarily only angers both parties further, leading to a deeper conflict instead of the desired compromise. Mercier's plays thereby illustrate the inability of a mediator—even one empowered by the law of the father—to compel a party to compromise against its wishes.

This failure inspires the notary in *L'Indigent* to change tactics. His volte-face begins with the expulsion from his chambers of de Lys's lawyer. Having silenced one legal authority, the notary then relinquishes his own claim to speak for the law. Instead of trying to impose on de Lys his father's will (in both senses of the term), he now encourages him to listen to his heart and follow his moral code—a recognition of the fact that a compromise, like all acts of virtue, must come from within.[109] To help de Lys rediscover his moral core, the notary uses a strategy straight out of *Le Fils naturel*: staging a re-enactment. Announcing that he will resurrect de Lys's father ("rise from the grave," to use his terms), he drags de Lys's uncle, Rémi, out from the secret cabinet where he had hidden him, along with Charlotte and her future husband.[110] This resurrection entails a significant transformation in the notary's function. Previously, it was he who spoke in the voice of the father, the latter having chosen him as his executor. In this role, he enforced the father's will, drawing on the patriarch's sacred laws and authority to declare de Lys guilty and demand obedience. As we saw, however, this threatened to divide the family even further. For a conciliation to be successful, Mercier's play suggests, mediators like the notary must surrender their right to judge (and the feeling of power that comes with it) and seek instead the intervention of fathers. This shift from a delegated, contractual authority to an inherent, paternal one transforms the performance of mediation. The uncle, or resurrected father, since de Lys sees him as such ("Uncle, I see my father in you"),[111] does not arrive on the scene to impose his will, as the notary had attempted to do in his name. Instead, he reminisces about the days when he carried an infant de Lys against his heart, adding that he no longer recognizes this child as one of his own.[112] His biological link to de Lys, which ensures their relationship is based not only on power but also on affection, allows him to foreground the suffering and disappointment that de Lys's disobedience is causing him. While he could, even more than the notary, legitimately seek to bend the young libertine to his will, he too refuses to do so, sacrificing his power over his progeny in a final, public display of affection.

For Mercier, as for Diderot, sacrifice is communicative (especially when it is properly staged!). Although in a position of power, with the law and the notary on her side, Charlotte follows the example set by her adoptive father and uncle. She refuses to impose her will on her brother by means of a trial and offers instead to forego nearly her entire share of the inheritance.[113] This supreme sacrifice, coming from a victim certain to win her case and yet moved by virtue to forfeit everything, is nearly always present in the successful conciliations described by Mercier. For instance, in *Le Juge*, the farmer expresses a willingness to part with his land—only moments after gaining indisputable ownership of it through his legal victory over the count. Indeed, the plays bear some striking similarities. As in *L'Indigent*, conciliation succeeds in *Le Juge* thanks to the refusal by a legal authority to adjudicate in the name of the father and his laws, at great personal cost, since he stands to lose his power to judge in a far more tangible and durable way than the notary, the count having threatened to dismiss him. By refusing to act as an instrument of his father's will, the judge sets the stage for the resurrection of a genuine father. The count is so deeply stirred by a melodramatic spectacle orchestrated by the farmer, in which the latter's wife and children soothe the judge's suffering through displays of their admiration and affection for him, that he cannot keep himself from recognizing the judge as his natural son. This embrace of true, biological fatherhood transforms the count: no longer does he seek to impose his power through laws and delegates; on the contrary, he willingly sacrifices his authority over his son, by rescinding his punishment, and over the farmer, by pledging not to pursue an appeal he would likely win.

It is this spectacle of a restored paternity, one based on virtue and affection rather than power, that motivates the farmer to consider selling his land. The count promptly rejects his offer but is moved to reproduce his sacrifice, not only by surrendering all claims to the contested land, but also by ceding the remainder of his estate to the judge, in the form of an inheritance. Indeed, the victim's supreme sacrifice operates in many of Mercier's plays as a vital step toward a compromise because, as the apex in a sequence of ever-greater sacrifices, it inspires all who see it to imitate it. Hence, in *L'Indigent*, de Lys turns down his sister's proposal, noting repeatedly that he is following her example ("I will imitate you" and "your generosity, which I admire, traces the path of my duty").[114] With the notary's help, they ultimately reach a compromise, one that, tellingly, follows neither the father's will nor the law of equity (both of which require an even split) but succeeds in making both parties happy. As in *Le Fils naturel*, the family's reunification is sealed with a meal, the exchange of food and pleasantries a fitting (if clichéd) image of the reciprocal sacrifices that have brought the family members closer together than the dictates of an external force, even a benevolent one, ever could have.

If this ending brings to mind *Le Fils naturel*, so too does the path that led to it. Like Diderot's play, *L'Indigent* illustrates the persuasive power of reenactment. In both plays, an initial attempt at resurrecting a father and imposing his will meets with failure, but out of that failure emerges a second reenactment that transforms the father from a symbol of law into a symbol of loss. Whereas the first performance commands a sacrifice, the second displays it, providing its participants with an example to imitate. Its success in inspiring emulation, even in the villain de Lys, reveals that *L'Indigent,* like *Le Fils naturel,* defines virtue not as a narrow obedience to external laws but as a willingness, cultivated through exposure to moral exemplars, to make sacrifices for the common good. This particular vision offers a solution to the liberal impasse over conciliation. Mercier's plays make clear that because compromise, like virtue, consists of a sacrifice, it cannot be imposed from without, neither through the encouragements of a well-meaning but powerless mediator (as in the contractual model) nor through the dictates and threats of a powerful arbitrator speaking in the name of the law. Parties must arrive at it from within, and for this, they must be inspired by a model. What better model can there be than a reenactment that exposes the great sorrow and disappointment of a patriarch at his relatives' litigiousness, yet does not culminate, as expected, in a punishment, but rather in the patriarch's voluntary surrender of his right to adjudicate and discipline—a sacrifice born of paternal love and of the knowledge that a punitive ruling would only produce further hatred and suffering? By renouncing his legitimate power to judge, in the name of harmony and forgiveness, the father moves even his most litigious relatives to make sacrifices of their own and embrace a mode of conflict resolution based on concession, not competition.

Mercier deviates from *Le Fils naturel,* however, as well as from the domestic tribunals imagined by liberals such as Lacretelle and Bernardi, in one essential way: his plays insist on the continued centrality of the family patriarch. *Le Fils naturel* and the liberal vision of domestic tribunals are consistent with Hunt's classic account of the weakening and effacement of the father in the second half of the eighteenth century and his replacement by a family of equals, unified through virtue and affection.[115] They can therefore be seen as illustrations of a broader transition from the absolute to the liberal and from the authoritarian to the contractual. One could try to fit Mercier's plays into this narrative, insofar as the patriarchs they portray perfectly illustrate the concept of the "good father," whose midcentury rise Hunt describes as a pivotal stage in the father's gradual loss of authority.[116] Yet unlike in *Le Fils naturel,* where the second reenactment truly erases Lysimond from the text and performance, obliterating the father as a source of law and fixity, Mercier's plays depict a very different outcome, as most end with a resurrection of the father. For instance, in *L'Indigent,* the second reenactment actually succeeds in instilling Rémi with the spirit and status of de Lys's father, precisely what Lysimond had hoped would happen to him after his death. In fact, as we saw earlier, Mercier's plays often stage a shift from delegated, institutional justice to natural, paternal authority—the inverse progression to the one we'd expect from Hunt's narrative. While *Le Fils naturel* ends with a meal where the father's now vacant place is taken by a virtuous spectator, extending the family beyond blood ties to symbolic, contractual ones, Mercier's plays typically conclude with the recreation of a family around a reinstated and thus re-empowered patriarch.

Mercier's theater therefore appears less an illustration of the movement toward weaker fathers than a reaction against it. Indeed, as I mentioned earlier, Mercier also wrote articles condemning the very transformations that Hunt offers as evidence for the waning of paternal authority, from judicial reforms curtailing the punitive power of fathers to the campaign against *lettres de cachet*. His fiction and nonfiction thus converge in their praise of domestic tribunals, the most fruitful site for conciliation in Mercier's opinion, so long, that is, as they exist in their natural form, under the direction (legal and theatrical) of a powerful patriarch. Such authoritarianism may seem odd coming from an anti-absolutist thinker like Mercier, but it reflects his faith in the value of sacrifice, for how can the sacrifice of one's right to judge and punish be worthy of imitation unless said right is recognized as irrefutable. This, ultimately, is what differentiates the father from other mediators. A liberal mediator derives his legitimacy from his selection, giving him an authority that is necessarily temporary and contingent. The power to judge is never truly his, making its sacrifice, in an attempt at conciliation, largely meaningless. By contrast, the father's legitimacy does not depend on the parties; it is natural, not contractual, and as such persists even posttrial. Only he can perform the supreme sacrifice, relinquishing his absolute authority as a child's first judge in a concession to domestic harmony that other family members are then inspired to imitate. In a typical Enlightenment paradox, self-sacrifice becomes a source of strength, not weakness. Hence, in *Jenneval*, the tyrannical patriarch Ducrone only pushes his heir Jenneval deeper and deeper into a life of dissolution and crime through his strict punishments, while the benevolent father Dabelle, through his often spectacular, tearful refusals to discipline Jenneval, gains ever more sway over the young man. In Mercier's eyes, then, the "good father" does not weaken patriarchal authority; on the contrary, he both depends upon and contributes to a strengthening of paternal influence.

In sum, Mercier goes against all expectations by seeing no incompatibility between authoritarianism and conciliation. The same holds true for Rétif, who not only champions a deeply authoritarian justice system modeled on the domestic tribunals of ancient Rome, but promotes conciliation as well, to the extent of reproducing in his *Thesmographe* the entirety of an eighty-page pamphlet in favor of amicable resolutions (Champlair's *L'Ami de la concorde*). This belief that (re)empowering fathers is central to the dream of widespread conciliation, rather than contradictory to it, reveals a fascinating unease with the contractual principles underlying liberal justice. Taken to its logical extreme, a contractual society destroys the very notion of permanent, immanent authority. In doing so, it narrows considerably the possibility for true sacrifice, thereby producing a society governed by law and judgment rather than mores and conciliation. It would thus be wrong to assume that equality helps nurture amicable resolutions, for instance by revealing a shared humanity. The inverse appears to be true: where all possess the same individual rights, all are equally (il)legitimate, leaving no one with any more power or incentive to compromise than anyone else. Hence the paradoxical conclusion that conciliation, that most egalitarian type of conflict resolution, is far more likely to succeed in an inegalitarian structure. Among authoritarian models, however, only one is acceptable to the likes of Mercier, because it is genuinely natural (and thus not arbitrary): the domestic tribunal of a powerful yet power-averse patriarch.

The Domestic Tribunals of the Revolution

In August 1790, the Revolutionaries established a domestic tribunal—*le tribunal de famille*. As a result of this law, it became mandatory for any relatives engaged in a conflict to present their case to four arbitrators before they could pursue a more traditional trial. The four arbitrators were selected by the parties from among their family members or, if need be, from their friends and neighbors. If the arbitrators failed to bring about an amicable resolution, they appointed a *surarbitre* with the authority to impose a verdict, albeit one that could then be appealed before a district court. That such a tribunal was instituted alongside and at the same time as profoundly dissimilar liberal reforms, such as public and adversarial criminal proceedings, shows the sincerity and influence of the domestic vision of justice that many thinkers turned to again and again in response to the theatricality of liberal justice.

Indeed, deputies applauded the very same nontheatrical attributes (overlooking the ways that they contradicted some of their liberal principles) that Mercier and others had highlighted. Notably, they praised the secrecy of domestic tribunals for averting public scandal and for improving social mores and familial ties through a benevolent and preventive surveillance.[117] They also noted the relative freedom from legalism found in domestic tribunals, without depicting it, as one may have anticipated, as a dangerous form of arbitrariness, but rather as an opportunity for simpler, faster, and more flexible proceedings, culminating in, at best, a conciliation, or, at worst, a more equitable verdict than the laws may have allowed.

Yet if the deputies recognized the value, in some instances at least, of secrecy and arbitrariness (understood as a degree of autonomy from fixed laws and procedures), they drew the line at authoritarianism. Following the example set by Lacretelle, Bernardi, and the authors of the *Dictionnaire de jurisprudence*, they fashioned their domestic tribunal in keeping with contractual ideals, instead of modelling it on primeval, agrarian or Roman antecedents. In fact, Mirabeau and other deputies openly presented domestic tribunals as a replacement for *lettres de cachet*, offering the same advantages arising from a private, flexible form of justice, but with the added benefit of stripping fathers of their despotic powers and turning them into just another family member. In that regard, as Hunt and others have shown, domestic tribunals consisted of a key component in a wider endeavor in the early years of the Revolution to reform the family into a small, autonomous republic of equals, united by mutual affection and obligations, not paternal authority.[118] So strong was the contractual pull, however, that it led to the extension of the new domestic tribunals beyond the family. The deputies considered but ultimately rejected limiting the choice of arbitrators to family members, citing as a justification the contractual dogma that arbitrators derive their legitimacy from their free selection by a party, not from blood ties.[119] In the end, not only was arbitration no longer restricted to fathers, but it was opened to essentially anyone, so vague were the terms "friends" and "neighbors" included in the law.

The result was all too predictable: lawyers suddenly discovered they had hundreds of new friends, all eager to appoint them as their arbitrators.[120] For instance, in her study of the domestic tribunals in Douai, Demars-Sion calculated that in less than 3 percent of cases were all four arbitrators family members, friends, or neighbors. The remaining 97 percent of cases included at least one lawyer, with 69 percent composed exclusively of legal professionals.[121] The benefits were mutual: for the lawyers, a much-needed source of revenue (indeed, lest we blame them for corrupting the deputies' dream of free domestic justice, it is worth remembering that the same deputies had recently abolished the lawyers' order and with it much of their livelihood), and for the parties, an arbitrator capable of defending their claim with an eloquence and judicial expertise far superior to anything Oncle Jacques or Tante Marie were likely to muster. Yet this came at a cost: the distortion of domestic tribunals into an institution virtually indistinguishable from ordinary liberal proceedings. The introduction of lawyers, paid to obtain the best possible outcome for their client, not the most beneficial one for the family, ensured that the proceedings took the form of agonistic debates, more likely to inflame existing antagonisms than to lead to an amicable resolution. To win, the lawyers turned to the kind of arguments they knew best, shifting the terms of the trials from questions of equity and harmony to ones of legality and guilt. As a result, the vast majority of domestic procedures did not end in a compromise but with a ruling in favor of a single party, one that revealed through its style (the use of legalese) and its content (obscure references to legal precedents) that it derived from a strict application of the law.[122]

In short, the deputies failed to heed the lessons contained in Mercier's plays. By transforming the domestic tribunal, an inherently paternal mode of justice, into a contractual negotiation between free and equal parties, they drastically diminished its ability to produce amicable settlements. Open arbitration, hailed as an antidote to authoritarianism, quickly gave way to representation, and all the dramatic elements of liberal justice that the domestic tribunal had been intended to avoid came galloping back with it. Although it is true that the proceedings remained largely private, they unfolded in the same theatrical fashion as a typical liberal trial, with professional representatives debating legal questions and precedents before a judge, not a mediator, that neither party had personally selected. Ironically, then, an institution created to reduce the number of trials between family members may have in fact nearly doubled them, by adding an extra layer of proceedings that nearly always failed to conciliate the parties and usually resulted in an appeal. Indeed, while the domestic tribunals of the Revolution were meant to prevent the rise in society of a lawsuit culture through the supposed goodwill and compassion found within families, they seem to have accomplished the very opposite and introduced instead a lawsuit culture within families.

Inquire about "eighteenth-century domestic tribunals" today and the response, if any comes, will almost certainly refer only to this failed experiment. Yet the domestic tribunals of the Revolution constitute a poor illustration—one might even say a liberal perversion—of an older dream that haunted the imagination of eighteenth-century thinkers of all stripes. For these thinkers, domestic tribunals were meant to revive the most natural, universal, and straightforward mode of conflict resolution known to man, from primitive tribes and the early Romans to isolated French villagers: the humble tableau of a benevolent patriarch calling to his side two bickering siblings or an errant son, chiding, cajoling, showing equal part anger and sorrow, until through his lectures and example he succeeds in inspiring his loved ones to amend their ways and voluntarily put the interests of the family above their own—or, failing that, justly disciplines them. The popularity of this vision has gone largely unnoticed, obscured in part by the domestic tribunals of the Revolution, but also, I suspect, by its unexpectedness, given it goes against so many principles—the right to a lawyer, the presumption of innocence, the contractual and democratic nature of judging, the publicity of proceedings, and the need for a clear, precise, exhaustive code of law—that first emerged in France during the second half of the eighteenth century. Yet this is precisely what makes the dream of paternal tribunals, however quixotic it may seem, so significant: it shows that the tenets of liberal justice that we take for granted today, or at least that seem to us the result of a rational, humanitarian progress, were a source of much anxiety and dispute, even among liberals. Dig a little deeper and one uncovers that the dream of domestic tribunals had the same roots as the longing for perfect reenactments that we saw in the first section of this book: a fear of theatricality. Presiding over a domestic tribunal, a benevolent patriarch tries to inspire his children to withdraw from the lawsuit culture that has taught them to see justice as a public, dramatic joust, rewarding those with the best skills at representation, the most adversarial approach, and the broadest knowledge of the arcane laws and procedures that have replaced natural equity. Like the partisans of a true reenactment, he dreams of finding a nontheatrical performance of justice, free of actors and lawyers, spectators and judges, playhouses and tribunals, and artistic rules and legal codes.

PART III

The Revolution's Performance of Justice

Chapter 6

Performing Justice in the Early Years of the Revolution

Courtroom Dramas: Toward a New Performance of Justice

On December 17, 1790, the ill-fated Jean Calas was brought back to life at the Théâtre du Palais Royal just long enough to be tried yet again for the murder of his son. The play premiering that night, Auguste-Jacques Lemierre d'Argy's *Calas, ou Le Fanatisme,*[1] reenacted on stage with great precision all of the principal incidents of the infamous Calas affair, from the discovery of Marc-Antoine's body and the siege of the Calas residence by a horde of zealots, convinced that he had been murdered by his family to prevent his conversion from Protestantism to Catholicism, to the ensuing trial, led by the intolerant capitoul David de Beaudrigue,[2] and ending with Jean Calas's torture and execution on the wheel in 1762,[3] all the while proclaiming his innocence. The very next day, the actors of the Théâtre de la Nation staged their own reenactment of the trial—a tragedy written by Jean-Louis Laya.[4] All told, in the space of only seven months, five plays, including one by the most celebrated playwright of the Revolution, Marie-Joseph Chénier,[5] transplanted to the stage the lives and hardships of the Calas family,[6] even as several others tagged on minor roles to unrelated plots for Calas and Voltaire, who had fought so hard to exonerate him posthumously.[7]

Such a flurry of plays on the Calas affair[8] partly reflects, in fact, the Revolutionaries' profound admiration for Voltaire, a mania that reached its peak in July 1791 with the transfer of his remains to the Panthéon. Throughout the funerary march, one of the largest France has ever known, the specter of Calas was omnipresent, most notably in the prominent role given to his two daughters, walking at the head of the procession, and in the plays performed that night (*La Bienfaisance de Voltaire* and Chénier's *Jean Calas*).[9] The Calas plays also bear witness, however, to a widespread fascination in the early years of the Revolution with the theatrical reenactment of trials, a craze never studied until now.

Indeed, between 1789 and 1793, many illustrious victims of legal injustices, from age-old martyrs such as Socrates to contemporary ones such as the Chevalier de La Barre,[10] were exhumed from their everlasting sleep. The craze for "courtroom dramas," as I will refer to them, extended even to lesser-known cases, as playwrights dug through collections of past causes célèbres,[11] as well as through the daily press, in search of *faits divers*.[12] So popular was this particular genre that it threatened to displace in the public's mind some of the then-standard references to classical myths and history—or so is suggested by the amusing misunderstanding that saw spectators riot during a performance of *Le Jugement de Pâris*, so disappointed were they that the play dramatized the tale of the Trojan prince and not the trial of Philippe de Pâris, the murderer of Louis Michel Le Peletier.[13] In fact, as early as July 1790, the insertion into dramatic works of legal affairs, such as crimes, trials, and executions, had grown into enough of a vogue to elicit scathing criticism in the press.[14] Reactionary angst at the emergence of new generic forms and subject matters is hardly surprising, but in reality, courtroom dramas were not as new as they appeared. They belonged to the broader genre of judicial theater championed decades earlier by dramatic reformers. The ever-prescient Mercier had in fact predicted as far back as 1770 that future generations of Frenchmen would come together to perform and watch reenactments of the Calas trial.[15]

Why this sudden craze for courtroom dramas? It seems improbable that their popularity derived from anything they revealed. Unlike the Aristophanes-inspired genre of judicial theater we saw earlier (and will see again in this chapter), courtroom dramas did not expose unknown crimes. Nor did they reveal the innocence of the famous figures they resuscitated, since very few of their spectators were likely to have doubted the innocence of Socrates, La Barre, and Calas—especially the latter, who had been officially exonerated in 1765. Far from offering new revelations, in fact, the Calas plays meticulously recreated a trial already widely known through the hugely popular pamphlets written by Voltaire and others. The playwrights did not seek to revise this standard account of the Calas trial; on the contrary, they trumpeted their plays' faithfulness to it and to the legal transcripts, down to the exact words spoken by the accused and his judges.[16] Accordingly, I contend that courtroom dramas grew so popular not because they were trials (revelations of guilt or innocence) but because they were trials of trials. By reflecting on the ways that legal proceedings unfold, and by inviting their audiences to follow suit, they struck a chord at a time—the early years of the Revolution—when finding a new performance of justice ranked as one of the most significant orders of the day. In October of 1789, mere months after the creation of the National Assembly, the deputies had fulfilled the wishes of nearly every Revolutionary by adding spectators, lawyers, and defense witnesses to criminal proceedings. Yet this decree was presented as a provisional measure, addressing some widely condemned flaws of ancien régime justice, but leaving most other aspects of its procedure untouched, despite the fact that, in the words of the deputy Bon-Albert Briois de Beaumez, "Publicity affects the entire procedure and changes, so to speak, its nature."[17] As Beaumez recognized, publicity and legal representation were transformative; they made it necessary to reimagine, from start to finish, how a trial would actually unfold—who would speak, when, and how. This quest for a new performance of justice, added to the belief, by Brissot and other liberals, that the legal system could and should seek models in the theater, no doubt explains the urge among playwrights to reproduce trials from the past, as well as the craving among spectators to watch the resulting plays, even when the case and its outcome were already well known. As we will see, courtroom dramas were not only a means of highlighting the failures of ancien régime proceedings, they also served as a kind of workshop, a chance for authors and spectators to invent and examine potential performances of justice.

It is telling, in that regard, that the press responded to the Calas plays by exploring the implications of publicly reenacting a heated conflict or traumatic loss in the name of justice. On December 20, 1790, the *Feuille du jour* pondered the wisdom, for the Calas family and for the nation as a whole, of resurrecting an event that had been the cause of such division and sorrow: "All these theaters, ringing with the name of Calas, will inevitably reopen the wound of his poor widow. She has been in Paris for the past fifteen years and resides on Rue Poissonnière with her two daughters. She has not come out of mourning since the death of her husband. Her watch, stopped at the time of his execution, has never been rewound." There are few images as powerfully emblematic of trauma as this stopped watch, beautifully capturing the inability by the Calas family to move beyond the "judicial murder" of its patriarch. The wound is partly closed (how else could it be reopened?), and yet it remains everywhere visible, as in the widow's black clothes and frozen watch. The Calas plays now threatened to unsettle this uneasy stasis by forcing a confrontation with the repressed event at the origin of the trauma. This worried the journalists, who expressed the concern that publicly reenacting a divisive or tragic event might revive the suffering and animosity of the parties—in this case, casting the widow into despair and fueling hatred between Catholics and Protestants, or toward magistrates. This anxiety is reminiscent of the fears triggered by the liberal vision of legal proceedings as public repetitions of the dispute that led to the trial. As we saw in Chapter 5, many warned that this conception of justice, by transforming quarrels into a popular spectacle and by channeling them through an adversarial, dramatic structure, risked prolonging and exacerbating the sorrow and resentment of both parties, rendering conciliation nearly impossible.

Yet the *Feuille du jour* had already responded to this anxiety two days earlier, after it was voiced by a spectator: "I could hear someone next to me asking angrily: 'Why recall on stage these dreadful events?' Why? To ensure that the blood of the innocent never again stains the scaffold. It is useful to show this corpse to all centuries, to forever draw blood from the wound humanity received, when cruel men, when laws perhaps even crueler, ordered this despicable crime." The imagery is the same as in the later article, except the Calas plays are here praised, not feared, for their ability to reopen wounds. Digging into old scars is presented, somewhat paradoxically, as an essential step toward achieving a much-needed sense of closure. In support of this belief, journalists could (and did) point to the decision by Calas's own daughters to attend some of the performances. As the *Journal de Paris* noted, the Calas plays consisted of a genuine "revision of the famous trial before the tribunal of the audience"—both a second viewing ("re-vision") and a correction of it.[18] Indeed, while Jean Calas had been exonerated by the Crown decades earlier, never before had he had the chance to defend himself and win an acquittal in a trial conducted before an audience of his peers. By reenacting the past, the Calas plays amended it, if for no other reason than because the structure and conventions of the theater provided Jean Calas with the public, agonistic trial that the "cruel laws" of the ancien régime had denied him. For the Calas daughters, the sight of their fellow citizens weeping, trembling with indignation, booing the capitouls, and cheering every mention of their father's innocence meant more than just vindication; it was a chance to relive the trial as it ought to have unfolded, to experience a different, fairer outcome, and with this, to finally move beyond it.

This story shares many assumptions with the liberal campaign for more theatrical trials, most notably the belief that the public repetition of a conflict or tragic loss is valuable not only for uncovering the truth but also for what it offers its spectators—solace for the victim's friends and family, deterrence for would-be criminals, and a vital sense of closure for the community as a whole. Tellingly, in fact, one finds in newspaper articles of the time a constant slippage and implicit equivalence between the personal scars of the Calas family and a more general wound, suffered by the entire French people or broader yet, humanity. Of course, considering the nearly three decades separating the Calas affair from its theatrical reenactments, it may strike us as rather unlikely that anyone besides the victim's family could still be traumatized by Jean Calas's execution. Yet one should not forget that the Calas trial was the first to genuinely reach—and affect—a truly broad audience, thanks to fictitious trial briefs that moved and outraged men and women throughout France.[19] So profound was this mix of pity and indignation that the *Moniteur universel* claimed in 1790 that "twenty-five years haven't diminished it."[20] Certainly, for five playwrights to have chosen, in under a year, to write on the same trial suggests that it retained a powerful hold on the French imagination. More than any other trial, it acted as a symbol of the secrecy, inequality, and cruelty of the legal system under the ancien régime.

As a result, even in the absence of any personal association with the Calas affair or of a firsthand encounter with the inequities of pre-Revolutionary justice, it remains possible—likely even, given the debate in the *Feuille du jour*—that many spectators experienced the plays as offering relief from what the sociologist Jeffrey Alexander has dubbed a "cultural trauma." In "Towards a Theory of Cultural Trauma," Alexander distinguishes between psychological trauma, which is personal and results from direct exposure to a specific event, and cultural trauma, which is rooted in the collective memories of a group and results from a cultural construction.[21] While few spectators of the Calas plays likely had a direct cause for psychological trauma, the grounds for developing a cultural trauma were plentiful in the first years of the Revolution.[22] As Jean-Clément Martin has noted, the early Revolutionaries, in an attempt to promote changes in the justice system, frequently reminded the general public, often with great hyperbole, of the barbaric traditions of ancien régime tribunals. For instance, soon after the storming of the Bastille, hundreds of pamphlets were published describing (and often inventing) victims of ancien régime injustices found rotting in dark cells despite having committed no crime.[23] Few Frenchmen had in fact faced such injustices, but it was politically advantageous, from the Revolutionaries' point of view, that all feel the same wounds as those who had. This explains why it was so important that the spectators be made aware of the presence of Calas's daughters. The reality of the daughters' wounds, coupled with the belief that the reenactment of their father's trial might offer them closure, gave a sense of concreteness and specificity to what was, for most of the spectators, a rather ill-defined, collective trauma. Indeed, what is fascinating about the Calas plays is that they show that trauma need not consist of a personal wound, the result of a single, inexpressible event. Rather, the Calas plays sought to heal a general, cultural trauma by condensing the many injustices of the ancien régime into a representative event (the trial and execution of Jean Calas). In doing so, they participated in the construction of said cultural trauma, summoned it into being, in fact, but only so as to then publicly exorcize it by allowing the spectators to correct the unjust verdict issued against Calas.

The press's focus on the individual and cultural impact of watching dramatic recreations is telling, as is the way that these debates mirror earlier ones on the value of public, adversarial trials. It reveals that the impulse to repeat ancien régime trials partly stemmed from the fact that these trials had already failed as repetitions in the first place—and thereby allowed wounds to fester. Owing to this failure, they had abdicated one of the main functions of legal proceedings—providing closure. In an insightful article on the O. J. Simpson trial, Soshana Felman argues that the ability to translate a traumatic event into a controlled and controllable narrative constitutes a significant meeting point between the arts and the law.[24] Modern trials, according to Felman, Antoine Garapon, and Pierre Legendre, unfold according to a particular logic of representation—a dramaturgy—that aims to make mute acts and sufferings expressible, so as to allow a decisive judgment upon them, thereby laying them to rest as historical past.[25] To that end, legal "actors" (lawyers, witnesses, accuser, and accused) are assigned roles in an agonistic clash between two diametrically opposed narratives, publicly repeating the conflict at the heart of the trial. This restaging of the conflict serves two purposes. First, by translating it into a verbal confrontation, it revives perilous emotions, such as anger and hatred, in its participants, but ensures that they are expressed in a nonviolent, controlled fashion—an emotional purging reminiscent of catharsis, as legal scholars have noted.[26] Second, it reopens the wounds of the watching victims, but unlike the initial event, its repetition in a tribunal offers the promise of public vindication, a definitive, impartial resolution able to heal the wounds and restore social peace.

The Calas trial, like all criminal proceedings in the ancien régime, could fulfill neither of these functions. The reason why is most obvious for the second: public vindication was made unattainable by the absence of spectators, including the victim's family, from the courtroom—a secrecy that the Calas plays explicitly lament.[27] As for the first function, the participants were unlikely to find much catharsis in procedures deliberately designed to prevent any repetition of the initial conflict. Indeed, as we saw earlier, criminal trials were not accusatorial—they did not stage an agonistic clash between two symmetrical yet opposed narratives—but were, rather, inquisitorial, with judges directing the proceedings from start to finish and composing, through secret interrogations, textual analyses, and mathematical calculations, a single narrative of guilt. The accused were granted an appearance before their judges, but only in the final stages of the trial and under strict instructions to respond solely to the magistrates' narrative, not to present a competing account of their own. So intent was this system on averting unscripted, agonistic debate (for fear it would revive the passion and disorder of the original conflict) that the accused were not allowed to call forth their own witnesses, to speak to those who had testified against them, and even to present arguments, including *faits justificatifs* (proof of their innocence), unless they directly answered a question posed by the judges. It is worth highlighting, therefore, that even had his trial been public, Jean Calas would still have been largely unable to recount (and relive) his version of his son's death. The Calas plays can thus be understood as an attempt to tell a story that his trial could not—in fact, was designed not to—tell: an account of the trauma of loss, intolerance, and estrangement from one's own nation.

Indeed, much of the effectiveness of the Calas plays came from their unique ability to both show and tell. Not only did they argue explicitly that trials ought to serve as the public repetition of a conflict or traumatic event, by having their characters repeatedly invoke all the standard liberal critiques of ancien régime justice, but they also illustrated the power of such a repetition through their impact on the spectators. More than simply decrying pre-Revolutionary proceedings, they presented themselves, and more broadly theater, as an alternative performance of justice, superior because public and dialogical. Yet in doing so, they raised the question of how, precisely, such a live, agonistic spectacle would unfold—who its main actors would be, when they would speak, and what rules and conventions they would be expected to follow. With the closeted justice of the ancien régime offering no such dramaturgy, the authors of courtroom dramas had to look elsewhere.

One option was French classical tragedies, which often took the form, as Robert Horville has noted, of a particular type of trial, opening with an exposition to present known facts and the two parties, followed by an oratorical joust notable for its rigorous, masterful use of rhetoric and its structured, orderly progress, and culminating in a decisive resolution.[28] Many elements of this dramaturgy are also characteristic of the liberal model of justice, as defined by François Ost, from its binary configuration (splitting the parties into two rival camps) to its reliance on trained orators (lawyers) and fixed forms to help translate complicated claims and emotions into organized, composed, judicable speech.[29] This faith in rational, rehearsed debate, common to classical theater and liberal justice, is evident throughout the Calas plays. Indeed, the plays give a voice to Jean Calas, allowing him to present arguments in his defense through coherent, well-crafted, uninterrupted speeches, even as they condemn the ancien régime procedures that had prevented him from doing so during his actual trial. In particular, they deplore the fact that Jean Calas was denied legal counsel, defense witnesses, and knowledge of the evidence against him and his family,[30] making it impossible for him to prepare a persuasive narrative to rival the capitoul's account of his guilt. Several scenes highlight the futility of even trying to compose such a narrative, by showing that the judges determined Calas's guilt, based on false testimonies tallied together like so many fractions of proof, before ever speaking with him—as illustrated by the fact that they began their first (and last) encounter by asking him to name his accomplices instead of offering him an opportunity to defend himself.[31] In many regards, then, the Calas plays are both a plea for and an example of the procedural performance most closely associated with liberal justice: a competition between two equal parties and their carefully prepared narratives, presented with the assistance of trained orators and in accordance with strict rules about who gets to speak, how, and when, thereby averting the cacophony, confusing interruptions, and emotional outbursts of extrajudicial disputes.

In other regards, however, courtroom dramas draw from a very different dramaturgy. In a fascinating article, Renaud Bret-Vitoz argues that eighteenth-century tragedies increasingly turned away from portraying justice as a rhetorical contest characterized by lengthy, eloquent, meticulously constructed pleas, preferring instead to stage interrogation scenes, because the latter allow more spontaneous, physical, passionate exchanges.[32] This progression from the verbal and the rational to the visual and the emotional undoubtedly reflects a broader aesthetic evolution (the rise of sentimentalism and of bourgeois drama, in particular). Yet it also entails a different vision of the ideal performance of justice, closer to what Ost calls "traditional justice" than to the liberal model.[33] Traditional justice, as described by Ost, bears strong similarities to the domestic tribunals so prevalent in the eighteenth-century imaginary. Simple, swift, and more "natural," traditional justice takes the form of a free discussion between the parties unhindered by rules and representation. The parties (not their lawyers) are allowed by a trusted, benevolent arbitrator to argue passionately and extemporaneously, even to interrupt each other to contest a claim or to disrupt a rival's narrative and composure. Sincere, heated, and unscripted, the resulting argument comes much closer to reenacting the original conflict, including in the emotions that the parties feel, potentially offering a more cathartic and accurate performance of justice.

Several scenes in the Calas plays illustrate the ability of spontaneous, physical and emotional proceedings to disclose signs of innocence and guilt normally hidden by the legal practices of the ancien régime. For instance, in all three plays, Jean Calas's friends and family throw themselves at the judges' feet and, crying profusely, beg to share the accused's fate. Such a gesture ought to be taken into consideration when reaching a verdict, the playwrights argue, for would a truly wicked man, especially one accused of exercising a tyrannical rule over his family, be likely to inspire so many tears and such a great sacrifice? Likewise, decades earlier, Voltaire had expressed sorrow that the judges had not seen Calas's tears during his first interrogation by the capitoul. In his "Déclaration de Pierre Calas," he explains that Jean Calas grew so emotional while recounting (and reliving) the discovery of his son's body that he broke down in tears and began stammering and hesitating, leading him to forget details and to invert the order of minor events.[34] In the ancien régime, any such discrepancies between the transcribed depositions, even inconsistencies unrelated to the crime, were treated as a sign of dishonesty and counted toward a guilty verdict. Emotions could thus hurt one's case but not help it, since the judges never witnessed them: they only saw the accused's words, not his body. To Voltaire, however, the fact that a heartbroken Jean Calas had found it impossible to be fully rational and persuasive immediately after his son's death should have been regarded as evidence of his innocence, not of his guilt.

What makes Calas's tears so revealing is not just that they express his sorrow but also that they are unmediated, unrehearsed, and uncontrollable.

Indeed, there runs throughout the Calas plays an underlying belief that the body is a supreme site of truth, because it exists, far more than speech, beyond the control of consciousness. For instance, the peacefulness of Jean Calas's sleep, indicative of a mind untroubled by guilt, is inadmissible in court, and yet, in Chénier's play, it singlehandedly convinces a Catholic priest of his innocence.[35] Likewise, in Lemierre's play, the fundamental expressiveness of the unconscious body prompts Calas's wife to cry out tearfully, "If only his judges could see him in this state! Is that, we would tell them, the sleep of a criminal?"[36] Nor was this, to eighteenth-century ears, such a strange idea: the great Cicero himself, two thousand years earlier, had praised the decision to acquit two young men of the crime of parricide on the grounds that the soundness of their sleep upon being found proved that they could not have committed such a horrible crime—a story then repeated by eighteenth-century writers in support of new, nontextual modes of judgment.[37] By foregrounding the hysterical and the sleeping body, the Calas plays depart from the standard liberal dramaturgy to reveal a different conception of the performance of justice best suited to revealing the truth. In the liberal model, truth emerges from the selection of a victor between two prepared narratives. In this view, composing, with great rhetorical care, specific arguments and pleas, practicing their spoken delivery, and gaining mastery over one's self do not obscure the truth; they make it even more indisputable. By contrast, in the scenes above, truth appears when the parties lose conscious control, whether from sleep or overpowering emotions. It is during these unscripted moments that signs of innocence or guilt become most clearly visible on the body of the parties.

For such moments of self-loss to occur, trials need a flexible, almost improvisational dramaturgy; they must eschew, at least in part, ordered, rehearsed debates led by professional magistrates and attorneys in favor of impromptu, largely unstructured exchanges between the parties and witnesses, thereby encouraging more genuine, emotional interactions and giving a more central, visible role to the litigants and their bodies. The Calas plays include several such scenes, in a telling departure from ancien régime proceedings, which were designed to prevent live arguments. In fact, many of the plays' most spontaneous, passionate encounters stem from the initiatives of a nonconformist judge: Joseph Mathieu de Lassalle. The playwrights did not invent this historical figure, who tried, in vain, to come to Calas's aid, but they eagerly seized the opportunity he offered to model for their audience the duties of a good judge—a didactic aim evident in the subtitle of Chénier's tragedy: "L'École des juges." In all three plays, "la salle" (the auditorium and the spectators within it) is given every incentive, including homonymic ones, to identify with the exemplary judge La Salle (the alternate spelling of Lassalle used, no doubt intentionally, in the Calas plays). Instead of reading transcribed depositions and compiling fragments of proof,[38] the good magistrate breaks protocol (a fact the plays by Laya and Chénier emphasize) by visiting Jean Calas in jail in order to interact with him personally, hear his story directly, and observe his conduct and that of his friends and family as they mourn the death of Marc-Antoine and fret over their own fate. The sight of these suffering bodies produces in La Salle an instinctual sympathy that becomes a key basis for his belief in Calas's innocence. Throughout the plays, he attempts to convince the other judges to follow his example by trusting in their own eyes and compassion instead of in transcripts and equations.[39] Like the playwrights, he appears to believe, in true sentimentalist fashion, that the experience of pity poses no threat to a judge's equity, because human beings experience an instinctual sympathy only in favor of persecuted virtue. Compassion can therefore act as a reliable indicator of innocence. What better evidence, indeed, of the validity of a judgment based on instinct, pathos, and visual cues than the genuine despair at Jean Calas's conviction experienced by the spectators of the three plays?

The Calas plays thus contain elements from two distinct and, in many ways, conflicting judicial dramaturgies. While both recognize, unlike the ancien régime, the necessity for a trial to repeat the conflict or trauma at its origin, they disagree about the nature of this repetition. The liberal model perceives it as a *representation*—a translation of the conflict or trauma into a controlled and controllable performance, with ordered, rational speeches, assigned roles, and a fixed sequence of events. The traditional model aims instead at a more authentic *reenactment*, a repetition closer to the original conflict or trauma in its spontaneity, physicality, and emotionality. By drawing from these two very different dramaturgies, the Calas plays enabled their spectators to witness and compare alternative performances of justice, to give each a trial run, in a sense, but without an actual trial. They thus set the stage, literally and figuratively, for a series of lengthy, passionate arguments at the National Assembly about the way that criminal proceedings ought to unfold—what type of script, if any, they should follow. Indeed, it seems anything but coincidental that this debate took place over the same seven-month period (from late 1790 to mid 1791) as the five Calas plays.

Strangely, considering the innumerable studies on the new forms of political spectacle (notably the festival) that emerged in the early years of the Revolution, scholars have paid little attention to the equally radical transformation of judicial spectacle, whether in the tribunal or in the theater. While legal scholars have studied the creation of new rights (presumption of innocence, public trial, etc.), new courts (Tribunal de famille, Tribunal de cassation, etc.), and new actors (juror, justice of the peace, etc.),[40] there has been no comparable work on the contentious birth, in the same period, of a new performance of justice. This lack of interest may be attributed to the longstanding misreading of the evolution of eighteenth-century justice that I noted in the Introduction. Indeed, debates about the ideal dramaturgy of justice have no clear place in a narrative that considers the years 1789 to 1791 to be a turning point in a vast cultural shift from the visual and theatrical to the textual and rational. In reality, however, the addition of spectators, lawyers, jurors, and rehearsed debates naturally brought criminal proceedings closer to a dramatic representation, a reality the deputies did not fail to notice. Some embraced this theatricality as an essential element of the liberal model of justice. Others worried about the impact it would have—the same fears that had resurfaced, as we saw in earlier chapters, in the final decades of the ancien régime. This fundamental disagreement expressed itself through a series of arguments over technical, seemingly marginal questions (such as: may the accused interrupt a witness and if so, when, how, and why?). Taken together, however, these questions form a larger debate about the proper performance of justice, one that merits study, as it shows the profound influence of the ideal of reenactment. Indeed, reenactment, the eighteenth-century dream of a performance free of lies and mimesis, emerged as a solution that would allow the deputies, in a variant on Marie-Antoinette's apocryphal words, to have their cake and eat it too: to stage public trials without them becoming (too) theatrical. It is striking, in fact, how many of the early Revolutionaries believed that this unique kind of performance—more resurrection than representation—possessed an unrivaled ability to reveal the truth and induce catharsis. Studying the rise and impact of this belief can, I contend, provide a fuller understanding of the famously militant theater of the Revolution and its greatest causes célèbres, such as *L'Ami des lois*, and of the evolution of Revolutionary justice, including its most notorious milestones, such as the king's trial and the rise of the Terror.

The Truth Of/Off the Script: Reenactment in the Courtroom

Some in the press sensed there had to be a connection between the craze for courtroom dramas and the radical overhaul of the justice system in the early years of the Revolution: "We are grateful to Chénier for having revived an event that will attach us to the new justice system by making us shudder at the sight of the horrible consequences of the procedure in our former tribunals."[41] One can understand the implicit triumphalism here, the belief that the Calas plays are primarily valuable as foils—that is, as poignant illustrations of now bygone errors, serving as the perfect advertisement for the new and improved judicial order. After all, hadn't the decree of October 8–9, 1789 resolved the principal critiques leveled at ancien régime justice by the Calas plays? In addition to making trials public, it had implemented a series of reforms with one principal objective: to ensure that the accused could produce the most convincing narrative possible. Lawyers, once forbidden, became all but mandatory (the law stipulated that when the defendants could not find a lawyer, presumably from indigence or a weak case, one would be assigned to them), thereby ensuring that professional orators were always on hand to offer their assistance, from visiting the accused in jail before their first interrogation and helping them prepare a compelling defense to watching the trial alongside their clients and delivering a final plea on their behalf. As further support, the accused also gained several new rights, entitling them to know before appearing in court the charges and evidence against them, to call forth their own witnesses, and to present any evidence they (not the judges) deemed significant, including *faits justificatifs*, at the start of the trial.[42]

Yet if these reforms made it easier for defendants to compose a persuasive defense, they did not make its delivery—and, more broadly, the performance of justice—any more dialogical. On the contrary, the decree of October 8–9 explicitly stipulated that, as under the ancien régime, the accused would not be allowed to respond to accusers and witnesses directly. If the accused noted inconsistencies, lies, or biases in the depositions, their only recourse was to request, after sitting silently through the entire testimony, that the judge ask some follow-up questions on their behalf.[43] Lawyers, meanwhile, were prohibited from even this vicarious participation: the law stated that they could not utter a single word until their final plea, after the last interrogation had concluded.[44] In fact, far from abolishing the monologism of ancien régime trials, the reforms of 1789 may have made it even more conspicuous by requiring that the accused and their lawyers be present and, with trials now public, highly visible during the depositions, thereby making their silence all the more troubling. It should come as no surprise, then, that the reforms were quickly deemed insufficient, with lawyers in particular demanding en masse to be allowed to participate in the interrogations, as reported to the National Assembly on April 21, 1790.[45] The very next day, the deputies responded with an "interpretative decree of the provisional law of 8–9 October 1789" containing a minor concession: lawyers would henceforth be allowed, like their clients, to bring contradictions or falsehoods in a deposition to the judges' attention. Still, the deputies persisted: "In no instance will the accused or his counsel be allowed to question a witness directly."[46] Such a prompt and perfunctory response (the "interpretative decree" was approved without debate) suggests that the deputies were not yet ready to undertake a complete overhaul of the way that justice had been performed for centuries.

The pressure was, however, mounting, for the simple reason that the provisional decree of October 8–9 had left the reformers' vision of justice only half realized. Prior to the Revolution, nearly all had agreed that trials ought to be not only public but also adversarial—a dialogical contest conducted on a level playing field. In lieu of an omnipotent judge interrogating terrified, confused parties, all speakers—accused, accuser, lawyers, and witnesses—would be free to ask questions and challenge opposing claims. Such was the way of the ancients, as Bernardi noted: "Among the Greeks and Romans, . . . the truth of a testimony revealed itself in the clash of reciprocal interrogations, through the witness's composure and exactitude when answering the questions and difficulties thrown at him."[47] It is, the ancients believed, through debate that truth appears, since the most assured and steadfast speaker is the most likely to be giving an accurate account of the facts. Most early Revolutionaries shared Bernardi's desire to model the new judicial order on antiquity.[48] In fact, when the deputies set out in late 1790 to replace the provisional decree of 1789, their debates made it immediately clear that they nearly all agreed on the need for greater, more direct interaction between the trial's participants. This entailed, however, a complete overhaul of the performance of justice: if the judge no longer directed the interrogations, who would? Who would determine who could speak, when, how, and for how long? The necessity of imagining, virtually from scratch, a new dramaturgy of justice is a truly unique situation for a culture to be in, one that explains the popularity and relevance of the Calas plays even better, I contend, than their usefulness as foils. They too grappled with the thorny question of how—and especially, how closely—to repeat a conflict.

The magnitude and contentiousness of this question came to the fore in the National Assembly during a debate on the pros and cons of writing in courtroom proceedings—or, to be more precise, on the advisability of transcribing the testimonies and arguments occurring before and during a trial. This lengthy debate, unfolding over many weeks, has only been studied by Laura Mason, primarily for what it shows about the deputies' conception of legal judgment (*conviction intime*, sentimentalism, nature of proof, etc.).[49] Yet the choice between textuality (pro-transcription) and pure orality (anti-transcription) shaped not only the reception of justice but also its dramaturgy. While such a debate may sound limited in scope, it quickly expanded, raising dozens of related questions about the pros and cons in a trial of emotion, physical signs, repetition, and fixed forms, until what was at stake was nothing less than the very nature of legal proceedings. Far from narrow and inconsequential, the debate on writing split the assembly in two, revealing the existence of a fundamental disagreement about the ideal performance of justice.

One of the principal characteristics of writing is that it leaves a trace, where speech does not. When a witness or a suspect's first testimony is transcribed before a trial, the resulting text, because it is physical and permanent, transforms the subsequent legal proceedings. It creates a script to which the witness or suspect can return in preparation for the trial as well as during it. To highlight the importance of this script, René Gaston Baco de la Chapelle asked his fellow deputies to imagine a trial between a refined, well-spoken urbanite and a simple villager. The latter's lack of experience and education puts him at a severe disadvantage: "the facts are well placed in his memory but arrange themselves with difficulty in his mouth. He gropes for the right expression. He needs time, indulgence." The clever city dweller offers him neither; he interrupts him at every phrase, peppering him with misleading questions and false accusations, shattering the poor villager's train of thought and narrative arc, and compelling him to stammer, hesitate, and undermine his own testimony.[50] Only by sticking to a prepared script can the villager hope to elude these attempts at rattling and confusing him. Thankfully, his first testimony, carefully worded and well-organized, can provide him with such a script, offering him "the support of a deposition he made in cold-blood."[51] The first testimony thus comes to serve as a rehearsal for his far more important performance during the trial. Indeed, for deputies in favor of transcription, writing allows—encourages, in fact—meticulous preparation (due to the knowledge that one's every word will be fixed in time, and read by the judges), as well as deliberate repetition (since transcripts make it easier to tell the same story, in the same order, and in the same words)—vital protections against the ruses of a nimbler orator.

Writing protects the villager in another way. It is its absence, in Baco de la Chapelle's example, that allows the urbanite to destabilize the villager through his constant interruptions. Baco de la Chapelle warns the deputies that when legal proceedings are not transcribed, they degenerate into a "cacophony" of endless questions and accusations, as the participants try to speak over one another, making it impossible for parties and judges alike to organize the facts into a coherent narrative.[52] This is a common argument among supporters of transcription, who express fear of "scandalous spectacles," "pandemonium," and "marketplace brawls."[53] Such chaotic scenes are inconceivable in a legal system that mandates the transcription of trial proceedings, because they cannot be recorded, even by the fastest stenographer. Although occurring after speech, writing thus transforms it by requiring that it be writable. It ensures that trials unfold slowly and that fixed forms are put in place to prevent constant interruptions, with questions asked only by specific people and at specific moments—preferably not until after the speaker has finished his entire deposition, so that he may do so "calmly."[54] This static structure prevents "natural" arguments, which, outside the tribunal, tend to be fast-paced, muddled, and digressive, but the partisans of transcription deem this an asset since truly impromptu, disorganized exchanges favor the most educated and manipulative, not the most truthful. Their ideal dramaturgy remains an agonistic dialogue, but one that is closely rehearsed and regulated to provide a level playing field to all parties.

This vision of justice was also behind the deputies' decree that the accused would be entitled to legal counsel even before their first interrogation, so as to compose the best possible defense. Indeed, Beaumez justified this new law by emphasizing how vital it was for the accused to be so well prepared that they never be "surprised" during the interrogation, as this might lead an innocent man to appear guilty by hesitating and offering vague answers to questions he did not expect.[55] Liberal reformers, before the Revolution, had made a similar case for lawyers, with several insisting on the latter's sangfroid, which could help calm the overly emotional, frightened defendants and show them how to narrate their case with order and composure.[56] Boucher d'Argis had in fact connected the two needs—for transcripts and for a lawyer—in a revealing passage. Warning that defendants often become flustered before an imposing magistrate, causing them to give poor answers, Boucher d'Argis proposes a solution: "If the accused were given a copy of the proceedings, he would mull over it in the silence of his cell. Returned to himself, his reflections would be surer, his ideas calmer; he would confer with his lawyers and prepare a more reasoned defense for the interrogation preceding the verdict."[57] Particularly telling is the phrase "returned to himself," as it shows that the accused's meticulous preparation and rehearsal, with the help of his counsel, are not perceived by liberals as a means of disguising one's true self, but rather as a way of more accurately revealing it.

It is striking to note, in fact, that nearly all of the examples above include an explicit rejection of "surprises" and of any other elements (such as imposing magistrates or interruptions by rival parties) that might cause defendants to lose self-control and stray from their script.[58] This rejection stems from the liberal belief that spontaneity too often leads defendants, especially the poor and uneducated, to hesitate and display too much emotion—physical reactions that are then misconstrued as signs of guilt: "The indigent who trembles gives off an air of dishonesty: his discomfort obscures the truth, and he is condemned."[59] The partisans of transcription share this belief, with François Denis Tronchet, in particular, warning that it would be a tragic mistake to base the judges' *conviction intime* on the hesitations and fluctuations of the accused, since "innocence itself can be flustered."[60] In fact, they go even further by presenting the body in general, not just specific reactions such as trembling and stammering, as a site of deep uncertainty. Hence, Joseph Prugnon casts doubt on the idea that facial expressions are "etchings of the soul" and "a path to truth,"[61] before extending the same skepticism, fifteen days later, to the entire body, when he ridicules the partisans of pure orality for believing that "the truth will pour out of the witnesses' and accused's every pore."[62] For the supporters of transcription, physical signs, even unconscious ones, cannot be trusted. When defendants lose control, what is revealed is usually not the truth, but rather their anxiety or inexperience—neither of which makes them guilty. Instead, the pro-transcription deputies believe that truth best emerges through the composition and repetition of a narrative until its persuasiveness surpasses its rivals'—a view that mirrors the liberal belief we saw in Chapter 3 that eloquence is a reliable indicator of truth.

A script. A rehearsal. A fixed, orderly dramaturgy. It would have been difficult for the partisans of transcription to ignore the theatricality of such a vision, and indeed, Tronchet, for instance, often employs dramatic imagery with terms like actor, scene, and stage.[63] Like many liberals before the Revolution, they seem untroubled by this parallel, even depicting it as a positive. Since public and agonistic proceedings are inevitably theatrical, it makes sense to embrace a written script and a fixed dramaturgy, which are at least egalitarian insofar as they turn all participants into actors with the same resources, instead of letting a naïve, unprepared villager fall prey to the chicanery of a more experienced and sophisticated performer. To pro-transcription deputies, in fact, writing serves not only as an equalizer but also as a means of harnessing the theatricality of liberal justice, steering it toward truth instead of deceit. This is evident in Prugnon's succinct but telling justification for his proposal that all witnesses and defendants be heard in private by a judge and their depositions transcribed before they are allowed to testify in court: "a witness whose testimony is not written, testifies with far less care; he does not bear witness, he recounts."[64] In the absence of a script (the transcript of an earlier deposition), witnesses are more inclined to indulge in the all-too-human desire to play to the crowd. The resulting testimonies skip over details lacking in narrative appeal but of potential forensic significance and embellish others, in the hope of eliciting a powerful reaction. As such, they reflect the witnesses' love of acting more than their love of truth, making them inferior to the initial depositions, which were given far more calmly and attentively because there was no audience present to inflame the witnesses' theatrical instinct.

Writing also deters an even more dangerous form of acting, motivated not by vanity but by greed. Many of the supporters of transcription, including Tronchet and Prugnon, warn obsessively about the risk of paid witnesses in the absence of a written record.[65] Transcripts, they explain, create webs of interconnected facts that entrap false witnesses. It is often from catching a small inconsistency that an entire deposition begins to unravel, but such details can only be spotted by carefully reading and comparing written depositions.[66] By restraining those who, seduced by the spotlight, would exaggerate, and by exposing those who, seduced by money, would flat-out lie, writing thus helps to ensure that the acting in a trial—the practiced act of self-presentation that everyone engages in when speaking publicly—remains a generally truthful kind of acting. Indeed, so much of what writing does, in the eyes of pro-transcription deputies, consists of establishing a controlled, revelatory (instead of deceptive) form of theatricality. It is vital to a performance of justice that seeks to avoid the unexpected, the chaotic, and the physical—that strives to represent, not reenact, the conflict at the heart of the trial.

Many deputies rejected this dramaturgy, however, and argued that there should be no transcription whatsoever, from the first deposition to the last plea (in fact, some deputies even questioned whether jurors should be allowed to take notes). Although they agreed with their adversaries on one key point—that transcribing courtroom proceedings would mean imposing upon them a fixed structure and a measured pace—they disagreed entirely about its implications. The smartest and most complete critique came from Jacques Guillaume Thouret, in a speech so long it had to be read over two days. Among its most significant claims was the following: "If the debates were as cold, as dragging, as lifeless, as would be necessary for every word to be transcribed, it is difficult to believe that they would then contain many of the strokes of truth that form moral conviction. These signs of truth can only be produced by movement and heat; they only escape in moments of self-forgetting."[67] There is much in this brief but rich excerpt that challenges the vision of the pro-transcription deputies, but one difference sticks out most clearly. The composed, ordered proceedings that supporters of writing praise as "measured" and "rational," Thouret portrays instead as "cold," "dragging," and "lifeless." As an alternative, he champions passionate, extemporaneous debates, full of "movement and heat," and thereby more likely to reveal the truth. Beaumez makes the same claim—"a lively confrontation reflects the truth from all sides onto the attentive eyes that seek it"—before adding, in the next sentence, that witnesses should therefore not be allowed to give their depositions "without interruption."[68] Indeed, the partisans of pure orality welcome strong emotions in a trial, not in spite of the threat they pose to orderly proceedings, but because of it, because true passions elicit fragmented, stichomythic disputes between the accuser and the accused that are far more sincere, spontaneous, and conducive to "strokes of truth."

The disagreement about whether to allow interruptions during depositions perfectly captures, in fact, the two different visions of a trial's temporality (its relationship to all that precedes it, as well as the way that it unfolds in the present). For pro-transcription deputies, interruptions are best avoided because they prevent witnesses and litigants from delivering their narratives as they practiced it—in one go. This is what writing allows: the near-perfect repetition during the trial of a prepared script. By contrast, partisans of pure orality condemn the creation of such a script as the source of an unnatural fixity in the unfolding of trials, since it makes it easier and safer for witnesses to stick to their initial, written accounts, even in the face of new evidence contradicting their stories.[69] In their eyes, the transcription of proceedings resembles the ancien régime practice of punishing witnesses who deviate from their initial statements (with penalties up to and including death), insofar as the two yield the same result: witnesses and litigants who refuse to make even minor adjustments to their narratives, turning honest mistakes into deliberate lies and making it impossible for the parties to reach a consensus, let alone conciliation.[70] Pro-orality deputies embrace instead the fallibility of witnesses and litigants and uphold their right to be fragile, sensitive, and human and to amend their stories as new facts come to light, because, to them, trials are not the ultimate performance of preexisting scripts but a collective, impromptu debate. Hence, according to Thouret, "the jurors see and hear the witnesses and accused hounding and pressing each other, making the truth appear through their agonistic debate. As the debate progresses and becomes more animated, they develop a 'conviction intime.'"[71] Truth here does not precede adversarial debate but emerges through it; it does not reside in the meticulous preparation and repetition of a script but in the movement of the trial itself, which grows increasingly lively and unscripted, until the jurors arrive at the correct conviction.

Yet how do, in fact, heated, fast-paced, oft-interrupted debates reveal the truth? Thouret provides an answer above, when he states that "signs of truth can only be produced by movement and heat; they only escape in moments of self-forgetting." Like his opponents, Thouret believes that unexpected, intense emotions can break down the speakers' script, disrupt their rehearsed self-presentation, and reveal, in that moment of self-loss, the "unconscious body." Yet whereas the pro-transcription deputies deem the unconscious body to be ambiguous, just as likely to show fear and inexperience as it is guilt, the supporters of pure orality view it as a reliable site of truth. Jean-Baptiste-Charles Chabroud, for instance, extols the legibility of the body when he argues that one gesture can change the perception of an entire deposition,[72] a vital source of knowledge that would be lost, Jérôme Pétion de Villeneuve warns, if transcripts, which cannot record "bearing, gaze, gestures, all the living expressions of the soul," were allowed to play any part in legal judgment.[73] This notion that the inner truth of subjects, their "soul," shines through most clearly in their gestures and other physical signs because, unlike speech, they are involuntary, is of course far from original. We saw it in the

Calas plays' emphasis on the moments when bodies escape conscious control, through sleep or overpowering emotions. And we could see it in countless other eighteenth-century texts, since the belief that a spontaneous gesture is more meaningful and powerful than anything mediated through reason, including speech, is a central tenet of sentimentalism. Never before, however, had the legibility of the body been enshrined as law.

In *The Sentimental Theater of the French Revolution*, Feilla echoes Anne Vila's call in *Enlightenment and Pathology* to "re-somatize" our understanding of eighteenth-century psychology, philosophy, politics, ethics, and aesthetics, and sets out to answer it by showing the centrality of the "sensitive, reactive and expressive body" in the theater and political oratory of the French Revolution.[74] This call, however, remains unanswered in other fields, including one so understudied that it tellingly goes unmentioned by Vila: the legal realm.[75] Regrettably, the importance of the body in eighteenth-century judicial thought and practice has been almost entirely overlooked. This may partly be a consequence of the long tradition in early modern justice, unlike in the other fields cited by Vila, of hiding the body through a focus on writing and secrecy. Yet this tradition makes the emergence of the body as a locus of judicial truth all the more contentious, complex, and interesting. Indeed, the rise of the "sensitive, reactive and expressive body" does not unfold in the legal realm in quite the same way that it does in the fields listed by Vila (with the exception, perhaps, of politics). This is due, I contend, to the fact that the pro-orality deputies were faced with a unique dilemma, stemming from their embrace of ideas regarding the body drawn from sentimentalism, a generally antitheatrical worldview, at precisely the same time they instituted openly theatrical criminal proceedings through the introduction of public trials, live debate, and legal representatives.

Indeed, their hostility to the preparation and repetition of scripts, akin in their eyes to a dangerous form of acting, mirrors the view of ancien régime jurists.[76] This shared belief could have inspired the partisans of pure orality to borrow from the antitheatrical system of their predecessors, for instance by rising against the defendants' new rights to a lawyer, advance knowledge of the charges and evidence against them, and a public trial. Yet never do any of them even consider sacrificing the publicity, agonistic debates, and legal representation so central to liberal justice. The challenge they face, as a result, is how to summon the sensitive, spontaneous, nontheatrical body that is, in their sentimental worldview, the surest source of truth, during a trial whose very structure encourages theatricality. Or, to put it in another way, how to defuse the threat of theatricality intrinsic to public speaking, given the witnesses' natural instinct to act and the incentive for litigants to compose, rehearse, and stick to a script. The rejection by the partisans of pure orality not only of writing but also of fixed forms, speaking orders, and every other attempt at curbing the emotions and spontaneity of the participants suggests a unique answer to this challenge: not to forbid the performance of justice (as in the ancien régime), nor to seek to control it (like the pro-transcription deputies), but on the contrary to free it from artificial rules, so that it would more closely resemble the original conflict at the heart of the trial. Actors—since, at the trial's start, they will almost inevitably be so—are encouraged to speak rapidly, interrupt each other, amend their stories as new facts come to light, and feel genuine emotions, until they gradually lose themselves in the heat and movement of the debate, forget their prepared scripts, and cease to act. At that moment, the trial turns into a true reenactment—a performance that, paradoxically, seeks its own dissolution as performance. It becomes a resurrection, not a representation, of the initial conflict, allowing the spectators (and, more importantly, the judges and jurors) to see the marks of guilt and innocence on the litigants' bodies as they relive, rather than narrate, the events leading to the trial.

After months of debate, this vision, and the partisans of pure orality, won the day. On September 29, 1791, the National Assembly adopted Beaumez's "Projet d'instruction sur la procédure criminelle," which completely revolutionized criminal procedure. It stated that nearly everyone, from the accused, accusers, and their counsel, to magistrates, jurors, and even "friends" of the accused (presumably a reference to *défenseurs officieux*, not to random acquaintances in the audience) would henceforth be allowed to interrogate and criticize the witnesses personally, in an attempt to discredit them and their testimonies. None of these exchanges, nor any other parts of the judicial process, would ever be transcribed.[77] As Mason has noted, this explicit rejection of writing is incompatible with the standard narrative of a broad cultural shift away from theatricality and toward textuality. In fact, she argues, the inverse was taking place, with legal proceedings becoming more like dramatic performances. This is undeniable, insofar as the decree of 1791 reaffirmed the provisional reforms of 1789: public trials, agonistic debates, and legal representation for all. As we have seen, however, the opposition to transcription signaled a rejection not only of textuality but of theatricality as well—a fascinating challenge to the usual, overly reductive textuality/theatricality dichotomy. Indeed, while justice certainly became, in the early years of the Revolution, more theatrical, that very fact led the deputies to attempt to turn that theatricality against itself, to create a kind of "atheatrical theater," an open-ended, fluid spectacle, consisting of spontaneous, passionate arguments, closer to a live reenactment of the original conflict or event than to a scripted representation of it.

The Aristophanic Revolution: Reenactment in the Theater

In January 1793, a single play, *L'Ami des lois*, proved so controversial that it provoked heated confrontations, pitting the Girondins against the Jacobins, the National Convention against the Commune, and thirty thousand citizens against several military divisions, possibly including two cannons. Few plays can claim to have had a comparable impact: not only did the dispute surrounding *L'Ami des lois* interrupt the king's trial, but it also inspired such significant developments as the incarceration and near execution of the actors of the Théâtre de la Nation and the reintroduction of dramatic censorship.[78] Before the premiere, two concerned actors visited Mercier to seek his counsel and protection, allegedly because he belonged to the Girondin party.[79] One wonders, however, why they chose Mercier, who had once clashed with the troupe of the Comédie-Française (now Théâtre de la Nation) and was not a particularly influential figure among the Girondins. Perhaps the actors felt that Mercier would have a unique insight into their situation, since the play they were about to perform—a transparent and virulent denunciation of two powerful politicians, Robespierre and Marat—perfectly exemplified the judicial theater that Mercier had long advocated. Indeed, *L'Ami des lois* constitutes the apex—the highest point, but also the beginning of the fall—of a dramatic genre that achieved great popularity between 1789 and 1793: satirical, accusatory plays in the style of Aristophanes. To study *L'Ami des lois* and, through it, other plays from the first years of the Revolution, is to see once more the depth of the period's faith in reenactment, both as a source of truth—a means of encouraging debate and revealing guilt or innocence—and as a source of closure—a means of resolving conflicts by repeating them.

Although Laya repeatedly denied any satirical intent, claiming instead to be a disciple of Molière, his play was immediately portrayed, by friends and foes alike, as the latest and greatest example of the rebirth in France of the judicial theater of antiquity.[80] For instance, the *Chronique de Paris*[81] and the

Correspondance littéraire[82] praised *L'Ami des lois* for having extended the law's reach to men (Robespierre and Marat) whose power placed them beyond it, replicating in the process Aristophanes's courageous denunciation of the demagogue Cleon in *The Knights*. The parallel was apt, as Laya's play clearly possessed the two principal attributes of judicial theater we saw in Chapter 2. First, it denounced odious criminals in a serious, indignant tone, thereby fulfilling Laya's wish, back in 1789, that the new theater of the Revolution become a battlefield "where war was waged on crime and tyranny, as it had once been on ridicule."[83] And second, it targeted real individuals, not fictional ones. Despite some doubts about the secondary characters, virtually everyone, including his own brother,[84] recognized Robespierre in Nomophage and Marat in Duricrâne.[85] More than just apt, in fact, the parallel to Aristophanes was, by 1793, something of a cliché. Starting in 1790, numerous newspapers described the transformations in the theater since the storming of the Bastille as a revival of ancient Greek drama. The *Chronique de Paris*, the *Mercure français* and the *Révolutions de Paris*, to name only a few, turned to Aristophanes and his comedies as a lens through which to examine the new theater of the Revolution, exactly as Palissot and his critics had done thirty years earlier in response to the premiere of *Les Philosophes*.[86]

There were, however, some significant differences in their portrayal of Aristophanes. Unlike in the 1760s, when Palissot's play sparked a genuine quarrel, comparisons to the Greek playwright in the early years of the Revolution were universally meant to be flattering, with newspapers of every political persuasion lavishing praise on the satirical comedies of ancient Greece—a telling sign that judicial theater had gained complete acceptance. Moreover, the Aristophanes eulogized in the Revolutionary press was always the same one: the intrepid author of *The Knights*, who had risked his life to expose corruption in the highest echelons of the Athenian state.[87] By contrast, the quarrel over *Les Philosophes* had primarily focused on a different Aristophanes, the creator of *The Clouds*, with Palissot and his supporters in one corner, trying to rehabilitate a vision of satirical theater as a governmental weapon against seditious freethinkers and, in the other corner, the *philosophes* condemning this vision, albeit uneasily given some of their past positions. The article in the *Correspondance littéraire* highlights this difference between 1760 and 1793. Like other reviews of *L'Ami des lois*, it begins by noting the similarities in content between Palissot's and Laya's plays, which both borrow their plots from Molière's *Femmes savantes*, but it argues that the two are ultimately incomparable, owing to their perfectly opposed aims—in the first, an official satirist targets private citizens; in the second, a private citizen targets public officials.[88] This second model, that of *The Knights* and *L'Ami des lois*, is the kind of judicial theater that Mercier and others had advocated in the 1770s but had never been able to bring to reality (even as audiences tried to summon it anyway, through their applications), precisely because, unlike Palissot's vision, it required that artists be protected from any governmental interference (whether through censorship or retaliation). It is not surprising, therefore, that these two developments—the unprecedented acceptance of judicial theater and its mutation into a single, especially democratic form—transpired in the early years of the Revolution, a period that also ended (albeit only temporarily) state interventionism in affairs of the stage.

Indeed, on January 13, 1791, a mere two days after a particularly heated quarrel on the proper dramaturgy of trials, the National Assembly passed a law prohibiting governmental oversight over the theater. Article 1 lifted previous restrictions on the number and variety of theaters in Paris, while article 6 officially put an end to censorship.[89] Some deputies opposed this loss of state control, from fear that liberating speech in this way would transform the theater into a political weapon in the hands of factions. L'abbé Maury even warned that such liberty "could put the Assembly at risk of seeing itself played on stage," although Mirabeau cleverly ridiculed this fear of reenactive theater with the flippant response that l'abbé Maury need not worry about Mélitus (the magistrate then believed to have paid Aristophanes to write *The Clouds*), as he was no Socrates.[90] To be fair, however, l'abbé Maury's fears were far from unreasonable. Like the judicial reforms of 1791, the abolition of censorship promoted orality over textuality, since playwrights could now alter their plays to comment on the latest scandals and celebrities, and actors could now stray from the script as they saw fit, without the risk of legal repercussions. As a result, theater became, like the new criminal proceedings, less of a controlled and controllable "reading" and more of an unpredictable "happening." The law of January 13 thus brought about similar changes in the dramatic world as would the reforms of 1791 in the justice system—a liberation of speech, an embrace of polyphony, improvisation, and difference, and an invitation to resurrect recent conflicts and events.

Above all, the theatrical and legal spheres merged because, thanks to the abolition of censorship, playwrights and actors gained the freedom to expose, by means of (purportedly) faithful reenactments, criminal or unjust actions sometimes only a few weeks old. This judicial theater, its popularity boosted by the discord and suspicion at the heart of Revolutionary politics, was soon employed by every party, be it to denounce the sinful secrets of Jacques Necker, Mirabeau, and the Marquis de Lafayette, as in *La Journée des dupes*, of the judges of the Châtelet, as in *Le Procès de Socrate*, of Robespierre and Marat, as in *L'Ami des lois*, or even of Louis XVI, as in *La Journée de Varennes*.[91] The latter, performed just one month (to the day) after the king's flight, caused the newspaper the *Feuille du jour* to lament: "Will the department suffer that the king appear on a theater as before a tribunal? Isn't this way of bringing him to judgment the lowest of them all and the most degrading for the throne?"[92] The judicial language in this article highlights the theater's acquisition of a new function in the early years of the Revolution, that of a national tribunal. Indeed, dramatic satires like *La Journée de Varennes*, although similar in some ways to courtroom dramas, entertained a different, even more daring relationship to justice, insofar as they reenacted on stage recent criminal acts, rather than already completed trials, and could be, as a result, legitimately considered to *be* trials.

The cynic in all of us may find it hard to believe that such reenactments were genuinely seen as trials and not just as political propaganda. Yet it should be remembered, as playwrights and journalists often noted, that dramatic accusations, like judicial ones, were not accepted uncritically but were subject to the judgment of an autonomous, highly participatory audience. For Louis-Marie Prudhomme, a judicial play meant the opening of a debate, not a guaranteed conviction: "If the author is wrong, the pure life and exemplary conduct of the accused official will be enough to refute him."[93] Indeed, much suggests that, contrary to conventional wisdom, Revolutionary drama, especially before 1793, functioned far better as a forum than it did as a rostrum or, in judicial terms, better as a tribunal than as a scaffold.[94] By reproducing the accusations, counteraccusations, and pleas of multiple parties, reenactments proved particularly successful in engaging their spectators in contemporary debates. For instance, Prudhomme welcomed the lengthy, fiery "debate" at the Opéra on the nature of a Frenchman's love for his queen and criticized the tenor Étienne Lainez for having taken it upon himself to be the queen's "lawyer" (note, once more, the judicial language), because his decision to (literally) sing the queen's praises had cut the debate short and deprived the spectators of their right to judge.[95] Nowhere is this vision of reenactments as deliberative and interactive more evident than in Prudhomme's plan for a specially built theater on which the debates of the National Assembly would be recreated verbatim by trained impersonators of the leading deputies. Tellingly, Prudhomme chooses as an example the 1791 debate on the inviolability of the king, following his flight to Varennes—a judicial question that would become central to his trial, a year and a half later. As Prudhomme makes clear, reenacting legislative sessions would encourage spectators to debate current issues and pass judgment on their representatives (in this case, not only the deputies but the king himself).[96]

Revolutionary audiences eagerly accepted this invitation to assume the role of legal, rather than aesthetic, judges. As we saw in Chapter 2, judicial theater incites its viewers to focus their attention on content rather than form—to judge, in the words of the Revolutionary Paul Perrière, as "citizens" rather than as "spectators."[97] Newspaper reports corroborate this rejection of aesthetic judgment, notably when they mention that audiences often abstained from applauding actors playing the role of villains, for fear that applause for the artist would be misconstrued as an endorsement of the character's principles.[98] On occasion, spectators would even demand that the actors playing villains return to the stage once the play had ended and they were no longer in character, so as to be sure to applaud only their craft.[99] Not surprisingly, this non-aesthetic reception of judicial theater found an echo in the relationship between actor and character. As Jean-Marie Collot d'Herbois boasted about his satirical play, *Le Procès de Socrate*, "in other plays, one applauds the actors as artists; in this play, one applauds them as good citizens."[100] Such praise is the mirror image of Perrière's: instead of the spectators becoming citizens, it is now the actors who do.[101] What makes the actors good citizens, Collot d'Herbois explains, is their complete identification with their characters and with the Revolutionary values of the play, which ensures that they are less acting than they are sincerely proclaiming their own beliefs. This vision of the theater as a true reenactment blurs the distinction between actor and character, who appear to become one and the same. This is true, as we saw above, in the spectators' eyes. It is true, as well, for the playwrights, who tried to narrow the gap between actor and character. For instance, Ruggieri's *La Prise de la Bastille*—one of more than a dozen reenactments of the storming of the Bastille—featured as performers men who had (allegedly) participated in the momentous event.[102] Lastly, it is true for the actors themselves. Hence, Jean-Baptiste-Jacques Grammont turned down the role of the capitoul in Laya's *Jean Calas*, even though he usually played villains, and even after Laya tried to reassure him that "the repulsiveness of these types of roles never stains the actor who performs them."[103] Grammont thus revealed his understanding that, in a reenactment, his performance would not be seen merely as a representation, but as a merging of his identity with that of the real-life fanatic responsible for Calas's execution. The same fear inspired the singer François Lay, better known as Lays, to send a letter to several newspapers, in which he asked that the journalist Prudhomme take better care to distinguish in his reviews between "*Lays the singer*" and "*Lays the citizen*"—that is, that Prudhomme recognize that the words sang or spoken by an actor while in character bore no relation to his beliefs.[104]

As a type of reenactment—a performance that seeks to negate its own theatricality—it is not surprising that judicial theater promoted such a nonaesthetic ideal for performers and viewers alike. Against expectations, however, this rejection of the aesthetic did not arise from a Diderotian absorption into the fiction. The inclusion of identifiable events and figures, far from leading to a greater illusion, actually had the inverse effect.[105] Indeed, however much a performer might try to truly incarnate a specific, real-life person rather than represent a generic character, as La Rochelle did in *L'Ami des lois* when he reproduced to perfection the clothes and gestures of Marat,[106] Revolutionary spectators were never going to believe that the real Marat was on stage, precisely because the actual existence of Marat meant they could not forget this was an imitation, and that they were in a theater. Yet that same proximity to reality encouraged the spectators to express their opinions on the real Marat, instead of on the artistic qualities of the play. Judicial theater thus established a unique relationship to the stage, in which the spectators came to the theater not to engage in an aesthetic judgment (of actors), nor to lose themselves in the story (of fictional characters), but rather to deliberate, like a jury, on guilt and innocence (of real-life individuals). For Prudhomme and others, the theater became a site, as it had been in ancient Greece, where citizens gathered to "debate and illuminate national causes and cases" in the hope of reaching a public consensus.[107]

Indeed, the supporters of judicial theater had great faith in its ability not only to expose the truth but also to bolster national unity. Such faith may seem strange to us, who can only imagine unchecked, often politically motivated accusations as an endless source of discord. This is to overlook, however, the sincere belief among many Revolutionaries in the infallibility and unanimity of public opinion. For Mercier, whose vision of judicial theater most closely mirrors the early Revolutionaries', and for Prudhomme, who insists, as we saw above, that a false accusation would never be entertained by the people,[108] individual spectators may disagree at first but when gathered in a group and asked to serve as a jury, they will come to speak in the single, virtuous voice of the nation. Hence, in an article written in January 1791 in response to the newly decreed end of censorship, Prudhomme reassures his readers that the public is "a tribunal more severe and virtuous than the courts ever were" and that it can be trusted to punish "any foolhardy writer who'd dare attack the sanctity of laws."[109] Theatrical accusations thus always unite their viewers in virtuous indignation, whether it is directed at the guilty official whose crimes are reenacted on stage or at the irresponsible playwright who made a baseless accusation.

Judicial theater further strengthens national unity by deliberately using its accusations to deter potential dissidents. This strategy can be summarized as such: denounce a few to convert the rest. In Mercier's eyes, judicial theater deters from crime by revealing to the people that criminals never succeed in staying hidden: always awaiting them is the shame of a public accusation and punishment. Even the mighty Robespierre and Marat will one day find a Laya to hold them accountable—an important lesson for would-be radicals in the parterre. But the judicial theater of the Revolution goes even further: often, the conversion to virtue is already staged within the play itself. For instance, Laya includes a generic, "good" Jacobin, Filto, alongside the immediately identifiable and utterly evil Jacobins, Nomophage and Duricrâne. Filto grows in importance throughout the play, until the last scene, when his outrage at the extremism, false patriotism, and greed of his accomplices finally moves him to join the more moderate, virtuous Forlis. Laya's inclusion of Filto is shrewd: it partly shields him from the inevitable accusation that his play is nothing more than Girondin propaganda by enabling his supporters to claim that he aims not to denounce all Jacobins, but only two, responsible for leading the party astray. Laya thus describes Filto in his preface as an invitation to Jacobins who share some of Robespierre's beliefs, but not his crimes, to follow Filto's example and dissociate themselves from their extremist leaders.[110] No Jacobins in the audience were likely to recognize themselves in Nomophage and Duricrâne—because they are so transparently evil, and because they already stand in for real individuals—but, Laya argues, some might yet identify with, and imitate, the generic, virtuous Filto.

Laya employs the same reasoning to justify his largely positive depiction of the Baron de Versac, the royalist counterpart to the Jacobin Filto: "How can I inspire the start of a conversion, if not by rendering likable this deceived but honest man? If I make him a villain instead, aristocrats will decry it as exaggerated and deceitful."[111] By portraying noblemen in a nuanced and realistic manner, not as imbeciles or monsters (caricatures that were, by 1793, increasingly common on the French stage), Laya hopes to promote the identification and, ultimately, the conversion of the royalists in the audience. In that regard, *L'Ami des lois* follows the example set by countless plays in the first years of the Revolution, notably Beaumarchais's *La Mère coupable*, which ends with the Count Almaviva—perhaps the character most synonymous with aristocratic arrogance in eighteenth-century drama—embracing the new egalitarian regime.[112] These plays, catalogued and studied by Marie-Laurence Netter in her article "L'Intégration de nouvelles valeurs par le théâtre," all include well-meaning, if misguided, aristocrats and priests, who are slowly moved, by appeals to their reason and virtue, to support the Revolution.[113] In this theater of the early Revolution, characterized by Judith Schlanger as "tolerant," "optimistic," and "dialogical," royalists are not debased; they are allowed to speak and make their case, if only so as to then better refute their arguments and more convincingly stage their gradual conversion to the new regime.[114] Likewise, in *L'Ami des lois*, the final scene shows the beginning of Versac's conversion, immediately after Filto's—a telling repetition that underscores Laya's aim to denounce both extremes, royalists and radicals, in the hope that all Frenchmen will meet in the middle ground between absolutism and anarchy that, he believes, the Girondins occupy. Both the preface and the ending to *L'Ami des lois* thus reveal that Laya, like Mercier, views judicial theater as a public forum, a site of debate vital to the unity of the nation, thanks to its ability to resolve conflicts by reenacting them.

Reenacting the King's Trial: The Last Courtroom Drama?

Underlining the complex ties that bound justice and theater together in the early years of the Revolution, *L'Ami des lois* constitutes the period's best-known example not only of judicial theater but also of courtroom drama, thanks to its transparent reenactment of one of the most important trials in French history: the judgment of Louis XVI. It is surprising that this side of *L'Ami des lois* has never been studied,[115] since, as we will see, journalists of every political persuasion commented on the parallels between Laya's play and the king's trial. In doing so, they highlighted one of the most daring aspects of *L'Ami des lois*, more audacious even than the Calas plays: the fact that it reenacted an ongoing trial, whose outcome it could therefore still influence. To that end, Laya integrated into his play the principal events and controversies of Louis XVI's trial.[116] Hence, when Duricrâne stumbles upon a list of names and monetary sums misplaced by Forlis, the play's hero, he uses these vague financial records to accuse Forlis of secretly funding the nation's enemies. Likewise, the king was charged with treason, yet in the absence of much material evidence, the case against him rested heavily on the discovery among his private papers of a register of pensions and donations—proof, to his accusers, of a vast conspiracy to bribe men into joining the counter-Revolution.[117] To this accusation, Forlis and the king offered the same response—namely, that they merely gave to those in need, without any political design.[118]

Despite this defense, and against proper procedure, the Legislative Assembly elected to publish the king's register, in hope, according to David P. Jordan, of turning public opinion against him.[119] This decision played right into the Jacobins' hands, as it cultivated popular support for their stance that the king should be executed summarily, without a formal trial. Tellingly, Nomophage and Duricrâne employ the same stratagem in *L'Ami des lois* when they disseminate copies of Forlis's financial records with the intention of provoking a popular insurrection against him. Filto feebly protests that justice should be allowed to proceed free of interference, but he is promptly silenced by Duricrâne's rant against the legal system and its sluggishness, which he blames on listless judges and procedural forms that allow even the clearly guilty to engage in lengthy debates.[120] In light of this parallel, the scene where a violent mob, misled and riled by the Jacobins, nearly executes Forlis takes on both a new significance and a new signification. Forlis avoids such a tragic fate by demanding and obtaining a formal trial in compliance with the procedures established by the Revolution. In particular, he reclaims his rights, as a defendant, to be informed by the magistrates of the charges against him, to produce exculpatory evidence (a missing piece of his financial records) as well as witnesses (the people listed in the register), and to confront his accusers directly and publicly through a live debate.[121] Forlis's subsequent legal victory over Nomophage and Duricrâne can therefore be understood as an attempt by Laya to write a conclusion to the other great drama then captivating the nation, the king's pending judgment. In Laya's eyes, Louis XVI faced the same threat as Forlis: a Jacobin plot to use a popular insurrection as a means of executing a rival without a fair trial.

It is indeed true that at the precise moment Laya was writing his play, the Jacobins were arguing loudly and widely that there was no need to give Louis XVI his day in court, since he had already been convicted by the highest tribunal in France, the people, during the 10 August insurrection.

According to the Jacobins, a popular insurrection constituted a sublime moment, when the people briefly recovered their sovereign powers and, speaking in a single voice, dispensed an infallible justice. In this instance, the people's ruling—death—had been thwarted by the king's escape, and it now behooved the National Convention to execute this sovereign judgment and send Louis, without delay, to the scaffold. By contrast, the Girondins, like Forlis, upheld the right of all defendants, however guilty, to a trial conducted in accordance with the due process of law. Like any other defendant, Louis was entitled to the performance of justice instituted in the early years of the Revolution. As the Girondins made clear, to the Jacobins' dismay, this included a public trial and all the building blocks of a compelling defense: lawyers, witnesses, advance knowledge of the evidence, and a chance to confront one's accusers directly. Adhering closely to the standard performance of justice would, the Girondins claimed, make visible both the legality of the king's trial and the illegality of his actions. A fair trial would prove that the new Republican order was founded on the principle that the law applied to all equally, and a public trial would expose the king's crimes, thereby helping to convert the remaining doubters of Louis's guilt—notably the European nations then at war with France.

In the end, the Girondins and the Jacobins reached a de facto compromise. An unusual trial took place before the National Convention, allowing the king to defend himself in person and in public, with the help of lawyers, as the Girondins had wanted. Yet if it included certain attributes of the new, theatrical justice established in 1789, it lacked the elements introduced in 1791 to produce a more reenactive, dialogical performance. When reading transcripts of the king's trial—themselves a violation of the orality-only law of 1791—it quickly becomes clear that in the absence of defense witnesses, any cross-examination, and impartial magistrates (the deputies were, as the king's lawyers noted, at once his accuser and his judge), the proceedings did not unfold as a free and unscripted debate between parties presumed innocent, but rather as a one-sided, summary interrogation, with two primary objectives: confirming a narrative of guilt already accepted as fact by the magistrates and uncovering more information about likely accomplices. Far from a spontaneous, dialogical reenactment of a conflict, then, the king's trial more closely resembled the inquisitorial proceedings of the ancien régime—the very type of justice that many of the deputies now serving as judges had once condemned as evidence of the king's tyranny.

Laya's play dramatizes the struggle between these two judicial visions by juxtaposing insurrectional justice (which it condemns) and a dialogical, reenactive trial (which it praises). The unwarranted violence against Forlis's person and property (his house, notably, is burnt to the ground) illustrates that in the absence of laws and fixed procedures, it becomes far too easy for factions to mislead the people into committing crimes in the name of vigilantism. Insurrection cannot serve as a mode of justice, Laya argues throughout *L'Ami des lois*, because it shares the same flaws that legal reformers and Revolutionaries had so often denounced in the inquisitorial system of the ancien régime. Both begin with a narrative hostile to the accused, which is accepted as true before any interaction with them—a presumption of guilt that makes a fair trial by impartial judges impossible. Both then develop in secret, unbeknownst to the accused, who cannot as a result prepare a defense. What's more, in an insurrection, as in the ancien régime, accusers are under no obligation to make themselves known. Hence, Nomophage and Duricrâne deny any knowledge of the accusation against Forlis, leaving it to their henchmen to whip up the crowd.[122] Such anonymity prevents the accused from entering into a debate with their accusers and from proving that the accusations are motivated by personal animosity. *L'Ami des lois* thus shows, again and again, that popular insurrections, like inquisitorial trials, are perilously one-sided, secretive, expeditious, and arbitrary.

Strangely, however, Laya's play also constantly reaffirms, through the mouth of Forlis, the people's infallibility as judge. The solution to this apparent contradiction lies in the work performed by formal trials, which are designed to slow the progression of justice and establish a temporary equality between the litigants so as to allow the magistrates and the people to encounter different narratives, observe their confrontation and evolution, and from this, reach a correct verdict. As Forlis explains, the people can be misled, in a fleeting moment of passion, into committing a crime, but given time, they always feel regret and weep for their victim.[123] Hence, the same mob that was about to lynch Forlis without letting him speak gradually becomes convinced of his innocence by watching him debate his adversaries in a formal trial. Tellingly, in fact, although Forlis possesses written proof of his innocence, in the form of a missing piece of his financial records, the judges and the public never read it, as a group of witnesses appear in court and speak in Forlis's favor (a defense strategy denied to Louis by the Jacobins), with such eloquence that they render all material evidence moot.[124] In this dramatic conclusion, Laya foregrounds the forensic value of publicity, orality, spontaneity, and sensibility. As *L'Ami des lois* makes clear, even material evidence, such as a written register, can be deceptive. Unlike speech, and unlike physical signs of innocence and guilt, the written word is removed from its author, and as such, lends itself to distortion and exploitation. The only truly effective way to ascertain the truth, the play suggests, is to look for its imprint on the speeches and bodies of the litigants as they engage in a public, agonistic debate. *L'Ami des lois* thus concludes with a tribute to the Revolution's dialogical, reenactive mode of justice. Even the clearly guilty deserve a formal trial: the people, still in insurrection but having learned their lesson, refuse to sully their hands with the blood of Nomophage and drag instead the Jacobin to jail, in anticipation of his trial.[125] Laya hoped that his play would teach its spectators the same lesson, inspiring them to become "friends of the law" and demand that the king be granted a fair and formal trial.

More than just a critique of the king's pseudo-trial, in fact, *L'Ami des lois* offered an alternative to it, a second trial (happening at the same time as the first) that enabled the king, through the character of Forlis, to confront his accusers directly and publicly. This placed the spectators in the position of jurors, a role they eagerly assumed, wildly applauding, according to Jean-Baptiste Cléry, "all the allusions to His Majesty's trial,"[126] especially passages refuting the Jacobins' justifications for circumventing the laws: "Nomophage having repeated the maxim that rings out every day from the tribune of the Convention ever since the start of Louis XVI's trial—*the people's safety is the supreme law*—Filto responded: 'No, no, whatever the people's interest may command / If it strikes innocence, it is nothing more than a crime.' The applause that highlighted this passage made clear the audience's opinion on the judgment of the king."[127] In fact, the spectators ruled not only *against* the Jacobins but also *for* the king, by affirming through their applause the innocence of Forlis and his list and, by extension, that of the king and his register: "The spectators seize every allusion with fervor. When *Forlis* gives to the furious people *the list* that his enemies wish to use as proof of his treason, and the people, seeing that this *list* only contains *the names of some unfortunate fathers, whom Forlis helped rescue from a painful existence*, come back from their fatal mistake, lavish blessings on *their true friend*, and demand his persecutors be punished, then, the auditorium resounds with applause."[128] This dual approach, both for and against, fulfilled Laya's wishes, by transforming the Théâtre de la Nation into a tribunal where there simultaneously unfolded the trial of the Jacobins, the trial of the king, and the trial of the latter's trial.

That Louis, like Forlis, was repeatedly and enthusiastically exonerated in this tribunal no doubt explains the claim, first made by the Duc de Lévis in a speech welcoming Laya to the Académie Française, and then repeated by Laya himself, as well as by some subsequent historians, that if the Théâtre de la Nation had been as vast as the amphitheaters of ancient Greece, or if there had been a true leader in the parterre, the king would have been saved.[129] However self-aggrandizing and improbable this claim might seem to us today, it contained, perhaps, a kernel of truth. The king was not only aware of *L'Ami des lois* but seemed to believe that it could help his case. Why else would he request that a copy of the play be smuggled, at considerable risk, into his jail, so that he could read it just days before his judgment?[130] More tellingly yet, the Jacobins themselves warned, as justification for banning Laya's play, that it might be powerful enough to save the king's head.[131]

As we all know, the king's head was not, in fact, saved. *L'Ami des lois* failed, both as a defense of the importance of reenactment in legal proceedings and as a reenactment in its own right (since the fates of Forlis and Louis were not, ultimately, repetitions of one another). Not long after the king met an untimely end, so too did the play that had tried to save him, united in their defeat at the hands of the Jacobins. Indeed, the narrow vote to execute the king marked a turning point in the struggle between the Jacobins and the Girondins, tilting the balance in the former's favor. Within months, the triumphant Jacobins had forbidden *L'Ami des lois*, and it was not long before they reintroduced dramatic censorship and launched new forms of state involvement in the theater even more intrusive than the ancien régime's. In fact, *L'Ami des lois* proved to be, in my view, the Revolution's last true example both of judicial theater and of courtroom drama.[132] The decline of these two genres (at least in the form that Mercier had envisioned them) had deeper roots than the most immediately obvious one: the Jacobins' irritation at becoming the targets, in *L'Ami des lois* and other plays, of accusations beyond their control. As we will see in the next chapter, it also reflected the Jacobins' broader loss of faith in reenactment—and in free, spontaneous, adversarial debate—as a source of truth and reconciliation. Instead, the Jacobins increasingly came to see reenactment as a perilous performance of justice—a disillusionment that, I contend, goes a long way toward explaining the rise of the dramatic propaganda most often associated (far too reductively) with Revolutionary theater and of the radical vision and practice of justice that emerged during the Terror.

Chapter 7

The Curtain Falls on Judicial Theater and Theatrical Justice

Louis's Ghost, or the New Calas

Seeking an illustration of the historical right of Frenchmen to try their kings, the deputy Jean-Baptiste Mailhe exhumed a strange tale: "A French citizen stopped the funeral procession of William-the-Conqueror, accused him of having stolen his field, and only allowed the king's body to be taken to its final resting place after this property had been returned to him."[1] Mailhe thus affirmed, inadvertently, the ability of trials to transcend death itself by interrupting funeral processions—two rituals in many ways perfectly opposed, insofar as trials seek to unearth the past, and memorial services, to bury it. Interestingly, it was precisely this necromantic power, implicitly praised by Mailhe, that increasingly came to motivate the Jacobins' opposition to the trial of Louis Capet. Instead of a trial, the Jacobins contended, the National Convention should stage a funeral mass, a ceremony through which the already deceased king would be cast into eternal oblivion. Medically speaking, of course, Louis was still alive in 1792, but the Jacobins often noted that he had essentially been killed during the 10 August insurrection, his escape having merely postponed the execution of the death sentence handed to him by the people.[2] On December 3, Robespierre first voiced the odd claim that the king, not just the monarchy, had been "annihilated by the people."[3] More explicitly yet, his brother Augustin labeled Louis a "cadaver"[4] before Pierre Philippeaux stripped the king of even more of his substance, dubbing him a "political ghost," the rotting corpse of which contributed, no doubt, to the "mortiferous emissions" poisoning the minds and bodies of the deputies.[5] Death seems, indeed, to have reigned over the Convention or, at least, over the minds of the Jacobins, who saw ghosts everywhere[6]—a clear indication that a proper burial was needed, starting with a ceremony conducted with "the solemnity of a funeral," to quote Bertrand Barère,[7] and closing with the king's summary execution. Only this final act could bring to an end Louis's existence as a ghost—that is, as a being at once dead and yet disturbingly alive.

Accordingly, the Jacobins feared granting Louis's ghost the public platform of a formal trial, pointedly asking, with Robespierre, "when a king has been annihilated by the people, who has the right to resurrect him to make him a new pretext for unrest and rebellion?"[8] In their eyes, to try the king signified nothing short of resurrecting him, particularly if the Convention observed the legal forms established two years earlier, as the Girondins wanted. Indeed, as we have seen, the reforms of 1791 were meant to encourage a sincere and spontaneous reenactment—a true resurrection, not just a repetition, of the conflict and antagonists at the heart of the trial. It was during the proceedings against the king that the Jacobins most clearly and decisively came to doubt this resurrectionist conception of justice. Their response to the Girondins' plea for a fair and formal trial reveals that they had begun to lose faith in a reenactment's ability to offer truth and reconciliation by countering the theatricality inherent in public proceedings.

For instance, they argued that a legal reenactment inevitably consisted of an inaccurate repetition, because it rested upon the erasure of precisely that which it was intended to reveal—culpability. To grant the king a trial was to presume him innocent,[9] thereby obliterating past and present crimes constitutive of his identity. For the Jacobins, the 10 August marked a decisive victory of good over evil; as such, it could not be reenacted in a trial, which is designed to stage, at least initially, a conflict between two morally neutral parties. This foundational principle of liberal justice—accused and accuser enter the tribunal as equals—thus failed to reproduce the reality of most conflicts, in which, according to the Jacobins, there existed moral absolutes, having less to do with particular events than with the participants' identities. This Manichean perspective found perhaps its best articulation in Louis Antoine de Saint-Just's famous aphorism: "One cannot reign innocently."[10] For Saint-Just, the king's guilt was intrinsic to his very being, to his social status at birth, rather than to any specific opinion or action. By 1793, this view was widely held by the Jacobins. Hence, in the midst of the king's trial, the deputy Prieur took the floor at the National Convention to reject Laya's claim that *L'Ami des lois* could inspire "honest aristocrats" to embrace the Revolution, on the grounds that one could not be both honest and an aristocrat.[11] Likewise, a few days later, Prudhomme ridiculed the notion that noblemen—"these suspicious and incurable men"—could ever be converted.[12] According to this essentialist worldview, guilt preceded not only the trial (no presumption of innocence), but crime itself. This made reenactment impossible, since there lacked a specific event to reenact. It also made it ineffective, whether as a source of reconciliation or of truth. Aristocrats in the audience, given their innate villainy, would never be converted by a legal or dramatic spectacle, thereby foreclosing any chance of reconciliation. Nor would a legal reenactment reveal the truth. Quite the opposite: instead of revealing the accused's culpability, it threatened to obscure it, or worse, to assign it, however briefly, to the accuser (since both are equally innocent and guilty at the start of the trial). It amounted to the blasphemous implication that innocence and the people, guilt and the nobility, might not be at all times, and for all time, synonymous.

The reenactment of a conflict also encouraged a dialogical approach that the Jacobins found objectionable. Indeed, it was not only individuals with no place in a republic (kings and aristocrats) who were resurrected, it was their arguments as well: "By opening an arena to the champions of Louis XVI, you are reviving the battle between despotism and liberty, you are consecrating the right to blaspheme against the Republic and the people."[13] The Jacobins often spoke of the public realm in religious terms ("consecrate," "blaspheme") because they believed, with the assuredness of the devout, in an absolute, dualistic opposition between good and evil, with the result that any disagreement, indeed, any polyphony at all, was instantly discarded as sacrilegious. For the Jacobins, the people's triumph on the 10 August had opened a new era of social and political homogeneity, a unity that could only be sustained through the exclusion of all forms of otherness. As a result, to reenact the crimes that preceded it would not, as the Girondins claimed, resolve residual tensions (unity via catharsis) but would on the contrary renew the quarrels of the pre-Republican era (disunity via repetition). Tribunals were to function less as arenas than as churches, in which the ceremonial eradication of those no longer members of society could be conducted.

This mortuary brand of justice irritated Nicolas de Condorcet, who alleged that "the secret partisans of the throne, by a rushed judgment of the king, are eager to *bury* with him all the crimes of the royalty."[14] To the Girondins, too expeditious a trial amounted to the burial not only of Louis but also of his crimes. By contrast, a meticulous, public reenactment of the king's transgressions would provide closure to those already convinced of Louis's guilt and help convert the others—essential steps toward a more unified nation. In response, Robespierre and the Jacobins argued that "to demand a trial for Louis XVI is to try the Revolution itself."[15] The 10 August had already united the people into a republic; to try the king anew would undermine this unity, by calling into question the permanence and legitimacy of the ruling that had brought the people together. It would, the Jacobins feared, transform justice into theater, into an act that can be endlessly reiterated, each new repetition bringing with it a new audience and, as a result, the possibility of a different verdict. Briefly stated, for the Girondins, unity could not precede repetition, whereas for the Jacobins, a trial's reproducibility meant an unsettled republic, forever on trial. As a result, for every attempt by the Girondins to replicate the trial, there was a counter-attempt by the Jacobins to bury it, as when they defeated the *appel au peuple*, a Girondins-led proposal to submit the Convention's judgment to the ratification of the municipal assemblies. To do so, the Jacobins argued, would be to renew the contentious deliberations of the Convention and thus sow factionalism and disunity throughout France.

Reenactment posed a grave threat in the eyes of the Jacobins, not only because it kept defeated enemies and their arguments alive, producing ghosts and endless, divisive trials, but also because it transformed the individuals and conflicts that it resurrected, obscuring the very truth it claimed to reveal. We already saw one such transformation—from "intrinsically guilty" to "presumed innocent"—but others were even more devious, due to the ease with which a supposedly spontaneous and objective resurrection of the past could be rehearsed and altered to help a particular side. As proof, the Jacobins could point to the theater. Indeed, *L'Ami des lois* may have been the most explicit and controversial example of a play seeking to influence the king's trial by reproducing elements of it on stage, but it was far from the only one. According to the press, spectators also found in *La Chaste Suzanne* an opportunity to show their support for the king by applauding the acquittal of the titular heroine, saved by Daniel (a doppelganger of the king's lawyer, Desèze) at the precise moment that the false accusations of old men (the Jacobins) appeared to have condemned her to death.[16] The authors of *La Chaste Suzanne* encouraged this interpretation by including a scene in which the old men tried to join Suzanne's judges but were rebuked with these words: "you are his accusers, you cannot be his judges"—a clear echo of Desèze's famous declaration during his plea in defense of the king, just ten days before the play's premiere: "I seek judges among you and only see accusers!"[17] Likewise, at the Théâtre des Italiens, the play *Raoul, sire de Créqui* received wild ovations from the king's supporters—first, because it staged the suffering of a family unjustly imprisoned, and second, because it ended with the innocent father regaining his freedom.[18] Similar motives caused the spectators at the Théâtre du Marais to exult when the protagonist of *Le Tribunal redoutable* survived his brush with the law.[19] The Jacobins had good cause, therefore, to accuse Parisian theaters of seeking to manipulate the public perception of the king's trial.[20]

In particular, the Jacobins often accused the Girondins of seeking, through plays, songs, and newspaper articles, to obscure the true story of the king's trial by deflecting attention from his crimes onto the suffering that his imprisonment was causing him. This accusation was not unwarranted: Aurore Chéry has noted the rise of a "staging of intimacy" in the press, leading to a partial eclipse of the trial's public, political elements by its more personal, human dimension: a man, anxious and alone in his cell, faced with his own mortality.[21] The Jacobins responded by suppressing all depictions of the king as an ordinary, sensitive human being. Whether it be his daily existence as a prisoner (the Commune decreed in December that there would no longer be reports "on that which regards the inmates personally")[22] or his demeanor during his execution (the Convention refused to publish a report on the king's last day), the Jacobins agreed that "the tyrant's private life must be *buried* in the deepest oblivion."[23] Interestingly, in both instances, Jacques Hébert warned that such reports would inspire pity for a tyrant. This shows a striking lack of confidence in the standard belief among French sentimental writers, notably Diderot, that a spectator only feels compassion toward a virtuous victim. Indeed, underpinning judicial theater and theatrical justice alike was the conviction that impartial beholders instinctively identify with (and thus identify) wronged parties. To the Jacobins, the king's trial revealed that the people could be manipulated into feeling pity for any individual, even the most unquestionably guilty, like the king, so long as he or she was shown to be suffering. This, in the Jacobins' eyes, constituted one of the central problems of modern liberal justice: it lavishes attention on the accused, displaying them throughout the trial in a position of weakness, danger, and captivity, which encourages the audience to identify with them, regardless of their guilt.

The Jacobins' disillusionment with pity, notably their growing sense that it could be stage-managed, explains their anger and concern at the omnipresence of a sentimental script hidden within supposedly exact, impartial reenactments. With each new maudlin tale of the king's anguish at being separated from his wife and children, or of his generosity toward a sickly servant,[24] the Jacobins grew more and more anxious that Louis was being resurrected not as a tragic tyrant but as a character in a bourgeois drama. Hence, in *La Mort de Louis XVI* (published, but not performed, in 1793), the king first appears as a peacefully sleeping figure, like Jean Calas in the plays by Chénier and Lemierre. In the next scenes, Louis acts as a loving and patient tutor to his son, with one especially apropos lesson on the execution of Charles I of England. The play ends with the tearful separation of Louis and his children, who, in a poignant moment, volunteer to take his place on the scaffold—another echo of the three Calas plays.[25] In fact, the recasting of the king into a new role may have begun to influence reality, since some of Louis's actual jailers supposedly became convinced of his innocence, like the priest in Chénier's play, simply from witnessing the serenity of his sleep.[26] A lengthy, broadly publicized trial, the Jacobins feared, would only give the king's partisans further opportunities to promote the image of Louis as a domestic everyman, stoic victim of a pitiless legal system—that is, of Capet as a reincarnated Calas.

Even before the king's trial, an intense dread of repetition had begun to haunt the Jacobins. As early as August 1792, just days after the 10 August insurrection, they set out to obliterate the ancien régime from living memory by destroying the symbols through which it had reproduced itself into a kind of immortality.[27] Starting with the trial, however, this policy of erasure and forgetting took on a new, macabre dimension, as the Jacobins' fear of resurrection led them to target the very bodies—not just the replicas—of the monarchy. Whereas up until the Revolution the remains of deceased kings and queens had been embalmed so as to preserve them after death, the corpses of Louis, Marie-Antoinette, and their son were covered with quicklime in order to hasten their disintegration. More tellingly yet, on July 31, 1793, the Convention endorsed Barère's proposal that the first anniversary of the 10 August insurrection be celebrated by disinterring the monarchs of France, dousing their remains with quicklime, and discarding them in unmarked graves.[28] Such a ceremony meant the corpses of the monarchy were treated much as the Jacobins had wished that Louis himself be handled—as cadavers that had not been properly disposed of, that retained a strange power over the living and, as such, needed to be buried once more, but this time in such a way as to ensure their utter oblivion. Indeed, the fears of the Jacobins—that the monarchs were not quite dead, that they could, like ghosts, rise from the grave—were confirmed by the astonishingly good state of preservation in which many of the bodies were found, notably that of Henri IV, who was displayed to passersby for several days, as well as reportedly struck by a woman for "having borne the scepter,"[29] and that of Louis XIV, whose features were unchanged but whose face had turned pitch black, a reflection of his soul, if not of his moniker (the Sun King). The destruction of these undead monarchs consisted of a fitting celebration for the 10 August insurrection because, unlike the trial of Louis, which had been forced upon the Jacobins, it served not as a reenactment of the 10 August, but rather as its finale—a burial ceremony in which the dead were not remembered but, on the contrary, obliterated once and for all.

Ending Judicial Theater

Yet it is a sad truth that one can disinter and destroy the bodies of monarchs only once. As a result, if this macabre ceremony offered a suitable answer to the question of how to commemorate the 10 August without reviving the very conflicts and foes that the insurrection had supposedly eradicated, it did not resolve the issue for subsequent anniversaries, be they of the 10 August or of other similarly pivotal but divisive events in the Republic's brief history. Hence, when the time came in January 1794 to determine how, if at all, the death of Louis XVI would be celebrated, the debate started anew. One member of the Jacobins club proposed a reenactment of the king's execution: "let us make effigies of every king at war against us and let us cut off their heads."[30] This parade of royal effigies is evocative of the burlesque procession in *Le Jugement dernier des rois*, Sylvain Maréchal's hugely popular play, widely seen, then as now, as a ritual reenactment of the king's trial and execution.[31] It comes as no surprise, then, that during the same debate, Saintexte demanded that Maréchal's play be performed on every Parisian theater on the anniversary of the king's death.[32] The same week, the *Révolutions de Paris* called for a "French Shakespeare" to create an even more accurate reenactment: a play reproducing Louis's trial, not that of foreign monarchs, to be staged throughout France on the date of the king's execution.[33] As a group, however, the Jacobins rejected these three distinct but similar proposals for a dramatic recreation of the king's trial and execution. The fact that they ultimately settled, as we will see, on a very different kind of commemoration reveals that the Jacobins' loss of faith in the forensic and cathartic value of reenacting recent conflicts extended beyond legal proceedings, stretching to the world of the stage in a manner that sounded the death knell of judicial theater.[34]

And yet, at first, judicial theater appeared to receive a boost from the king's trial. So high were the stakes and passions that dozens of irreverent, aggressive comedies soon emerged, often accusing specific priests, noblemen, kings, and Girondins of crimes against the nation.[35] *Le Jugement dernier des rois* perfectly exemplifies this trend of "sans-culottes theater," in which political and clerical icons are paraded, lampooned, adorned comically, often in the clothes of the wrong gender, beaten with sticks, and made to brawl for scraps of food, to the spectators' delight.[36] These plays, it is true, differ from the judicial theater typical of the early years of the Revolution. Most notably, sans-culottes satires deprive the accused (both the characters on stage and the real individuals off it) of the chance to respond by depicting them as silent, grotesque caricatures. Such plays do not seek to inspire debate and reconciliation; on the contrary, they present themselves explicitly as instruments of vengeance, as outlets through which largely plebeian and inexperienced spectators can release their hatred and indignation.[37] Nevertheless, they remain judicial acts. Jean-Marie Apostolidès thus notes that the famous procession scene in *Le Jugement dernier des rois*, with its litany of accusations against real, foreign monarchs, who stand silently while their crimes against the nation are booed by a popular jury (the spectators), evokes the Revolutionary Tribunal of the Terror.[38] Likewise, Mark Darlow finds in Maréchal's play a vision of justice consonant with terrorist ideology, notably in its elliptic erasure of a formal trial, replaced by the immediacy and infallibility of the general will.[39] In short, if *Le Jugement dernier des rois* and plays like it look nothing like *L'Ami des lois*, it is not because they aren't judicial theater, but rather because they grow out of a different conception of justice, not the accusatorial model of the early Revolution, but the insurrectional vision defended by the Jacobins during the king's trial, in which guilt is innate and absolute, debate and repetition mislead, and a trial consists of a summary purging of the nation's enemies.

The plays' undeniable Republicanism and their conformity to the vision of justice at the time make it all the more surprising and revealing, then, that the Jacobins actively opposed them. Indeed, from the Committee of Public Safety's interdiction of several anticlerical farces[40] and Robespierre's victorious struggle against *Le Jugement dernier des rois*[41] to the Commission of Public Instruction's forceful indictment of "Hébertism in the arts,"[42] it becomes possible to piece together a manifestly concerted effort by the Jacobins to bring an end to sans-culottes theater. As has often been noted, the dubious morality and artistry of these burlesque plays—particularly evident in their more farcical, popular attributes—were a significant reason for the Jacobins' opposition, but I wish to suggest another, more closely related to the plays' status as judicial theater. On what grounds, after all, did the Jacobins overwhelmingly reject Saintexte's proposal that *Le Jugement dernier des rois* be performed on the anniversary of the king's execution? Not on moral or aesthetic ones, but rather because they preferred that the king's trial be forgotten. In fact, they were far from alone in wishing this, according to Letassey, a secret agent for the Ministry of the Interior, who reports that unidentified citizens gathered at the National Convention to protest, "What's the use of reminding true Republicans of this monster?"[43] As kings, noblemen, and priests multiplied on stage, even if only as caricatures, the Jacobins expressed increasing astonishment and irritation at this theatrical life after death, notably in the *Feuille du Salut Public*, the official newspaper of the Committee of Public Safety: "These enemies of the people have been annihilated. Why should their characters survive on stage?"[44] The *Journal des Spectacles* echoed this critique in a series of articles, in which it warned that representing vanquished enemies of the people not only resurrected them, it revived their beliefs and their followers as well: "persecutions are only good at making converts for the persecuted."[45] Moreover, it added, trying priests and noblemen on stage had little utility, since they no longer existed as a social category and were, in any case, incurable.[46] Such critiques are particularly suggestive, for they do not concern the artistic or moral defects of the burlesque genre but expose a broader unease with judicial theater. They show that the Jacobins, like the early Revolutionaries, believed in the theater's ability to resurrect the past, not just represent it, but that, unlike them, they did not view such reenactments as an opportunity for correcting and reconciling with the past, but rather as frightening ceremonies, adept at bringing deceased enemies and forgotten conflicts back to life. Their opposition to judicial theater thus mirrored their condemnation of theatrical justice during the king's trial—in both instances, they feared the ghosts that reenactment would summon.

Judicial theater, in fact, raised an additional issue: its ghosts came to life through the performance of actors. We have seen, in previous chapters, the fears elicited by actors and their empty speech—anxieties that both inspired the dream of reenactment and never ceased to gnaw at it. Not surprisingly, given their devotion to Rousseauian transparency, the Jacobins worried about the actor's ability to deceive and manipulate. Yet it is fascinating to see that, at least in the context of judicial theater, the Jacobins expressed even greater concern at the possibility that the speech of actors might *not* be empty. For centuries, empty speech had given actors, while on stage, a sort of impunity, allowing them, like the jesters of old, to incarnate roles (such as that of princes) forbidden to other classes, and even to act as mild censors, without the risk of being held accountable before a court of law. This relative impunity largely disappeared in December of 1789, when the National Assembly granted actors, along with executioners, full citizenship, giving them new rights, certainly, but also legal responsibility for any idea they expressed, even while in character.[47] Indeed, according to the law of January 13, 1791, while a play could no longer be censored before its first performance, actors could now be held legally responsible for the disturbances it provoked.[48] No longer could actors hide behind their role or behind the script, for the law of the land now discerned, beneath their characters, an exercise of the actors' free will and, thus, evidence of their liability. In the eyes of the state, actors did not simply speak as their characters, they also spoke for them: insofar as they had chosen to incarnate them, they could be held liable for their words. The actors' new status dovetailed nicely with the early Revolution's embrace of reenactment, which, as we saw in Chapter 6, involved a closing of the gap between actor and character. Yet for a particular type of reenactment—judicial theater—it posed an insoluble problem. Indeed, for a play to faithfully reenact a recent conflict or crime, did there not need to be actors willing to take on the roles of national enemies and defend treasonous ideas, like the monarchy? But then, either the actors voiced sentiments other than their own, thereby violating a central tenet of the reenactive paradigm, or they spoke sincerely, as spectators often presumed, and should then be tried as monarchists.

While it may seem hard to believe that actors could be condemned for principles they had only expressed while in character, such could be their fate during the Revolution. For instance, in early 1794, the actor Arouch was sentenced to the guillotine for having shouted "Long live our noble king!" His eminently reasonable defense, "But it was in my part," fell on deaf ears, and he was executed.[49] Olympe de Gouges used a similar defense when she was asked by the judges of the Revolutionary Tribunal why, in her play *La France sauvée ou le tyran détroné*, Marie-Antoinette uttered such insidious lies and insults against true patriots (many of them famous Jacobins). It was, she responded, her responsibility as a playwright to make sure that the "Capet woman" spoke in character.[50] Although her play was highly critical of the queen, the fact that it gave Marie-Antoinette a chance to speak and depicted her as a complex individual rather than as a one-dimensional monster marked it as the kind of judicial theater of the early Revolution that the Jacobins had grown to fear. It came as little surprise, then, when the judges of the Revolutionary Tribunal ruled that de Gouges, like Arouch, would be put to death for the crime of resurrecting a monarch. In fact, just as an actor could be held liable for his character's principles, so could he also be blamed simply for staying silent, as the following report illustrates: "When an actor speaks of peace, if the one who is on stage next to him does not respond: *No peace so long as enemies sully our land; no peace so long as tyrants have not paid homage to our Republic; no peace until our Republic is avenged*—then the actor is wrong, and one can accuse him of a treasonous moderation."[51] In these instances, as in many others, the actors' sole transgression was to have "acted," that is, to have followed the script, to have stayed in character, when they ought to have expressed their own sentiments. Not surprisingly, many actors attempted to resist this alarming conflation of "role-playing" and "debating," notably by breaking the fourth wall and assuring the audience that they did not share their characters' opinions.[52] And yet, despite these precautions, actors remained, throughout the Revolution, one of the most closely monitored and frequently persecuted social groups.[53]

These incidents illustrate both the extent of the Jacobins' interest in reenactive theater and the depth of their ambivalence toward it. On the one hand, such accusations reveal that the Jacobins implicitly accepted one of the core principles of the reenactive paradigm, since they failed to distinguish between the actors' opinions and that of their characters. On the other hand, by punishing actors for playing the role of villains, the Jacobins enforced a strict monologism on stage, thereby altering the content and function of the earlier, more deliberative judicial theater. Convinced that dialogism would yield lies and discord, rather than truth and unity, and that allowing anyone, even actors, to endorse the cause of the monarchy would amount to granting it legitimacy, the Jacobins largely restricted topical plays to the reenactments of military or civic sacrifices by model Republicans. Hence, as early as August 2, 1793, the National Convention decreed that all theaters would perform plays with Republican themes at least three times a week.[54] In the days surrounding this decree, from July 29 to August 10, and then again between January 20 and 25, 1794, the Committee of Public Safety convoked the directors and troupes of nearly all the theaters in Paris to impress upon them the necessity of replacing the unpatriotic plays of the past with reenactments of heroic deeds by famous Republicans.[55] In March of 1794, the General Council of the Paris Commune opted for an even more direct involvement by ordering that all Parisian theaters submit their repertoires for expurgation. Two months later, it was the turn of yet another governmental body, the Commission of Public Instruction, to take over the surveillance and censorship of the repertoires.[56] Finally, in May 1794, the Committee of Public Safety again urged all playwrights to reproduce only positive events on stage, illustrating the bravery, devotion, and invincibility of the French army.[57] This long list of decrees and governmental interventions reveals the intensity of the Jacobins' obsession with eradicating the theater of the pre-Republican era, including judicial theater, not that such measures were unsuccessful. On the contrary, between August 1793 and July 1794, dozens of plays were written and performed to glorify the lives of newly anointed Republican heroes (Marat, Beaurepaire, Barra, Cange, and Agricol Viala, among others), as well as dozens more to celebrate military triumphs, such as the capture of Toulon.[58]

As these plays reveal, the Jacobins did not abandon the dream of reenactment, but they greatly restricted its scope, stripping it of any judicial function. By reenacting great moments of civic unity while forbidding mentions of the divisions, conflicts, and enemies that had played such a significant role leading up to these moments, they created a mythic past, consisting of a series of foundational moments of complete and spontaneous harmony. This mythic past was meant to take the place in the nation's memory occupied by the years prior to the Republic, thus bringing to a close the ancien régime's unsettling persistence into the present. Indeed, the type of reenactment championed by the Jacobins was as much an attempt to erase a "bad" past as it was an attempt to immortalize a "good" one. Legislative bodies, police administrators, and official newspapers were called into action in an unrelenting campaign not only to impose Republican topics but also to erase any reminder, however innocuous, of the nation's monarchical past, even in pre-Revolutionary plays. To quote the police informant Latour-Lamontagne, "One should banish completely from the stage anything that could remind us of our former errors."[59] The Commission of Public Instruction concurred and set out to, in its own words, "clear the stage of the rubbish of the ancien régime,"[60] to such a degree that it eventually became perilous for actors not only to incarnate princes and priests but also to employ the language of feudalism (titles such as Duc, Baron, and Monsieur) and even to utter a single syllable, "Louis," be it to designate a character or just a gold coin.[61] Once attracted to reenactment as a means of working through the past and reconciling it with the present, Revolutionary culture had, by 1793, come to embrace a new reenactive paradigm, one with the very opposite function, that of forgetting the past.

It was to this nonjudicial conception of reenactment that the Jacobins turned during the debate on whether, and how, to commemorate the king's execution. Last we spoke of this debate, citizens had descended upon the National Convention to protest a series of proposals that they believed would resurrect the monstrous Capet. Other citizens were quick to reassure them, however, that the commemorations would not take the form of a reenactment of the king's trial and execution but would instead consist of a generic festival celebrating the Revolution.[62] They proved to be correct, as the commemorations held throughout France displayed countless mannequins of such historical figures as Brutus, Rousseau, and Benjamin Franklin, as well as allegorical ones such as Liberty and Equality, yet almost none of the king, headless or otherwise.[63] By centering the festivals on uncontroversial heroes and ideals, instead of the figure and event they were meant to memorialize, the Jacobins followed the intent, if not exactly the letter, of the proposal by Antoine Simon that the celebrations reenact the death of a true Republican martyr, Le Peletier, rather than Louis's.[64] In doing so, they ensured the commemorations would serve the paradoxical function of exorcizing the very past they claimed to celebrate by replacing it with a more harmonious, less contentious one.

This creation of a mythic harmony built on erasure and replacement is a testament to the Jacobins' fear that reenacting conflicts merely prolonged them. It also suggests that the Jacobins ceased to see the reenactment of conflicts as a means of revealing hidden truths. Indeed, the complete erasure of one party, leaving only model heroes on stage, guaranteed that the characters would never engage in any debate, questioning, or reassessment and would therefore never challenge the Jacobins' simplistic division of the world into good and evil.[65] The same can be said for the spectators, who were expected to align their comportment with the Republican ideals routinely staged for their benefit, that is, to assent and imitate rather than to judge. Repeating a conflict, the Jacobins came to believe, opened it to manipulation, both factual and emotional, which threatened to mislead the audience, especially when it was reproduced on stage by actors. This loss of faith in public accusation and debate and in the infallibility of the watching people not only influenced the type of plays authorized by the Jacobins (by inspiring their censorship of judicial theater), it also shaped the content of the plays that were performed. This influence can be seen, in particular, in a series of plays that surprisingly borrowed their intrigue and many of their conclusions from the by-then-forbidden *L'Ami des lois.*

Eight months after the premiere of Laya's play, the Jacobin Nicolas Camaille-Saint-Aubin responded with the play *L'Ami du peuple*, a near perfect mirror image of *L'Ami des lois.* This rewriting tells of the struggle between a loyal Jacobin, Démophile, or "lover of the people," and Forcerame, an evil Girondin. Not surprisingly, Démophile praises insurrectional justice, stressing its immediacy, restraint, and infallibility. Indeed, the presence of so many eyes watching over one another's behavior ensures that there will be no excesses: "The people hunt a traitor and know not how to plunder. / If there appears in the crowd a reckless scoundrel, / He soon encounters a stricter judge."[66] This collective and instinctual sense of fairness frightens Forcerame, who professes instead his love for the law because forms and proceedings are more pliable than moral imperatives, making it easier to play with the truth and postpone its emergence, with a view toward concealing his crimes.[67] Therefore, for the inversion of *L'Ami des lois* to be truly perfect, one would expect Forcerame to level a formally sound but morally questionable accusation against Démophile in a courtroom in an attempt to use legal sophistry to eliminate his rival. The people, learning of this injustice and entering insurrection mode, would then invade the tribunal, absolve Démophile, and unveil the secret crimes of Forcerame.

Instead, *L'Ami du peuple* follows the plot of *L'Ami des lois* so closely that one suspects Camaille-Saint-Aubin of having simply reversed the political affiliations of the principal characters, with nary a thought for the contradictions that ensue. For instance, Forcerame's Girondin henchmen, Phrazette and Poumonin, rely on the same expedient as the Jacobins in *L'Ami des lois*: they disseminate a suspicious letter, along with rumors of Démophile's guilt, in an attempt to instigate an insurrection.[68] The ease with which the people are misled into nearly executing Démophile seems at odds with the play's earlier praise for the restraint and infallibility of popular justice. Even stranger is Démophile's request, identical to Forlis's in *L'Ami des lois*, that the people not punish Forcerame on the spot but respect instead his right to a formal trial: "They were about to kill him; I rush forward, next to him / 'A free people,' I say, 'renounces vengeance. / To celebrate virtue, it claims its rights; / But when a punishment is needed, it relies on the laws.'"[69] Démophile's eagerness to shield Forcerame from popular justice may seem to go against his political affiliation, yet it is in fact a fair reflection of the Jacobins' ambivalent stance toward insurrection. Indeed, while the Jacobins never ceased to praise insurrection as a form of collective justice superior to the laws, once in power, they also attempted to popularize the notion that a free people willingly forswears violence out of respect for the rule of law.[70]

To convey this notion, the Jacobins wrote dozens of plays showing the people being misled by false accusers. Many of these plays replicate the intrigue from *L'Ami des lois* and *L'Ami du peuple* with such exactitude that one could almost claim they constitute a distinct genre.[71] Nearly all include a villain who stirs up the anger of the people against an innocent man by publicly denouncing him. Then, despite a lack of conclusive evidence, a crowd of citizens invariably come within seconds of killing the protagonist before they are reminded of the rule of law, yield their would-be victim to the courtroom, and in so doing discover his innocence. These plays deserve our attention, because they disclose a profound ambivalence toward the two vital principles—the reliability of public accusation and debate, and the intrinsic ability of the people to serve as judge—on which rest not only judicial theater but also, and more broadly, the Jacobins' well-known embrace of denunciation as a fundamental civic virtue. These plays could not be any more different, in fact, from the contemporaneous set of plays dubbed "dramas of domestic surveillance" by Maslan, which were written and performed as tributes to the practice of denunciation.[72] Challenging the standard perception of the Jacobins and of their theater as unconditional supporters of denunciation, the plays modeled on *L'Ami des lois* depict denunciation less as a means of unveiling the truth than as a way of distorting it. This distrust of denunciation—for being too summary, violent, and easily manipulated—is evident not only in the plot of many plays of the period but also in general debates about the function of theater, which ceased almost entirely to include any mention of the ability of dramatic performances to serve as public accusations (Aristophanes's name, on everyone's lips from 1789 to 1793, was rarely if ever uttered). Hence, a little more than a month before the fall of Robespierre, one finds in the *Décade philosophique* a lengthy article arguing that while theatrical satires were once useful when battling corrupt kings and noblemen, they had become obsolete, dangerous even, in a republic that offered better ways, like the police and the courts, to expose the crimes of the powerful—crimes that warranted, in any case, a far more severe punishment than some poorly written dramatic fare.[73]

Yet if these misgivings about public accusation and swift, popular judgment inspired a surprising number of plays to replicate the plot of *L'Ami des lois* at a time when few plays were more ardently despised by the Jacobins, these anti-denunciation plays ultimately reached a different conclusion than their model. Indeed, Laya's play condemns insurrectional justice for lacking the theatrical qualities of a formal trial. Accordingly, as soon as Forlis is allowed to publicly confront his accusers, the sincerity and probity of his speech and demeanor persuade the people of his innocence. In contrast, the Jacobins' anti-denunciation plays implicitly cast doubt on the people's ability to distinguish between genuine and feigned innocence during a debate. For them, the problem with denunciation is less its secrecy than its theatricality. In these plays, public accusations and confrontations do not result in the emergence of the truth; on the contrary, the villain's eloquence and emotional appeals seem set to lead the people to the wrong conclusion. Ultimately, the truth is not revealed by the spectacle of an agonistic clash between accuser and accused but by the serendipitous intervention of an authority figure, as for instance a justice of the peace in *Charles et Victoire*, an officer in *Les Épreuves du Républicain*, and a mayor in *Il était temps*. Tellingly, in most cases, this representative of institutional justice delivers the final, correct verdict (thus rectifying the people's) thanks to his discovery of written evidence, such as letters and financial records (the very inverse of the ending to Laya's play, in which written evidence is superseded—erased, even—by an oral confrontation). In implying that official authority figures and textuality are better at determining the truth than public opinion and orality, the Jacobin playwrights portray the tribunal as a corrective to popular justice, not because it is more theatrical (as Laya claimed), but because it is less so. For the theater to call into question the forensic value of performance is to some extent paradoxical. In fact, such plays constitute the inverse of the courtroom dramas we saw in the preceding chapter. Whereas the latter had presented themselves—that is, the theater—as an ideal mode of justice, the Jacobin plays described above seemed intent instead on promoting a less theatrical model.

By challenging both the forensic and cathartic value of publicly performing a recent or ongoing conflict, the Jacobins sapped the very foundation of judicial theater, ensuring it would not return, even after they were no longer in a position to forbid particular plays or words. True, for a brief moment following the coup of 9 Thermidor, it looked as if the judicial theater of the early years of the Revolution might be reborn after all. In dozens of satirical plays with titles such as *L'Intérieur des comités révolutionnaires, Les Jacobins de Goa, Les Jacobins aux enfers*, and *La Mort de Robespierre*, the fallen Jacobins were subjected to a second trial and conviction. Audiences, too, appeared to welcome a return to the critical role that had been theirs in the early years of the Revolution. To quote Paul d'Estrée, "the conduct of theatrical audiences returned to what it had been from 1790 to 1792. The emotions in auditoriums still manifested themselves very intensely; but their combativeness and tyranny no longer were, as under the Terror, the monopoly of a single party."[74] As the theater opened its doors to a more politically diverse audience in the weeks following 9 Thermidor, the press began reporting frequent clashes between radicals, moderates, and reactionaries, notably in response to the Muscadins' repeated destruction of the busts of Marat and other Jacobins in Parisian auditoriums. All elements were thus in place for the theater to reclaim its role as a site of debate and judgment, after years of serving almost exclusively as an instrument of state propaganda.

The extent to which it failed to do so only fully comes to light when one reads police reports from the period in chronological order. These reports, handily compiled by Alphonse Aulard, reveal, in addition to the Directory's close surveillance of the theater, a radical shift in audience behavior.[75] Starting in April of 1795 and lasting until the fall of the Directory in 1799, glowing mentions of the parterre's tranquility come to replace almost entirely the once standard descriptions of political clashes among the spectators. One such report, dating from 1796, is particularly eloquent in its brevity: "Theaters. No applications, immobile spectators, and lots of indifference."[76] One should not infer from this description, however, that audiences under the Directory suddenly adopted the stillness and apathy of spectators from the modern era. Emotionally, intellectually, and aesthetically, they remained involved in the performance with an intensity and directness largely foreign to us. As the report suggests, the agents of the Directory were primarily interested in applications, that is, in topical judgments, often of political figures, and in the conflicts they provoked. It was mostly with regards to this form of involvement that a new passivity set in: "The theater is tending toward a veritable metamorphosis; public affairs are respected, and applications injurious to the government are omitted."[77] This report draws a line between the public and the private, with the theater, once seen as a vital public institution—indeed, as the very site where a public opinion was born—falling firmly on the side of the private. This returns the theater to its former state as a realm of aesthetic pleasure largely detached from public affairs. The disappearance of applications suggests that spectators contributed or at least consented to this evolution as they abandoned one of the principal means of exposing, debating, and condemning the crimes of the rich and powerful.

Several factors explain the gradual abandonment by Revolutionary audiences of a judicial vision of theater. Ling-Ling Sheu has noted the return of a more educated and wealthy audience following an increase in seat prices in 1795.[78] According to Serge Bianchi, this social revolution in the parterre led to the resurgence of a classical repertoire, more suited to the taste of the cultural elites, as well as more likely to ignite aesthetic arguments than debates about current affairs and figures.[79] Spectators were further encouraged to assume a more aesthetic relationship to the stage by the example and exhortations of the press. There emerged under the Directory an influential group of reactionary critics, who, as self-appointed guardians of good taste, published article after article advocating a return to classical plays, rules, and spectatorial codes of conduct. Newspapers such as the *Courrier des spectacles* and the *Censeur dramatique*, both founded in 1797, campaigned obsessively against the topical theater of the Revolution, which they blamed for promoting a non-aesthetic mode of judgment. Instead of applications, which focus on content, spectators should, they argued, reclaim the responsibility, abandoned during the Terror, of booing talentless actors and playwrights, as only this classical focus on formal qualities and rules could reverse the decadence of the dramatic arts.[80] Theatrical troupes also set out to limit opportunities for applications. Starting in April of 1797, according to Grimod de la Reynière, French theaters held off on performing Molière's *Les Femmes savantes* "because a minister's name had the same ending as a ridiculous character's in that comedy," creating a rhyme that invited impertinent applications.[81] *Les Femmes savantes* holds a significant place in the history of judicial theater, having served as the inspiration for both Palissot's *Les Philosophes* and Laya's *L'Ami des lois*. How telling, then, of the Directory's opposition to judicial theater that these openly satirical and denunciatory plays were once performed publicly, but the far more innocuous *Femmes savantes* was now suppressed for no rhyme or reason, or rather, for the sole reason of a rhyme!

In fact, several anecdotes suggest that spectators grew tired of playing any judicial role in the theater: not only that of accusers (through applications) but also that of jurors. Hence, when, in August 1795, members of the parterre began berating the actor Vallien for his past support of the Terror—a practice particularly common in the second half of 1794, when Muscadins frequently went to the theater to try, convict, and punish alleged Jacobin actors—the audience as a whole responded "we are not here to act as judges in a tribunal" and demanded that the play be performed, which it was, without further incidents.[82] Likewise, in September 1796, a spectator who threw his cane at an actor playing the role of a Jacobin was promptly identified by the other audience members, who had no desire to join him in his extrajudicial judgment, leading to his arrest by a more legitimate representative of the law, a police officer. This disagreeable scene, the police report concluded, really drove home "the necessity of putting an end to performances that rekindle hatred, and of returning theaters to their true principles—to instruct and entertain, to soften and correct mores."[83] With spectators, actors, journalists, and government officials all in agreement that the theater should no longer serve as a space of public accusation and popular judgment, it could now return to its former state as a means of entertainment and gentle, moral edification.

This reluctance to denounce public figures extended to the playwrights. As Jean-Marie-Bernard Clément noted in 1797, dramatists largely stopped targeting identifiable individuals, even in the historically subversive genre of vaudeville: "Those who govern today are more imposing or irreproachable, no doubt, since vaudeville spares them with a prudence it never showed under the reign of our former despots."[84] This must have pleased Jean-François Cailhava de L'Estandoux, who wrote an entire play, *Athènes Pacifiée*, to deter fellow dramatists from the lure of judicial theater.[85] In this fascinating text, Aristophanes—returned to the object of scorn he had been until the middle of the eighteenth century—decides without conclusive evidence to produce a play denouncing several high-ranking Athenians. Mercury, the voice of the Gods and of Cailhava, appears just in time to dissuade him through an eloquent condemnation of judicial theater, which he accuses of promoting slander, arrogance, factionalism, and vigilantism. Indeed, as Cailhava's play suggests, the aversion to judicial theater during the Directory stemmed from a deep weariness among playwrights, spectators, journalists, and politicians alike with the violent political brawls that it often provoked. The anti-Jacobins plays in the weeks following 9 Thermidor had been complicit in this violence. Like the sans-culottes satires after the king's execution, most offered only grotesque, malicious caricatures of their enemies, portraying all Jacobins as objects of ridicule or as embodiments of pure evil, not as misguided individuals in need of conversion. Spectators were invited to partake less in a trial than in a punishment—a collective outpouring of pent-up anger and vengeance. Such plays served as a rallying call for rival factions to battle in the parterre, not as attempts to unite different parties through a fair and public debate, culminating in a collective rejection of past crimes by specific individuals.

These punitive, overly Manichean plays conflicted with the "happy medium" style of politics promoted (if not always practiced) by the Directory as a response to the violent clashes between extremists on both ends of the political spectrum. These brawls, many taking place in theatrical auditoriums, inspired a growing distrust of popular accusation and judgment. In fact, these misgivings can even be seen in some of the last anti-Jacobins plays, which, before their disappearance in mid-1795, began to serve less as incitements to vengeance than as appeals for its sublimation. For instance, *Le Souper des Jacobins* refrains from incendiary caricatures and ends on the exhortation "Let us entrust to the law the punishment of crimes."[86] Its author, Armand Charlemagne, thus makes clear that he does not wish for his dramatic work to be seen as a judicial act, as an invitation to judge and punish, like the earlier anti-Jacobins plays, but rather as a warning to its spectators not to look at the theater as an appropriate space of accusation and deliberation, nor at themselves as legitimate judges. It is ironic, but also telling, that plays that initially served as denunciations of the Jacobins came to resemble the anti-denunciation plays of the Jacobins. Their praise of official over popular justice reveals that the Jacobins' loss of faith in public accusation and in the infallibility of the watching people—and, as a result, in judicial theater—outlived their reign by transcending ideological divisions.

It is in fact possible to retrace the gradual disappearance of judicial theater through the many transformations (twelve, by one eighteenth-century critic's count) of a single play—*Le Tartuffe*.[87] Molière's original masterpiece ends with a famous passage extoling the king as the fount of all justice, unique in his ability to expose the religious hypocrite Tartuffe. A report dating from January 1794 reveals that the play did not escape the Jacobins' campaign against ancien régime rubbish: its final scene was almost entirely rewritten, so as to erase the king from it. Fascinatingly, this new ending follows the script of the Jacobins' anti-denunciation plays. No longer is the focus on Tartuffe as a religious hypocrite (a social type that, like the king, no longer existed); instead, he is reborn a fraudulent denunciator, whose greed leads him to accuse his former benefactor, Orgon, of treasonous words in support of the nation's enemies. His slander is about to bear fruit when a municipal officer arrests him instead, before closing the play with a resounding attack on false informers: "Your odious schemes are uncovered, and the time is past when a vile slanderer had mastery over the lives of true patriots."[88] In subsequent years, the play's ending was again rewritten, perhaps because the municipal officer now seemed tainted with Jacobinism. He was replaced, along with every mention of "the king," by the more generic "the law." Mechele Leon has brilliantly shown the problems that this new ending raised, notably the fact that the king could not so easily be erased from the text and from the minds of the play's spectators: "he [the king] haunts the denouement—like a phantom limb."[89] The inevitable resurrection of kings and devout charlatans was, as we have seen, one of the most common criticisms of judicial theater. Indeed, the diverse attempts at rewriting *Tartuffe*'s ending echo the various actions taken against judicial theater, including: exorcising old enemies by replacing them with Republican figures, dramatizing the dangers of denunciation, and celebrating the law as a generic, immediate, infallible agent (instead of as an adversarial, theatrical process). The failure by these different strategies to truly obliterate the king explains why, post-1793, the Revolutionaries concluded that judicial theater—the most explicitly resurrective of dramatic genres—had to be completely eradicated.

An interesting exchange of letters in the *Journal des théâtres* in 1798 reveals another similarity between *Tartuffe* and judicial theater.[90] In Chapter 3, we saw the two principal elements that distinguish judicial theater from other genres: the inclusion of real, identifiable individuals among the characters and a denunciatory tone, leveling accusations at specific crimes, rather than generic vices. While the many rewritings of *Tartuffe* testify to the growing unease at the ghostly presence of a real individual (the king), the letters focus instead on the second element: the fact that Molière's play targets odious crimes rather than ridiculous traits. This debate about the nature and function of comedy—largely identical to the one we studied in the middle of the eighteenth century—pits against each other two anonymous contributors to the *Journal des théâtres*, the first calling himself "l'amateur" and the other "simplex." "L'amateur" criticizes the prevalence of prisons, scaffolds, and tribunals on stage and calls for a return to a time (the French classical era) when theaters only targeted moral faults and ridiculous traits, adding that only the legal system can and should punish criminal acts: "The playwright's influence ends where the law's authority begins." "Simplex" rejects this vision of the theater, pointing, not surprisingly, to the social benefits that the ancient Greeks found in the satirical comedies of Aristophanes. Tellingly, however, perhaps for the first time since the 1750s, the last word falls to the devotee of French classical comedy ("L'amateur"), who condemns *Tartuffe* and other plays like it with the sweeping generalization: "the law must never get tangled up with the stage"—a fitting epitaph for judicial theater!

Ending Theatrical Justice

Let us now return to the king's trial. The proceedings against Louis XVI have traditionally been depicted as the earliest and best-known example of the political show trials that would become common under the Terror, sending Marie-Antoinette, the Girondins, the Dantonists, and others to the guillotine. Jean-Pierre Royer thus writes: "The Convention was for the king of France a *vast funeral theater* in which the different roles were skillfully assigned and knowingly accepted, politically distributed, and gradually layered based on the parties and factions present and their distinct sensibilities."[91] On what grounds have scholars as diverse as Jules Michelet,[92] Marie-Hélène Huet,[93] and Royer, to name only a few, likened Louis's trial to a theatrical performance? First, the presence of a lively audience, disputing, jeering, and applauding, despite the president's repeated calls for gravitas. Second, the duplicity of the deputies, many of whom observed legal procedures in which they did not believe and for which they lacked training and credentials, meaning they only "acted" the part of judges. Third, the existence of a script, to the degree that all the deputies, regardless of party, openly acknowledged the guilt of Louis (only his penalty remained in doubt), making the trial a strictly ceremonial prelude to his condemnation. Spectators, actors, and a script—it is easy to see why nineteenth- and twentieth-century historiography has traditionally portrayed Louis's trial as a show trial. Whereas the Girondins had aspired to hold a trial in compliance with the due process of law, the story goes, the Jacobins coerced the deputies into staging a parody of justice. Such a narrative, however, should give us pause. A show trial aims, above all, to make a spectacle of the accused so as to publicize his or her guilt—precisely the stated aim of the Girondins, not the Jacobins, who, on the contrary, repeatedly opposed all attempts at publicizing the case and the accused, notably by means of a trial. In fact, the standard depiction of the king's trial as theater risks obscuring the true nature of the conflict in the Convention, which rested on an understanding of theatricality in the courtroom unlike the one employed today.

Indeed, when one reads the deputies' countless speeches on the king's trial, it becomes clear that it was the Jacobins, *not* the Girondins, who most frequently accused their adversaries of practicing a theatrical mode of justice. For the Jacobins, this theatricality originated, as we saw earlier, in the presumption of innocence, the right to a lawyer, the observance of fixed forms, and the staging of agonistic debates—that is, in precisely those attributes which, today, we deem essential to legal proceedings, and in the absence of which we see, in lieu of justice, only theater. The Jacobins' loss of faith in reenactment, in the very idea of a performance designed to end itself *as* performance, led them to see the accusatorial model of 1791 not as a catalyst for sincere, spontaneous debates and emotions but as an invitation to an even more insidious form of theatricality, one that made it possible for wily legal actors to cast their emotional appeals and rehearsed arguments as artless, impromptu revelations. Presumed innocent, given free rein to spin their tales, and abetted by trained performers, the nation's enemies would turn each trial into a sentimental drama, shedding fake tears and making baseless accusations to move the naïvely compassionate people to their side. This anxiety explains why, I contend, Louis's trial, often identified as marking the beginning of a "theatrical justice," signaled instead, in the Jacobins' eyes, the beginning of its end.

Indeed, the reforms, notably the creation of a Revolutionary Tribunal, that soon followed the king's trial and launched the Terror show a similar ambiguity, born of the same conflicting definitions of theatricality. On the one hand, the Terror is often presented as theatrical, due to a series of prosecutions that, to modern eyes, can only be described as show trials, given their predetermined and politically motivated verdicts.[94] On the other hand, Huet and others have shown that the Terror was conceived as a broad attempt to eliminate all theatricality from Revolutionary society.[95] The Revolutionary Tribunal served as a cornerstone in the Jacobin quest for transparency by promoting public denunciations and by unveiling, beyond tangible crimes, the subterfuges and masks of secret conspirators. Carol Blum goes even further when she argues that the Rousseauian ideals of transparency and immediate, emotional sincerity shaped not only the aim of the proceedings (to unveil) but also the proceedings themselves, in the very way that they unfolded.[96] Legal procedure under the Terror was, she contends, influenced by a pervasive "epistemology of sentiment," notably the belief that virtuous patriots possess a natural instinct toward justice, enabling them to look at an accused and know, immediately, intuitively, and infallibly, his or her guilt or innocence. Blum traces this mode of judgment, based on feeling and intuition, back to the king's trial and presents it as the source of the Revolutionary Tribunal's (supposedly new) embrace of *conviction intime*, as well as its distrust of "legal" (rather than "moral") proof, fixed forms, and language.

Yet as we have seen, these ideals already underpinned the legal reforms of 1791. Not only did the reformers place *conviction intime* at the very heart of their judicial vision, they demonstrated their faith in sentiment, sincerity, and spontaneity by endorsing passionate, unscripted, and unstructured debate as a means of revealing the truth beyond fixed forms and rehearsed language. Why, then, did the legal proceedings of the Revolutionary Tribunal differ so markedly from those of 1791? The answer, I contend, lies in the way that the Revolutionary Tribunal sought to achieve the transparency that the Jacobins craved: not, as Blum believes, through a sentimental mode of justice, which more accurately describes the ambitions of the 1791 reformers, but rather through a systematic campaign to strip trials of elements too reminiscent of a dramatic performance. Many of these elements had been introduced in 1791, and indeed, the evolution toward the special courts of the Terror can be tied to the Jacobins' loss of faith in reenactment, most notably in the trustworthiness of supposedly spontaneous, sincere gestures and in the forensic reliability of compassion and intuition. As we will see, the Jacobins' attempt to detheatricalize justice did not lead to the creation of legal proceedings founded on unmediated presence and emotion (in keeping with a Rousseauian "epistemology of sentiment"). On the contrary, it inspired the Jacobins to establish—paradoxically and, one suspects, unwittingly—a justice system that, in its focus on the legitimacy found in exclusivity and textuality, more closely resembled the inquisitorial model of the ancien régime.

Nowhere is this more evident, perhaps, than in the way that judgment was redefined by the National Convention during the debate that led to the creation of a Revolutionary Tribunal, on March 10, 1793. Several deputies, most notably Pierre Philippeaux, argued that the new special courts should not include jurors, because ordinary men were too "prone to indulgence," their "sensitive souls" too easily swayed by the "beautiful oratorical movements" of schemers and traitors.[97] This opposition to jurors is striking for many reasons, but above all for its equation of a natural, instinctual sensibility with faulty judgment. By contrast, the *conviction intime* central to the reforms of 1791 had largely rested on two sentimental assumptions: that compassion and a sense of right and wrong are universal, irrespective of rank, and that feelings and intuitions of the sort are reliable indicators of guilt and innocence. The king's trial had, in the Jacobins' eyes, made a mockery of these assumptions by revealing the ease with which real and figurative dramatists could manipulate naïve, ordinary citizens into feeling pity for even the most irrefutably guilty, like the king. This realization made it necessary to redefine judgment in a way that made it less dependent on sensibility, depicted above as synonymous with indulgence. The surprising opposition to jurors consisted of an attempt to do precisely that, by ensuring that only career magistrates, made wiser and harder by years of judgments, would be entrusted with determining the guilt of men and women who, as skilled conspirators, knew better than anyone how to play the role of innocent, pitiable victims.

The deputies rejected the proposal to do away with jurors altogether, but the fear that ordinary people were too susceptible to dramatic manipulation inspired them to settle on an equally startling compromise: the jurors of the Revolutionary Tribunal would not be elected or chosen at random but would be appointed by the National Convention. The infamous law of 22 Prairial further enshrined this decision, reducing the number of jurors to just fifty and decreeing that they would serve for an indeterminate time, rather than for a specific trial or set term.[98] This radical transformation of what was, then as now, understood by the term "juror" (a temporary position, for which one is randomly selected) had the same aim as the proposed abolition of juries: to ensure that those who judged were *not* the simple, ordinary citizens, governed by feeling and intuition, that had been the ideal jurors in the minds of the early Revolutionaries. The Jacobins feared this mode of judgment for two reasons, both linked to theatricality: first, as we have seen, because its sentimentality made it far too vulnerable to dramatic manipulation, and second, because its universality, its openness to any and everyone, threatened its perception as infallible, causing its verdicts to appear just as subjective and transient as one's emotional response to a play. Indeed, the insistence on the exclusivity of the new jurors was meant as an assurance that the state had carefully vetted them and, upon confirming their unique wisdom and ideological purity, had invested them with the legitimacy to judge in its name. By establishing quasi-permanent positions, the law of 22 Prairial inscribed this legitimacy even deeper within the identity of each juror, further driving home the point that the ability to judge was an essential attribute not shared by all. Truth be told, then, these jurors were such in name only; they more closely resembled the lifetime magistrates of the ancien régime, whose verdicts were held to be absolute because they did not express a subjective opinion but the will of the king, who had supposedly handpicked them. The Jacobins' fear of theatricality thus drove them back, perhaps unwittingly, to a conception of judgment founded on external legitimacy, rather than on sentiments and instincts internal to all human beings.

Precisely the same evolution can be seen with regards to lawyers. The institution of *défenseurs officieux*, like that of juries, had been an attempt by the early Revolutionaries to open the justice system to the participation of the general public. *Défenseurs officieux* and lay jurors were deemed to possess the same qualities, stemming from their lack of judicial training: spontaneity, compassion, and sincerity. Yet the lack of a lawyer's order did not simply ensure a more natural, artless performance of justice, it also eliminated the primary mechanism for punishing lawyers who, out of greed or pride, sought out and defended the notoriously guilty. Most early Revolutionaries had welcomed this shift from a vision of legal counsel founded on vouching to one founded on acting, so inspired were they by the ideal that everyone ought to be allowed a lawyer, and so convinced that public opinion (in the form of spectators and lay jurors) would inevitably distinguish between the false eloquence of swindlers and the true eloquence of Ciceronian orators moved to speak by compassion and love of justice. This makes it all the more telling, then, that before the oft-noted abolition of legal counsel from the Revolutionary Tribunal by the law of 22 Prairial, the Jacobins had tried instead to relegitimize lawyers by handpicking them and narrowing their ranks, much as they had jurors. Hence, on June 29, 1793, they passed a decree requiring that all lawyers obtain a *certificat de civisme*[99]—a clear attempt to reintroduce a type of exclusivity lost with the old Order of Barrister, so as to ensure that lawyers adhered to certain values (Jacobinism) and defended only the "right" accused (the most frequent argument in favor of the decree was that conspirators and traitors had no difficulty finding lawyers to represent them before the Revolutionary Tribunal). The deputies at the National Convention hoped that such a decree, by guaranteeing that lawyers would henceforth be seen as politically upstanding, card-carrying Jacobins, would lead to two positive outcomes. First, it would rob the nation's enemies of their most eloquent defenders, and second, it would give lawyers a renewed, exclusive legitimacy and, with it, the ability to better defend wrongly accused patriots by vouching for them.

In fact, the return to a system founded on vouching is also evident in the law of 22 Prairial that finally eliminated lawyers entirely from the Revolutionary Tribunal. Huet was the first to link this rejection of legal counsel to the Jacobins' broader distrust of representation and, more specifically, to their desire to detheatricalize the Revolutionary Tribunal.[100] It is instructive, however, to look at the law's precise wording for a better sense of the theatricality that it targeted: "To slandered patriots, the law gives patriotic jurors as defenders; it grants none to conspirators." Whereas one might have expected a Rousseauian critique of the lack of transparency and emotional sincerity that arises from allowing anyone to represent another (guilty or innocent), the law focuses instead on the ancien régime anxiety about the theatricality that results from the representation of clearly guilty individuals. Georges Couthon, the law's main architect, expands on this fear in the lengthy speech that he gave in its support at the National Convention: "Could we have expected anything else from a class of men bound by their trade to the defense of the nation's enemies, or rather, from an institution that presupposes an absolute lack of principles?"[101] Here, Couthon does not fear that lawyers will introduce the lies and cold eloquence of practiced deceivers—after all, those who will speak in the lawyers' absence, the accused conspirators, are equally adept at manipulation—but rather that the practice of defending guilty parties discloses the same absolute lack of principles, of fixed identity, that is at the heart of professional actors, transforming the Revolutionary Tribunal from a battle between good and evil into so much empty speech. As the text of the law ultimately shows, with its insistence that the guilty, unlike the innocent, should never be given a defender, Couthon implicitly adheres to a vision of legal counsel as a form of vouching. Why does this vision now lead him and others to call for the total eradication of lawyers, instead of a less drastic purging of their ranks until only the politically legitimate remain? No doubt for the same reason that inspired the ancien régime to both forbid lawyers in criminal cases and establish a powerful Order of Barristers in civil ones. By Prairial 1794, the Revolutionary Tribunal, like criminal ones before the Revolution, operated from a presumption of culpability, not innocence, with the accused appearing only once in court to respond to a preexisting narrative of their guilt. In such an inquisitorial model, a lawyer could not vouch for any accused, as this would mean taking on and legitimizing their probable guilt. The rejection of lawyers from the Revolutionary Tribunal thus resulted at least as much, if not more, from the antitheatricality found in the ancien régime vision of justice as it did from a Rousseauian sentimentality.

A final and especially telling parallel to ancien régime justice lies in the surprising centrality of writing to the Revolutionary Tribunal. Blum presents *conviction intime* as a feeling or intuition born from the sight of the accused's body, yet that definition more accurately fits the 1791 vision of justice, in which passionate, unscripted debates were meant to disclose physical and emotional signs obscured by language and practiced actio. By contrast, as Carla Hesse shows in an important article, textuality increasingly came to displace presence and orality in the Revolutionary Tribunal.[102] This was true, notably, with respect to an element of legal proceedings that, perhaps more than any others, lay at the very heart of *conviction intime*: the public testimony and confrontation of witnesses. By June 1794, according to Hesse, oral testimonies had been almost entirely replaced by written depositions. There were practical reasons for this, notably the costs and logistical difficulties raised by the transportation of far-flung witnesses to the Paris-based tribunal.[103] Above all, however, the disappearance of oral testimony reflected the Jacobins' growing anxiety about false witnesses, as seen in a series of laws that imposed ever stricter penalties, from twenty years of forced labor to capital punishment.[104] That the Jacobins even believed in the need for such draconian deterrence shows how completely they had lost faith in the people's ability to distinguish between true and false eloquence, rehearsed performance and sincere statement, and actor and victim. This distrust culminated in the exclusion of witnesses from the Revolutionary Tribunal following the law of 22 Prairial (except when the judges, in the absence of material proof, chose to summon them). An earlier letter sent to the National Convention by the Revolutionary Tribunal reveals the reasons behind this silencing of witnesses. Witnesses, the letter explained, introduced a dangerous theatricality into the courtroom, not only in the form of potential actors but also through their promotion of agonistic debate: "each witness, while testifying, wants to give a full history of the Revolution. The accused then respond to the witnesses, who reply in turn; this creates a discussion that the defendants' loquacity makes very long."[105] By excluding witnesses from the Revolutionary Tribunal, the Jacobins hoped to diminish the influence of physical presence and spontaneous speech in the exercise of justice.

This objective also explains why private letters became the most common and trusted type of evidence in the trials of the Revolutionary Tribunal. Hesse traces this practice back to the king's trial, during which his personal correspondence and financial records had been used to silence him, on account that "the letter speaks for itself."[106] She goes on to describe the tentacular bureaucracy that was created at the Committee of General Security to read and classify tens of thousands of private letters so that they could then be compiled into dossiers and submitted to the Revolutionary Tribunal.[107] It is true, as Hesse notes, that the Jacobins were particularly drawn to letters because they were deemed to be transparent expressions of the accused's most sincerely held beliefs. Yet it is essential to look at the ways in which the new centrality of textual evidence transformed the nature of legal judgment. The creation of dossiers composed of private letters and of the transcriptions of testimonies and accusations made by distant individuals who could, therefore, neither be seen nor cross-examined (a key reason why such transcripts had been forbidden since 1791 by the institution of purely oral proceedings) meant that verdicts were once more based, as they had been under the ancien régime, primarily on textual exegesis, rather than on the firsthand experience of emotional, spontaneous debates and physical signs. This is not entirely surprising, since Robespierre, during the 1791 debates, had already condemned the idea that *conviction intime* ought to rest more on "moral proofs" and orality than on "legal proofs" and textuality (he favored, notably, the transcription of testimonies). The vision of *conviction intime* that triumphed in 1791 struck Robespierre as dangerously arbitrary, as it put too great a power in the hands of the judges and jurors, without requiring (or, indeed, enabling) them to provide justification for their verdicts.[108] In fact, in recent years, historians such as Peter McPhee, Jean-Clément Martin, and Annie Jourdan have shown that, contrary to his reputation, Robespierre was a legalist who believed that justice, even in the special tribunals of the Terror, should be rooted in concrete evidence. The renewed importance of textuality in the Revolutionary Tribunal supports this interpretation by revealing that the Jacobins were uneasy with notions of judging as wholly subjective, sentimental, and instinctual.

The existence of written dossiers also transformed the performance of justice. As in the ancien régime, these dossiers were read by the judges before the actual trial and thus before their first interaction with the accused, especially after the law of 22 Prairial, which eliminated preliminary inquiries and interrogations of the suspect (legal proceedings were thus reduced, in their entirety, to a summons, an immediate appearance and interrogation before the court, and a verdict). This meant that judges created an account of the accused's guilt in advance of the trial, thereby encouraging them to view their role less as that of a neutral, inactive spectator, watching and assessing an oral, agonistic debate between two equal parties, and more as that of a highly involved interrogator, directing a one-sided examination meant to confirm and publicize a preestablished narrative. Indeed, many articles in the law of 22 Prairial recall the monologism of ancien régime criminal proceedings. As we saw, the abolition of witnesses was at least partly motivated by a rejection of debate. Likewise, by suppressing the right to a lawyer and eliminating preliminary inquiries and interrogations, the law of 22 Prairial ensured that the accused would have little to no advance knowledge of the case being built against them and would lack therefore both the assistance and the time to prepare answers to the judges' accusations, let alone a counter-narrative. In sum, by June 1794, the Revolutionary Tribunal had become nearly as inquisitorial as the king's justice, from the absence of lawyers, defense witnesses, and elected, impartial judges, to the end of the presumption of innocence and true, adversarial debate.

Yet if the procedure in the special courts of the Terror was inquisitorial and state driven, as in the ancien régime, there remained one key difference: it retained the publicity introduced in the early years of the Revolution. This unique mixture explains, I contend, the widespread perception of the Revolutionary Tribunal as a theatrical court created to stage show trials. Indeed, the very elements of the inquisitorial model that had served under the ancien régime to shield justice from theatricality (such as the lack of lawyers and adversarial debates) appeared, once public, to have the opposite function: to spectators, they looked like efforts by the government to stage-manage the performance of justice so as to ensure it never departed from a prewritten script with a fixed ending. This publicity-produced inversion is the reason why the Jacobins' vision of justice has been understood as both theatrical and antitheatrical. The Jacobins did not, as is commonly claimed, long for show trials and dramatic justice—their embrace of antitheatrical strategies from the ancien régime reveals as much—but, in an ironic twist of fate, the more they tried to detheatricalize justice, the more it appeared theatrical. This perception emerged early and spread swiftly: according to Mason, the trial of the Hébertists in March 1794 prompted (perhaps for the first time in French history) widespread accusations that it was little more than a show trial.[109] From then on, Robespierre and the Jacobins were increasingly depicted as tyrants secretly directing political trials to strengthen their grip on power.

In the face of such accusations, Robespierre and the Jacobins came to realize that the Terror's conspiracy trials, designed to eliminate, through their special procedures and targets, the bane of theatricality, were instead increasingly being dismissed as political spectacles. Perhaps the clearest sign of this realization can be seen in the Jacobins' surprising unease, in the latter stages of their reign, with the concept of denunciation as a supreme civic duty. The importance of denunciation to the Jacobins' worldview, and notably to their vision of justice, needs little introduction. As is well known, the more control the Jacobins achieved over the government, the more they endeavored to extend the reach of denunciation, making it increasingly indeterminate (based on suspicions, rather than solely on specific, provable crimes) and universal (anyone could denounce, and anyone could be denounced). They embraced the limitless, collective surveillance that this vision of denunciation entailed, hailing it, to quote Colin Lucas, as "the weapon with which radicalism pursued its goal of social and individual transparency."[110] Denunciation was thus intrinsically linked to the Revolutionary Tribunal, not only because the latter could scarcely function without the former, since it pursued hidden conspiracies and suspicions more often than tangible crimes, but also, and more importantly, because they were the two principal weapons in the Jacobins' crusade to tear down all masks and establish a transparent (that is, detheatricalized) society. It is therefore especially telling that the Jacobins grew increasingly convinced that denunciation, like the Revolutionary Tribunal, had begun to cultivate the very theatricality that it was meant to combat.

Indeed, in his famous *Rapport sur les principes de morale politique*, Robespierre expresses the same anxiety as the authors of the anti-denunciation plays discussed earlier. As noted, these Jacobin plays, against all expectations, depict denunciation as a theatrical accusation, deriving from the denouncer's guilt and duplicity more than from the denounced's. Likewise, in his address to the National Convention, Robespierre voices the fear that denunciation might actually mask more than it unmasks when he describes enemies of the people as avid denunciators: "He [the people's enemy] is severe toward innocence but indulgent toward crime; accusing the guilty who are not rich enough to purchase his silence nor important enough to merit his zeal, but taking care never to compromise himself to the point of defending slandered virtue; discovering from time to time plots already discovered, ripping the masks off traitors already unmasked and even decapitated, but extolling living and still influential traitors."[111] Fascinatingly, Robespierre here accuses the people's enemies of acting and not, as one might have expected, of lying, since their accusations target men and women who are genuinely guilty (even if relatively harmless, since penniless, powerless, or already unmasked). The paradoxical notion that unmasking the guilty could ever be a sign of culpability suggests a first reason for Robespierre's misgivings about denunciation. Ironically, insofar as it fails to reveal the accuser's intentions, the act of denunciation, a supposed instrument of transparency, is itself not transparent. In other words, denunciation lacks a fixed moral value, thus making it possible for enemies of the people to unmask fellow wrongdoers solely so as not to be themselves unmasked.

Furthermore, the ethical distinction that Robespierre draws between accusing the guilty and defending the innocent suggests that he had grown aware of the basic inability of denunciation to yield a positive value, unlike the defense of virtue, which reveals the truth about a man's character. Indeed, as Huet has noted, "what is disclosed when masks are removed and veils are torn is acting, duplicity, lies, untruth. Revolutionary rhetoric does not speak of unveiling the truth but of unveiling treason, bringing to light treachery and falsehood."[112] The act of unveiling does not yield truth or any fixed, positive value; instead, it only reveals more veils, a paradox perfectly illustrated by Robespierre's observation that the enemies of the people strive to unmask those already unmasked. The perception of denunciation as a means toward greater transparency, a standard belief among the Jacobins, was thus intrinsically flawed, as it failed to take into account the fact that unveiling never offers even the slightest glimpse at a deeper truth beneath the veil. On the contrary, frequent denunciations revealed the omnipresence of theatricality, fueling the paranoia of the Revolutionaries and prompting in return an exponential rise in the quantity and intrusiveness of denunciations.

Not only did the endless repetition of denunciations cultivate, rather than dispel, a sense of ubiquitous theatricality, it also brought the practice of denunciation itself closer to the theater. Indeed, because the act of unmasking does not yield a fixed truth but only further masks, it shares with theater the attribute of being eternally reiterable.[113] There is simply no end to denunciation, if all it unveils are veils. As a result, according to Robespierre, the practice of denunciation was easily co-opted by the enemies of the people, in a way that turned it into theater. In a speech at the Club des Jacobins in April 1794, Robespierre accused a former ally and avid denouncer of this very crime: "Fabre d'Églantine performed a play before the committees; the craft of this skillful deceiver was to make small denunciations against small conspirators with whom he got along but whom he denounced to hide his opinions. Through his trickery, he found ways to muddle the facts so that the denunciation came to nothing."[114] Instead of quivering in fear of denunciation, Fabre d'Églantine and other false patriots embraced it as a means of clogging up the justice system with a multitude of irrelevant or jumbled cases, thereby obscuring actual threats. Robespierre's claim is reminiscent of the Jacobins' condemnation of sans-culotte comedies such as *Le Jugement dernier des rois* on the grounds that their denunciations of already unmasked villains (kings and priests) were not only fruitless but also hid, through a farcical parody of justice, the true nature and peril posed by the nation's secret enemies. Likewise, the false patriots' incessant and insincere unveilings, targeting men and women of no consequence or already unmasked, ridiculed the Jacobins' desire for a detheatricalized justice by turning denunciation itself into theater.

The popularity of denunciation also altered the performance of justice in a way that brought it closer to theater. As we saw earlier, the Jacobins opposed the accusatorial system instituted in 1791 for the prominence it gave to debate, rehearsal, and subjective, sentimental judgment. These attributes, the Jacobins believed, cast doubt on the certainty, legitimacy, and fixity of legal decisions. In Robespierre's eyes, the iterability of denunciation, coupled with its lack of transparency, threatened to reintroduce the theatrical procedure of 1791 into the Revolutionary Tribunal, with the same disastrous consequences. Hence, when the deputy Jean-Baptiste Louvet de Couvray accused him of despotic ambitions, Robespierre ended his response with the following assertion: "What's left for me to say against accusers who accuse themselves? . . . I have renounced the easy advantage of responding to my opponents' calumnies with more formidable denunciations."[115] By defending his own virtue, while explicitly refusing to unmask his unmaskers, Robespierre sought to elude the iterability of denunciation, which so often expressed itself as a reversal in the roles of accuser and accused. Indeed, by seeking to universalize denunciation, the Jacobins had made it not only possible but almost inevitable that the accused, in an attempt to save his or her life, would become the accuser. Such a reversal, which saw the denounced systematically respond with an even more damning denunciation, transformed what ought to have been an individual act of unveiling into a public, oratorical contest between two masked parties—that is, into theater.

In fact, Robespierre and Saint-Just became increasingly aware that denunciation, one of the Jacobins' leading weapons against theatricality, was not only (1) itself theatrical and (2) a catalyst for theatrical proceedings, but also (3) guilty of encouraging in the whole of society, even beyond the courtroom, the very dissimulation that it was designed to combat. In one of his most illustrious claims, Saint-Just lamented this unprecedented expansion of theatricality: "The Revolution is frozen; all its principles are weakened; there remains only red caps worn by intriguers."[116] Strikingly, this assertion appears to exclude the possibility of a nontheatrical act, in that it suggests that everyone who wore the proper patriotic attire did so less from principle than from a desire to tend to their image in the public sphere. In a world where surveillance is generalized, even true patriots come to think of an action in terms of its public perception, rather than simply in terms of its intrinsic worth. Indeed, the act of unveiling, because it is concerned with veils, that is, with surface coverings, inspires a collective focus on exteriority and in so doing detaches outward signs and actions from the moral intentions traditionally associated with them. In such a world, therefore, even a virtuous deed can be a mask: "The good is often itself a means of intrigue."[117] Dissimulation is everywhere present because it is everywhere looked for. As a result, as Robespierre suggests in a speech on calumny, seeking to unmask those who exploit denunciation to parody the Revolution will only reinforce this spiral of theatricality. Instead, he advises his followers to "observe, in silence, their guilty maneuvers; let them betray themselves through their own excesses."[118] True to his word, Robespierre adopted that very strategy against Louvet de Couvray, painting him and the Girondins as "accusers who accuse themselves."[119] There is perhaps no clearer expression of the paradoxical truth lying at the heart of the Jacobins' anti-denunciation plays, as well as ubiquitous in Robespierre's writing: He who unmasks only unmasks himself.

Not surprisingly then, on 8 Thermidor, as in his earlier conflict with Louvet de Couvray, Robespierre appeared before the Convention beset by accusations, yet unwilling to respond in kind—a refusal to unmask his unmaskers that many historians have since portrayed as a direct cause of his downfall. Instead, Robespierre offered the Convention what he deemed to be simple truths, adding that he would rather suffer the fate of Socrates than resort to dissimulations and other theatrical deceptions: "If I must disguise these truths, bring me the hemlock."[120] In his last few days on earth, in fact, Robespierre constantly equated himself to the Athenian philosopher. After his appearance before the Convention, he hurried to the Jacobin club, where he delivered the same speech, adding to it what would remain his last words as an orator: "I leave you my memory: you will defend it! I will drink the hemlock!"[121] Then, once in his cell, he repeated almost obsessively: "I will empty Socrates's cup, I will end my days."[122]

This last statement is doubly ironic. As we saw in Chapter 2, Rousseau and other critics of the theater admired Socrates for his refusal to resort to dramatic tricks to persuade his judges. In an earlier pamphlet, Robespierre had made it clear that he considered himself a modern Socrates, locked in battle with the sophists of his time,[123] because he too had endeavored to bring into being a simpler, purer language, stripped of the metaphors and hyperboles that hid the truth behind linguistic veils.[124] Ironically, however, by consciously imitating the actions of another (and drawing attention to this imitation), he unwittingly reintroduced theatricality into the courtroom. In fact, Saint-Just had once criticized the Revolutionaries' fondness for modeling themselves on the great men of antiquity for precisely this reason: "One does not imitate virtue: one is virtuous in one's own way, or one is a hypocrite. . . . The same is true for those who have the modesty of usurping the names of antiquity's great men; this affectation hides a schemer whose conscience has been sold."[125]

The second irony of Robespierre's statement resides in the story of its survival. By an astonishing twist of fate, the individual responsible for recording it for posterity was none other than Laya, the same Laya who, less than two years prior to the coup of 9 Thermidor, had been widely praised as a modern Aristophanes, willing to put his life at risk to unmask ambitious politicians, chief among them Robespierre.[126] Time and again, Laya's supporters had equated his *L'Ami des lois* with the Greek satirist's *The Knights*, in which Aristophanes had courageously attacked and discredited a dangerous demagogue, Cleon. By claiming Socrates's mantle, Robespierre sought to preemptively write the history of his downfall, in the hope that, like Socrates, he would be remembered as the innocent victim of a rampant theatricality. In this version, Laya remained Aristophanes, but his *L'Ami des lois* was cast as *The Clouds*, not as *The Knights*. In order to comply in full with this Socratic narrative, it was essential that Robespierre refuse to denounce his accusers, as such a noble gesture amounted to a heroic last stand against the intermixing of theater and justice.

Indeed, a statement such as "I will drink the hemlock" at a time when his fate was far from decided suggests Robespierre not only foresaw but also willingly embraced a Socratic martyrdom. To his credit, in fact, Robespierre followed the Greek's example to the very last breath. After his arrest, forces of the Commune freed him and his closest allies. In response, the Convention promptly voted them *hors-la-loi*, which not only meant that the fugitives could be executed without a trial, but also underlined that any actions they took against the Convention would be, as Michelet eloquently put it, "to start a war against the Law."[127] Knowing this, but pressed by his allies to sign a letter to the Paris sections calling for a general insurrection, Robespierre hesitated before asking, "But in whose name?"—a sublime recognition that no man had the authority to challenge the legal system that had condemned him. To do so would have meant to question the law's legitimacy, infallibility, and irreproducibility—the very ideals that had inspired Robespierre to abstain from a theatrical defense. By turning down his followers' offer to mount a popular insurrection, Robespierre imitated Socrates's own refusal to escape from Athens, despite the pleas of his friends and the broad support of the people. Like most eighteenth-century thinkers, Robespierre viewed Socrates as more than simply the victim of a toxic mixture of justice and theater. Besides a cautionary tale, Socrates was a role model: by freely accepting the fate of a judicial martyr, he had reaffirmed submission to the law as the highest civic virtue, an essential source of legitimacy and stability in a society so often ruled by sophistry and theatricality.[128] Robespierre's identification with Socrates suggests that he too had reached the conclusion that the only way to defeat Aristophanes, and the noxious fusion of justice and theater for which he stood, was paradoxically to become his victim. The last rampart against the Revolution's rampant theatricality was the sole act that cannot be repeated—death.

Not surprisingly, this self-sacrifice proved futile. Theatrical justice no more ended with Robespierre's death than did the Terror or the Revolutionary Tribunal. In fact, according to Mason, the public grew especially disillusioned with conspiracy trials during the Directory, due to the widespread belief that they amounted to little more than political show trials. By opening criminal proceedings to the public, the Revolution had created an aporia it could not so easily escape. Too inquisitorial a justice system bred anxieties about one type of theatricality—state-directed parodies of justice, with a predetermined ending—while too accusatorial a model led to another type of theatricality, as the emphasis on open, oral debates and the absence of the state's legitimizing hand created a space for empty speech, manipulation, and overly subjective, sentimental judgments. This is no doubt why Napoleon Bonaparte struck a middle ground between these two systems, by preserving the public, accusatorial justice of the Revolution, complete with lawyers, lay jurors, and free, agonistic debate, while asserting control over it and its performance through inquisitorial practices typical of the ancien régime, notably by appointing permanent judges and giving them a hugely active role as lead interrogators, both during the trial, which they shaped through their questions, and before it, when they built a case through private interrogations of the accused and witnesses.[129] To this day, it seems to me, justice remains uneasily poised between these two theatrical extremes. Too controlled, too monological, and it risks being seen as a show trial, directed by the authorities; too free, too dialogical, and it becomes susceptible to theatrical manipulations, turning what should be an artless repetition of the conflict into a dramatic competition between trained playwrights and actors. With this equilibrium now disturbed and ancient fears and debates reignited by the ever-growing influence of American-style dramatic justice, it remains to be seen whether France will find a better response to the threat of a lawsuit culture, celebrity lawyers, and trial by media than Robespierre's silent death wish.

Notes

INTRODUCTION

1. On classical dogma, see René Bray, *La Formation de la doctrine classique en France* (Paris: Librairie Nizet, 1983); Jacques Truchet, *La Tragédie classique en France* (Paris: Presses universitaires de France, 1997). In addition, until the Revolution, royal censors dissected all new plays not only for references to contemporary or historical figures but also for any character or situation that could potentially lend itself to applications by the audience. The principal troupes in Paris were also compelled by law to submit to the censors a list of the old plays they intended to revive so as to avoid any potential coincidence with current events.

2. François-Hédelin, abbé d'Aubignac, *La Pratique du théâtre* (Amsterdam: Jean Frédéric Bernard, 1715), 1:40.

3. For their often-explicit mockery of contemporary figures and customs, the comedies of Molière immediately come to mind. On Molière's vision of satire, see Larry Norman, *The Public Mirror: Molière and the Social Commerce of Depiction* (Chicago: University of Chicago Press, 1999). I study what distinguishes Molière from the judicial theater of the eighteenth century in Chapter 2.

4. I expand on the seventeenth-century opposition to Old Comedy in Chapters 1 and 2.

5. Denis Diderot, *Le Fils naturel*, ed. Jean Goldzink (Paris: GF Flammarion, 2005).

6. Charles Palissot, *La Comédie des Philosophes et autres textes*, ed. Olivier Ferret (Saint-Etienne: Publications de l'Université de Saint-Etienne, 2002).

7. Nicolas-Edme Rétif de La Bretonne, *L'Andrographe* (The Hague: Gosse, 1782), 129.

8. Richard Schechner, *Performance Theory* (London: Routledge, 2003), 112–70.

9. Jody Enders, *Death by Drama and Other Medieval Urban Legends* (Chicago: University of Chicago Press, 2002); Sarah Beam, *Laughing Matters: Farce and the Making of Absolutism in France* (Ithaca, NY: Cornell University Press, 2007).

10. Schechner, *Performance Theory*, 135.

11. Denis Diderot, *Le Paradoxe sur le comédien*, ed. Raymond Laubreaux (Paris: Flammarion, 1981), 12.

12. By Schechner, of course, but also by the many twentieth-century avant-garde playwrights and theorists who set out to resurrect a more efficacious mode of performance, in a reaction against bourgeois and realist drama.

13. Michael Fried, *Absorption and Theatricality: Painting and Beholder in the Age of Diderot* (Berkeley: University of California Press, 1980); Paul Friedland, *Political Actors: Representative Bodies & Theatricality in the Age of the French Revolution* (Ithaca, NY: Cornell University Press, 2002).

14. Enrico Rufi, *Le Rêve laïque de Mercier*, Studies on Voltaire and the Eighteenth Century (Oxford: Voltaire Foundation, 1995); Alain Ménil, *Diderot et le drame: Théâtre et politique* (Paris: Presses universitaires de France, 1995).

15. Maria Teodora Comsa, "Society Theater: A Laboratory for Esthetic and Social Change (1715–1815)" (PhD diss., Stanford University, 2014).

16. Emmett Kennedy et al., *Theatre, Opera, and Audiences in Revolutionary Paris: Analysis and Repertory* (Westport, CT: Greenwood Press, 1996), 62.

17. Anne Boës-Anthouard, *La Lanterne magique de l'histoire: Essai sur le théâtre historique en France de 1750 à 1789*, Studies on Voltaire and the Eighteenth Century (Oxford: Voltaire Foundation, 1982), 47.

18. Kirsten Postert studies several seventeenth-century plays that reenact current events. However, these all date back to the early decades of the century, before the institution of French classicism, and represent therefore more a vestige of medieval, efficacious theater than a counterexample to my argument. Kirsten Postert, *Tragédie historique ou Histoire en tragédie? Les sujets d'histoire moderne dans la tragédie française (1550–1715)* (Tübingen, Ger.: G. Narr, 2010).

19. To every sweeping claim there are exceptions. I know of two, both fascinating. The first is the performance at the Comédie-Française in 1698 of a play entitled *Le Mari retrouvé*, which recreated on stage the events at the heart of the then ongoing trial of Louis de La Pivardière. For more, see Jeffrey Ravel, *The Would-Be Commoner: A Tale of Deception, Murder, and Justice in Seventeenth-Century France* (New York: Houghton Mifflin Company, 2008). The second play, entitled *Cartouche ou les brigands*, purported to dramatize the crimes of the famous bandit. It too was performed at the Comédie-Française, during Cartouche's trial in 1721. For more, see Christian Biet, "L'Affaire Cartouche (1721): Scène juridique/scène littéraire. L'opinion publique, le théâtre, le pouvoir et le droit," in *Représentations du procès: Droit, théâtre, littérature, cinéma*, ed. Christian Biet and Laurence Schifano (Paris: Université Paris X-Nanterre, 2003), 445–59. It should be noted that both plays were immediately criticized (by magistrates and by the crown), with the Cartouche play also banned.

20. Sarah Maza, *Private Lives and Public Affairs: The Causes Célèbres of Prerevolutionary France* (Berkeley: University of California Press, 1993), 314.

21. In a later article, Maza appears to amend her earlier conclusions, noting that "the transformation in public culture that took place at the end of the Old Regime is therefore somewhat more complex than that suggested by some scholars who describe it as a shift away from the primarily iconic (the body of the king) to the primarily textual (the word of the law)." She goes on to argue that there is "substantial evidence, in the writings of progressive thinkers of the later eighteenth century, of a belief that an ideally open courtroom . . . could fulfill the same exemplary function as this new form of drama—indeed, that the two could feed off one another." Sarah Maza, "The Theater of Punishment: Melodrama and Judicial Reform in Prerevolutionary France," in *From the Royal to the Republican Body: Incorporating the Political in Seventeenth- and Eighteenth-Century France*, ed. Sara E. Melzer and Kathryn Norberg (Berkeley: University of California Press, 1998), 182–97.

22. Katherine Taylor, *In the Theater of Criminal Justice: The Palais de Justice in Second Empire Paris* (Princeton, NJ: Princeton University Press, 1993), xviii–xix. Laura Mason makes a similar argument in "The 'Bosom of Proof': Criminal Justice and the Renewal of Oral Culture During the French Revolution," *Journal of Modern History* 76 (2004): 29–61.

23. Taylor, *In the Theater of Criminal Justice*, 6.

24. For a more detailed description of the modus operandi of criminal proceedings under the ancien régime, see Richard Mowery Andrews, *Law, Magistracy and Crime in Old Regime Paris, 1735–1789* (New York: Cambridge University Press, 1994). See also Michel Foucault, *Surveiller et punir: Naissance de la prison* (Paris: Gallimard, 1975), 45–46.

25. See Ravel, *Would-Be Commoner*, 69–73; Natalie Zemon Davis, *Fiction in the Archives: Pardon Tales and Their Tellers in Sixteenth-Century France* (Stanford, CA: Stanford University Press, 1990); Maza, *Private Lives*.

26. On the existence of liberal thought in the eighteenth century, see Andreas Kalyvas and Ira Katznelson, *Liberal Beginnings: Making a Republic for the Moderns* (Cambridge: Cambridge University Press, 2008).

27. Jean-Claude Farcy, *Histoire de la justice en France* (Paris: La Découverte, 2015); Emmanuel Berger, *La Justice pénale sous la Révolution: Les Enjeux d'un modèle judiciaire libéral* (Rennes, Fr.: Presses universitaires de Rennes, 2008).

28. For instance, see Maza, *Private Lives*, 238.

29. *Le Pour et le contre: Recueil complet des opinions prononcées à l'Assemblée Conventionnelle dans le procès de Louis XVI* (Paris: Buisson, 1792–93), 3:18–19, 5:86.

30. Ibid., 3:389.

31. Ibid., 1:144, 378–79, 2:161–62, 3:198.

32. Ibid., 4:153, 5:26–27.

33. Ibid., 2:270–71.

34. Ibid., 2:330, 372, 3:166.

35. Ibid., 3:20–21, 5:112.

36. Ibid., 4:223–24.

37. Pierre Frantz, "Pas d'entracte pour la Révolution," in *La Carmagnole des muses: L'Homme de lettres et l'artiste dans la Révolution*, ed. Jean-Claude Bonnet (Paris: Armand Colin, 1988), 381.

38. Susan Maslan, *Revolutionary Acts: Theater, Democracy, and the French Revolution* (Baltimore: Johns Hopkins University Press, 2005); Friedland, *Political Actors*.

39. Cecilia Feilla, *The Sentimental Theater of the French Revolution* (Burlington, VT: Ashgate, 2013). Kennedy et al., *Theatre, Opera, and Audiences in Revolutionary Paris*.

40. Kennedy et al. and Feilla aim in part to challenge this understanding of Revolutionary drama by showing that the popularity of ancien régime plays, genres, and forms surpassed that of the polemical, often political works for which the Revolution is primarily known. While such a corrective is a welcome one, in that it paints a more nuanced picture of the theater of the Revolution, it does not diminish the significance of the more illustrious topical plays. While the latter may have had fewer performances, their impact was far greater, both on the key debates and events of the Revolution and on subsequent depictions of Revolutionary culture and theater.

41. One recent exception: Philippe Bourdin links the "théâtre patriotique" of the Revolution to the rise of a "théâtre historique" during the Enlightenment. His explanation for this transition (from historical to patriotic and topical) largely remains a political one, however. Philippe Bourdin, *Aux Origines du théâtre patriotique* (Paris: CNRS, 2017).

42. Matthew Buckley likewise seeks to reintegrate Revolutionary drama into the history of French theater but focuses almost exclusively on its continuity with later forms (he finds in the theater of the Revolution "the making of modern drama") rather than with earlier ones. Matthew Buckley, *Tragedy Walks the Streets: The French Revolution in the Making of Modern Drama* (Baltimore: Johns Hopkins University Press, 2006).

43. See Chapter 3, as well as Barbara Villez, "Lawyers and Courts in French Popular Culture," *Oxford Research Encyclopedia of Criminology and Criminal Justice* (August 2017), doi: 10.1093/acrefore/9780190264079.013.187.

CHAPTER 1

1. Diderot, *Fils naturel*, 43.

2. On dramaturgy (and particularly the perplexing question of the creative process in Diderot), see Jacques Chouillet, *La Formation des idées esthétiques de Diderot: 1745–1763* (Paris: A. Colin, 1973), as well as Yvon Belaval, *L'Esthétique sans paradoxe de Diderot* (Paris: Gallimard, 1950). On scenography (notably the issue of realism and the tableau), see Pierre Frantz, *L'Esthétique du tableau dans le théâtre du XVIIIe siècle* (Paris: Presses universitaires de France, 1998). On acting (in particular on the topic of pantomime and sensibility), see Angelica Goodden, *Actio and Persuasion: Dramatic Performance in Eighteenth-Century France* (Oxford: Clarendon, 1986). Lastly, on reception (especially the shift from admiration to sympathetic identification and absorption), see Ménil, *Diderot et le drame*, as well as Fried, *Absorption and Theatricality*.

3. In fact, save for two psychoanalytic readings—James Creech, *Diderot: Thresholds of Representation* (Columbus: Ohio State University Press, 1986), and James E. Fowler, *Voicing Desire: Family and Sexuality in Diderot's Narrative*, Studies on Voltaire and the Eighteenth Century (Oxford: Voltaire Foundation, 2000)—I am unaware of any attempts at understanding Diderot's interest in the reenactment of events still present in living memory.

4. Reinhart Koselleck, *Futures Past: On the Semantics of Historical Time*, trans. Keith Tribe (Cambridge, MA: MIT Press, 1985).

5. In *Tragedy Walks the Streets*, Buckley notes that the shift in the perception of history first diagnosed by Koselleck may also provide an explanation for the emergence of new theatrical genres in the middle of the eighteenth century. Classical historiography, like classical genres (tragedy and comedy), defined a set of exemplary rules and forms, which ensured that differences were always contained within a restricted and unchanging space of potential experience. As Buckley suggests, the appearance of new genres was made possible by a conception of the future that stressed its radical newness and unpredictability, instead of its homology to the past. Although by no means incompatible with it, my analysis differs from Buckley's in that I am less interested in the generic history of the theater than in the changes in its perceived relationship to the past.

6. On historiography as a form of exorcism, see Michel de Certeau, *The Writing of History*, trans. Tom Conley (New York: Columbia University Press, 1988).

7. See especially sections 1451a and 1451b of the *Poetics*, in which Aristotle contrasts history and poetry. Aristotle, *Poetics*, trans. Anthony Kenny (Oxford: Oxford University Press, 2013).

8. For the most astute and influential advocacy of an indeterminate setting, see Pierre Corneille, *Trois discours sur le poème dramatique*, ed. Marc Escola and Bénédicte Louvat (Paris: GF Flammarion, 1999).

9. Renaud Bret-Vitoz, *L'Espace et la scène: Dramaturgie de la tragédie française, 1691–1759*, Studies on Voltaire and the Eighteenth Century (Oxford: Voltaire Foundation, 2008), 109.

10. Ménil, *Diderot et le drame*, 60.

11. Louis-Sébastien Mercier, *Du Théâtre ou essai sur l'art dramatique* (Amsterdam: chez E. Van Harrevelt, 1773), 42.

12. Diderot, *Fils naturel*, 43.

13. Ibid.

14. Gita May, "Diderot and Burke: A Study in Aesthetic Affinity," *PMLA* 75 (1960): 527–39.

15. Denis Diderot, *Lettre sur les aveugles à l'usage de ceux qui voient; Lettre sur les sourds et muets à l'usage de ceux qui entendent et qui parlent*, ed. Marian Hobson (Paris: Flammarion, 2000), 147.

16. Denis Diderot, *Essais sur la peinture*, in *Diderot, Œuvres*, ed. Laurent Versini (Paris: R. Laffont, 1996), 4:472.

17. Hence, in the *Essais sur la peinture*, little more than a glimpse of a statue's foot is enough to know it belongs to a hunchback, while the proportions of the limbs of a drawn figure can communicate his or her daily existence (habits, duties, and rank) to the experienced beholder. Ibid., 467–68.

18. Denis Diderot, *Salon de 1767*, in Versini, *Diderot, Œuvres*, 4:532.

19. Diderot, *Fils naturel*, 43.

20. Remond de Sainte-Albine, *Le Comédien*, in *Mémoires de Molé et Le Comédien*, ed. Charles-Guillaume Étienne (Paris: E. Ledoux, 1825), 105.

21. Ibid., 106.

22. On the development in the eighteenth century of an "aesthetic of the tableau," see Frantz, *L'Esthétique du tableau.*

23. Denis Diderot, *Les Entretiens sur le Fils naturel*, ed. Jean Goldzink (Paris: GF Flammarion, 2005), 80.

24. On Condillac and the eighteenth-century fascination with his *langage d'action*, see Sophia Rosenfeld, A *Revolution in Language: The Problem of Signs in Late Eighteenth-Century France* (Stanford, CA: Stanford University Press, 2001), 36–56.

25. Diderot, *Les Entretiens*, 84.

26. Ibid.

27. All of these conventions are cited and ridiculed by Diderot in his "Lettre à Madame Riccoboni," reprinted in ibid., 345–58.

28. Ibid., 352.

29. Diderot, *Le Paradoxe*, 136.

30. For more on the aesthetic differences between *Le Fils naturel* and *Le Paradoxe*, notably the reintroduction of distance, both between life and fiction and between the spectator and the stage, see Yann Robert, "De l'Absorption et de l'identification chez Diderot: Illusion et participation du spectateur au dix-huitième siècle," in *La Scène, la salle et la coulisse dans le théâtre du XVIIIe siècle en France*, ed. Pierre Frantz and Thomas Wynn (Paris: Presses de l'Université Paris-Sorbonne, 2011), 263–78.

31. Diderot, *Les Entretiens*, 358.

32. Sainte-Albine, *Le Comédien*, 105–6.

33. In his *Paradoxe*, Diderot describes the art of acting in antithetical terms, even designating repetition and self-mastery as essential elements in the development of a great actor.

34. Diderot, *Les Entretiens*, 359.

35. Diderot, *Fils naturel*, 42.

36. Creech, *Diderot*, 86. Creech stresses the significance of Rosalie's declaration that "in him [Dorval] I met myself constantly."

37. Like reenactments, commemorations first appeared as a notion in the second half of the eighteenth century and became tremendously popular during the Revolution, with the

institution of national festivals. For more, see Mona Ozouf, "Peut-on commémorer la révolution française?" *Le Débat* 26 (1983/4): 161–72, as well as Mona Ozouf, *La Fête révolutionnaire: 1789–1799* (Paris: Gallimard, 1976).

38. Jay Caplan, *Framed Narratives: Diderot's Genealogy of the Beholder* (Minneapolis: University of Minnesota Press, 1985), 18.

39. For instance, see David Marshall, *The Surprising Effects of Sympathy: Marivaux, Diderot, Rousseau and Mary Shelley* (Chicago: University of Chicago Press, 1988), as well as Caplan, *Framed Narratives.*

40. Béatrice Didier, *Diderot dramaturge du vivant* (Paris: Presses universitaires de France, 2001), 35.

41. On the artistic and political interventionism of the parterre, see Jeffrey Ravel, *The Contested Parterre: Public Theater and French Political Culture, 1680–1791* (Ithaca, NY: Cornell University Press, 1999).

42. Mercier, among others, hailed this idea for its ability to grant "eternal life" and relevance to the masterpieces of the past. Mercier, *Du Théâtre*, 126.

43. Lynn Hunt, *The Family Romance of the French Revolution* (Berkeley: University of California Press, 1992).

44. Diderot, *Salon de 1767*, 721.

45. Diderot, *Lettre sur les aveugles*, 147.

46. Vernon, *Apologie du théâtre adressée à Mlle. Clairon* (The Hague: n.p., 1762), 53.

47. Sainte-Albine, *Le Comédien*, 106.

48. Denis Diderot, *De la Poésie dramatique*, ed. Jean Goldzink (Paris: GF Flammarion, 2005), 195.

49. Margaret Gilman, "Imagination and Creation in Diderot," *Diderot Studies* 2 (1952): 200–220.

50. On the significance of the sketch in Diderot's thought, see Angelica Goodden, "Painting for the Eye and Painting for the Mind: Correspondences of the Arts in Eighteenth-Century France," *Oxford Art Journal* 7, no.1 (January 1984): 3–14; Herbert Dieckmann, *Cinq leçons sur Diderot* (Geneva: Droz, 1959), 106–8.

51. Diderot, *Salon de 1767*, 715. This quotation is a direct (and unattributed) translation of a passage in Edmund Burke's *Philosophical Enquiry*, from which Diderot borrowed a great deal. See May, "Diderot and Burke," 535–36.

52. Denis Diderot, *Salon de 1765*, in Versini, *Diderot, Œuvres*, 4:388.

53. Friedrich Melchior Grimm et al., *Correspondance littéraire, philosophique et critique*, ed. Maurice Tourneux (Paris: Garnier Frères, 1877–82), 4:176.

54. Diderot, *Salon de 1765*, 388.

55. Jean-Christophe Bailly, Denis Guénoun, and Bernard Stiegler, *Le Théâtre, le peuple, la passion* (Besançon, Fr.: Les Solitaires intempestifs, 2006).

56. Diderot, "Lettre à Madame Riccoboni," 347–48.

57. Diderot, *De la Poésie dramatique*, 249.

58. Ibid.

59. Denis Diderot, *Les Entretiens*, 90.

60. Fried, *Absorption and Theatricality.*

61. Diderot, *Fils naturel*, 105.

62. Hans Robert Jauss, "Levels of Identification of Hero and Audience," *New Literary History* 5, no. 2 (Winter 1974): 283–317.

63. Diderot, *Les Entretiens*, 132.

64. Marie-Hélène Huet, *Rehearsing the Revolution: The Staging of Marat's Death, 1793–1797*, trans. Robert Hurley (Berkeley: University of California Press, 1982), 32–33.

65. Denis Diderot, *Jacques le Fataliste* (Paris: Le Livre de Poche, 1972), 196.

66. Diderot, *Salon de 1767*, 610–11.

67. Diderot, *Les Entretiens*, 154.

68. Ibid., 155.

69. Diderot, *Fils naturel*, 105.

70. Diderot, *Les Entretiens*, 125.

71. Ibid., 77.

CHAPTER 2

1. Jean-Marie Clément and Joseph de La Porte, *Anecdotes Dramatiques* (Paris: veuve Duchesne, 1775), 2:67–68.

2. For a recent, in-depth study of the quarrel, which goes beyond the ideological content of the play to show its significance in the history of French theater, see Logan Connors, *Dramatic Battles in Eighteenth-Century France: Philosophes, Anti-philosophes and Polemical Theatre*, Studies on Voltaire and the Eighteenth Century (Oxford: Voltaire Foundation, 2012).

3. Many of these pamphlets can be found in Ferret's edition of *Les Philosophes.*

4. Louis Coste d'Arnobat, "Le Philosophe, ami de tout le monde," in Palissot, *La Comédie des Philosophes*, 169.

5. In the eighteenth century, "satire" was used in French to designate a wide range of texts, including any work displaying a variety of subjects and forms (verse, prose, dialogue, fable). To this day, "satire" remains a polysemic term, referring equally to texts ridiculing social ranks, character flaws, and specific individuals. Here, my usage of the term is limited to plays accusing and condemning individuals by name.

6. "Les Si et les mais," in Palissot, *La Comédie des Philosophes*, 165.

7. Élie-Catherine Fréron, *L'Année littéraire* (Geneva: Slatkine Reprints, 1966), 7:330–31. Fréron goes on to note that this distinguishes Palissot from Molière, who never used "odious colors" (7:331).

8. "Over 180 plays introducing an absurd 'philosophe' were written in eighteenth-century France." David Welsh, "'Philosophers' and 'Alchemists' in Some Eighteenth-Century Russian Comedies," *Slavic and East European Journal* 8, no. 2 (Summer 1964): 149.

9. Olivier Ferret, "Mises en scène satiriques des Encyclopédistes: Autour de la querelle des *Philosophes* de Palissot," in *Le Philosophe sur les planches: L'Image du philosophe dans le théâtre des Lumières (1680–1815)*, ed. Pierre Hartmann (Strasbourg, Fr.: Presses Universitaires de Strasbourg, 2004), 113–28.

10. Ibid., 126.

11. Charles Palissot, "Lettre de l'auteur de la comédie des *Philosophes* au public pour servir de préface à la pièce," in Palissot, *La Comédie des Philosophes*, 117.

12. Jean-Jacques Rousseau, *Lettre à d'Alembert*, ed. Marc Buffat (Paris: Flammarion, 2003), 85–95.

13. Mercier, *Du Théâtre*, 55.

14. Rousseau, *Lettre à d'Alembert*, 75.

15. Denis Diderot, *Le Neveu de Rameau*, in Versini, *Diderot, Œuvres*, 2:661.

16. Louis-François Nouel de Buzonnière, *Essai sur les moyens de rendre la comédie utile aux mœurs*, in *De la réformation du théâtre*, by Luigi Riccoboni (Paris: Debure père, 1767), 23.

17. Antoine de Baecque, *Les Éclats du rire: La Culture des rieurs au XVIIIe siècle* (Paris: Calmann-Lévy, 2000), 107.

18. Jean Goldzink, *Comique et comédie au siècle des Lumières* (Paris: L'Harmattan, 2000), 36.

19. Mercier, *Du Théâtre*, 55.

20. Rousseau, *Lettre à d'Alembert*, 175–76.

21. English Showalter has noted that until *Le Cercle*, Palissot's worldview most closely resembled that of the *philosophes*. Similarly, he would later abandon his former allies and defend liberal and irreligious views during the Revolution. Both the beginning and the end of his career thus show him to have been more of an opportunist than a staunch *anti-philosophe*. English Showalter, "'Madame a fait un livre': Madame de Graffigny, Palissot et *Les Philosophes*," *Recherches sur Diderot et sur l'Encyclopédie* 23 (1997): 109–25.

22. Although his focus is entirely different, Connors also notes certain similarities between Palissot and his rivals: "While *philosophes* and *anti-philosophes* strongly disagreed on content, both parties relied on similar strategies of pamphlet publication and theatrical persuasion to enlighten and convince the spectator into adopting their world-views." Connors, *Dramatic Battles*, 74.

23. Catherine Volpilhac-Auger singles him out as the "most mistreated" ancient dramatist in the early modern era. Catherine Volpilhac-Auger, "Aristophane, 'poète comique qui n'est ni comique ni poète,' mis en page et en français au XVIIIe siècle," in *Philologie et théâtre: Traduire, commenter, interpréter le théâtre antique en Europe (XVe–XVIIIe siècle)*, ed. Véronique Lochert and Zoé Schweitzer (Amsterdam: Rodopi, 2012), 144.

24. See Chapter 1.

25. Romain Piana, "Brumoy et l'interprétation satirique d'Aristophane," *Anabases* 14 (2011): 87–100.

26. Volpilhac-Auger, "Aristophane."

27. "Les Qu'est-ce? A l'auteur de la comédie des *Philosophes*," in Palissot, *La Comédie des Philosophes*, 127.

28. Cited in Connors, *Dramatic Battles*, 63.

29. Palissot, "Lettre de l'auteur," 115.

30. Anne Dacier, *Comédies grecques d'Aristophane* (Paris: D. Thierry et Cl. Barbin, 1692).

31. Pierre Brumoy, *Le Théâtre des Grecs* (Paris: Rollin père, J. B. Coignard et Rollin fils, 1730), vol. 3.

32. Ignace Hugary de Lamarche-Courmont, "Réponse aux différents écrits publiés contre la comédie des *Philosophes*, ou parallèle des *Nuées* d'Aristophane, des *Femmes savantes*, du *Méchant* et des *Philosophes*," in Palissot, *La Comédie des Philosophes*, 305.

33. Raymond Trousson, "Le Théâtre tragique grec au siècle des Lumières," *Studies on Voltaire and the Eighteenth Century* 155 (1976): 2114.

34. Brumoy, *Théâtre des Grecs*, 3:iii.

35. Piana, "Brumoy et l'interprétation satirique d'Aristophane," 99.

36. Grimm et al., *Correspondance littéraire*, 4:240–41.

37. Charles Palissot, "Dialogues historiques et critiques: Aristophane & le Père Brumoy," in *Œuvres complètes* (Geneva: Slatkine reprints, 1971), 3:302. Palissot borrows this argument, almost verbatim, from Lamarche-Courmont, "Réponse aux différents écrits," 302.

38. Louis Poinsinet de Sivry, *Théâtre d'Aristophane* (Paris: Chez Desray, 1790), 1:13.

39. Diderot, *De la Poésie dramatique*, 179.

40. Bertrand de Latour, *Réflexions morales, politiques, historiques et littéraires sur le théâtre*, in *Œuvres Complètes*, ed. L'Abbé Migne (Paris: Migne, 1855), 4:554.

41. Denis Diderot, *Mémoires pour Catherine II*, ed. Paul Vernière (Paris: Classiques Garnier, 1966), 263.

42. Ibid., 102.

43. Diderot, *Le Paradoxe*, 136.

44. Voltaire, *Dictionnaire philosophique*, ed. René Pomeau (Paris: Garnier-Flammarion, 1964), 51.

45. See Roland Mortier, "La Satire, ce *poison de la littérature*: Voltaire et la nouvelle déontologie de l'homme de lettres," in *Essays on the Age of Enlightenment in Honor of Ira O. Wade*, ed. Jean Macary (Geneva: Droz, 1977).

46. Louis de Jaucourt, "Libelle," in Diderot and d'Alembert, *Encyclopédie*, 9:459.

47. Volker Kapp, "Satire et injure au XVIIIe siècle: Le Conflit entre la morale et la politique dans le débat sur les libelles," *Cahiers de l'Association internationale des études francaises* 36, no. 1 (1984): 155–65.

48. Voltaire, "Poems by C. Churchill," in *Œuvres complètes* (Paris: Didot, 1861), 9:236.

49. On these two definitions of "public" in the early modern era—the first, designating the political body; the second, that which is exposed to general view—and on the shift from the first to the second, leading to the birth of a modern notion of privacy, see Antoine Lilti, *The Invention of Celebrity*, trans. Lynn Jeffress (Cambridge: Polity Press, 2017), 80–81.

50. Jean-François Marmontel, "Comédie," in Diderot and d'Alembert, *Encyclopédie*, 3:667.

51. Ibid., 3:666.

52. Ibid., 3:667; Jean-Jacques Barthélemy, *Voyage du jeune Anacharsis en Grèce* (Paris: de Bure, 1788), 3:579; Voltaire, "Poems by C. Churchill," 236.

53. Louis-Sébastien Mercier, *Tableau de Paris* (Geneva: Slatkine Reprints, 1979), 4:186; Louis Charpentier, *Causes de la décadence du goût sur le théâtre* (Paris: Dufour, 1768), 1:155–56.

54. Both Marmontel and Barthélemy fall into that category.

55. Mercier, *Tableau de Paris*, 1:ix.

56. Louis-Sébastien Mercier, *Satyres contre Racine et Boileau* (Paris: Hénée, 1808), vi–viii.

57. Mercier, *Tableau de Paris*, 4:237–38.

58. Hence, Maza states in her *Private Lives* that "in the later eighteenth century most political pamphlets, although usually written by impoverished hacks, were commissioned and paid for by members of the elite" (179). See also Jeremy Popkin, "Pamphlet Journalism at the End of the Old Regime," *Eighteenth-Century Studies* 22 (Spring 1989): 351–67.

59. Mercier, *Tableau de Paris*, 6:88, 7:148.

60. Cited in Rufi, *Le Rêve laïque de Mercier*, 192.

61. Mercier, *Du Théâtre*, 89–90.

62. Ibid., 60–62.

63. Ibid., 151–52.

64. Ibid., 62.

65. Ibid., 39.

66. Ibid., 3–4.

67. Diderot, *De la Poésie dramatique*, 173–74.

68. Louis-Sébastien Mercier, *L'An 2440* (n.p.: n.p., 1786), 2:11–12; Nicolas-Edme Rétif de la Bretonne, *La Mimographe* (Amsterdam: Changuion, 1770), 119–20; Jean Mauduit-Larive, *Réflexions sur l'art théâtral* (Paris: Rondonneau, 1800), 40; *Journal des savants*, April 1773, 512.

69. Jean-Baptiste-Antoine Suard, "Des Applaudissements au théâtre," in *Mélanges de littérature* (Geneva: Slatkine, 1971), 4:330.

70. Mercier, *Tableau de Paris*, 3:27.

71. Charpentier, *Causes de la décadence du goût*, 2:139.

72. Ibid., 2:138.

73. Grimm et al., *Correspondance littéraire*, 3:483.

74. Mercier, *Tableau de Paris*, 3:28.

75. Suard, "Des Applaudissements au théâtre," 330.

76. Indeed, according to Mercier, it is possible to judge a spectator's humanity by his or her reaction to a theatrical performance. *Du Théâtre*, 12.

77. Charpentier, *Causes de la décadence du goût*, 2:139–40.

78. Jean-François Marmontel, *Éléments de littérature*, in *Œuvres Complètes de Marmontel*, ed. René de Chazet (Paris: Verdiere, 1818), 14:500.

79. Ibid.

80. On the shift from a vision of dramatic judgment based on normative or prescriptive criteria to a more empirical model, based on the emotional experience of the spectator, see Suzanne Pucci, *Sites of the Spectator: Emerging Literary and Cultural Practice in Eighteenth-Century France*, Studies on Voltaire and the Eighteenth Century (Oxford: Voltaire Foundation, 2001).

81. Louis-Sébastien Mercier, *Nouvel examen de la tragédie française*, in *De la littérature et des littérateurs* (Yverdon, Switz.: n.p., 1778), 99; Marmontel, *Éléments de littérature*, 14:504–5.

82. Mercier, *Du Théâtre*, 62.

83. Pierre Frantz, "Appropriation bourgeoise et populaire de l'histoire nationale dans les drames historiques de Mercier," *Romanistische Zeitschrift* 3–4 (1979): 319–34.

84. Mercier, *Tableau de Paris*, 9:285.

85. Mercier, *Du Théâtre*, 203.

86. Few scholars have noted the rise of a more judicial theater. Maza is one of them, in "The Theater of Punishment," an article published after (and in some ways as an amendment to) her *Private Lives*. Scott Bryson is another, although his work focuses primarily on the link between bourgeois drama and public executions and, as a result, on theater as a disciplinary apparatus and deterrent (not as a trial or site of denunciation). Scott Bryson, *The Chastised Stage: Bourgeois Drama and the Exercise of Power* (Stanford, CA: Stanford University Press, 1991).

87. Louis-Sébastien Mercier, *Charles II, roi d'Angleterre en certain lieu* (Venice: n.p., 1789).

88. Mercier, *L'An 2440*, 1:287.

89. Grimm et al., *Correspondance littéraire*, 15:154–55.

90. Maza, *Privates Lives*.

91. Ravel, *Contested Parterre*.

92. Connors, *Dramatic Battles*, 19, 32.

93. Louis Petit de Bachaumont, *Mémoires secrets pour servir à l'histoire de la république des lettres en France* (London: John Adamson, 1788), 33:84–85.

94. Ibid. See also *Journal encyclopédique*, August 1786, 522–23. Gustave Desnoiresterres claims that the three verses were added to Mlle Contat's role, yet they are present in the second play, *L'Amant bourru*. Gustave Desnoiresterres, *La Comédie satirique au XVIIIe siècle* (Paris: Perrin, 1885), 259.

95. Jacques Marie Boutet de Monvel, *L'Amant bourru* (Paris: Duchesne, 1777), 74.

96. Mercier, *Du théâtre*, 153.

97. Louis Philipon de La Madelaine, "Des Moyens d'indemniser l'innocence injustement accusée et punie," in *Bibliothèque philosophique, du législateur, du politique, du jurisconsulte*, ed. Jacques Pierre Brissot (Paris: Desauges, 1782), 4:293.

98. Bachaumont, *Mémoires secrets*, 35:397–98.

99. Armand Fouquier, *Causes célèbres de tous les peuples* (Paris: Lebrun, 1867), 7:26.

100. Grimm et al., *Correspondance littéraire*, 10:398.

101. Ibid., 10:294. On the Morangiès affair, see Maza, *Private Lives*, 19–67.

102. Ibid., 10:398.

103. Desnoiresterres, *La Comédie satirique*.

104. Grimm et al., *Correspondance littéraire*, 10:398.

105. Ibid., 10:294.

106. Ibid.

107. Joseph-Marie Gros de Besplas, *Des Causes du bonheur public* (Paris: Batilliot, 1790), 299.

108. Latour, *Réflexions morales*, 4:123–24.

109. Ibid., 5:138.

110. Mercier, *Tableau de Paris*, 6:321.

111. Nicolas Veysman, *Mise en scène de l'opinion publique dans la littérature des Lumières* (Paris: Honoré Champion, 2004).

112. Ibid., 145. On Mercier's ambivalent portrayal of the people, see also Pierre Frantz, "L'Usage du peuple," in *Louis-Sébastien Mercier, un hérétique en littérature*, ed. Jean-Claude Bonnet (Paris: Mercure de France, 1995), 55–79, as well as Pierre Frantz, introduction to *Du Théâtre*, in Louis-Sébastien Mercier, *Mon Bonnet de nuit, suivi de Du Théâtre*, ed. Jean-Claude Bonnet and Pierre Frantz (Paris: Mercure de France, 1999), lxxvi–cvi.

113. Rousseau, *Lettre à d'Alembert*, 161.

114. Ibid., 162.

115. Ibid., 177.

116. Brumoy, *Théâtre des Grecs*, 3:303.

117. On the logic of the supplement, see Jacques Derrida, *De la grammatologie* (Paris: Les Editions de Minuit, 1967).

118. I borrow the phrase "politics of contestation," along with some of the ideas that follow, from Keith Baker's *Inventing the French Revolution: Essays on French Political Culture in the Eighteenth Century* (Cambridge: Cambridge University Press, 1990).

119. Jean-Jacques Rousseau, *Du Contrat social*, ed. Bruno Bernardi (Paris: Flammarion, 2001), 69.

120. Brumoy, *Théâtre des Grecs*, 3:302.

121. Latour, *Réflexions morales*, 5:138.

122. Veysman, *Mise en scène de l'opinion publique*, 158–59; Ravel, *Contested Parterre*, 214–17.

123. Mercier, *Du Théâtre*, 149, 234.

124. Ibid., x, 290; Mercier, *Tableau de Paris*, 8:109.

125. Mercier, *Tableau de Paris*, 8:109.

126. Julie C. Hayes hence makes the provocative claim that, in *Du Théâtre*, Mercier's "aggressively pursued fraternal ideal will not bring about an end to difference or inequity, but rather that it provides a grid for a powerful new authoritarianism. When the writer's pen becomes the equal of the monarch's scepter, the imbalance of power is not undone, but merely

reversed." Julie C. Hayes, "Changing the System: Mercier's Ideological Appropriation of Diderot," *Studies in Eighteenth-Century Culture* 18 (1988): 351.

127. Plutarch, *Les Vies des hommes illustres,* trans. Jacques Amyot (Paris: Michel Vascosan, 1565), 66. This passage is taken from Jacques Amyot's French translation of Plutarch's *Parallel Lives,* a volume that Rousseau not only owned but admired to the extent that, by the age of eight, he knew it by heart. As a result, even though Rousseau does not quote Solon's exact words in his *Lettre à d'Alembert,* we can safely assume that he knew them well. On Rousseau's debt to Plutarch, see Abraham C. Keller, "Plutarch and Rousseau's First Discours," *PMLA* 54 (March 1939): 212–22.

128. Jean-Baptiste-Antoine Suard, "Censure des théâtres," in *Mélanges de littérature,* 4:313.

129. Ibid., 4:314.

130. Gabriel-François Coyer, *Discours sur la Satyre contre les philosophes* (Athens: chez le libraire anti-philosophe, 1760), 70.

131. This passage is a translation by Barthélemy of Plato's description of Socrates's trial in his *Apology.* Barthélemy, *Voyage du jeune Anacharsis,* 3:514. See also Raymond Trousson, *Socrate devant Voltaire, Diderot, et Rousseau: La Conscience en face du mythe* (Paris: Minard, 1977), 58.

132. Convinced he was the victim of a conspiracy, Rousseau never ceased to demand greater accountability for political, legal, and literary accusers. In fact, he believed that his life had been thrown off course by the slanderous and illegal denunciation made against his father by a Mr. Gautier. Jean-Jacques Rousseau, *Les Confessions,* ed. Raymond Trousson (Paris: Imprimerie Nationale, 1995), 160.

133. Gros de Besplas, *Des Causes du bonheur public,* 332.

134. Rousseau, *Lettre à d'Alembert,* 179.

135. Charpentier, *Causes de la décadence du goût,* 2:149–50.

136. Latour, *Réflexions morales,* 5:559.

137. Friedland, *Political Actors.*

138. Rétif, *Mimographe,* 7–10.

139. Rétif, *L'Andrographe,* 129.

140. Rétif, *Mimographe,* 340.

141. See Nicolas-Edme Rétif de la Bretonne, *La Prévention nationale* (Paris: Regnault, 1784), 3:430.

142. This is no coincidence, as we know that Rétif read *Le Fils naturel* and borrowed heavily from it while writing *La Mimographe.* See Claude Jaëcklé-Plunian, *À propos des écrits sur le théâtre au dix-huitième siècle,* Studies on Voltaire and the Eighteenth Century (Oxford: Voltaire Foundation, 1999), 107.

143. Rétif, *L'Andrographe,* 189.

144. Ibid., 190.

145. Rétif, *Mimographe,* 378, 382.

146. Foucault, *Surveiller et punir.*

147. Bryson, *Chastised Stage*; Maza, *Private Lives.*

CHAPTER 3

1. Jacques Pierre Brissot, "De la décadence du barreau français," in Brissot, *Bibliothèque philosophique,* 6:359–409.

2. Ibid., 6:378.

3. On courtroom architecture, see Katherine Taylor, "Geometries of Power: Royal, Revolutionary, and Post-revolutionary French Courtrooms," *Journal of the Society of Architectural Historians* 72, no. 4 (December 2013): 434–74. On theatrical architecture, see Pannill Camp, *The First Frame* (Cambridge: Cambridge University Press, 2014).

4. Brissot, "De la décadence du barreau français," 377. François Philippe Gourdin also blames the narrow circle to which French lawyers are circumscribed for their inability to emulate the "corporal eloquence" of the ancients. *Considérations philosophiques sur l'action de l'orateur* (Amsterdam: Vve Desaint, 1775), 130–31.

5. Brissot, "De la décadence du barreau français," 378.

6. Ibid., 377.

7. Ibid., 378.

8. Ibid., 369.

9. Ibid., 374–75.

10. The Athenians often held important trials in the Theater of Dionysus. Thousands would gather in ancient Greece and Rome to watch a trial, as they might a theatrical performance. Actors and legal orators were held to practice a similar trade, and they often exchanged knowledge and even roles. Dianne Dutton, "Le Plaideur comme comédien: L'Art dramatique du procès," in Biet and Schifano, *Représentations du procès*, 127.

11. See the Introduction.

12. Brissot, "De la décadence du barreau français," 377.

13. Antoine-Louis Séguier, "Réquisitoire contre le mémoire pour les trois hommes condamnés à la roue," in *Barreau français. Collection des chefs-d'œuvre de l'éloquence judiciaire en France* (Paris: Panckoucke, 1822), 3:497.

14. Gérard Soulier, "Le Théâtre et le procès," *Droit & Société* 17–18 (1991): 16.

15. Brissot, "De la décadence du barreau français," 389–90.

16. See Dominique Margairaz, *François de Neufchâteau: Biographie intellectuelle* (Paris: Publications de la Sorbonne, 2005), 83.

17. Brissot, "De la décadence du barreau français," 376.

18. Ibid., 389.

19. For instance, see Maza, *Private Lives*, 238.

20. Dutton, "Le Plaideur comme comédien," 127.

21. Ibid.

22. In fact, Goodden has noted that the actio of public orators (like lawyers and preachers) was held in the seventeenth century to be fundamentally different from playacting (which was not, until the early eighteenth century, considered to be a form of actio, or an element of classical rhetoric). Goodden, *Actio and Persuasion*, 49.

23. As Dutton herself notes in "Concurrence et convergence: Le Sermon et le plaidoyer de l'âge classique" *Biblio 17* 166 (2006): 223–32.

24. Latour, *Réflexions morales*, 4:190–91.

25. The most frequently cited example is that of François de Neufchâteau, who was believed to have been expelled from the Order of Barristers for his marriage to the niece of the famous actor Préville. See Gaston Maugras, *Les Comédiens hors la loi* (Paris: C. Lévy, 1887), 221. Modern scholars have since challenged this account of Neufchâteau's disbarment as a myth concocted by Linguet and Palissot, yet its very credibility and lasting popularity speaks to the depth of the order's antagonism toward actors.

26. See Louis Hurtaut Dancourt, *L.-H. Dancourt, Arlequin de Berlin, à M. J.-J. Rousseau* (Amsterdam: Schneider, 1759), 200–201; Barthélemy-Claude Graillard de Graville, *L'Homme vrai* (Amsterdam: Dufour, 1761), 77–78.

27. Graville, *L'Homme vrai*, 77–78.

28. Pierre Biarnoy de Merville, *Règles pour former un avocat* (Paris: Durand, 1778), 358–59.

29. Gourdin, *Considérations philosophiques*, 144.

30. The first is Luigi Riccoboni, who answers Gourdin's question negatively at the end of *Pensées sur la déclamation* (Paris: Briasson, 1738). I could not identify the second (Philippe Poisson?) or the passage to which Gourdin alludes.

31. Gourdin, *Considérations philosophiques*, 147.

32. Pierre-Louis-Claude Gin, *De l'Eloquence du barreau* (Paris: Hérissant fils, 1767), 301.

33. Merville, *Règles pour former un avocat*, 372–73.

34. Gin hence states in *De l'Eloquence du barreau* that "all of the rules come down to one principle: *Feel intensely, and you will express likewise*," before adding that "the principal utility that the orator must extract from the theater is to gain mastery over his delivery, to moderate or increase its power" (300–301).

35. See Gourdin, *Considérations philosophiques*, 147; Gin, *De l'Eloquence du barreau*, 300.

36. David Bell, *Lawyers and Citizens: The Making of a Political Elite in Old Regime France* (Oxford: Oxford University Press, 1994), 47–48.

37. Ibid., 37.

38. Henri François d'Aguesseau, "L'Indépendance de l'avocat," in *Discours de Monsieur le chancelier d'Aguesseau* (Paris: Libraires associés, 1783), 126–27.

39. Bell, *Lawyers and Citizens*, 6.

40. Maza, *Private Lives*, 94. Maza also notes that famous lawyers were wined, dined, and paraded before aristocrats, who befriended them and, when needed, begged for their counsel (257).

41. Cited in Lauren Clay, *Stagestruck: The Business of Theater in Eighteenth-Century France and Its Colonies* (Ithaca, NY: Cornell University Press, 2013), 99.

42. Chavray de Boissy, *L'Avocat, ou Réflexions sur l'exercice du barreau* (Rome: L. Cellot, 1777), 244.

43. Lilti, *Invention of Celebrity*, 86–108.

44. Lenard R. Berlanstein, "Women and Power in Eighteenth-Century France: Actresses at the Comédie-Française," *Feminist Studies* 20, no. 3 (1994): 475–506.

45. Lilti, *Invention of Celebrity*, 58.

46. Armand-Gaston Camus, *Lettres sur la profession d'avocat*, ed. André Dupin (Brussels: H. Tarlier, 1833), 254.

47. *Consultation sur la discipline des avocats* (Paris: Knapen, 1775), 16.

48. Gros de Besplas, *Causes du bonheur public*, 291. Likewise, Louis Charpentier warns that modern love of theater is undermining "paternal authority," as it had in ancient Rome. *Causes de la décadence du goût*, 2:39.

49. On the political motivations behind Plato's exclusion of actors from his republic, see Philippe Lacoue-Labarthe, *Typography: Mimesis, Philosophy, Politics* (Cambridge, MA: Harvard University Press, 1989). See also Jacques Rancière, *Le Philosophe et ses pauvres* (Paris: Flammarion, 2007), 74–77.

50. Paul-Antoine-Nicolas Nolivos de Saint-Cyr, *Tableau du siècle* (Geneva: n.p., 1759), 215; Louis Hurtaut Dancourt, *Lettre de l'Arlequin de Berlin à M. Fréron* (Amsterdam: Schneider, 1760), 43.

51. Nolivos de Saint-Cyr, *Tableau du siècle*, 169.

52. See Chapter 2. For other examples of this anxiety, see Friedland, *Political Actors*.

53. Actors could not be tried in court. When an actor was suspected of a crime, the Gentilshommes de la Chambre assembled to settle on a verdict and punishment. Maugras, *Les Comédiens hors la loi*, 215–17.

54. The term *infâme* was also used in ancient Rome to designate actors,107 as well as all other groups lacking a legal status. Florence Dupont, "La Scène juridique," *Communications* 26 (1977): 62–77.

55. Jacques Pierre Brissot, *Théorie des lois criminelles* (Berlin: n.p., 1781), 2:112; Voltaire, *Prix de la justice et de l'humanité* (London: n.p., 1777), 99; Julien Dentand, *Essai de jurisprudence criminelle* (Lausanne, Switz.: n.p., 1785), 2:93–94.

56. Jean-Paul Marat, *Plan de législation criminelle* (Paris: Rochette, 1790), 133. See also Joseph de Bernardi, *Principes des lois criminelles* (Paris: Serviere, 1788), 244.

57. Maugras, *Les Comédiens hors la loi*, 221.

58. Brissot, *Théorie des lois criminelles*, 2:114. Likewise, Beccaria does not mention actors.

59. Dutton, "Le Plaideur comme comédien," 127.

60. Bell, *Lawyers and Citizens*, 36. For a transcription and translation of this oath, see Ambroise Falconnet, *Essai sur le barreau grec, romain et français* (Paris: Grangé, 1773), 133–34.

61. Merville, *Règles pour former un avocat*, 411. See also Charles Rollin, *Traité des études* (Paris: Estienne, 1741), 2:450–51; Chavray de Boissy, *L'Avocat*, 235.

62. Bell, *Lawyers and Citizens*, 36 and 124.

63. Merville, *Règles pour former un avocat*, 387.

64. Many other treatises and manuals make this point, notably Rollin, *Traité des études*, 2:445 and Joseph Lanjuinais, *Manuel des jeunes orateurs* (Moudon, Switz.: Société typographique, 1777), 1:341.

65. *Consultation sur la discipline des avocats*, 3.

66. Merville, *Règles pour former un avocat*, 393.

67. Jean Domat, *Les Lois civiles dans leur ordre naturel* (Paris: Veuve Cavelier, 1766), 2:152; Marmontel, *Éléments de littérature*, 12:317.

68. Merville, *Règles pour former un avocat*, 396–97.

69. Ravel, *Would-Be Commoner*, 153.

70. Among others: Jacques-Vincent Delacroix, *Réflexions philosophiques sur l'origine de la civilisation* (Amsterdam: Belin, 1781), 333; Marat, *Plan de législation criminelle*, 149.

71. Brissot, *Théorie des lois criminelles*, 2:203.

72. Bernardi, *Principes des lois criminelles*, 277–78; Delacroix, *Réflexions philosophiques*, 333.

73. Brissot, "De la décadence du barreau français," 393; Simon-Nicolas-Henri Linguet, *Discours destiné à être prononcé par Me Linguet dans l'Assemblée des avocats, le 3 février 1775* (Paris: Pierres, 1775), 24.

74. Giovanni Ferri, *De l'Eloquence et des orateurs anciens et modernes* (Paris: J.-G. Mérigot, 1789), 50–51.

75. Mercier, *L'An 2440*, 1:106.

76. Mercier, *Tableau de Paris*, 2:41–2; Simon-Nicolas-Henri Linguet, *Théorie des lois civiles* (London: n.p., 1774), 5–6.

77. Mézard, *Essai sur les réformes à faire dans l'administration de la justice* (n.p.: n.p., 1788), 101 and 131.

78. Rétif, *L'Andrographe*, 133; Chavray de Boissy, *L'Avocat*, 234.

79. Tellingly, the command to never defend unjust causes was only removed from the lawyer's oath in 1822. Camus, *Lettres sur la profession d'avocat*, 221.

80. Gin, *De l'Eloquence du barreau*, 50.

81. Ibid., 51–52.

82. Delacroix, *Réflexions philosophiques*, 330.

83. Ibid., 331–32.

84. Harry Frankfurt, *On Bullshit* (Princeton, NJ: Princeton University Press, 2005).

85. Merville, *Règles pour former un avocat*, 382–84; Falconnet, *Essai sur le barreau grec, romain et français*, 211; Daniel Jousse, *Traité de l'administration de la justice* (Paris: Debure père, 1771), 2:448.

86. Marmontel, *Éléments de littérature*, 14:468.

87. Ibid.

88. Ibid., 12:319.

89. Ibid.

90. For a different perspective on these plans, see Martine de Rougemont, "Quelques utopies théâtrales du XVIIIe siècle," *Romanica Wratislaviensia* 25 (1985): 59–70.

91. Dancourt, *Lettre de l'Arlequin de Berlin.*

92. Fréron, *L'Année littéraire*, 7:670–71.

93. Rabelleau, *Dissertation sur les spectacles* (Amsterdam: M.-M. Rey, 1769).

94. Rétif, *Mimographe.*

95. Louis Gachet, *Observations sur les spectacles en général, et en particulier sur le Colisée* (Paris: P.-A. Le Prieur, 1772).

96. Jean-Jacques Rousseau, *Considérations sur le gouvernement de Pologne* (London: n.p., 1782). Although published in 1782, it was written in 1771–72.

97. Pierre-Paul Lemercier de La Rivière, *L'Heureuse nation* (Paris: Creuze et Béhal, 1792), 2:60–65.

98. "I'm thinking about the influence theater would have on good taste and mores if actors were virtuous and their profession honored. Where is the poet who would dare ask men of high birth to repeat flat or vulgar speeches in public?" Diderot, *Le Paradoxe*, 165.

99. Jean-Baptiste de Boyer Marquis d'Argens, *Lettres juives* (The Hague: Pierre Paupie, 1737), 6:198.

100. Comsa, "Society Theater."

101. Rétif, *Mimographe*, 154.

102. Rousseau, *Considérations sur le gouvernement de Pologne*, 12.

103. Boës-Anthouard, *La Lanterne magique*, 78.

104. Rousseau, *Considérations sur le gouvernement de Pologne*, 24.

105. Rétif, *Mimographe*, 192.

106. See Chapter 1.

107. Rétif, *Mimographe*, 334.

108. Rétif, *Andrographe*, 128.

109. Rabelleau, *Dissertation sur les spectacles*, 170.

110. Rousseau, *Considérations sur le gouvernement de Pologne*, 146.

111. Nicolas-Edme Rétif de la Bretonne, *Le Thesmographe* (The Hague: Gosse-junior, 1789), 447. Rétif had already proposed this idea in *L'Andrographe* (164).

112. Rousseau, *Du Contrat social*, 157–58.

113. Rétif, *Thesmographe*, 447.

114. See for instance Jean-Baptiste-René Robinet, ed., *Dictionnaire universel des sciences morale, économique, politique et diplomatique* (London: Libraires Associés, 1778), 6:613; Merville, *Règles pour former un avocat*; Lanjuinais, *Manuel des jeunes orateurs*.

115. Lanjuinais, *Manuel des jeunes orateurs*, 1:157.

116. *Archives parlementaires de 1787 à 1860* (Paris: P. Dupont, 1867), 21:466.

117. "Eloquence in the defense of citizens will show in advance to the nation the men who will one day support its rights as legislators." Ibid., 21:440.

118. Ibid., 21:487.

119. Ibid., 21:510.

120. Ibid., 21:465.

121. Ibid., 21:473 and 484–85.

122. Lucien Karpik, *French Lawyers: A Study in Collective Action, 1274 to 1994* (Oxford: Oxford University Press, 1999), 101; Michael Fitzsimmons, *The Parisian Order of Barristers and the French Revolution* (Cambridge, MA: Harvard University Press, 1987), 87; Nicolas Derasse, "Les Défenseurs officieux: Une Défense sans barreaux," *Annales historiques de la Révolution française* 350 (October–December 2007): 49–67.

123. Cited in Derasse, "Les Défenseurs officieux," 54.

124. Fitzsimmons, *Parisian Order*, 87.

125. Derasse, "Les Défenseurs officieux," 59.

126. Ibid., 60.

127. Fitzsimmons, *Parisian Order*, 154–93; Jean-Pierre Royer, *Histoire de la justice en France* (Paris: PUF, 1995), 523–24.

128. "Réglement Intérieur National de la profession d'avocat—RIN," Conseil National des Barreaux, http://cnb.avocat.fr/Reglement-Interieur-National-de-la-profession-d-avocat-RIN_a281.html (Art.1.3).

129. Ibid., Art.8.1.

130. Ibid., Art.21.2.7.

131. Karpik, *French Lawyers*, 158.

132. Articles using that term (revolution) include: "Le Droit à la publicité et au démarchage est accordé aux avocats," LINKIN, L'agence spécialisée en communication juridique, last modified September 10, 2014, http://communication-juridique.linkin.fr/2014/droit-publicite-demarchage-avocats/; "Autorisation du démarchage des avocats: un décret qui fait débat," Grands Avocats, last modified December 16, 2013, http://www.grands-avocats.com/chronique-juridique/autorisation-du-demarchage-des-avocats-decret-qui-fait-debat/; and Camille Delran, "La Publicité des avocats: Enfin une évolution majeure pour les avocats," Réseau Eurojuris France, last modified March 5, 2015, https://www.eurojuris.fr/articles/la-publicite-des-avocats-enfin-une-evolution-majeure-pour-les-avocats-17685.htm.

133. Octave Hocher, "Le Démarchage et la publicité enfin ouverts aux avocats," *Le Figaro.fr*, last modified November 3, 2014, http://www.lefigaro.fr/conjoncture/2014/11/03/20002-20141103ARTFIG00186-le-demarchage-et-la-publicite-enfin-ouverts-aux-avocats.php.

134. Elsa Lourdeau, "Regard sur le décret du 28 octobre 2014 autorisant le démarchage pour les avocats," Village de la justice: La Communauté des métiers du droit, last modified November 10, 2014, http://www.village-justice.com/articles/Regard-sur-decret-octobre-2014,18260.html#47B6CJ7HS2upuHAf.99.

135. "Les Avocats et le démarchage, qu'est-ce-qui change?" Agoralys, last modified August 12, 2014, http://www.agoralys.com/les-avocats-et-le-demarchage-quest-ce-qui-change/.

CHAPTER 4

1. Gin, *De l'Eloquence du barreau*, 220.

2. Ibid., 216–17.

3. Mézard, *Essai sur les réformes*, 29.

4. On *conviction intime*, see Michel Foucault, "Cours du 8 janvier 1975," in *Les Anormaux: Cours au Collège de France, 1974–1975*, ed. François Ewald and Alessandro Fontana (Paris: Gallimard, 1999), 3–24; Mason, " 'Bosom of Proof.' "

5. Dentand, *Essai de jurisprudence criminelle*, 2:106.

6. Germain Rubigni, *Comment la législation influe-t-elle sur les mœurs?* (Auxerre, Fr.: L. Fournier, 1789).

7. Marat, *Plan de législation criminelle*, 152.

8. Brissot, *Théorie des lois criminelles*, 2:266–67; Bernardi, *Principes des lois criminelles*, 327.

9. Brissot, *Théorie des lois criminelles*, 2:231–39.

10. Ibid., 2:318.

11. Latour, *Réflexions morales*, 4:260. The magistracy's passion for private theaters is confirmed by Maurice Lever in *Théâtre et Lumières: Les Spectacles de Paris au XVIIIe siècle* (Paris: Fayard, 2001), 274–78.

12. *Très-humbles et très-respectueuses remontrances qu'il a été arrêté en Parlement le 4 Janvier 1753, de faire au roi* (n.p.: n.p., 1753), 15.

13. To give but one example: "It is through the administration of justice that the king rules over his subjects and makes himself present throughout his empire." Guillaume-François Le Trosne, "Discours sur l'état actuel de la magistrature, et sur les causes de sa décadence," in Brissot, *Bibliothèque philosophique*, 4:156.

14. Maza, *Private Lives*, 38.

15. Huet, *Rehearsing the Revolution*, 55–56.

16. Lever, in *Théâtre et Lumières*, notes that they were often written by lawyers and judges (142).

17. Likewise, Mercier blames plays that ridicule judges for desacralizing the magistracy. Mercier, *Du Théâtre*, 74.

18. Latour, *Réflexions morales*, 4:135.

19. Taylor, *In the Theater of Criminal Justice*, 33.

20. Latour, *Réflexions morales*, 4:135.

21. Ibid., 2:18–19.

22. Jean-François de La Harpe, *Correspondance littéraire*, in *Œuvres de La Harpe* (Paris: Verdière, 1820), 10:23–24.

23. Maza, *Private Lives*, 60.

24. Marmontel, *Éléments de littérature*, 12:304.

25. Ibid., 12:315.

26. Séguier, "Réquisitoire," 439–40, 472–73.

27. Latour, *Réflexions morales*, 4:1245.

28. Plato, *The Collected Dialogues of Plato*, ed. Edith Hamilton and Huntington Cairns (New York: Pantheon Books, 1961), 1294.

29. Ibid., 1294–95.

30. Ibid., 1295.

31. Latour, *Réflexions morales*, 4:1245. Anne-Gabriel Meusnier de Querlon makes a similar claim in an article in the *Journal des savants* of April 1773. He traces the downfall of theater in

ancient Rome to the conceit among lower-class spectators that they too could judge. Their superficial judgments destroyed the theater and imbued the people with excessive pride—a tableau that "seems to paint our mores" (511–12).

32. Jean-Marie Apostolidès, *Le Roi-machine* (Paris: Editions de Minuit, 1981), 8.

33. See Martine de Rougemont, *La Vie théâtrale en France au XVIIIe siècle* (Paris: Champion, 1988), 228–29; Maurice Descotes, *Le Public de théâtre et son histoire* (Paris: PUF, 1964), 101–2.

34. Mercier thus asserts: "All men are called to judge by themselves the expressive arts: they feel it." *Tableau de Paris*, 3:316–17.

35. Ravel, in *The Contested Parterre*, and Friedland, in *Political Actors*, provide excellent overviews of the numerous studies on the rise of public opinion. Reading through them, it becomes apparent that the link between the notion of public opinion and the political upheaval of the Revolutionary period has constituted the principal topic of interest and debate. Another strand of scholarship has concerned the feminist implications of a public sphere that was rapidly and aggressively gendered male. Coming closest to my own approach, Maza studies in *Private Lives* the contribution of trial briefs to the creation of a public sphere and the impact of this public sphere on political issues and on the Revolution. She is not, however, particularly interested in the reverse—that is, on the effect of the notion of public opinion and of new modes of judgment on the workings of justice and more generally on the rule of law.

36. Nevertheless, the notion of theatrocracy has been studied almost exclusively from a political, rather than judicial, perspective. See Rancière, *Le Philosophe et ses pauvres*, 74–77; Peter Hallward, "Staging Equality: On Rancière's Theatrocracy," *New Left Review* 37 (January–February 2006): 109–29; Samuel Weber, "Replacing the Body: An Approach to the Question of Digital Democracy," in *Public Space and Democracy*, ed. Marcel Hénaff and Tracy B. Strong (Minneapolis: University of Minnesota Press, 2001), 172–88.

37. Ravel, *Contested Parterre*, 191–92.

38. Grimm et al., *Correspondance littéraire*, 14:483.

39. Ibid., 9:172.

40. Ibid., 13:367.

41. Ravel is one notable exception. His brilliant study *The Contested Parterre* underlines the role played by the theater in the rise of public opinion. His approach follows the standard narrative on public opinion, however, in its political focus and outcome.

42. Latour, *Réflexions morales*, 4:477–80. In *The Family Romance of the French Revolution*, Hunt analyzes novels and paintings to show that the eighteenth century experienced a general crisis in paternal authority, and that this contributed to the desacralization of the king and, subsequently, to the Revolution.

43. Nicolas-Edme Rétif de la Bretonne, *Le Paysan perverti*, ed. François Jost (Lausanne, Switz.: L'Âge d'homme, 1977), 2:157.

44. See Ravel, *Contested Parterre*.

45. Indeed, for the vast majority of eighteenth-century thinkers, "public opinion" was synonymous with enlightened opinion, not popular opinion. See Mona Ozouf, " 'Public Opinion' at the End of the Old Regime," *Journal of Modern History* 60 (September 1988): S1–S21.

46. *L'Influence de la Révolution sur le théâtre français* (Paris: Debray, 1790), 12. For a similar argument in a pre-Revolutionary text, see *Mercure de France*, June 5, 1788.

47. See *Mercure de France*, June 14, 1788; Grimm et al., *Correspondance littéraire*, 15:200, 276, 387.

48. Nicolas-Edme Rétif de la Bretonne, *Les Nuits de Paris*, in *Paris le jour, Paris la nuit*, ed. Michel Delon and Daniel Baruch (Paris: Robert Laffont, 1990), 1070.

49. See Ravel, *Contested Parterre*.

50. See Jeffrey Ravel, "Seating the Public: Spheres and Loathing in the Paris Theaters, 1777–1788," *French Historical Studies* 18 (Spring 1993): 173–210.

51. Cited in Jacques Rittaud-Hutinet, *La Vision d'un futur: Ledoux et ses théâtres* (Lyon, Fr.: Presses universitaires de Lyon, 1982), 132–33.

52. Marmontel, *Éléments de littérature*, 14:500–501.

53. Mercier, *Du Théâtre*, 206.

54. Marmontel, *Éléments de littérature*, 14:500–501.

55. Charpentier, *Causes de la décadence du goût*, 2:132.

56. Jacques Antoine Mague de Saint-Aubin, *La Réforme des théâtres* (Paris: Guillot, 1787), 56; *Mercure de France*, June 14, 1788.

57. Rétif, *Mimographe*, 162.

58. Antoine Maillet-Duclairon, *Essai sur la connaissance des théâtres français* (Paris: Prault père, 1751), 102.

59. Rétif, *Mimographe*, 119–20; *Journal des savants*, April 1773, 508.

60. Plato, *Collected Dialogues*, 1294.

61. Friedland, *Political Actors*, 23.

62. On Diderot and his followers' understanding of "illusion" as a "forgetting of the theater," and the importance they placed on tears and laughter as forms of judgment, see Chapter 2.

63. According to Frederick Burwick, this vision of dramatic illusion is typical of the second half of the eighteenth century and of partisans of bourgeois drama: "Dramatic illusion was generally defined as the heightening of emotional response to the point that the reason is overwhelmed. The spectator is then affected by the dramatic imitation as if it were reality." Frederick Burwick, *Illusion and the Drama: Critical Theory of the Enlightenment and the Romantic Era* (University Park: Pennsylvania State University Press, 1991), 44.

64. Diderot, "Lettre à Madame Riccoboni," 349. See also Mercier's opposition to the presence of officers in the parterre, who even punish spectators for involuntary responses such as laughing and sobbing. Mercier, *Tableau de Paris*, 6:207.

65. Rétif, *Mimographe*, 328.

66. Ibid.

67. Ibid., 329.

68. Ibid., 119–20.

69. Rétif, *Nuits de Paris*, 1094–95.

70. Nicolas-Edme Rétif de la Bretonne, *La Paysanne pervertie*, ed. Béatrice Didier (Paris: Garnier-Flammarion, 1976), 293–94. Long before Rétif, it is true, the police regularly attempted to impose silence on rowdy audiences, but Rétif is unique in calling for the suppression of all sounds, including involuntary ones, and in portraying this silencing as a gift to the spectators.

71. Of course, one should never forget the disparity between the theories of Diderot and Rétif and the realities of attending the theater in the eighteenth century. From the start, in fact, spectators engaged in a struggle against the illusionist model, which would not truly come into existence until the mid to late nineteenth century.

72. Rétif, *Nuits de Paris*, 1070.

73. Mercier, *Tableau de Paris*, 9:282.

74. As did Beaumarchais, when he excised an entire act from *Le Barbier de Séville* as a result of the audience's unfavorable response to the premiere of his play. Similarly, actors were required to be prepared to perform a second play if the audience deemed the first one to have failed.

75. Grimm et al., *Correspondance littéraire*, 1:407.

76. For a summary of the benefits of public trials, see Bon-Albert Briois de Beaumez's report to the National Assembly, transcribed in the *Moniteur universel*, September 29–30, 1789.

77. Ibid.

78. *Moniteur universel*, March 1, 1791. Spectators had already been ordered to remain silent during preliminary inquiries by a law passed in October 1789. *Archives parlementaires*, 9:393.

79. Taylor, "Geometries of Power," 447–48. In her earlier book, *In the Theater of Criminal Justice*, Taylor shows that this passivity was short-lived, and that nineteenth-century trial spectators, like theatrical ones, retained a tradition of direct involvement, despite continued attempts by officials throughout the century to create a silent audience.

80. Antoine-Gaspard Boucher d'Argis, "Observations sur la nécessité de la procédure secrète," in Brissot, *Bibliothèque philosophique*, 10:341–42.

81. *Moniteur universel*, March 1, 1791.

82. In *Political Actors*, Friedland traces a similar evolution in the conception of the audience in the political sphere. He argues that the Revolutionaries devised a political system designed to ensure a public is present and at the same time prevent it from participating.

83. To this day, delayed judgment remains the standard mode of interaction between those who act and those who watch. This is particularly true in politics: representative democracy rests on the principle that the people deserve the right to judge their rulers, but only at predetermined times (during elections) and only in the form of a comprehensive vote coming as a belated verdict on events and decisions to which they were not allowed to contribute directly.

84. This peculiar process is described by liberals and reactionaries alike, in such texts as: Pierre-François Muyart de Vouglans, *Les Lois criminelles de France* (Paris: Merigot, 1780), 648–49; François-Michel Vermeil, *Essai sur les réformes à faire dans notre législation criminelle* (Paris: Demonville, 1781), 163–64; M. Le F***, "Plan de législation sur les matières criminelles," in Brissot, *Bibliothèque philosophique*, 5:320.

85. Guillaume-François Le Trosne, *Vues sur la justice criminelle* (Paris: Debure, 1777), 70–71.

86. Bernardi, *Principes des lois criminelles*, 287–88.

87. Jacques Pierre Brissot, "Discours couronné par l'Académie de Châlons-sur-Marne," in Brissot, *Bibliothèque philosophique*, 6:145–46.

88. Bernardi, *Principes des lois criminelles*, 250–51.

89. Joseph-Michel-Antoine Servan, "Réflexions sur quelques points de nos lois," in Brissot, *Bibliothèque philosophique*, 7:164; Joseph-Michel-Antoine Servan, "Discours sur l'administration de la justice criminelle," in *Œuvres de Servan*, ed. S.-Xavier de Portets (Paris: les éditeurs, 1825), 2:51–52; Vermeil, *Essai sur les réformes*, 196–98.

90. Servan, "Réflexions sur quelques points," 166; Le F***, "Plan de législation," 320–21; Vermeil, *Essai sur les réformes*, 194.

91. Dentand, *Essai de jurisprudence criminelle*, 2:41.

92. Vermeil, *Essai sur les réformes*, 166.

93. Dentand, *Essai de jurisprudence criminelle*, 2:248.

94. Marat, *Plan de législation criminelle*, 132.

95. Taylor, *In the Theater of Criminal Justice*, 44–60.

CHAPTER 5

1. Mercier, *Tableau de Paris*, 7:242–53, 8:245–58, 9:32–38, 367–69. In *L'An 2440*, however, he criticizes *lettres de cachet*, suggesting that his support in the *Tableau de Paris* is partly pragmatic, reflecting the present state of Parisian society without necessarily extending to a future, utopian world. Mercier, *L'An 2440*, 1:111–12.

2. In his *Tableau de Paris*, Mercier denounces politically motivated uses of *lettres de cachet*, especially against writers, but affirms they are extremely rare (7:246–48). This distinguishes him from his contemporaries, notably Mirabeau, whose *Des Lettres de cachet et des prisons d'état*, one of the best sellers of pre-Revolutionary France, depicts *lettres de cachet* solely as an instrument of despotic power. Mercier is in fact correct: only 4 to 5 percent of *lettres de cachet* involved affairs of state. Fred Fling, "Mirabeau, a Victim of the Lettres de Cachet," *American Historical Review* 3 (October 1897): 19.

3. Nina Gelbart, "'Frondeur' Journalism in the 1770s: Theater Criticism and Radical Politics in the Prerevolutionary French Press," *Eighteenth-Century Studies* 17 (Summer 1984): 218, 225.

4. Huet explicitly calls the Revolutionaries' new justice system "a kind of anti-*lettre de cachet*." *Rehearsing the Revolution*, 7.

5. Jürgen Habermas, *The Structural Transformation of the Public Sphere*, trans. Thomas Burger (Cambridge, MA: MIT Press, 1991), 95.

6. Mercier, *Tableau de Paris*, 9:369.

7. Historians have confirmed that the vast majority of *lettres de cachet* were requested by fathers and husbands, rather than imposed by the government. In fact, Mirabeau himself owes his life to the *lettres de cachet* he so passionately opposed. By demanding his internment, his father saved him from the death penalty he had received in absentia for the abduction of a married woman. See Brian E. Strayer, *Lettres de cachet and Social Control in the Ancien Régime, 1659–1789* (New York: Peter Lang, 1992); Arlette Farge and Michel Foucault, *Le Désordre des familles* (Paris: Gallimard, 1982).

8. Mercier, *Tableau de Paris*, 7:248.

9. Ibid., 249.

10. Maximilien Robespierre, *Discours couronné par la Société Royale des Arts et des Sciences de Metz* (Amsterdam: Merigot, 1785), 35; Pierre Louis de Lacretelle, *Discours sur le préjugé des peines infamantes* (Paris: Cuchet, 1784), 98–99.

11. Lacretelle, *Discours sur le préjugé des peines infamantes*, 19–20; Joseph de Bernardi, *Mémoire sur la question suivante, proposée par la Société Royale de Metz*, in *Principes des lois criminelles* (Paris: Serviere, 1788), 413–16. The *Encyclopédie* also tells a similar story: see Antoine-Gaspard Boucher d'Argis, "Juge," in Diderot and d'Alembert, *Encyclopédie*, 9:8.

12. Lacretelle, *Discours sur le préjugé des peines infamantes*, 20.

13. Ibid., 20–21.

14. Maza has noted that pamphlets attacking *lettres de cachet* usually culminate in a profession of faith in contractual forms of government. *Private Lives*, 279.

15. Robespierre, *Discours couronné*, 22–23. Robespierre never pursues this possibility, however, and would in fact oppose the creation of domestic tribunals during the Revolution.

16. Bernardi, *Mémoire sur la question suivante*, 425.

17. Ibid., 426

18. Lacretelle, *Discours sur le préjugé des peines infamantes*, 157–58.

19. Ibid.; Bernardi, *Principes des lois criminelles*, 346.

20. Lacretelle, *Discours sur le préjugé des peines infamantes*, 158–59.

21. Ibid., 157; Bernardi, *Mémoire sur la question suivante*, 427.

22. Mercier, *Tableau de Paris*, 4:104–5, 9:290. Likewise, Massimiliano Murena argues that the principal aim of justice should be public utility, not individual rights. As a result, sons must not be allowed to testify against their fathers, even if this means a crime will go unpunished, as to do so would overturn the natural order. Massimiliano Murena, *Du Devoir des juges*, in *Traité des violences publiques et particulières*, trans. Jean-Claude Pingeron (Paris: Delalain, 1769), 299.

23. Robespierre, *Discours couronné*, 22; Lacretelle, *Discours sur le préjugé des peines infamantes*, 83–84; Bernardi, *Mémoire sur la question suivante*, 417–18.

24. Rétif, *Thesmographe*, 502.

25. *Lettre d'un avocat à M. de L***, président à Mortier au Parlement de Paris, sur les devoirs des juges par rapport à leurs secrétaires* (n.p.: n.p., 1788), 27. See also Linguet, *Théorie des lois civiles*, 129.

26. Sylvain Maréchal, *Correctif à la Révolution* (Paris: Cercle Social, 1793), 116. See also Rubigni, *Comment la législation influe-t-elle sur les mœurs?*, 20.

27. Dan Edelstein, *The Terror of Natural Right: Republicanism, the Cult of Nature, and the French Revolution* (Chicago: University of Chicago Press, 2009).

28. Mézard, *Essai sur les réformes*, 18–19.

29. Montesquieu, *L'Esprit des lois*, in *Œuvres complètes de Montesquieu*, ed. Édouard Laboulaye (Paris: Garnier, 1876), 3:287–88. Montesquieu presents domestic tribunals as courts primarily concerned with the conduct of women, but other authors (including Rétif) reveal that they were viewed in the eighteenth century as targeting both wives and children. See Antoine Terrasson, *Histoire de la Jurisprudence Romaine* (Paris: Théodore de Hansy, 1750), 55.

30. One example among many: "Once married, the husband will have a power over his family as complete as during Roman Antiquity; this power being necessary to maintain order." Rétif, *L'Andrographe*, 165.

31. Ibid., 69–70.

32. Ibid., 109.

33. Ibid., 152–53. This is a recurrent theme: the justice of the committees is "absolutely paternal" (195); fathers teach their sons to regard the committees with "filial" respect (72); the committees are a "familial magistracy" (193).

34. Ibid., 133.

35. Grimm et al., *Correspondance littéraire*, 4:77.

36. Maza, *Privates Lives*, 15, 63.

37. Mercier, *Tableau de Paris*, 3:225.

38. *Mercure de France*, December 1774, 110.

39. Louis-Sébastien Mercier, *L'Indigent*, in *Théâtre Complet de M. Mercier* (Amsterdam: Vlam, 1778), 3:62.

40. *Journal encyclopédique*, May 1775, 506.

41. Louis-Sébastien Mercier, *Le Juge* (London: Ruault, 1774), vi.

42. Louis-Sébastien Mercier, *Jenneval* (Paris: Le Jay, 1769), 81.

43. Mercier, *Le Juge*, 62, 86–89.

44. There is one exception, in Mercier's *Le Gentillâtre*, but the trial depicted is a dystopic one, led by a tyrannical feudal lord.

45. Rubigni, *Comment la législation influe-t-elle sur les mœurs?*, 14, 20.

46. Rétif, *Thesmographe*, 44.

47. Ibid., 12. There is in fact evidence of an increase in trials in the French countryside in the second half of the eighteenth century. Maza, *Privates Lives*, 91.

48. Rubigni, *Comment la législation influe-t-elle sur les mœurs?*, 16.

49. Ibid.

50. See Bryson, *Chastised Stage*.

51. Mercier, *Tableau de Paris*, 1:205.

52. Ibid., 3:130. See also 11:314, and Murena, *Du Devoir des juges*, 301.

53. "When, for example, members of a ring of sodomites were punished in Paris in 1726, Barbier reports that the authorities struggled to find a way to punish the culprits without 'advertising [*illustrer*] this crime and rendering it more common, the majority of people not knowing what it is.'" Paul Friedland, *Seeing Justice Done: The Age of Spectacular Capital Punishment in France* (Oxford: Oxford University Press, 2012), 172.

54. *Journal encyclopédique*, January 1770, 252.

55. Séguier, "Réquisitoire contre le mémoire," 404. See also Vermeil, *Essai sur les réformes*, 147.

56. "The investigation would become as odious as the crime." Mercier, *Tableau de Paris*, 3:131.

57. Ibid., 11:314. See also 8:167–68.

58. Séguier, "Réquisitoire contre le mémoire," 404–5. Others make the same claim: Charles Auguste Hautefort, "Observations sur le *Traité des délits et des peines*," in Brissot, *Bibliothèque philosophique*, 1:277–78; Jacques Pierre Brissot, "Avis de l'éditeur," in Brissot, *Bibliothèque philosophique*, 1:2.

59. Julien Dentand, *Lettre de M. Julien Dentand de Genève, sur le réquisitoire de M. de Séguier* (Amsterdam: n.p., 1787), 23.

60. Ibid., 21. See also Dentand, *Essai de jurisprudence*, 1:16–17; Servan, "Discours sur l'administration de la justice criminelle," 75.

61. Dentand, *Essai de jurisprudence*, 1:11. See also Marat, *Plan de législation criminelle*, 38; Augustin Rouillé d'Orfeuil, *L'Ami des Français* (Constantinople: n.p., 1771).

62. Dentand, *Lettre de M. Julien Dentand*, 22.

63. Dentand, *Essai de jurisprudence*, 1:7–8.

64. Dentand, *Lettre de M. Julien Dentand*, 21. This critique of ancien régime justice is very common among liberal reformers. See Pierre Rosanvallon, *The Demands of Liberty: Civil Society in France Since the Revolution*, trans. Arthur Goldhammer (Cambridge, MA: Harvard University Press, 2007), 57.

65. Pierre-Jacques Brillon, Antoine-François Prost de Royer, and M. Riolz, *Dictionnaire de jurisprudence et des arrêts* (Lyon, Fr.: La Roche, 1787), 6:48.

66. Mercier, *Le Juge*, 55.

67. Ibid., 37.

68. Louis-Sébastien Mercier, *Fragments de politique et d'histoire* (Paris: Buisson, 1792), 1:94–95.

69. Mercier, *Le Juge*, 23.

70. One instance among many: "Where mores are gentle, a multiplicity of laws is dangerous." Mercier, *L'An 2440*, 2:261.

71. Mercier admired Montesquieu and wrote a play, *Montesquieu à Marseille*, about a (largely fictitious) event in his life.

72. Montesquieu, *L'Esprit des lois*, 288.

73. Mercier, *Tableau de Paris*, 4:87–88.

74. Maréchal, *Correctif à la Révolution*, 115; Mercier, *L'An 2440*, 2:261; Stanislaw Lubomirski, "De Vanitate consiliorum," in Brissot, *Bibliothèque philosophique*, 10:86. Rousseau also frequently argues that a surfeit of laws has weakened mores.

75. Mercier, *L'An 2440*, 1:103–4.

76. Mercier, *Le Juge*, vi–vii.

77. Ibid.

78. Montesquieu, *L'Esprit des lois*, 287.

79. Ibid., 289. See also *Encyclopédie de jurisprudence* (Brussels: J. L. de Boubers, 1777–1781), 3:296.

80. Lacretelle, *Discours sur le préjugé des peines infamantes*, 98. See also Terrasson, *Histoire de la Jurisprudence Romaine*, 55.

81. Montesquieu, *L'Esprit des lois*, 287–88.

82. François-Vincent Toussaint, "Arbitraire," in Diderot and d'Alembert, *Encyclopédie*, 1:578.

83. In his dictionary, Antoine Furetière makes a similar claim, although he notes that it is "dangerous" to call God arbitrary. Antoine Furetière, "Arbitraire," in *Dictionnaire universel, contenant généralement tous les mots français* (The Hague: Husson, 1727).

84. For instance, Brillon, Prost de Royer, and Riolz, *Dictionnaire de jurisprudence*, 6:45.

85. "Arbitraire," in *Dictionnaire de l'Académie française, Sixième edition* (Paris: F. Didot frères, 1835), 1:96. By contrast, the dictionaries of Furetière, Jean-François Féraud, and the Académie française (pre-1835) all define arbitrariness according to the first understanding. See Jean-François Féraud, "Arbitraire," in *Dictionnaire critique de la langue française* (Marseille: J. Mossy, 1787), as well as Furetière, "Arbitraire."

86. Montesquieu, *L'Esprit des lois*, 90. On arbitrariness in Montesquieu, see Norbert Campagna, "Arbitraire," in *Dictionnaire Montesquieu*, ed. Catherine Volpilhac-Auger (Lyon, Fr.: École normale supérieure de Lyon, 2013), http://dictionnaire-montesquieu.ens-lyon.fr/fr/article/1377722783/fr.

87. In fact, some ancient authors use the term "arbitraire" to refer to judgments reached through arbitration. Brillon, Prost de Royer, and Riolz, *Dictionnaire de jurisprudence*, 6:44.

88. Véronique Demars-Sion, "Une Expérience d'arbitrage forcé: Les Tribunaux de famille révolutionnaires," *Revue historique de droit français et étranger* 83 (2005): 385–420.

89. François-Vincent Toussaint, "Arbitre," in Diderot and d'Alembert, *Encyclopédie*, 1:579.

90. At the beginning of *L'Esprit des lois*, Montesquieu also claims that a sense of equity predates human positive law (91). Supporters of equity-based arbitration include: Jousse, *Traité*, 2:698; Brillon, Prost de Royer, and Riolz, *Dictionnaire de jurisprudence*, 6:94.

91. Demars-Sion, "Une Expérience d'arbitrage forcé," 395–98.

92. Brillon, Prost de Royer, and Riolz, *Dictionnaire de jurisprudence*, 6:51.

93. For instance: Rousseau, *Considérations sur le gouvernement de Pologne*, 103; Antoine Polier de Saint-Germain, *Du Gouvernement des moeurs* (Lausanne, Switz.: Jules Henri Pott, 1784), 297.

94. Toussaint, "Arbitre," 579.

95. Dentand, *Essai de jurisprudence*, 2:146–47; Philipon de La Madelaine, "Des moyens d'indemniser l'innocence," 287–88.

96. Brillon, Prost de Royer, and Riolz, *Dictionnaire de jurisprudence*, 6:92.

97. Ibid., 6:93.

98. Ibid., 6:52.

99. Ibid., 6:53.

100. Ibid., 2:26.

101. Ibid., 6:109–13.

102. Ibid., 6:113.

103. Ibid., 6:69.

104. In its primeval state, unlike in its modern, liberal form, conciliation is more than just one mode of conflict resolution among others; it is the sole definition of justice, to such an extent that a dispute can only be resolved through a compromise. Akuavi Adonon, "Justice et oralité: Le Fonctionnement d'une justice negociée," in *Le Droit en action, Cahiers d'anthropologie du droit* (Paris: Karthala, 2006), 267–82.

105. Mercier, *L'Indigent*, 92.

106. Ibid., 102.

107. Ibid., 97.

108. Ibid., 103.

109. Ibid., 102.

110. Ibid.

111. Ibid., 106.

112. Ibid., 102.

113. Ibid., 104.

114. Ibid., 106–7.

115. Hunt, *Family Romance*.

116. Ibid., 23.

117. *Archives parlementaires*, 8:447, 17:616.

118. Hunt, *Family Romance*, 40–41; Jacques Commaille, "Les Tribunaux de famille sous la Révolution. Recours à l'histoire comme contribution à une sociologie de la justice et des relations privé-public," in *Une autre Justice. 1789–1799*, ed. Robert Badinter (Paris: Fayard, 1989), 217.

119. Demars-Sion, "Une Expérience d'arbitrage forcé," 417.

120. Jean-Louis Halpérin, "La Composition des tribunaux de famille sous la Révolution," in *La Famille, la Loi, l'Etat. De la Révolution au Code Civil* (Paris: Imprimerie Nationale, 1989), 292–304.

121. Demars-Sion, "Une Expérience d'arbitrage forcé," 412. For similar findings in other districts, see Commaille, "Les Tribunaux de famille," 214–15.

122. Demars-Sion, "Une Expérience d'arbitrage forcé," 403–4 and 415–16; Commaille, "Les Tribunaux de famille," 215–16.

CHAPTER 6

1. Auguste-Jacques Lemierre d'Argy, *Calas, ou Le Fanatisme* (Paris: Imprimerie des Révolutions, 1791).

2. The capitouls were municipal judges unique to the city of Toulouse. Along with military and administrative duties, they also held the right to act as examining magistrates, as they did during the Calas affair.

3. Inexplicably, Jean Calas's alleged accomplices were dealt much lighter punishments. His son, Pierre, was banished; his two daughters were briefly incarcerated in a Catholic convent; and his wife, servant, and old friend, Lavaisse, were all acquitted.

4. Jean-Louis Laya, *Jean Calas* (Avignon, Fr.: Jacques Garrigan, 1791).

5. Marie-Joseph Chénier, *Jean Calas* (Paris: Moutard, 1793).

6. In addition to Lemierre, Laya, and Chénier, two minor playwrights, Jean-Baptiste Pujoulx and François-Jean Villemain d'Abancourt, produced dramatic works on the Calas affair. In contrast with the former three, both plays depict the aftermath of the condemnation and execution of Calas and as a result give a more central role to Voltaire. Jean-Baptiste Pujoulx, *La Veuve Calas à Paris, ou le Triomphe de Voltaire* (Paris: Brunet, 1791); François-Jean Villemain d'Abancourt, *La Bienfaisance de Voltaire* (Paris: Brunet, 1791).

7. Calas first appeared as a character on the Parisian stage on July 14, 1790, during a performance of *Le Journaliste des ombres*. Joseph Aude, *Le Journaliste des ombres, ou Momus aux Champs Elysées* (Paris: Gueffier, 1790).

8. In yet another example, the playwright Jean-Baptiste Desforges announced in a letter to the *Feuille du jour* dated December 27, 1790, that he would resume work on his own adaptation of the Calas trial, a task he had abandoned upon being informed of Chénier's parallel undertaking.

9. For a detailed description of the funeral procession, see the *Chronique de Paris*, July 12, 1791.

10. *Le Chevalier de la Barre, fait historique*, by Benoît Joseph Marsollier des Vivetières, was unfortunately never published. From newspaper reports, however, it is possible to ascertain that the play premiered on the same day as Chénier's *Jean Calas* and that it included many of the exact expressions reported to have been uttered by the Chevalier during his trial.

11. Hence, Laya acknowledges in his preface to *Les Dangers de l'opinion* having borrowed aspects of his play's intrigue from Nicolas-Toussaint Des Essarts's *Causes célèbres*. Jean-Louis Laya, *Les Dangers de l'opinion* (Paris: Maradan, 1790), xi.

12. For instance, the unpublished play *Gertrude ou Le Suicide* stages the recent, tragic death of Gertrude Mainville, a young woman who had killed herself upon discovering that her name had been added, libelously, to *L'Almanach des filles de Paris*. On January 27, 1792, the *Chronique de Paris* praised the play and asked that its performance initiate a trial against the author of *L'Almanach des filles de Paris*.

13. Victor Fournel, "Le Parterre sous la Révolution," *Revue d'art dramatique* 31 (July–September 1893): 12. Le Peletier instantly became one of the most illustrious martyrs of the Revolution when, soon after casting his vote in favor of Louis XVI's execution, he was assassinated by a former guard of the king.

14. Hence, on July 13, 1790, the *Feuille du jour* asked, "Will the French Mepolmene spare us at last from scaffolds and the wheel?" Almost a year later, on July 8, 1791, a similar request appeared in the *Affiches, annonces et avis divers*, which lamented that women could no longer attend the theater for fear of fainting at the sight of "tortures, scaffolds, confessors, executioners, etc."

15. Mercier, *L'An 2440*, 1:287–88.

16. Hence, Laya notes explicitly that "everything read by the clerk was copied from the inquest itself" (*Jean Calas*, 29); Laya and Lemierre preface their plays with a detailed account

of the trial (by Voltaire); and all three plays include variants of quotes popularly attributed to Jean Calas (for instance, his response, when asked to name his coconspirators, that "where there is no crime, there can be no accomplices").

17. *Archives parlementaires*, 9:214.

18. *Journal de Paris*, December 19, 1791.

19. That tears were shed throughout France for an obscure Protestant merchant owes much to Voltaire's gifts as a publicist. By means of trial briefs, fictional memoirs, hundreds of letters, printed images, and the parading of Jean Calas's grief-stricken widow and daughters, Voltaire succeeded in arousing considerable pity for the Calas family and in transforming their suffering into a national cause célèbre. See Elisabeth Claverie, "Procès, affaire, cause: Voltaire et l'innovation critique," *Politix* 26 (1994): 76–85.

20. *Moniteur universel*, December 29, 1790.

21. Jeffrey Alexander, "Towards a Theory of Cultural Trauma," in *Cultural Trauma and Collective Identity* (Berkeley: University of California Press, 2004).

22. Scholars have recently argued for the existence of a profound and pervasive trauma in the years of the French Revolution, although they have presented this trauma as the result of Revolutionary events and not, as I am doing, as the result of ancien régime injustices and inequalities. See Barry M. Shapiro, *Traumatic Politics: The Deputies and the King in the Early French Revolution* (University Park: Penn State University Press, 2009) and Katherine Astbury, *Narrative Responses to the Trauma of the French Revolution* (Oxford: Legenda, 2012).

23. Jean-Clément Martin, *Violence et révolution: Essai sur la naissance d'un mythe national* (Paris: Seuil, 2006), 62.

24. Shoshana Felman, "Forms of Judicial Blindness, or the Evidence of What Cannot Be Seen: Traumatic Narratives and Legal Repetitions in the O. J. Simpson Case and in Tolstoy's *The Kreutzer Sonata*," *Critical Inquiry* 23 (1997): 738–88.

25. Antoine Garapon, *Bien juger: Essai sur le rituel judiciaire* (Paris: Odile Jacob, 1997). For a good introduction to Legendre's work, see Pierre Legendre, *Law and the Unconscious: A Legendre Reader*, ed. Peter Goodrich (New York: St. Martin's Press, 1997).

26. Garapon, *Bien juger*, 220 and 277; Soulier, "Le Théâtre et le procès," 19.

27. Chénier, *Jean Calas*, 91.

28. Robert Horville, "La Justice dans le théâtre français du XVIIe siècle," in Biet and Schifano, *Représentations du procès*, 115–25.

29. François Ost, "Juge-pacificateur, juge-arbitre, juge-entraîneur: trois modèles de justice," in *Fonction de juger et pouvoir judiciaire*, ed. Philippe Gérard, François Ost, and Michel van de Kerchove (Brussels: Publications Fac St Louis, 1983), 1–70.

30. Respectively: Chénier, *Jean Calas*, 33; Laya, *Jean Calas*, 28 and 30.

31. Laya, *Jean Calas*, 30.

32. Renaud Bret-Vitoz, "Mise en forme et mise en critique du procès au théâtre: L'Exemple des scènes d'interrogatoire dans *Athalie*, *Œdipe*, *Brutus* et *Guillaume Tell*," in Biet and Schifano, *Représentations du procès*, 223–36.

33. Ost, "Juge-pacificateur, juge-arbitre, juge-entraîneur."

34. Voltaire, "Déclaration de Pierre Calas," in *Mélanges philosophiques, littéraires, historiques* (Geneva: Cramer, 1771), 3:510–11.

35. Chénier, *Jean Calas*, 53.

36. Lemierre, *Calas*, 105.

37. Marco Tulio Cicéron, *Œuvres complètes de Cicéron: Oraisons* (Paris: C. L. F. Panckoucke, 1837), 1:65; Murena, *Du Devoir des juges*, 315.

38. For a critique of this mode of judgment, see Lemierre, *Calas*, 94.

39. Chénier, *Jean Calas*, 45.

40. For a good compendium, see Robert Badinter, ed., *Une autre Justice. 1789–1799* (Paris: Fayard, 1989).

41. *Révolutions de Paris*, February 26–March 5, 1791, 390.

42. *Archives parlementaires*, 9:216.

43. Ibid., 9:395.

44. Ibid., 9:216.

45. Ibid., 13:165.

46. Ibid., 15:246.

47. Bernardi, *Principes des lois criminelles*, 251–52. See also Voltaire, "Commentaire sur le livre des délits et des peines," in *Des Délits et des peines*, by Cesare Beccaria (Paris: Brière, Libraire, 1822), 349.

48. In *Les Toges du pouvoir*, Jacques Bouineau claims to have identified as many as 190 allusions to antiquity in Revolutionary tracts and parliamentary debates on judicial issues. Jacques Bouineau, *Les Toges du pouvoir, ou la Révolution de droit antique* (Toulouse, Fr.: Editions Eché, 1986), 132. For more on antiquity's influence on the French Revolution, see Harold Talbot Parker, *The Cult of Antiquity and the French Revolutionaries* (New York: Octagon Books, 1965) and Claude Mossé, *L'Antiquité dans la Révolution française* (Paris: Albin Michel, 1989).

49. Mason, "'Bosom of Proof.'"

50. *Archives parlementaires*, 21:672.

51. Ibid.

52. Ibid.

53. Ibid., 22:33, 36.

54. Ibid., 22:33.

55. Ibid., 9:216.

56. Dentand, *Lettre de M. Julien Dentand*, 206. See also Jacques-Vincent Delacroix, "Discours sur les mémoires," in *Peinture des mœurs du siècle* (Amsterdam: Lejay, 1777), 2:330–31.

57. Boucher d'Argis, "Observations sur la nécessité de la procédure secrète," 345–46.

58. Or, in the words of Vermeil, in his *Essai sur les réformes*: "certainly, justice should not aim to surprise" (196).

59. Delacroix, "Discours sur les mémoires," 325. Servan likewise warns judges not to trust in equivocal signs like agitation and hesitation. "Discours sur l'administration de la justice criminelle," 50.

60. *Archives parlementaires*, 22:301.

61. Ibid., 22:4.

62. Ibid., 22:306.

63. Ibid., 22:33.

64. Ibid., 22:4.

65. Ibid., 22:4 and 29.

66. Ibid., 21:689.

67. Ibid., 22:134.

68. Ibid., 22:25.

69. Ibid., 22:294.

70. Vermeil, *Essai sur les réformes*, 210; Le Trosne, *Vues sur la justice criminelle*, 60–63.

71. *Archives parlementaires*, 22:133.

72. Ibid., 22:297.

73. Ibid., 22:293.

74. Feilla, *Sentimental Theater*, 198.

75. Anne C. Vila, *Enlightenment and Pathology: Sensibility in the Literature and Medicine of Eighteenth-Century France* (Baltimore: Johns Hopkins University Press, 1998).

76. Séguier, "Réquisitoire contre le mémoire," 497.

77. *Archives parlementaires*, 31:656.

78. For a detailed performance history, see the preface to Jean-Louis Laya, *L'Ami des lois*, ed. Mark Darlow and Yann Robert (London: MHRA Critical Texts, 2011).

79. Fleury, *Mémoires de Fleury* (Paris: Adolphe Delahays, 1847), 2:155–56.

80. On the comedic traditions to which *L'Ami des lois* belongs, see Laya, *L'Ami des lois*, 56–76.

81. *Chronique de Paris*, January 4, 1793.

82. Grimm et al., *Correspondance littéraire*, 16:173.

83. Jean-Louis Laya, *Voltaire aux Français sur leur constitution* (Paris: Maradan, 1789), 54.

84. *Mercure français*, January 16, 1793.

85. *Révolutions de Paris*, January 12–19, 1793.

86. *Chronique de Paris*, November 10, 1790; *Révolutions de Paris*, November 13–20, 1790, and December 4–11, 1790; *Mercure français*, December 1, 1791.

87. One exception to these two rules: Jacques Hébert likens *L'Ami des lois* to *The Clouds*, with Robespierre in the role of Socrates and Laya as the minion of powerful royalists in the government. Tellingly, however, he never condemns judicial theater as a concept, and his critique of the Aristophanes of *The Clouds* leads him to praise, a contrario, the public denunciation of political figures (as in *The Knights*). *Père Duchesne*, no. 208.

88. Grimm et al., *Correspondance littéraire*, 16:173.

89. *Archives parlementaires*, 22:213. *The Declaration of the Rights of Man* had guaranteed the freedom of the press but not of the theater. As a result, up until 1791, censorship remained in effect, even if much more leniently than under the ancien régime.

90. Ibid., 22:216.

91. This list is far from exhaustive, of course, but it gives a good indication of the range of satirical plays staged in Paris during the Revolution. An astonishing number of satirical plays were published in the first few years of the Revolution, although few were performed on a public stage before 1791. See Desnoiresterres, *La Comédie satirique* and Paul-Eugène Jauffret, *Le Théâtre révolutionnaire, 1788–1799* (Paris: Jouvet, 1869).

92. *Feuille du jour*, July 16, 1791.

93. *Révolutions de Paris*, December 4–11, 1790.

94. Martial Poirson reaches the same conclusion in his preface to Nicolas François de Neufchâteau, *Paméla, ou La Vertu récompensée*, ed. Martial Poirson, Studies on Voltaire and the Eighteenth Century (Oxford: Voltaire Foundation, 2007), 16.

95. *Révolutions de Paris*, December 11–18, 1790.

96. Ibid., December 3–10, 1791.

97. Cited in Adolf Schmidt, ed., *Tableaux de la révolution française* (Leipzig, Ger.: Veit, 1867), 2:65.

98. *Chronique de Paris*, December 1, 1790. See also *Décade philosophique*, March 20, 1795, and *Journal des spectacles*, August 19, 1793.

99. *Chronique de Paris*, August 17, 1793.

100. Jean-Marie Collot d'Herbois, *Le Procès de Socrate* (Paris: Veuve Duchesne, 1791), vii.

101. In addition to actors and spectators, playwrights also received praise solely for being "good citizens." *Moniteur universel*, February 14, 1790.

102. René Tarin, *Le Théâtre de la Constituante* (Paris: Champion, 1998), 121.

103. See Laya's letter to the Théâtre de la Nation on December 1, 1790. The letter is unpublished but can be consulted at the Bibliothéque de la Comédie-Française in Paris.

104. *Révolutions de Paris*, October 1–8, 1791.

105. The *Abréviateur universel* welcomed this deliberate disavowal of illusion, noting that "one can produce grand effects on the stage by explicitly renouncing all theatrical illusion." Cited in James H. Johnson, *Listening in Paris: A Cultural History* (Berkeley: University of California Press, 1995), 120.

106. *Révolutions de Paris*, January 12–19, 1793.

107. Ibid., December 4–11, 1790.

108. Ibid.

109. Ibid., January 15–22, 1791.

110. Laya, *L'Ami des lois*, 136.

111. Ibid., 135.

112. *La Mère coupable* is also interesting because, as Jeffrey Leichman shows in an astute reading, it shares with reenactment a paradoxical faith in performance as a remedy to theatricality. Jeffrey Leichman, *Acting Up: Staging the Subject in Enlightenment France* (Lewisburg, PA: Bucknell University Press, 2016), 145–61.

113. Marie-Laurence Netter, "L'Intégration de nouvelles valeurs par le théâtre," in *Actes du colloque Théâtre et Révolution*, ed. Lucile Garbagnati and Marita Gilli (Paris: Les Belles Lettres, 1988), 29.

114. Judith Schlanger, "Théâtre révolutionnaire et représentation du bien," *Poétique* 22 (1975): 276.

115. Never studied, that is, until my edition, with Darlow, of Laya, *L'Ami des lois*.

116. On the king's trial, see Albert Soboul, *Le Procès de Louis XVI* (Paris: Gallimard, 1973); Michael Walzer, *Regicide and Revolution: Speeches at the Trial of Louis XVI* (Cambridge: Cambridge University Press, 1974); David P. Jordan, *The King's Trial: Louis XVI vs. the French Revolution* (Berkeley: University of California Press, 2004).

117. Jordan, *King's Trial*, 56–57.

118. *Archives parlementaires*, 55:8.

119. Jordan, *King's Trial*, 57.

120. Laya, *L'Ami des lois*, 184–85.

121. Ibid., 246–47.

122. Ibid., 207.

123. Ibid., 225.

124. Ibid., 247.

125. Ibid., 253.

126. Jean-Baptiste Cléry, *Mémoires de Cléry* (Paris: Firmin Didot frères, 1856), 89.

127. Edmond Biré, *Journal d'un bourgeois de Paris pendant la Terreur* (Paris: Perrin et Cie, 1884), 1:389.

128. *Annales de la République française*, January 11, 1793.

129. See Laya's letter to the Comte de la Bourdonnaye on October 28, 1829, unpublished, located at the Bibliothéque de la Comédie-Française in Paris; Henri Welschinger, "*L'Ami des lois* sous la Terreur et la Restauration," *Revue d'art dramatique* 24 (October–December 1891): 80; and P. Michel, "*L'Ami des lois* par Laya," *Bulletin du Bouquiniste* 36 (1875): 489.

130. See Laya's letter to the Comte de la Bourdonnaye. See also Cléry, *Mémoires de Cléry*, 89.

131. See, for instance, the letter sent by the Section du Faubourg de Montmartre to Nicolas Chambon, then mayor of Paris, transcribed in Laya, *L'Ami des lois*, 311.

132. Dramatic satires did not entirely disappear in 1793, of course, but as we will see in the next chapter, they ceased to be dialogical, becoming more like state-mandated propaganda than invitations to debate—more like punishments, in other words, than trials. As for courtroom dramas, I have not found any examples post-1793 of a play reenacting a real trial; if some exist, they had nowhere near the popularity and influence of the Calas plays and *L'Ami des lois*.

CHAPTER 7

1. *Le Pour et le contre*, 1:120.

2. Ibid., 2:90, 349, 4:14, 113, 5:187.

3. Ibid., 3:390.

4. Ibid., 3:380.

5. Ibid., 4:3. Even the moderate deputy Armand Guy Kersaint admitted, albeit with different objectives, that "in the eyes of the philosopher, that man [Louis] died on August 10." Ibid., 6:313.

6. "I see him [Louis] surrounded by thousands of unfortunate ghosts who scream for vengeance and in whose blood he is covered!" Ibid., 5:50. Likewise, Jeanbon Saint-André argues that the trial will only be valid if the "generous ghosts" who fought and died on August 10 can be made to reappear and confront the tyrant. Ibid., 6:209. Lastly, several texts also refer more abstractly to a "phantom of the monarchy." Ibid., 3:144.

7. *Archives parlementaires*, 55:710.

8. *Le Pour et le contre*, 3:390.

9. Ibid., 3:384.

10. Ibid., 1:185.

11. *Archives parlementaires*, 56:722.

12. *Révolutions de Paris*, January 12–19, 1793.

13. *Le Pour et le contre*, 3:390.

14. Ibid., 2:37. Emphasis mine.

15. Ibid., 3:384.

16. *Annales patriotiques*, January 12, 1793.

17. André Tissier, *Les Spectacles à Paris pendant la Révolution* (Geneva: Droz, 2002), 29. For a different take on the *Chaste Suzanne* affair, linking it to Revolutionary surveillance, see Maslan, *Revolutionary Acts*, 183–215.

18. *Annales patriotiques*, January 2, 1793.

19. *Abréviateur universel*, no. 6.

20. *Journal universel*, January 9, 1793.

21. Aurore Chéry, "'Je ne veux pas les attendrir': La Question de la sensibilité niée et ses conséquences dans le procès et l'exécution de Louis XVI," in *La Culture Judiciaire: Discours, représentations et usages de la justice du Moyen Âge à nos jours*, ed. Lucien Faggion, Christophe Regina, and Bernard Ribémont (Dijon, Fr.: Presses Universitaires de Dijon, 2014), 420.

22. Ibid., 423.

23. Cited in Paul Girault de Coursac and Pierrette Girault de Coursac, *Enquête sur le procès du roi Louis XVI* (Paris: Œil, 1992), 674. Emphasis mine.

24. See Jules Michelet, *Histoire de la Révolution française* (Paris: Lemerre, 1888), 6:162.

25. Etienne Aignan, *La Mort de Louis XVI* (Paris: Marchands de nouveautés, 1793).

26. Michelet, *Histoire de la Révolution française*, 6:162.

27. Statues were torn down and converted into cannons; royal emblems, such as the fleur de lys, were chiseled off or painted over; and all signs of the monarchy or of the nobility were strictly forbidden. Serge Bianchi, *La Révolution culturelle de l'An II: Élites et peuple (1789–1799)* (Paris: Aubier, 1982), 159.

28. For more details, see Jules-Julien-Gabriel Berthevin, *Recherches historiques sur les derniers jours des rois de France, leurs funérailles, leurs tombeaux* (Paris: F. Louis, 1825), and Sophia Beale, *The Churches of Paris* (London: W. H. Allen and Co., 1893). For a modern account, see Suzanne Lindsay, "Mummies and Tombs: Turenne, Napoleon, and Death Ritual," *Art Bulletin* 82, no. 3 (September 2000): 476–502.

29. Lindsay, "Mummies and Tombs," 3.

30. *Archives parlementaires*, 83:270.

31. Jean-Marie Apostolidès, "La Guillotine littéraire," *French Review* 62 (May 1989): 991.

32. *Archives parlementaires*, 83:270. See also Beatrice F. Hyslop, "The Theater During a Crisis: The Parisian Theater During the Reign of Terror," *Journal of Modern History* 17 (December 1945): 347.

33. *Révolutions de Paris*, January 12–27, 1794.

34. Hunt contends that the debates surrounding the anniversary of the king's death expose a "tension between forgetting and commemorating, between feeling guilty and rejecting guilt." In contrast with Hunt, I study the debates less from the perspective of the Revolutionaries' guilt than from that of their shifting attitudes toward reenactment. This leads me to argue that the Jacobins, rather than seeing a strict opposition between forgetting and commemorating, as Hunt suggests, embraced a specific type of commemoration as an instrument of forgetting. Hunt, *Family Romance*, 62.

35. Among others: *Le Jugement dernier des rois, La Papesse Jeanne, La Folie de Georges,* and *Buzot, roi du Calvados.*

36. I borrow the terms "Jacobin theater" and "sans-culottes theater" from an article by Serge Bianchi, in which he argues for the existence of two clashing visions and genres of theater in 1793 and 1794. Serge Bianchi, "Théâtre et engagement sur les scènes de l'an II," in *Littérature et engagement pendant la révolution française*, ed. Isabelle Brouard-Arends and Laurent Loty (Rennes, Fr.: Presses universitaires de Rennes, 2007).

37. Pierre Frantz, "Rire et théâtre carnavalesque pendant la Révolution," *Dix-huitième siècle* 32 (2000): 299.

38. Apostolidès, "La Guillotine littéraire," 991.

39. Mark Darlow, "Staging the Revolution: The *Fait historique*," *Nottingham French Studies* 45 (Spring 2006): 77–88.

40. Adolphe Liéby, *Étude sur le théâtre de Marie-Joseph Chénier* (Paris: Lecène et Oudin, 1901), 146.

41. Emmet Kennedy, *A Cultural History of the French Revolution* (New Haven, CT: Yale University Press, 1989), 275, 363.

42. Paul d'Estrée, *Le Théâtre sous la Terreur* (Paris: Émile-Paul frères, 1913), 44.

43. Pierre Caron, ed., *Paris pendant la Terreur: Rapports des agents secrets du ministre de l'intérieur* (Paris: Honoré Champion, 1943), 3:80.

44. *Feuille du Salut Public*, August 31, 1793.

45. *Journal des Spectacles*, January 1, 1794.

46. *Journal des Spectacles*, July 17, 1793, and December 14, 1793.

47. For a summary of the debates, along with an analysis of Rousseau's influence on the dissenters, see René Tarin, "*La Lettre sur les Spectacles* dans les débats à l'Assemblée Nationale Constituante," *Revue d'histoire littéraire de la France* 96 (November–December 1996): 1128–36.

48. *Archives parlementaires*, 22:214.

49. See Johnson, *Listening in Paris*, 116.

50. Janie Vanpée, "Performing Justice: The Trials of Olympe de Gouges," *Theatre Journal* 51, no. 1 (March 1999): 64.

51. *Feuille du Salut Public*, October 30, 1793.

52. For instance, Paul d'Estrée recounts the following, by no means unusual, incident: "A Cardinal, speaking about the people in *La Nuit de Charles V*, says: 'Peasants, these animals!' and immediately the actor performing the role assures the audience of the strength of his patriotic sentiments." *Le Théâtre sous la Terreur*, 374.

53. Arthur Pougin provides a list of actors and directors tried and convicted during the Terror. The list spans several pages. Arthur Pougin, *L'Opéra-Comique pendant la Révolution* (Paris: A. Savine, 1891), 100–102.

54. *Moniteur universel*, August 5, 1793.

55. Kennedy, *Cultural History of the French Revolution*, 363.

56. Marc Régaldo, "Retour à l'antique et art républicain dans le Théâtre de la Révolution française," in *Der theatralische Neoklassizismus um 1800*, ed. Roger Bauer (Bern, Switz.: Peter Lang, 1986), 172.

57. Bianchi, *La Révolution culturelle de l'An II*, 188.

58. Desnoiresterres, *La Comédie satirique*, 414–15.

59. Cited in Caron, *Paris pendant la Terreur*, 1:69. Latour-Lamontagne's report is dated September 11, 1793. A few days earlier, Aristide Valcour had made a nearly identical proposal in the *Journal de la Montagne*, September 7, 1793.

60. Cited in d'Estrée, *Le Théâtre sous la Terreur*, 41.

61. On titles, see the letter written by police administrators on April 26, 1794, in Henri Welschinger, *Le Théâtre de la Révolution* (Paris: Charavay Frères, 1881), 106. On Louis, see Schlanger, "Théâtre révolutionnaire et représentation du bien," 274.

62. Caron, *Paris pendant la Terreur*, 3:80.

63. Ozouf, *La Fête révolutionnaire*, 291–92.

64. *Archives parlementaires*, 83:270.

65. Annette Graczyk has likewise noted the decline, starting in 1793, of the earlier, conflict-driven theater, with its genuinely two-sided discussions and complex characters. Annette Graczyk, "Le Théâtre de la Révolution française, média de masses entre 1789 et 1794," *Dix-huitième siècle* 21 (1989): 401.

66. Nicolas Camaille-Saint-Aubin, *L'Ami du peuple, ou les intrigants démasqués* (Paris: Maradan, 1793), 9.

67. Ibid.

68. Ibid., 32.

69. Ibid., 59.

70. Charles Walton, "*Charles IX* and the French Revolution: Law, Vengeance, and the Revolutionary Uses of History," *European Review of History: Revue européenne d'histoire* 4 (1997): 93–94.

71. These plays include: *L'Innocence reconnue*; *Les Épreuves du Républicain, ou l'Amour de la patrie*; *Le Véritable ami des lois, ou le Républicain à l'épreuve*; *Charles et Victoire, ou les Amours de Plailly*; *Il était temps, ou L'Heureuse découverte*; *La Veuve du Républicain*; and *Les Dangers de la calomnie*.

72. Maslan, *Revolutionary Acts*, 191–205.

73. *Décade philosophique*, June 18, 1794.

74. D'Estrée, *Le Théâtre sous la Terreur*, 406.

75. Alphonse Aulard, ed., *Paris pendant la réaction thermidorienne et sous le Directoire* (Paris: Cerf, 1902).

76. Schmidt, *Tableaux de la révolution française*, 3:232.

77. Aulard, *Paris pendant la réaction thermidorienne*, 4:384.

78. Ling-Ling Sheu, *Voltaire et Rousseau dans le théâtre de la révolution française* (Brussels: Éditions de l'Université de Bruxelles, 2005), 11.

79. Bianchi, "Théâtre et engagement," 43.

80. For more on dramatic criticism under the Directory, see Michel Biard, "Thalie et Melpomène face à leurs juges. La critique théâtrale sous le Directoire," in *La République directoriale*, ed. Philippe Bourdin and Bernard Gainot (Clermont-Ferrand, Fr.: Société des études robespierristes, 1998), 2:663–78.

81. *Censeur dramatique*, April 19, 1798.

82. Schmidt, *Tableaux de la révolution française*, 2:393.

83. Aulard, *Paris pendant la réaction thermidorienne*, 3:435.

84. Cited in Gabriel de Broglie, *Ségur sans cérémonie (1757–1825)* (Paris: Perrin, 1977), 216.

85. Jean-François Cailhava de L'Estandoux, *Athènes pacifiée* (Paris: Pougens, 1797).

86. Armand Charlemagne, *Le Souper des Jacobins* (Paris: Barba, 1795), 34.

87. Mechele Leon, "The Poet and the Prince: Revising Molière and *Tartuffe* in the French Revolution," *French Historical Studies* 28 (Summer 2005): 461. For more on the Revolutionary treatment of Molière and his oeuvre, see Mechele Leon, *Molière, the French Revolution, and the Theatrical Afterlife* (Iowa City: University of Iowa Press, 2009).

88. Caron, *Paris pendant la Terreur*, 2:143–44.

89. Leon, "Poet and the Prince," 463.

90. *Journal des théâtres*, December 1, 11, and 13, 1798.

91. Royer, *Histoire de la justice en France*, 359.

92. Michelet, *Histoire de la Révolution française*, vol. 6.

93. Huet, *Rehearsing the Revolution*, 3.

94. Jean-François Gayraud, *La Dénonciation* (Paris: Presses Universitaires de France, 1995), 82.

95. Marie-Hélène Huet, "Le Sacre du Printemps: Essai sur le sublime et la Terreur," *MLN* 103 (1988): 782–99.

96. Carol Blum, *Rousseau and the Republic of Virtue* (Ithaca, NY: Cornell University Press, 1986).

97. *Archives parlementaires*, 60:70.

98. Annie Jourdan, "Les Journées de Prairial an II: le tournant de la Révolution?," *La Révolution française* 10 (2016): http://lrf.revues.org/1591.

99. Jean Baptiste Duvergier, ed., *Collection complète des lois, décrets, ordonnances, règlements et avis du Conseil d'état* (Paris: Guyot et Scribe, 1825), 5:161.

100. Huet, "Le Sacre du Printemps," 796.

101. *Archives parlementaires*, 20:696.

102. Carla Hesse, "La Preuve par la lettre: Pratiques juridiques au tribunal révolutionnaire de Paris (1793–1794)," *Annales HSS* 3 (May–June 1996): 629–42.

103. Ibid., 631–32.

104. Ibid., 634.

105. *Moniteur universel*, October 30, 1793.

106. Hesse, "La Preuve par la lettre," 635.

107. Ibid., 638.

108. *Archives parlementaires*, 22:10–11.

109. Laura Mason made this claim during a presentation entitled "Conspiracy as Theater During the French Revolution" at the Annual Meeting of the Society for French Historical Studies, Nashville, TN, March 2016.

110. Colin Lucas, "The Theory and Practice of Denunciation in the French Revolution," *Journal of Modern History* 68 (1996): 783. Likewise, Albert Soboul argues that "denunciation became an extreme application of the principle of publicity." Albert Soboul, *Les Sans-culottes* (Paris: Seuil, 1968), 141.

111. Maximilien Robespierre, *Discours et rapports de Robespierre*, ed. Charles Vellay (Paris: Eugène Pasquelle, 1908), 337.

112. Marie-Hélène Huet, *Mourning Glory: The Will of the French Revolution* (Philadelphia: University of Pennsylvania Press, 1997), 63.

113. On the complex and sometimes counterintuitive relationship between masks and theatricality (both masking and unmasking are theatrical gestures, and masks offer at once an illustration of and an escape from social acting and displays), see James H. Johnson, *Venice Incognito: Masks in the Serene Republic* (Berkeley: University of California Press, 2011). On similar questions in the French context, see James H. Johnson, "Versailles, Meet Les Halles: Masks, Carnival, and the French Revolution," *Representations* 73 (Winter 2001): 89–116, and James H. Johnson, "Urban Development and the Culture of Masked Balls in Nineteenth-Century Paris," *Urban History* 40 (November 2013): 646–62.

114. *Moniteur universel*, April 9, 1794.

115. Robespierre, *Discours et rapports*, 210.

116. Louis Antoine de Saint-Just, *Œuvres choisies*, ed. Jean Gratien (Paris: Gallimard, 1968), 330.

117. Ibid., 324.

118. Maximilien Robespierre, *Discours de Maximilien Robespierre sur l'influence de la calomnie sur la Révolution* (Paris: Pierre-Jacques Duplain, 1792), 30.

119. Robespierre, *Discours et rapports*, 210.

120. Ibid., 413. Many other examples of Robespierre's identification with Socrates can be found in his speeches. See pages 136, 243, 361, 363, and 374 in the same volume.

121. To which the painter Jacques-Louis David reportedly shouted back: "I will drink the hemlock with you!" Thomas Carlyle, *The French Revolution: A History* (London: Chapman and Hall, 1848), 3:344.

122. Cited in Antoine de Baecque, "Le Tableau d'un cadavre, les récits d'agonie de Robespierre," in *Robespierre: figure-réputation*, ed. Annie Jourdan (Amsterdam: Rodopi, 1996), 187.

123. "Did the Athenian philosopher cause more offence to the great people, the ecclesiastics, the sophists, and the political charlatans, than I have?" Cited in Eli Sagan, *Citizens & Cannibals: The French Revolution, the Struggle for Modernity, and the Origins of Ideological Terror* (Lanham, MD: Rowman & Littlefield, 2001), 372.

124. For more on the Jacobins' relationship to language and oration, see Marc Blanchard, *La Révolution et les mots: Saint-Just & Cie* (Paris: A.-G. Nizet, 1979), 66–67.

125. Saint-Just, *Œuvres choisies*, 213.

126. Indeed, Laya was the principal, albeit uncredited, author of Edme Bonaventure Courtois's *Rapport fait au nom de la commission chargée de l'examen des papiers trouvés chez Robespierre*, from which this passage is taken. Many historians have speculated that this famous report was partly based on fabricated documents. Nevertheless, its portrait of Robespierre's final hours, based on a firsthand report rather than on documents allegedly found in Robespierre's private papers, certainly bears a semblance of truth, as it is consistent with the declarations of *l'incorruptible* in the days prior to his death.

127. Cited in Huet, *Mourning Glory*, 108.

128. In the words of Shoshana Felman, Socrates "accepts and legally assumes and consummates his role as victim of injustice so as to safeguard (and teach) the supreme principle of the rule of law." Shoshana Felman, *The Juridical Unconscious: Trials and Traumas in the Twentieth Century* (Cambridge, MA: Harvard University Press, 2002), 220.

129. See Taylor, "Geometries of Power."

Bibliography

Adonon, Akuavi. "Justice et oralité: Le Fonctionnement d'une justice negociée." In *Le Droit en action, Cahiers d'anthropologie du droit*, 267–82. Paris: Karthala, 2006.

Aguesseau, Henri François d'. "L'Indépendance de l'avocat." In *Discours de Monsieur le chancelier d'Aguesseau*, 122–43. Paris: Libraires associés, 1783.

Aignan, Etienne. *La Mort de Louis XVI*. Paris: Marchands de nouveautés, 1793.

Alexander, Jeffrey. "Towards a Theory of Cultural Trauma." In *Cultural Trauma and Collective Identity*, 1–30. Berkeley: University of California Press, 2004.

Andrews, Richard Mowery. *Law, Magistracy and Crime in Old Regime Paris, 1735–1789*. New York: Cambridge University Press, 1994.

Apostolidès, Jean-Marie. "La Guillotine littéraire." *French Review* 62 (May 1989): 985–96.

———. *Le Roi-machine*. Paris: Editions de Minuit, 1981.

"Arbitraire." In *Dictionnaire de l'Académie française, Sixième edition*, 1:96. Paris: F. Didot frères, 1835.

Archives parlementaires de 1787 à 1860. Paris: P. Dupont, 1867–

Argens, Jean-Baptiste de Boyer Marquis d'. *Lettres juives*. The Hague: Pierre Paupie, 1737.

Aristotle. *Poetics*. Translated by Anthony Kenny. Oxford: Oxford University Press, 2013.

Astbury, Katherine. *Narrative Responses to the Trauma of the French Revolution*. Oxford: Legenda, 2012.

Aubignac, François-Hédelin, abbé d'. *La Pratique du théâtre*. Amsterdam: Jean Frédéric Bernard, 1715.

Aude, Joseph. *Le Journaliste des ombres, ou Momus aux Champs Elysées*. Paris: Gueffier, 1790.

Aulard, Alphonse, ed. *Paris pendant la réaction thermidorienne et sous le Directoire*. Paris: Cerf, 1902.

Bachaumont, Louis Petit de. *Mémoires secrets pour servir à l'histoire de la république des lettres en France*. London: John Adamson, 1788.

Badinter, Robert, ed. *Une autre Justice. 1789–1799*. Paris: Fayard, 1989.

Baecque, Antoine de. *Les Éclats du rire: La Culture des rieurs au XVIIIe siècle*. Paris: Calmann-Lévy, 2000.

———. "Le Tableau d'un cadavre, les récits d'agonie de Robespierre." In *Robespierre: figure-réputation*, edited by Annie Jourdan, 169–202. Amsterdam: Rodopi, 1996.

Bailly, Jean-Christophe, Denis Guénoun, and Bernard Stiegler. *Le Théâtre, le peuple, la passion*. Besançon, Fr.: Les Solitaires intempestifs, 2006.

Baker, Keith. *Inventing the French Revolution: Essays on French Political Culture in the Eighteenth Century*. Cambridge: Cambridge University Press, 1990.

Barthélemy, Jean-Jacques. *Voyage du jeune Anacharsis en Grèce*. Paris: de Bure, 1788.

Beale, Sophia. *The Churches of Paris*. London: W. H. Allen and Co., 1893.

Beam, Sarah. *Laughing Matters: Farce and the Making of Absolutism in France*. Ithaca, NY: Cornell University Press, 2007.

Belaval, Yvon. *L'Esthétique sans paradoxe de Diderot*. Paris: Gallimard, 1950.

Bell, David. *Lawyers and Citizens: The Making of a Political Elite in Old Regime France*. Oxford: Oxford University Press, 1994.

Berger, Emmanuel. *La Justice pénale sous la Révolution: Les Enjeux d'un modèle judiciaire libéral*. Rennes, Fr.: Presses universitaires de Rennes, 2008.

Berlanstein, Lenard R. "Women and Power in Eighteenth-Century France: Actresses at the Comédie-Française." *Feminist Studies* 20, no. 3 (1994): 475–506.

Bernardi, Joseph de. *Mémoire sur la question suivante, proposée par la Société Royale de Metz*. In *Principes des lois criminelles*, 397–428. Paris: Serviere, 1788.

———. *Principes des lois criminelles*. Paris: Serviere, 1788.

Berthevin, Jules-Julien-Gabriel. *Recherches historiques sur les derniers jours des rois de France, leurs funérailles, leurs tombeaux*. Paris: F. Louis, 1825.

Bianchi, Serge. *La Révolution culturelle de l'An II: Élites et peuple (1789–1799)*. Paris: Aubier, 1982.

———. "Théâtre et engagement sur les scènes de l'an II." In *Littérature et engagement pendant la révolution française*, edited by Isabelle Brouard-Arends and Laurent Loty, 27–49. Rennes, Fr.: Presses universitaires de Rennes, 2007.

Biard, Michel. "Thalie et Melpomène face à leurs juges. La critique théâtrale sous le Directoire." In *La République directoriale*, edited by Philippe Bourdin and Bernard Gainot, 2:663–78. Clermont-Ferrand, Fr.: Société des études robespierristes, 1998.

Biet, Christian. "L'Affaire Cartouche (1721): Scène juridique/scène littéraire. L'opinion publique, le théâtre, le pouvoir et le droit." In Biet and Schifano, *Représentations du procès*, 445–59.

———, and Laurence Schifano, eds. *Représentations du procès: Droit, théâtre, littérature, cinéma*. Paris: Université Paris X-Nanterre, 2003.

Biré, Edmond. *Journal d'un bourgeois de Paris pendant la Terreur*. Paris: Perrin et Cie, 1884.

Blanchard, Marc. *La Révolution et les mots: Saint-Just & Cie*. Paris: A.-G. Nizet, 1979.

Blum, Carol. *Rousseau and the Republic of Virtue*. Ithaca, NY: Cornell University Press, 1986.

Boës-Anthouard, Anne. *La Lanterne magique de l'histoire: Essai sur le théâtre historique en France de 1750 à 1789*. Studies on Voltaire and the Eighteenth Century. Oxford: Voltaire Foundation, 1982.

Boucher d'Argis, Antoine-Gaspard. "Juge." In Diderot and d'Alembert, *Encyclopédie*, 9:8–9.

———. "Observations sur la nécessité de la procédure secrète." In Brissot, *Bibliothèque philosophique*, 10:333–47.

Bouineau, Jacques. *Les Toges du pouvoir, ou la Révolution de droit antique*. Toulouse, Fr.: Editions Eché, 1986.

Bourdin, Philippe. *Aux Origines du théâtre patriotique*. Paris: CNRS, 2017.

Boutet de Monvel, Jacques Marie. *L'Amant bourru*. Paris: Duchesne, 1777.

Bray, René. *La Formation de la doctrine classique en France*. Paris: Librairie Nizet, 1983.

Bret-Vitoz, Renaud. *L'Espace et la scène: Dramaturgie de la tragédie française, 1691–1759*. Studies on Voltaire and the Eighteenth Century. Oxford: Voltaire Foundation, 2008.

———. "Mise en forme et mise en critique du procès au théâtre: L'Exemple des scènes d'interrogatoire dans *Athalie*, *Œdipe*, *Brutus* et *Guillaume Tell*." In Biet and Schifano, *Représentations du procès*, 223–36.

Brillon, Pierre-Jacques, Antoine-François Prost de Royer, and M. Riolz. *Dictionnaire de jurisprudence et des arrêts*. Lyon, Fr.: La Roche, 1787.

Brissot, Jacques Pierre. "Avis de l'éditeur." In Brissot, *Bibliothèque philosophique*, 1:1–18.

———, ed. *Bibliothèque philosophique, du législateur, du politique, du jurisconsulte*. Paris: Desauges, 1782–1785.

———. "De la décadence du barreau français." In Brissot, *Bibliothèque philosophique*, 6:359–409.

———. "Discours couronné par l'Académie de Châlons-sur-Marne." In Brissot, *Bibliothèque philosophique*, 6:2–22.

———. *Théorie des lois criminelles*. Berlin: n.p., 1781.

Broglie, Gabriel de. *Ségur sans cérémonie (1757–1825)*. Paris: Perrin, 1977.

Brumoy, Pierre. *Le Théâtre des Grecs*. Paris: Rollin père, J. B. Coignard et Rollin fils, 1730.

Bryson, Scott. *The Chastised Stage: Bourgeois Drama and the Exercise of Power*. Stanford, CA: Stanford University Press, 1991.

Buckley, Matthew. *Tragedy Walks the Streets: The French Revolution in the Making of Modern Drama*. Baltimore: Johns Hopkins University Press, 2006.

Burwick, Frederick. *Illusion and the Drama: Critical Theory of the Enlightenment and the Romantic Era*. University Park: Pennsylvania State University Press, 1991.

Buzonnière, Louis-François Nouel de. *Essai sur les moyens de rendre la comédie utile aux mœurs*. In *De la réformation du théâtre*, by Luigi Riccoboni, 2–75. Paris: Debure père, 1767.

Cailhava de L'Estandoux, Jean-François. *Athènes pacifiée*. Paris: Pougens, 1797.

Camaille-Saint-Aubin, Nicolas. *L'Ami du peuple, ou les intrigants démasqués*. Paris: Maradan, 1793.

Camp, Pannill. *The First Frame*. Cambridge: Cambridge University Press, 2014.

Campagna, Norbert. "Arbitraire." In *Dictionnaire Montesquieu*, edited by Catherine Volpilhac-Auger. Lyon, Fr.: École normale supérieure de Lyon, 2013. http://dictionnaire-montesquieu.ens-lyon.fr/fr/article/1377722783/fr.

Camus, Armand-Gaston. *Lettres sur la profession d'avocat*. Edited by André Dupin. Brussels: H. Tarlier, 1833.

Caplan, Jay. *Framed Narratives: Diderot's Genealogy of the Beholder*. Minneapolis: University of Minnesota Press, 1985.

Carlyle, Thomas. *The French Revolution: A History*. London: Chapman and Hall, 1848.

Caron, Pierre, ed. *Paris pendant la Terreur: Rapports des agents secrets du ministre de l'intérieur*. Paris: Honoré Champion, 1943.

Certeau, Michel de. *The Writing of History*. Translated by Tom Conley. New York: Columbia University Press, 1988.

Charlemagne, Armand. *Le Souper des Jacobins*. Paris: Barba, 1795.

Charpentier, Louis. *Causes de la décadence du goût sur le théâtre*. Paris: Dufour, 1768.

Chavray de Boissy. *L'Avocat, ou Réflexions sur l'exercice du barreau*. Rome: L. Cellot, 1777.

Chénier, Marie-Joseph. *Jean Calas*. Paris: Moutard, 1793.

Chéry, Aurore. "'Je ne veux pas les attendrir': La Question de la sensibilité niée et ses conséquences dans le procès et l'exécution de Louis XVI." In *La Culture Judiciaire: Discours, représentations et usages de la justice du Moyen Âge à nos jours*, edited by Lucien Faggion, Christophe Regina, and Bernard Ribémont, 419–30. Dijon, Fr.: Presses Universitaires de Dijon, 2014.

Chouillet, Jacques. *La Formation des idées esthétiques de Diderot: 1745–1763*. Paris: A. Colin, 1973.

Cicéron, Marco Tulio. *Œuvres complètes de Cicéron: Oraisons*. Paris: C. L. F. Panckoucke, 1837.
Claverie, Elisabeth. "Procès, affaire, cause: Voltaire et l'innovation critique." *Politix* 26 (1994): 76–85.
Clay, Lauren. *Stagestruck: The Business of Theater in Eighteenth-Century France and Its Colonies*. Ithaca, NY: Cornell University Press, 2013.
Clément, Jean-Marie, and Joseph de La Porte. *Anecdotes Dramatiques*. Paris: Veuve Duchesne, 1775.
Cléry, Jean-Baptiste. *Mémoires de Cléry*. Paris: Firmin Didot frères, 1856.
Collot d'Herbois, Jean-Marie. *Le Procès de Socrate*. Paris: Veuve Duchesne, 1791.
Commaille, Jacques. "Les Tribunaux de famille sous la Révolution. Recours à l'histoire comme contribution à une sociologie de la justice et des relations privé-public." In *Une autre Justice. 1789–1799*, ed. Robert Badinter, 205–23. Paris: Fayard, 1989.
Comsa, Maria Teodora. "Society Theater: A Laboratory for Esthetic and Social Change (1715–1815)." PhD diss., Stanford University, 2014.
Connors, Logan. *Dramatic Battles in Eighteenth-Century France: Philosophes, Anti-philosophes and Polemical Theatre*. Studies on Voltaire and the Eighteenth Century. Oxford: Voltaire Foundation, 2012.
Consultation sur la discipline des avocats. Paris: Knapen, 1775.
Corneille, Pierre. *Trois discours sur le poème dramatique*. Edited by Marc Escola and Bénédicte Louvat. Paris: GF Flammarion, 1999.
Coste d'Arnobat, Louis. "Le Philosophe, ami de tout le monde." In Palissot, *La Comédie des Philosophes*, 167–76.
Coyer, Gabriel-François. *Discours sur la Satyre contre les philosophes*. Athens: chez le libraire anti-philosophe, 1760.
Creech, James. *Diderot: Thresholds of Representation*. Columbus: Ohio State University Press, 1986.
Dacier, Anne. *Comédies grecques d'Aristophane*. Paris: D. Thierry et Cl. Barbin, 1692.
Dancourt, Louis Hurtaut. *Lettre de l'Arlequin de Berlin à M. Fréron*. Amsterdam: Schneider, 1760.
———. *L.-H. Dancourt, Arlequin de Berlin, à M. J.-J. Rousseau*. Amsterdam: Schneider, 1759.
Darlow, Mark. "Staging the Revolution: The *Fait historique*." *Nottingham French Studies* 45 (Spring 2006): 77–88.
Davis, Natalie Zemon. *Fiction in the Archives: Pardon Tales and Their Tellers in Sixteenth-Century France*. Stanford, CA: Stanford University Press, 1990.
Delacroix, Jacques-Vincent. "Discours sur les mémoires." In *Peinture des mœurs du siècle*, 2:322–35. Amsterdam: Lejay, 1777.
———. *Réflexions philosophiques sur l'origine de la civilisation*. Amsterdam: Belin, 1781.
Demars-Sion, Véronique. "Une Expérience d'arbitrage forcé: Les Tribunaux de famille révolutionnaires." *Revue historique de droit français et étranger* 83 (2005): 385–420.
Dentand, Julien. *Essai de jurisprudence criminelle*. Lausanne, Switz.: n.p., 1785.
———. *Lettre de M. Julien Dentand de Genève, sur le réquisitoire de M. de Séguier*. Amsterdam: n.p., 1787.
Derasse, Nicolas. "Les Défenseurs officieux: Une Défense sans barreaux." *Annales historiques de la Révolution française* 350 (October–December 2007): 49–67.
Derrida, Jacques. *De la grammatologie*. Paris: Les Editions de Minuit, 1967.
Descotes, Maurice. *Le Public de théâtre et son histoire*. Paris: PUF, 1964.
Desnoiresterres, Gustave. *La Comédie satirique au XVIIIe siècle*. Paris: Perrin, 1885.

Diderot, Denis. *Les Entretiens sur le Fils naturel.* Edited by Jean Goldzink. Paris: GF Flammarion, 2005.

———. *Essais sur la peinture.* In Laurent Versini, *Diderot, Œuvres,* 4:467–516.

———. *Le Fils naturel.* Edited by Jean Goldzink. Paris: GF Flammarion, 2005.

———. *Jacques le Fataliste.* Paris: Le Livre de Poche, 1972.

———. "Lettre à Madame Riccoboni." In Diderot, *Les Entretiens sur le Fils naturel,* 345–58.

———. *Lettre sur les aveugles à l'usage de ceux qui voient; Lettre sur les sourds et muets à l'usage de ceux qui entendent et qui parlent.* Edited by Marian Hobson. Paris: Flammarion, 2000.

———. *Mémoires pour Catherine II.* Edited by Paul Vernière. Paris: Classiques Garnier, 1966.

———. *Le Neveu de Rameau.* In Versini, *Diderot, Œuvres,* 2:605–695.

———. *Le Paradoxe sur le comédien.* Edited by Raymond Laubreaux. Paris: Flammarion, 1981.

———. *De la Poésie dramatique.* Edited by Jean Goldzink. Paris: GF Flammarion, 2005.

———. *Salon de 1765.* In Versini, *Diderot, Œuvres,* 4:291–466.

———. *Salon de 1767.* In Versini, *Diderot, Œuvres,* 4:517–819.

———, and Jean le Rond d'Alembert, eds. *Encyclopédie, ou dictionnaire raisonné des sciences, des arts et des métiers.* University of Chicago: ARTFL Encyclopédie Project (Autumn 2017 Edition). Edited by Robert Morrissey and Glenn Roe. http://encyclopedie.uchicago.edu/.

Didier, Béatrice. *Diderot dramaturge du vivant.* Paris: Presses universitaires de France, 2001.

Dieckmann, Herbert. *Cinq leçons sur Diderot.* Geneva: Droz, 1959.

Domat, Jean. *Les Lois civiles dans leur ordre naturel.* Paris: Veuve Cavelier, 1766.

Dupont, Florence. "La Scène juridique." *Communications* 26 (1977): 62–77.

Dutton, Dianne. "Concurrence et convergence: Le Sermon et le plaidoyer de l'âge Classique." *Biblio 17* 166 (2006): 223–32.

———. "Le Plaideur comme comédien: L'Art dramatique du procès." In Biet and Schifano, *Représentations du procès,* 127–34.

Duvergier, Jean Baptiste, ed. *Collection complète des lois, décrets, ordonnances, règlements et avis du Conseil d'état.* Paris: Guyot et Scribe, 1825.

Edelstein, Dan. *The Terror of Natural Right: Republicanism, the Cult of Nature, and the French Revolution.* Chicago: University of Chicago Press, 2009.

Encyclopédie de jurisprudence. Brussels: J. L. de Boubers, 1777–81.

Enders, Jody. *Death by Drama and Other Medieval Urban Legends.* Chicago: University of Chicago Press, 2002.

Estrée, Paul d'. *Le Théâtre sous la Terreur.* Paris: Émile-Paul frères, 1913.

Falconnet, Ambroise. *Essai sur le barreau grec, romain et français.* Paris: Grangé, 1773.

Farge, Arlette, and Michel Foucault. *Le Désordre des familles.* Paris: Gallimard, 1982.

Farcy, Jean-Claude. *Histoire de la justice en France.* Paris: La Découverte, 2015.

Feilla, Cecilia. *The Sentimental Theater of the French Revolution.* Burlington, VT: Ashgate, 2013.

Felman, Shoshana. "Forms of Judicial Blindness, or the Evidence of What Cannot Be Seen: Traumatic Narratives and Legal Repetitions in the O. J. Simpson Case and in Tolstoy's *The Kreutzer Sonata.*" *Critical Inquiry* 23, no. 4 (Summer 1997): 738–88.

———. *The Juridical Unconscious: Trials and Traumas in the Twentieth Century.* Cambridge, MA: Harvard University Press, 2002.

Féraud, Jean-François. "Arbitraire." In *Dictionnaire critique de la langue française.* Marseille: J. Mossy, 1787.

Ferret, Olivier. "Mises en scène satiriques des Encyclopédistes: Autour de la querelle des *Philosophes* de Palissot." In *Le Philosophe sur les planches: L'Image du philosophe dans le théâtre des Lumières (1680–1815)*, edited by Pierre Hartmann, 113–28. Strasbourg, Fr.: Presses Universitaires de Strasbourg, 2004.

Ferri, Giovanni. *De l'Eloquence et des orateurs anciens et modernes.* Paris: J.-G. Mérigot, 1789.

Fitzsimmons, Michael. *The Parisian Order of Barristers and the French Revolution.* Cambridge, MA: Harvard University Press, 1987.

Fleury. *Mémoires de Fleury.* Paris: Adolphe Delahays, 1847.

Fling, Fred. "Mirabeau, a Victim of the Lettres de Cachet." *American Historical Review* 3 (October 1897): 19–30.

Foucault, Michel. "Cours du 8 janvier 1975." In *Les Anormaux: Cours au Collège de France, 1974–1975*, edited by François Ewald and Alessandro Fontana, 3–24. Paris: Gallimard, 1999.

———. *Surveiller et punir: Naissance de la prison.* Paris: Gallimard, 1975.

Fouquier, Armand. *Causes célèbres de tous les peuples.* Paris: Lebrun, 1867.

Fournel, Victor. "Le Parterre sous la Révolution." *Revue d'art dramatique* 31 (July–September 1893): 1–16.

Fowler, James E. *Voicing Desire: Family and Sexuality in Diderot's Narrative.* Studies on Voltaire and the Eighteenth Century. Oxford: Voltaire Foundation, 2000.

Frankfurt, Harry. *On Bullshit.* Princeton, NJ: Princeton University Press, 2005.

Frantz, Pierre. "Appropriation bourgeoise et populaire de l'histoire nationale dans les drames historiques de Mercier." *Romanistische Zeitschrift* 3–4 (1979): 319–34.

———. *L'Esthétique du tableau dans le théâtre du XVIIIe siècle.* Paris: Presses universitaires de France, 1998.

———. Introduction to *Du Théâtre*. In Louis-Sébastien Mercier, *Mon Bonnet de nuit, suivi de Du Théâtre*, ed. Jean-Claude Bonnet and Pierre Frantz, lxxvi–cvi. Paris: Mercure de France, 1999.

———. "Pas d'entracte pour la Révolution." In *La Carmagnole des muses: L'Homme de lettres et l'artiste dans la Révolution*, edited by Jean-Claude Bonnet, 381–99. Paris: Armand Colin, 1988.

———. "Rire et théâtre carnavalesque pendant la Révolution." *Dix-huitième siècle* 32 (2000): 291–306.

———. "L'Usage du peuple." In *Louis-Sébastien Mercier, un hérétique en littérature*, edited by Jean-Claude Bonnet, 55–79. Paris: Mercure de France, 1995.

Fréron, Élie-Catherine. *L'Année littéraire.* 37 vols. Geneva: Slatkine Reprints, 1966.

Fried, Michael. *Absorption and Theatricality: Painting and Beholder in the Age of Diderot.* Berkeley: University of California Press, 1980.

Friedland, Paul. *Political Actors: Representative Bodies & Theatricality in the Age of the French Revolution.* Ithaca, NY: Cornell University Press, 2002.

———. *Seeing Justice Done: The Age of Spectacular Capital Punishment in France.* Oxford: Oxford University Press, 2012.

Furetière, Antoine. "Arbitraire." In *Dictionnaire universel, contenant généralement tous les mots français.* The Hague: Husson, 1727.

Gachet, Louis. *Observations sur les spectacles en général, et en particulier sur le Colisée.* Paris: P.-A. Le Prieur, 1772.

Garapon, Antoine. *Bien juger: Essai sur le rituel judiciaire.* Paris: Odile Jacob, 1997.

Gayraud, Jean-François. *La Dénonciation.* Paris: Presses Universitaires de France, 1995.

Gelbart, Nina. "'Frondeur' Journalism in the 1770s: Theater Criticism and Radical Politics in the Prerevolutionary French Press." *Eighteenth-Century Studies* 17 (Summer 1984): 493–514.

Gilman, Margaret. "Imagination and Creation in Diderot." *Diderot Studies* 2 (1952): 200–220.
Gin, Pierre-Louis-Claude. *De l'Eloquence du barreau*. Paris: Hérissant fils, 1767.
Girault de Coursac, Paul, and Pierrette Girault de Coursac. *Enquête sur le procès du roi Louis XVI*. Paris: Œil, 1992.
Goldzink, Jean. *Comique et comédie au siècle des Lumières*. Paris: L'Harmattan, 2000.
Goodden, Angelica. *Actio and Persuasion: Dramatic Performance in Eighteenth-Century France*. Oxford: Clarendon, 1986.
———. "Painting for the Eye and Painting for the Mind: Correspondences of the Arts in Eighteenth-Century France." *Oxford Art Journal* 7, no. 1 (January 1984): 3–14.
Gourdin, François Philippe. *Considérations philosophiques sur l'action de l'orateur*. Amsterdam: Vve Desaint, 1775.
Graczyk, Annette. "Le Théâtre de la Révolution française, média de masses entre 1789 et 1794." *Dix-huitième siècle* 21 (1989): 395–409.
Graville, Barthélemy-Claude Graillard de. *L'Homme vrai*. Amsterdam: Dufour, 1761.
Grimm, Friedrich Melchior, Denis Diderot, Guillaume-Thomas Raynal, and Jakob Heinrich Meister. *Correspondance littéraire, philosophique et critique*. Edited by Maurice Tourneux. 16 vols. Paris: Garnier Frères, 1877–82.
Gros de Besplas, Joseph-Marie. *Des Causes du bonheur public*. Paris: Batilliot, 1790.
Habermas, Jürgen. *The Structural Transformation of the Public Sphere*. Translated by Thomas Burger. Cambridge, MA: MIT Press, 1991.
Hallward, Peter. "Staging Equality: On Rancière's Theatrocracy." *New Left Review* 37 (January–February 2006): 109–29.
Halpérin, Jean-Louis. "La Composition des tribunaux de famille sous la Révolution." In *La Famille, la Loi, l'Etat. De la Révolution au Code Civil*, 292–304. Paris: Imprimerie Nationale, 1989.
Hautefort, Charles Auguste. "Observations sur le *Traité des délits et des peines*." In Brissot, *Bibliothèque philosophique*, 1:267–323.
Hayes, Julie C. "Changing the System: Mercier's Ideological Appropriation of Diderot." *Studies in Eighteenth-Century Culture* 18 (1988): 343–57.
Hesse, Carla. "La Preuve par la lettre: Pratiques juridiques au tribunal révolutionnaire de Paris (1793–1794)." *Annales HSS* 3 (May–June 1996): 629–42.
Horville, Robert. "La Justice dans le théâtre français du XVIIe siècle." In Biet and Schifano, *Représentations du procès*, 115–25.
Huet, Marie-Hélène. *Mourning Glory: The Will of the French Revolution*. Philadelphia: University of Pennsylvania Press, 1997.
———. *Rehearsing the Revolution: The Staging of Marat's Death, 1793–1797*. Translated by Robert Hurley. Berkeley: University of California Press, 1982.
———. "Le Sacre du Printemps: Essai sur le sublime et la Terreur." *MLN* 103 (1988): 782–99.
Hunt, Lynn. *The Family Romance of the French Revolution*. Berkeley: University of California Press, 1992.
Hyslop, Beatrice F. "The Theater During a Crisis: The Parisian Theater During the Reign of Terror." *Journal of Modern History* 17 (December 1945): 332–55.
L'Influence de la Révolution sur le théâtre français. Paris: Debray, 1790.
Jaëcklé-Plunian, Claude. *À propos des écrits sur le théâtre au dix-huitième siècle*. Studies on Voltaire and the Eighteenth Century. Oxford: Voltaire Foundation, 1999.
Jaucourt, Louis de. "Libelle." In Diderot and d'Alembert, *Encyclopédie*, 9:459–60.
Jauffret, Paul-Eugène. *Le Théâtre révolutionnaire, 1788–1799*. Paris: Jouvet, 1869.

Jauss, Hans Robert. "Levels of Identification of Hero and Audience." *New Literary History* 5, no. 2 (Winter 1974): 283–317.

Johnson, James H. *Listening in Paris: A Cultural History*. Berkeley: University of California Press, 1995.

———. "Urban Development and the Culture of Masked Balls in Nineteenth-Century Paris." *Urban History* 40 (November 2013): 646–62.

———. *Venice Incognito: Masks in the Serene Republic*. Berkeley: University of California Press, 2011.

———. "Versailles, Meet Les Halles: Masks, Carnival, and the French Revolution." *Representations* 73 (Winter 2001): 89–116.

Jordan, David P. *The King's Trial: Louis XVI vs. the French Revolution*. Berkeley: University of California Press, 2004.

Jourdan, Annie. "Les Journées de Prairial an II: le tournant de la Révolution?" *La Révolution française* 10 (2016), http://lrf.revues.org/1591.

Jousse, Daniel. *Traité de l'administration de la justice*. Paris: Debure père, 1771.

Kalyvas, Andreas, and Ira Katznelson. *Liberal Beginnings: Making a Republic for the Moderns*. Cambridge: Cambridge University Press, 2008.

Kapp, Volker. "Satire et injure au XVIIIe siècle: Le Conflit entre la morale et la politique dans le débat sur les libelles." *Cahiers de l'Association internationale des études francaises* 36, no. 1 (1984): 155–65.

Karpik, Lucien. *French Lawyers: A Study in Collective Action, 1274 to 1994*. Oxford: Oxford University Press, 1999.

Keller, Abraham C. "Plutarch and Rousseau's First Discours." *PMLA* 54 (March 1939): 212–22.

Kennedy, Emmet. *A Cultural History of the French Revolution*. New Haven, CT: Yale University Press, 1989.

———, Marie-Laurence Netter, James P. McGregor, and Mark V. Olsen. *Theatre, Opera, and Audiences in Revolutionary Paris: Analysis and Repertory*. Westport, CT: Greenwood Press, 1996.

Koselleck, Reinhart. *Futures Past: On the Semantics of Historical Time*. Translated by Keith Tribe. Cambridge, MA: MIT Press, 1985.

Lacoue-Labarthe, Philippe. *Typography: Mimesis, Philosophy, Politics*. Cambridge, MA: Harvard University Press, 1989.

Lacretelle, Pierre Louis de. *Discours sur le préjugé des peines infamantes*. Paris: Cuchet, 1784.

La Harpe, Jean-François de. *Correspondance littéraire*. In *Œuvres de La Harpe*, 10:23–13:262. Paris: Verdière, 1820.

Lamarche-Courmont, Ignace Hugary de. "Réponse aux différents écrits publiés contre la comédie des *Philosophes*, ou parallèle des *Nuées* d'Aristophane, des *Femmes savantes*, du *Méchant* et des *Philosophes*." In Palissot, *La Comédie des Philosophes*, 300–311.

Lanjuinais, Joseph. *Manuel des jeunes orateurs*. Moudon, Switz.: Société typographique, 1777.

Latour, Bertrand de. *Réflexions morales, politiques, historiques, et littéraires, sur le théâtre*. In *Œuvres Complètes*, edited by L'Abbé Migne, 4:1–5:1164. Paris: Migne, 1855.

Laya, Jean-Louis. *L'Ami des lois*. Edited by Mark Darlow and Yann Robert. London: MHRA Critical Texts, 2011.

———. *Les Dangers de l'opinion*. Paris: Maradan, 1790.

———. *Jean Calas*. Avignon, Fr.: Jacques Garrigan, 1791.

———. *Voltaire aux Français sur leur constitution*. Paris: Maradan, 1789.

Le F***, M. "Plan de législation sur les matières criminelles." In Brissot, *Bibliothèque philosophique*, 5:291–462.

Legendre, Pierre. *Law and the Unconscious: A Legendre Reader*. Edited by Peter Goodrich. New York: St. Martin's Press, 1997.

Leichman, Jeffrey. *Acting Up: Staging the Subject in Enlightenment France*. Lewisburg, PA Bucknell University Press, 2016.

Lemercier de La Rivière, Pierre-Paul. *L'Heureuse nation*. Paris: Creuze et Béhal, 1792.

Lemierre d'Argy, Auguste-Jacques. *Calas, ou Le Fanatisme*. Paris: Imprimerie des Révolutions, 1791.

Leon, Mechele. *Molière, the French Revolution, and the Theatrical Afterlife*. Iowa City: University of Iowa Press, 2009.

———. "The Poet and the Prince: Revising Molière and *Tartuffe* in the French Revolution." *French Historical Studies* 28 (Summer 2005): 447–67.

Le Trosne, Guillaume-François. "Discours sur l'état actuel de la magistrature, et sur les causes de sa décadence." In Brissot, *Bibliothèque philosophique*, 4:121–67.

———. *Vues sur la justice criminelle*. Paris: Debure, 1777.

*Lettre d'un avocat à M. de L***, président à Mortier au Parlement de Paris, sur les devoirs des juges par rapport à leurs secrétaires*. N.p.: n.p., 1788.

Lever, Maurice. *Théâtre et Lumières: Les Spectacles de Paris au XVIIIe siècle*. Paris: Fayard, 2001.

Liéby, Adolphe. *Étude sur le théâtre de Marie-Joseph Chénier*. Paris: Lecène et Oudin, 1901.

Lilti, Antoine. *The Invention of Celebrity*. Translated by Lynn Jeffress. Cambridge: Polity Press, 2017.

Lindsay, Suzanne. "Mummies and Tombs: Turenne, Napoleon, and Death Ritual." *Art Bulletin* 82, no. 3 (September 2000): 476–502.

Linguet, Simon-Nicolas-Henri. *Discours destiné à être prononcé par Me Linguet dans l'Assemblée des avocats, le 3 février 1775*. Paris: Pierres, 1775.

———. *Théorie des lois civiles*. London: n.p., 1774.

Lubomirski, Stanislaw. "De Vanitate consiliorum." In Brissot, *Bibliothèque philosophique*, 10:83–89.

Lucas, Colin. "The Theory and Practice of Denunciation in the French Revolution." *Journal of Modern History* 68 (1996): 768–85.

Maillet-Duclairon, Antoine. *Essai sur la connaissance des théâtres français*. Paris: Prault père, 1751.

Marat, Jean-Paul. *Plan de législation criminelle*. Paris: Rochette, 1790.

Maréchal, Sylvain. *Correctif à la Révolution*. Paris: Cercle Social, 1793.

Margairaz, Dominique. *François de Neufchâteau: Biographie intellectuelle*. Paris: Publications de la Sorbonne, 2005.

Marmontel, Jean-François. "Comédie." In Diderot and d'Alembert, *Encyclopédie*, 3:665–69.

———. *Éléments de littérature*. In *Œuvres Complètes de Marmontel*, edited by René de Chazet, 12:1–15:566. Paris: Verdiere, 1818–20.

Marshall, David. *The Surprising Effects of Sympathy: Marivaux, Diderot, Rousseau and Mary Shelley*. Chicago: University of Chicago Press, 1988.

Martin, Jean-Clément. *Violence et révolution: Essai sur la naissance d'un mythe national*. Paris: Seuil, 2006.

Maslan, Susan. *Revolutionary Acts: Theater, Democracy, and the French Revolution*. Baltimore: Johns Hopkins University Press, 2005.

Mason, Laura. "The 'Bosom of Proof': Criminal Justice and the Renewal of Oral Culture During the French Revolution." *Journal of Modern History* 76 (2004): 29–61.

———. "Conspiracy as Theater During the French Revolution." Paper presented at the Annual Meeting of the Society for French Historical Studies, Nashville, TN, March 2016.

Mauduit-Larive, Jean. *Réflexions sur l'art théâtral.* Paris: Rondonneau, 1800.

Maugras, Gaston. *Les Comédiens hors la loi.* Paris: C. Lévy, 1887.

May, Gita. "Diderot and Burke: A Study in Aesthetic Affinity" *PMLA* 75 (1960): 527–39.

Maza, Sarah. *Private Lives and Public Affairs: The Causes Célèbres of Prerevolutionary France.* Berkeley: University of California Press, 1993.

———. "The Theater of Punishment: Melodrama and Judicial Reform in Prerevolutionary France." In *From the Royal to the Republican Body: Incorporating the Political in Seventeenth- and Eighteenth-Century France*, edited by Sara E. Melzer and Kathryn Norberg, 182–97. Berkeley: University of California Press, 1998.

Ménil, Alain. *Diderot et le drame: Théâtre et politique.* Paris: Presses universitaires de France, 1995.

Mercier, Louis-Sébastien. *L'An 2440.* N.p.: n.p, 1786.

———. *Charles II, roi d'Angleterre en certain lieu.* Venice: n.p., 1789.

———. *Fragments de politique et d'histoire.* Paris: Buisson, 1792.

———. *L'Indigent.* In *Théâtre Complet de M. Mercier*, 3:1–109. Amsterdam: Vlam, 1778.

———. *Jenneval.* Paris: Le Jay, 1769.

———. *Le Juge.* London: Ruault, 1774.

———. *Nouvel examen de la tragédie française.* In *De la littérature et des littérateurs*, 89–158. Yverdon, Switz.: n.p., 1778.

———. *Satyres contre Racine et Boileau.* Paris: Hénée, 1808.

———. *Tableau de Paris.* Geneva: Slatkine Reprints, 1979.

———. *Du Théâtre ou essai sur l'art dramatique.* Amsterdam: chez E. Van Harrevelt, 1773.

Merville, Pierre Biarnoy de. *Règles pour former un avocat.* Paris: Durand, 1778.

Mézard. *Essai sur les réformes à faire dans l'administration de la justice.* N.p.: n.p., 1788.

Michel, P. "L'*Ami des lois* par Laya." *Bulletin du Bouquiniste* 36 (1875): 487–90.

Michelet, Jules. *Histoire de la Révolution française.* Paris: Lemerre, 1888.

Montesquieu. *L'Esprit des lois.* In *Œuvres complètes de Montesquieu*, edited by Édouard Laboulaye, 3:83–382. Paris: Garnier, 1876.

Mortier, Roland. "La Satire, ce *poison de la littérature*: Voltaire et la nouvelle déontologie de l'homme de lettres." In *Essays on the Age of Enlightenment in Honor of Ira O. Wade*, edited by Jean Macary, 233–46. Geneva: Droz, 1977.

Mossé, Claude. *L'Antiquité dans la Révolution française.* Paris: Albin Michel, 1989.

Murena, Massimiliano. *Du Devoir des juges.* In *Traité des violences publiques et particulières*, translated by Jean-Claude Pingeron, 172–421. Paris: Delalain, 1769.

Muyart de Vouglans, Pierre-François. *Les Lois criminelles de France.* Paris: Merigot, 1780.

Netter, Marie-Laurence. "L'Intégration de nouvelles valeurs par le théâtre." In *Actes du colloque Théâtre et Révolution*, edited by Lucile Garbagnati and Marita Gilli, 25–34. Paris: Les Belles Lettres, 1988.

Neufchâteau, Nicolas François de. *Paméla, ou La Vertu récompensée.* Edited by Martial Poirson. Studies on Voltaire and the Eighteenth Century. Oxford: Voltaire Foundation, 2007.

Nolivos de Saint-Cyr, Paul-Antoine-Nicolas. *Tableau du siècle.* Geneva: n.p., 1759.

Norman, Larry. *The Public Mirror: Molière and the Social Commerce of Depiction.* Chicago: University of Chicago Press, 1999.

Ost, François. "Juge-pacificateur, juge-arbitre, juge-entraîneur: Trois modèles de justice." In *Fonction de juger et pouvoir judiciaire*, edited by Philippe Gérard, François Ost, and Michel van de Kerchove, 1–70. Brussels: Publications Fac St Louis, 1983.

Ozouf, Mona. *La Fête révolutionnaire: 1789–1799*. Paris: Gallimard, 1976.

———. "Peut-on commémorer la révolution française?" *Le Débat* 26 (1983/4): 161–72.

———. "'Public Opinion' at the End of the Old Regime." *Journal of Modern History* 60 (September 1988): S1–S21.

Palissot, Charles. *La Comédie des Philosophes et autres textes*. Edited by Olivier Ferret. Saint-Etienne: Publications de l'Université de Saint-Etienne, 2002.

———. "Dialogues historiques et critiques: Aristophane & le Père Brumoy." In *Œuvres complètes*, 3:211–32. Geneva: Slatkine reprints, 1971.

———. "Lettre de l'auteur de la comédie des *Philosophes* au public pour servir de préface à la pièce." In Palissot, *La Comédie des Philosophes*, 113–19.

Parker, Harold Talbot. *The Cult of Antiquity and the French Revolutionaries*. New York: Octagon Books, 1965.

Philipon de La Madelaine, Louis. "Des Moyens d'indemniser l'innocence injustement accusée et punie." In Brissot, *Bibliothèque philosophique*, 4:275–329.

Piana, Romain. "Brumoy et l'interprétation satirique d'Aristophane." *Anabases* 14 (2011): 87–100.

Plato. *The Collected Dialogues of Plato*. Edited by Edith Hamilton and Huntington Cairns. New York: Pantheon Books, 1961.

Plutarch. *Les Vies des hommes illustres*, translated by Jacques Amyot. Paris: Michel Vascosan, 1565.

Poinsinet de Sivry, Louis. *Théâtre d'Aristophane*. Paris: Chez Desray, 1790.

Polier de Saint-Germain, Antoine. *Du Gouvernement des mœurs*. Lausanne, Switz.: Jules Henri Pott, 1784.

Popkin, Jeremy. "Pamphlet Journalism at the End of the Old Regime." *Eighteenth-Century Studies* 22 (Spring 1989): 351–67.

Postert, Kirsten. *Tragédie historique ou Histoire en tragédie? Les sujets d'histoire moderne dans la tragédie française (1550–1715)*. Tübingen, Ger.: G. Narr, 2010.

Pougin, Arthur. *L'Opéra-Comique pendant la Révolution*. Paris: A. Savine, 1891.

Le Pour et le contre: Recueil complet des opinions prononcées à l'Assemblée Conventionnelle dans le procès de Louis XVI. 7 vols. Paris: Buisson, 1792–93.

Pucci, Suzanne. *Sites of the Spectator: Emerging Literary and Cultural Practice in Eighteenth-Century France*. Studies on Voltaire and the Eighteenth Century. Oxford: Voltaire Foundation, 2001.

Pujoulx, Jean-Baptiste. *La Veuve Calas à Paris, ou le Triomphe de Voltaire*. Paris: Brunet, 1791.

"Les Qu'est-ce? A l'auteur de la comédie des *Philosophes*." In Palissot, *La Comédie des Philosophes*, 120–31.

Rabelleau. *Dissertation sur les spectacles*. Amsterdam: M.-M. Rey, 1769.

Rancière, Jacques. *Le Philosophe et ses pauvres*. Paris: Flammarion, 2007.

Ravel, Jeffrey. *The Contested Parterre: Public Theater and French Political Culture, 1680–1791*. Ithaca, NY: Cornell University Press, 1999.

———. "Seating the Public: Spheres and Loathing in the Paris Theaters, 1777–1788." *French Historical Studies* 18 (Spring 1993): 173–210.

———. *The Would-Be Commoner: A Tale of Deception, Murder, and Justice in Seventeenth-Century France*. New York: Houghton Mifflin Company, 2008.

Régaldo, Marc. "Retour à l'antique et art républicain dans le Théâtre de la Révolution française." In *Der theatralische Neoklassizismus um 1800*, edited by Roger Bauer, 168–83. Bern, Switz.: Peter Lang, 1986.

Rétif de la Bretonne, Nicolas-Edme. *L'Andrographe*. The Hague: Gosse, 1782.

———. *La Mimographe*. Amsterdam: Changuion, 1770.

———. *Les Nuits de Paris*. In *Paris le jour, Paris la nuit*, edited by Michel Delon and Daniel Baruch. Paris: Robert Laffont, 1990.

———. *La Paysanne pervertie*. Edited by Béatrice Didier. Paris: Garnier-Flammarion, 1976.

———. *Le Paysan perverti*. Edited by François Jost. Lausanne, Switz.: L'Âge d'homme, 1977.

———. *La Prévention nationale*. Paris: Regnault, 1784.

———. *Le Thesmographe*. The Hague: Gosse-junior, 1789.

Riccoboni, Luigi. *Pensées sur la déclamation*. Paris: Briasson, 1738.

Rittaud-Hutinet, Jacques. *La Vision d'un futur: Ledoux et ses théâtres*. Lyon, Fr.: Presses universitaires de Lyon, 1982.

Robert, Yann. "De l'Absorption et de l'identification chez Diderot: Illusion et participation du spectateur au dix-huitième siècle." In *La Scène, la salle et la coulisse dans le théâtre du XVIIIe siècle en France*, edited by Pierre Frantz and Thomas Wynn, 263–78. Paris: Presses de l'Université Paris-Sorbonne, 2011.

Robespierre, Maximilien. *Discours couronné par la Société Royale des Arts et des Sciences de Metz.* Amsterdam: Merigot, 1785.

———. *Discours de Maximilien Robespierre sur l'influence de la calomnie sur la Révolution*. Paris: Pierre-Jacques Duplain, 1792.

———. *Discours et rapports de Robespierre*. Edited by Charles Vellay. Paris: Eugène Pasquelle, 1908.

Robinet, Jean-Baptiste-René, ed. *Dictionnaire universel des sciences morale, économique, politique et diplomatique*. London: Libraires Associés, 1778.

Rollin, Charles. *Traité des études*. Paris: Estienne, 1741.

Rosanvallon, Pierre. *The Demands of Liberty: Civil Society in France Since the Revolution*. Translated by Arthur Goldhammer. Cambridge, MA: Harvard University Press, 2007.

Rosenfeld, Sophia. A *Revolution in Language: The Problem of Signs in Late Eighteenth-Century France*. Stanford, CA: Stanford University Press, 2001.

Rougemont, Martine de. "Quelques utopies théâtrales du XVIIIe siècle." *Romanica Wratislaviensia* 25 (1985): 59–70.

———. *La Vie théâtrale en France au XVIIIe siècle*. Paris: Champion, 1988.

Rouillé d'Orfeuil, Augustin. *L'Ami des Français*. Constantinople: n.p., 1771.

Rousseau, Jean-Jacques. *Les Confessions*. Edited by Raymond Trousson. Paris: Imprimerie Nationale, 1995.

———. *Considérations sur le gouvernement de Pologne*. London: n.p., 1782.

———. *Du Contrat social.* Edited by Bruno Bernardi. Paris: Flammarion, 2001.

———. *Lettre à d'Alembert*. Edited by Marc Buffat. Paris: Flammarion, 2003.

Royer, Jean-Pierre. *Histoire de la justice en France*. Paris: PUF, 1995.

Rubigni, Germain. *Comment la législation influe-t-elle sur les mœurs?* Auxerre, Fr.: L. Fournier, 1789.

Rufi, Enrico. *Le Rêve laïque de Mercier*. Studies on Voltaire and the Eighteenth Century. Oxford: Voltaire Foundation, 1995.

Sagan, Eli. *Citizens & Cannibals: The French Revolution, the Struggle for Modernity, and the Origins of Ideological Terror*. Lanham, MD: Rowman & Littlefield, 2001.

Saint-Aubin, Mague de. *La Réforme des théâtres.* Paris: Guillot, 1787.

Sainte-Albine, Remond de. *Le Comédien.* In *Mémoires de Molé et Le Comédien,* edited by Charles-Guillaume Étienne, 95–330. Paris: E. Ledoux, 1825.

Saint-Just, Louis Antoine de. *Œuvres choisies.* Edited by Jean Gratien. Paris: Gallimard, 1968.

Schechner, Richard. *Performance Theory.* London: Routledge, 2003.

Schlanger, Judith. "Théâtre révolutionnaire et représentation du bien." *Poétique* 22 (1975): 268–83.

Schmidt, Adolf, ed. *Tableaux de la révolution française.* Leipzig, Ger.: Veit, 1867.

Séguier, Antoine-Louis. "Réquisitoire contre le mémoire pour les trois hommes condamnés à la roue." In *Barreau français. Collection des chefs-d'œuvre de l'éloquence judiciaire en France,* 3:287–520. Paris: Panckoucke, 1822.

Servan, Joseph-Michel-Antoine. "Discours sur l'administration de la justice criminelle." In *Œuvres de Servan,* edited by S.-Xavier de Portets, 2:1–104. Paris: les éditeurs, 1825.

———. "Réflexions sur quelques points de nos lois." In Brissot, *Bibliothèque philosophique,* 7:153–278.

Shapiro, Barry M. *Traumatic Politics: The Deputies and the King in the Early French Revolution.* University Park: Penn State University Press, 2009.

Sheu, Ling-Ling. *Voltaire et Rousseau dans le théâtre de la révolution française.* Brussels: Éditions de l'Université de Bruxelles, 2005.

Showalter, English. "'Madame a fait un livre': Madame de Graffigny, Palissot et *Les Philosophes.*" *Recherches sur Diderot et sur l'Encyclopédie* 23 (1997): 109–25.

"Les Si et les mais." In Palissot, *La Comédie des Philosophes,* 164–66.

Soboul, Albert. *Le Procès de Louis XVI.* Paris: Gallimard, 1973.

———. *Les Sans-culottes.* Paris: Seuil, 1968.

Soulier, Gérard. "Le Théâtre et le procès." *Droit & Société* 17–18 (1991): 9–24.

Strayer, Brian E. *Lettres de cachet and Social Control in the Ancien Régime, 1659–1789.* New York: Peter Lang, 1992.

Suard, Jean-Baptiste-Antoine. "Des Applaudissements au théâtre." In *Mélanges de littérature,* 4:330–52.

———. "Censure des théâtres." In *Mélanges de littérature,* 4:309–19.

———. *Mélanges de littérature.* Geneva: Slatkine Reprints, 1971.

Tarin, René. "*La Lettre sur les Spectacles* dans les débats à l'Assemblée Nationale Constituante." *Revue d'histoire littéraire de la France* 96 (November–December 1996): 1128–36.

———. *Le Théâtre de la Constituante.* Paris: Champion, 1998.

Taylor, Katherine. "Geometries of Power: Royal, Revolutionary, and Post-revolutionary French Courtrooms." *Journal of the Society of Architectural Historians* 72, no. 4 (December 2013): 434–74.

———. *In the Theater of Criminal Justice: The Palais de Justice in Second Empire Paris.* Princeton, NJ: Princeton University Press, 1993.

Terrasson, Antoine. *Histoire de la Jurisprudence Romaine.* Paris: Théodore de Hansy, 1750.

Tissier, André. *Les Spectacles à Paris pendant la Révolution.* Geneva: Droz, 2002.

Toussaint, François-Vincent. "Arbitraire." In Diderot and d'Alembert, *Encyclopédie,* 1:578.

———. "Arbitre." In Diderot and d'Alembert, *Encyclopédie,* 1:579.

Très-humbles et très-respectueuses remontrances qu'il a été arrêté en Parlement le 4 Janvier 1753, de faire au roi. N.p.: n.p., 1753.

Trousson, Raymond. *Socrate devant Voltaire, Diderot, et Rousseau: La Conscience en face du mythe.* Paris: Minard, 1977.

———. "Le Théâtre tragique grec au siècle des Lumières." *Studies on Voltaire and the Eighteenth Century* 155 (1976): 2113–36.

Truchet, Jacques. *La Tragédie classique en France*. Paris: Presses universitaires de France, 1997.

Vanpée, Janie. "Performing Justice: The Trials of Olympe de Gouges." *Theatre Journal* 51, no. 1 (March 1999): 47–65.

Vermeil, François-Michel. *Essai sur les réformes à faire dans notre législation criminelle*. Paris: Demonville, 1781.

Vernon. *Apologie du théâtre adressée à Mlle. Clairon*. The Hague: n.p., 1762.

Versini, Laurent, ed. *Diderot, Œuvres*. Paris: R. Laffont, 1994–1997.

Veysman, Nicolas. *Mise en scène de l'opinion publique dans la littérature des Lumières*. Paris: Honoré Champion, 2004.

Vila, Anne C. *Enlightenment and Pathology: Sensibility in the Literature and Medicine of Eighteenth-Century France*. Baltimore: Johns Hopkins University Press, 1998.

Villemain d'Abancourt, François-Jean. *La Bienfaisance de Voltaire*. Paris: Brunet, 1791.

Villez, Barbara. "Lawyers and Courts in French Popular Culture." *Oxford Research Encyclopedia of Criminology and Criminal Justice* (August 2017). doi: 10.1093/acrefore/9780190264079.013.187.

Volpilhac-Auger, Catherine. "Aristophane, 'poète comique qui n'est ni comique ni poète,' mis en page et en français au XVIIIe siècle." In *Philologie et théâtre: Traduire, commenter, interpréter le théâtre antique en Europe (XVe–XVIIIe siècle)*, edited by Véronique Lochert and Zoé Schweitzer, 143–54. Amsterdam: Rodopi, 2012.

Voltaire. "Commentaire sur le livre des délits et des peines." In *Des Délits et des peines*, by Cesare Beccaria, 277–358. Paris: Brière, Libraire, 1822.

———. "Déclaration de Pierre Calas." In *Mélanges philosophiques, littéraires, historiques*, 3:507–13. Geneva: Cramer, 1771.

———. *Dictionnaire philosophique*. Edited by René Pomeau. Paris: Garnier-Flammarion, 1964.

———. "Poems by C. Churchill." In *Œuvres complètes*. Paris: Didot, 1861.

———. *Prix de la justice et de l'humanité*. London: n.p., 1777.

Walton, Charles. "*Charles IX* and the French Revolution: Law, Vengeance, and the Revolutionary Uses of History." *European Review of History: Revue européenne d'histoire* 4 (1997): 127–46.

Walzer, Michael. *Regicide and Revolution: Speeches at the Trial of Louis XVI*. Cambridge: Cambridge University Press, 1974.

Weber, Samuel. "Replacing the Body: An Approach to the Question of Digital Democracy." In *Public Space and Democracy*, edited by Marcel Hénaff and Tracy B. Strong, 172–88. Minneapolis: University of Minnesota Press, 2001.

Welschinger, Henri. "*L'Ami des lois* sous la Terreur et la Restauration." *Revue d'art dramatique* 24 (October–December 1891): 65–80.

———. *Le Théâtre de la Révolution*. Paris: Charavay Frères, 1881.

Welsh, David. "'Philosophers' and 'Alchemists' in Some Eighteenth-Century Russian Comedies." *Slavic and East European Journal* 8, no. 2 (Summer 1964): 149–58.

Index

Numbers in italics refer to figures.

Acknowledgments

Thanks to the support of my mentors, colleagues, friends, and family, writing this book was more often "play" than "trial" . . . and when it felt like the latter, I found in them the finest counsels and most benevolent judges. This book owes everything to them, and it is a pleasure to acknowledge some measure of that debt here.

For igniting in me, with her enthusiasm and erudition, a passion for eighteenth-century literature and culture, and for fostering that spark with just the right mixture of encouragement, shrewd suggestions, and constructive criticisms, my warmest thanks go to Marie-Hélène Huet. If not for her, I might have, like many before me, never bothered to even look at the theater of the Revolution. Likewise, this book would be considerably different—and inferior—were it not for the keen insights and generosity of Göran Blix, Volker Schröder, and Natasha Lee. I also wish to express my sincere gratitude to Reginald McGinnis, Lise Leibacher, and Meg Lota Brown, whose shining example as scholars and teachers I try to live up to every day. While a fellow at the Stanford Humanities Center, I had the incredible good fortune of interacting with a close-knit community of superb intellectuals and human beings: I thank them all, especially Dan Edelstein, J. P. Daughton, and Lanier Anderson. My luck has been such that I have found colleagues at the University of Illinois at Chicago (UIC) every bit as welcoming, generous, and insightful: my profuse thanks to everyone in the School of Literatures, Cultural Studies, and Linguistics, particularly John Ireland, Margaret Miner, Dolly Weber, and Ellen McClure (who gave me invaluable feedback on countless pages and ideas in this book), as well as to my fellow *dix-huitièmistes*, Lisa Freeman and Nina Dubin.

This community was further enriched by other academics I met at conferences and workshops in France, Britain, and the U.S. I have been deeply fortunate to benefit from the perspicacity, erudition, and altruism of such prominent scholars as Pierre Frantz, Mark Darlow, Thomas Wynn, Denis Guénoun, Laura Mason, and Jeffrey Ravel. The annual convention of the *American Society for Eighteenth-Century Studies* has become a kind of pilgrimage for me, as it is there that I most often meet with a new generation of eighteenth-century French theater scholars: Logan Connors, Annelle Curulla, Jeffrey Leichman, Maria Comsa, Pannill Camp, Sophie Marchand, and Laurence Marie. Dynamic and supportive, they have shaped this book in more ways than they likely realize. Other friends have also provided vital encouragement and advice, and have forever left their mark on me and on the book: among them, Michelle Coghlan, Anne-Marie Alexander, Jennifer Solheim, Elizabeth McManus, Melanie Conroy, Brian Jacobs, Ève Morisi, Daniel Worden, and Jérôme Quelin.

In addition to individuals, I am indebted to many institutions and organizations for their support. By presenting chapters of my work at interdisciplinary workshops (notably the University of Chicago's "Modern France Workshop" and the "Eighteenth-Century Interdisciplinary Salon" hosted by the Washington University in St. Louis), I was fortunate to receive feedback and leads from experts in multiple fields. My heartfelt thanks to the participants in these workshops and to the organizers who invited me: Larry Norman (UofC), Tili Boon Cuillé (WUSTL), and Laurence Mall, who brought me to the University of Illinois at Urbana-Champaign.

I owe a particularly large debt to the Andrew W. Mellon foundation, which has funded significant portions of my research through several fellowships, enabling me to conduct years of extensive research and join scholarly communities in Princeton, Stanford, and, most recently, the Newberry Library. I am also grateful to the Mrs. Giles Whiting foundation and the Jacob K. Javits fellowship program for their generous, multi-year support as I first began to explore theater and justice in eighteenth-century France. What these fellowships started, UIC completed. The College of Liberal Arts and Sciences, the School of Literatures, Cultural Studies, and Linguistics, and the Department of French and Francophone Studies gave me the support that every scholar needs: time to read, reflect, and write; opportunities to share work-in-progress with bright colleagues; and funding to present at conferences and dig through archival collections in world-class libraries. Among these libraries, I wish to express my gratitude to the staff at the Bibliothèque

Nationale de France, the Princeton University Library, the Bibliothèque de la Comédie-Française, and, above all, the Newberry Library. The latter's astonishing collection of French Revolutionary pamphlets had a profound effect on my book and continues to shape my research and my teaching, thanks notably to the French Revolution Pamphlets Digital Initiative.

Parts of Chapter 3 were previously published in a French article: "Des Acteurs au barreau, ou comment le dix-huitième siècle inventa l'avocat moderne," *Dix-huitième siècle* 49 (2017). Sections of Chapters 6 and 7 first appeared in "The Everlasting Trials of Jean Calas: Justice, Theater and Trauma in the Early Years of the Revolution," in *Representing Violence in France, 1760–1820*, ed. Thomas Wynn, Oxford: Voltaire Foundation, 2013, and are reprinted here by permission of the Voltaire Foundation, University of Oxford (http://www.voltaire.ox.ac.uk/). Chapter 6 also draws from material initially published in the introduction to my critical edition, co-authored with Mark Darlow, of Jean-Louis Laya's *L'Ami des lois* (London: Modern Humanities Research Association, 2011). I am deeply grateful to these publishers for their permission to reuse this material.

Of course, I am even more grateful to one publisher in particular: the University of Pennsylvania Press, which has proved a joy to work with throughout the publication process. My most sincere thanks go to Jerry Singerman and his colleagues, as well as to the two anonymous reviewers, whose remarkably detailed and constructive feedback improved the book immeasurably.

Last but certainly not least, this book would not exist today were it not for the unconditional love and support of my family. My parents and sister, Danièle, Georges, and Magali, inculcated me with a lifelong love of reading, and I will never forget the years spent devouring books far too advanced for me, hidden with my sister among the stacks in my mother's bookstore, *Jeux de mots*. Today, my wife Lori and I share the same love of reading with a new generation, our children, Claire and Nicolas. Not a day goes by that I don't thank my lucky stars for the boundless joy they have brought me, and I cannot wait to write the next chapters of our life together.

PALEONTOLOGY

PALEONTOLOGY

Editor

Justus Scheer

scitus
academics

Paleontology
Edited by **Justus Scheer**

This Book is Printed on Acid-Free Paper. ♾

ISBN: 9781681179032
Library of Congress Control Number: 2017948931

616, Corporate Way, Suite 2, 4766,
Valley Cottage, NY 10989

www.scitusacademics.com

Notice

Printed in United States of America.

Preface

Today, as society faces global issues such as climate change, the rapid degradation of habitats and accelerated extinction of species, we turn for insight not to "futurists" but to paleontologists, who often can demonstrate with empirical data from the fossil record how Earth and its inhabitants have responded to great changes -- some of them catastrophic -- in the past. Paleontology is a rich field, imbued with a long and interesting past and an even more intriguing and hopeful future. Paleontology represents the desire of human beings to better understand the history of life on Earth, and in so doing to better understand themselves and the world around them, including fundamental principles governing changes. Many people think paleontology is the study of fossils. In fact, paleontology is much more. In short, paleontology is the study of what fossils tell us about the ecologies of the past, about evolution, and about our place, as humans, in the world. Paleontology incorporates knowledge from biology, geology, ecology, anthropology, archaeology, and even computer science to understand the processes that have led to the origination and eventual destruction of the different types of organisms since life arose. Paleontologists study prehistoric life, seeking to piece together the story of how species evolved and how ancient ecosystems developed in response to an ever-changing Earth. And researchers do so with only the tiniest drops of evidence: fossilized remains of ancient life, from which we can infer much about our world as it was millions of years ago, teeming with life. In documenting evolution, paleontologists often can link the changes they see in species over time with large-scale changes in the environment of the entire planet, or of specific regions.

This book presents original research of interest to the international community in the fields of palaeontology, taxonomy and systematic. It deals with the recovery and identification of plant remains from geological contexts and their place in the reconstruction of past environments and the history of life. It covers the study of fossil and extant spores and pollen dealing with the recovery and identification of multicellular animal remains and the use of these fossils in the reconstruction of prehistoric environments and ancient ecosystems. It also focuses on how to use data from fossils and subfossils to reconstruct the ecosystems of the past.

Table of Contents

CHAPTER 1

Growth, inter- and intraspecific variation, palaeobiogeography, taphonomy and systematics of the Cenozoic ghost shrimp Glypturus

Adiël A. Klompmaker[a], Matúš Hyžný[b], Roger W. Portell[c] & Michał Kowalewski[a]

[a]*Florida Museum of Natural History, University of Florida, 1659 Museum Road, PO Box 117800, Gainesville, FL 32611, USA*

[b]*Geological-Paleontological Department, Natural History Museum Vienna, Burgring 7, 1010 Vienna, Austri*

[c]*Department of Geology and Paleontology, Faculty of Natural Sciences, Comenius University, Mlynsk_a dolina G1, 842 15 Bratislava, Slovakia*

ABSTRACT

Studies in systematic palaeontology are greatly aided when numerous, well-preserved specimens are available so that quantitative methods can be used to substantiate qualitative observations. This is often not the case for fossil decapods crustaceans due to their relatively low preservation potential. Here, we examined primarily two large collections of the well-preserved ghost shrimp Glypturus from the Holo-Pleistocene of Panama and the late

Miocene of Florida. Using descriptive, bivariate, multivariate and geometric morphometric methods, two new species are described based on appendage material: Glypturus panamacanalensis sp. nov. and G. sikesi sp. nov. New characters are identified, and sizerelated and intraspecific variation are assessed for these taxa and modern G. acanthochirus. Taxonomic placement of single specimens from other localities was confirmed by multivariate methods. Furthermore, Glypturus is revised, especially with regard to Western Atlantic species that inhabited both carbonate and siliciclastic environments. Callianassa anguillensis, C. latidigata, and Neocallichirus? quisquellanus are referred to as Glypturus sp. until more material is available to determine the validity of these species. Diversity within Glypturus may thus be underestimated, thereby also impacting the assessment of phylogenetic relationships. Minor propodi appear under-represented relative to major propodi, suggesting a taphonomic bias. Single specimens of interest include a specimen of G. panamacanalensis sp. nov. exhibiting a peculiar swelling in the fixed finger and another showing damage on the propodal upper margin, suggesting failed predation or antagonistic behaviour. Glypturus is first found in the Oligocene in the Western Atlantic and may have expanded its palaeobiogeographical range since the Miocene. The genus was still present on the Pacific side of the Isthmus of Panama in the Holo-Pleistocene, but is only known from the Western Atlantic today, suggesting a relatively recent extinction on the Pacific side.

Keywords: Cenozoic; shrimp; biogeography; growth; systematics; intraspecific variation

1. INTRODUCTION

For fossil decapod crustaceans, a limited number of specimens are typically available for study because of their limited preservation potential compared to other marine invertebrates (e.g. Kidwell & Flessa 1995; Foote & Sepkoski 1999; Stempien 2005). As a result, the systematic of fossil decapods is typically based on qualitative or marginally quantitative descriptions. In addition, the small sample sizes typical of many fossil decapod species hamper rigorous testing of interspecific, intraspecific and sizerelated variation in morphology. Consequently, few studies address these critical systematic issues in the palaeontological literature devoted to decapods (for exceptions, see Starzyk et al. 2011; Klompmaker et al. 2012a, b; Jones 2013). The flipside is that species delineation may appear easier because variation is necessarily limited, provided that the preservation of the specimen(s) is adequate. Parataxonomies exist as decapods consist of multicomponent exoskeletons (e.g. Jagt et al. 2010; Fraaije et al. 2013), but this does not appear to pose substantial problems with respect to synonymies, at least for the Cretaceous (Klompmaker 2013). For ghost shrimp systematic parataxonomies are not problematical because, typically, only the appendages are preserved, especially the relatively strongly calcified chelipeds, on which taxonomy of fossil taxa is primarily based. No possible synonymies of this kind were encountered among Cretaceous callianassid shrimp (Klompmaker 2013). Since (a) parataxonomies are limited for ghost shrimp; (b) their propodi are well calcified; (c) they can occur in high numbers locally; and (d) their burrowing nature allows for preferential preservation (Bishop & Williams 2005), major propodi of fossil ghost shrimp are often common and can be used for assessing interspecific, intraspecific (HyŽný & Hud_a_ckov_a 2012) and size-related variations. Also, biogeographical patterns can be reconstructed because of the abundance of fossils, as in this example using extant and fossil specimens of Glypturus Stimpson, 1866.

Today, specimens of Glypturus inhabit the Western Atlantic [G. acanthochirus Stimpson, 1866; Glypturus sp. = Glypturus rabalaisae sensu Sakai, 2005], the Indian Ocean and the south-west Pacific [G. armatus (A. Milne- Edwards, 1870)], and the Red Sea [G. laurae (de Saint Laurent in de Vaugelas & de Saint Laurent, 1984)] (HyŽný & Muller 2012, fig. 11). Furthermore, Glypturus has a fairly extensive fossil record that commences in the Eocene (HyŽný & Muller 2012; HyŽný et al. 2013). Mostly resembling modern species distributions of the genus, fossil species have been found in the Indo-West Pacific, the Tethys region and the Western Atlantic. Currently, the taxonomy of fossil Glypturus spp. is based on the presence/absence and extent of tuberculation on the lateral sides of the major propodus (HyŽný & Muller 2012; HyŽný et al. 2013), characters which also can be applied to extant Glypturus spp. (HyŽný & Muller 2012).

Recently, two large assemblages of fossil Glypturus spp., one from the Holo-Pleistocene of Panama and the other from the late Miocene of Florida, were discovered and collected, respectively. Additionally, many isolated Cenozoic specimens from a variety of localities in the Western Atlantic have been recognized. The main goals of this paper are to assess the species-level taxonomic placement of the large collections of fossil and extant specimens of Glypturus, explore the utility of quantitative methods in systematic studies of fossil decapod crustaceans, comment on the sedimentary environment and phylogeny of Glypturus, and explore the Western Atlantic palaeobiogeography of Glypturus through time.

2. GEOLOGICAL SETTING

Specimens identified below as Glypturus panamacanalensis sp. nov. were collected on Amador and Farfan beaches near the entrance to the Panama Canal, Panama City, in 1959 by M. D. Burkenroad, who identified at least one specimen as 'Callianassa acanthochirus'. They were most likely dredged before being dumped onto the beaches, suggesting that the provenance of the material is from or near the Pacific entrance of the Panama Canal. The age of these decapods, based on a co-occurring, wellpreserved mollusc fauna, is Holo-Pleistocene (undifferentiated). All faunal elements were found in irregularly shaped siliciclastic concretions and/or burrows of sandstone and siltstone. Bivalves included Anadara nux (Sowerby, 1833a) (UF 233946), Anadara concinna (Sowerby, 1833a) (UF 233945), Trachycardium procerum (Sowerby, 1833b) (UF 233997), Caryocorbula ovulate (Sowerby, 1833c) (UF 233956), Lirophora mariae (d'Orbigny, 1846), Chionopsis amathusia (Philippi, 1844), Tenuicorbula tenuis (Sowerby, 1833c), Tellina regia Hanley, 1844, and Lamelliconcha paytensis (d'Orbigny, 1845) (UF 233957); gastropods included Cosmioconcha modesta (Powys, 1835) (UF 233955) and Prunum sapotilla (Hinds, 1844) (UF 233960). All these molluscs are extant and are known from shallow marine (< 100 m), sandy to muddy environments (Keen 1971; Coan & Valentich-Scott 2012; Portell et al. 2012; Paleo- Biology Database 2013). Co-occurring brachyuran decapods include Hepatus sp. and a portunid. Farfan and Amador beaches are surrounded by Holocene and Pleistocene sediments of the Pacific Muck (e.g. Jones 1950; Woodring 1957), further supporting a Holo-Pleistocene age and consistent with the age determination of Portell et al. (2012), who suggested a Holo_late Pleistocene age for fossils found from nearby Bique and other beaches.

Specimens identified as Glypturus sikesi sp. nov. below were collected at University of Florida's Sikes Sand Mine 02 locality in Washington County, Florida, USA. These shrimp remains, found in fine phosphatic, micaceous, sandy clay, are believed to be part of the upper Miocene (Tortonian_Messinian) Choctawhatchee Formation of the Alum Bluff Group. First described by Matson & Clapp (1909) from a ravine near the Choctawhatchee River, south-east of the town of Redbay, the Choctawhatchee Formation has subsequently been revised, renamed and restricted; no longer included are the mollusc-rich beds described by Mansfield (1930, 1932), which are now referred to the Jackson Bluff Formation. For a comprehensive discussion of the Choctawhatchee Formation, see Huddlestun (1976; see also Portell et al. 2006, for a brief summary of the nomenclatural history of this and other fossiliferous Miocene deposits of the Florida Panhandle). Based on planktonic foraminifera, Huddlestun (1976) considered the formation to be of late

Miocene age. Associated invertebrate taxa from Sikes Sand Mine 02 include the calcitic bivalve genera Nodipecten Dall, 1898 and Amusium R€oding, 1798, and internal moulds of the gastropod genera Persististrombus Kronenberg & Lee, 2007 and Conus Linnaeus, 1758. Fragments of echinoid tests, rare valves of the brachiopod genus Glottidia Dall, 1870, and common remains of portunid, calappid and especially hexapodid crabs were also collected.

Examined specimens of Glypturus toulai (Rathbun, 1919) originated from the middle_upper Miocene (Serravallian _Tortonian) Gatun Formation of Panama (see Hendy 2013 for detailed stratigraphy and associated mollusk fauna), the formation from which they were first described. This species has been reported from the lower (Hyzny et al. 2013) and middle (Todd & Collins 2005) Gatun Formation. Typically, siliciclastic sediments were deposited on an inner shelf at an estimated depth of < 75 m (Hendy 2013).

3. MATERIAL AND METHODS

The collections of the Division of Invertebrate Paleontology at the Florida Museum of Natural History (FLMNH) were searched for and expanded with specimens of fossil Glypturus spp. as a result of fieldwork at the Sikes Sand Mine 02 in Washington County, Florida. Collections in invertebrate zoology in the same museum and the Naturhistorisches Museum, Wien were used for modern G. acanthochirus. The latter museum also yielded specimensof G. toulai including the types. The number of specimens per species is detailed in Supplemental Table 1. The three assemblages containing the most Glypturus specimens are: Sikes Sand Mine 02, Farfan and Amador beaches near Panama City (Panama), and specimens of modern G. acanthochirus from a variety of sites in the Western Atlantic.

Institutional abbreviations used here are: NHMW: Naturhistorisches Museum Wien, Vienna, Austria; UF: Florida Museum of Natural History at the University of Florida, Gainesville, Florida, USA; BMNPH PI IC and NHM UK In: Department of Earth Sciences, Natural History Museum, London, UK; MNHNCu-P: National Museum of Natural History, Paleontological collection, Havana, Cuba; USNM: US National Museum, Smithsonian Institution, Washington, DC, USA; MNHN: Mus_eum national d'Histoire naturelle, Paris, France.

Statistical analyses were performed in PAST 2.17c (Hammer et al. 2001) and R 3.0.1 (R Developmen Team). A significance level of 5% was used for all tests.

In an attempt to distinguish the major propodi of the three assemblages mentioned above and to explore possible taxonomic placement of isolated specimens of other localities, the following data were obtained: (a) length of the manus at the outer side as measured from the notch above the proximalmost part of the finger to the rim of the manus at the centre of the concavity (Fig. 1); (b) height of the manus as measured perpendicular to the axis of the propodus from the proximalmost spine on the upper margin (Fig. 1); (c) the areas occupied by tubercles on the inner and outer sides; and (d) the number of tubercles on both sides. The tubercles on the margin toward the dactylus were not included for (c) or (d). The measurements and areas were obtained using ImageJ 1.46r. All tubercles were counted. Initially, bivariate analyses were carried out separately for the inner and outer sides to explore whether the two sides showed similar growth-related trends in length/height ratios, percentage of coverage by tubercles, and density of tubercles. The precision of measurement errors was estimated by measuring 10 times the length, height and area occupied by tubercles on the outer side of the manus of the same image of a specimen (UF 248937 from the Holo-Pleistocene of Panama). Furthermore, 10 images taken from a specimen (UF 248936) from the same locality were analysed using the same variables to explore the combined effect of measurement error and the possibly slightly different angles of the specimen as the specimen was positioned anew for every photograph. A Sony DSC-R1 (10 MP) was used for most digital macrophotography.

To test whether the percentage of tubercle coverage of the manus varied across the three assemblages, a nonparametric Kruskal_Wallis test was applied to the percentage estimates obtained separately for the outer and inner sides of the mani. Subsequently, Mann_Whitney tests were used (with and without a Bonferroni correction for multiple tests) to assess whether tubercle coverage differed significantly for any given pair of samples. However, because tubercle coverage may vary with growth, the relationship between specimen size (a proxy of ontogenetic age) and the percentage coverage of tubercles was evaluated using simple linear regression (both ordinary least square (OLS) and Reduced Major Axis regression models yielded comparable outcomes and only OLS results are reported here). When this correlation was significant, Mann_Whitney tests were carried out on restricted data to make samples comparable in terms of size range of specimens included in the analysis. The Kruskal_Wallis and Mann_Whitney tests are based on ranks rather than absolute values of the observations and thus require less stringent statistical assumptions than the equivalent parametric tests (ANOVA [analysis of variance] and *t*-test, respectively).

The significance of the regression lines of plots of the length/height ratios versus length for the three assemblages was determined for the outer and inner side of the propodi. Subsequently, the slopes of the l/h ratios versus length plots of assemblages from the late Miocene of Florida and the Holo-Pleistocene of Panama were compared using a one-way ANCOVA (analysis of covariance). A Mann_Whitney test was performed to assess whether l/h ratios of these two assemblages were significantly different for the data restricted to specimens within the length range 13.1_18.0 mm based on the outer part of the manus. Sufficient samples were present in this range and a size-related change of the l/w ratio does not appear substantial.

Bivariate analyses were also carried out for the number of tubercles per 10 mm^2 (tubercle density) versus the length of the manus to explore trends within and among assemblages. This was done for the outer and inner sides separately.

To compare the shape of the major propodus of the assemblages from the late Miocene of Florida and the Holo-Pleistocene of Panama, six landmarks were defined. Using standard schemes (Bookstein 1997; Zelditch et al. 2004) these landmarks can be classified as follows: Landmark 1, type II, at the distal base of the tooth on the fixed finger; Landmark 2, type II, at the notch marking the startof the fixed finger; Landmark 3, type II, at the base of the distalmost spine on the upper margin of the propodus, usually best visible on the inner side; Landmark 4, type II, at the proximal corner of the upper margin; Landmark 5, type II, at the proximal corner of the lower margin; Landmark 6, type III, on the lower margin straight below Landmar 2 using a propodal orientation as in Figure 1. Specimens with the fixed finger located to the right in outer lateral view were flipped horizontally in Adobe Photoshop CS5, so that all specimens had their fixed finger oriented to the left. Left and right major propodi did not differ in shape visually, implying that they could be put into one sample. Initially, 16 specimens from the Holo- Pleistocene of Panama and 14 from the late Miocene of Florida were used for morphometric analyses. Tps Utility program (tpsUtil) 1.56 and tpsDig 1.40 were used to generate tps files containing landmark data. The average shape of the three smallest specimens per assemblage was calculated to use as references to determine the relative Procrustes distance for other specimens (see Webster 2007; Vergara-Solana et al. 2013). This distance was obtained in MorphoJ 1.05f (Klingenberg 2011) using canonical variate analysis (CVA) after a Procrustes fit aligned by principal axes (superposition of landmarks) and after classifying the specimens (smallest three specimens arranged in one group). As there was a positive, significant relationship between the Procrustes distance and the log-10 of the centroid size of the specimens from the late Miocene of Florida, indicating an allometric effect (see below), specimens with a centroid size of 19_27 (= 1.28_1.43 log10 centroid size) were selected for both assemblages for further analyses to compare the shape of the two assemblages while minimizing allometric effects (see Vergara-Solana et al. 2013). There was no allometric effect observed for the Procrustes distances for specimens from the Holo-Pleistocene of Panama. Exclusion of specimens outside the range reduced the final dataset to seven specimens from the late Miocene of Florida and six from the Holo-Pleistocene of Panama. These specimen groups were further analysed using CVA (in MorphoJ with permutation tests) and a Generalized Goodall F-test (using tpsRegr 1.38).

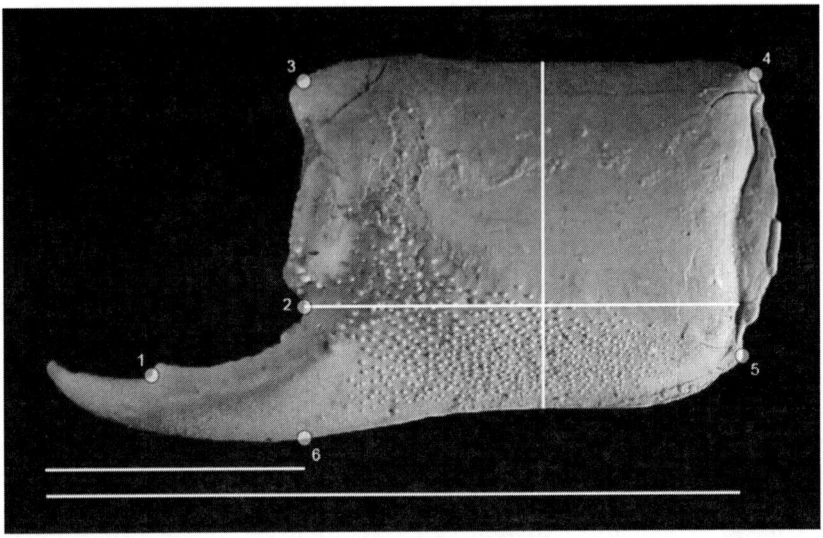

Figure 1. Placement of six landmarks on the outer side of the propodus of Glypturus sikesi sp. nov. (UF 235154, flipped horizontally). Method of measuring manus length, height and length of the fixed finger, and total propodus length are also shown. Lowermost scale bar width: 27.1 mm.

To compare further the two assemblages the six nonlandmark variables as defined above were used for multivariate analyses. To compare results to the abundant modern species in the Western Atlantic, five specimens of G. acanthochirus, 12 specimens of the late Miocene of Florida (Sikes Sand Mine 02), 13 specimens from the Holo- Pleistocene of Panama, and two specimens of G. toulai from the Miocene Gatun Formation were analysed. Additionally, five well-preserved specimens of Glypturus from other localities were included to determine to which species they could be ascribed. The data were obtained for only the best preserved specimens. Consequently, specimens from the lower Miocene Culebra Formation attributed to G. toulai (see Hyžný et al. 2013) were not included, as tubercles were not sufficiently preserved and the specimens are from a different age and assemblage than G. toulai from the Gatun Formation. As the morphometric variables used here are not all expressed in the same units, principal component analysis based on a correlation matrix was used to explore the ordination of the specimens of each assemblage on the log10-transformed data. Because strong size-dependence is suggested by the fact that PC1 explains most of the variance (71.3%) and all variables show strong positive correlations with PC1 (PCA loadings: 0.69_0.93), the withingroup allometric size component was minimalized by regressing all log10-transformed variables on PC1 (see Kowalewski et al. 1997). The residuals of this regression were used to perform multivariate tests including CVA and discriminant analysis (DA). Multivariate normality required for the reliable performance of DA was tested using the Dornik and Hansen omnibus test in PAST.

Using the same six non-landmark variables from above, allometric coefficients were computed per variable in PAST for the 12 specimens from the late Miocene of Florida and 13 specimens from the Holo-Pleistocene of Panama separately (> 10 specimens available), as well as for all specimens combined. The square root was taken from values of the two variables involving area before the data were log-transformed, after which the coefficient for each variable was estimated by dividing the PC1 loading for that variable by the average PC1 loading for all variables (Kowalewski et al. 1997). The 95% confidence intervals for the coefficients were calculated by bootstrapping (2000 replicates).

The same variables were used to determine the a posteriori error rate (= probability of misclassification) by the proportion of observations misclassified by DA (Kowalewski et al. 1997). Data were log-transformed after multiple 0-values in the data of G. acanthochirus were replaced by 0.0001, resulting in eight specimens instead of five for that species. All classificatory error rates are jackknife-corrected or jackknife cross-validated (e.g. Holdener 1994; Kowalewski & Novack-Gottshall 2010). The minimum required sample size needed for correct classification of a sample was assessed by resampling with replacement (bootstrapping) for n observations (n = 1_5) for all assemblages, except for G. toulai due to its low sample size (n = 2). Centroids of the samples were projected a posteriori (Kowalewski et al. 1997). Analyses were performed in R.

Since not a single minor propodus of Glypturus has been confirmed from the fossil record to date, we identified some of the characters that might be useful to distinguish minors from majors. First, the presence of tubercles on the minor was checked for all three extant species based on collections at FLMNH and NHMW, especially for G. acanthochirus, the species living in the West Atlantic region today. These minor propodi were also checked for the presence of spines on the upper margin. Third, the length of the fixed finger relative to the length of the propodus was determined for modern specimens of G. acanthochirus. A Mann_Whitney test was performed on the percentages of the relative fixed finger length of the minors and majors to determine whether the relative lengths of the fixed fingers differed statistically. Well-preserved specimens of the large assemblage from the late Miocene of Florida were used to explore whether potential minors were present in the sample using the same measurements. Specimens from the Holo-Pleistocene of Panama were not used as the tip of the fixed finger was rarely preserved.

4. RESULTS

4.1 Statistical and morphometric analyses

The dataset including all numerical measurements is found in Supplemental Appendix 1. Repeated measurements of the same specimen indicate relatively high precision: the standard deviations of repeated estimates of the length, height and area occupied by tubercles at the outer side of the manus were typically < 2% of the means (Supplemental Appendix 2). Thus, measurement errors are unlikely to have substantially influenced the results reported below.

The percentage of tubercle coverage on the outer side of the manus of Glypturus spp. does not increase with increasing size of the specimen (Fig. 2A). In contrast, for the inner side of the manus, larger specimens have a significantly higher percentage of tubercle coverage for the fossil species (Fig. 2B). The slope of the relation differs significantly for Glypturus spp. from the late Miocene of Florida when compared to the assemblage from the Holo- Pleistocene of Panama (one-way ANCOVA, $p = 0.01$).]

The Kruskal_Wallis test on the percentages of tubercle coverage of the outer side of the manus for the three large assemblages of Glypturus (modern, Holo-Pleistocene of Panama, and late Miocene of Florida) indicates that the medians are statistically different *(p* = 1.595×10^{-12}). The results are also highly significant for all pairwise assemblage comparisons of the outer side of the manus (Mann_Whitney tests; Table 1). In contrast, percentage based tubercle coverage of the inner side of the mani of the two Glypturus assemblages from the Holo-Pleistocene of Panama and the late Miocene of Florida is not significantly different (Mann_Whitney test: ($p = 0.83$). Here, the surface area of mani was restricted to 120_285 mm^2 to minimize growth effects on tubercle coverage (relatively more tubercles with size, see above). Mann_Whitney tests of these two assemblages with G. acanthochirus separately indicate that tubercle coverage is significantly different (($p = 0.0001$) for both pairs, suggesting a lower coverage of tubercles on the inner side for G. acanthochirus. There appears to be a trend towards decreasing tubercle coverage of the outer side of the manus through geological time (Fig. 2A). The inner side (Fig. 2B) seems o show a similar trend, where similar-sized specimens show a decrease in tubercle coverage from the oldest to the youngest assemblage.

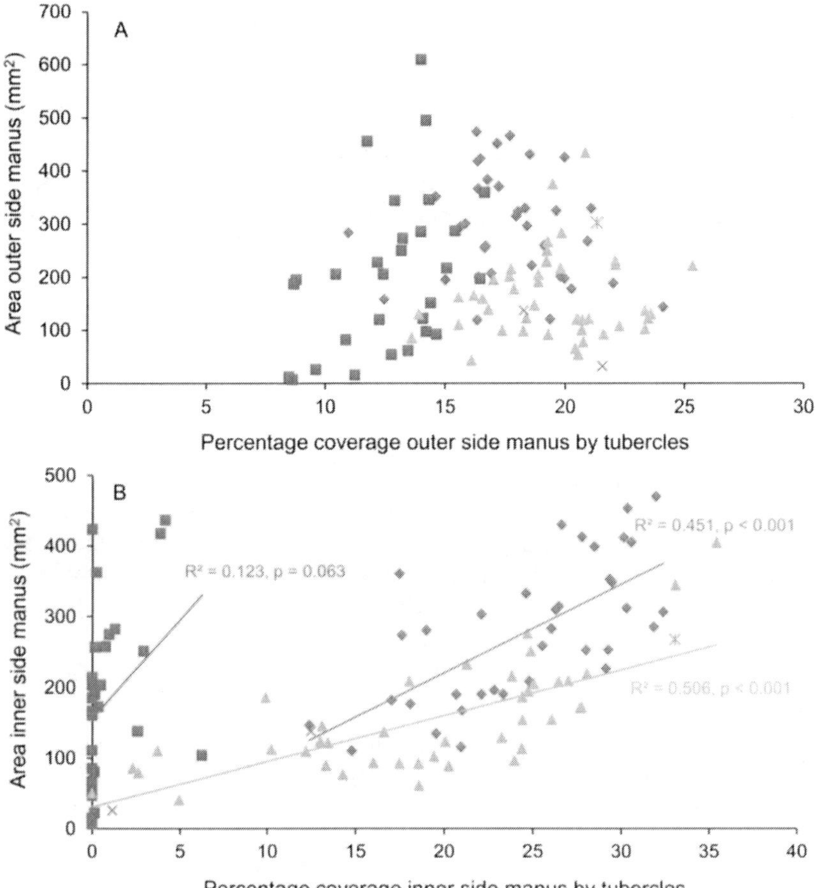

Figure 2. The influence of growth on the percentage of tubercle coverage of the manus of the propodus for species of Glypturus. A, outer side; B, inner side. Squares (red) = modern Glypturus acanthochirus; diamonds (blue) = G. panamacanalensis sp. nov. (Holo-Pleistocene of Panama); triangles (green) = G. skies sp. nov. (late Miocene of Florida, USA); cross (purple) = G. toulai (late Miocene of Panama); cross with vertical line (blue) = G. berryi (Oligocene of Mississippi, USA).

Length/height ratios versus length based on the outer side of the manus show that there is no significant sizerelated increase of l/h ratios for modern G. acanthochirus, whereas the fossil assemblages (late Miocene of Florida and Holo-Pleistocene of Panama) do show an increase in the l/h ratio as specimen size increases (Fig. 3). The slopes of the relationship between l/h ratio and size differ significantly for the two fossil assemblages (one-way ANCOVA, (p = 0.04). The l/h ratios for the late Miocene assemblage are generally higher than those from the Holo-Pleistocene assemblage for a restricted size range. For example, for the length range of 13.1_18.0 mm, a Mann_Whitney test shows that the two assemblages significantly differ ($p = 9.9 \times 10^5$). Similar results were obtained for measurements on the inner side of the manus, where the length of specimens is typically smaller compared to the outer side. Length/height ratios appear to increase faster throughout growth in geologically older assemblages (Fig. 3).

Although the number of tubercles increases throughout growth, the density of tubercles per unit area decreases as specimen size increases regardless of the species of Glypturus (Fig. 4). The trends closely follow a power function. All trend lines in Figure 4A are statistically significant ($p < 0.05$) when the y-data is $\log_{10}$-transformed and a linear trend line is chosen (all R^2 values _ 0.77). The spacing between the centres of the tubercles thus increases as specimens grow. Although not quantified here, tubercle size appears to increase throughout growth. Density of tubercles varies with geological age (Fig. 4A): the specimens from the oldest assemblage display highest tubercle densities on the outer side of the manus, whereas specimens of the modern G. acanthochirus exhibit lowest tubercle densities. Patterns are less obvious for the inner side of the manus, where Holo-Pleistocene assemblages from Panama and G. acanthochirus overlap (Fig. 4B).

After minimizing the allometric effect on the shape of the assemblage from the late Miocene of Florida (Fig. 5), by restricting the size range to 1.28_1.43 log10 centroid size for the assemblages from the Holo-Pleistocene of Panama and the late Miocene of Florida, the propodal shape of these assemblages were statistically distinguishable (Mahalanobis distance = 5.343; permutation test with 10,000 runs on Mahalanobis distance: p = 0.0002). Other tests (generalized Goodall F-test, permutation test on Procrustes distance) also returned significant differences.PCA on the log10-transformed dataset based on six non-landmark variables showed separation between G. acanthochirus and other species of Glypturus (Fig. 6A; Supplemental Appendix 3). Specimens of the assemblages from the Holo-Pleistocene of Panama and the late Miocene of Florida assemblage do not overlap substantially. The two specimens of G. toulai do not fall within any of the convex hulls. After minimizing the effect of size by regressing all variables on PC1, CVA on the residuals shows separation of all analysed Glypturus species (Fig. 7). Importantly, even the 95% confidence ellipses of assemblages from the Holo-Pleistocene of Panama and the late Miocene of Florida do not include the two specimens of G. toulai. Discriminant analysis separates the assemblages from the Holo-Pleistocene of Panama and the late Miocene of Florida (Hotelling's T^2 = 135.53; F = 17.45;p = 0.000002). The data do not depart significantly from a multivariate normal distribution

(Dornik and Hansen omnibus Ep = 10.89; $p = 0.53$). DA also separates the assemblage from the late Miocene of Florida and G. toulai (Hotelling's $T^2 = 191.02$; $F = 6.08$; $p = 0.035$; multivariate normality: Ep = 15.43, $p = 0.22$), and may distinguish the assemblage from the Holo-Pleistocene of Panama and G. toulai (Hotelling's $T^2 = 72.95$; $F = 7.48$; $p = 0.006$), although the compared datasets appear to not to follow a normal distribution (Ep = 33.78, $p = 0.0007$).

Table 1. The p-values of the Mann_Whitney pairwise comparison tests on the percentages of tubercle coverage of the outer side of the manus for three assemblages. Upper right: without a Bonferroni correction; lower left: with a Bonferroni correction.

	Glypturus acanthochirus (modern)	*G. panamacanalensis* sp. nov. (Holo-Pleistocene, Panama)	*G. sikesi* sp. nov. (late Miocene, Florida)
Glypturus acanthochirus (modern)	—	3.43×10^{-9}	4.58×10^{-11}
G. panamacanalensis sp. nov. (Holo-Pleistocene, Panama)	1.03×10^{-8}	—	0.00712
G. sikesi sp. nov. (late Miocene, Florida)	1.37×10^{-10}	0.02136	—

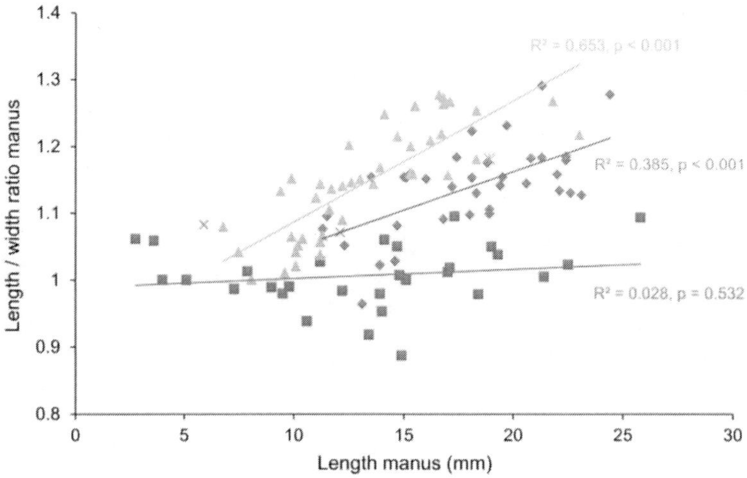

Figure 3. Length/height ratios throughout growth based on measurements on the outer side of the manus for species of Glypturus. Symbols as in Figure 2.

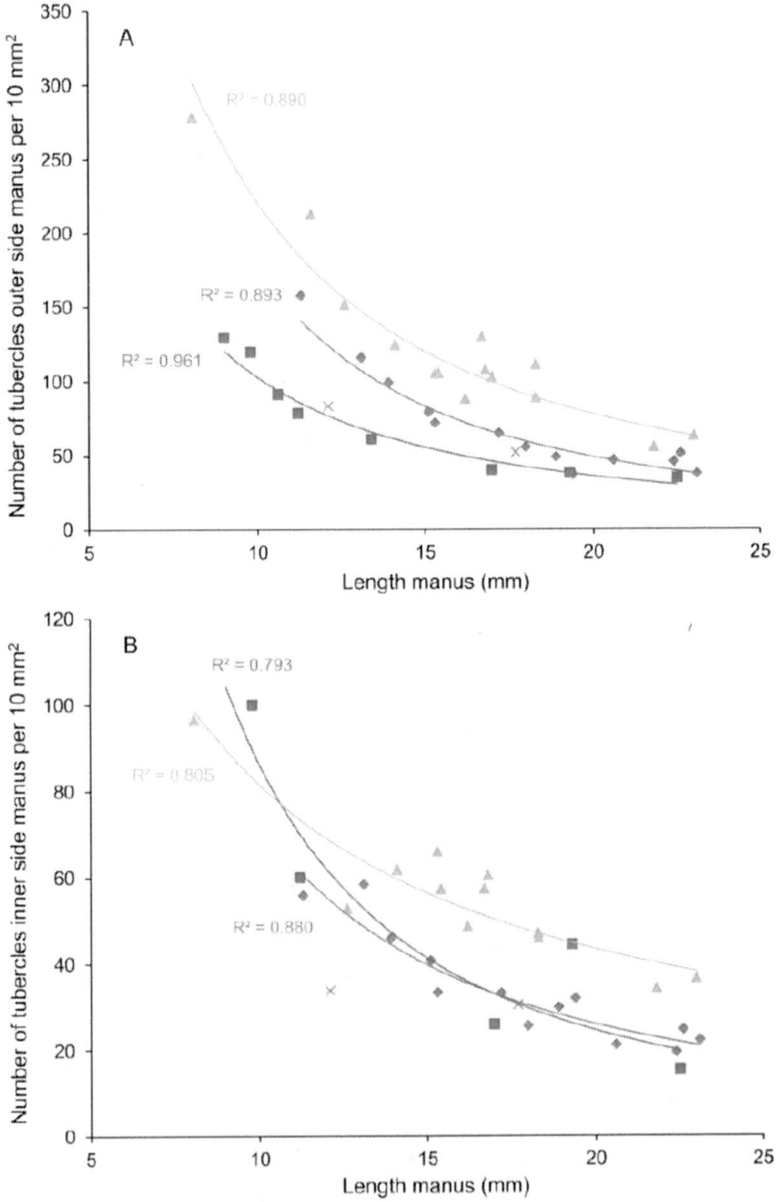

Figure 4. Tubercle density (number of tubercles per 10 mm²) versus length of the manus of Glypturus spp. A, outer side; B, inner side. Symbols as in Figure 2.

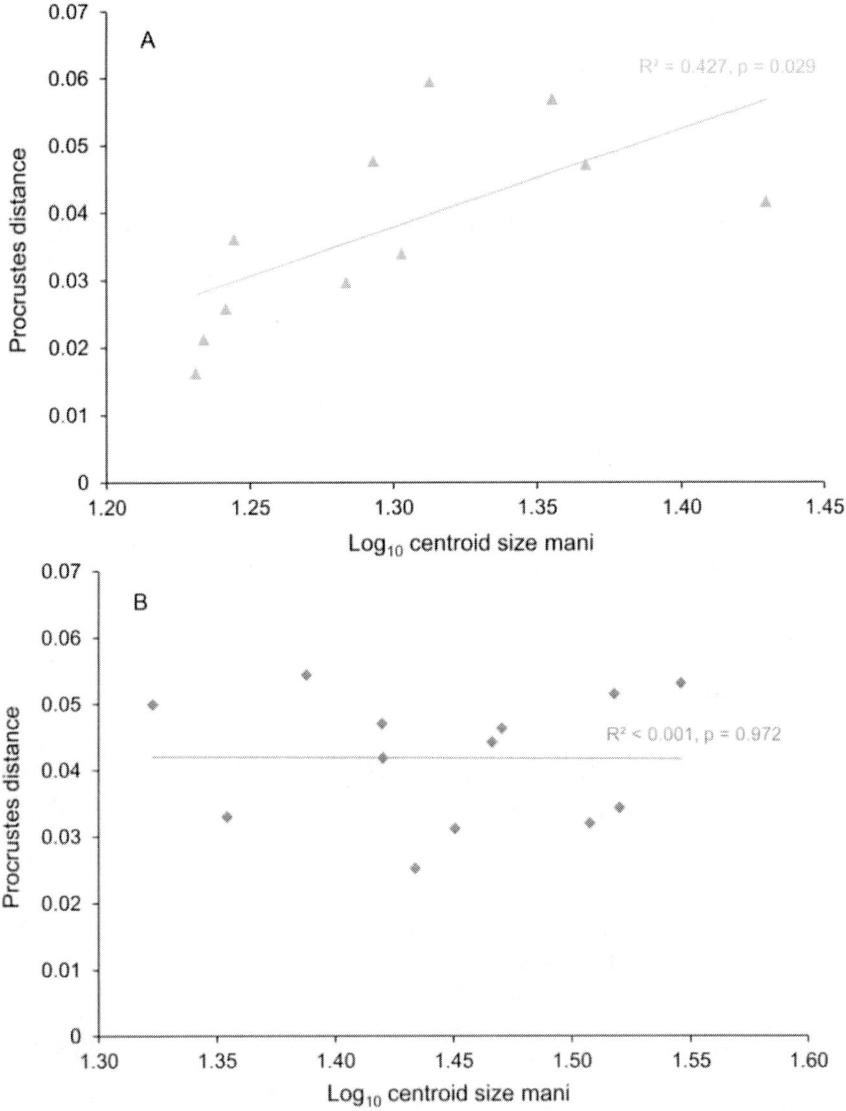

Figure 5. Procrustes distance relative to the three smallest specimens of each assemblage versus centroid size of the mani. A, Glypturus sikesi sp. nov. (late Miocene, Florida, USA); B, Glypturus panamacanalensis sp. nov. (Holo-Pleistocene, Panama)

In summary, the assemblages from the Holo-Pleistoceneof Panama and the late Miocene of Florida differ in the following aspects:

1) per cent coverage of tubercles on the outer side of the manus;
2) statistically different slopes of the regressions lines of (a) l/h versus length manus and (b) area manus versus percentage of inner side manus covered by tubercles;
3) higher l/h ratios for specimens from the late Miocene assemblage of Florida;
4) specimens from the late Miocene assemblage of Florida exhibit a higher tubercle density (outer and inner sides manus);
5) shape significantly differs using geometric morphometricanalyses;
6) separation using multivariate analyses: PCA, sizeindependent CVA, and DA.

Additionally, two minor morphological differences were found. The distalmost of the two dactylar teeth tends to be more pronounced (higher) in specimens from the Holo-Pleistocene assemblage of Panama for similar-sized specimens. Furthermore, the carpi of the Holo-Pleistocene assemblage of Panama exhibit tubercles near the lower margin of the outer side; tubercles are absent near the lower margin of the outer side of carpi from the late Miocene assemblage of Florida.

Differences with Glypturus toulai, the late Miocene species from Panama, roughly resembling the latter two in terms of tubercular coverage on the outer side of the propodus (Fig. 2A), are less numerous because of the lack of sufficient specimens precluding rigorous statistical testing of length/height ratios, percentage of tubercle coverage, and geometric morphometric analysis. Only two specimens from the Gatun Formation were available for multivariate analyses. Nevertheless, their location in PCA ordination space (Fig. 6A) and in size-independent CVA (Fig. 7) does suggest that the assemblages from the Holo-Pleistocene of Panama and the late Miocene of Florida differ from G. toulai. This seems further supported by DA. Morphological differences can also be found. For instance, the tuberculation pattern on the outer side shows a clearer reentrant close to the proximalmost part of the fixed finger in the case of G. toulai compared to other younger Cenozoic Glypturus spp. (Fig. 8). Additionally, the tubercular extent on the inner side seems to differ in that only the central portion of this side of G. toulai appears covered (Fig. 9), whereas the lower extent of the tubercular area of the assemblages from the Holo- Pleistocene of Panama and the late Miocene of Florida typically run diagonally towards the lower-proximal corner of the manus in medium- to large-sized specimens (Fig. 9).

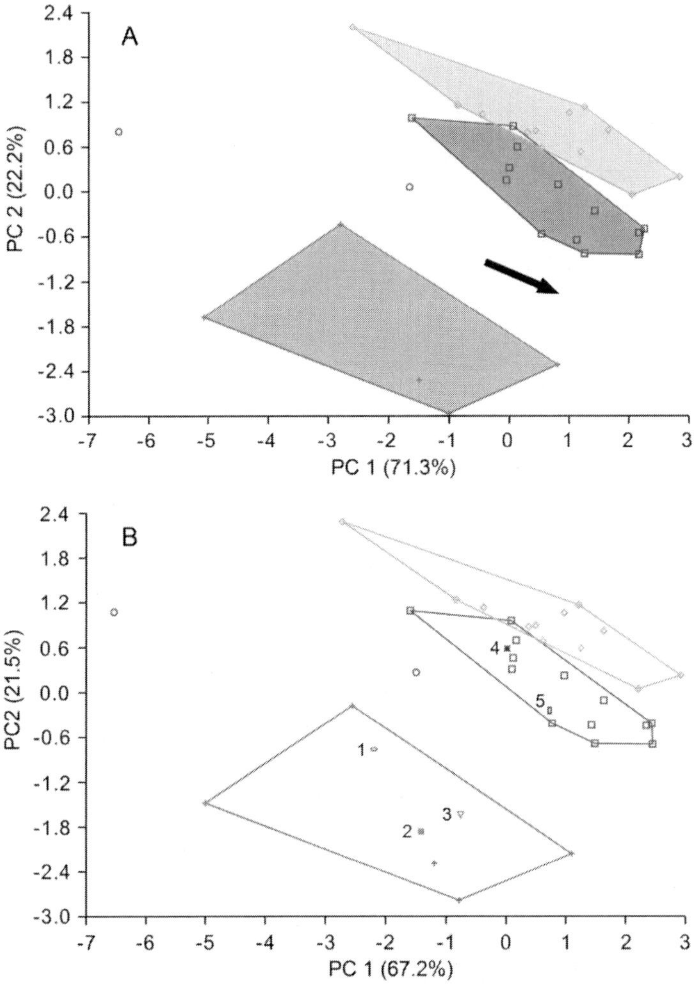

Figure 6. Principal component analysis on the log10-transformed dataset based on six variables extracted from the mani of Glypturus spp. A, PCA based on four collections; B, PCA based on four collections and five additional specimens from various localities (1_5). Red plus-sign = modern G. acanthochirus; blue squares = G. panamacanalensis sp. nov. (Holo-Pleistocene, Panama); green diamonds = G. sikesi sp. nov. (upper Miocene of Florida, Choctawhatchee Formation); purple circles = G. toulai (lower Miocene of Panama, Gatun Formation). Assemblages with > 2 individuals are surrounded by convex hulls. The arrow in A estimates the direction of size increase based on the shape of the convex hulls in conjunction with underlying specimen size. Numbers in B represent: 1, specimen from the upper Pliocene_lower Pleistocene Tamiami Formation (Pinecrest beds) of Florida (Mule Pen) (UF 42451); 2, specimen from the upper Pleistocene

Jaimanitas Formation of Cuba (Good Road 01) (UF 222839); 3, specimen from the Holo-Pleistocene of Jamaica (Falmouth 01) (UF 232383); 4, specimen from the upper Pleistocene Jaimanitas Formation of Cuba (Good Road 01) (UF 248008); 5, specimen from the middle Pleistocene Bermont Formation of Florida (Belle Glade 01) (UF 131471).

Although incomplete, the largest specimen of G. toulai from the Gatun Formation (UF 203348) does not show a clear trend of the lower tubercular margin directed toward the lower-proximal corner (Fig. 9; Hyžný et al. 2013, fig. 5). Lastly, the number of tubercles per 10 mm2 appears lower for medium-sized specimens of G. toulai for both sides compared to the assemblages from the Holo-Pleistocene of Panama and the late Miocene of Florida (Fig. 4). Given the numerous differences between the latter two assemblages and other congeneric species (see below), these two species are referred to as G. panamacanalensis sp. nov. and G. sikesi sp. nov., respectively, in the text from here onwards.

4.2 Taxonomic placement of isolated specimens

The tuberculation patterns on two specimens, UF 42451 from the late Pliocene_early Pleistocene of Florida and UF 232383 from the Holo-Pleistocene of Jamaica (see below), suggest they can be ascribed to G. acanthochirus. This is supported by their placement in the PCA ordination space within the area of modern G. acanthochirus (Fig. 6B). Another specimen (UF 131471, middle Pleistocene of Florida) morphologically resembles G. panamacanalensis sp. nov. from the Holo-Pleistocene of Panama. This is confirmed by the PCA ordination, which is why this specimen is referred to G. panamacanalensis sp. nov. The same applies for a specimen from the late Pleistocene of Cuba (UF 248008) (Fig. 6B). Another specimen (UF 222839) from the late Pleistocene of Cuba (see below), but from a different locality, plots in the space of G. acanthochirus, but does not show the typical tuberculation pattern on the outer side of the propodus. It is conservatively referred to Glypturus sp. here as not all tubercles may be preserved on the outer side or this may represent an anomalous specimen. The alternative is that both G. acanthochirus and G. panamacanalensis sp. nov. are present in the late Pleistocene of Cuba, which would not be surprising given the overlapping age ranges of the species (Supplemental Table 1).

4.3 Allometric coefficients and multiple-specimen classification

Figure 10 shows variables with negative (< 1.0) and positive allometry (> 1.0) relative to the PC1-based latent size proxy based on all six variables.

Figure 10A shows positive allometry for the variables measured on the inner side and negative allometry for the number of tubercles on the outer side.

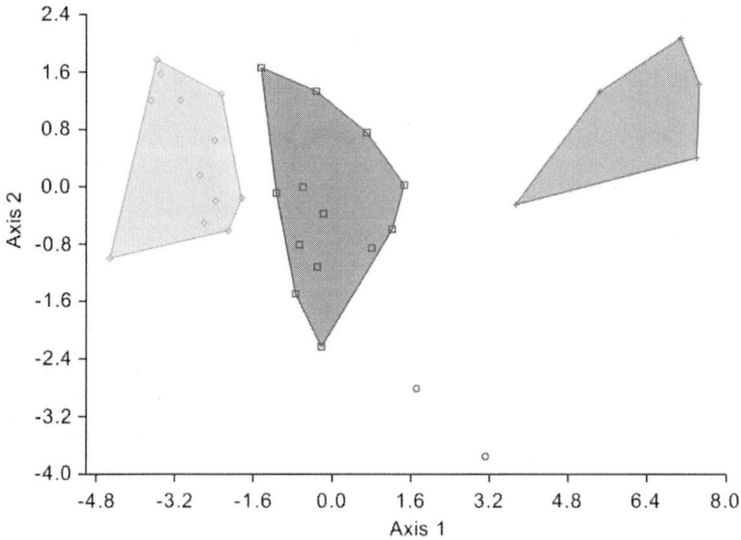

Figure 7. Canonical variate analysis on the residuals of the log10-transformed variables extracted from the mani of Glypturus spp. Symbols as in Figure 6. Assemblages with > 2 individuals are surrounded by convex hulls.

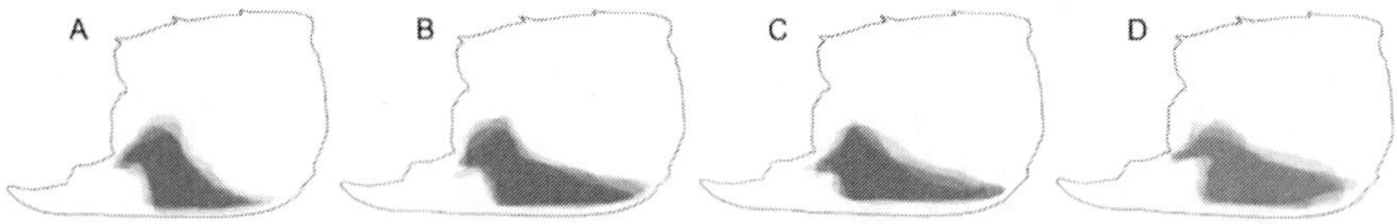

Figure 8. Tubercular extent on the outer side of the propodus highlighted by a grey, translucent shade for Glypturus spp. A, G. acanthochirus (modern); B, G. panamacanalensis sp. nov. (Holo-Pleistocene, Panama); C, G. sikesi sp. nov. (late Miocene, Florida, USA); D, G. toulai (late Miocene, Panama). All specimens were scaled to the same size. Five specimens were randomly selected for A_C. For G. toulai from the Gatun Formation only four specimens were available (NHMW 1933/0018/0159, NHMW 1933/0018/0160, UF 203348 and BMNPH PI IC 395). Possible tubercles directly above the notch above the fixed finger were not included.

The other variables do not display significant allometric departures from isometry. Isometry is observed for four variables in Figure 10B, whereas height and the number of tubercles on the inner side exhibit negative and positive allometry, respectively. For all specimens combined (Fig. 10C), the majority of the variables shows negative allometries, whereas positive allometries are seen for the variables measured on the inner side. Thus, the ratio of the number of tubercles and $\sqrt{}$ ATI to manus size increases as manus size increases.

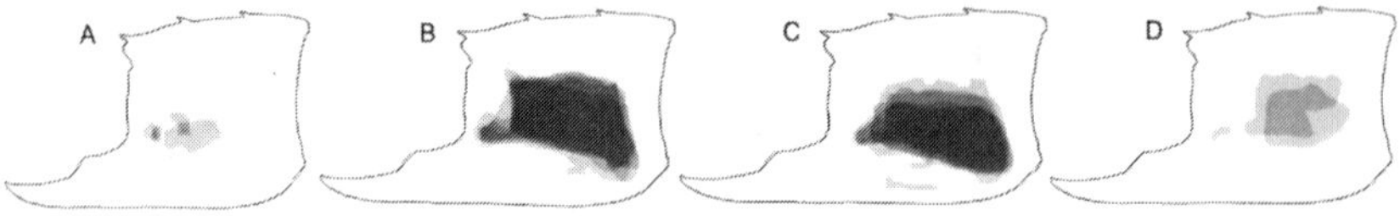

Figure 9. Tubercular extent on the inner side of the propodus highlighted by a grey, translucent shade for Glypturus spp. for specimens with a length of _ 20 mm including the fixed finger as tubercular patterns are better developed at larger sizes for the inner side. A, G. acanthochirus (modern); B, G. panamacanalensis sp. nov. (Holo-Pleistocene, Panama); C, G. sikesi sp. nov. (late Miocene, Florida, USA); D, G. toulai (late Miocene, Panama). All specimens were scaled to the same size. Five specimens were randomly selected for A_C. For G. toulai from the Gatun Formation only two specimens showed the inner tubercle pattern with this size restriction (NHMW 1933/0018/0159 and UF 203348), of which the latter was incomplete.

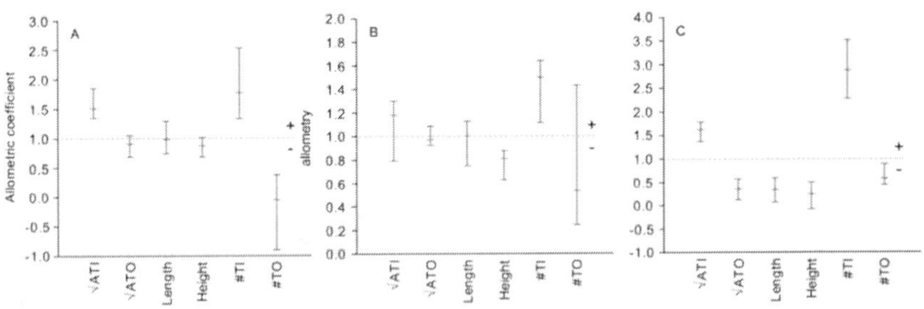

Figure 10. Allometric coefficients for six variables including 95% confidence intervals. ATI = area tubercles on inner side manus (mm^2); ATO = area tubercles on outer side manus (mm^2); length = length of manus (mm); height = height of manus (mm); #TI = number of tubercles on inner side manus; #TO = number of tubercles on outer side manus. A, Glypturus panamacanalensis sp. nov., 81.0% of variation in PC1; B, G. sikesi sp. nov., 90.8% of variation in PC1; C, All groups combined, 91.0% of variation in PC1.

The jackknife-corrected a posteriori classification using DA (Table 2) indicates that > 90% of specimens are classified correctly for the new species. When all taxa are combined > 85% of specimens are classified correctly. This is in line with the separation of the four taxa in Figures 6 and 7. The error rates for the three analysed groups decrease with increasing sample size (Table 3), to zero for a sample size of n = 5. Thus, a reliable classification of specimens should be possible for samples consisting of five or more well-preserved specimens for which all six non-landmark variables can be measured.

4.4 Major versus minor propodi in *Glypturus*

The minor propodi of the three extant species (Glypturus acanthochirus, G. armatus and G. laurae) based on specimens in collections at the FLMNH and NHMW contain no tubercles. Spines were always present on the upper margin of the minor and major propodus. The fixed fingers of G. acanthochirus are relatively large in minors compared to majors, and this proportion appears not to be influenced by growth (Fig. 11A). A Mann_Whitney test on the percentages shows that the relative lengths are significantly different ($p < 0.001$). Modern specimens of G. acanthochirus and specimens of G. sikesi sp. nov. from the late Miocene of Florida show no obvious size-related change (Fig. 11A, B). Data used for modern and late Miocene specimens are stored in Supplemental Appendix 4.

Table 2. Jackknife-corrected a posteriori classification of specimens of Glypturus using DA.

Taxon	Total number of specimens	% classified correctly	Number of misclassified specimens			
			G. panamacanalensis sp. nov.	*G. sikesi* sp. nov.	*G. acanthochirus*	*G. toulai*
G. panamacanalensis sp. nov.	13	92.3	—	1	0	0
G. sikesi sp. nov.	12	91.7	1	—	0	0
G. acanthochirus	8	75.0	1	0	—	1
G. toulai	2	50.0	1	0	0	—
Total	35	85.7	3	1	0	1

Table 3. Error rates as a function of sample size (n) in the Glypturus study.

	Total	*G. panamacanalensis* sp. nov.	*G. sikesi* sp. nov.	*G. acanthochirus*
$n = 1$	0.143	0.077	0.083	0.25
$n = 2$	0	0	0	0
$n = 3$	0.048	0	0	0.25
$n = 4$	0.056	0	0	0.333
$n = 5$	0	0	0	0

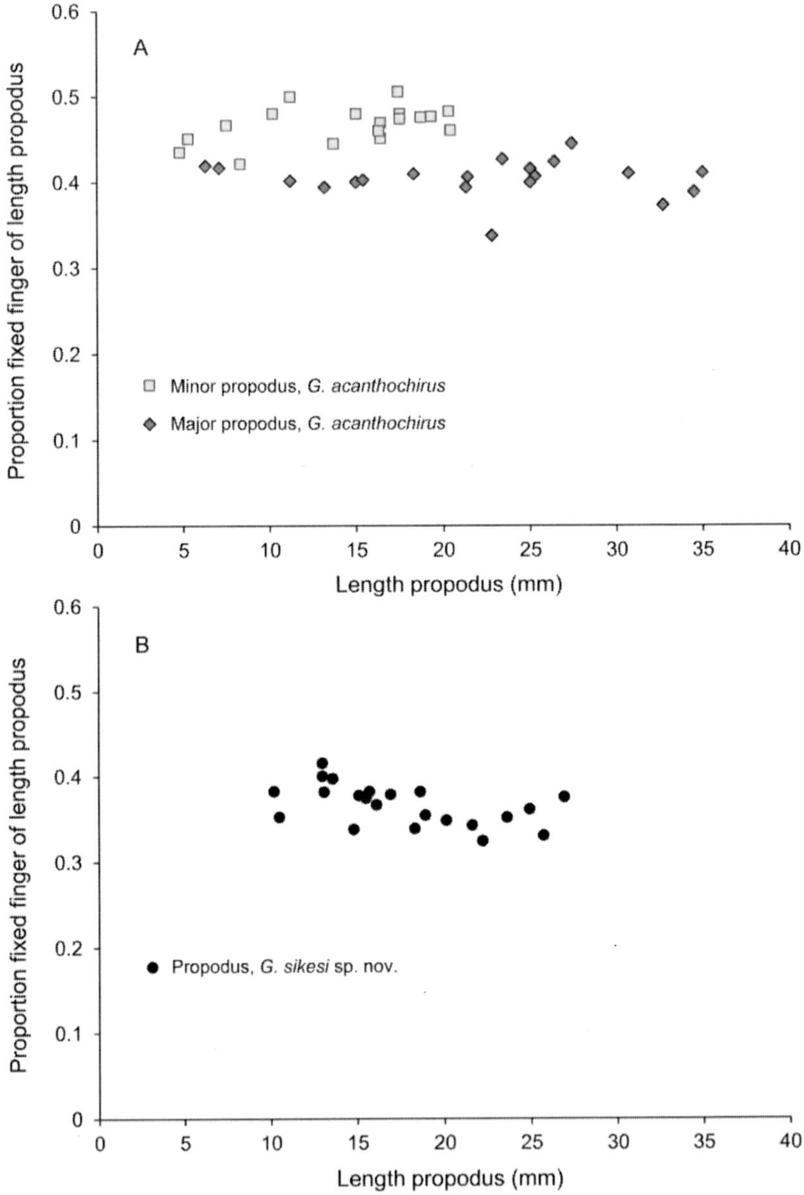

Figure 11. Proportion of the fixed finger of the total propodus length versus length propodus. A, modern Glypturus acanthochirus; B, late Miocene G. sikesi sp. nov. from Florida, USA.

Systematic palaeontology

Order **Decapoda** Latreille, 1802

Infraorder **Axiidea** de Saint Laurent, 1979

Family **Callianassidae** Dana, 1852

Subfamily **Callichirinae** Manning & Felder, 1991

Genus **Glypturus** Stimpson, 1866

Type species. Glypturus acanthochirus Stimpson, 1866, by monotypy.

Included species. (M = modern, F = fossil). Glypturus acanthochirus Stimpson, 1866 (M + F); G. armatus (A. Milne-Edwards, 1870) (= G. motupore Poore & Suchanek, 1988) (M + F); G. laurae (de Saint Laurent in de Vaugelas & de Saint Laurent, 1984) (M); Glypturus sp. (= Glypturus rabalaisae sensu Sakai, 2005) (M); G. berryi (Rathbun, 1935) (F); G. fraasi (Noetling, 1885) (F); G. munieri (Brocchi, 1883) (F); G. panamacanalensis sp. nov. (F); G. persicus HyŽný et al., 2013 (F); G. pugnax (BÖhm, 1922) (F); G. sikesi sp. nov. (F); G. spinosus (Lo_renthey, 1897) (F); G. toulai (Rathbun, 1919) (F).

Diagnosis. Carapace with rostral spine (anterior margin of carapace with three spines, median extending to cornea). Cornea dorsal, subterminal, disk-shaped. Al peduncle not longer and stouter than A2 peduncle. Mxp 3 without exopod, ischium-merus subpediform; merus not projecting beyond articulation with carpus. Chelipeds unequal, major without meral hook; [propodus usually with three distally directed spines near or on upper margin; lower margins of carpus and merus with spines; upper margin of merus with spines; keel present on outer side merus; tubercles usually present on outer side propodus and merus.] Plp l slender and uniramous, Plp 2 slender and biramous, Plp 3_5 foliaceous and biramous in both sexes; appendices intemae finger-like on Plp2 in both sexes, stubby, projecting from endopod of Plp 3_5 in both sexes (modified from Manning & Felder 1991, p. 778). [changes and/or additions in brackets]

Remarks. Manning & Felder (1991) provided a useful diagnosis that can be applied especially to modern species. However, other criteria are useful for palaeontologists and have been added here including tuberculation, spination, and a keel on the merus. Manning & Felder (1991, p. 778) stated "palm [= manus] with 3 spines on upper margin." This was modified as Hyžný & Muller (2012) mentioned exceptions (2_5 spines), and we found a specimen with only one spine (UF 248037, G. sikesi sp. nov.).

Until this study, the extent of tuberculation on the outer and inner sides of the propodus were sufficient to distinguish species of Glypturus (Hyžný & Muller 2012; Hyžný et al. 2013), and this character remains useful. However, as shown in Figures 8 and 9 the extent of the tuberculation on the propodus is not sufficient to distinguish between the new species, but other criteria clearly show they must be considered different taxa (see above).

The tubercular pattern of Glypturus sp. (= G. rabalaisae sensu Sakai, 2005) was neither figured nor described and, thus, cannot be compared to the new species below. A search did not result in locating the type material: the only specimen number mentioned in Rabalais et al. (1981) is USNM 172310, but this number does not correspond to a specimen of Glypturus in the USNM collection. Moreover, the same database does not yield specimens of Glypturus from the type locality as defined in Sakai (2005, 2011). An attempt to locate the un-numbered specimens including the types, probably stored in the University of Texas Marine Science Institute, was unsuccessful.

Glypturus panamacanalensis sp. nov.

(Figs 12, 13)

Diagnosis. Lateral tuberculation on outer propodal side from base of fixed finger diagonally to lower margin and proximal lower corner. Lateral tuberculation on inner propodal side covering large lower part of manus in medium to large specimens with lower margin of tuberculated area diagonally crossing from area of articulation of dactylus toward (but not reaching) proximal lower corner, tuberculation in small specimen more variable but mostly as in larger specimens. Occlusal margin of dactylus with two elongated, strong teeth exhibiting smooth top. Outer side carpus with tubercles near lower margin; inner side with tubercles on lower ~75%.

Derivation of name. Derived from the location where the type specimens were found: at beaches near the entrance of the Panama Canal near Panama City, Panama. The name also acknowledges the tremendous efforts in constructing, maintaining, and expanding the Panama Canal.

Material. Holotype: UF 248033 (Fig. 12F_H). Paratypes: UF 126585 (Fig. 12A, B), 248035 (Fig. 12C_E), 248032 (Fig. 12I_L), 126719 (Fig. 12Q, R), 246099 (Fig. 12S_U) and 246078 (Fig. 12Y).

Other material (P = propodus; D = dactylus; C = carpus; M = merus; FF = fixed finger): UF 246095 (Fig. 12M, N), 248030 (Fig. 12O, P), 246097 (Fig. 12V_X), 131471 (Fig. 12Z, A0), 248008 (Fig. 12B0, C0), 124236 (1P1C), 126571 (8D), 126572 (1D), 126573 (2P), 126574 (3P), 126575 (1D), 126576 (1FF), 126577 (2P), 126578 (13P), 126581 (1P), 126582 (2P), 126583 (1C), 126584 (2C), 126594 (5P), 126595 (8P), 126645_126646 (23P each), 126647 (16P), 126648 (28P), 126649 (23P), 126650 (24P), 126651 (19P), 126652 (20P), 126653 (13P), 126654_126655 (4FF each), 126663 (15P), 126664 (13P), 126665 (2FF), 126685_126686 (18P each), 126687 (11P), 126688 (20P), 126689 (21P), 126717 (4P), 126718 (1P), 126739 (3FF), 126740 (1FF), 126741 (12P), 126742 (2P), 230782 (1P),

230816_230841 (1P each), 246064 (2P), 246065_246070 (1P each), 246072_246076 (1P each), 246077 (1FF), 246079 (2P), 246080_246086 (1P each), 246087 (1C), 246088_246090 (1P each), 246091 (2P), 246092 (1P), 246093_246094 (1FF each), 246096 (1C), 246098 (1C), 246100_246101 (1C each), 248050_248053 (1P each), 248936_248937 (1P each), 250088 (2P), 251703_251725 (1P each), 251802_251803 (3P each), 251804 (1P), 251805_251807 (2P each), 251830_251833 (1P each), 251834 (7P), 251835 (4P), 251836_251839 (1P each), 251840 (2P), 251841 (3P), 251842_251843 (1P each) and 251844 (4P).

Occurrence. Collected (ex situ) on Amador and Farfan beaches (type locality) at the entrance of the Panama Canal near Panama City, Panama. The age is Holo-Pleistocene (see Geological setting); the formation is unknown. Additionally, the species is known from the middle Pleistocene Bermont Formation of Florida (Belle Glade 01 locality) and the upper Pleistocene Jaimanitas Formation of Cuba (Good Road 01 locality).

Description. Manus up to ~25 mm long and ~20 mm tall, length/height ratio ~1.0_1.3. Upper margin curving inward distally, proximally keeled, typically bearing three prominent spines pointing distally, proximalmost spine around mid-margin, keel terminating in blunt corner proximally. Lower margin sharp and keeled, lined with a row of setal pits on inner lateral side. Proximal margin convex on outer face, concave on inner; heightwise groove near proximal margin concave on inner side, concave to straight on outer side. Distal margin with protrusion just above fixed finger, hinge point with dactylus expressed as notch. Lateral tuberculation on outer side from base of fixed finger diagonally to lower margin and proximal lower corner. Lateral tuberculation on inner side covering large lower part of manus in medium to large specimens with lower margin of tuberculated area diagonally crossing from area of articulation of dactylus toward (but not reaching) proximal lower corner, tuberculation in small specimens more variable but mostly as in larger specimens. Fixed finger curving inward, triangular, sharply pointed, with distinct blunt tooth on occlusal margin around mid-length, tooth pointing distally. Dactylus stout; occlusal margin with two elongated, strong teeth exhibiting smooth top; tip hooked, curving downward. Carpus trapezoid, slightly taller than long; upper margin keeled and smooth with setal pits on inner part margin; lower margin keeled, shows bases of spines on inner side; distal margin straight to slightly concave; proximal margin concave on inner side, convex on outer side; outer side with tubercles near lower margin only; inner side with tubercles on lower ~75%. Outer side merus with longitudinal keel in centre, tuberculated below keel, spinose and convex lower margin. Other parts of species not preserved.

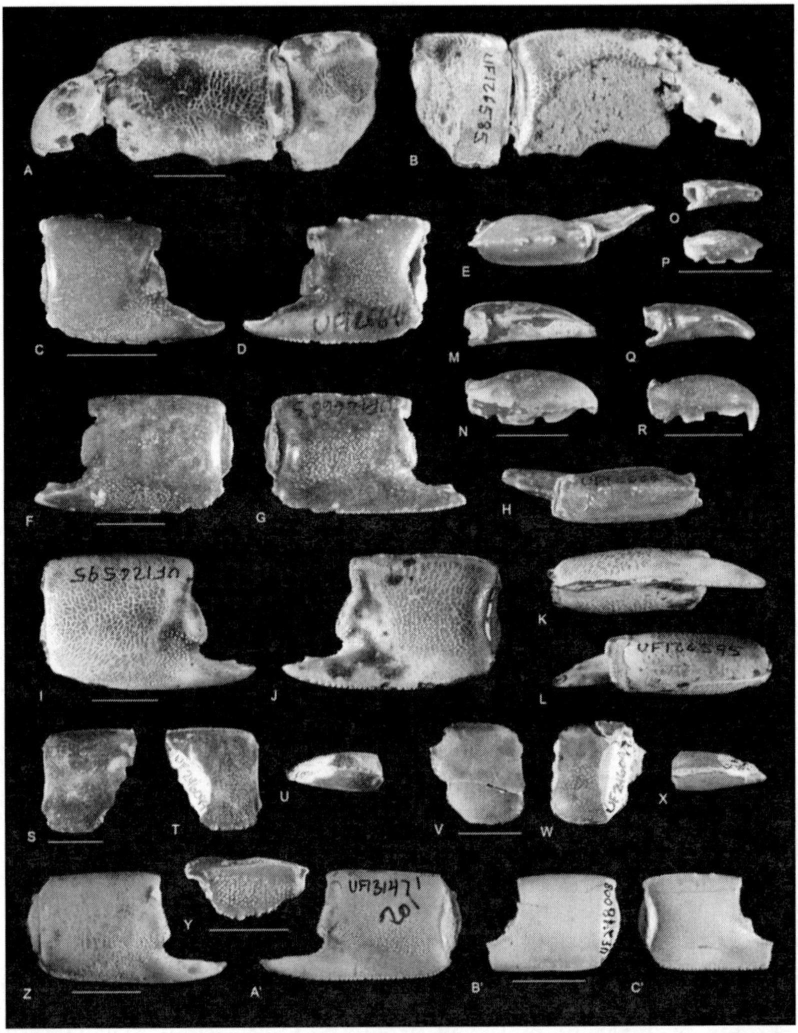

Figure 12. Glypturus panamacanalensis sp. nov. from: A_Y, Holo-Pleistocene of Panama (Farfan and Amador beaches); Z, A 0 , middle Pleistocene Bermont Formation of Florida (Belle Glade 01); B 0 , C 0 , upper Pleistocene Jaimanitas Formation in Cuba (Good Road 01). A, B, UF 126585, paratype: outer and inner sides of left dactylus, propodus, and carpus; C_E, UF 248035, paratype: outer side, inner side, and upper margin of right propodus; F_H, UF 248033, holotype: outer side, inner side, and upper margin of left propodus; I_L, UF 248032, paratype: outer side, inner side, lower margin, and upper margin of right propodus; M, N, UF 246095: occlusal surface and outer side of right dactylus; O, P, UF 248030: occlusal surface and outer side of right dactylus; Q, R, UF 126719, paratype: occlusal

surface and outer side of right dactylus; S_U, UF 246099, paratype: outer side, inner side, and lower margin of left carpus; V_X, UF 246097: outer side, inner side, and lower margin of right carpus; Y, UF 246078, paratype: part of outer side right merus; Z, A 0 , UF 131471: outer and inner sides of right propodus; B 0 , C 0 , UF 248008: outer and inner sides of right propodus. Scale bar widths: 10.0 mm. Note that images C_L were taken before specimens received new UF catalogue numbers.

Remarks. Intraspecific variation is observed in the strength of the teeth on the dactylus (Fig. 12A, B, M_R) and the tooth on the fixed finger (compare Fig. 12C to 12F, I). Furthermore, the number of spines on the upper margin of the propodus is typically three, but some (< 10%) specimens exhibit two (UF 248053) or four spines (UF 248050_248052). Size-related variation is particularly expressed in the tuberculation pattern on the inner side of small specimens as opposed to the more stable coverage in larger specimens, an increasing length/height ratio with size, and an increasing coverage of tubercles on the inner side with size. Although a higher number of major propodi (defined here: length manus ≥ 15 mm) are right-handed (193 versus 159 lefthanded), this is not statistically significant ($x^2 = 3.28; p = 0.07$).

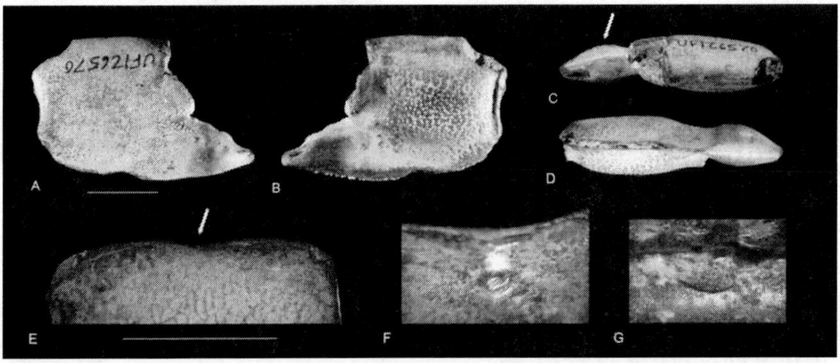

Figure 13. Anomalous specimens of Glypturus panamacanalensis sp. nov. A_D, outer side, inner side, upper margin, and lower margin of a specimen exhibiting a swelling in the fixed finger (UF 126570); E_G, upper part of a manus showing concavity on the margin, inner side near margin showing a subcircular indent, and a concave ridge on the outer side near the margin (UF 246071). Scale bar widths: 10.0 mm.

Glypturus panamacanalensis sp. nov. differs from G. acanthochirus, G. armatus, G. laurae, G. persicus, G. munieri and G. pugnax in that the tubercles cover a substantially greater area on the outer side of the propodus. Similarly, the inner side of the propodus of G. panamacanalensis sp. nov. has a greater coverage of tubercles compared to G. acanthochirus, G. armatus and G. laurae. Conversely, tubercular coverage on the inner side of G. fraasi is greater than in G. panamacanalensis sp. nov. The tubercles on the outer side of G. berryi reach above the lower proximal corner, which is not the case in G. panamacanalensis sp. nov. Glypturus spinosus bears much stronger spines on the upper margin compared to the new species, although spines may be variable (see HyŽnýc & Muller 2012, p. 982). Tubercular patterns are more difficult to use to distinguish G. toulai and G. sikesi sp. nov. from the new species, but sufficient differences were found to erect G. panamacanalensis sp. nov. (see above). One specimen (UF 126570) exhibits a swelling in the fixed finger (Fig. 13A_D). Isopod-induced swellings are known to occur in the branchial region of the carapace of decapod crustaceans including shrimp (Fran¸tescu 2014; Klompmaker et al. 2014), but not in the fixed finger. These ichnofossils were named Kanthyloma crusta Klompmaker et al., 2014. The origin of this particular swelling is unclear, but it may represent an example of a bacterial infection (Christopher Boyko, pers. comm. 11 February 2013). Another specimen (UF 246071) shows a concavity on the upper margin of the propodus accompanied by a subcircular indent on the inner side of the margin and a concave ridge on the outer side (Fig. 13E_G). The keel on the upper margin is somewhat offset. There are no signs of a fracture. It is speculated here that this could be a failed predation attempt or an attack by a conspecific individual (antagonistic behaviour), perhaps directly after the moulting phase when the cuticle was not fully hardened, which may explain why no fracture is observed. Antagonistic behaviour is known from modern ghost shrimps (e.g. Nihonotrypaea Manning & Tamaki, 1998), whereby the major cheliped is protruded and used to grapple with the chelipeds of another individual (Shimoda et al. 2005). Predators of fossil decapods are numerous (e.g. Klompmaker et al. 2013, table 1); those of modern ghost shrimp include fish, crabs, birds and juvenile grey whales (e.g. Posey 1986; Dworschak et al. 2012).

Glypturus skies sp. nov.

(Fig. 14)

Diagnosis. Lateral tuberculation on outer propodal side from base of fixed finger diagonally to lower margin and proximal lower corner. Lateral tuberculation on inner propodal side covering large lower part of manus in medium to large specimens with lower margin of tuberculated area diagonally crossing from area of articulation of dactylus toward (but not reaching) proximal lower corner, tuberculation in small specimens more variable but mostly as in larger specimens. Occlusal margin dactylus without teeth or exhibiting two weak to medium teeth. Outer side carpus without tubercles; inner side with tubercles on lower ~75%.

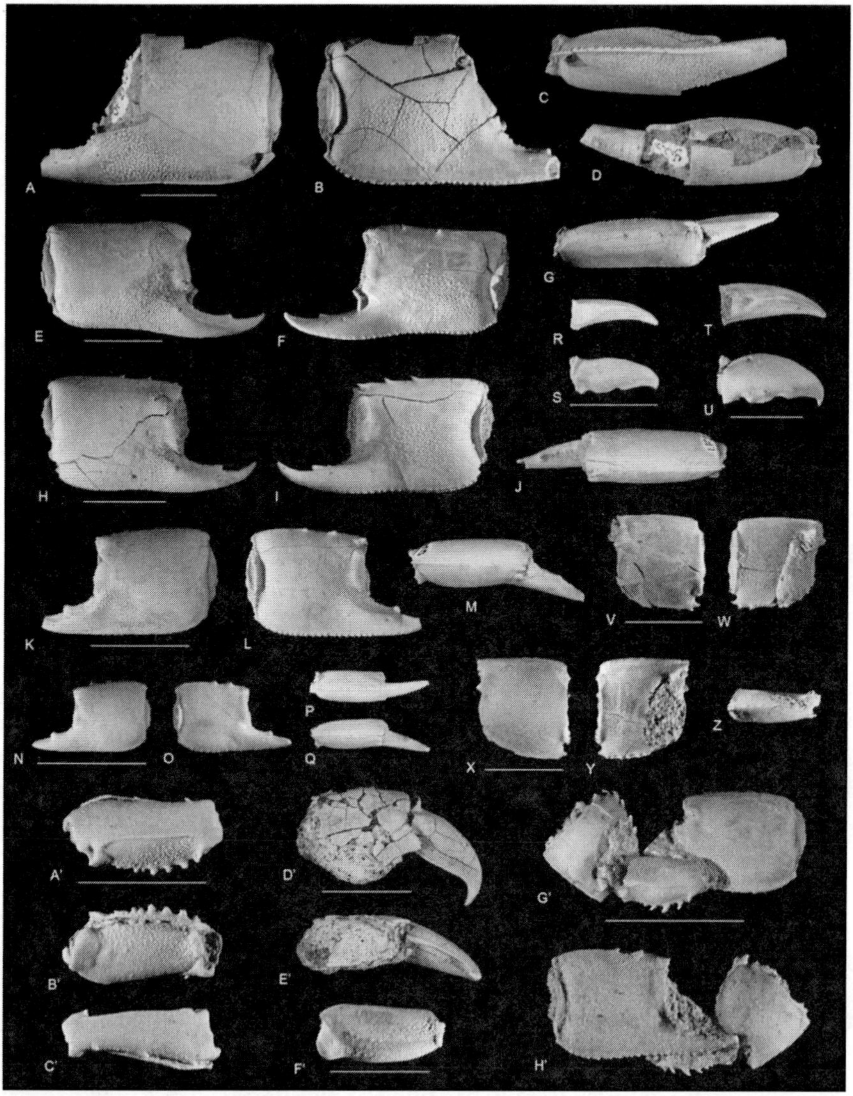

Figure 14. Glypturus sikesi sp. nov. from the upper Miocene Choctawhatchee Formation of Florida (Sikes Sand Mine 02). A_D, UF 235355, paratype, outer side, inner side, lower margin and upper margin of left propodus; E_G, UF 235154, paratype, outer side, inner side and upper margin of right propodus; H_J, UF 235152, holotype, outer side, inner side and upper margin of right propodus; K_M, UF 235370, paratype, outer side, inner side and upper margin of left propodus; N_Q, UF 235401, paratype, outer side, inner side, lower margin and upper margin of left propodus; R, S, UF 248044, occlusal surface and outer side of right dactylus; T, U, UF

235166, paratype, occlusal surface and outer side of right dactylus; V, W, UF 235420, outer and inner sides of right carpus; X_Z, UF 248029, paratype, outer side, inner side and lower margin of right carpus; A 0_C 0 , UF 248038, paratype, outer side, inner side and upper margin of left merus; D 0 , E 0 , UF 248041, paratype, outer and lower sides of partial propodus and dactylus; F 0 , UF 248028, part of inner side or plate of right merus; G 0 , UF 248042, paratype, inner side carpus, and outer sides of merus and propodus (from left to right); H 0 , UF 248042, paratype, inner sides of propodus and partially exposed merus, and outer side of carpus (from left to right). Scale bar widths: 10.0 mm.

Derivation of name. Named after the owner (Mr Lamar Sikes) of the Sikes Sand Mine in Florida, from which all currently known specimens originated.

Material. Holotype: UF 235152 (Fig. 14H_J); Paratypes: UF 235355 (Fig. 14A_D), 235154 (Fig. 14E_G), 235370 (Fig. 14K_M), 235401 (Fig. 14N_Q), 235166 (Fig. 14T, U), 248029 (Fig. 14X_Z), 248038 (Fig. 14A0_C0), 248041 (Fig. 14D0, E0) and 248042 (Fig. 14G0, H0).

Other material (P = propodus; D = dactylus; C = carpus; M = merus; FF = fixed finger): UF 248044 (Fig. 14R, S), 235420 (Fig. 14V, W), 248028 (Fig. 14F0), 232621 (1D), 232622_232632 (1P each), 232633 (14P), 232660 (1P), 232661 (8P), 232662 (2P), 235153 (1P), 235155_235164 (1P each), 235165 (1D), 235167_235168 (10P), 235169 (7P), 235356_235369 (1P each), 235371 (3P), 235372_235373 (15P each), 235374 (10P), 235399_ 235400 (1P each), 235402_235403 (1D each), 235404 (1FF), 235405_ 235419 (1P each), 235421_235432 (1P each), 235433 (33P), 248034 (1P), 248037 (1P), 248039 (1M), 248040 (4C), 248043 (10D), 248045_248049 (1P each), 251651 (1P), 251652 (1C), 251653_251658 (1P each) and 251901 (1C).

Occurrence. All specimens were collected at Sikes Sand Mine 02 (type locality) in Washington County, Florida,USA, and come from the upper Miocene Choctawhatchee Formation (see Geological setting).

Description. Manus up to ~23 mm long and ~19 mm tall, length/height ratio ~1.0_1.3. Upper margin curving inward distally, proximally keeled, typically bearing three prominent spines pointing distally, proximalmost spine around mid-margin, keel terminating in blunt corner proximally. Lower margin sharp and keeled, lined with a row of setal pits on inner lateral side. Proximal margin convex on outer face, concave on inner; heightwise groove near proximal margin concave on inner side, concave to straight on outer side. Distal margin with protrusion just above fixed finger, hinge point with dactylus expressed as notch. Lateral tuberculation on outer side from base of fixed finger diagonally to lower margin and proximal lower corner. Lateral tuberculation on inner side covering large lower part of manus in medium to large specimens with lower margin of tuberculated area diagonally crossing from area of articulation of dactylus toward (but not reaching) proximal lower corner, tuberculation in small specimens less prominent, largest specimens contain additional tubercles on lower margin below two distalmost spines on upper margin. Fixed finger curving inward, triangular, sharply pointed, with distinct blunt tooth on occlusal margin around mid-length, tooth pointing distally. Occlusal margin dactylus without teeth or exhibiting two weak to medium teeth with proximalmost one being largest; tip dactylus hooked, curving downward. Carpus subrectangular with rounded distalmost lower corner on outer side, slightly taller than wide; upper margin keeled and smooth with setal pits on inner part margin; lower margin keeled, exhibits spines on inner side; distal margin straight to slightly concave; proximal margin concave on inner side, convex on outer side with one tooth approximately one-third the distance from upper margin directed proximally; distalmost lower corner with one spine directed distally; outer side without tubercles; inner side with tubercles on lower ~75%. Outer side merus with longitudinal keel in centre; tuberculated below keel, especially proximally; spinose and convex lower margin; upper margin exhibiting three distally directed spines. Inner side merus flattened with tubercles on lower half and proximally. Other parts of species not preserved.

Remarks. Intraspecific variation is observed in the strength of the teeth on the dactylus (Fig. 14R_U, D0, E0) and the tooth on the fixed finger. Furthermore, the number of spines on the upper margin of the propodus is typically three, but some (< 10%) specimens exhibit more (four: UF 235424; five: UF 248034) or fewer spines (one: UF 248037; two: UF 232625, UF 235408). Size-related variation is particularly expressed in the tuberculation pattern on the inner side of small specimens as tubercle coverage is more variable in these specimens, an increasing length/height ratio with size, and an increasing coverage of tubercles on the inner side with size. A nearly equal number of major propodi (defined here: length manus ≥ 15 mm) is left-handed (34) and right-handed (36) ($x^2 = 0.06$; p D 0.81). The differences between Glypturus sikesi sp. nov. and G. acanthochirus, G. armatus, G. berryi, G. fraasi, G. laurae, G. persicus, G. munieri and G. pugnax are the same as described for G. panamacanalensis sp. nov. since the tubercular patterns of G. sikesi sp. nov. and G. panamacanalensis sp. nov. are nearly identical on the propodus. Glypturus spinosus bears much stronger spines on the upper margin compared to the new species. Tubercular patterns are more difficult to use to distinguish G. toulai and G. panamacanalensis sp. nov. from the new species, but sufficient differences were found to justify erection of G. sikesi sp. nov. (see above).

Glypturus acanthochirus Stimpson, 1866

(Fig. 15)

*1866 Glypturus acanthochirus Stimpson, 46. 2012 Glypturus acanthochirus Stimpson; Hyzny & Muller: 971, figs 1, 2A_C, 3A_C, I, 4C (cum syn.).

Diagnosis. Front trispinous. Manus of large cheliped usually with three well-developed spines along distal half of dorsal margin. Endopod of uropod elongate oval, about twice as long as wide. Outer side major propodus with tubercles arranged on lower half (~8_17% of manus), not reaching proximal corner. Tubercles on inner side major propodus absent to rare (< ~6% manus). Carpi without tubercles on outer side; part of specimens exhibit tubercles near lower-distal margin on inner side (< ~5% coverage). Minor chelipeds without tubercles (expanded from Biffar 1971, p. 655).

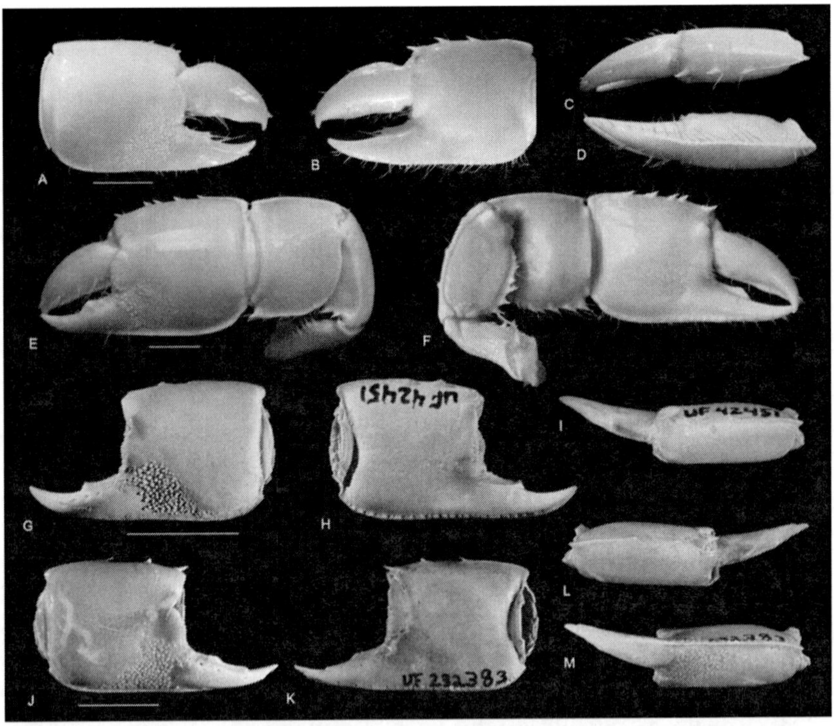

Figure 15. Modern and fossil specimens of Glypturus acanthochirus. A_D, NHMW 15340, outer side, inner side, upper margin and lower margin of right propodus of a modern specimen from Belize (Twin Cays, mangrove channel); E, F, NHMW 24967, outer and inner sides of left dactylus, propodus, carpus, merus and ischium of a modern specimen from Belize (Twin Cays) (modified from Hyzny &Muller 2012, fig. 2; courtesy of the Palaeontological Association); G_I, UF 42451, outer side, inner side and upper margin of left propodus from the upper Pliocene-lower Pleistocene

Tamiami Formation (Pinecrest beds) of Florida (Mule Pen); J_M, UF 232383, outer side, inner side, upper margin and lower margin of right propodus from the Holo-Pleistocene of Jamaica (Falmouth 01). Scale bar widths: 10.0 mm.

Material. F = fossil (propodi), remainder = modern (entire specimens). NHMW 6766 (Twin Cays, Belize), 6768_6770 (Twin Cays, Belize), 15338 (Twin Cays, Belize), 15340 (Fig. 15A_D; Twin Cays, Belize), 15341_15342 (Twin Cays, Belize), 19624 (Twin Cays, Belize), 19625 (South Water Caye, Belize), 19626_19627 (Twin Cays, Belize), 24967 (Fig. 15E, F; Twin Cays, Belize), 24968 (Twin Cays, Belize), 25261 (Pos Chiquito, Aruba), 25266 (Cayo Muerto, Morrocoy, Venezuela), 25635 (near STRI station, Bocas del Toro, Panama), 25636 (Panama, Bocas del Toro), 25637 (Panama, Bocas del Toro, San Cristobal, Punta Coco), 25638 (Panama, Bocas del Toro), 25639_25640 (Panama, Isla Grande). MNHN Th-1593 (Venezuela, Isla Margarita, Guamache). UF 32050 (French Antilles, Saint Martin, Le Galion), 32479 (French Antilles, Saint Martin, Little Key), 32113 (French Antilles, Saint Martin, Le Galion), 32131 (French Antilles, Saint Martin, Baie de l'Embrouchure), 32483 (French Antilles, Saint Martin, Little Key), 42451 (F, Fig. 15G_I; upper Pliocene_lower Pleistocene Tamiami Formation, Pinecrest beds, of Florida, Mule Pen), 232383 (F, Fig. 15J_M; Holo-Pleistocene of Jamaica, Falmouth 01), 232384_232385 (two fixed fingers, Holo-Pleistocene, Jamaica, Falmouth 01).

Occurrence. Western Atlantic region: Gulf of Mexico, Caribbean region, and northern part of the east coast of South America (Dworschak 1992; Sakai 2005; Hyzny & Muller 2012). Fossil specimens known from the Pleistocene and Holo-Pleistocene of Jamaica, and the late Pliocene _early Pleistocene of Florida (Collins et al. 1996; herein) (Supplemental Table 1).

Description. Additional to Biffar (1971, pp. 655_660): major propodus exhibiting tooth on fixed finger; tooth on fixed finger of minor reduced to absent. Upper margin minor and major propodus exhibit usually three forwardly oriented spines. Outer side major propodus with tubercles arranged on lower half (~8_17% of manus), not reaching proximal corner. Tubercles on inner side major propodus absent to rare (< ~6% manus). Carpi without tubercles on outer side; part specimens exhibit tubercles near lower-distal margin on inner side (< ~5% coverage). Meri with tubercles below longitudinal keel (especially proximally) on outer side of major propodus for larger specimens; inner side exhibiting tubercles, especially proximally and on lower margin inner plate for larger specimens. Minor chelipeds without tubercles. Fixed finger of minor comprises a statistically greater portion of propodal length compared to fixed finger of major (Fig. 11A).

Remarks. Biffar (1971, pp. 655_660) provided a detailed description of the entire body of the modern species. Details of tuberculation patterns, known to be important for fossil Glypturus spp., were not described in detail. Therefore, the description of the species is augmented.

Glypturus toulai (Rathbun, 1919)

(Fig. 16)

*1919 Callianassa toulai Rathbun, 146.

2013 Glypturus toulai (Rathbun); HyŽný et al.: 132, figs 4, 5 (cum syn.).

Diagnosis. Moderately tuberculated Glypturus; lateral tuberculation on outer side of propodus extending from near base of fixed finger diagonally to lower margin and reaching proximal lower corner; lateral tuberculation on inner side of the propodus restricted mainly to area of articulation with dactylus in small specimens, but covering [central portion of inner side of manus in large specimens.] (modified from HyŽný et al. 2013, pp. 132_133).

Material. UF 203348 (Fig. 16E, F). NHMW 1933/0018/ 0159 (Fig. 16A_D), 1933/0018/0160 (Fig. 16G_J C 3 fixed fingers). BMNPH PI IC 395 (Fig. 16K_M).

Occurrence. This species is known from the upper Miocene Gatun Formation in Panama (Supplemental Table 1).

Description. Manus length exceeding height (length/ height ratio ~1.1). Upper margin converging distally, proximally keeled, bearing three prominent spines pointing distally, proximalmost spine around mid-margin, keel terminating in blunt corner. Lower margin sharp and keeled, in larger specimens denticulate, lined with a row of setal pits on inner lateral side. Proximal margin convex on outer face, concave on inner, [heightwise groove near proximal margin concave on inner side, concave to straight on outer side]. Distal margin weakly convex. Lateral tuberculation on outer side from base of fixed finger diagonally to lower margin and proximal lower corner. Lateral tuberculation on inner side of propodus restricted mainly to area of articulation with dactylus in small specimens, but covering [central portion of inner side of manus in large specimens]. Fixed finger triangular, sharply pointed, with distinct blunt tooth on occlusal margin around mid-length, tooth pointing distally. Dactylus stout, occlusal margin [with or] without tooth [around mid-length], tip hooked (modified from HyŽný et al. 2013, pp. 134_135).

Glypturus aff. G. toulai (Rathbun, 1919)

2013 Glypturus toulai (Rathbun); HyŽný et al.: 132, fig. 6.

Remarks. Hyžný et al. (2013) ascribed specimens from the lower Miocene Culebra Formation in Panama to G. toulai based on the extent of the tuberculation on the propodus. The limited number of specimens and their inadequate preservation does not allow rigorous bi- and multivariate analyses to reassess their placement. One possible difference with G. toulai from the upper Miocene Gatun Formation in Panama is the extent of the tubercles on the inner side of the propodus (HyŽný et al. 2013, fig. 6). Also given the long interval between deposition of the Gatun and Culebra formations (~10 Ma, see Coates 1999; Kirby et al. 2008) relative to the other, younger species its ascription to G. toulai must be regarded as preliminary. Therefore, we herein propose the more conservative Glypturus aff. G. toulai until more material is studied.

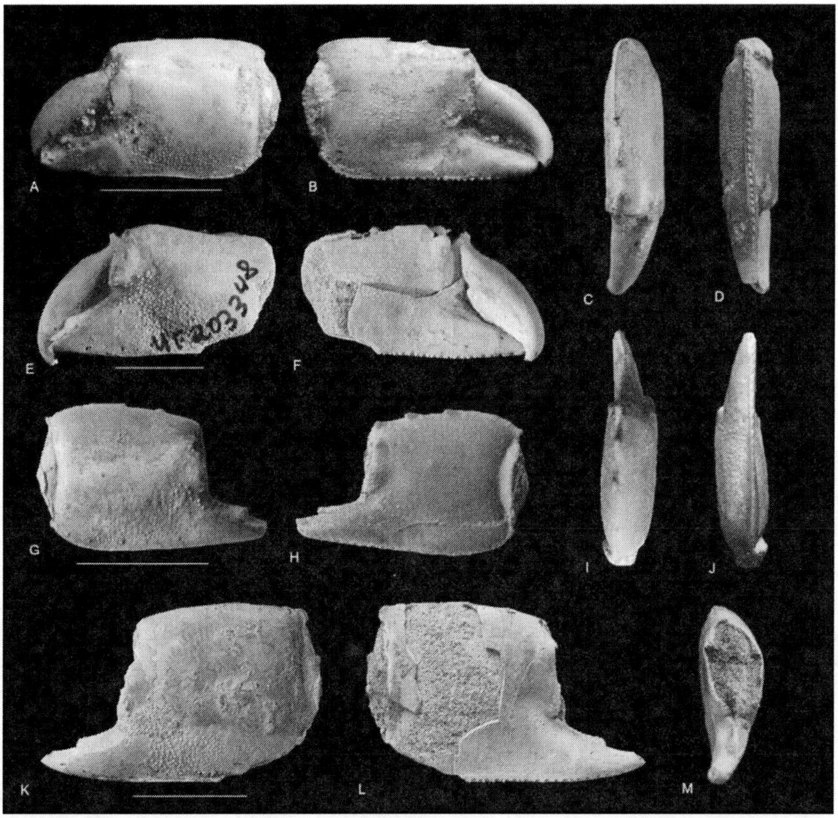

Figure 16. Glypturus toulai from the upper Miocene Gatun Formation of Panama. A_D, NHMW 1933/0018/0159, lectotype, outer side, inner side, upper margin and lower margin of left propodus; E, F, UF 203348, outer and inner sides of left propodus (from HyŽný et al. 2013, fig. 5; permission of Springer Science and Business Media); G_J, NHMW 1933/0018/0160, outer side, inner side, upper margin and lower margin of right propodus; K_M, BMNPH PI IC 395, outer side, inner side and frontal view of left propodus. Scale bar widths: A_F, K_M, 10.0 mm; G_J, 5 mm.

Glypturus sp.

(Fig. 17)

1919 Callianassa anguillensis Rathbun: 164, pl. 1.1_1.7. 1919 Callianassa latidigata Rathbun: 165, pl. 9.10, 9.11. 1924 Callianassa anguillensis Rathbun; Withers: 226, pl. 4.3_4.5. 2006 Neocallichirus? quisquellanus Schweitzer et al.: 115, fig. 3D. non 2008 ?Neocallichirus? quisquellanus Schweitzer et al.; Schweitzer et al.: 4, fig. 2.

Material. UF 222839 (Fig. 17N_Q), 248031 (Fig. 17R, S), 246508 (Fig. 17T), 77426 (Fig. 17U, V), 222383 (partial propodus, upper Pleistocene Jaimanitas Formation of Cuba, Caravela Road Fill Pit 01), 238826 (propodus, Pliocene Intracoastal Formation of Florida, Pickett Bay 01), 251883 (seven propodi, lower Miocene Chattahoochee Formation, Florida, Jim Woodruff Dam), 109960 & 109946 (propodus and two fixed fingers, lower Pleistocene Caloosahatchee Formation, Florida, De Soto Shell Pit 04), 35055 (fixed finger, upper Pliocene Tamiami Formation, lower Pinecrest beds, Florida, Macasphalt Shell Pit), 96809 (dactylus, Plio-Pleistocene, Florida, Macasphalt Shell Pit). MNHNCu-P5116 (Fig. 17A). USNM MO166941_166943 (in part Fig. 17B, C), MO324470 (Fig. 17D, E). NHM UK In 23770_23784 (in part Fig. 17F_M).

Remarks. Callianassa anguillensis Rathbun, 1919, from the Miocene of Anguilla (see Supplemental Table 1 for details), shows tubercles near the lower margin of the outer side of the propodus (Rathbun 1919, pl. 1.1, 1.3), tubercles in the centre of the inner side (pl. 1.2), and a spine is visible on the upper margin of the incompletely preserved holotype (pl. 1.4). Rathbun (1919, p. 164) mentioned that this spine ("tubercle") is directed forward and noted another spine at the distal extremity. A third spine on the upper margin, as in the far majority of wellpreserved specimens of Glypturus spp., was not observed, but the upper margin is incomplete. A tubercle on the upper margin is also noted for an incompletely preserved paratype (Rathbun 1919, pl. 1.2, 1.3). A finger appears to show a tooth (pl. 1.6). All these features suggest placement in Glypturus. Given the incomplete nature of the specimens, we refrain from a specific assignment, and refer the assemblage to Glypturus sp. Puzzling, however, are some of the tubercles shown near the upper margin of the outer side of the holotype (pl. 1.4), which would be unique for Glypturus. More specimens are needed to confirm whether or not this is an anomaly, but a paratype does not seem to show this feature (pl. 1.3). Five years later, Withers (1924) reported on 15 specimens (12 propodi, three dactyli) from a locality within a few kilometres of the type locality of the species (Crocus Bay), of which the best-preserved specimens are figured here (Fig. 17F_M). He did not mention a lithostratigraphical unit, but these specimens are very likely to have also originated from the Miocene Anguilla Formation.

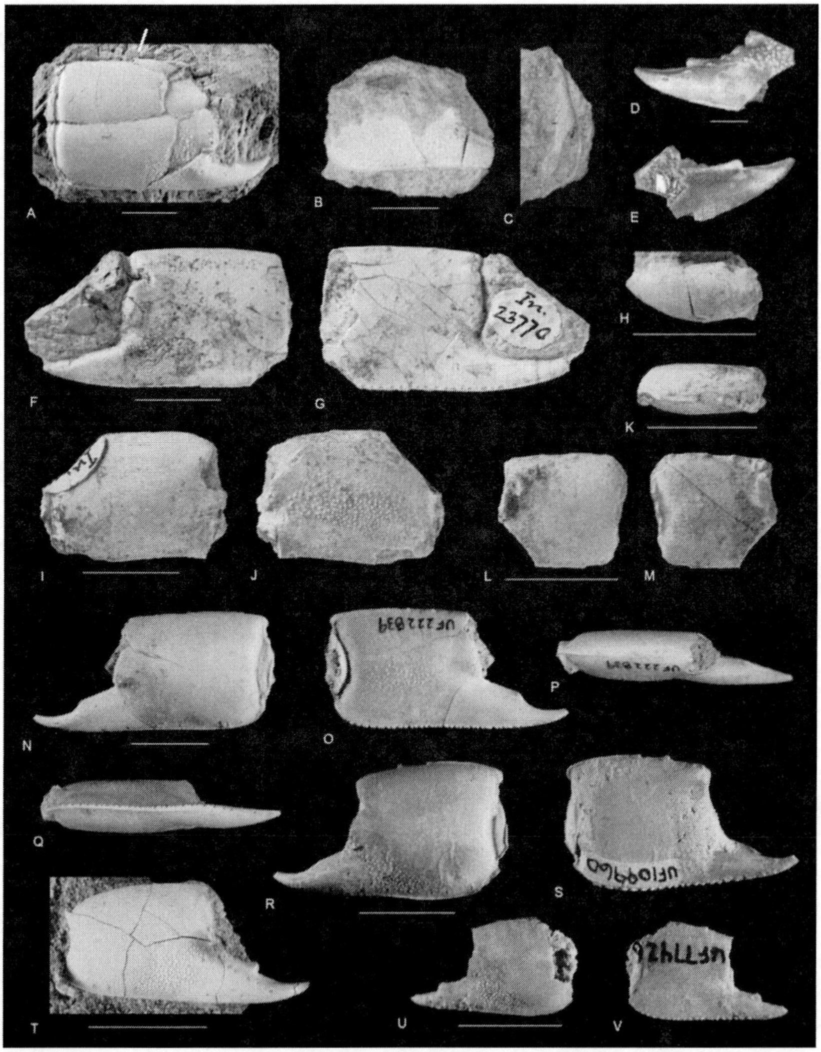

Figure 17. Western Atlantic Glypturus sp. A, MNHNCu-P5116, outer side of propodus of Glypturus sp. (= Neocallichirus? Quisquellanus Schweitzer et al., 2006) from the lower_middle Miocene Yanigua Formation of the Dominican Republic (R_ıo Camar_on) (refigured from Schweitzer et al. 2006, fig. 3D; permission of the Carnegie Museum of Natural History); B, C, USNM MO166941, outer side and upper margin of propodus of Glypturus sp. (= Callianassa anguillensis Rathbun, 1919, holotype) from the lower_middle Miocene Anguilla Formation of Anguilla (Crocus Bay) (courtesy of the Smithsonian Institution); D, E, USNM MO324470, outer and inner sides of fixed finger of Glypturus sp. (= Callianassa latidigata Rathbun, 1919) from the early Miocene of the Dominican Republic (Santo Domingo)

(courtesy of the Smithsonian Institution); F, G, NHM UK In 23770, outer and inner sides of propodus of Glypturus sp. (= Callianassa anguillensis) from the lower_middle Miocene Anguilla Formation of Anguilla (Cartouche Bay) (courtesy of the Natural History Museum, London); H, NHM UK In 23784, outer side of dactylus of Glypturus sp. (= Callianassa anguillensis) from the lower _middle Miocene Anguilla Formation of Anguilla (Cartouche Bay) (courtesy of the Natural History Museum, London); I, J, NHM UK In 23774, outer and inner sides of propodus of Glypturus sp. (= Callianassa anguillensis) from the lower_middle Miocene Anguilla Formation of Anguilla (Cartouche Bay) (courtesy of the Natural History Museum, London); K_M, NHM UK In 23777, upper margin and outer and inner sides of propodus of Glypturus sp. (= Callianassa anguillensis) from the lower_middle Miocene Anguilla Formation in Anguilla (Cartouche Bay) (courtesy Natural History Museum, London); N_Q, UF 222839, outer side, inner side, upper margin and lower margin of left propodus from the upper Pleistocene Jaimanitas Formation in Cuba (Good Road 01); R, S, UF 248031, outer and inner sides of left propodus from the lower Pleistocene Caloosahatchee Formation in Florida (De Soto Shell Pit 04); T, UF 246508, outer side of propodus of Glypturus sp. from the lower Miocene Chipola Formation in Florida (Tenmile Creek 12); U, V, UF 77426, outer and inner sides of left propodus from the upper Pleistocene Port Morant Formation in Jamaica (Port Morant Bay 01). All scale bar nwidths are 10.0 mm, except for D and E, which are 2 mm. Note that images R and S were taken before specimen received new UF catalogue number.

This was also assumed by Collins et al. (2009) and supported by outcrops of this formation in that part of Anguilla (e.g. Christman 1953; Budd et al. 1995). None of the specimens is well preserved on both lateral sides, which makes comparisons with other species difficult. Tubercles near the upper margin were not observed on these specimens. Well-preserved material is needed to determine whether this is a separate species or can be synonymized with an existing species. However, some preliminary suggestions can be made. The specimens seem different from the late Miocene G. sikesi sp. nov., given the smaller tubercles in the latter, and appear different from the late Miocene G. toulai in that the tubercles on the inner side appear to extend to the lower proximal corner.

Rathbun (1919) also described Callianassa latidigata from the early Miocene of the Dominican Republic based on a fixed finger and a dactylus. The fixed finger shows a tooth and tubercles (Rathbun 1919, pl. 9.11), consistent with Glypturus. Given the preservation and limited number of specimens we refer them to Glypturus sp. Withers (1924) suggested that this species resembled Callianassa anguillensis, but conclusive evidence cannot be provided.

Schweitzer et al. (2006) erected the species Neocallichirus? quisquellanus based on a Miocene specimen from the Dominican Republic (see also Supplemental Table 1). The presence of tubercles on the lower part of the outer side of the propodus, the tooth on the fixed finger and the presence of at least one spine on the upper margin (Schweitzer et al. 2006, fig. 3D) allows it to be ascribed to Glypturus with confidence. Given the preservation and the single photo provided showing only the outer side, specific assignment is premature and could be better addressed with additional specimens. Therefore, we refer N.? quisquellanus to Glypturus sp. The holotype and sole type specimen (MNHNCu- P511) could not be located in the Museo Nacional de Historia Natural (Havana, Cuba) when requested and may be lost. Later, Schweitzer et al. (2008) questionably referred specimens from the Oligocene of Puerto Rico to N.? quisquellanus. The notch above the fixed finger is much larger than the type specimen of N.? quisquellanus.

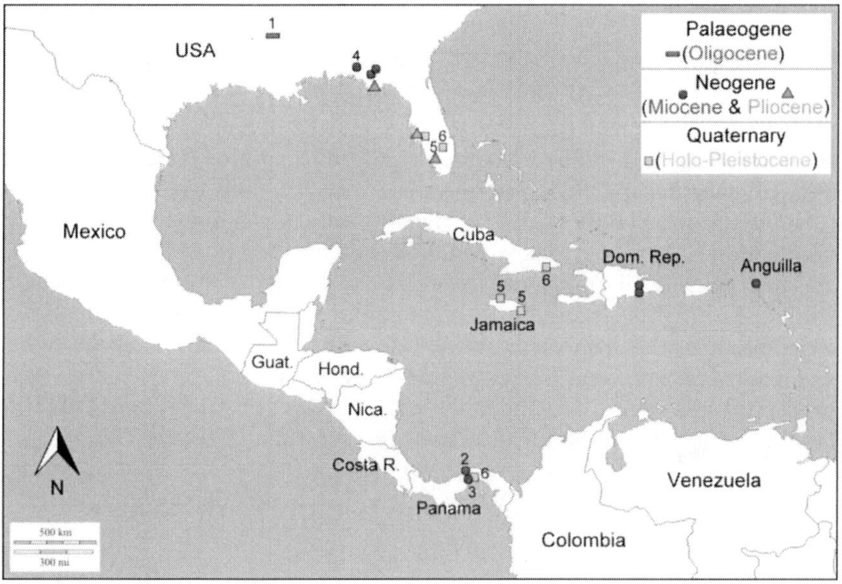

Figure 18. Known Cenozoic occurrences of fossil Glypturus spp. in the Western Atlantic by epoch. 1. G. berryi, 2. G. toulai, 3. G. aff. toulai, 4. G. sikesi sp. nov., 5. G. acanthochirus, 6. G. panamacanalensis sp. nov. Unnumbered dots represent occurrences of Glypturus sp. Note that G. acanthochirus from the Mule Pen Quarry in Florida is colour-coded as Pliocene, but the more conservative age is late Pliocene_early Pleistocene. For details of localities and more specific ages see Supplemental Table 1.

Moreover, there is no evidence of tubercles on one of the figured sides and no obvious evidence of spines on the upper margin are visible (Schweitzer et al. 2008, fig. 2), which could also be related to the poor preservation. Nevertheless, given the major difference in the size of the notch, the specimen is unlikely to be conspecific to the Miocene specimen from the Dominican Republic and, thus, assignment to Glypturus is not favoured here.

We refrained from referring these three taxa to nomen dubium so that the names remain available in case betterpreserved material becomes available from the respective localities, which may justify or refute these species names.

5. DISCUSSION

5.1 Diversity and use of characters

Distinguishing between species of Glypturus using the extent of the tuberculation pattern on the outer and inner lateral sides of the propodi has worked well and will continue to be useful to distinguish most species. However, two taxa studied herein are different species (G. sikesi sp. nov. and G. panamacanalensis sp. nov., see above), but the extent of the tuberculation on both sides is insufficient to distinguish them. The implication is that looking solely at the tubercular extent can underestimate species richness. The poor preservation and limited number of specimens from a variety of localities (Supplemental Table 1) severely hampers assessment of the true diversity and several existing taxa may be either synonyms or separate species (see Glypturus sp.). Since new, well-preserved specimens are needed for reliably evaluating the identity of these taxa, diversity within Glypturus may be underestimated further.

5.2 Use of geometric morphometric and multivariate methods

Traditional multivariate methods (based on non-landmark variables such as linear measurements) have been used in a variety of systematic studies to delineate new taxa and/or assess previously defined taxa (e.g. Hageman 1991, for Mississippian bryozoans; Geary 1992, for Miocene gastropods; Ausich & Meyer 1994, for Mississippian crinoids; Goldman 1995, for Ordovician graptolites; Kowalewski et al. 1997, for modern lingulide brachiopods; Graham et al. 2012, for modern scorpions). Landmark-based geometric morphometrics has been also used to distinguish among species (e.g. Budd et al. 1994, for modern corals; Vergara-Solana et al. 2013, for modern fish; Webster 2007, for Cambrian trilobites). However, the application of traditional multivariate morphometrics and/or geometric morphometrics in decapod palaeontology is unknown to us (except discriminant analysis in Starzyk et al. 2012). Furthermore, these methods have rarely been used for the systematic of extant decapods. The dearth of such studies is, at least in part, due to insufficient sample sizes and poorly preserved specimens. This study highlights the usefulness of these methods when sample sizes are sufficient and specimens are well preserved.

5.3 Where are the minors?

Palaeontological research on Glypturus has focused on the major propodus (HyŽný & Muller 2012; HyŽný et al. 2013). HyŽný & Muller (2012, p. 982) mentioned that the minor chela usually lack tuberculation in extant G. acanthochirus. We found that spines on the upper margin of the minor were present, no evidence of tubercles on the minor, and a significant difference of the proportion of the propodus length of the fixed finger comparing the major and the minor for G. acanthochirus. Minors may also be expected in the fossil record in large samples. They should be smaller than the majors (< ~20 mm propodus length), may have no tubercles, and may have a relatively long fixed finger compared to the major by analogy with modern G. acanthochirus. However, none of the several hundred specimens of G. sikesi sp. nov. from the late Miocene of Florida lacks tubercles and no specimen has a much longer fixed finger than other specimens (Fig. 11B), although some small specimens appear to have a higher proportion of the propodus represented by the fixed finger. Whether these specimens represent true minors is challenging to prove given that a marked increase in variance towards smaller specimens as shown in Figure 11A seems absent. Unless minors and majors exhibit exactly the same shape and tuberculation pattern for this species, which may be unlikely given the differences in the modern species, the implication is that minors are rarely preserved. This taphonomic bias is likely due to their small size and relative fragility compared to the majors of the same specimens, and perhaps also by the handling of moults by the animal. Schafer (1972) noted that the moult of Callianassa Leach, 1814 is taken outside the burrow except for the major claw, decreasing the preservation potential of minors. However, small-sized majors appear to be present in the sample (Fig. 11B). If all are majors, then minors are underrepresented, possibly suggesting that their cuticle is thinner than that of the majors of equal size. This is supported by the multiple functions of major chelipeds such as for feeding purposes, digging and fighting of ghost shrimp (e.g. Shimoda et al. 2005; Dworschak et al. 2006). To our knowledge, no neontological study is known that determines possible differences in the thickness of equal-sized majors and minors from the same taxon.

5.4 Sedimentary environment

Hyžný y & Muller (2012, p. 984) concluded that "extinct species of Glypturus are found in settings that are typical for modern relatives, that is, tropical to subtropical, nearshore carbonates of normal salinity." Our compilation of Western Atlantic specimens (Supplemental Table 1) indicates that Glypturus is also found frequently in siliciclastic sediments. In fact, the largest assemblages studied herein originated from siliciclastic settings and most localities contained siliciclastic sediments. Thus, Glypturus lived in a variety of sedimentary settings, at least in the Western Atlantic.

5.5 Biogeography

Prior to this research describing new occurrences and reassigning taxa to Glypturus, fossil specimens of this genus were only known from the USA, Jamaica and Panama (Fig. 18) in the Western Atlantic. This research thus expands the number of occurrences of the genus in the Western Atlantic to the extent that preliminary suggestions may be made about biogeographical patterns through time. As shown in Figure 18, the first known occurrence of Glypturus in the Western Atlantic region is in the USA (Mississippi) during the Oligocene. By the Miocene, occurrences are known from all over the Western Atlantic, perhaps suggesting a biogeographical expansion of the genus. Pliocene occurrences are only known from the USA (Florida), which may be related to limited collecting in other places. This is supported by the wider distribution in the Holo-Pleistocene all over the Western Atlantic and the modern distribution (HyŽný & Muller 2012, fig. 11). Today, Glypturus is only described from the Atlantic side of the Americas including Panama (e.g. Dworschak 1992; Sakai 2005; HyŽný & Muller 2012; herein). Importantly, this may not have been so in the recent past as Holo-Pleistocene specimens of G. panamacanalensis sp. nov. were found primarily on the Amador and Farfan beaches near Panama City, and their provenance is very likely sediments from the Pacific side (see Geological setting). Thus, Glypturus may have gone extinct on the Pacific side in the Holo-Pleistocene. This also suggests that Glypturus migrated into the Pacific prior to closure of the Central American Isthmus during the Cenozoic (e.g. Keigwin 1978; Coates et al. 1992; Montes et al. 2012). Interestingly, G. panamacanalensis sp. nov. was also found in the Pleistocene of Florida and Cuba on the Atlantic side of the isthmus, well after the closure isthmus. This suggests a wide distribution of the species prior to its relatively recent apparent extinction.

5.6 Phylogenetic relationships and morphological trends

Glypturus has been included in several phylogenetic analyses of extant ghost shrimps (Tudge et al. 2000; Felder & Robles 2009; Robles et al. 2009), but not all recognized taxa, implying that species-level phylogenetic relationships within Glypturus are unknown. Tudge et al. (2000) worked with a broadly defined Glypturus and the genus was resolved as a paraphyletic group. Following the concept of Glypturus as originally proposed by Stimpson (1866) and further emended by Manning (1987), Felder & Robles (2009) included two Glypturus species in their analyses, both from the Western Atlantic (G. acanthochirus and G. sp. = G. rabalaisae sensu Sakai, 2005). The sister group relationship of these two species resulting from their analysis is not surprising given their close geographical distribution. Robles et al. (2009) analysed relationships among the 'thalassinidean' families and several members of callianassid ghost shrimps were included.

5.6.1 Glypturus laurae was among them, however, without any other congeners.

Assuming a Tethyan origin of Glypturus and further division into several independent lineages (Hyžný & Muller 2012), G. armatus from the Indo-West Pacific and G. laurae from the Red Sea form a different lineage than the Western Atlantic species G. acanthochirus and G. sp. (see HyŽný & Muller 2012, fig. 11). Phylogenetic analyses evaluating members of both supposed lineages are desirable, if these are possible given the limited number of characters on fossil material.

Hyžný et al. (2013) noted an evolutionary trend in Glypturus with the most tuberculated species dating from the Palaeogene and less tuberculated species from today. As an example they mentioned the possible Western Atlantic lineage consisting of G. berryi_G. toulai_G. acanthochirus. However, the two new species described herein complicate the picture, as they are younger than G. toulai but clearly more tuberculated. In the Tethyan region, G. fraasi from the Eocene of Spain, Italy and Hungary is more tuberculated than G. munieri from the Miocene of Hungary, Austria and Malta (see HyŽný & Muller 2012, for details). Furthermore, Glypturus persicus from the Miocene of Iran possesses tubercles only on its inner propodal side (HyŽný et al. 2013, fig. 7d) and may be part of a lineage towards modern G. laurae and G. armatus. These species are less tuberculated (G. laurae) than G. acanthochirus, or have no tubercles at all (G. armatus). The pattern is not straightforward here either. The fossil record of the Indo-West Pacific region is patchy and the only known fossil species, G. pugnax from the early Miocene of Indonesia, is clearly more tuberculated than the slightly younger G. persicus from the middle_late Miocene of Iran (HyŽný et al. 2013).

Supposedly, the roots of the possible Western Atlantic lineage are in the Eocene assemblages of Europe (HyŽný & Muller 2012, fig. 13), i.e. its evolution could be independent from the Tethyan lineage, at least since the Oligocene from which the oldest Western Atlantic species is known. Another possibility is that there were several introductions of Glypturus into the Western Atlantic region via trans-Atlantic migrations during the Miocene (Harzhauser et al. 2002; HyŽný & Muller 2012). In such a case more tuberculated species (G. sikesi sp. nov. and G. panamacanalensis sp. nov.) would be more closely related to Tethyan G. munieri than to the roughly coeval G. toulai. Thorough analysis of the tuberculation pattern of G. munieri may resolve this issue in the future, as well as the documentation of Glypturus from more localities. Similarly, the analysis of the tuberculation pattern of G. sp. (= G. rabalaisae sensu Sakai, 2005) may shed light on the relationships within the Western Atlantic Glypturus species.

Results indicate that the length/height ratios increased faster throughout growth in geologically older assemblages based on three main assemblages (modern G. acanthochirus, Holo-Pleistocene G. panamacanalensis sp. nov. and late Miocene G. sikesi sp. nov.). This could represent an example of heterochrony, specifically paedomorphosis (e.g. McNamara 2001). However, phylogenetic relationships within Glypturus are unresolved and the oldest known specimen from the Western Atlantic, G. berryi from the Oligocene, does not plot above G. sikesi sp. nov. in Figure 3.

ACKNOWLEDGEMENTS

Peter Dworschak (Naturhistorisches Museum Wien) is thanked for useful information on modern Glypturus; the FLMNH Division of Invertebrate Zoology for access to modern specimens of G. acanthochirus; Alexis Rojas and Sahale Casebolt (both FLMNH) for information on geometric morphometrics; Austin Hendy (FLMNH) for literature and access to some Panamanian specimens and comments on part of the geological setting; Peter Ng (National University of Singapore) for important nomenclatural advice; and Manuel Iturralde-Vinent (Museo Nacional de Historia Natural, Havanna, Cuba) for attempting to locate the holotype of Neocallichirus? quisquellanus. We further acknowledge: Rafael Lemaitre and Thomas Jorstad (both Smithsonian Institution) for information on related specimens and permission to use Figure 17B_E, respectively; John Wible (Carnegie Museum of Natural History) for permission to use Figure 17A; Carrie Schweitzer (Kent State University) for providing the high resolution image used in Figure 17A; and Claire Mellish (Natural History Museum, London) for providing photos of G. anguillensis as described in Withers (1924). Field assistance at the Sikes Sand Mine 02 was provided by Harley

Means (Florida Geological Survey), Alex Kittle and Sean Roberts (both FLMNH), and Jon Bryan (Northwest Florida State College). Paul Huddlestun (retired stratigrapher from Georgia Geological Survey) visited the Sikes Sand Mine 02 and kindly offered his insights into the geology of the quarry and surrounding area. Fieldwork at Guantanamo Bay, Cuba by R.W.P. and James K. Toomey (FLMNH volunteer) was possible with the assistance, support and hospitality of Jos_e B. Montalvo (Natural Resource Officer) andMichael R.McCord (Public Works Department _ Environmental). Emily Vokes is thanked for facilitating the transfer of the Tulane University palaeontological collections. We also thank two anonymous reviewers for their useful comments that improved this manuscript substantially. This is University of Florida Contribution to Paleobiology 668. Disclosure statement: the funders had no role in study design, data collection and analysis, decision to publish, or preparation of the manuscript. This work was supported by the Jon L. and Beverly A. Thompson Endowment Fund to A.A.K.; National Science Foundation [grant 0966884, Partnerships for International Research and Education], the Florida Museum of Natural History (McGinty and Invertebrate Paleontology) endowments, and private funding by James K. Toomey to R.W.P.; the National Science Foundation [grant DBI 0645865] for curating the Tulane University Collection (including the Burkenroad Collection) into the collections of the FLMNH; the Austrian Science Fund [FWF; Lise Meitner Program M 1544-B25], [Scientific Grant Agency of the Slovak Republic VEGA 2/0068/11]; and the Slovak Research and Development Agency [under contracts no. APVV-0644-10; APVV-0436-12] to M.H.

REFERENCES

1. Ausich, W. I. & Meyer, D. L. 1994. Hybrid crinoids in the fossil record (Early Mississippian, Phylum Echinodermata). Paleobiology, 20, 362_367.
2. Biffar, T. A. 1971. The genus Callianassa (Crustacea, Decapoda, Thalassinidea) in South Florida, with keys to the western Atlantic species. Bulletin of Marine Science, 21, 637_715.
3. Bishop, G. A. & Williams, A. B. 2005. Taphonomy and preservation of burrowing thalassinidean shrimps. Proceedings of the Biological Society of Washington, 118, 218_236.
4. BÖohm, J. 1922. Crustacea. Pp. 521_538 in K. Martin (ed.) Die Fossilien von Java. I. Band, 2 Abteilung. E. J. Brill, Leiden.
5. Bookstein, F. L. 1997. Morphometric tools for landmark data: geometry and biology. Cambridge University Press, Cambridge, n435 pp.
6. Brocchi, P. 1883. Notes sur les Crustac_es fossiles des terres tertiaires de la Hongrie. Annales des Sciences G_eologiques, 14 (2), 1_8, pls 4, 5.
7. Budd, A. F., Johnson, K. G. & Potts, D. C. 1994. Recognizing morphospecies in colonial reef corals: I. Landmark-based methods. Paleobiology, 20, 484_505.
8. Budd, A. F., Johnson, K. G. & Edwards, J. C. 1995. Caribbean nreef coral diversity during the early to middle Miocene: An example from the Anguilla Formation. Coral Reefs, 14, 109_117.

9. Christman, R. A. 1953. Geology of St. Bartholomew, St. Martin, and Anguilla, Lesser Antilles. Geological Society of America Bulletin, 64, 65_96.
10. Coan, E. V. & Valentich-Scott, P. 2012. Bivalve seashells of tropical west America. Marine bivalve mollusks from Baja
11. California to Peru. Santa Barbara Museum of Natural History, Santa Barbara, California, Monographs, 6, 1_1258.
12. Coates, A. G. 1999. Lithostratigraphy of the Neogene strata of the Caribbean coast from Limon, Costa Rica, to Colon, Panama. Bulletins of American Paleontology, 357, 5_16.
13. Coates A. G., Jackson, J. B. C., Collins, L. S., Cronin, T. M., Dowsett, H. J., Bybell, L. M., Jung, P. & Obando, J. A. 1992. Closure of the Isthmus of Panama: The near-shore marine record of Costa Rica and western Panama. Geological Society of America Bulletin, 104, 814_828.
14. Collins, J. S. H., Donovan, S. K. & Dixon, H. L. 1996. Crabs and barnacles (Crustacea: Decapoda & Cirripedia) from the late Pleistocene Port Morant Formation of southeast Jamaica. Bulletin of the Mizunami Fossil Museum, 23, 51_63.
15. Collins, J. S. H., Portell, R. W. & Donovan, S. K. 2009. Decapod crustaceans from the Neogene of the Caribbean: diversity, distribution and prospectus. Scripta Geologica, 138, 55_111.
16. Dall, W. H. 1870. A revision of the Terebratulidae and Lingulidae, with remarks and descriptions of some recent forms. American Journal of Conchology, 6, 88_168.
17. Dall, W. H. 1898. Contributions to the Tertiary fauna of Florida, with especial reference to the Silex beds of Tampa and the Pliocene beds of the Caloosahatchie River, including in many cases a complete revision of the generic groups treated of and their American species. Part IV. I. Prionodesmacea. II. Teleodesmacea: Teredo to Ervilia. Transactions of the Wagner Free Institute of Science of Philadelphia, 3(4), viii C 571_947, pls 23_35.
18. Dana, J. D. 1852. Crustacea. Part I. United States Exploring Expedition, during the years 1838, 1839, 1840, 1841, 1842, under the command of Charles Wilkes, U.S.N.13. C. Sherman, Philadelphia, viii C 685 pp.
19. Dworschak, P. C. 1992. The Thalassinidea in the Museum of Natural History, Vienna; with some remarks on the biology of the species. Annalen des Naturhistorischen Museums in Wien, B, 93, 189_238.
20. Dworschak, P. C., Koller, H. & Abed-Navandi, D. 2006. Burrow structure, burrowing and feeding behaviour of Corallianassa longiventris and Pestarella tyrrhena (Crustacea, Thalassinidea, Callianassidae). Marine Biology, 148, 1369_1382.
21. Dworschak, P. C., Felder, D. L. & Tudge, C. C. 2012. Chapter 69. Infraorders Axiidea de Saint Laurent, 1979 and Gebiidea de Saint Laurent, 1979 (formerly known collectively as Thalassinidea). Pp. 109_219 in F. R. Schram, J. C. von Vaupel Klein, J. Forest & M. Charmantier-Daures (eds) Treatise on Zoology _ Anatomy, Taxonomy, Biology. The Crustacea. Complementary to the volumes translated from the French of the Trait_e de Zoologie [founded by P.-P. Grass_e], Volumee 9 Part B. Eucarida: Decapoda: Astacidea p.p. (Enoplometopoidea, Nephropoidea), Glypheidea, Axiidea, Gebiidea, and Anomura. Brill, Leiden.
22. Felder, D. L. & Robles, R. 2009. Molecular phylogeny of the family Callianassidae based on preliminary analysis of two mitochondrial genes. Pp. 327_342 in J. W. Martin, K. A. Crandall & D. L. Felder (eds) Decapod crustacean phylogenetics. Taylor & Francis/CRC Press, Boca Raton.
23. Foote, M. & Sepkoski, J. J. 1999. Absolute measures of the completeness of the fossil record. Nature, 398, 415_417.
24. Fraaije, R. H. B., Artal, P., Van Bakel, B. W. M., Jagt, J. W. M. & Klompmaker, A. A. 2013. An array of sixth abdominal tergite types of paguroid anomurans (Crustacea) from the mid-Cretaceous of Navarra, northern Spain. Netherlands Journal of Geosciences, 92, 109_117.
25. Fran¸tescu, O. D. 2014. Fossil mudshrimps (Decapoda: Axiidea) from the Pawpaw Formation (Cretaceous: Albian), northeast Texas, USA. Bulletin of the Mizunami Fossil Museum, 40, 13_22.
26. Geary, D. H. 1992. An unusual pattern of divergence between two fossil gastropods: ecophenotypy, dimorphism, or hybridization? Paleobiology, 18, 93_109.

27. Goldman, D. 1995. Taxonomy, evolution, and biostratigraphy of the Orthograptus quadrimucronatus species group (Ordovician, Graptolithina). Journal of Paleontology, 69, 516_540.
28. Graham, M. R., Ayrey, R. F. & Bryson Jr, R. W. 2012. Multivariate methods support the distinction of a new highland Vaejovis (Scorpiones: Vaejovidae) from the Sierra de los Ajos, Mexico. Journal of Arachnology, 40, 281_290.
29. Hageman, S. J. 1991. Approaches to systematic and evolutionary studies of perplexing groups: An example using fenestrate Bryozoa. Journal of Paleontology, 65, 630_647.
30. Hammer, ;., Harper, D. A. T. & Ryan, P. D. 2001. Past: Paleontological Statistics Software Package for Education and Data Analysis. Palaeontologia Electronica, 4(1), art. 4, 1_9.
31. Hanley, S. C. T. 1844_5. Descriptions of new species of the genus Tellina, chiefly collected by H. Cuming, Esq., in the Philippine Islands and Central America. Proceedings of the Zoological Society of London, 1844, 59_64.
32. Harzhauser, M., Piller, W. E. & Steininger, F. F. 2002. Circum- Mediterranean Oligo-Miocene biogeographic evolution _ the gastropods' point of view. Palaeogeography, Palaeoclimatology, Palaeoecology, 183, 103_133.
33. Hendy, A. J. W. 2013. Spatial and stratigraphic variation of marine paleoenvironments in the middle-upper Miocene Gatun Formation, Isthmus of Panama. Palaios, 28, 210_227.
34. Hinds, R. B. 1844_5. The zoology of the voyage of H. M. S. Sulphur, under the command of Capt. Sir Edward Belcher, . . .during the years 1836_42, vol. 2 [Mollusca]. Smith, Elder & Co., London. 72 pp., 21 pls.
35. Holdener, E. J. 1994. Numerical taxonomy of fenestrate bryozoans: evaluation of methodologies and recognition of intraspecific variation. Journal of Paleontology, 68, 1201_1214.
36. Huddlestun, P. F. 1976. The Neogene stratigraphy of the central Florida Panhandle. Unpublished PhD thesis, Florida State University, Tallahassee, 209 pp.
37. Hy_zn_y, M. & Hud_a_ckov_a, N. 2012. Redescription of two ghost shrimps (Decapoda: Axiidea: Callianassidae) from the Middle Miocene of the Central Paratethys: systematics, intraspecific variation, and in situ preservation. Zootaxa, 3210, 1_25.
38. Hy_zn_y, M. & M€uller, P. M. 2012. The fossil record of Glypturus Stimpson, 1866 (Crustacea, Decapoda, Axiidea, Callianassidae) revisited, with notes on palaeoecology and palaeobiogeography. Palaeontology, 55, 967_993.
39. Hy_zn_y, M., Bahrami, A., Klompmaker, A. A., Yazdi, M., Portell, R. W. & Neumann, C. 2013. The fossil record of Glypturus (Decapoda: Axiidea: Callianassidae) revisited with additional observations and description of a new species. Swiss Journal of Palaeontology, 132, 129_139.
40. Jagt, J. W. M., Fraaije, R. H. B., Van Bakel, B. W. M. & Artal, P. 2010. Necrocarcinus ornatissimus Forir, 1887, and Prehepatus werneri Fraaye and Collins, 1987 (Upper Maastrichtian, the Netherlands) revisited, with notes on other Cretaceous dynomenid crabs (Decapoda, Brachyura). Crustaceana Monographs, 11, 173_195.
41. Jones, S. M. 1950. Geology of Gatun Lake and Vicinity, Panama. Geological Society of America Bulletin, 61, 893_922.
42. Jones, A. 2013. Population dynamics of Dakoticancer overanus from the Pierre Shale, South Dakota. MS thesis, Kent State University, Ohio, 117 pp.
43. Keen, A. M. 1971. Sea shells of tropical West America: marine mollusks from Baja California to Peru. Stanford University Press, Stanford, 1064 pp.
44. Keigwin, L. D. 1978. Pliocene closing of the Isthmus of Panama, based on biostratigraphic evidence from nearby Pacific Ocean and Caribbean Sea cores. Geology, 6, 630_634.
45. Kidwell, S. M. & Flessa, K. W. 1995. The quality of the fossil record: Populations, species, and communities. Annual Review of Ecology and Systematics, 24, 433_464.
46. Kirby, M. X., Jones, D. S. & MacFadden, B. J. 2008. Lower Miocene stratigraphy along the Panama Canal and its bearing on the Central American Peninsula. PLOS ONE, 3(7), e2791. doi:10.1371/journal.pone.0002791
47. Klingenberg, C. P. 2011. MorphoJ: an integrated software package for geometric morphometrics. Molecular Ecology Resources, 11, 353_357.

48. Klompmaker, A. A. 2013. Extreme diversity of decapod crustaceans from the mid-Cretaceous (late Albian) of Spain: Implications for Cretaceous decapod paleoecology. Cretaceous Research, 41, 150_185.
49. Klompmaker, A. A., Feldmann, R. M. & Schweitzer, C. E. 2012a. A hotspot for Cretaceous goniodromitids (Decapoda: Brachyura) from reef associated strata in Spain. Journal of Crustacean Biology, 32, 780_801.
50. Klompmaker, A. A., Feldmann, R. M., Robins, C. M. & Schweitzer, C. E. 2012b. Peak diversity of Cretaceous galatheoids (Crustacea, Decapoda) from northern Spain. Cretaceous Research, 36, 125_145.
51. Klompmaker, A. A., Karasawa, H., Portell, R. W., Fraaije, R. H. B. & Ando, Y. 2013. An overview of predation evidence found on fossil decapod crustaceans with new examples of drill holes attributed to gastropods and octopods. Palaios, 28, 599_613.
52. Klompmaker, A. A., Artal, P., Van Bakel, B. W. M., Fraaije, R. H. B. & Jagt, J. W. M. 2014. Parasites in the fossil record: A Cretaceous fauna with isopod-infested decapods crustaceans, infestation patterns through time, and a new ichnotaxon. PLOS ONE, 9(3), e92551. doi:10.1371/journal. pone.0092551
53. Kowalewski, M., Dyreson, E., Marcot, J. D., Vargas, J., Flessa, K. W. & Hallman, D. P. 1997. Phenetic discrimination of biometric simpletons: paleobiological implications of morphospecies in the lingulide brachiopod Glottidia. Paleobiology, 23, 444_469
54. Kowalewski, M. & Novack-Gottshall, P. 2010. Resampling methods in paleontology. Paleontological Society Papers, 16, 19_54.
55. Kronenberg, G. C. & Lee, H. G. 2007. Genera of American strombid gastropods (Gastropoda: Strombidae) and remarks on their phylogeny. The Veliger, 49, 256_264. Latreille, P. A. 1802. Histoire naturelle, g_en_erale et particuli_ere des crustac_es et des insectes. Tome 3. Dufart, Paris, 467 pp.
56. Leach, W. E. 1814. Crustaceology. Pp. 383_437 in D. Brewster (ed.) The Edinburgh Encyclopedia. Blackwood, Edinburgh.
57. Linnaeus, C. von. 1758. Systema Naturae per Regna tria Naturae, secundum classes, ordines, genera, species, cum characteribus, differentiis, synonymis, locis, ed. 10. 1, 1_824. Laurentii Salvii, Holmiae [Stockholm].
58. Lo_renthey, E. 1897. Adatok Magyarorsz_ag harmadkor_u r_akfaun _aj_ahoz. Mathematikai _es Term_eszettudom_anyi _ Ertesito, 15, 149_169.
59. Manning, R. B. 1987. Notes on western Atlantic Callianassidae (Crustacea: Decapoda: Thalassinidea). Proceedings of the Biological Society of Washington, 100, 386_401.
60. Manning, R. B. & Felder, D. L. 1991. Revision of the American Callianassidae (Crustacea: Decapoda: Thalassinoidea). Proceedings of the Biological Society of Washington, 104, 764_792.
61. Manning, R. B. & Tamaki, A. 1998. A new genus of ghost shrimp from Japan (Crustacea: Decapoda: Callianassidae). Proceedings of the Biological Society of Washington, 111, 889_892.
62. Mansfield, W. C. 1930. Miocene gastropods and scaphopods of the Choctawhatchee Formation. Florida Geological Survey Bulletin, 3, 1_189.
63. Mansfield, W. C. 1932. Miocene pelecypods of the Choctawhatchee Formation. Florida Geological Survey Bulletin, 8, 1_240.
64. Matson, G. G. & Clapp, F. G. 1909. A preliminary report on the geology of Florida with special reference to the stratigraphy. Florida Geological Survey Annual Report, 2, 25_173.
65. McNamara, K. J. 2001. Importance of heterochrony. Pp. 180_188 in D. E. G. Briggs & P. R. Crowther (eds) Palaeobiology II. Wiley-Blackwell, Malden.
66. Milne-Edwards, A. 1870. R_evision du genre Callianassa (Leach) et description de plusieurs esp_eces nouvelles de ce groupe faisant partie de la collection du mus_eum. Nouvelles Archives du Mus_eum d'Histoire naturelle, Paris, 6, 75_101.
67. Montes, C., Cardona, A., McFadden, R., Mor_on, S. E., Silva, C. A., Restrepo-Moreno, S., Ram_ırez, D. A., Hoyos, N., Wilson, J., Farris, D., Bayona, G. A., Jaramillo, C. A., Valencia, V., Bryan, J. & Flores, J. A. 2012. Evidence for middle Eocene and younger land emergence in central Panama: Implications for Isthmus closure. Geological Society of America Bulletin, 124, 780_799.

68. Noetling, F. 1885. Uber Crustaceen aus dem Terti€ar Aegyptens. Sitzungsberichte der Koniglichen Preussischen Akademie der Wissenschaften, 26, 487_500, pl. 4.
69. Orbigny, A. d' 1845. Mollusques. Pp. 380 in R. de la Sagra (ed.) Histoire naturelle de l'ile de Cuba, Vol. 2. Bertrand, Paris.
70. Orbigny, A. d' 1846. Voyage dans l'Am_erique M_eridionale. Mollusques. Bertrand, Paris, 758 pp.
71. PaleoBiology Database. 2013. http://fossilworks.org, accessed 16 November 2013.
72. Philippi, R. A. 1844. Venus Tab. II. Abbildungen und Beschreibungen neuer oder wenig gekannter Conchylien, 1(5), 5_7, pl. 2. Fischer, Cassel.
73. Poore, G. C. & Suchanek, T. H. 1988. Glypturus motupore, a new callianassid shrimp (Crustacea: Decapoda) from Papua New Guinea with notes on its ecology. Records of the Australian Museum, 40, 197_204.
74. Posey, M. H. 1986. Predation on a burrowing shrimp: distribution and community consequences. Journal of Experimental Marine Biology and Ecology, 103, 143_161.
75. Powys, W. L. 1835. Characters of new species of shells collected by Mr. Cuming. Proceedings of the Zoological Society of London, 3, 94_96.
76. Portell, R. W., Polites, G. L. & Schmelz, G. W. 2006. Mollusca _ Shoal River Formation (middle Miocene). Florida Fossil Invertebrates, 9, 1_52.
77. Portell, R. W., Luque, J., Hendy, A. J. W. & Christy, J. 2012. Fidelity of marine invertebrate death and fossil assemblages in a coastal marine ecosystem, Bahia Bique, Panama. Geological Society of America, Abstracts with Programs, 44(7), 268.
78. Rabalais, N. N., Holt, S. A. & Flint, R. W. 1981. Mud shrimps (Crustacea, Decapoda, Thalassinidea) of the northwestern Gulf of Mexico. Bulletin of Marine Science, 31, 96_115.
79. Rathbun, M. J. 1919. West Indian Tertiary decapod crustaceans. Carnegie Institution of Washington Publication, 219, 159_184, pls 1_9.
80. Rathbun, M. J. 1935. Fossil Crustacea of the Atlantic and Gulf Coastal Plain. Geological Society of America, Special Paper, 2, i-viii, 1_160.
81. Robles, R., Tudge, C. C., Dworschak, P. C., Poore, G. C. B. & Felder, D. L. 2009. Molecular phylogeny of the Thalassinidea based on nuclear and mitochondrial genes. Pp. 309_326 in J. W. Martin, K. A. Crandall & D. L. Felder (eds) Decapod crustacean phylogenetics. Taylor & Francis/CRC Press, Boca Raton.
82. RÖding, P. F. 1798. Museum Boltenianum sive catalogus cimeliorum e tribus regnis naturæ quæ olim collegerat Joa. Fried Bolten, M. D. p. d. per XL. annos proto physicus Hamburgensis. Pars secunda continens conchylia sive testacea univalvia, bivalvia & multivalvia. Typis Johan Christi Trapii, Hamburg, viii C 119 pp.
83. Saint Laurent, M. de 1979. Sur la classification et la phylog_enie des Thalassinides: d_efinitions de la superfamille des Axioidea, de la sous-famille des Thomassiniinae et de deux genres nouveaux (Crustacea Decapoda). Comptes Rendus de l'Acad_emie des Sciences, Paris, S_erie D, 288, 1395_1397.
84. Sakai, K. 2005. Callianassoidea of the world (Decapoda: Thalassinidea). Crustaceana Monographs, 4, 1_285.
85. Sakai, K. 2011. Axioidea of the world and a reconsideration of the Callianassoidea (Decapoda, Thalassinidea, Callianassida). Crustaceana Monographs, 13, 1_520.
86. Schäfer, W. 1972. Ecology and Paleoecology of Marine Environments, Oertel, I., trans., G. Y. Craig (ed.). University of Chicago Press, Chicago, 568 pp.
87. Schweitzer, C. E., Iturralde-Vinent, M., Hetler, J. L. & Velez-Juarbe, J. 2006. Oligocene and Miocene decapods (Thalassinidea and Brachyura) from the Caribbean. Annals of Carnegie Museum, 75, 111_136.
88. Schweitzer, C. E., Velez-Juarbe, J., Martinez, M., Hull, A. C., Feldmann, R. M. & Santos, H. 2008. New Cretaceous and Cenozoic Decapoda (Crustacea: Thalassinidea, Brachyura) from Puerto Rico, United States Territory. Bulletin of the Mizunami Fossil Museum, 34, 1_15.
89. Shimoda, K., Wardiatno, Y., Kubo, K. & Tamaki, A. 2005. Intraspecific behaviors and major cheliped sexual dimorphism in three congeneric callianassid shrimp. Marine Biology, 146, 543_557.

90. Sowerby, G. B. 1833a. Characters of new species of shells from the collection formed by Mr. Cuming on the western coast of South America, and among the islands of the South Pacific Ocean. Proceedings of the Zoological Society of London, 1833, 16_22.
91. Sowerby, G. B. 1833b. Characters of new species of shells forming part of the collection made by Mr. Cuming on the western coast of South America, and among the islands of the South Pacific Ocean. Proceedings of the Zoological Society nof London, 1833, 82_85.
92. Sowerby, G. B. 1833c. Characters of new species of shells from the collection formed by Mr. Cuming on the western coast of South America and among the islands of the South Pacific Ocean. Proceedings of the Zoological Society of London, 1833, 34_38.
93. Starzyk, N., Krzemi_nska, E. & Krzemi_nski, W. 2011. Intraspecific variation in the Jurassic crab Bucculentum bucculentum (Decapoda: Homolodromioidea: Bucculentidae). Neues Jahrbuch f€ur Geologie und Pal€aontologie, Abhandlungen, 260, 203_210.
94. Starzyk, N., Krzemi_nska, E. & Krzemi_nski, W. 2012. A new crab species from the Oxfordian of Poland (Decapoda: Brachyura: Goniodromitidae). Neues Jahrbuch f€ur Geologie und Pal€aontologie, Abhandlungen, 263, 143_153.
95. Stempien, J. A. 2005. Brachyuran taphonomy in a modern tidalflat environment: Preservation potential and anatomical bias. Palaios, 20, 400_410.
96. Stimpson, W. 1866. Descriptions of new genera and species of macrurous Crustacea from the coasts of North America. Proceedings of the Chicago Academy of Sciences, 1, 46_48.
97. Todd, A. J. & Collins, J. S. H. 2005. Neogene and Quaternary crabs (Crustacea, Decapoda) collected from Costa Rica and Panama by members of the Panama Paleontology Project. Bulletin of the Mizunami Fossil Museum, 32, 53_85.
98. Toula, F. 1911. Die jungterti€are Fauna von Gatun am Panamakanal. Jahrbuch der kaiserlich-k€oniglichen Geologischen Reichanstalt Wien, 61, 487_530.
99. Tudge, C. C., Poore, G. C. B. & Lemaitre, R. 2000. Preliminary phylogenetic analysis of generic relationships within the Callianassidae and Ctenochelidae (Decapoda: Thalassinidea: Callianassoidea). Journal of Crustacean Biology, 20, Special Issue 2, 129_149.
100. Vaugelas, J. de & Saint Laurent, M. de 1984. Premi_eres donn_ees sur l'_ecologie de Callichirus laurae de Saint Laurent sp. nov. (Crustac_e d_ecapode Callianassidae): son action bioturbatrice sur les formations s_edimentaires du golfe d'Aqaba (Mer Rouge). Comptes Rendus des S_eances de l'Acad_emie des Sciences, Paris, S_erie 3, Sciences de la Vie, 298(6), 147_152.
101. Vergara-Solana, F. J., Garc_ıa-Rodr_ıguez, F. J. & De La Cruz- Ag€uero, J. 2013. Interspecific comparison of growth and shape within Diapterus (Gerreidae: Perciformes) using geometric morphometrics. Journal of Ichthyology, 53, 445_454.
102. Webster, M. 2007. Ontogeny and evolution of the Early Cambrian trilobite genus Nephrolenellus (Olenelloidea). Journal nof Paleontology, 81, 1168_1193.
103. Withers, T. H. 1924. Decapod crustaceans from the Oligocene of Anguilla. Annals and Magazine of Natural History, Series 9, 14, 225_233, pl. 6.
104. Woodring, W. P. 1957. Geology and paleontology of Canal Zone and adjoining parts of Panama. U.S. Geological Survey Professional Paper, 306(A), 1_145.
105. Zelditch, M. L., Swiderski, D. L., Sheets, H. D. & Fink, W. L. 2004. Geometric morphometrics for biologists: a primer. Elsevier Academic Press, San Diego, 443 pp

CHAPTER 2

Virtual reconstruction of endocast anatomy in early ray-finned fishes (Osteichthyes, Actinopterygii)

Author(s): Sam Giles and Matt Friedman

Department of Earth Sciences, University of Oxford, Oxford OX1 3AN, UK

ABSTRACT

Cranial endocasts, infillings of the skeletal void that once contained the brain and associated soft tissues, represent detailed anatomical structures that have long been the focus of paleontological investigation. We applied computed tomographics (CTs) in order to generate endocast models for the Paleozoic actinopterygian fishes *Mimipiscis* and *Kentuckia*, which serve as key representatives of anatomically primitive, early ray fins in analyses of early vertebrate relationships. The resultant endocranial models generally corroborate existing accounts of endocranial anatomy in these genera, drawn from descriptions of the inner face of the brain cavity. However, the endocasts also provide new anatomical details, the most significant of which are the presence in *Mimipiscis* of widely divergent olfactory tracts, small optic lobes, and anterior and posterior semicircular canals that extend dorsal to the roof of the endocranial chamber. By contrast, *Kentuckia* possesses a single, straight olfactory tract, wide optic lobes, and anterior and posterior semicircular canals that do not reach the dorsal surface of the endocast. In each of these features, *Kentuckia* resembles stratigraphically younger actinopterygians such as *Lawrenciella* and *Kansasiella*, whereas *Mimipiscis* more closely resembles sarcopterygians and other outgroups. This character distribution provides further support for earlier phylogenetic interpretations of these genera.

1. INTRODUCTION

THE OCCURRENCE of so-called "fossil brains" has fascinated vertebrate paleontologists since the earliest reports of such structures in the 1800s (e.g., Owen, 1841; Marsh, 1874; Owen, 1875; Moodie, 1915). When found, preserved brain and other nervous tissues are rich sources of morphological information, but such remains are exceedingly rare in the fossil record and sometimes difficult to interpret (Trinajstic et al., 2007; Pradel et al., 2009; Pradel, 2010). More typically, the sediment-filled void within the neurocranium provides the only clues about gross brain architecture. Such endocasts have been described for a diversity of groups (see discussion in Jerison, 1973; Coates, 1999; Walsh and Knoll, 2011), with Paleozoic fishes receiving considerable attention due to the early application of tomographic techniques by Erik Stensiö and other members of the 'Stockholm school' to a range of early vertebrate fossils (Stensiö, 1927, 1963a, 1963b; Jarvik, 1980).

Two key limitations apply to the study of neuroanatomy through the use of endocasts. The first of these arises from the mismatch between the endocast and brain in many groups of vertebrates. The brains of modern chondrichthyans and lobe-finned fishes can occupy as little as 1% of their associated cavities (Millot and Anthony, 1965; Kruska, 1988; Pradel, 2010), suggesting this disagreement might be primitive for jawed vertebrates. Important exceptions to this generality include birds, mammals, and, apparently, early ray-finned fishes (Edinger, 1929; Jerison, 1973). The high fidelity of brain anatomy captured by fossil actinopterygian endocasts is thought to reflect the presence of only a single layer of meningeal tissue separating the brain from the surrounding bone (Bjerring, 1991; Coates, 1999). This arrangement, combined with a relative abundance of well-preserved braincases (e.g., Nielsen, 1942; Rayner, 1951; Poplin, 1974; Schaeffer and Dalquest, 1978; Gardiner, 1984; Coates, 1998; Hamel, 2005), makes stratigraphically early fossil ray-finned fishes ideal targets for neuroanatomical study.

The second limitation associated with the study of vertebrate endocasts reflects the logistical difficulty in obtaining them. In the case of early ray-finned fishes, previous studies have often relied on the chance finding of ideally positioned or preserved specimens (e.g., Eastman, 1908; Moodie,

1915; Rayner, 1951; Coates, 1999). Although this permits description without recourse to more invasive procedures, such circumstances often allow only a cursory description of one face of the endocast or internal wall of the endocranial cavity (e.g., Eastman, 1908). More detailed approaches available to past researchers required a fossil to be serially destroyed and studied either through Sollas' grinding method (Sollas, 1904) or Poplin's more recent microtome technique (Poplin and de Ricqlès, 1970). In addition to being time-consuming, the destructive nature of these methods means that the specimen cannot be revisited, and the author's anatomical interpretations can only be corroborated through examination of original sections or associated photographs. Furthermore, such records are fragile and are prone to damage, as are the large wax models that are based upon them.

Virtual paleontology, through the use of computed tomographic (CT) techniques, provides a solution to the problems associated with mechanical tomographic techniques. Non-destructive CT methods generate datasets and resulting models that are long-lasting and portable (providing the files are stored in a way that can be accessible in the long term; Sutton et al., 2012). The results of such techniques are repeatable in the sense that the data can be revisited and the resultant hypotheses retested, and models can be digitally manipulated, sectioned and redescribed, with the ability to return to the original material as required. Furthermore, CT methods can be used to reinvestigate taxa previously studied via destructive or non-invasive methods, and to test existing interpretations in the literature (e.g., Gai et al., 2011). Importantly, specimens that were previously dismissed as too rare or fragile for destructive investigation can now be "virtually" dissected and studied, all in a process that takes days rather than decades.

Here we apply CT techniques to *Mimipiscis toombsi* Gardiner and Bartram, 1977, and *Kentuckia deani* Eastman, 1908, two Paleozoic ray-finned fishes that serve as key exemplars in analyses of interrelationships among early actinopterygians (Gardiner, 1984; Gardiner and Schaeffer, 1989; Coates, 1999; Arratia and Cloutier, 2004; Gardiner et al., 2005; Friedman and Blom, 2006; Long et al., 2008; Choo, 2011) and among Paleozoic gnathostomes more generally (Zhu et al., 1999, 2006; Friedman, 2007; Brazeau, 2009; Zhu et al., 2009; Davis et al., 2012). This prominence in phylogenetic analyses stems from the Late Devonian (Frasnian) and Mississippian (Tournaisian–Visean) age of these species, along with the fact that both preserve endoskeletal and dermal components of the skull in great detail.

The endocranial cavities of *Mimipiscis* Choo, 2011 and *Kentuckia* Rayner, 1951 have previously been described in the literature, and mid-sagittal sections through the endocavity have been presented for both (Fig. 1). This contribution provides the first endocast reconstructions for these taxa, which serve as a check on previous structural accounts (online

Supplemental Data file 1) and the phylogenetic interpretations drawn from them.

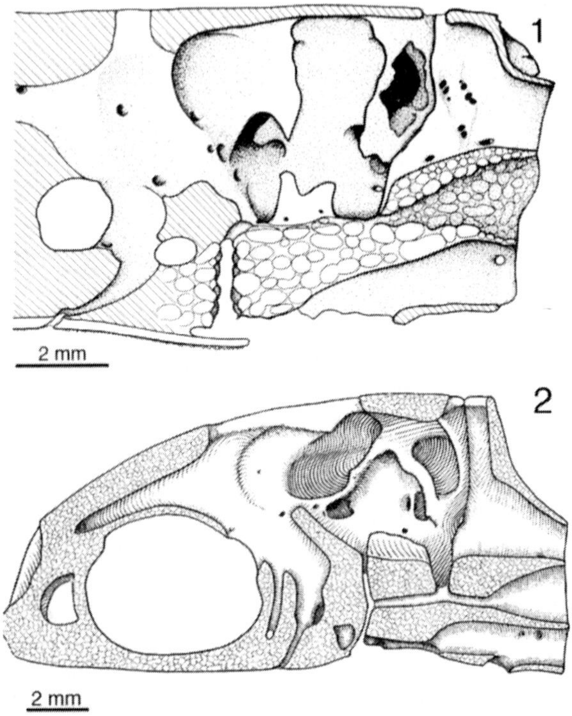

Figure 1—Existing illustrations of the cranial cavity of Mimipiscis toombsi Gardiner and Bartram, 1977 and Kentuckia deani Eastman, 1908. 1, sagittal section through post-ethmoid region of neurocranium of Mimipiscis toombsi; from Gardiner (1984, fig. 26); 2, sagittal section through neurocranium of Kentuckia deani; modified from Rayner (1951, fig. 9).

2. MATERIALS AND METHODS

2.1 Materials and taxonomic background

The first specimen examined is the near-complete skull roof and braincase of a large individual of *Mimipiscis* (Natural History Museum, London, UK [NHMUK] PV P.53247). The specimen is from the Gogo Formation, Western Australia, which is dated as late Givetian–early Frasnian on the basis of conodont biostratigraphy (Long and Trinajstic, 2010). The nodule-bearing horizons of the Gogo Formation lie within the *transitans* zone and are therefore of early Frasnian age. Originally described as *Mimia toombsi* (Gardiner and Bartram, 1977), *Mimipiscis* was erected as a replacement for the preoccupied *Mimia* Evans, 1953 by Choo (2011). He also recognized two distinct species of *Mimipiscis*: the type species *M. toombsi*, and the new species *M. bartrami* Choo, 2011. In his review of Gogo actinopterygian material housed at NHMUK, Choo regarded NHMUK PV P.53247 as *M. toombsi*. The specimen measures approximately 25 mm in length from snout to back of occiput and 15 mm at its widest point (Fig. 2.1). The specimen was previously acid prepared to remove surrounding matrix, and its dorsal surface embedded in a thin resin block. Although some sediment remains in the dorsal-most parts, the brain cavity itself is largely free of infillings and is preserved as void space.

Two individuals of *Kentuckia deani* were examined, both of which are deposited at Museum of Comparative Zoology, Harvard University, Cambridge, Massachusetts, U.S.A. (MCZ). These specimens derive from the New Providence Shale Member of the Stockdale Formation of Kentucky, U.S.A., which is referred to as the Waverley Shales in older accounts. This unit has been dated to the latest Tournaisian or early Visean on the basis of ammonoids and conodonts (Work and Mason, 2003). First named as *Rhadinichthys deani* Eastman, 1908, actinopterygians from the New Providence Shale Member were subsequently transferred to the new genus *Kentuckia* by Rayner (1951). She referred all but one of the specimens to *K. deani*, with one larger individual (MCZ 5257) identified as *Kentuckia* sp. A further species, *K. hlavini* Dunkle, 1964, was placed in the genus based on an articulated specimen from the Late Devonian (Famennian) Cleveland Shale Member of the Ohio Shale Formation. Dunkle (1964) himself noted that this attribution was far from certain, and we note that there are conspicuous differences between this older species and specimens from the Stockdale Formation. Following Friedman and Blom (2006), we do not regard *K. hlavini* as belonging to the genus *Kentuckia*, and advise against the use of composite codings for the genus that draws on evidence from both species (e.g., Arratia and Cloutier, 2004).

The first specimen of *Kentuckia* studied here (MCZ 8361) is contained within a broken nodule, splitting the fossil along an oblique mid-sagittal plane (Fig. 2.3, 2.4). The fossil represents a large individual, measuring 30 mm from the snout to the back of the skull. As internal parts of the cranium are visible, this specimen was one of two used by Rayner (1951) to describe the cranial cavity of *Kentuckia*. The second specimen (MCZ 5226) is contained within an unbroken nodule, the top of which has been prepared away to reveal the dorsal surface of the skull roof (Fig. 2.2). This individual is smaller than the first. The exposed part of the skull roof (from anterior margin of frontals to posterior margin of dermopterotics) measures 15 mm. A complete braincase and parasphenoid is preserved within the nodule. The two specimens exhibit clear morphological differences (see below), but we retain them within *Kentuckia* pending a much-needed taxonomic review of the genus. Specimen numbers are used when describing to morphological differences between these individuals.

Figure 2—Photographs of specimens used in this study. 1, Mimipiscis toombsi NHMUK PV P.53247; 2, Kentuckia deani MCZ 5226; 3, Kentuckia deani MCZ 8361, part; 3, Kentuckia deani MCZ 8361 counterpart.

2.1.1 Tomographic methods

All three specimens were scanned at the Imaging and Analysis Centre of NHMUK using a Metris X-Tek HMX ST 225 CT System with a 2,000 × 2,000 pixel detector panel. The two halves of the nodule comprising MCZ 8361 were secured together with a rubber band during scanning and 3,142 projections were made for each specimen. Other scan parameters are as follows: NHMUK PV P.53247: 150 kV, 169 μA, 1 mm thick copper filter, voxel size 27 μm; MCZ 8361: 210 kV, 200 μA, 2 mm thick copper filter, voxel size 26.5 μm; MCZ 5226: 210 kV, 200 μA, 2 mm thick copper filter, voxel size 14.5 μm.

2.2 Data segmentation and three-dimensional rendering

Following scanning, the resulting files ("vol") were manipulated in Avizo 7.1 (VSG Inc., Burlington, Massachusetts, U.S.A.). A workflow for the following method is provided in online Supplemental Data file 2. The segmentation editor in Avizo was used to generate a new label field. Bone material, distinguishable from the surrounding air by its different X-ray attenuation, visible as gray-values, was selected and added to a new mask. The mask was then locked, and the blow tool used to segment the void space representing the endocast, cranial nerves and canals. As this tool is semi-automated, it removes an element of worker subjectivity. This method can only be used where the tissue of interest is well mineralized and of a sufficiently different contrast than the surrounding matrix. Where this is not the case, as in some parts of MCZ 5226, segmentation must be completed by hand.

Once segmentation was complete, three-dimensional rendering was achieved by generating a surface view. The data object was saved ("ply" file) and exported to Blender (blender.org) for image and video acquisition (Garwood and Dunlop, 2014). The right side of the endocast of MCZ 5226 was resolved to a higher degree of completeness, but in order to follow standard practice when imaging endocasts this image has been flipped horizontally so as to resemble the left side of the endocast. Interpretive diagrams were drafted from virtual models. An animation of the endocast of *Mimipiscis* NHMUK PV P.53247 (online Supplemental Data file 3) and of *Kentuckia* MCZ 8361 (online Supplemental Data file 4) is provided. PLY 3D files of the endocast surfaces are also available (*Mimipiscis* NHMUK PV P.53247, online Supplemental Data file 5; *Kentuckia* MCZ 8361, online Supplemental Data file 6; *Kentuckia* MCZ 8361, online Supplemental Data file 7). Such files can be easily viewed and manipulated in free programs such as Meshlab (www.meshlab.sourceforge.net; Cignoni et al., 2008).

2.3 Comparative materials

The morphology of the endocasts of *Mimipiscis* and *Kentuckia* was compared with descriptive accounts of this structure in other extinct and extant jawed vertebrates (online Supplemental Data file 1). Particular emphasis was placed on Paleozoic actinopterygians: *Kansasiella* Poplin, 1974, *Lawrenciella* Poplin, 1984 (Hamel, 2005; Hamel and Poplin, 2008), *Mesopoma* Traquair, 1890 (Coates, 1999) and Paleozoic sarcopterygian fishes: *Diplocercides* Stensiö, 1922 (Jarvik, 1954; Stensiö, 1963b; Jarvik, 1980), *Dipnorhynchus* Jaekel, 1927 (Thomson and Campbell, 1971; Campbell and Barwick, 1982, 2000), *Ectosteorachis* Cope, 1880 (Romer, 1937), *Eusthenopteron* Whiteaves, 1881 (Bjerring, 1971; Jarvik, 1980); *Youngolepis* Chang and Yu, 1981 (Chang, 1982). Extant actinopterygians used for comparison are *Polypterus* Lacépède, 1803 (Senn, 1976; Nieuwenhuys, 1982); *Acipenser* Linneaus, 1758 (Nieuwenhuys, 1982; Rupp and Northcutt, 1998; Gómez et al., 2009); *Amia* Linneaus, 1766 (Nieuwenhuys, 1982); and *Lepisosteus* Linneaus, 1758 (Balfour and Parker, 1882).

2.4 Anatomical abbreviations

Acv, canal for anterior cerebral vein; ant.amp, ampulla of anterior semicircular canal; asc, anterior semicircular canal; aur, cerebellar auricle; bhc, bucco-hypophysial canal; b.oc.a, canal for branch of occipital artery; c.c, crus commune; ccc, communication between cranial cavity and notochordal canal; c.co, cerebellar corpus; die, diencephalon; esc, external semicircular canal; ext.amp, ampulla of external semicircular canal; ica, canal for internal carotid artery; l.c.c, lateral cranial canal; ldv, canal for longitudinal dorsal vein; mcv, canal for middle cerebral vein; nc, nasal capsule; olf.b, olfactory bulb; oof, otico-occipital fissure; opt.f, optic fenestra; opt.l, optic lobe; pdf, posterior dorsal fontanelle; pin.f, pineal foramen (anterior dorsal fontanelle); pit.f, pituitary fenestra; post.amp, ampulla of posterior semicircular canal; psc, posterior semicircular canal; sac, sacculus; s.oph.a, canal for small ophthalmic artery (branch of anterior cerebral artery); spio, canal for spino-occipital nerve; s.su, sinus superior; s.v, saccus vasculosus; tel, telencephalon; v.fon, vestibular fontanelle; I, canal for olfactory nerve; III, canal for oculomotor nerve; IV, canal for trochlear nerve; V, canal for trigeminal nerve; Vprof, canal for profundus nerve; VI, canal for abducens nerve; VII, canal for facial nerve; VIIlat, canal for lateralis branch of facial nerve; IX, canal for glossopharyngeal nerve; X, canal for vagus nerve. Dotted lines in figures indicate unresolved regions.

3. ANATOMICAL DESCRIPTION: MIMIPISCIS

3.1 General endocast morphology

The endocast is long and narrow, with elongate, anterolaterally-directed olfactory tracts (I, Figs. 3–5). The endocast of *Mimipiscis* has unusual proportions relative to that of other early extant and extinct actinopterygians listed above. The forebrain (excluding olfactory tracts) accounts for less than 20% of the total length, as opposed to the more usual 25–30%, and the hindbrain takes up over 60% of total brain length rather than around 50%.

3.2 Forebrain

This region of the endocast corresponds to the diencephalon, telencephalon and olfactory bulbs. The separation between the diencephalon (die) and the mesencephalon (mes) is marked by a constriction dorsally and laterally (Figs. 3, 4), and the diencephalon and telencephalon (tel) are continuous. As in most primitive extant and extinct actinopterygians, such as *Polypterus*, *Acipenser*, and *Lawrenciella*, the olfactory bulbs (olf.b, Figs. 3–5) are confluent with the telencephalon. However, it is almost impossible to distinguish two olfactory bulbs in *Mimipiscis*. This contrasts with the situation in the fossil taxa *Lawrenciella* and *Mesopoma*, as well as many extant chondrosteans and neopterygians, where the olfactory bulbs are well developed and clearly divided. The region of the olfactory bulbs is confined to the posterior part of the orbit (Coates, 1999). The roof of the telencephalic region is perforated by a single foramen for the anterior cerebral vein (acv, Figs. 3, 4). This anterior exit is unusual, as the more standard early actinopterygian arrangement is for it to exit from the roof of the diencephalon as in *Lawrenciella*, *Kentuckia*, and *Kansasiella*.

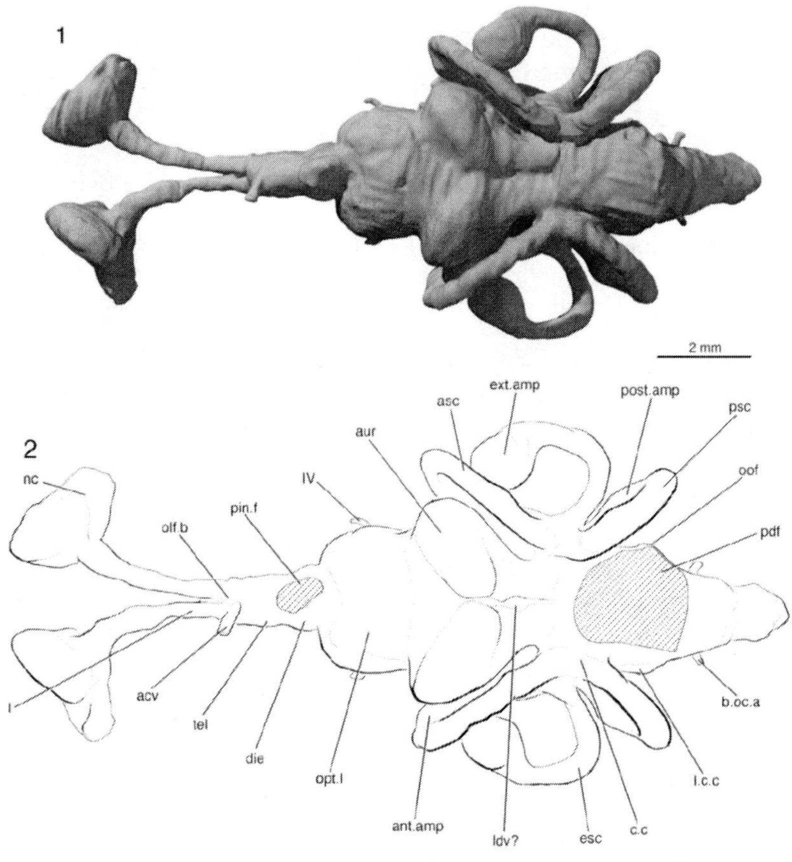

Figure 3—Reconstruction of the endocast of Mimipiscis toombsi, NHMUK PV P.53247, in dorsal view. 1, three-dimensional rendering of endocast; 2, interpretive drawing of endocast.

The diencephalon in NHMUK PV P.53247 is visible dorsally only as a slight swelling. Ventrally, however, it extends downwards and slightly posteriorly under the mesencephalon (die, Fig. 4), in a similar orientation to that of *Acipenser*. The diencephalon is mostly confined beneath the optic lobes, unlike in *Lawrenciella*, *Mesopoma*, and *Polypterus*, where it extends posteriorly beneath the cerebellar auricles. Anteriorly, the interorbital wall is unfinished and thus does not delimit the endocast (opt.f, Figs. 4, 5). The optic (II) nerves were likely transmitted through this opening, and foramina for the internal carotids are visible just beneath (ica, Fig. 5). Unlike in *Lawrenciella*, there is no groove or foramen for the small ophthalmic artery; the apparent opening in this region illustrated (but not identified) by Gardiner (1984, fig. 13) does not penetrate the bone. The hypophysial canal, carrying the pituitary vein, extends ventrally into the diencephalon. The saccus vasculosus is developed as a somewhat dorsally directed pouch on the caudal face of the diencephalon (s.v, Figs. 4, 5), and is of a similar relative size to that of *Lawrenciella* and *Kansasiella*, but smaller than that of *Mesopoma*. An anterior prolongation at the bottom of the diencephalic region marks the passage of the bucco-hypophysial canal through the parasphenoid (bhc, Figs. 4, 5).

As a whole, the endocranial cast of the forebrain in *Mimipiscis* is very narrow, being barely wider than the olfactory tracts. These tracts, transmitting the olfactory (I) nerves, diverge almost immediately upon leaving the olfactory bulbs and extend anterolaterally towards the nasal sacs (Figs. 3, 5). This differs from the condition seen in the fossils of almost all other early actinopterygians, where the two nerves share a common canal for most of their length. The anterolateral orientation of the tracts is also unusual, but is similar to that seen in sarcopterygian fishes such as *Youngolepis* and *Ectosteorachis*, as well as extant chondrosteans.

3.3 Midbrain

The mesencephalic region in *Mimipiscis* is about twice the width of the forebrain, but does not reach the maximum width of the cerebellum (Fig. 3). As with *Acipenser*, the two optic lobes (opt.l, Figs. 3–5) lack a well-defined median groove. In comparison to Carboniferous ray fins, the optic lobes of *Mimpiscis* are poorly developed. The root of the trochlear (IV) nerve pierces the lateral limit of each lobe (Fig. 4), a position somewhat higher than the corresponding foramen in *Lawrenciella*, *Mesopoma*, and *Kansasiella*. The oculomotor (III) nerve leaves the floor of each optic lobe and, as in *Lawrenciella*, bifurcates almost immediately to enter the orbit through two closely spaced foramina (III, Fig. 4).

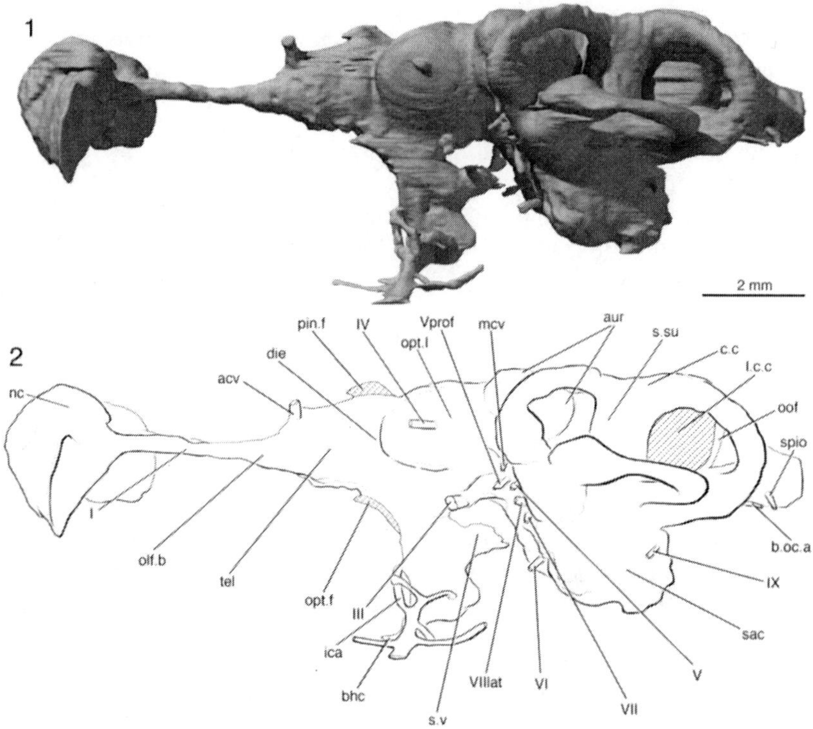

Figure 4—Reconstruction of the endocast of Mimipiscis toombsi, NHMUK PV P.53247, in left lateral view. 1, three-dimensional rendering of endocast; 2, interpretive drawing of endocast. The lateral cranial canal has been only been partially filled so as to avoid obscuring details of the labyrinth.

3.4 Hindbrain

This region of the endocast relates to the cerebellum and rhombencephalon. In *Mimpiscis*, the cerebellar auricles resemble those of *Acipenser* in being robust but short (aur, Figs. 3, 4). As in *Lawrenciella*, *Kansasiella*, and extant chondrosteans, they are separated from the optic lobes by a deep sulcus. In *Lawrenciella*, dorsal ridges within the sulcus are thought to be related to the middle cerebral vein. No such ridges are present in *Mimipiscis*; instead, a canal that exits from the bottom of the auricle and extends ventrally has been suggested to carry this vessel (Gardiner, 1984). A similar canal is reported in *Pteronisculus* White, 1933 (Nielsen, 1942), where it leaves the auricle and passes directly into the orbit above the trigeminofacialis chamber. Somewhat unusually, the canal in *Mimipiscis* appears to enter the trigeminofacialis chamber (mcv, Figs. 4,

5). Gardiner (1984) commented upon a similarly close relationship between the middle cerebral vein and trigeminal (V) nerve in teleosts, and it is likely that in *Mimipiscis* the vein entered the chamber and exited again almost immediately by way of an anterodorsally directed canal.

Relative to the placement seen in other ray fins, the auricles in *Mimipiscis* are positioned far anteriorly, with the anterior limits level with the ampulla of the anterior semicircular canal and the posterior extent no further than the external ampulla (Fig. 3). Dorsally, the auricles stand proud of the rest of the endocast, a condition uncommon in early fossil ray fins, as well as extant chondrosteans and neopterygians. It is hard to compare this with the condition seen in actinopterygian outgroups as the endocranial cavity typically does not conform well to the shape of the brain in this region. However, in *Ectosteorachis* and *Youngolepis*, there is a suggestion of an increase in depth of the endocavity in the region of the cerebellum. Similarly, in *Latimeria* Smith 1939, the cerebellum extends above the rest of the brain, although the auricles sit somewhat lower (Northcutt et al., 1978).

Beneath the auricles, the lateral limits of the endocast slope inwards to meet a short distance above the saccus vasculosus. This lateral wall is pierced by two foramina: the more medial for the anteriorly directed profundus (Vprof) nerve canal, and the more lateral for the trigeminal (V) nerve canal (Figs. 4, 5). The canal for the trigeminal nerve travels laterally to enter the trigeminofacialis chamber, intercepting and carrying the middle cerebral vein en route (see above). Lateral and slightly ventral to these two openings are two additional foramina. The more dorsal of these most likely transmitted the lateralis branch of the facial (VIIlat) nerve, which also travels into the trigeminofacialis chamber. The more ventral transmitted the facialis (VII) nerve ventrolaterally. The canal for the abducens (VI) nerve pierces the zygal plates and extends anterolaterally along the medial boundaries of the saccular recesses (Fig. 5). The glossopharyngeal (IX) nerve leaves the sacculus ventral to the ampulla for the posterior semicircular canal (Fig. 4).

A deep groove between the two auricles presumably marked the course of the longitudinal dorsal vein (ldv, Fig. 3; Coates, 1999). This groove extends posteriorly, but does not appear to continue forwards between the optic lobes, unlike the condition inferred for *Mesopoma*. There is no obvious cerebellar corpus projecting behind the auricles. The region posterior to the auricles is elongate and bilobed, and may represent the area octavolateralis. The lateral wall of the endocast between the sinus superior and oticocippital fissure is interrupted by a large foramen for the lateral cranial canal (l.c.c, Fig. 4). Although the canals are complete in the specimen, they have only been partially segmented so as to avoid obscuring any parts of the labyrinth. Behind the fissure the endocast sloped downwards to assume a cylindrical shape, from which canals issue for branches of the occipital arteries (b.oc.a, Figs. 3–5) and, further posteriorly, the spino-occipital nerves (spio, Figs. 3–5).

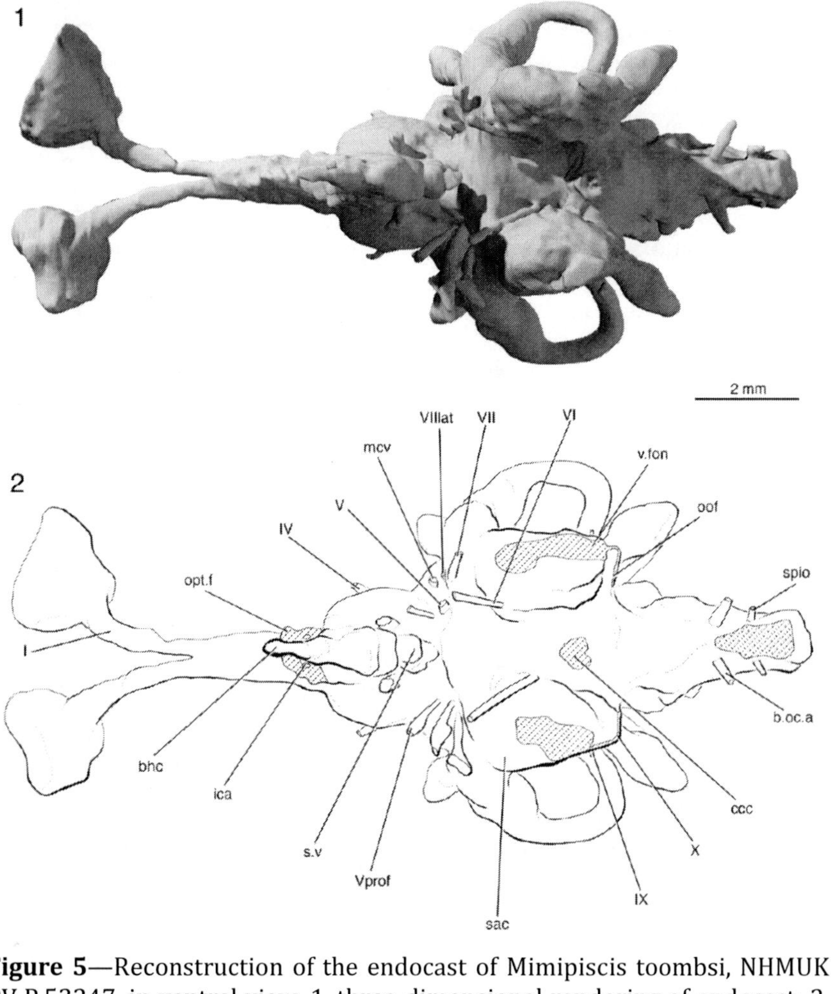

Figure 5—Reconstruction of the endocast of Mimipiscis toombsi, NHMUK PV P.53247, in ventral view. 1, three-dimensional rendering of endocast; 2, interpretive drawing of endocast.

3.5 Labyrinth

The overall morphology of the labyrinth region in *Mimipiscis* is as expected for an early actinopterygian (Figs. 3–5). The three semicircular canals (anterior, posterior, and external) are robust, with a relatively large separation between them and the lateral walls of the endocast. The sinus superior (s.su, Fig. 4) is wide and is underlain by a large saccular recess that lacks an obvious lagena (sac, Fig. 4). Despite being widespread among vertebrates, a separate lagenar pouch is also unknown in all other early actinopterygians, as well as in the extant *Acipenser*, *Amia*, and *Lepisosteus* (Popper, 1978; Mathiesen and Popper, 1987; Lovell et al., 2005). Its absence in early members of other groups, for example in some sarcopterygians (Jarvik, 1980; Platt et al., 2004) and chondrichthyans (de Burlet, 1934; Gauldie et al., 1987; Maisey, 2005, 2007; Pradel, 2010), suggests that a distinct lagenar pouch may have arisen independently several times in vertebrates. No otoliths are preserved within the saccular chambers of *Mimipiscis*, and were presumably dissolved during acid preparation, as otoliths have been found in other material examined by Gardiner (1984, p. 227). The curvature of the anterior and posterior canals is such that they rise above the level of the hindbrain, causing the crus commune to sit just above the level of the endocast roof (c.c, Fig. 4).

4. ANATOMICAL DESCRIPTION: KENTUCKIA

4.1 General endocast morphology

In both MCZ 5226 and MCZ 6381, the endocast is markedly less slender than that of *Mimipiscis* (Figs. 6–10). The relative proportions assumed are more typical of previously described endocasts of primitive extant and extinct ray-finned fishes (see references above); the forebrain constitutes around 25% of the total brain length and the hindbrain around 50%. Although the endocasts of the two specimens agree in these general proportions, they differ in a series of more specific features: the optic lobes are better developed and more spherical in MCZ 5226 than in MCZ 8361; the cerebellar auricles are proportionally longer in MCZ 5226 than in MCZ 8361; the posterior semicircular canal is more tightly curved and thus shorter in MCZ 8361 than MCZ 5226; and the canal for the third cranial nerve bifurcates in MCZ 5226 but remains undivided in MCZ 8361. These are reviewed in more detail in the relevant sections below.

4.2 Forebrain

Similar to in *Mimipiscis*, *Lawrenciella*, and *Kansasiella*, the cast of the forebrain of *Kentuckia* is narrow. The separation between the diencephalon (die) and the mesencephalon (mes) is marked by a constriction dorsally and laterally (Figs. 3, 4). As in *Mimipiscis*, olfactory bulbs cannot be identified in either MCZ 5226 or MCZ 8361, and it is difficult to distinguish between the diencephalon and telencephalon (Figs. 6, 9). The telencephalon can be identified with confidence only in MCZ 5226, where a slight bulge is visible laterally (tel, Fig. 10). In both *Kentuckia* specimens, the dorsal limit of the endocast is uncertain immediately in advance of the anterior dorsal fontanelle (pin.f, Fig. 9), and it seems likely that this region of the brain was not closely applied to the walls of the endocranial chamber. In MCZ 8361, a canal exits from the top of the diencephalic region. This corresponds to the single foramen for the anterior cerebral vein (acv, Figs. 6, 7). The bone in MCZ 5226 is poorly mineralized in this region, and no such passage is visible. In both specimens, the olfactory (I) nerves are carried through a single tract, which travels anteriorly before diverging into two anterolateral canals immediately before reaching the nasal capsules (Figs. 6, 9). Curiously, the shared tract extends ventrally as well as anteriorly (I, Figs. 7, 10). This is not reported in any other fossil actinopterygian, but is very similar to the condition in *Acipenser*.

The ventral portion of the diencephalon is poorly preserved in MCZ 8361, but can be described in more detail from MCZ 5226. A shared opening for the optic (II) nerves is visible anteriorly (opt.f), and above this lie two small anteriorly directed canals that likely transmitted the small ophthalmic arteries, as in *Lawrenciella* (s.oph.a, Fig. 10). In both specimens, the internal carotids (ica, Figs. 7, 10) extend downwards from the optic foramen. Posterior to this, the hypophysial stalk extends ventrally under the optic lobes, as in *Acipenser* and *Lepisosteus*, ending in the bucco-hypophysial canal (bhc, Fig. 10). The full extent of the saccus vasculosus is uncertain in either specimen of *Kentuckia*.

4.3 Midbrain

The mesencephalic region of the endocast is well developed, with the optic lobes over twice the width of the forebrain. Large optic lobes are known in *Mesopoma* and *Lawrenciella*, as well as extant chondrosteans and neopterygians. The lobes are relatively larger and more rounded in MCZ 5226 than in MCZ 8361, and extend dorsal to the more anterior parts of the endocast (opt.l, Figs. 6, 7, 9, 10). The trochlear (IV) nerve pierces the lobe in a slightly more ventral position than in *Mimipiscis*, although the oculomotor (III) nerve bifurcates before entering the orbits in the same way (III, Fig. 10). This bifurcation is not seen in MCZ 8361. The region between the optic lobes is occupied by a large anterior dorsal fontanelle (pin.f, Fig. 9), obscuring any median groove. In MCZ 5226 this extends from the front of the optic lobes to the posterior limit of the cerebellar auricles. This fontanelle has been traversed by a crack in MCZ 8361, and as a result much of the dorsal surface of the portion of the endocast relating to the mid- and hindbrain is obscured. A thin canal extends along the midline behind the fonanelle in MCZ 5226. Comparison with *Mesopoma* and teleosts (Zwehl, 1961; Coates, 1999) indicates that it transmitted the longitudinal dorsal vein (ldv, Fig. 9).

4.4 Hindbrain

The cerebellar region of the endocast is separated from the mesencephalon by a groove. Although this may have housed the middle cerebral vein (Hamel and Poplin, 2008), no supporting ridges are apparent. Dorsally, the cerebellar auricles display a similar morphology in both specimens of *Kentuckia*, extending from the ampulla of the anterior semicircular canal back to the crus commune of the anterior and posterior canals (aur, Figs. 6, 7, 9, 10). Rather than being laterally separated from the endocast, the anterior semicircular canal is set into a deep groove extending along the auricle, producing a ventral auricular lobe that continues towards the utriculus (Figs. 5, 6, 9). This unusual arrangement is seen elsewhere only in *Kansasiella*, where the auricles are so reduced that they only display this ventral lobe. The auricles are relatively larger in MCZ 5226 than in MCZ 8361, standing proud above the rest of the dorsal surface of the endocast.

The layout of the canals in the lateral region of the diencephalon is fairly similar in both specimens of *Kentuckia*. The most medial of the three canals leaves the lateral wall of the cranial cavity and extends laterally and slightly anteriorly to the trigeminofacialis chamber. This carried the profundus (Vprof) nerve. Its position is slightly more ventral in MCZ 5226. Two canals exit medial and ventral to the utriculus. The more dorsal of these is very short, and transmits the trigeminal (V) nerve and lateralis branch of the facial (VIIlat) nerve into the trigeminofacialis chamber (Fig. 8). The more ventral projects laterally to enter the orbit, and carried the facial (VII) nerve. The exit for the abducens (VI) nerve, on the anterior face of the sacculus, is visible only in MCZ 8361 (Fig. 8).

The posterior portion of the rhombencephalon is very poorly known in MCZ 8361, especially dorsally. The sinus superior (s.su) is incompletely resolved in both specimens, but appears to be similar in size to that of *Mimipiscis* and *Lawrenciella*, as is the saccular recess (sac). Only the upper portion of the saccular recess is known in detail, but it appears fairly extensive (sac, Figs. 7, 10), and a canal for the glossopharyngeal (IX) nerve exits the lateral edge of the sacculus in MCZ 8361 (Fig. 8). The opening for the lateral cranial canal is small (l.c.c, Figs. 7, 10), and appears to protrude through the posterior semicircular canal as a "pocket," as in *Lawrenciella*. The region is better resolved in MCZ 5226. As in *Boreosomus* Stensiö 1921 (Nielsen, 1942), *Mesopoma*, *Pteronisculus* (Nielsen, 1942), and *Polypterus*, the hind part of the cerebellum in this specimen of *Kentuckia* displays two lobes divided along the midline, and there is a suggestion that they are further subdivided transversely (c.co, Fig. 9). These lobes are smooth and confluent with the cerebellar auricles, and represent the cerebellar corpus. The endocast narrows to a cylinder behind the posterior dorsal fontanelle.

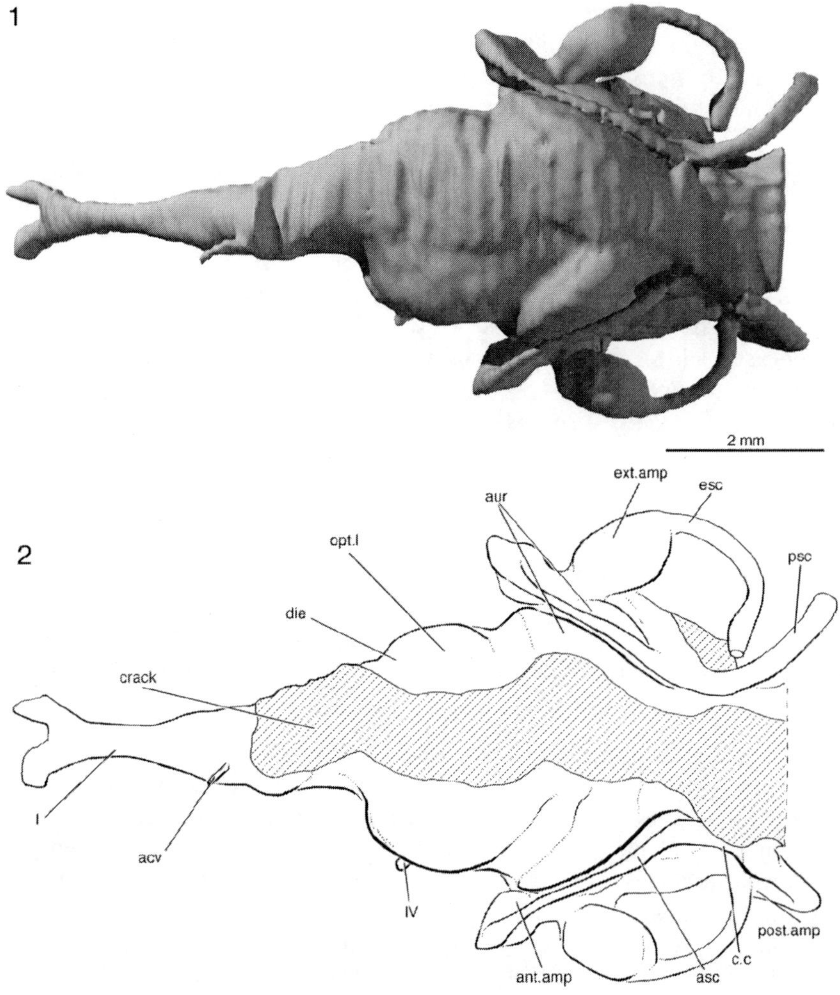

Figure 6—Reconstruction of the endocast of Kentuckia deani, MCZ 8361, in dorsal view. 1, three-dimensional rendering of endocast; 2, interpretive drawing of endocast

4.5 Labyrinth

At first glance, the morphology of the semicircular canals in MCZ 8361 and MCZ 5226 appears strikingly different. The canals in MCZ 8361 are very delicate and narrow in comparison to those of MCZ 5226. This, however, appears to be a preservational artifact; CT sections through the specimen reveal that the original bone material is not preserved. Instead, what is preserved is an infilling of the space that would have been occupied in life by the membranous labyrinth, a structure thinner than the osseus labyrinth preserved in MCZ 5226. As mentioned above, the anterior canal is set very closely into the auricle, appearing to divide it into two lobes (aur, Figs. 6, 7, 10). The ampullae of the anterior and external canals in MCZ 5226 are relatively larger than those of *Mimipiscis* and *Lawrenciella*, and the utriculus is much smaller than in *Mimipisicis*. All three canals in MCZ 8361 and MCZ 5226 are tightly curved and therefore short, as in *Lawrenciella* and *Kansasia*. The sinus superior is positioned below the upper surface of the endocast, and this gives the canals a flattened appearance, quite unlike the condition observe.

5. DISCUSSION

5.1 Validation of previous interpretations

The morphological data described in the previous section can be used to test the anatomical descriptions laid out by Gardiner (1984) for *Mimpiscis* and those of Moodie (1915), Rayner (1951) for *Kentuckia*.

The existing description of the endocast of *Mimipiscis* can largely be corroborated, but we are able to add several important features that have not previously been recognized. As part of his description of *Mimipiscis*, Gardiner included a short section on the morphology of the brain cavity, as well as referring to aspects of it elsewhere. He figured the dorsal structure of the endocast (anterior to the pineal foramen), but much of the morphology is obscured by the extension of the anterior myodome (Gardiner, 1984, figs. 33, 34). A sagittal section through the endocranial cavity was also illustrated (Gardiner, 1984, fig. 26). The description can largely be corroborated, with one or two exceptions in the region of the trigeminofacialis complex. Gardiner referred to the trigeminal (V) nerve and profundus (Vprof) nerve as entering the orbit independently but having a shared root, with the profundus branching from the anterior part of the facial canal. In fact, they appear to leave the cranial cavity through different openings and have entirely separate courses.

Consequently, the foramen referred to as "V" (fig. 26) can be reinterpreted as the opening for the root of the profundus nerve. The trigeminal nerve has a separate exit from the cranial cavity, which was misidentified by Gardiner (1984, fig. 26) as the lateralis branch of the facial nerve. The opening for the lateralis branch is not visible in sagittal section, being obscured from view by the ampulla for the anterior semicircular canal.

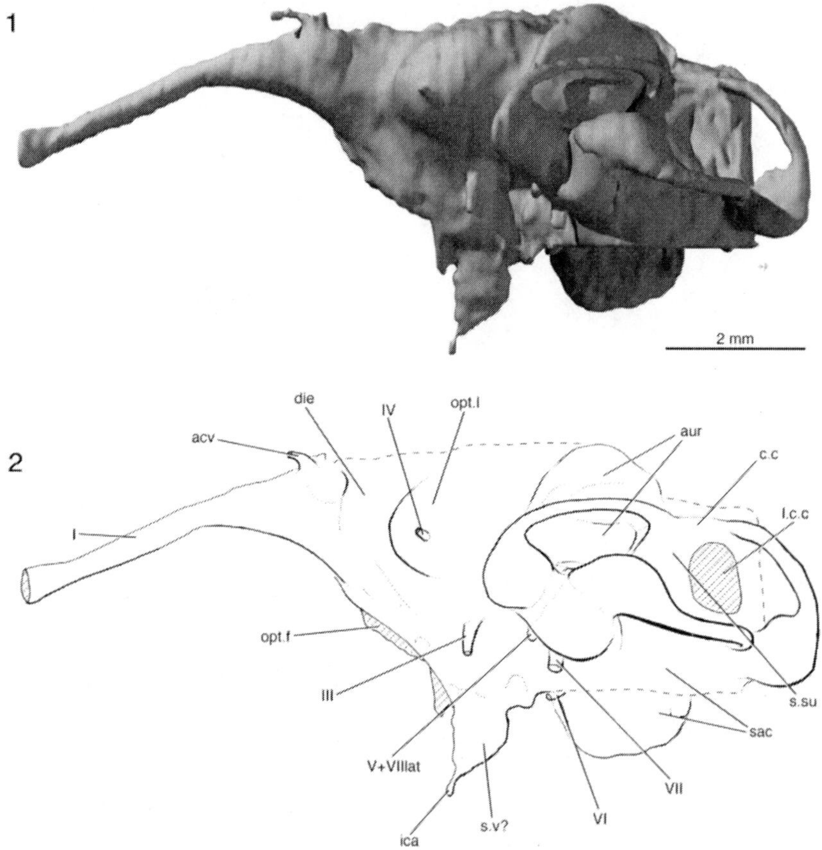

Figure 7—Reconstruction of the endocast of Kentuckia deani, MCZ 8361, in left lateral view. 1, three-dimensional rendering of endocast; 2, interpretive drawing of endocast. The pocket of the lateral cranial canal has been 'cut' to avoid obscuring parts of the labyrinth.

Gardiner's (1984) interpretation of the layout of nerves within the orbit is corroborated by our analysis. The middle cerebral vein enters the orbit via its own foramen in this specimen of *Mimipiscis*, situated dorsally and slightly anteriorly of the common opening for the trigeminal nerve and lateralis branch of the facial nerve.

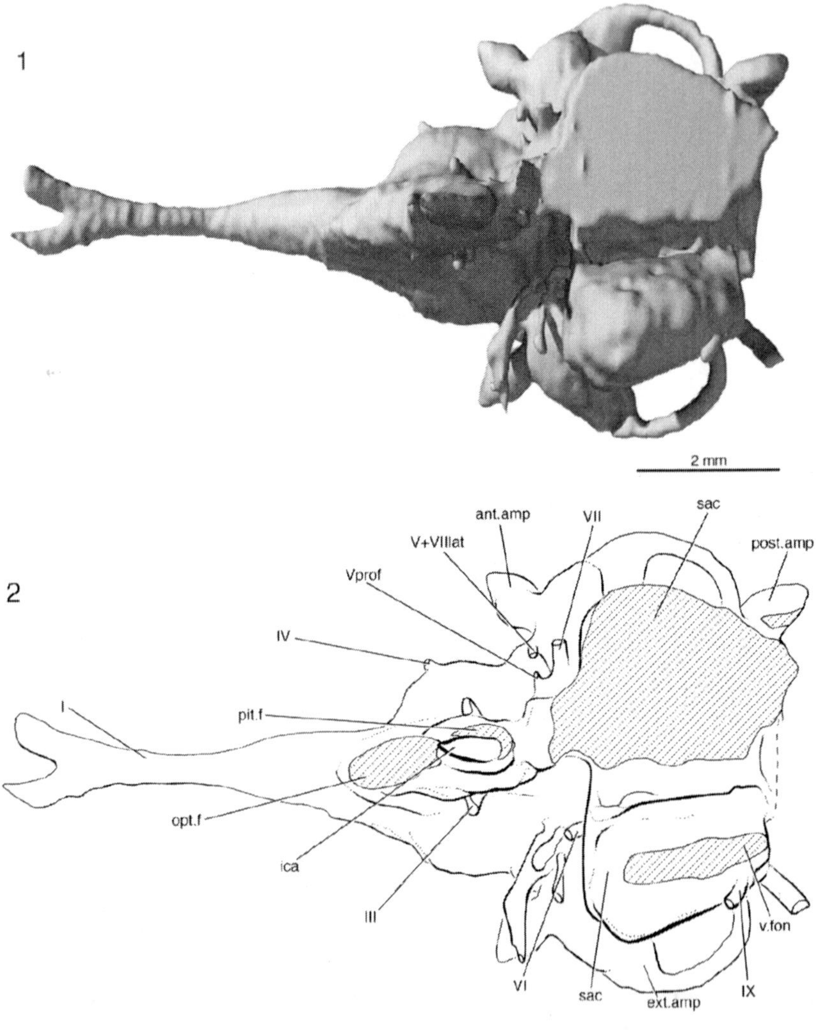

Figure 8—Reconstruction of the endocast of Kentuckia deani, MCZ 8361, in ventral view. 1, three-dimensional rendering of endocast; 2, interpretive drawing of endocast.

We are also able to correct some interpretations of the bony labyrinth. Gardiner (1984) described the posterior opening of the exterior semicircular canal as passing through the ampulla of the posterior canal, but it is clear that they enter the cranial cavity separately. This brings the structure in *Mimispicis* in line with that seen in *Kentuckia*, as well as the Triassic *Boreosomus* and *Pteronisculus* (Nielsen, 1942). A vertical separation between the external semicircular canal and posterior ampulla, with one opening sitting above the other, is evident in placoderms (Goujet, 1984) and chondrichthyans (Schaeffer, 1981; Maisey, 2007), as well as some sarcopterygians (e.g., *Chirodipterus*; Säve-Söderbergh, 1952). The alternative condition is seen in *Kansasiella* (Poplin, 1974) and a number of Triassic actinopterygians (Nielsen, 1942). On a more minor note, the recess for the saccus vasculosus is somewhat larger than that figured by Gardiner (1984, fig. 26).

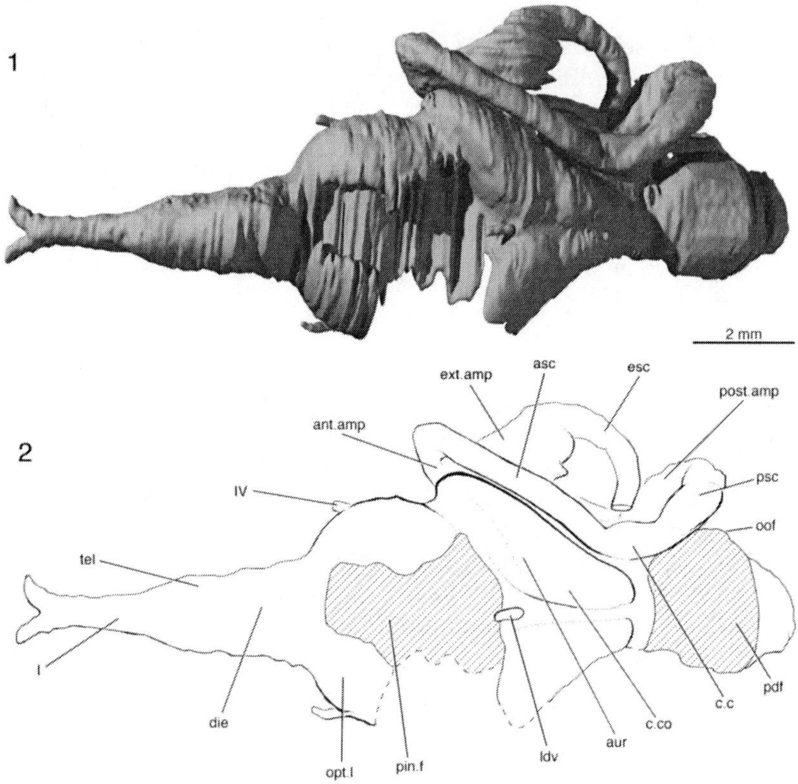

Figure 9—Reconstruction of the endocast of Kentuckia deani, MCZ 5226, in dorsal view. 1, three-dimensional rendering of endocast; 2, interpretive drawing of endocast.

This study is also able to confirm many of Rayner's tentative interpretations concerning the endocranial cavity of *Kentuckia* while revealing new morphological data concerning overall brain structure and proportions. We are also able to test the interpretations made by Moodie (1915) of the lectotype of *Kentuckia*, a natural endocranial cast. The written account of the endocranial cavity provided by Rayner is detailed, but only one figure (1951, fig. 9), a diagrammatic sagittal section through the braincase, provides illustration. While many of the interpretations are correct, the figure as a whole is misleading. The proportions of the braincase are incorrect, and the region behind the orbit needs to be stretched by approximately one third to reflect the true shape. Once the correct proportions are resolved, it becomes clear that the optic lobes are far larger than illustrated, and the arrangement of the utriculus and exits of the semicircular canals resembles that of *Mimipiscis* and other early ray-finned fishes. The root of the abducens (VI) nerve, which Rayner could not locate, emerges from the medial portion of the sacculus and travels forward to exit into the orbit.

Other minor amendments that can be made refer to openings that Rayner could not identify with certainty. The "deep hollow" (Rayner, 1951, fig. 9, "x") found in the loop of the posterior semicircular canal can be confirmed as the lateral cranial canal. A smaller pocket in the loop of the anterior canal is the ventral lobe of the cerebellar auricle, rather than part of the lateral cranial canal network. Segmentation of the complete course of the oculomotor (III) nerve confirms that the tract bifurcates distally to enter the orbit through two separate foramina in at least some specimens of *Kentuckia*, such as MCZ 5226.

As described and illustrated by Rayner, three canals leave the cranial cavity to enter the trigeminofacialis chamber before continuing into the orbit. The external configuration illustrated by Rayner (1951, fig. 8) largely matches that seen in MCZ 5226. The facial (VII) nerve canal (probably also carrying the trigeminal [V] nerve) is described as opening into the orbit from the floor of the trigeminofacialis chamber. This is largely accurate, although the opening is on the medial wall of the chamber rather than its roof. The profundus nerve (Vprof) enters the orbit via an opening just dorsal to the two oculomotor (III) foramina. Rayner's labeling of this opening in lateral view (1951, fig. 7) is misleading; the opening identified as "Vprof" is in fact a branch of the arterial/venous network. The true position of Vprof is somewhat more ventral, although no corresponding foramen is drawn in Rayner's figure.

The pattern of nerve exits from the cranial cavity proposed by Rayner is more difficult to ratify, particularly as the positioning of these canals differs between MCZ 5226 and MCZ 8361. This variation is even more apparent in sagittal section. Rayner's illustration (1951, fig. 9) identifies three exits: a canal for the facial nerve, leaving from the same region as the anterior ampulla; a slightly more anteriorly-placed canal for the profundus nerve; and the trigeminal nerve canal more anteriorly still. The relative position of these three nerves largely matches that of MCZ 5662, although the facial nerve exits the cranial cavity more medially than the exit from the ampulla shown by Rayner (1951, fig. 9).

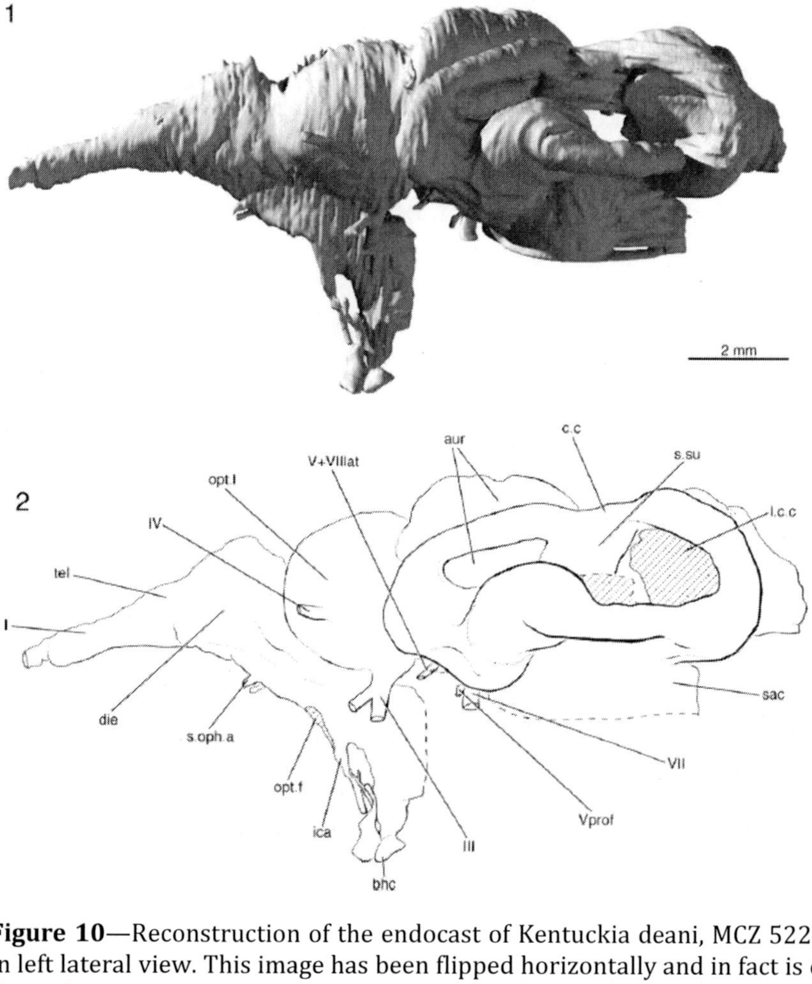

Figure 10—Reconstruction of the endocast of Kentuckia deani, MCZ 5226, in left lateral view. This image has been flipped horizontally and in fact is of the right side of the endocast. 1, three-dimensional rendering of endocast; 2, interpretive drawing of endocast. The pocket of the lateral cranial canal has been "cut" to avoid obscuring parts of the labyrinth.

This is not the case in MCZ 8361, where the canal for the trigeminal nerve does in fact exit from the region of the anterior ampulla. The facial nerve in MCZ 8361 exits more medially, and the canal for the profundus nerve is situated more anteriorly. Finally, the canal for the glossopharyngeal (IX) nerve exits the cranial cavity of MCZ 8361 considerably more ventrally than indicated by Rayner (1951, fig. 9). This region is not resolved in MCZ 5226, but the exit is assumed to be in a similar position.

The morphology of the lectotype (MCZ 5222) described by Moodie (1915, figs. 3, 4) largely matches that of our virtual endocast models. Despite the fact that many morphological details are obscured in the lectotype, Moodie's description can generally be corroborated, although his 'tuberculum acusticum' is in fact the bilobed cerebellum.

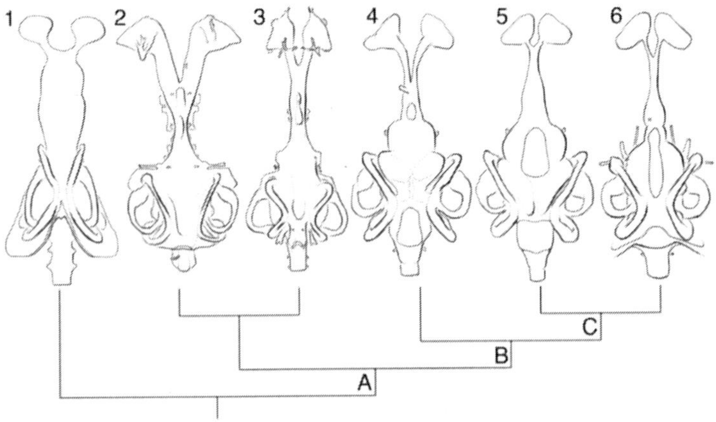

Figure 11—Cladogram showing distribution of potential apomorphies visible in the endocast, with an emphasis on osteichthyans, particularly actinopterygians. Cladogram based on Coates (1999), Hamel and Poplin (2008), and Zhu et al. (2009). Proposed endocast synapomorphies are drawn from this study and others (referenced accordingly). 1, Orthacanthus Agassiz, 1883, modified from Schaeffer, 1981; 2, Youngolepis, modified from Chang, 1982; 3, Eusthenopteron, modified from Jarvik, 1980; 4, Mimipiscis; 5, Kentuckia; 6, Lawrenciella, modified from Hamel and Poplin (2008). Node A: long olfactory tracts (Friedman and Brazeau, 2010); horizontal semicircular canal joins labyrinth level with the ampulla for the posterior semicircular canal (Davis et al., 2012). Node B: lateral cranial canal (Coates, 1999; although see Discussion); cerebral hemispheres formed by evagination of telencephalon (Nieuwenhuys, 1982). Node C: anteriorly directed olfactory tracts (Coates, 1999); olfactory nerves carried in a single tract; optic lobes as wide as cerebellum; crus commune of anterior and posterior semicircular canals ventral to endocranial roof.

5.2 Systematic and evolutionary implications

As well as representing critical tests of previous morphological interpretations of *Mimipiscis* and *Kentuckia*, the virtual endocasts produced by this study permit more direct comparison with similar reconstructions available for other early gnathostomes (Fig. 11). Although the endocasts of early fossil actinopterygians are thought to faithfully record brain structure (Edinger, 1929; Jerison, 1973; Bjerring, 1971; Coates, 1999), this is not the case for other groups of vertebrates. As a consequence, paleontological comparisons like those below are most accurately framed as being between the anatomy of endocasts rather than brains.

The endocasts of *Mimipiscis* and *Kentuckia* reveal characteristics consistent with previous phylogenetic placements of these genera. Their long olfactory tracts represent an osteichthyan synapomorphy (Friedman and Brazeau, 2010). The presence of a lateral cranial canal is thought to unite these genera with other actinopterans (Coates, 1999), although the discovery of a putative lateral cranial canal in *Meemannia*, *Psarolepis*, and *Ligulalepis* raises the possibility that this feature may be more widely distributed amongst osteichthyans (Zhu et al., 2010). At a finer phylogenetic scale, the endocasts of *Mimipiscis* and *Kentuckia* show some striking differences, especially in terms of overall geometry. The endocast of *Kentuckia* broadly resembles that of stratigraphically younger ray fins from the Pennsylvanian, particularly *Lawrenciella* (Hamel and Poplin, 2008) and *Kansasiella* (Poplin, 1974). All of these Carboniferous taxa are interpreted as branching from more crownward positions on the actinopteran stem than *Mimipiscis* (Coates, 1999; Gardiner et al., 2004). Our new endocast data supports this phylogenetic hypothesis by revealing generalized features shared by *Mimipiscis*, sarcopterygians and chondrichthyans, but which show apparently derived conditions in Carboniferous and younger actinopteran ray-finned fishes (Fig. 11). These relate to the morphology of the olfactory tracts, labyrinth, and mesencephalon.

As in sarcopterygians (e.g., Nieuwenhuys et al., 1977, fig. 1; Chang, 1982, figs. 17, 18; Clément and Ahlberg, 2010, fig. 7), the stem osteichthyan *Ligulalepis* (Basden et al., 2000, fig. 1; Basden and Young, 2001, figs. 1, 7), chondrichthyans (Schaeffer, 1981, figs. 14, 15; Maisey, 2005, fig. 27; Pradel, 2010, fig. 30), and placoderms (e.g., Stensiö, 1963b, figs. 26, 27, 29–33, 35), the olfactory canals of *Mimipiscis* are broadly separated along most of their length (Figs. 3, 5). This is opposed to the morphology seen in all other early actinopterygians, where the canal is present as a single midline tube (Fig. 11.5, 11.6, Node C). Related to this, the tracts of *Mimipiscis* are laterally divergent, again more closely resembling the condition in actinopterygian outgroups than that found in other Paleozoic ray fins (Fig. 11.1–11.4, Node C). A further generalized condition apparent in *Mimipiscis* relates to the geometry of the labyrinth region. In previously described ray-finned fish endocasts, the crus commune of the anterior and posterior semicircular canal is typically set into the lateral wall of the cranial cavity (Fig. 11, Node C; e.g., Hamel and Poplin, 2008, figs. 13, 14; Poplin, 1974, fig. 27). This is not the case in *Mimipiscis*; instead, the crus commune sits above the cranial cavity (Figs. 3, 4). This arrangement is seen elsewhere in early members of actinopterygian outgroups (e.g., Chang, 1982, fig. 19; Säve-Söderbergh, 1952, fig. 9), and is developed to such an extent in some Paleozoic chondrichthyans that the crus commune of the left canal almost meets with that of the right canal at the midline (Fig. 11.1; Schaeffer, 1981, fig. 14). Additionally, the general arrangement of the optic lobes in *Mimipiscis* appears to be primitive relative to *Kentuckia* and other Carboniferous actinopterygians. Whereas the optic lobes are conspicuously expanded in the endocasts of these stratigraphically younger ray fins, such that the optic lobes are the same width as the cerebellum (Fig. 11.5 and 11.6), the endocast of *Mimipiscis* increases gradually in width from the diencephalon to the cerebellum (Fig. 3). This matches the condition in sarcopterygians and chondrichthyans (Fig. 11.1–11.3) (e.g., Chang, 1982, fig. 17; Maisey, 2007, fig. 26), and is presumably the primitive arrangement for crown gnathostomes.

The unusual geometry of the brain seen in *Mimipiscis* reflects the small optic lobes of the genus in comparison to other actinopterygians. Enlargement of the optic lobes in ray fins is generally interpreted as reflecting the strong reliance on vision in this group (Goatley et al., 2010). The absence of large optic lobes in *Mimipiscis* is somewhat surprising, given its proportionally large eyes and presumed reefal ecology (Long and Trinajstic, 2010). An increased dependence on vision appears to have been derived within actinopterygians, based on the relatively small eyes found in the deepest branching members of the group, (e.g., *Cheirolepis* Agassiz, 1843 [Pearson and Westoll, 1979], *Osorioichthys* Casier, 1954 [Taverne, 1997]) and early sarcopterygians, (e.g., *Grossius* Schultze, 1973; *Guiyu* Zhu et al., 2009; *Miguashaia*Schultze, 1973; *Onychodus* Newberry, 1857 [Andrews et al., 2006]; *Osteolepis* Agassiz, 1843; *Porolepis* Woodward, 1891). Assuming that the modest optic lobes of *Mimipiscis* represent a primitive condition rather than a reversal, then enlargement of the eyes in actinopterygians preceded corresponding architectural modifications to the brain. Endocast data for other early ray-finned fishes would provide a critical test of this inference.

6. CONCLUSION

The study of endocast morphology in early fossil vertebrates has a long scientific history, with the majority of detailed reconstructions available in the literature representing the results of studies conducted several decades ago (online Supplemental Data file 1). We applied CT techniques in order to investigate endocranial anatomy of two phylogenetically significant genera of early ray-finned fishes, *Mimipiscis* and *Kentuckia*. Detailed accounts of the endocranial chamber had been presented for both (Rayner, 1951; Gardiner, 1984), but no endocasts had been produced that would permit more direct comparisons with similar reconstructions available for other early vertebrates. Our virtual endocasts provide a critical test of previous anatomical interpretations of structure in these Paleozoic ray-finned fishes. Apart from some details relating to specific patterns of innervation and proportions, these older accounts are largely accurate. However, our endocasts clearly show new features not apparent in existing descriptions. Key among these are the presence of long, separate olfactory tracts and small optic lobes in *Mimipiscis*. These conditions diverge from those found in other Paleozoic actinopterygians, but agree with those apparent in sarcopterygians, suggesting that they are general features of crown osteichthyans.

Details of the neurocranium in general and its internal structure in particular have great potential in early vertebrate systematics, especially because consistent endoskeletal comparisons can be drawn across groups with radically different dermal skeletons. Despite this promise, relatively few characters pertaining to endocast morphology are incorporated in cladistic analyses (but see Coates, 1999; Friedman, 2007; Friedman et al., 2007; Brazeau, 2009; Zhu et al., 2009; Coates and Friedman, 2010; Davis et al., 2012). In part, this reflects the historical difficulty in obtaining endocast data from fossil specimens, with the consequence that reconstructions are only available for a small number of taxa within each major group of early vertebrates (online Supplemental Data file 1). This problem is clearly illustrated by our contribution, which provides the first endocast models for pre-Pennsylvanian ray-finned fishes. However, the proliferation of tomographic techniques and virtual paleontology, combined with a wealth of excellently preserved neurocrania, provides the means of quickly and efficiently filling these gaps in our understanding of endocranial structure in early vertebrates. As in our analysis, we anticipate that the application of CT scanning to other previously studied taxa will offer a critical test of existing endocast reconstructions (e.g., Gai et al., 2011). The revisions and new discoveries from these classic specimens can be complemented with completely novel endocasts for previously uninvestigated materials. Both will represent important sources of raw morphological data that will provide an important addition to existing character sets for early vertebrates.

ACKNOWLEDGMENTS

Firstly, we thank I. Rahman and S. Smith for the invitation to contribute to this volume. We would also like to thank J. Cundiff and Z. Johanson for access to collections and the permission to borrow specimens. We are grateful to D. Sykes and Z. Johanson for help with the scanning of specimens, and to R. Garwood and S. Lautenschlager for advice on Blender. We thank M. Coates and an anonymous reviewer for providing helpful comments on an earlier version of this manuscript. Funding for this project was provided by NERC cohort NE/J500045/1, and travel to access specimens was made possible by an AMNH Collections Study Grant to SG

REFERENCES

1. Agassiz, L. 1838–1844. Recherches Sur Les Poissons Fossiles. Neuchatel 5 vols, 1420 p.
2. Andrews, S. M., J. Long, and P. Ahlberg. 2006. The structure of the sarcopterygian *Onychodus jandemarrai* n. sp. from Gogo, Western Australia: with a functional interpretation of the skeleton. Transactions of the Royal Society of Edinburgh Earth Sciences, 96:197–307.
3. Arratia, G. and R. Cloutier. 2004. A new cheirolepidid fish from the Middle–Upper Devonian of Red Hill, Nevada, U.S.A., p. 583–598. *In* G. Arratia, M. V. Wilson, and R. Cloutier (eds.). Recent Advances in the Origin and Early Radiation of Vertebrates. Verlag, Dr. Friedrich Pfeil, Munich.
4. Balfour, F. M. and W. N. Parker. 1882. On the structure and development of *Lepidosteus*. Philosophical Transactions of the Royal Society of London, 173:359–442.
5. Basden, A. M. and G. C. Young. 2001. A primitive actinopterygian neurocranium from the Early Devonian of Southeastern Australia. Journal of Vertebrate Paleontology, 21:754–766. BioOne
6. Basden, A. M., G. C. Young, M. I. Coates, and A. Ritchie. 2000. The most primitive osteichthyan braincase? Nature, 403:185–188.
7. Bjerring, H. C. 1971. The nerve supply to the second metamere basicranial muscle in osteolepiform vertebrates, with some remarks on the basic composition of the endocranium. Acta Zoologica, 52:189–225.
8. Bjerring, H. C. 1991. Two intracranial ligaments supporting the brain of the brachiopterygian fish *Polypterus senegalus*. Acta Zoologica, 72:41–47.
9. Brazeau, M. D. 2009. The braincase and jaws of a Devonian "acanthodian" and modern gnathostome origins. Nature, 457:305–308.
10. Campbell, K. S. W. and R. E. Barwick. 1982. The neurocranium of the primitive dipnoan *Dipnorhynchus sussmilchi* (Etheridge). Journal of Vertebrate Paleontology, 2:286–327.
11. Campbell, K. and R. E. Barwick. 2000. The braincase, mandible and dental structures of the Early Devonian lungfish *Dipnorhynchus kurikae* from Wee Jasper, New South Wales. Records of the Australian Museum, 52:103–128.
12. Casier, E. 1954. Contributions à l'étude des poissons fossiles de la Belgique. XI. Note additionelle relative à "*Stereolepis*" (=*Osorioichthys* nov. num) et à l'origine de

l'interoperculaire. Bulletin de l'Institut royal des Sciences naturelles de Belgique, 30:1–12.

13. Chang, M. 1982. The braincase of *Youngolepis*, a Lower Devonian crossopterygian from Yunnan, South-Western China. Unpublished Ph.D dissertation, Department of Geology, University of Stockholm, 113 p.
14. Chang, M. and X. B. Yu. 1981. A new crossopterygian, *Youngolepis praecursor*, gen. et sp. nov., from Lower Devonian of E. Yunnan, China. Scientia Sinica, 24:89–97.
15. Choo, B. 2011. Revision of the actinopterygian genus *Mimipiscis* (=*Mimia*) from the Upper Devonian Gogo Formation of Western Australia and the interrelationships of the early Actinopterygii. Earth and Environmental Science Transactions of the Royal Society of Edinburgh, 102:77–104.
16. Cignoni, P., M. Corsini, and G. Ranzuglia. 2008. Meshlab: An open-source 3D mesh processing system. Ercim News, 63:45–46.
17. Clément, G. and P. E. Ahlberg 2010. The endocranial anatomy of the early sarcopterygian *Powichthys* from Spitsbergen, based on CT scanning, p. 365–379. *In* D. K. Elliot, J. G. Maisey, X. Yu, and D. Miao (eds.), Morphology, Phylogeny and Paleobiogeography of Fossil Fishes. Verlag, Dr. Friedrich Pfeil, Munich.
18. Coates, M. I. 1998. Actinopterygians from the Namurian of Bearsden, Scotland, with comments on early actinopterygian neurocrania. Zoological Journal of the Linnean Society, 122:27–59.
19. Coates, M. I. 1999. Endocranial preservation of a Carboniferous actinopterygian from Lancashire, U.K., and the interrelationships of primitive actinopterygians. Philosophical Transactions of the Royal Society B, Biological Sciences, 354:435–462.
20. Coates, M. I. and M. Friedman. 2010. *Litoptychus bryanti* and characteristics of stem tetrapod neurocrania, p. 389–416. *In* D. K. Elliot, J. G. Maisey, X. Yu, and D. Miao (eds.), Morphology, Phylogeny and Paleobiogeography of Fossil Fishes. Verlag, Dr. Friedrich Pfeil, Munich.
21. Cope, E. D. 1880. Second contribution to the history of the vertebrata of the Permian Formation of Texas. Proceedings of the American Philosophical Society, 19:38–58.
22. Davis, S. P., J. A. Finarelli, and M. I. Coates. 2012. *Acanthodes* and shark-like conditions in the last common ancestor of modern gnathostomes. Nature, 486:247–250.
23. De Burlet, H. M. 1934 Vergleichende Anatomie des stato-akustischen Organs. Handbuch der vergleichenden Anatomie der Wirbeltiere. Berlin, Urban and Schwarzenberg, 2:1293–1432.
24. Dunkle, D. H. 1964. Preliminary description of a paleoniscoid fish from the Upper Devonian of Ohio. Cleveland Museum of Natural History, 3:1–16.
25. Eastman, C. R. 1908. Devonian fishes of Iowa, Iowa Geological Survey, 18:29–386.
26. Edinger, T. 1929. Die Fossilen Gehirne. Ergebnisse der Anatome und Entwicklungsgeschichte, 28:1–249.
27. Evans, W. H. 1953. A catalogue of the American Hesperiidae indicating the classification and nomenclature adopted in the British Museum. Part III. Pyrginae Section 2. British Museum (Natural History), London.
28. Friedman, M. 2007. *Styloichthys* as the oldest coelacanth: Implications for early osteichthyan interrelationships. Journal of Systematic Palaeontology, 5:289–343.
29. Friedman, M. and H. Blom. 2006. A new actinopterygian from the Famennian of East Greenland and the interrelationships of Devonian ray-finned fishes. Journal of Paleontology, 80:1186–1204. BioOne
30. Friedman, M., M. Coates, and P. Anderson. 2007. First discovery of a primitive coelacanth fin fills a major gap in the evolution of lobed fins and limbs. Evolution and Development, 9:329–337.
31. Friedman, M. and M. D. Brazeau. 2010. A reappraisal of the origin and basal radiation of the Osteichthyes. Journal of Vertebrate Paleontology, 30:36–56. BioOne
32. Gai, Z., P. C. J. Donoghue, M. Zhu, and P. Janvier. 2011. Fossil jawless fish from China foreshadows early jawed vertebrate anatomy. Nature, 476:324–327.

33. Gardiner, B. G. 1984. The relationships of the palaeoniscid fishes, a review based on new specimens of *Mimia* and *Moythomasia* from the Upper Devonian of Western Australia. Bulletin of the British Museum (Natural History), 37, 428 p.
34. Gardiner, B. G. and A. W. H. Bartram. 1977. The homologies of ventral cranial fissures in osteichthyans, p. 227–245. *In* S. M. Andrews, R. S. Miles, and A. D. Walker (eds.) Problems in Vertebrate Evolution. Academic Press, London.
35. Gardiner, B. G. and B. Schaeffer. 1989. Interrelationships of lower actinopterygian fishes. Zoological Journal of the Linnean Society, 97:135–187.
36. Gardiner, B., B. Schaeffer, and J. A. Masserie. 2005. A review of the lower actinopterygian phylogeny. Zoological Journal of the Linnean Society, 144:511–525.
37. Garwood, R. and J. Dunlop. The walking dead: Blender as a tool for palaeontologists. Journal of Paleontology, 88:735–746.
38. Gauldie, R. W., K. Mulligan, and R. K. Thompson. 1987. The otoliths of a chimaera, the New Zealand elephant fish *Callorhynchus milii*. New Zealand Journal of Marine and Freshwater Research, 21:275–280.
39. Goatley, C. H. R., D. R. Bellwood, and O. Bellwood. 2010. Fishes on coral reefs: Changing roles over the past 240 million years. Paleobiology, 36:415–427. BioOne
40. Gómez, A., E. Durán, F. M. Ocaña, and F. Jiménez-Moya. 2009. Observations on the brain development of the sturgeon *Acipenser naccarii*, p. 155–174. *In* R. Carmona, A. Domezain, M. G. Gallego, J. A. Hernando, R. Rodríguez, and M. Ruiz-Rejón (eds.), Biology, Conservation and Sustainable Development of Sturgeons. Springer, Netherlands.
41. Goujet, D. 1984. Les poissons placodermes du Spitsberg. Cahiers du Paléontologie C. N. R. S., Paris, 284 p.
42. Hamel, M.-H. 2005. A new lower actinopterygian from the Early Permian of the Paraná Basin, Brazil. Journal of Vertebrate Paleontology, 25:19–26. BioOne
43. Hamel, M-H. and C. Poplin. 2008. The braincase anatomy of *Lawrenciella schaefferi*, actinopterygian from the Upper Carboniferous of Kansas (U.S.A.). Journal of Vertebrate Paleontology, 28:989–1006. BioOne
44. Jaekel, O. 1927. Der Kopf der Wirbeltiere. Bergmann, 1927.
45. Jarvik, E. 1954. On the visceral skeleton in *Eusthenopteron* with a discussion of the parasphenoid and palatoquadrate in fishes. Kungliga Svenska Vetenskapsakademiens Handlingar, 5:1–104.
46. Jarvik, E. 1980. Basic Structure and Evolution of Vertebrates. Academic Press, London.
47. Jerison, H. 1973. Evolution of the Brain and Intelligence. Academic Press, New York.
48. Kruska, D. C. T. 1988. The brain of the basking shark (*Cetorhinus maximus*). Brain, Behavior and Evolution, 32:353–363.
49. Lacépède, B. G. 1798–1903. Histoire naturelle des poissons, 5 vols. Chez Plassan, Paris.
50. Linneaus, C. 1758. Systema naturae, Editio X. Holmiae. v. 1, 824 p.
51. Linneaus, C. 1766. Systema naturae sive regna tria naturae, secundum classes, ordines, genera, species, cum characteribus, differentiis, synonymis, locis. Laurentia Salvii, Holmiae, 12th ed., vol. 1, pt. 1., 532 p.
52. Long, J., B. Choo, and G. C. Young. 2008. A new basal actinopterygian fish from the Middle Devonian Aztec Siltstone of Antarctica. Antarctic Science, 20:393–412.
53. Long, J. and K. Trinajstic. 2010. The Late Devonian Gogo Formation Lägerstatte of Western Australia: exceptional early vertebrate preservation and diversity. Annual Review of Earth and Planetary Sciences, 38:255–279.
54. Lovell, J. M., M. M. Findlay, R. M. Moate, J. R. Nedwell, and M. A. Pegg. 2005. The inner ear morphology and hearing abilities of the Paddlefish (*Polyodon spathula*) and the Lake Sturgeon (*Acipenser fulvescens*). Comparative Biochemistry and Physiology Part A, Molecular and Integrative Physiology, 142:286–296.
55. Maisey, J. G. 2005. Braincase of the Upper Devonian shark *Cladodoides wildungensis* (Chondrichthyes, Elasmobranchii), with observations on the braincase in early Chondrichthyans. Bulletin of the American Museum of Natural History, p. 1–103. BioOne
56. Maisey, J. G. 2007. The braincase in Paleozoic symmoriiform and cladoselachian sharks. Bulletin of the American Museum of Natural History, p. 1–122. BioOne

57. Marsh, O. C. 1874. Small size of the brain in Tertiary mammals. American Journal of Science, 8:66–67.
58. Mathiesen, C. and A. N. Popper. 1987. The ultrastructure and innervation of the ear of the gar, *Lepisosteus osseus*. Journal of Morphology, 194:129–142.
59. Millot, J. and J. Anthony. 1965. Anatomy de *Latimeria chalumnae*. Vol. II. Système nerveux et organes de sens. Éditions du Centre National de la Recherche Scientifique, Paris. 131 p.
60. Moodie, R. L. 1915. A new fish brain from the Coal Measures of Kansas, with a review of other fossil brains. The Journal of Comparative Neurology, 25:135–181.
61. Newberry, J. S. 1857. New fossil fishes from the Devonian rocks of Ohio. American Journal of Science, 24:147–149.
62. Nielsen, E. 1942. Studies on Triassic Fishes from East Greenland I. *Glaucolepis* and *Boreosomus*. Meddelelser om Grønland, 146:1–309.
63. Nieuwenhuys, R. 1982. An overview of the organization of the brain of actinopterygian fishes. American Zoologist, 22:287–310.
64. Nieuwenhuys, R., J. P. M. Kremers, and C. van Huijzen. 1977. The brain of the crossopterygian fish *Latimeria chalumnae*: a survey of its gross structure. Anatomy and Embryology, 151:157–169.
65. Northcutt, R. G., T. J. Neary, and D. G. Senn. 1978. Observations on the brain of the coelacanth *Latimeria chalumnae*: External anatomy and quantitative analysis. Journal of Morphology, 155:181–192.
66. Owen, R. 1841. Report on British Fossil Reptiles, Pt II. Report of the British Association for the Advancement of Science, 11:60–204.
67. Owen, R. 1875. On fossil evidences of a sirenian mammal (*Eotherium aegypiacum*, Owen), from the Nummulitic Eocene of the Mokattam Cliffs, near Cairo. Quarterly Journal of the Geological Society of London, 31:100–104.
68. Pearson, D. M. and T. S. Westoll. 1979. The Devonian actinopterygian *Cheirolepis* Agassiz. Transactions of the Royal Society of Edinburgh, 70:337–399.
69. Poplin, C. M. 1974. Étude de quelques paléoniscidés pennsylvaniens du Kansas. Cahiers du Paléontologie C. N. R. S., Paris, 151 p.
70. Poplin, C. M. 1984. *Lawrenciella schaefferi* n. g., n. sp. (Pisces: Actinopterygii) and the use of endocranial characters in the classification of the palaeonisciformes. Journal of Vertebrate Paleontology, 4:413–421.
71. Poplin, C. M. and A. J. de Ricqlés. 1970. A technique of serial sectioning for the study of undecalcified fossils. Curator, 13:7–20.
72. Popper, A. N. 1978. Scanning electron microscopic study of the otolithic organs in the bichir (*Polypterus bichir*) and shovel-nose sturgeon (*Scaphirhynchus platorynchus*). The Journal of Comparative Neurology, 181:117–128.
73. Pradel, A. 2010. Skull and brain anatomy of Late Carboniferous Sibyrhynchidae (Chondrichthyes, Iniopterygia) from Kansas and Oklahoma (U.S.A.). Geodiversitas, 32:595–661. Link
74. Pradel, A., M. Langer, J. G. Maisey, D. Geffard-Kuriyama, P. Cloetens, P. Janvier, and P. Tafforeau. 2009. Skull and brain of a 300-million-year-old chimaeroid fish revealed by synchrotron holotomography. Proceedings of the National Academy of Sciences of the United States of America, 106:5224–5228.
75. Rayner, D. H. 1951. III.—On the cranial structure of an early palæoniscid, *Kentuckia*, gen. nov. Transactions of the Royal Society of Edinburgh, 62:53–83.
76. Romer, A. S. 1937. The braincase of the Carboniferous crossopterygian *Megalichthys nitidus*. Bulletin of the Museum of Comparative Zoology, 73 p.
77. Rupp, B. and G. Northcutt. 1998. The diencephalon and pretectum of the white sturgeon (*Acipenser transmontanus*): A cytoarchitectonic study. Brain, Behavior and Evolution, 51:239–262.
78. Säve-Söderbergh, G. 1952. On the skull of *Chirodipterus wildungensis* Gross, an Upper Devonian dipnoan from Wildungen. Kungliga Svenska Vetenskapsakademiens Handlingar, 4:1–28.
79. Schaeffer, B. 1981. The xenacanth shark neurocranium, with comments on elasmobranch monophyly. Bulletin of the American Museum of Natural History, 169:1–66.

80. Schaeffer, B. and W. W. Dalquest. 1978. A palaeonisciform braincase from the Permian of Texas, with comments on cranial fissures and the posterior myodome. Novitates, 2658:1–15.
81. Schultze, H.-P. 1973. Crossopterygier mit heterozerker Schwanzflosse aus dem Oberdevon Kanadas, nebst einer Beschreibung von Onychodontida-Resten aus dem Mitteldevon Spaniens und aus dem Karbon der U.S.A. Palaeontographica Abteilung A, 143:188–208.
82. Senn, D. G. 1976. Brain structure in *Calamoichthys calabaricus* Smith 1865 (Polypteridae, Brachiopterygii). Acta Zoologica, 57:121–128.
83. Smith, J. 1939. A surviving fish of the order Actinistia. Transactions of the Royal Society of South Africa, 27:47–50.
84. Sollas, W. J. 1904. A method for the investigation of fossils by serial sections. Philosophical Transactions of the Royal Society of London. Series B, Containing Papers of a Biological Character, 196:259–265.
85. Stensiö, E. A. 1921. Triassic Fishes from Spitzbergen, Vol. 1. A. Holshausen, Vienna.
86. Stensiö, E. A. 1922. Notes on certain crossopterygians. Proceedings of the Zoological Society of London, 92:1241–1271.
87. Stensiö, E. A. 1927. The Downtonian and Devonian vertebrates of Spitsbergen. 1. Family Cephalaspidae. Skrifter om Svalbard og Ishavet, 12:1–391.
88. Stensiö, E. A. 1963a. Anatomical studies on the arthrodiran head. Kungliga Svenska Vetenskapsakademiens Handlingar, 9:1–419.
89. Stensiö, E. A. 1963b. The brain and the cranial nerves in fossil, lower craniate vertebrates. Skrifter utgitt av Det Norske Videnskaps-Akademi i Oslo, Mat.-Naturv. Klasse. Ny serie 13. Oslo, Norway.
90. Sutton, M. D., R. J. Garwood, D. J. Siveter, and D. J. Siveter. 2012. SPIERS and VAXML: A software toolkit for tomographic visualisation and a format for virtual specimen interchange. Palaeontologia Electronica, 15, 15 p. palaeo-electronica.org/content/94-issue-2-2012-technical-articles/226-ct-toolkits.
91. Taverne, L. 1997. *Osorioichthys marginis*, "paléonisciforme" du Famennien de Belgique, et la phylogénie des Actinoptérygiens dévoniens (Pisces). Bulletin de l'Institut royal des Sciences naturelles de Belgique, 67:57–78.
92. Thomson, K. S. and K. S. W. Campbell. 1971. The structure and relationships of the primitive Devonian lungfish—*Dipnorhynchus sussmilchi* (Etheridge). Bulletin of the Peabody Museum of Natural History, Yale University, 38, 190 p.
93. Traquair, R. H. 1890. LXI.—Observations on some fossil fishes from the lower Carboniferous Rocks of Eskdale, Dumfriesshire. Annals and Magazine of Natural History, 6:491–494.
94. Trinajstic, K., C. Marshall, J. Long, and K. Bifield. 2007. Exceptional preservation of nerve and muscle tissues in Late Devonian placoderm fish and their evolutionary implications. Biology Letters, 3:197–200.
95. Walsh, S. A. and M. A. Knoll. 2011. Directions in palaeoneurology. Special Papers in Palaeontology, 86:263–279.
96. White, E. I. 1933. XIV.—New Trassic Palæoniscids from Madagascar. Annals and Magazine of of Natural History, 11:118–128.
97. Whiteaves, J. F. 1881. On some remarkable fossil fishes from the Devonian rocks of Scaumenac Bay, in the Province of Quebec. Annals and Magazine of Natural History, 8:159–162.
98. Woodward, A. S. 1891. 1. - The Devonian Fish Fauna of Spitzbergen. Annals and Magazine of Natural History, 8:1–15.
99. Work, D. M. and C. E. Mason. 2003. Mississippian (middle Osagean) ammonoids from the Nada Member of the Borden Formation, Kentucky. Journal of Paleontology, 77:593–596. BioOne
100. Zhu, M., X. Yu, and P. Janvier. 1999. A primitive fossil fish sheds light on the origin of bony fishes. Nature, 397:607–610.
101. Zhu, M., X. Yu, W. Wang, W. Zhao, and L. Jia. 2006. A primitive fish provides key characters bearing on deep osteichthyan phylogeny. Nature, 441:77–80.

102. Zhu, M., W. Wang, and X. Yu. 2010. *Meemannia eos*, a basal sarcopterygian fish from the Lower Devonian of China - expanded description and significance, p. 199–214. *In* D. K. Elliot, J. G. Maisey, X. Yu, and D. Miao (eds.), Morphology, Phylogeny and Paleobiogeography of Fossil Fishes. Verlag, Dr. Friedrich Pfeil, Munich.
103. Zhu, M., W. Zhao, L. Jia, J. Lu, T. Qiao, and Q. Qu. 2009. The oldest articulated osteichthyan reveals mosaic gnathostome characters. Nature, 458:469–474.
104. Zwehl, V. 1961. l: Über die Blutgewissversorgnung des Gehirns bei einigen Teleostiern. Zoologische Jahrbuch. Abteilung Anatomie, 79:371–438.

CHAPTER 3

A taxonomic reassessment of *Ichthyosaurus communis* and *I. intermedius* and a revised diagnosis for the genus

Judy A. Massare & Dean R. Lomax

[a]*Department of Earth Sciences, SUNY College at Brockport, Brockport, NY, USA*

[b]*School of Earth and Environmental Sciences, The University of Manchester, Manchester, UK*

ABSTRACT

Ichthyosaurus communis De la Beche & Conybeare, 1821 and I. intermedius Conybeare, 1822 have been considered synonymous by some researchers, but distinct species by others. The distinction between the two species was originally based on tooth morphology, which has been shown to vary ontogenetically as well as within an individual. Subsequent literature of the nineteenth century did not propose adequate diagnostic features to distinguish the two species. In addition, illustrations suggest that both species were confused with I. breviceps, which was defined over 50 years later. The type specimens of both species are missing, making the problem unresolvable. However, a neotype was designated for I. communis to retain the widely used species name and to stabilize the taxonomy. The species can be recognized by a symmetric, triangular maxilla with long processes and a large, broad, triradiate lacrimal, as well as a unique ombination of other characters. The neotype shares numerous features with the I. intermedius 'type figure', including the morphologies of the maxilla, prefrontal, lacrimal, jugal and postorbital, such that the two are nearly indistinguishable. Thus I. intermedius must be considered a synonym of I. communis. Ichthyosaurus communis can be identified from the Lyme Regis-Charmouth coast, west Dorset; the ?Whitby coast of Yorkshire; and probably from Street, Somerset. The stratigraphical range of I. communis is at least lower Hettangian to lower Sinemurian.

Keywords: Ichthyosaurus communis; Ichthyosaurus intermedius; Lower Jurassic; Dorset; Somerset

1. INTRODUCTION

Arguably, the first modern, scientific palaeontological study of an extinct marine reptile was of a large ichthyosaur (NHMUK PV R1158) collected by Mary and Joseph Anning from Lyme Regis, Dorset (Home 1814; Torrens 1995), although no name was proposed for it. A few years later, Home (1819a) proposed the name Proteosaurus to encompass all ichthyosaurs known at that time, however K€onig (1818) had previously mentioned the name Ichthyosaurus, and that was the genus name accepted by subsequent workers. The work of Home (1814, 1819a, 1819b) and the new fossils coming from the Dorset and Yorkshire coasts, the limestone quarries of Somerset, and elsewhere paved the way for the identification and scientific study of ichthyosaurs and plesiosaurs. De la Beche & Conybeare (1821) provided the first detailed description of Ichthyosaurus, based on several specimens. However, the skull illustrations (De la Beche & Conybeare 1821, figs 9–12) were composite sketches of several specimens (Conybeare 1822, p. 105). The type species for the genus, I. communis, was introduced by De la Beche & Conybeare (1821, p. 594). A year later, Conybeare (1822) further described the genus Ichthyosaurus and recognized four species from the UK: I. communis, I. platyodon (now Temnodontosaurus), I. tenuirostris (now Leptonectes) and I. intermedius. Subsequently, most new species of ichthyosaur from the Lower Jurassic were assigned to the genus Ichthyosaurus. Almost two decades later, Owen (1840) recognized 10 species of the genus, and later included an additional two (Owen 1881).

By 1900, over 50 species of Ichthyosaurus had been described (McGowan & Motani 2003), although subsequent studies synonymized some and assigned other species to new genera, e.g. Leptonectes and Temnodontosaurus. McGowan & Motani (2003) recognized three valid species: I. communis, I. breviceps and I. conybeari. Ichthyosaurus communis is by far the most common species of the three, and it is extremely variable (McGowan 1974; McGowan & Motani 2003). However, recent work (Lomax

& Massare 2015, 2017) has recognized three new species, I. anningae, I. larkini and I. somersetensis, based on specimens that were previously considered within the range of variation of I. communis.

Ichthyosaurus intermedius was described shortly after I. communis (Conybeare 1822), based largely on tooth morphology. Neither species was sufficiently described when the names were proposed, and the locations of what would have been the type specimens are unknown. However, some teeth assigned to I. communis by Conybeare (1822, pl. 15, figs 4, 8) may be those held at the BGS (Geol. Soc. Coll. 4476, Geol. Soc. Coll. 4477). Many, if not most, of the fairly complete skeletons in museum collections were originally identified as I. intermedius. The species was recognized at more localities than I. communis (Owen 1840, p. 112), and was more common than I. communis at Somerset locations, whereas the reverse occurred at Dorset locations (Owen 1840; Lydekker 1889). McGowan (1974) synonymized I. intermedius with I. communis, although Appleby (1979), Maisch (1997) and Maisch & Matzke (2000a) disagreed. McGowan & Motani (2003) argued that the characters proposed to distinguish the species were too variable to be useful. The research presented here examines the original, nineteenth century diagnoses of the two species in more detail than previously published. It supports the synonymy of McGowan (1974).

2. INSTITUTIONAL ABBREVIATIONS

AGC: Alfred Gillett Collection, cared for by the Alfred Gillett Trust (C & J Clark Ltd), Street, UK; ANSP: Academy of Natural Science of Drexel University, Philadelphia, PA, USA; BELUM: National Museums Northern Ireland (Ulster Museum), Cultra, Northern Ireland; BGS: British Geological Survey, Keyworth, Nottingham, UK; BU (BIRUG): Lapworth Museum of Geology, University of Birmingham, Birmingham, UK; CAMSM: Sedgwick Museum, Cambridge University, Cambridge, UK; CHMUS: Charterhouse School Museum, Surrey, UK; FMNH: Field Museum, Chicago, IL, USA; GSL: Geological Society of London, London, UK; MANCH: Manchester Museum, University of Manchester, Manchester, UK; MCZ: Museum of Comparative Zoology, Harvard University, Cambridge, MA, USA; NHMUK (formerly BMNH): The Natural History Museum, London, UK; NMW: National Museum of Wales, Cardiff, UK; OUMNH: Oxford University Museum of Natural History, Oxford, UK; PETMG: Peterborough Museum and Art Gallery, Peterborough, UK; SMNS: Staatliches Museum f€ur Naturkunde, Stuttgart, Germany; WOSMG: Worcester City Art Gallery and Museum, Worcester, UK; YORYM: Yorkshire Museum, York, UK.

2.1 Original diagnoses

The name Ichthyosaurus communis first appeared in the literature as a note at the end of De la Beche & Conybeare (1821) that briefly described a fairly complete specimen from Lyme Regis. Aside from providing measurements of certain features of the skeleton, the account did not specify any diagnostic characters. The specimen has been regarded as the holotype of I. communis, but it was reported lost by McGowan (1974), and we have notlocated it. The following year, Conybeare (1822) provided descriptions of I. communis and I. intermedius, and distinguished four species on the basis of tooth morphology, although he might not have intended that to be the sole criterion:

Mr. De la Beche, however, long since believed himself able, from the examination of the teeth, combined with some other characters, to establish three species, to which he has applied the names communis, platyodon, and tenuirostris: and to these our joint observations have recently added a fourth, Ichthyosaurus intermedius. (Conybeare 1822, p. 108).

Ichthyosaurus intermedius has "more acutely conical" teeth (presumably meaning that the tooth crowns were more slender) with less prominent longitudinal striations than I. communis (Conybeare 1822, p. 108). Teeth representing these species were illustrated, although, as was common at the time, neither the tooth of I. intermedius nor any other material was formally designated a type specimen (Conybeare 1822, pl. 15, figs 8, 9; Fig. 1). The figures also suggest that the longitudinal striations of the root are more prominent in I. communis than in I. intermedius, although this was not mentioned in the text. The figure of the tooth of I. intermedius (Fig. 1B) shows a slender crown, with a base that is much narrower than the root, a form which Maisch (1997) called 'waisted'; but again, the original diagnosis did not mention such a difference. Maxillary teeth often have crowns that are narrower than the root. Instead, we would argue that Conybeare (1822) was distinguishing between wider conical teeth with strong longitudinal striations (Smash guild of Massare 1987), and slender, more acute conical teeth with finer striations (Pierce I guild of Massare 1987). The former would include the teeth figured for I. communis, whereas the latter would include the teeth figured for I. intermedius.

Conybeare (1822, p. 112) also noted that Ichthyosaurus intermedius was distinguished from other species by differences in the lateral exposure of the angular and 'coronoid' (surangular) bones of the lower jaw. He contended that in I. communis, the surangular is partially hidden by the dentary such that the angular is visible further anteriorly than the surangular; whereas in I. intermedius, the surangular extends further anteriorly than the angular. However, the figured morphology of a skull of I. intermedius contradicts the description in the text (Conybeare 1822, pl.

17). Specifically, the angular extends slightly more anteriorly than the surangular (Fig. 2A).

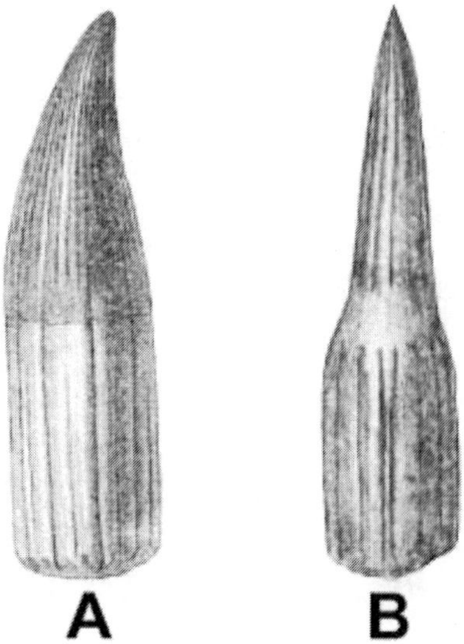

Figure 1. Original figures of teeth of A, Ichthyosaurus communis (Conybeare, 1822, pl. 15, fig. 8); and B, I. intermedius (Conybeare, 1822, pl. 15, fig. 9). No size information given in the original publication, so a scale bar cannot be provided.

Conybeare (1822, pl. 16, fig. 8) also included a drawing of a partial skull identified as I. communis (Fig. 3A), which belonged to the Oxford Museum according to the caption, but we could not locate it at the OUMNH. Thus, Conybeare provided the first illustrations of specimens assigned to I. communis and I. intermedius, in the form of drawings of skulls showing the details of sutures, mainly in the post-narial portion of the skull. The I. communis figure, however, is problematic. The large maxillary teeth with prominent grooves in the roots, the lack of an anterior process of the lacrimal, and especially the long subnarial process that makes up almost all of the ventral margin of the external naris, all suggest that this is a sketch of I. breviceps (Fig. 3), defined more than 50 years later by Owen (1881). Given the emphasis on tooth morphology at the time, it is not surprising that an I. breviceps specimen would have initially been assigned to I. communis, especially if the entire rostrum was not preserved. Furthermore, both I. communis and I. breviceps have broad forefins with numerous phalanges. Adding to the uncertainty, the skull diagrams are interpretations. Without the actual specimens, it is impossible to determine their accuracy. But it appears that, apart from the probable I. breviceps skull, I. communis was not actually illustrated except for some teeth that might or might not be the same as those of the holotype. Thus, I. intermedius was initially better defined, or at least better illustrated, than I. communis.

Another figure, of a fairly complete forefin, was identified only as Ichthyosaurus (Conybeare 1822, pl. 20, fig. 1). It shows a bifurcation of digit II in the metacarpal row, and a second bifurcation between the p3 and p4 rows, for a total of six primary digits. Two posterior accessory digits are also present. It is certainly a specimen of what is presently considered Ichthyosaurus (Motani 1999; McGowan & Motani 2003), and it might be an I. communis. We could not locate this forefin.

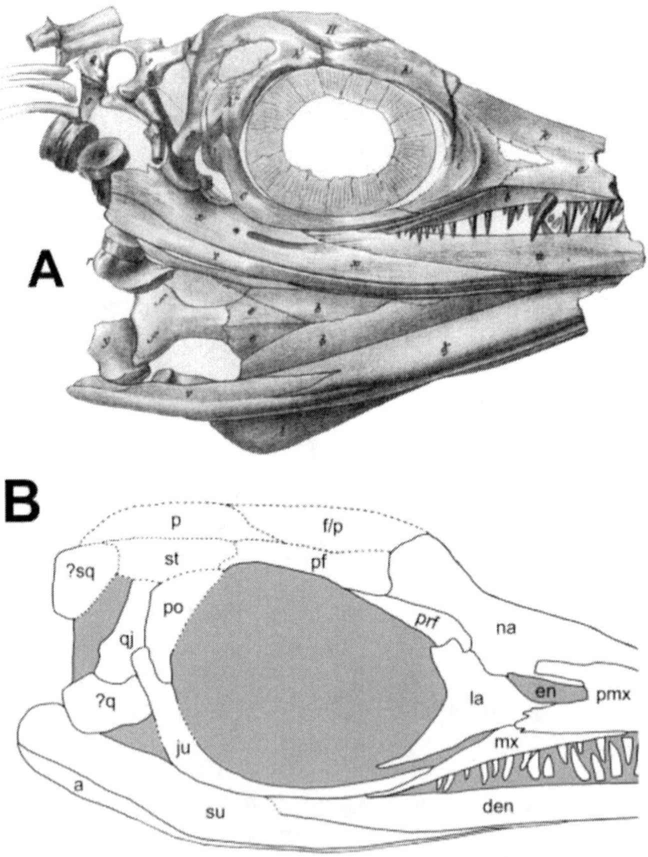

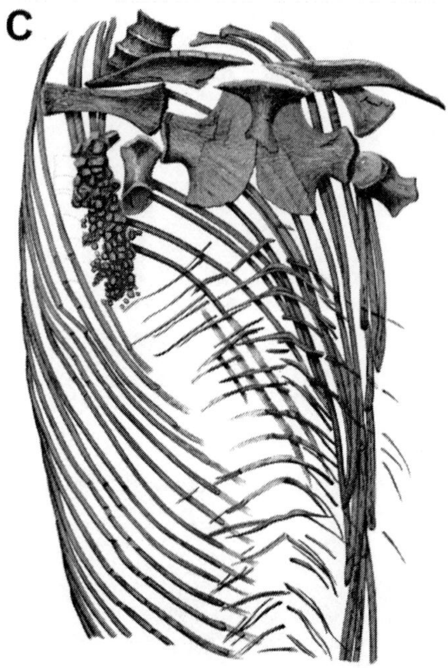

Figure 2. A, type skull of Ichthyosaurus intermedius as figured by Conybeare (1822, pl. 17); B, interpretive skull illustration of the neotype of I. communis (NHMUK PV R1162), reversed to show the same orientation; the dorsal skull roof of the neotype is poorly preserved due to crushing, so sutures and openings in the skull could not be determined with certainty; C, postcranial skeleton of the type specimen (A) of I. intermedius as figured by Home (1819b). Abbreviations: a, angular; den, dentary; en, external naris; f, frontal; ju, jugal; la, lacrimal; mx, maxilla; na, nasal; p, parietal; po, postorbital; pmx, premaxilla; pf, postfrontal; prf, prefrontal; q, quadrate; qj, quadratojugal; sq, squamosal; st, supratemporal; su, surangular. Light grey denotes matrix or openings in skull. Dashed lines indicate broken edge and possible sutures. Scale: A, C, no size information given in the original publications, B, specimen behind glass and inaccessible, so scale bars cannot be provided.

3. WHAT IS ICHTHYOSAURUS COMMUNIS?

The first published figure of a practically complete specimen identified as I. communis was the skeleton of a small specimen (jaw length »25 cm) in Buckland (1836, vol. 2, pl. 8, fig. 1). This could not have been the type specimen, because it is much smaller than the specimen mentioned in De la

Beche & Conybeare (1821; jaw length »47 cm). The figured specimen was described as the "Skeleton of a young Ichthyosaurus communis, in the collection of the Geological Society of London, found in the Lias at Lyme Regis" (Buckland 1836, p. 21).

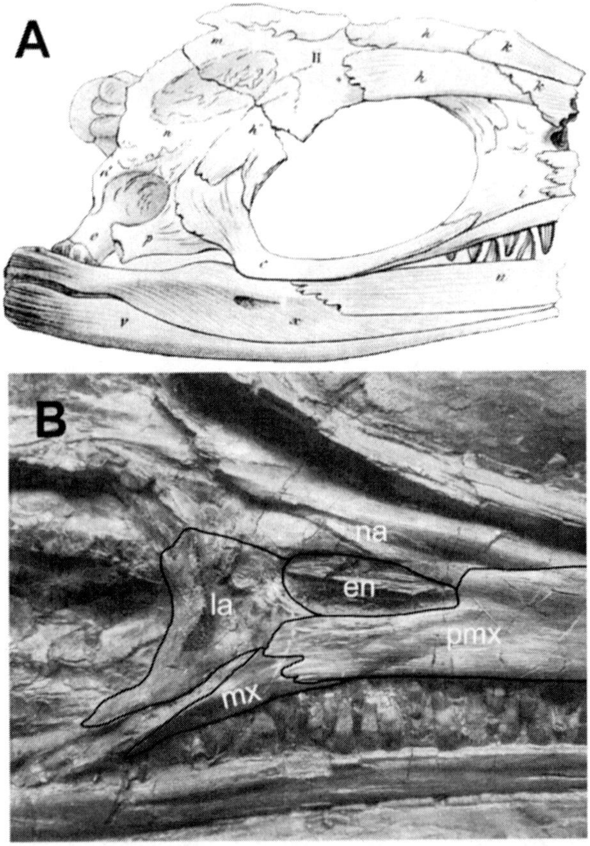

Figure 3. A, original figure by Conybeare (1822, pl. 16, fig. 8) of a specimen referred to as Ichthyosaurus communis. B, holotype specimen of I. breviceps (NHMUK PV OR43006) with lines indicating key sutures of the skull; the skull has been reversed to show the same orientation; note the similar extent of the subnarial process of the premaxilla and the reduced anterior process of the lacrimal; the medial portion of the lacrimal is damaged, and the dorsal extent is estimated. Abbreviations: en, external naris; la, lacrimal; mx, maxilla; na, nasal; pmx, premaxilla. Scale: A, no size information in the original publication, B, specimen behind glass and inaccessible, so scale bars cannot be provided.

Most of the GSL collection was transferred to BGS (Taylor & Clark in press), but we could not locate the specimen. However, OUMNH J.10341 and CAMSM X.50259 are plaster casts of the figured skeleton, which must have been considered an important specimen at the time. Interestingly, on the same plate, Buckland (1836, pl. 8, fig. 2) identifies a specimen of I. breviceps (NHMUK PV R8437; McGowan 1974; Taylor 2014) as I. intermedius, again showing inconsistency or confusion in the early literature.

Owen (1840) expanded the diagnosis of Ichthyosaurus communis, but again emphasized tooth form. He described the conical, slightly curved crown with 'longitudinal furrows' and noted the expanded roots with coarse, deep grooves that Conybeare (1822) figured but did not describe. Owen noted features of I. communis that are also characteristic of other parvipelvian ichthyosaurs (jugal forms entire ventral margin of the orbit; prefrontal and postfrontal only forming the dorsal margin of the orbit); features that eventually became characters of the genus (small frontals enclosing the pineal foramen; short, stout humerus relative to its length; broader forefins than are found in any of the other 'species', here encompassing all of the Lower Jurassic genera; phalanges 'transversely oblong', i.e. rectangular), and features of uncertain taxonomic utility (shallow depression on ventral basioccipital; basioccipital longer than wide; tooth count; number of sclerotic plates; mandibular symphysis about 1/4 of the length of the mandible). Characters that might be interpreted as diagnostic for the species itself include: (1) 18 maxillary teeth; (2) external naris straight dorsally and curved ventrally; and (3) about 40 presacral centra, based on the position of the ilium. Thus even this emended diagnosis did not provide many characteristics that are not also characteristics of the genus, perhaps not surprising considering that I. communis is the type species for the genus.

Owen (1881) reviewed the species of Ichthyosaurus from the 'Liassic Formations', and again noted that the main distinguishing features of I. communis were the morphologies of the teeth and forefin. His description of tooth morphology was essentially the same as Owen (1840), except that he pointed out that the teeth were proportionally larger than in most species. He also pointed out that the forefin has five primary digits and both an anterior and posterior accessory digit, for a total of seven (Owen 1881, p. 105). We have found that an anterior accessory digit occur frequently on specimens of I. breviceps, but very rarely on other Ichthyosaurus species. The early literature, however, sometimes confused a second digital bifurcation with an anterior accessory digit.

Owen (1881) also provided new information on other aspects of the morphology of I. communis. An important observation was that the external naris is bordered by the nasal dorsally, and by the lacrimal and premaxilla ventrally, excluding the maxilla from contact with the external naris. We take this to mean that the supranarial process of the premaxilla is short, if present at all. Of all of the species of Ichthyosaurus, only I. breviceps has a reduced supranarial process such that the nasal makes up practically the entire dorsal margin of the external naris (Fig. 3B). This again suggests confusion between I. communis and I. breviceps in the early literature. On all other species of Ichthyosaurus, the supranarial process extends one-third to half of the length of the external naris (Lomax & Massare 2017). Owen (1881) also indicated that the mandibular symphysis was composed mainly of the dentaries, with only a small contribution from the splenials. He also provided the first description of a tripartite pelvis in I. communis, noting that the ischium and pubis were about the same length (»7.0 cm), and slightly longer than the moderately curved ilium (»6.4 cm). Finally, he described the hind fin as having five primary digits, owing to a bifurcation of the anterior digit in the "fifth bone from the femur" (Owen 1881, p. 112; presumably the first phalangeal row) and a posterior accessory digit (Owen 1881, p. 105, pl. 28, fig. 5), although in the figure, the latter is represented by only a single element. He further noted that four elements were in the third (distal tarsal) row of the hind fin.

Lydekker (1889) relied heavily on tooth form and forefin width to assign specimens at the NHMUK to I. communis. He introduced four new characters for the species: (1) the rostrum length equal to or slightly less than three times the maximum orbit dimension; (2) cervical and dorsal centra with neural spines more than twice the centrum height; (3) small, indistinct vascular foramina on fin elements; and (4) lack of notching on the anterior digit of the fins. Fin notching, however, has only limited taxonomic utility (Maxwell et al. 2014; Massare & Lomax 2016a).

McGowan (1974) argued that the descriptions of I. communis in De la Beche & Conybeare (1821) and Conybeare (1822) were inadequate to erect a species. He synonymized I. intermedius and I. latimanus with I. communis because those species were also based on unreliable characters, although McGowan also considered I. communis to be a nomen dubium. However, because the name had been in use for so long, and had priority, McGowan (1974) retained the name I. communis by selecting a neotype (NHMUK PV R1162) that was consistent with the original definition and subsequent definitions in the early literature (Owen 1840, 1881). He emended the diagnosis of I. communis to include a presacral vertebral count of 41–47 (but usually <46), preflexural vertebral count of 75–79, several ratios of skull elements, four or more primary digits with 17 or more elements in the longest digit, and up to 18 maxillary teeth. Interestingly, the latter two are somewhat similar to what Owen (1840) proposed.

McGowan (1974) also noted 'two populations' of I. communis, one from Lyme Regis, Dorset and the other from Street, Somerset, that vary in forefin structure. The Somerset 'population' often has only five primary digits, has notching in one or two elements of the anterior digit, and has less than 20 elements in the longest digit; whereas the Dorset 'population' usually has six or seven primary digits, lacks notching of the anterior digit, and has more than 20 elements in the longest digit. McGowan (1974) further pointed out that forefin morphology is quite variable, and these differences could be within the normal range of variation within a species. He also noted that the Somerset 'population' has a larger maxilla, smaller orbit, and relatively smaller skull, but the differences are not statistically significant. McGowan (1974) concluded that these differences are too small to warrant a taxonomic distinction. Appleby (1979), however, disagreed, and argued that the high variation in relative skull size and the differences in the forefins were too great to be considered a single species. Recent work (Lomax & Massare 2017) has demonstrated that many of the Somerset specimens are a new species, I. somersetensis.

4. WHAT IS ICHTHYOSAURUS INTERMEDIUS?

Owen (1840) agreed with the assessment of I. intermedius as a distinct species (Conybeare 1822). He pointed out that the surangular is exposed further forwards than the angular in I. intermedius, but not as far forward as in I. communis, correcting the description of Conybeare (1822). He further stated that the fore and hind fins are not very broad in proportion to their length in I. intermedius.

Owen (1881) gave a more detailed account by expanding on previous characters of the species, stating that the teeth of I. intermedius are more numerous and relatively smaller and longer, which we interpret to mean narrower and longer. Specifically, the finely striated crown is acutely conical with a narrow base, and the root has longitudinal grooves that are not prominent (Owen 1881, p. 113). He also recognized differences in the pectoral girdle: the clavicles of I. intermedius are "long, and less strong than in I. communis", and the humero-scapular articulation of the coracoid "is of less relative extent than in I. communis" (Owen 1881, p. 114); but pectoral girdle morphology can vary within a species (Johnson 1979; Maxwell & Druckenmiller 2011). Owen (1881) again indicated that I. intermedius has a narrower forefin with fewer phalanges than I. communis, but that both species have five primary digits. He also noted notching on three anterior elements of the hind fin. Although providing the location of discovery and repository for other reptiles illustrated in his monograph, Owen (1881) did not specify which specimens his ichthyosaur descriptions were based upon, although he illustrated one skeleton that he identified as I. intermedius (Owen 1881, pl. 30, fig. 1), which is definitely NHMUK PV OR2013*. Although by the time of Owen's publication, many specimens had been identified in museum and private collections, this was only the second illustration of I. intermedius in the literature since Conybeare (1822) defined the species. However, this specimen differs from the illustrated 'type' of I. intermedius (Conybeare 1822, pl. 17) in several significant features including: the height and asymmetry of the maxilla; the size and anterior extent of the prefrontal; the shape and dorsal extent of the lacrimal; the anterior extent of the jugal; the shape and position of the postfrontal; the relative height of the posterior portion of the angular and surangular; and the prominent grooves in the tooth root. This specimen has recently been referred to a new species, I. somersetensis Lomax & Massare, 2017. The aforementioned Buckland (1836, pl. 8, fig. 2) illustration of 'I. intermedius', the first illustration in the literature after Conybeare (1822), was also incorrectly attributed to the species. This inconsistency in identifying specimens arguably occurred because the initial diagnoses were inadequate.

A brief but notable account of the species was provided by Lydekker (1889). He mentioned various features that had previously been considered distinct for the species, including the morphology of the paddles and clavicles, but did not discuss the tooth morphology. He proposed additional features of the species including a somewhat lower neural spine height on the cervical and dorsal vertebrae and the presence of notching on the anterior digit in the hind fin and sometimes the forefin. His emphasis on notching, especially in assigning specimens to the species, provided no clarification because nearly all specimens of Ichthyosaurus from Somerset have notched hind fins, and many have notched forefins as well (Massare & Lomax 2016a).

The most recent account of I. intermedius was by Maisch (1997), who identified the type specimen as the skull illustrated by Conybeare (1822, pl. 17; Fig. 2A) and the postcranial skeleton figured by Home (1819b, pl. 14; Fig. 2C), which is the same specimen, as noted in the plate explanations in Conybeare (1822). The skull was reported as specimen R7615 in the collection of the Geological Society of London by Blake (1902, p. 1), donated by De la Beche who originally owned it (Conybeare 1822, explanation of pl. 17). Although most of the GSL collection was transferred to BGS, this specimen probably was not (Taylor & Clark in press). The specimen was listed in the register when the collection was transferred, but its destination was listed as 'Staircase', presumably in the GSL rooms (P. Shepherd, pers. comm.). We have not located the specimen at BGS, NHMUK or GSL.

Maisch (1997) provided an emended diagnosis of the species, based on SMNS 13111, a well-preserved, isolated skull, apparently from the Lower Jurassic of Yorkshire. The additional features in his diagnosis included: only rudimentary fossae on the premaxilla and dentary; a very short fossa surangularis; a relatively high maxilla with a slightly concave ventral border and a delicate posterior process that extends to below the middle of the orbit; more than 20 maxillary teeth (possibly more than 25) that extend well below the orbit; distinctly curved posterior maxillary teeth; a dorsoventrally compressed dorsal ramus of the jugal, with a lateral ridge; a dorsoventrally shortened quadratojugal with a "well-developed and characteristically shaped processus quadratus"; and a delicately built quadrate with a narrow lateral edge (Maisch 1997, p. 4).

5. COMPARISON OF ICHTHYOSAURUS COMMUNIS AND I. INTERMEDIUS

Although the original diagnoses were inadequate, many characters were subsequently proposed to distinguish Ichthyosaurus intermedius from I. communis (Table 1). Researchers of the nineteenth century (Conybeare 1822; Owen 1840, 1881; Lydekker 1889) agreed that Ichthyosaurus communis was much larger than I. intermedius, the former being up to 3.8 m (15 ft) long whereas the latter was 1.8 m (7 ft) or less. Thus the supposed maximum size of I. intermedius is only slightly larger than I. breviceps, which is generally regarded as a small species (»1.6 m preflexural length, Massare & Lomax 2014). The specimen of I. communis first mentioned in De la Beche & Conybeare (1821), and presumed to be the holotype specimen, had a jaw length of 47 cm (18.5 in), which corresponds to an individual only about 2.4 m (7.9 ft) long, a rough estimate that assumes the skull length was about 20% of the total preflexural length. If the size difference is correct, one could argue that the two species are ontogenetic stages of a single species. The issue is complicated, however, by inconsistencies in species assignments based on size. One of the largest skeletons of Ichthyosaurus, NHMUK PV OR2013 _ (»2.7 m total length), was figured by Owen (1881) as an example of I. intermedius, although it is clearly within the supposed size range of I. communis, not I. intermedius. The basis for Owen's attribution is puzzling because the specimen also has little in common with Conybeare's (1822) 'type' figure. Another issue is that the maximum length given for I. communis in the early literature is too large, at least for specimens from the UK. The largest specimen measured by McGowan (1974, fig. 1) had a jaw length of about 55 cm, which corresponds to an individual about 2.8 m long, again assuming that the skull is about 20% of the preflexural length. Massare et al. (2015) estimated the maximum preflexural length for the genus in the UK as just under 3 m. Even allowing for a tail fluke, these estimates are quite a bit shorter than the size suggested for I. communis in the early literature; possibly other taxa were mixed up with I. communis, e.g. Temnodontosaurus. European specimens of the genus, however, are much larger (Godefroit 1996; Maisch 1997), although whether they represent I. communis cannot be determined. In any case, a difference in size between the two species does not seem to be a useful distinction.

Table 1. An assessment of previously proposed characters to distinguish Ichthyosaurus intermedius from I. communis. Additional details are in the text. Neotype refers to NHMUK PV R1162, the neotype of I. communis.

Character	Author	Assessment
Body length	Conybeare 1822; Owen 1840, 1881	Inconsistent with historical identifications of specimens.
Length of rostrum	Owen 1840; Lydekker 1889	Influenced by orientation and flattening; range overlaps among species.
Tooth crown morphology	Conybeare 1822; Owen 1840, 1881	Intermediate forms exist; ontogenetic in part; influenced by orientation.
Lack expanded tooth root; grooves not prominent	Owen 1840, 1881	No obvious difference from neotype.
'Waisted' tooth form	Maisch 1997	Varies within an individual.
Tooth count	Owen 1840	Uncertain taxonomic utility; depends on preparation and completeness in part.
Number of maxillary teeth	Owen 1840; Maisch 1997	Uncertain taxonomic utility; depends on preparation in part.
Curvature of maxillary teeth under orbit	Maisch 1997	Occurs in other species; depends on orientation.
Prominence of fossa on premaxilla, dentary, surangular	Maisch 1997	Uncertain taxonomic utility; range of variation has never been assessed.
Extent of surangular versus angular, lateral view	Conybeare 1822; Owen 1840	No obvious difference from neotype.
Relative length of mandibular symphysis	Owen 1840	Uncertain taxonomic utility; not commonly preserved so cannot be assessed.
Relative contributions of dentary and splenials to mandibular symphysis	Owen 1881	Uncertain taxonomic utility; not commonly preserved so cannot be assessed.
Morphology of maxilla	Maisch 1997	Noticeably lower, with shorter anterior process, on neotype.
Morphology of jugal dorsal ramus	Maisch 1997	No obvious difference from neotype.
Morphology of quadratojugal	Maisch 1997	No obvious difference from neotype.
Clavicle morphology	Owen 1881; Lydekker 1889	Highly variable within a species.
Extent of humero-scapular articulation of coracoid	Owen 1881	Highly variable within a species.
Forefin narrower with fewer phalanges	Owen 1881; Lydekker 1889	Highly variable; influenced by fin completeness and preparation.
Notching on anterior digit of hind fin/forefin	Lydekker 1889	Little taxonomic utility; ontogenetic in part.
Prominent vascular foramina in fin elements	Lydekker 1889	Little taxonomic utility; probably ontogenetic in part.
Neural spine height on cervical and dorsal centra	Lydekker 1889	Uncertain taxonomic utility; has never been assessed for most species.
Number of presacral centra	Owen 1840	Similar in all species of *Ichthyosaurus*.

Tooth form has been a major criterion for distinguishing the two species. The 'waisted' tooth form of I. intermedius has been a key argument for the retention of the species (Maisch 1997), although that feature was not in the original diagnosis (Conybeare 1822). We have seen individual specimens that have waisted teeth as well as those with a more gradual increase in the diameter of the root, i.e. not waisted (e.g. AGC 11; NMW 93.5G.2; CAMSM J35183). However, Conybeare (1822), and later Owen (1840), provided many other supposedly diagnostic features of the teeth: larger teeth with expanded roots; coarser, more prominent grooves in the roots; less slender, less acute crown; and fewer teeth in I. communis compared to I.

intermedius. These differences are recognizable, but seemingly intermediate morphologies also exist (pers. obs.). Furthermore, tooth morphology varies within a species (McGowan 1974, 1994; Dick et al. 2016; Lomax 2016). Recent work demonstrated that tooth size and morphology varies ontogenetically as well (Dick & Maxwell 2015; Dick et al. 2016), and that is certainly complicating the problem of recognizing distinct morphologies for a species. However, Lydekker (1889) recognized difference in tooth form between specimens of the same size, although he also pointed out that juveniles of the two species are difficult to distinguish. McGowan & Motani (2003, p. 92) argued that tooth morphology is not useful taxonomically, yet some general forms are clearly distinguishable among taxa (Massare 1987; Lomax 2016). Preservation, orientation and preparation can also complicate the recognition of distinct morphologies. So, although we recognize that different morphologies exist, we agree with McGowan & Motani (2003) that tooth morphology is not a reliable taxonomic character to distinguish these two species, at least with our current knowledge.

Owen (1840, p. 110) indicated that I. communis and I. intermedius can best be distinguished by the "form and relative size of the head and teeth", with a shorter rostrum in I. intermedius. Lydekker (1889) quantified this somewhat by stating that the rostrum of I. communis was greater than or equal to three times the length ('the maximum diameter') of the orbit whereas the rostrum length of I. intermedius was less than three times the length of the orbit. However, the ratio is affected by preservation, specifically by the skull orientation and how much the orbit is distorted by compaction or crushing. McGowan (1974) used a similar metric, the snout ratio, which is the preorbital length divided by the length of the mandible, to characterize the relative size of the rostrum. He did not find a separation into two distinct morphologies, so if both species are valid, then their respective ranges for snout ratio must overlap.

Owen (1840) also proposed that forefin morphology could distinguish between I. communis and I. intermedius. The forefin of I. communis is broader, has an additional digit, and "about 50 additional phalangeal ossicles" (Owen 1840, p. 109), although exactly what is meant by the latter is unclear. It could mean that the fin had more numerous, smaller phalanges, which is a distinction between 'populations' noted by McGowan (1974); or that the fin was longer overall; or that it had more accessory digits. Moreover, the number of phalanges is related to the completeness of the fin. In reality, what is often seen as a typical 'fairly complete' forefin on specimens from Somerset (McGowan & Motani 2003, fig. 80D) is incomplete; the fin is considerably longer than what is normally preserved (compare Fig. 4A with Fig. 4B, C).

In a later monograph, Owen (1881) again indicated that I. intermedius had a narrower forefin, but the subjective criteria of 'broad' versus 'narrow' are not tied to the number of primary digits nor to the number of accessory digits in the forefin. Owen (1881, pp. 105, 115) described both species as having five primary digits and both an anterior and posterior accessory digit, although the anterior accessory digit illustrated for I. intermedius (Owen 1881, pl. 33, fig. 1) is not an accessory, but a second distal bifurcation. This might have been the case for his interpretation of I. communis as well, but he did not figure the fin. Indeed, the fin width is not explicitly related to the number of primary digits. Fins with a proximal digital bifurcation (mc or p1 row) may be wider than ones with a more distal bifurcation (p3 or p4) even though the number of primary digits is the same (compare Fig. 4B, C). Some fins that have five primary digits (a single digital bifurcation; Fig. 4B) can appear as wide as or wider than fins with six primary digits (two digital bifurcations; Fig. 4D). The number of accessory digits and how proximally they originate also affects fin width. So Owen's distinction between 'broad' and 'narrow' fins is too poorly defined to apply consistently and objectively. Lydekker (1889) introduced fin notching as a character that distinguished the two species. However, Massare & Lomax (2016a) demonstrated that, although notching of the radius or tibia is useful in some taxa, notching has no taxonomic significance in more distal elements of either the forefin or hind fin in Ichthyosaurus. Furthermore, Maxwell et al. (2014) have shown that fin notching is, at least in part, ontogenetic in Stenopterygius.

Forefin morphology is extremely variable within and among species of Ichthyosaurus, differing in which digit bifurcates, the location of the bifurcation, the number of bifurcations, the relative size of the anterior and posterior branches of the bifurcation, and the number of accessory digits, among others. McGowan (1974) acknowledged that forefin morphology was different between specimens from Somerset and Dorset, but attributed it to intraspecific variation over time. Appleby (1979) argued that these were valid species differences. The problem is complicated by the frequent incompleteness of the forefin (Fig. 4), especially in recognizing a second or third digital bifurcation; and by unrecognized composites in historical collections (Massare & Lomax 2016b). Preparation can also be a factor. Some historical specimens have forefins that seem to be carved out of the matrix, so it is possible that some bone, such as isolated elements of accessory digits, could have been removed to make a cleaner, better defined fin, or even to make a more streamlined one, more aesthetically pleasing for display. Still other specimens have fins in which the elements were probably reset and rearranged (e.g. NHMUK PV R3372). The utility of forefin morphology for taxonomy will only become evident when species of Ichthyosaurus are better defined on the basis of other characters. At that time, forefin morphology can be examined for features characteristic of each species. The number of digital bifurcations or the location of the first (proximal) digital bifurcation may eventually prove to be significant. For now, however, forefin morphology appears too variable to use in distinguishing species, although it is reliable in distinguishing Ichthyosaurus from other genera.

Owen (1881) contended that Ichthyosaurus communis and I. intermedius could be distinguished by the extent of the contribution of the splenial to the mandibular symphysis. In ventral view, the dentaries form most of the mandibular symphysis in I. communis, with only a small contribution from the splenials; whereas the splenials comprise two thirds of the mandibular symphysis in I. intermedius (Owen 1881, pl. 21, figs 2, 4).

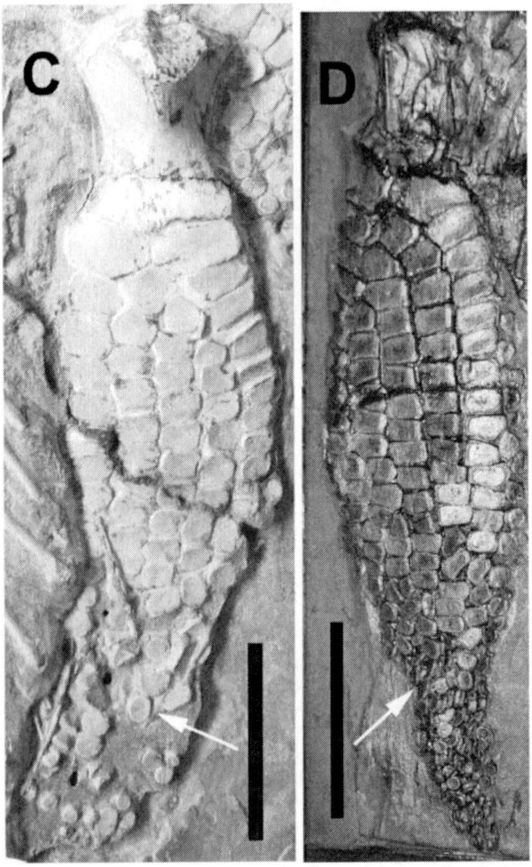

Figure 4. Examples of forefin morphology of Ichthyosaurus. A, CAMSM J35183 from Somerset, an example of what a 'typical' fin from Somerset looks like; B, CHMUS 2015.0102 possibly from Lyme Regis, an example of a wide, five-digit forefin; C, AGC 11 from Somerset, an example of a narrow, five digit forefin; D, YORYM 2006-3803 from Lyme Regis, an example of narrow, six digit forefin. Specimens B–D are exceptionally complete. The arrows indicate the point at which specimens from Somerset (such as A) are usually considered to be complete. Scale bars = 5 cm.

Relatively few specimens of Ichthyosaurus with complete rostra are preserved in ventral view, so it is difficult to assess whether the range of variation is bimodal, as Owen (1881) suggested. Furthermore, it has not been evaluated in other species of the genus, which also raises the issue of reliability. An additional question arises in exactly which features, independent of the symphysis morphology, were used in the assignment of a specimen to I. communis or I. intermedius. If it was based on tooth morphology or forefin morphology, then Owen's (1881) distinguishing character is questionable.

Maisch (1997) has provided the most extensive and specific list of characters in the literature to diagnose Ichthyosaurus intermedius. Most of the proposed diagnostic characters, however, can be seen on the neotype of I. communis (Fig. 5; Table 1). In lateral view, the maxilla has the same, symmetric triangular shape, including the slightly concave ventral border, with the anterior process extending well beyond the edge of the external naris, and the posterior process extending under the orbit (Maisch 1997, figs 1, 5). The maxilla is, however, noticeably higher in SMNS 13111. The lacrimal is large, but not as large as in the neotype. It has a similar triradiate shape, and the dorsal process makes up a large portion of the anterior margin of the orbit, as in the neotype. The dorsal ramus of the jugal of the neotype has a similar right-angle bend and the same dorsal extent as that of SMNS 13111, and like it, shows a lateral ridge. Only a portion of the quadrate is exposed in lateral view on the neotype, and it is similar to that of SMNS 13111. The well-developed processus quadratus of the quadratojugal and its extent are also very similar to those seen in the neotype. The neotype differs from SMNS 13111 in some characters that Maisch (1997) included in the emended diagnosis. The maxilla is lower and its anterior process does not extend as far anteriorly in the neotype as that of SMNS 13111. The neotype has only 12 maxillary teeth rather than 20+, although there is space for several more, and only three maxillary teeth are situated below the orbit.

Furthermore, the posterior maxillary teeth lack curvature, but the latter could be because of the orientation in which they are preserved or due to displacement. In fact, curved maxillary teeth occur on many species of Ichthyosaurus (e.g. I. breviceps, CAMSM X50187; I. larkini, CAMSM J59575; I. communis, MCZ 1079; I. somersetensis, MANCH L.5666), and it is especially noticeable if a portion of the root is also exposed. Finally, the premaxillary fossa are shorter, and the dentary fossa are longer and more continuous in the neotype than what is figured in Maisch (1997). However, intraspecific variation in fossa has never been assessed. The fossa surangularis, however, is similar on both.

In addition to the characters described by Maisch (1997) the neotype is similar to SMNS 13111 in a slender prefrontal that makes up less than half of the anterior border of the orbit; the subnarial process of the premaxilla that makes up half of the ventral margin of the naris; and an anterior process of the jugal that does not extend beyond the anterior margin of the orbit (Fig. 5). Our assessment is that SMNS 13111 has more similarities with the neotype of I. communis than differences, and we would assign it to that species.

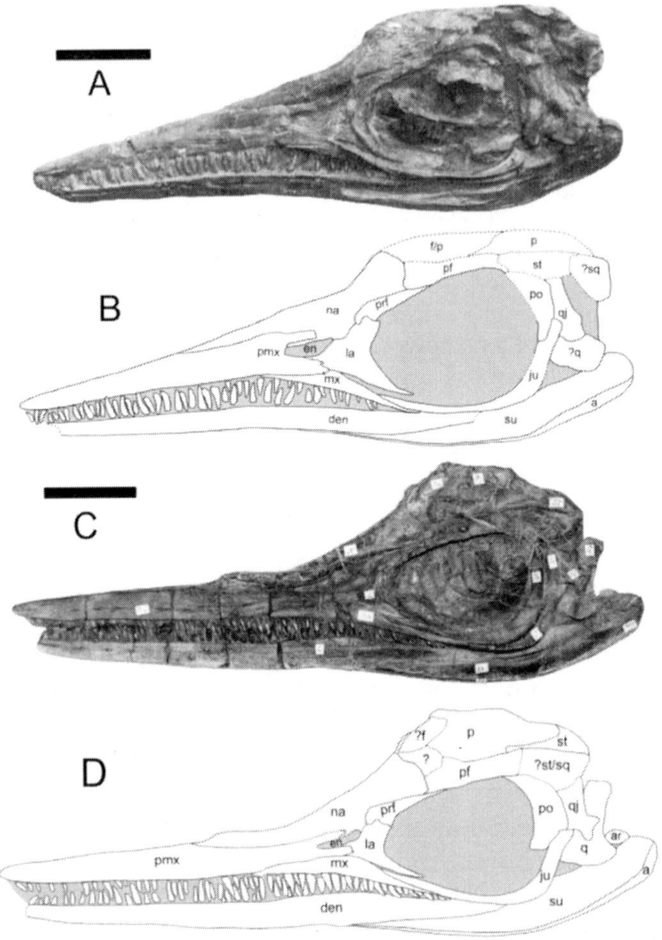

Figure 5. A, skull of Ichthyosaurus communis neotype (NHMUK PV R1162); B, interpretive illustration of the neotype; C, skull of SMNS 13111; D, interpretive illustration of SMNS 13111. Abbreviations: a, angular; den, dentary; en, external naris; f, frontal; ju, jugal; la, lacrimal; mx, maxilla; na, nasal; p, parietal; po, postorbital; pmx, premaxilla; pf, postfrontal; prf, prefrontal; q, quadrate; qj, quadratojugal; sq, squamosal; st, supratemporal; su, surangular. Light grey denotes matrix and openings in skull. Dashed lines indicate broken edge and possible sutures. The dorsal skull roof of the neotype is poorly preserved and the extent of the bones should be interpreted with caution as other bones and openings in the skull could not be identified. The parietal in SMNS 13111 is not well preserved and the shape and extent is deformed due to crushing. Scale bars = 5 cm. The scale bar for A is estimated because the specimen is behind glass and is inaccessible for measurement.

The illustrated skull of I. intermedius (Conybeare 1822, pl. 17, fig. 20) also shows features that are identical with the neotype specimen of I. communis (Fig. 2A, B), including the shape and extent of the maxilla, the shape of the lacrimal, a slender prefrontal making up less than half of the anterior border of the orbit, the shape and extent of the anterior portion of the jugal, the dorsal ramus of the jugal with a right-angle bend, the extent of the bones surrounding the external naris, and the tooth shape. Therefore, because the type 'illustration' of I. intermedius displays features consistent with the neotype of I. communis, we agree with the synonymy of McGowan (1974) and McGowan & Motani (2003).

Systematic palaeontology

Order Ichthyosauria de Blainville, 1835

Family Ichthyosauridae Bonaparte, 1841

Genus Ichthyosaurus De la Beche & Conybeare,

1821 1818 Ichthyosaurus K€onig: 54 [nomen nudum].

1819a Proteosaurus Home: 209.

1821 Ichthyosaurus De la Beche & Conybeare: 563.

1840 Polyostinus Hawkins: 12.

1840 Paramecostinus Hawkins: 15.

1904 Eurypterygius Jaekel: 32.

1979 Protoichthyosaurus Appleby: 492 [in part].

Emended diagnosis. Pineal enclosed within frontals at their posterior edge; large, wide nasals; maxilla excluded from margin of the external naris by subnarial process of premaxilla and anterior process of lacrimal; squamosal present; basioccipital with extensive extracondylar area and well-developed peg; angular with minimal exposure in lateral view; scapula with long shaft, slightly expanded distal end and expanded proximal end, but acromion process absent; coracoid with prominent anterior and posterior notches; humerus with nearly equal width distally and proximally, with slight constriction in the shaft; forefin with distal carpals 3 and 4 contacting the intermedium; metacarpal 5 in the distal carpal row, in contact with the ulnare; digit V as prominent or more prominent than digit IV; digital bifurcation anterior to the primary axis in forefin; forefin with at least five primary digits (although the fin must be preserved to at least p4 row to verify that a bifurcation is present); hind fin with at least four primary digits and an anterior digital bifurcation; rectangular, closely spaced phalanges on most of proximal to middle portion of forefin; pelvic girdle tripartite, without fusion between pubis and ischium; femur longer than wide, with distal end wider than proximal end; preflexural vertebrae <80 (modified from McGowan & Motani 2003; Ji et al. 2016).

Occurrence. The genus is very common from Dorset and Somerset, England, but additional unequivocal occurrences of the genus include: Leicestershire (Martin et al. 1986), Nottinghamshire (Lomax & Gibson 2015), Warwickshire (Smith & Radley 2007), Gloucestershire (e.g. BU 5289, formerly BIRUG 4175), Worcestershire (WOSMG:1, WOSMG:2), Yorkshire (Maisch 1997; Massare et al. 2015), Devon (NHMUK PV R5787), England; Glamorgan, Wales (NMW 2009.35G.1); County Antrim, Northern Ireland (e.g. BELUM K1643, BELUM K28052); Belgium (Godefroit 1996); Switzerland (Maisch et al. 2008); Portugal (Zbyszewski & Moitinho de Almeida 1952; Bardet et al. 2008); and Alberta, Canada (McGowan 1978). The genus was also reported from Scotland, bt contrary to Brusatte et al. (2015), these specimens (teeth and an impression of a lower jaw) are too fragmentary to be assigned to the genus. Similarly, a specimen from British Columbia, Canada (Dennison et al. 1990) shows no diagnostic characters of the genus, and the relative rostrum length would suggest that it is not Ichthyosaurus.

Ichthyosaurus has previously been reported from the uppermost Triassic (Rhaetian) of Somerset (McGowan & Motani 2003), but recent studies suggested that specimens from Somerset are probably from the lowermost Jurassic (Hettangian; Benson et al. 2012, 2015; Lomax & Massare 2017). However, DRL recently examined specimens of Ichthyosaurus currently held in a private collection that were collected in situ from the base of the Liassic Group (probably Rhaetian) of northern Somerset (Carpenter 2001). Thus it is plausible that some specimens of Ichthyosaurus in historical collections are from the Rhaetian. The genus has definitively been reported from the lowermost Jurassic (Hettangian), Pre-planorbis beds of Somerset and Leicestershire (McGowan 1974; Martin et al. 1986; also see discussion in Lomax & Massare 2017). The youngest occurrence of the genus is from the lower Pliensbachian (Lomax 2010; Lomax & Massare 2015).

Ichthyosaurus communis De la Beche & Conybeare, 1821

1821 Ichthyosaurus communis De la Beche & Conybeare: 594.

1822 Ichthyosaurus intermedius Conybeare: 108.

non 1834 Ichthyosaurus chiropolyostinus Hawkins: 25;pls 7–12 [nomen dubium].

non 1834 Ichthyosaurus chiroparamekostinus Hawkins: 32; pls 18–22 [nomen dubium].

non 1840 Ichthyosaurus latimanus Owen: 123 [nomen dubium].

non 1884 Ichthyosaurus fortimanus Owen: 176 [nomen dubium].

non 1911 Ichthyosaurus communis hyperdactyla Jaekel: fig. 154 [nomen dubium].

1922 Eurypterygius communis; Huene: 5 [in part].

1922 Eurypterygius intermedius; Huene: 9 [in part].

1979 Protoichthyosaurus prostaxalis Appleby: 942 [in part].

Neotype. NHMUK PV R1162 (McGowan 1974), a practically complete skeleton comprising the skull, an articulated vertebral column extending into the tail fluke, ribs and gastralia, some pectoral elements, forefin, hind fin, and pelvic girdle.

Emended diagnosis. Ichthyosaurus communis is diagnosed relative to other species of Ichthyosaurus by the following unique characters: symmetric, triangular maxilla with long processes, extending anteriorly beyond external naris and posteriorly well under orbit; large, broad, triradiate lacrimal making up at least half of the anterior orbit margin.

The species is further diagnosed relative to other species of Ichthyosaurus by the following unique combination of characters: snout ratio >0.60 but probably less than 0.65 (as in I. anningae and I. larkini; in the lower range of I. conybeari); premaxilla supranarial and subnarial processes about equal length, extending about half way across the dorsal and ventral margins of the external naris, with nasal about half of dorsal margin (as in all species except I. breviceps and possibly I. anningae); pointed anterior process of jugal extends only slightly beyond the orbit, if at all (as in I. breviceps, I. conybeari); jugal dorsal ramus with a right angle bend (as in all species except I. somersetensis) makes up about half of posterior margin of orbit; and relatively short, wide, crescentic postorbital makes up remainder of posterior margin (as in I. breviceps); lacrimal dorsal process participates in anterior orbit margin, with small prefrontal, contributing less than half of anterior orbit margin (as in I. breviceps, I. conybeari and I. anningae); humerus much longer than wide (as in all species except I. conybeari and I. anningae); irregular depression on articular surface of humerus (as in I. larkini and I. somersetensis); humerus dorsal process large, central, extends less than half way down the shaft (similar to I. larkini); four elements in third (distal tarsal) row of hind fin, with two digits contacting the astragalus (as in I. larkini and I. anningae); hind fin with five primary digits (as in I. conybeari, I. anningae, unknown in I. larkini).

Material. Only two specimens referred to the species by McGowan (1974), both from Lyme Regis, can be unequivocally referred to I. communis: NHMUK PV R1073, NHMUK PV OR36256. The following substantially complete skeletons can also be referred to the species: BU 5289, CAMSM J35187, FMNH P 25027, MCZ 1079, MCZ 1493, OUMNH J.10341/P (cast of specimen figured by Buckland 1836, pl. 8, fig. 1), PETMG R174 and ROM 12805. SMNS 13111, a skull discussed above, is also referred to the species.

Occurrence. The geographical and stratigraphical ranges given here are based only on the neotype and referred specimens listed above. The neotype was collected from Lyme Regis, Dorset. Other referred specimens have been collected from the Lyme Regis-Charmouth area in Dorset, possibly from the Whitby coast of Yorkshire (Maisch 1997, as discussed above), and Gloucestershire (BU 5289). The species is probably also from Street and the surrounding area in Somerset (see Discussion). The species has been reported from Europe (Zbyszewski & Moitinho de Almeida 1952; Godefroit 1996; Maisch et al. 2008; Bardet et al. 2008) and the Isle of Skye, Scotland (Brusatte et al. 2015; as discussed above) but the remains are too incomplete for species assignment.

Specimens from the west Dorset coast are most likely from the Blue Lias and Charmouth Mudstone formations (Page 2010). Historically, the 'Lyme Regis' location was often recorded for ichthyosaurs from several localities along the west Dorset coast. The stratigraphical range usually given for Lyme Regis strata is upper Hettangian– lower Sinemurian (McGowan 1974), although upper Sinemurian– lower Pliensbachian strata are also exposed at nearby localities, such as Charmouth and Seatown (Benton & Spencer 1995; Lomax 2010; Page 2010). It is likely that many historical specimens of Ichthyosaurus were collected from various localities along the west Dorset coast. However, I. communis has not been unequivocally reported from the upper Sinemurian or Pliensbachian (contrary to Bennett et al. 2011; Massare & Lomax 2016a). The uppermost Triassic (Rhaetian) White Lias Formation is also exposed along the coast, south west of Lyme Regis (Gallois 2007); however, we have not seen any specimens of I. communis from the 'White Lias'. Somerset specimens, however, are most likely from the lower Hettangian (McGowan 1974; Benson et al. 2012, 2015). Thus the species range is at least lower ettangian– lower Sinemurian.

Remarks. For most of the nineteenth century, all ichthyosaur specimens were identified as Ichthyosaurus, so old museum identifications and identifications from historical literature should be considered carefully. However, even more recent identifications need to be checked against the criteria presented here. Previous diagnoses of the species allowed for so much variation that all large (>1.5 m) specimens of Ichthyosaurus were assigned to I. communis. The species has been treated as a catch-all for specimens that could not be assigned to I. breviceps or I. conybeari, two small species (<1.6 m) within the genus. But not all larger specimens are I. communis. In particular, the Somerset specimens NHMUK PV OR2013*, NHMUK PV OR2013, NHMUK PV R44, CAMSM J59575, and probably CAMSM J35183, previously referred to the species by McGowan (1974), are not I. communis (Lomax & Massare 2017). In this analysis, we selected a few practically complete specimens that could be unequivocally assigned to the species based on the revised diagnosis. These were included in the geographical range summary above. Notably, I. communis is substantially more common from Dorset than from Somerset, as had been noted in the early literature (Owen 1840, 1881). In fact, fairly complete skeletons of I. communis from Somerset seem to be rare.

6. DISCUSSION

Because Ichthyosaurus communis is herein diagnosed largely by a unique combination of characters, a substantial portion of a skeleton or a well-preserved skull is required to distinguish I. communis from other species in the genus. Therefore our synonymy for Ichthyosaurus communis differs from those previously published (e.g. McGowan & Motani 2003) in considering many species nomina dubia rather than synonyms. Ichthyosaurus chiropolyostinus (Hawkins 1834, pls 7–12) and I. chiroparamecostinus (Hawkins 1834, pls 18–22) were not described in sufficient detail, nor are the figured specimens sufficiently complete to assign them to I. communis. In fact, one of the figured specimens of I. chiropolyostinus in Hawkins (1834, pl. 7) is actually an example of I. breviceps (NHMUK PV OR2001*). The holotype of I. latimanus Owen, 1840 was fairly complete, but it was destroyed in 1940 during the bombing of Bristol (M. A. Taylor, pers. comm.). Although nineteenth century casts of it exist (OUMNH J.10343/P, ANSP 17426, among others; Taylor & Clark in press), the quality is not sufficient to recognize features that can identify I. latimanus as I. communis or any other species of the genus. Moreover, the original published description of I. latimanus (Owen 1840) mixed the description of the holotype with that of another specimen (Taylor & Clark in press) and the validity of the species was questioned (Lydekker 1889; McGowan 1974). Ichthyosaurus fortimanus (Owen 1884) and I. communis hyperdactyla (Jaekel 1911) were each defined on the basis of forefin morphology. Within Ichthyosaurus, forefin morphology is extremely variable and does not appear to be species specific, at least with our current knowledge. Thus these species are herein considered nomina dubia rather than synonyms of I. communis.

The absence of a squamosal in Ichthyosaurus has been considered a characteristic of the genus (Motani 2005; Ji et al. 2016); however, Maisch & Matzke (2000b), Maisch et al. (2008) and Vincent et al. (2014) reported it from specimens of I. communis. The squamosal is present in the holotypes of I. larkini and I. somersetensis (Lomax & Massare 2017), on the holotype of I. anningae (mistaken for part of the supratemporal in Lomax & Massare

2015) and on I. conybeari (NMW 93.5G.2). The postorbital portion of the skull is damaged in the neotype of I. communis, so the presence of a squamosal cannot be verified. Maisch & Matzke (2000b) and Maisch et al. (2008) suggested that a well-preserved post-orbital portion of the skull is required to recognize the squamosal because it is a thin plate of bone that is easily damaged or disarticulated. Well-preserved skulls of most of the species have a squamosal, so its presence should be considered a feature of the genus. The morphology of the mesopodium of the hind fin has been suggested as a taxonomically useful feature (Lomax & Massare 2017). Ichthyosaurus communis has four elements in the third (distal tarsal) row, two of which contact the astragalus. In the neotype, the astragalus has an angular distal edge, and the contacts with digit III and digit IV are equally broad. On some specimens, however, particularly those from Somerset, the astragalus has a flat distal edge and the contact with digit III is much narrower than the contact with digi IV. If the fin elements are displaced or poorly articulated, the contacts are sometimes difficult to discern, even in specimens from Dorset. However, four elements in the third row can often identify a hind fin as belonging to either I. communis, I. larkini or I. anningae. Additional information is required to determine to which of the three species a particular specimen should be assigned. One such example is OUMNH J.13799, from Somerset, a nearly complete specimen of an old individual that is preserved mainly in ventral view, although the skull is in dorsal view. The articulated left hind fin, missing the femur, has four elements in the distal tarsal row and two digits in contact with the astragalus. The astragalus has a straight distal edge, and the contact with digit IV is about twice as broad as the contact with digit III. There is a facet on the astragalus, however, for both of the contacts, so this might be a variation on the pattern displayed on the neotype of I. communis. The humerus/femur ratio indicates that this is not a specimen of I. anningae. Ichthyosaurus larkini also has a contact between digit V and the astragalus, which is absent on this specimen. Thus OUMNH J.13799 is possibly I. communis solely on the basis of the hind fin morphology. If correct, then it would be the only complete skeleton of the species thus far identified from Somerset.

7. CONCLUSIONS

As recognized by McGowan (1974), initial definitions and illustrations of Ichthyosaurus communis and I. intermedius were insufficient to diagnose either species. Complicating the problem, the type specimen of I. communis was not illustrated, and the first illustration of the species (Conybeare 1822, pl. 16, fig. 8), aside from some teeth that may or may not be the same as those of the holotype, was probably an example of I. breviceps. This raises the question of whether the differences described between I. communis and I. intermedius were actually differences between I. breviceps and I. intermedius. Specimens that would have been the holotypes cannot be located, making the problem unresolvable based on the original literature and illustrations. Subsequent nineteenth century descriptions of the species (Owen 1840, 1881; Lydekker 1889) did not propose suitable diagnostic characters nor adequately distinguish between I. intermedius and I. communis. What had been considered the key character, namely tooth morphology, is part of a continuous spectrum of variation that is at least in part ontogenetic. Apparent variation in tooth morphology can also be due to the orientation of the tooth on specimens in lateral view, as well as the quality of preservation and care in preparation of the specimen. Other supposedly important characters were based on forefin morphology, which is also extremely variable.

The problems were more or less resolved by the designation of a neotype for Ichthyosaurus communis, which provides the basis for redefining the species (McGowan 1974). Ironically though, the neotype displays most of the features originally associated with I. intermedius, based on our interpretation of the illustration of the type specimen (Conybeare 1822). In retrospect, when the neotype was assigned, I. intermedius would probably have been a better name to select, given that the skull of the species was figured. However, the name 'I. communis' has been widely used in the literature and is historically significant. Changing the name at this point would only add confusion and destabilize the taxonomy. But regardless, I. communis has priority over I. intermedius, having been introduced a year earlier (De la Beche & Conybeare 1821). Because the neotype shares nearly all of the features originally proposed for I. intermedius, we agree with McGowan (1974) that the two species are the same.

ACKNOWLEDGEMENTS

We thank H. Ketchum and E. Howlett (OUMNH), E. Daeschler and E. Gilmore (ANSP), S. Chapman, P. Barrett and R. Hansen (NHMUK), M. Riley and S. Finney (CAMSM), J. Cundiff (MCZ), D. Gelsthorpe and K. Sherburn (MANCH), K. Seymour (ROM), J. Clatworthy (BU), I. Gladstone (formerly YORYM); C. Howells (NMW), G. Wass and J. Liston (PETMG), M. Simms (BELUM), G. Philips, R. Roden and D. Fox (WOSMG), E. Maxwell (SMNS) and W. Simpson (FMNH) for assistance with and access to specimens at their respective institutions. We also thank R. Clark, C. Berry and the Alfred Gillett Trust, Street, for access to the Alfred Gillett Collection. M. A. Taylor assisted us in trying to locate the figured specimens in Buckland (1836) and Conybeare (1822), C. Smith and S. Jackson supplied pictures of the CHMUS specimen,

N. Larkin called our attention to BU 5289, and B. Loudon provided lodging in London, for which we are grateful. We also thank M. A. Taylor, E. Maxwell and an anonymous reviewer for helpful comments on the manuscript. JAM travel was paid for in part by a Faculty Development Grant through United University Professions and a Faculty Travel Grant from SUNY College at Brockport. DRL's travel was covered in part by a Karl Hirsch Memorial Grant awarded by the Western Interior Paleontological Association (WIPS), a Dean's Doctoral Scholarship Award from the University of Manchester, and funding from RCUK.

REFERENCES

1. Appleby, R. M. 1979. The affinities of Liassic and later ichthyosaurs.*Palaeontology*, **22**, 921–946.
2. Bardet, N., Pereda Suberbiola, X. & Ruiz Omeñaca, J. I. 2008. Mesozoic marine reptiles from the Iberian Peninsula. *Geo-Temas*, **10**, 1245–1248.
3. Bennett, S. P., Barrett, P. M, Collinson, M. E., Moore-Fay, S., Davis, P. G. & Palmer,C. P. 2012. A new specimen of *Ichthyosaurus communis* from Dorset, UK, and its bearing on the stratigraphical range of the species. *Proceedings of the Geologists' Association*, **123**, 145–154.
4. Benson, R. B. J., Evans, M. & Druckenmiller, P. S. 2012. High diversity, low disparity and small body size in plesiosaurs (Reptilia, Sauropterygia) from the Triassic–Jurassic boundary. *PLoS ONE*, **7**, e31838.
5. Benson, R. B. J., Evans, M. & Taylor, M. A. 2015. The anatomy of *Stratesaurus*(Reptilia, Plesiosauria) from the lowermost Jurassic of Somerset, United Kingdom. *Journal of Vertebrate Paleontology*, **35**, e933739.
6. Benton, M. J. & Spencer, P. S. 1995. *Fossil Reptiles of Great Britain*. Chapman & Hall, London, 400 pp.
7. Blainville, H. M. D. de. 1835. Description de quelques espèces de reptiles de la Californie, précédée de l'analyse d'un systéme general d'herpetologie et d'amphibiologie. *Nouvelles Annales du Muséum d'Histore Naturelle*, **4**, 236–296.
8. Blake, J. F. 1902. *List of the types and figured specimens recognized by C. D. Sherborn, F.G.S. in the collection of the Geological Society of London.* Geological Society, London, 100 pp.
9. Bonaparte, C. L. 1841. A new systematic arrangement of vertebrated animals.*Transactions of the Linnean Society of London*, **18**, 247–304.
10. Brusatte, S. L., Young, M. T., Challands, T. J., Clark, N. D. L., Fischer, V., Fraser, N. C., Liston, J. L., MacFadyen, C. C. J., Ross, D. A., Walsh, S. & Wilkinson, M. 2015.Ichthyosaurs from the Jurassic of Skye, Scotland. *Scottish Journal of Geology*, **51**,43–55.
11. Buckland, W. 1836. *Geology and Mineralogy considered with reference to Natural Theology*. 2 volumes. Pickering, London, 128 pp.
12. Carpenter, S. 2001. Excavating a vertebrate-bearing horizon in the Upper Triassic sediments of North Mendip. *Geology Today*, **17**, 29–32.
13. Conybeare, W. D. 1822. Additional notices on the fossil genera *Ichthyosaurus* and*Plesiosaurus. Transactions of the Geological Society of London*, **1**, 103–123.
14. De la Beche, H. T. & Conybeare, W. D. 1821. Notice of the discovery of a new fossil animal, forming a link between the *Ichthyosaurus* and crocodile, together with general remarks on the osteology of the *Ichthyosaurus. Transactions of the Geological Society of London*, **5**, 559–594.
15. Dennison, S. S., Smith, P. L. & Tipper, H. W. 1990. An Early Jurassic ichthyosaur from the Sandilands Formation, Queen Charlotte Islands, British Columbia.*Journal of Paleontology*, **64**, 850–853.

16. Dick, D. G. & Maxwell, E. E. 2015. The evolution and extinction of the ichthyosaurs form the perspective of quantitative ecospace modelling. *Biological Letters*, **11**, 20150339.
17. Dick, D. G., Schweigert, G. & Maxwell, E. E. 2016. Trophic niche ontogeny and paleoecology of early Toarcian Stenopterygius (Reptilia: Ichthyosauria).*Palaeontology*, **59**, 423–431.
18. Gallois, R. W. 2007. The stratigraphy of the Penarth Group (Late Triassic) of the east Devon coast. *Geoscience in south-west England – Proceedings of the Ussher Society*, **11**, 287–297.
19. Godefroit, P. 1996. Un crane d'*Ichthyosaurus communis* (Reptilia, Ichthyosauria) du Sinemurien superieur de Lorraine Belge. *Bulletin de la Société belge de Géologie*, **104**, 77–89.
20. Hawkins, T. 1834. *Memoirs of Ichthyosauri and Plesiosauri, Extinct Monsters of the Ancient Earth*. Rolfe and Fletcher, London, 58 pp.
21. Hawkins, T. 1840. *The Book of the Great Sea-Dragons, Ichthyosauri and Plesiosauri*.W. Pickering, London, 27 pp.
22. Home, E. 1814. Some account of the fossil remains of an animal more nearly allied to fishes than any other classes of animals. *Philosophical Transactions of the Royal Society of London*, **101**, 571–577.
23. Home, E. 1819a. An account of the fossil skeleton of the *Proteosaurus.Philosophical Transactions of the Royal Society of London*, **108**, 24–32.
24. Home, E. 1819b. Reasons for giving the name *Proteo-Saurus* to the fossil skeleton which has been described. *Philosophical Transactions of the Royal Society of London*, **109**, 209–211.
25. Huene, F. von. 1922. *Die Ichthyosaurier des Lias und ihre Zusammenhänge. Monographien zur Geologie und Paläontologie, 1*. Verlag von Gebrüder Borntraeger, Berlin, 114 pp.
26. Jaekel, O. 1904. Eine neue Darstellung von *Ichthyosaurus*. Zeitschrift der Deutschen Geologischen Gesellschaft, **56**, 26–34.
27. Jaekel, O. 1911. *Die Wirbeltiere. Eine Übersicht über die fossilen un lebenden Formen*. Verlag von Gebrüder Borntraeger, Berlin, 252 pp.
28. Ji, C., Jiang, D.-Y., Motani, R., Rieppel, O., Hao, W.-C. & Sun, Z.-Y. 2016. Phylogeny of the Ichthyopterygia incorporating recent discoveries from South China.*Journal of Vertebrate Paleontology*, **36**, e1025956.
29. Johnson, R. 1979. The osteology of the pectoral complex of *Stenopterygius* Jaekel (Reptilia: Ichthyosauria). *Neues Jahrbuch für Geologie und Paläontologie, Abhandlungen*, **159**, 41–86.
30. König, C. D. E. 1818. *Synopsis of the contents of the British Museum*. 13th edition.British Museum, London, 146 pp.
31. Lomax, D. R. 2010. An *Ichthyosaurus* (Reptilia, Ichthyosauria) with gastric contents from Charmouth, England: First report of the genus from the Pliensbachian. *Paludicola*, **8**, 22–36.
32. Lomax, D. R. 2016. A new leptonectid ichthyosaur from the Lower Jurassic (Hettangian) of Nottinghamshire, England, UK, and the taxonomic usefulness of the ichthyosaurian coracoid. *Journal of Systematic Palaeontology*, doi:10.1080/14772019.2016.1183149, 15 pp.
33. Lomax, D. R. & Gibson, B. J. A. 2015. The first definitive occurrence of*Ichthyosaurus* and *Temnodontosaurus* (Reptilia: Ichthyosauria) in Nottinghamshire, England and a review of ichthyosaur specimens from the county. *Proceedings of the Geologists' Association*, **126**, 554–563.
34. Lomax, D. R. & Massare, J. A. 2015. A new species of *Ichthyosaurus* from the Lower Jurassic of west Dorset, England.*Journal of Vertebrate Paleontology*, **35**,e903260.
35. Lomax, D. R. & Massare, J. A. 2017. Two new species of *Ichthyosaurus* from the lowermost Jurassic (Hettangian) of Somerset, England, UK. *Papers in Palaeontology*, **3**, 1–20.
36. Lydekker, R. 1889. *Catalogue of the fossil Reptilia and Amphibia in the British Museum (Natural History). Part II. Containing the Orders Ichthyopterygia and Sauropterygia*. Taylor and Francis, London, 307 pp.

37. Maisch, M. W. 1997. The cranial osteology of *Ichthyosaurus intermedius*Conybeare, 1822 from the Lias of Great Britain. *Stuttgarter Beiträge zur Naturkunde, Serie B (Geologie und Paläontologie)*, **258**, 1–26.
38. Maisch, M. W. & Matzke, A. T. 2000a. The Ichthyosauria. *Stuttgarter Beiträge zur Naturkunde Serie B (Geologie und Paläontologie)*, **298**, 1–159.
39. Maisch, M. W. & Matzke, A. T. 2000b. New data on the cranial osteology of*Ichthyosaurus communis* Conybeare, 1822. *Geologica et Palaeontologica*, **34**, 137–143.
40. Maisch, M. W., Reisdorf, A. G., Schlatter, R. & Wetzel, A. 2008. A large skull of*Ichthyosaurus* (Reptilia: Ichthyosauria) from the Lower Sinemurian (Lower Jurassic) of Frick (NW Switzerland). *Swiss Journal of Geosciences*, **101**, 617–627.
41. Martin, J., Frey, E. & Riess, J. 1986. Soft tissue preservation in ichthyosaurs and a stratigraphic review of the Lower Hettangian of Barrow-Upon-Soar, Leicestershire. *Transaction of the Leicester Literary & Philosophical Society*, **80**, 58–73.
42. Massare, J. A. 1987. Tooth morphology and prey preference of Mesozoic marine reptiles. *Journal of Vertebrate Paleontology*, **7**, 121–137.
43. Massare, J. A. & Lomax, D. R. 2014. An *Ichthyosaurus breviceps* collected by Mary Anning: New information on the species. *Geological Magazine*, **151**, 167–182.
44. Massare, J. A. & Lomax, D. R. 2016a. A new specimen of *Ichthyosaurus conybeari*(Reptilia: Ichthyosauria) from Watchet, Somerset, UK and a re-examination of the species. *Journal of Vertebrate Paleontology*, **36**, e1163264.
45. Massare, J. A. & Lomax, D. R. 2016b. Composite specimens of *Ichthyosaurus* in historic collections. *Paludicola*, **10**, 207–240.
46. Massare, J. A., Lomax, D. R. & Klein, A. 2015. A large forefin of *Ichthyosaurus* from the UK, and estimates of the size of the genus. *Paludicola*, **10**, 119–135.
47. Maxwell, E. E. & Druckenmiller, P. S. 2011. A small ichthyosaur from the Clearwater Formation (Alberta, Canada) and a discussion of the taxonomic utility of the pectoral girdle. *Paläontologie Zeitschrift*, **85**, 457–463.
48. Maxwell, E. E., Scheyer, T. M. & Fowler, D. A. 2014. An evolutionary and developmental perspective on the loss of regionalization in the limbs of derived ichthyosaurs. *Geological Magazine*, **151**, 29–40.
49. McGowan, C. 1974. A revision of the latipinnate ichthyosaurs of the Lower Jurassic of England (Reptilia: Ichthyosauria). *Life Science Contributions of the Royal Ontario Museum*, **100**, 1–30.
50. McGowan, C. 1978. Further evidence for the wide geographical distribution of ichthyosaur taxa (Reptila: Ichthyosauria). *Journal of Paleontology*, **52**, 1155–1162.
51. McGowan, C. 1994. *Temnodontosaurus risor* is a juvenile of *T. platyodon* (Reptilia: Ichthyosauria). *Journal of Vertebrate Paleontology*, **14**, 472–479.
52. McGowan, C. & Motani, R. 2003. *Handbook of Paleoherpetology, Ichthyopterygia*.Verlag Dr. Friedrich Pfeil, Munich, 175 pp.
53. Motani, R. 1999. On the evolution and homologies of ichthyopterygian forefins.*Journal of Vertebrate Paleontology*, **19**, 28–41.
54. Motani, R. 2005. True skull roof configuration of *Ichthyosaurus* and *Stenopterygius*and its implications. *Journal of Vertebrate Paleontology*, **35**, 338–342.
55. Owen, R. 1840. Report on British fossil reptiles. Part I. *Report of the British Association for the Advancement of Science*, **9**, 43–96.
56. Owen, R. 1881. A Monograph of the fossil Reptilia of the Liassic formations. Part 3. Ichthyopterygia. *Monographs of the Palaeontographical Society*, 83–134.
57. Owen, R. 1884. *A History of British Fossil Reptiles, Volume III*. Cassell & Company Limited, London, 199 pp.
58. Page, K. 2010. Stratigraphical framework. Pp. 33–54 in A. R. Lord & P. G. Davis(eds), *Fossils from the Lower Lias of the Dorset coast*. The Palaeontological Association, London.
59. Smith, A. S. & Radley, J. D. 2007. A marine reptile fauna from the Early Jurassic Saltford Shale (Blue Lias Formation) of central England. *Proceedings of the Yorkshire Geological Society*, **56**, 253–260.
60. Taylor, M. A. 2014. Rediscovery of an *Ichthyosaurus breviceps* Owen, 1881 sold by Mary Anning (1799–1847) to the surgeon Astley Cooper (1768–1841) and figured by William

Buckland (1784–1856) in his Bridgewater Treatise. *Geoscience in South-West England*, **13**, 321–327.

61. Taylor, M. A. & Clark, R. D. In press. Ichthyosaurs from the Lower Lias (Lower Jurassic) of Banwell, Somerset. *Geoscience in South-West England*, **14**, 57–71.
62. Torrens, H. S. 1995. Mary Anning (1799–1847) of Lyme; 'the greatest fossilist the world ever knew'. *British Journal for the History of Science*, **28**, 257–284.
63. Vincent, P., Taquet, P., Fischer, V., Bardet, N., Falconnet, J. & Godefroit, P. 2014.Mary Anning's legacy to French vertebrate palaeontology. *Geological Magazine*,**151**, 7–20.
64. Zbyszewski, G. & Moitinho de Almeida, F. 1952. Restes d'ichtyosauriens dans le Lias de S. Pedro de Muel. *Comunicacoes Servicos Geologicos de Portugal*, **33**, 5–10.

CHAPTER 4

Palaeobiology of Silurian Leptaeninae (Brachiopoda) from Gotland, Sweden

Ole A. Hoel

Natural History Museum, University of Oslo, Blindern, P.O. Box 1172, 0318 Oslo, Norway

ABSTRACT

Leptaenine brachiopods are common and widespread on Gotland. *Lepidoleptaena poulseni and Leptaena rhomboidalis* retained a functional apical pedicle throughout ontogeny, and both had strong adductor muscles and robust ornamentation, allowing them to occupy shallow water and high energy environments. A pedicle-shortening muscle is present within the pedicle tube of *Leptaena rhomboidalis. Leptaena sperion, L. depressa visbyensis*, and *L. depressa* lata inhabited low energy environments, retaining very slender pedicles. *L. depressa depressa and L. parvorugata* atrophied the pedicle early and then lived ambitopically in deeper water. The presence or absence of the apical pedicle strongly influenced the cardinal process morphology. Leptaenine shells had a small gape. The lophophore was simple, similar to productids and *Leptaenoidea.* In closed valves, the inner epithelium of leptaenine trails remained exposed to the sea. This was probably important in gas exchange. The life position of pedically attached species was with the disc vertical. Some ambitopic specimens may have retained a similar attitude. Shells of L. *depressa depressa* and *Lepidoleptaena poulseni* commonly are encrusted by epibionts, apparently without problems for larger shells. Small shells are shown to have been killed by bryozoan epizoans. Repaired shell damage is rare on the disc but is common along the commisure.

1. INTRODUCTION

The genus *Leptaena* is one of the most widespread and taxonomically diverse strophomenide brachiopods, with more than 50 named species worldwide and many more occurrences placed in open nomenclature. The temporal distribution is also notable in that the genus extends from the Middle Ordovician (Llanvirn) (e.g., [1]) into the Lower Devonian (Emsian) (e.g., [2, 3]), which amounts to a longevity of about 75 million years. In the Silurian succession of Gotland, Leptaena is a very common component of most brachiopod faunas from the late Llandovery to the Middle Ludlow, after which its role is taken over by the closely related *Lepidoleptaena*. The taxonomy of these two genera on Gotland has been revised elsewhere [4], following which the recognised species present in the Silurian of Gotland are *Leptaena rhomboidalis, Wahlenberg* [5]; *L. depressa depressa Sowerby,* [6]; *L. depressa lata, Hoel* [4]; *L. depressa visbyensis, Hoel* [4]; *L. sperion, Bassett* [7]; *L. parvorugata*, Hoel [4]; *Lepidoleptaena poulseni*, Kelly [8]; *Lepidoleptaena sp.* A and sp. B. In the course of that study several aspects of functional morphology and ecology came to light, which prompted the present paper. Figured specimens belong to the following Swedish institutions: NRM: Swedish Museum of Natural History, Stockholm; PMU: palaeontological collections, Museum of Evolution, Uppsala University; SGU: Geological Survey of Sweden, Uppsala.

2. EXTERNAL MORPHOLOGY

2.1. Shell Form (Figure 1)

All leptaenines have a more or less semicircular outline, but often with laterally extended posterolateral margins, called alae. In profile the valves are initially concavoconvex, but later in ontogeny they become parallel and plane. At the margins, both valves often have a small ventral deflection, but then they both geniculate dorsally. The geniculation is usually abrupt (~90°).

Alae. Most specimens of Leptaena and Lepidoleptaena have somewhat expanded alae, but only in Leptaena depressa lata (Figure 1(e)) and some specimens of Lepidoleptaena poulseni (Figure 1(c)) is there great expansion both laterally and posteroanteriorly, with the result that the lateral parts of the trail form a "ledge" or "terrace."

Figure 1: Shell form in Gotland leptaenines. Scale bar = 1cm (= 0.5cm in detail pictures). (a)–(g): Conjoined valves in ventral view. (a) L. depressa visbyensis. NRM Br32290; Gnisvärd, Tofta parish; Upper Visby Formation. (b) L. rhomboidalis. NRM Br137849; Bals klint; Upper Visby Formation. (c) Lepidoleptaena poulseni. NRM Br121583; Lau Backar, Lau parish; Eke Formation. (d) L. sperion. NRM Br32368; unknown locality, possibly near Visby; Högklint Formation. (e) L. depressa lata. NRM Br32747; Västergarn, Sanda parish. (f) L. parvorugata. NRM Br32641, Follingbo parish. (g) L. depressa depressa. NRM Br112615; Djupvik, Eksta parish; Halla Formation, Djupvik Member. (h)–(j): Conjoined valves in median section. (h) L. rhomboidalis. PMU G1053; unknown locality; large internal volume. (i) L. depressa depressa. PMU G1052; Halla Formation, Fröjel; small internal volume. (j) L. depressa depressa. PMU G1051; Halla Formation, Fröjel; large internal volume. (k)–(o): Conjoined valves in lateral view. (k) L. depressa depressa. NRM Br32557; Visne Myr kanal, Fardhem parish; Hemse Group; note extremely long trail. (l) L. rhomboidalis. NRM Br116187; unknown locality; Upper Visby Formation; flat profile. (m) L. rhomboidalis. NRM Br116186; unknown locality; Upper Visby Formation; Ball-shaped profile. (n) Lepidoleptaena poulseni. NRM Br121581; Gansviken, Grötlingbo parish; Hamra Formation; Very long trail. (o) L. depressa depressa. NRM Br32441; Klintehamn, Klinte parish; Slite Group.

In other species, the lateral expansion is less, often only developed on one side of the animal and mostly involving only the hinge line and the immediately anterior area. As most adult *leptaenines* were ambitopic (*sensu*, Jaanusson [9]; see also [10]) and lost their attachment early in ontogeny, such wide alae are usually interpreted as an adaptation for stability on softer substrates. This is most certainly true for L. depressa lata, which occurs only in the deepest part of the Gotland marine basin, in the southwest area of the outcrop of the Slite Group (see map of species distribution in [4, Figure 12]). On the other hand, similar wide alae are also developed in specimens of the reef-dwelling species *L. rhomboidalis* and *Lepidoleptaena poulseni*, which both retained a functional pedicle (see [4, Figures 2(J), 8(A)]). In such a high energy environment, the wide hinge must have been advantageous for another purpose; it might have helped to stabilise the shell in strong currents, as has been suggested for some spiriferids with a wide hinge line [11], allowing the shell to "float" above the substrate. If this interpretation is correct, this would be an interesting adaptation of a preexisting morphology to accommodate a totally different function without much modification. Such interpretations require testing in flume tank experiments.

Trail. The distinctive trail of many leptaenines is usually interpreted as a functional morphology to elevate the commisure above the substrate (e.g. [12, 13]), with the shell resting on the convex ventral valve. In this attitude, the shell could even be buried within the sediment without the animal dying, as long as the growth of the trail maintained a rate at least equal to the sedimentation rate (see, e.g., [10, page 243]). Another possible function was that of separating the feeding currents. Emig [14] considered that the fold and sulcus of living brachiopods make filtering more effective by spatially separating inhalant from exhalant currents and precluding recycling. Analogous solutions have also been described in molluscs, for example, the Pennsylvanian bellerophontacean *Knightites multicornutus* (see [15, page 248]). The most important effect of the fold and sulcus, however, is to move the position of the inhalant currents to a more anterior position [14]. When the shell anterior is pointing into the current, this produces an increased inflow compared with rectimarginate forms, which have the intake laterally. These factors seem to be borne out by the observation that the volumetric flow rate per unit area is almost twice as great in plicate species than in rectimarginate forms ([14, page 299]). On a firm substrate, the geniculation of many strophomenides may have worked in a comparable way as the plicate commisure of other groups. If the shell were oriented in the conventional way, the trail would lift the anterior part of the commisure higher than the lateral parts and thus separate the exhalant and inhalant currents. In soft substrates, the geniculate shell of a leptaenide would tend to sink, especially anteriorly because of the thickening of the dorsal marginal rim. Thus the entire commisure would lie close to the substrate and the geniculation would only serve to keep the animal from sinking too far. The presence of a trail was therefore advantageous on both hard and soft substrates, and on a hard surface a shell could even survive being flipped over with the dorsal valve lowermost, as suggested by Lescinsky [16], although on a soft substrate the commisure would surely sink and the animal would die.

In several specimens of *Leptaena depressa depressa*, the trail is extremely long, and in these specimens the anterior commisure is plicate (Figure 1(k), see also [4, Figures 4(S)-4(T)] and [10, text-Figure 3]). This is not observed in specimens with shorter (lower) trails, except in one specimen of *L. rhomboidalis* (see [4, Figure 2(K)]). As noted by Bassett [10], it is probable that long trailed specimens lived quasi-infaunally and that the plication of the anterior commisure was the only way to separate the inhalant and exhalant currents, because the lateral part of the animal was buried in sediment. The plicate specimen of the normally high-energy species *L. rhomboidalis* may possibly have become detached and transported into softer sediment, which prompted the unusual trail development. Long-trailed specimens are comparatively few in the population and thus represent only the most extreme living conditions. Most other specimens would have lived at or just below the water-sediment interface. Young specimens with a thin and light shell would "float" on the substrate, while older specimens would have usually sunk into the soft sediment with the point of geniculation sinking deepest. The dorsal valve is the thickest, and it is especially thickened at the point of geniculation, with the development of a peripheral rim. Even so, leptaenines also appear to have been able to live in other orientations (see further discussion of this in the section on life position below), and this plasticity of behaviour may have been a reason for the success of the group. Most other ambitopic strophomenides were either relatively flat and thin shelled, "floating" on the substrate (most strophodontids) or with a deeply convexoconcave profile without geniculation, where the shell would have settled into the substrate (e.g., Strophonella and larger plectambonitoideans).

The change in mode of growth at the time of geniculation was fundamental; after this event, the animal can be said to have effectively stopped growing, because the area of the filtration chamber could not become larger. Even so, the animal still had the capacity to increase the internal volume of the shell. This was accomplished in many specimens by ventral growth of the dorsal valve at the peripheral rim, which elevated the dorsal valve, but at the same time rotated the still growing dorsal valve margin posteriorly. To keep the aperture as small as possible, the growing edge of the ventral valve thus had to grow posteriorly as well as dorsally. As the trail grew longer, this resulted in the shell becoming increasingly ball-shaped (see Figures 1(l)-1(m) and [4, Figures 2(F)-2(G)]). In specimens where the mantle cavity remained low, the trail was straight or oriented anteriorly.

2.2. Rugae

Rugae are an especially distinct character in leptaenide brachiopods. One of their functions was most probably that of strengthening the shell, which would be advantageous especially in higher energy water and which probably explains the association of several species with precisely this kind of environment. The reef-dwelling *L. rhomboidalis* has shells with extremely deep rugae, a shell thickness of 0.3–0.8 mm (thickest in the ridge part of the rugae, thinnest in the furrows.) *L. depressa and L. sperion* occurs in low energy marlstones, and their shells are 0.2–0.4 mm thick with quite subdued rugae. L. parvorugata, which occurs only in the presumably deepest environments of the Slite Group, is generally devoid of rugae. The radial sculpture of costellae is developed more or less equally in all these species. Dewing ([17, page 140]) interpreted the rugae of *Leptaena* and similar brachiopods as functioning as a plough in soft sediments. He suggested that the animal would have used the pedicle between the valves (see comments on this below) to pull the shell backwards, redistributing sediment with the steep posterior faces of the rugae, and then lets it glide forwards under the pull of gravity on the shallow-angled anterior faces. For this to work, the pedicle would need to be attached to the substrate above the level of the brachiopod and then would only serve to bury the animal. Most sessile animals have a primary need to avoid being buried during excessive sedimentation, and it would seem unnecessary to move even deeper into the sediment. Since most specimens of Leptaena found on Gotland appear to have been current-transported to some degree, a truly infaunal habit also seems unlikely, although some specimens must have lived thus [10].

Rugae may also disclose other aspects of the life of strophomenides. Timms and Brunton [18] inferred growth rate in productides based on numbers of rugae. They suggested that geniculation could have occurred at the onset of sexual maturity, because geniculation occurred at about half adult size; maturity at half adult size seems to be comparable with living brachiopods. They also presented the idea that the number of rugae on productid brachiopods could be related to the growth rate of the animal. They noted that the most likely periodicity in the production of rugae was the synodic month, thereby interpreting each ruga to have been produced in one month. In this interpretation the animals that they studied were between 19 and 33 months old at the time of geniculation. If this is applied similarly to leptaenids from Gotland, *Leptaena depressa visbyensis* from the late Llandovery lower Visby beds reached geniculation in from 5 to 17 months, the Middle Wenlock *Leptaena depressa depressa* from 5 to 21 months, and the Ludlow *Lepidoleptaena poulseni* from 4 to 19 months. Why such a fundamental morphological change would occur at seemingly very different times in the life history of different specimens of the same species is unclear, but seems to rule out the idea of sexual maturity; it is unlikely that a specimen could be mature at 4 months. The only published age of sexual maturity in brachiopods that I am aware of is about two years for the Recent *terebratulide Calloria* (Williams et al., [19, page 95]).

2.3. Phenotypic Variation

As noted by Spjeldnæs [20], the large collections of *L. depressa depressa* from the western outcrop of the Halla Formation (formerly Mulde beds, see [21]) in the Fröjel area demonstrate a clearly expressed dimorphism; type A has a semicircular, anteriorly rounded outline, and a long trail, which can be as long as the disc. Type B has a squared-off disc outline and very short trail. The significance of this dimorphism is as yet unclear, but it seems improbable that it is a sex differentiation, as there are specimens with intermediate morphologies. It may therefore be an ecological effect. Exactly which ecological factors that are involved is difficult to establish without new extensive, well-constrained collections, since most museum specimens have been collected from scree. They may therefore originate from slightly different stratigraphical levels at the same locality.

Phenotypic variation among Ordovician species of *Rafinesquina* was studied by Alexander [22], who found that the perimeter/volume ratio (perimeter being the length of the commisure from hinge margin to hinge margin) shows good correlation with the sedimentary environment inferred by other methods. A high ratio suggests a wide, flat shell with a minimum of oxygen-consuming biomass and maximum mantle surface for oxygen uptake and good "snow-shoe" effect keeping the shell "afloat" on soft, muddy substrates, which is where these specimens occur. Conversely, a low ratio indicates a deeper shell with more biomass, weighting the animal into the substrate and keeping it from overturning in stronger currents. A similar relationship may be valid for the specimens of *Leptaena* from the *Fröjel* area, but it is not possible to confirm this without further detailed study.

2.4. Life Position

Although concavoconvex shells of strophomenides are found usually with the convex ventral valve uppermost, most workers have advocated a life position with the ventral valve lowermost and the trail vertical, because this would have lifted the commisure above the substrate and minimized the influx of suspended mud particles. In a controversial paper, Lescinsky [16] argued that the life position was the other way round, with the ventral valve on top. In such a position the trail would have worked as an inclined plane and functioning as a sediment trap, hindering coarse suspended material from flowing into the commisure. In support of this view he studied a large sample of encrusted concavo-convex brachiopods from eleven localities across the USA of Ordovician and Devonian age. In these samples most of the epifauna was preserved on the ventral valve surface, which would be in contact with the substrate in the conventional view. This view has been discussed only briefly by later workers (e.g., [23, 24]), although it is refuted by the work of Leighton and Savarese [25], who showed that in a convex-upward attitude, the commisure sinks into the substrate if pore water content approaches 50%.

Another main argument against Lescinsky's idea is that the convex-up position is the most hydrodynamically stable state, to which any dead shell or an individual unable to otherwise right itself would probably end up because of hydrostatic constraints as opposed to biological strategies. The time spent by a dead shell on the surface before burial would generally be sufficient for settlement of encrusters on the ventral valve. Most specimens of *Leptaena* from Gotland in which the taphonomic attitude of the shell has been observed corroborate this view; they are lying convex-up, and if they are not filled completely with sediment, the lower surface of the geopetal fillings is parallel with the edge of the trail (Figure 2(a)).

From a similar study of conjoined shells of *Leptaena* and other brachiopods from the western outcrop of the Halla Formation (formerly Mulde beds) on Gotland, Spjeldnæs [20] found that the proportion of encrusters was similar on both valves, which could be interpreted in two ways: (1) the shells could have been exposed on the substrate and then been tumbled around by currents, ending up with epifauna on both valves. This is unlikely because the valves would almost certainly be separated from each other fairly quickly because of the weakly efficient interlocking function of their deltidiodont dentition; (2) they had lived in a vertical position, with the umbo down into the sediment. During fieldwork, I found a specimen of *L. depressa depressa* in this position in the Halla Formation (Mulde Brick clay Member) at Blåhäll, and the geopetal filling in the specimen of Figure 2(b) shows that the shell was buried with its ventral valve more or less vertical. Several specimens of *L. depressa visbyensis* from the Högklint beds (Figure 2(c)) are also buried with their disc vertical.

A method by which unattached strophomenides could remain vertical or escape burial was suggested by Dattilo [26], who suggested that the plectambonitoid *Sowerbyella* was able to move upwards in sediment and orienting itself vertically by valve snapping. A vertical position was probably the normal life orientation in those leptaenines that retained their pedicle throughout life (*L. rhomboidalis and Lepidoleptaena poulseni*) (see Figure 4).

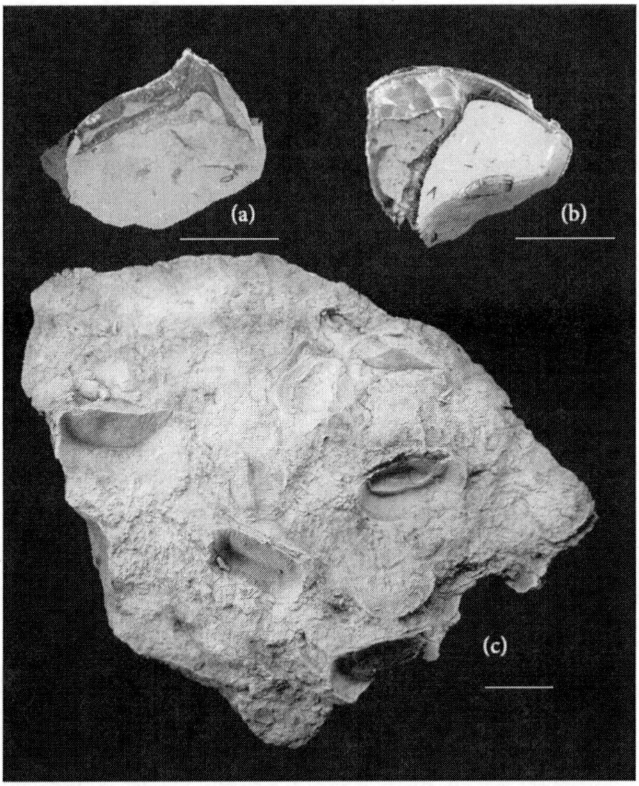

Figure 2: Life position versus postmortem orientation. Scale bar = 1cm (= 0.5cm in detail pictures). (a) L. depressa depressa. PMU G1055; Halla Formation, Fröjel. Section of conjoined valves buried with commisure horizontal. (b) L. depressa depressa. PMU G1051; Halla Formation, Fröjel. Section of conjoined valves apparently buried with disc in a more or less vertical attitude. (c) L. depressa visbyensis. SGU 9225; Visby Formation Underside of a slab from the Visby Formation showing several individuals of Leptaena depressa visbyensis buried with their umbo pointing downwards. Note that this subspecies had a small, open foramen.

It is interesting to note that the latter two species developed long trails, even though they were not in danger of being buried in sediment. When the shells are oriented in their supposed life orientation attached to the substrate by a short pedicle, the disc is often seen to have been vertical and the outer portion of the trail horizontal. This probably means that orienting the trail horizontal would impart an advantage to the animal in strong currents. Oriented in this way (as seen in Figure 1(m)), the shell would present a half-sphere shape towards the current, probably with the convex side facing into the current. *LaBarbera* [27] noted that in a unidirectional current, terebratulids orient the shell with their anteroposterior axis normal to the current. Since they have lateral inhalant currents, this would make filtration more effective. In another study [28], I have demonstrated that the cementing strophomenide *Leptaenoidea* must have had an anteromedial inhalant current. Assuming that the lophophore was essentially similar in *Leptaena* (see Figure 9), pointing the anteroposterior axis downstream, then gaping would result in eddies behind the commisure. The turbulence would have resulted in particles falling out of suspension, making filtration more effective than having the fast-moving water currents flow through the filtration cavity, maybe damaging the delicate lophophore tentacles in the process.

2.5. Anchored and Secondarily Free-Lying (Ambitopic) Strategies

As in all marine filter feeding invertebrates (such as bivalves), most living brachiopods have physical stability as a basic requirement. In surface-dwelling bivalves, this is achieved commonly initially by byssal fixation, and later in life by valve thickening (Stanley [29]). Such strategies are probably analogous to those of some ambitopic strophomenide taxa, such as late Palaeozoic productides [12], which had a functional pedicle (or were cementing) in early life, after which they lost their attachment and became thick-shelled. In the majority of strophomenide species, however, the loss of attachment did not entail dramatic thickening of the valves, and these relatively thin and light shells must have been in danger of being swept away by currents or buried by sediment. It is therefore not surprising that the greatest diversity of strophomenides is found in relatively low-energy environments, such as the midouter ramp marlstone areas of western Gotland. Even so, many strophomenides thrived in relatively high-energy environments. Of about 15 strophomenide genera present in the Silurian of Gotland, eight occur in high energy (shallow water) environments; four genera were generalists (*Leptaenoidea, Brachyprion, Leptostrophia,* and *Strophonella*), occurring in both high-, and low-energy settings; three genera are found almost exclusively in high energy sediments (*Lepidoleptaena, Shaleria*, and *Strophodonta*); and one normally low-energy genus (*Leptaena*) has a single species (*L. rhomboidalis*) which is specialized for high energy. Three of the generalists are ambitopic, without any trace of a pedicle in adult shells, while Leptaenoidea is pedically attached in early life and then becomes cementing in high-energy environments or ambitopic in lower-energy environments [28].

In the ambitopic species of *Leptaena,* thickening of the valves is observed in some specimens, but this is mostly confined to the visceral area and the bounding ridge around the dorsal disc. Otherwise, the valves are quite thin. Together with the long trail, this resulted in the mantle cavity being quite deep and the passage from the commisure to the mantle cavity becoming long and narrow, thus probably inhibiting influx of fouling sediment to the lophophore.

Both L. rhomboidalis and *Lepidoleptaena poulseni* have large apical pedicle foramina in their ventral valves throughout ontogeny. *L. rhomboidalis* occurs in high-energy limestones, predominantly in the Högklint Formation. It retained a functional pedicle throughout life, which grew to be quite thick, as attested by the large foramen, and the shell does not exhibit great thickening, except in the posteromedial area where the visceral mass was situated. Usually it also has a relatively shorter trail than *L. depressa*. The apical foramen is quite similar to that of one group of living lingulates (*Discinisca*, see [19, Figure 90[5]]), which has only a flat, adhesive pad as an attachment structure. One specimen of *Lepidoleptaena poulseni* (see [4, Figure 9(A)]) has an impression of the apical pedicle within a bryozoan colony, which apparently grew along and around the pedicle for several mm outside the shell. The pedicle was therefore longer than the adhesive patch of *Discinisca,* probably enabling the shell to rotate an appreciable amount, as necessary.

The pedicle of strophomenates was evidently a totally different structure than the pedicle of other rhynchonelliformeans. Rather than being a rod of connective tissue, the strophomenide "pedicle" was probably an outgrowth of the ventral body wall, similar in structure to living lingulates such as *Discinisca,* in which it contains a large part of the coelom and has a strongly muscular wall ([19, Figures 39, 90[5]]). This was probably the original pedicle structure in the Brachiopoda, which was retained in the Chileata, Obolellata, Kutorginata, and Strophomenata. A wholly new structure was developed in the Rhynchonellata, which originates from the mantle rudiment in larvae ([19, page 60]).

Some specimens of *Leptaena rhomboidalis* (Figures 3(b)–3(d)) were cut through vertically at the level of the foramen, showing a section of the tubular chamber connecting the delthyrial cavity and the foramen. On the anteroventral inner surface of this tube there are clear traces of a pedicle adjustor muscle attachment (white arrow in Figure 3(c)). This section of a scar is similar to those preserved in sections through the cardinal processes. A muscle attached here would probably have served to shorten the pedicle, thereby keeping the umbo as close as possible to the substrate. With an attachment close to the anterior wall of the pedicle, retraction of the muscle would have resulted in a rotational moment of the shell towards the ventral valve outer surface. Such a rotational moment could have been necessary to counter water current pressure if the shell presented the ventral valve towards the current (see Figures 4(a)-4(b)). As far as I know, this is the first direct evidence of how the muscular control of the strophomenide pedicle worked. Dewing ([17, pl. 2, Figure 6]) interpreted smooth areas on the dental plates of several strophomenide species from the late Ordovician of Anticosti, Canada, as attachment pads for adjustor muscles, implying a more normal articulate pedicle leaving the shell through the delthyrium. I am not convinced by his arguments; as already shown (Figure 3, see also [17, Figure 5]), the attachment points for muscles are preserved in section as fibres normal to the shell surface, not as layers parallel to it as figured by Dewing [17, Figure 10]. If most strophomenides with a small gap between the pseudodeltidium and chilidium had a pedicle, then surely these "adjustor scars" would be preserved in more than an extremely low number of specimens, especially from sequences with extremely good preservation such as those on Anticosti and Gotland. My interpretation of these structures is that they are layers of secondary shell material lining the delthyrial cavity for smooth operation of the diductor muscles. Such layers are often almost nacre-like in smoothness and are present in most well-preserved Leptaena from Gotland, especially in those that sealed off their interior pedicle tubes early (see Figures 3(e)-3(f)). Dewing [17, Pl. 2, Figure 6] also figures this type of feature (which he interpreted as adjustor scars) in Gunnarella fluctuosa.

2.6. Shell Damage, Predation, and Encrustation

In high energy environments, damage to the shell would have occurred often. When the animal died, the valves would be broken up, but a surprising number of strophomenides show repaired damage, indicating that the animal could survive extensive shell damage. Examples of repaired strophomenide shells can be seen in Alexander ([30] from the late Ordovician of north-central USA), Ebbestad and Högström ([31] from the late Ordovician of central Sweden) and (Dewing [32, pl. 5, Figures 5, 13]; from the late Ordovician of Anticosti, Canada). The incidence of successful shell repair is generally much higher in strophomenides than in other articulated stocks and an explanation for this may be that the close proximity of the two valves probably made damage to the valve edge less catastrophic for strophomenides than for species having more globular shell shapes [23]. Most leptaenids from Gotland display fairly minor damage, especially along the commisure, but in some cases a number of specimens show more extensive repair. Examples of such repair are illustrated in Figure 5. The specimen of *L. depressa visbyensis* (Figure 5(a)) from the Visby Formation has repaired a substantial injury after having a semicircular portion taken out of the shell, removing about 25% of the disc.

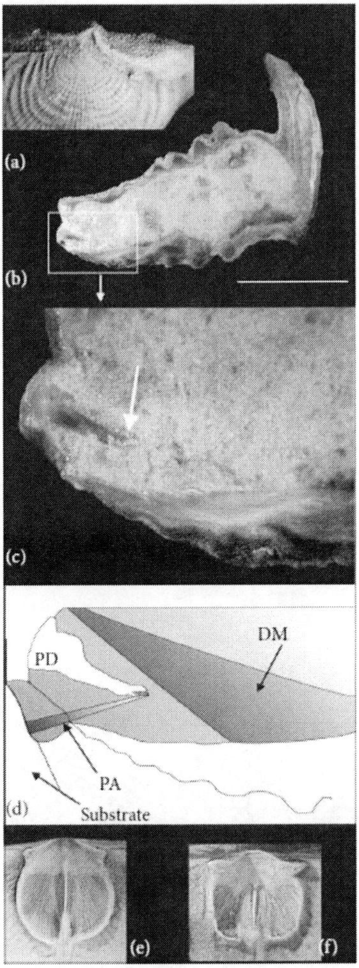

Figure 3: (a)–(d): Shape and function of the apical pedicle in attached species. Scale bar = 1cm (= 0.5cm in detail pictures). (a) *Lepidoleptaena poulseni.* NRM Br129751; Burgsvik, Öja parish; Hamra Formation; Pedicle length and thickness indicated by bryozoan overgrowth. (b)–(d) *L. rhomboidalis.* PMU G1054; Visby, Högklint Formation; section through open apical foramen showing scars after attachment of muscles within the pedicle tube (white arrow) and reconstruction of the intrapedicular muscle (PA) attaching to the ventral interarea (PD). DM is the diductor muscles. (e)-(f): Internal sealing of the apical foramen in free-lying species. (e) *L. parvorugata.* NRM Br138049a; Valleviken 1, Rute, Slite Group. (f) *L. depressa depressa*. NRM Br138045; Mulde Tegelbruk, Fröjel; Halla Formation. Both have covered the apical part of the muscle scars with thick secondary shell material.

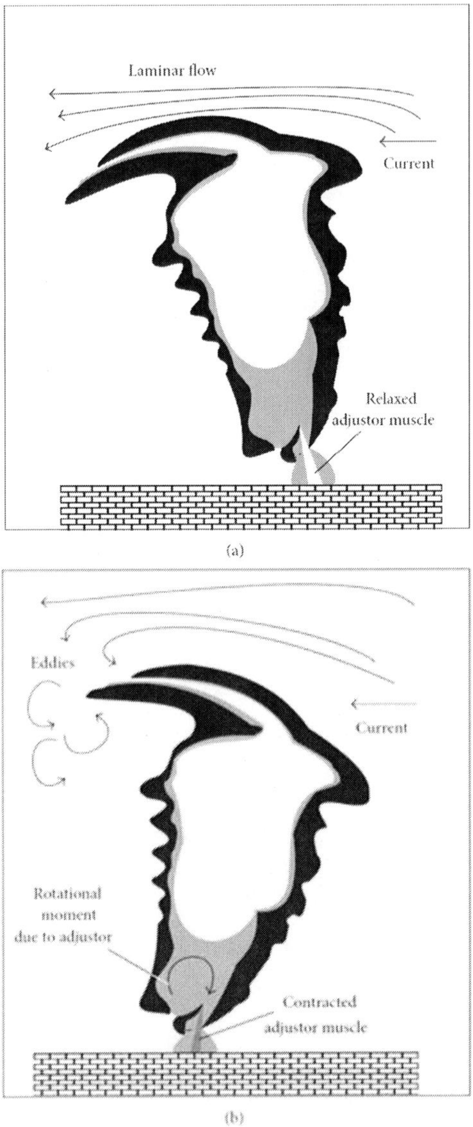

Figure 4: *Leptaena rhomboidalis*. PMU G1054; Visby, Högklint Formation. Reconstruction of the function of the pedicle retractor muscle inferred from the specimen in Figures 3(b)–3(d). (a) Muscle is relaxed; commisure is oriented down towards the substrate and the current that hits the ventral valve tends to flow past the commisure in a smooth flow. (b) Muscle is contracted; commisure points more upwards and the current becomes disturbed with eddies forming outside the commisure, which makes particle fall out of suspension to be collected by the brachiopod.

This was probably a result of predation, and it is not improbable that such a shape would be expected from a cephalopod beak. Cephalopods are common on Gotland; Hedström [33] described seven species of *Phragmoceras* from the Visby Formation alone. Figure 5(b) shows a specimen of *Lepidoleptaena poulseni* from the Eke Formation, which has lost both lateral portions of the shell, extending to the bounding ridges surrounding the disc. This could also have been a result of predation, but the shallow water, high energy environment in which it occurs, also suggests that the damage could have been a result of strong water buffeting, for example, during a storm. Both these specimens show that when the disc was damaged after the commencement of geniculation, the regrowing mantle was not able to mimic the bordering rugae on the disc; it could only regenerate the growth of the radial ornament of costellae similar to those on the trail. A dorsal valve of *Lepidoleptaena poulseni* (Figure 5(c)) displays a double disc-bounding ridge, possibly caused by some infection or impairment of growth control.

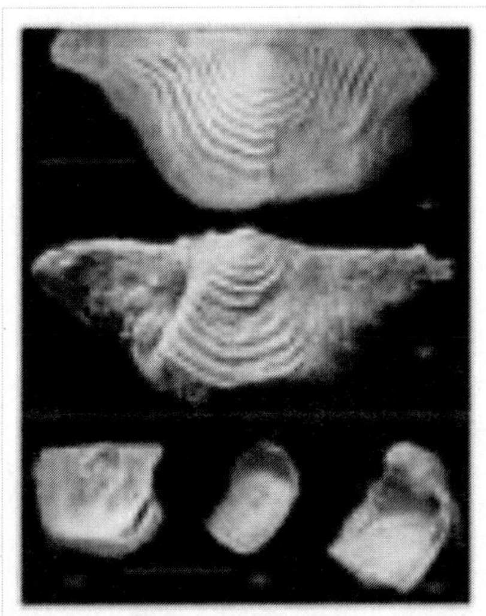

Figure 5: Damage and fouling by epibionts. Scale bar = 1cm (= 0.5cm in detail pictures). (a) *L. depressa* visbyensis. NRM Br32290; Gnisvärd, Tofta parish; Upper Visby Formation; repaired crescentic wound. (b)–(e): *Lepidoleptaena poulseni*. (b) NRM Br32699; Lau Backar, Lau parish; Eke Formation; abnormal sculpture on regrown parts of the shell after loss of entire lateral areas on both sides. (c) NRM Br131994; Kättelviken, Sundre parish; Hamra Formation; abnormal growth of dorsal trail on the right side. (d) NRM Br129748; without bryozoan encrustation the trail is low. (e) NRM Br128749; with bryozoan encrustation the trail grew tall in an unsuccessful attempt to escape being overgrown.

Evidence of predation is rare among the leptaenids; apart from the specimen noted above, only boring organisms have been noted. Two single valves (not illustrated) of Leptaena depressa depressa from the Halla Formation at Djupvik have been bored through the shell; a ventral valve (SMNH Br108919) has a hole penetrating obliquely through the extra-muscular area. This damage was repaired by the brachiopod. A dorsal valve (SMNH Br112648) has been bored vertically through its right adductor muscle. This damage is unrepaired, and the animal thus died from the wound. Alternatively, the shell might have been dead and buried when the boring occurred.

Specimens of *Lepidoleptaena poulseni* from the Ludlow of Gotland are often encrusted with epifauna. The larger specimens are often covered with oncolithic crusts, usually on the ventral valve. In smaller specimens the surface is more often unencrusted, with the trail often quite low, but when encrusted with bryozoan colonies, the trail becomes long. This may indicate that the brachiopod was trying to outgrow the bryozoan colony as the colonies approach the commisure. The overgrown commisure on such specimens suggests that the competition sometimes killed the brachiopod (Figures 5(d)-5(e)). Large specimens of the same species sometimes have bryozoan epifauna (see Figure 1(c)), but they do not seem to have been troubled by the encrustation. This might indicate a growth rate in large specimens much higher than the growth of the bryozoans. Modern bryozoan colonies have growth rates up to 3mm/year, which is about the same as that found in some living brachiopods (Terebratulina retusa initially grows at 4mm/year but slows down after three years. It lives for 7 years; [19, page 242]).

The populations of *Leptaena depressa depressa* from the Fröjel area also show a very large rate of infestation, mostly by bryozoans (about 90% [20]), where the rate is highest on the trails. Nevertheless, I have not found any specimens that have grown a longer trail because of the infestation. This may be explained by the much larger specimen size (width ~3-4cm) in this sample. Large specimens of *Lepidoleptaena poulseni* are often heavily encrusted seemingly without any problems, which indicate a refuge from the dangers of infestation above a certain size. This size may be about 15–18mm length, as there is a discontinuity in the size distribution in this area (see [4, Figure 11(g)]). A similar discontinuity is found in *Leptaena depressa depressa* at 10–15mm length and may be explained in a similar way.

Two small specimens of Lepidoleptaena poulseni from the Hamra beds at Burgsvik (Br129760 and Br129777) have specimens of Petrocrania sp. attached to their dorsal valves, while the most usual epifauna encrusting this species is *Spirorbis.*

3. INTERNAL MORPHOLOGY

3.1. Vascular System

In fossil brachiopods the visible trace of the vascular system comprises mantle canal impressions. In living species the canals are predominantly occupied by the gonads. In leptaenines the mantle canals are mostly confined to the trails. According to Williams et al. ([19, page 413]), *Leptaena* had gonocoelic tissues covering most of the disc area, while the circulation was controlled by the vascula media in the ventral valve and the *vascula myaria* in the dorsal valve. These are interpreted by these authors to turn laterally along the disc margin, and larger canals (~0.3mm diameter) branch off and continue on the trails to the commisure. In the ventral valves of Leptaena from Gotland, the mantle canals are usually not visible (an exception is shown on Figure 6(d)), but in the dorsal valves they are readily visible on the trail (Figure 6(a)). On the dorsal disc, the canals are usually not developed, but in a specimen of (Figure 6(c)), they can be seen to originate at several locations along the frontal scars (as defined by [8]) and branch repeatedly on the disc before crossing the peripheral rim. This pattern contradicts the interpretation of Williams et al. [19] in that the canals do not originate along the disc margin, but at the anterior body wall. It also shows that the mantle on the disc was not different in organization from that on the trail, although this may indicate that the mantle tissues were thicker on the disc than on the trail, since the mantle canals did not make depressions in the shell material. The large canals on the trail indicate that the mantle tissue was an important component of the circulation system, probably aiding in the uptake of oxygen. When the valves were closed, the mantle cavity was effectively closed by the dorsal disc peripheral ridge, which contacted the inner surface of the ventral valve trail, but even in closely shut shells, the mantle surfaces on the inner surfaces of the dorsal and ventral trails are separated by up to 0.6mm, which would have continually exposed the mantle tissue to the sea water (Figure 7). The animal could have thus acquired the necessary oxygen and released waste products without opening access to the mantle cavity and the lophophore. The pseudopunctae on the trail are strong and closely approach the opposing valve surface, and they point towards the commisure, so that any particles entering the narrow passage between the valves would have had difficulty entering very far and would have easily been expelled by a quick snapping of the valves (Figure 7).

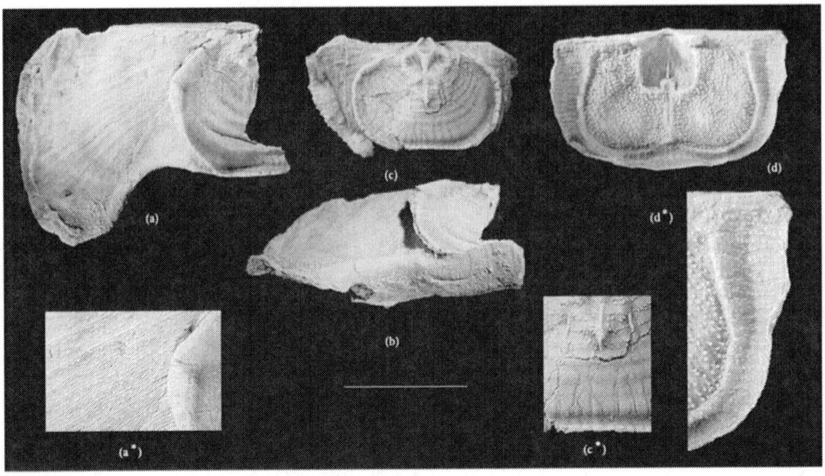

Figure 6: Mantle canals. Scale bar = 1cm (= 0.5cm in detail pictures). (a)-(b) *L. depressa lata*. NRM Br134087; Klintehamn, Klinte; strong mantle canals on the extremely large alae. (c) *L. depressa lata*. NRM Br32745; Västergarn, Sanda; note mantle canals on the disc as well as the trail. (d) *L. depressa depressa*. NRM Br138045; Mulde Tegelbruk, Fröjel; Halla Formation; rare example of visible mantle canals on the ventral trail.

3.2. Muscular Systems

3.2.1. Cardinal Process and Opening of the Shell

In all leptaenines, the strong development of both the notothyrial platform and the cardinal process lobes can be explained probably by the structure and function of the relatively large and heavy dorsal valve. This is especially clear in Lepidoleptaena poulseni, where the large shells often are heavily encrusted, which added significantly to the weight of the dorsal valve (Figure 1(c)). The ventral valve muscle field is deeply impressed, and also occupies a relatively large part of the disc, emphasising the strength of the diductor muscles. Externally, the base of the cardinal process is massive and is covered by a large chilidium. In Leptaena, the chilidium is much larger than the pseudodeltidium, which is normally very small. The possible opening angle of the shell seems to have been controlled by the large size of the chilidium; during opening, the dorsal valve would have rotated around the teeth until the upper surface of the chilidium contacted the lower edge of the pseudodeltidium. In Leptaena, the pseudodeltidium and chilidium were set a considerable distance posterior to the actual rotation axis of the hinge line.

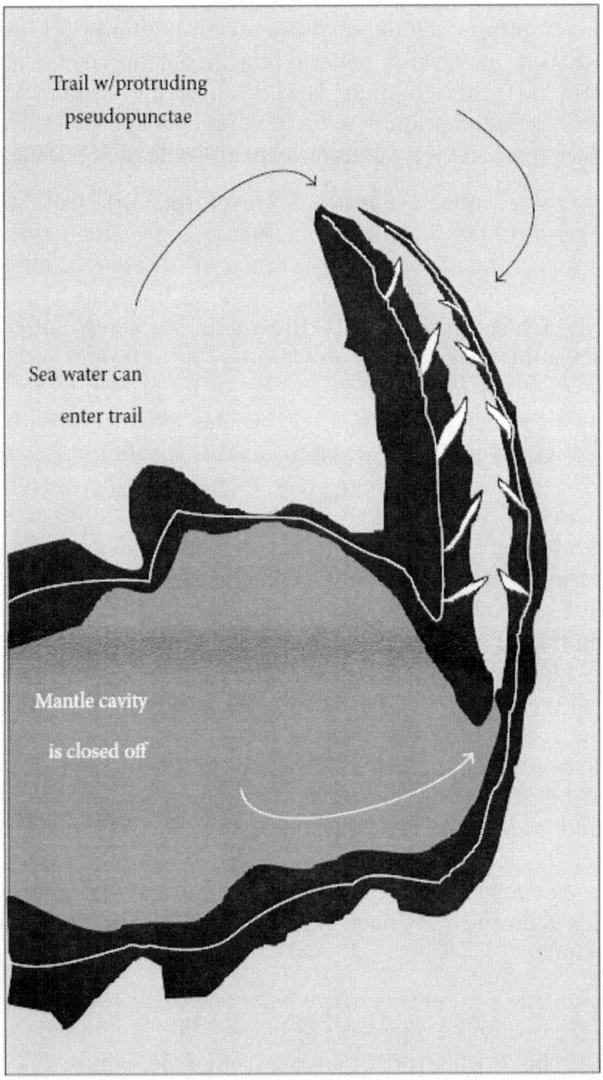

Figure 7: Reconstruction of a closed valve of *L. depressa depressa* showing the gap between the ventral and dorsal trails and how the taleolae (in white) are oriented towards the commisure and act like a sieve.

At the same time, the distance between them was very small, and thus the possible angle of rotation was small, probably not more than ~20°. In Lepidoleptaena, the pseudodeltidium is larger than the chilidium, which might indicate a larger gape, but the angle between the two interareas is quite small, so that it would also limit the gap in that genus. This is also the case in many other strophomenides from Gotland (especially the furcitellinids), but in several genera (e.g. Leptaenoidea, Liljevallia, and Mesoleptostrophia), the chilidium is very small and would have rotated under the large pseudodeltidium without contact at any point. These genera could thus have opened their shells at up to an angle of 65° [28].

The cardinal process lobes are of two distinct forms: (a) divergent and large (Figure 8(e)) and (b) parallel and small (Figure 8(g)). The occurrence of the two types are correlated with the presence or absence of an open apical foramen. Species which have an open foramen have the type A cardinal process lobes, which not only are divergent but have large, triangular muscle attachment facets facing posteriorly. A wide gap is also present between the cardinal process lobes in these forms, which is interpreted here as allowing space for tissue and muscles associated with the apical pedicle outgrowth. This tissue was presumably located in a cardinal pit, a bowl-shaped depression between and anterior to the cardinal process lobes. The species with type A cardinal process lobes are *Leptaena rhomboidalis* and *Lepidoleptaena poulseni*, which have large foramina, and *Leptaena sperion*, which has a tiny foramen. Type B occurs in *L. depressa depressa* and *L. parvorugata*, in which the evidently early loss of the pedicle and associated closing of the foramen allowed the cardinal process lobes to grow close together, and they are thus narrow and parallel, with rectangular posterior facets. The cardinal pit is small or absent. *L. depressa visbyensis* and *L. depressa lata* are intermediate in having a small foramen and large cardinal pit, but their cardinal process lobes are small and parallel. A similar pattern occurs in two species from the Ordovician-Silurian Boundary interval of Anticosti (Dewing [32], e.g., pls 23-24), where specimens of *Leptaena quadrilatera Shaler*, 1865 has type A cardinal process lobes, a deep cardinal pit, and open foramen, while those belonging to L. cf. valida Bancroft [34] have type B, a small or no cardinal pit, and a sealed foramen.

The reason for these differences may have been that the diductor muscles were most effective when operating as close to the midline of the animal as possible [35]. This is illustrated by Armstrong ([36, Figure 2]), and simple trigonometry shows that more the muscle force is used for actually rotating the shell, the closer the two lines of operation of the diductor muscles are to the midline. This interpretation is also supported by the type B cardinal process being developed whenever a species lost its apical attachment to the substrate and resorbed the pedicle tissue, that is, whenever the larvae settled in low-energy environments where an ambitopic life strategy was possible.

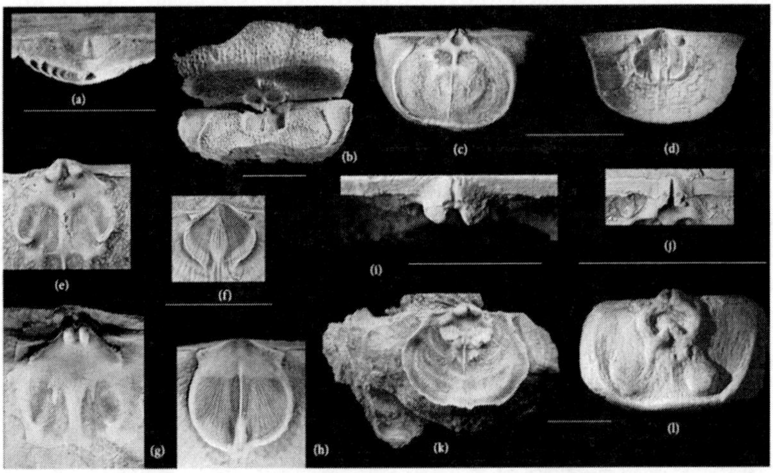

Figure 8: Muscle systems and gape. Scale bar = 1cm (= 0.5cm in detail pictures). (a) *L. rhomboidalis*. NRM Br116301; Stuguklint, Stenkyrka parish; Högklint Formation; open foramen and large chilidium. (b) NRM Br138045 + NRM Br138048; Mulde Tegelbruk, Fröjel; Halla Formation; two valves posed to illustrate the relationship between the muscle scars in the two valves. (c), (d), and (j) *L. depressa visbyensis*. (c), (j) NRM Br116262; Norderstrand, Visby; Lower Visby Formation; dorsal interior and posterior view of cardinalia. (d) NRM Br137848; Nyhamn, Lummelunda; Lower Visby Formation; ventral interior. (e)-(f) *L. sperion*. Ansarve, Tofta; Högklint Formation; (e) NRM Br116273; dorsal muscle field, note cardinal pit and diverging cardinal process lobes (f) NRM Br116271; ventral muscle field, note relatively large adductor scars. (g)-(h) *L. parvorugata*. Valleviken 1, Rute; Slite Group; (g) NRM Br138049b; dorsal muscle field, note no cardinal pit and small, parallel cardinal process lobes. (h) NRM Br138049a; ventral muscle field, note small adductor scars and secondary shell filling the delthyrial cavity. (i) *L. rhomboidalis*. NRM Br116161; Östra Vi, Visby; Slite Group; posterior view of cardinal process lobes. (k) *Lepidoleptaena poulseni* NRM Br121588; Lau Backar, Lau; Eke Formation; dorsal interior showing muscle scars elevated on a platform, and very strong, diverging cardinal process lobes. (l) . PMU G1056; probably Mulde tegelbruk, Fröjel; very gerontic specimen with greatly thickened transmuscle ridges.

3.2.2. Adductor Muscles

In those species that lived in soft, muddy environments (*L. depressa, L. parvorugata*), the diductor muscles occupy most of the ventral muscle field, while the adductor scars are relatively small. In high-energy environment species such as *L. rhomboidalis* and *Lepidoleptaena poulseni*, the scars of the adductor muscles occupy a much greater proportion of the ventral muscle field, implying that the need to keep the valves closed was more important. The shell could have experienced vigorous water current energy, and a shell shaped like *Leptaena* would be buffeted and rotated on the pedicle. In such circumstances, a tightly closed shell was probably the best survival strategy. Similar strong ventral adductors are developed in *L. sperion,* even though it is not considered to have been subjected to a very high energy environment. Rather, it is possible that the genetic makeup was more important for this character than the environment. L. sperion is closely related to L. rhomboidalis, and the two species could possibly be ecophenotypes of a single species, as they have very different size and outer morphology, but their interiors are very similar.

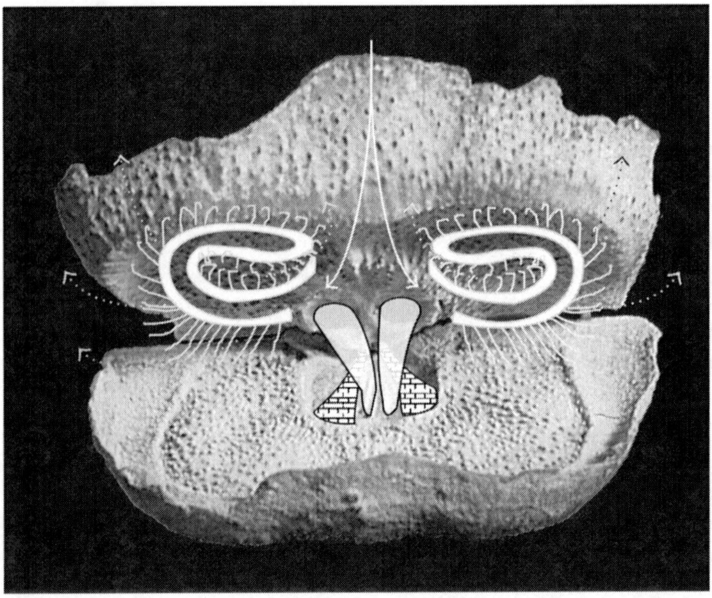

Figure 9: Reconstruction of the muscles and lophophore with feeding currents of *L. depressa depressa* based on Figure 8(b) and the reconstruction of the *lophophore* of *Leptaenoidea* in [28].

The dorsal adductor scars are usually divided by a ridge into anteromedian and posterolateral sectors. In Recent brachiopods (see [19, page 81]), the posterior pair of adductor muscles are long and have striated muscle fibres; they are referred to as the "quick" muscles for fast closing of the valve, while the anterior pair have short, smooth ("catch") muscle fibres, which close the valves tightly and can remain contracted for a long time. This anterior position of the catch muscles results in them having much stronger leverage for holding the valves together. Although the dorsal adductor scars of leptaenines are divided, it is not clear whether the same division of labour can be inferred. Although the scar-separating ridge is set at ~45° to the hinge line in *Leptaena*, most of the anteromedian pair of muscles would not strictly be anterior to the quick muscles, and in gerontic specimens they are not separated at all (Figure 8(l)). The short distance between the valves also did not necessitate long tendons between the muscles and their ventral attachment.

3.3. Lophophore Anatomy and Feeding Method

The configuration of the lophophore in *Leptaena* is unknown, but several ventral valves of *L. depressa* have traces that may throw some light on its structure. They have coiled, raised ridges (Figure 6(d), see also Davidson [37], pl. 39, Figure 15), not unlike the ridges in the dorsal valve of productides (see [38]), and also in the cementing strophomenide *Leptaenoidea* [39] from Gotland [28]. If the lophophore of *Leptaena* was suspended from the dorsal mantle just above this ridge (there is no preserved ridge on the inner surface of the dorsal valves of *Leptaena* itself), the shape could be reconstructed as quite similar to that of *Leptaenoidea*. As already noted, *leptaenines* could not open their shells very widely, so the anterior inhalant current would probably be more important than in *Leptaenoidea,* while the exhalant current would probably exit the shell quite far posterolaterally, probably just anterior to the posterolateral margins of the shell.

This feeding method would be quite similar to the method used by Recent brachiopods, which produce feeding currents by the rhythmic motion of cilia on the tentacles and the mantle surface. The tentacles are similar in size throughout life; in living forms there are about 20 tentacles per mm of lophophore, and the amount of food particles trapped is proportional to the absolute number of tentacles [40]. In small specimens of living species, the lophophore is simple, comprising a one-dimensional ring or a schizolophe, with a small number of tentacles. As the animal grows larger, the volume of the animal grows faster than the area of tentacles, and the need to increase the number of tentacles thus becomes greater and greater. Therefore the lophophore must be coiled in different ways, primitively as two spirals (vertical or horizontal). In the most successful modern group, the Terebratulida, the coiled lophophore first has a wide sweep along the lateral margins, then it swings backwards anteriorly and then into a medial vertical spiral. This is the most effective way of filling the available space in the mantle cavity. In most strophomenides, the valves remained close together during ontogeny, and even large specimens usually had a mantle cavity of small volume. The preserved lophophore traces seen in some genera (such as *Leptaenoidea, Leptaenisca, Christiania, Eoplectodonta*, and many productides) appear to indicate that the *lophophore* did not develop to more than a relatively small schizolophe. Because there would not be many tentacles present on the short brachia, the ciliary pumping action alone might not have been sufficient for adult (or in any case large) strophomenides [41]; it would suffice only in specimens up to a few mm in length. Zorn's alternative view, following Rudwick [12, 42], is that the valves opened and closed continuously during feeding. Due to the small interior volume when the valves were closed, opening the shell would draw water into the mantle cavity, where the lophophore could extract food particles. When the valves closed again, practically all the water would be expelled, so that the next time it opened its valves, new and undepleted water would enter the mantle cavity. This method would have made the water exchange more complete but would not then have made the extraction of particles from the water more effective because that would still depend on the number of tentacles. In addition, these "flapping valves" would need diductor muscles capable of repeated and fairly rapid movement to lift the dorsal valve sufficiently quickly to create the inflow. Modern brachiopods, even lingulides and craniides, have neither fast diductors nor adductor muscles capable of often repeated effort, so if the strophomenides used this system, a radically different muscle physiology must be inferred.

As an alternative, Westbroeck et al. [43] suggested that the mantle surface could have been effective in gas exchange, as I have already noted for the trails, and even in collecting dissolved nutrients directly from the water. In this scenario the reduced lophophore would only be involved in the large-particle catching. The mantle surface area of strophomenides was relatively larger than in other brachiopods because it would follow the surface of the protruding taleolae, which may support this hypothesis. Westbroeck et al. [43] also suggested that the ciliated mantle surface could have acted as a particle filtration device in its own right, but then for extracting mud particles and transporting them to the mantle edge. This would make the filtration by the lophophore more effective and make it possible for the animal to live in more turbid water than other brachiopods.

ACKNOWLEDGMENTS

This paper has benefited from helpful discussions and reviews by M. G. Bassett, National Museum of Wales; L. Holmer and J. S. Peel, both from Uppsala University. Facilities were provided by the Palaeobiology Program, Institute of Earth Sciences, Uppsala University. Technical support from J. O. R. Ebbestad, Uppsala University, is greatly appreciated.

REFERENCES

1. N. Spjeldnæs, The Middle Ordovician of the Oslo Region, Norway. 8. Brachiopods of the Suborder Strophomenida, vol. 37 of Norsk Geologisk Tidsskrift, 1957.
2. C. W. Merriam, Paleontology and Stratigraphy of the Rabbit Hill Limestone and Lone Mountain Dolomite of Central Nevada, vol. 808 of US Geological Survey Professional Paper, 1973.
3. Williams, S. J. Carlson, C. H. C. Brunton et al., Treatise on Invertebrate Paleontology. Part H: Brachiopoda, vol. 2-3, Geological Society of America, 2000.
4. O. A. Hoel, "Silurian Leptaeninae (Brachiopoda) from Gotland, Sweden," Paläontologische Zeitschrift, vol. 79, no. 2, pp. 263–284, 2005.
5. G. Wahlenberg, Petrificata Telluris Svecanae, Nova Acta Regiae Societatis Scientiarium Upsaliensis 8, 1821.
6. J. D. C. Sowerby, The Mineral Conchology of Great Britain, Meredith, London, UK.
7. M. G. Bassett, The Articulate Brachiopods from the Wenlock Series of the Welsh Borderland and South Wales: Part 4, Monographs of the Palaeontographical Society, 1977.
8. F. B. Kelly, "Silurian Leptaenids (Brachiopoda)," Palaeontology, vol. 10, pp. 590–602, 1967.
9. V. Jaanusson, "Ecology and faunal dynamics," in Lower Wenlock Faunal and Floral Dynamics—Vattenfallet Section, Gotland, V. Jaanusson, S. Laufeld, and R. Skoglund, Eds., vol. 762 of Sveriges Geologiska Undersökning C, pp. 253–294, 1979.
10. M. G. Bassett, "Life strategies of Silurian brachiopods," Special Papers in Palaeontology, vol. 32, pp. 237–263, 1984.
11. F. G. Blight and D. F. Blight, "Flying spiriferids: some thoughts on the life style of a Devonian spiriferid brachiopod," Palaeogeography, Palaeoclimatology, Palaeoecology, vol. 81, no. 1-2, pp. 127–139, 1990.
12. M. J. S. Rudwick, Living and Fossil Brachiopods, Hutchinson University Library, London, UK, 1970.
13. R. P. Richards, "Autecology of Richmondian brachiopods (late Ordovician of Indiana and Ohio)," Journal of Paleontology, vol. 46, pp. 386–405, 1972.
14. C. C. Emig, "Functional disposition of the lophophore in living Brachiopoda," Lethaia, vol. 25, no. 3, pp. 291–302, 1992.
15. J. S. Peel, "Systematics, ontogeny and functional morphology of Silurian trilobed bellerophontacean gastropods," Bulletin of the Geological Society of Denmark, vol. 23, pp. 231–264, 1974.
16. H. L. Lescinsky, "The life orientation of concavo-convex brachiopods: overturning the paradigm," Paleobiology, vol. 21, no. 4, pp. 520–551, 1995.
17. K. Dewing, "Hinge modifications and musculature of strophomenoid brachiopods: examples across the Ordovician-Silurian boundary, Anticosti Island, Quebec," Canadian Journal of Earth Sciences, vol. 38, no. 2, pp. 125–141, 2001.
18. E. Timms and C. H. C. Brunton, "Growth rates and periodicity in Antiquatonia and Plicatifera, lower carboniferous productacean brachiopods," in Proceedings of the 2nd International Brachiopod Congress, Brachiopods through Time, D. I. Mackinnon, D. E. Lee, and J. D. Campbell, Eds., pp. 41–47, Balkema, Dunedin, New Zealand, 1991.
19. Williams, S. J. Carlson, C. H. C. Brunton et al., Treatise on Invertebrate Paleontology. Part H: Brachiopoda, vol. 1, Geological Society of America, 1997.
20. N. Spjeldnæs, "Epifauna as a tool in autecological analysis of Silurian brachiopods," Special Papers in Palaeontology, vol. 32, pp. 225–235, 1984.
21. M. Calner and L. Jeppsson, "Carbonate platform evolution and conodont stratigraphy during the middle Silurian Mulde Event, Gotland, Sweden," Geological Magazine, vol. 140, no. 2, pp. 173–203, 2003.

22. R. R. Alexander, "Phenotypic lability of the Brachiopod Rafinesquina alternata (Ordovician) and its correlation with the sedimentologic regime," Journal of Paleontology, vol. 49, pp. 607–618, 1975.
23. R. R. Alexander, "Function of external skeletal characteristics of articulate brachiopods," in Functional Morphology of the Invertebrate Skeleton, E. Savazzi, Ed., pp. 371–398, Wiley & Sons, New York, NY, USA, 1999.
24. R. R. Alexander, "Functional morphology and biomechanics of articulate brachiopod shells," Paleontological Society Papers, vol. 7, pp. 145–169, 2001.
25. L. Leighton and M. Savarese, "Functional and taphonomic implications of Ordovician strophomenide brachiopod valve morphology," in Brachiopods, P. Copper and J. Jin, Eds., pp. 161–168, A. A. Balkema, Rotterdam, The Netherlands, 1996.
26. F. Dattilo, "A new angle on strophomenid paleoecology: trace-fossil evidence of an escape response for the plectambonitoid brachiopod Sowerbyella rugosa from a tempestite in the Upper Ordovician Kope Formation (Edenian) of Northern Kentucky," Palaios, vol. 19, no. 4, pp. 332–348, 2004.
27. M. LaBarbera, "Brachiopod orientation to Water movement: functional morphology," Lethaia, vol. 11, pp. 67–79, 1978.
28. O. A. Hoel, "Cementing strophomenide brachiopods from the Silurian of Gotland (Sweden): morphology and life habits," Geobios, vol. 40, no. 5, pp. 589–608, 2007.
29. S. M. Stanley, Relation of Shell form to Life Habits of the Bivalves (Mollusca), Geological Society of America Memoir 125, 1970.
30. R. R. Alexander, "Resistance to and repair of shell breakage induced by durophages in Late Ordovician brachiopods," Journal of Paleontology, vol. 60, no. 2, pp. 273–285, 1986.
31. J. O. R. Ebbestad and A. E. S. Högström, "Shell repair following failed predation in two Upper Ordovician brachiopods from central Sweden," Geologiska Föreningens I Stockholm Förhandlingar, vol. 122, no. 3, pp. 307–312, 2000.
32. K. Dewing, Late Ordovician and Early Silurian Strophomenid Brachiopods of Anticosti Island, Québec, Canada, vol. 17, Palaeontographica Canadiana, 1999.
33. H. Hedström, Über die Gattung Phragmoceras in der Obersilurformation Gotlands, vol. 15 of Sveriges Geologiska Undersoökning, 1917.
34. B. Bancroft, Welsh Valentian Brachiopods and the Strophomena Antiquata Group of Fossil Brachiopods, Privately printed, Mexborough, UK, 1949.
35. V. Jaanusson and H. Neuhaus, "Mechanism of the diductor muscles in articulate brachiopods," Stockholm Contributions in Geology, vol. 13, pp. 1–8, 1965.
36. J. Armstrong, "Analysis of the function of the diductor muscles in articulate brachiopods," Neues Jahrbuch für Geologie und Paläontologie, vol. 11, pp. 641–654, 1968.
37. T. Davidson, British Fossil Brachiopoda, vol. 3, part 7, no. 4, Monograph of the Palaeontological Society, London, UK, 1871, index and appendix for volume III, and general index to volume I-III.
38. H. C. Brunton, "The functional morphology and palaeoecology of the Dinantian brachiopod Levitusia," Lethaia, vol. 15, pp. 149–167, 1982.
39. H. Hedström, Ueber Einige mit der Schale Befestigte Strophomenidae aus dem Obersilur Gotlands, vol. 276 of Sveriges Geologiska Undersökning C, 1917.
40. Surlyk, "Life habit, feeding mechanism and population structure of the Cretaceous brachiopod genus Aemula," Palaeogeography, Palaeoclimatology, Palaeoecology, vol. 15, no. 3, pp. 185–203, 1974.
41. H. Zorn, "Form und funktion von Gehäuse und Lophophor der Strophomenida (Brachiopoda)," Neues Jahrbuch für Geologie und Paläontologie, pp. 49–64, 1979.
42. M. J. S. Rudwick, "The feeding mechanism of the Permian brachiopod Prorichthofenia," Palaeontology, vol. 3, pp. 450–471, 1961.
43. P. Westbroeck, J. Yanagida, and Y. Isa, "Functional morphology of brachiopod and coral skeletal structures supporting ciliated epithelia," Paleobiology, vol. 6, pp. 313–330, 1980.

CHAPTER 5

Micropaleontology of the lower Mesoproterozoic Roper Group, Australia, and implications for early eukaryotic evolution

Emmanuelle J. Javaux[1], and Andrew H. Knoll[2]

[1]*Department of Geology, UR Geology, University of Liège, 14 allée du 6 Août B18, Quartier Agora, Liège 4000, Belgium (ej.javaux@ulg.ac.be)*

[2]*Department of Organismic and Evolutionary Biology, Harvard University, Cambridge, Massachusetts 02138, USA (aknoll@oeb.harvard.edu)*

ABSTRACT

Well-preserved microfossils occur in abundance through more than 1000m of lower Mesoproterozoic siliciclastic rocks composing the Roper Group, Northern Territory, Australia. The Roper assemblage includes 34 taxa, five interpreted unambiguously as eukaryotes, nine as possible eukaryotes (including *Blastanosphaira kokkoda* new genus and new species, a budding spheromorph with thin chagrinate walls), eight as possible or probable cyanobacteria, and 12 incertae sedis. Taxonomic richness is highest in inshore facies, and populations interpreted as unambiguous or probable eukaryotes occur most abundantly in coastal and proximal shelf shales. Phylogenetic placement within the Eukarya is difficult, and molecular clock estimates suggest that preserved microfossils may belong, in part or *in toto*, to stem group eukaryotes (forms that diverged before the last common ancestor of extant eukaryotes, or LECA) or stem lineages within major clades of the eukaryotic crown group (after LECA). Despite this, Roper fossils provide direct or inferential evidence for many basic features of eukaryotic biology, including a dynamic cytoskeleton and membrane system that enabled cells to change shape, life cycles that include resting cysts coated by decay-resistant biopolymers, reproduction by budding and binary division, osmotrophy, and simple multicellularity. The diversity, environmental range, and ecological importance of eukaryotes, however, were lower than in later Neoproterozoic and Phanerozoic ecosystems.

1. INTRODUCTION

In classifying the past 541 million years as the Phanerozoic Eon, stratigraphers give formal recognition to the animal fossils commonly found in rocks of this age. In terms of evolution, the age of animals must form the latter part of a phylogenetically broader and historically deeper age of eukaryotes, but when protists emerged as major participants in marine ecosystems remains uncertain. Molecular clocks, calibrated largely by Phanerozoic fossils, nearly all suggest that crown group eukaryotes emerged during the Proterozoic Eon. The error bars are large, but even so, the oldest (ca. 2000 Ma) and youngest (800 Ma or a bit earlier) molecular estimates for the divergence of crown group eukaryotes do not overlap (e.g., Douzery et al., 2004; Hedges et al., 2004; Yoon et al., 2004; Berney and Pawlowski, 2006; Chernikova et al., 2011; Parfrey et al., 2011; Eme et al., 2014). Neither early nor late crown group emergence precludes the possibility of a substantial earlier record of stem group eukaryotes (Javaux et al., 2010; Javaux, 2011; Knoll, 2014; Sugitani et al., 2015; Butterfield, 2015).

Diverse eukaryotic microfossils occur in rocks 800 Ma and younger (Porter et al., 2003; Butterfield, 2004; Butterfield, 2005a, 2005b; Knoll et al., 2006; Cohen and Knoll, 2012), and these include at least a few populations assigned with confidence to extant eukaryotic clades (e.g., Butterfield et al., 1994; Porter et al., 2003). Accepting the ~1100-Ma fossil *Bangiomorpha pubescens* as a red alga (Butterfield, 2000), possibly a stem group rhodophyte (Yang et al., 2016), further requires that crown group eukaryotes evolved earlier than this. Older microfossils potentially push the eukaryotic crown group still deeper into the past (Moczydłowska et al., 2011; Butterfield, 2015), but only if these fossils can be confidently interpreted not only as eukaryotes but also as crown versus stem group taxa—a potentially challenging distinction in ancient rocks (Knoll, 2014).

Improved understanding of the timing and context of early eukaryotic divergence begins with careful systematic analysis of well-preserved fossil populations drawn from basins characterized by good age and environmental control. One such basin is recorded by the Mesoproterozoic Roper Group, Northern Territory, Australia. Abundant microfossils were discovered in coastal marine mudstones of the McMinn Formation, near the top of the group (Peat et al., 1978). Our investigations reveal that fossils are abundant and exceptionally well preserved throughout the Roper succession, enabling us to document the paleoenvironmental as well as stratigraphic distribution of microfossil assemblages (Javaux et al., 2001).

1.1 Geologic setting

The Roper Group is a ramp-like sedimentary succession developed in association with regional rifting following an episode of late Paleoproterozoic tectonism known locally as the Isan Orogeny (Betts and Gilles, 2006; de Vries et al., 2008). Although limited Roper outcrop is dominated by erosionally resistant sandstone units, an extensive and lithologically heterogeneous record of Roper deposition is available in drill core obtained during the 1970s and 1980s. The >1800m Roper succession consists almost entirely of siliciclastic rocks divided by Abbott and Sweet (2000) into half a dozen third-order sedimentary sequences. Environments recorded in each sequence range from basinal black shales deposited below storm wave base during maximum flooding to paralic and even fluviatile sandstones, as well as oolitic ironstones found as a marginal-marine facies in highstand systems tracts. Depositional age is constrained by a U-Pb zircon age of 1492±4Ma for a tuff in the Mainoru Formation, low in the Roper succession (Jackson et al., 1999), Re-Os shale dates of 1417±29Ma and 1361±21Ma for the Velkerri Formation in the upper part of the succession (Kendall et al., 2009), and a less reliable, but broadly consistent Rb-Sr illite date of 1429±31Ma for shale within the McMinn Formation, near the top of the group (Kralick, 1982). Thus, Roper deposition took place about 1500–1400Ma (Figure 1).

Surface waters in the Roper seaway were oxic, as determined by iron-speciation chemistry (Shen et al., 2003), but several lines of evidence indicate that within the Roper basin the oxygen minimum zone was commonly anoxic and ferruginous, and at times euxinic (Shen et al., 2003; Planavsky et al., 2011). Consistent with this, S isotopic data document an active microbial sulfur cycle (Shen et al., 2003; Johnston et al., 2008), with facies-specific differences in expressed fractionation suggesting that bacterial sulfate reduction occurred in the water column in basinal environments, but was confined to sediments in coastal settings (Shen et al., 2003). Mo abundance and isotope values for Roper samples point more broadly to early Mesoproterozoic oceans with widespread subsurface anoxia, including sulfidic water masses more extensive than today (Arnold et al., 2004; Kendall et al., 2009), with some exceptions locally (Sperling et al., 2014).

2. MATERIALS AND METHODS

Carbonaceous shales occur throughout the Roper succession in environmental settings that range from basinal to lagoonal (Abbott and Sweet, 2000; Javaux et al., 2001). A majority of these shales contain microfossils preserved as organic compressions, and in a subset of these, distributed throughout the succession, preservation is excellent. The fossils described here come from the following cores: Amoco (A) 82-3 and Golden Grove (GG) 1, reposited at the Northern Territory Geological Survey in Darwin, and Urapunga (U) cores 4, 5, and 6, reposited at the Australian Geological Survey Organization, Canberra. Collectively, these cores represent most of the Roper Group, save for the upper McMinn and Chambers River formations at the top of the succession.

All microfossils come from residues of static acid maceration and have been examined with transmitted light microscopy. For some taxa, detailed morphological observations with SEM, wall ultrastructure with TEM, and wall microchemistry are described elsewhere (Javaux et al., 2003, 2004; Marshall et al., 2005). Systematic description is focused on the genus and species levels, with taxa ordered alphabetically, and the International Code of Nomenclature for Algae, Fungi, and Plants is followed. Sample number includes core number and depth (e.g., U6 230.8m is sample from core Urapunga 6 at 230.8m depth). *Repositories and institutional abbreviations.*—All illustrated specimens are reposited in the Paleobotanical Collections of Harvard University (HU numbers).

3. SYSTEMATIC PALEONTOLOGY

Classification of Roper microfossils presents challenges at either end of the Linnean hierarchy, in both cases reflecting the limited availability of systematically useful characters and character states. At the fine scale, the challenge is to recognize discrete populations and classify them in light of previously diagnosed taxa. Populations can be demarcated in terms of general form (e.g., spheroidal versus cylindrical), size frequency distribution, surface ornamentation when present, and wall thickness and textures (when obvious ornamentation is absent).

Preliminary research shows that morphologically simple Mesoproterozoic microfossils can also preserve distinct wall ultrastructures (Javaux et al., 2004), but extensive TEM imaging would be prohibitive, and existing diagnoses do not take ultrastructural characters into account. Because of character limitations and the ways that observed traits have been used in classification, it can be easier to recognize populations as distinct than it is to assign them to formal taxa, especially for the abundant but simple spheroidal vesicles known as leiosphaerids. We recognize 34 distinct entities within the Roper assemblage.

The other systematic challenge is to relate Roper populations to higher taxa, which can be problematic even at the level of domain. For this reason, we find it useful to provide qualitative confidence estimates for phylogenetic interpretation—with what degree of certainty we recognize a given population as eukaryotic or bacterial. We show that five morphospecies can be classified with confidence as eukaryotes, including three distinct populations of ornamented spheromorphic acritarchs (*Dictyosphaera delicata*, *Satka favosa*, and *Valeria lophostriata*), one acanthomorphic acritarch (*Tappania plana*), and one population of large striated tubes (*Lineaforma elongata*). Nine additional taxa are considered possible eukaryotes (six smooth-walled spheromorphs: *Leiosphaeridia crassa*, *L. jacutica*, *L. minutissima*, *L. tenuissima*, *Leiosphaeridia* sp., and *L. ternata*; one spheromorph population with a granular wall texture (*L. atava*), and two populations of budding spheromorphs (cf., *Gemuloides doncookii* and *Blastanosphaira kokkoda*). Eight taxa of filaments (*Palaeolyngbya catenata*, five species of *Siphonophycus*, *Trachytrichoides* sp.) and vesicles with rounded bulges inferred to be imprints of internal cells (*Squamosphaera colonialica*), are interpreted as probable cyanobacteria, whereas 12 distinctive populations can be classified only as incertae sedis; this group includes five types of spheromorphs (Unnamed forms B to E), six colonial forms (*Chlorogloeaopsis contexta*, cf. *Coneosphaera arctica*, *Eomicrocystis magilca*, *Synsphaeridium* spp., *Symplassosphaeridium* spp., and a large compartmentalized multicellular form—unnamed form A), and two filamentous taxa (*Tortunema* sp. and unnamed form F). Some of the Roper colonial and filamentous microfossils are interpreted as probable cyanobacteria because of both their occurrence in shallow-water photic zone and their morphology.

Genus *Blastanosphaira* new genus

Type species.—Blastanosphaira kokkoda, by monotypy

Diagnosis.—As for type species.

Etymology.—From the greek βλασταυω, to bud or to germinate, σφαιρα, sphere, and κοκκωδη, granular

Blastanosphaira kokkoda new species Figure 2.1–2.11

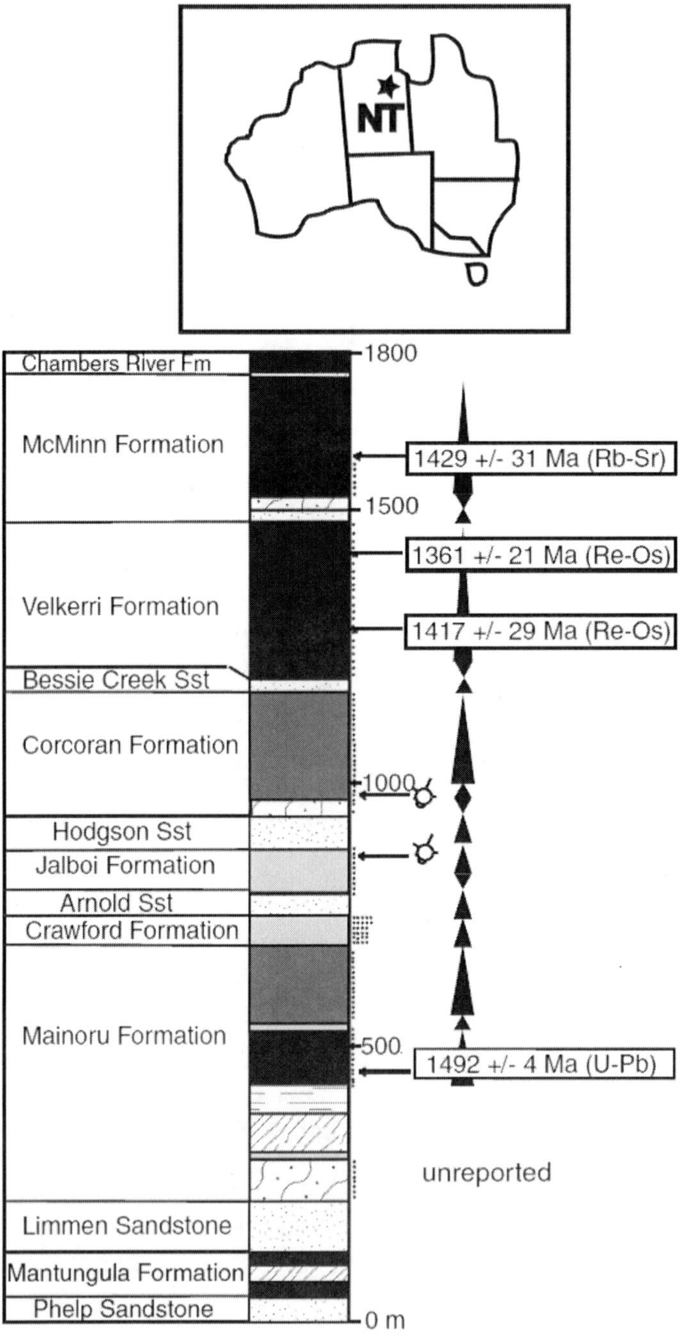
NT
Chambers River Fm
McMinn Formation
Velkerri Formation
Bessie Creek Sst
Corcoran Formation
Hodgson Sst
Jalboi Formation
Arnold Sst
Crawford Formation
Mainoru Formation
Limmen Sandstone
Mantungula Formation
Phelp Sandstone
1800
1500
1000
500
0 m
1429 +/- 31 Ma (Rb-Sr)
1361 +/- 21 Ma (Re-Os)
1417 +/- 29 Ma (Re-Os)
1492 +/- 4 Ma (U-Pb)
unreported

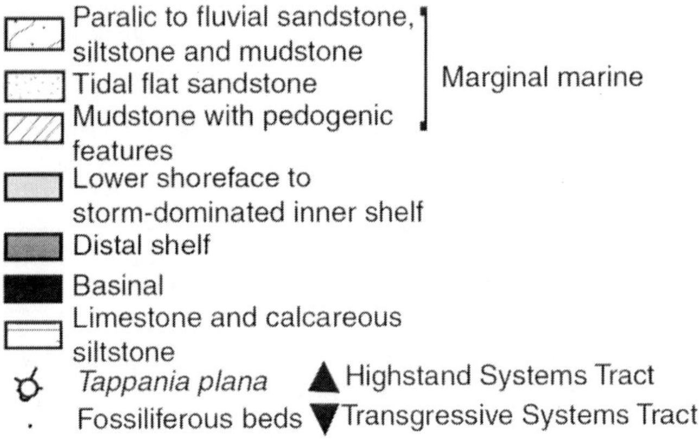

Figure 1. The Roper Group, showing location, facies distribution and stratigraphic column (modified from Javaux et al., 2001)

Holotype.—Specimen Figure 2.1, palynological slide U5 569.1 m, England finder coordinates R/S42, from the Wood Duck Member of the Mainoru Formation, Roper Group.

Diagnosis.—Spheromorph, a few up to ~100 μm in diameter, with very thin chagrinate wall, small sinuous folds, and one lanceolate fold predominantly near the margins of compressed vesicles. Division by budding, with one or several large spherical scars left by detaching buds; serial budding without cells detaching common, leading to a colonial habit. Commonly, taphonomic alteration results in the thin wall peeling off the vesicle from an equally tenuous internal layer.

Occurrence.—Mesoproterozoic, Wood Duck Member of the Mainoru Formation, Roper Group, Australia.

Description.—Spheromorph with very thin chagrinate wall and small sinuous folds, and one lanceolate fold predominantly near the margins of compressed vesicles. Size 3–93 μm in minimum diameter (mean: 28.7 μm, σ = 16.8 μm, N = 149). Two specimens oval shaped (52–104 μm long and 32–64 μm wide), and one specimen (27 μm in diameter) bears an elongate expansion (40 μm long x 8 μm wide) (Fig. 2.3). Division by budding, with cells staying attached and forming irregular colonies, cells rarely isolated, often attached to one to four other cells, commonly with large spherical scars left by detaching buds or adjacent cells. Range of diameter and morphology may vary greatly, from spherical to oval to filamentous. Commonly, taphonomic alteration results in the thin wall peeling off the vesicle from an equally tenuous internal layer.

Materials.—149 specimens measured, as clustered populations in basinal facies (samples U5 581.9m and 569.1m in the Wood Duck Member of the Mainoru Formation).

Remarks.—The Roper population forms an essentially monospecific assemblage in euxinic basinal shales, and is rare in other facies. It differs from *Gemmuloides* by the thin chagrinated wall, circular scars, and multiple attached buds forming colonies. It also differs from *Eosaccharomyces ramosus* Hermann, another budding spheromorph forming colonies, by the chagrinate ornamentation of the vesicle wall, and taphonomic features such as circular scars (Fig. 2.4) and one large lanceolate fold at periphery and very thin folds more centrally distributed (Fig. 2.1, 2.10). The attachment to a biofilm reported and illustrated by Hermann (1990, pl. 14) and Hermann and Podkovyrov (2012) is not observed for the Roper population, although it is not mentioned as a diagnostic character (Jankauskas et al., 1989). Growth of oval cells oriented in the direction of the "branches" of the colony do occur in the Lakhanda material, as underscored by Knoll et al. (2006), but this is not always the case (see Hermann 1990, pl. 14, figs. 5, 7), and is not reported as a diagnostic criterion in Jankauskas et al. (1989). The chagrinate spheromorphs commonly show evidence of budding (Fig. 2.2–2.8), forming spheres (Fig. 2.6–2.8) or elongate extensions (Fig. 2.3), with up to seven specimens attached. Some specimens bear a distinct circular hole rimmed by a fold in the wall (with a diameter up to more than 60% of the vesicle diameter) (Fig. 2.4). Because budding specimens may bear this hole (Fig. 2.7), it cannot be interpreted as a pylome (excystment structure), but rather as a scar left when connected individuals detached. Commonly, the thin wall has partially peeled off, exposing the lighter inner side of the vesicle wall (Fig. 2.6). Cells can be isolated, or more commonly attached to 1 to 4 other cells (Fig 2.7). *Blastanosphaira kokkoda* differs also from other spheromorphs with chagrinate walls, such as *L. obsuleta* and *L. atava*, by its prominent budding habit and consequent colonial association, very thin wall, and circular scars.

The chagrinate appearance seems to be an ornamentation rather than taphonomic alteration, suggesting eukaryotic affinity. SEM shows a granular wall and occasional taphonomic holes (Fig. 2.11). Budding is also consistent with eukaryotic affinities, resembling yeast behavior, but detailed ultrastructural and microchemical analyses will be required to confirm the affinity of this population. Due to its budding without cells detaching and forming colonies, *E. ramosus* has been interpreted as a possible fungus (yeast-like) by Hermann and Podkovyrov (2012) or as social amoebae, although these are difficult to preserve as compressions (Porter, 2006), except in stages of their life cycle when they can produce cellulose walls. Interestingly, cells of the modern yeast *Saccharomyces* may bear several circular scars, and when budding rapidly, form pseudomycelia. However, budding as a form of asexual reproduction also occurs in some bacteria (cyanobacteria, prosthecate proteobacteria; Angert, 2005), in addition to some protists, fungi (yeast), and animals. The chagrinate ornamentation of the wall combined with large size suggest the Roper fossils are probable eukaryotes, and their common budding and pseudocolonial habit shows they represent metabolically active, reproducing vegetative cells. Their restricted distribution in deeper anoxic facies may suggest an anaerobic metabolism (see Muller et al., 2012 for a review of modern anaerobic eukaryotes) or facultatively aerobic metabolism at low oxygen tensions. Alternatively, they could have been planktonic, but in this case, their limitation to deeper anoxic facies is difficult to explain.

Genus *Chlorogloeaopsis* Maithy, 1975, emend. Hofmann and Jackson, 1994

Type species.—Chlorogloeaopsis zairensis Maithy, 1975, from the Bushimay (now Mbuyi-Mayi) Supergroup, RDC, Meso-Neoproterozoic.

Other species.—Chlorogloeaopsis kanshiensis (Maithy, 1975), n. comb. Hofmann and Jackson, 1994;*Chlorogloeaopsis contexta* (Hermann, 1976) n. comb. Hofmann and Jackson, 1994

Chlorogloeaopsis contexta (Hermann in Timofeev, Hermann, and Mikhailova, 1976), emend. Hofmann and Jackson, 1994 Figure 2.12–2.13

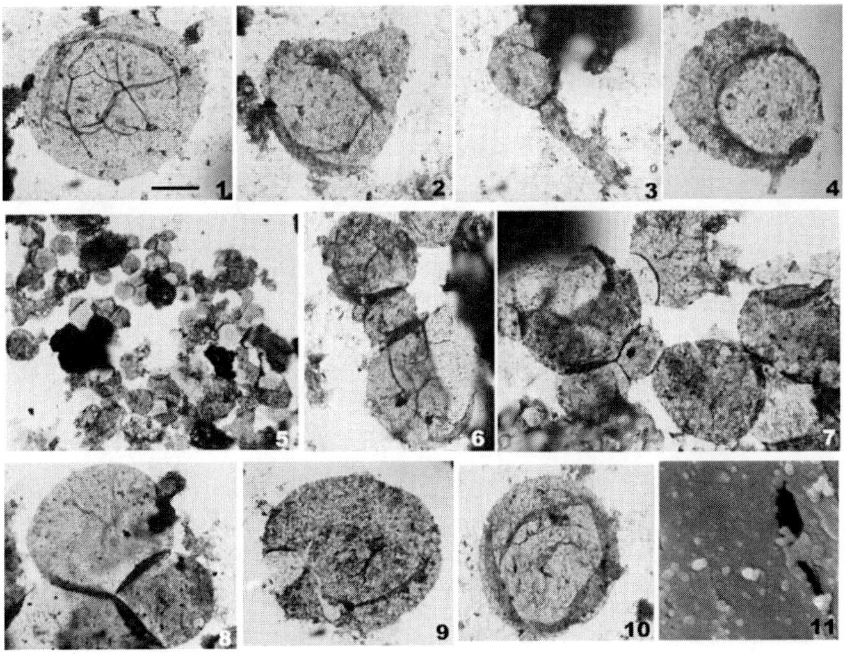

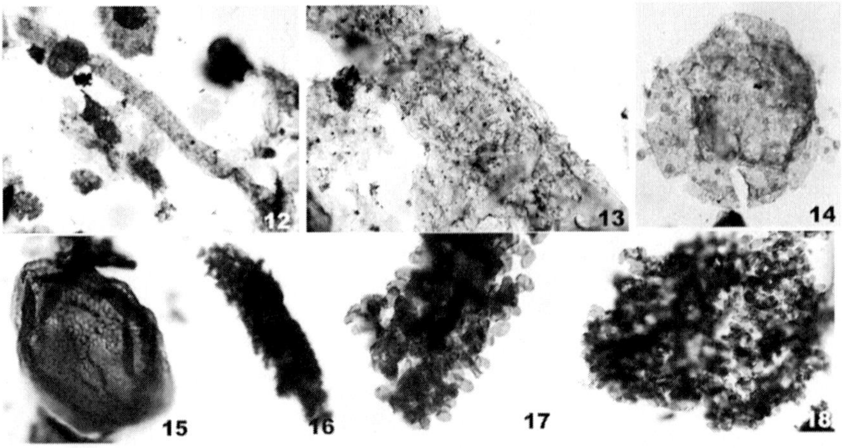

Figure 2. Photographs of Roper organic-walled microfossils: (**1–11**) *Blastanosphaira kokkoda* n. gen. n. sp.; (**2**) specimen starting budding; (**3**) specimen showing an elongate expansion; (**4**) specimen showing circular opening; (**6**) the bottom specimen's wall is peeling off the vesicle; (**8**) thick folds between attached specimens; (**5–8**) specimens showing multiple budding; (**11**) SEM picture showing details of granular wall. (**12–13**) *Chlorogloeaopsis contexta*. (**14**) *Coneosphaera artica*. (**15**) *Dictyosphaera delicata*. (**16–18**) *Eomicrocystis magilca*: (**17**) detail of (**16**) showing oval cells and absence of external envelope. Scale bar in **(1)** is: (**1, 2, 8, 9, 10**) 13μm; (**3, 14, 16, 18**) 20μm; (**4, 13, 17**) 10μm; (**5**) 80μm; (**6, 7**) 15μm; (**11**) 500 nm; (**12**) 50μm. Slides and England coordinates are (**1**) U5 569.1m .2 Q42, (**2, 3**) U5 569.1m .2 Q40/2, (**4**) U5 569.1m .2 R43, (**5**) U5 569.1m .2 R/S42, (**6**) U5 569.1m .2 R43, (**7–10**) U5 536.6m .2 P33, (**12, 13**) U6 240.2m .2 S16, (**14**) A82/3 311.3m O5/2, (**15**) GG1 48.75m .2 J43/4, (**16**) U5 125.1m .2 N33/2, (**18**) U6 230.8m H16

1976 *Polysphaeroides contextus* Hermann in Timofeev, Hermann, and Mikhailova, p. 42, pl. 14, fig. 3

1989 *Polysphaeroides contextus*; Jankauskas et al., p. 119, pl. 27, figs. 10a, b

1990 *Polysphaeroides contextus*; Hermann, p. 26, pl. 8, fig. 8

1994 *Chlorogloeaopsis contexta*; (Hermann in Timofeev et al., 1976), emend. Hofmann and Jackson, p. 19, figs. 12.13–12.15

Holotype.—Polysphaeroides contextus Hermann, 1976 in Timofeev, Hermann, and Mikhailova, p. 42–43, pl. 14, fig. 3; from the late Riphean (Tonian) Miroedikha Formation of the Turukhan Uplift, Siberia.

Occurrence.—Mesoproterozoic and Neoproterozoic successions worldwide, such as the Mbuyi-Mayi Supergroup, RDC; the Miroedikha Formation of the Turukhan Uplift, Siberia; the Roper Group, Australia; the Bylot Supergroup, Canada.

Description.—One cylindrical colony without envelope, composed of several indistinctly defined rows of cells 3–5 μm wide; colony 400 μm long and 25 μm wide.

Materials.—One specimen from sample U6 240.2m, Mainoru Formation.

Remarks.—The spelling of the genus was corrected by Hofmann and Jackson (1994, p. 18–19) and simultaneously (both in July 1994) by Butterfield et al. (1994, p. 72). Hofmann and Jackson (1994) recognized three species of *Chlorogloeaopsis*: *C. contexta* (Hermann, 1976) n. comb. Hofmann and Jackson, 1994, has indistinct rows of cells and cell diameter ranging from 1 to 5 μm; *C. zairensis* Maithy, 1975 with cells 8 to 10 μm in diameter, two to four in a row, while *C. kanshiensis* has cells 10–15 μm in diameter, two or three distinct rows of cells. The Roper population differs from *C. kanshiensis*, defined by two or three rows of cells, and from*Polysphaeroides* spp., which are loose aggregates of spheroidal dispersed cells or pairs, tetrads, octads, and spheroidal colonies of up to 10–20 cells in a sheath

Genus *Coneosphaera* Luo, 1991

Type species.—Coneosphaera inaequalalis Luo, 1991, from the Changlongshan Formation, Neoproterozoic, China.

Other species.—Coneosphaera artica Hofmann and Jackson, 1994; *Coneosphaera* sp. Hofmann and Jackson, 1994.

Coneosphaera sp.Figure 2.14

Description.—50–51 μm thin-walled light brown spheromorphs loosely associated with many smaller 2–4 μm vesicles on the wall surface and close to their periphery. Three specimens observed.

Materials.—Three specimens from sample U6 226.95 m, Mainoru Formation.

Remarks.—Our specimens differ from *C. artica*, which shows larger diameters of both large and small vesicles (79–130 μm and 8–11 μm, respectively) and a higher number of the loosely attached or closely associated small vesicles. It also differs from *C.* sp. in the Bylot Group (Hofmann and Jackson, 1994), which has a few vesicles firmly attached to a larger central one and resembles a specimen illustrated by Hermann (1990, p. 20, pl. 5.11) in the Miroedikha Formation, Siberia. It differs from *C. inaequalalis*, which is characterized by a large cell three or four times bigger than the attached smaller cells, and one cell much smaller than the others (Luo, 1991, p. 193).

Genus *Dictyosphaera* Xing and Liu, 1973

Type species.—Dictyosphaera macroreticulata Xing and Liu, 1973, from the Chuanlingguo Formation, Yenliao region; Chih County of Hopei, northern China, Mesoproterozoic.

Dictyosphaera macroreticulata Xing and Liu, 1973 Figure 2.15

1973 *Dictyosphaera macroreticulata* Xing and Liu, p. 22, 58, pl. 1, 16–17.

1982 *Dictyosphaera delicata*; Hu and Fu, p. 108, pl. 2, figs. 3–6.

2001 *Dictyosphaera* sp.; Javaux et al., fig 1e.

2003 *Dictyosphaera delicata*; Kaufman and Xiao, fig. 1.

2005 *Dictyosphaera delicata*; Yin et al., p. 52, fig. 2.1, 2.2, 2.4, 2.5, 2.7, 2.9, 2.10.

2007 *Dictyosphaera delicata*; Yin and Yuan, p. 351, fig. 1.1.

2009 *Dictyosphaera delicata*; Schiffbauer and Xiao, fig. 3f.

2011 "ellipsoidal vesicle with a micro-reticulate wall" Strother et al., fig. 1i, j.

2015 *Dictyosphaera macroreticulata*; Agic et al., p. 32, figs. 2–4.

Lectotype.—Specimen originally described as *Dictyosphaera sinica* Xing and Liu, 1973, from the Chuanlingguo Formation, Yenliao region, Chih County of Hopei, northern China, Mesoproterozoic, and junior synonym of *D. macroreticulata* Xing and Liu (1973, pl. I:18) (Agic et al., 2015).

Occurrence.—Paleoproterozoic and Mesoproterozoic of China (Ruyang and Gaoshanhe Groups) (Xing and Liu, 1973), Australia (Roper Group) (Javaux et al., 2001), Belt Supergroup (Adam, 2014).

Description.—Only three specimens observed in the Roper population, one specimen measured: 50 μm in diameter with polygonal plates less than 2 μm wide. No excystment structure observed.

Materials.—Three specimens in basinal mudstones of the Velkerri Formation (sample GG1 48.75 m).

Remarks.—Agic et al. (2015) revised the taxonomy of the genus *Dictyosphaera* and synonymized all the species previously described (*D. delicata, D. sinica, D. gyrorugosa, D. incrassata*) to the senior species *D. macroreticulata*, described as 10 to 300 μm vesicles ornamented by a reticulate polygonal pattern consisting of interlocking 1–6 μm polygonal plates. Excystment by pylome or medial split. Because the holotype was not available for re-examination, they selected a lectotype from the same material as the holotype. In their original diagnosis, Hu and Fu (1982) described a reticulate surface ornamentation, but did not comment on its fine structure. TEM analysis by Yin et al. (2005) subsequently demonstrated that the wall is made of interlocked polygonal plates 1–3 μm wide, perforated by nanopores observed with SEM on both the exterior and interior vesicle surfaces (Kaufman and Xiao, 2003). The wall ultrastructure is multilayered (FIB-EM analyses;Schiffbauer and Xiao, 2009), and excystment by partial rupture or a circular opening (pylome) has also been observed (Yin et al., 2005).

Dictyosphaera macroreticulata is reported from the ~1580–1460Ma Lower Belt Group, USA (Adam, 2014), as well as the 1400–1700 Ma Ruyang and broadly correlative Gaoshanhe groups of China, where it co-occurs with abundant *Shuiyousphaeridium macroreticulatum*, an acanthomorph with similar wall ornamentation but bearing many processes (Xiao et al., 1997; Schiffbauer and Xiao, 2009). In the Chinese assemblages, *Dictyosphaera* specimens may include life cycle or taphonomic variants of *Shuiyousphaeridium* (Xiao et al., 1997) that either lost or never formed the outer wall layer from which processes arise (Javaux et al., 2004). The Chinese population includes vesicles ranging from 28 to 240 μm in diameter, with 1–4 μm platelets (Agic et al., 2015). In the Roper Group, however, *D. macroreticulata* (= *D. delicata*) is rare and *Shuiyousphaeridium* absent. *Dictyosphaera* possibly occurs, as well, in the ~1000Ma Stoer and lower Torridon groups, Scotland (Javaux, personal observation, 2008), although it is unnamed in Strother et al. (2011), who described a population as ellipsoidal fossils with walls made of highly ordered circular pits, creating a reticulate pattern and, therefore, differing from the plate-like wall structure of the Mesoproterozoic *Dictyosphaera*.

Kaufman and Xiao (2003) suggested that *D. macroreticulata* (= *D. delicata*) was a photosynthetic eukaryote based on its complex morphology and C-isotopic composition. Neither morphology nor isotopic composition, however, is diagnostic with respect to energy metabolism, although the eukaryotic nature of this ornamented acritarch is convincing. Functionally, *D. macroreticulata* is most likely a cyst or resting stage common to the life cycles of metabolically diverse eukaryotes (see below).

Recently, Tang et al. (2015) described a new species, *D. tacita*, based on two specimens that differ from the other species by their smooth external surface and the presence of hexagonal platelets only on the interior vesicle surface. The hexagons are smaller (0.5–0.9 μm) and the vesicle diameter larger (100–120 μm) than those of *D. macroreticulata* (2–6 μm platelets, 10–20 μm vesicle diameter), *D. sinica* (0.5–1.5 μm platelets, 15–45 μm vesicle diameter), and *D. delicata* (1–3 μm platelets, 50–300 μm vesicle diameter). However, Agic et al. (2015) proposed a synonymy among *D.*

delicata, *D. macroreticulata*, and other species of the genus based on the overlapping size range of the vesicles and wall platelets, and similar morphologies. Tang et al. (2015) argued that this needs reevaluation.

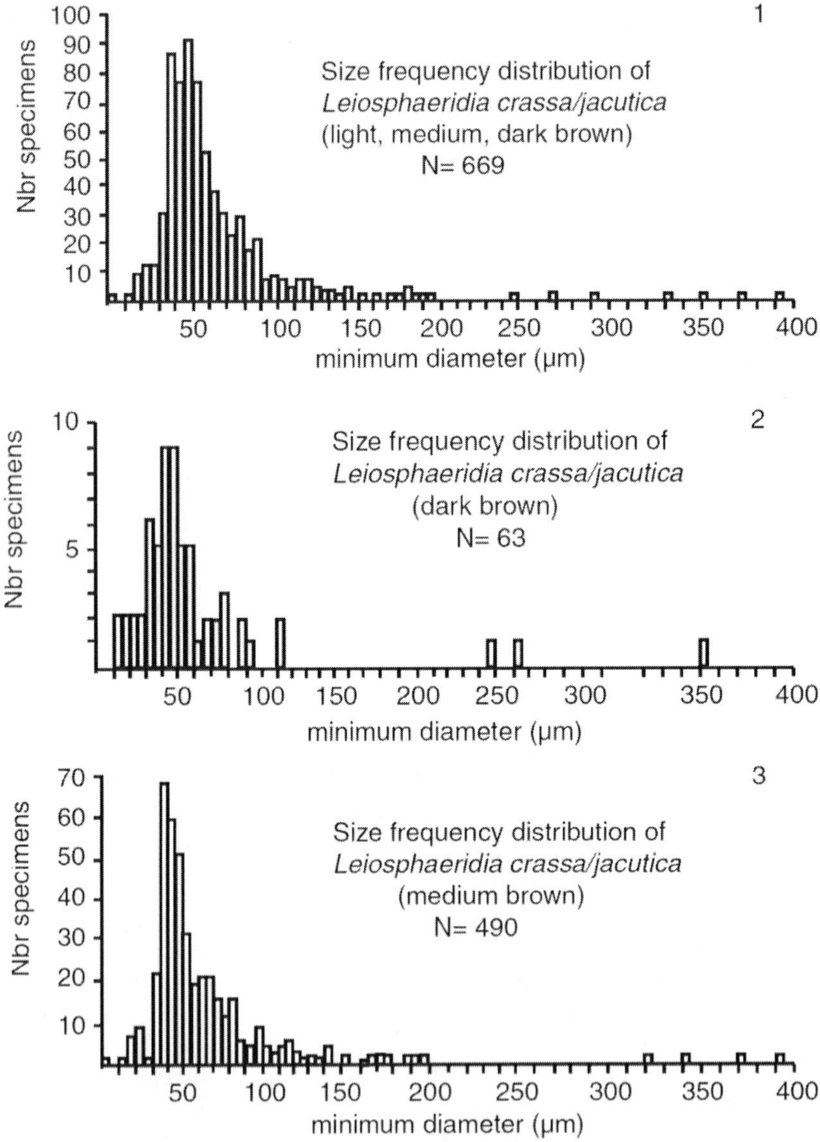

4

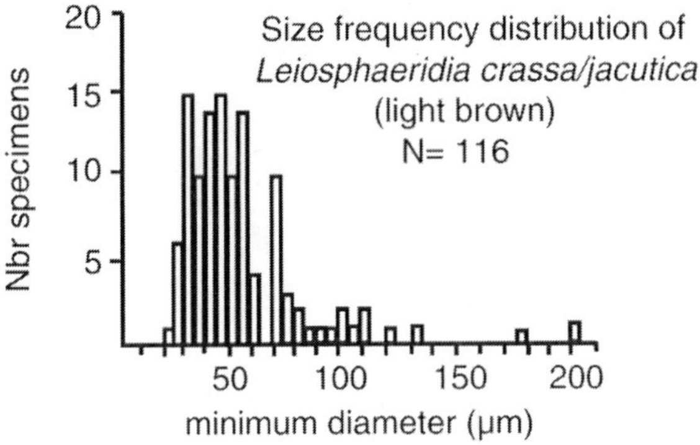
Size frequency distribution of
Leiosphaeridia crassa/jacutica
(light brown)
N= 116
Nbr specimens
20
15
10
5
50
100
150
200
minimum diameter (μm)

5

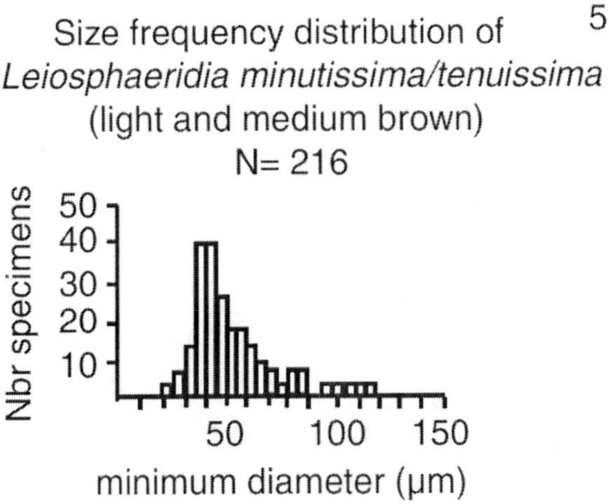
Size frequency distribution of
Leiosphaeridia minutissima/tenuissima
(light and medium brown)
N= 216
Nbr specimens
50
40
30
20
10
50
100
150
minimum diameter (μm)

6

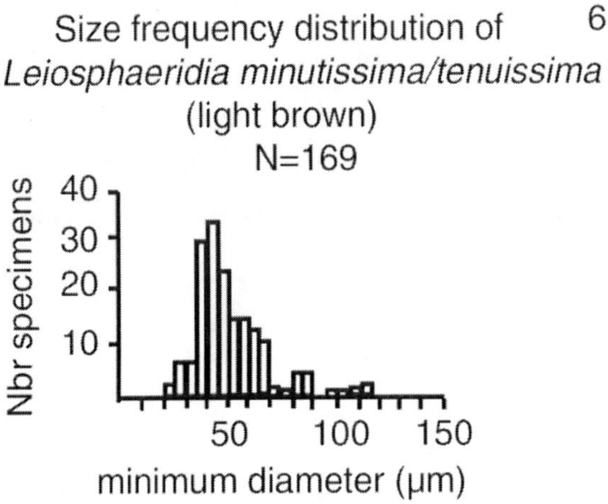
Size frequency distribution of
Leiosphaeridia minutissima/tenuissima
(light brown)
N=169
Nbr specimens
40
30
20
10
50
100
150
minimum diameter (μm)

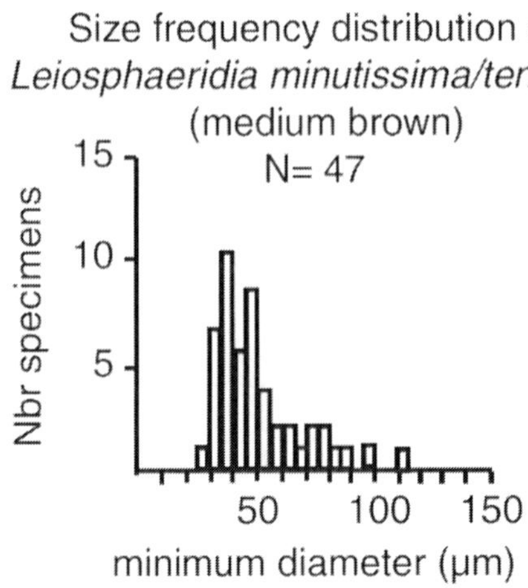

Figure 3. Size frequency distribution of leiospheres: (**1**) Size frequency distribution of all *Leiosphaeridia crassa/jacutica* (dark-, medium-, and light-brown walls); (**2**) Size frequency distribution of dark-brown *Leiosphaeridia crassa/jacutica*; (**3**) Size frequency distribution of medium-brown *Leiosphaeridia crassa/jacutica*; (**4**) Size frequency distribution of light-brown *Leiosphaeridia crassa/jacutica*; (**5**) Size frequency distribution of all *Leiosphaeridia minutissima/tenuissima* (medium- and light-brown walls); (**6**) Size frequency distribution of light-brown *Leiosphaeridia minutissima/tenuissima*; (**7**) Size frequency distribution of medium-brown *Leiosphaeridia minutissima/tenuissima.*

Genus *Eomicrocystis* Golovenok and Belova, 1986

Type species.—Eomicrocystis magilca Golovenok and Belova, 1986

Other species.—Eomicrocystis elegans Golovenok and Belova, 1986

Eomicrocystis magilca Golovenok and Belova, 1986 Figure 2.16–2.18

1986 *Eomicrocystis magilca* Golovenok and Belova, p. 95 [English version p. 89], pl. 7., figs. 5–7.

1989 *Eomicrocystis magilca*; Jankauskas et al., p. 91, pl. 19, fig. 7.

1994 *Eomicrocystis magilca*; Hofmann and Jackson, p. 25, pl. 18, figs. 2–4.

1997 *Eomicrocystis magilca*; Cotter, p. 258, fig. 7A, B.

2016 *Eomicrocystis magilca*; Baludikay et al., 2016, p. 179, fig. 12f.

Holotype.—Eomicrocystis malgica Golovenok and Belova, 1986, pl. 7, fig. 5, from the Malgina Formation in the Uchur-Maya region, eastern Siberia.

Description.—Small ovoid or spheroidal colonies of light brown, loosely packed, small spheroidal to ovoid vesicles of uniform size, sometimes dividing by binary fission, without enclosing envelope. Three colonies observed, with cells 3 μm wide and 6–7 μm long.

Occurrence.—Mesoproterozoic and early Neoproterozoic, Roper Group, Australia; Malgina Formation in the Uchur-Maya region, eastern Siberia (Golovenok and Belova, 1986); Bylot Supergroup, Canada (Hofmann and Jackson, 1994); Belt Supergroup, USA (Adam et al., 2016); Mbuyi-Mayi Supergroup, RDC (Baludikay et al., 2016).

Materials.—Three colonies in samples U5 125.1m from the Jalboi Formation and U6 230.8m from the Mainoru Formation.

Remarks.—Eomicrocystis differs from the genus *Coleogleba* (Strother et al., 1983) in lacking an organic matrix or distinct envelope enclosing the cell clusters, and from the genus *Coniunctiophycus* by the absence of a single dense mass less than a micron in diameter within cells, the smaller cell size (10 μm in *C.* sp), and the shape of the colony described in the Belt Supergroup as "spheroidal colony of tens of individuals, from which a wide, linear extension of more cells emerges and folds back onto itself to form a single reticulate fold" (Adam et al., 2016, p. 16). It also differs from described species of *Myxococcoides* (Schopf, 1968) in the size and organization of constituent cells. *Eomicrocystis malgica* differs from *E. elegans* by the smaller size of the cells' minimum diameter (3–5 μm versus 6–9 μm) and more regular shape of the aggregate. The Roper colonies have cell diameters intermediate between the two species, but also have an irregular aggregate shape, and therefore are identified as *E. malgica*.

Genus *Gemmuloides* Samuelsson and Butterfield, 2001

Type species.—Gemmuloides doncooki Samuelsson and Butterfield 2001

cf. *Gemmuloides doncooki* Samuelsson and Butterfield, 2001 Figure 4.1

2001 *Gemmuloides doncooki* Samuelsson and Butterfield, p. 248, fig 7, D–F.

2014 *Gemmuloides doncooki*; Adam, p. 35, fig. 13.

Holotype.—Gemmuloides doncooki Samuelsson and Butterfield, 2001, p. 248, 249, GSC 117042 (Fig. 7D), Lone Land Formation, NW flank of Cap Mountain (63°24′11″N, 123°14′12″W), Canada, approximately 2m above carbonate ledge. Sample 94-LL-8. GSC loc. C-404520.

Description.—Two spheromorphs, 260 and 85 μm diameter, with chagrinate wall were observed, each with a dark central sphere; only one shows evidence of budding. The presence of a dark central body is not included in the original description, but this may reflect taphonomic rather than systematic differences. The presence of a bud allies the Roper fossils with *Gemmuloides doncooki*.

Occurrence.—Roper Group, Australia; Lone Land Formation, Canada (Samuelsson and Butterfield, 2001); Belt Supergroup, USA (Adam, 2014).

Materials.—Two adjacent specimens in samples A82/3 328.35m from the Jalboi Member and U6 240.2m from the Mainoru Formation.

Remarks.—The Roper assemblage includes another budding spheromorph, *Blastanosphaira kokkoda*, which differs from cf. *G. doncooki* by its colonial habit, smaller diameter, thinner chagrinate wall with thin folds, and multiple buds of larger size relative to the mother cell, as well as by the presence of circular scars left by detached buds. *Coneosphaera* sp. in the Bylot Group (Hofmann and Jackson, 1994) has several smaller vesicles attached to a central one, resembling a specimen illustrated by Hermann (1990, p. 20, pl. 5.11) from the Miroedikha Formation, Siberia, which also differs from cf. *G. doncooki. Gemmuloides doncooki* is also reported in the Belt Supergroup, Montana, USA (Adam, 2014)

Genus *Leiosphaeridia* Eisenack, 1958, emend. Downie and Sarjeant, 1963, emend. Turner, 1984

Type species.—Leiosphaeridia baltica Eisenack, 1958.

Remarks.—Jankauskas (1989) revised the taxonomy of the genus *Leiosphaeridia* (see for detailed synonymy) and proposed an operational approach to species recognition within the genus *Leiosphaeridia*, essentially diagnosing species based on a combination of two characters: size and wall texture. Subsequent workers have tended to follow this scheme, with some modifications (e.g., Butterfield et al., 1994; Hofmann and Jackson, 1994). Jankauskas (1989) discriminated four smoothwalled *Leiosphaeridia* species: *L. crassa* and *L. jacutica* are thick-walled leiospheres, smaller or larger than 70 μm in diameter, respectively; *L. minutissima* and *L. tenuissima* are thin-walled vesicles, again smaller or larger than 70 μm in diameter, respectively. A fifth species, *L. ternata* differs from other species in having a distinctively rigid, opaque wall that fractures radially.*Chuaria circularis* is also a smooth-walled spheromorph, but can be discriminated from the leiospheres by its much thicker wall (at least 2 μm thick), concentric folds and wrinkles, and large diameter (0.43–3.5mm), leaving textured imprints on bedding surfaces (Butterfield et al., 1994).

The difficulty of applying the modified Jankauskas classification lies in the potential challenge of estimating wall thickness (underscored by Butterfield et al., 1994) and in classifying populations that do not fit neatly within the proposed size classes, as also noticed by Porter and Riedman (in press) in populations from the Neoproterozoic Chuar Group. Thus, while Butterfield et al. (2004) and Hofmann and Jackson (1994) reported a taxonomic break at 70 μm, there is little in the size frequency diagrams they present to justify this. Wall thickness has commonly been estimated on the basis of color or fold morphology, but wall color can vary as a function of taphonomy, thermal maturity, or original composition. Butterfield (in Butterfield et al., 1994, p. 11–12) has discussed the distinction between the thickness of folds and the thickness of the wall, which are not necessarily correlated. Previous study of wall ultrastructure in different *Leiosphaeridia* species from the Roper Group (Javaux et al., 2003, 2004) showed that *L. crassa* with thick lanceolate folds had a thinner wall than *L. tenuissima* with thin sinuous folds. We suggest that fold morphology, which reflects the taphonomy of walls with biological differences in flexibility, provides a more objective criterion than wall thickness or color. In this view, *L. crassa* and *L. jacutica* have thick lanceolate folds, whereas *L. minutissima* and *L. tenuissima* have thin sinuous folds.

Size frequency distribution presents a second complication, because many leiosphaerid populations transgress the 70 μm boundary taken to separate species. For example, we measured the minimum diameter of specimens of different color (dark brown, medium brown, light brown) and fold morphology (broad lanceolate or thin sinuous folds) within the Roper assemblage and observed no size break around 70 μm in these different morphotypes (Figs. 3.1–3.7, 4.4–4.8). This difficulty has also been underlined by Porter and Riedman (2016) for Chuar Group populations. We suggest that species should be distinguished on the basis of modal rather than maximum diameter, so that *Leiosphaeridia* with lanceolate folds and a modal size <70 μm would be assigned to *L. crassa*, whereas populations with lanceolate folds and a modal size >70 μm would be placed in *L. jacutica*. This has the advantage of removing ambiguity in size frequency distributions while retaining the species distinctions used in many previous publications.

Based on the presence of a multilayered recalcitrant wall, Roper leiospheres have been interpreted as eukaryotic (Javaux et al., 2004). In the absence of supporting TEM analyses of wall ultrastructure, this attribution cannot be extended to all Proterozoic leiospheres; very likely the genus *Leiosphaeridia* is polyphyletic and their simple morphologies may record both prokaryotes and eukaryotes. Occasionally, medial split excystment structures have been observed in Roper specimens, suggesting that at least some of these fossils were resting cysts; however, even here, caution is advisable, because baeocyte-producing cyanobacterial cells can split in ways that resemble medial split excystment (Waterbury and Stanier, 1978, p. 13, fig. 4).

Leiospheres may occur as isolated specimens assigned to *Leiosphaeridia*, compact colonies called *Synsphaeridium* spp., or loose colonies named *Symplassosphaeridium* spp., possibly reflecting cyst and vegetative stages of the same population or life stages of different organisms. Single leiospheres might also be detached specimens from a colony (Hofmann and Jackson, 1994). The simple morphologies of leiospheres make it difficult to choose among these hypotheses, but more detailed analyses of wall ultrastructure and chemistry may provide the requisite tests (Javaux et al., 2004; Javaux and Marshall, 2006).

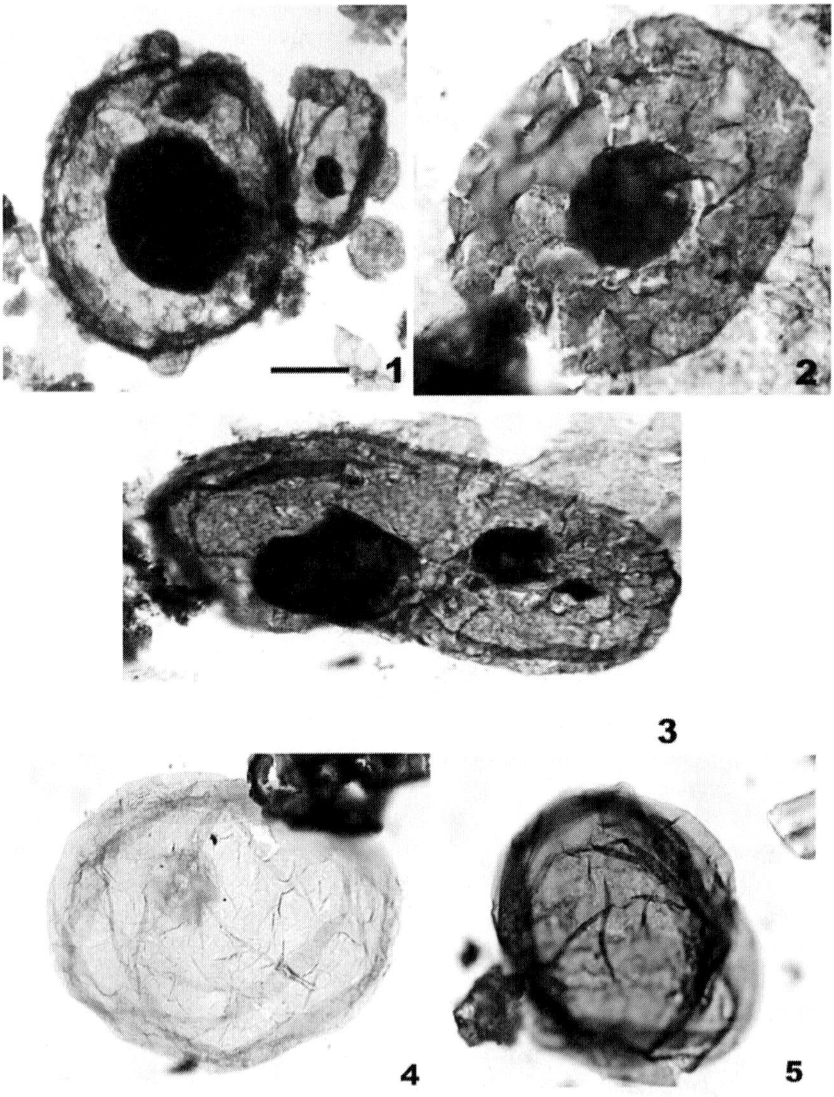

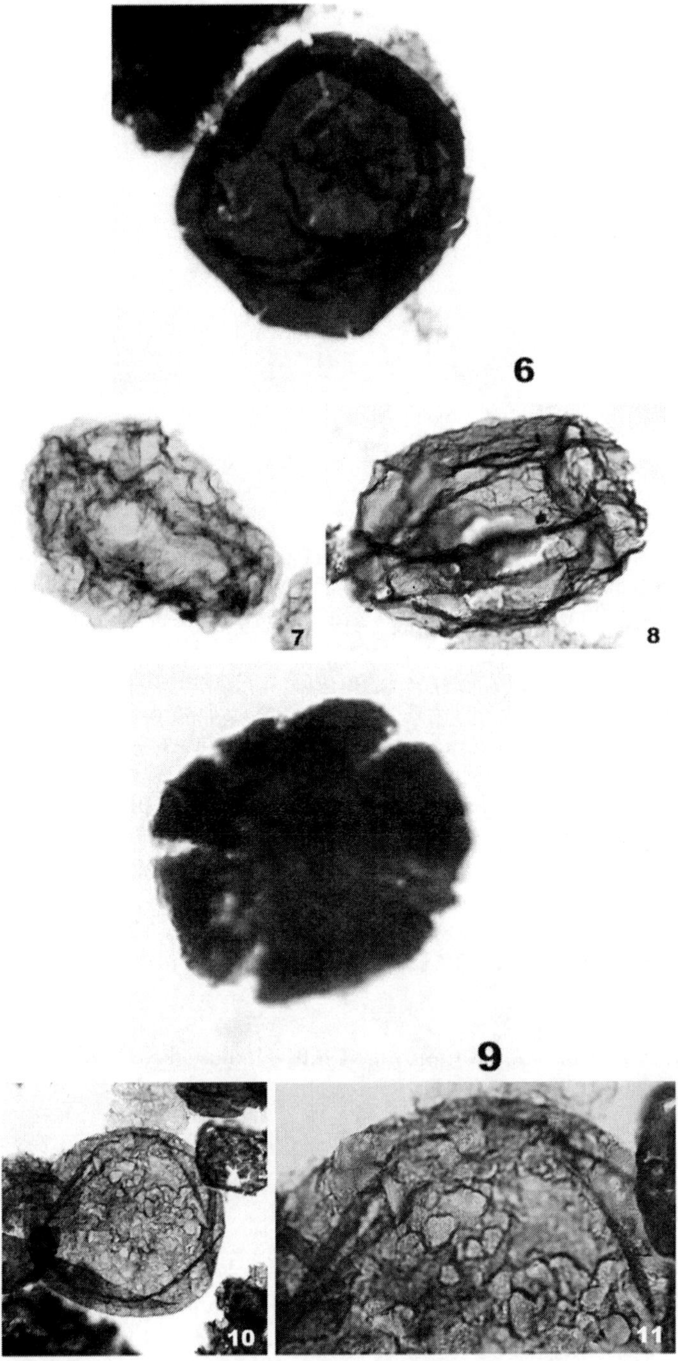
6
7
8
9
10
11

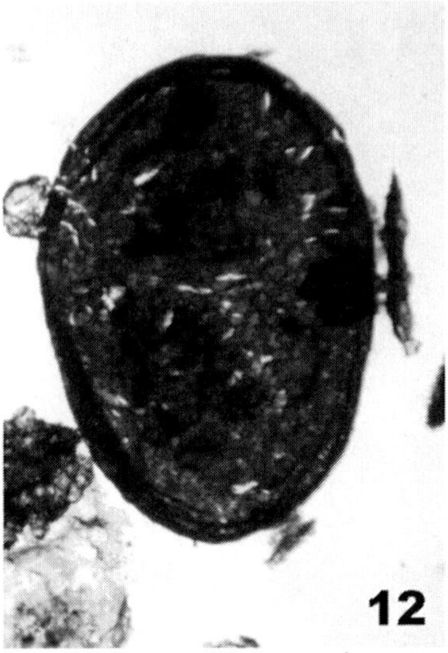

Figure 4. Photographs of Roper organic-walled microfossils (color figures are available in the online version of this paper): (**1**) cf. *Gemmuloides doncooki*. (**2, 3**) *Leiosphaeridia atava*. (**4**) Light-brown *Leiosphaeridia crassa/jacutica*. (**5**) Medium-brown *Leiosphaeridia crassa/jacutica*. (**6**) Dark-brown *Leiosphaeridia crassa/jacutica*. (**7**) Light-brown *Leiosphaeridia minutissima/tenuissima*. (**8**) Medium-brown *Leiosphaeridia minutissima/ tenuissima*. (**9**) *Leiosphaeridia ternata*. (**10–12**) *Leiosphaeridia* sp., (**11**) showing details of wall texture of specimen in (**10**). Scale bar in (**1**) is: (**1**) 85μm; (**2**) 12μm; (**3**) 15μm; (**4**) 14μm; (**5**) 17μm; (**6**) 10μm; (**7–8**) 6μm; (**9**) 90μm; (**10**) 30μm; (**11**) 60μm; (**12**) 10μm. Slides and England coordinates are (**1**) U6 230.8m .2 L2Y/1; (**2**) U6 305.1 m.2A O26 ¾; (**3**) U6 305.1 m.2A U37/1; (**4, 7**) U6 230.8m .2 H46/G46 (area); (**5**) U6 240.2m .2 O34/3; (**6**) U6 305.1m .2A T26/1; (**8**) U6 305.1m .2A U20; (**9**) U5 125.1 m; (**10, 11**) U6 305.1m 2A N20; (**12**) U6 230.8 m.2 S24/2.

Leiosphaeridia atava (Naumova, 1960) Jankauskas, Mikhailova, and Hermann, 1989 Figure 4.2–4.3

1960 *Megasacculina atava* Naumova, pl. 3, fig. 15.

1989 *Leiosphaeridia atava* (Naumova, 1960); Jankauskas et al., p. 74, pl. 10, figs. 4–7.

2016 *Leiosphaeridia atava*; Sergeev et al., fig. 4.5.

Holotype.—Preparation 452/1, paleontological collection at the Institute of Precambrian Geology and Geochronology, St. Petersburg, Russia, upper Riphean (Tonian), Lakhanda Group, Neryuen Formation, Uchur-Maya region, Siberia. (The holotype was lost, as mentioned by Sergeev and Lee, 2006).

Occurrence.—The Mainoru Formation, Roper Group, Australia; the Lakhanda Group, Neryuen Formation, Uchur-Maya region, Siberia (Jankauskas, 1989); the Koltasy Formation, Russia (Sergeev et al., 2016); the El Mreiti Group, Taoudeni Basin, Mauritania (Beghin et al., in review).

Description.—Spheroidal to oval vesicle with a fine granular, flexible wall, with numerous folds, 46 to 56 μm in diameter (N = 4); two specimens with a dark, internal bleb of organic matter. No excystment structures observed.

Materials.—Four specimens observed in sample U6 230.8m from the Mainoru Formation.

Remarks.—*Leiosphaeridia atava* differs from *L. obsuleta* by its diameter larger than 70 μm (Jankauskas, 1989).

Leiosphaeridia crassa (Naumauva, 1949), emend. Jankauskas in Jankauskas, Mikhailova, and Hermann, 1989 Figure 4.4–4.6

1949 *Leiotriletes crassus* Naumova, p. 54, pl. 1, figs. 5, 6; pl. 2, figs 5, 6.

1989 *Leiosphaeridia crassa*; Jankauskas in Jankauskas et al., p. 75, pl. 9, figs. 5–10.

1989 *Leiosphaeridia minutissima*; Jankauskas et al., p. 75, pl. 9, figs. 2, 3.

Holotype.—No holotype was designated by Naumova (1949), from the Lontova Formation, lower Cambrian, Estonia. A lectotype was designated by Jankauskas (*in* Jankauskas et al., 1989, p. 75) from Naumova (1949, pl. 1, fig. 3), but this specimen was part of *Leiotriletes simplicissimus*, which is a species that Jankauskas et al. (1989) synonymized with a different species of *L. minutissima* (Porter and Riedman, 2016).

Emended diagnosis.—A species of *Leiosphaeridia* with smooth, pliant walls with lanceolate folds and a modal diameter of less than 70 μm.

Occurrence.—Proterozoic and lower Paleozoic, worldwide.

Description.—Smooth-walled leiospheres with large lanceolate folds (Fig. 3.1–3.4). Minimum diameter ranges from 5 to 390 μm (mean: 58.1 ±40.2 μm, N = 669). No statistical differences among dark brown, medium, and light brown subpopulations, with mean diameters and standard deviations of, 54.5± 21.6 μm (N = 61), 55.3 ±30.7 μm (N = 191 μm), and 56.0± 27.7 μm (N = 116). Excystment by partial rupture and medial split.

Materials.—These are the most common microfossils in the Roper assemblage, especially in samples U6 305.1m from the Mainoru Formation and U5 125.1m from the Jalboi Member.

Remarks.—As noted above, the rationale for emending the diagnosis of this species stems from the desire to focus on observed rather than inferred wall characters and to articulate size distinctions in a way that will minimize ambiguity in observed populations. The emended diagnosis considers the presence of lanceolate folds on a smooth wall as a diagnostic character as opposed to the wall color, which is not considered as a valid character.

Leiosphaeridia jacutica (Timofeev, 1966), emend. Mikhailova and Jankauskas in Jankauskas, Mikhailova, and Hermann, 1989 Figure 4.4–4.6

1966 *Kildinella jacutica* Timofeev, p. 30, pl. 7, fig. 2.

1989 *Leiosphaeridia jacutica* (Timofeev, 1966); Mikhailova and Jankauskas in Jankauskas et al., 1989, p. 77, pl. 9, fig. 12; pl. 12, figs. 3, 6, 7, 9.

Holotype.—Preparation number 452/1, Biostratigraphy Laboratory, Maya River Collection, late Mesoproterozoic/early Neoproterozoic Lakhanda Group, Russia (Timofeev, 1966, pl. 7, fig. 2).

Emended diagnosis.—A species of *Leiosphaeridia* characterized by smooth, pliant walls with lanceolate folds and a modal diameter greater than 70 μm.

Occurrence.—Proterozoic worldwide.

Description.—A species of *Leiosphaeridia* characterized by smooth, pliant walls with lanceolate folds and a modal diameter greater than 70 μm. Excystment by partial rupture and medial split. While we cannot exclude the possibility that these represent a long right-hand tail of the *L. crassa* population, we suspect that, by comparison to other mid-Proterozoic assemblages, distinct populations of large leiosphaerids were present in the Roper seaway.

Materials.—The Roper assemblage contains a relatively small proportion of very large, smooth walled leiosphaerids, in samples U6 305.1m and 240.2m from the Mainoru Formation and sample GG1 326.2m from the Corcoran Formation.

Remarks.—As noted above, the rationale for emending the diagnosis of this species stems from the desire to focus on observed rather than inferred wall characters and to articulate size distinctions in a way that will minimize ambiguity in observed populations. The emended diagnosis considers the presence of lanceolate folds on a smooth wall as a diagnostic character, as opposed to wall color, which is not considered as a valid character.

Leiosphaeridia minutissima (Naumova, 1949), emend. Jankauskas in Jankauskas, Mikhailova, and Hermann, 1989 Figure 4.7–4.8

1949 *Leiotreletes minutissimus* Naumova, p. 52, pl. 1, figs. 1, 2; pl. 2, figs. 1, 2.

1989 *Leiosphaeridia minutissima* (Naumova); Jankauskas in Jankauskas et al., p. 79, pl. 9, figs. 1, 4, 11.

Lectotype.—No holotype was designated by Naumova (1949). Jankauskas (in Jankauskas et al., 1989, p. 80) designated a specimen of *Leiotriletes minutissimus* (pl. 1, fig. 1) from Naumova (1949) as lectotype.

Emended diagnosis.—A species of *Leiosphaeridia* characterized by smooth walls with sinuous folds and a modal diameter less than 70 μm.

Description.—Smooth-wall spheromorphs with sinuous folds and a modal diameter less than 70 μm. Minimum diameter 21–117 μm (mean: 50.6 ±18.2 μm, N = 216) (Figure 3.5–3.7). Light brown specimens 21–117 μm in minimum diameter (N = 116, mean: 50.8± 17.9 μm) and medium brown specimens 27–111 μm (N = 47, mean: 49.6± 19.1 μm). No dark brown specimens observed.

Occurrence.—Proterozoic worldwide.

Materials.—Common in inshore facies of the Roper Group, especially in samples U6 305.1 m, and U6 273.7m from the Mainoru Formation.

Remarks.—As noted above, the rationale for emending the diagnosis of this species stems from the desire to focus on observed rather than inferred wall characters and to articulate size distinctions in a way that will minimize ambiguity in observed populations. The emended diagnosis considers the presence of sinuous folds on a smooth, thin wall as a diagnostic character, as opposed to wall color, which is not considered as a valid character.

Leiosphaeridia tenuissima Eisenack, 1958 emend. Figure 4.7–4.8

1958 *Leiosphaeridia tenuissima* Eisenack, p. 391, pl. 1, figs. 2, 3.

1989 *Leiosphaeridia tenuissima*; Jankauskas et al., p. 81, pl. 9, fig. 13.

Holotype.—Preparation A3, 3 number 4 from the *Dictyonema*shales of the lower Ordovician, St Petersburg area, Russia (Eisenack, 1958, pl. 1, fig. 2).

Emended diagnosis.—A species of *Leiosphaeridia* characterized by smooth walls with sinuous folds and a modal diameter (rather than maximum diameter) greater than 70 μm; the wall color is not a diagnostic criteria.

Description.—Smooth wall spheromorphs with sinuous folds and a modal diameter greater than 70 μm. These may reflect a larger, uncommon population of *Leiosphaeridia* in Roper shales.

Occurrence.—Proterozoic worldwide.

Materials.—Uncommon specimens in samples U6 305.1m and U6 230.8m from the Mainoru Formation.

Remarks.—As noted above, the rationale for emending the diagnosis of this species stems from the desire to focus on observed rather than inferred wall characters and to articulate size distinctions in a way that will minimize ambiguity in observed populations. The emended diagnosis considers the presence of sinuous folds on a smooth, thin wall as a diagnostic character as opposed to wall color, which is not considered as a valid character.

Leiosphaeridia ternata (Timofeev, 1966), emend. Mikhailova and Jankauskas in Jankauskas et al., 1989 Figure 4.11

1966 *Turuchanica ternata* Timofeev, p. 45, pl. 9, fig. 8.

1989 *Leiosphaeridia ternata* (Timofeev); Mikhailova and Jankauskas in Jankauskas et al., p. 81, pl. 11, figs. 2–4; pl. 12, figs. 4, 5, 8.

2016 *Leiosphaeridia ternata*; Sergeev et al., fig. 4.3, 4.4.

Holotype.—Preparation 169/1, Biostratigraphical laboratory LAGED AN SSSR, Turukhansk collection, lower Tungunska, Turukhansk district; Miroedikhinsk series, Riphean (Mesoproterozoic and early Neoproterozoic boundary), rarely Ordovician (Timofeev, 1966).

Occurrence.—Found globally in worldwide Proterozoic successions.

Description.—Compressed opaque spheromorph with thick, rigid walls commonly showing characteristic radial fractures. Diameter 15 to 110 µm.

Materials.—A few specimens were observed in samples A82/3 157.5m in the Jalboi Member, GG1 326.2m in the Corcoran Formation, and U6 305.1m in the Mainoru Formation.

Leiosphaeridia sp. Figure 4.10–4.12

Description.—Large medium to dark brown spheroidal to oval vesicles with a characteristic cork-like wall texture made of 5–11 µm, irregular patchy areas of different colors and fabric; this texture may well be taphonomic, but if so, it reflects original differences in wall composition, compared to other leiosphaerids. Concentric folds at the periphery. The minimum diameter of 19 spheroidal specimens is 56–455 µm (mean: 159.8± 96.3 µm). Three oval specimens measured 75–210 µm wide and 160–330 µm long.

Materials.—22 specimens in the Gibb Member, samples U6 305.1 m, U6 230.8m of the Mainoru Formation, and in sample GG1 171.5m of the Corcoran Formation.

Remarks.—This species differs from another large leiosphere *L. jacutica* by its particular cork-like wall texture and a morphology that ranges from spheroidal to ovoidal. It also differs from *Chuaria circularis*, which has a thicker opaque, smooth wall. These specimens are left in open nomenclature until further characterization by SEM and TEM.

Genus *Lineamorpha* Vorob'eva, Sergeev, and Yu, 2015

Type species.—Lineamorpha elongata Vorob'eva, Sergeev, and Yu, 2015, by monotypy.

Lineamorpha elongata Vorob'eva et al., 2015

Figure 5.1–5.4

2004 "large striated tubes" Javaux et al., p. 126, fig 3 g–k.

2015 *Lineamorpha elongata*; Vorob'eva et al., p. 216, figs. 7 1–7.5.

2016 *Lineamorpha elongata*; Adam et al., fig. 9 A–D.

Holotype.—Figure 7.4, Vorob'eva et al., 2015, GINPC 14711-804, locality AK-14, Kotuikan River valley, Kotuikan Formation, Anabar Uplift, northern Siberia.

Occurrence.—Early Mesoproterozoic, Jalboi, Crawford, and upper Mainoru formations, Roper Group, Australia; Belt Supergroup, Montana, US (Adam, 2014); and Kotuikan Formation, northern Siberia (Vorob'eva et al., 2015).

Description.—Longitudinally striated hollow tubes (not a sheath around bundled filamentous sheaths) that often break into fragments, so maximum length is unknown but millimetric, 34 to 150 μm in diameter, fragment length: 131 to 473 μm (N = 25).

Materials.—562 specimens observed in maceration, in lowershoreface to inner shelf facies of the Jalboi, Crawford, and upper Mainoru formations, Roper Group; one observed in thin section, 25 measured specimens. Abundant specimens observed in samples U5 125.1m and U5 151.3m of the Jalboi Member; in samples U5 334.3m and U5 412.1m of the Arnold sandstone Member; in samples A82/3 311m of the Crawford Formation; and in samples U6 305.1 m, U6 230.8 m, and U6 240.2m from the basal Mainoru Formation, but rare elsewhere.

Remarks.—In the Roper population, there seems to be no relation between diameter and fragment length, nor dominant fragment length, suggesting random fragmentation of longer, probably millimetric, tubes. Light microscopy shows longitudinal, micron-scale striations along the tubes while SEM reveals a thick multilayered wall of densely packed granules, but no longitudinal striations. At the ultrastructural level (TEM), however, transverse sections of the wall show a clear alternation of electron-dense and electron-tenuous bands that correspond in size and distribution to the striations observed by light microscopy (Javaux et al., 2004). The wall is ~1 μm thick, occasionally with an outer, electron-dense layer. The striations, thus, are not wall sculpture, but reflect original compositional heterogeneities in the tube wall, indicating complex physiological controls on wall formation.

The Roper material appears to be indistinguishable from the type of *Lineaforma elongata* from the lower Mesoproterozoic Kotuikan Formation, northern Siberia (Vorob'eva et al., 2015). In the Roper Group, these filaments occur as transported fragments, contributing less than 3% to the entire assemblage, but up of 40% in lower-shoreface to innershelf shales. The rounded, closed tube ends observed in the Russian population were not observed in fragmental Roper specimens. The large size and complex wall ultrastructure of these microfossils suggest a eukaryotic affinity (Javaux et al., 2004).

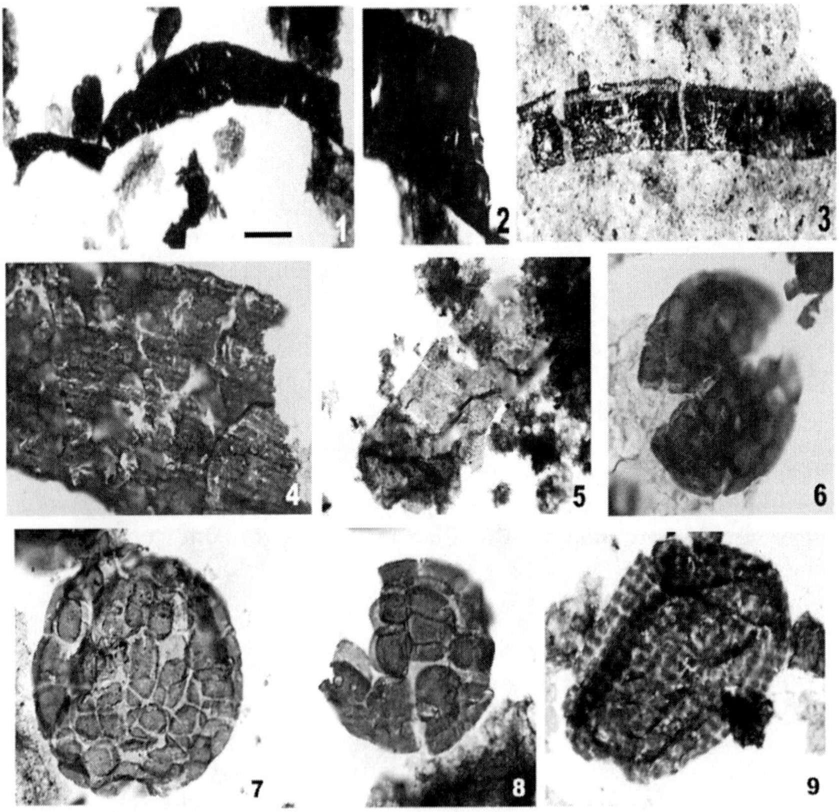

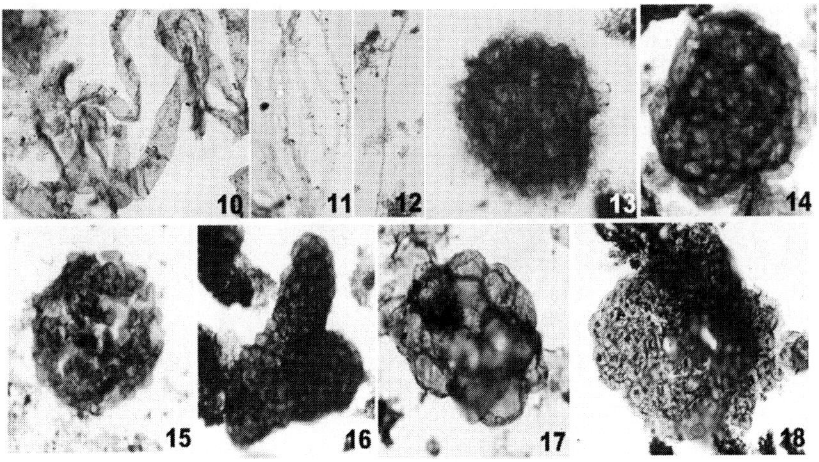

Figure 5. Photographs of Roper organic-walled microfossils: (**1–4**) *Lineaforma lineata*: (**2**) showing hollow extremity of specimen in (**1**), (**3**) specimen in situ in thin section. (**5**) *Paleolyngbya catenata*. (**6–9**) *Satka favosa*: (**6**) showing medial split and hollow interior, (**8**) showing hollow interior. (**10**) *Siphonophycus kestron* (bottom specimen) and *S. typicum* (top specimen). (**11**) *Siphonophycus robustum*. (**12**) *Siphonophycus septatum*. (**13**) *Siphonophycus thulenema*. (**14**) *Squamosphaera colonialica*. (**15**) *Symplassophaeridium* sp, (**16–18**) *Synsphaeridium* spp. Scale bar in (**1**) is: (**1**) 60μm; (**2**) 100 μm; (**3**) 50μm; (**4**) 110 μm; (**5, 7**) 15μm; (**6, 8)** 20 μm; (**9**) 40μm; (**10, 13**) 20μm; (**11, 12**) 10μm; (**14**) 50μm; (**15, 16**) 33μm; **(17, 18**) 15μm. Slides and England coordinates are (**1, 2**) U5 125.1m C13/3; (**3**) thin section 3785a R47/1; (**4**) A82/3 328.35 m.3 N41/4; (**5**) U5 130.5 ker E21; (**6**) U6 240.8m .2 K23/3; (**7**) U6 305.1m . E29; (**8**) U6 230.8 m.2 F14; (**9**) U6 230.8m .2 J26/4; (**10**) U6 240.2m .2 Z27/2; (**11**) U5 125.1m .2 X48/4; (**12**) GG1 340.2 m.3 M13; (**13**) U6 240.2m .2 Q18/3; (**14**) A82/3 328.35m .3 K/L35; (**15**) A82/3 311.3m .2 O5/2; (**16**) U5 125.1m .2 R34/3; (**17**) A82/3 311.3m .2 H40/4; (**18**) U5 151.3m .2 Q/R29.

Genus *Palaeolyngbya* Schopf, 1968

Type species.—Palaeolyngbya barghoorniana Schopf, 1968 *Palaeolyngbya catenata* Hermann, 1974 Figure 5.5

1974 *Palaeolyngbya catenata* Hermann, p. 8, pl. 6, fig. 5.

1980 *Oscillariopsis robusta*; Horodyski and Donaldson, p. 149, fig. 13H.

1994 *Palaeolyngbya catenata*; Butterfield et al., 1994, p. 61, fig. 25F–G.

Holotype.—No holotype designated by Hermann, 1974, p. 8, 9, pl. 6, fig. 5, Tonian, Miroedikha Formation, Russia.

Description.—Cellular trichome within a single encompassing sheath, cells 26 μm wide and 6 μm long.

Materials.—One fragmented specimen with ripped sheath in sample U5 130.5m from the Jalboi Member.

Genus *Satka* Jankauskas, 1979a

Type species.—*Satka favosa* Jankauskas, 1979a

Satka favosa Jankauskas, 1979a

Figure 5.6–5.9

1979a *Satka favosa* Jankauskas, pl. 4, fig. 2.

1980 "polygonally segmented sphaeromorphs" Horodyski, p. 658, pl. 2, figs. 8–12.

1989 *Satka favosa*; Jankauskas et al., p. 51, pl. 4, figs. 1, 2?

1989 *Satka elongata*; Jankauskas et al., p. 51, pl. 4, figs. 3, 5.

1989 *Satka granulosa*; Jankauskas et al., p. 51, pl. 4, fig. 8.

1994 *Satka* spp. Hofmann and Jackson, pl. 18, figs. 26–31.

2001 *Satka favosa*; Javaux et al., pl. 1e, f.

2003 *Satka favosa*; Javaux et al., figs. 1–10, 11.

2004 *Satka favosa*; Javaux et al., 2004, p. 125, fig. 3a–f.

Holotype.—Specimen pl. 4, fig. 2, preparation 16-1815-635, lower and middle Riphean (Mesoproterozoic) successions of the southern Urals, Russia (Jankauskas, 1989).

Description.—Hollow oval spheromorph, 24 to 100 μm wide and 29 to 100 μm long (N = 122), with walls made of tessellated 6 to 16 μm (minimum diameter) polygonal plates and with no external envelope. Excystment by medial split (Fig. 5.6).

Occurrence.—*Satka favosa*, as described here, seems to be restricted to Mesoproterozoic rocks, including lower Mesoproterozoic shales of the Belt Supergoup ("polygonally segmented sphaeromorphs" of Horodyski, 1980; Adam, 2014), the Bylot Supergroup of the Canadadian Arctic (Hofmann and Jackson, 1994, as *Satka* spp., pl. 18, figs. 26–31), and lower and middle Riphean (Mesoproterozoic) successions of the southern Urals (Jankauskas et al., 1989).

Materials.—Many specimens observed in shoreface facies of the Gibb Member, basal Mainoru Formation (samples U6 240.2 m, U6 273.7 m, U6 305.1 m), but rare elsewhere.

Remarks.—The wall construction of *S. favosa* identifies it as a eukaryote, most likely the resting stage of some protist. Great confusion exists in the literature concerning *Satka* and its species. Jankauskas (1989) differentiated *S. favosa* from *S. elongata* (40–70 μm) by its smaller size and the characteristic shape of its inward-curving plates; *S. colonialica* (up to 150 μm) was segregated because of its simpler regular shape and betterdefined plates; and *S. granulosa* (40–50 μm wide to 75–125 μm long) was differentiated by its smaller size and granular appearance (linked to the presence of internal bodies). The specimens illustrated by Jankauskas (1989) as *Satka elongata* (pl. 4, figs. 3, 5) and *Satka granulosa* (pl. 4, fig. 8) also resemble *Satka favosa* as described here. *Satka squamifera* is described as having rounded plates and an external envelope. From our observations, however, the "plates" of *S. squamifera* represent the imprints of spheroidal cells on an encompassing envelope; therefore, we interpret this population as a colonial microorganism, perhaps cyanobacterial, which is unlikely to be linked to *S. favosa* at the domain level, and recently placed within the new genus *Squamosphaera* (Tang et al., 2015).

Genus Siphonophycus Schopf, 1968, emend. Knoll, Swett, and Mark, 1991

Type species.—Siphonophycus kestron Schopf (1968).

Occurrence.—Widespread in Proterozoic assemblages, common throughout the Roper Group.

Description.—Fragments of smooth, non-septate tubes, commonly interpreted as the sheaths of oscillatorialean cyanobacteria.

Remarks.—Different species are distinguished on the basis of cross-sectional diameter (revision in Butterfield et al., 1994): *S. thulenema*: 0.5 μm; *S. septatum*: 1–2 μm; *S. robustum*: 2–4 μm; *S. typicum*: 4–8 μm; *S. kestron*: 8–16 μm; and *S. solidum*: 16–32 μm. Five species occur in Roper shales: *S. kestron, S. robustum, S. septatum*and *S. typicum* occur as transported fragments; and *S. thulenema* forms small balls of thin filamentous sheaths.*Siphonophycus* spp. are commonly interpreted as the sheaths of oscillatorialean cyanobacteria.

Siphonophycus kestron Schopf, 1968 Figure 5.10

1968 *Siphonophycus kestron* Schopf, p. 671, pl. 80, figs. 1–3.

1971 *Siphonophycus kestron*; Schopf and Blacic, pl. 109, figs. 3, 4.

1992 *Siphonophycus kestron*; Sergeev, p. 95, pl. 16, figs. 8, 9.

1992 *Siphonophycus kestron*; Schopf, pl. 31, fig. J.

1994 *Siphonophycus kestron*; Butterfield et al., fig. 21D.

2001 *Siphonophycus kestron*; Sergeev and Lee, p. 8, pl. 1, fig. 1

2006 *Siphonophycus kestron*; Sergeev and Lee, pl. 1, fig. 10.

2006 *Siphonophycus kestron*; Sergeev, p. 214, pl. 22, figs. 1, 2; pl. 28, fig. 3; pl. 36, fig. 3; pl. 44, fig. 11; pl. 45, figs. 3, 6.

Holotype.—Specimen pl. 80, fig. 1 (Schopf, 1968), thin section Bit. Spr. 6-3, Paleobotanical Collections, Harvard University number 58469, from Neoproterozoic Bitter Springs Formation, Amadeus Basin, Australia.

Description.—Fragments of smooth, non-septate tubes, 8–16 μm in diameter, most specimens 8–9 μm, a few up to 16 μm.

Materials.—Dozens of filamentous sheaths, abundant in samples GG1 340.2m of the Corcoran Formation, a few in sample GG1 48.75m from the Velkerri Formation. *Siphonophycus robustum* (Schopf, 1968) Knoll, Swett, and Mark, 1991 Figure 5.11

1968 *Eomycetopsis robusta* Schopf, p. 685, pl. 82, figs. 2–3; pl. 83, figs. 1–4.

1991 *Siphonophycus robustum*; Knoll et al., p. 565, fig. 10.3, 10.5.

1994 *Siphonophycus robustum*; Butterfield et al., p. 64, figs. 26A, G.

Holotype.—Specimen pl. 83, fig. 1 (Schopf, 1968), thin section Bit. Spr. 10-1, Paleobotanical Collections, Harvard University number 58491 from Neoproterozoic Bitter Springs Formation, Amadeus Basin, Australia.

Description.—Smooth filamentous sheaths 2–4 μm in diameter, most specimens 2–3 μm in diameter.

Materials.—Dozens of specimens, most abundant in sample GG1 340.2m of the Corcoran Formation and sample U6 240.6m of the Mainoru Formation.

Siphonophycus septatum (Schopf, 1968) Knoll, Swett, and Mark, 1991 Figure 5.12

1968 *Tenuofilum septatum* Schopf, p. 679, pl. 86, figs. 10–12.

1991 *Siphonophycus septatum*; Knoll et al., p. 565, fig. 10.2.

Holotype.—Specimen pl. 86, fig. 11 (Schopf, 1968), thin section Bit/Spr 6–3, Paleobotanical collections, Harvard University, number 58527 from the Neoproterozoic Bitter Springs Formation, Amadeus Basin, Australia.

Description.—Fragments of smooth, non-septate tubes, 1–2 μm in diameter. Common, as transported fragments.

Materials.—Common in the Roper Group, abundant in sample U5 508.6m of the Mainoru Formation.

Siphonophycus thulenema Butterfield, Knoll, and Swett, 1994 Figure 5.13

1994 *Siphonophycus thulenema* Butterfield et al., fig. 22I.

Siphonophycus thulenema Butterfield, Knoll, and Swett, 1994, fig. 22I

Holotype.—HUPC 62718, fig. 22I, slide 86-G-62-46, R-28-3, Algal Dolomite Member, Svanbergfjellet Foramtion, Geerabukta (79°35′30″N, 17°44″E), 55m above base of member.

Description.—Fragments of thin, smooth, non-septate tubes, 0.5 μm in diameter, forming small balls of enrolled filamentous sheaths.

Materials.—Rare, in sample U5 125.1m of the Jalboi Member.

Siphonophycus typicum (Hermann, 1974), Butterfield, Knoll, and Swett, 1994 Fig. 5.10

1974 *Leiothrichoides tipicus* Hermann, p. 7, pl. 6, figs. 1–2.

1994 *Siphonophycus typicum*; Butterfield et al., p. 66, figs. 23B–D, 26B, H, I.

Holotype.—Specimen pl. 6, figs. 1, 2 (Hermann, 1974), preparation number 49/2T, Neoproterozoic Miroyedikha Formation, Krasnoyarsk Krai in Turukhansk region, near Maya River, Siberia.

Description.—Fragments of thin smooth, non-septate tubes, 4–8 μm in diameter.

Materials.—Common; most abundant in samples U5 508.6m of the Mainoru Formation, GG1 46.75m of the Velkerri Formation and GG1 340.2m of the Corcoran Formation.

Genus *Squamosphaera* Tang et al., 2015

Type species.—Squamosphaera colonialica (Jankauskas, 1979b) Tang et al., 2015 by monotypy

Squamosphaera colonialica (Jankauskas, 1979b) Tang et al., 2015 Figure 5.14

1979b *Satka colonialica* Jankauskas, p. 192, pl. 1, figs. 4, 6.

1985 *Satka colonialica*; Knoll and Swett, p. 468, pl. 53, figs. 4–6, 8.

1989 *Satka colonialica*; Jankauskas et al., p. 51, pl. 4, figs. 4, 7.

1989 *Satka squamifera*; Jankauskas et al., p. 52, pl. 4, fig. 10; pl. 5, fig.1–8

1997 *Satka colonialica*; Samuelsson, p. 175, fig. 9A, B.

1999 *Satka colonialica*; Cotter, p. 77, fig. 7C.

1999 *Satka colonialica*; Samuelsson et al., fig. 4G.

2015 *Squamosphaera colonialica*; Tang et al., 2015, p. 312, fig. 12 A–C2, fig. 13 A–F2 in press *Squamosphaera colonialica*; Porter and Riedman, fig. 17, 1–7. [See for complete synonymy]

Holotype.—Number 16-62-4762/22, slide 1. Well Kabakovo-62, 4762-4765 m. Neoproterozoic Zigazino-Komarovo Formation, Ufa, Bashkirian Urals (Jankauskas, 1979, fig. 4).

Description.—Single-walled, spheroidal, tomaculate, or irregularly shaped vesicles with irregular outline characterized by numerous broadly domical bulges. Vesicles 29–166 μm wide and 66–184 μm long (N = 37); individual bulges 11 to 14 μm in diameter.

Materials.—Many specimens were observed in all facies except the most basinal and are particularly abundant in the lowershoreface to storm-dominated shelf facies of the Jalboi Member and Crawford Formation (samples A82/3 311 m, A82/3 166 m, U5 125.1 m, U5 151.3 m, U5 334.3 m, U5 412.1 m).

Remarks.—The Roper population closely matches the emended diagnosis provided by Porter and Riedman (in press). Populations assigned here to the genus *Squamosphaera* were originally classified as a species of the genus *Satka* (Jankauskas, 1979b). As discussed above, the type species of *Satka*, *S. favosa*, is characterized by a wall of tessellated plates, which is far different from the vesicles observed in *S. colonialica*. The two species should not be placed in the same genus and doubtfully belong to the same domain. Tang et al. (2015) gave formal recognition to this by segregating populations of *Satka colonialica* into the new genus. Tang et al.'s (2015) diagnosis and description suggest that *Squamosphaera* was a cyst wall ornamented by broadly domical processes, but this conflicts with the irregular morphology of individual vesicles, both within Tang et al.'s (2015) illustrated materials and populations observed elsewhere. For this reason, Porter and Riedman (in press) emended the diagnosis of *Squamosphaera*, identifying the domical surface features simply as bulges. Roper populations closely resemble those from the Chuar Group, and we interpret them as enveloped marked by imprints of internal cells no longer present.

Hofmann and Jackson (1994, p. 28) described *Satka colonialica* from the Bylot Supergroup, the Canadadian Arctic, as a colony of packaged cells in "distinct belt-like rows transverse to the long axis of the colony," with a smooth surface and distinct curvilinear folds. They further suggested that *S. squamifera*, *S. granulosa*, and *S. elongata* might be taphonomic variants of the same taxon, and mentioned *S. elongata* Jankauskas, 1989 as the senior synonym to which other species should be referred. *Satka favosa*, however, is actually the senior species of the genus *Satka* (Jankauskas, 1979b). Hofmann and Jackson (1994) also include in their suggestion of synonymy a Bylot population referred to *Satka* spp. that we interpret as *S. favosa* (see above). Several types of coccoidal cyanobacteria (Chroococcales and

Pleurocapsales) and green algae (such as *Pandorina*) can produce colonies of packed spheroidal cells embedded in an envelope of amorphous mucilage matrix. Less commonly, the individual cells have a single wall rather than a multilamellate envelope, are closely packed, and the colony is surrounded in a structurally defined envelope, such as in modern cyanobacteria that produce baeocytes (endospores) within a parental wall (*Chroococcidiopsis* and *Staniera/Dermocarpa*). *Squamosphaera colonialica* resembles these pleurocapsalean cyanobacteria, with the internal cells not preserved, only their imprints on the wall. *Squamosphaera* differs from *Synsphaeridium* spp., which are colonies without an envelope.

Genus *Symplassosphaeridium* Timofeev, 1959 *Symplassosphaeridium* sp. Figure 5.15

Description.—Aggregates of loosely packed, smooth-walled vesicles of variable size, but with similar morphology and size within a colony. Differs from *Synsphaeridum* by the loose packing of vesicles.

Materials.—Dozens of colonies observed.

Genus *Synsphaeridium* Eisenack, 1965

Type species.—Synsphaeridium gotlandicum Eisenack, 1965.

Synsphaeridium sp. Figure 5.16–5.18

Occurrence.—Widespread in Proterozoic and Phanerozoic rocks.

Description.—Aggregates of contiguous smooth-walled vesicles, sometimes with internal inclusions, without envelope. Vesicles are similar in morphology and size within a colony. Colonies have variable size, from broadly spherical to elongated and irregular. Cell diameter ranges from 4 to 40 μm, and colonies can be up to 180 μm or more in diameter.

Materials.—Dozens of colonies observed, especially in samples GG1 326.2 m, in the Corcoran Formation and in samples U5 125.1m and U5 151.3m of the Jalboi Member.

Genus *Tappania* Yin, 1997

Type species.—Tappania plana Yin, 1997.

Other species.—Tappania tubata Yin, 1997; *Tappania gangaei* Prasad and Asher, 2001. *Tappania plana* Yin, 1997 Figure 6.1–6.15

1997 *Tappania plana* Yin, p. 23, pl. 1, figs. 4, 6, 7.

1997 *Tappania tubata* Yin, p. 23, 24, pl. 2, figs. 1, 3, 4, 6.

1997 *Tappania plana*; Xiao et al., p. 205, fig. 3c.

2001 *Tappania plana*; Prasad and Asher, p. 73, pl. 2, figs. 1–3, 9; pl. 3, figs. 1–6.

2001 *Tappania tubata*; Prasad and Asher, p. 74, pl. 2, figs. 4–7.

2001 *Tappania gangaei*; Prasad and Asher, p. 74, pl. 2, figs. 8, 10.

2001 *Tappania plana*; Javaux et al., pl. 1a–c.

2004 *Tappania plana*; Javaux et al., p. 124, fig. 2a–e.

2009 *Tappania plana*; Nagovitsin, fig. 2 a–e.

Holotype.—Sample and slide M 9208-1, L4/37, Shuiyou section, southern Shanxi, North China; lower shales of Beidajian Formation of the Ruyang Group (Meso-Neoproterozoic) (Yin, 1997, pl. 1, fig. 7).

Description.—Size 15 to 158 μm (N = 48), irregularly spheroidal vesicle bearing zero to 21 tubular, heteromorphic, sometimes branching, sometimes septate processes with closed relatively dark, rounded ends; zero to four neck-like expansions; zero to three bulbous protrusions. Process length up to 8 μm; bulbous expansions 2 μm wide; neck up to 2 μm high and 2 μm wide; two specimens show septate processes (Fig. 6.2–6.4), two others with branching processes. One specimen with a neck-like expansion shows a concentration of small (~8 μm long) processes with dark ends in one area of the vesicle surface, and another has small (3–5 μm long), hair-like spines, which are probably developing processes (not shown). The vesicle occasionally includes a dark cytoplasmic remnant. Specimens may bear only broad neck-like extensions (Fig. 6.6, 6.7, 6.10), or only processes (zero to 21) (Fig. 6.2, 6.5, 6.9, 6.13), or both. Neck-like extensions usually have a dark rim. In one specimen without processes, this trapezoidal extension is open, possibly indicating excystment (Fig. 6.15). Some specimens also show bulbous expansions suggestive of division by budding (Fig. 6.1); buds have semi-circular to oval convex morphology, whereas neck-like expansions have a trapezoidal shape, with side walls flaring outward and a convex end.

Occurrence.—*Tappania plana* seems to be restricted to uppermost Paleoproterozoic and Mesoproterozoic rocks, including, in addition to the Roper Group, Australia (Javaux et al., 2001); the Ruyang Group, China (Xiao et al., 1997; Yin, 1997); the Bahraich and Kheinjua groups, India (Prasad and Asher, 2001; Prasad et al., 2005); the Kamo Group of Siberia (Nagovitsin 2009; Nagovitsin et al., 2010); and the Lower Belt Group, USA (Adam, 2014).

Materials.—48 specimens measured in samples, U5 151.3m and U5 130.5m from the Jalboi Formation (proximal shelf facies), and from GG1 340.2m and GG1 326.2m from the Corcoran Formation (TST, distal shelf facies).

Remarks.—We observed a wide range of morphologies within *Tappania*, ranging from specimens with only broad, neck-like extensions, or only processes, to individuals with both broad, neck-like extensions and processes. On one fragmented specimen bearing a neck-like expansion, very small processes with dark, rounded closed ends are locally grouped on the vesicle wall. This is the first time this morphology has been reported in*Tappania plana*, however a single fragmented specimen and the large variability of the species precludes the creation of a new species at this time. Rare specimens show processes with septa, suggesting *Tappania* was multicellular. Ultrastructural analyses show a unilayered homogenous wall (Javaux et al., 2004). The Roper population shows division by budding, and possible excystment through the opening of a neck-like extension. Specimens from the Kotuikan Formation illustrated by Nagovitsin (2009) suggest that *Tappania* could also reproduce by a simple binary division of the vesicle.

Yin (1997) described a second species of *Tappania*, *T. tubata*, that co-occurs with *T. plana* and has a broad tubelike extension but not trapezoidal neck-like extension, with a fimbriate distal margin and a few small processes on its extension surface. The Roper *Tappania* population displays the range of morphological characters originally ascribed to *T. plana* and *T. tubata*, occasionally on a single specimen. Therefore, we consider *T. tubata* to be a synonym of the senior species, *Tappania plana*. Prasad and Asher (2001) described a third species, *Tappania gangaei*, based on the rounded bulbous extension, rather than trapezoidal or tube-like. However, in the Roper population, specimens may bear both neck-like and rounded extension (interpreted as budding structures), therefore here too, we consider *T. plana* as the senior synonym.

Vesicles bearing neck-like expansions but no processes are reported as cf. *Tappania*? in the late Mesoproterozoic—early Neoproterozoic Mbuyi-Mayi Supergroup, RDC (Baludikay et al., 2016). However, the absence of processes on any of the six specimens observed so far and the younger age of these fossils leaves this occurrence ambiguous, even though *Tappania* populations elsewhere also include similar morphologies without processes. Indeed, so far, *Tappania plana* seems to be restricted to uppermost Paleoproterozoic to Mesoproterozoic rocks. Butterfield (2005a) described specimens from the mid-Neoproterozoic Wynniatt Formation, the Canadian arctic as *Tappania,* but these show a complex pattern of septation, peripheral branching and anastomosis not found in Mesoproterozoic populations and lack the neck-like expansions or the closed and rounded process terminations characteristic of older fossils. Therefore, the Neoproterozoic population might usefully be placed into a separate genus.

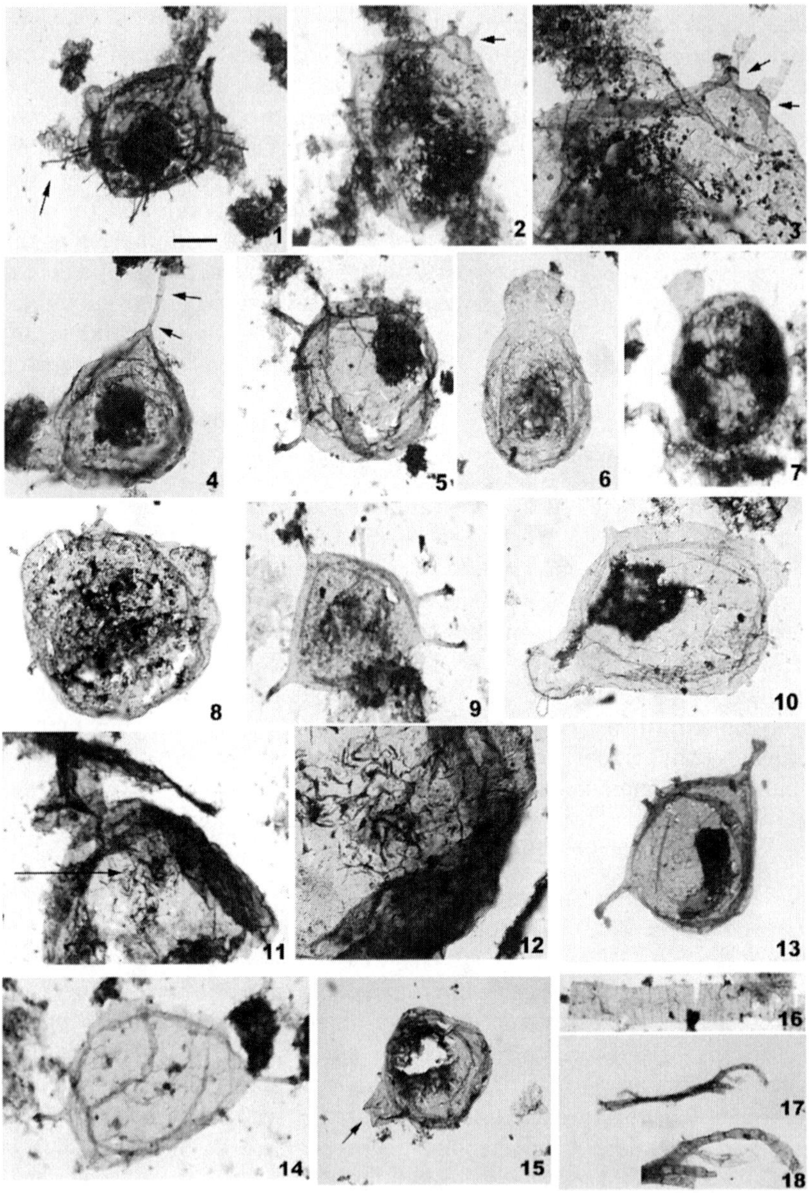

Figure 6. Photographs of Roper organic-walled microfossils: (**1–15**) *Tappania plana*: arrow in (**1**) showing furcating process, arrows in (**2–4**) showing septae in processes, (**3**) showing details from specimen in (**2**), arrow in (**11**) showing the area of locally grouped small processes shown in (**12**), arrow in (**15**) shows open neck-like expansion, suggesting excystment structure. (**16**) *Tortunema* sp. (**17, 18**) *Trachytrichoides* sp.: (**18**) showing

details of cells morphology in filaments in (**17**). Scale bar in (**1**) is: (**1, 2**) 40μm; (**3, 11**) 10μm; (**4, 8, 14**) 20μm; (**5, 9, 16, 17**) 30μm; (**6, 10, 12, 15, 18**) 15μm; (**7**) 27μm; (**13**) 25μm. Slide and England finder coordinates: (**1**) GG1 340.2m .3 B X36/2, (**2, 3**) GG1 340.2m .2 A J47/2, (**4**) GG1 340.2m .3B T40/2, (**5**) GG1 340.2m .2A E28/4, (**6**) U5 151.3m .2 Q28/3, (**7**) GG1 326.2m .2 V33/1, (**8**) U5 151.3m .2 Y14/2, (**9**) GG1 340.2m .3 H26/2, (**10**) GG1 326.2m .3 F39/1, (**11, 12**) GG1 340.2m .2 E17/1, (**13**) GG1 326.2 m .2 Y28/4, (**14**) GG1 340.2m .3 O19/1, (**15**) U5 130.5m .2 U9, (**16**) A82/3 379.1M G57/0, and (**17**) U6 240.2m .2B J34/1.

Genus *Tortunema* Hermann, 1976

Type species.—Tortunema wernadskii (Schepeleva, 1960) Butterfield et al., 1994.

Tortunema sp. Figure 6.16

Description.—Fragmental remains of compressed cylindrical sheaths, 250–300 μm long and 30 μm wide (N = 2), marked by thin, regularly spaced, transverse annulations that record cell boundaries of originally ensheathed trichomes. Spacing of prominent annulations 6 μm, commonly with less-pronounced annulations between them.

Materials.—Two specimens.

Discussion.—Pseudoseptate filaments, widely distributed in Proterozoic platform and inner-shelf shales, are generally interpreted as the empty sheaths of cyanobacteria (e.g., Jankauskas, 1989; Butterfield et al., 1994). These sheaths are larger than the type species of the genus, *T. wernadskii* (Schepeleva) Butterfield. Because they are rare, we have little sense of their size frequency distribution, so only identify them as *Tortunema* sp.

Genus *Trachytrichoides* Hermann in Timofeev, Hermann, and Mikhailova, 1976

Type species.—Trachytrichoides ovalis Hermann in Timofeev et al., 1976.

Trachytrichoides sp. Figure 6.17–6.18

Description.—Multicellular filaments with ovoid cells and thick intercellular septa, no external sheath, 157 μm long and 5 μm wide (N = 3), with individual ellipsoidal cells 5 μm wide x 6 μm long.

Materials.—Three filaments observed in sample U6 240.2m of the Mainoru Formation.

Remarks.—A rare component of the Roper Group, differs from other filamentous taxa by the oval shape of the cells and absence of ellipsoidal fold between the cells (as in *Arctacellularia*), and from the type species *T. ovalis* by the smaller cell size than those of the holotype (25–35 μm wide and 30–60 μm long).

Genus *Valeria* Jankauskas, 1982, emend. Nagovitsin, 2009

Type species.—Valeria lophostriata (Jankauskas, 1979b) Jankauskas, 1982.

Valeria lophostriata (Jankauskas, 1979b) Jakauskas, 1982 Figure 7.1–7.4

1979b *Kildinella lophostriata* Jankauskas, p. 153, fig. 1.13–1.15.

1982 *Valeria lophostriata*; Jankauskas, p. 109, pl. 39, fig. 2.

1983 *Kildinosphaera lophostriata*; Vidal and Siedlecka, p. 59, fig. 6A–G.

1985 *Kildinosphaera lophostriata*; Vidal and Ford, p. 361, fig. 4C, E–F.

1989 *Valeria lophostriata*; Jankauskas et al., p. 86, pl. 16, figs. 1–5. [See for additional synonymy]

1994 *Valeria lophostriata*; Hofmann and Jackson, 1994, p. 24, pl. 17, figs. 14–15; pl. 19, fig. 4.

1997 *Valeria lophostriata*: Xiao et al., p. 201, fig. 3e.

1999 *Valeria lophostriata*; Samuelsson et al., p. 15, fig. 8E.

2001 *Valeria lophostriata*; Javaux et al., fig. 1D.

2004 *Valeria lophostriata*; Javaux et al., fig. 2F–I.

2009 *Valeria lophostriata*; Nagy et al., fig. 1A, B.

2009 *Valeria lophostriata*; Nagovitsin, p. 144, fig. 4E.

2009 ovoidal acritarch with striated ornamentation Peng et al., fig. 4.

2009 ovoidal acriatrch with striated ornamentation Lamb et al., fig. 4 A.

?2012 “dark walled megasphaeric coccoid with a subradial striation” Battison and Brasier, fig. 8B.

2015 *Valeria lophostriata*; Tang et al., p. 315, fig. 11.

in press *Valeria lophostriata*; Riedman and Porter, p. 10, fig. 4.1.

in press *Valeria lophostriata*; Porter and Riedman, fig. 19.1–19.3.

(For additional synonymy see Jankauskas et al., 1989, and Hofmann and Jackson, 1994)

Holotype.—Number 16-62-4762/16, sp. 1, DH Kabakovo 62 drill core, depth 4762 to 4765 meters, Neoproterozoic Zigazino-Komarovo Formation, southern Urals (Jankauskas, 1979b, fig. 1.14).

Description.—Large vesicle, 104–160 μm in minimum diameter, with lanceolate folds and a distinctive ornamentation of concentric ridges, giving the appearance of a “target” (Fig. 7.3, 7.4).

Occurrence.—This taxon is found worldwide (Hofmann, 1999) from the late Paleoproterozoic Era (Javaux et al., 2004; Lamb et al., 2009; Peng et al., 2009) to the Cryogenian (Nagy et al., 2009).

Materials.—Several specimens observed, mostly in samples U6 305.1 m, U6 273.7 m, and U6 240.2m from the Mainoru Formation.

Remarks.—SEM analyses show that the striations are 1-μm ridges located on the inside of the vesicle wall (Javaux et al., 2004). Excystment by medial split gives rise to two half vesicles that commonly enroll onto themselves (Fig. 7.1, 7.2).

Unnamed form A Figure 7.5–7.6

Description.—A large ovoidal or irregular and globular envelope including several contiguous compartments, each surrounded by an envelope and containing closely packed spheroidal cells. Two fragmented specimens are 350 μm wide and 600–700 μm long, internal compartments surrounded by an inner envelope 39–85 μm in diameter, containing poorly defined, closely packed cells. The external envelope is 8–13 μm thick.

Materials.—Two specimens in sample U6 305.1m from the Mainoru Formation.

Unnamed form B Figure 7.7–7.8

Description.—Black opaque vesicles, 141 and 215 μm in diameter (N = 2), with medial split and folds at periphery.

Materials.—Two specimens in sample GG1 340.2m from the Corcoran Formation.

Remarks.—These vesicles differ from *Chuaria circularis* by the translucent margin showing folds.

Unnamed form C

Figure 7.9

Description.—Vesicles with smooth to chagrinate walls, 30 and 35m in diameter (N = 2), connected by a 14-μm-long filamentous expansion.

Materials.—Two vesicles in sample U5 125.1m from the Jalboi Member.

Unnamed form D Figure 7.10

Description.—Vesicle 40 μm in diameter, attached to a large 80 μm filamentous expansion, but not communicating with the cell interior (thus distinct from *Germinosphaera*).

Materials.—One specimen in sample GG1 326.2m from the Corcoran Formation.

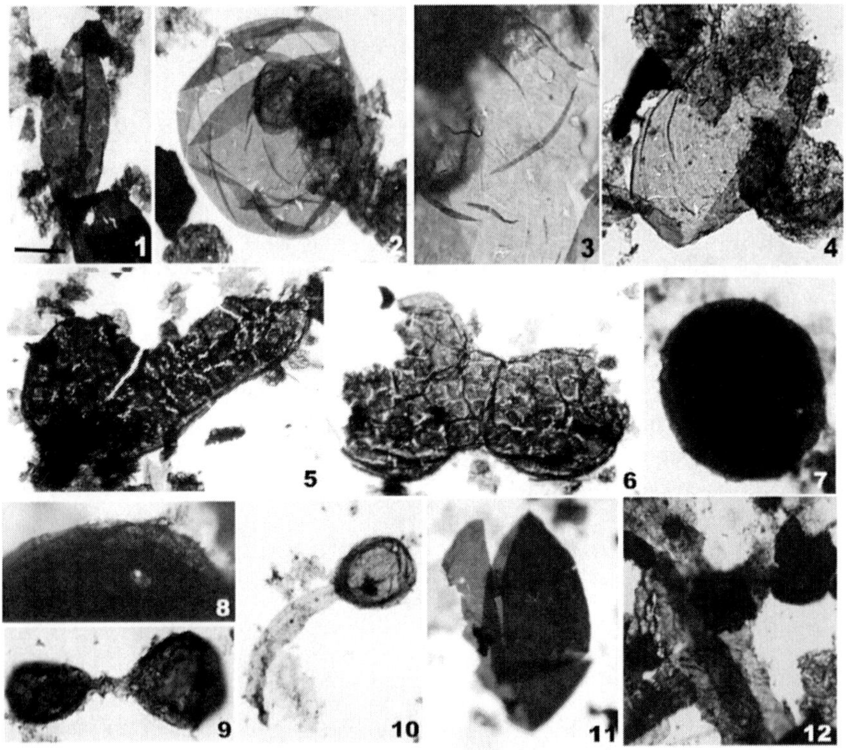

Figure 7. Photographs of Roper organic-walled microfossils: (**1–4**) *Valeria lophostriata*: (**1**) showing half enrolled vesicle following medial split, (**2**) showing start of medial split, (**3, 4**) showing wall ornamentation by characteristic concentric striations. (**5, 6**) Unnamed form A, large compartmentalized colonial forms. (**7, 8**) Unnamed form B, opaque spheromorph, (**8**) showing details of folds at periphery. (**9**) Unnamed form C, spheromorphs connected by a filamentous expansion. (**10**) Unnamed form D, spheromorph with a filamentous expansion. (**11**) Unnamed form E, large smooth thick brittle spheromorph. (**12**) Unnamed form F, large filament in indented sheath. Scale bar in (**1**) is: (**1**) 100 μm, (**2, 4, 8**) 25μm, (**3**) 10μm, (**5**) 70μm, (**6**) 120 μm, (**7**) 45μm, (**9**) 18μm, (**10, 15**) 30μm, (**11**) 80μm, and (**12**) 55μm. Slide and England finder coordinates: (**1**) U6 305.1m .2A S41, (**2**) U6 230.8m .2 N27/2, (**4**) U6 233.6 B45/0, (**5**) U6 305.1m .2A O/N39, (**6**) U6 305.1m B45/1, (**7**) GG1 340.2m .3B U30, (**9**) U5 125.1m .2 M41/3, (**10**) GG1 326.2m .2 E20/1, (**11**) U6 240.2m .2U27/2, (**12**) U5 436.7m .2 S51.

Unnamed form E Figure 7.11

Description.—Large, smooth-walled, thick, brittle, brownorange wall fragment of a spheromorph, 310 μm in diameter.

Materials.—One specimen in sample U6 240.2m from the Mainoru Formation.

Unnamed form F Figure 7.12

Description.—Large, 16 to 29 μm wide filament in a 72 μm × 171 μm smooth indented sheath.

Materials.—A single specimen in sample U5 437m from the Mainoru Formation (Showell Creek Member).

Remarks.—This large filamentous fossil differs from other sheathed filamentous taxa by the indentation of the sheath and absence of septae in the filament, although these characters could be taphonomic. Other taxa, such as *Rugosoopsis*, can reach large diameters, but have a distinct transverse fabric not observed here.*Palaeolyngbya* may also have a wide sheath, but is characterized by regular uniseriate array of well-preserved cells (Butterfield et al., 1994).

4. DISCUSSION

Paleoecology: the distribution of Roper fossils in space.— Abbott and Sweet (2000) interpreted Roper sequence stratigraphy in terms of four facies groups: (1) paralic to fluviatile redbeds characterized by heterolithic, iron-rich sandstones along with finer siliciclastics and oolitic ironstone, dessication cracks and paleosols; (2) tide-dominated shoreline sandstones dominated by trough cross-bedded quartz arenite; (3) shore-face to storm-dominated shelf deposits with alternating rippled and cross-bedded quartz arenites and laminated siltites and shales; and (4) basinal facies consisting of thinly laminated shales deposited below storm wave base. In a preliminary study, Javaux et al. (2001) suggested that Roper diversity peaked in coastal facies, and analysis of the entire sample suite confirms this view. Microfossils do not occur in tidal sandstones and ironstones, but are abundant in shaley intervals of shoreface and proximal shelf successions. Indeed, diversity is highest in shallow shelf environments characterized by interbedded shales and cross-bedded sandstones, with individual taxa peaking in abundance at different points along the shelf gradient (Fig. 8).

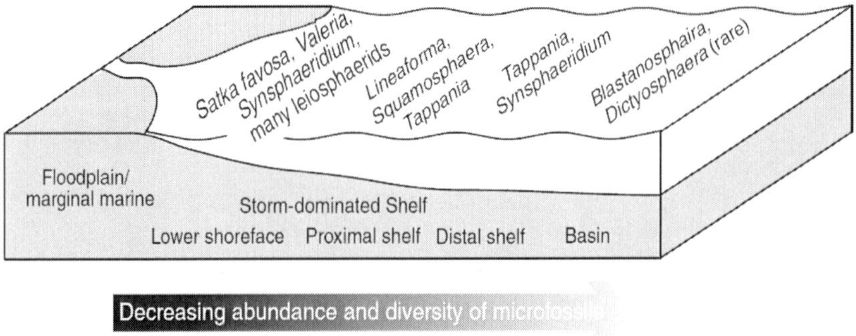

Figure 8. Paleoecological distribution of selected microfossils in the Roper Group.

Eukaryotes and probable eukaryotes are least abundant and diverse in basinal shales throughout the Roper succession, the exception being *Blastanosphaira kokkoda*, which locally forms a monospecific assemblage in basinal shales, and rare *Dictyosphaera*. It has long been apparent empirically that quality of microfossil preservation varies inversely with total organic content (Butterfield et al., 1994). Therefore the limited presence of eukaryotes in basinal shales could reflect, in part, the high organic content of many basinal samples. That noted, even where basinal shales contain reasonably preserved microfossils, diversity is low. Bitumens occur throughout the Roper Group, in part the result of migration from source beds in the Velkerri Formation (Jackson and Raiswell, 1991; Dutkiewicz et al., 2003). Biomarker analysis of carbonaceous shales in the underlying McArthur Group suggests strong dominance of open water primary production by bacteria, including anoxygenic photosynthetic bacteria that inhabited anoxic waters within the photic zone (Brocks et al., 2005).

Biostratigraphy: the distribution of Roper fossils in time.— Early work in Russia established a broad biostratigraphic framework for organic-walled microfossils in Proterozoic shales, with *Satka favosa* characterizing early Mesoproterozoic samples and *Valeria lophostriata* more common in Neoproterozoic successions (summaries in Jankauskas et al., 1989; Sergeev et al., 2010). More recent research shows that both of these morphospecies co-occur with *Tappania plana* and other Roper taxa in the Kamo Group, Siberia, and in correlative shales of the Debengda Formation (Nagovitsin, 2009; Stanevich et al., 2009; Nagovitsin et al., 2010). The fossiliferous shales are interspersed with stromatolitic carbonates and so represent shallow platform environments. Depositional age is constrained only broadly by shale dating techniques to be ca. 1000–1500 Myr. Another possible Mesoproterozoic index fossil includes *Lineaforma* from the Roper Group, the Kotuikan Formation of Siberia (Vorob'va et al., 2015), and Belt Supergroup of Montana, USA (Adam, 2014).

Tappania plana occurs as well in the Ruyang Group, China (Xiao et al., 1997; Yin, 1997; Yin et al., 2005); the Sarda Formation of the Bahraich Group, Ganga Basin (Prasad and Asher, 2001) and possibly correlative beds of the Kheinjua Group,Vindhyan Basin (Prasad et al., 2005) in northern India; and in the Lower Belt Group, Montana (Adam, 2014; Adam et al., 2016). Detrital zircons indicate that Ruyang deposition began no earlier than 1700 Ma (Hu et al., 2014), and xenotime Pb-Pb ages of about 1400 Ma for the overlying Luoyu Group constrain deposition from above (Lan et al., 2014). A U-Pb zircon date from an ash bed within the Luoyu Group potentially constrains Ruyang deposition to be older than 1611± 8 Ma, but the abundance of detrital grains in the dated bed and the wide range of ages for individual zircons (Su et al., 2012) suggest that the published date may provide only a maximum age constraint on Luoyu deposition (Lan et al., 2014). Belt microfossils, which share many taxa in common with the Roper Group (Horodyski, 1980, 1993; Adam, 2014; Adam et al., 2016), are similarly constrained by a 1576 ±13 Ma basement, 1460–1470 Ma sills that intrude into the fossiliferous stratigraphy and a U-Pb zircon date of 1454 ±9Ma for bentonite in the overlying Helena Formation (Lydon, 2007). U-Pb zircon dating of ash beds just below the Vindhyan succession containing unambiguous *Tappania* indicates that these fossils are ≤ 1631 ±1Ma (Ray et al., 2002). Thus, all known occurrences of *T. plana* fall within the latest Paleoproterozoic or Mesoproterozoic Era, with the Roper and Belt populations being the most tightly constrained by radiometric ages. The absence in Roper assemblages of distinctive taxa (e.g., the distinctive acanthomorphic taxon *Shuiyousphaeridium macroreticulatum* or the ornamented forms *Miroedichia* sp. and *Lophosphaeridium* sp.) that cooccur with *Tappania* elsewhere could reflect differences in either age or environment (e.g., Nagovitsin et al., 2010).

More broadly, the moderately diverse protist compressions of the Roper Group are intermediate in nature between the simple leiosphere-dominated assemblages found in most late Paleoproterozoic shales (e.g., Lamb et al., 2009; Peng et al., 2009) and the slightly more diverse (and taxonomically distinctive) assemblages reported from late Mesoproterozoic shales (e.g., Hermann, 1990; Samuelsson et al., 1999). Recently, Vorob'eva et al. (2015) reported a relatively diverse assemblage of microfossils in the ~1.5Ga Kotuikan Formation of Siberia. The assemblage includes 12–14 spheroidal and filamentous forms plausibly interpreted as eukaryotes, but no acanthomorphs. Notably, the Kotuikan assemblage contains the distinctively striated filament *Lineaforma elongata*, which is also found in the Roper Group. Sergeev et al. (2016) also reported well-preserved microfossils in shales of the 1.4–1.45 Ga Kaltasy Formation, East European

Platform, Russia. This assemblage includes a number of probable eukaryotic taxa, but also lacks conspicuously ornamented spheromorphic populations, which in this case possibly reflects the unusual (for Mesoproterozoic successions) combination of basinal deposition and oxic bottom waters. In general, then, the summed occurrences suggest that while many of the organic-walled microfossils in the Roper and other assemblages have long stratigraphic ranges, some can be used to identify uppermost Paleoproterozoic and Mesoproterozoic sedimentary successions and may, in time, permit the broad subdivision of Mesoproterozoic time.

The phylogenetic and functional interpretation of Roper fossils.—Because Roper fossils are both unusually well preserved and differentially well constrained by age and environment, they prompt questions of phylogenetic affiliation. In particular, can individual populations be identified with confidence as eukaryotes and, if so, can they further be assigned to extant eukaryotic clades?

In principle, Roper populations could include the polysaccharide sheaths and envelopes of cyanobacteria or other bacteria, the walls of metabolically active eukaryotic cells, and eukaryotic resting or reproductive cysts. Cyst walls are commonly reinforced with compounds that improve preservation potential, for example, sporopollenin in plant spores, dinosporin in some dinoflagellates, and algaenan in a few green algae and eustigmatophytes (de Leeuw et al., 2006; Kodner et al., 2009; Scholz et al., 2014). Known and assumed protistan cysts predominate in Phanerozoic marine shales, and this has understandably influenced the interpretation of older microfossils. We must recognize, however, that prospects for the preservation of vegetative walls would have been enhanced in the low-oxygen, bioturbation-free muds found widely in earlier seaways, as illustrated by the preservation of simple multicellular and coenocytic remains in Neoproterozoic shales (Butterfield et al., 1994; Butterfield, 2009) and carbonaceous seaweeds in Ediacaran and Paleozoic successions (e.g., Xiao et al., 2002; LoDuca et al., 2003; Kenrick and Vinther, 2006; Yuan et al., 2011).

Bacterial microfossils do occur in the Roper assemblage, especially *Siphonophycus* spp., which is found as minor components of Roper assemblages. Sheath-forming filaments occur in a number of bacterial clades, but given their relatively large size and occurrence in oxic waters within the shallow reaches of the photic zone, *Siphonophycus* populations are most readily interpreted as cyanobacteria comparable to modern *Lyngbya*, *Plectonema*, and *Phormidium* (Rippka et al., 1979). The Roper assemblage also includes rare trichomes and pseudoseptate filaments that may record cyanobacteria or other bacteria. Such an interpretation is fully in accord both with microfossil assemblages preserved in Proterozoic cherts and molecular clocks that indicate major cyanobacterial diversification before the time of Roper deposition (Tomitani et al., 2006, and references cited therein).

Cyanobacteria may also occur among spheromorphic forms. Horodyski (1993), for example, interpreted *Satka squamifera* as possible envelopes of colonial entophysalid cyanobacteria, a view formalized by the reassignment of this and other probable synonyms of *Satka colonialica* to *Squamosphaera* (Tang et al., 2015; Porter and Riedman, in press). Simple leiosphaerid compressions could also include the envelopes of colonial coccoidal cyanobacteria, some of which can have both a large diameter and medial splits similar to those commonly interpreted as excystment structures in microfossils (Waterbury and Stanier, 1978). TEM may be necessary to ascertain the affinities of leiospherids, especially those with very thin walls. In the limited number of Roper specimens examined to date, preserved complex multilayered wall ultrastructure suggests eukaryotic rather than cyanobacterial affinities (Javaux et al., 2004; see systematic paleontology section).

While comparisons to cyanobacteria are based principally on morphological similarities, constrained by paleoenvironmental setting (e.g., Knoll and Golubic, 1992), taphonomic experiments underscore the preservation potential of cyanobacterial sheaths and envelopes (e.g., Bartley, 1996). Recent microanalyses of modern and subfossil mats in Antarctic lakes provide strong evidence for the preservation of cyanobacterial morphologies and chemistries, including sheaths and the sheath pigment scytonemin (Lepot et al., 2014).

If eukaryotic, Roper microfossils must be viewed as the remains of cell walls, which places both functional and phylogenetic constraints on interpretation. Cell walls are best known from algae, especially the cellulosic cell walls of green, red, brown, dinoflagellate, and some golden-brown algae (Graham and Wilcox, 2000). Walls occur, as well, in osmotrophic eukaryotes, including the chitinous walls of fungi and the cellulosic walls of oomycetes (Melida et al., 2013). Moreover, a wall can form during a specific life cycle stage, even in organisms not otherwise characterized by cell wall synthesis (e.g., the cellulosic macrocyst walls of dictyostelid amoebozoans) (Saga and Yanagisawa, 1982; Blanton et al., 2000) and chemically uncharacterized walls synthesized by coccoidal cells in chlorarachniophyte rhizarians (Ishida and Hara, 1994).

Walled resting or reproductive cysts occur widely within the Eukarya, not only in algae, but also in heterotrophic clades. Ciliates, for example, make cyst walls that can be smooth or conspicuously ornamented (Beers, 1948, 1966; Foissner et al., 2007; Verni and Rosati, 2011), and so do many animals (e.g., Blades-Eckelbarger and Marcus, 1992). In many eukaryotes, cyst formation (commonly but not always associated with sexual fusion) is induced by conditions that inhibit growth, including desiccation, nutrient deprivation, and anoxia, and so one might expect a resting stage to occur in the life cycles of eukaryotes in oceans with anoxic water masses beneath a thin oxic mixed layer (Johnston et al., 2012). The broad phylogenetic distribution of cellulose and other wall compounds suggests that the ability to synthesize a protective wall evolved early in the Eukarya, perhaps before the earliest divergences of crown group taxa.

Tappania plana has been interpreted as a metabolically active microorganism on the basis of its irregularly placed, occasionally branching processes that extend outward from the main vesicle (Xiao et al., 1997; Javaux et al., 2003, 2004). Bulbous extensions on the same individuals may record vegetative reproduction. Cell walls that completely encompass individuals are common in photosynthetic and osmotrophic eukaryotes, but the cylindrical extensions provide a functional argument in favor of osmotrophy. These structures would increase the surface area for absorption and enable cells to probe nutrient-rich habitat patches, but would do little to enhance primary production. Butterfield (2005a), in fact, interpreted *Tappania* as a possible fungus, based on a population from Neoproterozoic shales of the Shaler Group, the Canadian Arctic (but see Butterfield, 2015). As noted in the systematic paleontology section, Shaler fossils differ in many ways from Roper and other Mesoproterozoic *Tappania*, but the functional argument holds. In eukaryote evolution, phagotrophy is the ancestral state (evolved at least at the time of LECA, Knoll and Lahr, 2016), while phototrophy required the evolution of chloroplast by endosymbiosis of a cyanobacteria, and thus is derived and evolved not later than 1.1 Ga—the age of *Bangiomorpha*. Today, many marine protists are mixotrophs (able to use both phagotrophy and phototrophy; Mitra et al., 2016).

The ability to absorb dissolved organic molecules (osmotrophy) is ubiquitous among protists (Mitra et al., 2016), but only a few clades, chiefly fungi and oomycetes, employ osmotrophy as the primary or sole means of obtaining food, having lost phagotrophy (Richards and Talbot, 2013). Recently, Knoll and Lahr (2016) investigated the phylogenetic distribution of major feeding modes within the Eukarya. While bacterivory is basal within the domain, other feeding modes evolved early, helping to explain the later Mesoproterozoic diversification of crown groups. Molecular clock estimates for the initial divergence of crown group fungi generally postdate Roper time (e.g., 800 Ma, Berney and Pawlowski, 2006; 730–820 Ma, Lücking et al., 2009; 1050 Ma, Parfey et al., 2011; 812 Ma, Floudas et al., 2012). Crown group Stramenopiles may also have late Mesoproterozoic or Neoproterozoic origins (e.g., Parfrey et al., 2011). For this reason, it is possible that early Mesoproterozoic *Tappania* fossils record stem group protists functionally, but not necessarily phylogenetically comparable to extant osmotrophic heterotrophs. In any event, the complex morphology of *Tappania* provides direct evidence for cell organization by a dynamic cytoskeleton and membrane system, which is a fundamental feature of eukaryotic biology (Javaux et al., 2001; Knoll et al., 2006).

Other Roper fossils find reasonable interpretation as cyst walls, for example, *Valeria lophostriata*, with its distinctive ornamentation of parallel ridges and opening by medial split (Javaux et al., 2003, 2004). Accepting *V. lophostriata* as a resting or reproductive cyst relaxes any constraint on its metabolism or placement within a specific subgroup of the eukaryotic domain (as noted above, cysts occur in many eukaryotic taxa that lack walls on metabolically active cells). Similarly, the ornamented spheromorphs *Dictyosphaera delicata*, with its reticulated wall, and *Satka favosa*, with its wall made of polygonal plates and (rare) opening by medial split, are best interpreted as eukaryotic cysts. *Blastanosphaira kokkoda* has a finely chagrinate wall, and intensive budding, both of which are evidence for vegetative reproduction.

Spheromorphic microfossils in Paleo- and Mesoproterozoic rocks have sometimes been interpreted as green algae, requiring an early origin of photosynthesis in the domain (Moczydłowska et al., 2011). Chlorophyte algae are sometimes recognized on the basis of a distinctive trilaminar structure (TLS) observed in TEM images of cell walls (Allard and Templier, 2000), and TLS has been documented in microfossils as old as Cambrian (Talyzina and Moczydłowska, 2000). TLS covaries phylogenetically with the biosynthetic capacity to make long-chain aliphatic molecules called algaenans (Allard and Templier, 2000), and a phylogenetic survey of this capacity suggests that it may be limited to two (now) non-marine clades within the Trebouxiophyceae and Chlorophyceae (Kodner et al., 2009), neither of which is likely to have diverged much earlier than the Ediacaran or Cambrian periods. In the Roper Group's taxa studied with TEM, the occurrence of TLS has not been observed to date and we have no indication for photosynthetic eukaryotic crown group taxa (Javaux et al., 2004).

Alternatively, prasinophyte algae, a paraphyletic group at the base of the green algal tree, can form thick-walled phycomata, which are found widely in Paleozoic shales (Colbath and Grenfell, 1995). Some phycomata have a diagnostic ultrastructure (Talyzina and Moczydłowska, 2000), but this has not been observed in Roper or other microfossils of comparable age. Thus, the argument that Roper and other early microfossil assemblages contain green algae must rely on broad comparisons of simple morphologies and the debatable assumption that preserved eukaryotic microfossils are likely to be algal.

Molecular estimates for the origin of crown group green algae vary widely (Fig. 10), but generally suggest late Mesoproterozoic or younger diversification (e.g., 1100 Ma, Heckman et al., 2001; 1200 Ma, Yoon et al., 2004; 1000–900 Ma, Parfrey et al., 2011; 936 Ma, Becker, 2013; and even ~700 Ma, Berney and Pawlowski, 2006). The ~800 Ma *Cladophora*-like fossil *Proterocladus* casts doubt on the youngest molecular clock estimates, and the early diverging red alga *Bangiomorpha* from 1100–1200 Ma cherts in the Canadian Arctic (Butterfield, 2000) further constrains the age of total (but not crown) group green algae. Nonetheless, if even the oldest of current molecular clock estimates is broadly correct, it is unlikely that Roper microfossils can be interpreted in terms of specific extant clades within the green algae.

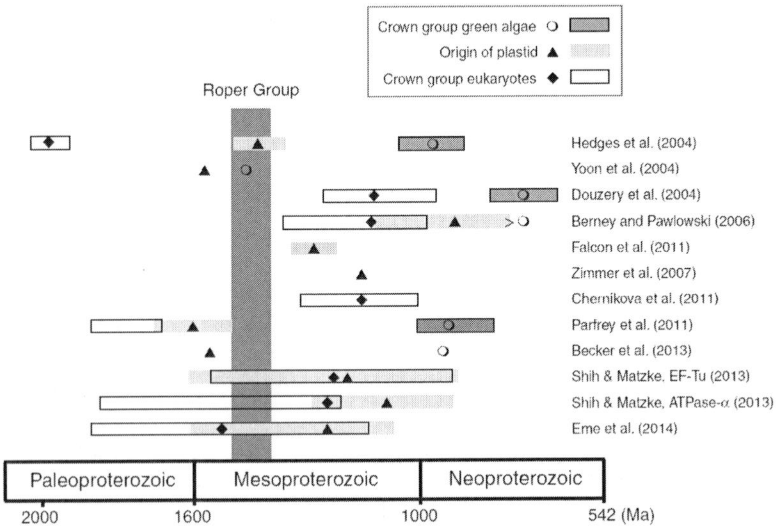

Figure 9. Comparison of Roper age with molecular clock estimates for the divergences of crown group green algae, photosynthetic eukaryotes, and crown group eukaryotes. Circle, diamond and triangles are the mean ages for the origin of crown group algae, plastid, crown group eukaryotes, respectively, and the dark gray, medium gray and white rectangles represent the errors on estimates, respectively.

If Roper leiosphaerids cannot be assigned to crown group green algal clades, what are the possibilities for phylogenetic placement? Not surprisingly, age estimates for the last eukaryotic common ancestor (LECA) of all extant eukaryotes vary among treatments, but those not rejected on the basis of *Bangiomorpha*'s age and interpretation suggest a late Paleoproterozoic or early Mesoproterozoic time of origin for the eukaryotic crown group (Fig. 9). Accepting this, Roper fossils could include the vegetative walls or resting cysts of stem-group green algae, stem-group taxa of the more inclusive Archaeplastida (green algae/embryophytes, red algae and glaucocystophytes, united by the presence of a chloroplast derived via primary endosymbiosis with a cyanobacterium), stem-group or morphologically unrecognizable crown-group members of other non-photosynthetic eukaryotic clades, or stem-group eukaryotes (before LECA). In the absence of additional data, we find it impossible to choose among these possibilities. Note, however, that it would not be unusual to have a biota dominated by stem-group members of a clade. For example, most arthropod diversity in early and mid-Cambrian oceans belonged to stem group members of the phylum, and the same is true of Cambrian echinoderms, Carboniferous seed plants, and many other clades. Stem-group taxa are common in the deep fossil record.

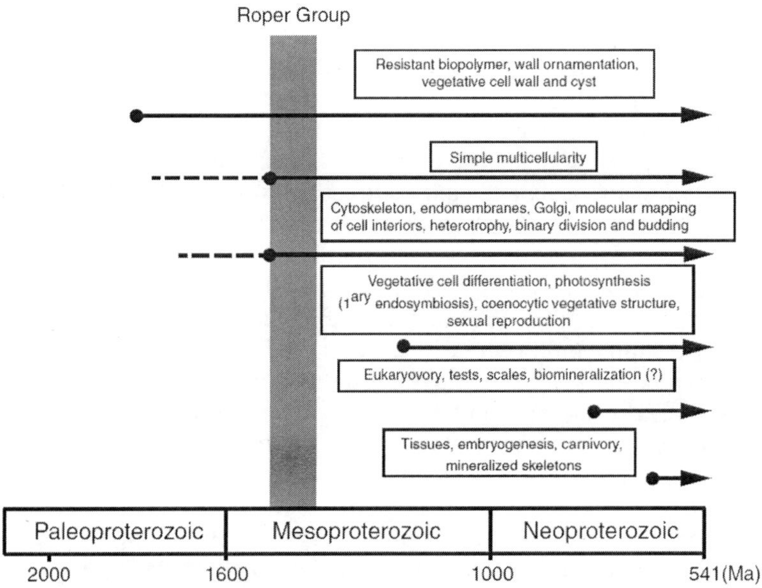

Figure 10. Biological innovations in early eukaryotes inferred from preserved microfossils (modified from Javaux, 2011).

Finally, there are the large, striated tubes of *Lineaforma elongata*, which commonly are fragmental but locally abundant in Roper samples. The size and complexity of these tubes favor a eukaryotic interpretation, but more specific attribution is impossible.

In general, then, eukaryotic remains are prominent, even dominant components of the Roper assemblage, but all are simple and, at lower taxonomic levels, problematic. Consistent with molecular clock inferences, Roper eukaryotes may include stem-group taxa; early, morphologically unattributable crowngroup species; or both. Missing from the Roper biota are highly ornamented cysts of the type found commonly in later Neoproterozoic and, especially, Phanerozoic shales. Cyst ornamentation can serve a number of purposes (see, for example, Cohen et al., 2009), one of which is defense against predation (e.g., Peterson and Butterfield, 2005). The last common ancestor of extant eukaryotes was probably a heterotroph capable of phagocytosing bacteria and other small particles; eukaryotes that eat other eukaryotic cells, however, are derived (Knoll and Lahr, 2016). The limited ornamentation of Roper microfossils is consistent with the hypothesis that predation on protists was low prior to the Neoproterozoic Era, because of the relatively late radiation of eukaryovorous protists (Knoll, 2014) and animals (Butterfield, 2015).

Taxonomy aside, the Roper assemblage documents biological innovations in early eukaryotes (Fig. 10; see also Javaux, 2006, 2011; Knoll et al., 2006). Reproductive modes in **Roper populations include simple binary division and budding** (e.g., *Tappania*, *Blastanosphaira*). We have no direct evidence for sex in Roper populations, but this reflects absence of evidence and not necessarily evidence of absence. Sex was present in the last common ancestor of extant eukaryotes, so any paleontological inference must rest on currently uncertain systematic interpretations of Roper fossils as stem- or crown-group eukaryotes. Whether associated with sexual fusion or not, Roper protists formed resting cysts, with excystment by medial split (*Valeria, Satka favosa*) and possibly by the opening of neck-like expansions (*Tappania*). Simple multicellularity is observed both in eukaryotes (septa in *Tappania* processes) and in prokaryotes (colonies of diverse types and filaments). The wall ornamentation of several taxa, especially *Tappania*'s heteromorphic processes and the plates of *Satka favosa* and *Dictyosphaera delicata*, implies the presence of a eukaryotic cytoskeleton. The tessellation of organic plates to make up the wall of these acritarchs further suggests the presence of an internal membrane system (including endoplasmic reticulum, or ER) and Golgi apparatus. The Golgi apparatus (or remnants of, in parasites) and the ER are essential for intracellular transport, occur in all extant eukaryotes, and are associated with the nuclear envelope (Jékely, 2006), although the relative timing of their appearance is unknown and the origin of the nucleus itself is far from constrained (see review in Lopez-Garcia and Moreira, 2015).

5. CONCLUSIONS

Roper microfossils contribute to an increasingly refined picture of life in Mesoproterozoic oceans, complementing the window opened by microfossils preserved in silicified carbonates. Chert assemblages largely illuminate peritidal environments dominated by diverse cyanobacteria and contain few recognizable eukaryotes (Muir, 1976, 1979; Oehler, 1978; Horodyski and Donaldson, 1980, 1983; Zhang, 1981; Golubic et al., 1995; Sergeev et al., 1995).

Stromatolites further indicate that microbial mat communities covered extensive portions of the Mesoproterozoic seafloor, extending from supratidal environments to the base of the photic zone (Bertrand-Sarfati and Walter, 1981; Walter et al., 1988). Cyanobacteria are generally accepted as the principal architects of Mesoproterozoic stromatolites, but whether eukaryotes participated in mat communities is difficult to know, given that few stromatolites contain well-preserved microfossils. Variation in macrostructure may well tell us mostly about the range of physical and chemical environments in which stromatolites accreted (e.g., Grotzinger and Knoll, 1999; Bosak et al., 2013), but microstructure, or petrofabric, can preserve clues to microbial community diversity (Knoll et al., 2013). Eukaryotes could be recorded by macroscopic chain-ofbeads impressions called *Horodyskia* (Grey and Williams, 1990; Fedonkin and Yochelson, 2002; review in Dong et al., 2008) and the Mesoproterozoic specimens of coiled centimeterscale septate compressions named *Grypania* (Walter et al., 1990), both exposed on siliciclastic bedding planes. The phylogenetic and functional nature of these organisms remains obscure.

Microfossils suggest that eukaryotic organisms were most common in the water column and non-mat benthos of welloxygenated, shallow-shelf environments. Because the last common ancestor of extant eukaryotes was a phagocytosing heterotroph that consumed bacteria and other small particles, Roper eukaryotes certainly would have played a role in completing the marine carbon cycle. This may have been true in anoxic as well as oxic environments, because many eukaryotes retain the capacity for anaerobic metabolism (Müller et al., 2012). Osmotrophic uptake of organic molecules must also have occurred, and appears to have the primary form of carbon acquisition in *Tappania plana*. As discussed above, phagotrophic protists were present in Mesoproterozoic oceans, but these may not have included protists able to eat other large eukaryotic cells.

Whether eukaryotes played an important role as primary producers is less clear. As noted above, microfossil morphologies are agnostic with respect to this metabolism, and limited organic geochemical data suggest that bacteria were the principal primary producers in Mesoproterozoic oceans (Brocks et al., 2005). Primary production by eukaryotes might well have been limited by fixed nitrogen availability (Anbar and Knoll, 2002; Reinhard et al., 2013), especially in oxic waters above sulfidic water masses (Boyle et al., 2013). The spatial distribution of presumed eukaryotes in the Roper Basin is consistent with isotopic inferences about Mesoproterozoic nitrogen cycling (Stüeken, 2013). Upward mixing of anoxic and sometimes sulfidic waters would also have constituted a persistent challenge for eukaryotes in the photic zone (Johnston et al., 2009, 2010; Guilbaud et al., 2015).

In short, Mesoproterozoic oceans supported diverse microbial communities that included early eukaryotes, some of them preserved in Roper shales. The diversity and ecological importance of these early protists, however, were much lower than in later Neoproterozoic and Phanerozoic ecosystems, which is a function, at least in part, of ecological constraints involving food web complexity and physical constraints imposed by marine redox profiles.

ACKNOWLEDGMENTS

We thank M. Walter and the core facility staffs at the Northern Territory Geological Survey in Darwin and the Australian Geological Survey Organization in Canberra for making it possible to sample Roper cores. We also thank Z. Adam, V.N. Sergeev, L.A. Riedman, and S. Porter for discussion and access to unpublished materials, and reviewers for helpful criticisms of an earlier draft. E.J acknowledges support from European Research Council Stg ELITE FP7/308074, Belspo IAP Planet Topers, and the Francqui Foundation research professorship. AHK acknowledges support from NASA Exobiology Grant NAG5-3645 and the NASA Astrobiology Institute.

REFERENCES

1. Abbott, S.T., and Sweet, I.P., 2000, Tectonic control on third-order sequences in a siliciclastic ramp-style basin: an example from the Roper Superbasin (Mesoproterozoic), northern Australia: Australian Journal of Earth Sciences, v. 47, p. 637–657.
2. Adam, Z.R., 2014, Microfossil Paleontology and Biostratigraphy of the Early Mesoproterozoic Belt Supergroup, Montana [Ph.D. dissertation]: Bozeman, Montana State University, 192 p.
3. Adam, Z.R, Skidmore, M.L., and Mogk, D.W., 2016, Paleoenvironmental implications of an expanded microfossil assemblage from the Chamberlain Formation, Belt Supergroup, Montana: The Geological Society of America Special Paper, v. 522, 20 p.
4. Agic, H., Moczydłowska, M., and Yin, L.-M., 2015, Affinity, life cycle, and intracellular complexity of organic-walled microfossils from the Mesoproterozoic of Shanxi, China: Journal of Paleontology, v. 89, p. 28–50.
5. Allard, B., and Templier, J., 2000, Comparison of neutral lipid profile of various trilaminar outer cell wall (TLS)-containing microalgae with emphasis on algaenan occurrence: Phytochemistry, v. 54, p. 369–380.
6. Anbar, A.D., and Knoll, A.H., 2002, Proterozoic ocean chemistry and evolution: a bioinorganic bridge?: Science, v. 297, p. 1137–1142.
7. Angert, E.R., 2005, Alternative to division in Bacteria: Nature Reviews Microbiology, v. 3, p. 214–224.
8. Arnold, G.L., Anbar, A.D., Barling, J., and Lyons, T.W., 2004, Molybdenum isotope evidence for widespread anoxia in mid-Proterozoic oceans: Science, v. 304, p. 87–90.

9. Baludikay, B.K., Storme, J.-Y., François, C., Baudet, D., and Javaux, E.J., 2016, A diverse and exquisitely preserved organic-walled microfossil assemblage from the Meso—Neoproterozoic Mbuji-Mayi Supergroup (Democratic Republic of Congo) and implications for Proterozoic biostratigraphy: Precambrian Research, v. 281, p. 166–184.
10. Bartley, J., 1996, Actualistic taphonomy of cyanobacteria: implications for the Precambrian fossil record: Palaios, v. 11, p. 571–586.
11. Battison, L., and Brasier, M.D., 2012, Remarkably preserved prokaryote and eukaryote microfossils within 1 Ga-old lake phosphates of the Torridon Group, NW Scotland: Precambrian Research, v. 196–197, p. 204–217.
12. Becker, B., 2013, Snow ball earth and the split of Streptophyta and Chlorophyta: Trends in Plant Sciences, v. 18, p. 180–183.
13. Beers, C.D., 1948, Excystment in the ciliate *Bursaria truncatella*: Biological Bulletin, v. 94, p. 86–98.
14. Beers, C.D., 1966, The excystment process in the ciliate *Nassula ornata* Ehrbg.: Journal of Protozoology, v. 13, p. 79–83.
15. Beghin, J., Storme, J.-Y., Blanpied, C., Gueneli, J., Brocks, J., Poulton, S., and Javaux, E.J., in review, Microfossils from the late Mesoproterozoic (1.1 Ga) Atar/El Mreïti Group, Taoudeni Basin, Mauritania, northwestern Africa: Precambrian Research.
16. Berney, C., and Pawlowski, J., 2006, A molecular time-scale for eukaryote evolution recalibrated with the continuous microfossil record: Proceedings of the Royal Society, London, v. 273B, p. 1867–1872.
17. Bertrand-Sarfati, J., and Walter, M.R., 1981, Stromatolite biostratigraphy: Precambrian Research, v. 15, p. 353–371.
18. Betts, P.G., and Gilles, D., 2006, The 1800–1100 Ma tectonic evolution of Australia: Precambrian Research, v. 144, p. 92–125.
19. Blades-Eckelbarger, P.I., and Marcus, N.H., 1992, The origin of cortical vesicles and their role in egg envelope formation in the spiny eggs of a calanoid copepod, *Centropages velificatus*: Biological Bulletin, v. 182, p. 41–53.
20. Blanton, R.L., Fuller, D., Iranfar, N., Grimson, M.J., and Loomis, W.F., 2000, The cellulose synthase gene of *Dictyostelium*: Proceedings of the National Academy of Sciences, USA, v. 97, p. 2391–2396.
21. Bosak, T., Knoll, A.H., and Petroff, A.P., 2013, The meaning of stromatolites: Annual Review of Earth and Planetary Sciences, v. 41, p. 21–44.
22. Boyle, R.A., Clark, J.R., Poulton, S.W., Shields-Zhou, G., Canfield, D.E., and Lenton, T.M., 2013, Nitrogen cycle feedbacks as a control on euxinia in the mid-Proterozoic ocean: Nature Communications, Article 4:1533, doi: 10.1038/ncomms2511.
23. Brocks, J.J., Love, G.D., Summons, R.E., Knoll, A.H., Logan, G.A., and Bowden, S., 2005, Biomarker evidence for green and purple sulfur bacteria in an intensely stratified Paleoproterozoic ocean: Nature, v. 437, p. 866–870.
24. Butterfield, N.J., 2000, *Bangiomorpha pubescens* n. gen., n. sp.: Implications for the evolution of sex, multicellularity, and the Mesoproterozoic/Neoproterozoic radiation of eukaryotes: Paleobiology, v. 26, p. 386–404.
25. Butterfield, N.J., 2004, A vaucherian alga from the Middle Neoproterozoic of Spitsbergen: implications for the evolution of Proterozoic eukaryotes and the Cambrian explosion: Paleobiology, v. 30, p. 231–252.
26. Butterfield, N.J., 2005a, Probable Proterozoic fungi: Paleobiology, v. 31, p. 165–182. Butterfield, N.J., 2005b, Reconstructing a complex Early Neoproterozoic eukaryote, Wynniatt Formation, Arctic Canada: Lethaia, v. 38, p. 155–169.
27. Butterfield, N.J., 2009, Modes of pre-Ediacaran multicellularity: Precambrian Research, v. 173, p. 201–211.
28. Butterfield, N.J., 2015, Early evolution of the Eukaryota: Palaeontology, v. 58, p. 5–17.
29. Butterfield, N.J., Knoll, A.H., and Swett, K., 1994, Paleobiology of the Neoproterozoic Svanbergfjellet Formation, Spitsbergen: Fossils and Strata, v. 34, p. 1–84.
30. Chernikova, D., Motamedi, S., Csueroes, M., Koonin, E.V., and Rogozin, I.B., 2011, A late origin of the extant eukaryotic diversity: divergence time estimates using rare genomic changes: Biology Direct, v. 6. Article Number: 26, doi: 10.1186/1745-6150-6-26.

31. Cohen, P.A., and Knoll, A.H., 2012, Neoproterozoic scale microfossils from the Fifteen Mile Group, Yukon Territory: Journal of Paleontology, v. 86, p. 775–800. BioOne
32. Cohen, P.A., Kodner, R., and Knoll, A.H., 2009, Large spinose acritarchs in Ediacaran rocks as animal resting cysts: Proceedings of the National Academy of Sciences, USA, v. 106, p. 6519–6524.
33. Colbath, G.K., and Grenfell, H.R., 1995, Review of biological affinities of Paleozoic acid-resistant, organic-walled eukaryotic algal microfossils (including "acritarchs"): Review of Palaeobotany and Palynology, v. 86, p. 287–314.
34. Cotter, K., 1997, Neoproterozoic microfossils from the Officer Basin, Western Australia: Alcheringa, v. 21, p. 247–270, doi: 10.1080/031155197 08619166.
35. Cotter, K.L., 1999, Microfossils from Neoproterozoic Supersequence 1 of the Officer Basin, Western Australia: Alcheringa, v. 23, p. 63–86.
36. De Leeuw, J.W., Vesteegh, J.M., and van Bergen, P.F., 2006, Biomacromolecules of algae and plants and their fossil analogues: Plant Ecology, v. 182, p. 209–233.
37. de Vries, S.T., Pryer, L.L., and Fry, N., 2008, Evolution of Neoarchaean and Proterozoic basins of Australia: Precambrian Research, v. 166, p. 39–53.
38. Dong, L., Xiao, S., Shen, B., and ZhouC., 2008, Silicified *Horodyskia* and *Palaeopascichnus* from upper Ediacaran cherts in South China: tentative phylogenetic interpretation and implications for evolutionary stasis: Journal of the Geological Society, v. 165, p. 367–378.
39. Douzery, E.J.P., Snell, E.A., Bapteste, E., Delsuc, F., and Philippe, H., 2004, The timing of eukaryotic evolution: Does a relaxed molecular clock reconcile proteins and fossils?: Proceedings of the National Academy of Sciences, v. 101, p. 15386–15391.
40. Downie, C., and Sarjeant, W.A.S., 1963, On the interpretation and status of some hystrichosphere genera: Palaeontology, v. 6, p. 83–96.
41. Dutkiewicz, A., Volk, H., Ridley, J., and George, S., 2003, Biomarkers, brines and oil in the Mesoproterozoic, Roper Superbasin, Australia: Geology, v. 31, p. 981–984.
42. Eisenack, A., 1958, *Tasmanites* Newton 1875 und *Leiosphaeridia* n.g. als Gattungen der Hystrichosphaeridea: Palaeontographica Abteilug A, v. 110, p. 1–19.
43. Eisenack, A., 1965, Mikrofossilien aus dem Silur Gotlands. Hystrichosphären, Problematika: Neues Jahrburch für Geologie und Paläontologie Abhandlungen, v. 122, p. 257–274.
44. Eme, L., Sharpe, S.C., Brown, M.W., and Roger, A.J., 2014, On the age of eukaryotes: Evaluating evidence from fossils and molecular clocks: Cold Spring Harbor Perspectives in Biology, v. 6, doi: 10.1101/cshperspect. a016139
45. Fedonkin, M.A., and Yochelson, E.L., 2002, Middle Proterozoic (1.5 Ga) *Horodyskia moniliformis* Yochelson and Fedonkin, the oldest known tissue-grade colonial eukaryote: Smithsonian Contributions to Paleobiology, v. 94, p. 1–29.
46. Floudas, I., et al., 2012, The Paleozoic origin of enzymatic lignin decomposition reconstructed from 31 fungal genomes: Science, v. 336, p. 1715–1719, doi: 10.1126/science.1221748.
47. Foissner, W., Mueller, H., and Agatha, S., 2007, A comparative fine structural and phylogenetic analysis of resting cysts in oligotrich and hypotrich Spirotrichea (Ciliophora): European Journal of Protistology, v. 43, p. 295–314.
48. Golovenok, M.K., and Belova, M.Y., 1986, The Riphean microflora in the cherts from the Malgin Formation in the Yudoma-Maya basin: Paleontological Journal, v. 2, p. 85–90.
49. Golubic, S., Sergeev, V.N., and Knoll, A.H., 1995, Mesoproterozoic *Archaeoellipsoides*: akinetes of heterocystous cyanobacteria: Lethaia, v. 28, p. 285–298.
50. Graham, L.E., and Wilcox, L.W., 2000, Algae: Upper Saddle River NJ, Prentice Hall, 640 p.
51. Grey, K., and Williams, I.R., 1990, Problematic bedding-plane markings from the Middle Proterozoic Manganese Subgroup, Bangemall Basin, Western Australia: Precambrian Research, v. 46, p. 307–327.
52. Grotzinger, J.P., and Knoll, A.H., 1999, Proterozoic stromatolites: evolutionary mileposts or environmental dipsticks?: Annual Review of Earth and Planetary Science, v. 27, p. 313–358.

53. Guilbaud, R., Poulton, S.W., Butterfield, N.J., Zhu, M., and Shields-Zhou, G.A., 2015, Global transition to ferruginous conditions in the early Neoproterozoic oceans: Nature Geosciences, v. 8, p. 466–470.
54. Heckman, D.S., Geiser, D.M., Eidell, B.R., Stauffer, R.L., Kardos, N.L., and Hedges, S.B., 2001, Molecular Evidence for the Early Colonization of Land by Fungi and Plants: Science, v. 293, p. 1129–1133.
55. Hedges, B.S., Blair, J.E., Venturi, M.L., and Shoe, J.L., 2004, A molecular timescale of eukaryote evolution and the rise of complex multicellular life: BMC Evolutionary Biology, v. 4, article 2, doi: 10.1186/1471-2148-4-2.
56. Hermann, T.N., 1974, Finds of massive accumulation of trichomes in the Riphean, *in* Timofeev, B.V., ed., Microfitofossilii Proterozoia I Rannego Paleozoia SSSR: Leningrad, Nauka, p. 6–10.
57. Hermann, T.N., 1990, Organic world one billion years ago: Leningrad, Nauka, 50 p. [in Russian with English summary]
58. Hermann, T.N., and Podkovyrov, V.N., 2012, Fungal Remains from the Late Riphean: Paleontological Journal, v. 40, p. 207–214.
59. Hofmann, H.J., 1999, Global distribution of the Proterozoic sphaeromorph acritarch *Valeria lophostriata* (Jankauskas): Acta Micropaleontologica Sinica, v. 16, p. 215–224.
60. Hofmann, H.J., and Jackson, G.D., 1994, Shale-facies microfossils from the Proterozoic Bylot Supergroup, Baffin Island, Canada: Paleontological Society Memoir, v. 37, p. 1–39.
61. Horodyski, R.J., 1980, Middle Proterozoic shale-facies microbiota from the Lower Belt Supergroup, Little Belt Mountains, Montana: Journal of Paleontology, v. 54, p. 649–663.
62. Horodyski, R.J., 1993, Paleontology of Proterozoic shales and mudstones: examples from the Belt Supergroup, Chuar Group and Pahrump Group, western USA: Precambrian Research, v. 61, p. 247–278.
63. Horodyski, R.J., and Donaldson, J.A., 1980, Microfossils from the Middle Proterozoic Dismal Lakes Groups, Arctic Canada: Precambrian Research, v. 11, p. 125–159.
64. Horodyski, R.J., and Donaldson, J.A., 1983, Distribution and Significance of Microfossils in Cherts of the Middle Proterozoic Dismal Lakes Group, District of Mackenzie, Northwest Territories, Canada: Journal of Paleontology, v. 57, p. 271–283.
65. Hu, Y., and Fu, J., 1982, Micropalaeoflora from the Gaoshanhe Formation of the Upper Precambrian in Luonan of Shaanxi Province and its stratigraphic significance: Bulletin Xi'an Institute Geology and Mineral Resources, Chinese Academy of Geological Sciences, v. 4, p. 102–113.
66. Hu, G., Zhao, T., and Zhou, Y., 2014, Depositional age, provenance and tectonic setting of the Proterozoic Ruyang Group, southern margin of the North China Craton: Precambrian Research, v. 246, p. 296–318.
67. Ishida, K., and Hara, Y., 1994, Taxonomic studies on the Chlorarachniophyta *Chlorarachnion globosum* sp. nov.: Phycologia, v. 33, p. 351–358.
68. Jackson, M.J., and Raiswell, R., 1991, Sedimentology and carbon-sulfur geochemistry of the Velkerri Formation, a mid-Proterozoic potential oil source in northern Australia: Precambrian Research, v. 54, p. 81–108.
69. Jackson, M.J., Sweet, I.P., Page, R.W., and Bradshaw, B.E., 1999, The South Nicholson and Roper Groups: evidence for the early Mesoproterozoic Roper Superbasin, *in* Bradshaw, B.E., and Scott, D.L., eds., Integrated Basin Analysis of the Isa Superbasin using Seismic, Well-log, and Geopotential Data: An Evaluation of the Economic Potential of the Northern Lawn Hill Platform: Canberra, Australia, Australian Geological Survey Organisation Record 1999/19. [unpaginated]
70. Jankauskas, T.V., 1979a, Nizhnerifeiskie mikrobioty Iuzhnogo Urala (Lower Riphean microbiotas of the southern Urals): Akademii Nauk SSSR, Doklady (Proceedings of the USSR Academy of Sciences), v. 247, p. 1465–1467.
71. Jankauskas, T.V., 1979b, Srednerifeyski microbiota Yuzhnogo Urala i Bashkirskogo Priural'ya (Middle Riphean microbiota of the southern Urals and the Ural region in Bashkiria): Akademii Nauk SSSR, Doklady (proceedings of the USSR Academy of Sciences), v. 248, p. 190–193. [in Russian]

72. Jankauskas, T.V., 1982, Mikrofossilii rifeya Yuzhnogo Urala [Microfossils of the Riphean of the South Urals], *in*Keller, B.M., ed., Stratotype of the Riphean: Paleontology and Paleomagnetics: Moscow, Nauka, p. 84–120.
73. Jankauskas, T.V., Mikhailova, N., and Hermann, T.N., 1989, Mikrofossilii dokembriya SSSR (Precambrian microfossils of the USSR): Leningrad, Trudy Instituta Geologii i Geochronologii Dokembria SSSR Akademii Nauk. Nauka, 188 p. [In Russian]
74. Javaux, E.J., 2006, The early eukaryote fossil record, *in* Jékely, G., ed., Evolution of the Eukaryotic Endomembrane System and Cytoskeleton: Austin, Texas, Landes Biosciences Publishers, p. 1–19.
75. Javaux, E.J., 2011, Evolution of early eukaryotes in Precambrian oceans, *in* Gargaud, M., Lopez-Garcia, P., and Martin, H., eds., Origins and Evolution of Life: an astrobiology perspective: Cambridge, UK, Cambridge University Press, p. 414–449.
76. Javaux, E.J., and Marshall, C.P., 2006, A new approach in deciphering early protist paleobiology and evolution: combined microscopy and microchemistry of single Proterozoic acritarchs: Review of Palaeobotany and Palynology, v. 139, p. 1–15.
77. Javaux, E.J., Knoll, A.H., and Walter, M.R., 2001, Ecological and morphological complexity in early eukaryotic ecosystems: Nature, v. 412, p. 66–69.
78. Javaux, E.J., Knoll, A.H., and Walter, M.R., 2003, Recognizing and interpreting the fossils of early eukaryotes: Origins of Life and Evolution of the Biosphere, v. 33, p. 75–94.
79. Javaux, E.J., Knoll, A.H., and Walter, M.R., 2004, TEM evidence for eukaryotic diversity in mid-Proterozoic oceans: Geobiology, v. 2, p. 121–132.
80. Javaux, E.J., Marshall, C.P., and Bekker, A., 2010, Organic-walled microfossils in 3.2-billion-year-old shallow-marine siliciclastic deposits: Nature, v. 463, p. 934–938.
81. Jékely, G., 2006, Evolution of the Eukaryotic Endomembrane System and Cytoskeleton: Advances in Experimental Medicine and Biology, v. 607: Austin, Texas, Landes Biosciences Publishers, 145 p.
82. Johnston, D.T., Farquhar, J., Summons, R.E., Shen, Y., Kaufman, A.J., Masterson, A.L., and Canfield, D.E., 2008, Sulfur isotope biogeochemistry of the Proterozoic McArthur Basin: Geochimica et Cosmochimica Acta, v. 72, p. 4278–4290.
83. Johnston, D.T, Wolfe-Simon, F., Pearson, A., and Knoll, A.H., 2009, Anoxygenic photosynthesis modulated Proterozoic oxygen and sustained Earth's middle age: Proceedings of the National Academy of Sciences, USA, v. 106, p. 16925–16929.
84. Johnston, D.T, Poulton, S., Dehler, C., Porter, S., Husson, J., and Canfield, D.E., 2010, An emerging picture of Neoproterozoic ocean chemistry: Insights from the Chuar Group, Grand Canyon, USA: Earth and Planetary Science Letters, v. 290, p. 64–73.
85. Johnston, D.T., Goldberg, T., Poulton, S.W., Sergeev, V.N., Podkovyrov, V., Vorob'eva, N.G., Bekker, A., and Knoll, A.H., 2012, Late Ediacaran redox stability and metazoan diversification: Earth and Planetary Science Letters, v. 335–336, p. 25–35.
86. Kaufman, A.J., and Xiao, S., 2003, High CO_2 levels in the Proterozoic atmosphere estimated from analyses of individual microfossils: Nature, v. 425, p. 279–282. CrossRef, PubMed
87. Kendall, B., Creaser, R.A., Gordon, G.W., and Anbar, A.D., 2009, Re-Os and Mo isotope systematics of black shales from the Middle Proterozoic Velkerri and Wollogorang Formations, McArthur Basin, northern Australia: Geochimica et Cosmochimica Acta, v. 73, p. 2534–2558.
88. Kenrick, P., and Vinther, J., 2006, *Chaetocladus gracilis* n. sp., a non-calcified Dasycladales from the Upper Silurian of Skåne, Sweden: Review of Palaeobotany and Palynology, v. 142, p. 153–160.
89. Knoll, A.H., 2014. Paleobiological perspective on early eukaryotic evolution: Cold Spring Harbor Perspectives in Biology, doi: 10.1101/cshperspect.a016121.
90. Knoll, A.H., and Golubic, S., 1992, Living and Proterozoic cyanobacteria, *in* Schidlowski M., Golubic, S., and Kimberley, M.M., eds., Early Organic Evolution: Implications for Mineral and Energy Resources: Berlin, Springer-Verlag, p. 450–462.
91. Knoll, A.H., and Lahr, D.J.G., 2016, Fossils, feeding, and the evolution of complex multicellularity, *in* Niklas, K.J., Newman, S., and Bonner, J.T., eds., Multicellularity, Origins and Evolution, The Vienna Series in Theoretical Biology: Boston, Massachusetts Institute of Technology, p. 1–16.

92. Knoll, A.H., and Swett, K., 1985, Micropalaeontology of the Late Proterozoic Veteranen Group, Spitsbergen: Palaeontology, v. 28, p. 451–473.
93. Knoll, A.H., Swett, K., and Mark, J., 1991, Paleobiology of a Neoproterozoic tidal flat/lagoonal complex: the Draken Conglomerate Formation, Spitsbergen: Journal of Paleontology, v. 65, p. 531–570.
94. Knoll, A.H., Javaux, E.J., Hewitt, D., and Cohen, P., 2006, Eukaryotic organisms in Proterozoic oceans: Philosophical Transactions of the Royal Society, London, v. 361B, p. 1023–1038.
95. Knoll, A.H., Wörndle, S., and Kah, L., 2013, Covariance of microfossil assemblages and microbialite textures across a late Mesoproterozoic carbonate platform: Palaios, v. 28, p. 453–470.
96. Kodner, R., Knoll, A.H., and Summons, R.E., 2009, Phylogenetic investigation of the aliphatic, non-hydrolyzable biopolymer algaenan, with a focus on the green algae: Organic Geochemistry, v. 40, p. 854–862.
97. Kralik, M., 1982, Rb—Sr age determinations on Precambrian carbonate rocks of the Carpentarian McArthur Basin, Northern Territories, Australia: Precambrian Research, v. 18, p. 157–170.
98. Lamb, D.M., Awramik, S.M., Chapman, D.J., and Zhu, S., 2009, Evidence for eukaryotic diversification in the similar to 1800 million-year-old Changzhougou Formation, North China: Precambrian Research, v. 173, p. 93–104.
99. Lan, Z., Li, X., Chen, Z.Q., Li, Q., Hofmann, A., Zhang, Y., Liu, Y., Tang, G., Ling, X., and Li., J., 2014, Diagenetic xenotime age constraints on the Sanjiaotang Formation,Luoyu Group, southern margin of the North China Craton: Implications for regional stratigraphic correlation and early evolution of eukaryotes: Precambrian Research, v. 251, p. 21–32.
100. Lepot, K., Compère, P., Gérard, E., Namsaraev, Z., Verleyen, E., Tavernier, I., Hodgson, D.A., Vyverman, W., Gilbert, B., Wilmotte, A., and Javaux, E.J., 2014, Organic and mineral imprints in fossil photosynthetic mats of an East Antarctic lake: Geobiology, v. 12, p. 424–450.
101. LoDuca, S.T., Kluessendorf, J., and Mikulic, D.G., 2003, A new noncalcified dasycladalean alga from the Silurian of Wisconsin: Journal of Paleontology, v. 77, p. 956–962.
102. Lopez-Garcia, P., and Moreira, D., 2015, Open Questions on the Origin of Eukaryotes: Trends in Ecology and Evolution, v. 30, p. 697–708.
103. Lücking, R., Huhndorf, S., Pfister, D.H., Plata, E.R., and Lumbsch, H.T., 2009, Fungi evolved right on track: Mycologia, v. 101, p. 810–822.
104. Luo, Q.-L., 1991, New data on the microplants from Changlongshan Formation of Upper Precambrian in western Yanshan Range: Tianjin Instute of Geology and Mineral Resources, v. 25, p.107–118.
105. Lydon, J.W., 2007, Geology and metallogeny of the Belt-Purcell Basin, *in* Goodfellow, W.D., ed., Mineral Deposits of Canada: A Synthesis of Major Deposit-Types, District Metallogeny, the Evolution of Geological Provinces, and Exploration Methods: Geological Association of Canada, Mineral Deposits Division, Special Publication No. 5, p.581–607.
106. Maithy, P.K.,1975,Microorganisms from the Bushimay System (Late Precambrian) of Kanshi, Zaire: The Paleobotanist, v. 22, p.133–149.
107. Marshall, C.P., Javaux, E.J., Knoll, A.H., and Walter, M.R., 2005, Combined micro-Fourier transform infrared (FTIR) spectroscopy and micro-Raman spectroscopy of Proterozoic acritarchs: a new approach to palaeobiology: Precambrian Research, v. 138, p. 208–224.
108. Melida, H., Sandoval-Sierra, J.V., Dieguez-Uribeondo, J., and Bulone, V., 2013, Analyses of extracellular carbohydrates in oomycetes unveil the existence of three different cell wall types: Eukaryotic Cell, v. 12, p. 194–203.
109. Mitra, A., et al., 2016, Defining Planktonic Protist Functional Groups on Mechanisms for Energy and Nutrient Acquisition: Incorporation of Diverse Mixotrophic Strategies: Protist, v. 167, p. 106–120.
110. Moczydłowska, M., Landing, E., Zang, W., and Palacios, T., 2011, Proterozoic phytoplankton and timing of Chlorophyte algae origins: Palaeontology, v. 54, p. 721–733.
111. Muir, M.D., 1976, Proterozoic microfossils from the Amelia Dolomite, McArthur Basin, Northern Territory: Alcheringa, v. 1, p. 143–158.

112. Muir, M.D., 1979, A sabkha model for the deposition of part of the Proterozoic McArthur Group of the Northern Territory, and its implications for mineralization: BMR Journal of Australian Geology and Geophysics, v. 4, p. 149–162.
113. Müller, M., Mentel, M., van Hellemond, J.J., Henze, K., Woehle, K., Gould, S. B., Yu, R.-Y., van der Giezen, R.M., Tielens, A.G.M., and Martin, W.F., 2012, Biochemistry and evolution of anaerobic energy metabolism in eukaryotes: Microbiology and Molecular Biology Reviews, v. 76, p. 444–495.
114. Nagovitsin, K., 2009, *Tappania*-bearing association of the Siberian platform: Biodiversity, stratigraphic position and geochronological constraints: Precambrian Research, v. 173, p. 137–145.
115. Nagovitsin, K.E., Stanevich, A.M., and Kornilova, T.A., 2010, Stratigraphic setting and age of the complex *Tappania*-bearing Proterozoic fossil biota of Siberia: Russian Geology and Geophysics, v. 51, p. 1192–1198.
116. Nagy, R.M., Porter, S.M., Dehler, C.M., and Shen, Y., 2009, Biotic turnover driven by eutrophication before the Sturtian low-latitude glaciation: Nature Geoscience, v. 2, p. 415–418.
117. Naumova, S.N., 1949, Spory nizhnego kembriya [spores from the Lower Cambrian]: Izvestiya Akademiy Nauk, v. 4, p. 49–56.
118. Naumova, S.N., 1960, Spore-pollen assemblages in the Riphean and Lower Cambrian deposits of the USSR: Proceedings of the 21st International Geological Congress, Reports of Soviet Scientists, v. 8, p. 109–117. [in Russian]
119. Oehler, D.Z., 1978, Microflora of the middle Proterozoic Balbirini Dolomite (McArthur Group) of Australia: Alcheringa, v. 2, p. 269–309.
120. Parfrey, L., Lahr, D., Knoll, A.H., and Katz, L.A., 2011, Estimating the timing of early eukaryotic diversification with multigene molecular clocks: Proceedings of the National Academy of Sciences, USA, v. 108, p. 13624–13629.
121. Peat, C.J., Muir, M.D., Plumb, K.A., McKirdy, D.M., and Norwick, M.S., 1978, Proterozoic microfossils from the Roper Group, Northern Territory, Australia: BMR Journal of Australian Geology and Geophysics, v. 3, p. 1–17.
122. Peng, Y., Bao, H., and Yuan, X., 2009, New morphological observations for Paleoproterozoic acritarchs from the Chuanlinggou Formation, North China: Precambrian Research, v. 168, p. 223–232.
123. Peterson, K.J., and Butterfield, N.J., 2005, Origin of the Eumetazoa: Testing ecological predictions of molecular clocks against the Proterozoic fossil record: Proceedings of the National Academy of Sciences, USA, v. 102, p. 9547–9552.
124. Planavsky, N.J., McGoldrick, P., Scott, C.T., Li, C., Reinhard, C.T., Kelly, A.E., Chu, X., Bekker, A., Love, G.D., and Lyons, T.W., 2011, Widespread ironrich conditions in the mid-Proterozoic ocean: Nature, v. 477, p. 448–452.
125. Porter, S., 2006, The Proterozoic fossil record of heterotrophic eukaryotes, *in* Xiao, S., and Kaufman, A.J., eds. Neoproterozoic Geobiology and Paleobiology: Dordrecht, The Netherlands, Springer, p. 1–21.
126. Porter, S., and Riedmann, L.A., in press, Systematics of organic-walled microfossils from the ~780–740 Ma Chuar Group, Grand Canyon, Arizona: Journal of Paleontology.
127. Porter, S., Meisterfeld, R., and Knoll, A., 2003, Vase-shaped microfossils from the Neoproterozoic Chuar Group, Grand Canyon: a classification guided by modern testate amoebae: Journal of Paleontology, v. 77, p. 409–429, doi: http://dx.doi.org/10.1017/S0022336000044140.
128. Prasad, B., and Asher, R., 2001, Acritarch biostratigraphy and lithostratigraphic classification of Proterozoic and Lower Paleozoic sediments (Preunconformity sequence) of Ganga Basin, India: Paleontographica Indica, v. 5, 151 p.
129. Prasad, B., Uniyal, S.N., and Asher, R., 2005, Organic-walled microfossils from the Proterozoic Vindhyan Supergroup of Son Valley, Madhya Pradesh, India: Palaeobotanist, v. 54, p. 13–60.
130. Ray, J.S., Martin, M.W., Veizer, J., and Bowring, S.A., 2002, U—Pb zircon dating and Sr isotope systematics of the Vindhyan Supergroup, India: Geology, v. 30, p. 131–134.

131. Reinhard, C.T., Planavsky, N.J., Robbins, L.J., Partin, C.A., Gill, B.C., Lalonde, S.V., Bekker, A., Konhauser, K.O., and Lyons, T.W., 2013, Proterozoic ocean redox and biogeochemical stasis: Proceedings of the National Academy of Sciences, USA, v. 110, p. 5357–5362.
132. Richards, T.A., and Talbot, N.J., 2013, Horizontal gene transfer in osmotrophs: playing with public goods: Nature Reviews Microbiology, v. 11, p. 720–727.
133. Riedman, L.A., and Porter, S.M., in press, High morphological diversity of organic-walled microfossils from the Neoproterozoic Alinya Formation, Officer Basin, Australia: Journal of Paleontology.
134. Rippka, R., Deruelles, J., Waterbury, J.B., Herdman, M., and Stanier, R.Y., 1979, Generic assignments, strain histories and properties of pure cultures of cyanobacteria: Journal of General Microbiology, v. 111, p. 1–61.
135. Saga, Y., and Yanagisawa, K., 1982, Macrocyst development in *Dictvostelium discoideum*. 1. Induction of synchronous development by giant cells and biochemical analysis: Journal of Cell Science, v. 55, p. 341–352.
136. Samuelsson, J., 1997, Biostratigraphy and paleobiology of early Neoproterozoic strata of the Kola Peninsula, northwest Russia: Norsk Geologisk Tidsskrift, v. 77, p. 16–192.
137. Samuelsson, J., and Butterfield, N., 2001, Neoproterozoic fossils from the Franklin Mountains, northwestern Canada: stratigraphic and palaeobiological implications: Precambrian Research, v. 107, p. 235–251.
138. Samuelsson, J., Dawes, P.R., and Vidal, G., 1999, Organic-walled microfossils from the Proterozoic Thule Supergroup, Northwest Greenland: Precambrian Research, v. 96, p. 1–23.
139. Schepeleva, E.D., 1960, Nakhodki sinezelenykh vodoroslej v nizhnekembrijskikh otlozheniyakh Leningradskoj oblasti [Finds of blue-green algae in Lower Cambrian deposits of the Leningrad region]. *in*., Problemy Neftyanoj Geologii i Voprosy Metodiki Laboratornykh Issledovanij: Moscow, Nauka, p. 170–172.
140. Schiffbauer, J.D., and Xiao, S., 2009, Novel application of focused ion beam electron microscopy (FIB-EM) in preparation and analysis of microfossil ultrastructures: a new view of complexity in early eukaryotic organisms: Palaios, v. 24, p. 616–626.
141. Scholz, M.J., Weiss, T.L., Jinkerson, R.E., Jing, J., Roth, R., Goodenough, U., Posewitz, M.C., and Gerkene, H.G., 2014, Ultrastructure and composition of the *Nannochloropsis gaditana* cell wall: Eukaryotic Cell, v. 13, p. 1450–1464.
142. Schopf, W., 1968, Microflora of the Bitter Springs Formation, late Precambrian, central Australia: Journal of Paleontology, v. 42, p. 651–688.
143. Schopf, J.W., 1992, Atlas of representative Proterozoic microfossils, *in* Schopf, J.W., and Klein, C., eds., The Proterozoic Biosphere: Cambridge, Cambridge University Press, p. 1057–1117.
144. Schopf, J.W., and Blacic, J., 1971, Microorganisms from the Bitter Springs Formation (Late Precambrian) of the North-Central Amadeus Basin, Australia: Journal of Paleontology, v. 45, p. 925–960.
145. Sergeev, V.N., 1992, Silicified Microfossils of the Precambrian and Cambrian in the Urals and central Asia: Moscow, Nauka, 139 p.
146. Sergeev, V.N., 2006, Precambrian Microfossils in Cherts : Their Paleobiology, Classification, and Biostratigraphic Usefulness: Moscow, Geos, 280
147. Sergeev, V.N., and Lee, S.-J., 2001, Microfossils from Cherts of the Middle Riphean Svetlyi Formation, the Uchur-Maya Region of Siberia, and Their Stratigraphic Significance: Stratigraphic Geological Correlation, v. 9, p. 3–12.
148. Sergeev, V.N., and Lee, S.-J., 2006, Real Eukaryotes and Precipitates First Found in the Middle Riphean Stratotype, Southern Urals: Stratigraphy and Geological Correlation, v. 14, p. 1–18.
149. Sergeev, V.N., Knoll, A.H., and Grotzinger, J.P., 1995, Paleobiology of the Mesoproterozoic Billiakh Group, Anabar Uplift, Northeastern Siberia: Paleontological Society Memoir, v. 39, 37 p.
150. Sergeev, V.N., Semikhatov, M.A., Fedonkin, M.A., and Vorob'eva, N.G., 2010, Principal stages in evolution of Precambrian organic world: 2. The late Proterozoic: Stratigraphy and Geological Correlation, v. 18, p. 561–592.

151. Sergeev, V.N, Knoll, A.H., Vorob'eva, N., and Sergeeva, N., 2016, Microfossils from the lower Mesoproterozoic Kaltasy Formation, East European Platform: Precambrian Research, v. 278, p. 87–107, doi: 10.1016/j.precamres.2016.03.015.
152. Shen, Y., Knoll, A.H., and Walter, M.R., 2003, Evidence for low sulphate and deep water anoxia in a mid-Proterozoic marine basin: Nature, v. 423, p. 632–635.
153. Sperling, E.A., Rooney, A.D., Hays, L., Sergeev, V.N., Vorob'eva, N.G., Sergeeva, N.D., Selby, D., Johnston, D.T., and Knoll, A.H., 2014, Redox heterogeneity of subsurface waters in the Mesoproterozoic ocean: Geobiology, v. 12, p. 373–386.
154. Stanevich, A.M., Maksimova, E.N., Kornilova, T.A., Gladkochub, D.P., Mazukabzov, A.M., and Donskaya, T.V., 2009, Microfossils from the Arymas and Debengde Formations, the Riphean of the Olenek Uplift: Age and presumable nature: Stratigraphy and Geological Correlation, v. 17, p. 20–35.
155. Strother, P.K., Knoll, A.H., and Barghoorn., E.S., 1983, Microorganisms from the late Precambrian Narssârssuk Formation, north-western Greenland: Palaeontology, v. 26, p. 1–32.
156. Strother, P., Battison, L., Brasier, M.D., and Wellman, C.H., 2011, Earth's earliest non-marine eukaryotes: Nature, v. 473, p. 505–509.
157. Stüeken, E.E., 2013, A test of the nitrogen-limitation hypothesis for retarded eukaryote radiation: Nitrogen isotopes across a Mesoproterozoic basinal profile: Geochimica et Cosmochimica Acta, v. 20, p. 121–139.
158. Su, W., Li, H., Xu, L., Jia, S., Geng, J., Zhou, H., Wang, Z., and Pu, H.-Y., 2012, Luoyu and Ruyang Group at the south margin of the North China Craton (NCC) should belong in the Mesoproterozoic Changchengian System: direct constraints from the LA-MC-ICPMS U-Pb age of the tuffite in the Luoyukou Formation, Ruzhou, Henan, China: Geological Survey and Research, v. 35, p. 96–108.
159. Sugitani, K., Mimura, K., Takeuchi, M., Lepot, K., Ito, S., and Javaux, E.J., 2015, Early evolution of large micro-organisms with cytological complexity revealed by microanalyses of 3.4 Ga organic-walled microfossils: Geobiology, v. 13, p. 522–545.
160. Talyzina, N., and Moczydłowska, M., 2000, Morphological and ultrastructural studies of some acritarchs from the Lower Cambrian Lukati Formation, Estonia: Review of Palaeobotany and Palynology, v. 112, p. 1–21.
161. Tang, Q., Pang, K., Yuan, X., Wan, B., and Xiao, S., 2015, Organic-walled microfossils from the Tonian Gouhou Formation, Huaibei region, North China Craton, and their biostratigraphic implications: Precambrian Research, v. 266, p. 296–318.
162. Timofeev, B.V., 1959, Dreveneyshaya flora Pribaltiki i ee stratigraficheskoe znachenie (Oldest flora of the Baltic area and its stratigraphic significance): Trudy Vsesoyuznogo Neftyanogo Nauchno-Issle-dovatel'skogo Geologorazvedochnogo Instituta (VNIGRI), v. 129, 320 p. [in Russian]
163. Timofeev, B.V., 1966, Mikropaleofitologicheskoe isslodovanie drevnikh svit (Microphytological investigations of ancient formations): Akademiya Nauk SSSR, Nauka, Moscow, 147 p. [in Russian]
164. Timofeev, B.V., Hermann, T.N., and Mikhailova, N.S., 1976, Mikrofitofossilii Dokembriia, Kembriia i Ordovika (Plant Microfossils of the Precambrian, Cambrian, and Ordovician): Leningrad, Scientific Institute of Precambrian Geology and Geochronology, 106 p. [in Russian]
165. Tomitani, A., Knoll, A.H., Cavanaugh, C.M., and Ohno, T., 2006, The evolutionary diversification of cyanobacteria: Molecular—phylogenetic and paleontological perspectives: Proceedings of the National Academy of Sciences, v. 103, p. 5442–5447.
166. Turner, R.E., 1984, Acritarchs from the type area of the Ordovicain Caradoc Series, Shropshire, England: Palaeontographica, Abteiling B, v. 190, p. 87–157.
167. Verni, F., and Rosati, G., 2011, Resting cysts: a survival strategy in Protozoa Ciliophora: Italian Journal of Zoology, v. 78, p. 134–145.
168. Vidal, G., and Ford, T.D., 1985, Microbiotas from the late Proterozoic Chuar Group (northern Arizona) and Uinta Mountain Group (Utah) and their chronostratigraphic implications: Precambrian Research, v. 28, p. 349–389.

169. Vidal, G., and Siedlecka, A., 1983, Planktonic, acid-resistant microfossils from the Upper Proterozoic strata of Barents Sea region of Varanger Peninsula, East Finnmark, Northen Norway: Norges Geologiske undersøkelse Bulletin, v. 382, p. 45–79.
170. Vorob'eva, N.G., Sergeev, V.N., and Yu, P., 2015, Kotuikan Formation assemblage: a diverse organic-walled microbiota in the Mesoproterozoic Anabar succession, northern Siberia: Precambrian Research, v. 256, p. 201–222.
171. Waterbury, J.M., and Stanier, R.Y., 1978, Patterns of growth and development in pleurocapsalean cyanobacteria: Microbiological Reviews, v. 42, p. 2–44.
172. Walter, M.R., Krylov, I.N., and Muir, M.D., 1988, Stromatolites from Middle and Late Proterozoic sequences in the McArthur and Georgina Basins and the Mount Isa Province, Australia: Alcheringa, v. 12, p. 79–106.
173. Walter, M.R., Du, R.L., and Horodyski, R.J., 1990, Coiled carbonaceous megafossils from the Middle Proterozoic of Jixian (Tianjin) and Montana: American Journal of Science, v. 290A, p. 133–148.
174. Xiao, S.H., Knoll, A.H., Kaufman, A.J., Yin, L.M., and Zhang, Y., 1997, Neoproterozoic fossils in Mesoproterozoic rocks? Chemostratigraphic resolution of a biostratigraphic conundrum from the North China Platform: Precambrian Research, v. 84, p. 197–220.
175. Xiao, S.H., Yuan, X.L., Steiner, M., and Knoll, A.H., 2002, Macroscopic carbonaceous compressions in a terminal Proterozoic shale: A systematic reassessment of the Miaohe biota, south China: Journal of Paleontology, v. 76, p. 347–376.
176. Xing, Y., and Liu, K., 1973, On Sinian microflora in Yenliao region of China and its geographic significance: Acta Geologica Sinica, v. 1, p. 1–64.
177. Yang, E.C., Boo, S.M., Battacharya, D., Saunders, G.W., Knoll, A.H., Fredericq, S., Graf, L., and Yoon, H.S., 2016. Divergence times estimates and the evolution of major lineages in the florideophyte red algae: Scientific Reports, 2016 Feb 19;6:21361, doi: 10.1038/srep21361.
178. Yin, L.M., 1997, Acanthomorphic acritarchs from Meso-Neoproterozoic shales of the Ruyang Group, Shanxi, China: Review of Palaeobotany and Palynology, v. 98, p. 15–25.
179. Yin, L., and Yuan, X., 2007, Radiation of Meso-Neoproterozoic and Early Cambrian protists inferred from the microfossil record of China: Palaeogeography, Palaeoclimatology, Palaeoecology, v. 254, p. 350–361.
180. Yin, L.M., Yuan, X.L., Meng, F.W., and Hu, J., 2005, Protists of the Upper Mesoproterozoic Ruyang Group in Shanxi Province, China: Precambrian Research, v. 141, p. 49–66.
181. Yoon, H.S., Hackett, J.D., Ciniglia, C., Pinto, G., and Bhattacharya, D., 2004, A molecular timeline for the origin of photosynthetic eukaryotes: Molecular and Biological Evolution, v. 21, p. 809–818.
182. Yuan, X., Chen, Z., Xiao, S., Zhou, C.M., and Hua, H., 2011, An early Ediacaran assemblage of macroscopic and morphologically differentiated eukaryotes: Nature, v. 470, p. 390–393.
183. Xiao, S., Knoll, A.H., Kaufman, A.J., Yin, L., and Zhang, Y., 1997, Neoproterozoic fossils in Mesoproterozoic rocks? Chemostratigraphic resolution of a biostratigraphic conundrum from the North China Platform: Precambrian Research, v. 84, p. 197–220.
184. Zhang, Y., 1981, Proterozoic stromatolite microfloras of the Gaoyuzhuang Formation (Early Sinian: Riphean), Hebei, China: Journal of Paleontology, v. 55, p. 485–506.

CHAPTER 6

Laser-Stimulated Fluorescence in Paleontology

Thomas G. Kaye[1*], Amanda R. Falk[2] Michael Pittman[3], Paul C. Sereno[4], Larry D. Martin[5] †, David A. Burnham[6], Enpu Gong[7], Xing Xu[8], Yinan Wang[9]

1 Burke Museum of Natural History and Culture, Seattle, Washington, United States of America

2 Southwestern Oklahoma State University, Department of Biology, Weatherford, Oklahoma, United States of America

3 Vertebrate Palaeontology Laboratory, Department of Earth Sciences, University of Hong Kong, Pokfulam, Hong Kong, China

4 Department of Organismal Biology and Anatomy, University of Chicago, Chicago, Illinois, United States of America

5 Division of Vertebrate Paleontology, Biodiversity Institute, Natural History Museum, University of Kansas, Lawrence, Kansas, United States of America

6 Division of Vertebrate Paleontology, Biodiversity Institute, Natural History Museum, University of Kansas, Lawrence, Kansas, United States of America

7 Department of Geology, Northeastern University, Shenyang, Liaoning, China

8 Institute of Vertebrate Paleontology and Paleoanthropology, Beijing, China

9 1111 Army Navy Drive, Arlington, Virginia, United States of America

ABSTRACT

Fluorescence using ultraviolet (UV) light has seen increased use as a tool in paleontology over the last decade. Laser-stimulated fluorescence (LSF) is a next generation technique that is emerging as a way to fluoresce paleontological specimens that remain dark under typical UV. A laser's ability to concentrate very high flux rates both at the macroscopic and microscopic levels results in specimens fluorescing in ways a standard UV bulb cannot induce. Presented here are five paleontological case histories that illustrate the technique across a broad range of specimens and scales. Novel uses such as back-lighting opaque specimens to reveal detail and detection of specimens completely obscured by matrix are highlighted in these examples. The recent cost reductions in medium-power short wavelength lasers and use of standard photographic filters has now made this technique widely accessible to researchers. This technology has the potential to automate multiple aspects of paleontology, including preparation and sorting of microfossils. This represents a highly cost-effective way to address paleontology's preparatory bottleneck.

1. INTRODUCTION

Highlighting and identifying fossilized structures can be difficult whether it is bone, soft tissue such as skin, muscle and internal organs, or integument such as scales and feathers. Historically, multiple methods have been used to highlight structures for photography, including cross-lighting, polarized light [1], camera filters, and ultraviolet (UV) light [2–6]. Cross-lighting can highlight structures that are difficult to see in direct light. Polarized light can help to enhance image contrast. UV light is capable of causing minerals (e.g. bone [hydroxyapatite]) to fluoresce, and can even highlight soft tissue to some extent [7]. This paper describes a next-generation method of fluorescing minerals using specific wavelengths of light produced by a laser and corresponding imaging through the use of laser-blocking longpass camera filters (see Methods). This method is herein named Laser-stimulated fluorescence (LSF).

For many decades UV light has been used at night to find and collect fluorescent mineral specimens, which are prized for their wide variation in color [8]. The field of biology has made tremendous scientific advances through the use of laser-induced fluorescence mostly through the widespread use of confocal laser microscopes [9–12]. In paleontology, UV light has seen increasing use in recent years where the resulting fluorescence can often reveal structures and patterns not seen under white light [13, 14]. The typical UV light source consists of commonly available standard fluorescent lamps with low wattage and a wavelength of 364 nanometers (nm) [7]. Greater amounts of UV flux on the specimen will cause fluorescent minerals to become more conspicuous, allowing for easier photographic documentation, sometimes with the aid of UV filters (e.g. Hoya brand) [6]. The limited variety of detectable fluorescence in fossils has been a primary limitation in the past using standard UV bulbs [14].

The technique presented here utilizes laser illumination to stimulate fluorescence which offers an order of magnitude improvement in the signal-to-noise ratio over standard UV light. The irradiance of a 20 watt UV fluorescent lamp is about 510 milliwatts per square centimeter (mWcm-2) at a distance of 20 centimeters from the target [15], but the irradiance of a ½ watt laser is on the order of 4000–8000 mWcm-2 [16]. This results in detectable fluorescence of many hard-to-fluoresce mineral types which typically remain dark under standard UV. This advantage can be leveraged when other factors are accounted for. For instance, matching the correct laser line with one of the specimen's absorption bands provides more effective excitation of the fluorescence in a sample. Furthermore, using the right optical filter that matches one of the fluorescence bands of the specimen would improve contrast in the fluorescence image.

Each color of laser emits a different wavelength of light, which will excite fossils and matrix from different rock units in different ways, as the case histories that follow will indicate. Again, LSF techniques depend on the wavelength of light used, the filter used, and the inherent fluorescent properties of the rocks under study. The exact methodology used, therefore, is going to vary depending on these properties.

Laser-induced fluorescence imaging performed through confocal laser-scanning microscopy (CLSM) has been used in micropaleontology to study the morphology and cellular anatomy of fossils *in situ*, at micron-scale resolution, and even in three-dimensions [17–19]. LSF is a simplified and more accessible version of CLSM that uses simpler laser beam scanning and data acquisition systems, and lacks a confocal hole. However, the LSF technique provides its own unique advantages in studying macroscopic paleontological specimens including the compactness and low cost of its setup, its fast data acquisition rate and its high sensitivity compared to UV-stimulated fluorescence. The purpose of this paper is to describe the laser-stimulated fluorescence (LSF) imaging technique and to formalize its use in paleontology in the hope that new and more efficient modes of discovery will be possible.

2. METHODS

Laser-stimulated fluorescence (LSF) imaging is a versatile observational technique that has a multitude of paleontological applications. Both automated and manual systems can be used to scan or otherwise observe fossils under laser illumination. A series of common steps apply to any LSF work, these are detailed below.

Laser light is concentrated on a specimen either as a point source for microscopic work, as a divergent light cone for smaller-sized specimens (with the aid of a laser diffuser), or a collimated beam (in which all light rays are parallel) is raster scanned over very large specimens. Since the laser is very bright, it must be blocked with an appropriate filter that still allows the longer wave fluorescence signal to pass through. Proper precautions using laser-blocking protective glasses and manufacturer's safety protocol should be followed.

The equipment used with this methodology depends on the exact wavelength of light produced by the laser. Specialized light-blocking longpass filters, often used in astronomy, are best-suited for these methods. These particular filters will allow all wavelengths of light longer than a certain wavelength to pass through the filter, however, it will stop all shorter wavelengths. For instance, a red-orange longpass filter (LP580, MidOpt) will allow 91–95% of light between the wavelengths of 600–1100 nm, however, the transmission sharply decreases between 600–520 nm, and by 510 nm, no light passes through the filter (www.midopt.com). A 477 nm blue laser would be efficiently blocked by this filter, but will still allow imaging of longer fluorescent wavelengths. The laser wavelengths and filters for each particular specimen were chosen experimentally via the trial and error method, a procedure that we believe is reasonable given the simplicity of this technique. The setup parameters for each of the five case histories presented in this study are given in Table 1.

Table 1. Setup parameters for five case histories

Case history	Laser wavelength / nm	Lasercolor	Laser wattage /mW	Filter	Wavelength blocked / nm
1	532	green	300	O-54	<540
2	532	green	300	O-54	<540
	457	blue	500	Y-48	<480
3	532	green	150	O-54	<540
4	532	green	250	O-54	<540
5	408	violet	500	Y-44	<440
	532	green	500	O-54	<540

Listing of laser wavelength and wattage plus filter type for five case histories.

Standard UV bulbs can be used in addition to lasers in order to cover a broad range of the light spectrum. Imaging is done in both UVA from 315–400 nm and UVB from 280–315 nm. When working with UV light, photographs can be taken both with and without filters due to the low UV sensitivity of digital camera CCD (charge-coupled device) chips.

No special digital cameras are needed to photograph specimens using laser fluorescence. Typically, digital single lens reflex cameras (DSLRs) capable of manual time exposures (e.g. Nikon D610) with either wide angle or macro lenses are sufficient. Ideally, the photography should be done in a darkroom, basement, or office without windows or with blackout curtains, as any influence of natural light will reduce the clarity of the fluorescence. The use of a tripod is necessary, as the exposure time during photography is typically long—up to several minutes, although this may not be the case for close macro photography. The aperture setting (f-value) should be as low as possible for long-exposure shots.

Multiple types of laser light sources can be used. The more powerful the laser, the better and brighter the fluorescence. For the experiments outlined here, class III lasers in the 300–500 mW category were used. These were well below the threshold that results in radiation damage to the specimens studied. A lab laser, which plugs into the wall and is fairly static, and a high-powered laser pointer that runs off of CR123A lithium batteries, have both been used successfully depending on the locality of the specimen. The benefit of using a lab laser is that it can be used for hours at a time without overheating. It is typically used for precision work and photographing larger specimens. A high-power laser pointer is more portable and adjustable than a lab laser, however it can only be used for ~5 minutes, or else it will overheat and become damaged. If the photographer knows what f-value and shutter speeds are necessary for photography, a laser pointer can be used to great effect. It is excellent for macro photography in the field due to its portability.

A laboratory setup for table-top-sized specimens would typically hold the laser on a fixed mount (Fig 1). The laser itself emits a collimated beam, which results in only a small dot of illumination. This beam can be used as is for maximum flux or be expanded using a diffuser (ARF used a 20-degree diffraction diffuser from Thorlabs). The smaller the angle of the diffuser, the better—i.e. 20 degrees would be better than 50 degrees, as it restricts the beam to a narrower angle and results in a brighter and smaller area of illumination, even if the laser is placed further away from the specimen. The laser should illuminate as much of the specimen as possible, and the diffuser's cone angle changes the area covered by the laser depending on the laser-to-specimen distance.

Larger specimens can be scanned using a custom device (Fig 2A and 2B). A Powel laser line lens projects a laser line in the Y direction that evenly distributes the laser energy over the length of the line (Fig 2C). A motor scans the entire assembly in the X direction (Fig 2A and 2B). This allows specimens of almost any size to be imaged. The exposure time of the DSLR camera should cover one or more of the X direction scans of the specimen.

For a microscope setup, the collimated laser beam is directed through one of the illumination ports or projected directly onto the specimen. The emitted light, laser and fluorescence, comes back through the microscope's optical train where a longpass filter is placed either before the objective lens or internally in a filter slot to block the intense laser light. The fluorescence can then be observed and photographed in detail.

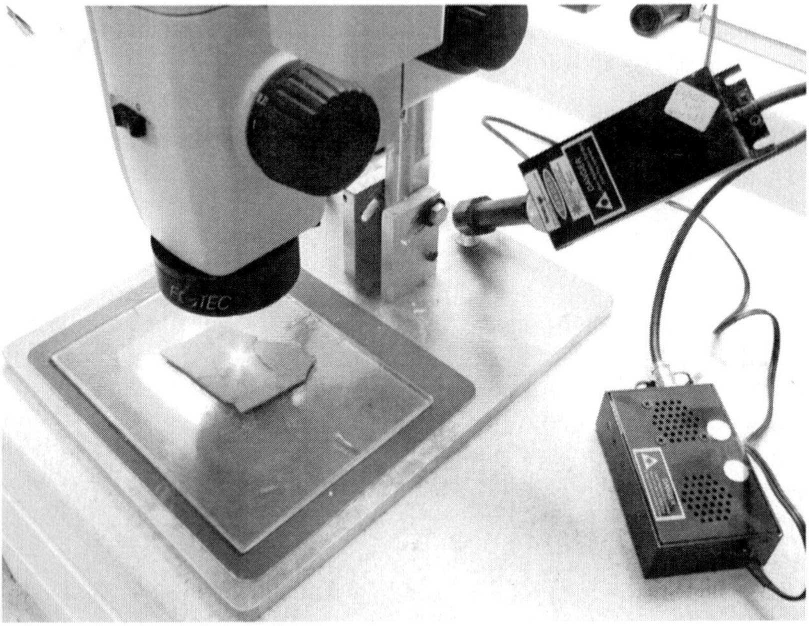

Figure 1. Laser mounted on a stereo microscope. mounted to the side of a stereo microscope. The blocking filter is mounted in front of the objective lens. No diffuser is used here for maximum effect with a smaller spot.

Specimen sources for each case history:

Case history 1: Burke Museum of Natural History and Culture, UWBM 103073—feather from Green River Fm.; UWBM 103074—feather from Parachute Member of Green River Fm.

Case history 2: Department of Land and Resources of Liaoning Province, LVH 0026—fish specimen from Jiufotang Fm. [20]

Case history 3: UWBM 103075—microfossils from Brule Fm.; UWBM 103076—microfossils from Hell Creek Fm.

Case history 4: Gobero specimen housed in the University of Chicago Research Collection, G1B2—juvenile female skeleton from mid-Holocene lake deposits

Case history 5: Institute of Vertebrate Paleontology and Paleoanthropology, Beijing, China, IVPP V13320—*Microraptor* skull from Jiufotang Fm. [21]

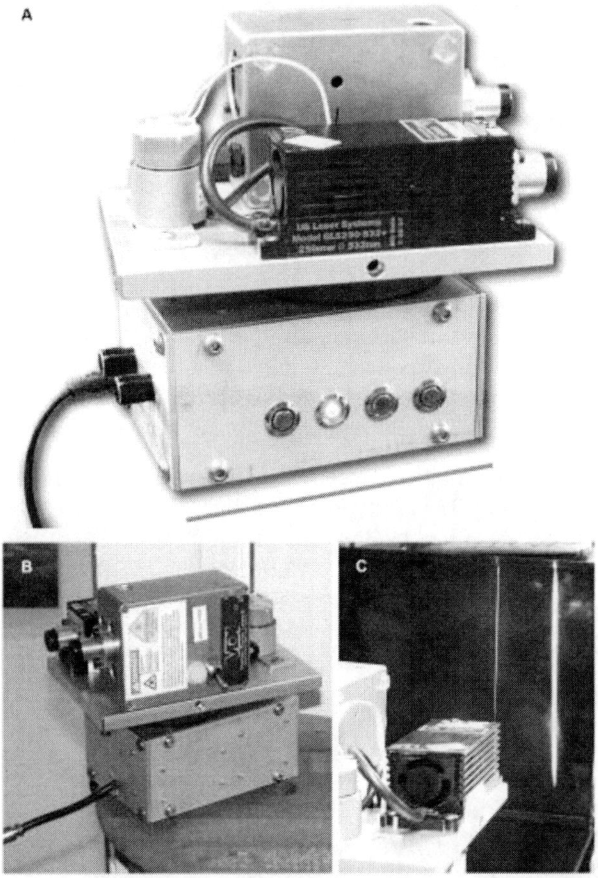

Figure 2. Laser scanning system.A, Custom-built laser scanning device. B, Blue and green laser modules are mounted onto the scanning plate. A variable speed DC motor scans the plate back and forth laterally and is adjustable for degrees covered. C, Removable line lenses convert the laser spot to a more diffuse vertical line. Scale bar in Fig 2A equals 15 cm.

3. CASE HISTORIES

The setup parameters for all case histories are given in Table 1 of the Methods section.

3.1 Case history 1: Silhouette illumination of carbon films

Feathers and other carbonized structures—like ichthyosaur body outlines and fossil leaves—offer unusual insight into certain soft tissues preserved in the fossil record. Usual methods of reflected light microscopy and scanning electron microscopes (SEM) detail surface topography only. The vastly preferred method for microscopy uses transmitted rather than reflected light, but carbon films are typically never thin-sectioned to allow for back illumination. Completely carbonized organic matter is typically not fluorescent, but immature carbonaceous matter of fossilized organisms may fluoresce [18]. In this case, and in similar cases encountered so far, the background matrix is composed of a highly fluorescent mineral that silhouettes the carbon films so that they show up in stark contrast to the matrix around them—the fluorescence intensity of the matrix contrasts with the apparent non-fluorescence of the carbonaceous matter. However, the latter can fluoresce to a small degree in some specimens.

Fig 3 shows a feather from the Green River Formation under the microscope in reflected (Fig 3A) and polarized light (Fig 3B). It clearly shows the barbs, but no barbules are immediately apparent. Fig 3C shows the same field using a smaller laser spot to fluoresce the matrix under the carbon film. It is clear that barbules are in fact present and widely distributed in this specimen. Multiple specimens from the same formations showed these results (Fig 4). Back side illumination also removes topography from the image and makes partially buried barbules visible.

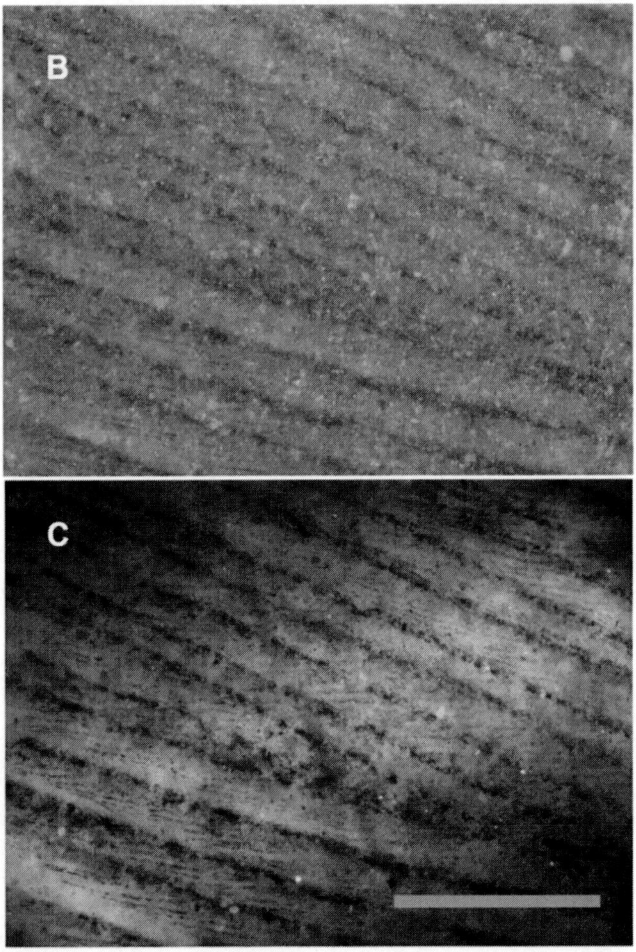

Figure 3. Feather under reflected and matrix fluoresced illumination. Green River Formation feather using identical images under different lighting conditions. A, Reflected light microscopy, only barbs are visible. B, Polarized light, some traces of barbules. C, Laser-stimulated fluorescence of matrix behind the carbon film backlights the feather and renders barbules visible across the entire field of view. Scale bar 0.5 mm white light and fluorescence results revealing new details on the surface of the specimen and within its matrix.

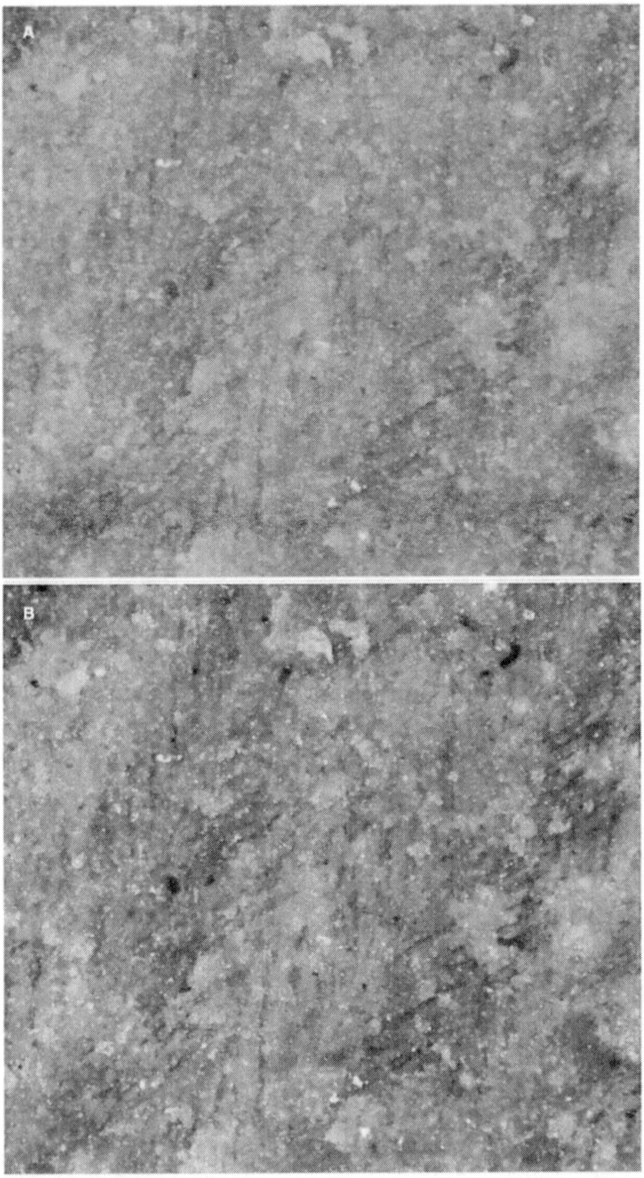
A
B

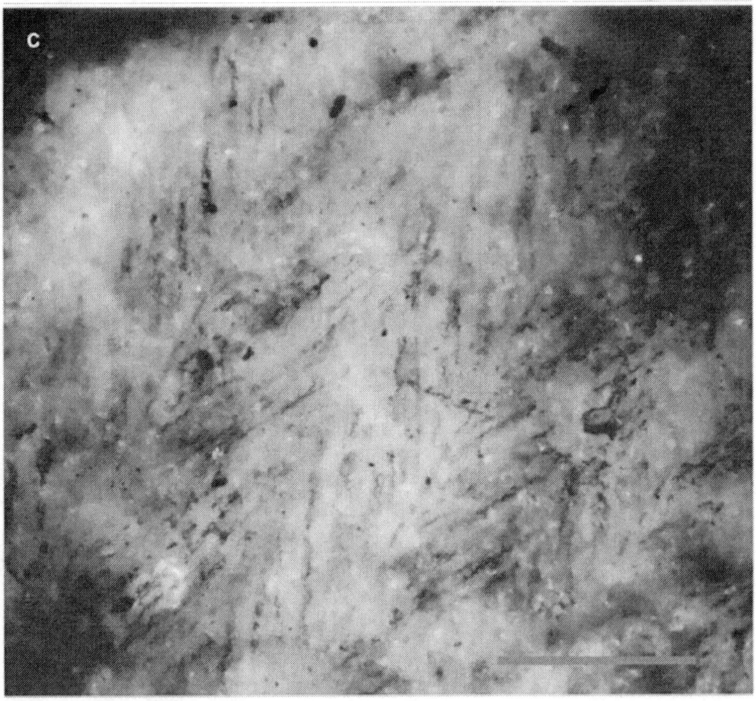

Figure 4. Feather structure comparison using white light, polarized and laser illumination. A second Green River Formation feather specimen under: A, white light, B, polarized light, and C, laser illumination. Scale bar 0.2 mm

A very small specimen (Fig 6) was discovered on the same slab as a Microraptor specimen (Theropoda: Dromaeosauridae [20]) discovered in Liaoning province, China (LVH 0026). The visible bones were not sufficient to identify the specimen, so it was submitted for laser analysis as a last resort. Laser fluorescence identified the specimen as a fish within minutes. In this case the hydroxyapatite in the bones and teeth fluoresced at a higher intensity than the surrounding matrix. The higher intensity fluorescent reaction of the specimen, in comparison to the matrix, revealed teeth below the surface and transparent scales on the surface that were virtually invisible in reflected light (Fig 7). Note that the bone fragment on the right in Fig 7 actually lies under the scale. Laser fluorescence of the formerly translucent scale shows enough detail to count the scale's growth rings.

The laser has a unique ability not seen using lower intensity UV fluorescent bulbs, which is to penetrate a short distance into the matrix and fluoresce buried specimens (Fig 8A and 8B).

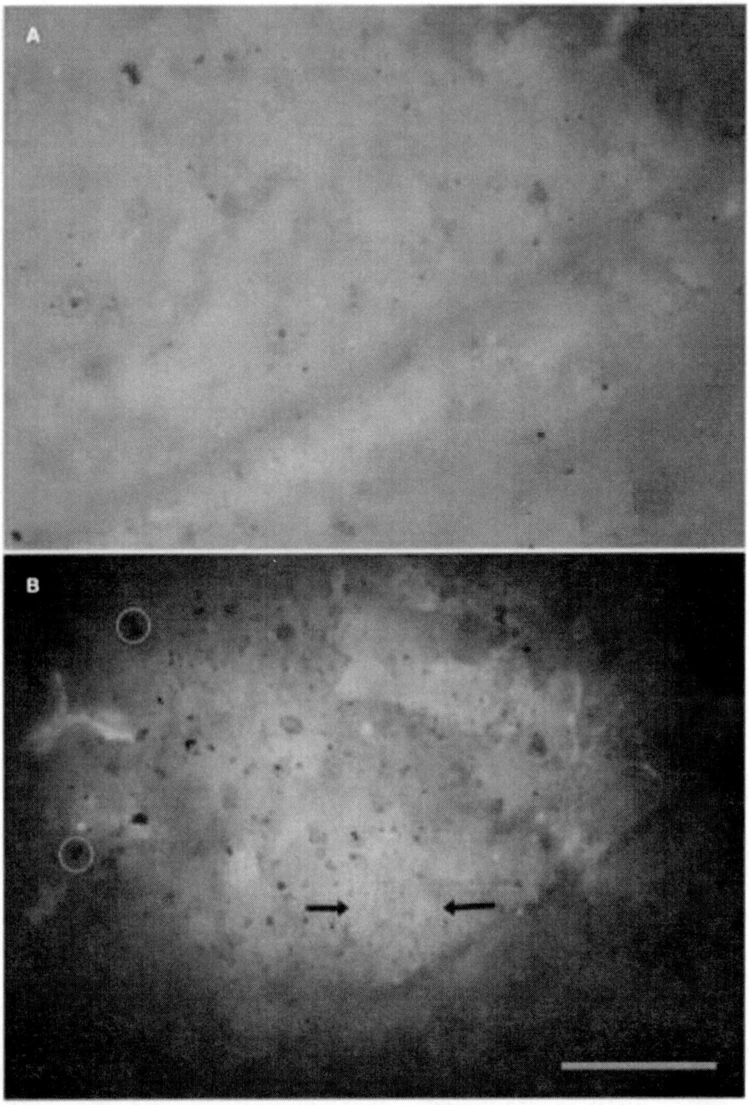

Figure 5. Micro-imaging—visible light vs. laser fluorescence. Identical views of the same field. A, Reflected white light image of a purposely nondescript field. B, Same field illuminated with a 532 nm laser. Some features are at the specimen's surface, but lack color contrast, others are visible within the matrix of the specimen. Black arrows indicate teeth found coincidentally in this image. Circles indicate reference landmarks. Scale bar 0.15 mm

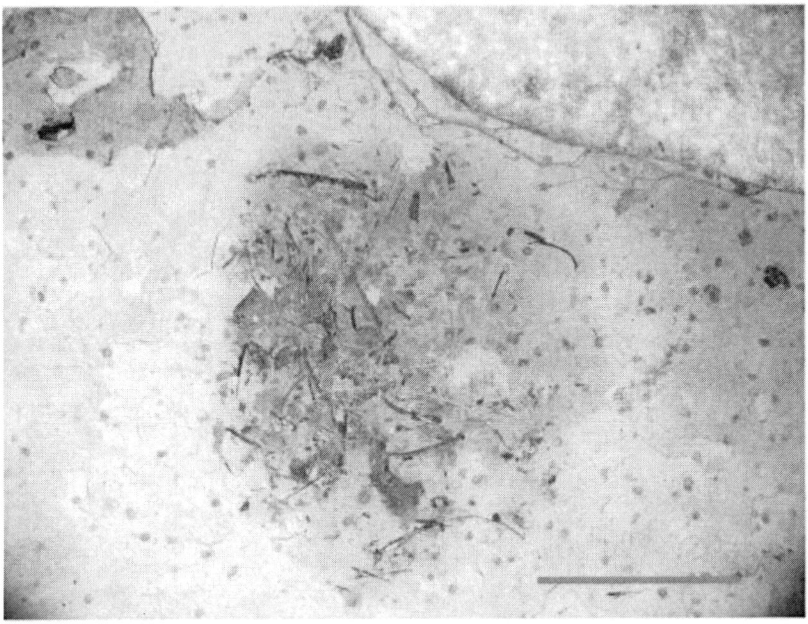

Figure 6. Unidentified Liaoning fossil specimen. An unidentifiable specimen from a Liaoning rock slab containing a Microraptor specimen (LVH 0026). No diagnostic bones are visible on the specimen surface, but laser penetration into the matrix induced fluorescence in multiple teeth and scales, making the identification of a fish possible. Scale bar 1 cm

The top image shows a partially buried bone fragment on the right in white light. Fig 8B shows the margins of the fragment in stark detail. The ability of the intense laser to penetrate into the matrix to reveal hidden specimens is a technique previously only available through regular Xrays and expensive computer tomography (CT) scans [22]. However, this laser property has already been utilized via laser-Raman and CLSM methods to characterize microscopic specimens buried within matrix [18, 19, 23]. The laser has limited penetration, but for specimens buried in finely-laminated sedimentary rocks, material may be limited to the first lamination, as was the case with this specimen. This makes the technique valuable for this and potentially many other Liaoning specimens. Specimens with a uniform matrix that is translucent to laser, fluorescent and scattered light are especially ideal for this technique. This is because the laser beam will be experience less distortion from inhomogeneities in the matrix and will achieve a greater penetration depth.

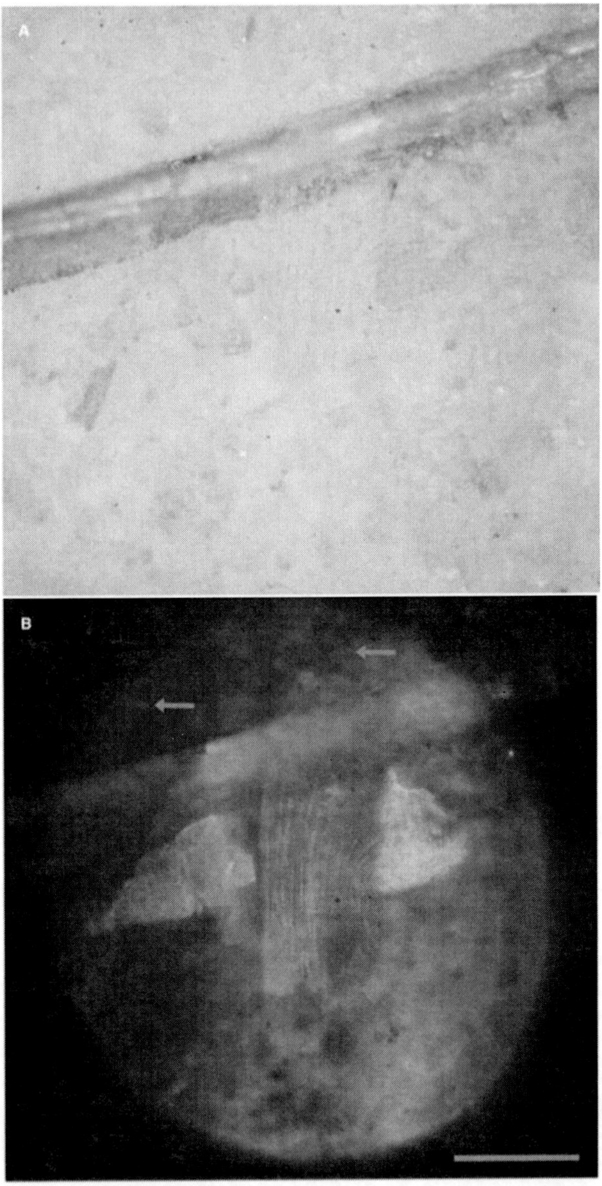

Figure 7. Details enhanced with laser fluorescence. A, White light photo. B, Fluoresced with a 457 nm blue laser. Fish scale on the surface is translucent and barely perceivable under white light. Growth rings on the scale are revealed under fluorescence and can be counted. Bone fragments are brought out in sharp detail. Arrows point to teeth in the matrix. Scale bar 0.5 mm.

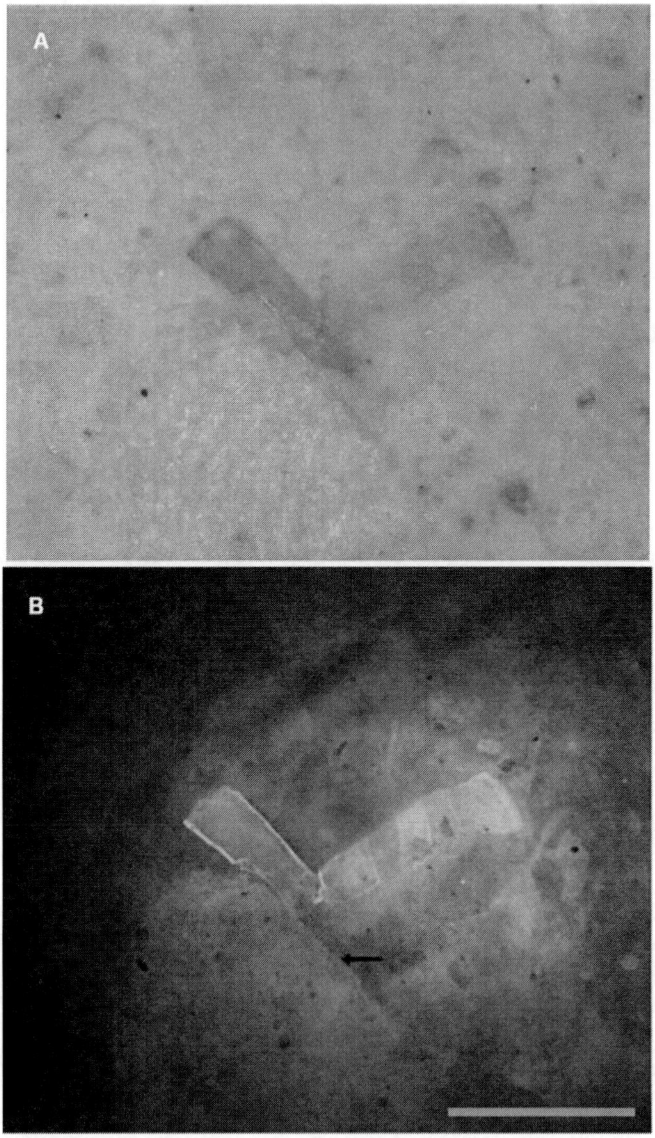

Figure 8. Sub-surface imaging. A, White light micrograph shows the bone fragment on the right entombed within matrix. B, Specimen under laser fluorescence. Photograph shows a high level of detail invisible under white light. Note that another much larger fragment also becomes visible (arrow). Scale bar 0.5 mm

3.3 Case history 3: Automated sorting of micro-fossils

In testing, fossil teeth and bone from formations such as the Eocene Chadron Formation and Oligocene Brule Formation (White River Group) fluoresce well under fluorescent bulb UV light, but small specimens from the Late Cretaceous Lance and Hell Creek Formations do not. Lance and Hell Creek microfossils are prized because of the rarity of mammals and small dinosaurs from these formations. Typical methodologies for recovering these specimens utilize screen washing or anthill collecting. Ants select specific grain sizes to build an anthill over their colony exit and inadvertently concentrate small fossils (usually no more than a few mm across). In either case, the resulting concentrate is historically manually scanned under a microscope by an operator, which in virtually all cases takes weeks to years to go through just a few kilograms of concentrate.

Experiments were conducted on Lance and Hell Creek specimens using a non-dispersed 300 mW, 532nm green laser beam to induce maximum flux. Results indicated that specimens from both formations would indeed fluoresce under these conditions (Fig 9). A stereo microscope was set up with a longpass filter attached to the objective, and a laser beam was directed to the middle of the visual field (Fig 1). A one layer deep pan of concentrate was then raster scanned by hand under the microscope in search of specimens that fluoresced. Given the high contrast of the fluorescing specimens, these could be identified very quickly compared to the conventional approach of identifying specimens based on their color, texture and morphology

This inexpensive setup allows concentrate to be worked through much faster than conventional microscopic sorting.

The success of the manual method was followed by an experimental setup to automatically sort fluorescing fossils from concentrate without human intervention [24]. The entire experimental apparatus consisted of an industrial feeder bowl, green laser, video camera, computercontrolled air puff, and two bins for reject material and candidate specimens (Fig 10). See Supplemental Information for a more detailed description of the system (S1 Fig).

A vibratory bowl feeder was set up to feed a continuous narrow stream of material that was completely illuminated by the laser. A video camera with an appropriate longpass filter viewed the material moving under the laser. When the brightness of a specified group of pixels exceeded a preset threshold, a computer, linked to the video camera, would trigger a short puff of air that would move the specimen into the side tube so it can fall into the "super concentrate" bin.

Figure 9. Fluorescent black light vs. blue laser. A direct comparison between a 15 watt fluorescent UV light illuminating all the fossils at a distance of 7cm, and a 447nm 500mw laser stimulating the specimens in the upper left corner. A, Specimens from the Lance Formation exhibit very low reactivity under fluorescent UVA bulbs. B, Specimens from the White River Formation typically fluoresce very well. This demonstrates that the intensity of laser stimulation can influence low reactivity specimens to fluorescence several orders of magnitude better than specimens known to fluoresce well under UV bulbs. Scale bar 1 cm

3.3 Case history 4: In situ analysis with minimal equipment

This example focuses on the use of minimal equipment for in situ evaluation of a difficult-toexamine specimen. A mid-Holocene-aged skeleton of a young girl from the Sahara desert of Gobero, Niger (Fig 11) was found with an intact bracelet around her arm (G1B2; ~2835 B.C.E.) [25]. It was not possible to move the skeleton or remove the artifact. The circumstances surrounding the specimen necessitated a rapid investigation, and proper laser scanning equipment was not available. A 532 nm green laser was raster scanned by hand over the artifact in a dark room during a timed exposure of a DSLR camera fitted with a yellow longpass filter. The resulting fluorescence exposed a crack pattern (Fig 12) that was one of several lines of evidence used to identify the bracelet material as coming from a hippopotamus tusk (hippo ivory).

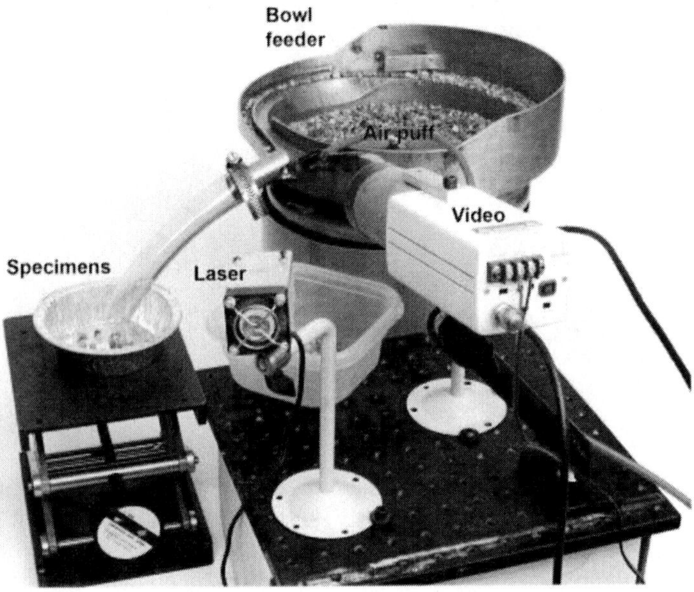

Figure 10. Automated fossil sorter. Proof-of-concept prototype automated micro-fossil picker. The feeder bowl guides a stream of matrix under the laser while a video camera detects 'blobs' of a certain size and brightness. Fluorescing fossils are guided down a tube into a tray by a puff of compressed air.

3.4 Case history 5: Using LSF to spot potential composite "Two faced" Microraptor specimen

The skull of a Microraptor specimen (IVPP V13320 [21]) was first examined under white light conditions. Although there are subtle color differences in the fossil, nothing unusual stands out on first inspection (Fig 13A). Subsequent imaging using LSF reveals dramatic differences in fluorescence between the proximal and distal portions of the skull prompting further investigation (Fig 13B). These results could relate to different skull ossification centers as theropods show postnatal elongation of the rostrum [26–28]. However, this hypothesis is discounted because the fluorescence pattern does not follow bone boundaries, but a break in the slab (Fig 13B).

Figure 11. In situ investigation. A mid-Holocene-aged Gobero skeleton of a small girl preserved wearing an arm bracelet (G1B2; ~2835 B.C.E.) [25]. Due to the impossibility of removing the bracelet, analysis required portable, non-invasive techniques.

These mineralogical differences may instead reflect variability in the specimen's depositional environment (source minerals and pore water composition) and taphonomic history (microbial activity and diagenesis). At a finer scale within the proximal and distal portions of the skull, cartilage and different bone types all fluoresce with different colors e.g. the scleral ring and some premaxillary tooth roots have a lighter fluorescence color than the rest of the darker-colored proximal portion of the skull (Fig 13B). Both the proximal and distal skull portions belong to Microraptor (see Supporting Information for more details, S2 Fig), but a shared dorsal margin for the frontal and most of the teeth as well as a shared ventral margin for the suspected postorbital, splenial and prearticular, suggests that the ventral margin of the proximal skull portion is strangely positioned dorsally. Taken together with the fluorescence results, these observations indicate that the skull of IVPP V13320 might be a composite specimen; this will need to be confirmed by future work using more immobile, higher-cost chemical mapping techniques such as synchrotron rapid scanning X-ray fluorescence (SRS-XRF) [29].

Figure 12. Bracelet fluorescing under laser stimulation. A, The bracelet (G1B2 [25]) under normal light, and B, The bracelet fluorescing under a handscanned laser. The cracking pattern in the upper left corner is only visible under fluorescence and aided in the identification of the bracelet material as hippopotamus tooth. Scale bar 2 cm.

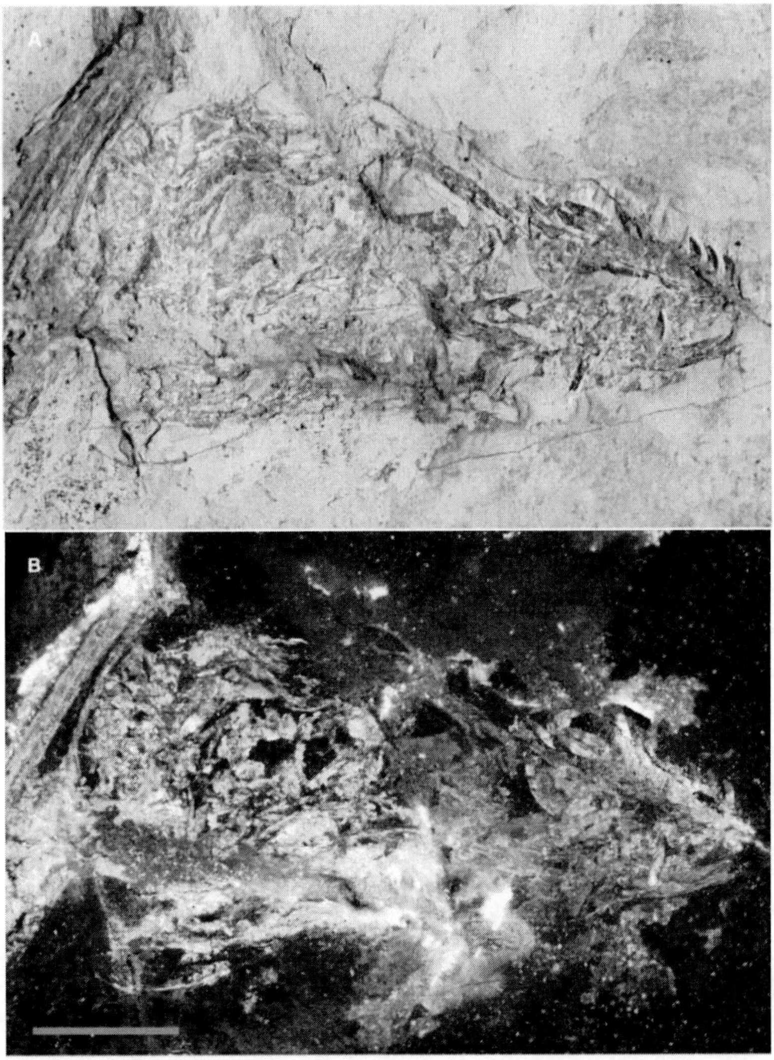

Figure 13. Is the skull of Microraptor IVPP V13320 a composite? A, the skull of IVPP V13320 under white light conditions shows subtle color differences in the bone across a break in the slab—darker bone proximally and lighter bone distally. B, Under laser light stimulation, the bone fluoresces with the same color pattern observed under white light conditions (see A) indicating that the color differences relate to differences in fossil mineralogy. The latter indicates that the skull is a composite specimen, but it is also possible—but less likely—that the pattern observed reflects variable depositional and taphonomic conditions. Scale bar 1 cm. S2 Fig is a labelled version of this figure (see Supporting Information).

LSF can improve the efficiency with which potential composite fossils are identified because it is more mobile than CT scanning and produces more vivid fluorescence images than UV light stimulation (see Introduction and Methods) [30–33]. However, as mentioned, LSF is also a useful tool for identifying differences in bone type which can reveal information about an animal's bone ossification centers and ontogeny. LSF can also uncover heterogeneity in a specimen's depositional environment and taphonomic history.

4. DISCUSSION

There is a short list of non-destructive techniques that are both affordable and accessible for use in paleontology. Laser-stimulated fluorescence (LSF) is a new addition to this list. It provides an instantaneous, non-invasive, geochemical fingerprint of fossilized bone, soft tissue, integument and the surrounding matrix. LSF is also valuable for uncovering anomalies in specimens that direct the user towards more detailed investigations using other methods such as Raman spectroscopy—LSF is not presently quantifiable as to the precise elemental or molecular nature of the material. In addition to the aforementioned fossilized structures, anomalies can also relate to the use of glue, differences in matrix and bone composition, and the potential presence of composite skeletons. With higher sensitivity than UV lamp-based fluorescence imaging, and the compactness and low cost of the setup, LSF promises to become a diagnostic paleontological technique for everyday use. LSF imaging therefore has great potential for use in future descriptive work, particularly of fossils from well-preserved assemblages (konservatlagerstätten) like those of the Mesozoic of northeastern China, which can have incomplete provenance information.

In the examples given in this paper, new information was revealed using relatively inexpensive and rapid techniques that would otherwise have not been discovered without the use of much more expensive and/or time-intensive methods. Setups start from around US$500 and process within seconds to minutes making LSF easily accessible.

The ability to look into the matrix for hidden specimens with simple techniques like the ones described here (Case history 2), was previously only possible using X-rays, CT scans, CLSM and RAMAN which have high cost and low accessibility [18, 23]. Micro-CT has certainly revolutionized the way small specimens are dealt with, but in virtually all cases the specimens are already known and CT is not likely to be used as a basic discovery process due to its expense. Silicates can often diffuse a concentrated laser beam several millimeters into the matrix. Future experiments may quantify the depth of matrix penetration using more powerful lasers and may extend the detection depth further than expected. This technique is particularly useful for fossils that are too large to fit onto a standard microscope stage or into regular CT scanners. It is also useful for fossils with an insufficient density contrast with their host matrix, which cannot produce meaningful CT images. The technique can therefore help to bridge a number of important knowledge gaps relating to such fossils.

LSF can also be used in a novel way as a light source behind non-fluorescing features, such as carbon films (Figs 3 and 4). These soft-tissue remains have become progressively more important and are improving our understanding of fossil morphologies, but the techniques to investigate them have been slow to develop. Small details in carbon films can be missed using reflective light microscopy, however, the use of LSF will often backlight carbonized films both on and slightly below the surface. This clarifies the image and creates extra contrast that makes carbonized structures easier to see, especially smaller structures (e.g. the feather barbules in Figs 3 and 4). If LSF is adopted as a standard investigative tool, we may be able to further investigate carbonized films and other non-fluorescing soft tissues. The backlighting technique can also highlight material defects, which could be phylogenetically informative e.g. the distinctive cracking pattern of hippo ivory (Case history 4). Such defects may also reveal useful biomechanical and behavioral information if they relate to tooth, tusk and bone loading and wear.

Multi-spectral imaging with different wavelengths highlights the fact that various minerals and compounds fluoresce with different intensity, according to wavelength. This is an important property as it may not always be desirable to fluoresce the entire specimen. In the case of the auto-picker, only bone specimens were of interest and the green laser was an ideal choice. Had a method such as UVB been employed the bone fragments would have been overwhelmed by other common minerals and organics, which also fluoresce under UVB, defeating the purpose of the machine.

5. CONCLUSIONS

The advent of low cost, high power lasers including blue, green and violet wavelengths, means that the laser-stimulated fluorescence (LSF) technique can become widely available. The filters can be sourced from the photography industry or astronomy suppliers again at reasonable cost. The compactness and portability of the system combined with its efficiency in scanning large and extremely small fossils fills a gap in our ability to quickly and easily analyze specimens. It provides instant geochemical comparisons over a wide range of specimens, including specimens that previously exhibited very low fluorescence activity. At the microscopic level, LSF has already proven its worth in revealing unseen details in many specimens. The use of fluorescence is already in common use in multiple subdisciplines of biology, and is clearly a technique that is useful in paleontology as well. We have only scratched the surface of the ability of fluorescence to contribute to paleontology. LSF already holds a 'first' in the automation of micro-fossil sorting and this could theoretically be extended into automated preparation of specimens which is the single biggest bottleneck in paleontology. Overall, LSF is a discovery process geared toward uncovering unusual features of interest for follow up examination with more specialized tools.

ACKNOWLEDGMENTS

The authors wish to thank Peter and Debra Ceravolo, Chris Lively, Bob Davis and Zheng Wenjie. Craig Byron and an anonymous reviewer are thanked for their feedback, which resulted in significant improvements to this manuscript

REFERENCES

1. Cook SF, Brooks ST, Ezra-Cohn HE. Histological studies on fossil bone. Journal of Paleontology. 1962:483–94.
2. Chen JY, Oliveri P, Li CW, Zhou GQ, Gao F, Hagadorn JW, et al. Precambrian animal diversity: putative phosphatized embryos from the Doushantuo Formation of China. Proceedings of the National Academy of Sciences. 2000;97(9):4457–62. pmid:10781044
3. Eichler B, Werneburg R. Neufunde von Branchiosauriern aus dem Rotliegend von Freital bei Dresden im UV-Licht New specimens of branchiosaurs from the Rotliegend (Sakmarian) of Freital near Dresden in ultra-violet light. Journal of Central European Geology. 2010;56(2):137–57.
4. Frey E, Tischlinger H. The Late Jurassic pterosaur *Rhamphorhynchus*, a frequent victim of the ganoid fish *Aspidorhynchus*? PloS one. 2012;7(3):e31945. pmid:22412850
5. Tischlinger H. Ultraviolet light investigations of fossils from the Upper Jurassic Plattenkalks of Southern Frankonia. Zitteliana B. 2005;26:26.
6. Tischlinger H, Arratia G, editors. Ultraviolet light as a tool for investigating Mesozoic fishes, with a focus on the ichthyofauna of the Solnhofen archipelago. Mesozoic Fishes 5—global diversity and evolution; 2010; Saltillo2013.
7. Hone DWE, Tischlinger H, Xu X, Zhang FC. The extent of the preserved feathers on the four-winged dinosaur *Microraptor gui* under ultraviolet light. PloS one. 2010;5(2):e9223. pmid:20169153
8. Warren TS, Gleason S, Bostwick RC, Verbeek ER. Ultraviolet light and fluorescent minerals: understanding, collecting and displaying fluorescent minerals. Gem Guides Book. 1999.
9. Hibbs AR. Confocal microscopy for biologists: Kluwer Academic/Plenum Publishers New York 2004.

10. Schomacker KT, Frisoli JK, Compton CC, Flotte TJ, Richter JM, Nishioka NS, et al. Ultraviolet laser-induced fluorescence of colonic tissue: basic biology and diagnostic potential. Lasers in surgery and medicine. 1992;12(1):63–78. pmid:1614265
11. Donnert G, Keller J, Medda R, Andrei MA, Rizzoli SO, Lührmann R, et al. Macromolecular-scale resolution in biological fluorescence microscopy. Proceedings of the National Academy of Sciences. 2006;103(31):11440–5. pmid:16864773
12. Matsumoto B. Cell biological applications of confocal microscopy: Academic Press; 2003.
13. Kaye TG, Martin L, Burnham D, Gong E. Multispectral imaging and analysis of a Liaoning 'mystery specimen'. 70th Annual Meeting of the Society of Vertebrate Paleontology 2010;Abstracts of papers, 28(3):114A. PubMed Central PMCID: PMC2010.
14. Croft DA, Kaye TG, Panko L. A new method for finding small vertebrate fossils: ultraviolet light at night. Palaeontology. 2004;47(4):795–800.
15. Electric G. UVA Blub Catalog. In: Electric G, editor. UVA Blub Catalog2014.
16. Effects of Low Doses of Radiation on Crop Plants. Vienna: International Atomic Energy Agency,; 1966. 58 p.
17. Birkmann H, Lundin RF. Confocal microscopy: potential applications in micropaleontology. Journal of Paleontology. 1996;70:1084–7.
18. Schopf JW, Tripathi AB, Kudryavtsev AB. Three-dimensional confocal optical imagery of Precambrian microscopic organisms. Astrobiology. 2006;6:1–16. pmid:16551223
19. Schopf JW, Kudryavtsev AB. Confocal laser scanning microscopy and raman (and fluorescence) spectroscopic imagery of permineralized Cambrian and Neoproterozoic fossils. In: Laflamme M, Schiffbauer JD, Dornbos SQ, editors. Quantifying the evolution of early life. Topics in Geobiology. 36: Springer Netherlands; 2011. p. 241–70.
20. Gong EP, Martin LD, Burnham DA, Falk AR, Hou LH. A new species of *Microraptor*from the Jehol Biota of northeastern China. Palaeoworld. 2012;21(2):81–91. Available: http://dx.doi.org/10.1016/j.palwor.2012.05.003.
21. Xu X, Zhou Z, Wang X, Kuang X, Zhang F, Du X. Four-winged dinosaurs from China. Nature. 2003;421(6921):335–40 pmid:12540892
22. Endo H, Frey R, editors. Anatomical imaging: towards a new morphology. Tokyo: Springer-Verlag; 2008.
23. Schopf JW, Kudryavtsev AB. Three-dimensional Raman imagery of Precambrian microscopic organisms. Geobiology. 2005;3:1–12.
24. Kaye TG. Fully automated sorting of microfossils from sediment using laser-stimulated fluorescence. 67th Annual Meeting of the Society of Vertebrate Paleontology. 2007;Abstracts of papers, 27 (S3):98A.
25. Sereno PC, Garcea EAA, Jousse H, Stojanowski CM, Saliege JF, Maga A, et al. Lakeside cemeteries in the Sahara: 5000 years of Holocene population and environmental change. PLoS One. 2008;3(8):1–22.
26. Bever GS, Norell MA. The perinate skull of *Byronosaurus* (Troodontidae) with observations on the cranial ontogeny of paravian theropods. American Museum Novitates. 2009;3657:1–52.
27. Carr TD. Craniofacial ontogeny in the Tyrannosauridae (Dinosauria, Coelurosauria). Journal of Vertebrate Paleontology. 1999;19:497–520.
28. Rauhut OWM, Fechner R. Early development of the facial region in a non-avian theropod dinosaur. Proceedings of the Royal Society of London B. 2005;272:1179–83.
29. Bergmann U, Morton RW, Manning PL, Sellers WI, Farrar S, Huntley KG, et al. *Archaeopteryx* feathers and bone chemistry fully revealed via synchrotron imaging. Proceedings of the National Academy of Sciences. 2010;107(20):9060–5. pmid:20457935
30. Miethe A, Born A. Die fluorographie von fossilien. Paläontologische Zeitschrift. 1928;9: 343–56.
31. Tischlinger H, Arratia G. Ultraviolet light as a tool for investigating Mesozoic fishes, with a focus on the ichthyofauna of the Solnhofen archipelago. In: Arratia G, Schultze HP, Wilson MVH, editors. Mesozoic fishes 5—global diversity and evolution. München: Verlag Dr. Friedrich Pfeil; 2013. p. 549–60. pmid:24423941

32. Rowe T, Ketcham RA, Denison C, Colbert M, Xu X, Currie PJ. Forensic palaeontology: the Archaeoraptor forgery. Nature. 2001;410(6828):539–40. Available: http://www.nature.com/nature/journal/v410/n6828/suppinfo/410539b0_S1.html. pmid:11279483
33. Mateus O, Overbeeke M, Rita F. Dinosaur frauds, hoaxes and "Frankensteins": how to distinguish fake and genuine vertebrate fossils. Journal of Paleontological Techniques. 2008;2:1–5.

CHAPTER 7

Molecular and Paleontological Evidence for a Post-Cretaceous Origin of Rodents

Shaoyuan Wu[1*], Wenyu Wu[2], Fuchun Zhang[3], Jie Ye[2], Xijun Ni[2], Jimin Sun[4], Scott V. Edwards[1], Jin Meng[5*], Chris L. Organ[1]

1 Department of Organismic and Evolutionary Biology and Museum of Comparative Zoology, Harvard University, Cambridge, Massachusetts, United States of America,

2 Institute of Vertebrate Paleontology and Paleoanthropology, Chinese Academy of Sciences, Beijing, China

3 Xinjiang Key Laboratory of Biological Resources and Genetic Engineering, Xinjiang University, Urumqi, Xinjiang, China

4 Key Lab of Cenozoic Geology and Environment, Institute of Geology and Geophysics, Chinese Academy of Sciences, Beijing, China

5 Division of Paleontology, American Museum of Natural History, New York, New York, United States of America

ABSTRACT

The timing of the origin and diversification of rodents remains controversial, due to conflicting results from molecular clocks and paleontological data. The fossil record tends to support an early Cenozoic origin of crown-group rodents. In contrast, most molecular studies place the origin and initial diversification of crown-Rodentia deep in the Cretaceous, although some molecular analyses have recovered estimated divergence times that are more compatible with the fossil record. Here we attempt to resolve this conflict by carrying out a molecular clock investigation based on a nine-gene sequence dataset and a novel set of seven fossil constraints, including two new rodent records (the earliest known representatives of Cardiocraniinae and Dipodinae). Our results indicate that rodents originated around 61.7–62.4 Ma, shortly after the Cretaceous/Paleogene (K/Pg) boundary, and diversified at the intraordinal level around 57.7–58.9 Ma. These estimates are broadly consistent with the paleontological record, but challenge previous molecular studies that place the origin and early diversification of rodents in the Cretaceous. This study demonstrates that, with reliable fossil constraints, the incompatibility between paleontological and molecular estimates of rodent divergence times can be eliminated using currently available tools and genetic markers. Similar conflicts between molecular and paleontological evidence bedevil attempts to establish the origination times of other placental groups. The example of the present study suggests that more reliable fossil calibration points may represent the key to resolving these controversies.

1. INTRODUCTION

Molecular clocks and fossil record are the two major approaches to date evolutionary divergence times, which are crucial for using the Tree of Life to understand evolutionary processes and mechanisms. In the case of major divergences among groups of placental mammals, the general tendency has been for paleontological studies to suggest that these events took place in the Paleocene, while molecular ones place them deep in the Cretaceous [1, 2], although some molecular studies have recovered estimated divergence times that are more compatible with the fossil record [3, 4, 5, 6]. The general pattern of disagreement has confounded our ability to discern the influence of the K/Pg extinction event on the radiation of extant mammals. This problem is particularly evident in rodents, a group that accounts for approximate 42% of extant mammalian diversity [7]. The oldest known fossil that can be clearly identified as a member of the rodent lineage, the fragmentary possible crown-rodent *Acritoparamys*, has a Late Paleocene age of about 57 million years (Ma) [8, 9]. However, early molecular studies almost unanimously supported a Cretaceous radiation of rodents [5, 6, 10, 11, 12, 13, 14, 15, 16], although Douzery et al. [3] and Kitazoe et al. [4] obtained molecular results that placed the earliest divergences within crown-Rodentia in the Paleocene and was therefore compatible with the fossil record. Despite these exceptions, a strong discrepancy still persists between the fossil record and the preponderance of results from molecular clock studies. Resolving this discrepancy is therefore critical not only for understanding the evolutionary history and dynamics of rodents, but also for assessing the reliability of molecular clocks and fossils to accurately estimate divergence times.

Molecular clocks attempt to pinpoint divergence events whereas the fossil record alone can yield minimum estimates given by the first known fossil occurrence for a given group [1, 2]. The problem of molecular rate heterogeneity, a major source undermining the accuracy of molecular clock estimates, has been addressed by applying relaxed molecular clocks across sequences [17]. The availability of reliable fossils that can be used as calibration points, therefore, may hold the key to obtaining an accurate time estimate of the origin and radiation of rodents. In this study, we employed five rodent calibrations based on recent fossil discoveries, including two new fossils that are chronologically constrained with palaeomagnetic chrons. The earliest known fossils of Dipodinae (three-toed jerboas) is dated to 10.5 Ma from the beginning of the Late Miocene of China (Fig. S1 and Fig. S2), providing an upper (more recent) bound for the divergence time between Dipodinae and Allactaginae (five-toed jerboas). The earliest known fossils of the two extant genera of Cardiocraniinae (dwarf jerboas), *Cardiocranius* and *Salpingotus*, are dated to 9 Ma [18]. The lower (more ancient) bound of each of these divergence events is 13 Ma, in the middle part of the Middle Miocene, based on recent biostratigraphic and paleomagnetic data. The earliest known myodont, *Erlianomys*, was discovered from the Early Eocene (54 Ma) [19], providing a reliable lowest known bound for the divergence time between the two primary myodont groups, Dipodoidea and Muroidea (Fig. S3) [20]. The upper bound of this divergence can be constrained to 43 Ma, based on the earliest known dipodoids [21] and muroids [22] from China. We therefore use the split between mice and rats [23] as well as between octodontids and erethizontids [24, 25] as calibration points, because of their improved fossil record and stratigraphic data. In order to achieve a balanced distribution of calibration points within the phylogeny, we also applied two well-defined non-rodent calibrations in successive sister lineages to rodents, including the split of marsupials and placentals [26, 27], and feliforms and caniforms [28].

We use the fossils noted above to create seven fossil calibrations with a nine-gene sequence dataset to re-evaluate the timing of rodent origin and diversification. For taxon sampling, we included major lineage across rodents, and sampled comprehensively within Dipodoidea to include all six subfamilies, an approach we referred to as "bottom-up" taxon sampling (i.e. building up an analytic model from a foundation of many individual data samples, versus the "top-down" approach of inferring an analytic model from relatively few data points). This sampling approach allowed us to accurately incorporate these new calibration points based on Chinese dipodoid fossils that are comparatively recent in geological time. Our analysis implements a relaxed molecular clock model using Bayesian and maximum likelihood approaches. Our results suggest that rodents originated and diversified after the K/Pg boundary at the beginning of the Cenozoic, a finding consistent with patterns found in the fossil record.

2. RESULTS

2.1 Test of molecular rate heterogeneity

The BEAST [29] analysis shows that substantial rate variation across the data set was only found in the CNR1 locus, with an ucld.stdev parameter of 1.788 (95% confidence interval (CI) 1.35–2.19). The ucld.stdev values of all other loci lie between 0 and 1, indicating that these loci have a moderate level of rate variation (see Table S1). The ucld.stdev parameter of the concatenated partitioned data set is 0.57 (95% CI 0.45–0.71), which is lower than that of all other individual genes except IRBP. These results demonstrate the necessity of utilizing a relaxed molecular clock mode on the DNA dataset for the molecular dating estimates.

2.2 Molecular dating with complete fossil constraints

We inferred a time-calibrated phylogenetic tree for 41 mammal species focusing on the superfamily Dipodoidea (jerboas and relatives) for which we sampled 18 species, representing all six subfamilies. Nine unlinked nuclear genes were used to construct the tree using Bayesian [30] and likelihood [31] criteria. Topologically, the Bayesian and maximum likelihood approaches gave identical, highly resolved phylogeny, supporting Hystricomorpha as the most basal rodent clade (bootstrap support = 71, posterior probability = 0.98, Fig. 1). For time-calibrated trees, we estimated divergence times using Bayesian [29] (Fig. 2) and likelihood [32] approaches, which returned similar results (Table 1). Our estimated divergence times are much younger than those estimated in previous molecular analyses, and are more congruent with the fossil record.

We estimate that the divergence between rodents and lagomorphs occurred about 61.7 Ma (Bayesian, Bayesian credibility interval (BCI) 52.8–71) or 62.4 Ma (likelihood). The basal divergence of rodents was estimated to be 57.7 Ma (Bayesian, BCI 50.1–66) or 58.9 Ma (likelihood). These estimates are roughly consistent with recent interpretations of the early gliran fossil record. The oldest known Glires, *Heomys* and *Mimotona*, may both fall on the lagomorph stem [33], although Meng et al. [9] recovered *Heomys* as a stem-rodent rather than a stem-lagomorph. However, both analyses agree that *Heomys* and *Mimotona* belong to the gliran lineage. Both genera are placed in the early Late Paleocene [9, 34], an age close to the rodent-lagomorph divergence time estimated by our study. The appearance of sciuromorphs was estimated at 55.6 Ma (Bayesian, BCI 48.4–63.2) or 57 Ma (likelihood). The divergence between castorimorphs and myodonts was estimated at 52.9 Ma (Bayesian, BCI 46.5–59.9) or 54.6 Ma (likelihood). In addition, we estimate the basal divergence of hystricomorphs to be 50.2 Ma (Bayesian, BCI 41.6–58.7) or 52.3 Ma (likelihood), a result consistent with the oldest hystricomorph fossils, which date to ~50 Ma [35]. We estimate the origin of crown Hystricognathi to be 36.9 Ma (Bayesian, BCI 31.6–43) or 35.2 Ma (likelihood), compatible with the occurrence of the oldest hystricid fossils at ~34 Ma [36].

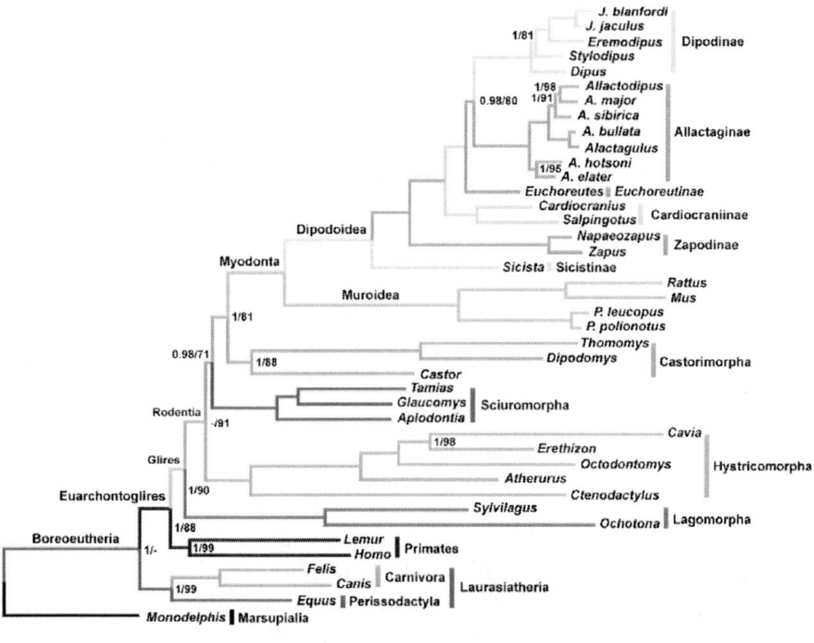

Figure 1. Phylogenetic relationships for rodents and outgroups estimated using Bayesian and maximum likelihood algorithms. The Bayesian posterior probability and the maximum likelihood bootstrap values for each of the nodes are provided from the left to the right of the slash, respectively. Support scores are not shown for nodes that receive a full support of both posterior probability and bootstrap value. https://doi.org/10.1371/journal.pone.0046445.g001

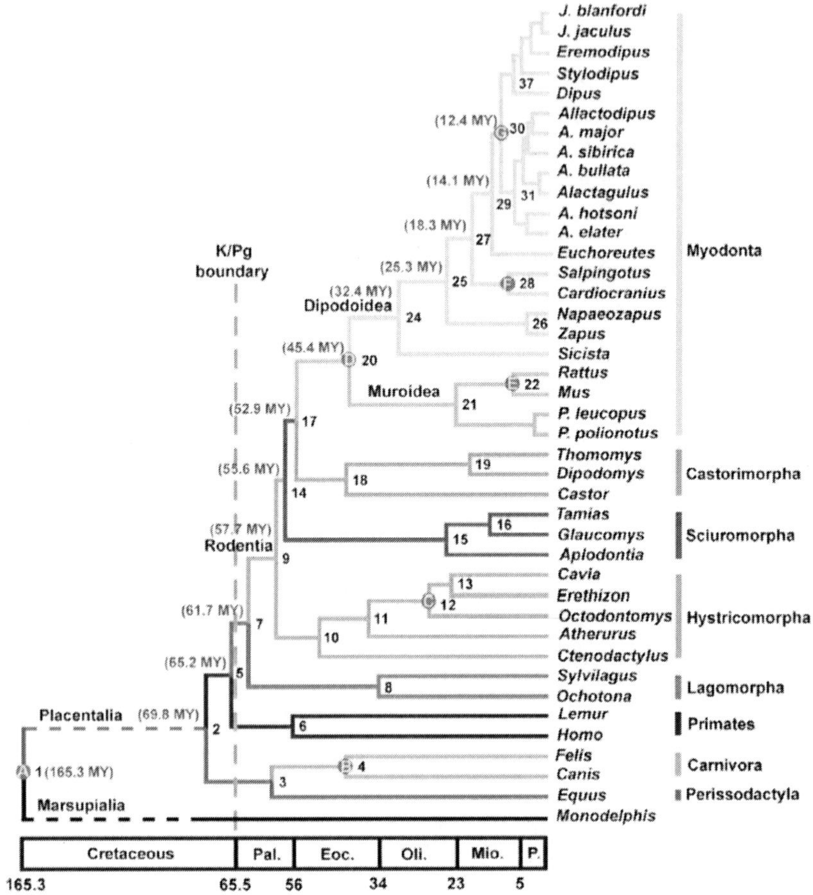

Figure 2. Molecular time scale for the orders of Rodentia, Lagomorpha, Primates, Carnivora and Perissodactyla obtained from the Bayesian estimates based on seven fossil calibration points and relaxed molecular clock model. Fossil constraints are indicated by circle A to G on the corresponding nodes: A. 160–190 Ma for the split between Placentalia and Marsupialia; B. 38–61.7 Ma for the split between Caniformia and Feliformia; C. 28.5–37 Ma for the split between *Octodontomys* and *Erethizon*; D. 43–54 Ma for the basal split of Myodonta; E. 7.3–12.2 Ma for the split between mice and rats; F. 9–13 Ma for the split between *Cardiocranius* and *Salpingotus*; G. 10.5–13 Ma for the split between Dipodinae and Allactaginae. https://doi.org/10.1371/journal.pone.0046445.g002

Table 1. Support values of divergence dates for Bayesian and penalized likelihood estimates using seven fossil calibration points.

Nodes	Description of Nodes	Bayesian estimates	Foss. Cons. Exp. Dist.				Likelihood estimates	Uniform constraint	
			ESS	Mean	offset	95% cre. int.		Mini.	Maxi.
1	Marsupialia-Placentalia	165.3 (160–175.7)	8861	3.9	124.6	160–190	-	160	160
2	Base of Boreoeutheria	69.8 (58.6–81.9)	257	-	-	-	69.71	-	-
3	Perissodactyla-Carnivora	56.5 (44.2–69.5)	691	2.5	62.3	62.36–71.52	60.7	-	-
4	Caniformia-Feliformia	41.6 (38–48.4)	1992	6.5	38	38–61.98	42.55	38	61.7
5	Primates-Glires	65.2 (55–75.4)	254	-	-	-	65.35	-	-
6	Hominoidea-Lemuroidea	55.6 (40.4–70)	697	-	-	-	57.86	-	-
7	Lagomorpha-Rodentia	61.7 (52.8–71)	251	-	-	-	62.37	-	-
8	Ochotonidae-Leporidae	34.6 (18.8–50.7)	386	-	-	-	38.11	-	-
9	Base of Rodentia	57.7 (50.1–66)	245	-	-	-	58.89	-	-
10	Base of Hystricomorpha	50.2 (41.6–58.7)	445	-	-	-	52.32	-	-
11	Hystricidae-Caviomorpha	36.9 (31.6–43)	1095	-	-	-	35.19	-	-
12	*Octodontomys-Erethizon*	29.8 (28.5–32.2)	4214	2.3	28.5	28.56–36.98	28.5	28.5	37
13	*Cavia-Erethizon*	24.6 (17.6–30)	876	-	-	-	25.52	-	-
14	Myodonta-Sciuromorpha	55.6 (48.4–63.2)	251	-	-	-	56.98	-	-
15	Base of Sciuromorpha	25.4 (11.9–38.6)	245	-	-	-	35.87	-	-
16	*Glaucomys-Tamias*	17.8 (7.3–29.9)	228	-	-	-	27.54	-	-
17	Myodonta-Castorimorpha	52.9 (46.5–59.9)	268	-	-	-	54.57	-	-
18	Base of Castorimorpha	45.5 (33.9–55.3)	408	-	-	-	49.96	-	-
19	Heteromyidae-Geomyidae	20.6 (9.9–32.2)	453	-	-	-	22.31	-	-
20	Muroidea-Dipodoidea	45.4 (43–49.4)	539	3	43	43.08–54.07	46.08	43	54
21	Cricetidae-Muridae	23.4 (14.7–32.2)	561	-	-	-	20.93	-	-
22	Mouse-Rat	9.5 (7.3–12.9)	1206	1.4	7.3	7.335–12.46	10.96	7.3	12.2
24	Base of Dipodoidea	32.4 (25.2–39.7)	515	-	-	-	28.85	-	-
25	Zapodidae-Dipodidae	25.3 (19.1–31.7)	528	-	-	-	22.47	-	-
26	*Zapus-Napaeozapus*	5.7 (1.9–10.1)	1063	-	-	-	3.5	-	-
27	Base of Dipodidae	18.3 (13.9–22.8)	664	-	-	-	16.15	-	-
28	*Salpingotus-Cardiocranius*	10.2 (9–12.4)	4295	1.1	9	9.028–13.06	11.27	9	13
29	Euchoreutinae-Allactaginae	14.1 (11.2–17.3)	693	-	-	-	12.24	-	-
30	Dipodinae-Allactaginae	12.4 (10.5–14.9)	747	0.7	10.5	10.52–13.08	11.29	10.5	13
31	Base of Allactaginae	7.7 (5.4–9.9)	562	-	-	-	4.53	-	-
37	Base of Dipodinae	7.5 (5–9.8)	627	-	-	-	4.25	-	-

Values in parentheses are the 95% credibility intervals. - indicates that the corresponding node was not present in the corresponding analyses. Abbreviations: Foss. Cons. Exp. Dist., fossil constraints set as exponential distribution; ESS, effective sample size; Cre. Int., credibility interval; Mini, minimum; Maxi, Maximum.

doi:10.1371/journal.pone.0046445.t001

We tested for the Node Density Effect (NDE) [37], [38] using the online utility available at (http://www.evolution.reading.ac.uk/pe/index.html), which is based on the method outlined by Venditti et al. (2006) [39]. The results of this test indicate that the NDE is present in our tree (β significantly greater than zero). By successively pruning clades in the tree, we find that the NDE is present because of the correlation between nodes and branch lengths associated with the increasing sampling of Dipodinae and Allactaginae in relation to the rest of the tree. Reducing the numbers of taxa within Dipodinae and Allactaginae or pruning out Dipodinae removes the NDE. The NDE may have the effect of causing our estimates of divergence time to appear more recent, because unsampled lineages could downwardly bias the molecular divergences. To test this, we re-analyzed our data set using BEAST with reduced taxon sampling in the subfamilies Dipodinae and Allactaginae. For these two subfamilies, we sampled two taxa for each, including *Dipus sagitta* and *Jaculus blanfordi* for Dipodinae, and *Allactaga elater* and *Allactodipus bobrinskii* for Allactaginae, because such taxon sampling removes the NDE from our tree. Our results show that the BEAST analysis based on the reduced tree produced divergence times for major nodes that are similar to those for the full taxa (Table S6), and statistically we found no significant difference between these two estimates (t-test, p-value=0.954). These results suggest that the impact of the NDE on the estimated divergence times for the rest of the tree is limited.

Although the confidence intervals attached to our Bayesian estimates are relatively wide, as is often the cases for studies like this one that employ a limited number of genes [6], the fact that our Bayesian and maximum likelihood estimates generally agree with one another reinforces the results of both analyses and suggests that the dates are reliable.

2.3 Sensitivity test of fossil age constraints

We tested the sensitivity of applying different fossil constraints for their impact on the estimated times of divergence within rodents.

2.4 Bayesian

Compared with the estimated dates using all constraints, omitting constraint D for the divergence between Dipodoidea and Muroidea has limited impact on the estimated times for all nodes. The estimated date of 44 Ma (BCI 33.9–54.9) for Dipodoidea-Muroidea divergence is close to 45.4 Ma (BCI 43–49.3) when this fossil constraint was employed (Table 2). When constraints on tip rodent nodes of calibration point E, F and G were relaxed, the estimates for most nodes increased remarkably, pushing the basal divergence of Glires into the Cretaceous at 68.4 Ma (BCI 55.6–82.6) (Table 2). When only using constraint E, the most commonly used rodent calibration for mouse-rat divergence, and the two non-rodent constraints A and B, as expected [12], estimates for all nodes in Euarchontoglires incleased dramatically: 84.3 Ma (BCI 57.6–116.5) for the base of Boereoeutheria, 79 Ma (BCI 53.2–108.6) for the base of Euarchontoglires, 66.4 Ma (BCI 41–95.7) for the base of Primates, 74.7 Ma (BCI 50.6–103) for the base of Glires, and 69.7 Ma (BCI 46.5–96.1) for the base of Rodentia (Table 2). In addition, we test an alternative constraining of a minimum age of 124.6 Ma and a maximum age of 138.4 Ma for the split between placentals and marsupials to assess the sensitivity of descendant nodes to this date. The minimum age assignments were based on the Early Cretaceous *Eomaia* [40], which was previously regarded as the oldest known eutherian before the recent discovery of *Juramaia sinensis* [27] from the Late Jurassic. The maximum age was based on the basal therian

Vincelestes [41]. The analysis shows that the change of this age resulted in slightly younger estimates of divergence times for deep nodes, but had little impact on recent nodes (Table 2). One major uncertainty in the rodent phylogeny is the position of the root of Rodentia. Based on dental morphology, Marivaux et al. [42] places Hystricomorpha as the basalmost clade of rodents. However, molecular phylogenetic studies support either Sciuromorpha, Hystricomorpha or the clade formed by Sciuromorpha and Hystricomorpha as the most basal clade of rodents, but all of these placements received relatively weak statistical support [11, 15, 43, 44]. To test whether acceptance of the alternative topologies would strongly affect our dating estimates, we conducted two alternative BEAST analyses by changing the root of Rodentia from Hystricomorpha to (1) Sciuromorpha and (2) the clade formed by Sciuromorpha and Hystricomorpha. The results showed that neither permutation had an important impact on the results, so our major conclusions remain unchanged (Figs. S4, S5).

Table 2. Summary of results of sensitivity test of fossil age constraints.

Nodes	Description of Nodes	Bayesian estimates	Foss. Cons. Exp. Dist.				Likelihood estimates	Uniform constraint	
			ESS	Mean	offset	95% cre. int.		Mini.	Maxi.
1	Marsupialia-Placentalia	165.3 (160–175.7)	8861	3.9	124.6	160–190	-	160	160
2	Base of Boreoeutheria	69.8 (58.6–81.9)	257	-	-	-	69.71	-	-
3	Perissodactyla-Carnivora	56.5 (44.2–69.5)	691	2.5	62.3	62.36–71.52	60.7	-	-
4	Caniformia-Feliformia	41.6 (38–48.4)	1992	6.5	38	38–61.98	42.55	38	61.7
5	Primates-Glires	65.2 (55–75.4)	254	-	-	-	65.35	-	-
6	Hominoidea-Lemuroidea	55.6 (40.4–70)	697	-	-	-	57.86	-	-
7	Lagomorpha-Rodentia	61.7 (52.8–71)	251	-	-	-	62.37	-	-
8	Ochotonidae-Leporidae	34.6 (18.8–50.7)	386	-	-	-	38.11	-	-
9	Base of Rodentia	57.7 (50.1–66)	245	-	-	-	58.89	-	-
10	Base of Hystricomorpha	50.2 (41.6–58.7)	445	-	-	-	52.32	-	-
11	Hystricidae-Caviomorpha	36.9 (31.6–43)	1095	-	-	-	35.19	-	-
12	*Octodontomys-Erethizon*	29.8 (28.5–32.2)	4214	2.3	28.5	28.56–36.98	28.5	28.5	37
13	*Cavia-Erethizon*	24.6 (17.6–30)	876	-	-	-	25.52	-	-
14	Myodonta-Sciuromorpha	55.6 (48.4–63.2)	251	-	-	-	56.98	-	-
15	Base of Sciuromorpha	25.4 (11.9–38.6)	245	-	-	-	35.87	-	-
16	*Glaucomys-Tamias*	17.8 (7.3–29.9)	228	-	-	-	27.54	-	-
17	Myodonta-Castorimorpha	52.9 (46.5–59.9)	268	-	-	-	54.57	-	-
18	Base of Castorimorpha	45.5 (33.9–55.3)	408	-	-	-	49.96	-	-
19	Heteromyidae-Geomyidae	20.6 (9.9–32.2)	453	-	-	-	22.31	-	-
20	Muroidea-Dipodoidea	45.4 (43–49.4)	539	3	43	43.08–54.07	46.08	43	54
21	Cricetidae-Muridae	23.4 (14.7–32.2)	561	-	-	-	20.93	-	-
22	Mouse-Rat	9.5 (7.3–12.9)	1206	1.4	7.3	7.335–12.46	10.96	7.3	12.2
24	Base of Dipodoidea	32.4 (25.2–39.7)	515	-	-	-	28.85	-	-
25	Zapodidae-Dipodidae	25.3 (19.1–31.7)	528	-	-	-	22.47	-	-
26	*Zapus-Napaeozapus*	5.7 (1.9–10.1)	1063	-	-	-	3.5	-	-
27	Base of Dipodidae	18.3 (13.9–22.8)	664	-	-	-	16.15	-	-
28	*Salpingotus-Cardiocranius*	10.2 (9–12.4)	4295	1.1	9	9.028–13.06	11.27	9	13
29	Euchoreutinae-Allactaginae	14.1 (11.2–17.3)	693	-	-	-	12.24	-	-
30	Dipodinae-Allactaginae	12.4 (10.5–14.9)	747	0.7	10.5	10.52–13.08	11.29	10.5	13
31	Base of Allactaginae	7.7 (5.4–9.9)	562	-	-	-	4.53	-	-
37	Base of Dipodinae	7.5 (5–9.8)	627	-	-	-	4.25	-	-

Values in parentheses are the 95% credibility intervals. - indicates that the corresponding node was not present in the corresponding analyses. Abbreviations: Foss. Cons. Exp. Dist., fossil constraints set as exponential distribution; ESS, effective sample size; Cre. Int., credibility interval; Mini, minimum; Maxi, Maximum.
doi:10.1371/journal.pone.0046445.t001

The above analyses demonstrate that changes of the age of non-rodent constraints have limited impact on the estimated divergence times of nodes in the rodent tree. By contrast, removal of all three recent rodent constraints results in dramatic increase of ages for other nodes, reverting to the older divergence times estimated by earlier studies. Moreover, these results indicate that the use of a single mouse-rat constraint for the divergence time estimates for rodents can result in overestimates for all nodes in Glires.

2.5 Likelihood

When constaints on tip rodent nodes E, F and G were relaxed, the estimated dates for all nodes change little (Table 2). This is not surprising, since age constraints on the root and deep nodes have a much bigger influence on the divergence estimates of other nodes in the program r8s [32]. Setting the age of the root to 180 Ma only caused a slight increase of the date estimates for nodes, including 64.8 Ma for the basal split of Glires, and 61.1 Ma for the basal diversification of Rodentia (Table 2). These analyses show that the influence of the root's age on the estimated dates of major rodent lineages is limited.

3. DISCUSSION

Three hypotheses have been proposed to characterize the evolutionary radiation of placental mammals: the Explosive Model puts the origin of placental orders and their intraordinal diversification shortly after the K/Pg boundary, whereas the Short Fuse Model places the origin of placental orders and intraordinal diversification in the Cretaceous, and the Long Fuse Model posits Cretaceous origins of placental orders but intraordinal diversification after the K/Pg boundary. Paleontological evidence favors the Explosive Model, suggesting that the origin and diversification of placental mammals occurred following the K/Pg extinction event that wiped out the non-avian dinosaurs and opened up many ecological niches. By contrast, recent molecular studies support either the Short Fuse or the Long Fuse Models, which suggests that continental breakup in the Late Cretaceous contributed to the origin and/or diversification of placental mammals, rather than the opening of ecological niches by differential extinction among groups. For rodents, most previous molecular studies consistently support a Short Fuse Model for them, making rodents one of the oldest placental orders which originated and diversified in the Cretaceous [11, 12, 13, 14, 15]. Because rodents lack a Cretaceous fossil record, however, there is no evidence to indicate whether their postulated diversification in the Cretaceous would have been driven by tectonic events or by other factors.

Recent phylogenetic studies, based on extensive sampling of fossil mammals, have placed all Cretaceous eutherians outside the placental crown groups [9, 33, 45]. Our estimated divergence times are consistent with a rapid radiation of major rodent lineages during the Paleocene. Therefore, our results agree with those of a few other recent molecular studies [3, 4] in supporting the hypothesis that the origin and intraordinal diversification of rodents occurred after the K/Pg Boundary about 65 Ma, following the extinction of non-avian dinosaurs. These diversification patterns are consistent with the Explosive Model as applied to mammalian orders generally, rather than with the Short Fuse Models for radiation within the orders of Rodentia.

Our study is methodologically similar to others that employed the relaxed molecular clock and multiple fossil calibration points [6, 11, 12, 14, 15, 20] (Fig. 3a). However, the divergence times we obtained, particularly those for rodents, are significantly younger than those in some recent studies that considerably predate the K/Pg boundary (Fig. 3b). Compared to the results of previous studies, our younger estimates are probably attributable to the fact that we employed multiple, internal rodent fossil constraints, which are well documented stratigraphically in a continuous sequence dated with convincing paleomagnetic chrons (see Figs. S2, S3). The study of Springer et al. (2003) [12] applied one rodent constraint, the split of mouse and rat, with a minimum age of 12 Ma (Fig. 3b). But recent increased resolution of the fossil record has decreased the minimum age constraint for mouse-rat to be around 7.3 Ma [23]. Additionally, our sensitivity test shows that the use of a single rodent calibration point can result in overestimates for all nodes in rodents. Several recent studies employed multiple rodent fossil constraints [6, 11, 15, 20]. However, their estimated divergence times for rodents are still similar to that of Springer et al. (2003), supporting the Short Fuse Model of rodent diversification (Fig. 3b).

The major difference between the fossil constraints used in this study and those used by Huchon et al. (2007) [11] and Meredith et al. (2011) [15] is that the minimum and maximum age constraints for many rodent calibration points used in both the latter studies are farther apart than the constraints for points used in our study (Fig. 3a), because of uncertainty in the paleontological and stratigraphic data associated with the fossils in question. For example, the youngest rodent fossil constraint used by Meredith et al. (2011), the split between Ctenomyidae and Ocodontidae, has a minimum age of 9.07 Ma and a maximum age of 34 Ma, for a range of 24.93 Ma. Our fossil calibration points are well constrained, with smaller amounts of time between the minimum and maximum ages (Fig. 3a).

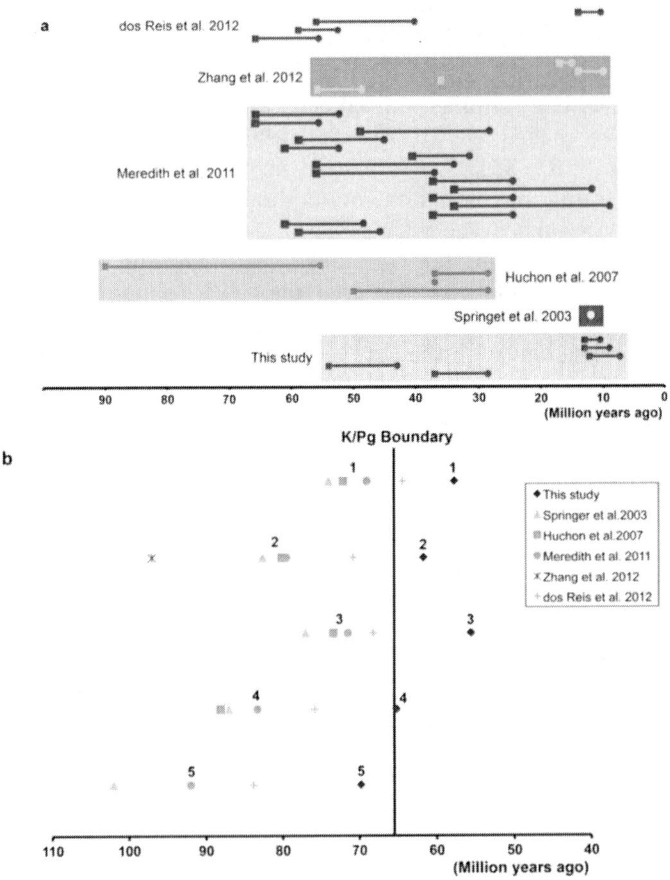

Figure 3. Comparisons among rodent fossil constraints used and divergence times estimated. A. The temporal distribution of rodent fossil constraints used. The circles and squares represent the minimum and maximum age constraints for each of the fossil calibration points, respectively. The bar connecting the circle and square shows the range between the minimum and maximum age constraints. Note that most calibration points used by Huchon et al. 2007 and Meredith et al. 2011 have much larger gap between the minimum and maximum age constraints, compared to that used by this study. **B**. Divergence time estimates obtained for major boreoeutherian lineages. The estimates of Springer et al. 2003, Huchon et al. 2007 and Meredith et al. 2011 are close to each other, and predate the K/Pg boundary. However, the divergence estimates obtained by the present study are much younger and very close to the K/Pg boundary. Numbers from 1 to 5 indicate: **1**. Base of Rodentia; **2**. Base of Glires (rodents and lagomorphs); **3**. Base of Primates; **4**. Base of Euarchontoglires; **5**. Base of Boreoeutheria. https://doi.org/10.1371/journal.pone.0046445.g003

By contrast, the Zhang et al. (2012) [20] study was similar to ours in that dipodoids were densely sampled, but differed from ours in that sampling of major rodent lineages outside Dipodoidea was very limited. This lack of extensive sampling of rodent lineages may account for the fact that Zhang et al. (2012) recovered a comparatively early divergence time for the rodent-lagomorph node, consistent with earlier studies rather than with our results. Conversely, dos Reis et al. (2012) [6] carried out a study with extensive genomic sampling and broad taxonomic sampling across Placentalia, but sampled relatively few rodents of any kind. dos Reis et al. (2012) estimated the rodent-lagomorph divergence to have occurred at 70.8 Ma (Confidence Interval: 69.9–71.8), considerably earlier than the estimate recovered by our study, and the discrepancy may arise from either the lack of dense sampling within Rodentia by dos Reis et al. (2012) or the lack of extensive genomic sampling and/or broad sampling outside Rodentia in our analysis. The strengths and weaknesses of these different sampling approaches remain to be fully explored.

Our results show that reconciliation between estimates of divergence times based on molecular clock and paleontological data is possible with standard tools and genetic markers, at least for the Rodentia, the most speciose of all mammalian orders. Achieving this consistency requires a reasonable number of reliable fossil calibration points supported by a well-constrained paleontological and stratigraphic record. The consistency between our results and the paleontological record suggests that similar controversies regarding the origin and diversification of other major biological groups, including the post-K/Pg diversification of various orders of modern mammals and birds [2] and the "Cambrian Explosion" of animal phyla [46] are potentially resolvable given adequate and reliable fossil calibration points.

5. MATERIALS AND METHODS

5.1 Taxon and genomic sampling

This study includes 33 rodent species across major rodent lineages and eight outgroup taxa. The taxa examined and their classification are provided in Table S2. Portions of nine unlinked the nuclear genes were sampled, including alpha 2B adrenergic receptor (A2AB), cannabinoid receptor 1 (CNR1), growth hormone receptor (GHR), interphotoreceptor retinoid binding protein (IRBP), breast cancer susceptibility (BRCA1), von Willebrand factor (vWF), ATPase, Cu++ transporting, alpha polypeptide (ATP7A), 3′-UTR region of cAMP responsive element modulator (Crem), recombination activating gene 2 (RAG2). Detailed information of these loci is provided in Table S3.

Genomic DNA was prepared from either muscle or liver tissue samples using DNeasy Tissue Kit (Qiagen, inc). PCR reactions were undertaken in 25-μL volumes with the following conditions: 94°C (5–10 min); 35 cycles of 94°C (45 s); 55°C (45 s); 72°C (40–60 s); 72°C (5–10 min). Sequence data were collected on ABI 3730 DNA Analyzers for both directions subsequent to Big Dye chemistry. The primers for both PCR and sequencing reactions are identified in Table S4.

DNA sequences were aligned using Kalign as implemented in the program eBioX (http://www.ebioinformatics.org) under default conditions, and refined manually using MacClade 4.06 [47]. Ambiguous sites including potentially heterozygous sites were encoded based on IUPAC Ambiguity protocol. The GenBank accession numbers for each of the sequence data are provided in Table S5.

5.2 Phylogenetic analysis

Phylogenetic trees were constructed using maximum likelihood and Bayesian criteria. The Akaike information criterion was used to determine the best substitution models of sequence evolution based on the results from MODELTEST 3.07 [48] (Table S3). The maximum likelihood estimates for the best tree were performed with the program PhyML 3.0 [31] for the concatenated dataset with 100 bootstrap replicates.

Bayesian inference of phylogeny was performed with the program MrBayes 3.1.2 [49]. We performed four independent runs under identical conditions with partitions defined for each of the nine loci evolving with independent model parameters. For each analysis, one run was performed with four chains, and was sampled every 2000 generations for fifty million generations after a burn-in cycle of 5000 trees. The convergence of each run was examined with the program Tracer 1.5 [29].

5.3 Test of molecular rate heterogeneity

The levels of molecular rate heterogeneity for the concatenated dataset and for each of the loci were examined in the program BEAST 1.5.4 [29]. When running under the uncorrelated relaxed lognormal clock model, BEAST can measure the ucld.stdev parameter, which can determine how clock-like the DNA dataset is. The dataset is strictly clock-like if the ucld.stdev parameter is 0, and the dataset has substantial rate heterogeneity among lineages if the parameter is greater than 1. The dataset has a moderate level of heterogeneity if the ucld.stdev parameter lies between 0 and 1 [29]. For each individual locus, the test incorporated in BEAST was performed using five million generations sampled every 500 generations. For the concatenated dataset, BEAST run was performed using 40 million generations, sampled every 500 generations for two independent runs.

5.4 Molecular estimates of divergence times

We employed two approaches to estimates divergence times of each node: a Bayesian method as implemented in the program BEAST 1.5.4, and a penalized likelihood method in the program r8s 1.71 [32].

Bayesian analyses of molecular dating were estimated for the combined dataset with the substitution models for each gene partition. The relaxed molecular clock model was chosen for all BEAST analyses [50], since the estimated value of ucld.parameter is 0.57 for the concatenated DNA dataset. Each run of BEAST analyses comprised forty million generations, sampled either every 500 generations or 1000 generations for two independent runs. The output files of the two independent analyses were combined using LogCombiner 1.5.4 [29] to produce the final results. Each run was examined with the program Tracer 1.5 [29] for convergence.

The program r8s [32] was used to compare maximum likelihood results with those obtained from BEAST. The r8s analyses were performed using the best maximum likelihood tree calculated in PhyML. We used the penalized likelihood model, the log penalty function and the truncated Newton algorithm based on the recommendation of the developer [32]. The optimal smoothing parameter was determined by a cross-validation run with r8s. For the nodes used as fossil age constraints, the check-gradient function was conducted to determine if the estimated values of divergence timings of these nodes fall beyond the age constraints. The date of root (marsupial-placental) was fixed at 160 and 180 Ma in order to assess the sensitivity of descendant nodes to the age of the root. Since the use of the two different root ages do not have significant impact on the estimated ages of other nodes (Table 2), this study used 160 as the age of the root for all r8s analyses.

5.5 Fossil constraints

We applied seven fossil age constraints for the molecular dating analyses in this study. Minimum age constraints were based on the earliest known fossil record of a member of one of the divergent lineages. Where possible, the maximum age constraints are based on the age of the youngest well-sampled horizon that does not contain any members of the divergent lineages, in a stratigraphic sequence in which members of these lineages subsequently appear. When a stratigraphic sequence suitable for setting a particular upper bound by this method was not available, the age of the oldest member of the stem lineage leading up to the divergence was used as the upper bound. For the program BEAST, these calibration points were set as soft constraints with upper and lower bounds that allow for a 2.5% chance of lying beyond each user-input bound. The r8s program only allows the fossil calibrations to be set as a hard bound. Fossil constraints are as follows (Fig. 2):

a) We assigned a minimum age of 160 Ma and a maximum age of 190 Ma for the divergence between marsupials and placentals, based on the earliest known placental mammal *Juramaia sinensis* [27] and the basal mammal *Hadrocodium* [26].

b) We assigned a minimum age of 38 Ma and a maximum age of 61.7 Ma for the divergence between caniforms and feliforms, based on the oldest known crown carnivoran *Hesperocyon* and *Daphoenus* from the Late Eocene [28] and the oldest stem carnivore *Protictis schaffi* from the early Paleocene [28], respectively.

c) We assigned a minimum age of 28.5 Ma and a maximum age of 37 Ma for the divergence between *Octodontomys* and the clade formed by *Cavia* and *Erethizon*, based on the oldest fossil record of Caviomorpha from the Late Eocene [25] and the oldest fossil erethizontid (*Steiromys* sp.) from the mid-Oligocene [24].

d) The earliest muroid is *Pappocricetodon* [22], and the earliest dipodoid is *Primisminthus* and *Banyuesminthus* [21]. All the above species emerge in the middle part of the Eocene of China. *Erlianomys*, which is from the lower part of the Arshanto Formation in Nuhetingboerhe of Inner Mongolia, China, represents the earliest fossil record of myodonts [19]. Based on recent magneto-stratigraphic analyses, the Nuhetingboerhe section was dated to the early part of the Early Eocene [51] (Fig. S3). Consistent with these fossil and stratigraphic results, we assigned a minimum age of 43 Ma and a maximum age of 54 Ma for the divergence between muroids and dipodoids.

e) We assigned a minimum age of 7.3 Ma and a maximum age of 12.2 Ma for the divergence between mice and rats, based on the occurence of the earliest known mouse *Mus* sp. and the earliest known *Prognomys* from the late Miocene of Pakistan [23].

f) We assigned a minimum age of 9 Ma for the divergence between the two cardiocraniine genera *Cardiocranius* and *Salpingotus*, based on the occurence of the earliest known *Cardiocranius* (*C. pussillus*) and the earliest known *Salpingotus* (*S. primitivus*) from the Late Miocene of China [18].

g) We assigned a minimum age of 10.5 Ma for the divergence between the two dipodoid subfamilies Dipodinae and Allactaginae, based on the occurence of the earliest known dental fossils of Dipodinae from the middle bed of the Dingshanyanchi Formation, Xinjiang, China (Fig. S1). The cheek teeth of the Dingshanyanchi species lack the mesoloph and mesocone on the upper molars, and have no mesolophid and mesoconid on the lower molars. Cusps on the labial and lingual sides of each molar show an alternating, rather than opposite, arrangement. The anteroloph of M2 and ectolophid of the lower molars are oriented oblique to the longitudinal axis. These dental features represent synapomorphies of dipodine molars. According to stratigraphic and palaeomagnetic results, the middle bed of the Dingshanyanchi Formation falls toward the base of the long normal magnetic chron C5n.2n, and thus dates to the earliest part of the Late Miocene [52] (Fig. S2).

We set a maximum age of 13 Ma for the divergence between Dipodinae and Allactaginae and the divergence between *Salpingotus* and *Cardiocranius*. The Middle Miocene deposits are well exposed and have been extensively sampled in northern China and surrounding areas [53, 54, 55, 56]. The only Dipodidae that can be found during the Middle Miocene is *Protalactaga*, a primitive genus. These deposits produce no species of extant dipodid subfamilies – Dipodinae, Allactaginae, Euchoreutinae and Cardiocraniinae – not even in the northern Junggar Basin of Xinjiang, which has a continuous geological sequence ranging from the Late Oligocene to the Late Miocene and where screen washing has been applied for decades [52, 53, 55]. On this basis, the maximal boundary for these two divergence events was placed in the middle part of the Middle Miocene.

ACKNOWLEDGMENTS

We are grateful to D. Kramerov of the Russian Academy of Sciences, and A. Shahin of the Minia University of Egypt for donating DNA and tissue samples. We would like to thank F. Jenkins, L. Flynn and C. Sullivan for comments. We thank the Museum of Comparative Zoology (MCZ), Harvard University, the Museum of Vertebrate Zoology, University of California at Berkeley, the American Museum of Natural History, New York, and the National Museum of Natural History, Smithsonian Institution for the loan of tissues.

REFERENCES

1. Bromham L, Penny D (2003) The modern molecular clock. Nat Rev Genet 4: 216–224.
2. Smith AB, Peterson KL (2002) Dating the time of origin of major clades: Molecular clocks and the fossil record. Ann Rev Earth Planet Sci 30: 65–88.
3. Douzery EJP, Delsuc F, Stanhope MJ, Huchon D (2003) Local molecular clocks in three nuclear genes: divergence times for rodents and other mammals and incompatibility among fossil calibrations. J Mol Evol 57: S201–S213.
4. Kitazoe Y, Kishino H, Waddell PJ, Nakajima N, Okabayashi T, et al. (2007) Robust time estimation reconciles views of the antiquity of placental mammals. PLos one 2: e384.
5. Hallstrom BM, Janke A (2010) Mammalian evolution may not be strictly bifurcating. Mol Biol Evol 27: 2804–2816.
6. dos Reis M, Inoue J, Hasegawa M, Asher RJ, Donoghue MJ, et al. (2012) Phylogenomic datasets provide both precision and accuracy in estimating the timescale of placental mammal phylogeny. Proc R Soc B. doi:10.1098/ rspb.2012.0683.
7. Wilson DE, Reeder DM (2005) Mammal Species of the World: A Taxonomic and Geographic Reference. Baltimore, MD: Johns Hopkins University Press.
8. Dawson MR, Beard CK (1996) New Late Paleocene rodents (Mammalia) from Big Multi Quarry, Washakie Basin, Wyoming. Palaeovertebrata 25: 301–321.
9. Meng J, Hu Y-M, Li C-K (2003) The osteology of Rhombomylus (Mammalia, Glires): Implications for phylogeny and evolution of Glires. Bull Amer Mus Natl Hist 275: 1–247.
10. Huchon D, Catzeflis FM, Douzery EJP (2000) Variance of molecular datings, evolution of rodents and the phylogenetic affinities between Ctenodactylidae and Hystricognathi. Proc Zool Soc London B 267: 393–402.
11. Huchon D, Chevret P, Jordan U, Kilpatrick CW, Ranwez V, et al. (2007) Multiple molecular evidences for a living mammalian fossil. Proc Natl Acad Sci 104: 7495–7499.
12. Springer MS, Murphy WJ, Eizirik E, O'Brien SJ (2003) Placental mammal diversification and the Cretaceous-Tertiary boundary. Proc Natl Acad Sci 100: 1056–1061.
13. Kumar S, Hedges SB (1998) A molecular timescale for vertebrate evolution. Nature 392: 917–920.
14. Bininda-Emonds ORP, Cardillo M, Jones KE, MacPhee RDE, Beck RMD, et al. (2007) The delayed rise of present-day mammals. Nature 446: 507–512.
15. Meredith RW, Janecka JE, Gatesy J, Ryder OA, Fisher CA, et al. (2011) Impacts of the Cretaceous terrestial revolution and KPg extinction on mammal diversification. Science 334: 521–524.
16. Adkins RM, Gelke EL, Rowe D, Honeycutt RL (2001) Molecular phylogeny and divergence time estimates for major rodent groups: Evidence from multiple genes. Mol Biol Evol 18: 777–791.
17. Rutschmann F (2006) Molecular dating of phylogenetic trees: a brief review of current methods that estimate divergence times. Divers Distrib 12: 35–48.
18. Li Q, Zheng S-H (2005) Note on four species of dipodids (Dipodidae, Rodentia) from the Late Miocene Bahe Formation, Lantian, Shaanxi. Vert PalAsiat 43: 283–296.
19. Li Q, Meng J (2010) Erlianomys combinatus, a primitive myodont rodent from the Eocene Arshanto Formation, Nuhetingboerhe, Nei Mongol, China. Vert PalAsiat 48: 133–144.
20. Zhang Q, Xia L, Kimura Y, Shenbrot G, Zhang Z-Q, et al. (2012) Tracing the origin and diversification of Dipodoidea (Order: Rodentia): Evidence from fossil record and molecular phylogeny. Evol Biol. doi: 10.1007/s11692-11012-19167-11696.
21. Tong Y-S (1997) Middle Eocene small mammals from Liguanqiao Basin of Henan Province and Yuanqu Basin of Shanxi Province, central China. Paleont Sinica, N S C 26.
22. Tong Y-S (1992) Papporicetodon, a pre-Oligocene cricetid genus (Rodentia) from central China. Vert PalAsiat 30: 1–16.
23. Jacobs LJ, Flynn LJ (2005) Of mice again: the Siwalik rodent record, murine distribution, and molecular clocks. In: Lieberman DE, Simth RJ, Kelley SJ, editors. Interpreting the past:

Essays on human, primate, and mammal evolution in honor of David Pilbeam. Boston, MA: Brill Academic Publishers. pp. 63–80.
24. Walton AH (1997) Rodents. In: Kay RF, Madden RH, Cifelli RL, Flynn JJ, editors. Vertebrate paleontology in the Neotropics The Miocene Fauna of La Venta, Colombia. Washington, DC: Smithsonian Institution Press. pp. 392–409.
25. Wyss AR, Flynn JJ, Norell MA, Swisher CC, Charrier R, et al. (1993) South America's earliest rodent and recognition of a new interval of mammalian evolution. Nature 365: 434–437.
26. Luo Z-X, Crompton AW, Sun A-L (2001) A New Mammaliaform from the Early Jurassic and Evolution of Mammalian Characteristics. Science 292: 1535–1540.
27. Luo Z-X, Yuan C-X, Meng Q-J, Ji Q (2011) A Jurassic eutherian mammal and the divergence of marsupials and placentals. Nature 476: 442–445.
28. Tomiya S (2011) A new basal Caniform (Mammalia: Carnivora) from the middle Eocene of North America and remarks on the phylogeny of early carnivorans. PLoS one 6: e24146.
29. Drummond AJ, Rambaut A (2007) BEAST: Bayesian evolutionary analysis by sampling trees. BMC Evol Biol 7: 214.
30. Ronquist F, Huelsenback JP (2003) Bayesian phylogenetic inference under mixed models. Bioinformations 19: 1572–1574.
31. Guindon S, Gascuel O (2003) A simple, fast and accurate algorithm to estimate large phylogenies by maximum likelihood. Syst Biol 52: 696–704.
32. Sanderson MJ (2003) r8s: inferring absolute rates of molecular evolution and divergence times in the absence of a molecular clock. Bioinformatics 19: 301–302.
33. Asher RJ, Meng J, Wible JR, McKenna MC, Rougier GW, et al. (2005) Stem Lagomorpha and the Antiquity of Glires. Science 307: 1091–1094.
34. Li C-K, Chow M-C (1994) The origin of rodents. In: Tomida Y, editor. Rodent and lagomorph families of Asian origins and diversification. Tokyo, Japan: National Science Museum.
35. Hartenberger JL (1982) A review of the Eocene rodents of Pakistan. Univ Mich Mus Paleo Contr 26: 19–35.
36. Sallam HM, Seiffert ER, Steiper ME, Simons EL (2009) Fossil and molecular evidence constain scenarios for the early evolutionary and biogeographic history of hystricognathous rodents. Proc Natl Acad Sci 106: 16722–16727.
37. Fitch WM, Beintema JJ (1990) Correcting parsimonious trees for unseen nucleotide substitutions: The effect of dense branching as exemplified by ribnuclease. Mol Biol Evol 7: 438–443.
38. Fitch WM, Bruschi M (1987) The evolution of prokaryotic ferredoxins-with a general method correcting for unobserved substitutions in less branched lineages. Mol Biol Evol 4: 381–394.
39. Venditti C, Meade A, Pagel M (2006) Detecting the node-sensity artifact in phylogeny reconstruction. Syst Biol 55: 637–643.
40. Ji Q, Luo ZX, Yuan CX, Wible JR, Zhang JP, et al. (2002) The earliest known eutherian mammal. Nature: 816–822.
41. Kielan-Jaworowska Z, Cifelli RL, Luo ZX (2004) Mammals from the age of dinosaurs: origin, evolution, and structure. New York: Columbia University Press.
42. Marivaux L, Vianey-Liaud M, Jaeger J (2004) High-level phylogeny of early Tertiary rodents: dental evidence. Zool J Linnean Soc 142: 105–134.
43. Huchon D, Madsen O, Sibbald MJJB, Ament K, Stanhope MJ, et al. (2002) Rodent phylogeny and a timescale for the evolution of Glires: Evidence from an extensive taxon sampling using three nuclear genes. Mol Biol Evol 19: 1053–1065.
44. Blanga-Kanfi S, Miranda H, Penn O, Pupko T, DeBry RW, et al. (2009) Rodent phylogeny revised: analysis of six nuclear genes from all major rodent clades. BMC Evol Biol 9: 71.
45. Wible JR, Rougier GW, Novacek MJ, Asher RJ (2007) Cretaceous eutherians and Laurasian origin for placental mammals near the K/T boundary. Nature 447: 1003–1006.

46. Cartwright P, Collins A (2007) Fossil and phylogenies: integrating multiple lines of evidence to investigate the origin of early major metazoan lineages. Integr Comp Biol 47: 744–751.
47. Maddison DR, Maddison WP (2003) MacClade 4: analysis of phylogeny and character evolution, version 4.06. Sunderland, MA: Sinauer Associates.
48. Posada D, Crandal K (1998) MODELTEST: testing the model of DNA substitution. Bioinformatics 14: 817.
49. Ronquist F, Huelsenbeck JP (2003) MrBayes 3: Bayesian phylogenetic inference under mixed models. Bioinformatics 19: 1572.
50. Drummond AJ, Ho SYW, Phillips MJ, Rambaut A (2006) Relaxed phylogenetics and dating with confidence. PLos Biology 4: e88.
51. Sun B, Yue L-P, Wang Y-Q, Meng J, Wang J-Q, et al. (2009) Magnetostratigraphyof the Early Paleogene in the Erlian Basin. J Stratigraphy 33: 62–68.
52. Sun J-M, Ye J, Wu W-Y, Ni X-J, Bi S-D, et al. (2010) Late Oligocene-Miocene mid-latitude aridification and wind patterns in Asian interior. Geology 38: 515– 518.
53. Meng J, Ye J, Wu W-Y, Ni X-J, Bi S-D (2008) The Neogene Dingshanyanchi Formation in northern Junggar basin of Xinjiang and its stratigraphic implications. Vertebrata PalAsiat 46: 90–110.
54. Qiu Z-D (1996) Middle Miocene micromammalian fauna from the Tunggur, Nei Mongol. Beijing: Science Press.
55. Wu W-Y, Meng J, Ye J, N iX-J, Bi S-D, et al. (2009) The Miocene mammals from Dingshanyanchi Formation of northern Junggar Basin, Xinjiang. Vertebrata PalAsiat 47: 208.
56. Zazhigin VS, Lopatin AV (2000) The history of the Dipodoidea (Rodentia, Mammalia) in the Miocene of Asia: 3. Allactaginae. Paleont J 34: 553–565.

CHAPTER 8

A silicified Early Triassic marine assemblage from Svalbard

William J. Foster, Silvia Danise & Richard J. Twitchett

[a]*Jackson School of Geosciences, University of Texas, Austin, TX 78712, US*

[b]*Earth Sciences, Plymouth University, Plymouth, PL4 8AA, UK*

[c]*Department of Earth Sciences, Natural History Museum, London, SW7 5BD, UK*

[d]*Department of Geology, University of Georgia, Athens, GA 30602, USA*

ABSTRACT

Understanding how the marine biosphere recovered from the late Permian mass extinction event is a major evolutionary question. The quality of the global fossil record of this interval is, however, somewhat poor due to preservational, collection and sampling biases. Here we report a new earliest Induan (*Hindeodus parvus* Zone) marine assemblage from the Deltadalen Member of the Vikinghøgda Formation, central Spitsbergen, which fills a critical gap in knowledge. The fully silicified fossils comprise the oldest silicified assemblage known from the Triassic and provide critical new systematic data. For its age, the assemblage is exceptionally diverse with 14 species of bivalves and gastropods, as well as conodonts and ammonoids. Four new bivalve species (*Austrotindaria antiqua*, *A. svalbardensis*, *Nucinella taylori* and *N. nakremi*) and one new gastropod species (*Glabrocingulum parvum*) are described, and five families are recorded in the Induan for the first time. Some of the common and globally widespread Early Triassic taxa, such as *Unionites*, are also present, and their exceptional preservation reveals key morphological characters that are documented for the first time. Taxonomic and ecological revisions based on these new data suggest that shallow-infaunal deposit-feeders were a dominant component of pre-Spathian benthic communities. The gastropods and bivalves all possessed a planktotrophic larval stage, which may have been a particular advantage in the wake of the late Permian mass extinction.

Keywords: extinction, Early Triassic, diversification, Mollusca, Protobranchia, chemosymbiosis

1. INTRODUCTION

The aftermath of the late Permian mass extinction represents a key interval in the diversification of marine biota. Even though 78% of marine genera are estimated to have gone extinct during the late Permian event, no novel phyla or classes and only one new mode of life originated during the extinction aftermath (Erwin et al. 1987; Foster & Twitchett 2014). The re-diversification of benthic groups in the wake of the extinction, such as bivalves (Nakazawa & Runnegar 1973; Komatsu et al. 2004; Fraiser & Bottjer 2005; Hautmann 2007; Posenato 2008) and gastropods (Erwin & Pan 1996; Nützel 2005; Gründel & Nützel 2012), is typically described as occurring in the Middle Triassic, resulting in the traditional view of a 'delayed' post-Permian recovery. The Early Triassic fossil record is, however, notoriously poor, as evidenced by an unusually high number of Lazarus taxa, due to the typical mouldic preservation of shells (Nakazawa & Runnegar 1973; Wheeley & Twitchett 2005) and their small, easily overlooked sizes (Hautmann & Nützel 2005), as well as the substantial regional and latitudinal sampling bias towards low (tropical) palaeolatitudes of the Palaeotethys (Foster & Twitchett 2014).

Better preserved benthic fossil assemblages have been reported from the Induan of South China (Kaim et al. 2010; Hautmann et al. 2011, 2015) and Primorye, Russia (Shigeta et al. 2009), and from the Olenekian of the western USA (Batten & Stokes 1986; Hautmann & Nützel 2005; Nützel & Schulbert 2005; Pruss et al. 2015) and Pakistan (Wasmer et al. 2012; Kaim et al. 2013). In addition, a partially silicified fauna is known from the Griesbachian of Oman (Twitchett et al. 2004; Wheeley & Twitchett 2005; Oji & Twitchett 2015). Studies of those assemblages have shown that a greater number of bivalve, gastropod and crinoid lineages survived the late Permian mass extinction event and/or were present in the Early Triassic than previously thought. These partially silicified and better preserved assemblages still lack key diagnostic characters of many taxa, however, especially the internal morphology of bivalve shells, making taxonomic assignments often equivocal. Better preserved early Induan (Griesbachian) fossil assemblages from palaeotropical localities have been critical in demonstrating that taxonomically and ecologically diverse benthic ecosystems reappeared locally in some settings by the second conodont zone of the Triassic in the Neotethys (Twitchett et al. 2004). At higher latitudes, however, early Induan shelly benthic assemblages are rarely reported and typically consist of poorly preserved cosmopolitan generalists, such as Claraia, Unionites, Lingularia and Warthia (Spath 1930; Mørk et al. 1999; Zonneveld et al. 2007). In these regions, trace fossils are typically used as a measure of documenting ecosystem collapse and recovery (following Twitchett 2006) and demonstrate that rapid local recovery of the infauna took place within the earliest Induan (Twitchett & Barras 2004; Beatty et al. 2008; Zonneveld et al. 2010). From their analysis of global fossil occurrences, Foster & Twitchett (2014) also concluded that during the Induan the benthic fauna of the extratropical northern palaeolatitudes contained a greater ecological diversity than that of the palaeotropics.

Here, we describe the first silicified fossil assemblage from the Lower Triassic of the northern palaeolatitudes. The assemblage was recovered from the lower Griesbachian of central Spitsbergen, Svalbard, making it the oldest silicified assemblage known from the Mesozoic. It is the first fully silicified assemblage of Early Triassic age to be found, and the exquisite preservation of the internal and external morphology of the bivalve and gastropod shells provides critical new taxonomic data that have major implications for our understanding of the response of marine ecosystems to the late Permian mass extinction event and of the stratigraphical ranges of several molluscan families.

2. MATERIAL AND METHODS

The fossil assemblage described herein was recovered from two carbonate concretions, collected by WJF and RJT in 2013 from 11.9 and 12.6 m above the base of the Deltadalen Member of the Vikinghøgda Formation, Lusitaniadalen, Svalbard (N78_17054.800, E016_43059.300; Fig. 1). The fossils were extracted in the laboratory by first mechanically disaggregating 3 kg samples to expose larger fossils. Remaining rock fragments were then dissolved using the buffered formic acid technique of Jeppsson & Anehus (1995). To maximize yield, the residue was collected at c. 12 hour intervals, washed thoroughly with tap water to remove any excess solution and to avoid crystal growth, and dried. The buffered solution was renewed every

48 hours. Heavy liquid separation (Mitchell & Heckert 2010) was used to separate the fossils from the remaining residue. The specimens are housed in the Natural History Museum, London (NHMUK).

3. GEOLOGICAL SETTING

During the Early Triassic, the Svalbard archipelago was situated at c. 45–50^{0}N in the southern part of the Boreal Ocean (Fig. 1; Hounslow et al. 2008). In central Spitsbergen, the Vikinghøgda Formation, described by Mørk et al. (1999), records deposition through the latest Permian and entire Early Triassic in a siliciclastic, open-marine, shelf setting. It is divided into three members, of which the Deltadalen Member is the lowest (Mørk et al. 1999). At the study site in Lusitaniadalen, the basal 1.6 m of the Deltadalen Member is composed of bedded, well-bioturbated, fine- to medium-grained, glauconitic sandstones that are very similar to the underlying Kapp Starostin Formation except that they lack diagenetic chert nodules (Mørk et al. 1999; Nabbefeld et al. 2010). These sandstones contain a diverse trace fossil assemblage, indicating a fully functional benthic ecosystem that was living under well-oxygenated conditions (Nabbefeld et al. 2010). In contrast, the body fossil assemblage is limited, comprising mainly the phosphatic-shelled lingulid brachiopods, which may indicate preservational bias.

The sandstones record the onset of marine transgression (Mørk et al. 1999; Nabbefeld et al. 2010), with the base of the overlying laminated, silty mudstones marking significant deepening. Several horizons of cemented siltstones and tabular concretions are found in the lower few metres of this mudstone-dominated interval and contain coarser laminae with abundant ichthyoliths and disarticulated lingulid shells. Occasional, 1–5 cm thick, fine-grained, pyritic and glauconitic, graded, cemented sandstones, interpreted as distal tempestites, also occur within the laminated silty mudstones. Biomarker data support the interpretation based on field observations that deposition took place under anoxic and periodically euxinic conditions during transgression and maximum flooding, with evidence of phytoplankton blooms in the surface waters likely driven by nutrient influx (Nabbefeld et al. 2010).

From c. 10 m above the base of the mudstones, the lithologies become noticeably coarser with a greater proportion of interbedded siltstones and very fine sandstones, presumably due to progradation or sea level fall. The coarser, heterolithic beds are bioturbated, initially by millimetre-diameter Planolites and then with the addition of Skolithos and Arenicolites about 1.5 m higher, indicative of environmental amelioration and deposition under more persistently oxygenated conditions.

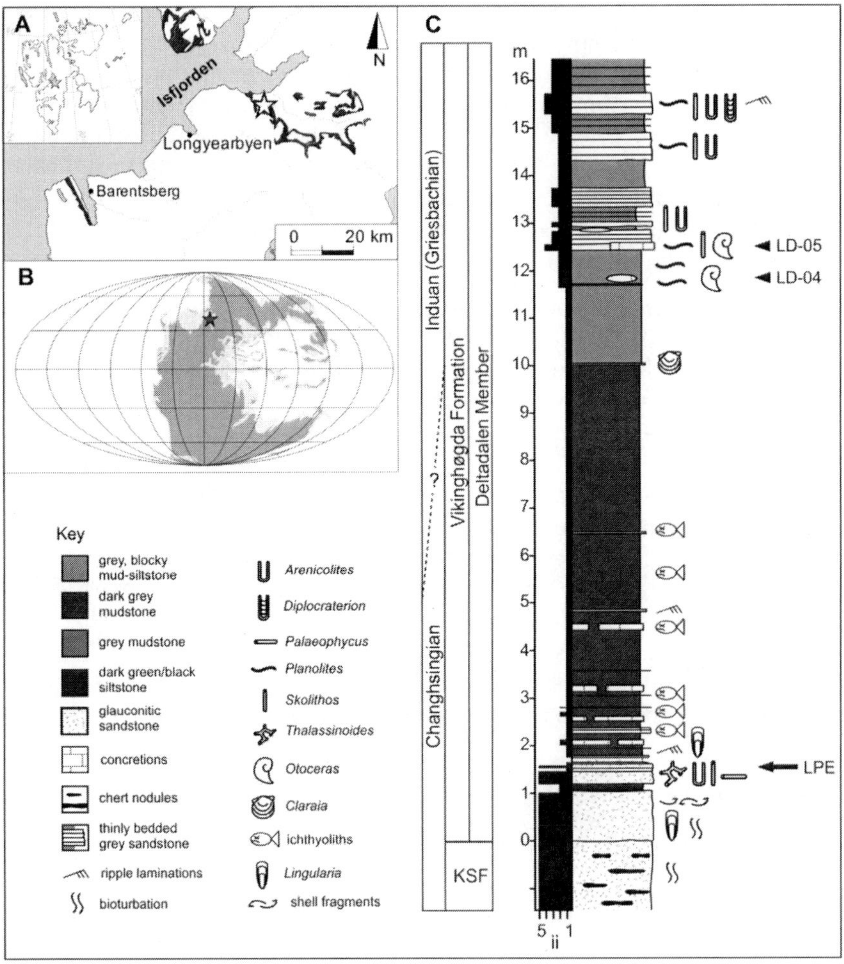

Figure 1. Locality and stratigraphy of the studied section in Lusitaniadalen. A, locality map of the Lusitaniadalen section; B, palaeogeographical position; C, stratigraphical column indicating the position of the sampled concretionary levels (LD-04 and LD-05) and disappearance of bioturbation associated with marine ecosystem collapse and the Late Permian mass extinction (LPE; modified from Nabbefeld et al. 2010). Abbreviations: KSF, Kapp Starostin Formation; ii, ichnofabric index. Palaeogeography after Blakey (2012).

The ichnofabric index remains low (ii2–3), however, and the burrows are small (diameters <5 mm) and do not penetrate deeply, indicating that the environment was probably still not fully optimal for benthic colonization. Earliest Triassic ammonoids, conodonts and a moderate benthic assemblage have already been recorded from the Planolitesdominated interval (Mørk et al. 1999). One of the concretions that yield the silicified assemblage documented in this study derives from that same horizon, 12.6 m above the base of the formation. The second concretion was collected from c. 65 cm lower (Fig. 1)

The age of the Deltadalen Member is well constrained by biostratigraphy (ammonoids and conodonts) and magnetostratigraphy, with deposition recorded from the upper Changhsingian, prior to the late Permian mass extinction event, through most of the Induan (Mørk et al. 1999; Hounslow et al. 2008; Nakrem et al. 2008). Locally, the late Permian extinction event is recorded by the disappearance of prolific bioturbation just below the top of the glauconitic sandstones, 1.6 m above the base of the member (Nabbefeld et al. 2010). From conodont evidence, Nakrem et al. (2008) inferred that the Permian/Triassic boundary occurs between 5 and 11 m above the base of the Deltadalen Member. Claraia cf. wangi is recorded 10.1 m above the base of the member at Lusitaniadalen, indicative of a Griesbachian age. The silicified assemblages described herein are of earliest Griesbachian (earliest Induan) age, and are assigned to the upper part of the Otoceras boreale Zone, which corresponds to the basal Triassic Hindeodus parvus Conodont Zone (Orchard 2007).

Systematic palaeontology

Phylum Brachiopoda Dum_eril, 1805

Class Lingulata Goryansky & Popov, 1985

Order Lingulida Waagen, 1885 Family Discinidae Gray, 1840

Genus Orbiculoidea d'Orbigny, 1847

Type species. Orbicula forbesii Davidson, 1848; Silurian, Wenlock; West Midlands, England.

Diagnosis. The generic diagnosis follows Mergl (2006). Shell thin, strongly dorsibiconvex, subcircular, with subtrapezoidal outline of the posterior part. Ornament on both valves composed of regular raised concentric fila separated by broader interspaces. Dorsal valve is conical to subconical with subcentral apex; ventral valve with subcentral apex. Ventral valve depressed conical with subcentral apex. Pedicle track narrow, tapering posteriorly and anteriorly closed by shallow listrium; foramen in posterior end of listrium with short internal tube.

Orbiculoidea winsnesi Gobbet, 1963 (Fig. 2A)

1963 Orbiculoidea winsnesi Gobbett: 46, pl. 1, figs 4, 5.

Material. One dorsal valve from LD-04 (NHMUK PI BE 3238).

Description. Shell outline is subcircular, with its length slightly greater than the width. The dorsal valve is inflated to an apex, which is located about a third of the diameter from the anterior margin. Shell smooth, except for fine concentric growth lines.

Remarks. Extant solitary discinids are sessile, epifaunal invertebrates that attach to hard surfaces with a suckerlike pedicle (Mergl 2010). They have been attaching to shelled invertebrates since the Ordovician (Mergl 2010), and one of the specimens described herein is attached to an ammonoid. Discinids are suspension feeders, and their co-occurrence with lingulids in laminated black shales has led some authors to interpret them as being tolerant of low-oxygen conditions (Savoy 1992; Hallam 1995; Mergl 2010).

Figure 2. A, Orbiculoidea winsnesi Gobbet, 1963, NHMUK PI BE 3238, dorsal view, dorsal valve; B, Austrotindaria? Canalensis (Catullo, 1846), NHMUK PI MB 1198, external view, left valve; C–G, Promyalina schamarae (Bittner, 1899), external view; C, D, NHMUK PI MB 1204; C, right valve; D, left valve. E, F, NHMUK PI MB 1203; E, right valve; F, left valve. G, NHMUK PI MB 1202, right valve. Scale bars: A, B, G = 2 mm, C–F = 1 mm.

Mode of life. Surficial, stationary, attached, suspension feeder (Mergl 2010).

Phylum Mollusca Linnaeus, 1758

Class Bivalvia Linnaeus, 1758

Order Pterioida Newell, 1965

Family Myalinidae Frech, 1891

Genus Promyalina Kittl, 1904

Type species. Promyalina hindi Kittl, 1904; Permian, Changhsingian; near Sarajevo, Bosnia-Herzegovina.

Diagnosis. Outline mytiliform and less triangular than Myalina; dorsal margin slightly convex, moderately thickened; narrow beak present. Left valve inflated below the umbo. Inequivalve with the right valve being less inflated and less curved.

Promyalina schamarae (Bittner, 1899) (Fig. 2C–G)

1899 Myalina schamarae Bittner 19, pl. 4, figs 20–25.

2009 Promyalina schamarae (Bittner); Kumagae & Nakazawa: 157, fig. 144, 4–5.

Material. Three specimens from LD-04 (NHMUK PE PEI 5484; NHMUK PI MB 1202; NHMUK PI MB 1205) and seven specimens from LD-05 (NHMUK PI MB 1188; NHMUK PI MB 1203–1204; NHMUK PE PEI 5475– 5476; NHMUK PE PEI 5500; NHMUK PE PEI 5503).

Description. Shell is small, mytiliform, inequilateral, prosocline, higher than long, and moderately inflated. Umbo is small, terminal and prosogyrate. Posterior dorsal margin is straight. Posterior margin is slightly convex, forming a rounded posteroventral margin. Anterior margin is long, nearly straight or weakly acute and partly depressed near the umbo.

Remarks. The internal characters of the shells cannot be observed because all the specimens are articulated. Externally, the shells resemble Promyalina schamarae from the Griesbachian Lazurnaya Bay Formation, Russia (Shigeta et al. 2009), and are therefore assigned to this species. These specimens differ from P. groenlandica (Newell, 1955), as the beak does not project beyond the dorsal margin, and from P. spathi in having a more convex anterior margin. **Mode of life.** Surficial, stationary, attached, suspension feeder (Stanley 1972).

Order Solemyoida Dall, 1889

Family Nucinellidae Vokes, 1956

Diagnosis. Shell nuculoid, obliquely oval, higher than long, monomyarian with anterior adductor muscle scar only. Hinge with subumbonal taxodont teeth and single elongate lateral tooth on the anterior dorsal margin. Ligament mostly opisthodetic, wholly external or in a sunken resilifer.

Remarks. Although living nucinellids are sometimes classified in the family Manzanellidae, which extends back into the Permian (e.g. Coan & Valentich-Scott 2012), Oliver & Taylor (2012) argued that the Nucinellidae and Manzanellidae should be separated on morphological grounds and their conclusions are followed here. Manzanella, the type genus of Manzanellidae, is dimyarian and subcircular in outline, with its taxodont teeth lying posterior to the beak. In contrast, Nucinella and Huxleyia (i.e. the Nucinellidae) are both monomyarian and elliptical, with their teeth positioned anterior to the beak (Oliver & Taylor 2012).

Genus Nucinella Wood, 1851

Type species. Pleurodon ovalis Wood, 1840; Neogene, Pliocene; Suffolk, England.

Diagnosis. Nucinellids with external ligament.

Remarks. Of the two genera described for the Nucinellidae, Huxleyia has a mostly internal ligament set in a sunken resilifer, whereas Nucinella has an external ligament. The specimens described herein have an opisthodetic or amphidetic ligament and so are assigned to Nucinella.

Nucinella taylori sp. nov. (Fig. 3)

Diagnosis. A small Nucinella having a nuculoid shape, smooth shell except for growth lines with three subumbonal and two anterior pointed blade-like teeth, with no triangular flat area below the dentition; opisthodetic ligament.

Holotype. Disarticulated left valve, NHMUK PI MB 1206, L=-04; length = 1.6 mm, height = 1.6 mm.

Paratypes. Disarticulated right valve, NHMUK PI MB 1209, LD-04; length = 1.6 mm, height = 1.6 mm; disarticulated right valve, NHMUK PI MB 1210, LD-05; length = 2.1 mm, height = 2.3 mm.

Other material. Two specimens from LD-04 (NHMUK PI MB 1207–1208) and three specimens from LD-05 (NHMUK PE PEI 5500; NHMUK PE PEI 5506; HMUK PE PEI 5517). Fifty-three prodissoconch valves from LD- 04 (NHMUK PI MB 1211–1217; NHMUK PE PEI 5481) and 36 prodissoconch valves from LD-05 (NHMUK PI MB 1218).

Derivation of name. Named after Dr John Taylor (Natural History Museum, London, UK) in recognition of his work on chemosymbiotic bivalve molluscs.

Description. Shell is small, thin, inequilateral, equivalve, with a nuculoid, suboval outline. Posterior dorsal margin is slightly incurved; anterior margin almost straight. Opisthogyrate, beaks close to posterior margin, umbo prominent. Smooth shell, except for concentric, irregularly spaced growth lines. Monomyarian: posterior adductor muscle scar absent; anterior adductor large, oval. Opisthodetic ligament, prominent, external does not invade the hinge plate. Hinge made by five pointed blade-like teeth as a single arched series, with the anterior subumbonal teeth being smaller and wider than the posterior ones. A single, long lateral tooth. Left valve with a secondary ridge creating a shallow socket.

Figure 3. Nucinella taylori sp. nov. A, holotype, NHMUK PI MB 1206, external view, left valve; B, paratype, NHMUK PI MB 1209, external view, right valve; C, paratype, NHMUK PI MB 1210, internal view, right valve; D, holotype, NHMUK PI MB 1206, internal view, left valve; E, F, paratype, NHMUK PI MB 1209, internal view, right valve; G–J, prodissoconchs of N. taylori; G, NHMUK PI MB 1213, external view, left valve; H, NHMUK PI MB 1211, external view, right valve; I, NHMUK PI MB 1214, internal view, left valve; J, NHMUK PI MB 1211, internal view, right valve. Scale bars: A–F = 500 mm; G–J = 100 mm.

Prodissoconch valves: outline nuculoid and suboval. Posterior margin is distinct, long and slightly incurved. Inequilateral, with beaks close to posterior margin, and sculpture consists of irregularly spaced growth laminae. Ventral valve margin has a narrow flat platform. Five anterior and 11 posterior hinge teeth. Amphidetic ligament, lying between the beak and anterior hinge plate.

Remarks. These specimens are most similar to the extant nucinellid Nucinella serrei in their small size, number of posterior and anterior hinge teeth and opisthodetic ligament. However, they lack a flat triangular area below the teeth dentition and a small circular pit at the end of the lateral tooth, which supports their separation.

The majority of extant Nucinella range from intertidal to 500 m deep (La Perna 2005), but some species have been described from water depths exceeding 3000 m (Oliver & Taylor 2012). A large fossil Nucinella species has been described from a Late Cretaceous cold-seep deposit (Amano et al. 2007), showing that this genus may inhabit a wide range of sulphide-rich environmental settings. Bacterial symbiosis with sulphur-oxidizing bacteria is confirmed for N. owenensis and has been inferred for all species of the Nucinellidae (Oliver & Taylor 2012). Nucinella taylori sp. nov. supplants N. birkelundi from the Late Jurassic (Clausen & Wignall 1990) and Nucinella? sp. from the Late Triassic (Nützel & Kaim 2014) as the oldest known species of Nucinella, and extends the range of the genus to the basal Triassic H. parvus Conodont Zone.

The prodissoconch valves are very similar to adult specimens of Nucinella taylori sp. nov. except that they have more hinge teeth, which appears to reflect their premetamorphosis stage of development. The position of the ligament in the prodissoconch valves also differs from adult specimens of N. taylori sp. nov. in being amphidetic rather than opisthodetic, but this character is known to change after metamorphosis (Bernard 1898). The prodissoconch valves most resemble N. taylori sp. nov. rather than N. nakremi sp. nov., but may represent larval stages for either or both species.

Mode of life. Shallow infaunal, fully motile, slow, chemosymbiotic (Oliver & Taylor 2012).

Nucinella nakremi sp. nov. (Fig. 4)

Diagnosis. A small Nucinella having a nuculoid shape, smooth shell except for growth lines. Prosogyrate beak, one to three subumbonal teeth. Ligament amphidetic and does not invade the hinge plate.

Holotype. Disarticulated left valve, NHMUK PI MB 1219, LD-04; length = 1.1 mm, height = 1.1 mm.

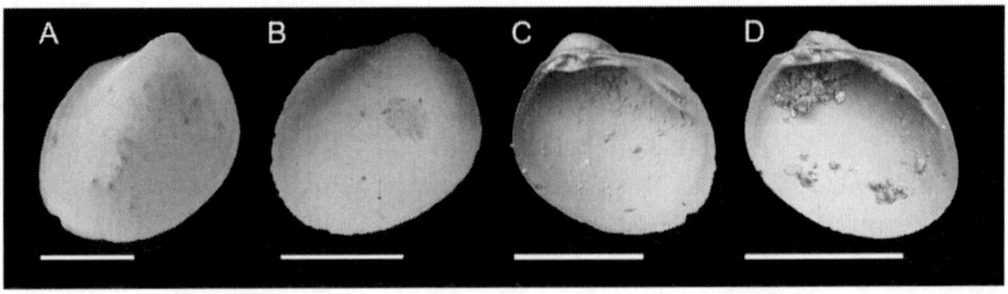

Figure 4. Nucinella nakremi sp. nov. A, holotype, NHMUK PI MB 1219, external view, left valve; B, paratype, NHMUK PI MB 1220, external view, left valve; C, holotype, NHMUK PI MB 1219, interior view, left valve; D, paratype, NHMUK PI MB 1220, interior view (transposed hinge), left valve. Scale bars = 500 μm.

Paratype. Disarticulated left valve, NHMUK PI MB 1220, LD-04; length = 0.9 mm, height = 0.8 mm (transposed hinge).

Other material. Two specimens from LD-04 (NHMUK PI MB 1221–1222). Derivation of name. Named after Dr Hans Arne Nakrem in recognition of his work on Permian and Triassic fossils from Svalbard.

Description. Shell small, nuculoid and ovate. Posterior dorsal margin distinct, slightly incurved; posterior margin rounded. Inequilateral, prosogyrate, with beaks close to anterior margin. Umbo prominent. Smooth, thin shell with very weak growth lines. Monomyarian: posterior adductor muscle scar absent; anterior adductor large, oval. One to two subumbonal, pointed blade-like teeth plus one anterior tooth. Ligament amphidetic, prominent, external does not invade the hinge plate.

Remarks. These specimens differ from other described nucinellid species in having fewer hinge teeth, a more elliptical shape and a prosogyrate beak. Such differences may occur during the ontogeny of Nucinella (e.g. Bernard 1898) and so are not sufficient for assignment to a separate genus. These specimens are, however, considered to represent a separate species rather than an intermediate ontogenetic stage between the protoconch and adult stage of Nucinella taylori. During ontogeny, the shape, size and position of nucinellid subombonal teeth also vary: in earlier stages of development they are more rounded and later they develop a chevron-blade shape with the older teeth making space below the beak for thinner, newer ones (Bernard 1898; La Perna 2004). In contrast, the subumbonal teeth of specimens assigned to N. nakremi and N. taylori have comparable shapes, and so indicate a similar stage of development. Furthermore, because the position of the ligament in nucinellids is fixed after metamorphosis (Bernard 1898; La Perna 2004), and the only subsequent ontogenetic change is an increase in ligament size with age, the differences in ligament position between N. nakremi and N. taylori cannot be ontogenetic. If the specimens assigned to N. nakremi were included as an intermediate ontogenetic stage of N. taylori, the ontogenetic pattern would not match any known nucinellid (cf. Bernard 1898; La Perna 2004), and, therefore, the differences in the subumbonal teeth and the position of the ligament support their separation.

A specimen of Nucinella nakremi sp. nov. includes an example of a transposed hinge on a left valve (Fig. 4D). Instead of the normal left valve arrangement of three hinge teeth and a lateral secondary ridge creating a secondary socket, this specimen has two hinge teeth and a lateral tooth (i.e. the normal right valve arrangement). An alternative interpretation is that this specimen represents an earlier ontogenetic stage, but this is rejected because even though the specimen is slightly smaller, its lateral tooth is more prominent than in a typical left valve arrangement and both the subumbonal and lateral teeth appear to fit with the expected corresponding valve arrangement. In addition, it has been reported that in the early stages of nucinellid development the second lateral tooth is very small and closer to the subumbonal teeth than later in ontogeny (Bernard 1898), which is not the case with this specimen. Transposed hinges have been reported in a number of bivalve families, but this is the first reported occurrence in a species of Nucinellidae.

Mode of life. Shallow infaunal, fully motile, slow, chemosymbiotic (Oliver & Taylor 2012).

Order Nuculanoida Carter et al., 2000

Family Neilonellidae Schileyko, 1989

Diagnosis. Hinge plate with taxodont teeth in two series, sometimes separated by narrow, plain area, without resilifer; ligament predominantly external, opisthodetic to amphidetic, weak. **Remarks.** The Neilonellidae are very similar to the Nuculanidae, but the lack of a resilifer in mature adults supports their separation (Coan & Valentich-Scott 2012). The new specimens described herein differ from the Malletiidae in lacking conspicuous gapes, and from the Tindariidae in having a short gap in the dentition below the beaks (Di Geronimo & La Perna 1997). The family is currently known from the Jurassic to the present in all oceans, especially in deep water and soft substrates (Coan & Valentich- Scott 2012).

Genus Austrotindaria Fleming, 1948

Type species. Austrotindaria wrighti Fleming 1948; Holocene, Quaternary; Southland, New Zealand. Diagnosis. Delicate almost smooth shell, with weak concentric sculpture. A short, edentulous gap between the posterior and anterior hinge plates. No pallial sinus and without rostrum.

Remarks. The Neilonellidae comprises three valid genera: Neilonella, Austrotindaria and Pseudoneilonella (La Perna 2007). The convex shape of the posterior margin and the presence of an opisthodetic ligament in our specimens indicate better agreement with Austrotindaria than Neilonella (Di Geronimo & La Perna 1997; La Perna 2007). Austrotindaria differs from Neilonella and Pseudoneilonella by having a delicate, almost smooth shell rather than a sturdy, sculptured shell, and by having a small elongate pit below the posterior and anterior teeth (La Perna 2007). This genus is currently known from the Miocene to Recent (La Perna 2007; Coan & Valentich-Scott 2012), and the specimens identified in his study extend the range of the genus to the beginning of the Triassic.

Austrotindaria antiqua sp. nov. (Fig. 5)

1899 Anodontophora (Myacites) fassaensis (Wissmann); Bittner: 22, pl. 3, figs 28–33.

1908 Anoplophoria (Myacites) fassaensis (Wissmann); von Wittenburg: 33, fig. 15.

1926 Anodontophora fassaensis (Wissmann); Matsushita: pl. 8, fig. 11.

1963 Unionites fassaensis (Wissmann); Ciriacks: 81, pl. 16, fig. 13.

1988 Unionites fassaensis var. brevis Neri & Posenato: 94, pl. 2, fig. 8.

2009 Unionites fassaensis (Wissmann); Kumagae & Nakazawa: 166, fig. 145, 5–9.

2014 Unionites? fassaensis (Wissmann); Pan et al.: 151, fig. 5G, H.

2015 Unionites fassaensis (Wissmann); Hofmann et al.: 8, fig. 4K.

2015 cf. Unionites fassaensis (Wissmann); Foster et al.: 381, fig. 4L.

Diagnosis. Shell small, smooth except for concentric growth lines, subtrigonal, inequilateral, prosogyrate; taxodont hinge dentition with more than 50% fewer anterior than posterior ones, obtusely chevron-shaped teeth, hinge plate interrupted below the beak by an edentulous gap, a small rounded triangular pit below the edentulous gap; ligament opisthodetic.

Holotype. Disarticulated right valve, NHMUK PI MB 1240, LD-04; length = 4.0 mm, height = 3.0 mm. Paratype. Disarticulated left valve, NHMUK PI MB 1241, LD-04; length = 4.6 mm, height = 3.4 mm.

Other material. Eight specimens from LD-04 (NHMUK PI MB 1194; NHMUK PE PEI 5479; HMUK PE PEI 5486–5488; NHMUK PE PEI 5513; NHMUK PE PEI 5520) and 18 specimens from LD-05 (NHMUK PI MB 1191; NHMUK PI MB 1196–1197; NHMUK PI MB 1199; NHMUK PI MB 1242; NHMUK PE PEI 5475– 5476; NHMUK PE PEI 5483; NHMUK PE PEI 5494; NHMUK PE PEI 5497; NHMUK PE PEI 5499–5501; NHMUK PE PEI 5504;

NHMUK PE PEI 5506; NHMUK PE PEI 5515). Two prodissoconch valves from LD-04 (NHMUK PI MB 1243–1244).

Derivation of name. Latin, antiqua (ancient) referring to this species being the oldest known of the genus.

Description. Equivalve, inequilateral shell with a subtrigonal outline and a beak positioned approximately 30% along the length of the dorsal margin from the posterior; H/L ratio 0.6–1. Conspicuously tumid. Umbo prosogyrate, prominent, moderately broad, rounded and projects above the hinge margin. Slightly rounded and gently sloping anterodorsal margin. Posterodorsal margin almost straight to slightly rounded, gently sloping, with a slight angled junction with the posterior margin. Ventral margin deeply rounded. Escutcheon short, relatively broad, elliptical; lunule narrow. Shell smooth with fine concentric growth lines; entire inner margin smooth. mall ligament, external, opisthodetic, with a well-defined margin and wellrounded triangular pit seated beneath the edentulous gap. Hinge plate with taxodont teeth in two series, sometimes separated by a narrow, plain area, without resilifer, that is narrow below the beak, broadening towards the anterior and posterior ends. Robust teeth, moderately long and blunt, with more than 50% fewer anterior than posterior ones. Smooth ventral margin. No pallial line, sinus or muscle scars are present. As the size of the shell increases the edentulous gap becomes proportionally smaller and more central, and moves externally.

Remarks. The external morphology of these specimens is identical to most Early Triassic specimens previously described as 'Unionites' fassaensis, which is one of the most widespread bivalve species from the Lower Triassic and is also a problematic dustbin taxon that includes a range of different morphologies. These specimens differ from the original description and figures of 'Myacites' fassaensis Wissmann, 1841 in having a less elongated posterior margin and a more prosogyrate beak. Due to poor preservation, however, little is known about the internal morphology of Early Triassic specimens assigned to U. fassaensis, which has created some uncertainty (Hautmann et al. 2013). Internally, these new specimens lack the following characters that Geyer et al. (2005) determined were diagnostic of Unionites: a nymph extending nearly half of the posterior margin; an impressed adductor muscle scar; an overlap of the anterior hinge; and a deeply impressed lunule and posterior keel. Thus, these specimens cannot be assigned to Unionites. The presence of taxodont hinge dentition, an opisthodetic ligament and lack of ornamentation are, however, characteristic of the genus Austrotindaria.

The more prosogyrate beak means that these specimens have a similar external morphology to Middle Triassic Unionites specimens (e.g. Geyer et al. 2005), but apart from possessing a faint posterior keel they lack the diagnostic criteria of Unionites. Furthermore, the Unionites specimens described by Geyer et al. (2005) and from this study (see below) all have a strong posterior keel. Thus, these specimens are not assigned to Unionites. These specimens, and all previous specimens assigned to Unionites fassaensis that possess a prosogyrate beak and lack a well-defined posterior keel, are therefore assigned to Austrotindaria antiqua sp. nov.

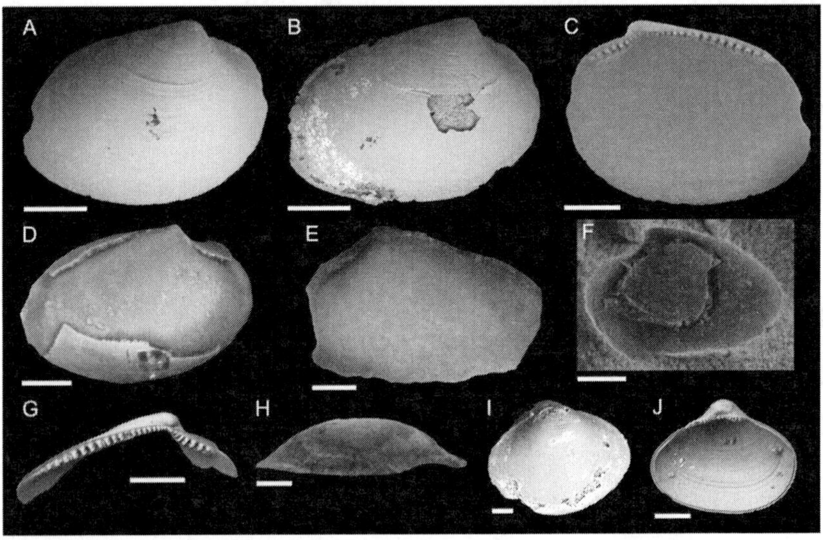

Figure 5. Austrotindaria antiqua sp. nov. A, holotype, NHMUK PI MB 1240, external view, right valve; B, paratype, NHMUK PI MB 1241, external view, right valve; C, holotype, NHMUK PI MB 1240, internal view, right valve; D, NHMUK PI MB 1191, external view, right valve; E, NHMUK PI MB 1199, external view, left valve; F, NHMUK PI MB 1196, external view, right valve; G, NHMUK PI MB 1242, hinge plate of left valve; H, NHMUK PI MB 1194, dorsal view, right valve; I, articulated specimen, NHMUK PI MB 1243; J, larval shell, NHMUK PI MB 1244, left valve. Scale bars: A–C, G = 500 mm; D–F D 1 mm; I, J = 100 μm

Mode of life. Shallow infaunal, fully motile, slow, miner (Stanley 1968).

Austrotindaria svalbardensis sp. nov. (Fig. 6)

1864 Anoplophora fassaensis (Wissmann); Alberti: 137, pl. 3, fig. 8.

1930 Nucula sp. juv. ind; Spath: 53, pl. 7, fig. 12.

2013a Unionites fassaensis (Wissmann); Hofmann et al.: 887, fig. 8, 17–18.

2015 Unionites cf. fassaensis; Hautmann et al.: 890, fig. 10H.

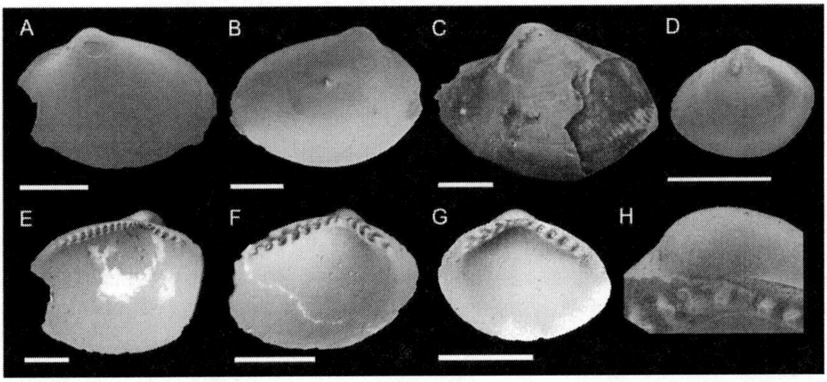

Figure 6. Austrotindaria svalbardensis sp. nov. A, paratype, NHMUK PI MB 1231, external view, left valve; B, holotype, NHMUK PI MB 1223, external view, right valve; C, NHMUK PI MB 1190, left valve, external view; D, larval shell, NHMUK PI MB 1234, external view, right valve; E, NHMUK PI MB 1225, internal view, left valve; F, NHMUK PI MB 1227, internal view, left valve; G, larval shell, NHMUK PI MB 1237, internal view, right valve; H, paratype, posterior and anterior hinge plate junction, NHMUK PI MB 1231. Scale bars = 500 μm.

Diagnosis. Shell small, smooth except for concentric growth lines, subtrigonal, inequilateral, orthogyrate; taxodont hinge dentition with more posterior than anterior teeth, obtusely chevron-shaped teeth, hinge plate interrupted below the beak by an edentulous gap, a small rounded triangular pit below the edentulous gap; ligament opisthodetic.

Holotype. Disarticulated right valve, NHMUK PI MB 1223, LD-04; length = 1.8 mm, height = 1.3 mm.

Paratype. Disarticulated left valve, NHMUK PI MB 1231, LD-04; length = 1.5 mm, height = 1.0 mm.

Other material. Twenty-one specimens from LD-04 (NHMUK PI MB 1190; NHMUK PI MB 1192–1193; NHMUK PI MB 1224–1230; NHMUK PI MB 1232– 1233; NHMUK PI MB 1235–1236; NHMUK PE PEI 5478; NHMUK PE PEI 5482; NHMUK PE PEI 5489; NHMUK PE PEI 5505; NHMUK PE PEI 5509–5510; NHMUK PE PEI 5512; NHMUK PE PEI 5520) and 12 specimens from LD-05 (NHMUK PI MB 1189; NHMUK PI MB 1197; NHMUK PI MB 1200; NHMUK PE PEI 5476; NHMUK PE PEI 5491–5492; NHMUK PE PEI 5496; NHMUK PE PEI 5498; NHMUK PE PEI 5503– 5504; NHMUK PE PEI 5517). Twenty-four prodissoconch valves from LD-04 (NHMUK PI MB 1234; NHMUK PI MB 1237; NHMUK PI MB 1238; NHMUK PE PEI 5520) and five prodissoconch valves from LD-05 (NHMUK PI MB 1239).

Derivation of name. Named after the Svalbard archipelago.

Description. Shell outline subtrigonal, equivalve, inequilateral with beak positioned approximately 60% of the distance along the dorsal margin from the posterior; Height/Length (H/L) ratio 0.6–1; conspicuously tumid. Orthogyrate umbo, prominent, moderately broad, rounded and projected above the hinge margin. Anterodorsal margin slightly rounded and gently sloping. The posterodorsal margin is almost straight to slightly rounded and gently sloping. Ventral margin is smooth and deeply rounded. Escutcheon is short, relatively broad, elliptical; lunule narrow. No sculpture except for fine concentric growth lines; entire inner margin is smooth. Prodissoconch is smooth, broadly subovate, with H/L ratio of 0.6–0.9. Ligament small, external with well-defined margin, opisthodetic, with a well-rounded triangular pit seated beneath the edentulous gap. Hinge plate with taxodont teeth in two series; separated by narrow, plain area, without resilifer, narrow below the beak, broadening towards the anterior and posterior ends. Teeth are robust, moderately long and blunt, with more posterior than anterior teeth, separated by an edentulous gap. As the size of the shell increases the edentulous gap becomes proportionally smaller, more central and moves externally. No pallial line, sinus or muscle scars present.

Remarks. These specimens differ from Austrotindaria antiqua sp. nov. in having a more equal number of anterior to posterior teeth and an orthogyrate beak. The direction of the beak also separates these specimens from unequivocal species of Unionites. In the specimens described here and other Austrotindaria species the beak is orthogyrate to posteriorly opisthogyrate, whereas in Unionites it is prosogyrate. Based on this key character, most specimens previously assigned to Unionites fassaensis, and similar Early Triassic specimens with an orthogyrate beak and no internal morphological detail preserved, are herein assigned to Austrotindaria svalbardensis sp. nov.

These specimens have a very similar shape, size and ornamentation to the type species of Austrotindaria (A. wrighti Fleming); however, they differ in possessing a small, rounded, triangular pit below the edentulous gap, and differ from other Austrotindaria species, such as A. mawheraensis, in lacking a weak posterior rostrum. For these reasons, they are therefore considered a separate species.

Mode of life. Shallow infaunal, fully motile, slow, miner (Stasek 1961; Stanley 1968).

Austrotindaria? canalensis (Catullo, 1846) (Fig. 2B)

1846 Tellina canalensis Catullo: 56, pl. 4, fig. 4.

1899 Anodontophora (Myacites) canalensis (Catullo); Bittner: 23, pl. 3, figs 34–38.

1908 Anoplophoria canalensis (Catullo); von Wittenburg: 281, pl. 5, fig. 6.

1963 Unionites canalensis (Catullo); Ciriacks: 81, pl. 16, figs 11, 12.

1988 Unionites canalensis (Catullo); Neri & Posenato: 94, pl. 2, fig. 8.

2004 Unionites aff. canalensis (Catullo); Kashiyama & Oji: 214, fig. 8F.

2009 Unionites canalensis (Catullo); Kumagae & Nakazawa: 166, fig. 145, 1–4.

2015 Unionites canalensis (Catullo); Hofmann et al.: 481, fig. 4J.

2015 cf. Unionites canalensis (Catullo); Foster et al.: 381, fig. 4K.

Material. Three specimens from LD-05 (NHMUK PI MB 1198; NHMUK PE PEI 5493; NHMUK PE PEI 5500).

Description. Outline subovate to elongate, equivalve, inflated below the umbo; inequilateral with beak lying approximately 62% along the dorsal margin length from posterior; H/L ratio 0.4–0.7. Posterior margin elongated and almost straight, anterior margin narrowly rounded. Escutcheon and lunule indistinct. Umbo orthogyrate, prominent, moderately broad, rounded, projecting above the hinge margin. Ornamented externally with fine concentric growth lines; entire inner margin smooth.

Remarks. The internal characters and hinge in these specimens were not observed and have not been reported for Unionites canalensis. Externally, the shell is virtually identical to those that are typically assigned to U. canalensis (e.g. Hofmann et al. 2015), with a medially placed umbo that is a diagnostic feature of U. canalensis (Catullo, 1846) and an orthogyrate beak. In contrast, all other species of Unionites have a more anteriorly located umbo, and the beak in Unionites is prosogyrate (Geyer et al. 2005). Thus, these Early Triassic specimens clearly do not belong to the genus Unionites. The external features of these specimens are most similar to species of Neilonellidae, such as Austrotindaria benthicola (Dell, 1956). Austrotindaria is the only genus of the Neilonellidae that is reported from the Early Triassic, and these specimens are, therefore, tentatively assigned to it. Without observation of the internal characters, an unequivocal generic assignment cannot be made. The posterior margin is more elongate than in Austrotindaria svalbardensis sp. nov., and these specimens are therefore considered to represent a separate species.

Mode of life. Shallow infaunal, fully motile, slow, miner (Stanley 1968). Family Malletiidae Adams & Adams, 1858 gen. et sp. indet. (Fig. 7) Diagnosis. Subequilteral to inequilateral; usually with elongate, compressed posterior end; sculpture of commarginal striae or ribs; anterior and posterior gapes present; hinge plate weak, with fine taxodont teeth in two series, sometimes separated by plain area, without resilifer; ligament external, opisthodetic to amphidetic, weak; pallial sinus large. Material. Three larval shells from LD-04 (NHMUK PI MB 1248–1250).

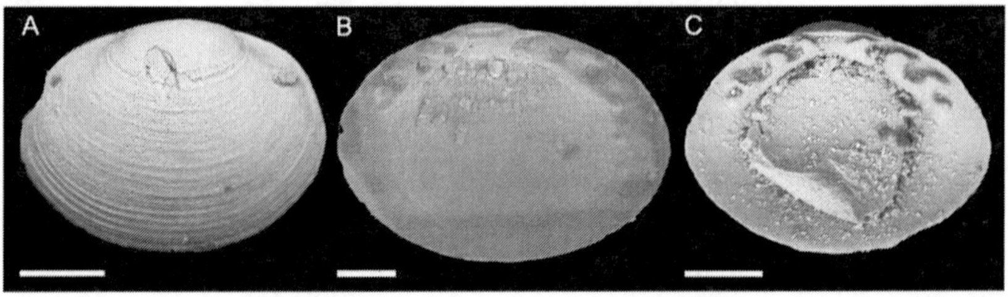

Figure 7. Malletiidae gen et sp. indet., larval shells. A, NHMUK PI MB 1249, external view; B, NHMUK PI MB 1249, internal view; C, NHMUK PI MB 1248, internal view. Scale bars = 100 μm.

Description. Shell is equilateral, elliptical, H/L ratio of 0.7, and moderately inflated. Umbo is broad, orthogyrate, with beak positioned centrally. Shell smooth except for concentric growth lines. Hinge plate has three anterior and three posterior teeth in two series separated by a large plain area with a groove. Ligament is predominantly external, amphidetic and weak.

Remarks. Malletiidae are very similar to Nuculanidae, but the lack of a resilifer in mature adults supports their separation (Coan & Valentich-Scott 2012). These specimens do not belong to the Neilonellidae because they possess a small conspicuous gape between the valves. The Malletiidae is a long-ranging family known from the Ordovician to the Recent, and three genera (Malletia, Palaeoneilo and Taimyrodon) belonging to the family have previously been reported from the Lower Triassic (e.g. He et al. 2007; Wasmer et al. 2012). Externally, these specimens resemble the larval shells of Paleoneilo? fortistriata figured by Wasmer et al. (2012), but they have far fewer hinge teeth. There are also equal numbers of anterior to posterior hinge teeth in these specimens, whereas in P. fortistriata there are many more posterior than anterior teeth (Wasmer et al. 2012).

Mode of life. Shallow infaunal, fully motile, slow, miner (Stanley 1968).

Order Unionoida Stoliczka, 1871

Family Anthracosiidae Amalizky, 1892

Genus Unionites Wissmann, 1841

Type species. Unionites muensteri Wissmann, 1841; Carnian, Late Triassic; South Tyrol, Italy.

Diagnosis. The generic diagnosis follows Geyer et al. (2005). Shell suboval to elongate-elliptical or rectangular to trapeziform; equivalve, inequilateral. Umbo prosogyrate. Shell surface smooth except for growth rugae, or with rather fine commarginal riblets and, rarely, a faint radial ornamentation. Anterior hinge margin of right valve projects beyond the plane of commissure, fitting into a recess in the opposite valve. Small subumbonal groove limits this shell projection posteriorly. Posterior lateral tooth of right valve generally distinct, engaging below posterior dorsal margin of left valve. Hinge of left valve with anterior platform that bears depression for corresponding anterior hinge margin of right valve, followed posteriorly by small, tuberculiform subumbonal tooth. Narrow groove extends parallel to margin at distal part of anterior hinge margin and corresponds to anterior lateral tooth of right valve. Lower part of posterior dorsal margin slightly projects beyond plane of commissure, fitting above posterior lateral tooth of right valve. Ligament fixed on nymph, which extends about half the length of the posterior dorsal margin.

Unionites aff. subrectus (Bittner, 1901) (Fig. 8)

aff. 1901 Anodontophora subrecta Bittner: 100, pl. 7, figs 28–30.

aff. 2003 Unionites subrectus (Bittner); Szente & V€or€os: 131, pl. Biv-II, figs 25, 26.

2009 Triaphorus aff. multiformis Kiparisova; Kumagae & Nakazawa: 171, fig. 145, 18–25.

Material. Seven specimens from LD-04 (NHMUK PI MB 1245–1247; NHMUK PE PEI 5480; NHMUK PE PEI 5485; NHMUK PE PEI 5507; NHMUK PE PEI 5519), and nine specimens from LD-05 (NHMUK PI MB 1195; NHMUK PI MB 1197; NHMUK PI MB 1201; NHMUK PE PEI 5495; NHMUK PE PEI 5506; NHMUK PE PEI 5508; NHMUK PE PEI 5516).

Description. Outline elongate-elliptical. Shell equivalved, inflated below the umbo, and inequilateral with beak positioned approximately 85% along the length of the dorsal margin from the posterior. Lower part of anterior dorsal margin projects slightly beyond plane of commissure. Posterodorsal margin is almost straight to slightly round and gently sloping. Lunule is long and narrow, with deeply impressed escutcheon. Umbo is prosogyrate and rises above the hinge margin. Ornamented with fine concentric growth lines. The entire inner margin is smooth. Prodissoconch is smooth and orbicular.

A small subumbonal groove limits the shell projection posteriorly. Short lateral tooth, left valve possesses weak secondary ridge creating a shallow socket. Hinge of left valve has an anterior platform that bears a depression for the corresponding anterior hinge margin of the right valve; posterior to this is a small, tuberculiform subumbonal tooth fitting above posterior lateral tooth of right valve. Ligament is fixed to a nymph, which extends about half the length of the posterior dorsal margin. Isomyarian muscle scars with a deeply impressed anterior adductor muscle scar.

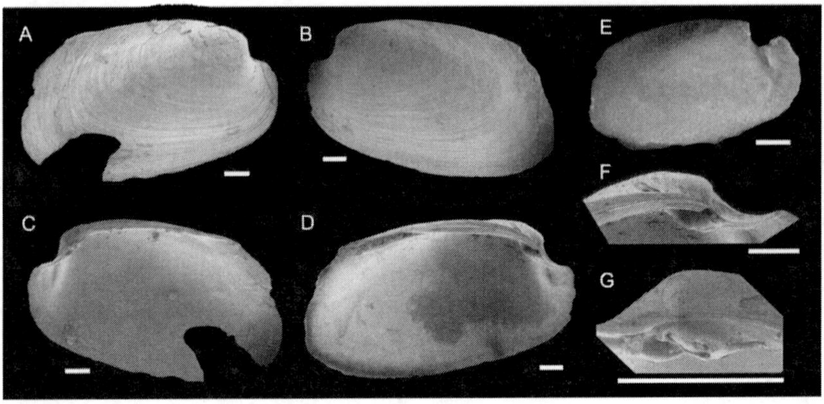

Figure 8. Unionites aff. subrectus (Bittner, 1901). A, NHMUK PI MB 1246, external view, right valve; B, NHMUK PI MB 1245, external view, left valve; C, NHMUK PI MB 1246, internal view, right valve; D, NHMUK PI MB 1245, internal view, left valve; E, NHMUK PI MB 1195, external view, right valve; F, hinge margin, NHMUK PI MB 1245, left valve; G, hinge margin, NHMUK PI MB 1246, right valve. Scale bars = 1 mm.

Remarks. Insufficient knowledge of the internal morphology of Early Triassic bivalves in general, and Unionites in particular, has created uncertainty regarding their systematic position. Based on their external morphology alone these specimens would be assigned to Triaphorus aff. multiformis (Kumagae & Nakazawa 2009), but they possess the following characters that are diagnostic of Unionites: the anterior hinge margin of the right valve overlaps that of the left; a nymph that extends nearly half the length of the posterior hinge margin; an impressed anterior adductor muscle scar; a deeply impressed lunule; and a long and narrow escutcheon. Thus, these specimens are assigned to Unionites.

These specimens differ from U. brevis, U. fassaensis, U. letticus, U. griesbachi, U. borealis and U. rhomboidalis because their length greatly exceeds their height. They are most similar to U. subrectus described from the Middle Triassic of Hungary by Szente & V€or€os (2003), except for their more elliptical outline.

Mode of life. Shallow infaunal, facultatively motile, unattached, suspension feeder (Hautmann et al. 2013).

Order Trigoniida Dall, 1889

Family Myophoriidae Bronn, 1849

Genus Neoschizodus Giebel, 1855

Type species. Lyrodon laevigatum (Goldfuss, 1837), Anisian, Middle Triassic, Rüdersdorf, Germany.

Diagnosis. The diagnosis follows Newell & Boyd (1975). Orthogyrous to moderately prosogyrous shell with slightly incurved beak. Posterior ridge angular to subangular in transverse profile. Myophorian hinge; teeth and sockets smooth or bearing transverse striations.

Remarks. These specimens have most of the required diagnostic criteria for assignment to Neoschizodus: an orthogyrate to moderately prosogyrate shell with an incurved beak and a posterior ridge angular to subangular in transverse. The nymph, teeth and umbonal platform were not present in these specimens so it is not known whether these specimens possess the myophorian hinge that is also diagnostic of this genus. These specimens do, however, have a similar external morphology to other Early and Middle Triassic specimens assigned to Neoschizodus (e.g. Kumagae & Nakazawa 2009) and are, therefore, referred to this genus.

Neoschizodus laevigatus (Goldfuss, 1837) (Fig. 9)

Material. Five specimens from LD-04 (NHMUK PI MB 1251; NHMUK PE PEI 5489; NHMUK PE PEI 5519; NHMUK PE PEI 5522), and eight specimens from LD-05 (NHMUK PE PEI 5476–5477; NHMUK PE PEI 5499; NHMUK PE PEI 5501; NHMUK PE PEI 5518; NHMUK PE PEI 5521). Fifty-nine prodissoconch valves from LD- 04 (NHMUK PI MB 1252; NHMUK PI MB 1254; NHMUK PI MB 1255–1260; NHMUK PE PEI 5480; NHMUK PE PEI 5484; NHMUK PE PEI 5486; NHMUK PE PEI 5511; NHMUK PE PEI 5513; NHMUK PE PEI 5520), and 14 prodissoconch valves from LD-05 (NHMUK PI MB 1253; NHMUK PE PEI 5514).

Description. Shell is trigonally subovate, equivalve, inflated below the umbo, inequilateral, slightly higher than long. Umbo is small and orthogyrate, with an elevated, subangular to rounded, umbonal ridge. Indistinct posterior ridge. Anterodorsal margin recurvate, passing to widely arched ventral margin, posterodorsal margin straight, entire inner margin smooth. Smooth sculpture except for faint concentric growth lines.

The larval shells have a similar external morphology to the adult shells, with a short and subumbonal hinge and short, narrow nymphs running down the anterior and posterior margins. The prodissoconch is smooth with fine concentric growth lines.

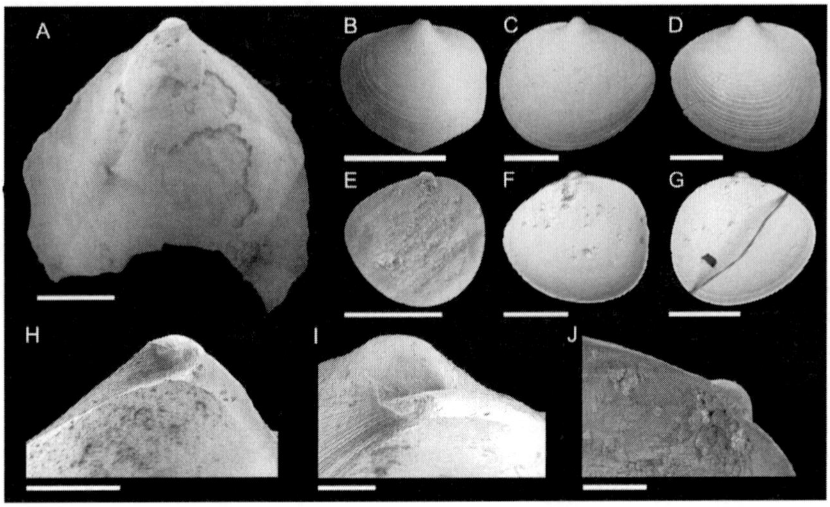

Figure 9. Neoschizodus laevigatus (Goldfuss, 1837). A, NHMUK PI MB 1251, external view, left valve; B–G, J, larval shells; B, NHMUK PI MB 1256, external view, right valve; C, NHMUK PI MB 1259, external view, left valve; D, NHMUK PI MB 1257, external view, right valve; E, NHMUK PI MB 1260, internal view, left valve; F, NHMUK PI MB 1258, internal view, left valve; G, NHMUK PI MB 1255, internal view, right valve; H, I, beak of adult specimen, NHMUK PI MB 1251; J, hinge plate of a larval shell, NHMUK PI MB 1260. Scale bars: A = 2 mm; B–G, I = 200 μm; H = 1 mm; J = 50 μm.

Remarks. Neoschizodus laevigatus is a cosmopolitan Early and Middle Triassic species with high variability in its morphological characters. The shell shape and indistinct posterior ridge mean that the present specimens agree with the characters of N. laevigatus, and similar specimens identified from the Early Triassic (e.g. Kumagae & Nakazawa 2009; Hautmann et al. 2011).

One of the adult specimens preserves a prodissoconch (Fig. 9I) and its morphology is identical to that of the other prodissoconchs that were found as isolated specimens. The hinge plate of the prodissoconchs was not observed to be myophorian – instead the hinge dentition is typical of a taxodont – but it is not known how a myophorian hinge plate develops through ontogeny (Newell & Boyd 1975). Hautmann & Nützel (2005) suggested that, in bivalves, the presence of a small prodissoconch I and a relatively large prodissoconch II indicates a planktotrophic larval stage. Therefore, a planktotrophic larval stage is interpreted for these specimens.

Mode of life. Shallow infaunal, facultatively motile, unattached, suspension feeder (Hautmann et al. 2013).

Class Gastropoda Cuvier, 1795

Order Amphigastropoda Simroth, 1906

Family Euphemitidae Knight, 1956

Genus Warthia Waagen, 1880

Type species. Warthia brevisinunata Waagen, 1880; Middle Permian, Salt Range, Pakistan.

Diagnosis. The generic diagnosis follows Waterhouse(1963). Deeply involute planispirally coiled bellerophont gastropod, distinguished by absence of spiral ornament. Sinus is broad, usually with a short slit. Selenizone obscured by inductural layer. Ornament of faint growth lines and growth wrinkles. Umbilicus generally filled.

Warthia zakharovi Kaim, 2009 (Fig. 10)

2009 Warthia zakharovi Kaim: 141, figs 132–134.

Material. One hundred and thirty-eight specimens from LD-04 (NHMUK PI MG 1468–1473; NHMUK PI MG 1495–1496; NHMUK PI MG 1502–1511; NHMUK PE PEI 5478–5482; NHMUK PE PEI 5484–5490; NHMUK PE PEI 5505; NHMUK PE PEI 5507; NHMUK PE PEI 5509–5513; NHMUK PE PEI 5519–5520; NHMUK PE PEI 5522), and 193 specimens from LD-05 (NHMUK PI MG 1467; NHMUK PI MG 1474–1481; NHMUK PI MG 1483; NHMUK PI MG 1485–1494; NHMUK PI MG 1497–1499; NHMUK PI MG 1512; NHMUK PE PEI 5475–5477; NHMUK PE PEI 5483; NHMUK PE PEI 5491–5504; NHMUK PE PEI 5506; NHMUK PE PEI 5508; NHMUK PE PEI 5514–5518; NHMUK PE PEI 5521).

Diagnosis. Warthia with wide shell in comparison to its thickness and weakly depressed selenizone. Description. Shell globular, almost as long as wide. Slit short and broad at base of U-shaped sinus. Weakly depressed selenizone. In well-preserved specimens growth lines can be observed. Aperture is arched around earlier whorls, and curved inwards by the selenizone.

Remarks. The shell of Warthia is usually entirely involute and overgrows the umbilicus. In some of our smaller specimens, the umbilicus is still visible, but in larger specimens it has become overgrown during subsequent growth. Even though our specimens lack an inductural layer and have growth lines that have not previously been recorded in Early Triassic Warthia species, in Permian species of Warthia visible growth lines or wrinkles have been recorded (e.g. W. micromphala and W. stricta; Waterhouse 1963) and, therefore, we consider our specimens to belong to Warthia.

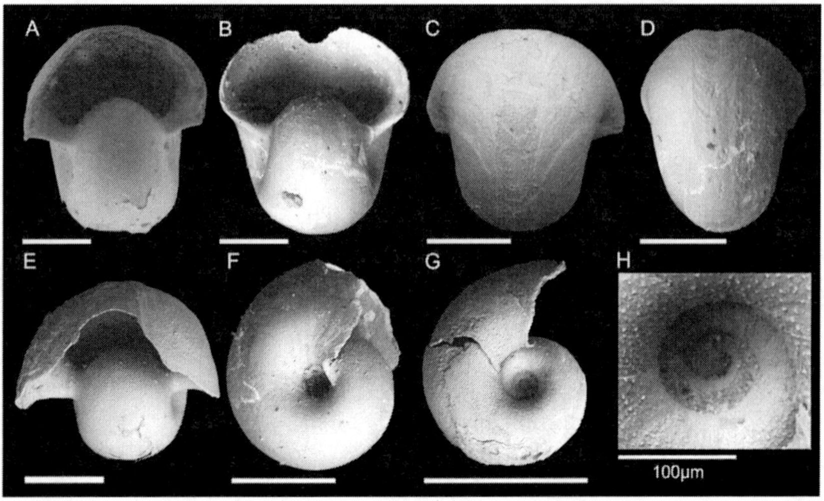

Figure 10. Warthia zakharovi Kaim, 2009. A, NHMUK PI MG 1502, apertural view; B, C, NHMUK PI MG 1505; B, apertural view; C, lateral view; D, E, NHMUK PI MG 1509; D, lateral view; E, apertural view; F, NHMUK PI MG 1508, apical view; G, H, NHMUK PI MG 1504; G, apical view; H, protoconch. Scale bars = 500 μm, except H.

The question of whether bellerophontids had a planktonic larval stage is unresolved (Nützel & Mapes 2001). The protoconch in bellerophontids may be very small, less than one whorl, and is succeeded by the teleoconch (Fr_yda 1999), and in our specimens the initial whorl is overgrown almost immediately. The small size (<0.05 mm), bilateral symmetry and lack of ornamentation in the initial whorls of Warthia zakharovi recorded in this study (Fig. 10H) are comparable to the embryonic shells of Bellerophon from the late Silurian that Fr_yda (1999) interpreted as indicating planktotrophy. A planktotrophic larval stage is, therefore, inferred for Warthia zakharovi.

Mode of life. Surficial, fully motile, slow, surface deposit feeder (Linsley 1977).

Order Vetigastropoda Salvini-Plawen, 1980

Family Eotomariidae Wenz, 1938

Subfamily Eotomariinae Wenz, 1938

Genus Glabrocingulum Thomas, 1940

Type species. Glabrocingulum beggi Thomas, 1940;Carboniferous, Scotland.

Diagnosis. Low- to moderately high-spired and turbiniform shell shape. The upper whorl surface forming an angle of <45_ with the selenizone located on the upper edge of whorl face. Sutures sharply defined. Upper whorl face with both spiral and collabral ornament; most strongly developed near the suture, weakest near the selenizone. Anomphalus to widely phaneromphalus, with or without funicle.

Remarks. These specimens resemble the Permian genera Wannerispira, Ananias and Glabrocingulum, and the Triassic genus Kamupena. They differ from Wannerispira by possessing a selenizone in the upper third of the whorl, and only having two rather than three strong spiral ribs; from Ananias by being low- rather than high-spired and having a less conspicuous and thinner concave band below the selenizone; and from Kamupena by lacking a strong umbilical callus plug. These specimens also differ from other neilsoniines by having spiral ribs and no axial ornamentation, and by being less elongated. Another genus with a comparable whorl profile is Rhaphistomella, which has been considered a synonym of Glabrocingulum (Batten 1989; Erwin & Pan 1996), but it differs from these specimens by the absence of a prominent medial concave band and a more strongly nodulose keel under the suture. These specimens are therefore assigned to the genus Glabrocingulum.

Wannerispira is the only other unequivocal eotomariid genus to have been reported from the Early Triassic (Kaim et al. 2010; Hautmann et al. 2015), and belongs to the Subfamily Neilsoniinae. Since Glabrocingulum, in contrast, is dextral, low- rather than high-spired, and with a moderately deep slit developing into a selenizone with rounded margins, it belongs within the Subfamily Eotomariinae. These specimens represent the first Early Triassicrecord of the Subfamily Eotomariinae and are the first Early Triassic record of the genus Glabrocingulum, which is rarely recorded after the Permian period.

Glabrocingulum parvum sp. nov. (Fig. 11)

Diagnosis. Moderately low-spired shells with faint spiral ornament without sutural nodes. Broad selenizone in relation to whorl height with sharp edges. Deeply concave selenizone. Funicle absent or weakly formed.

Holotype. Dextral shell, NHMUK PI MG 1531; height = 2.5 mm, width = 3.0 mm.

Paratype. Dextral shell, NHMUK PI MG 1518; height = 2.0 mm, width = 2.0 mm.

Other material. Ten specimens from LD-04 (NHMUK PI MG 1468; NHMUK PI MG 1471; NHMUK PI MG 1495; NHMUK PI MG 1500–1501; NHMUK PI MG 1513–1515; NHMUK PE PEI 5519–5520), and 14 specimens from LD-05 (NHMUK PI MG 1476; NHMUK PI MG 1482; NHMUK PI MG 1484; NHMUK PI

MG 1493; NHMUK PI MG 1530; NHMUK PE PEI 5493; NHMUK PE PEI 5502; NHMUK PE PEI 5514). Fourteen juvenile shells from LD-04 (NHMUK PI MG 1516–1517; NHMUK PI MG 1519–1529; NHMUK PE PEI 5486). Derivation of name. Latin, parvum (small), referring to its small size.

Description. Shell is dextral, turbiniform, low-spired, with simple sutures. The upper whorl surface is slightly concave and gently sloping, and bears the selenizone between sharply protruding edges, with the lower of the edges on the shell periphery. Selenizone is concave and moderately deep. Narrow, concave band immediately below the lower rib. Whorl profile below the lower rib is gently convex. Basal angulation is relatively sharply defined, but convex; base with a rounded circum-umbilical shoulder; small umbilical chink. Aperture is a rounded trapezoid; inner lip is reflexed; peristome interrupted by a slit in the outer lip. Shell ornamented with closely, irregular spaced fine spiral lirae. Growth lines visible with small knobs at the intersection of spiral ribs, otherwise no axial ornamentation observed. On the top of the keel, near the suture, the growth lines form small nodules.

Figure 11. Glabrocingulum parvum sp. nov. A, B, apertural view; A, holotype, NHMUK PI MG 1531; B, paratype, NHMUK PI MG 1518; C–E, NHMUK PI MG 1531; C, lateral view; D, side view of initial whorls; E, apical view; F, apertural view of a larval shell, NHMUK PI MG 1520. Scale bars = 1 mm, except F.

Protoconch: openly coiled; first two whorls smooth; third whorl possesses »15 evenly spaced, rounded, spiral threads; peristome uninterrupted (Fig. 11F).

Remarks. These specimens resemble Glabrocingulum texanum Batten, 1989 with the selenizone being located in the upper third of the whorl and lacking axial ornamentation. They differ from G. texanum in having a broader selenizone in relation to whorl height; a more concave selenizone with sharper edges; a weakly developed funicle or none at all; and in being moderately low-spired. The uncoiling that has been described for some G. texanum specimens from the Permian of the south-western US

(Batten 1989) was not observed. These specimens are also considerably smaller (max. size: H = 3.6 mm, W = 4.6 mm) than the type material of G. texanum (max. size: H = 8.7 mm, W = 9.9 mm), which may be a consequence of environmental stress in the immediate aftermath of an extinction event and an expression of the Lilliput effect in this genus (cf. Twitchett 2007). Due to their excellent preservation, these specimens reveal the morphology of the larval stages, which show a similar ontogenetic development to other species of Glabrocingulum (e.g. Pan & Shen 2008).

The Vetigastropoda have a diverse range of living habits including being described in association with woodfall communities (Kiel et al. 2008). The specimens in this study do occur in association with wood; however, no direct relationship was observed. Eotomariidae recorded from Zechstein reefs are described as motile algal grazers that were probably confined to a hard substrate (Hollingworth & Pettigrew 1988). The lack of evidence of a hard substrate in their depositional environment, however, suggests that these specimens probably had a similar life habit to deep-sea vetigastropods that typically consume sediment (Hickman 1988).

Mode of life. Surficial, fully motile, slow, surface deposit feeder. Order Ptenoglossa Gray, 1853 Family Pseudozygopleuridae Knight, 1930 gen. et sp. indet. (Fig. 12)

Material. Three larval shells from LD-04 (NHMUK PI MG 1532–1534). Description. Teleoconch not observed. Protoconch is conical, elongate and composed of five whorls. The initial whorl is smooth and has a diameter of 0.08 mm. Collabral ornamentation is initiated on the second whorl, continues to the base of the protoconch, and consists of narrow costellae that intersect at or just below the mid-whorl. Costellae are sigmoidal: on the upper part of the whorls they are slightly curved and oriented at 40_ to the shell axis, and on the lower part of the whorls they are oriented at 200_ to the shell axis. Growth lines are visible as faint collabral ribs between, and perpendicular to, the costellae. Aperture is circular, with a small columellar fold. Four whorls are present in these specimens.

Figure 12. Pseudozygopleuridae gen et sp. indet., larval shell. A, B, NHMUK PI MG 1532; A, apertural view; B, lateral view; C, NHMUK PI MG 1533, apical view; D, side view of initial whorl, NHMUK PI MG 1532. Scale bars D 100 mm.

Remarks. Hoare & Sturgeon (1978) showed that protoconchs of species of Pseudozygopleuridae are very similar, but can be readily differentiated from those of the Zygopleuridae. Diagnostic characters of pseudozygopleurid protoconchs that are present in these specimens include an elongate, conical shape with 3–5 whorls; smooth initial whorl with collabral ornamentation from the second whorl; and narrow opisthocline to sigmoidal transverse costellae that are equally spaced, extend up and below from the suture and curve uniformly to the midwhorl (Hoare & Sturgeon 1978). In contrast, protoconchs of the Zygopleuridae have smooth whorls with fine riblets at the sutures (Nützel & Mapes 2001; Kaim 2004) orstraight ribs in the Ampezzopleurinae (Nützel 1998, 2005). Protoconchs of the Ladinulidae are similar to those of the Pseudozygopleuridae but can be differentiated due to their vertical costellae (Bandel 2006). These specimens are, therefore, representatives of the Pseudozygopleuridae. No teleoconch is apparently present in these specimens as the sculpture of the prodissoconch is uninterrupted.

Pseudozygopleuridae is primarily a Palaeozoic family. Apart from the Early Triassic specimens described herein, the only other Mesozoic pseudozygopleurid is Plocezyga from the Jurassic of Poland (Kaim 2004). The specimens attributed to Plocezyga by Kaim (2004), however, lack aprotoconch with the diagnostic sigmoidal pseudozygopleurid ornamentation described by Hoare & Sturgeon (1978, 1980). Instead they have a reticulate pattern, shouldered whorls and transverse costae on the protoconch, indicating that they belong to a different genus and family.

Nützel (1998) used the diameter, ornamentation and whorl number of the protoconch to separate planktotrophic from non-planktotrophic pseudozygopleurid species. The specimens recorded in this study have small protoconch I diameters (0.12–0.14 mm), and the same ornamentation and number of whorls as pseudozgopleurid larval shells interpreted as planktotrophic by Mapes & Nützel (2009), suggesting that they too had a planktotrophic larval lifestyle. A teleoconch was not developed in any of the specimens, which may indicate that the adults were unable to live in this environment.

Order Architectibranchia Haszprunar, 1985

Family Tubiferidae Cossmann, 1895

Genus Sinuarbullina Gründel, 1997

Type species. Sinuarbullina ansorgi Gründel, 1997; Jurassic, Bathonian, NE Germany, NW Poland.

Diagnosis. The generic diagnosis follows Gründel & Nützel (2012). The shell is fusiform with a distinctly elevated spire. The teleoconch whorls have a subsutural ramp. The transition from the ramp to the outer whorl face is either rounded or angular, sometimes demarcated abapically by a spiral concavity. Whorls are smooth in most species, although faint spiral furrows occur on the base in a few of them. Growth lines are prosocyrt on the outer whorl face but strongly curving in an abapertural direction and opisthocyrt at the ramp. The aperture is relatively low for the group, teardrop-shaped and lacks a columnellar fold. The protoconch is trans- to medioaxial.

Remarks. Pan et al. (2003) described Jiangxispira as a new genus using the following diagnostic features: (1) a small, high-spired, slender, fusiform shell; (2) teleoconch whorls with narrow shoulder; and (3) a heterostrophic, discoidal, transaxial protoconch. These characters are all within the diagnostic features of the genus Sinuarbullina Gründel (1997), and Jiangxispira is, therefore, a junior synonym of Sinuarbullina.

Figure 13. Sinuarbullina yangouensis (Pan et al., 2003). A, B, lateral views; C, D, views of the protoconch. Scale bars D 1 mm, except D. Note: specimen lost by WJF after photography.

Sinuarbullina yangouensis (Pan, Erwin, Nützel, & Xiang-Shui, 2003) comb. nov. (Fig. 13)

2003 Jiangxispira yangouensis Pan, Erwin, Nützel, & Xiang-Shui: 44, fig. 3, 1–7.

Material. Specimen lost by WJF after photography.

Description. The shell is high-spired, slender and fusiform. Teleoconch whorls have a subsutural ramp. The ramp from the outer whorl face is rounded with a rib on the shell periphery. Whorls are smooth, except for growth lines which are prosocyrt on the outer whorl face curving in an apertural direction and become opisthocyrt towards the ramp. The surface of the shell shows a coloured spiral band around the subsutural ramp. The aperture is an elongated teardrop shape. Protoconch is heterostrophic, sinistral, nearly discoidal with lightly elevated spire 30_ offset from the shell axis; protoconch has 1–2 round whorls.

Remarks. Seven species are included in Sinuarbullina, and S. convexa (= 'Cylindrobullina' convexa) is the only accepted species from the Lower Triassic (Gundel & Nützel 2012). These specimens are more slender than S. convexa, described from the Sinbad Limestone of the western USA by Batten & Stokes (1986), and better resemble Jiangxispira yangouensis from the Induan Dayie Formation, China. The shell morphology is similar to that of Meekospira, which has been interpreted as a slow-moving shell dragger (Hughes 1986), but could have also been a burrower (Hollingworth & Pettigrew 1988). Interpreting the feeding strategy of fossil gastropods is difficult because information on the organ system, including the ctenidium, is not usually preserved. The ancestral ecology of high-spired gastropods is presumably as algal grazers on hard substrates (Declerck 1995). Given the absence of hard substrates in this study, the specimens described herein were probably detritus feeders or possibly micro-carnivorous on sedentary prey, like many modern shelled opisthobranchs (e.g. Lobo da Cunha et al. 2009).

Mode of life. Surficial, fully motile, slow, deposit feeder.

4. DISCUSSION

Implications for Permian–Triassic extinction and diversification

The fully silicified, diverse, earliest Triassic assemblage described herein includes gastropod and bivalve taxa that have not previously been recognized from the Early Triassic. Some occurrences extend stratigraphical ranges back to the basal Triassic (Fig. 14), with implications for timing and rates of diversification, whereas others show unequivocally that some taxa that were previously thought to have become extinct during the late Permian mass extinction event actually survived.

Three of the four gastropod taxa represent families that originated in the Palaeozoic, of which two (Warthia and Wannerispira) have previously been recognized from the earliest Griesbachian and have been interpreted as 'dead clades walking' (sensu Jablonski 2002) by Kaim et al. (2010) and Kaim & Nützel (2011). The family Pseudozygopleuridae is recorded in the Triassic for the first time (Fig. 14), confirming that it too survived the late Permian extinction, and could also be interpreted in this way. As noted above, the Jurassic specimens assigned to the Pseudozygopleuridae by Kaim (2004) do not have the expected suite of diagnostic characters and it may be that they represent a different family. If so, then the specimens described herein from Svalbard would represent the youngest occurrence of the Pseudozygopleuridae.

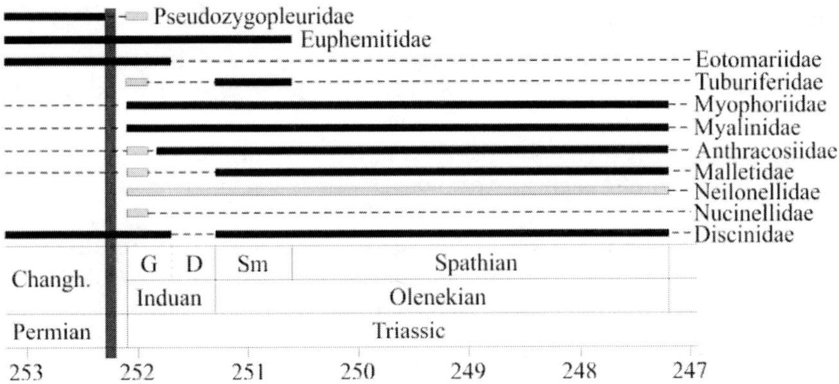

Figure 14. Ranges of benthic invertebrate families identified from the base of the Vikinghøgda Formation. Grey bars = range extensions based on this study; black bars = previously known unequivocal ranges of families; dashed lines = ghost ranges. Chang. = Changhsingian. G = Griesbachian = Dienerian, Sm = Smithian. Radiometric ages (bottom) after Lehrmann et al. (2006), Galfetti et al. (2007) and Shen et al. (2011). Late Permian mass extinction event is indicated by a vertical dark grey bar.

The other gastropod described in this study, Sinuarbullina yangouensis, represents one of the oldest occurrences of the architectibranchs (sensu Gründel & Nützel 2012), a group that diversified in the late Triassic and Jurassic. Although architectibranchs have been described from the Carboniferous, the Carboniferous specimens do not have a heterostrophic protoconch, which means that they are not true architectibranchs (Gründel & Nützel 2012). Thus, while the oldest unequivocal architectibranchs occur in the first conodont zone of the Triassic (this study; Pan et al. 2003), as hypothesized for other benthic invertebrate groups, such as the articulate crinoids (Baumiller et al. 2010; Oji & Twitchett 2015), their origin may have been Palaeozoic.

Of the five bivalve genera identified in this study, Promyalina, Unionites and Neoschizodus have previously been recorded in the earliest Induan (e.g. Hautmann et al. 2015). The occurrences of the protobranchs Nucinella and Austrotindaria represent significant range extensions back to the Induan and are the oldest occurrences of the Nucinellidae and Nuculanida, respectively. Recent phylogenetic analyses show that the protobranchs rapidly diversified in the late Triassic and Jurassic (Bieler et al. 2014), but these new occurrences demonstrate that the Nucinellidae and Neilonellidae appeared c. 50 million years before that, in the basal Triassic, which better supports the view of Sharma et al. (2013) that the late Permian mass extinction event triggered protobranch diversification. Future phylogenetic analyses will need to take into account our new findings in order to better calibrate molluscan evolutionary trees.

The excellent preservation of the fossil assemblage described in this study has been critical in recognizing that most specimens previously assigned to Unionites fassaensis and U. canalensis (Palaeoheterodonta) from Lower Triassic rocks worldwide are likely to have been misidentified and better resemble the protobranch Austrotindaria. Other specimens from this study are, however, unequivocally identified as Unionites, confirming its presence in Svalbard during the earliest Triassic. The palaeoheterodonts Unionites and Neoschizodus represent two lineages that were part of a major Early Triassic diversification of the Palaeoheterodonta (Newell & Boyd 1975; Ros et al. 2011; Sharma et al. 2013; Bieler et al. 2014).

The re-assignment of most Early Triassic 'Unionites' specimens to Austrotindaria has important implications for understanding how benthic marine ecosystems functioned in the wake of the late Permian mass extinction event, as pre-Spathian shelly benthic assemblages are typically described as being dominated by 'Unionites' (Fraiser & Bottjer 2007; Hofmann et al. 2013a, 2014, 2015; Foster et al. 2015). Our taxonomic re-assignment has implications for the functional interpretation of those specimens previously described as 'Unionites' because the motility and feeding of Unionites and Austrotindaria are significantly different – that is, the former is a facultatively motile suspension feeder and the latter is a motile deposit feeder. Other non-protobranch taxa with a similar morphology, such as Tellina, also have a deposit-feeding mode of life, so this ecological reinterpretation will still be valid even if the tentative generic reassignment from 'Unionites' canalensis to Austrotindaria? canalensis is subsequently revised. This new functional interpretation means that the palaeoecology of Early Triassic benthic shelly assemblages is in better agreement with the ichnofaunal record than previously thought (cf. Twitchett 2006), and that in many post-extinction, pre-Spathian benthic communities the dominant functional group was infaunal, motile, deposit-feeders.

The Middle and, especially, the Late Triassic are frequently described as being key intervals in the radiation of extant marine invertebrate groups from both fossil and molecular evidence (e.g. Nakazawa & Runnegar 1973; Nützel 2005; Hautmann 2007; Posenato 2008; Gründel & Nützel 2012; Rouse et al. 2013; Bieler et al. 2014; Hausmann & Nützel 2014). The poor quality of the Early Triassic fossil record is, however, widely recognized (Fraiser & Bottjer 2005) and it is demonstrably biased towards certain regions, palaeolatitudes and depositional settings (Foster & Twitchett 2014). As shown by other studies (e.g. Hautmann & Nützel 2005; Oji & Twitchett 2015), taxa may be overlooked because they are small or poorly preserved, or inhabited particular depositional settings, and there is significant hidden diversity in the Early Triassic. The present study reinforces that view as the assemblage documented herein is the first fully silicified Early Triassic fauna, comes from a remote location, comprises mainly small-sized fossils, and demonstrates that Early Triassic diversity was higher than previously recognized.

The high-fidelity silicification, which has preserved shells that were originally aragonitic in exquisite detail, is a key factor. A significant post-Permian reduction in the number of silicified assemblages has been attributed to a decline and movement offshore of siliceous sponges (Schubert et al. 1997), driven by changes in climate, ocean circulation and productivity (Kidder & Erwin 2001). Although partially silicified assemblages are known from the Early Triassic (e.g. Twitchett et al. 2004), which Fraiser & Bottjer (2005) argued are adequate for palaeoecological analyses, the present study has demonstrated the necessity of early, complete and highfidelity silicification for detailed taxonomic and ecological analysis. Thus, it appears that there is significant hidden biodiversity in the Early Triassic and that the diversification of many extant marine groups probably began earlier than is presently recognized, with implications for both the timing and rate of evolution. The most diverse silicified assemblages of the earliest Induan are known from offshore settings (Twitchett et al. 2004; this study), consistent with the hypothesis of Schubert et al. (1997) that siliceous sponges moved offshore after the late Permian extinction event, and so a search strategy focussing on those depositional settings is likely to yield critical new information, especially if regions that are currently underrepresented are prioritized.

5. THE IMPORTANCE OF PLANKTOTROPHY

The exceptionally preserved prodissoconchs and protoconchs in this study provide valuable insights into the early ontogeny of these taxa. Valentine & Jablonski (1983, 1986) suggested that during the late Permian extinction event there was selection against benthic invertebrates with planktotrophic larval stages. More recently, however, planktotrophic larval shell development has been inferred for many Early Triassic gastropods (Nützel & Erwin 2002; Pan et al. 2003; Nützel & Schulbert 2005) and this selectivity has been questioned (Nützel 2014). All gastropod taxa recorded in the present study (i.e. Warthia, Glabrocingulum, Sinuarbullina and the Pseudozygopleuridae) are inferred to have had planktotrophic larvae (Nützel & Mapes 2001; this study), and in addition, the bivalves Nucinella, Austrotindaria, Unionites and Neoschizodus all possess a small prodissoconch I and a relatively large prodissoconch II which imply planktotrophic larval development (cf. Hautmann & Nützel 2005). Thus, we infer that the possession of planktotrophic larvae was a particular advantage for benthic molluscs inhabiting shelf settings of the Boreal Ocean in the earliest Triassic. This may simply be a consequence of sampling this particular depositional setting, as benthic taxa with plankotrophic larvae were common in similar mid-outer shelf settings during the Palaeozoic (e.g. Fr_yda 2001; Nützel & Mapes 2001; Bandel et al. 2002). Alternatively, it may be a consequence of the extinction event and associated environmental changes.

One possible advantage of a planktotrophic larval development is protection from benthic predation (Nützel & Fr_yda 2003). Although predators are rarely identified in Early Triassic benthic assemblages (e.g. Schubert & Bottjer 1995; Twitchett et al. 2004; Hautmann et al. 2011; Hofmann et al. 2013a, b, 2014, 2015; Foster & Twitchett 2014; Foster et al. 2015), it is possible that some nektobenthic conodonts, ammonoids or fish may have fulfilled this role or that the predators were largely non-mineralized. Fish with durophagous dentitions, such as Bobasatrania, are locally common in the lowest Triassic of the Boreal Ocean (e.g. East Greenland; Stensi€o 1932), and trace fossil evidence of vagile crustaceans has been recorded from the Induan of north-west Canada (Beatty et al. 2008; Zonneveld et al. 2010) and central Spitsbergen (WJF & RJT pers. obs.).

An alternative advantage is that planktotrophic larvae enable more effective dispersal and a wide geographical distribution. The cosmopolitan opportunists that thrived in the wake of the late Permian mass extinction (e.g. Lingularia and Claraia) all have an inferred planktotrophic larval stage (Hammond & Poiner 1984; Yang et al. 2001). Possession of planktotrophic larvae would have been particularly useful for Early Triassic benthic invertebrates given the spatial and temporal fluctuations in benthic oxygen concentrations that have been inferred for the earliest Triassic seafloor (Wignall & Twitchett 1996; Thomas et al. 2004; Nabbefeld et al. 2010). Effective dispersal and wide distribution would have afforded greater protection from extinction and enabled rapid colonization of vacated seafloor once harsh environmental conditions had ameliorated. The late Permian mass extinction did not select against animals with planktotrophic larval development (Nützel 2014; Posenato et al. 2014), and possession of that character may have been a key factor in the survival and radiation of certain groups.

The occurrence of well-preserved planktotrophic larval shells in this newly described benthic assemblage has additionalpalaeoenvironmental implications. First, it implies that primary production in surface waters was adequate to sustain planktic food webs. Second, the exquisite preservation of the earliest formed larval stages and the complete absence of any signs of shell dissolution or repair (cf. Garilli et al. 2015) demonstrates that neither the surface waters nor benthic habitat in this particular region were affected by ocean acidification at this time, and the pH was not low enough to have curtailed biomineralization.

6. CONCLUSIONS

The fossil assemblage from the Lusitaniadalen section, Svalbard, is the first fully silicified fauna to have been described from the Early Triassic and provides new critical systematic data. The fauna includes four new bivalve species: Nucinella taylori, N. nakremi, Austrotindaria antiqua and A. svalbardensis and a gastropod species: Glabrocingulum parvum. The silicified fauna from Svalbard demonstrates that the aftermath of the late Permian mass extinction was a key interval for the diversification of the Architectibranchs, Protobranchia and Palaeoheredonta. The assignment of Early Triassic specimens previously identified as Unionites to Austrotindaria has important palaeoecological implications demonstrating that infaunal deposit-feeders dominated benthic assemblages prior to the Spathian. The gastropod and bivalve taxa recorded in the present study are inferred to have had planktotrophic larvae, and it is likely that this was an important adaptation for bivalves and gastropods in midouter shelf settings of the Boreal Ocean during the earliest Triassic.

ACKNOWLEDGEMENTS

We would like to thank the Governor of Svalbard for granting permission for the fieldwork, and Alistair McGowan, Tom Challands, Torran Purchase and Zoe Langford for their assistance in the field. Research in Svalbard (RiS) Portal ID 6336.WJF would also like to thank John Taylor (NHMUK) for his discussions concerning the Nucinellidae; James Wheeley for his hospitality whilst the samples were being processed at the University of Birmingham; and Alex Ball (NHMUK), Tomasz Goral (NHMUK), Ann Molineux (University of Texas) and Angella Thompson (University of Texas) for their assistance with photography. We are also grateful to Jon Todd and Zoe Hughes (NHMUK) for accessioning the material, and to the former for improving the manuscript. Alexander Nützel and Michael Hautmann are thanked for their helpful reviews that have enhanced the manuscript. This work was supported by Natural Environment Research Council (NERC) grant [NE/I005641].

REFERENCES

1. Adams, H. & Adams, A. 1858. The genera of recent Mollusca arranged according to their organization. John van Voorst, London, 661 pp.
2. Alberti, F. von. 1864. Uberblick uber die Trias, mit Berucksichtigung ihres Vorkommens in den Alpen. J. G. Cottasche Buchhandlung, Stuttgart, 353 pp.
3. Amalizky, W. 1892. Ueber die Anthracosien der Permformation Russlands. Palaeontographica, **39**, 125–213.
4. Amano, K., Jenkins, R. G. & Hikida, Y. 2007. A new gigantic *Nucinella* (Bivalvia: Solemyoida) from the Cretaceous cold-seep deposit in Hokkaido, northern Japan. Veliger, **49**, 8–90.
5. Bandel, K. 2006. Families of the Cerithioidea and related superfamilies (Palaeo-Caenogastropoda; Mollusca) from the Triassic to the recent characterized by protoconch morphology-including the description of new taxa. Freiberger Forschungshefte C, **511**, 59–138.
6. Bandel, K., Nützel, A. & Yancey, T. E. 2002. Larval shells and shell microstructures of exceptionally well preserved late Carboniferous gastropods from the Buckhorn Asphalt deposit (Oklahoma, USA). Senckenbergiana Lethaea, **82**, 639–689.
7. Batten, R. L. 1989. Permian gastropods of the southwestern United States. 7. Pleurotomariacea: Eotomariidae, Lophospiridae, Gosseletinidae. American Museums Novitates, **2958**, 1–64.
8. Batten, R. L. & Stokes, W. L. 1986. Early Triassic gastropods from the Sinbad Member of the Moenkopi Formation, San Rafael Swell, Utah. American Museum Novitates, **1864**, 1–33.
9. Baumiller, T. K., Salamon, M. A., Gorzelak, P., Mooi, R., Messing, C. G & Gahn, F. J.2010. Post-Paleozoic crinoid radiation in response to benthic predation preceded the Mesozoic marine revolution. Proceedings of the Natural Academy of Sciences, **107**, 5893–5896.
10. Beatty, T. W., Zonneveld, J-P. & Henderson, C. M. 2008. Anomalously diverse Early Triassic ichnofossil assemblages in northwest Pangea: a case for a shallow-marine habitable zone. Geology, **36**, 771–774.

11. Bernard, F. 1898. Recherches ontogénetiques et morphologiques sur la coquille des lamellibranches. Première partie. Taxodontes et Anisomyaires. Annales des Sciences Naturelles. Zoologie et Paléontologie, **8**, 1–208.
12. Bieler, R., Mikkelsen, P. M., Collins, T. M., Glover, E. A., Gonzalez, V. L., Graf, D. L.,Harper, E. M., Healy, J., Kawauchi, G. Y., Sharma, P. P., Staubach, S., Strong, E. E.,Taylor, J. D., Temkin, I., Zardus, J. D., Clark, S., Guzman, A., McIntyre, E., Sharp, P. &Giribet, G. 2014. Investigating the bivalve tree of life – an exemplar-based approach combing molecular and novel morphological characters. Invertebrate Systematics, **28**, 32–115.
13. Bittner, A. 1899. Versteinerungen aus den Trias-Ablagerungen des Süd-Ussuri-Gebietes in der ostsibirischen Küstenprovinz. Mémoires du Comité Géologique, **7**,1–35.
14. Bittner, A. 1901. Lamellibranchiaten aus der Trias des Bakonyerwaldes. In: Resultaten der Wissenschaftlichen Erforschung des Balatonsees, 1.Palaeontologie der Umgebung des Balatonse, **2**, 1–107.
15. Blakey, R. 2012. *Global Paleogeography*. [updated at:http://www2.nau.edu/rcb7/globaltext2.html, accessed July 2014]
16. Bronn, H. G. 1849. *Index Palaeontologicus oder Übersicht der bis jetzt bekannten fossilen Organismen*. Zweite Abtheilung. Enumerator palaeontologicus: systematische Zusammenstellung und geologische Entwickelungs-Gesetze der organischen Reiche.Schweizerbart, Stuttgart, 776 pp.
17. Carter, J. G., Campbell, D. C., & Campbell, M. R. 2000. Cladistic perspectives on early bivalve evolution. Pp. 44–79 in E. M. Harper, J. D. Taylor & J. A. Crame (eds) The Evolutionary Biology of the Bivalvia. The Geological Society of London, London.
18. Catullo, T. A. 1846. Memoria geognostico-paleozoica sulle Alpi Venete. Memorie della Societ'a Italiana delle scienze residente in Modena, **24**, 1–158.
19. Ciriacks, K. W. 1963. Permian and Eotriassic bivalves of the Middle Rockies.Bulletin of the American Museum of Natural History, **125**, 1–98.
20. Clausen, C. K. & Wignall, P. B. 1990. Early Kimmeridgian bivalves of southern England. Mesozoic Research, **2**, 97–149.
21. Coan, E. V. & Valentich-Scott, P. 2012. Bivalve seashells of tropical West America. Marine bivalve mollusks from Baja California to northern Peru. Santa Barbara Museum of Natural History Monographs 6, Santa Barbara, CA, 1258 pp.
22. Cossmann, M. 1895. Essais de paléontologie comparée, Vol. 1. Comtoir Géologique, Paris, 159 pp.
23. Cuvier, G. 1795. Second mémoire sur l'organisation et les rapports des animaux à sang blanc, dans lequel on traite de la structure des Mollusques et de leur division en ordre. Magazin Encyclopédique, ou Journal des Sciences, des Lettres et des Arts, **2**, 433–449.
24. Dall, W. H. 1889. On the hinge of pelecypods and its development with an attempt toward a better subdivision of the group. American Journal of Sciences, Series 3, **38**, 445–462.
25. Davidson, T. 1848. Mémoire sur les brachiopods du Système silurien supérieur de l'Angleterre. Bulletin de la Société géologique de France, série 2, **5**, 309–338, 370–374.
26. Declerck, C. H. 1995. The evolution of suspension feeding in gastropods.Biological Reviews, **70**, 549–569.
27. Dell, R. K. 1956. The archibenthal Mollusca of New Zealand. Dominion Museum Bulletin, **18**, 1–235.
28. Di Geronimo, I. & La Perna, R. 1997. Pleistocene bathyal molluscan assemblages from southern Italy. Rivista Italiana di Paleontologia e Stratigrafia, **103**, 1–10.
29. Dumeril, A. M. C. 1805. Zoologie analytique ou method naturelle de classification des animaux. Allais, Paris, xxiv, 364 pp.
30. Erwin, D. H. & Pan, H-Z. 1996. Recoveries and radiations: gastropods after the Permo-Triassic mass extinction. Geological Society, London, Special Publications,**102**, 223–229.
31. Erwin, D. H., Valentine, J. W. & Sepkoski, J. J. 1987. A comparative study of diversification events; the early Paleozoic versus the Mesozoic. Evolution, **41**,1177–1186.
32. Fleming, C. A. 1948. New species and genera of marine Mollusca from the Southland fiords. Transactions of the Royal Society of New Zealand, **77**, 72–92.
33. Foster, W. J. & Twitchett, R. J. 2014. Functional diversity of marine ecosystems after the late Permian mass extinction. Nature Geoscience, **7**, 233–238.

34. Foster, W. J., Danise, S., Sedlacek, A., Price, G. D., Hips, K. & Twitchett, R. J. 2015.Environmental controls on the post-Permian recovery of benthic, tropical marine ecosystems in western Palaeotethys (Aggtelek Karst, Hungary). Palaeogeography, Palaeoclimatology, Palaeoecology, **440**, 374.
35. Fraiser, M. L. & Bottjer, D. J. 2005. Restructuring in benthic level-bottom shallow marine communities due to prolonged environmental stress following the end-Permian mass extinction. Comptes Rendus Palevol, **4**, 583–591.
36. Fraiser, M. L. & Bottjer, D. J. 2007. When bivalves took over the world.Paleobiology, **33**, 397–413.
37. Frech, F. 1891. Die devonischen Aviculiden Deutschlands, ein Beitrag zur Systematik und Stammesgeschichte der Zweischaler. Abhandlungen zur Geologischen Spezialkarte von Preußen und den Thüringischen Staaten, **9**, 1–253.
38. Frýda, J. 1999. Higher classification of Paleozoic gastropods inferred from their shell ontogeny. Journal of Czech Geological Society, **44**, 137–154.
39. Frýda, J. 2001. Discovery of a larval shell in Middle Paleozoic subulitoidean gastropods with description of two new species from the Early Devonian of Bohemia. Bulletin of the Czech Geological Survey, **76**, 29–37.
40. Galfetti, T., Bucher, H., Ovtcharova, M. Schaltegger, U., Brayard, A., Brühwiler, T.,Goudemand, N., Weissert, H., Hochuli, P. A., Cordey, F. & Guodun, K. 2007. Timing of the Early Triassic carbon cycle perturbations inferred from new U-Pb ages and ammonoid biochronozones. Earth and Planetary Science Letters, **258**, 593–604.
41. Garilli, V., Rodolfo-Metalpa, R., Scuderi, D., Brusca, L., Parrinello, D., Rastrick, S. P.,Foggo, A., Twitchett, R. J., Hall-Spencer, J. M. & Milazzo, M. 2015. Physiological advantages of dwarfing and surviving extinctions in high-CO_2 oceans. Nature Climate Change, **5**, 678–682.
42. Geyer, G., Hautmann, M., Hagdorn, H., Ockert, W. & Streng, M. 2005. Well-preserved mollusks from the Lower Keuper (Ladinian) of Hohenlohe (Southwest Germany). Paläontogische Zeitschrift, **79**, 429–460.
43. Giebel, C. 1855. Kritisches über die Myophorien des Muschelkalkes. Zeitschrift für die gesamten Naturwissenschaften, **5**, 34.
44. Gobbett, D. J. 1963. Carboniferous and Permian brachiopods of Svalbard. Norsk Polarinstitutt Skrifter, **127**, 1–201.
45. Goldfuss, G. A. 1837. Petrefacta Germaniae tam ea, quae in museo universitatis regiae Borussicae Fridericae Wilhelmiae Rhenanae servantur quam alia quaecunque in museis Hoeninghusino, Muensteriano aliisque extant, iconibus et descriptionibus illustrata. Verlag lithographische Anstalt Arnz and Co, Düsseldorf, 312 pp.
46. Goryansky, V. Y. U. & Popov, L. E. 1985. Morphology, systematic position and origin of the inarticulate brachiopods with calcareous shells. Paleontologicheskii Zhurnal, **1985**, 3–14.
47. Gray, J. E. 1840. Synopsis of the contents of the British Museum. British Museum,London, 370 pp.
48. Gray, J. E. 1853. On the division of ctenobranchous gastropodous Mollusca into larger groups and Familys. Annals and Magazine of Natural History, (2), **11**, 124–132.
49. Gründel, J. 1997. Heterostropha (Gastropoda) aus dem Dogger Norddeutschlands und Nordpolens. III. Opisthobranchia. Berliner geowissenschatliche Abhandlungen, **25**, 177–223.
50. Gründel, J. & Nützel, A. 2012. On the early evolution (Late Triassic to Late Jurassic) of the Architectibranchia (Gastropoda: Hetereobranchia), with a provisional classification. Neues Jahrbuch für Geologie und Palaontologie Abhandlungen, **264**, 31–59.
51. Hallam, A. 1995. Oxygen-restricted facies of the basal Jurassic of North West Europe. Historical Biology, **10**, 247–257.
52. Hammond, L. & Poiner, I. R. 1984. Genetic structure of three populations of the 'living fossil' brachiopod *Lingula* from Queensland, Australia. Lethaia, **17**, 139–143.
53. Haszprunar, G. 1985. The Heterobranchia – a new concept of the phylogeny of the higher Gastropoda. Zeitschrift für zoologische Systematik und Evolutionsforschung, **23**, 15–37.
54. Hausmann, I. M. & Nützel, A. 2015. Diversity and palaeoecology of a highly diverse Late Triassic marine biota from the Cassian Formation of north Italy.Lethaia, **48**, 235–255.

55. Hautmann, M. 2007. Steuerungsfaktoren globaler Biodiversifizierungsmuster am Beispiel frühmesozoischer Muscheln. Beringeria, **37**, 61–74.
56. Hautmann, M. & Nützel, A. 2005. First record of a heterodont bivalve (Mollusca) from the Early Triassic: palaeoecological significance and implications for the 'Lazarus Problem'. Palaeontology, **48**, 1131–1138.
57. Hautmann, M., Smith, A. B., McGowan, A. J. & Bucher, H. 2013. Bivalves from the Olenekian (Early Triassic) of south-western Utah: systematics and evolutionary significance. Journal of Systematic Palaeontology, **11**, 263–293.
58. Hautmann, M., Bucher, H., Brühwiler, T., Goudemand, N., Kaim, A. & Nützel, A.2011. An unusually diverse mollusc fauna from the earliest Triassic of South China and its implications for benthic recovery after the end-Permian biotic crisis. Geobios, **44**, 71–85.
59. Hautmann, M., Bagherpour, B., Broose, M., Frisk, Å., Hofmann, R., Baud, A.,Nützel, A., Goudemand, N. & Bucher, H. 2015. Competition in slow motion: the unusual case of benthic marine communities in the wake of the end-Permian mass extinction. Palaeontology, **58**, 871–901.
60. He, W., Feng, Q., Weldon, E. A., Gu, S., Meng, Y., Zhang, F. & Wu, S. 2007. A late Permian to Early Triassic bivalve fauna from the Dongpan section, southern Guangxi, South China. Journal of Paleontology, **81**, 1009–1019.
61. Hickman, C. S. 1988. Archaeogastropod evolution, phylogeny and systematics: a re-evaluation. Malacological Review, **4**, 17–34.
62. Hoare, R. D. & Sturgeon, M. T. 1978. The Pennsylvanian a gastropod genera*Cyclozyga* and *Helminthozyga* and the classification of the Pseudozygopleuridae.Journal of Paleontology, **52**, 850–858.
63. Hoare, R. D. & Sturgeon, M. T. 1980. The Pennsylvanian pseudozygopleurid gastropod genus *Gamizyga* n. gen. from Ohio and West Virginia. Journal of Paleontology, **54**, 159–187.
64. Hofmann, R., Hautmann, M. & Bucher, H. 2013a. A new paleoecological look at the Dinwoody Formation (Lower Triassic, western USA): intrinsic versus extrinsic controls on ecosystem recovery after the end-Permian mass extinction. Journal of Paleontology, **87**, 854–880.
65. Hofmann, R, Hautmann, M. & Bucher, H. 2015. Recovery dynamics of benthic marine communities from the Lower Triassic Werfen Formation, northern Italy.Lethaia, **48**, 474–496.
66. Hofmann, R., Hautmann, M., Wasmer, M. & Bucher, H. 2013b. Palaeoecology of the Spathian Virgin Formation (Utah, USA) and its implications for the Early Triassic recovery. Acta Palaeontologica Polonica, **58**, 149–173.
67. Hofmann, R., Hautmann, M., Brayard, A., Nützel, A., Bylund, K. G, Jenks, J. F.,Vennin, E., Olivier, N. & Bucher, H. 2014. Recovery of benthic marine communities from the end-Permian mass extinction at the low latitudes of eastern Panthalassa. Palaeontology, **57**, 547–589.
68. Hollingworth, N. & Pettigrew, T. 1988. Zechstein reef fossils and their palaeoecology. The Palaeontological Association Field Guides to Fossils, **3**, 1–72.
69. Hounslow, M. W., Peters, C., Mørk, A., Weitschat, W & Vigran, J. O. 2008.Biomagnetostratigraphy of the Vikinghøgda Formation, Svalbard (Arctic Norway), and the geomagnetic polarity timescale for the lower Triassic. Geological Society of America Bulletin, **120**, 1305–1325.
70. Hughes, R. N. 1986. A functional biology of marine gastropods. Crook Helm, London, 245 pp.
71. Jablonski, D. 2002. Survival without recovery after mass extinctions. Proceedings of the Natural Academy of Sciences, **99**, 8139–8144.
72. Jeppsson, L. & Anehus, R. 1995. A buffered formic acid technique for conodont extraction. Journal of Paleontology, **69**, 790–794.
73. Kaim, A. 2004. The evolution of conch ontogeny in Mesozoic open sea gastropods. Acta Palaeontologica Polonica, **62**, 3–183.
74. Kaim, A. 2009. Gastropods. National Museum of Nature and Science Monographs,**38**, 141–155.

75. Kaim, A. & Nützel, A. 2011. Dead bellerophontids walking – the short Mesozoic history of the Bellerophontoidea (Gastropoda). Palaeogeography, Palaeoclimatology, Palaeoecology, **308**, 190–199.
76. Kaim, A., Nützel, A., Hautmann, M. & Bucher, H. 2013. Early Triassic gastropods from Salt Range, Pakistan. Bulletin of Geosciences, **88**, 505–516.
77. Kaim, A., Nützel, A., Bucher, H., Brühwiler, T. & Goudemand, N. 2010. Early Triassic (Late Griesbachian) gastropods from south China (Shanggan, Guangxi).Swiss Journal of Geosciences, **103**, 121–128.
78. Kashiyama, Y. & Oji, T. 2004. Low-diversity shallow marine benthic fauna from the Smithian of northeast Japan: paleoecologic and paleobiogeographic implications. Paleontological Research, **8**, 199–218.
79. Kidder, D. L. & Erwin, D. H. 2001. Secular distribution of biogenic silica through the Phanerozoic: comparison of silica-replaced fossils and bedded cherts at the series level. The Journal of Geology, **109**, 509–522.
80. Kiel, S., Amano, K. & Jenkins, R. G. 2008. Bivalves from Cretaceous cold-seep deposits on Hokkaido, Japan. Acta Palaeontologica Polonica, **53**, 525–537.
81. Kittl, E. 1904. Geologie der Umgebung von Sarajevo. Jahrbuch der Geologischen Reichsanstalt, **53**, 707–738.
82. Knight, J. B. 1930. The gastropods of the St. Louis, Missouri, Pennsylvanian outlier: the Pseudozygopleurinae. Journal of Paleontology, **4**, 1–89.
83. Knight, J. B. 1956. New families of Gastropoda. Journal of the Washington Academy of Sciences, **46**, 41–42.
84. Komatsu, T., Chen, J-H., Cao, M-Z., Stiller, F. & Naruse, H. 2004. Middle Triassic (Anisian) diversified bivalves: depositional environments and bivalve assemblages in the Leidapo Member of the Qingyan Formation, southern China.Palaeogeography, Palaeoclimatology, Palaeoecology, **208**, 207–223.
85. Kumagae, T. & Nakazawa, K. 2009. Bivalves. National Museum of Nature and Science Monographs, **38**, 156–172.
86. La Perna, R. 2004. *Nucinella alibrandi* (Conti, 1864) and *N. seguenzae* (Dall, 1898), the last European nucinellids (Bivalvia, Protobranchia). Rivista Italiana di Paleontologica e Stratigrafia, **110**, 571–577.
87. La Perna, R. 2005. A gigantic deep-sea Nucinellidae from the tropical West Pacific (Bivalvia: Protobranchia) Zootaxa, **88**, 1–10.
88. La Perna, R. 2007. Taxonomy of the family Neilonellidae (Bivalvia, Protobranchia): Miocene and Plio–Pliestocene species of *Pseudoneilonella* Laghi, 1986 from Italy. Veliger, **49**, 196–208.
89. Lehrmann, D. J., Ramezani, J., Bowring, S. A., Martin, M. W., Montgomery, P., Enos,P., Payne, J. L., Orchard, M. J., Hongmei, W. & Jiayong, W. 2006. Timing of recovery from the end-Permian extinction: geochronologic and biostratigraphic constraints from south China. Geology, **34**, 1053–1056.
90. Linnaeus, C. 1758. *Systema Naturae per Regna Tria Naturae, Secundum Classes, Ordines, Genera, Species, cum Characteribus, Differentiis, Synonymis, Locis*. Tomus I (Tenth Edition). Laurentius Salvius, Stockholm, 824 pp.
91. Linsley, R. M. 1977. Some 'laws' of gastropod shell form. Paleobiology, **3**, 196–206.
92. Lobo da Cunha, A., Ferreira, I., Coehlo, R. & Calado, G. 2009. Light and electron microscopy study of the salivary glands of the carnivorous opisthobranch*Philinopsis depicta* (Mollusca, Gastropoda). Tissue and Cell, **41**, 367–375.
93. Mapes, R. H., & Nützel, A. 2009. Late Palaeozoic mollusc reproduction: cephalopod egg-laying behavior and gastropod larval palaeobiology. Lethaia, **42**,341–356.
94. Matsushita, S. 1926. Lower Triassic fossils of Kurotaki, Tosa province. Chikyu, **5**,420–429.
95. Mergl, M. 2006. A review of Silurian discinoid brachiopods from historical British localities. Bulletin of Geosciences, **81**, 215–236.
96. Mergl, M. 2010. Discinid brachiopod life assemblages: fossil and extant. Bulletin of Geosciences, **85**, 27–38.

97. Mitchell, J. S. & Heckert, A. B. 2010. The setup, use and efficacy of sodium polytungstate separation methodology with respect to microvertebrate remains.Journal of Paleontological Techniques, **7**, 1–12.
98. Mørk, A, Elvebakk, G., Forsberg, A. W., Hounslow, M. W., Nakrem, H. A., Vigran, J. O. & Weitschat, W. 1999. The type section of the Vikinghøgda Formation: a new Lower Triassic unit in central and eastern Svalbard. Polar Research, **18**, 51–82.
99. Nabbefeld, B., Grice, K., Twitchett, R. J., Summons, R. E., Hays, L., Böttcher, M. E &Asif, M. 2010. An integrated biomarker, isotopic and palaeoenvironmental study through the late Permian event at Lusitaniadalen, Spitsbergen. Earth and Planetary Science Letters, **291**, 84–96.
100. Nakazawa, K. & Runnegar, B. 1973. The Permian–Triassic boundary: a crisis for bivalves? Memoirs of the Canadian Society of Petroleum Geologists, **2**, 608–621.
101. Nakrem, H. A., Orchard, M. J., Weitschat, W., Hounslow, M. W., Beatty, T. W. &Mørk, A. 2008. Triassic conodonts from Svalbard and their Boreal correlations.Polar Research, **27**, 523–539.
102. Neri, C. & Posenato, R. 1988. New biostratigraphical data on uppermost Werfen Formation of Western Dolomites (Trento, Italy). Geologisch-Paläontologische Mitteilungen, **14**, 83–107.
103. Newell, N. D. 1965. Classification of the Bivalvia. American Museum Novitates,**2206**, 1–25.
104. Newell, N. D. 1955. Permian pelecypods of east Greenland. Meddelelser om Grønland, **110**, 1–36.
105. Newell, N. D. & Boyd, D. W. 1975. Parallel evolution in early Trigoniacean bivalves. Bulletin of the American Museum of Natural History, **154**, 1–158.
106. Nützel, A. 1998. Über die Stammesgeschichte der Ptenoglossa (Gastropoda).Berliner Geowissenschaafliche Abhandlungen, Reihe E, **26**, 1–229.
107. Nützel, A. 2005. A new Early Triassic gastropod genus and the recovery of gastropods from the Permian/Triassic extinction. Acta Palaeontologica Polonica,**50**, 19–24.
108. Nützel, A. 2014. Larval ecology and morphology in fossil gastropods.Palaeontology, **57**, 479–503.
109. Nützel, A. & Erwin, D. H. 2002. *Battenizyga*, a new Early Triassic gastropod genus with a discussion of the caenogastropod evolution at the Permian/Triassic boundary. Paläontologische Zeitschrift, **76**, 21–27.
110. Nützel, A. & Frýda, J. 2003. Paleozoic plankton revolution: evidence from early gastropod ontogeny. Geology, **31**, 829–831.
111. Nützel, A & Kaim, A. 2014. Diversity, palaeoecology and systematics of a marine fossil assemblage from the Late Triassic Cassian Formation at Settsass Scharte, N Italy. Paläontol Z, **88**, 406–431.
112. Nützel, A. & Mapes, R. H. 2001. Larval and juvenile gastropods from a Carboniferous black shale: palaeoecology and implications for the evolution of the Gastropoda. Lethaia, **34**, 143–162.
113. Nützel, A. & Schulbert, C. 2005. Facies of two important Early Triassic gastropod lagerstätten: implications for diversity patterns in the aftermath of the end-Permian mass extinction. Facies, **51**, 480–500.
114. Oji, T. & Twitchett, R. J. 2015. The oldest post-Palaeozoic crinoid and Permian–Triassic origins of the Articulata (Echinodermata). Zoological Science, **32**, 211–215.
115. Oliver, P. G. & Taylor, J. D. 2012. Bacterial symbiosis in the Nucinellidae (Bivalvia: Solemyida) with descriptions of two species. Journal of Molluscan Studies, **78**, 81–91.
116. d'Orbigny, A. 1847. Considérations zoologiques et géologiques sur les Brachiopodes ou Palliobranches. Comptes Rendus Hebdomadaires des Séances de l'Académie des Sciences, **25**, 193–195, 266–269.
117. Orchard, M. J. 2007. Conodont diversity and evolution through the latest Permian and Early Triassic upheavals. Palaeogeography, Palaeoclimatology, Palaeoecology, **252**, 93–117.

118. Pan, H-Z. & Shen, S-Z. 2008. Late Permian (Lopingian) gastropods from the Qubuerga Formation at the Qubu section in the Mt. Everest (Qomolangma) region, Southern Tibet (Xizang), China. Journal of Paleontology, **82**, 1038–1042.
119. Pan, H-Z., Erwin, D. H., Nützel, A. & Xiang-Shui, Z. 2003. *Jiangxispira*, a new gastropod genus from the Early Triassic of China with remarks on the phylogeny of the heterostropha at the Permian/Triassic boundary. Journal of Paleontology,**77**, 44–49.
120. Pan, Y. H., Hu, S. X., Sha, J. G., Zhang, Q. Y., Wang, Y. Q., Zhou, C. Y., Wen, W.,Huang, J. Y. & Xie, T. 2014. Early Triassic bivalves from the Feixianguan Formation in Xingyi, Guizhou and the Ximatang Formation in Qiubei, Yunnan (southern China). Palaeoworld, **23**, 143–154.
121. Posenato, R. 2008. Patterns of bivalve biodiversity from Early to Middle Triassic in the Southern Alps (Italy): regional vs. global events. Palaeogeography, Palaeoclimatology, Palaeoecology, **261**, 145–159.
122. Posenato, R., Holmer, L. E. & Prinoth, H. 2014. Adaptive strategies and environmental significance of lingulid brachiopods across the late Permian extinction. Palaeogeography, Palaeoclimatology, Palaeoecology, **399**, 373–384.
123. Pruss, S., Payne, J. L. & Westacott, S. 2015. Taphonomic bias of selective silicification revealed by paired petrographic and insoluble analysis. Palaios, **30**,620–626.
124. Ros, S., De Renzi, M., Damborenea, S. E. & Márquez-Aliaga, A. 2011. Coping between crises: Early Triassic–Early Jurassic bivalve diversity dynamics.Palaeogeography, Palaeoclimatology, Palaeoecology, **311**, 184–199.
125. Rouse, G. W., Jermiin, L. S., Wilson, N. G., Eeckhaut, I., Lanterbecq, D., Oji, T.,Young, C. M., Browning, T., Cisternas, P., Helgen, L. E., Stuckey, M. & Messing, C. G. 2013. Fixed, free, and fixed: the fickle phylogeny of extant Crinoidea (Echinodermata) and their Permian–Triassic origin. Molecular Phylogenetics and Evolution, **66**, 161–181.
126. Salvini-Plawen, L. von. 1980. A reconsideration of systematics in the Mollusca (phylogeny and higher classification). Malacologia, **19**, 249–278.
127. Savoy, L. E. 1992. Environmental record of Devonian–Mississippian carbonate and low-oxygen facies trnasitions, southernmost Canadian Rocky Mountains and northwesternmost Montana. Geological Society of America Bulletin, **104**,1412–1432.
128. Schileyko, A. A. 1989. Morfologicheskaia evolutsiia nodotriada Protobranchia (Bivalvia) and peculiarities of abyssal members of the group [Morphological evolution of superorder Protobranchia and peculiarities of abyssal members of the group]. Trudy Instituta Okeanologii, **123**, 81–101.
129. Schubert, J. K. & Bottjer, D. J. 1995. Aftermath of the Permian-Triassic mass extinction event: paleoecology of Lower Triassic carbonates in the western USA.Palaeogeography, Palaeoclimatology, Paleoecology, **116**, 1–39.
130. Schubert, J. K., Kidder, D. L. & Erwin, D. H. 1997. Silica-replaced fossils through the Phanerozoic. Geology, **25**, 1031–1034.
131. Sharma, P. P., Zardus, J. D., Boyle, E. E., Gonzalez, V. L., Jennings, R. M., McIntyre,E., Wheeler, W. C., Etter, R. J. & Giribet, G. 2013. Into the deep: a phylogenetic approach to the bivalve subclass Protobranchia. Molecular Phylogenetics and Evolution, **69**, 188–204.
132. Shen, S.-Z., Crowley, J. L., Wang, Y., Bowring, S. A., Erwin, D. H., Sadler, P. M., Cao,C.-Q., Rothman, D. H., Henderson, C., Ramezani, J., Zhang, H., Shen, Y., Wang, X.-D., Wang, W., Mu, L., Li, W.-Z., Tang, Y.-G., Liu, X.-L., Liu, L.-J., Zeng, Y., Jiang, Y.-F. &Jin, Y.-G. 2011. Calibrating the end-Permian mass extinction. Science, **334**, 1367–1372.
133. Shigeta, Y., Zakharov, Y. D., Maeda, H. & Popov, A. M. 2009. Concluding remarks.National Museum of Nature and Science Monographs, **38**, 202.
134. Simroth, H. 1906. Versuch einer neuen Deutung der Bellerophontiden.Sitzungsberichte der naturforschenden Gesellschaft zu Leipzig, **1905**, 3–8.
135. Spath, L. F. 1930. The Eotriassic invertebrate fauna of east Greenland.Meddelelser Om Grønland, **83**, 1–89.
136. Stanley, S. M. 1968. Post-Paleozoic adaptive radiation of infaunal bivalve molluscs: a consequence of mantle fusion and siphon formation. Journal of Paleontology, **42**, 214–229.

137. Stanley, S. M. 1972. Functional morphology and evolution of bysally attached bivalve mollusks. Journal of Paleontology, **46**, 165–212.
138. Stasek, C. R. 1961. The ciliation and function of the labial palps of *Acila castrensis*(Protobranchia, Nuculidae), with an evaluation of the role of the protobranch organs of feeding in the evolution of the Bivalvia. Journal of Zoology, **137**, 511–538.
139. Stensiö, E. 1932. Triassic fishes from east Greenland collected by the Danish expeditions in 1929–1931. Meddelelser om Grønland, **83**, 1–305.
140. Stoliczka, F. 1871. Cretaceous fauna of southern India, v. 3. The Pelecypoda, with a review of all known genera of this class, fossil and Recent. Palaeontologia Indica, Series 6, **3**, 1–537.
141. Szente, I. & Vörös, A. 2003. The Pelsonian Bivalvia fauna of the Balaton Highland.Geologica Hungarica Series: Palaeontologica, Fasciculus, **55**, 123–138.
142. Thomas, E. G. 1940. Revision of the Scottish Carboniferous Pleurotomariidae. Transactions of the Geological Society of Glasgow, **20**, 30–72.
143. Thomas, B. M., Willink, R. J., Twitchett, R. J., Purcell, R. R., Archbold, N. W., George,A. D., Tye, S., Alexander, R., Foster, C. B. & Barber, C. J. 2004. Unique marine Permian–Triassic boundary section from Western Australia. Australian Journal of Earth Sciences, **51**, 423–430.
144. Twitchett, R. J. 2006. The palaeoclimatology, palaeoecology and palaeoenvironmental analysis of mass extinction events. Palaeogeography, Palaeoclimatology, Palaeoecology, **232**, 190–213.
145. Twitchett, R. J. 2007. The Lilliput effect in the aftermath of the end-Permian extinction event. Palaeogeography, Palaeoclimatology, Palaeoecology, **252**, 132–144.
146. Twitchett, R. J & Barras, C. G. 2004. Trace fossils in the aftermath of mass extinction events. Geological Society, London, Special Publications, **228**, 397–418.
147. Twitchett, R. J., Krystyn, L., Baud, A., Wheeley, J. R. & Richoz, S. 2004. Rapid marine recovery after the end-Permian mass-extinction event in the absence of marine anoxia. Geology, **32**, 805–808.
148. Valentine, J. W. & Jablonski, D. 1983. Larval adaptations and patterns of brachiopod diversity in space and time. Evolution, **37**, 1052–1061.
149. Valentine, J. W. & Jablonski, D. 1986. Mass extinctions: sensitivity of marine larval types. Proceedings of the National Academy of Sciences, **83**, 6912–6914.
150. Vokes, H. E. 1956. Notes on the Nucinellidae (Pelecypoda) with description of a new species from the Eocene of Oregon. Journal of Paleontology, **30**, 652–671.
151. Waagen, W. 1880. Salt-range fossils. Vol. I, Productus-limestone fossils. Part II, Pisces—Cephalopoda: supplement. Gasteropoda. Palaeontologia Indica, **13**, 73–183.
152. Waagen, W. 1885. Salt–Range fossils, Vol. 2: fossils from the Ceratite Formation. Pisces–Ammonoidea (Cephalopoda). *Memoirs of the Geological Survey of India*,Palaeontologia Indica, **13**, 1–323.
153. Wasmer, M., Hautmann, M., Hermann, E., Ware, D., Roohi, G., Ur-Rehman, K.,Yaseen, A. & Bucher, H. 2012. Olenekian (Early Triassic) bivalves from the Salt Range and Surghar Range, Pakistan. Palaeontology, **55**, 1043–1073.
154. Waterhouse, J. B. 1963. Permian gastropods of New Zealand. Part 1 – Bellerophontacea and Euomphalacea. New Zealand Journal of Geology and Geophysics, **6**, 88–112.
155. Wenz, W. 1938. Gastropoda. Teil 1: Allgemeiner Teil und Prosobranchia. Pp. 1–1639 in O. H. Schindewolf (ed.) Handbuch der Paläozoologie, Band 6. Borntraeger,Berlin.
156. Wittenburg, P. von. 1908. Beitrage zur Kenntnis der Werfener Schichten Sudtirols. Geologische und Palaontologische Abhandlungen, Neue Folge, **8**, 251–289.
157. Wheeley, J. R. & Twitchett, R. J. 2005. Palaeoecological significance of a new Griesbachian (Early Triassic) gastropod assemblage from Oman. Lethaia, **38**, 37–45.
158. Wignall, P. B. & Twitchett, R. J. 1996. Oceanic anoxia and the end Permian mass extinction. Science, **272**, 1155–1159.
159. Wissman, H. L. 1841. Beiträge zur Geognosie und petrefactenkunde des Südöstlichen Tirol's. Beiträge zur Petrefactenkunde, **4**, 1–152.
160. Wood, S. V. 1840. A catalogue of shells from the Crag. Annals and Magazine of Natural History, **6**, 243–253.

161. Wood, S. V. 1851. Monograph of the Crag Mollusca with descriptions of shells from the Upper Tertiaries of the British Isles. Palaeontographical Society Monographs, **4**, 1–150.
162. Yang, F., Peng, Y. & Gao, Y. 2001. Study on the late Permian *Claraia* in south China. Science in China (Series D), **44**, 797–807.
163. Zonneveld, J.-P., Beatty, T. W. & Pemberton, S. G. 2007. Lingulide brachiopods and the trace fossil *Lingulichnus* from the Triassic of western Canada: implications for faunal recovery after the end-Permian mass extinction. Palaios,**22**, 74–97.
164. Zonneveld, J.-P., Gingras, M. K. & Beatty, T. W. 2010. Diverse ichnofossil assemblages following the P–T mass extinction, Lower Triassic, Alberta and British Columbia, Canada: evidence for shallow marine refugia on the northwestern coast of Pangea. Palaios, **25**, 368–392.

CHAPTER 9

Stratigraphy, mammalian paleontology, paleoecology, and age correlation of the Wasatch Formation, Fossil Butte National Monument, Wyoming

Gregg F. Gunnell,[1] John-Paul Zonneveld,[2] and William S. Bartels[3]

[1]*Division of Fossil Primates, Duke University Lemur Center, Durham, North Carolina 27705, USA (gregg.gunnell@duke.edu)*

[2]*Department of Earth and Atmospheric Sciences, University of Alberta, Edmonton, AB, T8N 7B2, Canada (zonnevel@ualberta.ca)*

[3]*Department of Geological Sciences, Albion College, Albion, MI 49224, USA (wbartels@albion.edu)*

ABSTRACT

Fieldwork conducted in the Wasatch Formation in and around Fossil Butte has yielded a diverse assemblage of early Eocene vertebrates. Fossil vertebrates are distributed through three discrete stratigraphic intervals within the uppermost 180 m of the main body of the Wasatch Formation underlying the Green River Formation. These assemblages were derived primarily from fluvial overbank mudstone units overprinted with variably well-developed paleosols. The lowest (20 m) and highest (60 m) sections are characterized by less mature and more hydromorphic paleosols, whereas the middle section (100 m) is typified by more mature paleosols and more abundant channel sandstones.

The combined assemblages contain at least 46 species of mammals. Faunal characteristics include high abundances of equid perissodactyls and a relatively high abundance and diversity of notharctines primates, an apparent absence of omomyid primates, relatively high rodent diversity, and relatively diverse and abundant artiodactyls. One new genus (*Eoictops* new genus) and three new species (*Eoictops novaceki* new species, *Palaeosinopa lacus* new species, and ?*Notoparamys blochi* new species) are included in the Fossil Butte assemblage. Also recorded are late occurrences of two hyopsodontid condylarths and an early occurrence of a rare phenacodontid condylarth. The relatively high abundances of equids and notharctines suggest that vertebrate samples were derived from relatively open paleohabitats that included forested areas along water courses.

All three assemblages contain characteristic Lysitean (Wasatchian biochron Wa-6) elements, but the occurrence of the palaeotheriid perissodactyl *Lambdotherium* in the uppermost horizon indicates a Lostcabinian (Wa-7) age for at least the top of the Wasatch Formation. The overlying predominantly fish-bearing Fossil Butte Member of the Green River Formation also contains*Lambdotherium* and is therefore Wa-7 in age as well.

1. INTRODUCTION

Fossil vertebrates from Fossil Butte National Monument (FBNM), Wyoming were first discovered in the mid-1800s (Leidy, **1856**; Hayden, **1871**). Thinly bedded micrite layers in the lacustrine Green River Formation in the central part of Fossil Basin have produced an amazing variety of fish, crocodylians, turtles, birds, rare mammals, and invertebrates (including ostracodes, decapods, gastropods, pelecypods, and insects) (Grande, **1984**, **2001**, **2013**; Buchheim, **1994**; Buchheim and Eugster, **1998**; Buchheim et al., **2011**). Despite numerous reports on the paleontology of aquatic vertebrate assemblages in the Green River Formation (particularly the fish; e.g., Leidy, **1856**; Thorpe, **1938**; Grande, **1984**, **2013**; Grande and Bemis, **1998**), little attention has been given to fossils in the alluvial strata with which the lacustrine beds are interstratified.

This study documents the mammalian faunal assemblage of the Eocene Wasatch Formation in the area of Fossil Butte collected by a joint Albion College-University of Michigan-University of Alberta expedition in conjunction with Fossil Butte National Monument. These fossils are important as they provide insight into the ecology and environment of the lowlands adjacent to Fossil Lake during the early Eocene. Additionally, they provide well-defined age constraints on Eocene fluvial-lacustrine strata in Fossil Basin and firmly establish the middle to late early Eocene age (Wa-6–Wa-7) of the Wasatch Formation (Gingerich, **2001**; Gunnell et al., **2009**).

2. GEOLOGIC SETTING

Eocene strata at Fossil Butte National Monument were deposited in Fossil Basin, a small, north-south trending, structurally controlled sedimentary basin within the Wyoming Overthrust Belt (**Fig. 1**). Fossils mammals reported here were recovered from the uppermost 180 m of the main body of the Wasatch Formation (**Fig. 2**), which stratigraphically underlies the Fossil Butte Member of the Green River Formation (Oriel and Tracy, **1970**). In Fossil Basin, the Wasatch Formation consists primarily of brightly variegated mudstone with subordinate interbedded siltstone, sandstone, and conglomerate (Hayden, **1869**; Oriel and Tracy, **1970**) and represents deposition on an intermontane alluvial plain (Oriel and Tracy, **1970**; Zonneveld et al., **2006**).

Distribution of vertebrate fossils in the Wasatch Formation.— Eocene vertebrates are well known from Fossil Basin. Most of these fossils come from the Green River Formation (Grande, **1984**, **2001**, **2013**); however, fossil vertebrates are also known from the Wasatch and Fowkes formations (Gazin, **1952**, **1961**, **1962**; Nelson, **1973**).

Within the Wasatch Formation at FBNM, vertebrate fossils are known only from the lower member, main body, and Bullpen Member. A single tooth of the condylarth *Meniscotherium* cf. *M. robustum* was collected from the lower member near the northwestern margin of the Monument. Fish bones and scales (*Asineops* and *Lepisosteus*), common in the Green River Formation, also occur in the lower and Bullpen members.

Fossil vertebrates are considerably more common in the main body of the Wasatch Formation in and around FBNM. Small faunal assemblages have been described from Knight Station (near Evanston), Elk Mountain (~20 km south of FBNM) and from the Monument itself (Hayden, **1869**; Cope, **1872**, **1873**; Gazin, **1952**, **1961**, **1962**). Recent fieldwork at FBNM has resulted in a diverse collection of mammal fossils from 29 localities in the 180 m of the main body of the Wasatch Formation (**Fig. 1**, **Table 1**).

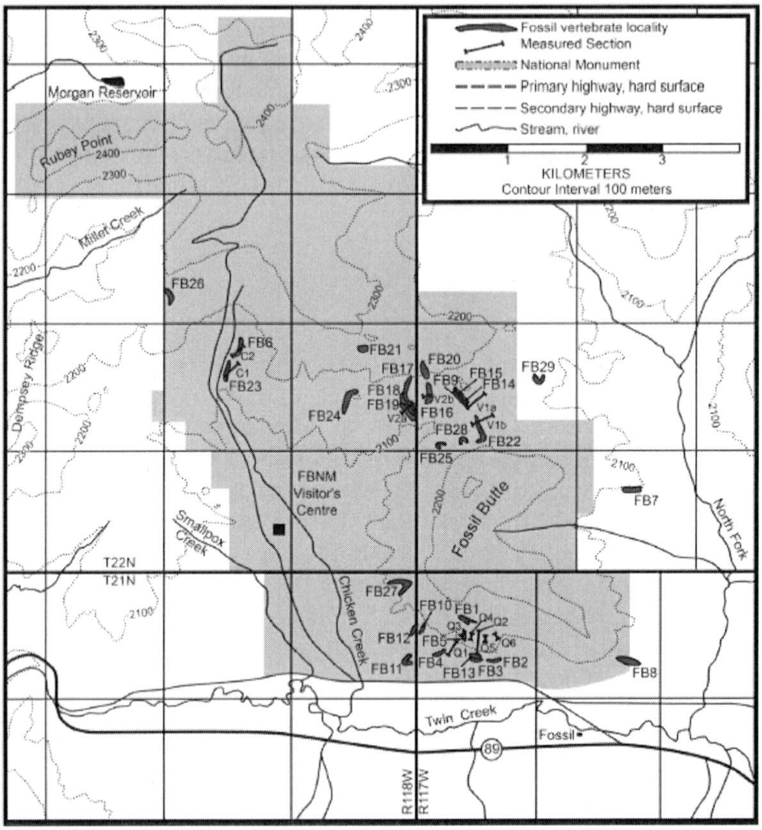

Figure 1 Map showing fossil vertebrate localities and measured sections in the Wasatch Formation at Fossil Butte National Monument, Lincoln County, southwestern Wyoming.

3. MATERIALS AND METHODS

Repositories and institutional abbreviations.— Most of the fossil materials described in this paper are housed and cataloged at storage facilities of the National Park Service, Fossil Butte National Monument, near Kemmerer, Wyoming, USA (FBF = old Fossil Butte catalog number; FOBU = new Fossil Butte catalog number). Those few specimens not housed at Fossil Butte can be found in the collections at the University of Michigan, Museum of Paleontology, Ann Arbor (UM); the United States National Museum, Smithsonian Institution, Washington, DC (USNM); or the Yale Peabody Museum of Natural History, Princeton Collection, Yale University, New Haven, Connecticut, USA (YPM-PU).

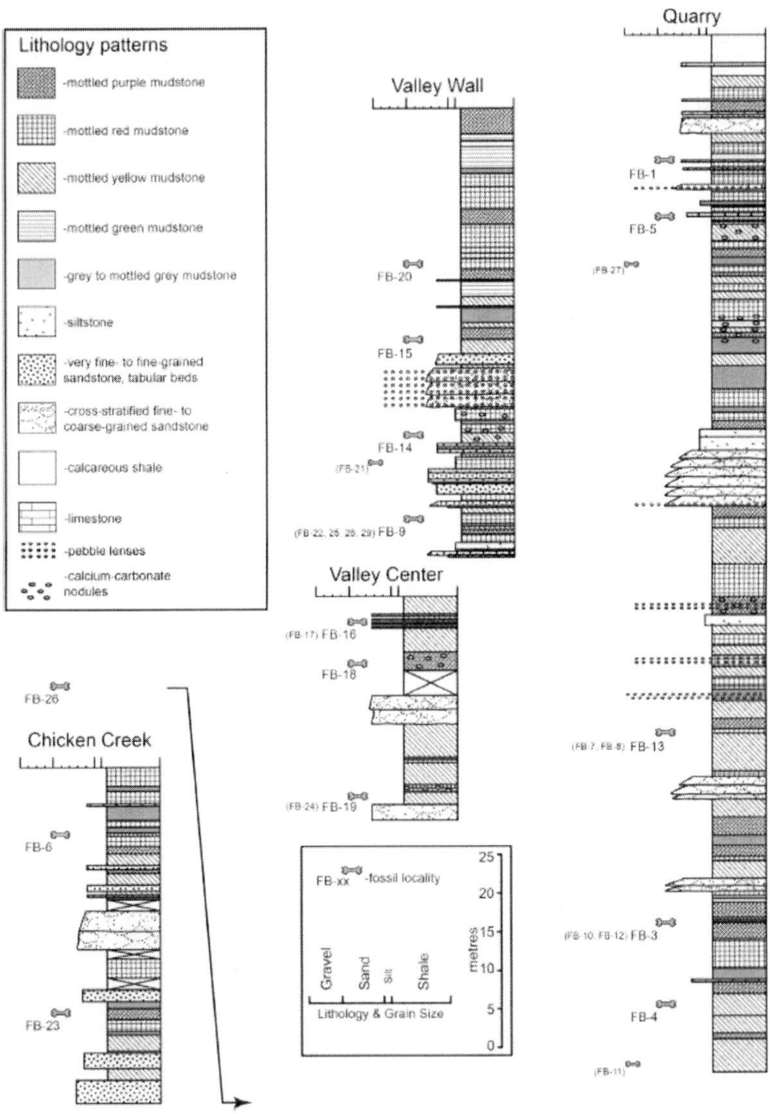

Figure 2 Composite measured sections at Fossil Butte National Monument and stratigraphic distribution of important Fossil Butte (FB) fossil localities. Sections were measured in the three main areas of Wasatch outcrop exposure: (1) near the historic quarry trail on the south face of Fossil Butte (Quarry); (2) through the valley on the north side of Fossil Butte (Valley Wall, Valley Center); and (3) near the head of Chicken Creek (arrow indicates position of Chicken Creek section below Valley section). General locations of composite sections are shown on Figure 1.

Table 1. Wasatch Formation mammalian faunal list – Fossil Butte National Monument.

- Mammalia
  - Didelphimorphia
    - Didelphidae
      - *Copedelphys innominatum*
  - Leptictida
    - Leptictidae
      - ***Eoictops novaceki*, new genus and species**
  - Cimolesta
    - Suborder?
      - Palaeoryctidae
        - Palaeoryctid indet.
    - Apatotheria
      - Apatemyidae
        - *Apatemys* cf. *A. whitakeri*
      - Pantolesta
        - Pantolestidae
          - ***Palaeosinopa lacus*, new species**
      - Tillodontia
        - Esthonychidae
          - *Esthonyx* cf. *E. bisulcatus*
      - Taeniodonta
        - Stylinodontidae
          - *Ectoganus* sp. indet.
      - Pantodonta
        - Coryphodontidae
          - *Coryphodon* sp. indet.
  - Pholidota
      - Palaeanodonta
        - Metacheiromyidae
          - *Palaeanodon* sp. indet. (small and large species)
  - ?Primates
        - Microsyopidae
          - *Microsyops latidens*
          - *Microsyops knightensis*
        - Paromomyidae
          - *Phenacolemur* sp.
  - Primates
        - Notharctidae
          - *Cantius frugivorus*
          - *Copelemur australotutus*
          - *Copelemur tutus*
  - Condylarthra
        - Hyopsodontidae
          - *Hyopsodus minor*
          - *Hyopsodus powellianus*
          - *Apheliscus* cf. *A. insidiosus*
          - *Haplomylus* cf. *H. scottianus*

Phenacodontidae
Phenacodus trilobatus
Ectocion superstes
Meniscotheriidae
Meniscotherium cf. *M. robustum.*
Mesonychia
Mesonychidae
Mesonychid sp. indet.
Rodentia
Ischyromyidae
Reithroparamys cf. *R. debequensis*
?*Notoparamys blochi* new species
Paramys excavates
Paramyine sp. indet.
Sciuravidae
Knightomys depressus
Knightomys huerfanensis
Oxyaenodonta
Oxyaenidae
Oxyaena forcipata
Hyaenodonta
Hyaenodontidae
Prototomus secundarius
Hyaenodontid sp. indet.
Carnivora
Viverravidae
Viverravus sp. indet.
Didymictis cf. *D. protenus*
Miacidae
Vulpavus australis
Miacid sp. A & B indet.
Perissodactyla
Equidae
Protorohippus venticolum
Xenicohippus craspedotum
Equid sp. indet.
Helaletidae
Heptodon calciculus
Palaeotheriidae
Lambdotherium popoagicum
Artiodactyla
Dichobunidae
Bunophorus grangeri
Diacodexis secans
Homacodontidae
Hexacodus uintensis

Systematic paleontology

Nomenclature abbreviations.— Wa = Wasatchian biochronologic zone; FB = Fossil Butte field number (for specimen references); **FB** = University of Michigan Fossil Butte field locality (for locality references). Lower teeth are indicated by a lowercase letter and tooth position number (e.g., m1 = lower first molar), upper teeth by an uppercase letter and tooth position number (e.g., P3 = upper third premolar). All measurements are provided in millimeters.

Class Mammalia Linnaeus, **1758**

Order Didelphimorphia Gill, **1872**

Family Didelphidae Gray, **1821**

Tribe Didelphini Crochet, **1979**

Genus *Copedelphys* Korth, **1994a**

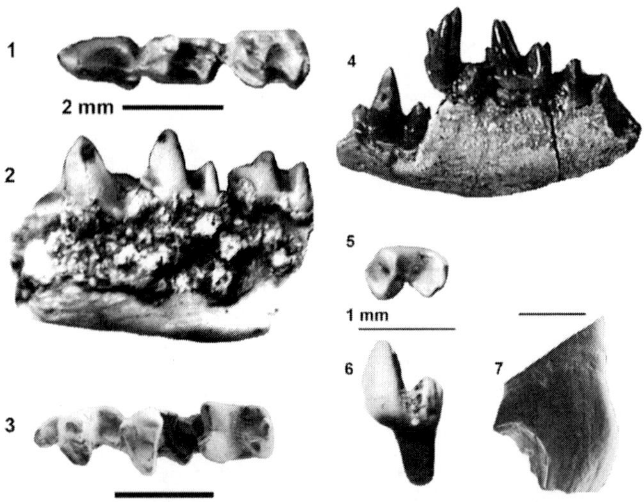

Figure 3 Images 3 and 7 are SEM photographs; others are standard photographs. (1–2) FOBU 6338, Copedelphys innominatum, left dentary p3-m2 in occlusal (top) and lateral (bottom) views. (3–4) YPM-PU 16171, Eoictops novaceki n. gen. n. sp. (Holotype), left dentary with p5 (erupting), m1-2, and broken m3 in occlusal (top, m3 not shown in this view) and lateral (bottom) views. (5–6) FOBU 6094, Palaeoryctid sp. indet., left broken m1 in occlusal (top) and buccal (bottom) views. (7) FOBU 6189, Apatemys cf. A. whitakeri, right I1 in lateral view. Scale bars=2mm, except for images 5 and 6 where scale bars=1mm.

Type species.—Peratherium titanelix Matthew, 1903, Renova Formation, Montana.

Copedelphys innominata (Simpson, **1928**)

Figure 3.1–3.2

1928 *Peratherium innominatum* **Simpson**, p. 6, fig. 5

Holotype

AMNH 11493, left dentary m1-4, Bridgerian biochron Br2, Bridger Formation, Millersville, Uinta County, Wyoming.

Occurrence

Locality **FB**-19, late middle early Eocene, Wasatchian biochronologic zone Wa-6, main body, Wasatch Formation, Fossil Basin, Lincoln County, Wyoming.

Materials

FOBU 6338, left dentary p3-m2.

Remarks

The referred specimen is in the size range of both *Copedelphys innominatum* and *Peradectes chesteri*. It differs from *Peradectes* in having a distinct lower molar entoconid and well-developed entoconid notch with a low hypoconulid. It also has p3 smaller than m1 and m1 with a widely open trigonid lingually. This combination of characters differentiates FOBU 6338 from both *Peradectes* and *Herpetotherium* (Korth, **2008**).

Rothecker and Storer (**1996**) moved the species *Peratherium innominatum*, from *Peratherium* to *Copedelphys* based mostly on its very small size, upper molars with tiny conules and similar sized stylar cusps, and open lower molar trigonids, especially on m1. The specimen referred here is even smaller than those from Lac Pelletier described by Rothecker and Storer (**1996**), but the lower molars do have open trigonids lingually. This specimen could conceivably represent a new species of *Copedelphys*, but given the lack of any known upper molars at present a new name seems premature. Nonetheless this record represents one of the earlier known occurrences of this tiny marsupial outside of the seemingly anomalous earliest Wasatchian record at Castle Gardens in the Bighorn Basin (see Strait, **2001**).

Measurements

FOBU 6338: p3 = 1.29 x 0.72, m1 = 1.36 x 0.79; m2 = 1.40 x 0.89

Order Leptictida McKenna, **1975**

Family Leptictidae Gill, **1872**

Genus *Eoictops* new genus

Type species

Eoictops novaceki new species by monotypy.

Diagnosis

As for type species by monotypy.

Etymology

Eos, Greek for early or dawn and *Ictops* (= *Leptictis*), a common North American Oligocene leptictid genus, in reference to the earlier occurrence of a related species (and in keeping with *Palaeictops*, another related taxon, as proposed by Matthew, **1899**).

Remarks

Recognition of true *Diacodon* as an erinaceomorph (Novacek, **1982**; Novacek et al., **1985**) necessitates a new generic name for Fossil Butte a specimen once assigned to *Diacodon* since it is clear (see below) that this specimen is a leptictid that differs from all previously known North American members of this order.

Eoictops novaceki new species

Figure 3.3–**3**.4

1952 *Diacodon*, cf. *alticuspis*; **Gazin**, p. 20

1962 *Diacodon*, cf. *alticuspis*; **Gazin**, p. 22

Holotype

Type and only specimen, YPM-PU 16171, left dentary with p5 (erupting), m1-2, and broken m3, found "Three miles northwest of Fossil, Wyoming, Wasatch Formation, about 100 feet below the Green River Formation" Gazin, **1952**, p. 20 (approximately equivalent to UM Localities **FB**-7, **FB**-8, **FB**-13, **FB**-19, and **FB**-24).

Diagnosis

Differs from all other North American leptictids in having p5 the same length as m1 (other leptictids have p5 longer to much longer than m1), p5 with more trenchant talonid exhibiting a very reduced, anteriorly shifted and low entoconid connected via a postentocristid to a small hypoconulid that is appressed to the posterolingual aspect of the hypoconid, and m3 relatively smaller than other lower molars; further differs from *Palaeictops* by having relatively higher and anteriorly angled molar trigonids and relatively shorter molar talonids.

Occurrence

Late middle early Eocene, Wasatchian biochronologic zone Wa-6, main body, Wasatch Formation, Fossil Basin, Lincoln County, Wyoming.

Description

p5 is in its crypt, but the crown is fully formed. It had a prominent protoconid, the tip of which is now broken away. The p5 paraconid is robust, isolated from the anterior flank of the protoconid, centered on the tooth and positioned very low, forming the anterior base of the tooth. The metaconid appears as if it is somewhat smaller relative to the protoconid, but was probably nearly as tall and distinct. The protoconid and metaconid are positioned directly opposite each other and together form a high and prominent loph. The p5 talonid is trenchant and is dominated by a distinct and robust hypoconid that is placed just labial of center. A much lower and smaller entoconid is present as is a small hypoconulid. A weakly formed postcristid extends from the hypoconid to the hypoconulid and then continues as a curving postentocristid to reach the entoconid. The prehypocristid is steep and does not reach the postvallid, leaving the talonid open labially. Similarly, the preentocrisitd is absent, leaving the talonid open lingually through the entoconid notch. The talonid is shallowly basined due to the presence of the postcristid. There are no cingulids developed on p5.

The lower m1-2 of *Eoictops novaceki* n. sp. are nearly identical morphologically with m2 being only slightly smaller than m1. Both have tall and acute protoconids and metaconids with the metaconid being somewhat more robust than the protoconid and both being nearly equal height. These cusps are aligned labiolingually and are separated from each other by a fairly deep, v-shaped postprotocristid. The paraconid is much lower and relatively much smaller. It is placed just lingual of center on the prevallid, has an acute tip, and juts slightly anteriorly. A small precingulid is formed just labial and beneath the paraconid and constitutes the only cingulid developed on either tooth. Both teeth have high talonid cusps (not as high as the protoconid and metaconid, however) that are aligned in a slight arc along the posterior margin of the talonid. The hypoconid and hypoconulid are equally as tall and robust with the entoconid being only somewhat lower and smaller. Unlike p5, the prehypocristid extends to the base of the postvallid, joining that surface centrally and closing the talonid labially. The talonid is open lingually through a relatively broad entoconid notch. The talonid is narrowly basined with its occlusal surface sloping rather severely from labial to lingual (as it does in p5).

The lower third molar crown is damaged, but it is clear that m3 would have been smaller than either m1 or m2.

Etymology

Specific name for Michael J. Novacek who untangled the confusing systematics of Cenozoic leptictids and additionally for his many contributions towards the understanding of early insectivorans and the origins of placental mammals.

Remarks

Gazin (**1952**, **1962**) noted the presence of a leptictid dentary from near Fossil Butte in the collections at Princeton University (now housed at the Yale Peabody Museum). He did not figure or describe this specimen in detail, but assigned it to *Diacodon*, cf. *alticuspis*. Novacek (**1977**) placed *Diacodon*, Gazin, **1952** in synonymy with *Prodiacodon* Matthew, **1929**, although he did not specifically mention the Fossil Butte specimen under any of the synonymies he provided for *Prodiacodon* (also see Gunnell et al., **2008b**). Novacek (**1977**) did specifically place *Diacodon pineyensis* Gazin, **1952** within *Prodiacodon tauri-cinerei* (Jepsen, **1930**).

Following detailed analyses by Novacek (**1982**) and Novacek et al. (**1985**), *Diacodon alticuspis* is now recognized as an erinaceomorph (McKenna and Bell, **1997**; Gunnell et al., **2008c**). Gazin (**1952**) had previously stated that *D. alticuspis* was unlike other species of the genus in its p4 (= p5) morphology, suggesting that perhaps *Palaeictops* should be resurrected to accommodate the species of *Diacodon* other than *D. alticuspis* (Gazin identified these specimens as *Palaeictops* in 1962). While Gazin (**1952**) assigned YPM-PU 16171 to *Diacodon*, cf. *alticuspis*, it is clear from his discussion that he viewed this specimen to be a leptictid.

While similar to *Diacodon alticuspis* in some ways (e.g., simpler p5 talonid, anteriorly sloping molar trigonids, especially notable on m2), YPM-PU 16171 is clearly distinguishable from this New Mexican taxon. *Eoictops novaceki* differs from *Diacodon alticuspis* in the following ways: (1) m3 smaller relative to m1-2 (m3 larger in *D. alticuspis*); (2) lower molar paraconids relatively higher, more cuspate and distinct (not lower, loph-like and less distinct); (3) p5 paraconid larger, higher, and more distinct; (4) p5 metaconid relatively larger and higher; and (5) p5 talonid more sloping (labially to lingually), less basined, and with a very tiny and low entoconid and a small hypoconulid that is positioned close to the posterior aspect of the hypoconid.

As Gazin noted (**1952**), YPM-PU 16171 has relatively high molar trigonids, which is one of the characters cited by Novacek (**1977**) distinguishing *Prodiacodon* from *Palaeictops*, but the differences in p5 structure cited above clearly differentiate this specimen from both *Prodiacodon* and *Palaeictops*.

Measurements

YPM-PU 16171: p5 = 3.0 x 1.7, m1 = 3.0 x 2.1, m2 = 2.8 x 1.9.

Order Cimolesta McKenna, **1975**

Family Palaeoryctidae Winge, **1917**

Palaeoryctid indet.

Figure 3.5–**3**.6

Occurrence

Locality **FB**-16, late middle early Eocene, Wasatchian biochronologic zone Wa-6, main body, Wasatch Formation, Fossil Basin, Lincoln County, Wyoming.

Materials

FOBU 6094, left m1.

Remarks

This slightly broken m1 represents a palaeoryctid based on its relatively high and compressed trigonid and low, lingually open talonid (Gunnell et al., **2008a**). It differs from *Eoryctes* (Thewissen and Gingerich, **1989**) in having a broader talonid basin that is open lingually and in having a more lingually placed entoconid. It differs from *Palaeoryctes* in having a less compressed trigonid with relatively larger and more inflated protoconid and metaconid, a more mesially directed and stronger paracristid, a relatively lower trigonid, and in having a small but distinct hypoconulid centered between the hypoconid and entoconid. This specimen differs from *Pararyctes* (Van Valen, **1966**) in having a relatively higher trigonid, a less distinct entoconid, and in lacking an entocristid. It is similar to *Ottoryctes* (Bloch et al., **2004**) in having a relatively broad talonid and may represent that genus, but definitive identification awaits better specimens.

Measurements

FOBU 6094: m1 = 2.4 x 1.5.

Suborder Apatotheria Scott and Jepsen, **1936**

Family Apatemyidae Matthew, **1909**

Genus *Apatemys* Marsh, **1872**

Type species

Apatemys bellus Marsh, **1872**, Bridger Formation, Henrys Fork, Wyoming.

Apatemys cf. *A. whitakeri* (Simpson, **1954**)

Figure 3.7

1954 *Teilhardella whitakeri* **Simpson**, p. 1, fig. 1

Holotype

AMNH 48004, left dentary p4-m2, Wasatchian Biochron Wa7, San Jose Formation, Almagre Facies, San Juan Basin, New Mexico.

Occurrence

Locality **FB**-8, late middle early Eocene, Wasatchian biochronologic zone Wa-6, main body, Wasatch Formation, Fossil Basin, Lincoln County, Wyoming.

Materials

FOBU 6189, right I1.

Remarks

Apatemys is relatively rare in biochrons Wa-6 and Wa-7 (Gunnell et al., **2008a**). *A. whitakeri* apparently is the only valid species of the genus now recognized from Wa-6 (Guthrie, **1967**), therefore FB 96-093 is tentatively assigned to that taxon.

Suborder Pantolesta McKenna, **1975**

Family Pantolestidae Cope, **1884**

Genus *Palaeosinopa* Matthew, **1901**

Type species

Palaeosinopa veterrima Matthew, **1901**, Willwood Formation, Bighorn Basin, Wyoming.

Palaeosinopa lacus new species

Figure 4.1–**4**.3

Holotype

FOBU 6205, left dentary p2-m1, only known specimen, from Locality **FB**-5.

Diagnosis

Differs from all other species of *Palaeosinopa* in having a very broad and bulbous P/4 with a basined talonid possessing small but distinct hypoconid and entoconid cusps. Further differs from other species of *Palaeosinopa* in having a relatively smaller (but still distinct) mental foramen placed beneath p4 rather than a larger foramen beneath m1. *Palaeosinopa lacus* n. sp. is intermediate in size between *Palaeosinopa lutreola* and *Palaeosinopa didelphoides* (?= *Palaeosinopa veterrima*), being larger (about 25%) than the former and smaller (about 30%) than the latter.

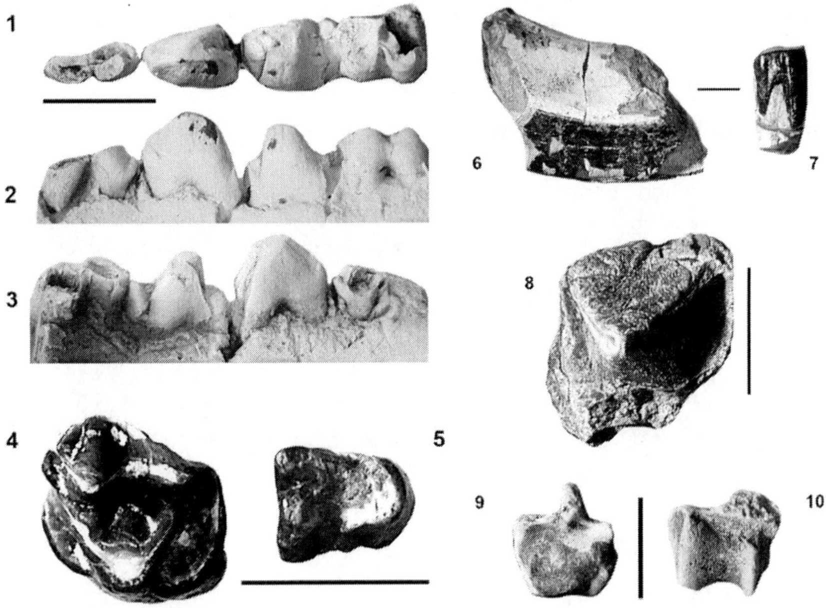

Figure 4 (1–3) FOBU 6205, Palaeosinopa lacus n. sp. (Holotype), left dentary with roots of p2 and slightly broken p3-m1 in occlusal (top), lateral (middle) and medial (bottom) views. (4) UM 102585, Esthonyx cf. E. bisulcatus, left Mx (labial portion missing) in occlusal view. (5) FOBU 6389, Esthonyx cf. E. bisulcatus, right mx trigonid in occlusal view. (6–7) FOBU 6361, Ectoganus sp. indet., incisor fragment (left) and isolated molar (right) in lateral views. (8) FOBU 6356, Coryphodon sp. indet., upper molar fragment in occlusal view. (9) FOBU 6097, Palaeanodon sp. indet., right distal radius in distal view. (10) FOBU 6198, Palaeanodon sp. indet., left broken astragalus in dorsal view. Scale bars=5 mm for images 1–5 and 9–10; 1 cm for images 6–8.

Occurrence

Late middle early Eocene, Wasatchian biochronologic zone Wa-6, main body, Wasatch Formation, Fossil Basin, Lincoln County, Wyoming.

Description

The p2 is broken, preserving only its posterior-most part. This tooth is long and relatively narrow and has a tiny, centered talonid cuspule. The talonid is very short and narrow. Compared to *P. didelphoides*, the p2 of *P. lacus* is more elongate.

The p3 is broken posteriorly. It has no paraconid or metaconid and lacks an anterior basal cuspule (unlike *P. didelphoides*). The p3 paracristid is weakly defined and curves antero-lingually. The postvallid is flat and lacks a central ridge unlike *P. didelphoides*. Overall, p3 is relatively robust and heavily constructed with a blunt, rounded protoconid.

The p4 is broken anteriorly, so the disposition of the paraconid and paracristid cannot be determined. The protoconid is bulbous and robust with a flattened postvallid (lacking the central ridge present in *P. didelphoides*). There is no metaconid developed. The buccal and lingual margins of the postvallid are more vertical and less flared and sloping compared to *P. didelphoides*. Overall, p4 has a short and broad talonid with small, but distinct, hypoconid and entoconid cusps, the latter being slightly larger. There is a small basined area developed between these two cusps and the postvallid. Like all of the premolars of *P. lacus*, p4 lacks cingulid development.

The enlarged p4 of *P. lacus* is superficially similar to those seen in Paleocene pentacodontines (Gunnell et al., **2008a**), but it differs from these taxa in being relatively less bulbous and enlarged, in lacking a metaconid, and in having a shorter, less well-developed talonid basin.

The lower first molar is somewhat broken and worn. It differs from other species of *Palaeosinopa* in having the talonid distinctly broader than the trigonid. The cristid obliqua joins the postvallid centrally as in most other *Palaeosinopa* species, but unlike the other species, nearly reaches the crest of the postvallid. The trigonid is worn into a flat triangle, the typical wear pattern exhibited by many pantolestids.

The dentary of *P. lacus* lacks the enlarged mental foramen beneath m1 typical of many pantolestids, instead having a relatively small mental foramen placed under the p4. The dentary, as in most pantolestids, is relatively shallow and tapers anteriorly.

Etymology

Specific name from "*lacus*", Latin for lake, in reference to Fossil Lake, the shores of which provided the habitat for the mammals from Fossil Butte.

Remarks

Matthew (**1909, 1918**) recognized three (perhaps four) species of *Palaeosinopa* and five species of *Pantolestes*. Gazin (**1962**) named an additional early Eocene pantolestid, *Amaramnis* (based on a single lower jaw with m2-3). While all three genera are probably valid, it seems nearly certain that there were fewer species present than have been previously recognized (Rose, **2006**; Gunnell et al., **2008a**). Matthew (**1918**) hinted at this when he tentatively suggested that *Palaeosinopa didelphoides* and *P. veterrima* may be conspecific. Further work is required to sort out the diversity of North American Eocene pantolestids.

Measurements

FOBU 6205: p2 = 4.2 x 1.7, p3 = 4.4 x 2.6, p4 = 4.6 x 3.2, m1 = 3.9 x 3.3.

Suborder Tillodontia Marsh, **1875**

Family Esthonychidae Cope, **1883**

Genus *Esthonyx* Cope, **1874**

Type species

Esthonyx bisulcatus Cope, **1874**, San Jose Formation, New Mexico.

Esthonyx cf. *E. bisulcatus* Cope, **1874**

Figure 4.4–**4**.5

1874 *Esthonyx bisulcatus* **Cope**, p. 6

Holotype

USNM 1103, left dentary p3, m1-3, from Arroyo Blanco, Wasatchian Biochron Wa7, San Juan Basin, New Mexico.

Occurrence

Localities **FB**-6, 7, 16, 19, late middle early Eocene, Wasatchian biochronologic zone Wa-6, main body, Wasatch Formation, Fossil Basin, Lincoln County, Wyoming.

Materials

FB-6: FOBU 6190, left p4 trigonid; **FB-7**: UM 102585, left Mx fragment; UM 108144, left m1-2 (broken). **FB-16**: FOBU 6419, right mx fragment. **FB-19**: FOBU 6389, right mx trigonid.

Remarks

These fragmentary teeth confirm the presence of *Esthonyx* at Fossil Butte. Estimating tooth size from the fragments preserved indicates that these specimens are in the size range of *E. bisulcatus* and probably represent that species.

Measurements

All of these teeth are too broken to provide accurate measurements.

Suborder Taeniodonta Cope, **1876**

Family Stylinodontidae Marsh, **1875**

Genus *Ectoganus* Cope, **1874**

Type species

Ectoganus gliriformis Cope, **1874**, San Jose Formation, New Mexico.

Ectoganus sp. indet.

Figure 4.6–**4**.7

1962 *Ectoganus* sp. **Gazin**, p. 44, Pl. 12, fig. 7

Occurrence

Locality **FB**-16, late middle early Eocene, Wasatchian biochronone Wa-6, main body, Wasatch Formation, Fossil Basin, Lincoln County, Wyoming.

Materials

FOBU 6361, incisor and molar fragments.

Remarks

While fragmentary, this specimen confirms the presence of *Ectoganus* in the Fossil Butte sample.

Measurements

FOBU 6361 is too fragmentary to be certain of tooth position or to provide accurate measurements. Gazin (**1962**) figured three fragmentary teeth (USNM 22785) of *Ectoganus* sp. from Fossil Butte.

Suborder Pantodonta Cope, **1873**

Family Coryphodontidae Marsh, **1876**

Genus *Coryphodon* Owen, **1845**

Type species

Coryphodon eocanus Owen, **1845**, London Clay, Essex, United Kingdom.

Coryphodon sp. indet.

Figure 4.8

1952 *Coryphodon*, cf. *radians* (in part); **Gazin**, p. 63, Pl. 9

1962 *Coryphodon radians* (in part); **Gazin**, p. 70, Pl. 11, figs. 1–5, Pl. 12, figs. 1–2

Occurrence

Localities **FB**-6, 7, 9–12, 18, late middle early Eocene, Wasatchian biochronologic zone Wa-6, main body, Wasatch Formation, Fossil Basin, Lincoln County, Wyoming.

Materials

FB-6: FOBU 6135, associated teeth and tooth fragments; FB 96-014, canine. **FB-7**: UM 102582, tooth fragments; UM 102586, tooth fragments; UM 102592, tooth fragments. **FB-9**: FB 96-062, canine; FB 96-067, tooth fragments; FB 96-068, canine; FB 97-023, tooth fragments. **FB-10**: FB 96-082, canine fragments. **FB-11**: FOBU 6356, upper molar fragment; FOBU 6363, tooth fragments; FB 96-086, postcrania; FB 96-088, tooth fragments. **FB-12**: FB 96-091, ulna. **FB-18**: FOBU 6286, postcrania.

Remarks

There are two species of *Coryphodon* recognized from Wa-6 in Wyoming (Uhen and Gingerich, **1995**), the larger *C. lobatus* and the smaller *C. armatus*. Most of the Fossil Butte *Coryphodon* specimens are too fragmentary to assign to either of these species. The relatively large size of the one measurable specimen, FOBU 6135, indicates that this individual probably represents *Coryphodon lobatus*. In a table (p. 9) published in 1952, Gazin indicated that *Coryphodon* sp. was present at Fossil Butte, but he did not mention any specific specimens in his discussion (Gazin, **1952**, p. 63). Gazin (**1962**, p. 70) noted the presence of scattered, fragmentary remains of *Coryphodon* from the lower slopes at Fossil Butte and included these specimens under his discussion of *Coryphodon radians*, a taxon now recognized as being restricted to Wasatchian biochron Wa-3 (Uhen and Gingerich, **1995**).

Measurements

FOBU 6135: p4 = 26.1 x 20.8.

Order Pholidota Weber, **1904**

Suborder Palaeanodonta Matthew, **1918**

Family Metacheiromyidae Wortman, **1903**

Genus *Palaeanodon* Matthew, **1918**

Type species

Palaeanodon ignavus Matthew, **1918**, Willwood Formation, Wyoming.

Palaeanodon sp. indet.

Figure 4.9–**4**.10

Occurrence

Localities **FB**-1, 9, 19, late middle early Eocene, Wasatchian biochronologic zone Wa-6 (**FB**-9, 19) and late early Eocene, Wasatchian biochronologic zone Wa-7 (**FB**-1), main body, Wasatch Formation, Fossil Basin, Lincoln County, Wyoming.

Materials

FB-1: FOBU 6163, right metacarpal II fragment; FOBU 6198, left astragalus. **FB-9**: FOBU 6097, right distal radius. **FB-19**: FOBU 6315, right dentary.

Remarks

There are two different sizes of palaeanodonts present at Fossil Butte. The small sample size and fragmentary nature of the remains preclude specific determinations.

Order ?Primates Linnaeus, **1758**

Suborder Plesiadapiformes Simons and Tattersall in Simons, **1972**

Superfamily Microsyopoidea Osborn and Wortman, **1892**

Family Microsyopidae Osborn and Wortman, **1892**

Genus *Microsyops* Leidy, **1872**

Type species

Limnotherium elegans Marsh, **1871**, Bridger Formation, Wyoming.

Microsyops latidens (Cope, **1882a**)

Figure 5.1–**5**.2

m1 in occlusal view. (2) FOBU 6287, Microsyops latidens, left dentary m2-3 in occlusal view. (3) FOBU 10011, Phenacolemur sp., left I1 in postero-occlusal view. (4) FOBU 6362, Cantius frugivorus, right dentary m2-3 in occlusal view. (5) UM 102587, Copelemur australotutus, right dentary p4-m3 in occlusal view. (6) FOBU 6193, Copelemur tutus, right dentary with p3 talonid, p4-m1, and partial trigonid of m2 showing distinct paraconid in occlusal view. Scale bars=5 mm for images 1–2 and 4–6; 2 mm for image 3.

1882a *Cynodontomys latidens* **Cope**, p. 151

Holotype

AMNH 4195, left dentary p4, right dentary m1-2, from Wasatchian Biochron Wa6, Bighorn Basin, Wyoming.

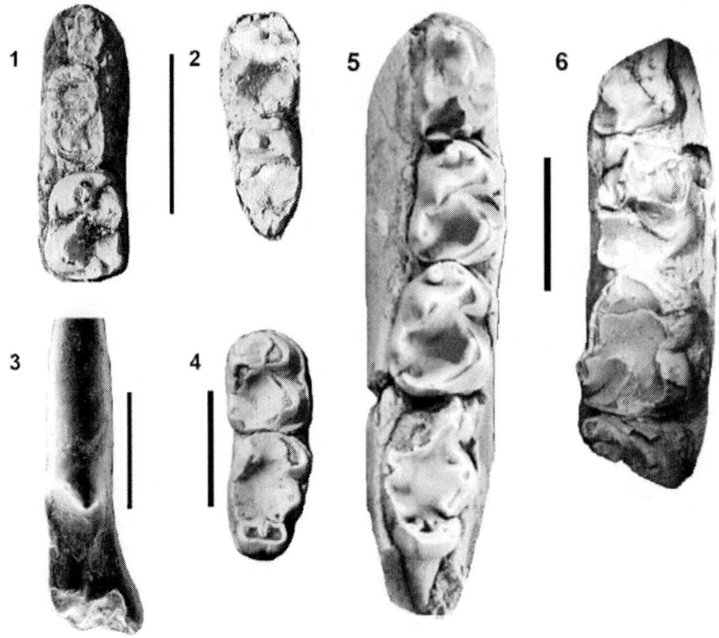

Figure 5 (1) FOBU 6366, Microsyops latidens, left dentary

Occurrence

Localities **FB**-9, 16, 18, late middle early Eocene, Wasatchian biochronologic zone Wa-6, main body, Wasatch Formation, Fossil Basin, Lincoln County, Wyoming.

Materials

FB-9: FB 97-020, left m1; **FB-16:** FOBU 6281, left dentary m1-2 talonids; FOBU 6366, left dentary m1-m/2 talonid. **FB-18:** FOBU 6287, left dentary m2-3.

Remarks

Microsyops latidens is the most common species of *Microsyops* from Wa-6 (Gunnell, **1989**). All of these specimens fall in the size range of *M. latidens*.

Measurements

FOBU 6366: m1 = 3.4 x 2.6; FOBU 6287: m2 = 3.2 x 2.5, m3 = 3.7 x 2.4.

Microsyops knightensis (Gazin, **1952**)

1952 *Cynodontomys knightensis* **Gazin**, p. 20, Pl. 2, fig. 1

Holotype

USNM 19314, left dentary p4-m3, from Knight Beds (=Wasatch Formation), LaBarge Fauna, Green River Basin, Wyoming.

Occurrence

Locality **FB**-16, late middle early Eocene, Wasatchian biochronologic zone Wa-6, main body, Wasatch Formation, Fossil Basin, Lincoln County, Wyoming.

Materials

FOBU 6199, left dentary m1-3 (teeth fragmentary; includes associated miscellaneous fragments cataloged as FOBU 6198).

Remarks

This single specimen represents a species of *Microsyops* larger than *M. latidens*. It can be identified as the common Wa-7 species of *Microsyops—M. knightensis*. As such, it represents the earliest known (Lysitean = Wa6) occurrence of this species.

Measurements

FOBU 6199: m2 = 4.2 x 3.3.

Superfamily Paromomyoidea Simpson, **1940**

Family Paromomyidae Simpson, **1940**

Genus *Phenacolemur* Matthew, **1915b**

Type species

Phenacolemur praecox Matthew, **1915b**, Willwood Formation, Wyoming.

Phenacolemur sp.

Figure 5.3

Occurrence

Horizon equivalent to locality **FB**-11 late middle early Eocene, Wasatchian biochronologic zone Wa-6, main body, Wasatch Formation, Fossil Basin, Lincoln County, Wyoming.

Materials

FOBU 10011, left I1.

Remarks

There is a single specimen representing *Phenacolemur* from Fossil Butte. It is not currently possible to identify this isolated upper incisor to the species level.

Order Primates Linnaeus, **1758**

Infraorder Adapiformes Szalay and Delson, **1979**

Family Notharctidae Trouessart, **1879**

Subfamily Notharctinae Trouessart, **1879**

Genus *Cantius* Simons, **1962**

Type species

Protoadapis eppsi Cooper, **1932**, Blackheath beds, Abbey Wood, Woolwich, Kent, United Kingdom.

Cantius frugivorus (Cope, **1875**)

Figure 5.4

1875 *Pelycodus frugivorus* **Cope**, p. 14

1962 *Pelycodus*, near *P. jarrovii*; **Gazin**, p. 28

Holotype

Unnumbered (specimen now lost), right dentary m2-3, from San Jose Formation, San Juan Basin, New Mexico (Neotype designated by Beard, **1988**: CM 37448, right dentary p3-m3, CM Almagre Locality 2, Sandoval County, New Mexico).

Occurrence

Localities **FB**-1, 4, 6, 7, 11, 19, 25, 26, late middle early Eocene, Wasatchian biochronologic zone Wa-6 (**FB**-4, 6-7, 11, 19, 25-26) and late early Eocene, Wasatchian biochronologic zone Wa-7 (**FB**-1), main body, Wasatch Formation, Fossil Basin, Lincoln County, Wyoming.

Materials

FB-1: FB 95-002, right m2 trigonid; FB 96-048, right m2; FB 97-006, navicular. **FB-4**: FOBU 6362, right dentary p4, m2-3; FOBU 9864, right maxilla M3. **FB-6:** FB 97-062, right M2. **FB-7:** UM 102588, right dentary m2, left m1. **FB-11**: FOBU 6373, left dentary m2-3; FOBU 6381, right dentary m2-3; FOBU 6391, right dentary p4-m3; FOBU 9895, left dentary p4-m2. **FB-19**: FOBU 6114, right dentary m3. **FB-25**: FOBU 6116, right dentary p3-m3. **FB-26**: FOBU 6112, right dentary m2-3.

Remarks

Cantius frugivorus is the most common species of Wa-6 adapiform known from southern Wyoming (Gunnell, **2002**). These referred specimens agree in size and morphology with that species. Gazin (**1962**, p 28) noted the presence of five adapiform specimens in the USNM collections from the "slopes of Fossil Butte" (including USNM 22259) that are larger than "*Pelycodus*" *trigonodus*. One of these specimens (USNM 22261) is the holotype of *Copelemur australotutus* (see below), while the others likely represent *Cantius frugivorus*.

Measurements

FOBU 6362: p4 = 3.9 x 2.7, m2 = 4.2 x 3.7, m3 = 5.1 x 3.4; FOBU 6373: m2 = 4.0 x 3.5; FOBU 6381: m2 = 4.6 x 4.2, m3 = 6.8 x 3.7; FOBU 6391: m3 = 5.2 x 3.5; FB 96-048: m2 = 4.5 x 3.6; FOBU 6114: m3 = 5.4 x 3.3; FOBU 6116: p3 = 3.5 x 2.5, p4 = 3.8 x 3.0, m1 = 4.1 x 3.6, m2 = 4.3 x 3.8; FOBU 6112: m3 = 5.5 x 3.4; UM 102588: m2 = 4.4 x 4.1.

Genus *Copelemur* Gingerich and Simons, **1977**

Type species

Tomitherium tutum Cope, **1877**, San Jose Formation, New Mexico.

Copelemur australotutus Beard, **1988**

Figure 5.5

Holotype

USNM 22261, left dentary p3-m1, from north face of Fossil Butte, Wasatch Formation, Fossil Basin, Wyoming.

Occurrence

Localities **FB**-1, 7, 8, 11, 19, 21, late middle early Eocene, Wasatchian biochronologic zone Wa-6 (**FB**-7-8, 11, 19, 21) and late early Eocene, Wasatchian biochronologic zone Wa-7 (**FB**-1), main body, Wasatch Formation, Fossil Basin, Lincoln County, Wyoming.

Materials

FB-1: FB 96-042, left m3 (enamel eroded); FB 96-096, right m1 fragment. **FB-7:** UM 102587, right dentary p4-m3; UM 102589, left maxilla M2-3, C1, right dentary m3; UM 108138, left m1. **FB-8:** FB 96-026, left m1 trigonid. **FB-11**: FOBU 9893, right dentary m1-2. **FB-19**: FB 97-089, left dentary m2. **FB-21**: FBF 150, right dentary m2-3.

Remarks

Beard (**1988**) named *C. australotutus* based on a relatively poorly preserved specimen from Fossil Butte (USNM 22261). These newly referred specimens corroborate Beard's recognition of *C. australotutus* as a distinct species of *Copelemur*. Relatively large samples of *C. australotutus* from the Washakie Basin (Gunnell, **2002**), in combination with those from Fossil Butte, make *C. australotutus* the best-known species of the genus.

Measurements

FB 97-089: m2 = 4.5 x 3.7; UM 102587: p4 = 4.1 x 3.0, m1 = 4.5 x 3.6, m2 = 4.8 x 4.0; UM 102589: M2 = 4.6 x 6.4, M3 = 4.8 x 5.7, m3 = 6.0 x 4.0.

Copelemur tutus (Cope, **1877**)

Figure 5.6

1877 *Tomitherium tutum* **Cope**, p. 141, Pl. 39, fig. 19

1881 *Pelycodus tutus* (in part); **Cope**, p. 187

1915b *Pelycodus tutus*; **Matthew**, p. 441, fig. 15

1962 *Pelycodus*? *tutus*; **Gazin**, p. 29

1977 *Copelemur tutus*; **Gingerich and Simons**, p. 271, Pl. 1, fig. 3, text fig. 6b

1988 *Copelemur tutus*; **Beard**, p 454, **Fig. 8, 9**

Holotype

Unnumbered (specimen now lost), right dentary p3-m1, from San Jose Formation, San Juan Basin, New Mexico (Neotype designated by Beard, **1988**: UALP 10233, right dentary p3-m2, UALP Locality 7745, Regina Member, Sandoval County, New Mexico).

Occurrence

Locality **FB**-13, late middle early Eocene, Wasatchian biochronologic zone Wa-6, main body, Wasatch Formation, Fossil Basin, Lincoln County, Wyoming.

Materials

FOBU 6193, right dentary p4-m1.

Remarks

Copelemur tutus is relatively common in the San Juan Basin in New Mexico but is rare from southern Wyoming (Gingerich and Simons, **1977**; Gunnell, **2002**). While this specimen is somewhat worn and broken, the clear presence of a distinct paraconid on m2, the presence of a short, lingually bowed entocristid and entoconid notch on m1, and the presence of a distinct, high metaconid and a strong paracristid on p4 identify it as *Copelemur*. Its large size confirms its identification as *C. tutus*.

Measurements

FOBU 6193: p4 = 5.0 x 3.8, m1 = 5.6 x 4.0.

Order Condylarthra Cope, **1881**

Family Hyopsodontidae Trouessart, **1879**

Genus *Hyopsodus* Leidy, **1870**

Type species

Hyopsodus paulus Leidy, **1870**, Bridger Formation, Wyoming.

Hyopsodus minor Loomis, **1905**

Figure 6.1–**6**.2

1962 *Hyopsodus*, cf. *H. miticulus* (in part); **Gazin** p. 63

Holotype

AC 3492, right dentary m1-3, from Wasatchian Biochron Wa6, Wind River Formation, Wind River Basin, Wyoming.

Occurrence

Localities **FB**-4, 5, 6, 7, 9, 10, 15, 16, 18, 19, 24-27, late middle early Eocene, Wasatchian biochronologic zone Wa-6, main body, Wasatch Formation, Fossil Basin, Lincoln County, Wyoming.

Materials

FB-4: FOBU 6370, left maxilla M1-2; FOBU 6412, left dentary m1-2; FOBU 6434, right mx fragment. **FB-5**: FB 97-015, right P3. **FB-6**: FB 96-006, right dentary m2-3; FB 96-013, left mx talonid. **FB-7:** UM 102594, right M2. **FB-9**: FB 96-063, right dentary m2-3; FOBU 6213, left dentary m1-3. **FB-10**: FB 96-078, right m1. **FB-15**: FB 97-026, left maxilla P4-M1; FB 97-028, right dentary m1-3; FB 97-068, left dentary p4. **FB-16**: FB 97-033, right m3; FOBU 6392, left maxilla M1-2. **FB-18**: FB 97-075, right M2; FB 97-076, right dentary p4-m1; FB 97-081, right m2. **FB-19**: FB 97-095, right dentary m3; FB 97-099, left M2. **FB-24**: FB 97-108, right dentary m1-3. **FB-25**: FB 97-110, left M2. **FB-26**: FB 97-115, right dentary m2-3. **FB-27**: FOBU 6398, left M2.

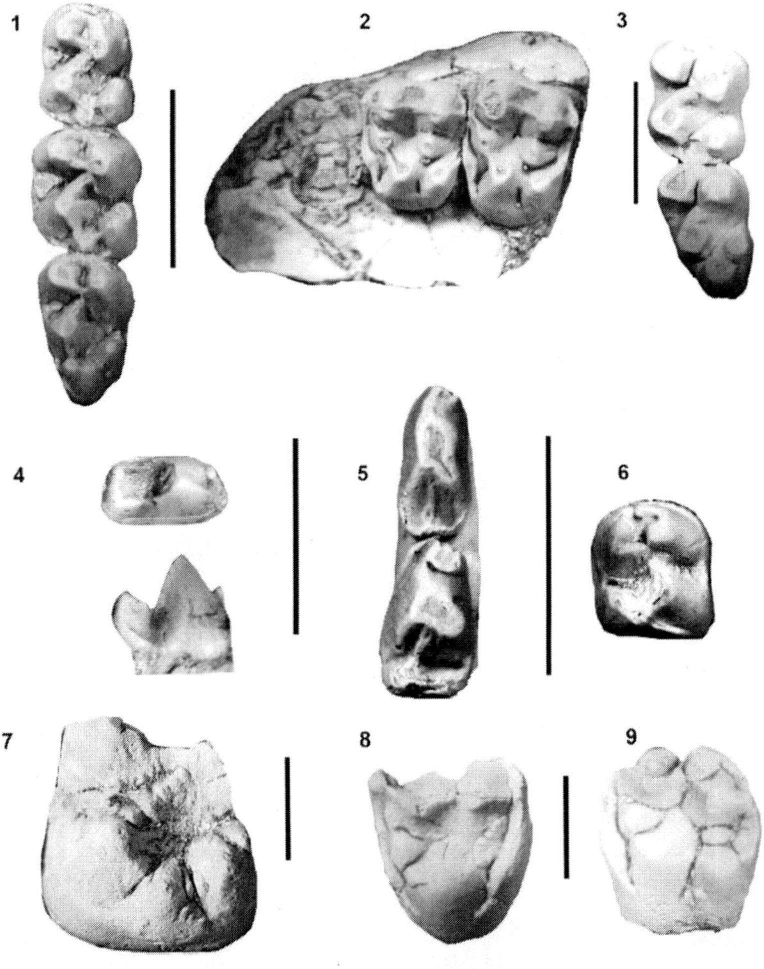

Figure 6 (1) FOBU 6213, Hyopsodus minor, left dentary m1-3 in occlusal view. (2) FOBU 6370, Hyopsodus minor, left maxilla M1-2 in occlusal view. (3) FOBU 6129, Hyopsodus powellianus, left dentary m2-3 in occlusal view. (4) FOBU 6297, Apheliscus cf. A. insidiosus, right p4 in occlusal (top) and buccal (bottom) views. (5) FOBU 6318, Haplomylus cf. H. scottianus, left dentary p3-4 in occlusal view. (6) FOBU 6437, Haplomylus cf. H. scottianus, right m2 in occlusal view. (7) FOBU 6365, Phenacodus trilobatus, left lower molar fragment (most of trigonid and a portion of the lingual margin missing) in occlusal view. (8–9) FOBU 6229, Ectocion superstes, left broken P4 (left, labial edge missing) and M1 (right, broken labially) in occlusal views. Scale bars=5 mm.

Remarks

These specimens are consistent in size and morphology with the relatively small species of *Hyopsodus, H. minor*, documented from several areas in the Green River Basin (Gazin, **1968**), other areas in Wyoming, the San Juan Basin in New Mexico, and the Piceance Basin in Colorado (Redline, **1997**). Gazin tentatively referred several specimens in the USNM collections from Fossil Butte (numbers not cited) to a relatively small species of *Hyopsodus, H. miticulus* but it is more likely, given the size of these specimens, that they represent *H. minor* instead.

Measurements

FOBU 6370: M1 = 3.1 x 3.8, M2 = 3.2 x 4.4; FOBU 6398: M2 = 3.6 x 5.0; FOBU 6412: m1 = 3.2 x 2.5, m2 = 3.3 x 2.7; FOBU 6392: M1 = 3.4 x 4.3, M2 = 3.6 x 4.7; FB 96-063: m2 = 3.5 x 3.1, m3 = 3.6 x 2.7; FB 96-078: m1 = 3.2 x 2.6; FOBU 6213: m1 = 3.2 x 2.7, m2 = 3.5 x 3.0, m3 = 3.7 x 2.8; FB 97-026: P4 = 3.3 x 4.3, M1 = 3.7 x 4.9; FB 97-033: m3 = 3.9 x 2.6; FB 97-068: p4 = 3.8 x 2.6; FB 97-076: p4 = 3.1 x 2.8, m1 = 3.5 x 3.2; FB 97-081: m2 = 3.4 x 3.1; FB 97-099: M2 = 3.2 x 4.8; FB 97-108: m1 = 3.0 x 2.6, m2 = 3.3 x 2.9, m3 = 3.6 x 2.6; FB 97-110: M2 = 3.4 x 4.6; UM 102594: M2 = 3.6 x 5.1.

Hyopsodus powellianus Cope, **1884**

Figure 6.3

1962 *Hyopsodus browni* (in part); **Gazin**, p. 65

Lectotype

AMNH 4147, dentary m1-3, from unknown locality, Bighorn Basin, Wyoming.

Occurrence

Localities **FB**-1, 15 late middle early Eocene, Wasatchian biochronologic zone Wa-6 (**FB**-15) and late early Eocene, Wasatchian biochronologic zone Wa-7 (**FB**-1), main body, Wasatch Formation, Fossil Basin, Lincoln County, Wyoming.

Materials

FB-1: FOBU 6129, left dentary m2-3; FB 96-035, left maxilla P4-M2. **FB-15**: FB 97-066, left maxilla M2-3.

Remarks

These teeth are intermediate in size between *Hyopsodus powellianus* and *Hyopsodus paulus* (Redline, **1997**). The M2 is within the size range of *Hyopsodus paulus*, but P4 is larger than the observed range for this species (Redline, **1997**), falling instead within the size range of *H. powellianus*. The lower teeth are within the lower size range for *H. powellianus*, therefore we identify all of these specimens as that species. Large species of *Hyopsodus* are relatively rare from biochron Wa-6 in the Green River Basin (Gazin, **1962**). Gazin (**1962**, p. 65) identified two large *Hyopsodus* specimens as *H. browni*, a maxilla with partial M2 and M3 from "high on the southwest slope of Fossil Butte," in the deeper red beds just beneath the Green River (near UM Localities **FB**-1 and **FB**-27) and a dentary with m2 and part of m3 from "the saddle on the north side of Fossil Butte" (near UM Locality **FB**-22). We consider these specimens to represent *H. powellianus*.

Measurements

FOBU 6129: m2 = 5.1 x 4.1, m3 = 5.9 x 3.7; FB 96-035: P4 = 4.0 x 4.7; FB 97-066: M2 = 4.1 x 5.5.

Genus *Apheliscus* Cope, **1875**

Type species

Prototomus insidiosus Cope, **1874**, San Juan Basin, New Mexico.

Apheliscus cf. *A. insidiosus* (Cope, **1874**)

Figure 6.4

1874 *Prototomus insidiosus* **Cope**, p. 14

Holotype

Unnumbered, dentary p4-m3 (specimen lost), from unknown locality, Biochron Wa7, San Jose Formation, New Mexico.

Occurrence

Locality **FB**-16, late middle early Eocene, Wasatchian biochronologic zone Wa-6, main body, Wasatch Formation, Fossil Basin, Lincoln County, Wyoming.

Materials

FOBU 6297, right dentary p4.

Remarks

This p4 is in the size range of *A. insidiosus* but differs from that species by possessing a small, anterior basal cuspule. *Apheliscus* is never especially abundant and is exceedingly rare in Wa-6, being represented in this biochron only by: (1) the type specimen of *A. insidiosus* from the San Juan Basin in New Mexico (the type has been lost for over 80 years, and no other specimens of *Apheliscus* have been reported from the San Juan Basin; see Rose, **1981**); (2) the above specimen from Fossil Butte; (3) a few specimens from the Bighorn Basin in northwestern Wyoming (personal communication, K.D. Rose, 2015); and (4) a single reported specimen from the Wind River Basin in south-central Wyoming (Guthrie, **1967**). *Apheliscus* apparently disappeared by the end of Wa-6 elsewhere (Woodburne et al., **2009**).

Measurements

FOBU 6297: p4 = 3.1 x 1.7.

Genus *Haplomylus* Matthew, **1915a**

Type species

Microsyops sperianus Cope, **1880**, Bighorn Basin, Wyoming.

Haplomylus cf. *H. scottianus* Gingerich, **1994**

Figure 6.5–**6**.6

1994 *Haplomylus scottianus* **Gingerich**, p. 126, figs. 3c, 3g, 4

Holotype

UM 92489, left dentary p4-m3, Wasatchian Biochron Wa5, Willwood Formation, Bighorn Basin, Wyoming.

Occurrence

Localities **FB**-11, 18, 19, late middle early Eocene, Wasatchian biochronologic zone Wa-6, main body, Wasatch Formation, Fossil Basin, Lincoln County, Wyoming.

Materials

FB-11: FOBU 6437, right dentary m2. **FB-18**: FOBU 6304, right dentary with talonid of p4 and m1 with broken trigonid. **FB-19**: FOBU 6318, left dentary p3-4.

Remarks

These specimens are in the size range of *H. scottianus* (Gingerich, **1994**), but differ from that species in having a simpler, relatively shorter p4 talonid, a weaker paracristid on m2, and a much weaker hypoconulid on m1-2. These specimens may prove to represent a species distinct from *H. scottianus* when better samples are discovered. These records (Wa-6) of *Haplomylus* are the latest known occurrences of the genus, whereas it apparently disappears by the end of Wa-5 elsewhere (Gazin, **1962**; Gingerich, **1994**).

Measurements

FOBU 6437: m2 = 2.7 x 2.5; FOBU 6304: m1 = 2.6 x 2.1; FOBU 6318: p3 = 3.2 x 1.6, p4 = 3.4 x 1.9.

Family Phenacodontidae Cope, **1881**

Genus *Phenacodus* Cope, **1873**

Type species

Phenacodus primaevus Cope, **1873**, Green River Basin, Wyoming.

Phenacodus trilobatus Cope, **1882b**

Figure 6.7

Holotype

AMNH 4679, left dentary m1-3, locality unknown, middle to late Wasatchian, Willwood Formation, Bighorn Basin, Wyoming.

Occurrence

Locality **FB**-11, late middle early Eocene, Wasatchian biochronologic zone Wa-6, main body, Wasatch Formation, Fossil Basin, Lincoln County, Wyoming.

Materials

FOBU 6365, left lower molar trigonid (worn).

Remarks

This specimen preserves only enough morphology to indicate that it represents a relatively large species of *Phenacodus*. *Phenacodus trilobatus* is similar in size and is known from the late Wasatchian (Thewissen, **1990**), therefore this specimen is accordingly identified as that species.

Measurements

No standard measurements are possible on this broken specimen.

Genus *Ectocion* Cope, **1882c**

Type species

Oligotomus osbornianus Cope, **1882c**, Bighorn Basin, Wyoming.

Ectocion superstes Granger, **1915**

Figure 6.8–**6**.9

Holotype

AMNH 233A, dentary c1, p3-m3, Bridgerian Biochron Br1a, Wind River Formation, Wind River Basin, Wyoming.

Occurrence

Locality **FB**-16, late middle early Eocene, Wasatchian biochronologic zone Wa-6, main body, Wasatch Formation, Fossil Basin, Lincoln County, Wyoming.

Materials

FOBU 6229, left P4 and M1, both broken.

Remarks

Besides these two fragments of *E. superstes* from Fossil Butte, the only other known sample of this rare phenacodontid comes from the earliest Bridgerian (Br1a) in the Wind River Basin of Wyoming (Thewissen, **1990**). These two fragmentary teeth from Wa-6 at Fossil Butte represent the earliest known occurrence of this species.

Measurements

No measurements are possible.

Family Meniscotheriidae Cope, **1882d**

Genus *Meniscotherium* Cope, **1874**

Type species

Meniscotherium chamense Cope, **1874**, San Juan Basin, New Mexico.

Meniscotherium cf. *M. robustum* Thorpe, **1934**

1934 *Mensicotherium robustum* **Thorpe**, p. 401, figs. 1–4

1962 *Meniscotherium robustum* (in part); **Gazin**, p. 68

Holotype

YPM 10101, skull, dentary, Knight beds (= Wasatch Formation), middle to late Wasatchian, near Aspen, Wyoming.

Occurrence

Locality **FB**-15, late middle early Eocene, Wasatchian biochronologic zone Wa-6, main body, Wasatch Formation, Fossil Basin, Lincoln County, Wyoming.

Materials

FB-15: FBF 155 (= USNM 22670), left dentary p4-m2, right dentary m1, left maxilla M1-2, associated postcranial fragments.

Remarks

As discussed by Gazin (**1962**), *Meniscotherium* is extremely rare in Fossil Basin, which seems odd given that it is abundant from correlative beds in the adjacent Green River Basin. Gazin (**1962**, p. 68) noted the presence of this one specimen of *Meniscotherium* from "high on Fossil Butte" (UM **FB**-15) that he hesitantly assigned to *M. robustum*.

Measurements

FBF 155: p4 = 8.0 x 5.5, m1 = 8.0 x 5.8, m2 = 9.0 x 6.8.

Order Mesonychia Matthew, **1937**

Family Mesonychidae Cope, **1875**

Mesonychid sp. indet.

Occurrence

"Low on slope of Fossil Butte" (Gazin, **1962**, p. 51; probably in the vicinity of UM localities **FB**-4, **FB**-11, and **FB**-26), late middle early Eocene, Wasatchian biochronologic zone Wa-6, main body, Wasatch Formation, Fossil Basin, Lincoln County, Wyoming.

Remarks

Gazin (**1962**, p. 51) noted the presence of a fragmentary lower cheek tooth of a mesonychid from Fossil Butte. He identified this tooth as *Pachyaena gracilis*, but noted that it seemed rather small and reminiscent of *Dissacus* as well. In either case, it represents the only known record of a mesonychid from Fossil Butte.

Order Rodentia Bowdich, **1821**

Family Ischyromyidae Alston, **1876**

Subfamily Reithroparamyinae Wood, **1962**

Genus *Reithroparamys* Matthew, **1920**

Type species

Paramys delicatissimus Leidy, **1871**, Green River Basin, Wyoming.

Reithroparamys cf. *R. debequensis* Wood, **1962**

1962 *Reithroparamys debequensis* **Wood**, p. 134, fig. 45D–G

1962 *Reithroparamys* sp., **Gazin**, p. 46

Holotype

FMNH (CNHM) P-26726, left dentary i1, m1-3, Wasatchian Biochron Wa6, Debeque Formation, near Rifle, Colorado.

Occurrence

Saddle north of Fossil Butte (near UM Localities **FB**-22 and **FB**-28), late middle early Eocene, Wasatchian biochronologic zone Wa-6, main body, Wasatch Formation, Fossil Basin, Lincoln County, Wyoming.

Materials

USNM 22380, left dentary i1, m1.

Remarks

A single specimen of *Reithroparamys* is represented at Fossil Butte, questionably identified as *R. debequensis* by Wood (**1962**). He noted that it was similar to *R. debequensis* but that the molar was much narrower than other specimens.

Subfamily Paramyinae Haeckel, **1895**

Genus ?*Notoparamys* Korth, **1984**

Type species

Leptotomus costilloi Wood, **1962**, Huerfano Basin, Colorado.

?*Notoparamys blochi* new species

Figure 7.1–**7**.4

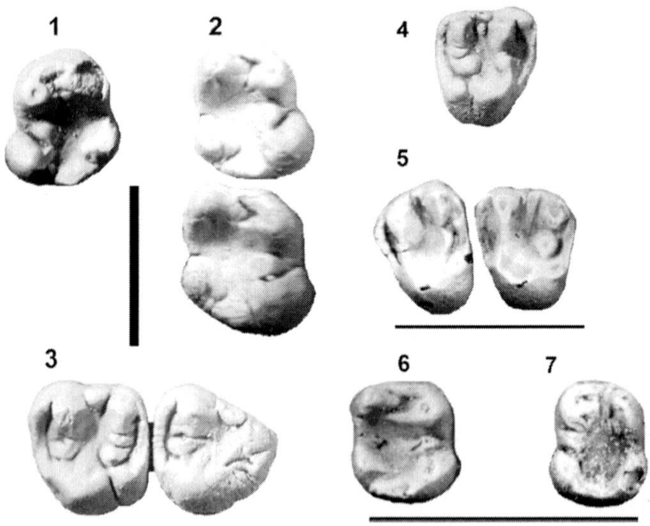

Figure 7 (1–2) FOBU 6092, ?Notoparamys blochi n. sp. (Holotype), left m1 (left) and right dentary m1-2 (right) in occlusal view. (3–4) FOBU 6092, ?Notoparamys blochi n. sp. (Holotype), left maxilla M2-3 (top) and right M1 (bottom) in occlusal view. (5) FOBU 6182, Paramys excavatus, left maxilla P4-M1 in occlusal view. (6–7) FOBU 6161, Knightomys depressus, right m2 (left) and FOBU 6408, Knightomys depressus, left m1 (right) in occlusal view. Scale bars=5 mm.

Holotype

Holotype and only specimen, FOBU 6092, associated left dentary m1, right dentary m1-2, left maxilla M2-3, right maxilla M1, and postcranial fragments, found by Jonathan I. Bloch, July 30, 1997, from locality **FB**-15, late middle early Eocene, Wasatchian biochronologic zone Wa-6, main body, Wasatch Formation, Fossil Basin, Lincoln County, Wyoming.

Diagnosis

?*Notoparamys blochi* n. sp. differs from *Notoparamys costilloi* in having an unreduced M3, a less transversely elongate hypoconulid on lower molars, an m1-2 mesoconid that is connected to the base of the protoconid and to the anterolingual base of the hypoconid (i.e., complete ectolophid), in lacking a protoconid loph that extends into the trigonid basin, and in lacking full development of the distinctive double-ridged connection between the hypoconulid and entoconid that is apparently typical of *Notoparamys* (Korth, **1984** and discussion below); differs from *N. arctios* in being substantially larger in tooth dimensions (on average 25% larger in linear dimensions), but does resemble this species in lacking a protoconid extension into the trigonid basin.

Description

The holotype (and only) specimen of ?*Notoparamys blochi* n. sp. is known from upper and lower molars. Lower m1 and m2 are similar in having bulbous and marginally placed proto-, meta-, hypo-, and entoconids, with the hypoconid being the most robust cusp, followed by the metaconid. The hypoconid bulges buccally towards its base and is essentially separated from the protoconid by a distinct, low mesoconid (the mesoconid is connected to both the proto- and hypoconid on m1). There is a distinct, crescentic hypoconulid present that is centered on posterolophid of each tooth (not more lingually placed as noted for *Notoparamys* by Korth, **1984**) and separated from both the hypoconid and entoconid by narrow valleys. There is a short crest that extends from the buccal base of the entoconid posterobuccally toward the hypoconulid but does not reach that cusp. The hypoconulid is not connected to the entoconid by an additional crest posterior to the one from the entoconid, instead being separated posteriorly from the entoconid by a tiny cuspule. Lower m2 differs from m1 in being slightly larger with a slightly more anteroposteriorly compressed metalophid.

Upper molars are all similar to one another and share the following morphological features. Protocones are rounded and robust and paracones. Metacones are distinct and relatively smaller than the protocone, especially on M1-2. A distinct hypocone is present on M1 and M2 (absent on M3) that is separated from the protocone by a sharply defined groove as in *Notoparamys* . Hypocones do not extend as far lingually as the protocones.

Robust and bulbous mesostyles are present on all molars, with M3 having at least three small mesostylar cusps. Incipiently doubled potoconules (best seen on M2-3) and distinctly doubled metaconules are found on all three molars, the latter feature being shared with *Notoparamys* (and other paramyines as well, see Rose and Von Koenigswald, **2007**for discussion). Pre- and postcingula are well developed and anteroposteriorly broad.

M1 differs from M2 in being somewhat smaller and anteroposteriorly narrower with a less broad trigon fovea (basin). M3 differs from both M1 and M2 in lacking a hypocone and in having a more robust and relatively larger protocone. It also differs from the other molars in having a rounded and posteriorly directed metacone, a double-crested metaloph with the posterior branch reaching the postcingulid and forming a small cuspule there, and in being somewhat more triangular in shape rather than more rhomboidal like M1-2.

Etymology

For Jonathan I. Bloch, who discovered the type specimen and for his many contributions to the recovery and study of fossil mammals from Wyoming and elsewhere.

Remarks

Rose and Von Koenigswald (**2007**) discussed the complicated history of *Notoparamys* and described a highly variable sample of what they referred to as *N. costilloi* from Wa-6 in the Bighorn Basin of northwestern Wyoming. They noted that many (most) of the distinctive characters used to diagnose this genus (hypocone distinct and adjacent to metaconule on M1-2, M3 smaller than M1-2, mesoconid large and isolated on lower molars, hypoconulid wide and connected to entoconid by a pair of ridges enclosing a tiny basin that may be open posteriorly, accessory lophid extends from metaconid into trigonid fovea, low incisor flattened medially, rounded laterally, see Korth, **1984**, **1994b**; Anderson, **2008**) are variably present or absent and variably developed or not in the Bighorn Basin sample.

?*Notoparamys blochi* n. sp. is no exception, with only a distinct hypocone and an accessory lophid extending from the metaconid into the trigonid fovea on the lower molars being definitively shared in common with the genotype species, *N. costilloi.* The double-ridge connection of the hypoconulid to the entoconid is only incipient (see description above) on the m1-2 of ?*N. blochi*. Korth (**1984**) indicated that both of these ridges originated from the lingual end of the hypoconulid in *Notoparamys* but it is apparent from the m1-2 of ?*N. blochi* that the more mesial of these ridges likely originated from the entoconid and extended posterobucally to eventually reach the hypoconulid. The more posterior of these ridges is described as being "broken at its center by narrow valley" (Korth, **1984**, p. 21). In ?*N. blochi*, the posterior ridge is clearly differentiated from the entoconid by a rather distinct valley on m1 while that valley is partially bridged by a small cuspule located between the entoconid and hypoconulid on m2.

We tentatively assign this new species to ?*Notoparamys*. However, we note that, aside from the type sample from Huerfano (Wood, **1962**; Robinson, **1966**; Korth, **1984**), it is questionable whether or not any of the other specimens assigned to *Notoparamys* (Korth, **1984**; Rose and Chinnery, **2004**; Rose and Von Koenigswald, **2007**) actually belong to that genus, and if they do, whether or not the genus can be sustained as defined given that virtually every character cited in the diagnosis is so variable as to often be completely absent. We believe that, at the generic level especially, diagnostic characters must be those that are present in all specimens whether or not they are weakly or more strongly formed.

Measurements

FOBU 6092: M1 = 3.7 x 4.3, M2 = 3.8 x 4.3, M3 = 4.3 x 3.9, m1 = 4.1 x 3.5, m2 = 4.5 x 3.8.

Genus *Paramys* Leidy, **1871**

Type species

Paramys delicatus Leidy, **1871** (as designated by Wood, **1962**), Green River Basin, Wyoming.

Paramys excavatus Loomis, **1907**

Figure 7.5

Holotype

ACM 327, right dentary p4-m3, Wasatchian Biochron a6, Wind River Formation, Bridger Creek, Wyoming.

Occurrence

Localities **FB**-1, 10, 18, 19, late middle early Eocene, Wasatchian biochronologic zone Wa-6 (**FB**-10, 18-19) and late early Eocene, Wasatchian biochronologic zone Wa-7 (**FB**-1), main body, Wasatch Formation, Fossil Basin, Lincoln County, Wyoming.

Materials

FB-1: FB 96-038, left dentary i1; FB 96-039, left m1. **FB-10**: FOBU 6182, left maxilla P4-M1. **FB-18**: FB 97-079, left p4. **FB-19**: FB 97-096, left maxilla P4.

Remarks

These specimens are in the size range of the relatively common taxon *Paramys excavatus* (Wood, **1962**) and probably all represent that species.

Measurements

FB 96-039: m1 = 3.1 x 3.0; FOBU 6182: P4 = 2.7 x 3.3, M1 = 2.7 x 3.3; FB 97-079: p4 = 2.6 x 2.1.

Paramyinae sp. indet.

Occurrence

Locality **FB**-16, late middle early Eocene, Wasatchian biochronologic zone Wa-6, main body, Wasatch Formation, Fossil Basin, Lincoln County, Wyoming.

Materials

FOBU 6283, right M2.

Remarks

This tooth represents a small paramyine, larger than *Microparamys*, but smaller than other known paramyines. M2 is almost square with a relatively small, indistinct, posteriorly placed hypocone, a relatively strong, isolated metaconule, and a tiny mesostyle. This tooth may represent a new paramyine genus, but more complete specimens are required to be certain.

Measurements

FB 6283: M2 = 2.1 x 2.2

Family Sciuravidae Miller and Gidley, **1918**

Genus *Knightomys* Gazin, **1961**

Type species

Tillomys senior Gazin, **1952**, Green River Basin, Wyoming.

Knightomys depressus Loomis, **1907**

Figure 7.6–**7**.7

Holotype

ACM 432, skull with right M1-3, left I1, Wasatchian Biochron Wa6, Wind River Formation, Wyoming.

Occurrence

Localities **FB**-1, 4, late middle early Eocene, Wasatchian biochronologic zone Wa-6 (**FB**-4) and late early Eocene, Wasatchian biochronologic zone Wa-7 (**FB**-1), main body, Wasatch Formation, Fossil Basin, Lincoln County, Wyoming.

Materials

FB-1: FOBU 6161, right m2. **FB-4:** FOBU 6408, left m1.

Remarks

These two specimens represent a sciuravid larger than *Knightomys senior* (Gazin, **1952**) and are similar in size to *K. depressus* (Loomis, **1907**). The type sample of *K. depressus* is from the Wa-6 horizon in the Wind River Basin (Wood, **1965**), but the species may range into the Bridgerian (Korth, **1994b**).

Measurements

FOBU 6161: m2 = 2.0 x 1.9; FOBU 6408: m = 2.0 x 1.7.

Knightomys huerfanensis (Wood, **1962**)

1962 *Paramys huerfanensis* **Wood**, p. 62

1966 *Paramys huerfanensis*; **Robinson**, p. 45

Holotype

AMNH 55114, right dentary p4-m3, Bridgerian Biochron Br1a, Locality II, Huerfano Formation, Colorado.

Occurrence

Locality **FB**-19, late middle early Eocene, Wasatchian biochronologic zone Wa-6, main body, Wasatch Formation, Fossil Basin, Lincoln County, Wyoming.

Materials

FOBU 6397, left M2.

Remarks

This single tooth represents a relatively large species of *Knightomys*. It is of similar size to *K. huerfanensis* and, like that species, has relatively robust and rounded cusps, especially the protocone and hypocone (Korth, **1984**). This specimen represents the earliest known occurrence (Wa-6) of *K. huerfanensis*, otherwise only known from the latest Wasatchian (Wa-7) and earliest Bridgerian (Br-1a).

Measurements

FOBU 6397: M2 = 2.3 x 2.5.

Order Oxyaenodonta Van Valen, **1971**

Family Oxyaenidae Cope, **1877**

Subfamily Oxyaeninae Cope, **1877**

Genus *Oxyaena* Cope, **1874**

Type species

Oxyaena lupina Cope, **1874**, San Juan Basin, New Mexico.

Oxyaena forcipata Cope, **1874**

Figure 8.1–**8**.2

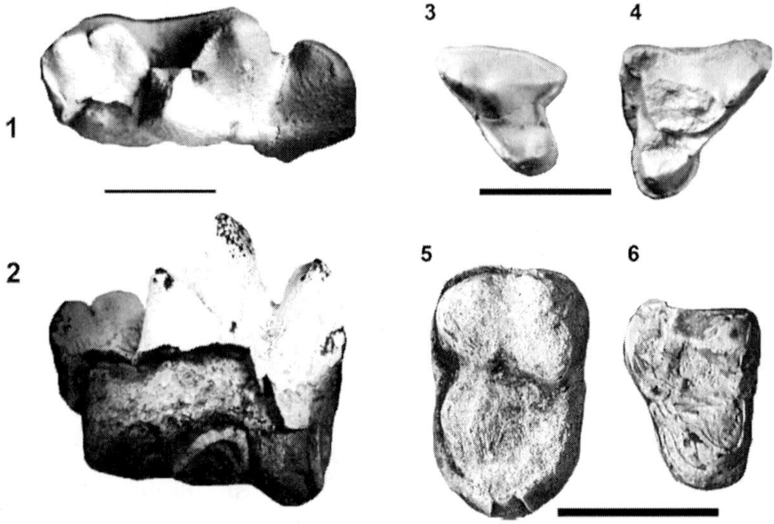

Figure 8 (1–2) UM 102584, Oxyaena forcipata, left dp4 with broken labial trigonid and lingual talonid in occlusal (top) and lingual (bottom) views. (3) FOBU 6380, Prototomus secundarius, right P4 in occlusal view. (4) FOBU 6380, Prototomus secundarius, left broken M1 in occlusal view. (5) FOBU 6385, Didymictis cf. D. protenus, left m2 in occlusal view. (6) UM 108143, Didymictis cf. D. protenus, left M1 (broken) in occlusal view. Scale bars=5 mm.

Holotype

USNM 1029, left and right dentaries, Wasatchian Biochron Wa7, San Jose Formation, San Juan Basin, New Mexico.

Occurrence

Locality **FB**-7, late middle early Eocene, Wasatchian biochronologic zone Wa-6, main body, Wasatch Formation, Fossil Basin, Lincoln County, Wyoming.

Materials

UM 102584, left dp4.

Remarks

This specimen represents a relatively large species of *Oxyaena*. The Wa-6 form, *O. forcipata*, is of the right size and morphology, and we identify UM 102584 as this species.

Measurements

UM 102584: dp4 length = 13.9 mm (a width measurement is not possible on this broken specimen).

Order Hyaenodonta Van Valen, **1967**

Genus *Prototomus* Cope, **1874**

Type species

Prototomus viverrinus Cope, **1874**, San Juan Basin, New Mexico.

Prototomus secundarius Cope, **1875**

Figure 8.3–**8**.4

1962 *Sinopa*, cf. *S. multicuspis* (in part); **Gazin**, p. 55

Holotype

USNM 1025, left and right dentary fragments, Wasatchian Biochron Wa7, San Jose Formation, San Juan Basin, New Mexico.

Occurrence

Locality **FB**-27, late middle early Eocene, Wasatchian biochronologic zone Wa-6, main body, Wasatch Formation, Fossil Basin, Lincoln County, Wyoming.

Materials

FOBU 6380, right P4, left maxilla P3-M1.

Remarks

These specimens represent an intermediate-sized hyaenodontid and are of appropriate size and morphology to be identified as *P. secundarius*. An additional specimen, probably referable to *P. secundarius*, from "high on Fossil Butte" (Gazin, **1962**, p. 55; near UM Localities **FB**-1 and **FB**-27), is USNM 22460, a fragmentary right maxilla with two broken molars.

Measurements

FOBU 6380: P3 = 5.0 x 2.7, P4 = 5.5 x 5.0, M1 = 6.0 x 7.2.

Hyaenodontid sp. indet.

Occurrence

Localities **FB**-13, 18, late middle early Eocene, Wasatchian biochronologic zone Wa-6, main body, Wasatch Formation, Fossil Basin, Lincoln County, Wyoming.

Materials

FB-13: FB 97-004, right maxilla, P2 fragment. **FB-18**: FB 97-077, postcrania.

Remarks

These two specimens represent hyaenodontids, but it is not possible to identify either to genus or species.

Order Carnivora Bowdich, **1821**

Family Viverravidae Wortman and Matthew, **1899**

Genus *Viverravus* Marsh, **1872**

Type species

Viverravus gracilis Marsh, **1872**, Green River Basin, Wyoming.

Viverravus sp. indet.

Occurrence

Localities **FB**-8, 9, late middle early Eocene, Wasatchian biochronologic zone Wa-6, main body, Wasatch Formation, Fossil Basin, Lincoln County, Wyoming.

Materials

FB-8: FOBU 6148, right P4 fragment. **FB-9**: FOBU 6177, left dentary p4-m2, teeth broken.

Remarks

These two specimens confirm the presence of *Viverravus* at Fossil Butte. They are too fragmentary for specific determination.

Genus *Didymictis* Cope, **1875**

Type species

Limnocyon protenus Cope, **1874**, San Juan Basin, New Mexico.

Didymictis cf. *D. protenus* (Cope, **1874**)

Figure 8.5–**8**.6

1874 *Limnocyon protenus* **Cope**, p. 15

1882a *Didymictis curtidens* **Cope**, p. 160

1962 *Didymictis altidens* (in part); **Gazin**, p. 57

Holotype

USNM 1092, left and right dentaries, Wasachian Biochron Wa7, San Jose Formation, San Juan Basin, New Mexico.

Occurrence

Localities **FB**-1, 5, 7, late middle early Eocene, Wasatchian biochronologic zone Wa-6 (**FB**-5, 7) and late early Eocene, Wasatchian biochronologic zone Wa-7 (**FB**-1), main body, Wasatch Formation, Fossil Basin, Lincoln County, Wyoming.

Materials

FB-1: FOBU 6120, left m1 trigonid. **FB-5**: FOBU 6385, left m2. **FB-7**: UM 108143, left M1.

Remarks

These specimens represent a medium-sized species of *Didymictis*. They are similar in size to *D. protenus* and smaller than *D. altidens*. Gazin (**1962**, p. 57) tentatively assigned some tooth fragments from the "higher slopes of Fossil Butte" (probably near UM Localities **FB**-1 and **FB**-27) to *D. altidens*. We believe it is more probable that they represent *D. protenus*.

Measurements

FOBU 6385: m2 = 8.0 x 4.7; UM 108143: M1 = 7.0 x 9.9.

Family Miacidae Cope, **1880**

Genus *Vulpavus* Marsh, **1871**

Type species

Vulpavus palustris Marsh, **1871**, Green River Basin, Wyoming.

Vulpavus australis Savagea

1962 cf. *Vulpavus australis*; **Gazin**, p. 60

Holotype

AMNH 16226, left dentary p4-m3, Wasatchian Wa7, San Jose Formation, San Juan Basin, New Mexico.

Occurrence

"High on the slope of Fossil Butte" (Gazin, **1962**, p. 60; probably near UM Localities **FB**-1 and **FB**-27), late middle early Eocene, Wasatchian biochronologic zone Wa-6 (**FB**-27) or late early Eocene, Wasatchian biochronologic zone Wa-7 (**FB**-1), main body, Wasatch Formation, Fossil Basin, Lincoln County, Wyoming.

Materials

USNM 22474, right M1.

Remarks

Gazin (**1962**, p. 60) noted the presence of a single tooth of *Vulpavus* from Fossil Butte. This specimen conforms in size and morphology with *V. australis*.

Miacid sp. A & B indet.

Occurrence

Localities **FB**-1, 5, 7, late middle early Eocene, Wasatchian biochronologic zone Wa-6 (**FB**-5, 7) and late early Eocene, Wasatchian biochronologic zone Wa-7 (**FB**-1), main body, Wasatch Formation, Fossil Basin, Lincoln County, Wyoming.

Materials

FB-1: FOBU 6109, right m1 trigonid. **FB-5**: FOBU 6110, right m2 talonid. **FB-7**: UM 102593, left m2 talonid.

Remarks

These fragmentary specimens represent two different miacid carnivorans, but are too incomplete to be assigned to any particular genus or species.

Order Perissodactyla Owen, **1848**

Family Equidae Gray, **1821**

Genus *Protorohippus* Wortman, **1886**

Type species

Hyracotherium venticolum Cope, **1881**, Wind River Basin, Wyoming.

Protorohippus venticolum (Cope, **1881**)

Figure 9.1–**9**.2

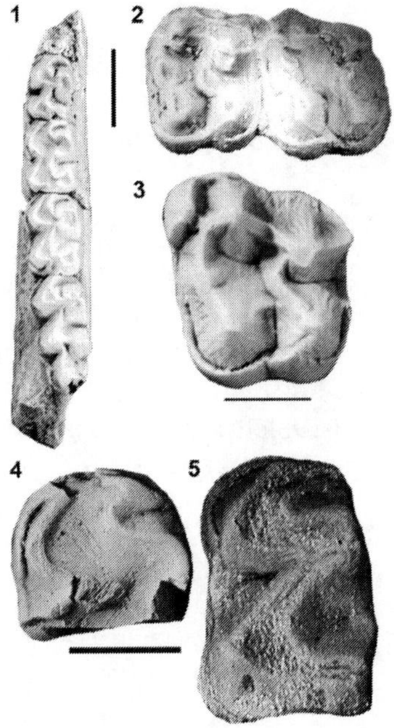

Figure 9 (1) FOBU 6378, Protorohippus venticolum, left dentary p4-m3 in occlusal view. (2) FOBU 6325, Protorohippus venticolum, left maxilla M2-3 in occlusal view. (3) FOBU 6179, Heptodon calciculus, left M1 in occlusal view. (4) FOBU 6154, Lambdotherium popoagicum, left m1 trigonid in occlusal view. (5) DPC 14810, Lambdotherium popoagicum, left m1 in occlusal view. Scale bars=5 mm.

1881 *Hyracotherium venticolum* **Cope**, p. 198

1886 *Protorohippus venticolus*; **Wortman**, p. 105

1908 *Eohippus venticolus*; **Granger**, p. 244

1952 *Hyracotherium index* (in part); **Gazin**, p. 66

1956 *Hyracotherium vasacciense venticolum*; **Kitts**, p. 50

1962 *Hyracotherium vasacciense* (in part); **Gazin**, p. 73

1967 *Hyracotherium vasacciense*; **Guthrie**, p. 43

2002 *Protorohippus venticolum*; **Froehlich**, p. 180

Holotype

AMNH 4832, skull and skeleton, Wasatchian Biochron Wa7, Wind River Formation, Wind River Basin, Wyoming.

Occurrence

Localities **FB**-4, 5, 7–9, 11, 14–16, 18, 19, 21, 22, 26, 27, 29, late middle early Eocene, Wasatchian biochronologic zone Wa-6, main body, Wasatch Formation, Fossil Basin, Lincoln County, Wyoming.

Referred specimens

FB-4: FOBU 6387, left Mx. **FB-5**: FB 95-006, left m1-2; FOBU 6404, right Mx. **FB-7**: UM 102583, right maxilla dP3-4-M1; UM 102590, right P3; UM 108137, left P2; UM 108139, right p4; UM 108140, left p3; UM 108141, right P4; UM 108142, right maxilla P2-M1. **FB-8**: FB 96-017, right dentary m2; FB 96-020, right P3, Mx. **FB-9**: FB 96-064, right p4; FB 96-073, left M3; FB 96-074, right P4; FB 97-019, left m2. **FB-11**: FOBU 6358, right dentary m3 (broken); FOBU 6374, left dp4, m2; FOBU 6375, left dentary, postcrania; FOBU 6378, left and right dentaries, right maxilla; FOBU 6383, left m3. **FB-14**: FB 97-025, left m1. **FB-15**: FB 97-027, left M3, left m3; FB 97-067, right M1. **FB-16**: FB 97-031, left maxilla M1-2, right m1; FB 97-032, right dentary m3; FB 97-034, left p4; FB 97-042, right dentary p3-m2, Mx; FB 97-071, left dentary m2; FOBU 6372, right dentary m1-2 (teeth broken); FOBU 6418, left m1. **FB-18**: FB 97-078, right m1. **FB-19**: FB 97-084, left dentary m2; FB 97-087, left maxilla M1-3; FB 97-090, right maxilla M1; FB 97-093, right dentary dp4-m3; FOBU 6382, right dentary p3-4, m2-3. **FB-21**: FB 97-103, left M3. **FB-22**: FOBU 6325, palate. **FB-26**: FB 97-114, left dentary m1; FB 97-117, right M2-3. **FB-27**: FOBU 6428, left p3. **FB-29**: FB 97-124, left dentary m1.

Remarks

Equids are by far the most common mammals found at Fossil Butte. While there is some variation in tooth size, all of these specimens can be accommodated in *Protorohippus venticolum*, the most common Wa-6–Wa-7 species of North American equid (Froehlich, **2002**). Gazin (**1952**, p 66) referred YPM-PU 16172 from three miles north of Fossil, Wyoming to *Hyracotherium index*. In 1962, Gazin noted that Kitts (**1956**) synonymized *H. index* with *H. vasacciense*. Gazin (**1962**, p. 73) reallocated all of the specimens he had assigned to *H. index* in 1952 to *H. vasacciense*, but noted that he still believed that two species were included within these samples and that *H. index* was still valid even though he was uncertain how to definitively separate the samples into two distinct species. Froehlich (**2002**) assigned this species to *Protorohippus*, and we follow that designation here. It seems clear that *P.venticolum* is a highly variable species, both in size and morphology. We concur with Gazin (**1962**) that two species probably are represented within the various samples, but we have chosen to include all of the Fossil Butte specimens referred above in this single species given the fragmentary nature of most specimens and the difficulty in isolating trends in either size or morphology.

Table 2 Tooth measurements of Protorohippus venticolum; L=maximum length, W=maximum width, d indicates deciduous tooth.

Specimen	p3L	p3W	p4L	p4W	dp4L	dp4W	m1L	m1W	m2L	m2W	m3L	m3W	P2L	P2W	P3L	P3W	P4L	P4W	M1L	M1W	M2L	M2W	M3L	M3W
FOBU 6325													5.3	3.8			6	7.8	6.9	8.3	7.8	9.6	7.9	9.3
FOBU 6374					6.2	3.9			8.1	5.6														
FOBU 6378			5.6	4.1			6.4	4.5	7.1	5.1	9.9	5	4.7	3.4	5.3	5.6	5.6	6.7	6.5	8.1	7.5	8.9		
FOBU 6382	5.4	3.3	5.4	3.8					6.6	4.4	8.7	4.3												
FOBU 6383											11.1	6												
FOBU 6387																					7.2	8.6		
FOBU 6404																					7	8.5		
FOBU 6418							6.2	4.5																
FOBU 6428	5	3.3																						
FB 95-006							7.7	5																
FB 96-017									6.7	4.4														
FB 96-064			5.6	4.1																				
FB 96-073																							7.8	8.3
FB 96-074																	5.7	6.2						
FB 97-117																							6.4	7.9
FB 97-025							7.2	4.7																
FB 97-027											10.6	5.9											7.9	9
FB 97-031							6.7	4.5																
FB 97-034			5.8	3.9																				
FB 97-042	5.7	3.7	6.2	4.4			6.9	5.2	7.7	5.4														
FB 97-071									9.1	5.7														
FB 97-078							7.3	5																
FB 97-084									8.5	5.4														
FB 97-093					6.6	3.9			8.3	5.2														
FB 97-103																							6.5	8.8
UM 102590															5.5	6.8								
UM 108137													4.4	3.5										
UM 108139			5.8	4.2																				
UM 108140	5.1	3.4																						
UM 108141																	5.8	6.9						

Measurements

See **Table 2** for tooth measurements of *Protorohippus venticolum.*

Genus *Xenicohippus* Bown and Kihm, **1981**

Type species

Xenicohippus grangeri Bown and Kihm, **1981**, Bighorn Basin, Wyoming.

Xenicohippus craspedotum (Cope, **1880**)

1880 *Hyracotherium craspedotum* **Cope**, p. 747

1908 *Eohippus craspedotum*; **Granger**, p. 244

1952 *Hyracotherium*, cf. *H. venticolum* (in part); **Gazin**, p. 66

1962 *Hyracotherium*, cf. *H. craspedotum* (in part); **Gazin**, p. 74, Pl. 13, fig. 11

1966 *Hyracotherium craspedotum*; **Robinson**, p. 61, Pl. IV, fig. 3

Holotype

AMNH 4830, left and right dentaries, Wasatchian Biochron Wa6, Wind River Formation, Wind River Basin, Wyoming.

Occurrence

Localities **FB**-1, 6, 25.

Materials

FB-1: FB 96-040, left p2. **FB-6**: FB 96-008, right dentary p3-m1. **FB-25**: FB 97–111, left dentary p3-4, late middle early Eocene, Wasatchian biochronologic zone Wa-6 (**FB**-6, 25) and late early Eocene, Wasatchian biochronologic zone Wa-7 (**FB**-1), main body, Wasatch Formation, Fossil Basin, Lincoln County, Wyoming.

Remarks

Three equid specimens from Fossil Butte are outside the tooth size range of *H. vasacciense* (=*P. venticolum*) as documented by Kitts (**1956**). They can be recognized as the larger Wa-6–Wa-7 equid species, *Xenicohippus craspedotum*. Gazin (**1952**) identified YPM-PU 16173 from near Fossil, Wyoming as *Hyracotherium* cf. *H. venticolum*. In 1962, Gazin moved this specimen into *Hyracotherium* cf. *H. craspedotum* a decision with which we concur. Froehlich (**2002**) assigned this species to *Xenicohippus*, and we follow that designation here.

Measurements

FB 96-040: p2 = 6.6 x 3.4; FB 96-008: p3 = 6.5 x 4.3, p4 = 7.4 x 5.9, m1 = 8.2 x 6.2; FB 97-111: p3 = 6.6 x 3.9, p4 = 7.5 x 4.9.

Equid sp. indet.

Occurrence

Localities **FB**-1, 4–9, 11, 16, 19, 27, late middle early Eocene, Wasatchian biochronologic zone Wa-6 (**FB**-4–9, 11, 16, 19, 27) and late early Eocene, Wasatchian biochronologic zone Wa-7 (**FB**-1), main body, Wasatch Formation, Fossil Basin, Lincoln County, Wyoming.

Materials

FB-1: FB 96-028, left Mx fragment; FB 96-031, left maxilla P4; FB 96-034, left Mx; FB 96-036, postcrania; FB 96-043, postcrania; FB 96-047, left P4; FB 96-050, postcrania. **FB-4**: FB 97-009, right Mx fragment. **FB-5**: FB 96-056, postcrania; FB 96-060, right Mx. **FB-6**: FB 96-004, left astragalar body; **FB-7**: UM 108136, postcrania. **FB-8**: FB 96-016, tooth fragments. **FB-9**: FB 96-066, postcrania. **FB-11**: FB 96-087, postcrania; FB 96-089, left Mx; FOBU 6357, postcrania; FOBU 6364, left m3 talonid; FOBU 6450, postcrania. **FB-16:** FB 97-035, tooth fragments; FOBU 6367, left astragalus; FOBU 6431, right mx trigonid. **FB-19**: FB 97-085, left dentary dp3; FB 97-086, left maxilla dP3; FB 97-091, right astragalus. **FB-27**: FOBU 6369, left and right Mx (broken), canine fragment; FOBU 6411, postcrania.

Remarks

These equid specimens are not complete enough for further identification.

Family Helaletidae Osborn and Wortman, **1892**

Genus *Heptodon* Cope, **1882e**

Type species

Lophiodon ventorum Cope, **1880**, Wind River Basin, Wyoming.

Heptodon calciculus (Cope, **1880**)

Figure 9.3

1880 *Lophiodon calciculus* **Cope**, p. 747

1952 *Heptodon* cf. *H. ventorum* (in part); **Gazin**, p. 70

1962 *Heptodon ventorum* (in part); **Gazin**, p. 78, Pl. 13, fig. 12

Holotype

AMNH 4858, left and right dentaries p3-m3, Wasatchian Biochron Wa7, Wind River Formation, Wind River Basin, Wyoming.

Occurrence

Localities **FB**-9, 12, 26, late middle early Eocene, Wasatchian biochronologic zone Wa-6, main body, Wasatch Formation, Fossil Basin, Lincoln County, Wyoming.

Materials

FB-9: FOBU 6179, left M1; FOBU 6291, right dP4. **FB-12**: FB 96-092, left M1. **FB-26**: FOBU 6333, left dentary mx fragment.

Remarks

Heptodon is the most common tapiroid known from Wa-6–Wa-7 in Wyoming and Colorado. These specimens agree in size and morphological detail with *H. calciculus* and are smaller than *Heptodon posticus* (Radinsky, **1963**). Gazin (**1952**) tentatively identified YPM-PU 16174, a dP/4 from near Fossil, Wyoming, as *Heptodon ventorum*. In 1962, Gazin again identified this specimen, along with four lots of fragmentary teeth from Fossil Butte (no specimen numbers cited), as *H. ventorum*, although he noted that all of these specimens corresponded more closely to the holotype of *H. calciculus*. We recognize all specimens of *Heptodon* from Fossil Butte as *H. calciculus*.

Measurements

FOBU 6179: M1 = 10.9 x 12.3; FOBU 6291: dP4 = 11.0 x 11.2.

Family Palaeotheriidae Bonaparte, **1850**

Genus *Lambdotherium* Cope, **1880**

Type species

Lambdotherium popoagicum Cope, **1880**, Wind River Basin, Wyoming.

Lambdotherium popoagicum Cope, **1880**

Figure 9.4

Holotype

AMNH 4863, left dentary p2-m3, Wasatchian Biochron Wa7, Wind River Formation, Wind River Basin, Wyoming.

Occurrence

Locality **FB**-1, late early Eocene, Wasatchian biochronologic zone Wa-7 (**FB**-1), main body, Wasatch Formation, Fossil Basin, Lincoln County, Wyoming.

Materials

FOBU 6154, left m1 trigonid.

Remarks

Although this specimen is fragmentary, it can be confidently identified as *Lambdotherium*. *Lambdotherium* is the primary index taxon of the Lostcabinian, indicating that the top of the Wasatch section at Fossil Butte represents Wa-7.

Order Artiodactyla Owen, **1848**

Family Dichobunidae Turner, **1849**

Genus *Bunophorus* Sinclair, **1914**

Type species

Mioclaenus etsagicus Cope, **1882a**, Bighorn Basin, Wyoming.

Bunophorus grangeri (Sinclair, **1914**)

Figure 10.1–**10**.2

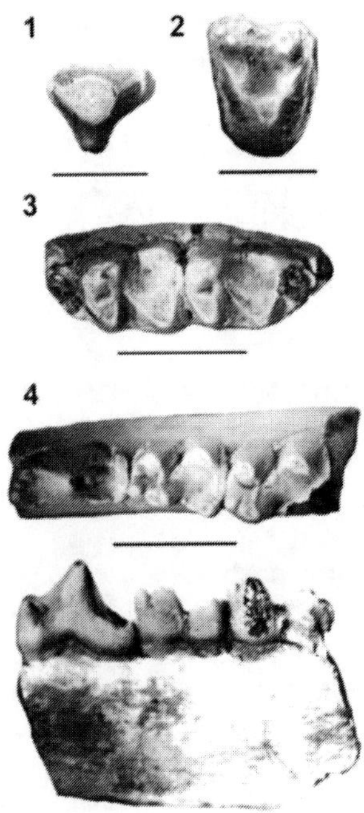

Figure 10 (1) FOBU 6441, Bunophorus grangeri, left P3 in occlusal view. (2) FOBU 6410, Bunophorus grangeri, right M1 in occlusal view. (3) FOBU 6122, Diacodexis secans, left dentary m2-3 in occlusal view. (4) FOBU 6123, Hexacodus uintensis, right dentary p4-m2 in occlusal (top) and lingual (bottom) views. Scale bars=5 mm.

1914 *Wasatchia grangeri* **Sinclair**, p. 269

Holotype

AMNH 15516, left and right dentaries, Gray Bull beds, middle Wasatchian (Wa3-5), Willwood Formation, Bighorn Basin, Wyoming.

Occurrence

Localities **FB**-11, 13, 16, 19, 27, late middle early Eocene, Wasatchian biochronologic zone Wa-6, main body, Wasatch Formation, Fossil Basin, Lincoln County, Wyoming.

Materials

FB-11: FOBU 6394, left m2 fragment. **FB-16**: FOBU 6280, left m2 fragment, M/3. **FB-19**: FOBU 6441, left P3. **FB-27**: FOBU 6410, right M1. Also FOBU 6194, a right dentary fragment with c1 from **FB-13** is questionably assigned to *Bunophorus*.

Remarks

These specimens represent a relatively small species of *Bunophorus*. They agree in size and morphology with *B. grangeri* (Stucky and Krishtalka, **1990**).

Measurements

FOBU 6410: M1 = 5.8 x 6.8; FOBU 6441: P3 = 5.4 x 4.6.

Genus *Diacodexis* Cope, **1882e**

Type species

Pantolestes secans Cope, **1881**, Wind River Basin, Wyoming.

Diacodexis secans (Cope, **1881**)

Figure 10.3

1881 *Pantolestes secans* **Cope**, p. 187

Holotype

AMNH 4899, left and right dentaries p4-m3, Wasatchian Biochron Wa6, Wind River Formation, Wind River Basin, Wyoming.

Occurrence

Localities **FB**-1, 5, 16, 19, 27, late middle early Eocene, Wasatchian biochronologic zone Wa-6 (**FB**-5, 16, 19, 27) and late early Eocene, Wasatchian biochronologic zone Wa-7 (**FB**-1), main body, Wasatch Formation, Fossil Basin, Lincoln County, Wyoming.

Materials

FB-1: FOBU 6182, left mx trigonid. **FB-5**: FOBU 6421, left M1. **FB-16**: FOBU 6122, left dentary m2-3; FOBU 6226, right dentary m3; FOBU 6279, left M1; FOBU 6432, left Mx (worn); FOBU 6447, left dentary m1 fragment. **FB-19**: FOBU 6416, left m1; FOBU 6446, right M3. **FB-27**: FOBU 6337, left M1.

Remarks

Diacodexis secans is the most common dichobunid artiodactyl known in Wa-6–Wa-7 (Krishtalka and Stucky, **1985**). These specimens agree in size and morphology with this species.

Measurements

FOBU 6122: m2 = 4.2 x 3.5; FOBU 6279: M1 = 4.1 x 4.9; FOBU 6337: M1 = 4.2 x 5.2; FOBU 6416: m1 = 4.2 x 3.5; FOBU 6421: M1 = 4.3 x 5.3; FOBU 6446: M3 = 3.4 x 5.1.

Family Homacodontidae Marsh, **1894**

Genus *Hexacodus* Gazin, **1952**

Type species

Hexacodus pelodes Gazin, **1952**, Green River Basin, Wyoming.

Hexacodus uintensis Gazin, **1952**

Figure 10.4

1952 *Hexacodus uintensis* **Gazin**, p. 76, Pl. 11, fig. 4

1962 *Hexacodus uintensis*, **Gazin**, p. 85, Pl. 14, fig. 5

Holotype

USNM 16175, left dentary m1-2, Wasatchian Biochron Wa6, Wasatch Formation, Green River Basin, 3 miles NW of Fossil Station, Wyoming.

Occurrence

Localities **FB**-11, 16, 19, 24, 27, late middle early Eocene, Wasatchian biochronologic zone Wa-6, main body, Wasatch Formation, Fossil Basin, Lincoln County, Wyoming.

Materials

FB-11: FOBU 6449, right dentary m1 talonid-m2. **FB-16**: FOBU 6228, left M1. **FB-19**: FOBU 6123, right dentary p4-m2. **FB-24**: FOBU 6327, left maxilla M1. **FB-27**: FOBU 6402, right mx (broken).

Remarks

Hexacodus uintensis was described by Gazin (**1952**) based on a single specimen (YPM-PU 16175) from three miles northwest of Fossil, Wyoming. Gazin (**1962**) later described another specimen of *H. uintensis* (USNM 22250) from Fossil Butte and noted that two other specimens, one from Knight Station and the other from the Bighorn Basin, might represent this species as well. The specimens assigned here expand the sample of this rare artiodactyl.

FOBU 6123 includes the first p4 known for *H. uintensis*. It differs from p4 in *H. pelodes* in being laterally compressed anteriorly, with the talonid being broader than the anterior part of the tooth. It also has a stronger paracristid that developed a small accessory cuspule close to the anterior flank of the protoconid unlike *H. pelodes*. The p4 of *H. uintensis* has a small anterobuccal cingulid, which is lacking in *H. pelodes*. Unlike that species, the p4 of *H. uintensis* lacks an entoconid cusp.

Measurements

FOBU 6449: m2 = 4.4 x 3.6; FOBU 6228: M1 = 4.2 x 5.1; FOBU 6123: p4 = 4.9 x 2.7, m1 = 4.4 x 3.1; FOBU 6327: M1 = 4.6 x 5.6.

4. FAUNAL COMPARISONS, PALEOECOLOGY AND AGE

The mammalian assemblage from the Wasatch Formation at Fossil Butte (**Table 1**) presents interesting similarities and contrasts with other Wa-6 and Wa-7 samples from Wyoming. **Figure 11.1** compares diversity as expressed by species per order between the Fossil Butte sample, a Wa-6 sample from the Bighorn Basin in northwestern Wyoming (UM collections), and a Wa-7 sample from the Pinnacles area of the northeastern Green River Basin, southwestern Wyoming (Gunnell et al., **2004**; UM collections). Although a limited Wa-7 fauna occurs 30 km to the southeast, on Little Muddy Creek near the hamlet of Cumberland Gap (Zonneveld et al., **2000**), this fauna is too limited, in both diversity and abundance to facilitate useful comparison to the Fossil Butte material.

The Fossil Butte sample is similar to the Wa-6 sample in having relatively high diversity of Cimolesta, Condylarthra, and Carnivora, but differs in having a lower diversity of Primates, "Creodonta", and Perissodactyla, and a much higher diversity of Rodentia. In comparison to the Wa-7 sample, Fossil Butte exhibits higher diversity of Cimolesta, Condylarthra, Rodentia, and Carnivora, but lower diversity of Primates and Perissodactyla. Perhaps the most unusual aspect of Fossil Butte mammalian diversity is the relatively low diversities of primates and perissodactyls (especially given the high abundance of perissodactyls, see below) and the very high diversity of rodents.

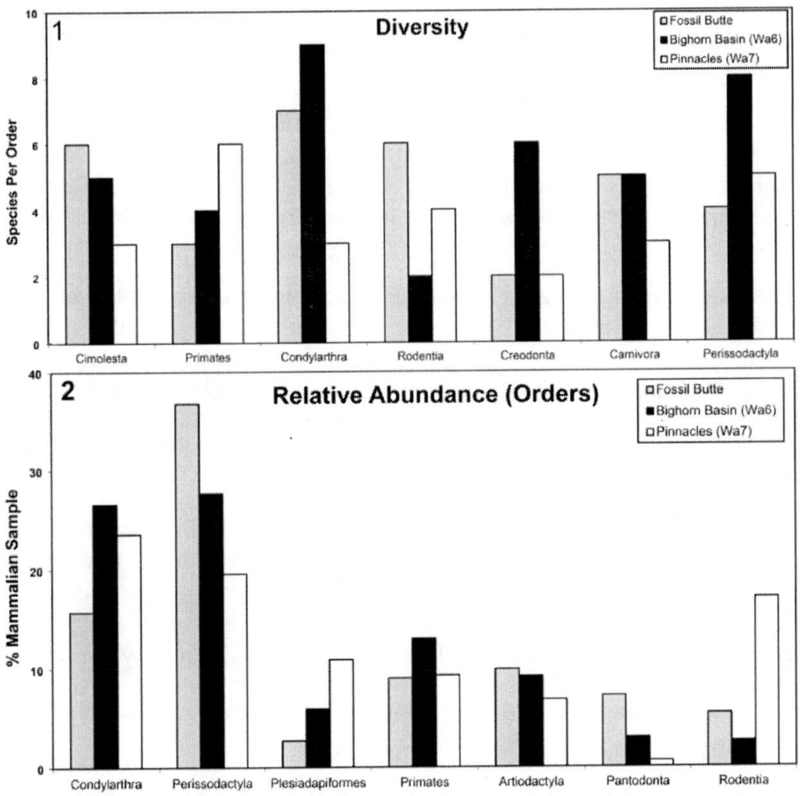

Figure 11 (1) Mammalian species-level diversity (number of species per selected orders) at Fossil Butte compared to a Wa-6 sample from the Bighorn Basin in northwestern Wyoming and a Wa-7 sample from the Pinnacles area near South Pass, southwestern Wyoming. (2) Mammalian abundance (percent total number of specimens representing selected orders) at Fossil Butte compared with same faunal samples as in 1.

Relative abundances of Fossil Butte mammals can be compared to assemblages from the Bighorn Basin and the Pinnacles in northwestern and southwestern Wyoming, respectively. Since sample size for the Fossil Butte assemblage is relatively low, these comparisons will be made using percent of specimens in each sample. **Figure 11.2** compares relative abundance for eight orders of Fossil Butte mammals with assemblages from the Bighorn

Basin and the Pinnacles. Compared to Fossil Butte, both the Bighorn Basin and Pinnacles samples have higher abundances of condylarthans, almost entirely due to the very high abundance of *Hyopsodus* in the latter two basins. While relatively common at Fossil Butte, *Hyopsodus* only represents 14% of the mammalian sample compared to 21.5% in the Bighorn Basin and 22.3% at the Pinnacles. Both of these samples also have higher abundances of plesiadapiforms compared to Fossil Butte, almost entirely represented by *Microsyops*.

In contrast to the Bighorn and Pinnacles samples, perissodactyls are more common at Fossil Butte, almost entirely due to the high abundance of equids. At Fossil Butte, *Xenicohippus* and *Protorohippus* account for 32.7% of all mammal specimens, while in the Bighorn Basin the relative abundance of equids is at 23% and 17.6% at the Pinnacles.

Primates exhibit similar specimen abundance in all three samples, but there are substantial differences in the taxonomic composition of primates among the three areas. Primate taxonomic composition at Fossil Butte consists entirely of notharctid primates—there are no omomyid primates yet known from any Fossil Butte locality. Omomyids make up 36% of all primate specimens from Wa-6 localities in the Bighorn Basin and 26.7% of Wa-7 primate specimens from the Pinnacles.

The apparent absence of omomyid primates at Fossil Butte is probably at least partly because of the relatively poor preservation in the Wasatch Formation locally. Specimens are fragmentary with few documented associations. There are no vertebrate bone concentrations and screen washing for smaller members of the vertebrate community has proven unproductive. Omomyids are all relatively small and are difficult to find by surface prospecting. However, paleoecological factors also may be partially responsible for the lack of Fossil Basin omomyids.

Early Eocene (Wasatchian) omomyid primates from both the Fossil and greater Green River basins are extremely rare. Outside of a single series of localities in the Washakie Basin (Savage and Waters, **1978**), published records of omomyids from the rest of the early Eocene of southwestern Wyoming consist of fewer than 75 specimens (Gazin, **1952**, **1958**, **1962**; West, **1973**; Szalay, **1976**; Stucky, **1984**; Bown and Rose, **1987**; Zonneveld et al., **2000**; Muldoon and Gunnell, **2002**; Holroyd and Strait, **2008**; Nachman et al., **2010**). The paucity of omomyids from early Eocene strata in the greater Green River Basin suggests that ecological conditions were not suitable for anaptomorphine omomyids, the subfamily most common in the Wasatchian (Gunnell, **1997**). However, by the middle Eocene (Bridgerian biochrons Br1b–Br3), omomyine omomyids are common elements in mammalian faunal assemblages of the Bridger Formation in the Green River Basin.

Overall, mammalian faunal community structure at Fossil Butte, combined with geological evidence, suggests paleohabitats consisting of both forested and more open areas. The extremely high abundance of the equid perissodactyls *Protorohippus* and*Xenicohippus* argue for open, broken forest habitats. The modestly high abundance of artiodactyls also suggests the presence of some open habitats. The relatively high abundance of notharctine primates indicates that forested areas occurred nearby, perhaps along river and stream courses.

The abundant presence of hydromorphic paleosols (sensu Kraus and Aslan, **1993**) at the base of the exposed main body of the Wasatch Formation at Fossil Butte suggests that the lower portion of the section was deposited during relatively wet and poorly drained conditions. The middle part of the section (with better developed paleosols) was probably deposited during an interval with better drainage deposition. The upper part of the section was deposited under more poorly drained conditions and was followed by the onset of lake-sediment deposition as Fossil Lake formed during the Lostcabinian (Grande, **1984**, **2013**; Lillegraven and Ostresh, **1988**).

Differences between the mammalian faunal sample at Fossil Butte and those in other areas are almost certainly due to the differing paleoecological condition. The fact that Fossil Basin was geomorphically isolated from other areas to the east by the Wyoming Overthrust Belt and to the west by the Tunp Range, may have contributed to some of the unusual occurrences in the Fossil Butte sample. The presence of *Knightomys huerfanensis*, *Copelemur tutus*, and *Reithroparamys debequensis*, all more common from southern areas (Colorado and New Mexico), suggests some interchange between Fossil Basin and these southern communities.*Meniscotherium*, which is common in both New Mexico and the adjacent Green River Basin, is nearly absent from Fossil Basin, suggesting that *Meniscotherium* preferred habitats different from those available in the Fossil Basin.

Given the location of Fossil Basin within the Overthrust Belt, it might be expected that the sample would include faunal indications of basin-margin habitats (Gunnell and Bartels, **2001**). Included among basin-margin faunal indicators are the presence of unique species, such as the rodent *Adaetoparamys blochi*, the artiodactyl *Hexacodus uintensis*, the leptictid *Eoictops novaceki*, and the pantolestid *Palaeosinopa lacus*. The occurrences of the rare Wa-6 taxa *Apheliscus* and *Haplomylus*, and the anachronistically early appearance of the very rare *Ectocion superstes* may also suggest basin-margin influences.

Figure 12 summarizes the stratigraphic ranges of mammalian taxa in the Fossil Butte Wasatch Formation sequence. The Wa6 index taxon *Heptodon calciculus* is first found 135 m below the base of the Fossil Butte Member of the Green River Formation at locality **FB**-26. There is only one locality (**FB**-6) below the level of **FB**-26 that has yielded any identifiable mammals.

None of the taxa recovered from this level suggests any pre-Wa-6 Eocene horizons existing at Fossil Butte. *Lambdotherium* appears at locality **FB**-1, within 15 m of the base of the Fossil Butte Member of the Green River Formation.

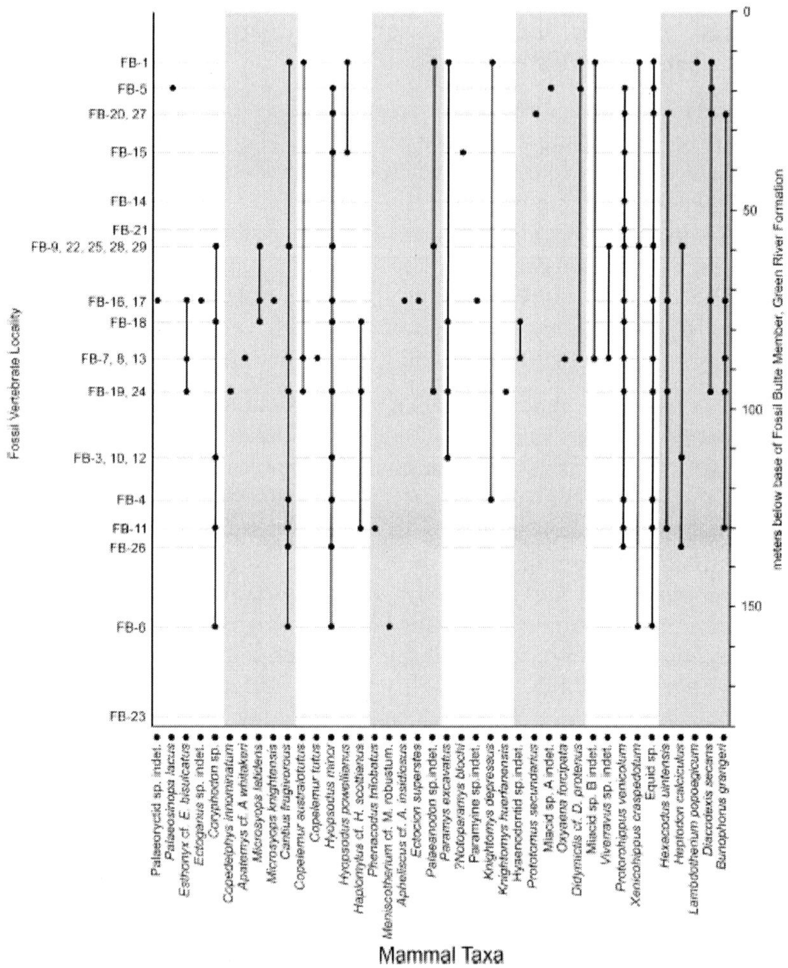

Figure 12 Stratigraphic ranges of mammalian taxa in the Wasatch Formation at Fossil Butte, not including specimens found previous to this work (Mesonychid indet., Reithroparamys cf. R. debequensis, Vulpavus australis) because it was not possible to precisely fit them into proper stratigraphic position. Left axis shows the distribution of fossil localities in the Fossil Butte section. Right axis shows section measured in m below the base of the overlying Fossil Butte Member of the Green River Formation.

This indicates that the top of the Fossil Butte section of the Wasatch Formation represents the Lostcabinian (Wa-7), as does the Fossil Butte Member of the Green River Formation, wherein *Lambdotherium* has also been found (Froehlich and Breithaupt, **1997**). Based on the ranges of mammalian taxa at Fossil Butte, all of the Wasatch Formation represents at least Wa-6, with the top 15 m of the section representing Wa-7.

5. SUMMARY

The mammalian faunal assemblage from the Wasatch Formation at Fossil Butte National Monument consists of 36 genera and as many as 46 species. Two genera and three species are new and, along with *Hexacodus uintensis*, are unique to the Fossil Butte sample. Most of the other members of the assemblage are well known from other Wa-6 sediments in Wyoming and New Mexico. The top 15 m of the local section samples the beginning of the succeeding Wasatchian biochron (Wa-7), as indicated by the first appearance of the immigrant perissodactyl *Lambdotherium*. However, some taxa represent relatively rare forms (*Ectocion superstes*) or unusually late Wasatchian occurrences (*Apheliscus*, *Haplomylus*), suggesting that Fossil Basin may have provided a refugium for some taxa. Also, some taxa are more common from southern basins within North America (*Knightomys huerfanensis*, *Copelemur tutus*, and *Reithroparamys debequensis*), indicating that Fossil Basin exchanged faunal elements with these areas during the early Eocene. The most abundant mammals living in Fossil Basin during Wa-6 were equid perissodactyls representing over 30% of the total number of specimens. The relatively high percentage occurrence of fossil horses at Fossil Butte suggests that well-drained, open-forest habitats were common in the area during the early Eocene.

ACKNOWLEDGMENTS

The authors thank A.L. Brandes, K.M. Christenson, J.M. Lavigne, S. Zack, R.J. Walker, J.I. Bloch, and A.R. Bair for their work in describing and measuring the stratigraphic sections and fossil collecting. We thank R.L. Anemone for providing access to unpublished data from the southern Red Desert. We also thank the staff at Fossil Butte National Monument, especially Superintendent D. McGinnis, R. Benton, P. Ambrose, V. Santucci, and A. Aase, for their assistance during our work. We thank J.A. Lillegraven, J.E. Storer, D. Anderson, and the late S.L. Walsh for many helpful comments on previous versions of this manuscript. This research was supported by National Park

Service and NSF grants to WSB and GFG and an NSERC Discovery grant to JPZ.

REFERENCES

1. Alston E.R., 1876, On the classification of the order Glires*: Proceedings of the Zoological Society of London, v.* 1876, *p.* 61–98.
2. Anderson D., 2008, *Ischyromyidae, in Janis, C.M., Gunnell, G.F., and Uhen, M.D., eds., Evolution of Tertiary Mammals of North America, Volume 2:*Cambridge, Cambridge University Press, *p.* 311–325.
3. Beard K.C., 1988, New notharctine primate fossils from the early Eocene of New Mexico and southern Wyoming and the phylogeny of Notharctinae*: American Journal of Physical Anthropology, v.* 75, *p.* 439–469.
4. Bloch J.I., Secord R., *and* Gingerich P.D., 2004, Systematics and phylogeny of late Paleocene and early Eocene Palaeoryctinae (Mammalia, Insectivora) from the Clarks Fork and Bighorn Basins, Wyoming*: Contributions from the Museum of Paleontology, University of Michigan, v.* 31, *p.* 119–154.
5. Bonaparte C.L., 1850, 1. *Conspectus Systematis Mastozoologiae. Editio altera reformata,* Leiden, Conspectus Systematum, 372 *p.*
6. Bowdich T.E., 1821, *An Analysis of the Natural Classifications of Mammalia for the use of Students and Travelers,* Paris, J. Smith, 115 *p.*
7. Bown T.M., *and* Kihm A.J., 1981, *Xenicohippus*, an unusual new hyracothere (Mammalia, Perissodactyla) from the lower Eocene rocks of Wyoming, Colorado and New Mexico*: Journal of Paleontology, v.* 55, *p.* 257–270.
8. Bown T.M., *and* Rose K.D., 1987, Patterns of dental evolution in early Eocene anaptomorphine primates (Omomyidae) from the Bighorn Basin, Wyoming*: The Paleontological Society Memoir, v.* 23, *p.* 1–151.
9. Buchheim H.P., 1994, Paleoenvironments, lithofacies and varves of the Fossil Butte Member of the Eocene Green River Formation, southwestern Wyoming*: Contributions to Geology, University of Wyoming, v.* 3, *p.* 3–14.
10. Buchheim H.P., *and* Eugster H.P., 1998, Eocene Fossil Lake: the Green River Formation of Fossil Basin, southwestern Wyoming: *Utah Geological Association Publication, v. 26, p.* 191–208.
11. Buchheim H.P., Cushman R.A. Jr.., *and* Biaggi R.E., 2011, Stratigraphic revision of the Green River Formation in Fossil Basin, Wyoming: Overfilled to underfilled lake evolution*: Rocky Mountain Geology, v.* 46, *p.* 165–181.
12. Cooper C.F., 1932, On some mammalian remains from the Lower Eocene of the London Clay*: Annals and Magazine of Natural History, London, v.*1901, *p.* 129–153.
13. Cope E.D., 1872, Third account of new Vertebrata from the Bridger Eocene of Wyoming Territory*: Paleontological Bulletin, v.* 3, *p.* 1–4.
14. Cope E.D., 1873, Fourth notice of extinct Vertebrata from the Bridger and Green River Tertiaries*: Paleontological Bulletin, v.* 17, *p.* 1–4.
15. Cope E.D., 1874, *Report upon vertebrate fossils discovered in New Mexico with descriptions of new species: Geographical Exploration and Survey West of the 100th Meridian, Appendix FF, Chief of Engineers for 1874, Washington, D.C., p. 1–18.*
16. Cope E.D., 1875, *Systematic catalogue of Vertebrata of the Eocene of New Mexico, collected in 1874: Report to Engineer Department, U. S. Army (Wheeler Survey), Washington, D.C., p. 5–37.*
17. Cope E.D., 1876, On the Taeniodonta, a new group of Eocene Mammalia*: Proceedings of the Academy of Natural Sciences, Philadelphia, v.* 28, *p.*39.
18. Cope E.D., 1877, *Report upon the extinct Vertebrata obtained in New Mexico by parties of the expedition of 1874: Chapter XII, Fossils of the Eocene period: Geographical Surveys West*

of the 100th Meridian, Corps of Engineers (Wheeler Survey), U. S. Army, Washington, D.C., p. 37–282.

19. Cope E.D., 1880, The bad lands of the Wind River and their fauna*: The American Naturalist, v.* 14*, p.* 745–748.
20. Cope E.D., 1881, On the Vertebrata of the Wind River Eocene beds of Wyoming*: Bulletin of the U. S. Geological and Geographical Survey of the Territories, v.* 6*, p.* 183–202.
21. Cope E.D., 1882*a*, Contributions to the history of the Vertebrata of the lower Eocene of Wyoming and New Mexico made in 1881. I. The fauna of the Wasatch beds of the Basin of the Big Horn River*: Proceedings of the American Philosophical Society, v.* 20*, p.* 139–197.
22. Cope E.D., 1882*b*, On the Vertebrata of the Wind River Eocene Beds of Wyoming*: Bulletin of the U. S. Geographical and Geological Survey of the Territories, v.* 6*, p.* 183–202.
23. Cope E.D., 1882*c*, Notes on Eocene Mammalia*: The American Naturalist, v.* 16*, p.* 522.
24. Cope E.D., 1882*d*, New characters of the Perissodactyla Condylartha*: The American Naturalist, v.* 16*, p.* 334.
25. Cope E.D., 1882*e*, Two new genera of Mammalia from the Wasatch Eocene*: The American Naturalist, v.* 16*, p.* 1029.
26. Cope E.D., 1883, On the mutual relations of the bunotherian Mammalia*: Proceedings of the Academy of Natural Sciences, Philadelphia, v.* 1883*, p.*77–83.
27. Cope E.D., 1884, The Vertebrata of the Tertiary formations of the west: Book I*: Report to the U.S. Geological Survey of the Territories (Hayden Survey), v.* 3*, p.* 1–1009.
28. Crochet J.-Y., 1979, Données nouvelles sur l'histoire paléogéographique des Didelphidae (Marsupialia)*: Comptes Rendus de l'Academie des Sciences, Paris, v.* 288*, p.* 1457–1460.
29. Froehlich D.J., 2002, Quo vadis *Eohippus*? The systematics and taxonomy of the early Eocene equids (Perissodactyla)*: Zoological Journal of the Linnean Society, v.* 134*, p.* 141–256.
30. Froehlich D.J., *and* Breithaupt B.H., 1997, A *Lambdotherium* specimen from the Fossil Butte Member of the Green River Formation, with comments on its biostratigraphic and paleoenvironmental importance and the phylogenetic significance of its postcrania*: Journal of Vertebrate Paleontology, Abstracts, Supplement to v, v.* 17*, p.* 47A.
31. Gazin C.L., 1952, The lower Eocene Knight Formation of western Wyoming and its mammalian faunas*: Smithsonian Miscellaneous Collections, v.*117*, p.* 1–82.
32. Gazin C.L., 1958, A review of the middle and upper Eocene primates of North America*: Smithsonian Miscellaneous Collections, v.* 136*, p.* 1–112.
33. Gazin C.L., 1961, New sciuravid rodents from the lower Eocene Knight Formation of western Wyoming*: Proceedings of the Biological Society of Washington, v.* 74*, p.* 193–194.
34. Gazin C.L., 1962, A further study of the lower Eocene mammalian faunas of southwestern Wyoming*: Smithsonian Miscellaneous Collections, v.* 144*, p.* 1–98.
35. Gazin C.L., 1968, A study of the Eocene condylarthran mammal *Hyopsodus : Smithsonian Miscellaneous Collections, v.* 153*, p.* 1–90.
36. Gill T., 1872, Arrangement of the families of mammals with analytical tables*: Smithsonian Miscellaneous Collections, v.* 2*, p.* 1–98.
37. Gingerich P.D., 1994, New species of *Apheliscus*, *Haplomylus*, and *Hyopsodus* (Mammalia, Condylarthra) from the late Paleocene of southern Montana and early Eocene of northwestern Wyoming*: Contributions from the Museum of Paleontology, University of Michigan, v.* 29*, p.* 119–134.
38. Gingerich P.D., 2001, *Biostratigraphy of the continental Paleocene-Eocene boundary interval on Polecat Bench in the northern Bighorn Basin, inGingerich, P.D., ed., Paleocene-Eocene Stratigraphy and Biotic Change in the Bighorn and Clarks Fork Basins,* Wyoming, University of Michigan, Papers on Paleontology, *v.* 33*, p.* 37–71.
39. Gingerich P.D., *and* Simons E.L., 1977, Systematics, phylogeny, and evolution of early Eocene Adapidae (Mammalia, Primates) in North America*:Contributions from the Museum of Paleontology, University of Michigan, v.* 24*, p.* 245–279.
40. Grande L., 1984, Paleontology of the Green River Formation, with a review of the fish fauna*: The Geological Survey of Wyoming, Bulletin, v.* 63*, p.*1–333.
41. Grande L., 2001, *An updated review of the fish faunas from the Green River Formation, the world's most productive freshwater Lagerstätten, inGunnell, G.F., ed., Eocene Biodiversity—*

Unusual Occurrences and Rarely Sampled Habitats, New York, Kluwer Academic/Plenum Publishers, *p.* 1–38.

42. Grande L., 2013, *The Lost World of Fossil Lake—Snapshots from Deep Time,* Chicago, The University of Chicago Press, 425 *p.*
43. Grande L., *and* Bemis W.E., 1998, A comprehensive phylogenetic study of amiid fishes (Amiidae) based on comparative skeletal anatomy. An empirical search for interconnected patterns of natural history*: Society of Vertebrate Paleontology, Memoir 4 (Supplement to v. 18), p.* 1–690.
44. Granger W., 1908, A revision of the American Eocene horses*: Bulletin of the American Museum of Natural History, v.* 24, *p.* 221–264.
45. Granger W., 1915, A revision of the lower Eocene Wasatch and Wind River faunas. Part III. Order Condylarthra. Families Phenacodontidae and Meniscotheriidae*: Bulletin of the American Museum of Natural History, v.* 34, *p.* 329–361.
46. Gray J. E., 1821, On the natural arrangement of vertebrose animals*: London Medical Repository, v.* 15, *p.* 296–310.
47. Gunnell G.F., 1989, Evolutionary history of Microsyopoidea (Mammalia, ?Primates) and the relationship between Plesiadapiformes and Primates*:Papers on Paleontology, University of Michigan, v.* 27, *p.* 1–157.
48. Gunnell G.F., 1997, Wasatchian–Bridgerian (Eocene) paleoecology of the western interior of North America: changing paleoenvironments and taxonomic composition of omomyid (Tarsiiform) primates*: Journal of Human Evolution, v.* 32, *p.* 105–132.
49. Gunnell G.F., 2002, Notharctine primates (Adapiformes) from the early to middle Eocene (Wasatchian-Bridgerian) of Wyoming: transitional species and the origins of *Notharctus* and *Smilodectes : Journal of Human Evolution, v.* 43, *p.* 353–380.
50. Gunnell G.F., *and* Bartels W.S., 2001, *Basin margins, biodiversity, evolutionary innovation, and the origin of new taxa, in Gunnell, G.F., ed., Eocene Biodiversity—Unusual Occurrences and Rarely Sampled Habitats,* New York, Kluwer Academic/Plenum Publishers, *p.* 404–432.
51. Gunnell G.F., Bartels W.S., *and* Zonneveld J.-P., 2004, A late Wasatchian (late early Eocene) vertebrate assemblage preserved in meandering stream channel deposits, northern Red Desert, Wyoming*: Geological Society of America, Abstracts with Programs, v.* 36, no. 5, *p.* 92.
52. Gunnell G.F., Bown T.M., Bloch J.I., *and* Boyer D.M., 2008*a, "Proteutheria", in Janis, C.M., Gunnell, G.F., and Uhen, M.D., eds., Evolution of Tertiary Mammals of North America, Volume 2:* Cambridge, Cambridge University Press, *p.* 63–81.
53. Gunnell G.F., Bown T.M., *and* Bloch J.I., 2008*b, Leptictida, in Janis, C.M., Gunnell, G.F., and Uhen, M.D., eds., Evolution of Tertiary Mammals of North America, Volume 2:* Cambridge, Cambridge University Press, *p.* 82–88.
54. Gunnell G.F., Bown T.M., Hutchison J.H., *and* Bloch J.I., 2008*c, Lipotyphla, in Janis, C.M., Gunnell, G.F., and Uhen, M.D., eds., Evolution of Tertiary Mammals of North America, Volume 2,* Cambridge, Cambridge University Press, *p.* 89–125.
55. Gunnell G.F., Murphey P.C., Stucky R.K., Townsend K.E.B., Robinson P., Zonneveld J.-P., *and* Bartels W.S., 2009, *Biostratigraphy and biochronology of the latest Wasatchian, Bridgerian, and Uintan North American Land Mammal "Ages", in Albright, L.B., III, ed., Papers on Geology, Vertebrate Paleontology, and Biostratigraphy in Honor of Michael O. Woodburne:* Museum of Northern Arizona Bulletin, *v.* 65, *p.* 279–330.
56. Guthrie D.A., 1967, The mammalian fauna of the Lysite Member, Wind River Formation (early Eocene) of Wyoming*: Memoirs of the Southern California Academy of Sciences, v.* 5, *p.* 1–53.
57. Haeckel E., 1895, *Systematische Phylogenie der Wirbelthiere (Vertebrata),* Berlin, Dritter Theil des Entwurfs einer systematischen Phylogenie, 660*p.*
58. Hayden F.V., 1869, Preliminary field report of the United States Geological Survey of Colorado and New Mexico. 3, *p.* 1–144.
59. Hayden F.V., 1871, Preliminary report of the United States Geological Survey of Wyoming*: United States Geological and Geographical Survey of the Territories 4th Annual Report, v.* 1871, *p.* 142–144.

60. Holroyd P.A., *and* Strait S.G., 2008, *New data on Loveina (Primates: Omomyidae) from the early Eocene Wasatch Formation and Implications for washakiin relationships, in Fleagle, J.G., and Gilbert, C.C., eds., Elwyn Simons, A Search for Origins,* New York, Springer, *p.* 243–257.
61. Jepsen G.L., 1930, New vertebrate fossils from the lower Eocene of the Bighorn Basin, Wyoming*: Proceedings of the American Philosophical Society, v.* 64, *p.* 117–130.
62. Kitts D.B., 1956, American *Hyracotherium* (Perissodactyla, Equidae)*: Bulletin of the American Museum of Natural History, v.* 110, *p.* 1–60.
63. Korth W.W., 1984, Earliest Tertiary evolution and radiation of rodents in North America*: Bulletin of Carnegie Museum of Natural History, v.* 24, *p.* 1–71.
64. Korth W.W., 1994*a*, Middle Tertiary marsupials (Mammalia) from North America*: Journal of Paleontology, v.* 68, *p.* 376–397.
65. Korth W.W., 1994*b*, *The Tertiary Record of Rodents in North America,* New York, Plenum Press, 319 *p.*
66. Korth W.W., 2008, *Marsupialia, in Janis, C.M., Gunnell, G.F., and Uhen, M.D., eds., Evolution of Tertiary Mammals of North America, Volume 2.*Cambridge, Cambridge University Press, *p.* 39–47.
67. Kraus M.J., *and* Aslan A., 1993, Eocene hydromorphic paleosols: significance for interpreting ancient floodplain processes*: Journal of Sedimentary Petrology, v.* 63, *p.* 453–463.
68. Krishtalka L., *and* Stucky R.K., 1985, Revision of the Wind River faunas, early Eocene of central Wyoming. Part 7. Revision of *Diacodexis* (Mammalia, Artiodactyla)*: Annals of Carnegie Museum, v.* 54, *p.* 413–486.
69. Leidy J., 1856, Notice of some remains of fishes discovered by Dr. John E. Evans*: Proceedings of the Academy of Natural Sciences, Philadelphia, v.* 6, *p.* 256–257.
70. Leidy J., 1870, Report on the vertebrate fossils of the Tertiary Formations of the west*: U. S. Geological Survey of the Territories (Hayden Expedition), v.* 1870, *p.* 340–370.
71. Leidy J., 1871, Notice of some extinct rodents*: Proceedings of the Academy of Natural Sciences, Philadelphia, v.* 22, *p.* 230–232.
72. Leidy J., 1872, On the fossil vertebrates in the early Tertiary formations of Wyoming*: U.S. Geological Survey of Montana and Adjacent Territories (Hayden Survey), 5th Annual Report, Washington DC, US Government Printing Office, v.* 5, *p.* 353–377.
73. Lillegraven J.A., *and* Ostresh L.M. Jr.., 1988, Evolution of Wyoming's early Cenozoic topography and drainage patterns*: National Geographic Research, v.* 4, *p.* 303–327.
74. Linnaeus C., 1758, *Systema Naturae, Volume I,* 10th Edition*:* Stockholm, Laurentius Salvius, 824 *p.*
75. Loomis F.B., 1905, Hyopsodontidae of the Wasatch and Wind River basins*: American Journal of Science, v.* 19, *p.* 416–424.
76. Loomis F.B., 1907, Wasatch and Wind River rodents*: American Journal of Science, v.* 23, *p.* 123–130.
77. Marsh O.C., 1871, Notice of some new fossil mammals and birds from the Tertiary formations of the West*: American Journal of Science, v.* 2, *p.*120–127.
78. Marsh O.C., 1872, Preliminary description of new Tertiary mammals. Parts I through IV*: American Journal of Science, v.* 4, *p.* 122–128, *202–224.*
79. Marsh O.C., 1875, On a new order of Eocene mammals*: American Journal of Science, v.* 9, *p.* 221.
80. Marsh O.C., 1876, On some characters of the genus *Coryphodon* Owen*: American Journal of Science, v.* 3, *p.* 425–428.
81. Marsh O.C., 1894, Description of Tertiary artiodactyls*: American Journal of Science, v.* 48, *p.* 259–274.
82. Matthew W.D., 1899, A provisional classification of the fresh-water Tertiary of the West*: Bulletin of the American Museum of Natural History, v.* 12, *p.* 19–75.
83. Matthew W.D., 1901, Additional observations on the Creodonta*: Bulletin of the American Museum of Natural History, v.* 14, *p.* 1–38.
84. Matthew W.D., 1903, The fauna of the *Titanotherium* beds at Pipestone Springs, Montana*: Bulletin of the American Museum of Natural History, v.*19, *p.* 197–226.

85. Matthew W.D., 1909, Carnivora and Insectivora of the Bridger Basin, middle Eocene: *Memoirs of the American Museum of Natural History, v.* 9, *p.*291–567.
86. Matthew W.D., 1915*a*, A revision of the Lower Eocene Wasatch and Wind River faunas. Part II. Order Condylarthra, Family Hyopsodontidae: *Bulletin of the American Museum of Natural History, v.* 34, *p.* 311–328.
87. Matthew W.D., 1915*b*, A revision of the lower Eocene Wasatch and Wind River faunas: Part IV. Entelonychia, Primates, and Insectivora (Part):*Bulletin of the American Museum of Natural History, v.* 34, *p.* 429–483.
88. Matthew W.D., 1918, A revision of the Lower Eocene Wasatch and Wind River faunas. Part V. Insectivora (continued), Glires, Edentata: *Bulletin of the American Museum of Natural History, v.* 38, *p.* 565–657.
89. Matthew W.D., 1920, A new genus of rodents from the middle Eocene: *Journal of Mammalogy, v.* 1, *p.* 168–169.
90. Matthew W.D., 1929, Preoccupied names: *Journal of Mammalogy, v.* 10, *p.* 171.
91. Matthew W.D., 1937, Paleocene faunas of the San Juan Basin, New Mexico: *Transactions of the American Philosophical Society, v.* 30, *p.* 1–510.
92. McKenna M.C., 1975, *Toward a phylogenetic classification of the Mammalia, in Luckett, W.P., and Szalay, F.S., eds., Phylogeny of the Primates,* New York, Plenum Press, *p.* 21–46.
93. McKenna M.C., *and* Bell S.K., 1997, *Classification of Mammals Above the Species Level,* New York, Columbia University Press, 631 *p.*
94. Miller G.S., *and* Gidley J.W., 1918, Synopsis of the supergeneric groups of rodents: *Journal of the Washington Academy of Sciences, v.* 8, *p.* 431–448.
95. Muldoon K.M., *and* Gunnell G.F., 2002, Omomyid primates (Tarsiiformes) from the early middle Eocene at South Pass, Greater Green River Basin, Wyoming: *Journal of Human Evolution, v.* 43, *p.* 479–511.
96. Nachman B., Beard K.C., *and* Anemone R., 2010, New Primates (Omomyidae) from the Great Divide Basin, Wyoming: *Journal of Vertebrate Paleontology, Program and Abstracts, v.* 2010, *p.* 138A.
97. Nelson M.E., 1973, Age and stratigraphic relations of the Fowkes Formation, Eocene of southwestern Wyoming and northeastern Utah:*Contributions to Geology, University of Wyoming, v.* 12, *p.* 27–31.
98. Novacek M.J., 1977, A review of Paleocene and Eocene Leptictidae (Eutheria: Mammalia) from North America: *PaleoBios, v.* 24, *p.* 1–42.
99. Novacek M.J., 1982, *Diacodon alticuspis*, an erinaceomorph insectivore from the early Eocene of northern New Mexico: *Contributions to Geology, University of Wyoming, v.* 20, *p.* 135–149.
100. Novacek M.J., Bown T.M., *and* Schankler D., 1985, On the classification of the early Tertiary Erinaceomorpha (Insectivora, Mammalia): *American Museum Novitates, v.* 2813, *p.* 1–22.
101. Oriel S.S., *and* Tracy J.I., 1970, Uppermost Cretaceous and Tertiary stratigraphy of Fossil Basin, southwest Wyoming: *U.S. Geological Survey Professional Paper, v.* 635, *p.* 1–53.
102. Osborn H.F., *and* Wortman J.L., 1892, Fossil mammals of the Wasatch and Wind River beds. Collected in 1891: *Bulletin of the American Museum of Natural History, v.* 4, *p.* 80–147.
103. Owen R., 1845, *Odontography; a treatise on the comparative anatomy of teeth,* London, Hippolyte Bailliere, 655 *p.*
104. Owen R., 1848, Description of teeth and portions of jaws of two extinct Anthracotherioid quadrupeds (*Hyopotamus vectianus* and *Hyop. bovinus*) discovered by the Marchioness of Hastings in the Eocene deposits on the NW coast of the Isle of Wight: with an attempt to develop Cuvier's idea of the Classification of Pachyderms by the number of their toes: *Quarterly Journal of the Geological Society of London, v.* 4, *p.* 103–141.
105. Radinsky L., 1963, Origin and early evolution of North American Tapiroidea: *Bulletin of the Peabody Museum of Natural History, v.* 17, *p.* 1–106.
106. Redline A.D., 1997, Revision of the Wind River faunas, early Eocene of central Wyoming. Part 13. Systematics and phylogenetic pattern of early Eocene *Hyopsodus* (Mammalia: Condylarthra): *Annals of Carnegie Museum, v.* 66, *p.* 1–81.

107. Robinson P., 1966, Fossil Mammalia of the Huerfano Formation, Eocene, of Colorado: *Bulletin of the Peabody Museum of Natural History, v.* 21, *p.*1–95.
108. Rose K.D., 1981, The Clarkforkian Land-Mammal Age and mammalian faunal composition across the Paleocene-Eocene boundary: *University of Michigan Papers on Paleontology, v.* 26, *p.* 1–197.
109. Rose K.D., 2006, *The Beginning of the Age of Mammals,* Baltimore, The Johns Hopkins University Press, 428 *p.*
110. Rose K.D., *and* Chinnery B.J., 2004, The postcranial skeleton of early Eocene rodents: *Bulletin of Carnegie Museum of Natural History, v.* 36, *p.* 211–244.
111. Rose K.D., *and* Von Koenigswald W., 2007, The marmot-sized paramyid rodent *Notoparamys costilloi* from the early Eocene of Wyoming, with comments on dental variation and occlusion in paramyids: *Bulletin Carnegie Museum of Natural History, v.* 39, *p.* 111–125.
112. Rothecker J., *and* Storer J.E., 1996, The marsupials of the Lac Pelletier Lower Fauna, middle Eocene (Duchesnean) of Saskatchewan: *Journal of Vertebrate Paleontology, v.* 16, *p.* 770–774.
113. Savage D.E., *and* Waters B.T., 1978, A new omomyid primate from the Wasatch Formation of southern Wyoming: *Folia Primatologica, v.* 30, *p.* 1–29.
114. Scott W.B., *and* Jepsen G.L., 1936, The mammalian fauna of the White River Oligocene—Part I. Insectivora and Carnivora: *Transactions of the American Philosophical Society (New Series), v.* 28, *p.* 1–153.
115. Simons E.L., 1962, A new Eocene primate genus, *Cantius*, and a revision of some allied European lemuroids: *Bulletin, British Museum of Natural History (Geology), v.* 7, *p.* 1–36.
116. Simons E.L., 1972, *Primate Evolution, an introduction to man's place in nature,* New York, Macmillan, 322 *p.*
117. Simpson G.G., 1928, American Eocene didelphids: *American Museum Novitates, v.* 307, *p.* 1–7.
118. Simpson G.G., 1940, Studies on the earliest primates: *Bulletin of the American Museum of Natural History, v.* 77, *p.* 185–212.
119. Simpson G.G., 1954, An apatemyid from the early Eocene of New Mexico: *American Museum Novatates, v.* 1654, *p.* 1–4.
120. Sinclair W.J., 1914, A revision of the bunodont Artiodactyla of the middle and lower Eocene of North America: *Bulletin of the American Museum of Natural History, v.* 33, *p.* 267–295.
121. Strait S.G., 2001, *New Wa-0 mammalian fauna from Castle Gardens in the southeastern Bighorn Basin, in Gingerich, P.D., ed., Paleocene–Eocene Stratigraphy and Biotic Change in the Bighorn and Clarks Fork Basins, Wyoming:* University of Michigan, Papers on Paleontology, *v.* 33, *p.* 127–143.
122. Stucky R.K., 1984, Revision of the Wind River faunas, early Eocene of central Wyoming. Part 5. Geology and biostratigraphy of the upper part of the Wind River Formation, northeastern Wind River Basin: *Annals Carnegie Museum, v.* 53, *p.* 231–294.
123. Stucky R.K., *and* Krishtalka L., 1990, Revision of the Wind River faunas, early Eocene of central Wyoming. Part 10. *Bunophorus* (Mammalia, Artiodactyla): *Annals of Carnegie Museum, v.* 59, *p.* 149–171.
124. Szalay F.S., 1976, Systematics of the Omomyidae (Tarsiiformes, Primates): taxonomy, phylogeny, and adaptations: *Bulletin of the American Museum of Natural History, v.* 156, *p.* 159–449.
125. Szalay F.S., *and* Delson E., 1979, *Evolutionary History of the Primates,* New York, Academic Press, 580 *p.*
126. Thewissen J.G.M., 1990, Evolution of Paleocene and Eocene Phenacodontidae (Mammalia, Condylarthra): *University of Michigan Papers on Paleontology, v.* 29, *p.* 1–107.
127. Thewissen J.G.M., *and* Gingerich P.D., 1989, Skull and endocranial cast of *Eoryctes melanus*, a new palaeoryctid (Mammalia: Insectivora) from the early Eocene of western North America: *Journal of Vertebrate Paleontology, v.* 9, *p.* 459–470.
128. Thorpe M.R., 1934, Meniscotherium robustum sp. nov. and a discussion of *Hyracops socialis* Marsh: *American Journal of Science, v.* 27, *p.* 401–409.

129. Thorpe M.R., 1938, Wyoming Eocene fishes in the Marsh collection: *American Journal of Science, v.* 36, *p.* 279–295.
130. Trouessart E.-L., 1879, Catalogue des mammifères vivants et fossiles. I. Primates: *Revue et Magasin de Zoologie (Paris), v.* 6, *p.* 108–140, *162–169.*
131. Turner H.N. Jr.., 1849, On the evidence of affinity afforded by the skull in the ungulate Mammalia: *Proceedings of the Zoological Society, London, v.*1849, *p.* 147–158.
132. Uhen M.D., *and* Gingerich P.D., 1995, Evolution of *Coryphodon* (Mammalia, Pantodonta) in the late Paleocene and early Eocene of northwestern Wyoming: *Contributions from the Museum of Paleontology, University of Michigan, v.* 29, *p.* 259–289.
133. Van Valen L., 1966, Deltatheridia, a new order of mammals: *Bulletin of the American Museum of Natural History, v.* 132, *p.* 1–126.
134. Van Valen L., 1967, New Paleocene insectivores and insectivore classification: *Bulletin of the American Museum of Natural History, v.* 135, *p.* 219–284.
135. Van Valen L., 1971, Adaptive zones and the orders of mammals: *Evolution, v.* 25, *p.* 420–428.
136. Weber M., 1904, *Die Säugetiere. Einführing in die Anatomie und Systematik der recenten und Fossilen Mammalia,* Jena, Gustav Fischer, 866 *p.*
137. West R.M., 1973, Geology and mammalian paleontology of the New Fork-Big Sandy Area, Sublette County, Wyoming: *Fieldiana Geology, v.* 29, *p.* 1–193.
138. Winge H., 1917, Udsigt over Insektaedernes indbyrdes Slaegtskab: *Videnskabelige Meddelelser Dansk Naturhistorisk Forening, Copenhagen, v.* 68, *p.* 83–203.
139. Wood A.E., 1962, The Early Tertiary rodents of the family Paramyidae: *Transactions of the American Philosophical Society, v.* 52, *p.* 1–261.
140. Wood A.E., 1965, Small rodents from the early Eocene Lysite Member, Wind River Formation of Wyoming: *Journal of Paleontology, v.* 39, *p.* 124–134.
141. Woodburne M.O., Gunnell G.F., *and* Stucky R.K., 2009, Land mammal faunas of North America rise and fall during the Early Eocene Climatic Optimum: *Denver Museum of Nature & Science Annals, v.* 1, *p.* 1–74.
142. Wortman J.L., 1886, Species of *Hyracotherium* and allied perissodactyls from the Wahsatch and Wind River Beds of North America: *Bulletin of the American Museum of Natural History, v.* 8, *p.* 81–110.
143. Wortman J.L., 1903, Studies of Eocene Mammalia in the Marsh collection, Peabody Museum. Part II. Primates, Suborder Cheiromyoidea: *American Journal of Science, v.* 16, *p.* 345–368.
144. Wortman J.L., *and* Matthew W.D., 1899, The ancestry of certain members of the Canidae, the Viverridae, and Procyonidae: *Bulletin of the American Museum of Natural History, v.* 12, *p.* 109–139.
145. Zonneveld J.-P., Gunnell G.F., *and* Bartels W.S., 2000, Early Eocene fossil vertebrates from the southwestern Green River Basin, Lincoln and Uinta Counties, Wyoming: *Journal of Vertebrate Paleontology, v.* 20, *p.* 369–386.
146. Zonneveld J.-P., Lavigne J.M., Bartels W.S., *and* Gunnell G.F., 2006, *Lunulichnos tuberosus* (ichnogen. and ichnosp. nov.) from the Early Eocene Wasatch Formation, Fossil Butte National Monument, Wyoming: an arthropod-constructed trace fossil associated with alluvial firmgrounds: *Ichnos, v.* 13, *p.*87–94.

Accepted 18 April 2016

CHAPTER 10

Palaeopopulations of Late Pleistocene Top Predators in Europe: Ice Age Spotted Hyenas and Steppe Lions in Battle and Competition about Prey

Cajus G. Diedrich

Private Research Institute Paleologic, Petra Bezruce 96, 26751 Zdice, Czech Republic

ABSTRACT

Late Pleistocene spotted hyena Crocuta crocuta spelaea (Goldfuss, 1823) and steppe lion Panthera leo spelaea(Goldfuss, 1810) were top predators in Central Europe. The fossil record (2.303 hyena/1.373 lion bones = ratio 3/1) from 106 cave and open air sites demonstrates comparable associations to modern African hyenas/lions resulting in competition about prey and territory. Cannibalism within extinct spotted hyenas is well documented, including two individual skeletons. Those hyenas produced bone accumulations at dens. Feeding specializations on different megamammal groups are demonstrated for Late Pleistocene hyenas whose prey partly overlaps (e.g., cave bears) with those of lions and wolves. At most fossil sites, 1–3% of the lion remains indicate scavenging of lions by hyenas. The larger Late Pleistocene felids focussed on cervids (reindeers specialization during the high glacial = LGM), on bovids (steppe bison/aurochs), and possibly on saiga antelope and on the cave bear, hunting deep in caves during their hibernations and targeting cubs. The cave bear feeding was the target of all three top predators (lions, hyenas, and wolves) in the Late Pleistocene boreal forests which caused deathly conflicts in caves between them, especially with lions/hyenas and herbivorous cave bears that have no modern analogue.

1. INTRODUCTION

Pleistocene top predator research started in Europe with the first discoveries of "foreign animal finds" in the Zoolithen Cave (Germany) in 1774 when the German Priest Esper discovered some hyena (Figures 1–3), lion (Figures 4–6), wolf, and cave bear remains and explained them resulting from the "great deluge" [1]. Rosenmüller collected a large amount of cave bear remains including the Ursus spelaeus holotype skull [2] and the largest amount of lion material in the same cave [3]. This collection survived until today [2]. The French zoologist Cuvier interpreted in 1805 [4] some skull fragments from the German Zoolithen Cave as "hyena". It was the German Paleontologist Goldfuss who described and named the first top predator of the Pleistocene with the holotype skull of the "cave lion Felis spelaea" in 1810 [5, 6]. In 1823 he published on the second large predator with the holotype skull of the "cave hyena Hyaena spelaea" [7]. Both of these skulls from the Zoolithen Cave were described in more detail after their rediscovery in 2009 [8]. Finally, also the "cave wolf Canis spelaeus" was described in 1823 based on a cub skull found also in the Zoolithen Cave [7].

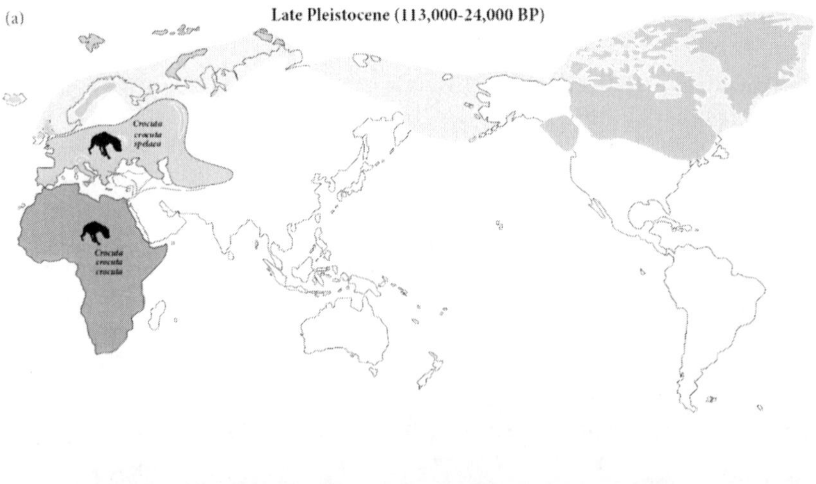

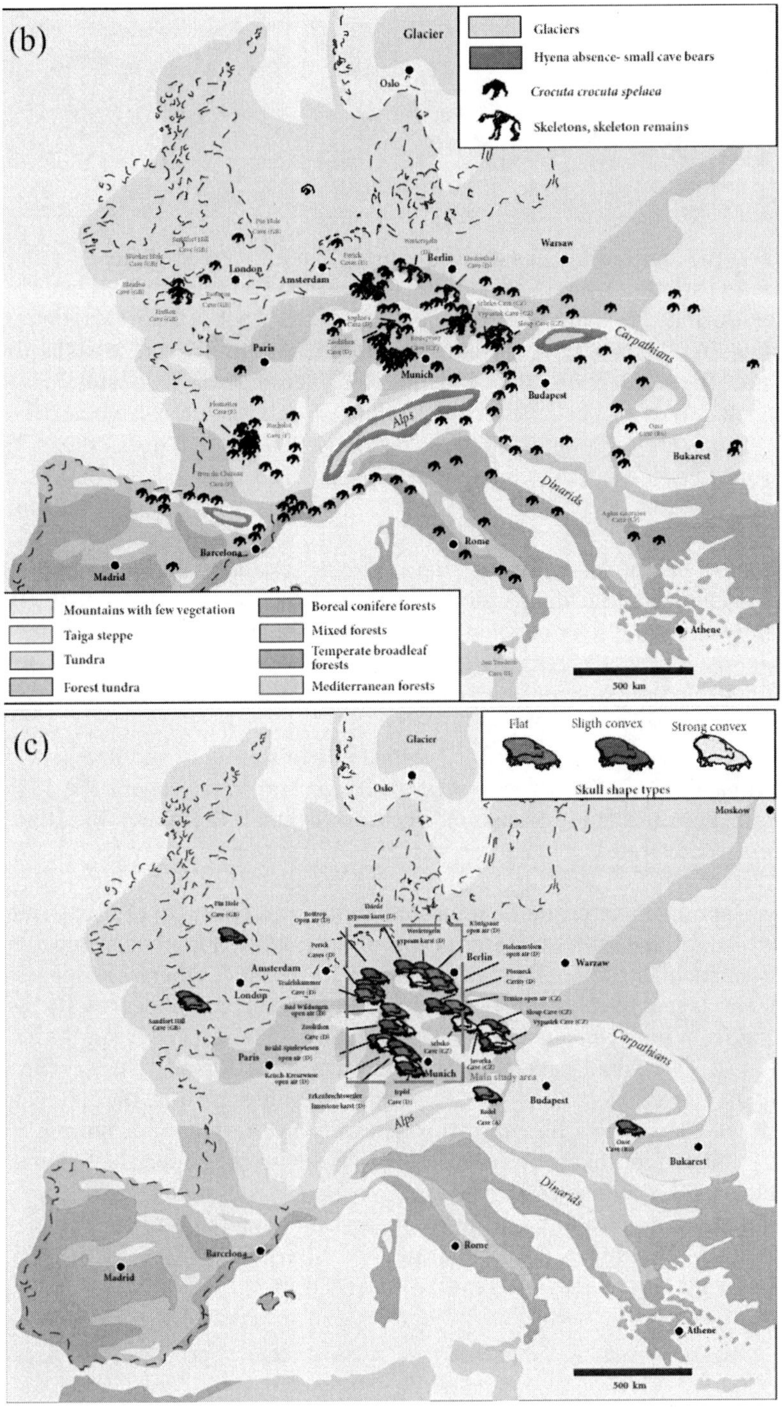
(b)
Glacier
Glaciers
Hyena absence- small cave bears
Crocuta crocuta spelaea
Skeletons, skeleton remains
Oslo
Warsaw
Berlin
London
Amsterdam
Paris
Munich
Budapest
Carpathians
Alps
Bukarest
Dinarids
Rome
Barcelona
Madrid
Athene
Mountains with few vegetation
Taiga steppe
Tundra
Forest tundra
Boreal conifere forests
Mixed forests
Temperate broadleaf forests
Mediterranean forests
500 km
(c)
Glacier
Flat
Sligth convex
Strong convex
Skull shape types
Oslo
Moskow
Berlin
Warsaw
Amsterdam
London
Paris
Munich
Main study area
Budapest
Carpathians
Alps
Bukarest
Dinarids
Barcelona
Rome
Madrid
Athene
500 km

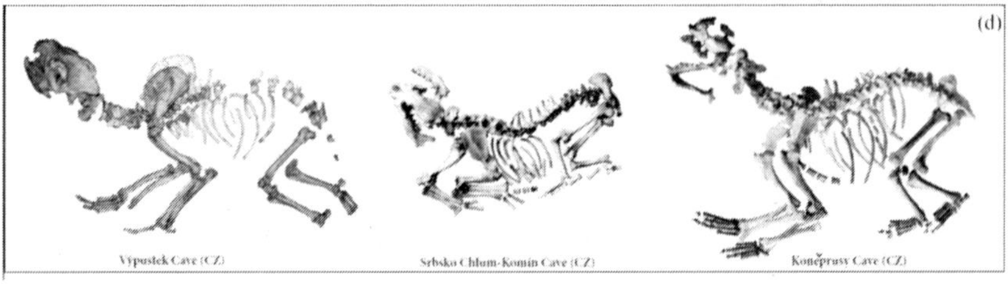

Figure 1: (a) Spotted hyenas globally during the Late Pleistocene. ((b) and (c)) Ice Age spotted hyena Crocuta crocuta spelaea (Goldfuss, 1823) sites in Europe during the Late Pleistocene before the Last Glacial Maximum (113.000–24.000 BP) with absence in alpine regions (= red areas). (d) Skeletons from Europe: adult individual skeleton from Výpustek Cave (Moravian Karst, CZ, coll. NHMW); composed cub skeleton from Srbsko Chlum-Komín Cave (Bohemian Karst, coll. NHMP); adult individual skeleton from Koněprusy Cave (Bohemian Karst, CZ, coll. NHMP).

The modern era of "cave hyena" den research started in 1823, when the English Geologist Buckland published his "Reliquiae Diluvianae" [9]. Modern hyena den interpretation from historic times was based on mainly the famous Kent's Caverns (E) and the König-Ludwigs Cave (D, there mentioned as "Kuhstall or Rabenstein Cave") [9]. The German Biologist Giebel excavated hyena [10] and other faunal remains from Perick Caves (= Sundwig Cave, Sauerland Karst) in 1849–1852 in Germany and hyena and prey fauna remains from the Sewecken-Berge and Westeregeln (D) [11] open air gypsum karst areas of northern-central Germany. In 1863, Dawkins discovered the hyena bone-rich (467 remains, mainly teeth) and Neanderthal artefact bearing (e.g., bifaces) Wookey Hole Cave hyena den and overlapping Pleistocene Neanderthal human camp site (E) [12, 13]. Den research continued with the descriptions of the faunas of famous hyena den cave sites such as the Lindental Cave Gera (D) in 1867, where phosphatic excrement layers were reported and where fractured rhinoceros bones resulting from hyenas have been misidentified as "Pleistocene Neanderthal tools" [14]. This small cave also had artefacts from Neanderthals, which lead to historical conclusions that these nontool bones must be the "kitchen rubbish" of Pleistocene humans who "chewed on the bones" leaving bite marks (= "Osteodontokeratic culture" [15]). Nehring continued the German Late Pleistocene hyena research and collected some skulls and several postcranial hyena remains and prey bones from a new open air gypsum karst den site Thiede (D) [16] and at the Rösenbeck Cave (D) [17]. In 1892 Haarlé started the "hyena den" research in SE-France [18].

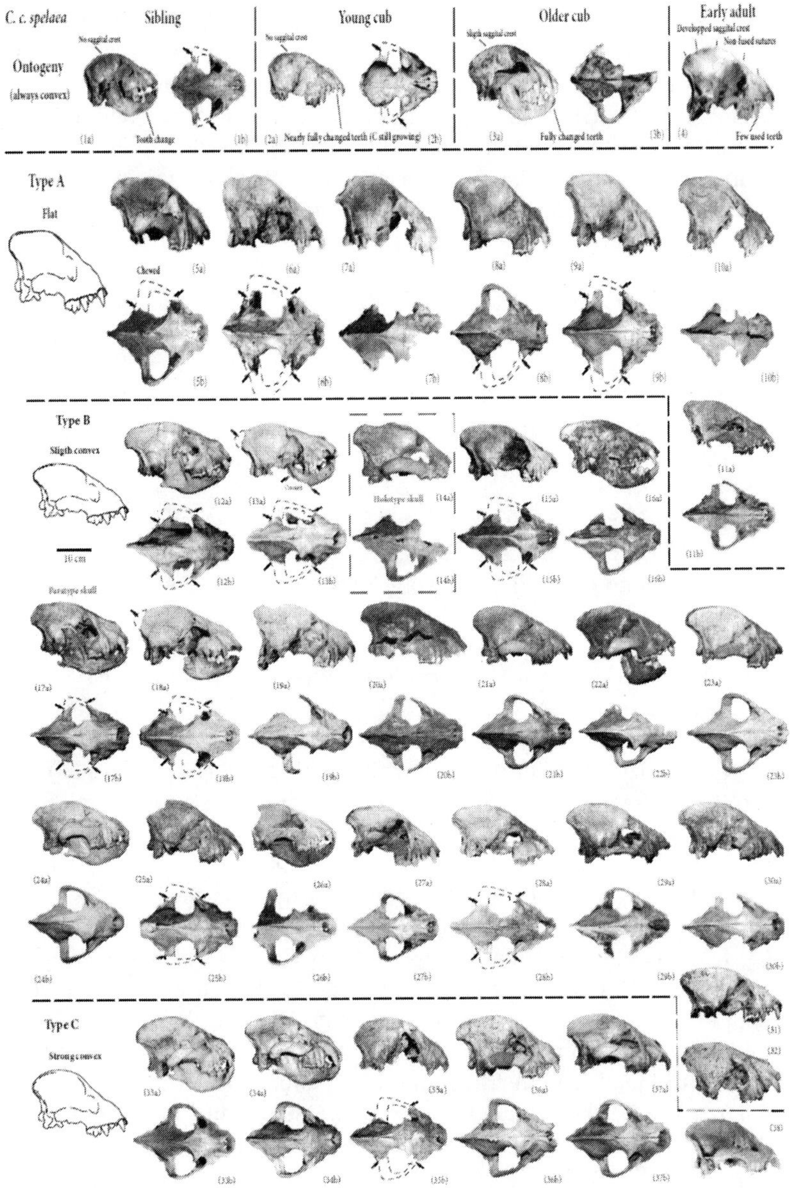

Figure 2: Crocuta crocuta spelaea (Goldfuss, 1823) ontogenetically skull shape change and three main skull shape types across Europe (composed from [17] and new material). (1) Sibbling skull (with cannibalistic damage) in tooth change from Srbsko Chlum-Komín Cave, Czech Republic (NMP No. R3779), (a) lateral and (b) dorsal. (2) Young cub with last tooth change of

the canine from Ukraine (UZM without no.), (a) lateral and (b) dorsal. (3) Skull of an older cub with fully changed permanent dentition from Perick Caves, Germany (SNSD No. Sundwig-15), (a) lateral and (b) dorsal. (4) Skull of an early adult with few used teeth and still unfused brain case sutures from Badel Cave, Austria (MOM No. F1), dorsal. (5) Skull (with cannibalistic damage) of a male from Perick Caves, Germany (BMNHL No. 28557), (a) lateral and (b) dorsal. (6) Skull (with cannibalistic damage) from Perick Caves, Germany (SNSD Sundwig-14), (a) lateral and (b) dorsal. (7) Skull from Teufelskammer Cave, Germany (RE No. 554 791 A1005), (a) lateral and (b) dorsal. (8) Skull (with cannibalistic damage) from Erkenbrechtsweiler open air karst site, Germany (SMNS No. 19062a), (a) lateral mirrored and (b) dorsal. (9) Early adult female skull (with cannibalistic damage) from Bad Wildungen-Biedensteg open air site, Germany (HMBW No. Bi-52/45), (a) lateral mirrored and (b) dorsal. (10) Skull of a male from Trmice open air loess site, Czech Republic (MB.Ma.902), (a) lateral and (b) dorsal. (11) Adult skull from Königsaue, Germany (LSDA No. HK-62 : 248), (a) lateral and (b) dorsal. (12) Old adult female skull (with cannibalistic damage) from Döbritz Cave, Germany (MB No. Ma.44381), (a) lateral and (b) dorsal. (13) Old adult skull (with cannibalistic damage) of a female from Perick Caves, Germany (NMB No. Heinr-1), (a) lateral and (b) dorsal. (14) Adult skull from Zoolithen Cave, Germany (GMB No. M.2609; Holotype in Goldfuss, 1823), (a) lateral and (b) dorsal. (15) High adult skull (with cannibalistic damage) of a female from Perick Caves, Germany (BMNHL No. 28558), (a) lateral and (b) dorsal. (16) Adult skull, with lower jaw, of a female from Sloup Cave, Czech Republic (NHMW No. 2008z0087/0000), (a) lateral mirrored and (b) dorsal. (17) Old adult skull of a female with lower jaw (with cannibalistic damage) from Zoolithen Cave, Germany (UE No. GL 77/203 and 28/509; Paratype in Diedrich, 2011e). (18) Old adult skull (with cannibalistic damage) from Sandfort Hill Cave, England (TM No. 44/1995/695; original to Reynolds, 1902), (a) lateral and (b) dorsal. (19) Old adult skull (with cannibalistic damage) from Sandfort Hill Cave, England (TM No. 45/1995/407; original to Reynolds, 1902), (a) lateral and (b) dorsal. (20) High adult skull from Thiede open air gypsum karst site, Germany (MB No. Ma.49139.1), (a) lateral mirrored and (b) dorsal. (21) High adult skull of a male from Ketsch-Kreuzwiese Rhine River terrace open air site, Germany (SMNS No. 6617.7.3.62.1), (a) lateral and (b) dorsal. (22) Old adult skull-composite from Bottrop open air site and Emscher River terrace open air site, Germany (MFUOB without No.), (a) lateral and (b) dorsal. (23) High adult skull of a female from Oase Cave, Romania (SIRB No. Oases crocuta-1), (a) lateral and (b) dorsal. (24) High adult skull from Irpfel Cave, Germany (SMNS No. AH262), (a) lateral mirrored and (b) dorsal. (25) Adult skull (with cannibalistic damage) from Sloup Cave, Czech Republic (NHMW No. 2008z0087/0002), (a) lateral mirrored and (b) dorsal. (26) High adult skull of a male from Westeregeln gypsum karst open air site (MLU.IFG No.

WEgeln-13A-B), (a) lateral and (b) dorsal. (27) Adult skull from Badel Cave, Austria (WMM No. F2), (a) lateral and (b) dorsal. (28) Deformed high adult skull (with cannibalistic damage) of a female from Bad Wildungen-Biedensteg open air site, Germany (HMBW No. Bi-10at), (a) lateral and (b) dorsal. (29) High adult skull of a female from Gernsheim, Germany (MSG without no.), (a) lateral (mirrored) and (b) dorsal. (30) High adult skull from Doesburg near Arnheim, Germany (RE without no.), (a) lateral (mirrored) and (b) dorsal. (31) Young adult skull from Pin Hole Cave, England (MMU No.65/7), lateral mirrored. (32) Adult skull from the Mladeč Cave, Czech Republic (AMB No. 2644), lateral. (33) Young adult skull of a female from Srbsko Chlum-Komín Cave, Czech Republic (NMP No. R1067), (a) lateral and (b) dorsal. (34) Old adult skull from the female skeleton of Výpustek Cave, Czech Republic (NHMW No. A5529), (a) lateral mirrored and (b) dorsal. (35) Adult skull (with cannibalistic damage) from the Javorka Cave, Czech Republic (AMB No. OK114891), (a) lateral and (b) dorsal. (36) High adult skull (with frontal bite impact in the process of healing) from Irpfel Cave, Germany (SMNS No. 7.801), (a) lateral and (b) dorsal. (37) High adult skull of a male from Gernsheim, Germany (MSG without no.), (a) lateral (mirrored) and (b) dorsal. (38) Senile skull with dental pathology from Crumstadt, Germany (HLMD without no), lateral.

Reynolds published in 1902 [19] by far the best monograph on the English Late Pleistocene hyena remains of its time, but he confused some material as "individual skeletons" which are actually from at least two different caves, Wookey Hole [19, 20] and Sandfort Hill [19, 20] Caves (E). Two rediscovered skulls [17] from these two localities and a large collection which was hidden during the second World War under coals in the Somerset Museum [20] have not been analysed yet at present. The Teufelslucken Cave (A) was another hyena cave den and the first described from Austria in 1937 [21]. Zapfe presented in 1939 a paper on damaged bones by hyenas from different cave and open air sites, especially from Austria [22]. After the Second World War, new Late Pleistocene hyena dens were discovered in 1957 with the Torbryan Cave and Tonewton Cave (E) [20, 23]. In 1961, Thenius presented hyena damaged and chewed bones from Austria and critically discussed the "Osteodontokeratic culture" of the Tertiary Australopithecines (Hominidae), which were thought incorrectly to have produced hominid bite damage on bones, which were indeed made by hyenas [15]. The Czech Moravian Paleontologist Musil presented a further important monograph about the hyenas and their prey from the Sveduv Stůl Cave hyena den (Moravian Karst, CZ) in 1962 [24]. In 1968 some articulated hyena prey remains from open air loess sites (= mammoth steppe) were mentioned from the site of Achenheim (D) [25], which convincingly demonstrated hyena activities outside the caves for the first time.

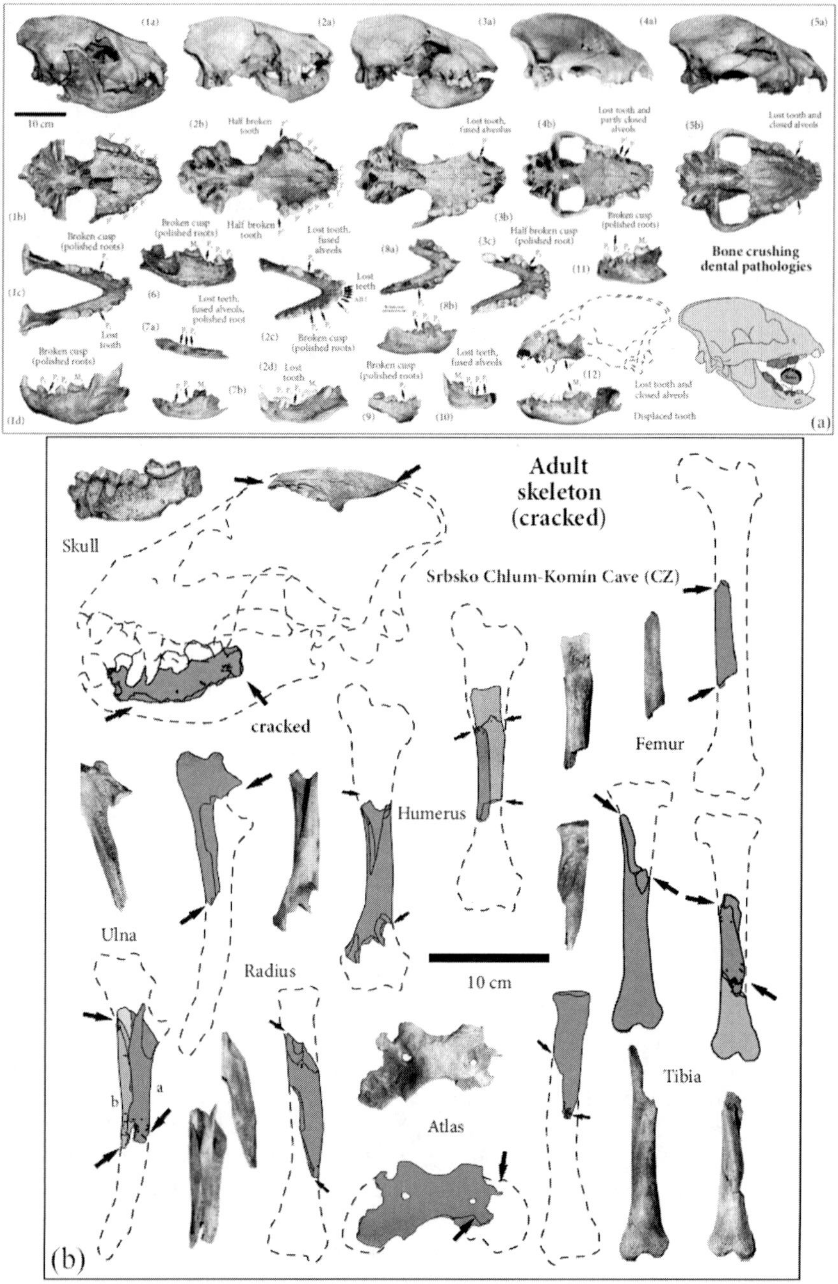
10 cm
Bone crushing
dental pathologies
(a)
Adult
skeleton
(cracked)
Skull
Srbsko Chlum-Komín Cave (CZ)
cracked
Femur
Humerus
Ulna
Radius
10 cm
Tibia
Atlas
(b)

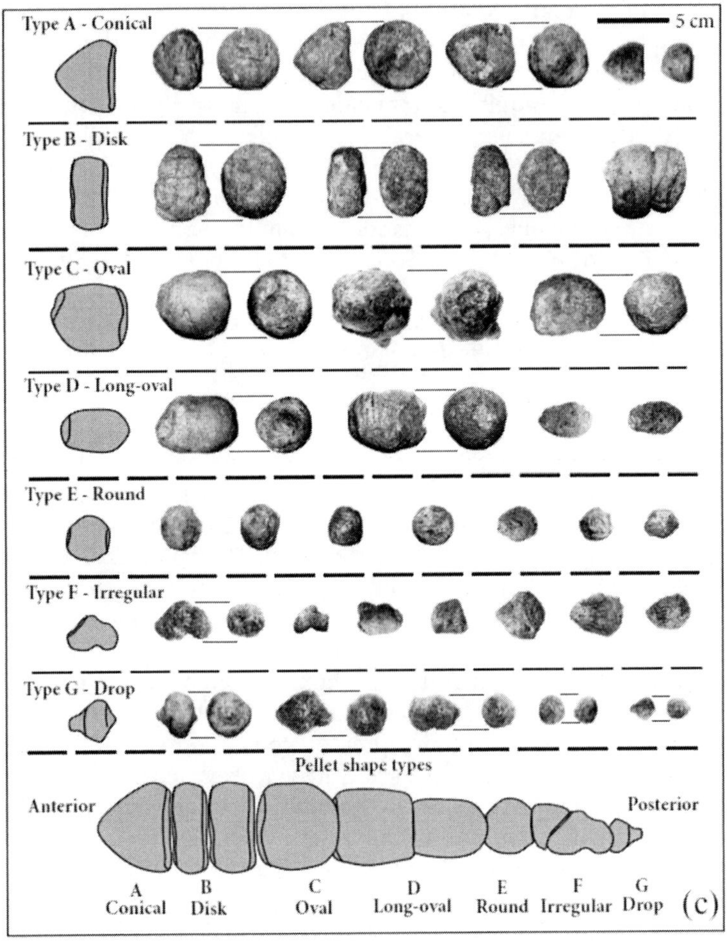

Figure 3: (a) Crocuta crocuta spelaea (Goldfuss, 1823) dental pathologies on skulls and lower jaws. Main damages are found on the premolars (bone crushing) and the incisives/canines (nibbling) (composed after [59]). (1) Paratype skull of an adult with lower jaw from the Zoolithen Cave, Germany (UE No. GL 77/203 and 28/509), (a) lateral, (b) ventral, (c) lower jaw dorsal, and (d) lower jaw lateral. (2) Skull with lower jaw of a senile from Perick Caves, Germany (NMB No. Heinr-1), (a) lateral, (b) ventral, (c) lower jaw dorsal, and (d) lower jaw lateral. (3) Skull of an old adult from Sandfort Hill Cave, England (TM No. 44/1995/695; original to Reynolds, 1902), (a) lateral, (b) ventral, and (c) lower jaw dorsal. (4) Senile skull from Crumstadt, Germany (HLMD without no), (a) lateral and (b) ventral. (5) High adult skull from Gernsheim, Germany (MSG without no.), (a) lateral (mirrored) and (b) ventral. (6) High adult right mandible from the Perick Caves, Germany (GMB no. M2565), lateral. (7) Senile left mandible from the

Wilhelms Cave, Germany (GMB no. M5999 (Mandible)/GPIM no. A5F1281 (M1), (a) lateral and (b) dorsal. (8) High adult mandible from the Seweckenberge open air gypsum karst, Germany (MB no. Ma 29606), (a) dorsal and (b) lateral. (9) High adult right mandible from the Grürmann's Cave, Germany (GMB without no.), lateral. (10) Senile rigth mandible from the Perick Caves, Germany (SNSD no. Sundwig-44), lateral. (11) High adult left mandible from the Wilhelms Cave, Germany (EMSCH No. Frettertal-1), lateral. (12) Adult maxillary and mandible from the Reporje Kalvarie Cave, Czech Republic (NMP no. 5473/R 12 and 111), lateral. (b) By Ice Age spotted hyenas cannibalistic scavenged and cracked hyena carcass from the Srbsko Chlum-Komín Cave hyena den, Czech Republic (modified after [41]). (c) Ice Age spotted hyena coprolite type shape types (modified after [60]).

Another southern German hyena den cave, the Aufhauser Cave, was 1982 shortly presented but remained not analysed [26]. In 1983, the first hyena remains were recovered with other Late Pleistocene bones on the seafloor of the North Sea by fishing boats [27]. In 1989, the Late Pleistocene hyena den Camiac Cave (F) was presented [28] and in 1992 another important hyena den from Agios Georgios Cave (Gr) [29]. The latter cave contained many Late Pleistocene horse and donkey remains that were the main prey of hyenas in a cub raising den site, but this was not well analysed in "hyena den context." In 1996 in SW-France, especially Tournepiche began studies on "bone assemblages" to separate their human from carnivore genesis (or overlap) mainly at cave sites. He identified 16 Late Pleistocene hyena cave dens but did not follow qualitative prey or population structure analyses [30–33]. These include the cold period hyena prey fauna from Trou du Cluzeau Cave [30], Plumettes Cave [30], and the Eemian warm period prey fauna from Rochelot Cave [34]. In the latter hyena den, even Neanderthal human remains (teeth and crushed longbone fragments) were found within the bovid/equid/suid dominated prey bone accumulation [34]. The most eastern known Late Pleistocene hyena den was reported in 2000 from the Prolom II Cave [35] in the Crimea, where there are hyena dens overlapping with human camp sites at cave entrances/portals. The overlapping often does not enable clear attribution to hyena prey or human kitchen rubbish. Interestingly, other hyena dens with possibly overlapping wolf dens were published for some Late Pleistocene Italian caves in 2004 [36]. Most probably instead the wolves were also prey and imported by hyenas, which is unsolved yet. The San Teodoro Cave on Sicily (I) was then presented in 2011, demonstrating the low marine sea level during the glacial of the Late Pleistocene which allowed the migration of hyenas to the island of present day [37]. Currant compiled several forgotten and new hyena dens from England in 2004, including the rediscovered Reynolds collections from World War II describing further caves as hyena dens such as Bleadon, Cavern, or Hutton Cavern [20]. A skull from Pin Hole [17] was added for English sites. In 2008 Polish hyena remains were compiled [38].

In the Czech Republic in 2004, the author's "European Late Pleistocene spotted hyena project" provided an overview of Late Pleistocene hyena den types, mainly caves, which was presented for the Bohemian Karst mountainous region (= between 150 and 650 a.s.l.) near Prague [39]. In addition the most famous Czech Late Pleistocene caves and hyena remains, and first individual hyena skeletons, were reported from the Koněprusy Cave [40] and Srbsko Chlum-Komín Cave [41].

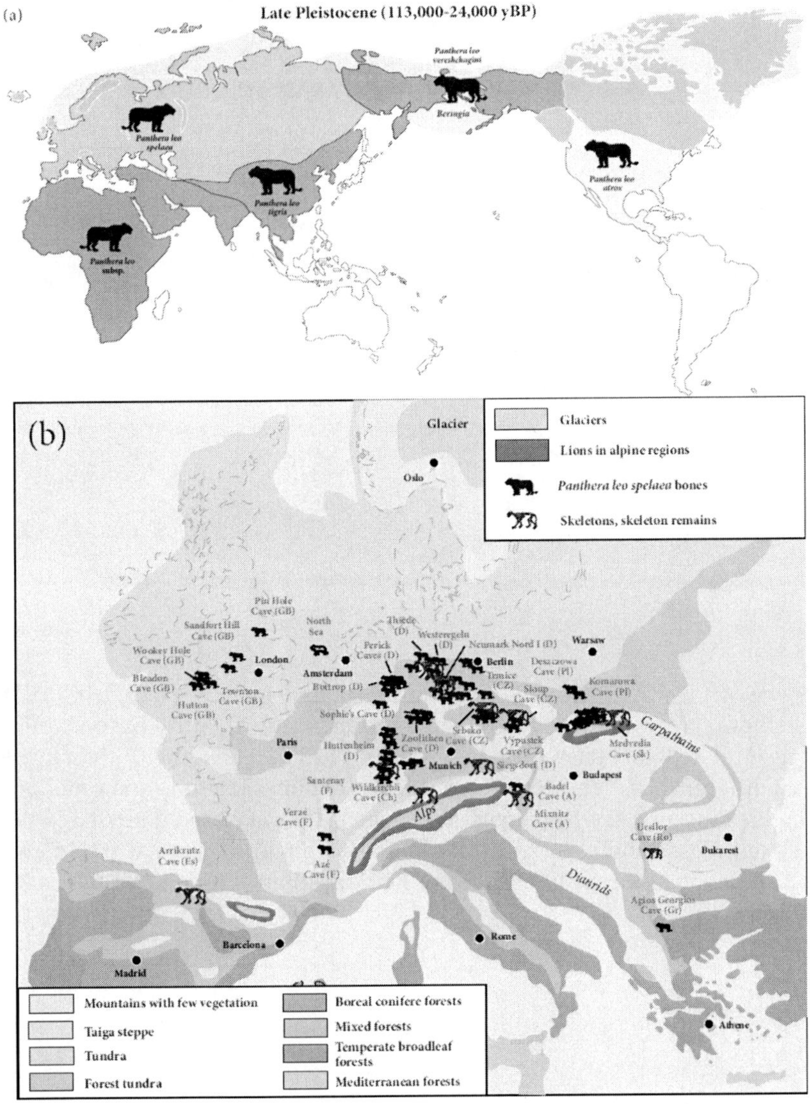

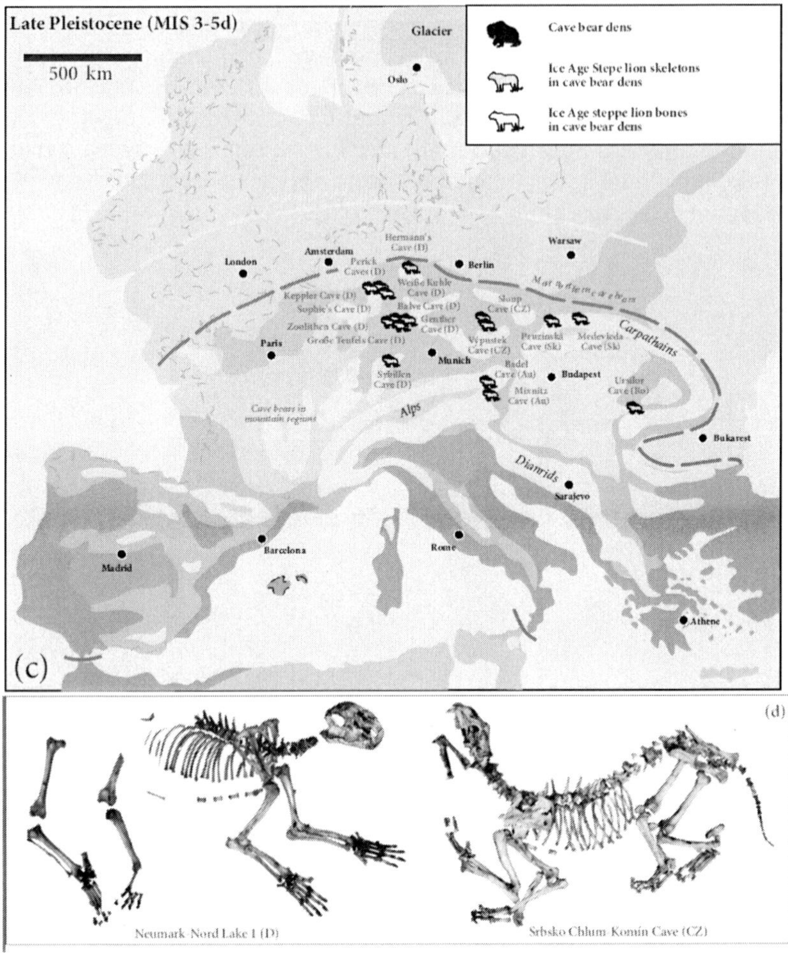

Figure 4: Ice Age steppe lion Panthera leo spelaea (Goldfuss, 1810) distribution (a) worldwide and (b) important sites in central Europe during Early/Middle Late Pleistocene before LGM (113.000–24.000 BP) (composed from different sources; see reference list). (c) Lion skeletons and remains in Late Pleistocene cave bear dens of Europe. (d) Articulated diseased lioness skeleton from Neumark-Nord Lake I (D) elephant graveyard (from [61]) and subadult diseased lioness from Srbsko Chlum-Komín Cave hyena den (CZ) (from [62]).

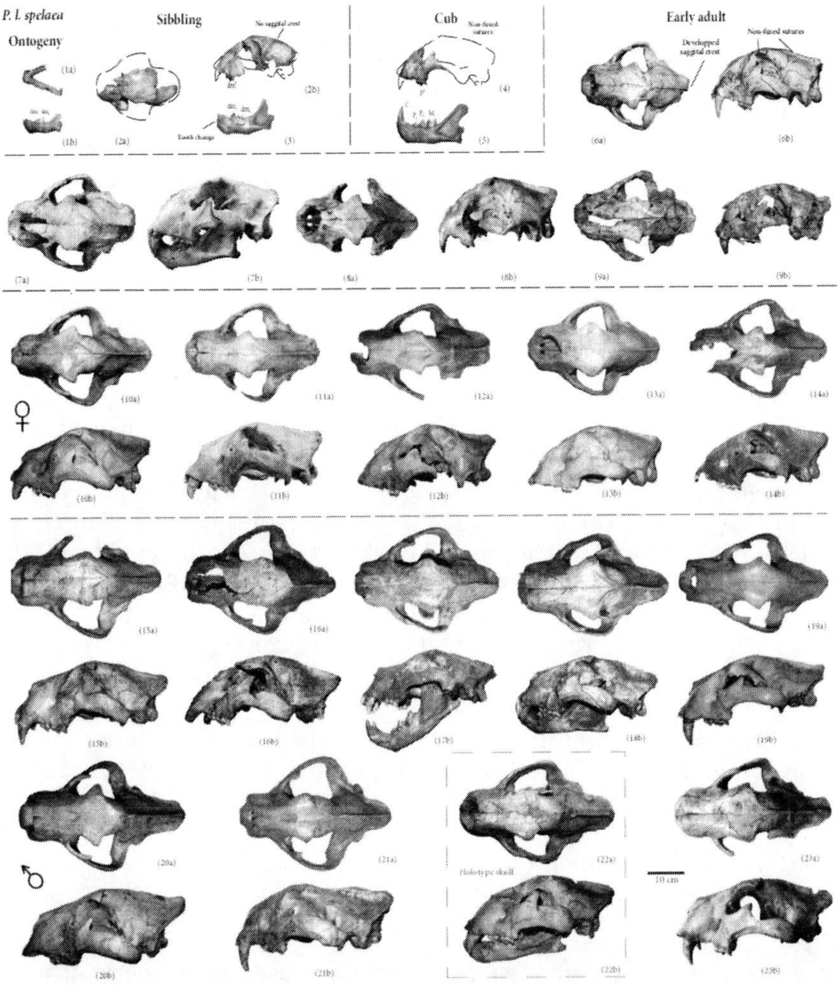

Figure 5: Panthera leo spelaea (Goldfuss, 1810) ontogenetically skull shape change and three main skull shape types across Europe (composed from [8, 46, 62–66] and herein added new material: 1–3, 10, 13, 16 and 20). (1) Sibbling lower jaw from the Mixnitz Cave cave bear den, Austria (RE no. NMB 108a), (a) dorsal and (b) lateral. (2) Incomplete sibling skull from Aufhauser Cave hyena den, Germany (SMNS without no.), (a) dorsal and (b) lateral. (3) Sibling mandible with milk dentition from Hohlenstein Cave hyena den, Germany (SMNS no. 33226), lateral. (4) Cub maxillary with permanent dentition from Zoolithen Cave hyena and cave bear den, Germany (UE no. Sp 42/14), lateral. (5) Cub mandible with permanent dentition from Zoolithen Cave hyena and cave bear den, Germany (UE no. GL 77/85), lateral. (6) Early adult skull from a skeleton of Urşilor Cave cave

bear den, Romania (SIER no. PU/0001), (a) dorsal and (b) lateral. (7) Early adult skull with lower jaw from a skeleton of Srbsko Chlum-Komín Cave hyena den, Czech Republic (NMP no. R4406), (a) dorsal and (b) lateral. (8) Early adult skull from the Perick Caves hyena and cave bear den, Germany (BMNHL no. 28553), (a) dorsal and (b) lateral. (9) Early adult skull from Beroun-Hýskov open air river terrace site, Czech Republic (MBKB no. 363a), (a) dorsal and (b) lateral. (10) Adult skull from Zoolithen Cave hyena and cave bear den, Germany (MB no. Ma.50947), (a) dorsal and (b) lateral. (11) Adult skull from Badel Cave hyena and cave bear den, Austira (MOM no. F1), (a) dorsal and (b) lateral. (12) Adult skull from Sloup Cave hyena and cave bear den, Czech Republic (AMB no. OK130570), (a) dorsal and (b) lateral. (13) Senile skull from Campusal Cave, Romania (SIER without no.), (a) dorsal and (b) lateral. (14) Adult skull from Bobenheim-Roxheim open air river terrace, Germany (RE no. PCC 132), (a) dorsal and (b) lateral. (15) Adult skull from Zoolithen Cave hyena and cave bear den, Germany (UM-O no. BT5421), (a) dorsal and (b) lateral. (16) Senile skull with several dental pathologies from Hermann's Cave cave bear den, Germany (NMB no. 1794-M), (a) dorsal and (b) lateral. (17) Adult skull (mounted in composite skeleton) from Sloup Cave hyena and cave bear den, Czech Republic (AMB without no.), (a) dorsal and (b) lateral. (18) Adult skull (mounted in composite skeleton) from Sloup Cave hyena and cave bear den, Czech Republic (NHMV no. 1885/0014/4302), (a) dorsal and (b) lateral. (19) Adult skull of a skeleton from Huttenheim open air river terrace site, Germany (SMNS no. 6816.5.6.73.1), (a) dorsal and (b) lateral. (20) Adult skull of a skeleton from Edingen (Brühl) open air river terrace site, Germany (SMNS no. 6617.1.9.72.2), (a) dorsal and (b) lateral. (21) Adult skull from Mixnitz Cave cave bear den, Austria (RE no. NMB 107), (a) dorsal and (b) lateral. (22) Holotype skull with bite mark damage pathology of an adult male from Zoolithen Cave, Germany (MB no. Ma.50948), (a) dorsal and (b) lateral. (23) Adult skull from Zoolithen Cave hyena and cave bear den, Germany (MB no. Ma.48155.1), (a) dorsal and (b) lateral.

Recent hyena populations and prey analyses based on modern African spotted hyena ethology were used for the famous Sloup Cave [42] and the Výpustek Cave [42] in the Moravian Karst (CZ). In Germany, several important forgotten or overlooked hyena den cave (10 sites) and open air sites (2 sites) have been described in the past decade. These include the Sauerland Karst cave-rich region in northwestern Germany and 750 bones and 13 skulls mainly from the Perick Caves [10], Teufelskammer Cave [43], Balve Cave [44], and Rösenbeck Cave [17]. The most important Zoolithen Cave in the German Franconian Karst was also reviewed for its hyena [45] and hyena prey and lion [46] content, whereas the Franconian Sophie's Cave [47] in that region supported the complex taphonomy solving between top predators and their scavenging and hunt of cave bears in Europe.

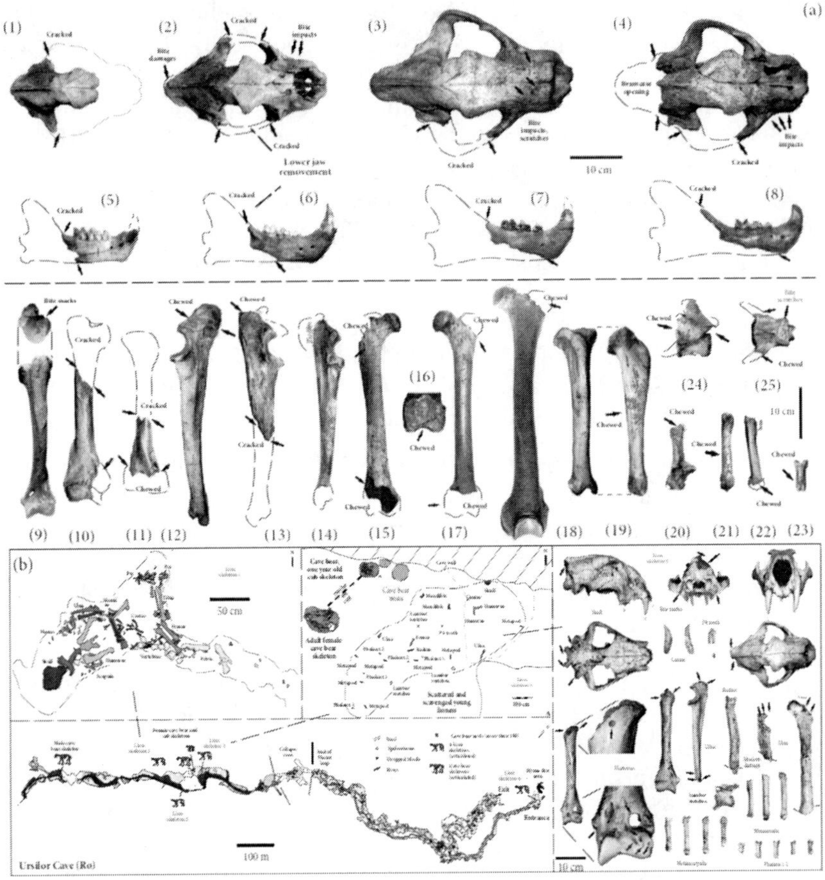

Figure 6: Ice Age steppe lion postmortal bite damages on (a) cranial and postcranial bones and (b) skeleton of a subadult (scavenged and scattered besides mother and cub on place skeletons on hibernation plateau) deep in the Urşilor Cave (Ro) (composed from [65, 67]).

To understand the life of extinct Late Pleistocene spotted hyenas outside the caves in lowlands of the Upper Rhine Valley [48], isolated remains were presented from river terrace gravel pit sites similar to the Münsterland Bay lowlands [49], whereas a population and its prey from the river terrace site Bottrop [50] is a key site with more then 3.000 bones to understand open air bone accumulations or dens and life of Late Pleistocene spotted hyenas, especially along rivers (river terrace den types). There, bones from gravel pit sites have been simply incorrectly attributed to "fluvial transport," but perfect preserved bite damage and high amounts of chewed large mammal bones, such as those found in Bottrop or Selm-Ternsche and Herne along the Lippe and Emscher Rivers, demonstrate that these bone accumulations are similar as those in modern African from spotted hyenas along water bodies. Other German open air hyena den and bone accumulation sites along ancient rivers and in loess mammoth steppe palaeoenvironments have been published. These include Bad Wildungen (there hyena birth den = recycled badger/fox dens in loess) [51] and Königsaue (overlapping Neanderthal camp site) [52], whereas more recent studies have analyzed open air gypsum karst (Westeregeln [53], Sewecken-Berge [54]) and limestone karst dens (Fuchsluken Cavity [55], Wüste Scheuer Cavity [56]) to cover all morphological den types, especially those outside caves. Hyena scavenging sites with remains of their largest prey (woolly rhinoceros carcass-Krölpa [56], woolly mammoth carcass-Siegsdorf [57], and forest elephant carcasses-Neumark-Nord Lake 1 [58]) demonstrate the top predator butchering technique and deathly conflict with lions over prey.

Late Pleistocene lions were described for the first time in 1810 based on a skull (Figure 5) from the Zoolithen Cave hyena and cave bear den (D) [5]. Because these initial finds were from caves, they were historically named "cave lions," which was revised recently to "steppe lion" [8]. In 1900, the most northern single tooth and bone remains of lions from English hyena den caves were presented in a monograph [69]. In 1906, "cave lion" remains from France were published [70]. A single skull was then reported from the Genther Cave, a cave bear den in Upper Franconia (D) in 1953 [71]. In 1968, a discussion between the comparison of lion remains from the German/European "Pleistocene" and modern African lions resulted in the determination that the "Pleistocene" forms (it was generalized) must have been slightly larger (1/4) than modern ones [72], which is the truth only for the Middle Pleistocene (Saalian glacial) P. leo fossilis subspecies, indeed. In 1957, Late Pleistocene lions were then attributed to the modern lion subspecies, as P. leo spelaea, osteometrically based on new material from France [73]. In 1983, fishing boats recovered many Pleistocene mammal bones, including lion remains, on the seafloor of the North Sea [27]. The first Late Pleistocene individual lion skeleton was then discovered in Arrikrutz (Es) in 1981 [74], with an additional skeleton in Austria [75]. Lion skulls and postcranial remains were published by Argant in 1988 from the cave bear den Aze Cave (F), which contained Middle/Late Pleistocene material mixed, including some Middle Pleistocene P. leo fossilis remains [76]. Another skeleton from a large male lion was found before 1992 beside a mammoth carcass at the open air site of Siegsdorf (D) [77]. Cranial and postcranial bones followed from a cave excavation in the German cave bear den site of Hermann's Cave [78]. From Croatia, lions were compiled with single remains from several cave sites without clear taphonomic context [79]. Further to the east in Yakutia, the first "cave lions" (not even "steppe lions," instead another subspecies P. leo vereshchagini) were reported from open air localities [80]. Another single P. l. spelaea lion skull was recovered in Zandobbio (It) dating to the Eemian interglacial [81]. From Czech Republic, remains were compiled in 2007 from several open air (e.g., Praha) and hyena den cave sites [63]. In 2008, an overview of Polish lion remains was presented, again without a clear understanding of their taphonomy [38]. The first European "skeletons" were published from the Sloup Cave hyena and cave bear den (CZ), which new studies revealed both composite skeletons of different individuals [62]. The only individual skeleton is from the Srbsko Chlum-Komín Cave, representing an early adult lioness (Figure 4) with evidence of a brain case trauma injured animal [62]. This skeleton is important for understanding the conflict between both top predators, especially at cave den sites. Several skulls and postcranial remains were analyzed for sexual dimorphism and taphonomic context, especially from cave bear and hyena den sites in Germany, where for the first time the hyena-lion antagonism and scavenging of lion carcasses by hyenas were discussed [64, 82, 83]. The most important new discoveries in 2009 were three lion skeletons in different taphonomic situations found deeply within the entrance of a cave bear hibernation plateaus in the Romanian Urşilor Cave [84]. This discovery yielded a clear evidence for the active hunting of hibernating cave bears by lions deep in larger and complex cave systems [65]. Further important is the open air site discovery of a diseased older lioness (Figure 4) in between the Eemian interglacial elephant graveyard Neumark-Nord Lake 1. This skeleton was interpreted to have resulted from a hyena/lion conflict over their largest prey [61]. The incorporation of lion remains at overlapping hyena den and human camp sites was discussed critically for the Balve Cave (D) [85], where it was incorrectly believed that Neanderthals/Aurignacian modern Pleistocene Late Palaeolithic humans imported "lion furs" after their kills to the camp site. Indeed, those lion remains were later demonstrated to have resulted from hyena and cave bear conflicts. A listing and analysis of some material without clear taphonomy, including a single skull (Bešeňová Cave), were compiled from ten Slovakian caves [86]. The largest European Late Pleistocene lion fossil record (= palaeopopulation) was recently described in 2011 for Zoolithen Cave, where evidence for cave bear hunting by lions was established by taphonomic studies [44]. Open air lion material was then reviewed for northern Germany for all kind of sites (Figure 4), of which several bones had also bite damages indicating scavenging and even importation of lion body parts to their dens by Late Pleistocene spotted hyenas [67]. In northern Germany, the only known Late Pleistocene lion trackway has been documented with other Late Pleistocene megafauna tracks at Bottrop, where additionally partly chewed and damaged lion remains have been described [67]. From the Upper Rhine Valley (D) three more skeleton remains and several bones have been reported in 2012 [66]. Here, a new unpublished skull is added of a lioness from the Austrian Badel Cave, another hyena and cave bear den, but also a skull from the Austrian Mixnitz Cave, or Upper Rhine Graen open air sites, such as finally the smallest and most rare cranial material of sibling and cub remains from Swabian caves of southwestern Germany (Figure 5).

Additionally, in the Late Pleistocene, there were large wolf "ecomorphs" [87] which glacial subspecies Canis lupus spelaeus Goldfuss, 1823) [6] was not yet revised, as third largest carnivores. Their ecology is still only beginning to be understood, especially for their cave occupation: den use for cub raising or import as prey by hyenas especially in boreal forest environments [36, 47, 87]. At the Sophie's Cave (D), clear evidence for cave bear scavenging activity was presented based on bone fragments found in excrements and within a faecal place where wolves even used a part of a cave bear den (several meters deep from the entrance area) over a short period obviously as den [47].

2. MATERIALS AND METHODS

2.303 hyena and 1.373 lion bones of Late Pleistocene age from 106 studied cave and open air localities in Central Europe were analysed mainly from prey bone assemblages of several German and Czech hyena dens (Table 1). This study and review used an interdisciplinary approach apart from classical "bite mark analyses on single bones", rather it used the newly developed "butchering decomposition and bone damage stage" analyses. New results started with the rediscovery of many historically collected bones of the Late Pleistocene predators and prey remains, which were reidentified for the first time as hyena den origin. Hyena populations were analysed, along with the bone assemblages. The study of all animal groups based on NISP (= number of identified specimens per taxon) and partial MNI (= minimum number of individuals) analyses were also the basis to distinguish den site types using the modern hyena/lion ethology comparison. Important for the results was the study of different topographic related hyena den morphotypes: caves open air, river terrace, loess, and gypsum karst sites. The historical collections are highly useful for these analyses, and in several cases two things were important for their modern analyses use: (1) bones from different collections were compiled from different museums; this often demonstrated the anthropogenic selection of "good bones" and "bad bones" (bone fragments), but in hyena den analyses the complete assemblage is required for interpretations. In some cases the historical sites were completely restudied at the existing sites such as the Zoolithen Cave, Sophie's Cave, Srbsko Chlum-Komín Cave, Sloup Cave, Westeregeln open air, and Sewecken-Berge open air, where additional excavations and stratigraphic/sedimentological and C14 dating work were important to understand the age, bone taphonomy, and site genesis in general. In total, several tens of thousands of bones were analysed since 2004 from three main study areas (Sauerland Karst, Thuringian Karst, Bohemain and fewer Moravian Karst, Franconian Karst, small area in the Carpathian Apuseni Mountain karst, and open air sites in Germany/Czech Republic). As part of those studies the holotype skulls of C. c. spelaea, P. l. spelaea, and U. s. spelaeus were rediscovered in the famous Rosenmüller 1794 collection. Other forgotten rediscovered German hyena den site collections are from Giebel 1844–1848 (Westeregeln, Sewecken-Berge), Nehring 1872 (Thiede, Westeregeln), or Müller 1902 (Fuchsluken Cavity). This large amount of material studied is no more at the former Preußische Geologische Landesanstalt Berlin (now coll. MB). Additionally, all the mostly overlooked individual skeletons of hyenas/lions have been identified, prepared, and composed by the author in the past years in various collections. The main important and relevant sites are listed (Table 1) at which material is housed in the following institutions of different countries: Austria: NHMV = Natural History Museum Vienna; Czech Republic: AMB = Anthroposmuseum Brno, MBKB = Museum of the Bohemian Karst Beroun, and NMP = National Museum Prague; England: BMNHL = British Museum of Natural History London, England, SM = Somerset Museum; Germany: BM = Balve Museum, GMB = Goldfussmuseum Bonn, GPIM = Geological-Paleontological Museum of the Westphalian Wilhelms University Münster, GZG = Geolocical Centrum Göttingen, HC = Heinrichs Cave Hemer, LDA = Landesmuseum for Archaeology Saxony-Anhalt, LM = Löbbecke Museum Aquazoo Düsseldorf, ME = private collection Menger, MLUIFG = Matin-Luther-University Institute for Geosciences Halle/Saale, MMS = Mammut-Museum Siegsdorf, MNB = Museum for Nature and Humans Bielefeld, MUOB = Museum Pre- and Local History Bottrop, MSG = Museum Schöfferstadt Gernsheim, RE = private collection Reiss, SNMB = Staatliche Naturhistorische Museum Brunswig, SMNS = Staatliche Museum Naturkunde Stuttgart, SNSD = Staatliche Naturhistorische Sammlungen Dresden, UE = University Erlangen, UZM = Urzeitmuseum Taufkirchen, U-MO = Oberfränkische Urweltmuseum Bayreuth, and ZO = Forschungsgruppe Höhle und Karst Franken e.V., Nürnberg; Romania: USC = Urşilor Cave, SIER = Speleological Institute Emil Racvita Bucharest; USA: MOM = Museum of Man.

3. LATE PLEISTOCENE SPOTTED HYENAS

The hyenas of the European Late Pleistocene were popularised historically as "cave hyenas" with the latin binomial name "*Hyaena spelaea*," because of their initial discoveries in the Zoolithen Cave (D) [6] and other caves in Europe. Recent revision according to modern taxonomic [89] and DNA [90] studies has considered these Late Pleistocene spotted hyenas as Crocuta crocuta spelaea (Goldfuss, 1823) [45]. These Late Pleistocene hyenas are slightly differed to modern spotted hyena subspecies, with those in the Eemian interglacial being smaller and the Weichselian glacial larger [91, 92]. Similar to modern spotted hyenas, the females in the extinct species [93] are larger [45, 94], which is also reflected in the skull record of Europe for the Late Pleistocene spotted hyenas (Figure 2) [17].

Table 1: 2.303 hyena and 1.373 lion bones of Late Pleistocene age from 105 studied cave and open air localities in Central Europe with Ice Age spotted hyena and steppe lion remains (details about the material, locality positions, and housing in collections can be found in the references).

Locality	Site type	Age	Hyenas (NISP)	Lions (NISP)	Bone assemblage (NISP)	References
Ahlen (D)	Open air loess, mammoth skeleton scavenging site	Weichselian (glacial)	Indirect by scavenging marks	0	Mammoth skeleton scavenging site	[55]
Alfter (D)	Open air loess on river terrace	Weichselian (glacial)	0	2	? unclear	[61]
Altlussheim, Almendwiesen (D)	Open air loess on river terrace	Weichselian (glacial)	1	1	562	[61]
Altlussheim, Eichelgarten (D)	Open air loess on river terrace	Weichselian (glacial)	0	1	? unclear	[61]
Altlussheim, Silzwiesen (D)	Open air loess on river terrace	Weichselian (glacial)	0	1	? unclear	[61]
Altrip, Neuhofener Altrhein (D)	Open air loess on river terrace	Weichselian (glacial)	0	1	? unclear	[61]
Bad Köstritz (D)	Zechstein gypsum karst hyena den (prey depot and communal den)	Weichselian (glacial)	2	4	? unclear	[61]
Bad Kösen (D)	Open air loess	Weichselian (glacial)	0	1	? unclear	[61]
Bad Lauchstädt (D)	Open air loess	Weichselian (glacial)	0	6 (from an adult female individual skeleton)	? unclear	[61]
Bad Wildungen (D)	Open air loess on river terrace	Weichselian (glacial)	11 (and 15 coprolites)	0	233	[49]
Balve Cave (D)	Carboniferous limestone cave (cave bear den, hyena cub raising and communal den/overlapping Neanderthal, and Aurignacian camp site)	Eemian-Weichselian (interglacial, mainly glacial)	34	56 (2 skulls)	? unclear	[42, 65]
Baumann's Cave (D)	Carboniferous limestone cave (cave bear den, short time hyena den, ? temporary wolf den)	? Saalian-Eemian, mainly-Weichselian (interglacial, mainly glacial)	10	148	? unclear, half Million cave bear bones	Unpublished
Berlin-Kreuzberg (D)	Open air river terrace	Weichselian (glacial)	0	1	? unclear	[61]
Beroun (CZ)	Open air river terrace	Weichselian (glacial)	0	1 (skull)	? unclear	[80]
Bilstein Cave (D)	Carboniferous limestone cave (cave bear den, short time hyena den, ? temporary wolf den)	Weichselian (glacial)	2	39	? unclear, many cave bear remains	[82]
Brühl (Koller), Schlangenwinkel (D)	Open air river terrace	Weichselian (glacial)	0	12 bones of a male skeleton	? unclear	[85]

Table 1: Continued.

Locality	Site type	Age	Hyenas (NISP)	Lions (NISP)	Bone assemblage (NISP)	References
Brühl, Spieswiesen-Ost (D)	Open air river terrace	Weichselian (glacial)	0	1	? unclear	[61]
Brühl, Spieswiesen-West (D)	Open air river terrace	Weichselian (glacial)	8 (2 skulls)	4	1.255	[61]
Brühl (Koller), Rheingewann (D)	Open air river terrace	Weichselian (glacial)	1	3	511	[61]
Burgtonna (D)	Travertin	Eemian (interglacial)	1 (unclear amount)	3 (unclear amount)	? unclear	[61]
Bochum (D)	? Open air river terrace	? Weichselian (glacial)	0	1 (skull)	? unclear	[61]
Bottrop (D)	Open air river terrace (hyena communal den, partly cub raising den and prey depot)	Weichselian (glacial)	50	26 (and one trackway)	?, about 3.000 bones, many of hyena den origin (especially woolly rhinoceros)	[48, 61]
Deutmecker Cave (D)	Carboniferous limestone cave (hyena den)	Weichselian (glacial)	2	0	? unclear	[65]
Edingen (Brühl), Edinger Ried (D)	Open air river terrace	Weichselian (glacial)	2 (skulls)	2 and 8 bones of a male skeleton, including skull	1.111	[85]
Flörsheim (D)	Open air loess on river terrace	Weichselian (glacial)	1	0	? unclear	Unpublished
Fuchsluken Cavities Saalfeld (D)	Zechstein limestone karst cavities hyena den (cub raising and communal den)	Eemian-Weichselian (interglacial, mainly glacial)	218	9	1.035	[61]
Freiburg a. d. U. (D)	Open air loess on river terrace, most probably Middle Palaeolithic site	Weichselian (glacial)	0	13 (from an adolescent individual skeleton)	?	[63]
Geddin (D)	Open air river terrace	Weichselian (glacial)	0	1	? unclear	[61]
Genther Cave (D)	Upper Jurassic dolomite cave (cave bear den)	Weichselian (glacial)	0	1 (skull)	? unclear	[71]
Göttingen (D)	Open air river terrace	Weichselian (glacial)	0	1	? unclear	[61]
Grürmanns Cave (D)	Carboniferous limestone cave (hyena den)	Weichselian (glacial)	11	1	? unclear	[65]
Halle/Saale (D)	Open air loess	Weichselian (glacial)	0	1	? unclear	[50]
Haltern (D)	Open air river terrace	Weichselian (glacial)	0	1	? unclear	[61]
Heddesheim, Neuwiesen (D)	Open air river terrace	Weichselian (glacial)	0	2	? unclear	[61]
Hermann's Cave (D)	Carboniferous limestone cave (cave bear den)	Weichselian (glacial)	0	47 (one skull, two individual skeleton remains)	? unclear, many cave bear bones	[76]

Table 1: Continued.

Locality	Site type	Age	Hyenas (NISP)	Lions (NISP)	Bone assemblage (NISP)	References
Herne (D)	Open air river terrace	Weichselian (glacial)	1	0	? unclear	[47]
Herten-Stuckenbusch (D)	Open air river terrace	Weichselian (glacial)	0	2	? unclear	[61]
Hohenmölsen (D)	Open air loess	Weichselian (glacial)	1 (skull)	0	? unclear	[50]
Hohle Stein Cave (D)	Carboniferous limestone cave (hyena prey depot)	Weichselian (glacial)	1	1	35	[65]
Holedeč near Žatec (CZ)	?	Weichselian (glacial)	0	2	? unclear	[80]
Hostim (CZ)	Open air river terrace	Weichselian (glacial)	0	4	? unclear	[80]
Huttenheim-Huttenheimer Kammer (D)	Open air river terrace	Weichselian (glacial)	0	3 and 37 bones of one lioness individual skeleton including skull	? unclear	[85]
Huttenheim, Sandfeld (D)	Open air river terrace	Weichselian (glacial)	0	1	? unclear	[61]
Johannes Cave (D)	Carboniferous limestone cave (hyena prey depot)	Weichselian (glacial)	3	2	31	[65]
Karlsruhe, Neureut (D)	Open air river terrace	Weichselian (glacial)	0	1	? unclear	[61]
Keppler Cave (D)	Carboniferous limestone cave (cave bear den)	Weichselian (glacial)	0	33	? unclear, many cave bear remains	[65]
Ketsch, Kreuzwiese (D)	Open air river terrace	Weichselian (glacial)	2 (skulls)	1	447	[61]
Ketsch, Hohwiesen (D)	Open air river terrace	Weichselian (glacial)	0	2	? unclear	[61]
Kleinbesten (D)	Open air river terrace	Weichselian (glacial)	0	1	? unclear	[61]
Königsaue (D)	Open air river terrace (hyena den/overlapping Neanderthal camp site)	Weichselian (glacial)	13 (skull)	2	? unclear	[50, 61]
Körbisdorf (D)	Open air river terrace	Weichselian (glacial)	0	4	? unclear	[61]
Körbiskrug (D)	Open air river terrace	Weichselian (glacial)	0	1	? unclear	[61]
Koněprusy Cave (CZ)	Carboniferous limestone cave (hyena prey depot den)	Weichselian (glacial)	12 (25 coprolites, 114 bones from individual skeleton)	23	611	[38]
Kreuz Cave (D)	Carboniferous limestone cave (unclear site, ? cave bear den)	? Weichselian (glacial)	0	2	? unclear	[65]
Lahntal Cave (D)	Karst cave (cub raising den)	Weichselian (glacial)	82	0	13	[65]
Lampertheim, In der Tanne (D)	Open air river terrace	Weichselian (glacial)	0	2	? unclear	[61]

Table 1: Continued.

Locality	Site type	Age	Hyenas (NISP)	Lions (NISP)	Bone assemblage (NISP)	References
Lampertheim, Lüderitzbucht (D)	Open air river terrace	Weichselian (glacial)	0	1	? unclear	[61]
Lichtenau, Hasenkopf (D)	Open air river terrace	Weichselian (glacial)	0	1	? unclear	[61]
Lipperode (D)	Open air river terrace	Weichselian (glacial)	1	0	? unclear	[47]
Martins Cave (D)	Carboniferous limestone cave (cave bear den, hyena cub raising and communal den, wolf den)	Weichselian (glacial)	147	17	16 (real amount unclear), many cave bear remains	[65]
Medvedia Cave near Liptovský (Sk)	Limestone cave (cave bear den)	Weichselian (glacial)	0	Skeleton of a subadult	? unclear	[86]
Minice (CZ)	?	Weichselian (glacial)	0	1	? unclear	[80]
Mücheln (D)	Lake	? Eemian/ Weichselian	0	1	? unclear	[61]
Neumark-Nord Lake 1 (D)	Lake, forest elephants at a graveyard surrounded by Middle Palaeolithic camps	Eemian (interglacial)	6 (4 coprolites)	4 (and 172 bones from ill lioness individual skeleton)	Many hyena/lion scavenged elephant carcasses	[56, 84]
Niederlehme (D)	Open air river terrace	Weichselian (glacial)	1	7	? unclear	[61]
Oberneissen Cave (D)	Karst cave (cub raising den)	Weichselian (glacial)	14	0	? unclear	Unpublished
Oberröblingen (D)	Open air loess	Weichselian (glacial)	0	1	? unclear	[61]
Oberrohn (D)	Open air loess	Weichselian (glacial)	0	1	? unclear	[61]
Otterstadt, Altrhein-Süd (D)	Open air river terrace	Weichselian (glacial)	0	2	? unclear	[61]
Otterstadt, Altrhein-Nord (D)	Open air river terrace	Weichselian (glacial)	0	3	? unclear	[61]
Otterstadt, Waldwiesen (D)	Open air river terrace	Weichselian (glacial)	0	3	? unclear	[61]
Osteroden (D)	Zechstein gypsum karst hyena den (type unclear)	? Weichselian (glacial)	1	0	? unclear	[50]
Perick Caves (D)	Carboniferous limestone cave (hyena cub raising and communal den)	Weichselian (glacial)	147 (5 skulls)	59	373	[10, 62]
Petershagen (D)	Open air river terrace	Weichselian (glacial)	0	1	Woolly rhinoceros skeleton, unscavanged	[61, 88]
Pfefferburg Cave (D)	Carboniferous limestone cave (hyena den, cave bear den, ? temporary wolf den)	Weichselian (glacial)	37 (and 8 coprolites)	2	31 (real amount ? unclear)	[65]
Phoeben (D)	Open air river terrace	Weichselian (glacial)	0	1	? unclear	[61]

Table 1: Continued.

Locality	Site type	Age	Hyenas (NISP)	Lions (NISP)	Bone assemblage (NISP)	References
Praha-Podbaba (CZ)	Open air river terrace	Weichselian (glacial)	0	16 (from two individual skeletons)	? unclear	[80]
Praha-Košíře (CZ)	Open air river terrace	Weichselian (glacial)	0	1	? unclear	[80]
Praha-Libeň (CZ)	Open air river terrace	Weichselian (glacial)	0	6	? unclear	[80]
Questenberg (D)	? unclear	? Weichselian (glacial)	1	0	? unclear	[50]
Rösenbeck Cave (D)	Carboniferous limestone cave (hyena communal and cave bear den)	Weichselian (glacial)	83 (5 skulls)	0	? unclear, many cave bear remains	[17]
Selm-Ternsche (D)	Open air river terrace	Weichselian (glacial)	3	0	? unclear	[47]
Siegsdorf (D)	River branch, river terrace site	Weichselian (glacial)	(3 coprolites)	62 bones of one male individual skeleton including skull	Mammoth bull carcass scavenging site	[75]
Speyer, Deutschof (D)	Open air river terrace	Weichselian (glacial)	0	1	? unclear	[61]
Svobodné Dvory near Hradec Králové (CZ)	? open air	Weichselian (glacial)	0	1	? unclear	[80]
Sewecken-Berge Quedlinburg (D)	Triassic gypsum karst hyena den (prey depot and communal den)	Eemian-Weichselian (interglacial, mainly glacial)	115 (1 skull of cub)	17	660	[52, 61]
Senzig (D)	Open air river terrace	? Weichselian (glacial)	0	1	? unclear	[61]
Sloup Cave (CZ)	Carboniferous limestone cave (hyena den, cave bear den, ? wolf den)	Weichselian (glacial)	85 (2 skulls)	4	52	[40]
Sophie's Cave (D)	Jurassic limestone cave (hyena cub raising and communal, cave bar, and wolf den)	Weichselian (glacial)	1	2	6, many cave bear remains (often carnivore damaged)	[45]
Speyer, Binsfeld-Südost (D)	Open air river terrace	Weichselian (glacial)	0	1	? unclear	[61]
Srbsko Chlum-Komín Cave (CZ)	Carboniferous limestone cave (hyena prey depot and commuting den)	Weichselian (glacial)	366 (from 6 individual skeletons, including cubs, 4 coprolites)	Two individual skeletons: 149 bones from an adolescent ill lioness, and 107 bones of a juvenile	2,947 (mainly Przewalski horse remains)	[39]
Teufelskammer Cave (D)	Carboniferous limestone cave (hyena den, cave bear den, ? temporary wolf den)	Weichselian (glacial)	71	1	97	[41]
Thiede (D)	Zechstein gypsum karst hyena den (prey depot and communal den)	Weichselian (glacial)	30 (1 skull of adult)	14	120 (even more, unclear amount at this stage)	[67]

Table 1: Continued.

Locality	Site type	Age	Hyenas (NISP)	Lions (NISP)	Bone assemblage (NISP)	References
Türmitz (CZ)	Open air loess	Weichselian (glacial)	2 (1 skull)	2	? unclear	[17]
Ústí nad Labem (CZ)	Open air river terrace	Weichselian (glacial)	0	1	? unclear	[80]
Výpustek Cave (CZ)	Carboniferous limestone cave (hyena den, cave bear den, ? temporary wolf den)	? Eemian/ Weichselian (interglacial/ glacial)	236 (3 skulls, one individual skeleton)	36	? unclear	Unpublished, skeleton in [39]
Wanne (D)	Open air river terrace	Weichselian (glacial)	0	1	? unclear	[61]
Westeregeln (D)	Zechstein gypsum karst hyena den (prey depot and communal den) and overlapping Neanderthal camp site	Weichselian (glacial)	84 (10 skulls, and 20 coprolites)	12	488	[51, 61]
Wildkirchli Cave (Ch)	Limestone cave (cave bear den)	Weichselian (glacial)	0	23	?, many cave bear remains	Unpublished
Wiesental, Allmendweg (D)	Open air river terrace	Weichselian (glacial)	0	1	? unclear	[61]
Wiesental, Viehweg (D)	Open air river terrace	Weichselian (glacial)	0	1	? unclear	[61]
Wilhelms Cave (D)	Carboniferous limestone cave (hyena cub raising and communal den)	Weichselian (glacial)	169	15 (sibling skeleton remain)	126	[65]
Wörth, Geisbögel (D)	Open air river terrace	Weichselian (glacial)	0	1	? unclear	[61]
Wörth, Rheinanlagen (D)	Open air river terrace	Weichselian (glacial)	0	1	? unclear	[61]
Wüste Scheuer Abri (D)	Zechstein limestone abri/small cavity	Weichselian (glacial)	27 (1 skull)	0	61	[54]
Zechovice near Volyně (CZ)	? open air Loess	Weichselian (glacial)	0	1	? unclear	[80]
Zoolithen Cave (D)	Jurassic limestone cave (hyena cub raising and communal, cave bar, and wolf den)	Saalian to Eemian/ Weichselian (interglacial/ glacial)	207 (2 skulls)	229 (9 skulls)	Few bones, mainly damaged cave bear bones in unclear amount (about half Million cave bear bones)	[43, 44]

3.1. Hyena Populations over Europe

In the study area of Germany and Czech Republic, the Late Pleistocene fossil record includes 2,303 bones and 2 skeletons from hyenas (Table 1). These predators must have migrated from Africa to the North and were distributed all over Eurasia up to northern England (most northern den in Pit Hole Cavern (GB)) during the Late Pleistocene (Eemian interglacial to Weichselian/Wuermian glacial, 126.000–24.000 BP). The last hyenas of Europe must have become extinct just before the Last Glacial Maximum (= LGM, around 22,000 BP) [93] at least in northern Europe. A retreat to the south is not really expected, while an eastern migration is not yet supported by studies from Asia with most eastern records in the Altai Mountains. In most cases except in the well studied regions of Germany and Czech Republic, where hyena remains are found, they occur at den sites even though they have been mostly overlooked (Figure 1). An overview of more than 120 Late Pleistocene hyena den sites (Figure 1) indicates much more small caves and entrances of larger caves to have been used, whereas the rare open air record is mostly a result of bone taphonomy accumulation misidentification. Not all sites are dated properly, but they likely represent the Late Pleistocene interval.

3.2. Holotype, Paratype Skulls, and Skeletons

The recently rediscovered holotype skull of "Hyeana spelaea" was found in the Zoolithen Cave of Bavaria (D) [6]. Besides this toothless, old individual, and historically damaged skull, a paratype skull was selected from a large hyena palaeopopulation of this cave [44]. From this cave, similar to many other sites of Europe, articulated skeletons are absent due to two reasons: (a) nonprofessional excavation and collecting and (b) hyena cannibalism. More recently, a fairly complete individual skeleton of an adult animal was rediscovered and composed from the Koněprusy Cave (CZ) [40] (Figure 1). Another skeleton with a better preserved skull was chosen from the Výpustek Cave (CZ) [41] (Figure 1). Skelton remains of three different cub/sibling individuals were used from the Srbsko-Chlum-Komín Cave [41], to build a first composite cub skeleton of this species (Figure 1), which is important for the identification of overlooked cub bones in various collections. Further incomplete hyena skeletons seem to have been present also in the Perick Caves, Hutton Cavern, and Zoolithen Cave, but cannibalism, river floods, or historical excavations destroyed their articulation context.

3.3. Skull Shape Types

Recent studies on both, modern African spotted hyenas [94] and more than 35 European Late Pleistocene spotted hyena skulls (mainly grown up individuals, but also few sibling and cub skulls) [17], have yielded similar results. The saggital crest is absent in infants and develops within juveniles after their teeth change and is strongly high in adults (Figure 2), which serves as the attachment for the massive bone crushing lower jaw musculature. Three different general skull shape variants similar in C. c. spelaea and in C. c. crocuta include (a) flat and (b) slight convex saggital crest shapes (Figure 2). As demonstrated in Europe for the Late Pleistocene spotted hyenas, those types overlap and do not allow a clear separation of "races" (Figures 1(c) and 2). The third, (c) strong convex shape (only 5% of the skulls), was demonstrated for the Late Pleistocene and modern spotted hyenas to be rare and pathologic and partly the result of cranial bite damages caused by top predators in conflicts (other hyenas or lions or cave bears; see Figures 2 and 7) [17]. The best and most impressive damaged skull is from the Zoolithen Cave (Figure 7(b)), which historically [92] astonished scientists, because the brain case was not damaged, and the individual survived at least couples of days with strong skull bite trauma damage (two centimeter deep saggital crest damage, Figure 7(b)). Full healing of such traumas resulted in high-convex saggital crest shapes similar to those found at the open air site of Brühl-Spielwiesen (D) (Figure 7(b)) [48].

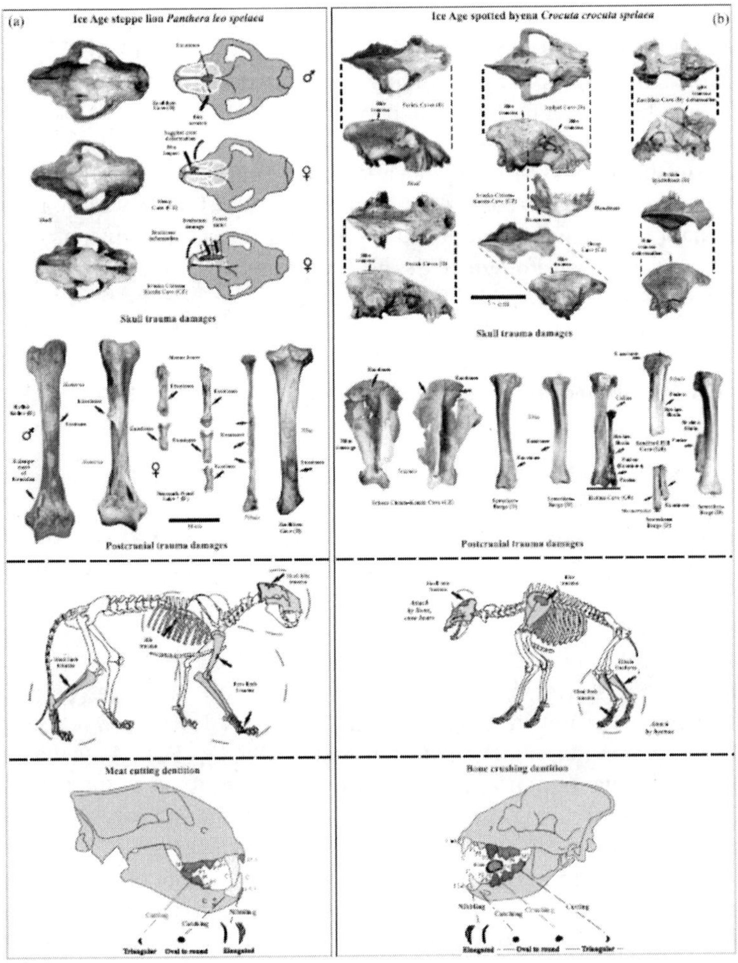

Figure 7: (a) Ice Age steppe lion and (b) Ice Age spotted hyena alive trauma pathologies (bite damages mainly) from different sites caused by hyenas, lions, and cave bears due to bite damages in battles in and outside of caves (compiled partly from [59, 68]).

3.4. Ontogeny and Sexual Dimorphism

The ontogeny in C. c. spelaea was best known only from its teeth, which were determined with milk, cub, and adult teeth of all jaw positions by Reynolds 1900 [19]. Here, the ontogenetic stages are demonstrated for the skull with three stages, (a) sibling with milk dentition, (b) cub with fully changed permanent teeth, (c) and adult with already worn teeth (Figure 2). Also compiled are skeletons in sibling (composite skeleton) and adult ages (individual skeletons, Figure 1(d)) from Czech Republic caves. From some caves milk teeth and dentition such as a few rare brain cases and nearly complete skulls are figured [19, 24, 26, 29, 32, 37, 39, 41, 45, 51]. Often postcranial sibling and cub remains were misidentified in overlapping hyena/cave bear dens, because their bones look very similar, and also the brain cases. Postcranial bones have been figured from a few caves and open air sites of Europe [41, 45, 51], because often those are strongly damaged and remained often unrecognized with fragments in the prey bone martial. The sexual dimorphism in modern [94–97] and Pleistocene hyenas [17, 89, 91] in general is well known with the larger females, whose statistics are presented for several caves of Germany and Czech Republic [45], whereas in many cases the sex identification remains unclear, especially if the site is not well-dated to be interglacial (smaller forms) or glacial (larger forms), or in the close overlap of small females and larger males.

3.5. Cannibalism

The documented and illustrated record of bone damage in the Late Pleistocene spotted hyenas is recently much better [59] than the modern record. There are two types of bone damage: (a) cracked bones, which even fit, are demonstrated best for the Srbsko Chlum-Komín Cave (CZ) [41] where an old hyena carcass in the den cave itself was consumed and crushed into pieces (Figure 3(b)); (b) chewed and nibbled bones with many bite marks, especially at longbones, and cracked lower jaws are more typical at communal and birth den sites [39–43, 51]. At cave sites, postcranial hyena remains are more common, whereas cranial remains (especially skulls) are more represented at open air sites (e.g., Bad Wildungen, Bottrop, Upper Rhine Valley sites, Westeregeln, and others) [48–56], which is similar to some modern spotted hyena open air dens in Africa [94–96]. Hyenas dens contain similarly damaged bones (similar damages as their prey bones). The removal of the lower jaws of their own species skulls was only possible due to breakage of the jugal arches and breakage of the jaws behind the last teeth; therefore lower jaws are very often found without the ramus and skulls without jugal arches [17, 59, 97, 98], which is similar to damage on lion or cave bear skulls. Scavenging is reported in all age classes from several cave dens, whereas even infant and cub remains (cranial and postcranial) very often show patterns of cannibalism damage, similar to that on juvenile remains from a modern African spotted hyena den [39]. The common kills especially in siblings [99] are after new studies of modern spotted hyenas not related to the maternal rank and not correlated with cub survival in the modern spotted hyena [100]. The damage exhibited of their own species longbones is similar to other carnivores (lions, wolves) and also to cave bears [61].

3.6. Den Types

There are three different Late Pleistocene types of dens in Europe to distinguish based on (A) landscape morphology (Figures 7 and 8): (a) cave dens, (b) gypsum/limestone karst open air dens, and (c) river terrace/loess open air dens [39, 51, 52, 54–56] which are mapped in detail in the case study area of Germany/Czech Republic in both, lowlands and mountainous regions (Figures 1 and 8). Hyena population structure and bone assemblage analyses (both after NISP) suggest that those morphotypes of dens are comparable to modern African spotted hyena den types similarly based on the (b) ethology and demography of populations [101–104], which is more difficult to compare to palaeopopulations and their fossil record. Three main types are distinguished in the Late Pleistocene of Europe (Figure 8): (a) birth/natal den (similar to Africa [103]: sibling bones/milk teeth, abundant "nibbling sticks", and few prey fauna remains which are strongly damaged, e.g., [37, 43, 49, 53]); (b) communal den (similar to Africa and most common den type [24, 35, 39, 41, 43, 45, 53, 54]: cub and mainly adult to senile hyena bones, often cannibalistic damaged, prey remains more fragmented and chewed, and abundant coprolites for den marking); (c) prey depot den (mainly/only adult remains and even articulated skeletons, abundant prey remains partly body parts in articulation and less bone damage, and few coprolites), which is more typical type of the Late Pleistocene cold period and cave-rich regions of Europe [34, 40].

3.7. Prey Remain "Bone" Accumulators

Hyenids of the Miocene to Early Pleistocene (including diffeent ecomorphs: bone crushing, hunting, civet-like, and others) seem to have started to develop bone accumulations (especially Crocuta) with bone damage due to prey import to dens (and less single bones). The earliest European Crocuta records date back to the Pliocene [102, 103, 105] with few sites known from the Early [106–108] and Middle Pleistocene [109]. Only bone-cracking ecomorph hyenids persisted in Europe to the Late Pleistocene. The most famous European Early Pleistocene Untermassfeld (D) site with a Pachycrocuta population [108]—here identified as a very typical "hyena open air and bone accumulation den site" on a river terrace position (high amount of Pachycrocutaremains, coprolites, many chew-damaged prey bones, often leg bone overrepresentation), with possible local short-distance transport after the carnivore prey remain depositions—was even incorrectly interpreted as resulting "only by floods accumulated" bone assemblage, which demonstrate that open air communal hyena den sites are still often overlooked. As herein compiled, the best and most dense fossil record of large carnivores and their activities and bone assemblages is from the Late Pleistocene (Figure 8).

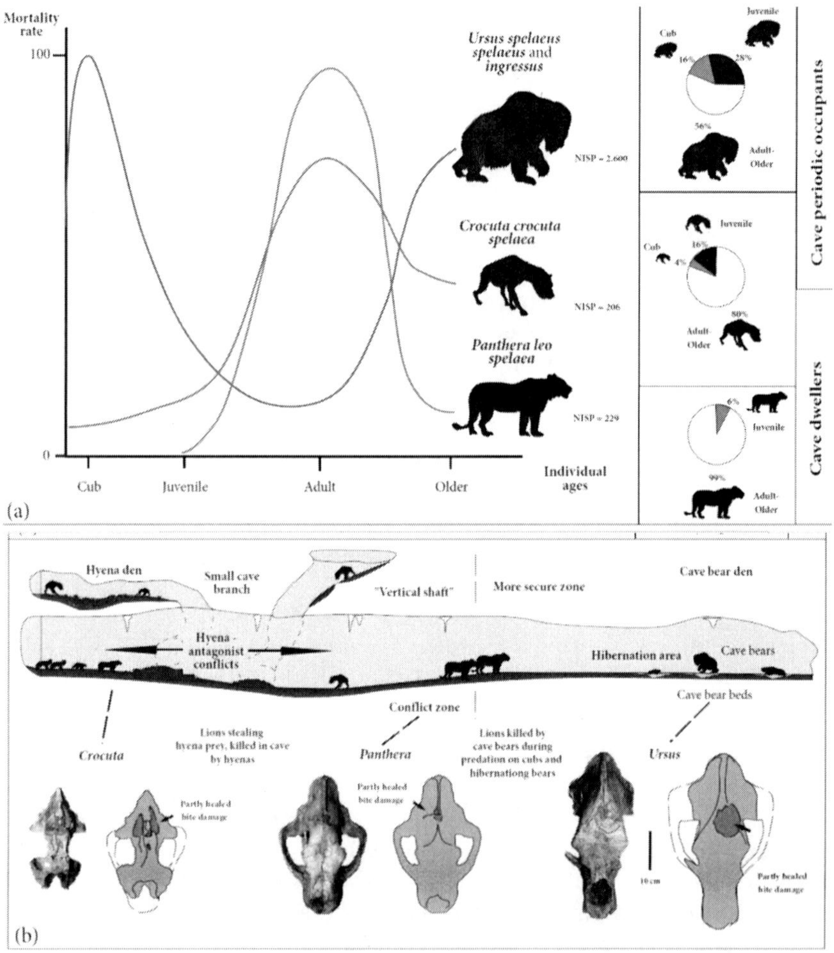

Figure 8: Late Pleistocene spotted hyenas, steppe lions, and cave bear ethology (cave dwellers or inhabitants) and conflict model for larger cave systems (here Zoolithen Cave, composed from [40, 41], cave-imaging illustrations G. Teichmann).

To understand those fossil "carnivore bone assemblages" most bone taphonomy studies dealt more recent only with the question about "anthropogenic or carnivore bone assemblage identification" [110–116] but did not consider the palaeoecology of extinct hyenas and the complex cave bone taphonomy, especially in caves. Bone accumulations caused by modern spotted hyenas, to avoid conflict with lions and other carnivores and to feed their cubs at the den site, are studied in several small caves and open air locations in Africa in some cases at least by their NISP and MNI [96, 107–122]. In Europe there was not a standard to analyse hyena den prey bone assemblages, and often only single animal groups were published from sites and are listed without NISP and MNI reports [30], while more recent works include the prey bone quantitative analyses. These quantitative statistics allow a first general hyena den site (versus human site) identification, because, at most Late Pleistocene spotted hyena den sites, 10–35% of the bones are hyena remains [32, 54] (Figure 8). In a second qualitative/quantitative study, less the "classical bite mark analyses" [123, 124] supports a hyena den bone accumulation origin, as furthermore the "repeating bone damage stage analyses" [125–130], which is best made with elephant and rhinoceros remains [50, 57] and bone element abundance [126, 127] whereas the schlepp effect [129] (= selection of body parts at scavenging site and nonimportation of all types from prey body, such as vertebral columns) is included in such studies. Finally the general "damage degree" is important simply to distinguish human "kitchen rubbish" (= mainly bone fragments at sites), and "carnivore sites" (= abundant complete and partly articulated remains) [110–130].

3.8. Bone Damage Stages

Modern and Late Pleistocene spotted hyenas are "bone crushers" [22, 130] with their specialized bone cracking jaws and dentition [89, 131] (Figure 6). Remains of old aged individuals show crown damage or the loss of mainly the lower jaw premolar teeth (bone crushing teeth) and fully used incisive teeth (bone nibbling teeth) which is demonstrated both for modern [132] and now for the Late Pleistocene spotted hyenas of Europe. There are two main groups of bones/prey types: (a) elephants and rhinoceros with unbreakable bones and (b) bovid, equid, cervid, ursid and antelope herbivorous, and carnivore bones which can be crushed by hyenas. For extinct elephant (Mammuthus [57], Palaeoloxodon [58]) and rhinoceros (Coelodonta [50]), in each taxon, three bone damage stages were presented being nearly identical as those of similar hyena butchering/decomposition techniques on the largest prey and of similar spongious filled bone structure of "uncrushable massive bones." In other Late Pleistocene megafauna mammal prey, those stages are not yet well distinguished, such as for horses, bovids, or cervids, but typically more abundant distal leg elements were left often untouched at den sites [53–55, 133, 134], similar to those known from modern spotted hyena dens [125, 126, 129]. At some sites even those distal leg bones (metapodials and phalanges mainly) of deers, horses, or steppe bisons were also crushed as best documented at the Perick Caves (D) hyena den [134–136] or Srbsko Chlum Komín Cave (CZ) [41] and Fuchsluken Cavity (D) [137]. Only two stages are described for modern bone shafts and bone fragments of cracked longbones. Also the cervid bones were much more easier to crush into pieces (similar as antelope bones [136]), and, therefore, longbones are mostly present fragmented and not chewed at Late Pleistocene spotted hyena den sites all over Europe. The nonelephant/rhinoceros bones were finally often used as "nibbling sticks" [130–136].

3.9. Nibbling Sticks and Play Bones

The socalled "nibbling sticks" are very typical at birth dens and less common at communal dens, though absent at prey storage dens [39]. These are any kind of bone fragments (mainly nonelephant/rhinoceros bones) which were first unipolar, then bipolar chewed mainly by siblings and cubs for teething purposes. They are best represented at the Nad Kačakem Cave (CZ) [39] where more than 60 strongly chewed bone fragments have been found. These nibbling sticks include less mammoth [57] and rhinoceros [50] and are known from other Late Pleistocene spotted hyena cave and open air den sites as useful for hyena den identification but are not yet published well from modern sites, however. Besides those, play bones are present, especially of elephants [57, 58], which are pieces mainly from the pelvis and scapula (= "Neanderthal pseudo hand axes" [57]) or femur joint heads of young elephants [58] which were also strongly chewed over longer periods.

3.10. Den Marking by Faeces

The fossil record is problematic, because coprolites have not been recovered or crumbled to "dust" over the centuries in many collections. Hyena dens and territorial boundaries are marked by extant hyenas [138] and were marked in the Late Pleistocene as documented best at communal den sites [60, 139]. In some European caves hyenas trampled even complete phosphatic horizons, historically described for Lindental Cave [14] or König-Ludwigs Cave (D) [9], whereas in Srbsko Chlum-Komín Cave (CZ) the phosphate pieces built a high percentage of the sediment [41]. At Czech Sloup Cave, Srbsko Chlum-Komín or Koněprusy Cave [40–42], and French caves (e.g., Rochelot Cave [34] and others) or Spanish caves [140], coprolites have been reported to be partly abundant, whereas also at the open air site Westeregeln (D) two faecal places with coprolite concentrations were documented at an open air communal gypsum karst den within the sinkhole [60]. An overview of the few surviving material has been published for the German and Czech hyena den and carcass scavenging sites whereas the different typical hyena shaped pellets built aggregates (Figure 3(c)), which are well compared to modern spotted hyena excrements [60]. Modern hyenas mark their dens and territory against other clans and even lions [138, 139] which must be expected for the Pleistocene record, too. Such early cemented coprolites can survive even water transport [141], especially if cemented and encrusted, for example, by caliche, and even survive salt water as reported from the North Sea [142]. Extractions of pollen from such excrements were used to reconstruct the vegetation and palaeoenvironment [143], but those studies did not take into account that these plant remains are not consumed by hyenas and seem to result more from intestine/inner organ feeding by hyenas of their prey. Therefore, the pollen from hyena faeces can completely reflect the diet of hyena's prey (= last plant food of the prey), which itself was selective in plant feeding [60]. To reconstruct "vegetation and landscape" based only by this is problematic, but in combination with hyena prey analyses, it might help to understand the prey of hyenas using their coprolites based on pollen and bone fragment DNA analyses.

3.11. Horse and Donkey Hunters

The main prey found at hyena den sites all over Europe is from horses. According to the latest revision of the Late Pleistocene European horse "Equus germanicus Nehring, 1884" based on those from Westeregeln (D) hyena den, it is determined that they are synonymous to the modern small Przewalski horse Equus caballus przewalskii Poljakov, 1881 [53]. Even at the Sewecken-Berge (D) hyena den, the "unicorn holotype skeleton" was demonstrated to have been composed of Przewalski horse skeleton remains [54]. At this site hyenas hunted additionally a "larger horse" Equus caballus cf. fossilis (taxonomy still unrevised) within the Eemian interglacial times [54]. At several caves, including the Wookey Hole hyena den (GB) [13], horses are the most abundant prey. At den sites abundant teeth were found which resulted from the crushing of the thin-walled skulls and moderately massive lower jaws. Additionally, also as best documented at Rochelot Cave [34], bones at den sites are dominated by distal leg elements, which where found partly in anatomical connections (= leg import). The horse hunting specialization of the Late Pleistocene spotted hyenas is best and most impressively documented at the Srbsko-Chlum-Komín Cave (CZ), where 51% of the NISP are small caballoid E. c. przewalskii horse bones (more than 1,500 bones). For modern spotted hyenas, equid (zebra) predation is well documented at two African hyena den bone assemblages of the Amboseli [119] and Syokimanu [96] dens sites (23% and 13% zebras) and zebras can reach up to 70% of hunted remains [133]. Within the Srbsko-Chlum-Komín Cave, remains of three foetal horses (one nearly complete foetus skeleton) suggested that hunting time occurred in the spring time; therefore mother horses were imported as carcasses to the den [133]. The Late Pleistocene record there indicates that the hunt was targeting mainly grown up horses (92%), which is similar to zebra hunting in African hyenas

[133]. The hunting of horses does depend on the different Late Pleistocene landscapes (Figure 8(b)), as they are more abundant in mammoth steppe environments but can be highly abundant in valleys of mountainous regions where there are much fewer cave bears as a possible food (e.g., Bohemian Karst [39]). This again is similar to modern hyenas, which also depend on landscape differences (woodland, mountain, and savannah) for different prey, and therefore prey abundance can be very different in modern spotted hyena bone accumulations [59, 88, 95–97, 106, 115, 117–122, 133, 144]. Late Pleistocene donkeys Equus hemionus hemionus were also targeted mainly in the steppe environments, as demonstrated well by two sites which have their remains in the hyena dens, the Fuchsluken Cavity (D) [137], and Agios Georgios Cave (Gr) [29]. In other caves and open air dens of Europe, these donkeys are generally rarer in the hyena den bone assemblages (1–3%).

3.12. Bovid Hunters or Scavengers

The steppe bison Bison priscus was targeted in the cold periods only in some areas or periods by Late Pleistocene spotted hyenas, especially where hyena dens were abundant, but cave bears (and elephants) were rare such as in the Thuringian Karst [56, 137]. There are only few examples where steppe bison hunting specialization developed as reaction to cave bear/mammoth prey absence or rareness, such as at Fuchsluken Cavity (D) [137]. At this hyena den, a high abundance (32% NISP) of bovid, mainly steppe bison, is unique for the German and Czech hyena den record. In Camiac Cave (F), the steppe bison (and/or bovid) remains were calculated to represent 39% of the prey fauna [27]. Also in Rochelot Cave (F), bovids were the second abundant prey remain [34]. In Italy San Teredo Cave (Sicily) even higher amounts (up to 50% NISP in some layers) were from bovids [37], also indicating a specialization there. Generally, steppe bisons are represented in similar abundance as horses in the mammoth steppe bone assemblages and are more rare in boreal or mountain forest hyena den bone assemblages (Figure 5(b)). The less important role (few NISP) of steppe bison at most hyena den sites in lowland den sites (e.g., Westeregeln, Bottrop) also indicates a competition/prey overlap, probably with the Late Pleistocene steppe lions and wolves, which were the active hunters, hyenas more the scavengers (Figure 8(b)). This suggestion is also supported by rare bison NISP amount at the Srbsko Chlum-Komín Cave hyena prey depot, where as in this most large European hyena den bone assemblage (NISP = 3,695) only few steppe bison remains (2% of NISP) are found [41]. Also, in the same landscape at the hyena prey depot of Koněprusy Cave, only 6% of the bone assemblage material was from the steppe bison [40]. The habitat variability in mountain regions with limited cave bear/mammoth seems to have determined either the bovid or equid hunting specialization—and logically those had to be hunted in higher amounts to reach the nutrition biomass. This explains the best high bovid/equiid prey percentages at both sites (Fuchsluken Cavity and Srbsko Chlum-Komín Cave). This is similar to African lions, which also specialize in hunting of buffalo in wetland areas (e.g., African Amboseli hyena den) [119], whereas Canadian wolf clans target woodland bison in mountain woodland regions of Canada [137, 145]. The same hyena/lion/wolf prey role occurs, though much less frequently, with Bos primigenius mainly in warm age periods. Scavenging is comparable to the modern spotted hyenas scavenging in "elephant-free" areas as documented in two modern African hyena den bone assemblages of the Amboseli [119] (buffalo/domestic cattle = 6%, wildbeest = 33%) and Syokimanu [96] dens sites (domestic cattle = 30%, wildbeest = 7%) [133].

3.13. Deer Scavenges and Shed Antler Collectors

Fast running cervids were not a main hunted food source for slow spotted hyenas (Figures 8(b) and 8(c)) similar to that gazelles are not the main hunted (but scavenged) prey in modern African spotted hyenas [59, 88, 95–97, 106, 115, 117–122, 133, 144]. Their rarity in the bone record of all studied hyena den bone assemblages must be interpreted carefully, because their bones are easy to crush and to swallow for bone collagen use. For the Perick Caves, the Megaloceros giganteus bone record demonstrates that cranial remains and distal leg elements dominate the bone record at den sites [136], as represented at the Sewecken-Berge [54] and Fuchsluken Cavity [137]. At all sites studied, the record of red and giant deer is always limited and bones are highly fragmented, whereas the remains of reindeer are variable in amounts and preservation, especially at hyena dens/overlapping human camp sites [53]. Compared to bovids and equiids or rhinoceroses, isolated teeth of the hunted cervid prey are more useful to estimate the MNI. Even with this, cervids are rarely represented by the tooth record at the dens. Obviously, cervids (Megaloceros, Cervus, Dama, and Capreolus) were not an important or main food source for the Late Pleistocene spotted hyenas at all (e.g., nearly absence even in boreal forest den sites like Srbsko Chlum-Komín Cave [41], where reindeer remains were possibly imported by wolves). Very interesting and only typical for hyenas in the European Late Pleistocene is the collecting of shed deer antlers, which is partly comparable to collected horns of gazelles found at African den sites [96]. The study of all hyena den antler records from Late Pleistocene dens in central Europe indicates that the importation of antlers (1–10 antlers only on each den site) by hyenas always left similar damage marks to the remains: the base with strong bite scratch marks at the chewed end and those on antler fragments of older individuals. The rough lower attachment part was never chewed, because it could have damaged the tooth meat.

3.14. Woolly Rhinoceros Carcass Decomposers

Only a single woolly rhinoceros carcass has been found in Petershagen of northern Germany and was found in articulation untouched by carnivores [146]. There is one scavenged skeleton from the Krölpa (D) open air gypsum karst scavenging site [56] and most probably another skeleton from the Bad Wildungen hyena open air loess den [51]. Both carcasses demonstrate carcass decomposition stage 2 (of 3), where the anatomical context is moderately to mostly destroyed, and parts have been already removed. In most hyena dens sites the bones are isolated or body parts are partly in anatomical context (mainly legs). The damage on rhinoceros bones of the Late Pleistocene is the best "hyena den marker" at all, because bones found at dens or open air scavenging sites follow a consistent damage pattern [50]. Coelodonta antiquitatis skulls (e.g., Koněprusy Cave, Srbsko Clum-Komin Cave, Krölpa) [39–41, 56] are documented to have been damaged similar as cannibalistic damaged hyena skulls (cracked jugals and ramus damage). In situations such as communal den sites, the skulls exhibit even greater damage, and only teeth are left, and in several cases were even compiled in dentition rows (e.g., Westeregeln [53], Sewecken-Berge [54]). There and at open air carcass scavenging sites, hyenas left excellent examples of brain case opening on calf to adult individual skulls (Bad Wildungen [51], Selm-Ternsche [50], and Krölpa [56]). All over Europe, Late Pleistocene spotted hyenas caused three main and similar bone damage stages on the pelvis, scapula, and longbones. Such are documented in greater amounts at open air dens (Bottrop [50], Bad Wildungen [51]) or cave den sites (Lindental Cave [14], Sveduv Stůl Cave [24], Teufelskammer Cave [43], Balve Cave [44], Srbsko Chlum-Komín Cave [41], Koněprusy Cave [40], or Sloup Cave [42]). With the carcass scavenging sites (carcass decomposition stages 1–3), a butcher technique for carcass decompositions on the second largest hyena prey is now demonstrated, which only is hyena-related. This has not been studied yet on modern African rhinoceros carcasses. Within the rhinoceros carcass butcher/decomposing technique, hyenas moved body parts to the den sites to avoid conflicts with lions/wolves. This is nearly identical to the carcass decomposition and bone damage stages of elephant bones (mammoth, forest elephants). At many cave sites, the woolly rhinoceros was imported abundantly which indicate that these were important food sources for meat and bones (e.g., Teufelskammer Cave [43], Bottrop [50], Bad Wildungen [51], Westeregeln [53]) being mostly on second position within the NISP (e.g., Lindenthal Cave [14], Wookey Hole [15], and Sewecken-Berge [54]) (Figures 9(b) and 9(c)), also as result of robustness of the uncrushable bones.

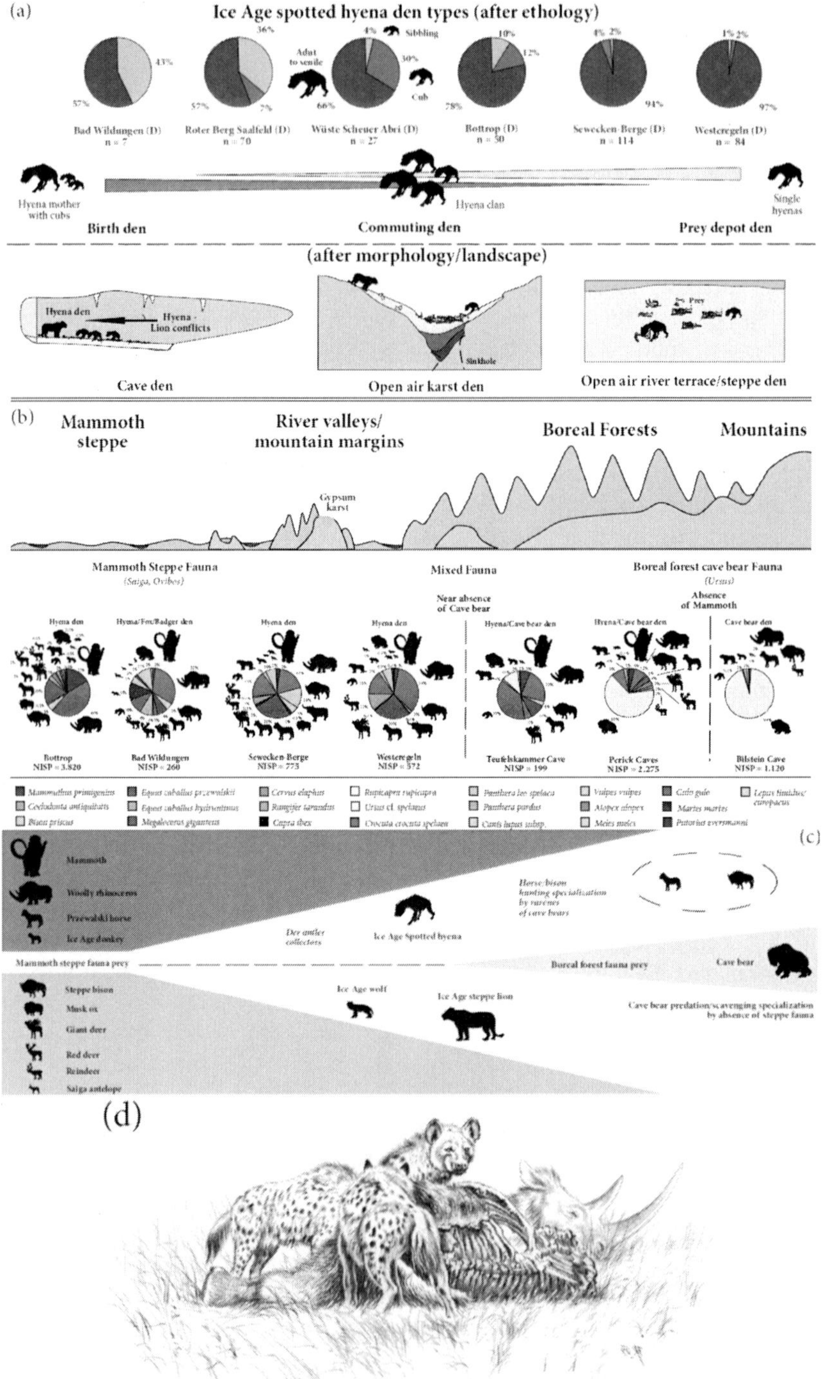
(a)
Ice Age spotted hyena den types (after ethology)
Bad Wildungen (D)
Roter Berg Saalfeld (D)
Wüste Scheuer Abri (D)
Bottrop (D)
Sewecken-Berge (D)
Westeregeln (D)
Hyena mother with cubs
Hyena clan
Single hyenas
Birth den
Commuting den
Prey depot den
(after morphology/landscape)
Hyena den
Hyena - Lion conflicts
Sinkhole
Cave den
Open air karst den
Open air river terrace/steppe den
(b)
Mammoth steppe
River valleys/ mountain margins
Boreal Forests
Mountains
Gypsum karst
Mammoth Steppe Fauna
Mixed Fauna
Boreal forest cave bear Fauna
Near absence of Cave bear
Absence of Mammoth
Bottrop
Bad Wildungen
Sewecken-Berge
Westeregeln
Teufelskammer Cave
Perick Caves
Bilstein Cave
(c)
Mammoth
Woolly rhinoceros
Przewalski horse
Ice Age donkey
Ice Age Spotted hyena
Mammoth steppe fauna prey
Boreal forest fauna prey
Cave bear
Steppe bison
Musk ox
Giant deer
Red deer
Reindeer
Saiga antelope
Ice Age wolf
Ice Age steppe lion
(d)

(e)

Figure 9: (a) Ice Age spotted hyena den types after ethology and landscape and morphology. (b) Hyena prey bone assemblages and (c) prey specialization in mammoth steppe lowland and boreal forest mountains. (d) Ice Age spotted hyenas decomposing in butcher technique a woolly rhinoceros carcass. (e) Ice Age spotted hyena clan hunting Przewalski horse (illustrations G. "Rinaldino" Teichmann).

3.15. Woolly Mammoth Carcass Butcher Technique

The decomposition of extinct and extant elephants (Loxodonta [46], Palaeoloxodon [58], and Mammuthus [57]) by modern and Late Pleistocene spotted hyenas is now being studied in detail. Lions and hyenas feeding on elephant carcasses overlap (Figure 9(c)) but are recognized only once in the initial stage 1 of carcass decomposition of a woolly mammoth at the Siegsdorf (D) bull carcass (intestine/inner organ, trunk, and feet feeding [57, 58, 147]). The destruction of the bones is similar to rhinoceros, because of similar prey size and similar bone structure. In elephant and rhinoceros, the bones are filled by spongiosa and are nearly unbreakable, even for hyenas [57, 58]. They only can chew their longbones and larger bones starting from the soft distal joins. The elephant feeding starts similarly in both top predators quite often on the inner organs/intestines, which body cavity they reach often over the anus [148]. Canine bite scratches on the inner side of the thoracic/lumbar vertebral columns on three Palaeoloxodon skeletons of Neumark-Nord Lake 1 demonstrated that top predators went into the body cavity eating from inside [58], which is even known from modern hyenas and lions in documentary films [149]. This is simple to explain, because the very thick skin is even hard to cut by top predators. The skin at the anus is thin and feeding from behind allows to consume intestines first. Also the trunk is initially eaten in elephant carcasses or the feet mainly by hyenas which was monitored at an African elephant carcass [148]. There are three main decomposition stages on elephant carcass documented in the fossil record. Hyenas are the only predators that start the second stage on elephants, especially on the legs. With this, the carcass is damaged and demonstrates why there are only few mammoth/forests elephant skeleton remains found complete in Europe. Exceptions are carcasses which were found in shallow lakes or river branches partly covered by water, such as at Neumark-Nord Lake 1 (several skeletons of P. antiquitatis [58]). The best example of initial feeding on M. primigenius is the large bull from Siegsdorf (D) [57]. The Ahlen (D) or Klinge (D) skeletons are further damaged (decomposition stage 2 [57]), whereas in all there is also typical damage to the skull, which is thin-walled and spongae-like in construction and easy to damage by hyenas. The final damage of the larger bones happened at communal or birth den sites where mainly bones of mammoth calves to subadults were found [57], simply a reason of transportation selection of smaller animal and body parts of less weight (= schlepp effect [129]). In some cases hyenas fed on mammoth remains, which Neanderthal humans left at cave camp sites (Weinberg Caves [149]), or stole fragments which they imported to their dens (Perick Caves [57]). The greater amount of calf remains cannot only be simply interpreted as "hunted mammoth calves" by hyena clans, which indeed cannot be excluded. Modern lions (or even Late Pleistocene subspecies) are the more successful elephant calf killers [148]. In all bone accumulations at hyena dens mainly teeth and bones from mammoth calves and subadults have been found, whereas their percentage in the NISP is always not that high (Figure 9(b)), but the body mass and weight are indeed much higher. Obviously, elephants were lowland inhabitants, and therefore they are very rare or absent in boreal forest hyena den cave faunal assemblages (Bohemian Karst [39], Thuringian Karst [137], and Sauerland Karst [57]), because of seasonal migration within the valleys of the mountain slopes.

3.16. Cave Bear Scavengers in Caves

The scavenging of cave bears (and bone damage) was initially believed to be a result of "cannibalism within cave bears" [11, 52]. This can only be understood by including megafauna quantitative and qualitative analyses and the hyena and lion (also wolf) bone record, including their taphonomy and ethology [61]. Many arguments against this "bear cannibalism" hypothesis have been published, such as the tooth morphology changes as adaptations to plant feeding (increasing of enamel cones and molar tooth size [150]); the nitrogen isotope record demonstrating a fully-herbivorous cave bears in the Late Pleistocene [151]; similar damage patterns left on cave bear skulls, jaws and long bones mainly, in addition to puncture and marks and chewing present on cave bear bones in every cave bear den of Europe [61]. The puncture marks were especially misinterpreted to have resulted from "noncarnivorous" cave bear canines, with round-oval holes in cave bear cub longbones also misidentified as "Neanderthal pseudo-bone flutes"—but those results are certainly from the molar crushing teeth of hyenas [61]. Hyenas were unable to crush cave bear cub femorae and longbones into pieces, because those were not calcified enough, and only subadult to adult longbones were crushed successfully to pieces in larger amounts in some caves [61]. The first evidence of hyena impacts on cave bear populations was published in 2005 based on bone taphonomy studies and full analyses of overlapping hyena and cave bear dens of the Perick Caves [152]. Still after this, cave bear researchers believed in "bone consumption" of cave bears, which was again incorrectly published for the Oase Cave (Ro) [153], where the hyena skull [17] find was first overlooked (also overlapping hyena/cave bear den). Hyena presence explain also there the large amounts of bone fragments (up to 21% of cave bear bones damaged). Hyenas specialized without a doubt in boreal mountain forest regions all over Europe, where cave bear populations were well represented in possibly higher densities as believed ("one cave bear family per cave" [150]). Evidence for their carcass feeding (possibly also killing of cubs = overlap with lion prey; Figure 9(c)), as a result of absence or rareness of the mammoth and its steppe megafauna abundance variability (especially horse/steppe bison) in those landscapes, is demonstrated for several caves such as best illustrated for the Perick Caves [152] or Zoolithen Cave [45].

3.17. Neanderthal Human Exhumers and Scavengers

There are two obvious examples where Late Pleistocene spotted hyenas must have exhumed and eaten Neanderthal human carcasses. The first convincing record is from the Rochelot Cave (F), where some teeth and cracked longbone fragments were found in a classical hyena den between Eemian interglacial equiid/bovid prey remains [34]. The interpretation of the nonhuman camp or burial in smaller caves documents the consuming of humans by Late Pleistocene spotted hyenas [154]. Fractured bone remains of several Neanderthal humans found in the Divje Babe I Cave (Hr) interpreted to have resulted from human cannibalism [155] are herein reconsidered for several reasons. Firstly, the cave was obviously not a well studied hyena den (own observations on carnivore bone material). Secondly, the human longbone fragments which have no evidence of "hit marks" suggesting they result from hyena bone crushing activities. The most important argument comes from comparing modern human bone material, which was exhumed from more than one meters in depth beside a hospital in Africa by spotted hyenas (unpublished Sutcliffe-modern hyena den collection in the BMNHL), where there is evidence for human body parts and crania imported into a small cave den. There, skulls were crushed in fragments similarly as all the long bones, and this material is a key for the understanding of hyenas scavenging on Neanderthals and humans/apes in general. Also, the Croatian Divje Babe I Cave is another overlapping hyena den/Neanderthal camp site. It is plausible that hyenas exhumed humans which were not deeply buried and left behind only crania pieces, teeth, and longbone fragments. The breakage patterns and selective presence of crania and longbone fragments correlate with the hyena den site of Rochelot Cave (F) and the modern African den sites, and therefore Neanderthals must have been on the list of the hyena prey, at minimum as carcasses. However, attacks on humans by these predators, especially on large portal caves where hyenas and humans occupied both of those, must be expected because both used those seasonally at the same or even different times, which complex situation has also been discussed for the overlapping hyena/Neanderthal site at Balve Cave (D) [44].

4. LATE PLEISTOCENE STEPPE LIONS

The lions of the Eurasian Late Pleistocene (Figures 4–6) were called historically "cave lions" because they were first found in the Zoolithen Cave (D) [5] and other caves in Europe. However, they were recently revised according to DNA [156, 157] studies to the Late Pleistocene steppe lion Panthera leo spelaea (Goldfuss, 1810). The holotype skull has composed lower jaws from other individuals [46]. Those Late Pleistocene steppe lions from the Eemian interglacial were smaller (e.g., modern males were nearly similar in size to Eemian males, which represent possibly even another warm period subspecies), but those of the Weichselian glacial were larger using the largest skulls [46, 79]. Similar to the modern African lions [77] the cold period males in the extinct species [77] are few larger [46, 77], which is also reflected in the skull record of Europe, wheras sibling to early adult skulls can not be attributed well to the sex (Figure 5).

4.1. Palaeopopulations over Europe

Lions were thought to be "rare" in the Late Pleistocene fossil record of Europe, but this was only because of a lack of research, mainly. In the past five years the addition of new unpublished material and revision of lion remains in Germany [46, 64, 66, 67, 83–86] and Czech Republic [62, 82] (1.373 bones, including remains of 9 skeletons) and new finds (4 skeletons) in Romania [61, 65] demonstrate "dens palaeopopulations" in the Late Pleistocene (Figure 3, Table 1) with a bone record ratio of 1 lion/3 hyenas. Some individual skeletons (Figure 3) and hundreds of bones have been described over the past years from Germany and Czech Republic, demonstrating more hyenas in the bone record, which does not reflect the real individual animal amounts because the mortality and taphonomy situation for both is different, especially in the cave dens. Lions were found instead less at open air sites [62, 66, 67, 85] and are more abundant in cave bear or hyena dens [46, 61, 65, 82–84, 86] (Table 1).

4.2. Holotype Skulls and Skeletons

The recently rediscovered holotype skull of "Felis spelaea" was originally found in the Zoolithen Cave of Bavaria (D) [5]. The lower jaws from this skull are actually composed from different individuals, with one mandible from a female incorrectly attributed to the male skull [8]. The largest palaeopopulation (possibly including different subspecies) was found in the European Zoolithen Cave [46]. Also from this Zoolithen Cave, similar to as many localities in Europe, articulated skeletons are absent because of three reasons: (a) historically nonprofessional excavation and collecting, (b) rare lion cannibalism (except of cubs), and (c) transportion by floods (third position). Most recently, a fairly complete skeleton of an individual subadult lioness with braincase damage was described from the Weichselian glacial Srbsko Chlum-Komín Cave hyena den (CZ) [82] (Figure 4). Another skeleton with a more heavily modern damaged pelvic area (Figure 4) of another strong ill lioness was found within the Neumark-Nord Lake 1 open air elephant graveyard site dating to the Eemian interglacial (D) [61]. Remains of three glacial aged skeletons from the Urşilor Cave cave bear den (Ro) (Figure 4) [65, 84] are the most spectacular finds at all. Other glacial lion skeletons have been found at various German (Siegsdorf [77], Huttenheim, Edingen, Brühl [66]), and Czech (Praha-Podbaba [63]) open air river terrace sites. Further skeletons have also been reported in unclear taphonomic context from Spain (Arrikrutz) [74] and Austria (Salzburg) [75]. The only known cub skeleton was found within a hyena den (Wilhelms Cave, D) and seem to have been imported as "hyena prey" or was killed by hyenas at their den site during prey stealing or cub killing purposes [85].

4.3. Ontogeny and Sexual Dimorphism

The ontogeny in P. l. spelaea was originally confusing and young individual material from the Zoolithen Cave was incorrectly attributed to a "cave tiger," which was revised [46]. Cub individual remains are rare in contrast to hyenas and have only been found with a partial skeleton in the Wilhelms Cave (D) hyena den [85], which demonstrates that this animal was not a cave "inhabitant", nor periodically "cave user," but only a dweller (Figure 8). Skeletons are only of subadult to senile in age (Figure 4). The sexual dimorphism in modern [77, 158–160] and Pleistocene lions [46, 77] is well known best from the teeth [160], crania, but also in postcranial comparisons [66]. In contrast to hyenas, male lions are known to be larger based on data presented for several caves and open air sites of Germany and Czech Republic [46]. There, the sex identification remains often unclear in cubs/subadults, especially if the site is not well-dated to be interglacial (smaller forms) or glacial (larger forms) or in the close overlap of small females and larger males [46, 66, 77].

4.4. Steppe Lions as Cave Dwellers

Additional to the taphonomic and nitrogen isotope record, the fossil record data on lion remains from cave bear dens indicate that only subadult to adult lion individuals died in the caves [46, 84]. Clearly the use of caves by lions can be excluded in comparison to the mortality of cave bears and hyenas (Figure 8) [6]. Late Pleistocene steppe lions were open environment inhabitants ranging in their territories from mammoth steppe to boreal forest environments, similar in ethology to their modern relatives in Africa [46, 66, 84]. Therefore, the historically named "cave lion" was recently renamed the "steppe lion" [8] according to DNA, taphonomic, and behavioural information.

4.5. Reindeer and Bison Hunters

Nitrogen isotopic studies on the Late Pleistocene steppe lions indicate that they seem to have switched to reindeer hunting at the end of the Late Pleistocene [161] as a result of extinction of the mammoth steppe megafauna and cave bears [158]. This is comparable to modern lions which typically hunt gazelles [158, 159]. Lions, as fast runners, seem to have specialized more in fast prey such as cervids (Cervus, Megaloceros, and Dama) or bovids (Bos, Bison) in the Late Pleistocene similar to the large wolf subspecies, possibly both hunting in packs. It must also be expected that the rare steppe bison/aurochs remains in most hyena dens reflect the prey competition with lions/wolves. As known in Africa, bovids are the main target of lions in many regions [158].

4.6. Mammoth and Forest Elephant Initial Feeders

Specialized predation on young-subadult elephants [162] cannot be demonstrated in the Late Pleistocene record of hyena den bone assemblages. At these sites the mammoth presence/absence depends more on the landscape morphology [57] (Figure 9(b)). Information of the lion's largest prey comes best from the fossil elephant carcass sites Siegsdorf (M. primigenius skeleton, glacial) and the Neumark-Nord Lake 1 site (Palaeoloxodon skeletons, interglacial). As documented in Africa, modern lions start to consume the trunk, and from the anus from where they eat the intestines of the body cavity finally from inside [58]. This is also well shown from modern hyenas and lions in documentary films [148] and a monitored Loxodonta carcass [147]. Modern hyenas feed on elephant carcasses at the killing site in the carcass decomposition stage 1 [147].

4.7. Cave Bear Cub Killers

In contrast to the Late Pleistocene spotted hyenas, the prey of the lions is much more difficult to reconstruct, because they did not [158, 159] accumulate prey or bone remains of their prey or do not leave consistenly damaged bones. The theory about lions killing cave bears even in deep caves resulted from taphonomic studies, whereas convincing evidence has recently emerged from Urşilor Cave cave bear den (Ro, Figure 4) [61, 65]. Further evidence from taphonomic studies is demonstrated from several caves in the Sauerland Karst [86]. Similar results were found finally at the Zoolithen Cave with the largest steppe lion population found ever in a large cave bear den (about a half million cave bear bones), where a feeding specialization on cave bears was argued due to the absence of mammoth steppe fauna in mountainous regions [61]. The latest nitrogen isotope data supports the cave bear hunting interpretation, whereas others even went further to declare that only "cubs" were a main food source [161]. More recent taphonomic studies at Sophie's Cave support this. The hunting of cave bears by lions explains that cave bears hibernated as deep as possible in larger cave systems even in dangerous passages to protect themselves against lion attacks [46]. Hunting cave bears in the caves seems to have been done mainly by females. There are some larger cave bear dens in Europe (e.g., Keppler Cave, Urşilor Cave, and possibly also Hermann's Cave), where two third of the lion bone material belongs to females. This is a similar behaviour as in modern lions, where dominant lionesses hunt in packs [158, 159]. A pair or pack hunt by Late Pleistocene steppe lions in the caves must be expected.

4.8. Deathly Battles with Cave Bears

The lion bone record in caves might simply demonstrate that females were more easy killed by grown up cave bears during conflicts in the cave dens [65]. Interestingly the amount at overlap at hyena/cave bear den sites of the male/female ratio is opposite to that of lions (Bilstein Cave [83], Perick Caves [64], and Zoolithen Cave [46]) with only one third of the bones from female hyenas. Lions must have been unsuccessful sometimes while hunting in the cave (Figure 8(d)). There are three examples of lion skeletons which seem to be the result of lost fights: (a) Sloup Cave "skeletons" (at minimum 2) [62], (b) Urşilor Cave skeletons (at minimum 3, Figure 6), and (c) Zoolithen Cave [46] (unclear amount, but remains are from originally partially articulated skeletons [46]). The lion remains in bone-rich cave bear dens never exceed 1–3% off the total NISP bone amount [46, 61, 67, 83, 84]. This calculates to only one dead lion per 10,000 years at maximum, which suggests often successful hunting on the "hibernating" and easy to kill cubs over ten thousands of years. The aforementioned "normal mortality" in cave bears of Europe [163–165] does not exist; instead, the high mortality in cave bear cubs (also here Zoolithen Cave: Figure 8(a)) seems to be a combination of both: natural dying and predation mortality (Figure 8), which is demonstrated by the percentage of bite damaged cub bones, whereas most of the bite damages clearly are of postmortal times (e.g., chewed joints). Also the picture of the cave bears life and death was presented incorrectly [150], such as in the bone taphonomy (cave bears as "cannibals" [166]), by not taking the predators into any account in any cave bear population statistics/mortality analyses. However, because of the lack of modern lion/bear population overlap, there are no possibilities to compare this very unique situation of lions hunting cave bears deep in caves during the Late Pleistocene.

4.9. Permanent War with Hyenas

Modern spotted hyenas (the leading female) are normally killed by the leading lion while male lions are rarely killed by hyenas [148]. Late Pleistocene spotted hyenas were feeding at least on dead lions (as similar as their modern relatives) and imported their remains to cave and open air den sites (also similar to modern [94]) which is well documented in the Late Pleistocene of Germany [64, 67] (Table 1). The conflicts are/were about territory, cub protection, and prey [95, 158], but in the Late Pleistocene, battles in hyena den caves are more frequent, which has only limited modern comparison due to lack of extensive caves present in Africa. The cave "battle model" of the Late Pleistocene predators established for the Zoolithen Cave [45, 46] (Figure 8(b)) demonstrates the cave use by hyenas (entrance area as den) and cave bears (deeper for hibernation). It remains unclear, if both synchronously used cave branches at least at some large cave systems [45]. In the Zoolithen Cave, skull bite trauma pathologies are present at all three animals, hyenas, lions, and cave bears (Figure 8(b)) [68]. Also a misinterpretation was made before here [167] that the damage to cave bear skulls resulted from "Neanderthal hunts" [168] which suggested not to have occurred at all in Europe for the Middle Palaeolithic, but only later with new weapon technology of modern humans in the Aurignacian/Gravettian (projectile fragment in vertebra, cut marks on cave bear bones, projectiles deep in cave bear dens, and pathological cave bear bones with bone projectile damage) [169, 170]. The cranial damage on the Zoolithen Cave lion skull is similar to that which has also been found on other skulls from cave bear dens (Sloup Cave) and hyena dens (Srbsko Chlum-Komín Cave) in Czech Republic (Figure 7) which are also attributed to battles between lions and cave bears or between lions and hyenas [62, 68]. In all these overlapping hyena/cave bear dens there seems to have been two main "war zones." The first (zone 1) is at the entrance of a hyena den (battle with hyenas while stealing prey, or killing their cubs), which resulted also in lion kills by hyenas, which is best demonstrated by the ill young lioness skeleton find from the Srbsko Chlum-Komín Cave hyena prey depot den (Figure 4) [62]. It was proposed that the young lioness with a bite trauma damage, which was possibly excluded from the pride, tried to steal prey from a hyena den prey storage site and was killed by the hyena clan (or it has been imported as complete carcass) [62]. A similar but different site type (scavenging open air site) battle situation was presented for the ill lioness from Neumark-Nord Lake I, which had only one lost upper jaw canine and hind leg trauma illness. There, a scenario is reconstructed where the outnumbered weak lioness was killed because of prey battles with a hyena clan [62]. Most of the cranial trauma damage seems to have resulted by these battles and not from cave bear battles, which also must have happened. Those can be determined by the pathological bones of both top predators (Figure 7). Newly studied traumatic pathologies in lions [68] and hyenas (herein) are different (Figure 7) and are even different from those of the cave bears, which latter abundant and very different types of pathologies must be revised and studied in future with predation and hunting background. As already discussed for lions [68], bite damage causing exostoses bone growth are caused by lions and are found mainly on their skull saggital crest, the fore, and much less the hind limbs (Figure 7) [68]. Lions struggle with the prey with the forelimbs and attack mainly on the head of the carnivore antagonist [68, 158]. This explains the damage on hyena skulls too, including on their saggital crest as has been found on at least six skulls (Figure 7). As mentioned in the skull shape types before, healing after strong bite damages causes strong-convex crests such as seen at remains from the Zoolithen Cave and Brühl-Spieswiesen open air sites. In Late Pleistocene spotted hyenas, other trauma pathologies on the shoulder area are also found in a single example (Srbsko Chlum-Knomín Cave—also possible battle with the afore mentioned lioness) and most often on their distal hind legs (Figure 7). In comparison, modern African spotted hyenas instead attack lions and other hyenas by biting them on the hind legs. The fact that they are much more common on hyenas than lion hind limbs demonstrates that these are results from mainly intraspecies conflicts of hyenas. The war between lions and hyenas is also documented with remains found in larger hyena den bone assemblages (see Table 1) where bones might result either from a kill or only scavenged carcass which hyenas found and imported to the den. Compared to modern African lion and hyenas, their battles result in 50% in each species mortality [148, 171], which must be expected to be similar but with cave bear mortality impact in the Late Pleistocene.

4.10. Late Pleistocene Steppe Lion Cannibalism

In the Late Pleistocene, there was also the war (zone 2 deep in the cave) with the cave bears. These attacks were made mainly on cubs (Figure 7) and from time to time lions must have been killed by the male or females protecting their cubs. These carcasses were not consumed by herbivorous cave bears which explains why lion skeletons in caves are often complete, such as those found in Urşilor Cave (Figure 6). However, one of these subadult lioness skeletons was scavenged by a large top predator (hyena or lion) as suggested by the bite mark sizes. The slight damage on bone joints only and absence of cracked bones might indicate a cannibalistic scavenging by a lion, rather than by a hyena. In this cave area about 800 meters far from the entrance in a second cave level where lions were possibly trapped, and possibly this situation in Urşilor, Cave is the only indication for possible lion cannibalism under stress situations, which stress cannibalism was also rarely observed in modern African lions [158]. If this is true, then we have another argument for "lions hunting in packs or pairs" whereas the youngest and weakest one was finally the target of other lions.

5. CONCLUSIONS

Late Pleistocene spotted hyena Crocuta crocuta spelaea (Goldfuss, 1823) and steppe lion Panthera leo spelaea(Goldfuss, 1810) are represented in Central Europe by a ratio of 3 hyenas/1 lion remain which is estimated on material from 106 mainly cave and in lesser amount of open air sites. One to three percent of the lion remains at hyena den sites indicate at minimum their scavenging by hyenas, which possibly even killed time by time cubs, adolescents, lioneses, or/and weak individuals, similar as well reported by the African relatives. The extant last hyenas and lions of Europe have similarities in their ecologies to modern African hyenas/lions resulting in competition about prey and territory, whereas only hyenas used caves as den sites. However there are differences to modern African hyenas/lions, because there caves are less abundant, and cave bears (or other bears) are absent, as are the prey group of cervids. Cannibalism within Late Pleistocene spotted hyenas is documented at many dens, whereas only two individual skeletons from Europe reflect special taphonomic site conditions (vertical-diagonal shafts or prey storage sites). Late Pleistocene spotted hyenas left bone accumulations at three different den types: (1) birth/natal dens, (2) communal dens, and (3) prey storage dens. None of the lion and wolf competitors produced bone accumulations, nor such massive bone damages found within hyena den bone assemblages. Only hyenas developed at all magamammal groups a similar butchering technique, to decompose carcasses, whose body parts (even Neanderthal/Cromagnon human remains of exhumed shallow burials) were imported to dens to avoid conflicts with other predators. Feeding specializations by hyenas, lions, and wolves on different megamammal groups partly overlap (e.g., cave bears). Lions and wolves were specialized cervid (fast running prey) and bovid (large herds) hunters, whereas hyenas were the main meat colossus scavengers and carcass decomposers of woolly mammoth and woolly rhinoceros, which subadults/adults have even for hyenas uncrushable bones. Late Pleistocene spotted hyenas left repeatedly similar damaged large prey bones all over Europe. Similar to modern spotted hyenas, Late Pleistocene ones are expected to have hunted in clans equids (Przewalski horses in the Late Pleistocene-zebras modern). Foetal Przewalski horse remains prove quite uniquely the hunt in spring times at one Czech hyena cave prey storage and communal den site. Steppe lions as open environment (mammoth steppe to boreal forests) felids focused on cervids with reindeer targeting specialization during the Last Glacial Maximum around 22.000 BP., when other megafauna became rarer or extinct. They also must have hunted possibly in packs bovids (steppe bison/aurochs) or saiga antelopes in the steppe or valley environments. Late Pleistocene lions never used caves even for short-term periods; they only dwelled for cave bears, mainly cub hunting. All three top predators (lions, hyenas, and wolves) fed (hunted or scavenged) on cave bears in boreal forest of middle high elevated (150–650 a.s.l) mountain regions (lions even up to elevations of 1,500 a.s.l.) which caused deathly conflicts in caves between all of them (inter-/intraspecies fights) that have no modern analogue. Those battles caused bite damages especially on their skulls and legs, which produced different postcranial, but similar cranial bite damage pathologies. Some of the bite marks also found at lion skeletons and bones cannot be separated clearly in their alive or postmortal origin.

ACKNOWLEDGMENTS

The author thanks all the museums and institutions mentioned and their curators for their support to study bone material from various sites in Germany, Czech Republic, Austria, and England. The company and private research institute Paleologic (http://www.paleologic.eu/) sponsored the science to the "European Ice Age Spotted Hyena Project." A first critical review and spell check was made thankfully by Dr. G. Zazula from the Beringeria Center, Canada. Dr. M. Sabol also commented on a first draft. J. McNamara (World Museum of Man, http://www.worldmuseumofman.org/) supported the paper with photos of the Austrian Badel Cave lion and hyena skulls and made a paper spell check. Finally G. Teichmann contributed the hyena, lion, and cave bear illustrations.

REFERENCES

1. J. F. Esper, "Ausf¨uhrliche Nachricht von neuentdecktenZoolithen unbekannter vierf¨ußiger Thiere, und denen sieenthaltenden, so wie verschiedenen andern denkw¨urdigenGr¨uften der Obergeb¨urgischen Lande des MarggrafthumsBayreuth," Knorrs, N¨urnberg, Germany, 1774.
2. C. G. Diedrich, "The rediscovered cave bear "*Ursus spelaeus*Rosenm¨uller 1794" holotype of the Zoolithen Cave (Germany)from the historic Rosenm¨uller collection," *Acta CarsologicaSlovacia*, vol. 47, no. 1, pp. 25–32, 2009.
3. J. C. Rosenm¨uller, "Quedam de ossibus fossilibus animaliscuiusdam, historiam eius et cognitionem accuratiorem illustrantia,dissertatio, quam d. 22. Octob. 1794 ad disputandumproposuit Ioannes Christ. Rosenm¨uller Heßberga-Francus,LL.AA.M," in *Theatro Anatomico Lipsiensi Prosector AssumtoSocio Io. Chr. Aug. Heinroth Lips. Med. Stud*, pp. 1–34, Cumtabula aenea, Leipzig, Germany, 1794.
4. G. L. C. F.D. Cuvier, "Sur les ossements fossiles des Hy`enes,"*Annales du Mus´ee Histoire Naturelle Paris*, vol. 6, p. 127, 1805.
5. G. A. Goldfuss, "Die Umgebungen von Muggendorf. EinTaschenbuch f¨ur Freunde der Natur und Altertumskunde,"Erlangen, Germany, 1810.
6. G. A. Goldfuss, "Osteologische Beitraege zur Kenntnis verschiedenerSaeugethiere der Vorwelt—IV. Ueber den Schaedeldes Hoehlenloewen," *Verhandlungen der Kaiserlichen LeopoldinischenCarolinaeischen Akademie der Naturfreunde*, vol. 10,no. 2, pp. 489–494, 1821.
7. G. A. Goldfuss, "Osteologische Beitraege zur Kenntnis verschiedenerSaeugethiere der Vorwelt—VI. Ueber die Hoehlen-Hy¨ane (*Hyaena spelaea*)," *Nova Acta Physico-Medica AcademieaCaesarae Leopoldino-Carolinae Naturae Curiosorum*, vol. 3, no.2, pp. 456–490, 1823.
8. C.G.Diedrich, "The holotypes of the upper Pleistocene *Crocutacrocuta spelaea* (Goldfuss, 1823: Hyaenidae) and *Panthera leospelaea* (Goldfuss, 1810: Felidae) of the Zoolithen Cave hyenaden (South Germany) and their palaeo-ecological interpretation,"*Zoological Journal of the Linnean Society*, vol. 154, no. 4,pp. 822–831, 2008.
9. W. Buckland, "Reliquiae Diluvianae, or observations on theorganic remains contained in caves, fissures, and diluvial gravel,and other geological phenomena, attesting the action of anuniversal deluge," J. Murray, London, UK, 1823.
10. C. G. Diedrich, "Eine oberpleistoz¨ane Population von *Crocutacrocuta spelaea* (Goldfuss, 1823) aus dem eiszeitlichen Fleckenhy¨anenhorst Perick-H¨ohlen von Hemer (Sauerland, NWDeutschland) und ihr Kannibalismus," *Philippia*, vol. 12, no. 2,pp. 93–115, 2005.
11. C. G. Giebel, "Die antediluvialianische SaeugethierfaunaDeutschlands," *Jahresberichte der NaturwissenschaftlichenVereinigung Halle*, vol. 3, pp. 219–236, 1852.
12. W. Boyd Dawkins and B. A. Oxen, "On a hyæna-den atWookeyhole, near wells. no. II," *Quarterly Journal of the GeologicalSociety of London*, vol. 19, no. 1-2, pp. 260–274, 1863.
13. E.K. Tratman, D. T. Donovan, and J. B. Campbell, "The hyenaden (Wookey Hole)Mendip Hills, Somerset," *Proceedings of theUniversity Bristol Spelaeological Society*, vol. 12, no. 3, pp. 245–279, 1971.
14. K. T. Liebe, "Die LindentalerHy¨anenh¨ohle und andere diluvialeKnochenfunde in Ostth¨uringen," *Arch¨aologisches und AnthropologischeOrgan der Deutschen Gesellschaft f¨ur AnthropologieEthnographie und Urgeschichte*, vol. 9, p. 155, 1876.
15. E. Thenius, "Hy¨anenfrassspuren aus dem Pleistoz¨an vonK¨arnten. Ein Beitrag zur Frage der sog. "osteodontokeratischenKultur" der Australopithecinen (Hominidae)," *Carinthia II*, vol.72, pp. 88–101, 1961.
16. Nehring, "Ausgrabungen bei thiede und westeregeln," *Verhandlungender Berliner Gesellschaft f¨ur Anthropologie, Ethnographieund Urgeschichte*, vol. 1876, pp. 206–209, 1876.

17. [C. G. Diedrich, "A clan of Late Pleistocene hyenas, *Crocutacrocuta spelaea* (Goldfuss 1823), from the R¨osenbeck Cave(Germany) and a contribution to cranial shape variability,"*Biological Journal of the Linnean Society*, vol. 103, no. 1, pp. 191–220, 2011.
18. E. Haarl´e, "Pr´esentation dos de repas d'hy`ene tachet´ees," *Bulletinde la Soci`et´e d'Histoire Naturelle de Toulouse*, vol. 26, pp.22–25, 1892.
19. S. H. Reynolds, "A monograph of the British PleistoceneMammalia—Volume II—Part II. The Cave Hyena," *PalaeontologicalSociety Monographs*, vol. 1902, pp. 1–25, 1902.
20. Currant, "The Quaternary mammal collections at the Sommerset Country Museum Taunton," in *The Quaternary Mammalsof Southern and Eastern England, Field Guide*, D. C.Schreve, Ed., pp. 101–109, 2004.
21. K. Ehrenberg, O. Sickenberg, and A. Stifft-Gottlieb, "DieFuchs- oder Teufelslucken bei Eggenburg, Niederdonau. 1 Teil,"*Abhandlungen der Zoologisch-Botanischen Gesellschaft*, vol. 17,no. 1, pp. 1–130, 1938.
22. H. Zapfe, "Die Lebensspuren der eiszeitlichen H¨ohlenhy¨ane.Die urgeschichtliche Bedeutung der Lebensspuren knochenfressenderRaubtiere," *Palaeobiologica*, vol. 7, pp. 111–146, 1939.
23. A.J. Sutcliffe and F. E. Zeuner, "Excavations in the TorbryanCave, Devonshire I Tonewton Cave," *Proceedings of the DevonArachaeological Explorations Society*, vol. 5, pp. 127–145, 1958.
24. R. Musil, "Die H¨ohle "Sved°uv stul", ein typischerH¨ohlenhy¨anenhorst," *Anthropos New Series*, vol. 5, no. 13, pp.97–260, 1962.
25. P. Wernert, "Beutetierst¨ucke der H¨ohlenhy¨anen im anatomischenVerband aus Achenheimer L¨ossen," *Quart¨ar*, vol. 19, pp.55–64, 1968.
26. T. Rathgeber, "Neue jungpleistoz¨ane S¨augetier-Reste aus derAufhauserH¨ohle (Kat.-Nr. 7424/13) beiGeislingen an der Steige(Schw¨abische Alb)," *Mitteilungen des Verbandes der deutschenH¨ohlen- und Karstforscher*, vol. 28, no. 1, pp. 9–12, 1982.
27. D. P. B. Erdbrink, "Eleven bones: more fossil remains of cavelions and cave hyenas from the North Sea area," *Bijdragen tot deDierkunde*, vol. 53, no. 1, pp. 1–12, 1983.
28. J. L. Guadelli, "´Etude taphonomique du repairesd'hy`enes deCamiac (Gironde, France), ´elements de comparisation entr´ee30 Paleontology Journalun site naturel et un gisement pr´ehistorique," *Bulletin del'Association Franc¸aise pour l' ´ Etude du Quaternaire*, vol. 2, pp.91–100, 1989.
29. E. S. Tsoukala, "The Pleistocene large mammals from the AgiosGeorgios Cave, Kilkis (Macedonia,N.Greece)," *Geobios*, vol. 25,no. 3, pp. 415–433, 1992.
30. J. F. Tournepiche, "Les grand mammiferes Pleistocenes dePoitou-charentes," *Pal´eo*, vol. 8, pp. 109–141, 1996.
31. P. Fosse, "Variabilit´e des assamblages osseux cr´e´es par l'hyenades cavernes," *Pal´eo*, vol. 9, pp. 15–54, 1997.
32. P. Fosse, J. P. Brugal, J.L. Guadelli, P. Michel, and J. F.Tournepiche, "Les repaires d'hyenes des cavernes en Europeoccidentale: presentation et comparisons de quelques assemblagesosseux," in *Economie Prehistorique, Les ComportementsDe Substance Au Paleolithique*, XVIII Rencontres Internationalesd'Archeologie et d'Historie d'Antibes, pp. 44–61, EditionsAPDCA, Sophia Antipolis, 1998.
33. P. Fosse, "Cave occupation during Palaeolithic times: manand/or Hyena?" *Verlag des R¨omisch-Germanischen ZentralmuseumsBonn Monographien*, vol. 42, pp. 73–88, 1999.
34. J. F. Tournepiche and C. Couture, "The hyena den of RochelotCave (Charente, France)," *Monographien des R¨omisch-Germanischen Zentralmuseums*, vol. 42, pp. 89–101, 1999.
35. J. G. Enloe, F. David, and G. Baryshnikov, "Hyenas and hunters:zooarchaeological investigations at Prolom II Cave, Crimea,"*International Journal of Osteoarchaeology*, vol. 10, no. 5, pp. 310–324, 2000.
36. M. C. Stiner, "Comparative ecology and taphonomy of spottedhyenas, humans, and wolves in Pleistocene Italy," *Revue dePaleobiologie*, vol. 23, no. 2, pp. 771–785, 2004.
37. G. Mangano, "An exclusively hyena-collected bone assemblagein the Late Pleistocene of Sicily: taphonomy and stratigraphiccontext of the large mammal remains from San Teodoro Cave(North-Eastern Sicily, Italy)," *Journal of Archaeological Science*,vol. 38, no. 12, pp. 3584–3595, 2011.

38. E. Barycka, "Middle and late Pleistocene Felidae andHyaenidaeof Poland. Fauna Poloniae. Fauna Polski 2ns," Museum andInstitute of Zoology Polish Academy of Science, Warszawa,Poland, 2008.
39. C. G. Diedrich and K. ˇZ´ak, "Prey deposits and den sites ofthe Upper Pleistocene hyena *Crocuta crocuta spelaea* (Goldfuss,1823) in horizontal and vertical caves of the Bohemian Karst(Czech Republic)," *Bulletin of Geosciences*, vol. 81,no. 4, pp. 237–276, 2006.
40. C. G. Diedrich, "Europe's first Upper Pleistocene *Crocutacrocuta spelaea* (Goldfuss, 1823) skeleton from the KonˇeprusyCaves: a hyena cave prey depot site in the Bohemian Karst(Czech Republic)," *Historical Biology*, vol. 24, no. 1, pp. 63–89,2012.
41. C. G. Diedrich, "The largest Late Pleistocene hyena populationfrom the Srbsko Chlum-Kom´ın Cave (Czech Republic) andits prey in a commuting and prey depot cave den of Central Europe," *Historical Biology*, 2014.
42. C. G. Diedrich, "An Ice Age spotted hyena *Crocuta crocuta spelaea* (Goldfuss, 1823) population, their excrements and preyfrom the Late Pleistocene hyena den of the Sloup Cave in theMoravian Karst, Czech Republic," *Historical Biology*, vol. 24, no.2, pp. 161–185, 2012.
43. C. G. Diedrich, "The *Crocuta crocuta spelaea* (Goldfuss, 1823)population and its prey from the Late Pleistocene teufelskammerCave hyena den besides the famous Paleolithic NeandertalCave (NRW, NWGermany)," *Historical Biology*, vol. 23, no. 2-3,pp. 237–270, 2011.
44. C. G. Diedrich, "Periodical use of the Balve Cave (NW Germany)as a Late Pleistocene *Crocuta crocuta spelaea* (Goldfuss,1823) den: Hyena occupations and bone accumulations vs.human Middle Palaeolithic activity," *Quaternary International*,vol. 233, no. 2, pp. 171–184, 2011.
45. C. G. Diedrich, "The Late Pleistocene spotted hyena *Crocutacrocuta spelaea* (Goldfuss, 1823) population with its type specimensfrom the Zoolithen Cave at Gailenreuth (Bavaria, SouthGermany): a hyena cub raising den of specialised cave bear scavengers in boreal forest environments of Central Europe,"*Historical Biology*, vol. 23, no. 4, pp. 335–367, 2011.
46. C. G. Diedrich, "The largest european lion *Panthera leo spelaea*(Goldfuss, 1810) population from the zoolithen cave, germany:specialised cave bear predators of Europe," *Historical Biology*,vol. 23, no. 2-3, pp. 271–311, 2011.
47. C. G. Diedrich, "Late Ice Age wolves as cave bear scavengersin the Sophie's Cave of Germany—extinctions of cave bears asresult of climate/habitat change and large carnivore predationstress in Europe," *ISRN Zoology*, 2013.
48. C. Diedrich, "Late Pleistocene hyenas *Crocuta crocuta spelaea*(Goldfuss, 1823) fromUpper Rhine valley open air sites and thecontribution to skull shape variability," *Cranium*, vol. 25, no. 2,pp. 31–42, 2008.
49. C. G. Diedrich, "Oberpleistoz¨ane fleckenhy¨anenreste (*Crocutacrocuta spelaea* (Goldfuss, 1823)) aus flussterrassenablagerungenin der m¨unsterl¨ander bucht (NW Deutschland)," *Philippia*,vol. 11, no. 3, pp. 227–234, 2004.
50. C. G. Diedrich, "The Late Pleistocene *Crocuta crocuta spelaea*(Goldfuss, 1823) populationfrom the Emscher River terracehyena open air den Bottrop and other sites in NW-Germany—woolly rhinoceros scavengers and their bone accumulationsalong rivers in lowland mammoth steppe environments," *QuaternaryInternational*, vol. 276-277, pp. 93–119, 2012.
51. C. G. Diedrich, "The Late Pleistocene spotted hyena *Crocutacrocuta spelaea* (Goldfuss, 1823) open air birth and communalden site Bad Wildungen-Biedensteg (Hesse, NW Germany)—woolly rhinoceros killers and scavengers in a mammoth steppeenvironment of Europe—recycling of badger/fox burrows inloess by hyenas in the Ice Age," *Journal of Geological Research*,vol. 276-277, pp. 93–119, 2013.
52. C. G. Diedrich, "Seltene Freilandfunde der sp¨ateiszeitlichenFleckenhy¨ane *Crocuta crocuta spelaea* (Goldfuss, 1823) inSachsen-Anhalt und Beitrag zu Horsttypen der letzten Hy¨anenim Jung-Pleistoz¨an von Mitteldeutschland," *Zeitschrift f¨ur MitteldeutscheVorgeschichte*, vol. 93, 2011.

53. C. G. Diedrich, "Late Pleistocene *Crocuta crocuta spelaea*(Goldfuss, 1823) clans as prezewalski horse hunters and woollyrhinoceros scavengers at the open air commuting den andcontemporaryNeanderthal camp siteWesteregeln (centralGermany),"*Journal ofArchaeological Science*, vol. 39,no. 6, pp. 1749–1767, 2012.
54. C. G. Diedrich, "The *Unicornu fossile* Valentini, 1714 "holotype"skeleton from the Ice Age spotted hyena commuting den at theopen air gypsum karst Quedlinburg Sewecken-Berge (CentralGermany)," *Earth Science Reviews*, 2012.
55. C. G. Diedrich, "Late Pleistocene*Hystrix (Acanthion) brachyura*Linnaeus, 1758 from the Fuchsluken cave at the Rote Bergnear Saalfeld (Thuringia, Germany)—a porcupine and hyenaden and contribution to their palaeobiogeography," *The OpenPalaeontological Journal*, vol. 1, pp. 33–41, 2008.
56. C. G. Diedrich, "TheLate Pleistocene spotted hyena populationsand their den sites in the Thuringian Mountains—rhino scavengersduring Neanderthal settlement times in the Zechsteinkarst near P¨oßneck,Thuringia (Central Germany)," *Eiszeitalterund Gegenwart. Quaternary Science Research*, 2014.
57. C. G. Diedrich, "Mammoth scavengers in Europe—the last IceAge spotted hyenas and steppe lions and their feeding strategieson their largest prey," *Journal of Archaeological Science*, 2014.
58. C. G. Diedrich, "Late Pleistocene Eemian Ice Age spotted hyenafeeding strategies and steppe lions on their largest prey—*Palaeoloxodon antiquus* Falconer and Cautley, 1845 at the straight-tusked elephant graveyard and Neanderthalian siteNeumark-Nord Lake 1, Central Germany," *Archaeological andAnthropologcal Sciences*, 2013.
59. C. G. Diedrich, "Cannibalism and inter-/intraspecies fightpathologies within Late Pleistocene spotted hyena *Crocuta crocutaspelaea* (Goldfuss, 1823) populations of Europe," *Pal Arch*,2014.
60. C. G. Diedrich, "An Ice Age spotted hyena *Crocuta crocutaspelaea* (Goldfuss, 1823) population, their excrements and preyfrom the Late Pleistocene hyena den of the Sloup Cavin theMoravian Karst, Czech Republic," *Historical Biology*, vol. 24, no.2, pp. 161–185, 2012.
61. C. G. Diedrich, "Adiseased *Panthera leo spelaea* (Goldfuss, 1810)lioness from a forest elephant graveyard in the Late Pleistocene(Eemian) interglacial lake atNeumark-Nord, central Germany,"*Historical Biology*, vol. 23, no. 2-3, pp. 195–217, 2011.
62. C. G. Diedrich, "Late Pleistocene *Panthera leo spelaea* (Goldfuss,1810) skeletons fromthe Czech Republic (centeral Europe);their pathological cranial features and injuries resulting fromintraspecific fights, conflicts with hyenas, and attacks on cavebears," *Bulletin of Geosciences*, vol. 86, no. 4, pp. 817–840, 2011.
63. C. G. Diedrich, "Upper Pleistocene *Panthera leo spelaea* (Goldfuss,1810) skeleton remains from Praha-Podbaba and otherlion finds from loess and river terrace sites in Central Bohemia(Czech Republic)," *Bulletin of Geosciences*, vol. 82, no. 2, pp. 99–117, 2007.
64. C. G. Diedrich, "Steppe lion remains imported by Ice Age spottedhyenas into the Late Pleistocene Perick Caves hyena den innorthernGermany," *Quaternary Research*, vol. 71,no. 3, pp. 361–374, 2009.
65. C. G. Diedrich, "Cave bear killers and scavengers from the lastice age of central Europe: feeding specializations in responseto the absence of mammoth steppe fauna from mountainousregions," *Quaternary International*, vol. 255, pp. 59–78, 2012.
66. C. G. Diedrich and T. Rathgeber, "Late Pleistocene steppe lion*Panthera leo spelaea* (Goldfuss 1810) skeleton remains of theUpper Rhine Valley (SW Germany) and contributions to their sexual dimorphism, taphonomy and habitus," *Historical Biology*,vol. 24, no. 1, pp. 1–28, 2012.
67. C. G. Diedrich, "Late Pleistocene steppe lion *Panthera leospelaea* (Goldfuss, 1810) footprints and bone records from open air sites in northern Germany—evidence of Hyena-lion antagonismand scavenging in Europe," *Quaternary Science Reviews*,vol. 30, no. 15-16, pp. 1883–1906, 2011.
68. B. M. Rothschild and C. Diedrich, "Comparison of pathologiesin the extinct Pleistocene Eurasian steppe lion *Pantherea leospelaea* (Goldfuss, 1810) to those in the modern lion,

Panthera leo—results of fights with hyenas, bears and lions and otherecological stress," *International Journal of Paleopathology*, 2012.

69. W. D. Dawkins and A. Sandfort, "A monograph of the Britishpleistocene mammalia," in *The British Pleistocene Felidae.Palaeontographical Society Monographs*, vol. 1(1866–1872), pp.1–194, 1900.
70. M. Boule, "Les grands chats des caverns," *Annales dePal´eontologie*, vol. 1, pp. 69–95, 1906.
71. F. Heller, "Ein Sch¨adel von *Felis spelaea* Goldf. aus der Frankenalb,"*Erlanger Geologische Abhandlungen*, vol. 7, pp. 1–24, 1953.
72. W.O. Dietrich, "Fossile L¨owen im Europ¨aischen und AfrikanischenPleistoz¨an," *Pal¨aontologische Abhandlungen A*, vol. 3, no. 2,pp. 323–366, 1968.
73. R. Ballesio, "´Etude de *Panthera (leo) spelaea* (Goldfuss) nov.subsp. (Mammalia, Carnivora, Felidae) du gisement du Pleistoc`ene moyen des Abimes de la Fage `a Noailles (Corr`eze),"*NouveauxArchaeologie duMus´eeHistoireNaturelle Lyon*, vol. 13,pp. 47–55, 1975.
74. J. Altuna, "Fund eines Skelettes des H¨ohlenl¨owen (*Panthera leospelaea* Goldfuss) in Arrikrutz, Baskenland," *Bonner ZoologischeBeitr¨age*, vol. 32, no. 1-2, pp. 31–46, 1981.
75. G. Tichy, " ¨ Uber der Fund eines H¨ohlenl¨owen (*Panthera felisspelaea* Goldfuss) aus dem Tennengebirge bei Salzburg," *Mitteilungender Gesellschaft f¨ur Salzburger Landeskunde*, vol. 125,pp. 845–864, 1985.
76. Argant, "´Etude de ʻexemplaire de *Panthera spelaea* (Goldfuss,1810) (Mammalia, Carnivora, Felidae) du gisement Pleistoc`enemoyen recent de la grotte d" Aze (Saone et Loire)," *Revue dePal´eobiologie*, vol. 7, no. 2, pp. 449–466, 1988.
77. Gross, *Das Skelett des H¨ohlenl¨owen (Panthera leo spelaea,Goldfuss, 1810) aus Siegsdorf/Ldkr. Traunstein im Vergleich mit anderen Funden aus Deutschland und den Niederlanden [dissertation]*,Tier¨arztliche Fakult¨at der Ludwig-Maximilians-Universit¨at M¨unchen, 1992.
78. K. Fischer, "Neufunde von jungpleistoz¨anenH¨ohlenl¨owen Pantheraleo spelaea (Goldfuss, 1810) in R¨ubeland, Harz," *BraunschweigerNaturkundliche Schriften*, vol. 4, no. 3, pp. 455–471,1994.
79. G. Guˇzvica, "Panihera spelaea (Goldfuss, 1810) from North-Western Croatia," *Geologia Croatica*, vol. 51, no. 1, pp. 59–73,1998.
80. G. F. Baryshnikov and G. Boeskorov, "The Pleistocene cave lion,*Panthera spelaea* (Carnivora, Felidae) from Yakutia, Russia,"*Cranium*, vol. 18, pp. 7–24, 2001.
81. F. Bona, "Systematic position of a complete lion-like cat skullfrom the Eemian ossiferous rubble near Zandobbio (Bergamo,North Italy)," *Rivista Italiana di Paleontologia e Stratigrafia*, vol.112, no. 1, pp. 157–166, 2006.
82. C. G. Diedrich, "Upper Pleistocene *Panthera leo spelaea* (Goldfuss,1810) remains from an open air loess bone accumulationand human campsite in Freyburg a. d. U. (Saxony-Anhalt),"*Jahresschrift f¨ur Mitteldeutsche Vorgeschichte*, vol. 92, pp. 9–24,2008.
83. C. G. Diedrich, "Upper Pleistocene *Panthera leo spelaea* (Goldfuss,1810) remains from the Bilstein Caves (Sauerland Karst)and contribution to the steppe lion taphonomy, palaeobiologyand sexual dimorphism," *Annales de Paleontologie*, vol. 95, no3, pp. 117–138, 2009.
84. C. G. Diedrich, M. Robu, O. Moldovan et al., "New UpperPleistocene steppe lion skeleton finds between the cave bearhibernation plateaus of the Urs,ilor Cave bear den, Romania,"in *Proceedings of the 15th International Cave Bear Symposium*, p.10, Bratislava, Slovakia, 2009.
85. C. Diedrich, "Pleistocene *Panthera leo spelaea* (Goldfuss, 1810)remains from the Balve Cave (NW Germany)—a cave bear,
86. hyena den and Middle Palaeolithic human cave, and review ofthe Sauerland Karst lion sites," *Quaternaire*, vol. 22, no. 2, pp.105–127, 2011.
87. M. Sabol, "A record of pleistocene lion-like felids in the territoryof Slovakia," *Quaternaire*, no. 4, pp. 215–228, 2011.

88. J. A. Leonard, C. Vil`a, K. Fox-Dobbs, P. L. Koch, R. K. Wayne,and B. Van Valkenburgh, "Megafaunal extinctions and the disappearance of a specialized wolf ecomorph," *Current Biology*,vol. 17, no. 13, pp. 1146–1150, 2007.
89. S. K. Bearder, "Feeding habits of spotted hyaenas in a woodlandhabitat," *East AfricanWildlife Journal*, vol. 15, pp. 263–280, 1977.
90. L. Werdelin and N. Solounias, "The Hyaenidae: taxonomy,systematics and evolution," *Fossils & Strata*, vol. 30, pp. 1–104,1991.
91. N. Rohland, J. L. Pollack,D.Nagel et al., "Thepopulation historyof extant and extinct hyenas," *Molecular Biology and Evolution*,vol. 22, no. 12, pp. 2435–2443, 2005.
92. R. G. Klein and K. Scott, "Glacial/interglacial size variation infossil spotted hyenas (*Crocuta crocuta*) from Britain," *QuaternaryResearch*, vol. 32, no. 1, pp. 88–95, 1989.
93. G. F. Baryshnikov, "Chronological and geographical variabilityof *Crocuta spelaea* (Carnivora,Hyaenidae) fromthe Pleistocene of Russia," *Deinsea*, vol. 6, pp. 155–174, 1999.
94. C. G. Diedrich, "Disappearance of the last hyenas and lionsof Europe in the Late Quaternary—a chain reaction of largemammal mammoth and woolly rhino prey extinction," in*Proceedings of the EuropeanGeoscienceUnionGeneralAssembly*,Vienna, Austria, 2010.
95. T. Lynn,*Morphological variation in a durophagous carnivore, thespotted hyena Crocuta crocuta [dissertation]*, Michigan University, Michigan, Ill, USA, 2009.
96. H. Kruuk, "The spotted hyena," in *A Story of Predation andSocial Behavior*, p. 335, The University of Chicago Press,Chicago, Ill, USA, 1972.
97. Y. M. Lam, "Variability in the behaviour of spotted hyaenas astaphonomic agents," *Journal of Archaeological Science*, vol. 19,no. 4, pp. 389–406, 1992.
98. H. Hofer and M. East, "Population dynamics, population size,and the commuting system of Serengeti spotted hyenas," in*Serengeti II: Dynamics, MAnagement, and Conservation of anEcosystem*, A. R. E. Sinclair and P. Arcese, Eds., pp. 332–363,University of Chicago Press, Chicago, Ill, USA, 1995.
99. S. T. Von Soemmerring, "Ueber die geheilte Verletzung einesfossilen Hyaenensch¨adels," *Nova Acta Physico-Medica AcademiaeCaesar Leopoldiana*, vol. 14, pp. 1–44, 1828.
100. L. G. Frank, "When hyenas kill their own," *New Scientist*, vol.141, pp. 38–41, 1994.
101. P. A. White, "Maternal rank is not correlated with cub survivalin the spotted hyena, *Crocuta crocuta*," *Behavioral Ecology*, vol.16, no. 3, pp. 606–613, 2005.
102. S. M. Cooper, "Denning behavior of spotted hyaenas (*Crocutacrocuta*) in Botswana," *African Journal of Ecology*, vol. 31, pp.178–180, 1993.
103. C. Stuart and T. Stuart, *Field Guide to the Larger Mammals ofAfrica*, Struik, Cape Town, South Africa, 1997.
104. M. L. East, H. Hofer, and A. T¨urk, "Functions of birth dens inspotted hyaenas (*Crocuta crocuta*)," *Journal of Zoology London*,vol. 219, pp. 690–697, 1989.
105. J. T. Pokines and J. C. Kerbis Peterhans, "Spotted hyena (*Crocutacrocuta*) den use and taphonomy in the Masai Mara NationalReserve, Kenya," *Journal of Archaeological Science*, vol. 34, no.11, pp. 1914–1931, 2007.
106. J. Brunner, "Beobachtungen zu den Lebensspuren der Hy¨anenan den Knochen der Huftiere aus dem Unter-Plioz¨an vonPikermi," *Palaeobiologica*, vol. 8, pp. 120–126, 1944.
107. J. P. Brugal, P. Fosse, and J. P. Guadeli, "Comparative studyof bone assemblages made by recent and Plio-PleistoceneHyaenids (*Hyena, Crocuta*)," *Hot Springs South Dakota OccasionalPublications*, vol. 1, no. 1, pp. 158–187, 1997.
108. Arribas and P. Palmqvist, "Taphonomy and palaeoecology ofan assemblage of large mammals: Hyaenid activity in the lowerPleistocene site at Venta Micena (Orce, Guadix-Baza basin,Granada, Spain)," *Geobios*, vol. 31, no. 3, pp. 3–47, 1998.
109. R.-D. Kahlke, "Untermassfeld—a late Early Pleistocene (Epivillafranchian)fossil site near Meiningen (Thuringia, Germany)and its position in the development of the European mammalfauna," *BAR International Series*, vol. 1578, pp. 1–114, 2006.
110. P. Fosse, "La grotte no. 1 de Lunel-Viel (H´erault, France): repaired'hy`enes du Pleistoc`ene Moyen," *Pal´eo*, vol. 8, pp. 47–81, 1996.
111. J. Lindly, "Hominid and carnivore activity atMiddle and UpperPalaeolithic cave sites in eastern Spain," *Munibe*, vol. 40, pp. 45–70, 1988.

112. K. Cruz-Uribe, "Distinguishing hyena from hominid boneaccumulations," *Journal of Field Archaeology*, vol. 18, pp. 467–486, 1991.
113. H. T. Bunn, "Comparative analyses of modern bone assemblagesfroma San hunter-gatherer camp in the Kalahari Desert,Botswana, and froma spotted hyena den near Nairobi, Keynia,"*British Archaeological Reports*, vol. 283, pp. 143–148, 1983.
114. T. R. Pickering, "Reconsideration of criteria for differentiatingfaunal assemblages accumulated by hyenas and hominids,"*International Journal of Osteoarchaeology*, vol. 12, no. 2, pp. 127–141, 2002.
115. P. Villa, J.-C. Castel, C. Beauval, V. Bourdillat, and P. Goldberg,Human and carnivore sites in the European Middle and UpperPaleolithic: similarities and differences in bone modificationand fragmentation," *Revue de Paleobiologie*, vol. 23, no. 2, pp.705–730, 2004.
116. S. W. Lansing, S. M. Cooper, E. E. Boydston, and K. E.Holekamp, "Taphonomic and zooarchaeological implications of spotted hyena (*Crocuta crocuta*) bone accumulations inkenya: a modern behavioral ecological approach," *Paleobiology*,vol. 35, no. 2, pp. 289–309, 2009.
117. B. F. Kuhn, L. R. Berger, and J. D. Skinner, "Examining criteriafor identifying and differentiating fossil faunal assemblagesaccumulated by hyenas and hominins using extant hyenidaccumulations," *International Journal of Osteoarchaeology*, vol.20, no. 1, pp. 15–35, 2010.
118. M. G. L. Mills and M. Mills, "An analysis of bones collected athyaena breeding dens in the Gemsbok National Parks," *Annalesof the Transvaal Museum*, vol. 30, pp. 145–155, 1977.
119. J. R. Henschel, R. Tildin, and F. von Blottnitz, "Implications ofa spotted hyaena bone assemblage in the Namib Desert," *SouthAfrican Archaeoligical Bulletin*, vol. 34, pp. 127–131, 1979.
120. Hill, "A modern hyena den in Amboseli National Park,Kenya," in *Proceedings of the 8th Panafrican Congress of Prehistoryand Quaternary Studies*, vol. 1980, pp. 137–138, 1980.
121. L. Scott and R.G.Klein, "Ahyena accumulated bone assemblagefrom late Holocene deposits at Deelpan, Orange Free State,South Africa," *Annals of the South African Museum*, vol. 86, pp.217–227, 1981.
122. G. Avery, D. M. Avery, S. Braine, and R. Loutit, "Bone accumulationby hyenas and jackals a taphonomic study," *South AfricanJournal of Science*, vol. 80, pp. 186–187, 1984.
123. E. E. Boydston, K.M. Kapheim, and K. E. Holekamp, "Patternsof den occupation by the spotted hyaena (*Crocuta crocuta*),"*African Journal of Ecology*, vol. 44, no. 1, pp. 77–86, 2006.
124. J. T. Faith, "Sources of variation in carnivore tooth-markfrequencies in a modern spotted hyena (*Crocuta crocuta*) denassemblage, Amboseli Park, Kenya," *Journal of ArchaeologicalScience*, vol. 34, no. 10, pp. 1601–1609, 2007.
125. G. Harnes, "A guide for differentiating mammalian carnivoretaxa responsible for gnaw damage to herbivore limb bones,"*Paleobiology*, vol. 9, no. 2, pp. 164–172, 1983.
126. P. R. K. Richardson, "Carnivore damage to antelope bones andits archaeological implications," *Palaeontologica Africana*, vol.23, pp. 109–125, 1980.
127. C.W.Marean and L. M. Spencer, "Impact of carnivore revengingon zooarchaeological measures of element abundance," *American Antiquity*, vol. 56, pp. 645–658, 1991.
128. R. J. Blumenschine, "An experimental model of the timingof hominid and carnivore influence on archaeological bone assemblages," *Journal of Archaeological Science*, vol. 15, no. 5, pp.483–502, 1988.
129. A.Hill, "Bone modification bymodern spotted hyenas," in *BoneModification*, R. Bonnichsen andM. H. Sorg, Eds., pp. 169–178,Center for the Study of the First Americans, Maine, Canada 1989.
130. C. W. Marean, L. M. Spencer, R. J. Blumenschine, and S. D.Capaldo, "Captive hyaena bone choice and destruction, the Schlepp effect and olduvai archaeofaunas," *Journal of ArchaeologicalScience*, vol. 19, no. 1, pp. 101–121, 1992.
131. J. Sutcliffe, "Spotted hyaena: crusher, Gnawer, digester andcollector of bones," *Nature*, vol. 227, no. 5263, pp. 1110–1113, 1970.
132. R. F. Ewer, "Some adaptive features in the dentition of hyenas,"*Annals and Magazine of Natural History*, vol. 12, no. 7, pp. 188–194, 1954.

133. S. Van Jaarsveld, J. D. Skinner, and M. Lindeque, "Growth,development and parental investment in the spotted hyaena,Crocuta crocuta," *Journal of Zoology*, vol. 216, no. 1, pp. 45–53,1988.
134. G. Diedrich, "Specialized horse killers in Europe: foetalhorse remains in the Late Pleistocene Srbsko Chlum-Kom´ınCave hyena den in the Bohemian Karst (Czech Republic) and actualistic comparisons to modern African spotted hyenas aszebra hunters," *Quaternary International*, vol. 220, no. 1-2, pp.174–187, 2010.
135. G. Diedrich, "Benagte und zerknackte Knochen des eiszeitlichen Pferdes *Equus ferus przewalskii* Poljakoff, 1881 aus einem oberpleistoz¨anen Fleckenhy¨anenhorst des Nordsauerlandes und westf¨alischen Freilandfundstellen," *Philippia*, vol. 12,no. 1, pp. 47–62, 2005.
136. G. Diedrich, "Von eiszeitlichen Fleckenhy¨anen eingeschleppteReste des Steppenwisents *Bison priscus* Bojanus 1827aus dem oberpleistoz¨anen Fleckenhy¨anenhorst des Perick-H¨ohlensystems (NW Deutschland)," *Philippia*, vol. 12, no. 1, pp.21–30, 2005.
137. C. G. Diedrich, "Von oberpleistoz¨anen Fleckenhy¨anen gesammelte,versteckte, verbissene, zerknackteKnochen undGeweihe des Riesenhirsches *Megaloceros giganteus* (Blumenbach, 1799)aus den Perick-H¨ohlen im Nordsauerland (NW Deutschland),"*Philippia*, vol. 12, no. 1, pp. 31–46, 2005.
138. C. Diedrich, "The Late Pleistocene Crocuta crocuta spelaea(Goldfuss, 1823) population and its prey from the FuchslukenCavities near Saalfeld (Thuringia, Central Germany)—a specializedbovid and equuid hunters commuting and cub raisinghyena and porcupine overlapping den site," *Pal Arch*, 2014.
139. S. K. Bearder and R. M. Randal, "The use of fecal marking sitesby spotted hyaenas and civets," *Carnivore*, vol. 1, pp. 32–48, 1978.
140. L. K. Horwitz and P. Goldberg, "A study of Pleistocene and Holocene hyaena coprolites," *Journal of Archaeological Science*,vol. 16, no. 1, pp. 71–94, 1989.
141. C. F. Rodr´ıguez, P. R. Rego, and A. M. Cortizas, "Characterization and depositional evolution of Hyaena (*Crocuta crocuta*) coprolites from La Valina Cave (Northwest Spain)," *Journal of Archaeological Science*, vol. 22, no. 5, pp. 597–607, 1995.
142. N. R. Larkin, J. Alexander, andM. D. Lewis, "Using experimentalstudies of recent faecalmaterial to examine hyaena coprolitesfrom theWest Runton freshwater bed, Norfolk, U.K," *Journal of Archaeological Science*, vol. 27, no. 1, pp. 19–31, 2000.
143. J. Reumer, D. Mol, and W. Borst, "The first Late Pleistocenecoprolite of *Crocuta crocuta spelaea* from the North Sea,"*Deinsea*, vol. 14, pp. 15–18, 2010.
144. J. S. Carri´on, J. A. Riquelme, C. Navarro, and M. Munuera,"Pollen in hyaena coprolites reflects late glacial landscape isouthern Spain," *Palaeogeography, Palaeoclimatology, Palaeoecology*,vol. 176, no. 1–4, pp. 193–205, 2001.
145. C. Sillero-Zubiri and D. Gottelli, "Feeding ecology of spottedhyaena (Mammalia: *Crocuta crocuta*) in a mountain foresthabitat," *Journal of African Zoology*, vol. 106, no. 2, pp. 169–176,1992.
146. L. D. Mech, *The Arctic Wolf: Living With the Pack*, VoyageurPress, Stillwater, Minn, USA, 1988.
147. C.G.Diedrich, "Askeleton of an injured *Coelodonta antiquitatis*(Blumenbach 1807) from the Upper Pleistocene of northwesternGermany," *Cranium*, vol. 25, no. 1, pp. 1–16, 2008.
148. P. White and C. G. Diedrich, "Taphonomy story of a modern African elephant *Loxodonta africana* carcass on a lakeshore inZambia (Africa)," *Quaternary International*, vol. 276-277, pp.287–296, 2012.
149. D. Joubert and B. Joubert, *Eternal Enemies: Lions & Hyenas*,Wildlife Films Botswana for National Geographic, 2003.
150. W. von Koenigswald, H. M¨uller-Beck, and E. Pressmar,"Arch¨aologie und pal¨aontologie in den weinbergh¨ohlen von Mauern (Bayern), Grabungen 1937–1967," *Archaeologica Venatoria*, vol. 3, pp. 1–152, 1999.
151. G. Rabeder,D.Nagel, andM. Pacher, *DerH¨ohlenb¨ar*,ThorbeckeSpecies 4, Stuttgart, Germany, 2000.
152. D. E. Nelson, A. Angerbj¨orn, K. Lid´en, and I. Turk, "Stableisotopes and the metabolism of the European cave bear,"*Oecologia*, vol. 116, no. 1-2, pp. 177–181, 1998.

153. C. G. Diedrich, "Cracking and nibbling marks as indicators forthe Upper Pleistocene spotted hyaena as a scavenger of cave bear (*Ursus spelaeus* Rosenm¨uller, 1794) carcasses in the PerickCaves den ofNorthwestGermany," *Abhandlungen der NaturhistorischenGesellschaft N¨urnberg*, vol. 45, pp. 73–90, 2005.
154. J. Quil`es, C. Petrea, O. Moldovan et al., "Cave bears from P. cuOase (Banat, Romania): taphonomy and paleobiology," *ComptesRendus-Palevol*, vol. 5, no. 8, pp. 927–934, 2006.
155. J. F. Tournepiche, "Un Neandertalien devore par des hyenas?*Paleo*, vol. 6, pp. 319–321, 1994.
156. Turk, J. Dirjec, and G. Bastiani, "Nove analize piscali iz Divjibab I (Slovenija)," *Archeolo˘ski Vestnik*, vol. 52, pp. 25–79, 2001.
157. J. Burger,W. Rosendahl,O. Loreille et al., "Molecular phylogenyof the extinct cave lion *Panthera leo spelaea*," *Molecular Phylogeneticsand Evolution*, vol. 30, no. 3, pp. 841–849, 2004.
158. R. Barnett, B. Shapiro, I. Barnes et al., "Phylogeography of lions(*Panthera leo* ssp.) reveals three distinct taxa and a late Pleistocenereduction in genetic diversity,"*Molecular Ecology*, vol. 18,no. 8, pp. 1668–1677, 2009.
159. G. Schaller, *The Serengeti Lion. A Study of Predator-Prey Relations*,University of Chicago Press, Chicago, Ill, USA, 1972.
160. R. Estes, *The Safari Companion: A Guide to Watching AfricanMammals*,Chelsea Green PublishingCompany,Vermont,USA,1999.
161. Turner, "Dental sex dimorphism in European lions (*Pantheraleo* L.) of the Upper Pleistocene: palaeoecological and palaeoethological implications," *Annales Zoologici Fennici*, vol. 21, pp. 1–8, 1984.
162. H. Bocherens, D. G. Drucker, D. Bonjean et al., "Isotopicevidence for dietary ecology of cave lion (*Panthera spelaea*) inNorth-Western Europe: prey choice, competition and implications for extinction," *Quaternary International*, vol. 245, no. 2,pp. 249–261, 2011.
163. D. Joubert, "Hunting behaviour of lions (*Panthera leo*) onelephants (*Loxodonta africana*) in the Chobe National Park,Botswana," *African Journal of Ecology*, vol. 44, no. 2, pp. 279–281, 2006.
164. Grandal-D'Anglade and J. R. Vidal Roman´ı, "A populationstudy on the Cave Bear (*Ursus spelaeus* Ros.-Hein.) from CovaEir´os (Triacastela, Galicia, Spain)," *Geobios*, vol. 30, no. 5, pp. 723–731, 1997.
165. P. Argenti and P. P. A. Mazza, "Mortality analysis of the LatePleistocene bears from Grotta Lattaia, central Italy," *Journal ofArchaeological Science*, vol. 33, no. 11, pp. 1552–1558, 2006.
166. Debeljak, "Fossil population structure and mortality of thecave bear from the Mokrica cave (North Slovenia)," *ActaCarsologica*, vol. 36, no. 3, pp. 475–484, 2007.
167. C. Pinto Llona and P. J. Andrew, "Scavenging behaviourpatterns in cave bears *Ursus spelaeus*," in *14`eme congr`es UISPP,Hommes et Carnivores au Pal´eolithique*, J.-P. Brugal and P. Fosse, Eds., Revue de Pal´eobiologie 23, pp. 845–853, Gen`eve, Switzerland,2004.
168. J. T. Groiss, "¨ Uber pathologische bildungen an skelettrestenjungquart¨arer s¨augetiere aus der zoolithenh¨ohle bei burggeilenreuth,"*Geologische Bl¨atter NO-Bayern*, vol. 28, no. 1, pp. 1–21,1978.
169. C. G. Diedrich, "Pleistocene Stratigraphy and bone taphonomyin the Zoolithen Cave—and new theory about Esper's "biblic flood" with a first geomorphological Wiesent Valley and river terrace evolution model—small glaciers and high/postglacial flood events in Upper Franconia. Eiszeitalter und Gegenwart," *Quaternary Science Journal*, 2013.
170. S. C. M¨unzel, M. Stiller, M. Hofreiter, A. Mittnik, N. J. Conard,and H. Bocherens, "Pleistocene bears in the Swabian Jura (Germany):genetic replacement, ecological displacement, extinctionsand survival," *Quaternary International*, vol. 245, no. 2,pp. 225–237, 2011.
171. C. G. Diedrich, "Oldest and most Northern late palaeolithiccave bear hunters in Europe," *Archaeology, Ethnology andAnthropology of Eurasia*, 2014.
172. F. Palomares and T. M. Caro, "Interspecific killing amongmammalian carnivores," *American Naturalist*, vol. 153, no. 5, pp.492–508, 1999.

INDEX